To view the official video of
The World of Professional Golf 2020,
which reviews the highlights of the 2019 year in golf,
please go to:

www.rwopg2020.com and enter the password: **Rolex2020**

Presents

The World of Professional Golf 2020

Founded by
Mark H. McCormack

IMG

Editor: Jan Davis
Publication Coordinator: Sarah Wooldridge
Contributors: Andy Farrell, Doug Ferguson, Donald (Doc) Giffin, Marino Parascenzo

All rights reserved
First published 2020
© IMG WORLDWIDE LLC 2020

Designed and produced by Davis Design

ISBN-13: 978-0-9914858-6-4

Printed and bound in the United States.

Contents

Rolex Rankings		1
Official World Golf Ranking		6
World's Winners of 2019		13
Multiple Winners of 2019		22
World Money List		23
World Money List Leaders		31
Career World Money List		32
Women's World Money List		33
Senior World Money List		37
1	The Year In Retrospect	41

THE MAJOR CHAMPIONSHIPS

2	Masters Tournament	58
3	PGA Championship	65
4	U.S. Open Championship	72
5	The 148th Open Championship	79
6	Women's Major Championships	86

WORLDWIDE TOURS

7	American Tours	105
8	European Tours	162
9	Asia/Japan Tours	187
10	Australasian Tour	221
11	African Sunshine Tour	231
12	Women's Tours	246
13	Senior Tours	301

APPENDIXES

U.S. PGA Tour	344
Special Events	409
Korn Ferry Tour	413
Mackenzie Tour–PGA Tour Canada	430
PGA Tour Latinoamerica	436
European Tour	445
Challenge Tour	487
Asian Tour	502
PGA Tour Series–China	516
China Golf Association Tour	523
Japan Tour	530
ISPS Handa PGA Tour of Australasia	545
African Sunshine Tour	555
U.S. LPGA Tour	572
Ladies European Tour	592
Japan LPGA Tour	604
Korea LPGA Tour	625
Australian Ladies Tour	641
Champions Tour	646
Staysure Tour	667
Japan PGA Senior Tour	677

Foreword
(Written in 1968)

It has long been my feeling that a sport as compelling as professional golf is deserving of a history, and by history I do not mean an account culled years later from the adjectives and enthusiasms of on-the-spot reports that have then sat in newspaper morgues for decades waiting for some patient drudge to paste them together and call them lore. Such works can be excellent when insight and perspective are added to the research, but this rarely happens. What I am talking about is a running history, a chronology written at the time, which would serve both as a record of the sport and as a commentary upon the sport in any given year—an annual, if you will....

When I embarked on this project two years ago (the first of these annuals was published in Great Britain in 1967), I was repeatedly told that such a compendium of world golf was impossible, that it would be years out of date before it could be assembled and published, that it would be hopelessly expensive to produce and that only the golf fanatic would want a copy anyway. In the last analysis, it was that final stipulation that spurred me on. There must be a lot of golf fanatics, I decided. I can't be the only one. And then one winter day I was sitting in Arnold Palmer's den in Latrobe, Pennsylvania, going through the usual motions of spreading papers around so that Arnold and I could discuss some business project, when Arnold happened to mention that he wanted to collect a copy of each new golf book that was published from now on, in order to build a golf library of his own. "It's really too bad that there isn't a book every year on the pro tour," he said. "Ah," I thought. "Another golf fanatic. That makes two of us." So I decided to do the book. And I have. And I hope you like it. If so, you can join Arnold and me as golf fanatics.

Mark H. McCormack
Cleveland, Ohio
January 1968

Mark H. McCormack
1930 – 2003

In 1960, Mark Hume McCormack shook hands with a young golfer named Arnold Palmer. That historic handshake established a business that would evolve into today's IMG, the world's premier sports and lifestyle marketing and management company —representing hundreds of sports figures, entertainers, models, celebrities, broadcasters, television properties, and prestigious organizations and events around the world. With just a handshake Mark McCormack had invented a global industry.

Sean McManus, President of CBS News and Sports, reflects, "I don't think it's an overstatement to say that like Henry Ford and Bill Gates, Mark McCormack literally created, fostered and led an entirely new worldwide industry. There was no sports marketing before Mark McCormack. Every athlete who's ever appeared in a commercial, or every right holder who sold their rights to anyone, owes a huge debt of gratitude to Mark McCormack."

Mark McCormack's philosophy was simple. "Be the best," he said. "Learn the business and expand by applying what you already know." This philosophy served him well, not only as an entrepreneur and CEO of IMG, but also as an author, a consultant and a confidant to a host of global leaders in the world of business, politics, finance, science, sports and entertainment.

He was among the most-honored entrepreneurs of his time. *Sports Illustrated* recognized him as "The Most Powerful Man in Sports." In 1999, ESPN's Sports Century listed him as one of the century's 10 "Most Influential People in the Business of Sport."

Golf Magazine called McCormack "the most powerful man in golf" and honored him along with Arnold Palmer, Gerald Ford, Dwight D. Eisenhower, Bob Hope and Ben Hogan as one of the 100 all-time "American Heroes of Golf." *Tennis* magazine and *Racquet* magazine named him "the most powerful man in tennis." Tennis legend Billie Jean King believes, "Mark McCormack was the king of sports marketing. He shaped the way all sports are marketed around the world. He was the first in the marketplace, and his influence on the world of sports, particularly his ability to combine athlete representation, property development and television broadcasting, will forever be the standard of the industry."

The London *Sunday Times* listed him as one of the 1000 people who influenced the 20th century. Alastair Cooke on the BBC said simply that "McCormack was the Oracle; the creator of the talent industry, the maker of people famous in their profession famous to the rest of the world and making for them a fortune in the process … He took on as clients people already famous in their profession as golfer, opera singer, author, footballer, racing car driver, violinist—and from time to time if they needed special help, a prime minister, or even the Pope."

McCormack was honored posthumously by the Golf Writers Association of America with the 2004 William D. Richardson Award, the organization's highest honor, "Given to recognize an individual who has consistently made an outstanding contribution to golf."

Among McCormack's other honors were the 2001 PGA Distinguished Service Award, given to those who have helped perpetuate the values and ideals of the PGA of America. He was also named a Commander of the Royal Order of the Polar Star by the King of Sweden (the highest honor for a person living outside of Sweden) for his contribution to the Nobel Foundation.

Journalist Frank Deford states, "There have been what we love to call dynasties in every sport. IMG has been different. What this one brilliant man, Mark McCormack, created is the only dynasty ever over all sport."

Through IMG, Mark McCormack demonstrated the value of sports and lifestyle activities as effective corporate marketing tools, but more importantly, his lifelong dedication to his vocation—begun with just a simple handshake—brought enjoyment to millions of people worldwide who watch and cheer their heroes and heroines. That is his legacy.

Rolex has been an integral partner of golf for more than 50 years. Our support extends to all aspects of the sport – from its custodians, The R&A and the USGA, to the elite professional men's and women's tours and tournaments, as well as junior, amateur and senior ranks worldwide. As part of this enduring commitment, we have been presenting *The World of Professional Golf* since 2006.

In 2019, we witnessed many outstanding performances by our family of golf Testimonees — there were 27 victories in all — and other innovative developments that further enhanced our alliance with this great game.

A highlight was the incredible comeback of Tiger Woods. In April, after an 11-year gap, he won his 15th Major championship at the Masters Tournament and claimed a record-equalling 82nd victory on the PGA TOUR later in the year. His sustained excellence and sportsmanship over more than two decades continues to inspire the next generation of golfers.

Brooks Koepka was another Testimonee to enjoy a stellar season, claiming his fourth Major by defending his title at the PGA Championship and finishing the year ranked World No. 1.

Rolex supported the inaugural Augusta National Women's Amateur, which was a tremendous success, attracting live television coverage and creating an opportunity for women golfers to fulfil their dream of playing at the revered Augusta National Golf Club. Mexico's Maria Fassi finished a very creditable second before turning professional and becoming a Rolex Testimonee.

In another first, The Evian Championship Prize for a Better Tomorrow presented by Rolex was awarded to Lorena Ochoa, the former World No. 1 and two-time Major winner, in recognition of her work with underprivileged children in her native Mexico.

Elsewhere in the women's game, the Solheim Cup at Gleneagles produced the most sensational finish in the competition's history, with Europe prevailing by a single point to capture the trophy from the United States for the first time in six years. Rolex has sponsored the pre-eminent team event since 1994.

The brand welcomed two new Testimonees to the fold: American Cameron Champ and his fellow countryman Matthew Wolff, who, prior to turning professional, was among the world's finest college golfers and competed at the 2018 Arnold Palmer Cup, partnered by Rolex. Both players have won on the PGA TOUR and are part of the New Guard, the rising stars ready to assume the mantle of excellence from the game's legends.

The year concluded with the Presidents Cup at the Royal Melbourne Golf Club, where Woods, only the second playing captain in the competition's 25-year history, inspired his U.S. team to an incredible comeback victory against their international counterparts.

Since 1967 when we formed our seminal partnership with Arnold Palmer — who was joined by fellow members of The Big Three, Jack Nicklaus and Gary Player — Rolex's partnership with golf has flourished, permeating all levels. The 2019 season produced many memorable highlights, which we trust you will savour in the pages that follow.

Jean-Frédéric Dufour
Rolex SA
Chief Executive Officer

Rolex and Golf

Rolex, the leading brand of the Swiss watch industry, enjoys an unrivalled reputation for quality and expertise the world over. The company's partnership in excellence with golf began with Arnold Palmer in 1967. He, along with fellow Rolex Testimonees Jack Nicklaus and Gary Player — otherwise known as The Big Three — contributed to modernizing golf and giving it a worldwide dimension. Since 1967, the relationship between Rolex and golf has continuously grown and prospered. Today, Rolex is golf's leading supporter and is associated with the most important and prestigious entities governing the game worldwide, as well as with golf's principal professional tours, competitions and players.

Brooks Kopeka, winner of the PGA Championship

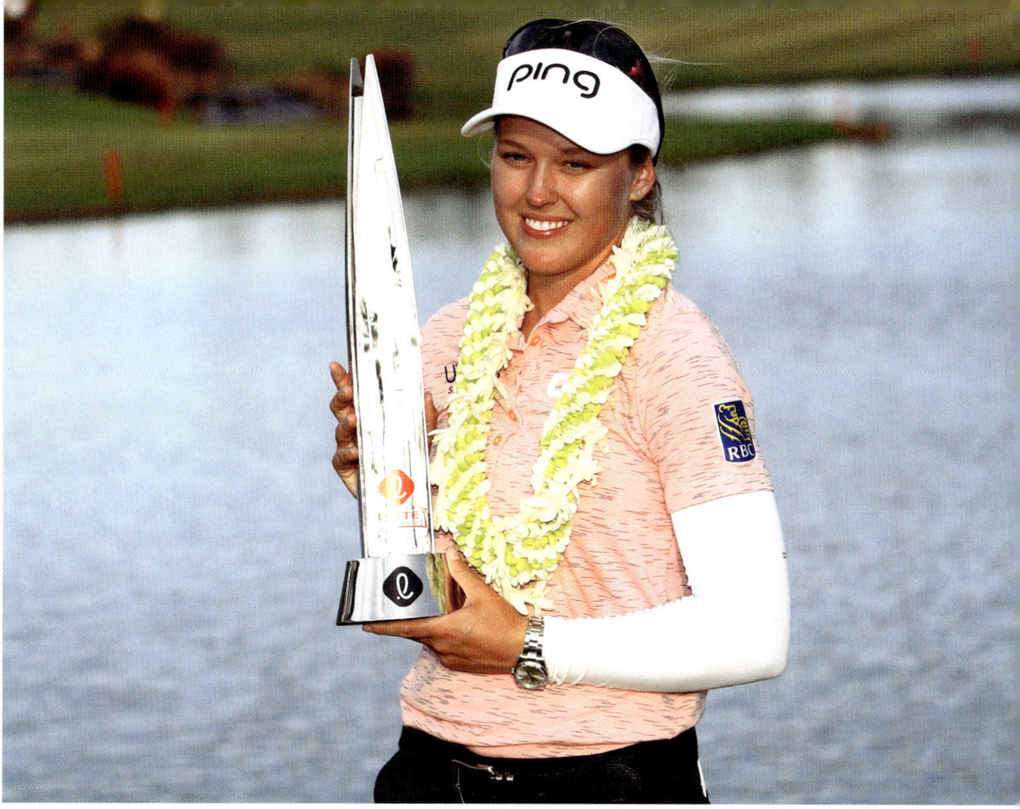

Gregory Shamus/Getty Images

Brooke M. Henderson, winner of the Lotte Championship

Harry How/Getty Images

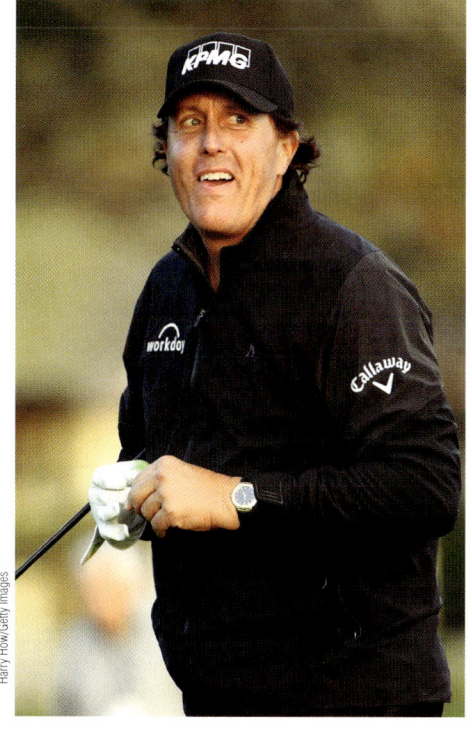

Phil Mickelson, winner of the AT&T Pebble Beach Pro-Am

Michael Reaves/Getty Images

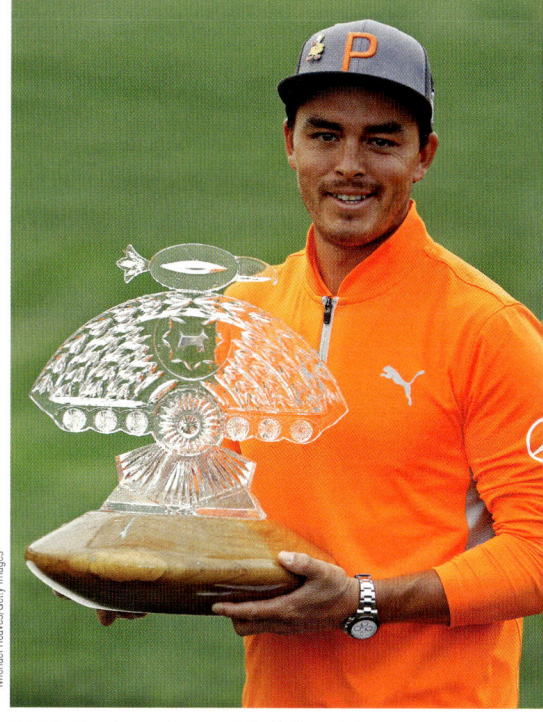

Rickie Fowler, winner of the Waste Management Phoenix Open

Tiger Woods, winner of the Zozo Championship

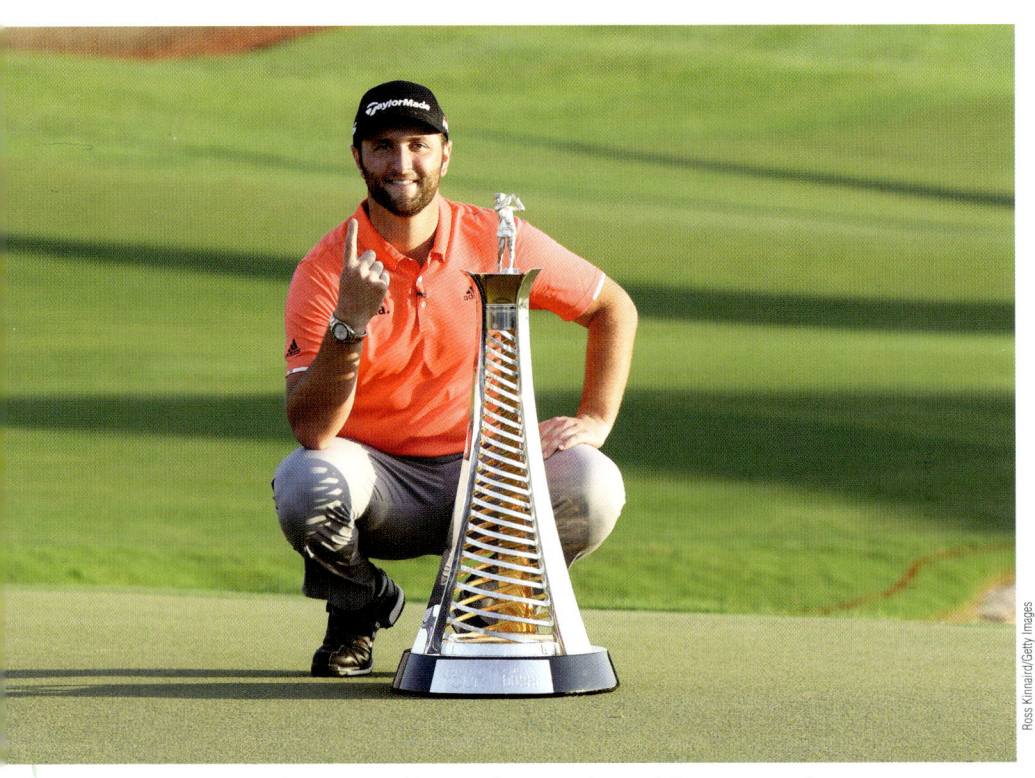

Jon Rahm, winner of the DP World Tour Championship and the Race to Dubai

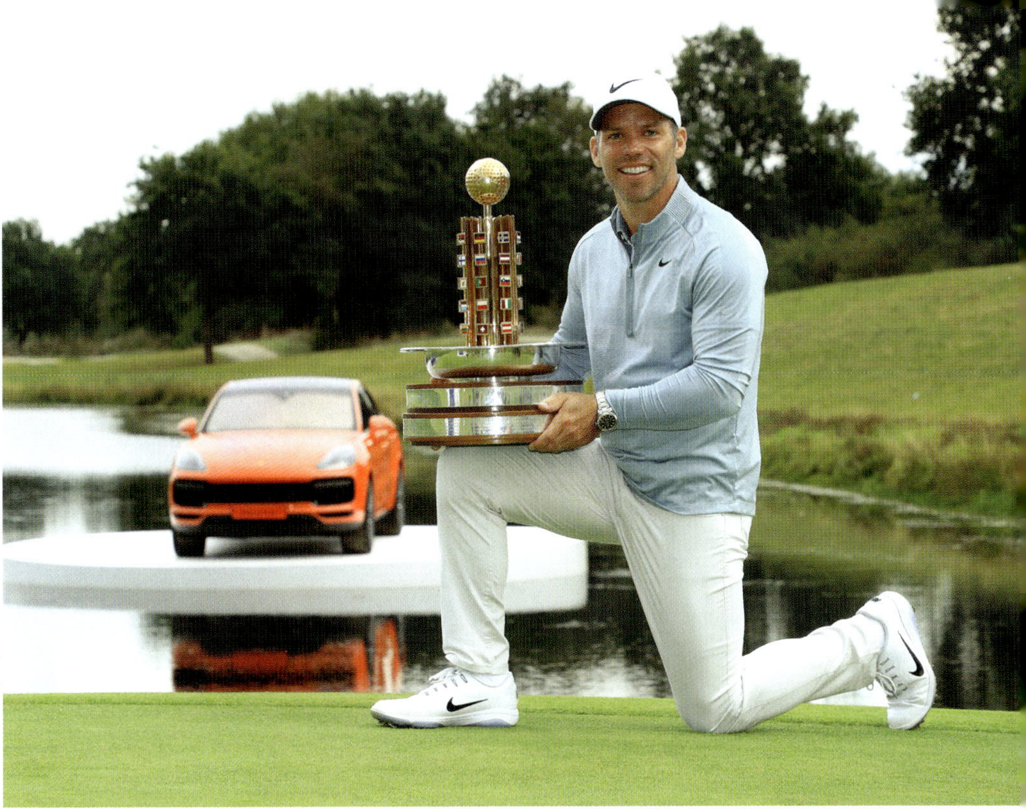
Matthew Lewis/Getty Images

Paul Casey, winner of the Porsche European Open

Ross Kinnaird/Getty Images

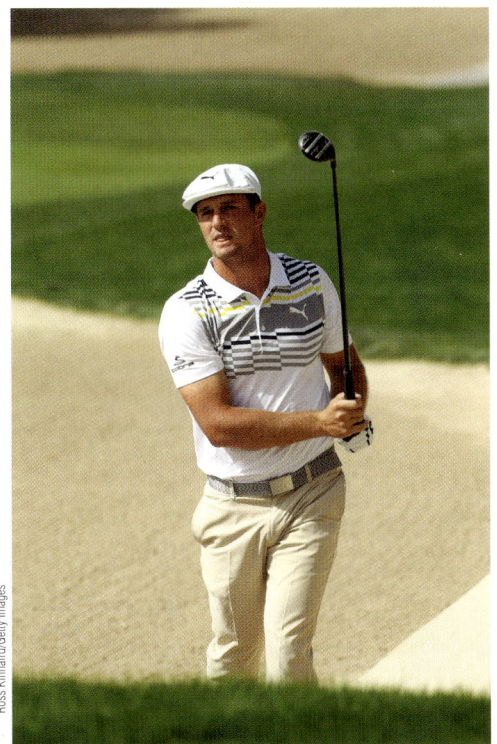

Bryson DeChambeau at the Dubai Desert Classic

Jonathan Ferrey/Getty Images

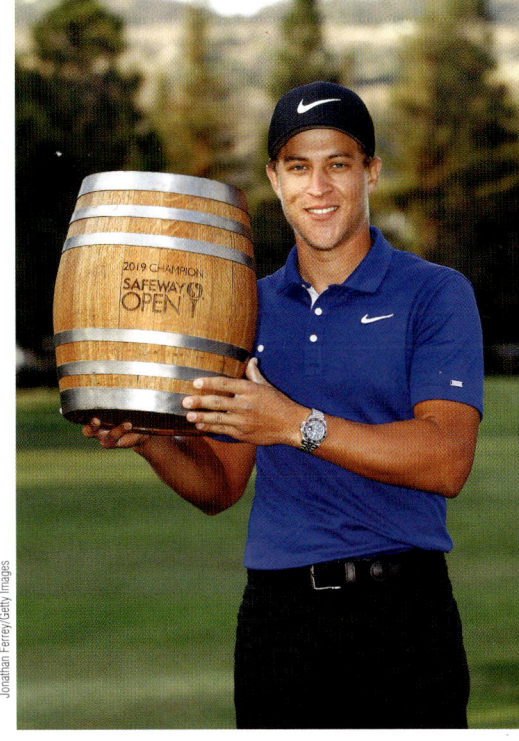

Cameron Champ, winner of the Safeway Open

Joaquin Niemann, winner of the Greenbrier Classic

Nicolas Colsaerts, winner of the Open de France

Thomas Pieters, winner of the D+D Real Czech Masters

Lexi Thompson, winner of the ShopRite LPGA Classic

Justin Thomas, winner of the BMW Championship

Bernhard Langer, winner of the Senior Open Championship

Hall of Fame inductee Retief Goosen

Colin Montgomerie at the Staysure PGA Seniors Championship

2019 Rolex Rankings Top 3

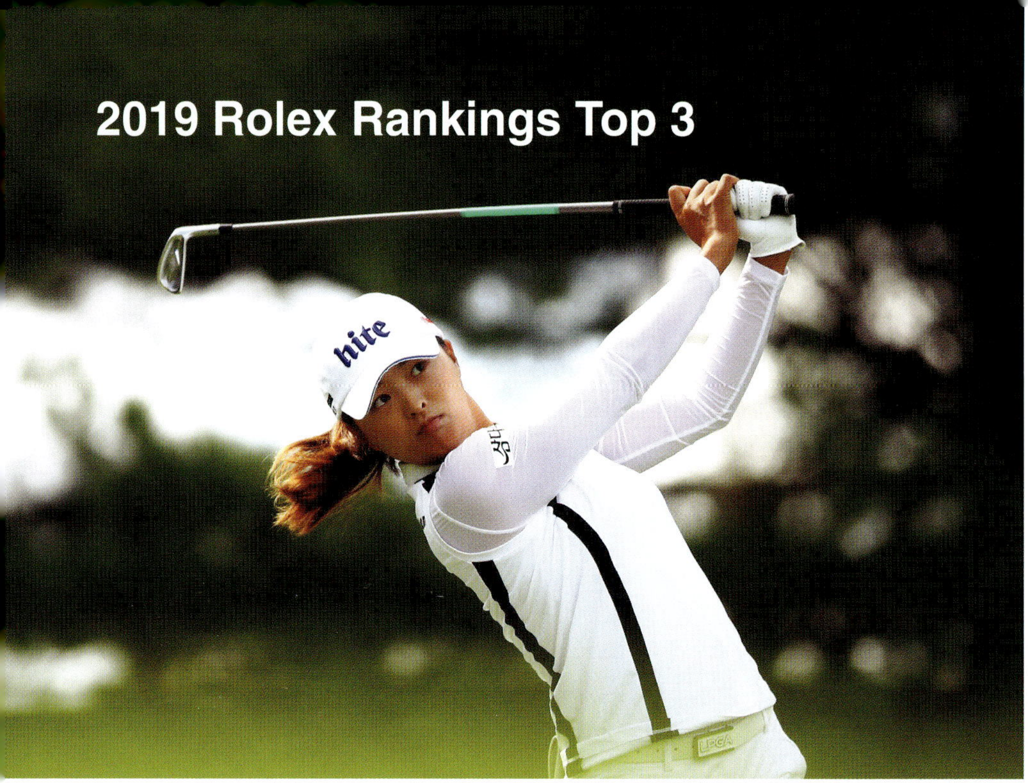

Vaughn Ridley/Getty Images

Jin Young Ko (Korea) 9.45 points

Stuart Franklin/Getty Images

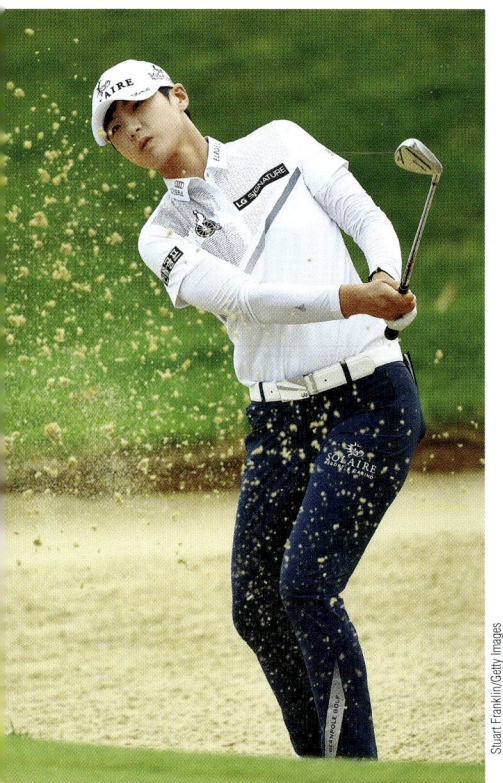

Sung Hyun Park (Korea) 6.77 points

Han Myung-Gu/Getty Images

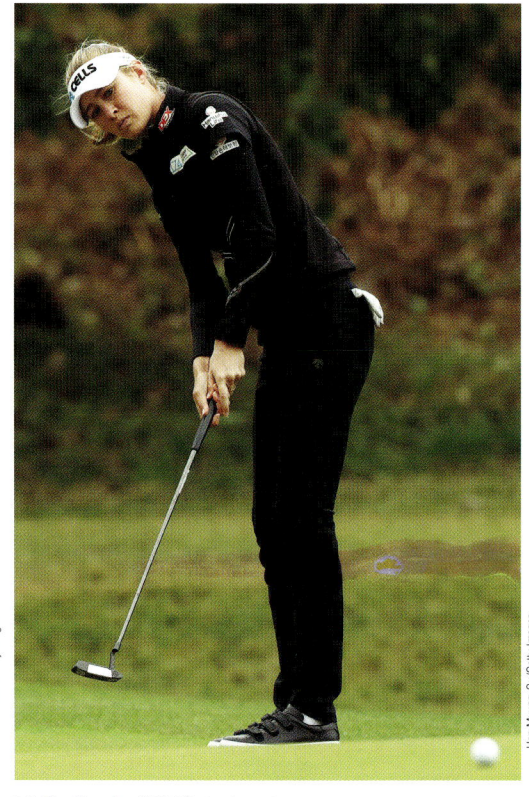

Nelly Korda (USA) 6.53 points

Rolex Rankings

For the third time in a row, a different player ended the year as the No. 1 on the Rolex Rankings from the one who started it. Following Shanshan Feng in 2017 and Ariya Jutanugarn in 2018, it was Jin Young Ko who finished 2019 in the top spot. Ko became the third Korean to enjoy the honor following Jiyai Shin in 2010 and Inbee Park in 2013 and 2014.

With five victories worldwide, Ko dominated the women's game and topped the Rankings for a total of 35 weeks. Having started the year ranked 10th, Ko won the first of four LPGA titles at the Bank of Hope Founders Cup before claiming the No. 1 spot for the first time with her maiden major victory at the ANA Inspiration in April. "To win a major championship and be called the best player in the world is absolutely a great honor," Ko said at the time. Winning the Evian Championship in July took Ko back to the top of the Rankings for the rest of the year.

While Jutanugarn fell to 12th place after a winless 2019, Ko's compatriot, and former Rankings leader, Sung Hyun Park had two brief stints as the world No. 1 after her wins at the HSBC Women's World Championship in March and the Walmart NW Arkansas Championship at the end of June.

Park ended the year as she had started it, in second place, with Nelly Korda becoming the leading American in third, jumping up from 23rd. Three new major winners all made significant leaps on the Rankings with U.S. Open champion Jeongeun Lee$_6$ moving from 17th to seventh; Hannah Green, the KPMG WPGA champion, moving up to 22nd from 143rd; and Japanese rookie Hinako Shibuno, the AIG Women's British Open champion, finishing the year in 11th place after starting it in 563rd.

The Rolex Rankings — which was developed at the May 2004 World Congress of Women's Golf — is sanctioned by 10 women's professional golf tours: the Ladies Professional Golf Association (LPGA); Ladies European Tour (LET); Ladies European Access Series (LETAS); Ladies Professional Golfers' Association of Japan (JLPGA); Ladies Professional Golfers' Association of Japan Step Up Tour (JSU Tour); Korea Ladies Professional Golf Association (KLPGA); Australian Ladies Professional Golf (ALPG); Symetra Tour; China Ladies Professional Golf Association Tour (CLPGA) and Chinese Taipei Ladies Professional Golf Association (TLPGA) - as well as The Royal and Ancient (R&A) and the United States Golf Association (USGA).

The major golf tours developed the rankings and the protocol that governs the ranking, while R2IT, an independent software development company, was retained to develop the software and to maintain the rankings on a weekly basis. The official events from all of the tours are taken into account and points are awarded according to the strength of the field, with the exception of the five major championships on the LPGA Tour, which have a fixed points distribution. The players' points averages are determined by taking the number of points awarded over a two-year rolling period, with the points awarded in the most recent 13-week period carrying a stronger value, and then dividing that by the number of tournaments played, with a minimum divisor of 35.

The Rolex Rankings are updated and released following the completion of the previous week's tournaments around the world.

Rolex Rankings
(As of December 31, 2019)

Rank	Player	Country	No. of Events	Average Points	Total Points
1	Jin Young Ko	Korea	51	9.45	481.98
2	Sung Hyun Park	Korea	47	6.77	318.08
3	Nelly Korda	USA	44	6.53	287.30
4	Danielle Kang	USA	47	5.77	271.38
5	Sei Young Kim	Korea	53	5.63	298.44
6	Nasa Hataoka	Japan	50	5.62	280.90
7	Jeongeun Lee[6]	Korea	50	5.51	275.69
8	Brooke M. Henderson	Canada	54	5.49	296.70
9	Minjee Lee	Australia	55	5.45	299.54
10	Lexi Thompson	USA	40	5.30	211.87
11	Hinako Shibuno	Japan	47	4.76	223.56
12	Ariya Jutanugarn	Thailand	56	4.64	259.66
13	Hyo Joo Kim	Korea	50	4.47	223.58
14	Inbee Park	Korea	38	4.31	163.61
15	Ai Suzuki	Japan	53	4.28	227.10
16	Carlota Ciganda	Spain	50	4.27	213.48
17	Jessica Korda	USA	36	4.26	153.18
18	So Yeon Ryu	Korea	46	3.88	178.26
19	Lizette Salas	USA	47	3.75	176.14
20	Amy Yang	Korea	47	3.69	173.38
21	Mi Jung Hur	Korea	44	3.63	159.58
22	Hannah Green	Australia	51	3.45	175.80
23	Shanshan Feng	China	49	3.34	163.86
24	Jiyai Shin	Korea	60	3.17	190.19
25	HeeJeong Lim	Korea	33	3.14	109.74
26	Charley Hull	England	47	3.02	141.84
27	Hye Jin Choi	Korea	61	2.97	181.09
28	Brittany Altomare	USA	53	2.90	153.70
29	Seonwoo Bae	Korea	60	2.81	168.71
30	Da Yeon Lee	Korea	48	2.79	133.77
31	Bronte Law	England	48	2.76	132.33
32	Ha Na Jang	Korea	55	2.75	151.12
33	Marina Alex	USA	47	2.71	127.44
34	Eun-Hee Ji	Korea	48	2.58	124.01
35	A Yean Cho	Korea	37	2.53	93.46
36	Yu Liu	China	54	2.52	135.85
37	Caroline Masson	Germany	52	2.42	125.74
38	Moriya Jutanugarn	Thailand	56	2.40	134.18
39	In-Kyung Kim	Korea	33	2.36	82.47
40	Lydia Ko	New Zealand	51	2.35	119.74
41	Georgia Hall	England	47	2.33	109.53
42	Angel Yin	USA	50	2.33	116.41
43	Azahara Munoz	Spain	57	2.26	128.86
44	Megan Khang	USA	52	2.23	116.21
45	Kristen Gillman	USA	27	2.13	74.72
46	Minyoung Lee[2]	Korea	60	2.12	127.38
47	Sun Ju Ahn	Korea	50	2.12	105.91
48	In Gee Chun	Korea	45	2.12	95.28
49	Mi Hyang Lee	Korea	54	2.04	110.40
50	Min Ji Park	Korea	53	2.01	106.34

ROLEX RANKINGS / 3

Rank	Player	Country	No. of Events	Average Points	Total Points
51	Jennifer Kupcho	USA	19	1.97	68.82
52	So Mi Lee	Korea	28	1.90	66.63
53	Morgan Pressel	USA	46	1.86	85.55
54	Mone Inami	Japan	33	1.85	64.89
55	Su-Hyun Oh	Australia	56	1.81	101.35
56	Gaby Lopez	Mexico	52	1.80	93.63
57	So Young Lee	Korea	58	1.75	101.54
58	Celine Boutier	France	57	1.74	99.33
59	Ally McDonald	USA	49	1.74	85.38
60	Jeong Min Cho	Korea	58	1.74	100.65
61	Momoko Ueda	Japan	60	1.73	103.59
62	Yui Kawamoto	Japan	51	1.72	87.53
63	Austin Ernst	USA	43	1.71	73.50
64	Annie Park	USA	45	1.68	75.60
65	Amy Olson	USA	48	1.68	80.43
66	Mamiko Higa	Japan	68	1.65	112.00
67	Nanna Koerstz Madsen	Denmark	53	1.65	87.26
68	A Lim Kim	Korea	55	1.59	87.58
69	Minami Katsu	Japan	71	1.58	112.50
70	Ji Yeong Kim$_2$	Korea	57	1.55	88.23
71	Chae Yoon Park	Korea	55	1.49	81.75
72	Sakura Koiwai	Japan	76	1.46	110.82
73	Eri Okayama	Japan	63	1.44	90.68
74	Jenny Shin	Korea	53	1.44	76.18
75	Chella Choi	Korea	56	1.43	79.97
76	Angela Stanford	USA	46	1.42	65.54
77	Ji Hyun Kim	Korea	56	1.41	78.81
78	Nicole Broch Larsen	Denmark	54	1.41	75.94
79	Cheyenne Knight	USA	38	1.37	52.12
80	Misuzu Narita	Japan	63	1.37	86.38
81	Pornanong Phatlum	Thailand	51	1.37	69.88
82	Ayaka Furue	Japan	22	1.37	47.89
83	Jing Yan	China	50	1.37	68.39
84	Teresa Lu	Chinese Taipei	64	1.35	86.57
85	Mirim Lee	Korea	49	1.35	66.16
86	Jodi Ewart Shadoff	England	46	1.32	60.89
87	Lala Anai	Japan	75	1.30	97.27
88	Ah-Reum Hwang	Korea	67	1.30	86.89
89	Anna Nordqvist	Sweden	51	1.28	65.36
90	Ryann O'toole	USA	47	1.28	60.20
91	Jaye Marie Green	USA	51	1.28	65.21
92	Ji Young Park	Korea	55	1.26	69.24
93	Seung Yeon Lee	Korea	33	1.26	44.03
94	Anne Van Dam	Netherlands	46	1.25	57.54
95	Hyun Kyung Park	Korea	30	1.23	43.11
96	Wei-Ling Hsu	Chinese Taipei	60	1.23	73.82
97	Ga Young Lee	Korea	29	1.22	42.71
98	Jung Min Lee	Korea	55	1.16	63.57
99	Erika Hara	Japan	62	1.14	70.87
100	Song Yi Ahn	Korea	53	1.14	60.58

4 / ROLEX RANKINGS

Rank	Player	Country	No. of Events	Average Points	Total Points
101	Stacy Lewis	USA	30	1.14	39.85
102	Melissa Reid	England	42	1.12	47.07
103	Jennifer Song	USA	45	1.11	49.73
104	Ashleigh Buhai	South Africa	60	1.10	66.25
105	Yealimi Noh	USA	14	1.10	38.47
106	Mo Martin	USA	35	1.09	38.23
107	Brittany Lincicome	USA	28	1.08	37.67
108	Mi Jeong Jeon	Korea	63	1.08	67.79
109	Bo Ah Kim	Korea	55	1.07	58.93
110	Cristie Kerr	USA	42	1.07	44.86
111	Jane Park	USA	43	1.07	45.84
112	Erika Kikuchi	Japan	67	1.06	71.26
113	Alena Sharp	Canada	48	1.06	50.95
114	Asuka Kashiwabara	Japan	70	1.06	74.27
115	Katherine Kirk	Australia	54	1.05	56.89
116	Gerina Piller	USA	22	1.03	36.21
117	Ji Hyun Oh	Korea	50	1.03	51.70
118	Madelene Sagstrom	Sweden	46	1.03	47.53
119	Hee-Kyung Bae	Korea	64	1.03	66.01
120	Ji Hee Lee	Korea	57	1.00	57.19
121	Ju Young Pak	Korea	55	1.00	55.05
122	Hae Ran Ryu	Korea	17	0.98	34.18
123	Xiyu Lin	China	48	0.98	46.88
124	Jin Seon Han	Korea	56	0.97	54.51
125	Caroline Hedwall	Sweden	44	0.96	42.46
126	Min Sun Kim$_5$	Korea	53	0.96	50.66
127	Jeong Eun Lee	Korea	44	0.94	41.55
128	Gyo Rin Park	Korea	27	0.93	32.70
129	Hina Arakaki	Japan	65	0.93	60.57
130	Sakura Yokomine	Japan	58	0.92	53.54
131	Jasmine Suwannapura	Thailand	59	0.92	54.14
132	Esther Henseleit	Germany	19	0.92	32.12
133	Kana Mikashima	Japan	64	0.91	58.10
134	So Yeon Park	Korea	55	0.90	49.31
135	Pajaree Anannarukarn	Thailand	42	0.89	37.41
136	Rei Matsuda	Japan	69	0.89	61.29
137	Ye Rim Choi	Korea	53	0.88	46.86
138	Maria Fernanda Torres	Puerto Rico	48	0.87	41.55
139	Hee Won Na	Korea	59	0.85	50.35
140	Char Young Kim$_2$	Korea	52	0.85	44.36
141	So Yi Kim	Korea	54	0.85	46.02
142	Sarah Schmelzel	USA	45	0.85	38.05
143	Aditi Ashok	India	53	0.84	44.65
144	Saki Asai	Japan	56	0.84	46.93
145	Sayaka Takahashi	Japan	66	0.84	55.18
146	Bo Mee Lee	Korea	55	0.82	45.29
147	S. Langkul	Thailand	53	0.82	43.23
148	Mika Miyazato	Japan	34	0.79	27.54
149	Shiho Oyama	Japan	47	0.78	36.63
150	Chae-Young Yoon	Korea	60	0.77	46.10

Rank	Player	Country	No. of Events	Average Points	Total Points
151	Ji Hyun Kim$_2$	Korea	50	0.76	38.15
152	Patty Tavatanakit	Thailand	15	0.76	26.53
153	Marianne Skarpnord	Norway	34	0.76	26.47
154	Hikaru Yoshimoto	Japan	61	0.76	46.08
155	Bo Mi Kwak	Korea	27	0.74	26.03
156	Pernilla Lindberg	Sweden	52	0.74	38.47
157	Lindy Duncan	USA	51	0.73	37.12
158	Saki Nagamine	Japan	69	0.73	50.22
159	Chie Arimura	Japan	60	0.71	42.76
160	Haeji Kang	Korea	45	0.71	31.76
161	Ayako Uehara	Japan	57	0.69	39.39
162	Mami Fukuda	Japan	66	0.68	45.16
163	Olivia Cowan	Germany	34	0.67	23.52
164	Kana Nagai	Japan	74	0.67	49.63
165	Sandra Gal	Germany	42	0.67	28.13
166	Ha Neul Kim	Korea	53	0.67	35.48
167	Eun Woo Choi	Korea	49	0.67	32.74
168	Harukyo Nomura	Japan	32	0.66	23.15
169	Mariajo Uribe	Colombia	42	0.65	27.40
170	Serena Aoki	Japan	73	0.65	47.35
171	Yuka Yasuda	Japan	19	0.65	22.61
172	Hana Wakimoto	Japan	45	0.65	29.04
173	Seung Hyun Lee	Korea	48	0.63	30.28
174	Tiffany Joh	USA	47	0.61	28.75
175	Rumi Yoshiba	Japan	75	0.61	45.84
176	Ritsuko Ryu	Japan	64	0.61	38.81
177	Gyeol Park	Korea	50	0.60	30.20
178	Emma Talley	USA	50	0.60	29.87
179	Haruka Morita Wanyaolu	China	66	0.59	39.14
180	Seul Gi Jeong	Korea	53	0.59	31.19
181	Weiwei Zhang	China	39	0.59	22.90
182	Hee Young Park	Korea	36	0.59	21.13
183	Pavarisa Yoktuan	Thailand	44	0.58	25.69
184	Sarah Kemp	Australia	39	0.58	22.74
185	Ji Hyun Lee$_2$	Korea	45	0.58	26.15
186	Min Kyung Choi	Korea	49	0.58	28.45
187	Daniela Darquea	Ecuador	39	0.58	22.55
188	Katherine Perry	USA	35	0.57	20.06
189	Linnea Strom	Sweden	44	0.57	25.19
190	Eimi Koga	Japan	58	0.57	33.13
191	Su Ji Kim	Korea	55	0.57	31.29
192	Min Song Ha	Korea	57	0.57	32.33
193	Mind Muangkhumsakul	Thailand	34	0.56	19.69
194	Mayu Hamada	Japan	65	0.56	36.17
195	Paula Creamer	USA	38	0.55	20.85
196	Reika Usui	Japan	37	0.54	20.09
197	Mariah Stackhouse	USA	46	0.53	24.54
198	Seo Hyeon Youn	Korea	25	0.53	18.67
199	Na-Ri Lee	Korea	50	0.53	26.54
200	Brittany Lang	USA	43	0.53	22.81

Official World Golf Ranking
(As of December 29, 2019)

Ranking		Player	Country	Average Points	Total Points	No. of Events	2019 Points Lost	2019 Points Gained
1	(1)	Brooks Koepka	USA	10.429	427.61	41	-366.74	380.49
2	(8)	Rory McIlroy	NIR	9.350	467.52	50	-285.39	496.25
3	(6)	Jon Rahm	ESP	8.091	396.46	49	-300.57	374.47
4	(4)	Justin Thomas	USA	7.078	332.67	47	-357.99	312.68
5	(3)	Dustin Johnson	USA	6.923	290.78	42	-373.01	301.38
6	(13)	Tiger Woods	USA	6.578	263.12	40	-181.71	230.85
7	(18)	Patrick Cantlay	USA	6.280	276.35	44	-175.04	270.36
8	(2)	Justin Rose	ENG	6.122	287.74	47	-380.15	206.63
9	(10)	Xander Schauffele	USA	5.679	289.64	51	-259.20	263.54
10	(12)	Tommy Fleetwood	ENG	5.588	290.58	52	-251.75	260.48
11	(21)	Webb Simpson	USA	4.976	233.88	47	-195.59	206.39
12	(15)	Patrick Reed	USA	4.868	253.18	52	-222.79	220.28
13	(41)	Adam Scott	AUS	4.858	213.79	44	-118.87	219.38
14	(5)	Bryson DeChambeau	USA	4.709	244.88	52	-282.54	168.13
15	(22)	Paul Casey	ENG	4.601	230.08	50	-206.07	249.86
16	(9)	Tony Finau	USA	4.594	238.93	52	-224.74	177.64
17	(31)	Gary Woodland	USA	4.587	238.56	52	-173.58	238.40
18	(7)	Francesco Molinari	ITA	4.584	201.73	44	-258.44	160.35
19	(75)	Shane Lowry	IRL	4.370	222.87	51	-118.92	247.19
20	(25)	Louis Oosthuizen	RSA	4.194	197.15	47	-137.49	178.09
21	(28)	Hideki Matsuyama	JPN	4.118	214.15	52	-171.56	214.68
22	(185)	Bernd Wiesberger	AUT	4.061	162.47	40	-52.47	178.21
23	(11)	Rickie Fowler	USA	3.913	168.26	43	-248.91	166.41
24	(34)	Matt Kuchar	USA	3.862	200.84	52	-196.87	230.87
25	(39)	Matthew Fitzpatrick	ENG	3.712	193.03	52	-139.18	187.83
26	(26)	Henrik Stenson	SWE	3.468	156.08	45	-135.52	139.12
27	(48)	Kevin Na	USA	3.400	163.22	48	-114.42	151.64
28	(20)	Marc Leishman	AUS	3.291	164.59	50	-206.90	147.37
29	(81)	Danny Willett	ENG	3.200	166.43	52	-57.27	142.14
30	(44)	Matt Wallace	ENG	3.064	159.35	52	-124.23	150.46
31	(53)	Shugo Imahira	JPN	3.052	158.71	52	-87.10	132.94
32	(23)	Tyrrell Hatton	ENG	3.033	157.76	52	-159.93	133.65
33	(36)	Billy Horschel	USA	2.931	152.43	52	-120.97	120.48
34	(98)	Sungjae Im	KOR	2.930	152.36	52	-87.35	163.04
35	(38)	Kevin Kisner	USA	2.890	150.32	52	-152.68	157.07
36	(63)	Chez Reavie	USA	2.859	148.68	52	-116.27	165.09
37	(14)	Jason Day	AUS	2.806	115.07	41	-200.66	93.52
38	(56)	Abraham Ancer	MEX	2.759	143.48	52	-86.08	120.32
39	(24)	Sergio Garcia	ESP	2.720	136.04	50	-159.11	123.20
40	(123)	Jazz Janewattananond	THA	2.682	139.51	52	-71.94	143.54
41	(29)	Rafa Cabrera Bello	ESP	2.659	138.31	52	-162.65	121.40
42	(52)	Byeong Hun An	KOR	2.472	128.56	52	-104.36	112.22
43	(40)	Ian Poulter	ENG	2.442	127.03	52	-146.65	129.44
44	(17)	Jordan Spieth	USA	2.428	118.99	49	-214.96	113.53
45	(132)	Victor Perez	FRA	2.415	118.36	49	-42.63	99.23
46	(50)	Brandt Snedeker	USA	2.344	121.91	52	-90.47	109.10
47	(16)	Bubba Watson	USA	2.331	104.93	45	-181.08	76.34
48	(70)	Andrew Putnam	USA	2.325	118.62	51	-88.00	111.21
49	(141)	Erik van Rooyen	RSA	2.318	120.54	52	-62.73	121.73
50	(69)	Adam Hadwin	CAN	2.309	115.49	50	-95.07	111.83

( ) Ranking in brackets indicates position as of December 31, 2018.

OFFICIAL WORLD GOLF RANKING / 7

Ranking		Player	Country	Average Points	Total Points	No. of Events	2019 Points Lost	2019 Points Gained
51	(30)	Keegan Bradley	USA	2.265	117.78	52	-137.54	80.26
52	(35)	Eddie Pepperell	ENG	2.257	101.58	45	-112.68	75.79
53	(27)	Cameron Smith	AUS	2.230	115.99	52	-145.64	79.53
54	(77)	Tom Lewis	ENG	2.120	110.24	52	-65.82	91.91
55	(58)	Charles Howell	USA	2.103	109.36	52	-96.73	105.41
56	(71)	Shaun Norris	RSA	2.072	107.77	52	-71.86	84.22
57	(223)	Jim Furyk	USA	2.058	82.36	40	-48.38	99.25
58	(155)	Joaquin Niemann	CHI	2.058	96.74	47	-39.20	92.74
59	(62)	Lee Westwood	ENG	2.027	85.14	42	-71.32	64.45
60	(267)	Corey Conners	CAN	2.025	105.31	52	-45.26	116.53
61	(271)	Chan Kim	USA	2.003	80.12	40	-31.05	85.39
62	(129)	Jason Kokrak	USA	1.981	101.05	51	-73.90	110.76
63	(2006)	Brendon Todd	USA	1.965	78.63	40	-2.10	80.73
64	(247)	Robert MacIntyre	SCO	1.947	101.25	52	-26.55	99.81
65	(2006)	Collin Morikawa	USA	1.940	77.60	40	-8.83	86.44
66	(1589)	Scottie Scheffler	USA	1.937	77.52	40	-15.28	91.58
67	(121)	Mike Lorenzo-Vera	FRA	1.922	86.50	45	-55.54	82.50
68	(42)	Haotong Li	CHN	1.919	99.82	52	-128.51	88.97
69	(100)	C.T. Pan	TPE	1.917	99.73	52	-73.91	96.70
70	(32)	Phil Mickelson	USA	1.903	89.46	47	-156.70	92.79
71	(136)	Lucas Glover	USA	1.888	90.63	48	-61.23	96.79
72	(85)	Justin Harding	RSA	1.878	97.69	52	-82.33	95.99
73	(225)	Paul Waring	ENG	1.862	83.82	45	-39.70	85.12
74	(99)	Andrea Pavan	ITA	1.852	96.31	52	-56.37	78.41
75	(19)	Alex Noren	SWE	1.833	93.51	51	-166.99	53.43
75	(190)	Kurt Kitayama	USA	1.833	89.85	49	-33.15	84.36
77	(347)	J.T. Poston	USA	1.810	94.14	52	-38.00	106.44
78	(92)	Cameron Champ	USA	1.778	92.48	52	-42.08	72.12
79	(228)	Matthias Schwab	AUT	1.771	92.14	52	-31.52	86.52
80	(220)	Ryo Ishikawa	JPN	1.760	80.98	46	-32.61	72.30
81	(45)	Lucas Bjerregaard	DEN	1.752	91.13	52	-99.78	61.94
82	(72)	Thomas Pieters	BEL	1.737	90.34	52	-77.86	78.69
83	(154)	Marcus Kinhult	SWE	1.736	83.37	48	-48.78	78.50
84	(200)	Rory Sabbatini	SVK	1.689	87.83	52	-48.98	95.93
85	(111)	Joost Luiten	NED	1.686	67.44	40	-63.51	76.62
86	(203)	Sunghoon Kang	KOR	1.659	86.30	52	-62.53	103.86
87	(521)	C. Bezuidenhout	RSA	1.625	84.54	52	-22.63	90.49
88	(477)	Nate Lashley	USA	1.620	71.29	44	-27.27	80.92
89	(197)	Benjamin Hebert	FRA	1.614	80.73	50	-42.08	81.73
90	(94)	Danny Lee	NZL	1.607	83.56	52	-61.19	63.44
91	(78)	Ryan Palmer	USA	1.596	70.23	44	-63.23	57.52
92	(43)	Thorbjorn Olesen	DEN	1.578	63.13	40	-102.53	32.26
93	(1157)	Viktor Hovland	NOR	1.559	62.37	40	-9.31	68.52
94	(169)	Junggon Hwang	KOR	1.548	80.51	52	-43.97	70.97
95	(96)	J.B. Holmes	USA	1.539	72.34	47	-82.36	80.56
96	(80)	Ryan Moore	USA	1.535	69.09	45	-73.44	59.22
97	(61)	Siwoo Kim	KOR	1.521	79.12	52	-104.49	81.60
98	(150)	Keith Mitchell	USA	1.509	78.51	52	-69.28	89.96
99	(278)	Matt Jones	AUS	1.509	78.47	52	-34.91	81.25
100	(102)	Jorge Campillo	ESP	1.508	78.45	52	-76.98	80.92

( ) Ranking in brackets indicates position as of December 31, 2018.

8 / OFFICIAL WORLD GOLF RANKING

Ranking		Player	Country	Average Points	Total Points	No. of Events	2019 Points Lost	2019 Points Gained
101	(206)	Joel Dahmen	USA	1.489	77.44	52	-47.99	81.46
102	(76)	Dylan Frittelli	RSA	1.471	76.50	52	-88.89	68.81
103	(305)	Vaughn Taylor	USA	1.465	76.20	52	-37.62	84.53
104	(298)	Juan Sebastian Munoz	COL	1.455	75.69	52	-32.45	78.78
105	(37)	Kiradech Aphibarnrat	THA	1.441	74.96	52	-137.20	63.10
106	(164)	Rikuya Hoshino	JPN	1.438	74.78	52	-41.32	64.02
107	(47)	Emiliano Grillo	ARG	1.437	73.31	51	-99.27	46.43
108	(152)	Scott Piercy	USA	1.436	73.26	51	-54.27	75.46
109	(530)	Guido Migliozzi	ITA	1.431	61.56	43	-21.94	71.02
110	(68)	Russell Knox	SCO	1.422	73.99	52	-85.59	59.36
111	(192)	Romain Langasque	FRA	1.416	73.67	52	-35.61	62.64
112	(392)	Calum Hill	SCO	1.398	55.93	40	-15.16	53.25
113	(51)	Aaron Wise	USA	1.394	68.33	49	-88.50	44.91
114	(33)	Kyle Stanley	USA	1.391	72.37	52	-132.90	38.60
115	(135)	Adri Arnaus	ESP	1.378	71.68	52	-41.13	62.10
116	(414)	Adam Long	USA	1.369	71.24	52	-38.07	88.61
117		Matthew Wolff	USA	1.360	54.43	40	-7.43	61.86
118	(138)	Thomas Detry	BEL	1.350	70.24	52	-46.60	55.85
119	(395)	Lanto Griffin	USA	1.324	68.85	52	-25.90	72.02
120	(569)	Francesco Laporta	ITA	1.308	60.18	46	-12.44	58.91
121	(238)	Graeme McDowell	NIR	1.306	63.99	49	-44.00	69.48
122	(187)	Kevin Streelman	USA	1.298	67.50	52	-54.68	75.26
123	(54)	Brian Harman	USA	1.282	66.70	52	-112.27	65.53
124	(157)	Harold Varner	USA	1.281	66.62	52	-49.12	59.06
125	(172)	Martin Kaymer	GER	1.278	66.48	52	-52.16	67.48
126	(64)	Pat Perez	USA	1.275	58.68	46	-90.99	46.79
127	(49)	Branden Grace	RSA	1.271	66.10	52	-120.83	65.05
128	(89)	Kevin Tway	USA	1.265	65.81	52	-65.75	48.25
129	(153)	Scott Vincent	ZIM	1.263	65.71	52	-48.48	59.01
130	(843)	Max Homa	USA	1.262	65.67	52	-24.22	82.36
131	(442)	Zhang Xinjun	CHN	1.237	64.35	52	-28.92	72.37
132	(299)	Brian Stuard	USA	1.221	63.51	52	-37.86	70.54
133	(211)	Mikumu Horikawa	JPN	1.210	62.95	52	-26.19	51.53
134	(180)	Brad Kennedy	AUS	1.205	55.45	46	-38.06	51.60
135	(250)	Sebastian Soderberg	SWE	1.200	62.41	52	-27.10	57.47
136	(117)	Sanghyun Park	KOR	1.191	61.95	52	-53.21	48.37
137	(134)	Andy Sullivan	ENG	1.173	58.67	50	-52.52	49.56
138	(128)	Brendan Jones	AUS	1.171	49.22	42	-37.87	34.00
139	(410)	Harry Higgs	USA	1.170	55.03	47	-15.00	53.27
140	(186)	Troy Merritt	USA	1.168	58.43	50	-41.88	52.76
141	(109)	Mikko Korhonen	FIN	1.160	55.70	48	-53.68	45.16
142	(382)	Carlos Ortiz	MEX	1.132	58.90	52	-25.09	60.83
143	(57)	Luke List	USA	1.129	58.75	52	-95.46	45.16
144	(181)	Matthew Southgate	ENG	1.128	58.69	52	-40.76	51.29
145	(176)	Denny McCarthy	USA	1.121	58.33	52	-38.76	47.05
146	(137)	Joachim B. Hansen	DEN	1.105	57.48	52	-47.46	43.91
147	(168)	Jason Scrivener	AUS	1.103	57.36	52	-45.01	48.91
148	(91)	Ryan Fox	NZL	1.102	57.31	52	-73.67	49.36
149	(131)	Jordan L Smith	ENG	1.099	57.15	52	-55.47	48.63
150	(112)	Ryuko Tokimatsu	JPN	1.093	56.86	52	-57.32	43.75

( ) Ranking in brackets indicates position as of December 31, 2018.

OFFICIAL WORLD GOLF RANKING / 9

Ranking		Player	Country	Average Points	Total Points	No. of Events	2019 Points Lost	2019 Points Gained
151	(639)	Gunn Charoenkul	THA	1.080	56.21	52	-13.84	60.27
152	(198)	Andrew Johnston	ENG	1.067	42.70	40	-31.52	38.94
153	(391)	Kazuki Higa	JPN	1.066	51.17	48	-17.25	50.56
154	(125)	Jhonattan Vegas	VEN	1.046	53.35	51	-75.29	61.09
154	(60)	Daniel Berger	USA	1.046	47.08	45	-85.83	40.40
156	(1356)	Doc Redman	USA	1.035	41.41	40	-7.88	47.27
157	(2006)	Joohyung Kim	KOR	1.023	40.92	40	-4.13	45.06
158	(55)	Charley Hoffman	USA	1.017	51.87	51	-109.79	49.69
159	(478)	Robby Shelton	USA	1.014	52.73	52	-22.16	60.78
160	(218)	Pablo Larrazabal	ESP	0.994	48.72	49	-37.69	47.98
161	(364)	Wyndham Clark	USA	0.986	51.28	52	-25.02	57.58
162	(90)	Yuta Ikeda	JPN	0.975	50.71	52	-70.79	38.95
163	(2006)	Zack Sucher	USA	0.974	38.99	40	-7.83	46.81
164	(386)	Tyler Duncan	USA	0.962	50.06	52	-22.81	48.80
165	(202)	Hosung Tora San Choi	KOR	0.958	49.84	52	-27.02	34.20
166	(1169)	Kristoffer Ventura	NOR	0.958	38.33	40	-7.46	42.73
167	(276)	Richard Sterne	RSA	0.952	44.77	47	-38.70	53.77
168	(65)	Chesson Hadley	USA	0.944	49.12	52	-88.06	34.66
169	(222)	Bud Cauley	USA	0.944	38.72	41	-38.48	43.20
170	(118)	Aaron Rai	ENG	0.941	48.98	52	-50.07	28.13
171	(143)	Brian Gay	USA	0.940	48.89	52	-54.12	43.56
172	(212)	Masahiro Kawamura	JPN	0.937	48.75	52	-33.37	39.41
173	(199)	Joakim Lagergren	SWE	0.928	45.52	49	-31.78	36.10
174	(1240)	Matthew Jordan	ENG	0.923	36.92	40	-5.81	40.11
175	(234)	J.C. Ritchie	RSA	0.921	37.80	41	-36.28	42.68
176	(466)	Darius van Driel	NED	0.918	40.42	44	-14.48	39.49
177	(239)	Kalle Samooja	FIN	0.918	45.90	50	-25.03	39.63
178	(59)	Alexander Bjork	SWE	0.908	44.52	49	-80.69	20.09
179	(184)	Nicolas Colsaerts	BEL	0.897	46.65	52	-40.29	39.38
180	(559)	Antoine Rozner	FRA	0.894	46.53	52	-17.86	51.25
181	(139)	Nick Watney	USA	0.885	46.06	52	-47.34	34.86
182	(87)	Beau Hossler	USA	0.881	45.81	52	-67.67	30.40
183	(333)	Harris English	USA	0.879	45.75	52	-27.77	47.92
184	(84)	Julian Suri	USA	0.878	38.66	44	-71.57	26.12
185	(104)	Bronson Burgoon	USA	0.876	42.94	49	-39.10	25.98
186	(1051)	Mark Hubbard	USA	0.875	45.54	52	-12.30	52.99
187	(115)	Ryan Armour	USA	0.870	45.25	52	-60.91	36.51
188	(600)	Sebastian Heisele	GER	0.869	36.51	42	-14.85	37.51
189	(205)	George Coetzee	RSA	0.868	45.14	52	-44.45	45.28
190	(309)	Zander Lombard	RSA	0.861	44.80	52	-25.72	38.60
191	(46)	Satoshi Kodaira	JPN	0.860	44.76	52	-105.78	25.01
192	(2006)	Rasmus Hojgaard	DEN	0.858	34.33	40	-2.72	37.06
193	(67)	Adrian Otaegui	ESP	0.855	44.50	52	-79.79	23.96
194	(189)	David Lipsky	USA	0.854	44.44	52	-42.19	38.52
195	(105)	Brandon Stone	RSA	0.852	44.34	52	-47.79	19.65
196	(108)	John Catlin	USA	0.850	44.22	52	-47.44	25.54
197	(314)	Yikeun Chang	KOR	0.845	33.82	40	-18.98	30.38
198	(130)	Seungsu Han	USA	0.837	43.53	52	-53.68	36.51
199	(119)	Shota Akiyoshi	JPN	0.836	41.84	50	-39.47	28.18
200	(86)	Stewart Cink	USA	0.832	36.65	44	-63.12	15.91

( ) Ranking in brackets indicates position as of December 31, 2018.

World Golf Rankings 1968-2019

Year	No. 1	No. 2	No. 3	No. 4	No. 5
1968	Nicklaus	Palmer	Casper	Player	Charles
1969	Nicklaus	Player	Casper	Palmer	Charles
1970	Nicklaus	Player	Casper	Trevino	Charles
1971	Nicklaus	Trevino	Player	Palmer	Casper
1972	Nicklaus	Player	Trevino	Crampton	Palmer
1973	Nicklaus	Weiskopf	Trevino	Player	Crampton
1974	Nicklaus	Miller	Player	Weiskopf	Trevino
1975	Nicklaus	Miller	Weiskopf	Irwin	Player
1976	Nicklaus	Irwin	Miller	Player	Green
1977	Nicklaus	Watson	Green	Irwin	Crenshaw
1978	Watson	Nicklaus	Irwin	Green	Player
1979	Watson	Nicklaus	Irwin	Trevino	Player
1980	Watson	Trevino	Aoki	Crenshaw	Nicklaus
1981	Watson	Rogers	Aoki	Pate	Trevino
1982	Watson	Floyd	Ballesteros	Kite	Stadler
1983	Ballesteros	Watson	Floyd	Norman	Kite
1984	Ballesteros	Watson	Norman	Wadkins	Langer
1985	Ballesteros	Langer	Norman	Watson	Nakajima
1986	Norman	Langer	Ballesteros	Nakajima	Bean
1987	Norman	Ballesteros	Langer	Lyle	Strange
1988	Ballesteros	Norman	Lyle	Faldo	Strange
1989	Norman	Faldo	Ballesteros	Strange	Stewart
1990	Norman	Faldo	Olazabal	Woosnam	Stewart
1991	Woosnam	Faldo	Olazabal	Ballesteros	Norman
1992	Faldo	Couples	Woosnam	Olazabal	Norman
1993	Faldo	Norman	Langer	Price	Couples
1994	Price	Norman	Faldo	Langer	Olazabal
1995	Norman	Price	Langer	Els	Montgomerie
1996	Norman	Lehman	Montgomerie	Els	Couples
1997	Norman	Woods	Price	Els	Love
1998	Woods	O'Meara	Duval	Love	Els
1999	Woods	Duval	Montgomerie	Love	Els
2000	Woods	Els	Duval	Mickelson	Westwood
2001	Woods	Mickelson	Duval	Els	Love
2002	Woods	Mickelson	Els	Garcia	Goosen
2003	Woods	Singh	Els	Love	Furyk
2004	Singh	Woods	Els	Goosen	Mickelson
2005	Woods	Singh	Mickelson	Goosen	Els
2006	Woods	Furyk	Mickelson	Scott	Els
2007	Woods	Mickelson	Furyk	Els	Stricker
2008	Woods	Garcia	Mickelson	Harrington	Singh
2009	Woods	Mickelson	Stricker	Westwood	Harrington
2010	Westwood	Woods	Kaymer	Mickelson	Furyk
2011	Donald	Westwood	McIlroy	Kaymer	Scott
2012	McIlroy	Donald	Woods	Rose	Scott
2013	Woods	Scott	Stenson	Rose	Mickelson
2014	McIlroy	Stenson	Scott	B. Watson	Garcia
2015	Spieth	Day	McIlroy	B. Watson	Stenson
2016	Day	McIlroy	D. Johnson	Stenson	Spieth
2017	D. Johnson	Spieth	Thomas	Rahm	Matsuyama
2018	Koepka	Rose	D. Johnson	Thomas	DeChambeau
2019	Koepka	McIlroy	Rahm	Thomas	D. Johnson

(The World of Professional Golf 1968-1985; World Ranking 1986-2019)

OFFICIAL WORLD GOLF RANKING / 11

Year	No. 6	No. 7	No. 8	No. 9	No. 10
1968	Boros	Coles	Thomson	Beard	Nagle
1969	Beard	Archer	Trevino	Barber	Sikes
1970	Devlin	Coles	Jacklin	Beard	Huggett
1971	Barber	Crampton	Charles	Devlin	Weiskopf
1972	Jacklin	Weiskopf	Oosterhuis	Heard	Devlin
1973	Miller	Oosterhuis	Wadkins	Heard	Brewer
1974	M. Ozaki	Crampton	Irwin	Green	Heard
1975	Green	Trevino	Casper	Crampton	Watson
1976	Watson	Weiskopf	Marsh	Crenshaw	Geiberger
1977	Marsh	Player	Weiskopf	Floyd	Ballesteros
1978	Crenshaw	Marsh	Ballesteros	Trevino	Aoki
1979	Aoki	Green	Crenshaw	Ballesteros	Wadkins
1980	Pate	Ballesteros	Bean	Irwin	Player
1981	Ballesteros	Graham	Crenshaw	Floyd	Lietzke
1982	Pate	Nicklaus	Rogers	Aoki	Strange
1983	Nicklaus	Nakajima	Stadler	Aoki	Wadkins
1984	Faldo	Nakajima	Stadler	Kite	Peete
1985	Wadkins	O'Meara	Strange	Pavin	Sutton
1986	Tway	Sutton	Strange	Stewart	O'Meara
1987	Woosnam	Stewart	Wadkins	McNulty	Crenshaw
1988	Crenshaw	Woosnam	Frost	Azinger	Calcavecchia
1989	Kite	Olazabal	Calcavecchia	Woosnam	Azinger
1990	Azinger	Ballesteros	Kite	McNulty	Calcavecchia
1991	Couples	Langer	Stewart	Azinger	Davis
1992	Langer	Cook	Price	Azinger	Love
1993	Azinger	Woosnam	Kite	Love	Pavin
1994	Els	Couples	Montgomerie	M. Ozaki	Pavin
1995	Pavin	Faldo	Couples	M. Ozaki	Elkington
1996	Faldo	Mickelson	M. Ozaki	Love	O'Meara
1997	Mickelson	Montgomerie	M. Ozaki	Lehman	O'Meara
1998	Price	Montgomerie	Westwood	Singh	Mickelson
1999	Westwood	Singh	Price	Mickelson	O'Meara
2000	Montgomerie	Love	Sutton	Singh	Lehman
2001	Garcia	Toms	Singh	Clarke	Goosen
2002	Toms	Harrington	Singh	Love	Montgomerie
2003	Weir	Goosen	Harrington	Toms	Perry
2004	Harrington	Garcia	Weir	Love	Cink
2005	Garcia	Furyk	Montgomerie	Scott	DiMarco
2006	Goosen	Singh	Harrington	Donald	Ogilvy
2007	Rose	Scott	Harrington	Choi	Singh
2008	Karlsson	Villegas	Stenson	Els	Westwood
2009	Furyk	Casey	Stenson	McIlroy	Perry
2010	McDowell	Stricker	Casey	Donald	McIlroy
2011	Stricker	D. Johnson	Day	Schwartzel	W. Simpson
2012	Oosthuizen	Westwood	B. Watson	Dufner	Snedeker
2013	McIlroy	Kuchar	Stricker	Z. Johnson	Garcia
2014	Rose	Furyk	Day	Spieth	Fowler
2015	Fowler	Rose	D. Johnson	Furyk	Reed
2016	Matsuyama	Scott	Reed	Noren	B. Watson
2017	Rose	Fowler	Koepka	Stenson	Garcia
2018	Rahm	F. Molinari	McIlroy	Finau	Schauffele
2019	Woods	Cantlay	Rose	Schauffele	Fleetwood

Age Groups of Current Top 70 World Ranked Players

Under 25	25-28	29-32	33-36	37-40	Over 40
	3. Rahm				
	4. Thomas				
	7. Cantlay				
	9. Schauffele				
	10. Fleetwood				
	14. DeChambeau	1. Koepka			
	21. Matsuyama	2. McIlroy			
	25. Fitzpatrick	12. Reed	5. D. Johnson		
	31. Imahara	16. Finau	11. W. Simpson		
	32. Hatton	19. Lowry	17. Woodland		
	38. Ancer	23. Fowler	22. Weisberger	8. Rose	6. Woods
	42. B-H An	29. Willett	27. Na	13. Scott	15. Casey
34. Sunjae Im	44. Spieth	30. Wallace	28. Leishman	18. F. Molinari	24. Kuchar
40. Janewattananond	45. Perez	33. Horschel	35. Kisner	20. Oosthuizen	26. Stenson
58. Niemann	52. Pepperell	37. Day	41. Cabrera Bello	36. Reavie	43. Poulter
64. MacIntyre	53. C. Smith	48. Putnam	51. Bradley	39. Garcia	47. B. Watson
65. Morikawa	54. Lewis	49. van Rooyen	62. Kokrak	46. Snedeker	57. Furyk
66. Scheffler	60. Conners	50. Hadwin	63. Todd	55. Howell	59. Westwood
68. Haotong Li	69. C.T. Pan	61. Chan Kim	67. Lorenzo-Vera	56. Norris	70. Mickelson

2019 World Ranking Review

Major Movements

Upward

Name	Net Points Gained	Position 2018	Position 2019
Rory McIlroy	210	8	2
Shane Lowry	128	75	19
Bernd Wiesberger	125	185	22
Adam Scott	100	41	13
Patrick Cantlay	95	18	7
Danny Willett	84	81	29
Brendon Todd	78	2006	63
Collin Morikawa	77	2006	65
Scottie Scheffler	76	1589	66
Sungjae Im	75	98	34
Jon Rahm	74	6	3
Robert MacIntyre	73	247	64
Jazz Janewattananond	71	123	40
Corey Conners	71	267	60
J.T. Poston	68	347	77
Christiaan Bezuidenout	67	521	87
Gary Woodland	64	31	17
Viktor Hovland	59	1157	93
Eric van Rooyen	59	141	49
Victor Perez	56	132	45

Downward

Name	Net Points Lost	Position 2018	Position 2019
Justin Rose	173	2	8
Bryson DeChambeau	114	5	14
Alex Noren	113	19	75
Jason Day	107	14	37
Bubba Watson	104	16	47
Jordon Spieth	101	17	44
Francesco Molinari	98	7	18
Kyle Stanley	94	33	114
Rickie Fowler	82	11	23
Satoshi Kodaira	80	46	191

World's Winners of 2019

U.S. PGA TOUR

Sentry Tournament of Champions	Xander Schauffele
Sony Open in Hawaii	Matt Kuchar
Desert Classic	Adam Long
Farmers Insurance Open	Justin Rose
Waste Management Phoenix Open	Rickie Fowler
AT&T Pebble Beach Pro-Am	Phil Mickelson
Genesis Open	J.B. Holmes
WGC - Mexico Championship	Dustin Johnson (2)
Puerto Rico Open	Martin Trainer
Honda Classic	Keith Mitchell
Arnold Palmer Invitational	Francesco Molinari
The Players Championship	Rory McIlroy
Valspar Championship	Paul Casey
WGC - Dell Technologies Match Play	Kevin Kisner
Corales Puntacana Resort & Club Championship	Graeme McDowell
Valero Texas Open	Corey Conners
Masters Tournament	Tiger Woods
RBC Heritage	C.T. Pan
Zurich Classic of New Orleans	Ryan Palmer/Jon Rahm
Wells Fargo Championship	Max Homa
AT&T Byron Nelson	Sung Kang
PGA Championship	Brooks Koepka
Charles Schwab Challenge	Kevin Na
Memorial Tournament	Patrick Cantlay
RBC Canadian Open	Rory McIlroy (2)
U.S. Open Championship	Gary Woodland
Travelers Championship	Chez Reavie
Rocket Mortgage Classic	Nate Lashley
3M Open	Matthew Wolff
John Deere Classic	Dylan Frittelli
Barbasol Championship	Jim Herman
WGC - FedEx St. Jude Invitational	Brooks Koepka (2)
Barracuda Championship	Collin Morikawa
Wyndham Championship	J.T. Poston

PGA TOUR PLAYOFFS FOR THE FEDEXCUP

The Northern Trust	Patrick Reed
BMW Championship	Justin Thomas
Tour Championship	Rory McIlroy (3)

START OF 2019-2020 SEASON

A Military Tribute at The Greenbrier	Joaquin Niemann
Sanderson Farms Championship	Sebastian Munoz
Safeway Open	Cameron Champ
Shriners Hospitals for Children Open	Kevin Na (2)
Houston Open	Lanto Griffin (2)
The CJ Cup @ Nine Bridges	Justin Thomas (2)
WGC - HSBC Champions	Rory McIlroy (4)
Bermuda Championship	Brendon Todd
Mayakoba Golf Classic	Brendon Todd (2)
The RSM Classic	Tyler Duncan

SPECIAL EVENTS

CVS Health Charity Classic	Brooke M. Henderson (3)/ Keegan Bradley/Billy Andrade
TaylorMade Pebble Beach Invitational	Kevin Sutherland (3)
Hero World Challenge	Henrik Stenson
PNC Father Son Challenge	Bernhard Langer (3)/Jason Langer
The Presidents Cup	United States
QBE Shootou	Kevin Tway/Rory Sabbatini

KORN FERRY TOUR

Bahamas Great Exuma Classic	Zecheng Dou
Bahamas Great Abaco Classic	Rafael Campos
Country Club de Bogota Championship	Mark Anderson
Panama Championship	Michael Gligic
LECOM Suncoast Classic	Mark Hubbard
Chitimacha Louisiana Open	Vince Covello
Savannah Golf Championship	Dan McCarthy
Robert Trent Jones Golf Trail Championship	Lanto Griffin
Dormie Network Classic	Xinjun Zhang
Nashville Golf Open	Robby Shelton
KC Golf Classic	Michael Gellerman
Knoxville Open	Robby Shelton (2)
Evans Scholars Invitational	Scottie Scheffler
Rex Hospital Open	Sebastian Cappelen
BMW Charity Pro-Am	Rhein Gibson
Lincoln Land Championship	Xinjun Zhang (2)
Wichita Open Supporting Wichita's Youth	Henrik Norlander
Utah Championship	Kristoffer Ventura
LECOM Health Challenge	Ryan Brehm
TPC Colorado Championship at Heron Lakes	Nelson Ledesma
Pinnacle Bank Championship	Kristoffer Ventura (2)
Price Cutter Charity Championship	Harry Higgs
Ellie Mae Classic	Zac Blair
WinCo Foods Portland Open	Bo Hoag

KORN FERRY TOUR FINALS

Nationwide Children's Hospital Championship	Scottie Scheffler (2)
Albertsons Boise Open	Matthew NeSmith
Korn Ferry Tour Championship	Tom Lewis

MACKENZIE TOUR–PGA TOUR CANADA

Canada Life Open	Jake Knapp
Bayview Place DCBank Open	Paul Barjon
GolfBC Championship	Jake Knapp (2)
Lethbridge Paradise Canyon Open	Alex Chiarella
Windsor Championship	Dawson Armstrong
Osprey Valley Open	Paul Barjon (2)
HFX Pro-Am	Lorens Chan
1932byBateman Open	Taylor Pendrith
ATB Financial Classic	Hayden Buckley
Players Cup	Derek Barron
Mackenzie Investments Open	Taylor Pendrith (2)
Canada Life Championship	Patrick Fishburn

PGA TOUR LATINOAMERICA

Buenaventura Classic	Jared Wolfe
Molino Canuelas Championship	Andres Echavarria
Abierto de Chile	John Somers
Abierto OSDE del Centro	Tom Whitney

Puerto Plata Open	Cristobal Del Solar
BMW Jamaica Classic	Evan Harmeling
Abierto Mexicano de Golf	Drew Nesbitt
Bupa Match Play	Patrick Flavin
Sao Paulo Golf Club Championship	Chandler Blanchet
JHSF Aberto do Brasil	Shad Tuten
Banco del Pacifico Open	Augusto Nunez
Diners Club Peru Open	Leandro Marelli
Termas de Rio Hondo Invitational	Alejandro Tosti
Neuqeun Argentina Classic	Puma Dominguez
VISA Open de Argentina	Ricardo Celia
Shell Championship	Augusto Nunez (2)

EUROPEAN TOUR

Abu Dhabi HSBC Championship	Shane Lowry
Omega Dubai Desert Classic	Bryson DeChambeau
Saudi International	Dustin Johnson
Oman Open	Kurt Kitayama
Commercial Bank Qatar Masters	Justin Harding
Magical Kenya Open	Guido Migliozzi
Trophee Hassan II	Jorge Campillo
Betfred British Masters	Marcus Kinhult
Made in Denmark	Bernd Wiesberger
Belgian Knockou	Guido Migliozzi (2)
GolfSixes Cascais	Thailand (Thongchai Jaidee/ Phachara Khongwhatmai)
BMW International Open	Andrea Pavan
Estrella Damm N.A. Andalucia Masters	Christiaan Bezuidenhout
Dubai Duty Free Irish Open	Jon Rahm (2)
Aberdeen Standard Investments Scottish Open	Bernd Wiesberger (2)
The 148th Open Championship	Shane Lowry (2)
D+D Real Czech Masters	Thomas Pieters
Scandinavian Invitation	Erik van Rooyen
Omega European Masters	Sebastian Soderberg
Porsche European Open	Paul Casey (2)
KLM Open	Sergio Garcia
BMW PGA Championship	Danny Willett
Alfred Dunhill Links Championship	Victor Perez
Mutuactivos Open de Espana	Jon Rahm (3)
Italian Open	Bernd Wiesberger (3)
Amundi Open de France	Nicolas Colsaerts
Portugal Masters	Steven Brown
Turkish Airlines Open	Tyrrell Hatton
DP World Tour Championship, Dubai	Jon Rahm (4)

CHALLENGE TOUR

Turkish Airlines Challenge	Connor Syme
Challenge de Espana	Antoine Rozner
Prague Golf Challenge	Antoine Rozner (2)
D+D Real Czech Challenge	Ross McGowan
Swiss Challenge	Ricardo Santos
Hauts de France - Pas de Calais Golf Open	Robin Roussel
Andalucía - Costa del Sol Match Play 9	Eirik Tage Johansen
Italian Challenge Open Eneos Motor Oil	Matthew Jordan
D+D Real Slovakia Challenge	Rhys Enoch
Le Vaudreuil Golf Challenge	Steven Tiley
Euram Bank Open	Calum Hill
Vierumaki Finnish Challenge	Jose-Filipe Lima
Made in Denmark Challenge	Calum Hill (2)

16 / WORLD'S WINNERS OF 2019

ISPS Handa World Invitational	Jack Senior
Rolex Trophy	Darius van Driel
KPMG Trophy	Dale Whitnell
Open de Bretagne	Sebastian Heisele
Open de Portugal	Adrian Meronk
Hopps Open de Provence	Lars van Meijel
Lalla Aicha Challenge Tour	Oliver Farr
Stone Irish Challenge	Emilio Cuartero Blanco
Challenge Tour Grand Final	Francesco Laporta (2)

ASIAN TOUR

SMBC Singapore Open	Jazz Janewattananond
Maybank Championship	Scott Hend
Hero Indian Open	Stephen Gallacher
Bangabandhu Cup Golf Open	Sadom Kaewkanjana
Volvo China Open	Mikko Korhonen
GS Caltex Maekyung Open	Tae Hee Lee
Kolon Korea Open	Jazz Janewattananond (2)
Sarawak Championship	Andrew Dodt
Bank BRI Indonesia Open	Miguel Carballo
Yeangder Tournament Players Championship	Yikeun Chang
Classic Golf & Country Club International	Rory Hie
Shinhan Donghae Open	Jbe' Kruger
Mercuries Taiwan Masters	Suradit Yongcharoenchai
Thailand Open	John Catlin
Panasonic Open India	Joohyung Kim
Sabah Masters	Pavit Tangkamolprasert
BNI Indonesian Masters	Jazz Janewattananond (3)
Thailand Masters	Jazz Janewattananond (4)

PGA TOUR SERIES-CHINA

Chongqing Championship	Taihei Sato
Sanya Championship	Trevor Sluman
Haikou Championship	David Kocher
Beijing Championship	Richard Jung
Qinhuangdao Championship	Luke Kwon
Nantong Championship	Kevin Techakanokboon
Suzhou Open	Cyril Bouniol
Huangshan Championship	Zhengkai Bai
Guangzhou Open	Max McGreevy
Dongguan Open	Joey Lane
Haikou Classic	Quincy Quek
Zhuzhou Classic	Motin Yeung
Macau Championship	Justin Shin

CHINA GOLF ASSOCIATION TOUR

Bo Ao Open	Maverick Antcliff
Shenzhou Peninsula Open	Maverick Antcliff (2)
Wuhan Optics Valley Open	Woojin Jung
Lushan Open	Shun Yat Hak
Beijing Open	Maverick Antcliff (3)
Tianjin Binhai Forest Open	Nicolas Paez
Huangshan Open	Kieran Muir
Hangzhou International Championship	Haimeng Chao
Hunan Taohuayuan Open	Huilin Zhang
Hainan Open	Francesco Laporta
Foshan Open	Zhengkai Bai (2)
China Tour Championship	Suteepat Prateeptienchai

JAPAN TOUR

Token Homemate Cup	Brendan Jones
The Crowns	Katsumasa Miyamoto
Asia-Pacific Diamond Cup	Yosuke Asaji
Kansai Open	Tomoharu Otsuki
Gateway to The Open Mizuno Open	Yuta Ikeda
Japan Golf Tour Championship	Mikumu Horikawa
Dunlop Srixon Fukushima Open	Rikuya Hoshino
Japan PGA Championship	Ryo Ishikawa
Shigeo Nagashima Invitational	Ryo Ishikawa (2)
RIZAP KBC Augusta	Kazuki Higa
Fujisankei Classic	Sanghyun Park
ANA Open	Yosuke Asaji (2)
Panasonic Open	Toshinori Muto
Tokai Classic	Shaun Norris
Bridgestone Open	Shugo Imahira
Japan Open Championship	Chan Kim
Zozo Championship	Tiger Woods (2)
Mynavi ABC Championship	Junggon Hwang
Heiwa PGM Championship	Hosung Choi
Mitsui Sumitomo VISA Taiheiyo Masters	Takumi Kanaya [A]
Dunlop Phoenix	Shugo Imahira (2)
Casio World Open	Kyungtae Kim
Golf Nippon Series JT Cup	Ryo Ishikawa (3)

ISPS HANDA PGA TOUR OF AUSTRALASIA

ISPS Handa Vic Open	David Law
ISPS Handa World Super 6 Perth	Ryan Fox
Coca-Cola Queensland PGA Championship	Daniel Nisbet
100th New Zealand Open	Zach Murray
SEC New Zealand PGA Championship	Kazuma Kobori [A]
SP PNG Golf Open	Peter Cooke
Tailor-made Building Services NT PGA	Brett Rankin
TX Civil & Logistics WA PGA Championship	Darren Beck
Victorian PGA Championship	Campbell Rawson
Gippsland Super 6	Tom Power Horan
AVJennings NSW Open	Josh Younger
Emirates Australian Open	Matt Jones
Australian PGA Championship	Adam Scott

AFRICAN SUNSHINE TOUR

Eye of Africa PGA Championship	Louis de Jager
RAM Cape Town Open	Benjamin Follett-Smith
Dimension Data Pro-Am	Philip Eriksson
Team Championship	Jaco Prinsloo/J.C. Ritchie
Limpopo Championship	J.C. Ritchie (2)
Sunshine Tour Championship	Jean-Paul Strydom
Mopani Redpath Greendoor Logistics Zambia	Daniel van Tonder
Zanaco Masters	J.C. Ritchie (3)
Investec Royal Swazi Open	Martin Rohwer
Lombard Insurance Classic	Jake Redman
Sun City Challenge	Garrick Higgo
KBC Karen Masters	Toto Thimba
Royal Swazi Spa Challenge	Ruan Conradie
Vodacom Origins of Golf - Sishen	Ockie Strydom
King's Cup	Jaco Ahlers
Vodacom Origins of Golf - Humewood	Merrick Bremner
Vodacom Origins of Golf - Stellenbosch	Thriston Lawrence
Sun Wild Coast Sun Challenge	Jean Hugo

Vodacom Origins of Golf - Selborne	Jaco Ahlers (2)
Sibaya Challenge	Hennie Otto
Vodacom Origins of Golf Final	George Coetzee
Nedbank Golf Challenge	Tommy Fleetwood
Alfred Dunhill Championship	Pablo Larrazabal
AfrAsia Bank Mauritius Open	Rasmus Hojgaard

U.S. LPGA TOUR

Diamond Resorts Tournament of Champions	Eun-Hee Ji
Honda LPGA Thailand	Amy Yang
HSBC Women's World Championship	Sung Hyun Park
Bank of Hope Founders Cup	Jin Young Ko
Kia Classic	Nasa Hataoka
ANA Inspiration	Jin Young Ko (2)
Lotte Championship	Brooke M. Henderson
Hugel-Air Premia LA Open	Minjee Lee
LPGA Mediheal Championship	Sei Young Kim
Pure Silk Championship	Bronte Law
U.S. Women's Open Championship	Jeongeun Lee$_6$
ShopRite LPGA Classic	Lexi Thompson
Meijer LPGA Classic for Simply Give	Brooke M. Henderson (2)
KPMG Women's PGA Championship	Hannah Green
Walmart NW Arkansas Championship	Sung Hyun Park (2)
Thornberry Creek LPGA Classic	Shanshan Feng
Marathon Classic	Sei Young Kim (2)
Dow Great Lakes Bay Invitational	Cydney Clanton/ Jasmine Suwannapura
CP Women's Open	Jin Young Ko (4)
Cambia Portland Classic	Hannah Green (2)
Indy Women in Tech Championship	Mi Jung Hur (2)
Volunteers of America Classic	Cheyenne Knight
Buick LPGA Shanghai	Danielle Kang
Taiwan Swinging Skirts LPGA	Nelly Korda (3)
CME Group Tour Championship	Sei Young Kim (3)

LADIES EUROPEAN TOUR

Fatima Bint Mubarak Ladies Open	Charley Hull
Investec South African Women's Open	Diksha Dagar
Jordan Mixed Open	Daan Huizing
Lalla Meryem Cup	Nuria Iturrios
Omega Dubai Moonlight Classic	Nuria Iturrios (2)
La Reserva de Sotogrande Invitational	Celine Herbin
Jabra Ladies Open	Annabel Dimmock
Ladies European Thailand Championship	Atthaya Thitikul [A]
Evian Championship	Jin Young Ko (3)
AIG Women's British Open	Hinako Shibuno (3)
Aberdeen Standard Investments Scottish Open	Mi Jung Hur
Tipsport Czech Ladies Open	Carly Booth
The Solheim Cup	Europe
Lacoste Ladies Open de France	Nelly Korda (2)
Estrella Damm Mediterranean Ladies Open	Carlota Ciganda
Hero Women's Indian Open	Christine Wolf
Andalucia Costa del Sol Open de Espana	Anne van Dam (2)
Magical Kenya Ladies Open	Esther Henseleit

JAPAN LPGA TOUR

Daikin Orchid Ladies	Mamiko Higa
Yokohama Tire PRGR Ladies Cup	Ai Suzuki
T-Point Eneos Ladies	Momoko Ueda
AXA Ladies	Yui Kawamoto
Yamaha Ladies Open	Misuzu Narita
Studio Alice Ladies Open	Jiyai Shin
Vantelin Ladies Open KKT Cup	Ji-Hee Lee
Fujisankei Ladies Classic	Jiyai Shin (2)
Panasonic Open Ladies	Minami Katsu
World Ladies Championship Salonpas Cup	Hinako Shibuno
Hoken no Madoguchi Ladies	Min-Young Lee
Chukyo TV Bridgestone Ladies Open	Minami Katsu (2)
Resort Trust Ladies	Erika Hara
Yonex Ladies	Momoko Ueda (2)
Ai Miyazato Suntory Ladies Open	Ai Suzuki (2)
Nichirei Ladies	Ai Suzuki (3)
Earth Mondahmin Cup	Jiyai Shin (3)
Shiseido Anessa Ladies Open	Hinako Shibuno (2)
Nippon Ham Ladies Classic	S. Langkul
Samantha Thavasa Girls Collection Ladies	Sakura Koiwai
Century 21 Ladies	Mone Inami
Daito Kentaku Eheyanet Ladies	Misuzu Narita (2)
Hokkaido Meiji Cup	Seonwoo Bae
NEC Karuizawa 72	Lala Anai
CAT Ladies	Saki Asai
Nitori Ladies	Ai Suzuki (4)
Golf 5 Ladies	Min-Young Lee (2)
Japan LPGA Championship Konica Minolta Cup	Nasa Hataoka (2)
Descente Ladies Tokai Classic	Hinako Shibuno (4)
Miyagi TV Cup Dunlop Ladies Open	Asuka Kashiwabara
Japan Women's Open Championship	Nasa Hataoka (3)
Stanley Ladies	Ah-Reum Hwang
Fujitsu Ladies	Ayaka Furue (A)
Nobuta Group Masters Golf Club Ladies	Asuka Kashiwabara (2)
Mitsubishi Electric/Hisako Higuchi Ladies	Ai Suzuki (5)
Toto Japan Classic	Ai Suzuki (6)
Itoen Ladies	Ai Suzuki (7)
Daio Paper Elleair Ladies Open	Hinako Shibuno (5)
Japan LPGA Tour Championship Ricoh Cup	Seonwoo Bae (2)

KOREA LPGA TOUR

Taiwan Women's Golf Open	Mi Jeong Jeon
Lotte Rent a Car Ladies Open	Ayean Cho
Celltrion Queens Masters	Jeongmin Cho
Nexen Saint Nine Masters	Seong Yeoun Lee
CreaS F&C KLPGA Championship	Hye Jin Choi
Kyochon Honey Ladies Open	So Yeon Park
NH Investment & Securities Championship	Hye Jin Choi (2)
Doosan Match Play Championship	Ji Hyun Kim
E1 Charity Open	Eun Bin Lim
Lotte Cantata Ladies Open	Bo Ah Kim
S-Oil Championship	Hye Jin Choi (3)
Kia Motors Korea Women's Open	Da Yeon Lee
BC Card HanKyung Ladies Cup	Jeongmin Cho (2)
McCol Youngpyong Resort Open	Hye Jin Choi (4)
Asiana Airlines Open	Da Yeon Lee (2)
MY Moonyoung Queens Park Championship	A Lim Kim
Jeju Samdasoo Masters	Hae Ran Ryu

Bogner MBN Ladies Open	Min Ji Park
High1 Resort Ladies Open	HeeJeong Lim
Hanwha Classic	Chae Yoon Park
KG-Edaily Ladies Open	Gyo Rin Park
All for You. Renoma Championship	HeeJeong Lim (2)
OKSavingsBank Se Ri Pak Invitational	Ayean Cho (2)
Hana Financial Group Championship	Ha Na Jang
Hite Jinro Championship	Jin Young Ko (5)
KB Financial Group Star Championship	HeeJeong Lim (3)
BMW Ladies Championship	Ha Na Jang (2)
SK Networks Seokyung Ladies Classic	Hye Jin Choi (5)
ADT CAPS Championship	Song Yi Ahn
Hyosung Championship	Da Yeon Lee (3)

AUSTRALIAN LADIES TOUR

Ballarat Icons ALPG Pro-Am	Marianne Skarpnord
ISPS Handa Vic Open	Celine Boutier
ISPS Handa Women's Australian Open	Nelly Korda
Pacific Bay Resort Australian Ladies Classic	Marianne Skarpnord (2)
ActewAGL Canberra Classic	Anne van Dam
Worrells NSW Women's Open	Meghan MacLaren
Sheraton Deva New Caledonia International	Brooke Baker
Trust Golf Thailand LPGA Masters	Weiwei Zhang
NZ PGW Pro-Am in Memory of Anita Boon	Breanna Gill

CHAMPIONS TOUR

Mitsubishi Electric Championship	Tom Lehman
Oasis Championship	Bernhard Langer
Chubb Classic	Miguel Angel Jimenez
Cologuard Classic	Mark O'Meara
Hoag Classic	Kirk Triplett
Rapiscan Systems Classic	Kevin Sutherland
Mitsubishi Electric Classic	Scott McCarron
Bass Pro Shops Legends of Golf	Scott Hoch/Tom Pernice, Jr.
Insperity Invitational	Scott McCarron (2)
Regions Tradition	Steve Stricker
KitchenAid Senior PGA Championship	Ken Tanigawa
Principal Charity Classic	Kevin Sutherland (2)
Mastercard Japan Championship	Scott McCarron (3)
American Family Insurance Championship	Jerry Kelly
U.S. Senior Open Championship	Steve Stricker (2)
Bridgestone Senior Players Championship	Retief Goosen
Dick's Sporting Goods Open	Doug Barron
Boeing Classic	Brandt Jobe
Shaw Charity Classic	Wes Short, Jr.
Ally Challenge	Jerry Kelly (2)
Sanford International	Rocco Mediate
PURE Insurance Championship	Kirk Triplett (2)
SAS Championship	Jerry Kelly (3)
Dominion Energy Charity Classic	Miguel Angel Jimenez (2)
Invesco QQQ Championship	Colin Montgomerie
Charles Schwab Cup Championship	Jeff Maggert

STAYSURE TOUR

Senior Italian Open	Barry Lane
Senior Open Hauts de France	Peter Baker
Farmfoods European Legends Championship	Jean-Francois Remesy
Swiss Seniors Open	Jose Coceres
European Tour Destinations Senior Classic	Jose Manuel Carriles
WINSTONgolf Senior Open	Clark Dennis
The Senior Open Championship	Bernhard Langer (2)
Staysure PGA Seniors Championship	Phillip Price
Scottish Senior Open	Paul Lawrie
The Sinclair Invitational	David Shacklady
Paris Legends Championship	David Shacklady (2)
Murhof Legends – Austrian Senior Open	Jose Coceres (2)
Farmfoods European Senior Masters	Thomas Levet
MCB Tour Championship - Madagascar	Barry Lane (2)
MCB Tour Championship - Seychelles	Peter Fowler
MCB Tour Championship - Mauritius	Jarmo Sandelin

JAPAN PGA SENIOR TOUR

Kanehide Senior Okinawa Open	Taichi Teshima
Nojima Champion Cup Hakone Senior	Shinichi Akiba
Fubon Yeangder Senior Cup	Eiji Mizoguchi
Sumaiida Cup	Masayoshi Yamazoe
Starts Senior	Masahiro Kuramoto
Kumamoto Aso Senior Open	Gregory Meyer
Fancl Classic	Prayad Marksaeng
Hiroshima Senior	Shinsuke Yanagisawa
Maruhan Cup Taiheiyo Club Senior	Prayad Marksaeng (2)
Komatsu Open	Thaworn Wiratchant
Japan Senior Open Championship	Toru Taniguchi
Seven Hills Cup KBC Senior Open	Akira Teranishi
Japan PGA Senior Championship	Hidezumi Shirakata
Trust Group Cup Sasebo Senior Open	Shinichi Akiba (2)
Fukuoka Senior Open	Toshimitsu Izawa
Fujifilm Senior Championship	Thaworn Wiratchant (2)
Elite Grip Senior Open	Eiji Mizoguchi (2)
ISPS Handa Cup Philanthropy Senior	Suk Joug Yul

Multiple Winners of 2019

PLAYER	WINS	PLAYER	WINS	PLAYER	WINS
Ai Suzuki	7	Jaco Ahlers	2	Min-Young Lee	2
		Shinichi Akiba	2	Shane Lowry	2
Hye Jin Choi	5	Yosuke Asaji	2	Prayad Marksaeng	2
Jin Young Ko	5	Seonwoo Bae	2	Guido Migliozzi	2
Hinako Shibuno	5	Zhengkai Bai	2	Eiji Mizoguchi	2
		Paul Barjon	2	Kevin Na	2
Jazz Janewattananond	4	Paul Casey	2	Misuzu Narita	2
Rory McIlroy	4	Ayean Cho	2	Augusto Nunez	2
Jon Rahm	4	Jeongmin Cho	2	Sung Hyun Park	2
		Jose Coceres	2	Taylor Pendrith	2
Maverick Antcliff	3	Hannah Green	2	Antoine Rozner	2
Nasa Hataoka	3	Lanto Griffin	2	Scottie Scheffler	2
Brooke M. Henderson	3	Calum Hill	2	David Shacklady	2
Ryo Ishikawa	3	Mi Jung Hur	2	Robby Shelton	2
Jerry Kelly	3	Shugo Imahira	2	Marianne Skarpnord	2
Sei Young Kim	3	Nuria Iturrios	2	Steve Stricker	2
Nelly Korda	3	Ha Na Jang	2	Justin Thomas	2
Bernhard Langer	3	Miguel Angel Jimenez	2	Brendon Todd	2
Da Yeon Lee	3	Dustin Johnson	2	Kirk Triplett	2
HeeJeong Lim	3	Asuka Kashiwabara	2	Momoko Ueda	2
Scott McCarron	3	Minami Katsu	2	Anne van Dam	2
J.C. Ritchie	3	Jake Knapp	2	Kristoffer Ventura	2
Jiyai Shin	3	Brooks Koepka	2	Thaworn Wiratchant	2
Kevin Sutherland	3	Barry Lane	2	Tiger Woods	2
Bernd Wiesberger	3	Francesco Laporta	2	Xinjun Zhang	2

World Money List

This list of the 400 leading money winners in the world of professional golf in 2019 was compiled from the results of men's (excluding seniors) tournaments carried in the Appendixes of this edition. This list includes tournaments with a minimum of 36 holes and four contestants and does not include such competitions as pro-ams and skins or skills contests. It does not include annual performance bonuses such as for the FedExCup (U.S.) and the Race to Dubai (Europe).

In the 54 years during which World Money Lists have been compiled, the earnings of the player in the 200th position have risen from a total of $3,326 in 1966 to $745,082 in 2019. The top 200 players in 1966 earned a total of $4,680,287. In 2019, the comparable total was $561,760,418.

The World Money List includes the official money lists of the U.S. PGA Tour, PGA European Tour, PGA Tour of Japan, Asian Tour, PGA Tour–China, China Golf Association Tour, African Sunshine Tour, PGA Tour of Australasia, PGA Tour Latinoamerica and Mackenzie Tour–PGA Tour Canada, along with winnings in established unofficial tournaments when reliable figures could be obtained. The conversion rates used for 2019 were: Euro = US$1.12; Japanese yen = US$0.009; South African rand = US$0.07; Australian dollar = US$0.70; Canadian dollar = US$0.75.

POS.	PLAYER, COUNTRY	TOTAL MONEY
1	Rory McIlroy, N. Ireland	$10,820,759
2	Jon Rahm, Spain	10,764,829
3	Brooks Koepka, USA	8,013,993
4	Tommy Fleetwood, England	7,783,429
5	Justin Thomas, USA	7,178,639
6	Dustin Johnson, USA	6,117,123
7	Patrick Cantlay, USA	5,968,695
8	Gary Woodland, USA	5,306,605
9	Matt Kuchar, USA	5,296,904
10	Xander Schauffele, USA	5,291,136
11	Shane Lowry, Ireland	5,266,758
12	Webb Simpson, USA	5,215,597
13	Tiger Woods, USA	5,129,615
14	Hideki Matsuyama, Japan	5,006,738
15	Paul Casey, England	4,658,727
16	Patrick Reed, USA	4,487,455
17	Justin Rose, England	4,482,995
18	Bernd Wiesberger, Austria	4,469,961
19	Adam Scott, Australia	4,246,127
20	Tyrrell Hatton, England	4,074,647
21	Sungjae Im, Korea	4,038,660
22	Matthew Fitzpatrick, England	4,032,592
23	Kevin Kisner, USA	3,743,258
24	Francesco Molinari, Italy	3,708,887
25	Rickie Fowler, USA	3,673,477
26	Kevin Na, USA	3,614,883
27	Tony Finau, USA	3,606,462
28	Chez Reavie, USA	3,557,295
29	Louis Oosthuizen, South Africa	3,505,502

WORLD MONEY LIST

POS.	PLAYER, COUNTRY	TOTAL MONEY
30	Corey Conners, Canada	3,251,011
31	Billy Horschel, USA	3,227,525
32	Bryson DeChambeau, USA	3,077,219
33	J.T. Poston, USA	3,076,146
34	Matt Wallace, England	3,061,002
35	Byeong Hun An, Korea	3,054,833
36	Rory Sabbatini, South Africa	3,051,290
37	Henrik Stenson, Sweden	3,032,879
38	Marc Leishman, Australia	3,009,517
39	Sung Kang, Korea	2,957,843
40	Ian Poulter, England	2,949,029
41	Sebastian Munoz, Colombia	2,935,633
42	Danny Willett, England	2,887,754
43	Joaquin Niemann, Chile	2,816,954
44	Sergio Garcia, Spain	2,799,523
45	Abraham Ancer, Mexico	2,787,191
46	Jason Kokrak, USA	2,783,590
47	Adam Hadwin, Canada	2,692,358
48	Ryan Palmer, USA	2,690,714
49	Brendon Todd, USA	2,675,893
50	Jim Furyk, USA	2,644,998
51	Rafa Cabrera Bello, Spain	2,593,378
52	Charles Howell, USA	2,569,884
53	Jordan Spieth, USA	2,567,907
54	Brandt Snedeker, USA	2,557,940
55	Phil Mickelson, USA	2,507,155
56	Adam Long, USA	2,495,404
57	Keith Mitchell, USA	2,427,612
58	Lucas Glover, USA	2,420,608
59	Erik van Rooyen, South Africa	2,395,799
60	Vaughn Taylor, USA	2,384,030
61	Nate Lashley, USA	2,370,972
62	Andrew Putnam, USA	2,339,623
63	Jason Day, Australia	2,270,885
64	Joel Dahmen, USA	2,270,873
65	Dylan Frittelli, South Africa	2,258,513
66	C.T. Pan, Chinese Taipei	2,250,487
67	Robert MacIntyre, Scotland	2,213,711
68	Max Homa, USA	2,176,767
69	Lanto Griffin, USA	2,157,111
70	Collin Morikawa, USA	2,083,948
71	Scott Piercy, USA	2,066,401
72	Marcus Kinhult, Sweden	2,062,748
73	Benjamin Hebert, France	2,062,679
74	Kevin Streelman, USA	2,035,814
75	Victor Perez, France	2,021,025
76	Keegan Bradley, USA	2,005,537
77	Carlos Ortiz, Mexico	1,992,877
78	Brian Harman, USA	1,979,322
79	Si Woo Kim, Korea	1,939,884
80	Brian Stuard, USA	1,939,702
81	Kurt Kitayama, USA	1,934,341
82	Danny Lee, New Zealand	1,928,640

POS.	PLAYER, COUNTRY	TOTAL MONEY
83	Eddie Pepperell, England	1,913,680
84	Matthias Schwab, Austria	1,910,645
85	Graeme McDowell, N. Ireland	1,910,259
86	Bubba Watson, USA	1,865,571
87	Cameron Smith, Australia	1,858,043
88	Tyler Duncan, USA	1,848,739
89	Mike Lorenzo-Vera, France	1,827,570
90	Matthew Wolff, USA	1,761,723
91	Cameron Champ, USA	1,759,911
92	Christiaan Bezuidenhout, South Africa	1,752,404
93	Harris English, USA	1,748,874
94	J.B. Holmes, USA	1,740,834
95	Shugo Imahira, Japan	1,700,234
96	Paul Waring, England	1,699,519
97	Jazz Janewattananond, Thailand	1,689,854
98	Justin Harding, South Africa	1,648,177
99	Jhonattan Vegas, Venezuela	1,639,283
100	Ryan Moore, USA	1,638,584
101	Kevin Tway, USA	1,608,768
102	Scottie Scheffler, USA	1,604,564
103	Charley Hoffman, USA	1,593,903
104	Jorge Campillo, Spain	1,584,580
105	Kiradech Aphibarnrat, Thailand	1,574,499
106	Harold Varner, USA	1,556,370
107	Haotong Li, China	1,540,767
108	Joost Luiten, Netherlands	1,514,118
109	Wyndham Clark, USA	1,505,620
110	Brian Gay, USA	1,501,819
111	Martin Kaymer, Germany	1,493,168
112	Russell Knox, Scotland	1,486,090
113	Tom Lewis, England	1,467,260
114	Branden Grace, South Africa	1,463,823
115	Lucas Bjerregaard, Denmark	1,452,333
116	Denny McCarthy, USA	1,444,885
117	Cameron Tringale, USA	1,422,155
118	Shaun Norris, South Africa	1,414,277
119	Matt Every, USA	1,410,425
120	Troy Merritt, USA	1,395,804
121	Talor Gooch, USA	1,392,830
122	Richard Sterne, South Africa	1,384,223
123	Matt Jones, Australia	1,382,038
124	Lee Westwood, England	1,370,332
125	Andrea Pavan, Italy	1,368,301
126	Doc Redman, USA	1,338,768
127	Tom Hoge, USA	1,338,699
128	Mark Hubbard, USA	1,315,845
129	Romain Langasque, France	1,295,669
130	Michael Thompson, USA	1,292,724
131	Viktor Hovland, Norway	1,287,493
132	Kyoung-Hoon Lee, Korea	1,267,952
133	Pat Perez, USA	1,262,581
134	Ryo Ishikawa, Japan	1,242,817
135	Thomas Pieters, Belgium	1,216,695

WORLD MONEY LIST

POS.	PLAYER, COUNTRY	TOTAL MONEY
136	Bud Cauley, USA	1,216,116
137	Alex Noren, Sweden	1,206,223
138	Sepp Straka, Austria	1,204,654
139	Chris Stroud, USA	1,200,552
140	Scott Stallings, USA	1,184,769
141	Adam Schenk, USA	1,175,469
142	Russell Henley, USA	1,172,975
143	Andy Sullivan, England	1,166,672
144	Scott Brown, USA	1,144,571
145	Nick Taylor, Canada	1,136,900
146	Roger Sloan, Canada	1,124,959
147	Xinjun Zhang, China	1,121,682
148	Nick Watney, USA	1,121,101
149	Thomas Detry, Belgium	1,116,194
150	Emiliano Grillo, Argentina	1,111,207
151	Luke List, USA	1,083,087
152	Kyle Stanley, USA	1,040,669
153	Scott Harrington, USA	1,035,620
154	Jason Scrivener, Australia	1,031,854
155	Mackenzie Hughes, Canada	1,021,271
156	Wes Roach, USA	1,008,113
157	Daniel Berger, USA	1,004,017
158	Adri Arnaus, Spain	1,002,955
159	Jordan Smith, England	991,086
160	Zack Sucher, USA	990,663
161	Matthew Southgate, England	981,438
162	Mikko Korhonen, Finland	975,548
163	Aaron Wise, USA	958,400
164	Chan Kim, USA	952,923
165	Guido Migliozzi, Italy	941,357
166	Ryan Armour, USA	934,662
167	Scott Hend, Australia	933,035
168	Pablo Larrazabal, Spain	929,914
169	Robby Shelton, USA	928,106
170	Brice Garnett, USA	925,488
171	Andrew Landry, USA	912,473
172	Patton Kizzire, USA	899,976
173	Hank Lebioda, USA	893,914
174	Fabian Gomez, Argentina	879,749
175	Andrew Johnston, England	873,566
176	Harry Higgs, USA	867,034
177	Peter Malnati, USA	861,459
178	Junggon Hwang, Korea	854,872
179	Sam Burns, USA	854,701
180	Sebastian Soderberg, Sweden	847,506
181	Shawn Stefani, USA	831,923
182	Jason Dufner, USA	829,180
183	Richie Ramsay, Scotland	826,959
184	Kelly Kraft, USA	823,558
185	Bronson Burgoon, USA	821,026
186	Chesson Hadley, USA	811,887
187	Austin Cook, USA	798,030
188	David Lipsky, USA	795,379

WORLD MONEY LIST / 27

POS.	PLAYER, COUNTRY	TOTAL MONEY
189	Joachim B. Hansen, Denmark	793,308
190	Masahiro Kawamura, Japan	782,269
191	Ryan Fox, New Zealand	782,141
192	Mikumu Horikawa, Japan	774,927
193	Aaron Baddeley, Australia	769,075
194	Jonas Blixt, Sweden	768,010
195	Shubhankar Sharma, India	756,912
196	Beau Hossler, USA	754,198
197	Martin Laird, Scotland	747,733
198	Seamus Power, Ireland	747,214
199	Dominic Bozzelli, USA	745,741
200	Robert Streb, USA	745,082
201	Jim Herman, USA	738,094
202	George Coetzee, South Africa	729,964
203	Zac Blair, USA	726,977
204	Richy Werenski, USA	722,467
205	Josh Teater, USA	716,774
206	Peter Uihlein, USA	696,046
207	Yosuke Asaji, Japan	695,991
208	Nacho Elvira, Spain	690,771
209	D.J. Trahan, USA	682,871
210	Martin Trainer, USA	678,203
211	Gavin Green, Malaysia	677,966
212	Joakim Lagergren, Sweden	673,597
213	Kalle Samooja, Finland	666,189
214	Sanghyun Park, Korea	664,268
215	Nicolas Colsaerts, Belgium	651,961
216	Zander Lombard, South Africa	639,828
217	Kramer Hickok, USA	639,288
218	Scott Vincent, Zimbabwe	638,623
219	Nino Bertasio, Italy	630,735
220	Brad Kennedy, Australia	623,594
221	Alvaro Quiros, Spain	620,019
222	Zach Johnson, USA	618,242
223	Roberto Diaz, Mexico	618,217
224	Sam Horsfield, England	614,730
225	David Hearn, Canada	613,876
226	Rikuya Hoshino, Japan	609,945
227	Ho-Sung Choi, Korea	603,747
228	Henrik Norlander, Sweden	599,255
229	Chris Paisley, England	587,055
230	Kyung-Tae Kim, Korea	582,234
231	Edoardo Molinari, Italy	579,355
232	Renato Paratore, Italy	572,177
233	Julian Suri, USA	567,640
234	Yuta Ikeda, Japan	562,414
235	Ted Potter, Jr., USA	561,847
236	Scott Jamieson, Scotland	551,689
237	Bill Haas, USA	548,605
238	Johnson Wagner, USA	547,435
239	Scott Langley, USA	543,590
240	Oliver Wilson, England	539,368
241	Wade Ormsby, Australia	532,796

WORLD MONEY LIST

POS.	PLAYER, COUNTRY	TOTAL MONEY
242	Trey Mullinax, USA	523,510
243	Ryuko Tokimatsu, Japan	519,733
244	Roberto Castro, USA	516,670
245	Kazuki Higa, Japan	516,611
246	Satoshi Kodaira, Japan	516,386
247	Jonathan Byrd, USA	515,089
248	Soren Kjeldsen, Denmark	512,830
249	Cameron Percy, Australia	511,634
250	Jimmy Walker, USA	505,893
251	Steven Brown, England	505,803
252	Stewart Cink, USA	501,059
253	Ross Fisher, England	500,400
254	Bo Hoag, USA	498,693
255	Brendan Jones, Australia	497,612
256	Fabrizio Zanotti, Paraguay	496,796
257	Gunn Charoenkul, Thailand	491,308
258	Thorbjorn Olesen, Denmark	487,518
259	Sam Ryder, USA	484,276
260	Matthew NeSmith, USA	481,750
261	Justin Walters, South Africa	479,030
262	Joey Garber, USA	477,963
263	J.J. Spaun, USA	474,793
264	Sean Crocker, Usa	471,744
265	Kristoffer Ventura, Norway	471,212
266	Adrian Otaegui, Spain	470,423
267	Toshinori Muto, Japan	460,840
268	Katsumasa Miyamoto, Japan	453,628
269	Seungsu Han, USA	452,023
270	Curtis Luck, Australia	451,980
271	Cameron Davis, Australia	451,718
272	Nicolai Hojgaard, Denmark	445,020
273	Hudson Swafford, USA	444,601
274	Stephan Jaeger, Germany	440,345
275	Alexander Bjork, Sweden	436,944
276	Brendan Steele, USA	436,922
277	Grant Forrest, Scotland	436,553
278	Robert Rock, England	429,780
279	Doug Ghim, USA	428,428
280	Y.E. Yang, Korea	425,047
281	Francesco Laporta, Italy	424,322
282	David Horsey, England	422,801
283	Maverick McNealy, USA	418,422
284	Padraig Harrington, Ireland	413,731
285	George McNeill, USA	412,080
286	Jeunghun Wang, Korea	410,853
287	Luke Donald, England	407,531
288	Alex Prugh, USA	402,472
289	Maximilian Kieffer, Germany	401,324
290	Sam Saunders, USA	398,535
291	Andres Romero, Argentina	397,445
292	Lucas Herbert, Australia	397,044
293	Ashley Chesters, England	394,532
294	Min Woo Lee, Australia	394,439

POS.	PLAYER, COUNTRY	TOTAL MONEY
295	Tae Hee Lee, Korea	393,457
296	Stephen Gallacher, Scotland	392,521
297	Adam Svensson, Canada	391,607
298	Oliver Fisher, England	390,223
299	Tapio Pulkkanen, Finland	389,509
300	Jeff Winther, Denmark	383,599
301	Ryan Blaum, USA	378,906
302	Tomoharu Otsuki, Japan	378,227
303	Jose de Jesus Rodriguez, Mexico	375,563
304	Matthew Griffin, Australia	374,753
305	Rhein Gibson, Australia	373,195
306	Callum Shinkwin, England	372,801
307	Ollie Schniederjans, USA	372,438
308	Dean Burmester, South Africa	370,112
309	Matthew Jordan, England	365,857
310	Jbe' Kruger, South Africa	365,209
311	Aaron Rai, England	358,074
312	Hiroyuki Fujita, Japan	357,356
313	Victor Dubuisson, France	355,700
314	Shota Akiyoshi, Japan	354,589
315	Ryan Brehm, USA	353,578
316	Calum Hill, England	349,063
317	David Law, Scotland	346,254
318	Anirban Lahiri, India	341,945
319	Lee Slattery, England	340,251
320	Niklas Lemke, Sweden	338,637
321	Jim Knous, USA	337,376
322	Louis de Jager, South Africa	336,943
323	Ernie Els, South Africa	335,993
324	K.J. Choi, Korea	334,737
325	James Morrison, England	334,460
326	Paul Dunne, Ireland	334,036
327	Haydn Porteous, South Africa	333,878
328	Jack Singh Brar, England	330,862
329	Brandon Stone, South Africa	330,852
330	Gaganjeet Bhullar, India	328,866
331	Mark Anderson, USA	317,215
332	Anthony Quayle, Australia	315,122
333	Tyler McCumber, USA	314,786
334	Antoine Rozner, France	314,757
335	Johannes Veerman, USA	314,544
336	Gonzalo Fernandez-Castano, Spain	313,103
337	Rafael Campos, Puerto Rico	310,873
338	Brandon Harkins, USA	306,531
339	Charl Schwartzel, South Africa	306,080
340	Joseph Bramlett, USA	304,255
341	Chase Seiffert, USA	302,546
342	Hugo Leon, Chile	302,413
343	Patrick Rodgers, USA	300,030
344	Nelson Ledesma, Argentina	295,406
345	Alexander Levy, France	291,554
346	Rob Oppenheim, USA	291,407
347	Richard Jung, Canada	284,706

30 / WORLD MONEY LIST

POS.	PLAYER, COUNTRY	TOTAL MONEY
348	Clement Sordet, France	284,264
349	Jamie Donaldson, Wales	284,173
350	John Chin, USA	281,653
351	Max Schmitt, Germany	280,886
352	Bradley Dredge, Wales	280,547
353	Suradit Yongcharoenchai, Thailand	277,461
354	Dongkyu Jang, Korea	276,063
355	Shingo Katayama, Japan	274,831
356	Bernd Ritthammer, Germany	274,405
357	Sebastian Cappelen, Denmark	272,981
358	Ashun Wu, China	272,553
359	Jake McLeod, Australia	272,047
360	Chris Baker, USA	268,610
361	Joel Sjoholm, Sweden	268,075
362	Sean O'Hair, USA	266,988
363	Wil Besseling, Netherlands	263,033
364	Chad Campbell, USA	258,149
365	Paul Peterson, USA	258,064
366	Yikeun Chang, Korea	256,393
367	Michael Gligic, Canada	256,228
368	Koumei Oda, Japan	256,183
369	Hiroshi Iwata, Japan	256,122
370	Matthieu Pavon, France	255,766
371	Boo Weekley, USA	254,613
372	Darren Fichardt, South Africa	254,372
373	Sihwan Kim, USA	253,268
374	Ben Silverman, USA	252,001
375	Billy Hurley, USA	250,826
376	Ben Taylor, England	249,096
377	Grayson Murray, USA	248,747
378	Romain Wattel, France	246,838
379	Michael Hendry, New Zealand	246,406
380	Julian Etulain, Argentina	245,453
381	Jinichiro Kozuma, Japan	241,076
382	Ben Crane, USA	240,926
383	Chris Kirk, USA	240,599
384	Eduardo De La Riva, Spain	237,290
385	Cody Gribble, USA	235,773
386	Darius van Driel, Netherlands	233,755
387	Charlie Danielson, USA	232,879
388	Kyle Jones, USA	231,562
389	Thongchai Jaidee, Thailand	230,967
390	Zecheng Dou, China	230,871
391	Cormac Sharvin, N. Ireland	229,902
392	Ryosuke Kinoshita, Japan	229,342
393	Alejandro Canizares, Spain	228,452
394	Sang-Hee Lee, Korea	227,883
395	Michael Gellerman, USA	225,907
396	Dylan Perry, Australia	225,311
397	Alex Cejka, Germany	224,769
398	Tim Wilkinson, New Zealand	224,682
399	Robert Karlsson, Sweden	220,584
400	John Catlin, USA	220,157

World Money List Leaders

YEAR	PLAYER, COUNTRY	TOTAL MONEY
1966	Jack Nicklaus, USA	$168,088
1967	Jack Nicklaus, USA	276,166
1968	Billy Casper, USA	222,436
1969	Frank Beard, USA	186,993
1970	Jack Nicklaus, USA	222,583
1971	Jack Nicklaus, USA	285,897
1972	Jack Nicklaus, USA	341,792
1973	Tom Weiskopf, USA	349,645
1974	Johnny Miller, USA	400,255
1975	Jack Nicklaus, USA	332,610
1976	Jack Nicklaus, USA	316,086
1977	Tom Watson, USA	358,034
1978	Tom Watson, USA	384,388
1979	Tom Watson, USA	506,912
1980	Tom Watson, USA	651,921
1981	Johnny Miller, USA	704,204
1982	Raymond Floyd, USA	738,699
1983	Seve Ballesteros, Spain	686,088
1984	Seve Ballesteros, Spain	688,047
1985	Bernhard Langer, Germany	860,262
1986	Greg Norman, Australia	1,146,584
1987	Ian Woosnam, Wales	1,793,268
1988	Seve Ballesteros, Spain	1,261,275
1989	David Frost, South Africa	1,650,230
1990	Jose Maria Olazabal, Spain	1,633,640
1991	Bernhard Langer, Germany	2,186,700
1992	Nick Faldo, England	2,748,248
1993	Nick Faldo, England	2,825,280
1994	Ernie Els, South Africa	2,862,854
1995	Corey Pavin, USA	2,746,340
1996	Colin Montgomerie, Scotland	3,071,442
1997	Colin Montgomerie, Scotland	3,366,900
1998	Tiger Woods, USA	2,927,946
1999	Tiger Woods, USA	7,681,625
2000	Tiger Woods, USA	11,034,530
2001	Tiger Woods, USA	7,771,562
2002	Tiger Woods, USA	8,292,188
2003	Vijay Singh, Fiji	8,499,611
2004	Vijay Singh, Fiji	11,638,699
2005	Tiger Woods, USA	12,280,404
2006	Tiger Woods, USA	13,325,949
2007	Tiger Woods, USA	12,902,706
2008	Vijay Singh, Fiji	8,025,128
2009	Tiger Woods, USA	10,998,054
2010	Graeme McDowell, N. Ireland	7,371,586
2011	Luke Donald, England	9,730,870
2012	Rory McIlroy, N. Ireland	11,301,228
2013	Tiger Woods, USA	9,490,217
2014	Rory McIlroy, N. Ireland	10,526,012
2015	Jordan Spieth, USA	12,477,758
2016	Dustin Johnson, USA	9,347,352
2017	Justin Thomas, USA	10,300,894
2018	Bryson DeChambeau, USA	9,231,811
2019	Rory McIlroy, N. Ireland	10,820,759

Career World Money List

Here is a list of the 50 leading money winners for their careers through 2019. It includes players active on both the regular and senior tours of the world. The World Money List from this and the 53 previous editions of the annual and a table prepared for a companion book, *The Wonderful World of Professional Golf* (Atheneum, 1973) form the basis for this compilation. Additional figures were taken from official records of major golf associations. Conversion of foreign currency figures to U.S. dollars is based on average values during the particular years involved.

POS.	PLAYER, COUNTRY	TOTAL MONEY
1	Tiger Woods, USA	$139,545,316
2	Phil Mickelson, USA	96,077,541
3	Ernie Els, South Africa	88,884,576
4	Vijay Singh, Fiji	88,776,387
5	Jim Furyk, USA	80,539,516
6	Sergio Garcia, Spain	72,200,021
7	Justin Rose, England	71,840,969
8	Rory McIlroy, N. Ireland	65,611,618
9	Adam Scott, Australia	62,923,720
10	Lee Westwood, England	61,469,604
11	Bernhard Langer, Germany	59,181,209
12	Dustin Johnson, USA	58,972,391
13	Padraig Harrington, Ireland	55,379,684
14	Davis Love, USA	55,189,844
15	Luke Donald, England	55,027,432
16	Retief Goosen, South Africa	53,979,800
17	Matt Kuchar, USA	51,848,287
18	Steve Stricker, USA	51,182,781
19	Colin Montgomerie, Scotland	50,857,474
20	Zach Johnson, USA	50,016,998
21	Ian Poulter, England	47,885,012
22	David Toms, USA	47,379,643
23	Kenny Perry, USA	47,142,440
24	Paul Casey, England	46,971,469
25	Jason Day, Australia	46,755,675
26	Fred Couples, USA	43,675,718
27	Graeme McDowell, N. Ireland	42,727,892
28	Bubba Watson, USA	41,975,374
29	Stewart Cink, USA	41,672,149
30	Miguel Angel Jimenez, Spain	40,797,899
31	Jordan Spieth, USA	40,555,533
32	Henrik Stenson, Sweden	40,225,514
33	Rickie Fowler, USA	40,037,822
34	Charles Howell, USA	39,107,094
35	Tom Lehman, USA	38,988,413
36	Nick Price, Zimbabwe	37,857,153
37	K.J. Choi, South Korea	37,842,501
38	Hale Irwin, USA	37,746,804
39	Justin Leonard, USA	37,534,807
40	Mark Calcavecchia, USA	37,196,468

POS.	PLAYER, COUNTRY	TOTAL MONEY
41	Robert Allenby, Australia	36,959,467
42	Fred Funk, USA	36,549,266
43	Jay Haas, USA	36,361,527
44	Rory Sabbatini, South Africa	35,066,987
45	Geoff Ogilvy, Australia	35,018,531
46	Jerry Kelly, USA	34,983,141
47	Charl Schwartzel, South Africa	34,533,362
48	Francisco Molinari, Italy	34,239,947
49	Stuart Appleby, Australia	34,144,187
50	Darren Clarke, N. Ireland	33,815,986

These 50 players have won $2,658,257,863 in their careers.

Women's World Money List

This list includes official earnings on the U.S. LPGA Tour, Ladies European Tour, Japan LPGA Tour, Korea LPGA Tour and Australian Ladies Tour, along with other winnings in established unofficial events when reliable figures could be obtained.

POS.	PLAYER, COUNTRY	TOTAL MONEY
1	Jin Young Ko, Korea	$3,126,955
2	Sei Young Kim, Korea	2,753,099
3	Jeongeun Lee$_6$, Korea	2,097,103
4	Hinako Shibuno, Japan	2,048,529
5	Brooke M. Henderson, Canada	1,836,017
6	Nelly Korda, USA	1,807,506
7	Lexi Thompson, USA	1,729,792
8	Minjee Lee, Australia	1,546,232
9	Nasa Hataoka, Japan	1,538,577
10	Sung Hyun Park, Korea	1,536,070
11	Danielle Kang, USA	1,529,668
12	Ai Suzuki, Japan	1,508,965
13	Hyo Joo Kim, Korea	1,372,879
14	Jiyai Shin, Korea	1,317,922
15	Ariya Jutanugarn, Thailand	1,242,838
16	Hye Jin Choi, Korea	1,182,962
17	Seonwoo Bae, Korea	1,168,734
18	Shanshan Feng, China	1,093,154
19	Hannah Green, Australia	1,064,395
20	Carlota Ciganda, Spain	1,049,054
21	Ha Na Jang, Korea	1,041,951
22	Lizette Salas, USA	1,038,152
23	Mi Jung Hur, Korea	1,030,252
24	So Yeon Ryu, Korea	992,418

WOMEN'S WORLD MONEY LIST

POS.	PLAYER, COUNTRY	TOTAL MONEY
25	Min-Young Lee, Korea	951,796
26	Amy Yang, Korea	949,719
27	Da Yeon Lee, Korea	942,061
28	Charley Hull, England	928,650
29	Yu Liu, China	880,048
30	Brittany Altomare, USA	878,369
31	Jessica Korda, USA	874,588
32	Inbee Park, Korea	846,874
33	HeeJeong Lim, Korea	806,474
34	Celine Boutier, France	793,190
35	Minami Katsu, Japan	792,871
36	Yui Kawamoto, Japan	792,233
37	Eun-Hee Ji, Korea	789,695
38	Moriya Jutanugarn, Thailand	785,105
39	Lala Anai, Japan	782,807
40	Angel Yin, USA	755,784
41	Sakura Koiwai, Japan	746,839
42	Momoko Ueda, Japan	744,395
43	Mamiko Higa, Japan	728,208
44	Caroline Masson, Germany	715,544
45	Azahara Munoz, Spain	692,264
46	Morgan Pressel, USA	680,872
47	Ayean Cho, Korea	676,775
48	Asuka Kashiwabara, Japan	674,659
49	Eri Okayama, Japan	668,249
50	Bronte Law, England	666,836
51	Chae Yoon Park, Korea	655,649
52	Mone Inami, Japan	646,860
53	Megan Khang, USA	646,367
54	Su Oh, Australia	640,703
55	Mi Hyang Lee, Korea	639,491
56	Ally McDonald, USA	638,014
57	Erika Hara, Japan	636,929
58	Jeongmin Cho, Korea	628,130
59	Marina Alex, USA	609,290
60	Ah-Reum Hwang, Korea	596,174
61	Nanna Koerstz Madsen, Denmark	594,712
62	Misuzu Narita, Japan	594,656
63	Mi-Jeong Jeon, Korea	577,209
64	Teresa Lu, Chinese Taipei	526,485
65	Jennifer Kupcho, USA	525,432
66	Min Ji Park, Korea	519,205
67	Jing Yan, China	517,412
68	Ji Yeong Kim$_2$, Korea	507,878
69	Gaby Lopez, Mexico	507,171
70	Sayaka Takahashi, Japan	497,603
71	Jasmine Suwannapura, Thailand	497,171
72	Lydia Ko, New Zealand	494,584
73	Kristen Gillman, USA	492,466
74	Nicole Broch Larsen, Denmaark	479,546
75	Sun-Ju Ahn, Korea	478,137
76	A Lim Kim, Korea	475,817
77	Bo-Mee Lee, Korea	475,171

WOMEN'S WORLD MONEY LIST / 35

POS.	PLAYER, COUNTRY	TOTAL MONEY
78	Mirim Lee, Korea	472,118
79	Ji Hyun Kim, Korea	468,498
80	Somi Lee, Korea	467,374
81	Jenny Shin, Korea	464,094
82	Hee-Kyung Bae, Korea	454,607
83	Chella Choi, Korea	452,719
84	Kana Mikashima, Japan	448,905
85	So Young Lee, Korea	440,777
86	Ashleigh Buhai, South Africa	434,696
87	Jaye Marie Green, USA	427,801
88	Hina Arakaki, Japan	423,761
89	Erika Kikuchi, Japan	417,939
90	Annie Park, USA	407,836
91	Georgia Hall, England	403,490
92	In-Kyung Kim, Korea	402,109
93	Anna Nordqvist, Sweden	393,685
94	Hikaru Yoshimoto, Japan	392,312
95	Alena Sharp, Canada	382,396
96	Wei-Ling Hsu, Chinese Taipei	379,875
97	S. Langkul, Thailand	366,491
98	Ji-Hee Lee, Korea	356,297
99	Ritsuko Ryu, Japan	353,063
100	Katherine Kirk, Australia	350,857
101	Song Yi Ahn, Korea	345,228
102	Jung Min Lee, Korea	343,217
103	So Yeon Park, Korea	341,599
104	Jodi Ewart Shadoff, England	340,914
105	Rei Matsuda, Japan	339,068
106	Amy Olson, USA	335,819
107	Saki Asai, Japan	333,363
108	Jin Seon Han, Korea	332,649
109	Stacy Lewis, USA	329,191
110	Mel Reid, England	323,450
111	Gerina Piller, USA	320,502
112	Cydney Clanton, USA	318,980
113	Pornanong Phatlum, Thailand	318,027
114	Ji Young Park, Korea	315,835
115	Mika Miyazato, Japan	314,377
116	Sakura Yokomine, Japan	313,978
117	Seung Yeon Lee, Korea	311,524
118	Bo Ah Kim, Korea	311,137
119	Min Sun Kim$_5$, Korea	308,681
120	So Yi Kim, Korea	305,013
121	Serena Aoki, Japan	300,599
122	Kana Nagai, Japan	295,569
123	Cheyenne Knight, USA	295,493
124	Chie Arimura, Japan	291,570
125	In Gee Chun, Korea	278,673
126	Hyun Kyung Park, Korea	278,129
127	Momoko Osato, Japan	276,699
128	Rumi Yoshiba, Japan	275,652
129	Gayoung Lee, Korea	273,037
130	Mami Fukuda, Japan	269,850

WOMEN'S WORLD MONEY LIST

POS.	PLAYER, COUNTRY	TOTAL MONEY
131	Esther Henseleit, Germany	269,423
132	Eimi Koga, Japan	268,259
133	Anne van Dam, Netherlands	265,689
134	Hee Won Na, Korea	262,199
135	Ju Young Pak, Korea	260,456
136	Caroline Hedwall, Sweden	260,362
137	Xiyu Lin, China	254,926
138	Chae-Young Yoon, Korea	254,183
139	Aoi Ohnishi, Japan	252,445
140	Sarah Schmelzel, USA	251,284
141	Ye Rim Sakai, Japan	250,216
143	Tiffany Joh, USA	249,154
144	Pajaree Anannarukarn, Thailand	249,049
145	Hana Wakimoto, Japan	238,973
146	Madelene Sagstrom, Sweden	236,128
147	Austin Ernst, USA	235,727
148	Saki Nagamine, Japan	234,757
149	Maria Shinohara, Japan	232,320
150	Satsuki Oshiro, Japan	230,859
151	Maria Fernanda Torres, Puerto Rico	227,557
152	Aditi Ashok, India	225,616
153	Jane Park, USA	218,147
154	Shiho Oyama, Japan	216,977
155	Mayu Hamada, Japan	216,149
156	Paula Creamer, USA	215,472
157	Char Young Kim$_2$, Korea	214,742
158	Shina Kanazawa, Japan	213,854
159	Ayako Uehara, Japan	211,832
160	Gyo Rin Park, Korea	208,649
161	Karis Davidson, Australia	207,806
162	Haruka Morita, Japan	207,076
163	Na-Ri Lee, Korea	206,093
164	Ryann O'Toole, USA	199,641
165	Sarah Kemp, Australia	198,722
166	Marianne Skarpnord, Norway	198,540
167	Eun Bin Lim, Korea	197,118
168	Linnea Strom, Sweden	187,257
169	Ayaka Furue, Japan	186,570
170	Haru Nomura, Japan	186,559
171	Ha-Neul Kim, Korea	185,377
172	Hiroko Azuma, Japan	185,055
173	Minami Hiruta, Japan	183,011
174	Charlotte Thomas, England	181,596
175	Cristie Kerr, USA	181,456

Senior World Money List

This list includes official earnings from the U.S. Champions Tour, European Staysure Tour and Japan Senior Tour, along with other winnings in established official and unofficial tournaments when reliable figures could be obtained.

POS.	PLAYER, COUNTRY	TOTAL MONEY
1	Scott McCarron, USA	$2,534,090
2	Jerry Kelly, USA	2,382,675
3	Bernhard Langer, Germany	2,076,695
4	Retief Goosen, South Africa	1,927,710
5	Woody Austin, USA	1,733,517
6	Steve Stricker, USA	1,669,997
7	Kirk Triplett, USA	1,608,298
8	David Toms, USA	1,599,700
9	Colin Montgomerie, Scotland	1,597,130
10	Scott Parel, USA	1,522,956
11	Billy Andrade, USA	1,518,238
12	Miguel Angel Jimenez, Spain	1,393,508
13	Kevin Sutherland, USA	1,327,714
14	Paul Broadhurst, England	1,212,605
15	Ken Tanigawa, Japan	1,208,194
16	Jeff Maggert, USA	1,111,529
17	Tom Lehman, USA	1,038,483
18	Steve Flesch, USA	1,029,288
19	Brandt Jobe, USA	985,123
20	Wes Short, Jr., USA	981,961
21	Marco Dawson, USA	949,931
22	Paul Goydos, USA	946,650
23	Tim Petrovic, USA	910,578
24	Joe Durant, USA	844,554
25	Vijay Singh, Fiji	788,094
26	Rocco Mediate, USA	780,911
27	Lee Janzen, USA	743,389
28	Stephen Ames, Canada	722,938
29	Kent Jones, USA	700,569
30	Fred Couples, USA	692,508
31	Tom Byrum, USA	689,230
32	Bob Estes, USA	689,066
33	Ken Duke, USA	684,579
34	Darren Clarke, N. Ireland	669,945
35	Doug Barron, USA	647,429
36	Jay Haas, USA	623,124
37	David McKenzie, Australia	611,698
38	Duffy Waldorf, USA	602,389
39	Tom Pernice, Jr., USA	601,439
40	Prayad Marksaeng, Thailand	597,433
41	Tom Gillis, USA	571,155
42	Mark O'Meara, USA	558,037
43	Gene Sauers, USA	554,980
44	Tommy Tolles, USA	546,602
45	Doug Garwood, USA	527,042
46	Kenny Perry, USA	493,913
47	Corey Pavin, USA	479,401

POS.	PLAYER, COUNTRY	TOTAL MONEY
48	Thaworn Wiratchant, Thailand	464,764
49	David Frost, South Africa	427,004
50	Billy Mayfair, USA	421,054
51	Chris DiMarco, USA	404,412
52	Olin Browne, USA	395,058
53	Jeff Sluman, USA	392,007
54	John Daly, USA	390,357
55	Glen Day, USA	362,546
56	Bart Bryant, USA	325,274
57	Esteban Toledo, Mexico	325,202
58	Stephen Leaney, Australia	316,089
59	Masahiro Kuramoto, Japan	313,458
60	Phillip Price, Wales	303,465
61	Barry Lane, England	292,380
62	Davis Love, USA	280,932
63	Willie Wood, USA	274,485
64	Jesper Parnevik, Sweden	261,989
65	Carlos Franco, Paraguay	255,875
66	Toru Taniguchi, Japan	243,735
67	James Kingston, South Africa	243,570
68	Shinichi Akiba, James	230,961
69	Jean-Francois Remesy, France	230,280
70	Fran Quinn, USA	228,002
71	Gregory Meyer, USA	218,742
72	David Shacklady, England	213,996
73	Tommy Armour, USA	212,753
74	Peter Fowler, Australia	210,114
75	Clark Dennis, USA	207,030
76	Paul Lawrie, Scotland	206,190
77	Gibby Gilbert, USA	203,428
78	Scott Hoch, USA	202,239
79	Jerry Smith, USA	199,734
80	Hidezumi Shirakata, Japan	195,373
81	John Huston, USA	186,348
82	Michael Allen, USA	177,089
83	Michael Bradley, USA	174,059
84	Jose Coceres, Argentina	173,839
85	Taichi Teshima, Japan	171,669
86	Steve Jones, USA	171,909
87	Peter Baker, England	170,622
88	Toru Suzuki, Japan	169,966
89	Tom Watson, USA	164,002
90	Cliff Kresge, USA	163,324
91	Tsuyoshi Yoneyama, Japan	161,461
92	Masayoshi Yamazoe, Japan	160,289
93	John Riegger, USA	160,200
94	Eiji Mizoguchi, Japan	158,252
95	Toshimitsu Izawa, Japan	158,199
96	Mark Calcavecchia, USA	156,978
97	Rod Pampling, Australia	148,827
98	Jarmo Sandelin, Sweden	148,529
99	Chien-Soon Lu, Chinese Taipei	147,182
100	Markus Brier, Austria	146,200

1. The Year in Retrospect

Golf had the biggest overhaul of the rules book in centuries. The PGA Championship moved to May for the first time in 70 years. Golf's oldest championship was held outside Britain for the first time since 1951. Women competed at Augusta National for the first time ever. The PGA Tour ended its season with a radical scoring system at the Tour Championship in which players began with a score under par before the first shot was struck. Change was so abundant in 2019 that at times it was hard to keep up.

And yet for so much that felt new, the year was defined by something gloriously old: A bright red shirt under a Masters green jacket.

Big moments in sport become colossal when comparisons are immediate. Tiger Woods winning the Masters after all he had been through — calamity in his personal life, four surgeries on his lower back, the unseen struggle to cope with the pain — fit that description. Was it the greatest comeback in sport? Ben Hogan winning the U.S. Open at Merion a year after a near fatal car accident gave pause to the hyperbole. Was it the greatest Masters ever? Jack Nicklaus winning a sixth green jacket at age 46 remains a special moment in golf history. This was simply Tiger Woods, Masters champion. And that was enough.

He was not the best player in 2019. Rory McIlroy was voted the PGA Tour Player of the Year by his peers for three victories and consistency that only Woods could appreciate in the last decade. Brooks Koepka had another astounding run through the majors by winning the PGA Championship, finishing second in the Masters and U.S. Open and tying for fourth in the Open Championship. Nicklaus, Woods and Jordan Spieth are the only other players to have finished no worse than fourth in all four majors. Koepka easily won the PGA of America award as Player of the Year, which is based on points. The Golf Writers Association of America also voted Koepka a narrow winner over McIlroy. The Associated Press gave its male athlete of the year to NBA star LeBron James. Woods wasn't even on the ballot.

Woods would be the first to say it wasn't his best year. He won only two times, the Masters and the inaugural Zozo Championship in Japan, and really only had a fleeting chance at one other title in the WGC-Dell Technologies Match Play. He missed the cut in two majors and wasn't a factor in the other, the U.S. Open at Pebble Beach, where he won in 2000 with what many consider the greatest performance in golf. Woods didn't even make it to the Tour Championship. "The rest of the tournaments I didn't really play as well as I wanted. But at the end of the day, I'm the one with the green jacket," he said. Never has he smiled so wide after failing to meet a goal.

Woods still owned the year for that moment so many thought they would never see again, and that explained his appeal that touched young and old, and transcended the sport as only he can. The younger generation really only knew Woods from video highlights, so powerful that over time it felt more like Hollywood than real life. On this Sunday at Augusta National, memories turned into reality. The older generation, which saw him win the

Masters by 12 shots and the U.S. Open by 15 shots, which remembered when he held all four majors at the same time, was mesmerized because there was reason to doubt it would ever see him win another major.

Augusta National was oozing with history this year even before Woods took the stage. Under the leadership of chairman Billy Payne, the club invited its first female members, created a youth initiative called the "Drive, Chip and Putt," and established amateur championships in Asia and Latin America. In his first year as chairman, Fred Ridley announced the Augusta National Women's Amateur, which featured two days of competition at nearby Champions Retreat, a practice round at Augusta National for all 72 players, and the final round at the home of the Masters for the 30 players who made the cut. Jennifer Kupcho and Maria Fassi delivered a duel on the Saturday before the Masters that added a chapter of lore to the back nine at the most famous tournament course in the world. Kupcho emerged the winner with an eagle and three birdies over the last six holes for a four-shot victory.

The rest of golf's biggest events tried to leave their mark. They were always going to be in the shadow of Woods at the Masters. Koepka and McIlroy showed early signs of a rivalry that took an entire year to marinate. Koepka joined Woods as the only back-to-back winners of the PGA Championship in stroke play, but not before nearly making the wrong kind of history when he lost all but one shot of a seven-stroke lead in the final day. "I was going to make history one way or another," Koepka said later.

He also won his first World Golf Championship at the FedEx St. Jude Invitational by rallying to beat McIlroy in the final round. McIlroy, who won The Players Championship in March, returned the favor by coming from behind to beat Koepka in the Tour Championship for the $15 million prize that comes with the FedExCup.

Jon Rahm won the Dubai Duty Free Irish Open again and closed out the year with consecutive victories in the Mutuactivos Open de Espana and the DP World Tour Championship in Dubai, that latter offering the biggest official check in golf at $3 million. Much like McIlroy, his year was built around consistency. McIlroy had a 76 percent rate of finishing in the top 10 around the world, 19 out of 25 tournaments. Rahm was at 69 percent, with 18 top-10s out of 26 events. Both won four times, which includes a team title for Rahm in New Orleans.

Koepka ended the year at No. 1 in the Official World Golf Ranking, the first player to end consecutive years at No. 1 since Woods in 2008 and 2009. McIlroy was closing in when he finished up the year. But there is no longer talk of a modern Big Three, or a big anything. Golf was getting too deep — with early signs of emergence down the road in Asia — for any group to remain at or near the top for longer than a year. Jordan Spieth drove home that point at the start of the year. He had gone through a winless 2018 (with another winless year to follow) when he said to reporters it was only a few years ago that everyone was mentioning a "Big Three." Spieth said none of those players was being mentioned as much. A few reporters in the room that day, some of whom had written about this new Big Three, looked at each other to figure out which players he meant. It was Spieth, McIlroy and Jason Day. On the day he spoke, they were No. 8 (McIlroy), No. 11 (Day) and No. 17 (Spieth). Time moves quickly.

What doesn't move as quickly is the game inside the ropes. All it took was a few anecdotal moments to bring more outrage on the pace of play, whether it was J.B. Holmes during a rain-delayed, 36-hole Sunday at Riviera in the Genesis Open, Koepka pointing to his watch as Holmes played Royal Portrush during the final round of the Open Championship, and Bryson DeChambeau taking more than two minutes to hit an eight-foot putt (and missing). Those ill-timed TV moments were enough for the PGA Tour to begin working on new pace-of-play measures expected to start in early 2020. The European Tour got ahead of it quicker, announcing a four-point plan for 2020 that included stronger vigilance of players who take too long and perhaps limiting field sizes.

There is nothing in the Rules of Golf, the previous version or the modern version, that mandates how long golf should take to play. Everything else about the rules were revamped. The changes getting the most attention were the knee-high drop instead of shoulder-length and the option for players to leave in the flagstick while putting on the green. One was modified early involving caddies lining up their players. Because of the way the rule was written, Haotong Li was penalized in Dubai and Adam Schenk was penalized in the Honda Classic because their caddies were standing in the wrong place at the wrong time.

The caddie alignment ruling, oddly enough, was not an issue on the LPGA Tour. It was odd because it was most prevalent in women's golf, with caddies standing behind players to check their alignment on the tee, the fairway, sometimes the green. Rules were only an issue in men's golf, it seemed.

The attention on women's golf was on Jin Young Ko, the latest player to dominate the LPGA Tour. She won four times, two of them majors at the ANA Inspiration and the Evian Championship. She might have won the Race to the CME Globe any other year, except for a change to the season-long competition that made the goal reaching the CME Group Tour Championship, and any of the top 60 players in the field only had to win the tournament to capture the bonus. That fell to Sei Young Kim, whose birdie on the last hole gave her the victory and $1.5 million in official money, the largest payoff in women's golf.

Even that wasn't the biggest moment for women's golf. Suzann Pettersen was thought to be retired after having her first child. She was a vice captain to Catriona Matthew for the Solheim Cup, and then Matthew suggested Pettersen practice in case Europe needed her at Gleneagles. Pettersen went from vice captain to captain's pick. And on the final shot of the Solheim Cup, Pettersen had a seven-foot putt. Make it and Europe wins. Miss it and the Americans win for the third straight time. Pettersen holed the putt, and then announced her retirement. It was the ultimate walk-off.

It's always a show whenever the U.S. plays Europe, even though Asian-born players continue to dominate in the world of women's golf. There were signs Asia was starting to really take hold as a golfing power in the men's game, too. Jazz Janewattananond of Thailand won the Asian Order of Merit and challenged for the money title in Japan. Perhaps the best evidence was the International team on the Presidents Cup, where five Asian players filled out the 12-man team — two from South Korea (Sungjae Im and Byeong Hun

An), one from Japan (Hideki Matsuyama), one from China (Haotong Li) and one from Chinese Taipei (C.T. Pan).

The biggest buzz in Thailand had nothing to do with golf. Woods caused a lot of commotion when he returned to Thailand on vacation with his two children and his girlfriend, all of them dressed in yellow. Twenty years earlier, when Woods was at his peak and defeated Ernie Els in an epic playoff at Kapalua to start the year, Els said, "He's 24. He'll probably be bigger than Elvis when he's in his 40s." At times in golf, it felt that way.

Even with another win — finally — under his belt after all his injuries and mishaps, there remained some curiosity about Woods at the start of the year. Sure, he won the Tour Championship in the fall of 2018, but then he turned in a dud at the Ryder Cup during another U.S. loss away from home, and he was out of the public eye until his Hero World Challenge, where he finished 17th against an 18-man field. Torrey Pines used to be a good barometer for Woods because he had won there eight times as a pro, including his last major in 2008 at the U.S. Open. This didn't give much reason for hope because he already was 11 shots behind going into the weekend and tied for 20th. It was like that for the next two months — a rugged start, one good round to raise hopes, a Sunday in red finishing well before the leaders. And then he missed the Arnold Palmer Invitational at Bay Hill citing a neck strain. He said it was not related to his fused lower back, though that didn't quell speculation that yet another injury was going to get in the way. He returned at The Players Championship and didn't break 70 until the final day, which helped him to a tie for 30th. The Masters was approaching. Woods was in neutral.

His final tune-up for Augusta National was the WGC-Dell Technologies Match Play in Austin, his first time competing in Texas since 2005. It also was his first time competing in the Match Play since 2013. Since then, the event had changed courses twice and the format once. What had not changed was how to advance — by winning — and Woods did just enough to get out of the group stage to set up a fourth-round duel against McIlroy. It lived up to the hype until McIlroy had a pitching wedge into the par-five 16th with a chance to square the match, except he missed it badly, hit his next shot out-of-bounds and didn't even finish the hole. Woods was on to the quarter-finals where he lost to Lucas Bjerregaard of Denmark. Even so, Woods had seen enough of his game and the shots he was hitting that he was in a perfect place heading to Augusta National.

Nothing fuels optimism more than Woods winning, especially in a major. In a *Golf Digest* survey from 2002, after Woods won the Masters and U.S. Open for his eighth major at age 26, the overwhelming vote was he was going to break Jack Nicklaus's record of 18 professional majors. Two years later, when he had gone 10 majors without winning, a similar survey revealed an overwhelming number saying the Nicklaus record was safe. During the worst crisis of his career, when Woods went from not winning majors to not contending in majors to not even playing in them, the general belief was that Woods could no longer get there. The sight of him in a green jacket was enough to put him squarely back into the race, and soon. The question in some corners was how much ground he would cover by the end of the year. The PGA Championship was at Bethpage Black, where Woods won the

U.S. Open in 2002. The U.S. Open was at Pebble Beach, site of his historic 15-shot victory in 2000. The Open Championship? Woods didn't know Royal Portrush — not many did — but links golf was perfect for his short game, imagination and creativity. The game was on.

Slowly, it fizzled out, and it wasn't until the end of the year that anyone understood why. The emotions of winning a major for the first time in 11 years took a toll on Woods, and he chose not to play between the Masters and PGA Championship. He played a practice round at Bethpage Black a week before the PGA Championship. He played nine holes in nasty weather on Monday — temperatures barely reached 50 degrees — had light practice on Tuesday and then chose not to come to the course on Wednesday. Woods was in the same group as Koepka and Francesco Molinari, and couldn't keep up. With rounds of 72-73, he missed the cut at the PGA Championship for the third time in his last four attempts. Perhaps more daunting was watching Koepka, the modern golfer Woods now had to beat, posting a major championship record for 36 holes at 128.

At the Open Championship he opened with a 78, matching his third-worst score in a major. Then again, Woods had played only 10 rounds since his Masters victory. "Playing at this elite level is a completely different deal. You've got to be spot on. These guys are too good. There are too many guys that are playing well and I'm just not one of them," Woods said in a somber assessment. And then it got worse.

Combined with a light schedule, the mediocre results put Woods at No. 28 in the FedExCup going into the postseason. At the Northern Trust he promptly opened with a 75 to fall 13 shots behind and withdrew the next day with what he described as a mild oblique strain. At that point, he looked done for the year. He was a long shot to make the Presidents Cup team — Woods was the U.S. captain — much less advance to the Tour Championship. He showed up at the BMW Championship, but didn't have enough firepower to advance to the top 30 and reach East Lake for the FedExCup finale.

Instead of being in Atlanta, Woods had arthroscopic surgery on his left knee that week to repair minor cartilage damage. He later would say it kept him from practice, from squatting to read putts and from moving gracefully to his left side. It was his fifth surgery on his left knee. Alarm bells sounded. And when he returned 10 weeks later at the Zozo Championship — the first PGA Tour event in Japan — the hype machine was purring.

Woods looked indifferent in a Skins Game streamed live around the world by Discovery-owned Golf TV with McIlroy, Matsuyama and Day. And then he won the Zozo going away. He began the rain-soaked tournament with three straight bogeys. The PGA Tour said it was rare for a player to finish in the top 10 after starting a 72-hole event with three straight bogeys. Woods was the first to win, and it was another big moment. It was his 82nd career victory, tying him with Sam Snead for most all-time on the PGA Tour. And it was another number to associate with Woods. There was the 15-shot win at the U.S. Open, the 142 consecutive cuts on the PGA Tour, the 11 times he has won PGA Tour Player of the Year, and now 82 victories. "It's just hard to imagine anybody doing that again," PGA Tour commissioner Jay Monahan said. Except that Woods wasn't finished.

The victory was a week before Woods — the U.S. captain for the Presidents

Cup — had to make his four wild-card selections. He had no choice but to select himself. He was the first playing captain since Hale Irwin in the inaugural Presidents Cup in 1994, and the first playing captain who made himself a captain's pick. And he didn't disappoint. Woods won his opening two matches with Justin Thomas. He sat out all of Saturday. And then he won in singles for a 3-0 mark, and another U.S. victory.

While a strong finish for Woods built anticipation for the next year, Koepka was going the opposite direction.

Unlike the previous year, when he was slowed by injury, Koepka appeared to be slowed by indifference. He was at No. 1 in the world. He already had three majors, including his repeat titles in the U.S. Open. The knock against Koepka, if it could be called criticism, was that he wasn't winning enough regular tournaments. In 2018 when he won the CJ Cup at Nine Bridges in South Korea to reach No. 1 for the first time, it was only his fifth PGA Tour title, three of them major. He also won twice in Japan and in Turkey. Koepka hardly featured at all except for his hometown Honda Classic, where he missed a playoff by one shot when Keith Mitchell birdied the final hole. He revealed at The Players Championship in March that he had been on a strict diet to lose weight, and it was only learned later that was to pose partially nude for ESPN's annual nudity issue in its magazine. Did he care more for vanity than trophies? Koepka never cares what anyone thinks, and he quieted any critics with his close call at the Masters, another major. One month later, he delivered what he later said were the best two rounds he has ever had in his career, and probably ever will, during his wire-to-wire win at the PGA Championship.

That made it four majors, along with five "regular" victories on the PGA Tour, European Tour and Japan Golf Tour. And then after a bottom-of-the-pack performance at the RBC Canadian Open, Koepka chased Gary Woodland to the finish line in the U.S. Open for another runner-up finish in a major. He played two more PGA Tour events, the Travelers Championship and the new 3M Open in Minnesota, and didn't crack the top 50.

Maybe it took the majors to bring out his focus. Or maybe, as Koepka had suggested during the PGA Championship, the majors were the easiest to win. Speaking about the fields at majors, Koepka said, "You figured at least 80 of them I'm just going to beat. From there, you figure about half of them won't play well from there, so you're down to about 35. And then from 35, some of them just … pressure is going to get to them. It only leaves you with a few more, and you've just got to beat those guys. I think one of the big things I've learned over the last few years is you don't need to win it. If you hang around, good things are going to happen."

It might have sounded brash, but he backed it up with results. When he headed to Northern Ireland for the final major of the year, Koepka had gone 1-2-1-2 in the previous four majors. Koepka laughed when he was asked at Royal Portrush whether he would have expected more or less if told that he would have two runner-up finishes and a victory in the majors that year. Yes, it was incredible. He also spoke to the disappointment of not winning the other two majors. More disappointment followed, at least by his standards, when he couldn't get a putt to fall on the links of Royal Portrush and tied for fourth.

That disappointment lasted all of a week. Back in America, Koepka overpowered the TPC Southwind with a 64-65 weekend to capture his first World Golf Championships event at the FedEx St. Jude Invitational. His lead atop the World Ranking kept growing. He was the best in golf, and there was no debate, and the PGA Tour Player of the Year should have been an easy choice. But it apparently wasn't after Koepka failed to win the Tour Championship, leaving McIlroy with a stronger record for the entire year, and Koepka with a superior record — an unreal record, to be fair — in the four events that matter the most.

McIlroy won the vote of his peers for the Jack Nicklaus Award, and that left plenty of questions. The PGA Tour chooses not to release the vote totals, not wanting anyone to focus on anything other than who won. Left unsaid was the margin of victory, and perhaps more importantly, how many PGA Tour players even voted. If Koepka considered that a slap, he wasn't saying. He showed up in Las Vegas six weeks later and said he doesn't play for awards, only to win tournaments. And then he left one little nugget, drawing comparisons to LeBron James and the NBA's Most Valuable Player award. "LeBron has only won four MVPs, and I'm pretty sure he's been the best player for more than just four years," Koepka said. Point taken.

If his comments about not having many players to beat at the majors rubbed some the wrong way, he made another coy reference to his ability at Las Vegas with a surprising revelation that he had stem cell treatment on his left knee during his short offseason. Koepka says his patella tendon was partially torn and he had spent the last several weeks in rehab. He never mentioned his injury during the season. But he says the knee hurt enough that "I didn't practice at all."

He won the PGA Tour money title with $9,684,006 dating to the start of the tour season in October. For 2019, he was third on the World Money List at $8,013,992. Imagine what he might have done if fully healthy. "I finally feel good enough where I can actually practice and feel prepared coming into golf tournaments, not trying to find it on Tuesday or Wednesday," he said. Maybe he spoke too soon. Two weeks later, Koepka was walking down a slope off the tee at the par-five third hole in the second round of the CJ Cup when his right foot hit a wet piece of concrete and he landed hard on his left knee for support. He shot 75 and withdrew after the round, returning to Florida for treatment. That was his final round of the year. He withdrew from the Presidents Cup and spent a big part of December in treatment, preparing for a return.

Koepka played three rounds over the last four months of the year — a missed cut in Las Vegas, the withdrawal in South Korea. His World Ranking average was 12.65 after the Tour Championship, and the closest player to him was McIlroy at 9.63.

McIlroy's victory in the Tour Championship under any scoring format at least allowed for consideration on who had the better year. If anything, it might have been a referendum on The Players Championship and how PGA Tour members view it. The records between Koepka and McIlroy each had strong points. Koepka was bullish in the majors, while McIlroy didn't really come close to winning one. But he did win The Players Championship, which features the strongest, deepest field in golf on a demanding course at the TPC Sawgrass. Koepka won a World Golf Championship. McIlroy won the FedExCup. Both won three times for the tour's October-to-August season (McIlroy added a fourth title at the WGC-HSBC Champions). McIlroy, however, showed alarming consistency.

McIlroy started the year with seven consecutive top-10s, including his win at The Players and a runner-up finish in the WGC-Mexico Championship. He played in the final group three times in his first six events. For the year, he finished out of the top 10 only six times in 25 events worldwide. McIlroy won the Vardon Trophy for the lowest adjusted season average. So consistent was his year that he captured the World Money title at $10,820,758, a scant $65,930 more than Rahm. And because he finished just as strong as he started — a tie for third in the Zozo Championship, a playoff victory in the HSBC Champions, fourth in the DP World Tour Championship — he nearly replaced Koepka at No. 1 in the world. Instead, Koepka finished the year at No. 1 for the second straight year. McIlroy was close enough that a return to No. 1, where he hasn't been since September 14, 2015, appeared to be a matter of time.

Was it his best year? No. McIlroy won two majors in 2014, the year he won four times and was runner-up five times. He was no less pleased because he was consistently great for so much of the year. McIlroy pays close attention to the "strokes gained total" statistic provided by the PGA Tour since 2004 through its ShotLink scoring system. It measures the average number of strokes per round a player is better than the field average that day. Woods is the only player to have an average greater than 3, which he achieved three times. McIlroy was at 2.55 this year, the best total by anyone outside Woods. "The Holy Grail is 3. I'm not going to stop until I get to 3 because Tiger has done that multiple seasons, and when you get three strokes gained, you're just in another league," McIlroy said. "One of my goals every year is plus-3. I'm getting closer. It's my best season to date."

Typical of the reaction to McIlroy, a solid start to the year was not without some level of negativity. He had gone nine months without winning. And when he arrived in Hawaii for his debut in the Sentry Tournament of Champions, he pointed out that he had played in the final group six times and had given himself 10 realistic chances to win tournaments. "The more you keep knocking on the door and putting yourself in those positions, sooner or later you're going to get really comfortable and rack up the wins," he said. By the end of the week, he played in the final group and tied for fourth. He played in the final group at the WGC-Mexico Championship and finished second to Dustin Johnson. He played in the final group at the Arnold Palmer Invitational and tied for sixth. Focus shifted from consistently good play to whether he could close.

Maybe it was just his luck that McIlroy was in the penultimate group at The Players Championship, one shot behind Jon Rahm, his best at the tournament and the golf course that had vexed him over the years. In a final round that featured eight players with at least a share of the lead at some point, McIlroy was tied with four holes to play when he delivered his best swing — a six iron from a bunker to 15 feet, which he later called his best shot of the year; a 347-yard drive down the par-five 16th to set up an easy birdie; and a tee shot drilled down the 18th fairway for the one-shot win over Jim Furyk.

The timing was ideal. It ended talk about his ability to close, and the Masters was only a month away, the missing piece of the career Grand Slam. Alas, it remains that way. He didn't break 70 until the final round, and by then he was 12 shots behind. For such a great year, the majors were where McIlroy was lacking. He was an afterthought at the PGA Championship (14 shots behind after three rounds) and the U.S. Open (five shots back going to Sunday). And at his home Open in Northern Ireland, he didn't even make it to Sunday. McIlroy missed the cut. It was the first time since 2013 that he was never closer than eight shots of the winner in all four majors. That he was voted PGA Tour Player of the Year speaks to the overall quality of his game in 2019.

Rahm wasn't too far behind. He made a late push for the World Money List and had a lead late in his final event at the Hero World Challenge until Henrik Stenson made an eagle and wound up winning by one shot. Rahm headed home to Spain for his wedding, and there was plenty of good tidings had he chosen to look back on his year. For the third straight year, he won three times worldwide in tournaments that offer World Ranking points. His fourth victory was shared with Ryan Palmer at the Zurich Classic in New Orleans, the PGA Tour's only team event. Rahm turned pro after the U.S. Open at Oakmont in 2016. In the 86 events he has played, he has 10 victories and 45 finishes in the top 10, a rate of 52 percent. In that respect, this year was no different from the others.

Even so, Rahm has started so consistently well that even having celebrated his 25th birthday by the end of the year, he is looked up to as the next player who needs to break through for his first major. The Spaniard became one of the favorites for the Open Championship when he won the Irish Open for the second time in his career. Rahm did well in the majors, except for missing the cut in the PGA Championship, just not enough to seriously challenge. He had top-10s in the Masters and U.S. Open, and he was just outside the top 10 at Royal Portrush, the tournament that Shane Lowry turned into a one-man race.

The second half of the year was worth watching because he was always part of the action, or at least it seemed that way. From his tie for third in the U.S. Open, Rahm finished no worse than third in eight of his last 13 tournaments. That included victories in the Irish Open, the Spanish Open and the DP World Tour Championship with its handsome payday. He was runner-up at the Hero World Challenge and the BMW PGA Championship at Wentworth. With each victory came more comparisons with his idol, the late Seve Ballesteros, and he was close to tears when told in Dubai that he joined Ballesteros as the only Spanish players to finish a season as Europe's top player. That seemed to be as valuable as the $5 million he had just won — $3 million for the tournament, $2 million for the Race to Dubai. "Seve is such an idol for all of us, and so are Sergio [Garcia] and Ollie [Jose Maria Olazabal] and so many of the great Spanish players. And to think that I'm putting my name there before they do is hard to believe. I can't believe some of the things I've accomplished." The pressure to perform figures to increase with every major going forward.

The majors come quickly now. This year was the first in coping with a rapid-fire playing of the four biggest events on the golfing calendar, which required moving parts by three organizations. The PGA Tour was eager to finish their reason before the American football played the first game. The PGA of America was growing weary of its PGA Championship being referred to as the last of the majors, and jokingly referred to as the least of them. It needed energy, and a move to May would allow it to be in the heart of the major championship season instead of the end. It also positioned the PGA Championship away from changes during Olympic years. That required the PGA Tour to move The Players Championship back to March, where it had been until 2006. Left behind was the European Tour, which typically stages its flagship event in May at Wentworth. It appeared to work well for everyone involved. The BMW PGA Championship attracted most of Europe's best, along with Americans such as Patrick Reed, Tony Finau and Billy Horschel. The Rolex Series on the European Tour saw significantly stronger fields, especially with the BMW PGA Championship and the Italian Open moved to later in the year. The only potential problem would have been the PGA Championship in May because it already was set for Long Island in New York. The weather was cold early in the week — not any colder than Pebble Beach in February — and delivered heat inside and outside the ropes. Still, it was an adjustment for the players. Justin Rose spoke what several players were thinking. There used to be a chance for players to catch their breath after the Masters until the next major in June. There was no time for that in 2019.

The other change was far more significant. Sometime after the Open Championship at St. Andrews in 2010, top rules experts from around the world began meeting privately to discuss blowing up the Rules of Golf and essentially starting over. The Royal and Ancient game needed to adapt to a modern culture. They wanted rules that made sense without losing the tradition or ethos of a game with six centuries behind it. After releasing a proposed draft, and then confirming it, the modern Rules of Golf went into effect at the start of the year. It was not the smoothest transition, at least by appearance.

The two changes getting most of the attention were leaving the flagstick in during putts on the green, and how to get a ball back in play. The first took getting used to by the fans. The other was a problem for the players.

To get the ball in play quicker, the new rule was to drop it from the height of a player's knee instead of the shoulder. Players from tours around the world had been dropping it the same way their entire lives. Rickie Fowler never liked the look of it, and then he paid a steep price in the WGC-Mexico Championship when he was penalized one shot for using the shoulder-level drop. Fowler knew he made a mistake but was no less furious, calling it a "terrible change" and suggesting such rules gave golf a bad look. It got even worse the following week at the Honda Classic.

The rule change that met with so much approval during the draft wound up causing the biggest stir. The intent was to keep caddies from lining up their players, but it was written in such a way that players were unclear how and when it was enforced. And it didn't take long for the outrage to spill over. First, Haotong Li received a two-shot penalty on the 18th green at the Omega Dubai Desert Classic because his caddie stood on a line behind his ball. The penalty knocked him from a tie for third to a tie for 12th. A week later in the Waste Management Phoenix Open, Denny McCarthy was penalized two shots for his caddie standing behind him during practice swings. Officials adjusted the rule so caddies could stand behind the players as long as the players stepped away and started over with the pre-shot routine. But a month later, Adam Schenk was penalized because his caddie was standing behind him in a bunker to discuss a tough shot.

Justin Thomas, maturing into a strong voice at age 26, took to Twitter to say the rules were terrible. Someone at the USGA tweeted back to accuse Thomas of skipping planned rules meetings and suggesting that he call. Thomas said no meetings were ever scheduled, making the USGA look worse, and this genteel sport was losing its civility. PGA Tour commissioner Jay Monahan delivered a stern memo to players to be patient, still be vocal, and to realize everyone was in this together. Besides, according to ShotLink data, only three penalties under the new rules had been assessed to tour members out of roughly 258,000 shots hit in the first 10 tournaments of the year. It wasn't long afterward that the firestorm was put out, and the attention returned to birdies and bogeys instead of the rule book.

Thomas, meanwhile, joined a growing list of injuries in golf. By the end of the year, Woods, Johnson and Koepka all had procedures on their knees. Johnson wound up missing the WGC-HSBC Champions in Shanghai and the Hero World Challenge a week before he returned at the Presidents Cup. Koepka lost out on the HSBC Champions and the Presidents Cup. Thomas had to sit out during a more crucial part of the year. He tried to hit a shot off a tree root at the Honda Classic in early March, shook his wrist and kept going. What followed were mediocre performances, and after the Masters, he chose to sit out for nearly two months to let it heal. That meant missing the PGA Championship. And when he returned, he missed the cut in two of his next four starts, including the U.S. Open. From there, he continued to emerge as the best of an age group that includes Jordan Spieth and Xander Schauffele. Thomas won the BMW Championship for his second FedExCup Playoffs victory. He won the CJ Cup in South Korea for the second time. Starting with the Aberdeen Standard Investments Scottish Open, he never finished worse than a tie for 17th in his last 10 tournaments of the year.

The slow start and the injury kept him from a chance to win the PGA Tour money list for the third straight year. Thomas was No. 5 in the World Money List at just over $7 million. He finished behind Tommy Fleetwood, who finished at No. 4 with $7,783,428. Fleetwood made most of his money in five tournaments while winning just once, the fewest victories among the top five on the World Money List. The biggest payoff for Fleetwood was winning the Nedbank Challenge for $2.5 million. Add that to a runner-up finish in the DP World Tour Championship, the Open Championship, a tie for third in the Arnold Palmer Invitational and a tie for fifth in The Players Championship, and those five tournaments represented 70 percent of his earnings for the year.

While arguments could be made for the best of the men in 2019, there was no debating who ruled the world of women's golf. Jin Young Ko turned pro when she was 18 and won 10 times on the LPGA of Korea Tour in a four-year span. She was runner-up in the Women's British Open in 2015, and her victory in the LPGA KEB Hana Bank Championship in Korea was her ticket to America. Ko won the ISPS Handa Women's Australian Open in 2018, finished in the top 10 at slightly more than half of her tournaments and was the Louis Suggs Rolex Rookie of the Year. That was the warm-up act.

After winning the Bank of Hope Founders Cup, Ko captured her first major championship at the ANA Inspiration and moved to No. 1 in the Rolex Women's World Golf Rankings. In the summer, she closed with a four-under 67 for a two-shot victory in the Evian Championship for her second major of the year. And with a tournament-record 262 in the CP Women's Open in Canada for a five-shot victory, she picked up her LPGA-best fourth victory of the year. Her short game, particularly her putting, carried her to a dominant year. Even without winning the CME Group Tour Championship and its $1.5 million prize, Ko still won the LPGA Tour money tile and the Vare Trophy for the lowest scoring average. The LPGA Rolex Player of the Year is based on points. Ko clinched that with a month to go in the season.

Her year painted a broader picture of women's golf. Yes, the Koreans remained the force on the LPGA Tour by winning 15 of the 32 official events on the schedule by eight players. Ko, Kim, Sung Hyun Park and M.J. Hur won multiple times. But sustaining dominance over a year was shown to be more difficult. The previous year, Ariya Jutanugarn won the U.S. Women's Open among her three LPGA titles, was the LPGA Rolex Player of the Year, won the Vare Trophy and the money title with nearly more money than the next two players on the list. In 2019, Jutanugarn didn't win a single LPGA event. In 2017, the player of the year was shared between Park and So Yeon Ryu. Park shared player-of-the-year honors as the rookie of the year. And to think it was only four years ago when the future belonged to Lydia Ko. It was more evidence that great depth and parity had arrived on the LPGA Tour. The Americans showed some strength with four winners. Nelly Korda led the way with two victories, and she was in the mix for the Race to the CME Globe at the end of the year. Korda finished the year at No. 3 in the world.

The best American performance might have belonged to the commissioner, Mike Whan. The LPGA Tour was losing sponsors and tournaments during the recession when Whan came along with high energy and big plans in 2010. The LPGA had 24 tournaments with official prize money of $41.4 million, and only one tournament — the U.S. Women's Open, run by the USGA — had a purse of $3 million or more. This year, the LPGA had 32 official events with $70.2 million in prize money. Five tournaments offered $3 million or more, and the CME Group Tour Championship to wrap up the season had a $5 million purse. Whan, who signed a long-term extension as commissioner at the end of the year, says it wasn't only numbers that allowed him to measure how far women's golf had come. "It was putting women on a platform that had never been seen before. I'm not sure we're there yet. And there's certainly a long way to go. But some really cool signs," he said.

The future of women's golf was blossoming, too. Paving the way was the Augusta National Women's Amateur, which brought women to the home of the Masters for the first time to compete. Along with illustrating progressive thinking by Augusta National, it brought more attention to the women's game by showcasing potential stars for the future. Jennifer Kupcho and Maria Fassi were among those who took advantage of a new LPGA Tour policy by earning cards at the Q-Series — a qualifying tournament of eight rounds stretched over consecutive 72-hole tournaments — by deferring their membership. By staying an amateur, they were able to compete at Augusta National, and they put on a show. Fassi is a powerful, dynamic personality from Mexico, and she appeared to take control in the final round. Kupcho developed a migraine in the middle of the final round, so severe she had trouble seeing. But she recovered just in time with a back-nine charge that was memorable, mostly the two shots she hit with a three-hybrid — to six feet on the 13th for eagle, and a hard draw around the trees and over the water to the 15th that set up birdie. They turned pro for the U.S. Women's Open, and despite only having just over five months, both kept their LPGA cards. Kupcho advanced to the CME Group Tour Championship.

The LPGA Tour has been looking beyond American shores for a while — it was the first truly international tour. Whan took an extraordinary step late in the year by promoting a partnership with the Ladies European Tour. The members of the LET agreed to the 50-50 joint venture to pool resources without it being an American takeover. Each tour will have six members on the board. The LET has been struggling for years to keep tournaments and sponsors. Whan saw it as a way to build opportunities for European countries, knowing there would be a path to the LPGA Tour. "If you read the mission of the LPGA, it's to provide women the opportunity to pursue their dreams in the game of golf, period. I don't see a boundary or a fence around that statement," Whan said. "So I said to my board, I think we should do this because we can. And I think it's our responsibility. Our founders would have done it, so why shouldn't we?"

Europe's greatest achievement this year was winning the Solheim Cup for the first time since 2013 in Colorado. Golf continued to thrive in Asia, too. Ai Suzuki won seven times on the Japan LPGA, the most victories by a professional in the world this year, male or female. Hinako Shibuno won five times — four in Japan, and one on the road. But that was a big one. Shibuno, with her charming style and devil-may-care attitude, won the AIG Women's British Open in her first major. Instead of taking up LPGA Tour membership, she decided to remain at home in Japan, still not sure — even after a major — her game was ready for the LPGA Tour. Ko, meanwhile, had five victories by adding another title on the Korean LPGA Tour.

There also was a growing trend toward putting men and women together, sometimes at the same golf complex, sometimes on the same golf course, playing for the same prize money and even competing against each other. One such occasion was the ISPS Handa Vic Open, co-sanctioned by the LPGA Tour and the European Tour. It featured men and women competing on the same course, with winners from each tour receiving equal prize money. The Jordan Mixed Open in April featured players from Europe's senior Staysure Tour, the Challenge Tour and the Ladies European Tour. Daan Huizing of the Netherlands, who plays on the Challenge Tour, won by two shots over Meghan MacLaren of the LET. The Challenge Tour also had the ISPS Handa World Invitational for men and women, who competed for separate trophies on the same course at Massereene Golf Club in Northern Ireland. Women were invited again to play in the GolfSixes event on the European Tour, while the European Tour and LET staged events in Morocco on the same golf resort, but different courses.

And it wasn't stopping there. Henrik Stenson and Annika Sorenstam got involved by announcing they will host the Scandinavian Mixed in 2020 in which players from the European Tour and LET will compete for one trophy, a prize fund of 1.5 million euros and world ranking points. Missing were the details, but not the momentum. "The European Tour has been leading the way in terms of innovative formats, and I believe this is certainly one that can be part of the way golf is played in the future," Stenson said.

Innovation was on the mind of the PGA Tour when it tried to find a cleaner end to is points-based system. The FedExCup has been around since 2007, and the system has been tweaked over the years. But there still was some confusion on the reset of points, along with the possibility of having two winners in one day — the winner of the Tour Championship, and the winner of the FedExCup. So it went for perhaps its most radical idea. The idea was to reward the best, most consistent season, but also to make the Tour Championship the deciding event for the FedExCup and the $15 million bonus. So it went with a staggered start. Whoever was leading the FedEx-Cup after the regular season and two postseason events — Thomas in this case — started the Tour Championship at 10 under par. Patrick Cantlay was second, so he started at eight under. It went all the way down the list for the top 30 until the last five players started at even par. And then the first shot was struck. It was odd, mainly because of the chance that whoever shot the lowest 72-hole score might not win the tournament. The upside for the tour was that fans could keep track of one score — whoever was lowest to par at the end. For one year, it worked out fine. McIlroy played so well that he would have won either way. He shot 13-under 267, which was three shots better than anyone else. With his head start at five under (he was No. 5 in the standings), he was credited with 18 under for a four-shot victory. The math still wasn't easy, except for counting the $15 million he won.

Youth showed itself around the world, an increasing trend in golf. Joaquin Niemann of Chile won A Military Tribute at The Greenbrier by five shots, and then was chosen by International captain Ernie Els to become the first Chilean to play in the Presidents Cup. Jazz Janewattananond of Thailand featured at the PGA Championship at Bethpage Black until he faded to a 77 in the final round and tied for 14th. Janewattananond easily won the Order of Merit on the Asian Tour by winning four tournaments, including the last two to crack the top 50 in the world and earn his first trip to the Masters.

On the PGA Tour, three players who turned pro after the NCAAs made an immediate impact. One month after Matthew Wolff won the Jack Nicklaus Award as the top player in college at Oklahoma State, he rolled in an eagle putt on the final hole of the TPC Twin Cities to win the 3M Open by one shot over Collin Morikawa, whose eagle attempt to force a playoff narrowly missed. Morikawa, who graduated from California, grew up with Wolff north of Los Angeles. Not to worry. Morikawa won the Barracuda Championship in Reno, Nevada, a month later. The other was Viktor Hovland of Norway, another star at Oklahoma State. Hovland did well enough to earn his PGA Tour card without winning, but he got everyone's attention with 19 consecutive rounds in the 60s, starting with a 64 in the final round of the Rocket Mortgage Classic in June, ending with a 74 in the third round of the CJ Cup in October.

One of those young stars used to be Jordan Spieth, who in 2019 went from the "Who's Who?" of golf to "Remember Them?" It wasn't that bad for Spieth. He accomplished so much so quickly — 14 wins worldwide (11 on the PGA Tour) and three legs of the career Grand Slam at age 23 — that he became one of the biggest stars in the game. That made his slump all the more pronounced. Coming off a year when he failed to win or even reach the Tour Championship, Spieth suddenly began to struggle on the weekend as he worked to get his swing back to where it once was. He was in contention going into the weekend of the AT&T Pebble Beach Pro-Am until closing with rounds of 74-75. He had a shot at the Genesis Open the following week at Riviera and shot 81 in the final round. There was a 74-75 weekend at the RBC Heritage, a final round over par (71) at the AT&T Byron Nelson. He played in the final group of the third round at the PGA Championship with Koepka and fell back with a 72. The result was the same — no victories, no trip to East Lake for the Tour Championship. Spieth began 2019 at No. 17 in the world and was at No. 44 when it ended, in danger of falling out of the top 50 for the first time since his rookie year in 2013. He wasn't alone. Spieth and Jason Day once battled for No. 1 in the world, and the Australian also took a tumble in the ranking. Coming off a two-win season, Day started with promise until his back began to act up again. He tied for fifth in the Masters, and then had only one top-10 the rest of the year as his World Ranking fell to No. 37 and he didn't make it to the Tour Championship. He was a captain's pick for the Presidents Cup, but then withdrew because of another back injury.

Dustin Johnson was nowhere near that category. It just seemed that way the second part of the year. He won the WGC-Mexico Championship for his 20th career victory on the PGA Tour, this after winning the inaugural Saudi International. He had his best finish in the Masters as a runner-up. He nearly made history at the PGA Championship when he tried to overcome a seven-shot deficit to Koepka, a rally that ended on the 16th hole. And then he went quiet. Johnson didn't record another top-10 the rest of the year — eight tournaments, his longest streak without a top-10 since the end of 2011 and the start of 2012. It made sense when he revealed he had surgery on his left knee, which had been bothering him most of the year and made him hang back on his right side instead of getting through the shot. Johnson said that led to a straight ball. Is that so bad? "It is when you're aiming for a cut," he said.

The other disappearing act after a victory belonged to Phil Mickelson. For starters, he disappeared from the world top 50. Mickelson really is an ageless wonder who remains as enthused about competition at age 49 as when he turned pro at age 22. When he won the WGC-Mexico Championship in 2018, Mickelson said he was certain he would reach his goal of 50 wins on the PGA Tour. That was his 43rd. And in February, he made it No. 44 with his fifth victory at the AT&T Pebble Beach Pro-Am. It was there that

Mickelson peeled back the curtain of reality. "The fact is it's very difficult to win out here, and to win seven more times — now it's only six — is not going to be easy," he said at Pebble. "It's still a goal of mine. But I also need to be realistic. That's going to be a tough goal to attain. But that's why it's such a fun challenge." The more immediate goal was a U.S. Open to complete the career Grand Slam. He missed again, this time at Pebble Beach. Then, it was to make his 25th consecutive team, Ryder Cup or Presidents Cup, already a record and one that might not be matched again. That seemed easy enough after Pebble Beach. It wasn't.

Mickelson only cracked the top 20 one time over his next 19 tournaments worldwide, a tie for 18th at the Masters. He was resigned to being left off the Presidents Cup team. More resignation arrived in Shanghai for the WGC-HSBC Champions, when Mickelson tied for 28th. It was enough for him to fall out of the top 50 for the first time since the last week in November in 1993. That adds to nearly 26 years of being among the top 50, a record so impressive that the OWGR board recognized Mickelson during the Open Championship at Royal Portrush. It requires perspective. The last time Mickelson was not in the top 50, Justin Thomas and Jordan Spieth were still in diapers. Jose Maria Olazabal had yet to win the Masters. Deane Beman was still commissioner of the PGA Tour. It was the first time Mickelson looked his age. Undeterred as ever, he pledged to return. "It was a good run. Unfortunately, the last eight months I played terribly and I've fallen out. But I'll get back in there," Mickelson said. He didn't play again the rest of the year and slipped all the way to No. 70. It looked like a tough road back.

Bernhard Langer also saw his streak come to an end. The two-time Masters champion had won the Charles Schwab Cup on the PGA Tour Champions a record five times. Even with his 62nd birthday approaching in the summer, he was considered the player to beat. Langer won his second start of the year, and then lost in a playoff the following week. He extended his senior record with his 11th major championship in the Senior Open Championship at Royal Lytham & St. Annes, his 40th victory on the PGA Tour Champions. But he only had three top-10s until the Charles Schwab Cup Playoffs, and at No. 7 he was too far behind to make up ground. Langer wound up at No. 4 in the final standings, his lowest since he was 24th in 2011.

Instead, the PGA Tour Champions became a one-man show, at least in terms of points, from Scott McCarron. He went to No. 1 with his victory in the spring at the Mitsubishi Electric Classic outside Atlanta, and he stayed there the rest of the year. McCarron won twice more — but no majors — and built such a big lead that not even a slump toward the end of the year could keep him from the $1 million annuity. Jerry Kelly tried to keep it close, but couldn't get it done in the final event. Retief Goosen had a chance to win the Schwab Cup, but the former U.S. Open champion missed a three-foot birdie putt in a playoff loss to Jeff Maggert at the Schwab Cup Championship in Arizona, and Goosen had to win the tournament to win the cup. Steve Stricker didn't play the PGA Tour Champions after July, but he still had a big year with two senior majors. One of them was the U.S. Senior Open, which makes him exempt for the U.S. Open return to Winged Foot.

Woods turned 44 at the end of the year, and he has often said he is closer to players like Stricker and Fred Couples and other PGA Tour Champions players than to his peers on the PGA Tour. But it was clear, especially in his final act of a special year, what the younger players meant to him. It was Thomas and Rickie Fowler, in particular, who encouraged Woods when he was struggling with his back. They played several practice rounds in Florida. He was their idol when they were teenagers, and it was inspiring to be around him on the same level. Most striking about Woods winning the Masters were the players who waited outside the scoring room to greet him. That didn't happen a generation ago, the last time Woods had won a major. Woods always had the awe of the public and the utmost respect of the players he beat. At this stage in his career, he was embraced by players who for years knew him best from highlights or video games.

He came to life this year, at least for one week at Augusta National to become a major champion again, and again in Japan to match a record that no one will touch for a long time, if ever. And until he stops playing, who knows what that PGA Tour career victory record will be?

2. Masters Tournament

Each generation would be left to choose its own greatest golf story, in the context of its own time — Bobby Jones winning the Grand Slam in 1930; Byron Nelson in 1945, scoring 11 consecutive wins, 18 overall; Arnold Palmer and the electrifying rally in the 1960 U.S. Open and his monumental effect on the game; Jack Nicklaus and his towering skills, winner of a record 18 majors, et al.

And, of course, Tiger Woods — his immense talent, the numerous victories, and then just when his incandescent career seemed to be burning out, recovering from painful and disabling physical problems to win the 2019 Masters. It was his fifth, at age 43, and it came against a host of new and young talent. Woods won his first Masters in 1997 at age 21, the youngest champion, with an 18-under 270 total, and by 12 strokes — all records. He won in 2001 by two, 2002 by three, 2005 in a playoff and now 2019 by one. Where would Masters 2019 fit in Woods' memory?

"There were so many different scenarios that could have transpired on that back nine," said Woods, reflecting on the double bogey at the 12th that erased Francesco Molinari's lead and changed the face of this Masters. "There were so many guys that had a chance to win. Leaderboard was absolutely packed and everyone was playing well. You couldn't have had more drama than we all had out there.

"I was grinding hard trying to chase Francesco," said Woods, marveling at the abrupt change, "and then all of a sudden the leaderboard flipped and there were a bunch of guys up there who had a chance to win."

Masters 2019 will always be thought of as the comeback of Tiger Woods, but it was actually more than that. Medically and physically, it was a rebirth, as well. It had been 11 years since his previous win in a major, the 2008 U.S. Open, and 14 years since his last Masters, in 2005. Since 2007, he'd had surgery five times on his left knee and four times on his back.

"I had serious doubts after what transpired a couple years ago," Woods said. "I could barely walk. I couldn't sit. Couldn't lay down. I really couldn't do much of anything. Luckily, I had the procedure on my back, which gave me a chance at having a normal life. But then all of a sudden, I realized I could actually swing a golf club again. I felt if I could somehow piece this together that I still had the hands to do it. The body's not the same as it was a long time ago, but I still have good hands."

His win had an impact on the golfers he'd just beaten.

"It's hard to really feel bad about how I played because I just witnessed history," said Xander Schauffele, 26, who led for about 30 seconds before tying for second, a stroke behind Woods. "Coming down the stretch Tiger making the roars. I got the full Masters experience."

Said Brooks Koepka, who also tied for second: "You want to play against the best ever to play … go toe-to-toe with them. I can leave, saying I gave it my all. He's just good, man."

And Molinari, who tied for fifth: "It was great to see … his story, his comeback, and to be a witness in first person, it's nice."

And said Tiger Woods: "Everyone was playing well at the same time, and it could have gone so many different ways. Just happened to hang in there and persevere."

FIRST ROUND

The 2019 Masters got off to a rousing start that perhaps could be heard over in Aiken, South Carolina, some 18 miles to the east. What with Brooks Koepka shooting a sizzling, birdie-only 66 and Bryson DeChambeau tying him, but on a wild ride in which he parred only six holes, and with Phil Mickelson taking third and saying that what didn't happen may have been more critical than what did happen in his 67 — his best start since 2010, when he won his third green jacket.

For the galleries, a catching of the breath was advisable.

Mickelson had birdied Nos. 2 and 8, then made the turn and immediately dodged a full-fledged disaster. He artfully saved a bogey out of the trees at the 10th and saved another out of the water at the 11th. His point: The bogeys were what did happen, but what didn't happen? "I made two great bogeys that should have and could have been doubles," he said. Round-killing, confidence-killing double bogeys. After the close calls, he roared home, birdieing five of the last seven holes — 12, 13, 15, 16 and 18 — for the 67.

The Masters book, noting his wizardry and his age — just weeks from 49 — called him Methuselah of the Masters and Merlin the Magician of the Masters.

If the 66s by Koepka and DeChambeau, both seeking their first Masters, came down to a question of degree-of-difficulty, it probably was a coin toss. Koepka, playing in the final group, authored the only bogey-free round of the day. DeChambeau rode the wild wind.

Koepka started with one birdie on the front nine, at No. 2, and then on the back five birdies in six holes. First at the 10th, then at the treacherous par-three 12; "...an easy two-putt birdie on 13 … then 14, a nice little putt; … then on 15, blasted it long right of the green and got it up and down." It was pretty much vintage Koepka, the one who won the U.S. Open in 2017 and 2018, and the 2018 PGA Championship.

"I just enjoy the big stage," Koepka said. "I enjoy major championships. I mean, that's what you're remembered by."

DeChambeau had a wild ride that started birdie-bogey-birdie from No. 2. He loosened up with birdie-bogey from No. 8, then roared over the last seven holes in six under, going birdie-eagle-bogey from the 12th, then birdieing the last four. And he came within two tap-ins of going two strokes lower. His eight-iron tee shot at the par-three 16th barely missed being an ace, and at the 18th, his six-iron uphill approach from behind the bunker rolled right to the hole and glanced off the flagstick. Said DeChambeau, ever the physics major out of Stanford: "My terminal velocity was too high."

Most of this happened before Tiger Woods even teed off in the next-to-last threesome with China's Haotong Li and Spain's Jon Rahm. Woods shot a halting two-under 70, going birdie-bogey-birdie at Nos. 2, 5 and 9, then birdie-birdie-bogey at 13, 14 and 17.

"I feel like I played well today and I controlled my golf ball all day," said Woods, whose last Masters was in 2005 and whose last major was the 2008

U.S. Open. "I've shot this number and won four coats, so hopefully I can do it again." The sentiment was laudable but the facts were askew. When he won his last green jacket in 2005, he'd opened with a 74. "The whole idea," Woods said, "is to try and peak for four times a year. And so I feel like my body's good and my game's good, it's sharp, so just got to go out there and execute."

Some wry twists opened this 2019 Masters. Rory McIlroy, going for the last leg of his personal career Grand Slam, didn't quite balance the books. "I made five birdies — that wasn't the problem," he said. "I just made too many mistakes." Meaning six bogeys. He shot 73. Justin Rose was among the favorites because he had returned to No. 1 in the Official Golf World Ranking and also because of his play in recent Masters. He shot 75. "Drove it left the first few holes," Rose said. "Never really found my rhythm." Thailand's Kiradech Aphibarnrat posted a hard-won 69. After a bogey at No. 4, he patiently battled the course for pars. "I've been waiting for my first birdie for quite a while," he said. Then at the par-five 13th, he put a three-iron second from the right rough 16 feet from the cup and made the eagle, a warm-up for birdies at 15 and 16.

Six amateurs got the thrill of playing in the Masters.

South Africa's Jovan Rebula, an Auburn University standout, on finally being on the first tee at Augusta National: "I mean, it was nerve-racking, for sure," he said. "The butterflies were going..."

Norway's Viktor Hovland, by way of Oklahoma State, found a new way of describing the experience. "So it was kind of surreal ... I almost had to kind of get out of my own head."

First-round leaders: Brooks Koepka 66, Bryson DeChambeau 66, Phil Mickelson 67, Dustin Johnson 68, Ian Poulter 68, Kevin Kisner 69, Kiradech Aphibarnrat 69, Justin Harding 69, Adam Scott 69, Jon Rahm 69.

SECOND ROUND

Tiger Woods had escaped some tight situations before, but nothing like the one in the second round. He'd just hit a low punch shot out of the trees at No. 14 and as he was walking toward the fairway, down a rain-slick slope, a security officer trying to keep the gallery back slipped on the wet grass and slid into his lower right leg. Woods didn't go down, but he limped a bit and flexed his ankle. "I'm fine," Woods said. "It's all good. Accidents happen, and move on."

He turned the potential disaster into a birdie, and ended the day just a stroke out of the biggest second-round tie for the lead ever in the Masters. Fully five players were tied at seven-under 137 — Francesco Molinari, with a 67, Jason Day (67), Brooks Koepka (71), Adam Scott (68) and Louis Oosthuizen (66). Then a shot behind came Woods, Dustin Johnson (70), Justin Harding (69) and Xander Schauffele (65).

"This is really stacked," said Scott, the 2013 Masters champion. "I think it's going to be an incredible weekend ... As a golf fan, I like it. As a player, I'd rather be like six in front or something."

Scott, who hadn't won in three years, eagled the par-five 15th on a two iron to five feet and was the only player to get to eight under. But he bogeyed the par-three 16th, missing his par from three feet.

Looking forward to third-round strategy? Oosthuizen cautioned prudent play. "Not try too much and play yourself out of the tournament," he said. "You just want to have a decent round and then Sunday there are a lot of holes where you want to be very aggressive."

Day considered himself fortunate that he could even get through two rounds with his painful back. He recounted bending to kiss his little daughter just before his tee time in the first round, then barely making it to the tee. And then on the way between holes telling his caddie, "Luke, I said, 'If this stays the same pain as it was on the putting green, I'll probably end up withdrawing.'" But he hung on for a courageous 67, matching Molinari, the 2018 Open champion. Molinari worked Augusta National from the ground up when he caddied for his older brother, Edoardo, the 2005 U.S. Amateur champion, in the 2006 Masters. Said Molinari, the only one of the top nine to go bogey-free in the round: "I know that I need to keep doing what I do ... and see if anyone can beat me."

Koepka twitted himself on the wild start to his 71. After a birdie at No. 1: "Just kind of No. 2 — I don't know what happened there. Pulled a drive and hit it a little off the toe and went in the trees. But stayed in the trees for a while and made seven." Someone noted that Jack Nicklaus warned against going left at No. 2.

"What's down there?" a writer asked. "There's a creek," Koepka said. "Were you in the creek?" "No. I was in the pine straw, then hit the tree, bounced on the cart path, went all the way down into the hazard ... and then you know, took a drop, punched out and hit on the green and two-putted."

Dustin Johnson, World No. 2, was doing an impressive job of broncobusting, pulling his fractious colt of a game back into line. He hit only six of the 14 driving fairways and nine greens in the second round, bogeyed just once and birdied three times for that 70, a shot out of the logjam lead. Rory McIlroy, after that six-bogey 73 in the first round, regrouped for a fragmented 71 that included two birdies, an eagle and three bogeys and trailed by seven shots, but also by 35 players. "To be here on the weekend and only be seven back," McIlroy said, "I'm really pleased."

Woods was one under on the front after alternating three birdies and two bogeys over six holes from No. 4. Coming in, he birdied the 11th, then holed the 30-footers at 14 and 15. He had a heart-stopping 68 that shattered the soft Georgia air. He missed two eight-footers for birdie on the back nine, but rolled in back-to-back 30-footers for birdies at 14 and 15. "It feels like I played my own way back into the tournament," Woods said. "I was just very patient today, felt very good."

The second round came to a close with Woods just one stroke out of the lead — the closest after 36 holes in a major since the 2013 Open Championship.

"The last three majors," Woods said, feeling the quickening, "I've been right there."

Second-round leaders: Francesco Molinari 67-137, Jason Day 67-137, Brooks Koepka 71-137, Adam Scott 68-137, Louis Oosthuizen 66-137, Dustin Johnson 70-138, Justin Harding 69-138, Xander Schauffele 65-138, Tiger Woods 68-138.

THIRD ROUND

It would go down as one of the grand ironies in the history of golf that two kids, thousands of miles apart, who were inspired by Tiger Woods at the same time, would be battling him for the Masters championship more than two decades later.

Saturday at the 2019 Masters, the third round, was the 22nd anniversary of Woods' victory in the 1997 Masters, a breathtaking, historic 12-stroke rampage by the 21-year-old.

In Utah that day, Tony Finau, only seven, was riveted to the television set. "Just watching Tiger dominate the way that he did was very inspiring for me, as a kid," he said, "and I took up the game." In Italy, Francesco Molinari, 14, was watching his hero, countryman Costantino Rocca. Then he fixed on Woods. "He was someone I looked up to," Molinari said. "He's one of those sporting icons that you don't need to be American to appreciate."

Then on that Saturday in the 2019 Masters, Molinari, Finau and Woods were fed into some kind of cosmic collision course that would bring them together in the final round the next day.

But this wasn't a three-man chase, not by a long shot. There were 11 golfers crammed within five shots of the lead at day's end.

Saturday at Augusta glowed. "The conditions were perfect — light wind, very scorable," said Dustin Johnson. Even so, the playful sprite that was golf slipped away from some. Johnson started the day one stroke off the lead, shot two-under 70, and finished five behind.

For Adam Scott, who started tied for the lead, it was the greens. "I tried to read the pace of the greens ... maybe the slowest I've ever seen them here," he said. "Early on I just didn't have enough pace on putts and then I had too much." He shot par 72 and fell six behind. For fellow Aussie Jason Day, who also had shared the lead, it was the tees. "I just couldn't get it on the fairways," he said. A 73 dropped him seven behind. South Africa's Louis Oosthuizen, another from the tie, shot 71 and fell five behind.

For Rory McIlroy, the career Grand Slam fell pretty much out of sight on his 71, 12 off the lead. "It's not as if I'm playing bad golf," he said. In the three rounds, he'd made 11 birdies and two eagles, but also 14 bogeys.

Molinari was leading going into the third round at seven under, Woods trailed by one and Finau by four, and the steeplechase was on.

Finau would be remembered as tying for 10th in the 2018 Masters despite fighting the pain of a severe ankle injury suffered in the par-three contest. This time he started the third round with a sprint, birdieing the first three holes. Another birdie at No. 6, and then an eagle at the par-five No. 8 — his four-iron approach stopped just inches from the cup — gave him a record-tying, six-under 30 on the front nine. Birdies at 13 and 15 gave him an eight-under 64, one of an unprecedented three for the day, with those of Patrick Cantlay and Webb Simpson.

Finau, leading for the moment at 11-under 205, frolicked on Augusta's par-fives. He'd played Nos. 2, 8, 13 and 15 in birdie-eagle-birdie-birdie. "Hitting it with length and hitting it in the fairway — they are very reachable for me," he said. "At Augusta National, you have to play the par-fives well to win."

Woods started 40 minutes after Finau and bogeyed No. 1 — the only bogey among the three in the third round. Then he raced to six birdies the rest of the way for a 67, tying Finau at 11 under.

"It's been a while since I've been in contention here," Woods said. "But then again, the last two majors count for something. I've been in the mix with a chance to win major championships in the last two years, and so that helps. I'm just thankful to be able to come back here and play again."

Woods tied for the lead — briefly — when he holed a seven-foot putt for birdie at the 16th, under the thunder of the gallery. He was tied with Molinari and Finau — the latter already finished — at 11 under. But shortly thereafter, Molinari rolled in an eight-footer at the 14th for the third of his four straight birdies, getting to 12 under. Another birdie at the 15th gave him a 66, a 13-under 203, and a two-stroke lead. Woods and Finau were tied for second, two behind. They would play the last round as the final group. But it was not a three-man race. Brooks Koepka shot 69 and was three behind, and Webb Simpson, after that 64, and Ian Poulter (68) were four behind.

Third-round leaders: Francesco Molinari 66-203, Tony Finau 64-205, Tiger Woods 67-205, Brooks Koepka 69-206, Webb Simpson 64-207, Ian Poulter 68-207, Matt Kuchar 68-208, Justin Harding 70-208, Xander Schauffele 70-208, Dustin Johnson 70-208, Louis Oosthuizen 71-208.

FOURTH ROUND

"It fits," Tiger Woods said.

And wearing a huge smile and the coveted green jacket he'd just slipped into, Tiger Woods emerged as the 2019 Masters champion.

He had just won his fifth Masters (second to Jack Nicklaus's six) and 15th major (second to Nicklaus's 18). The man who was in danger of never playing again had just won his first major in nearly 11 years, since the 2008 U.S. Open, and his first Masters in 14 years. It felt as good as all the others, in 1997, 2001, 2002 and 2005. Maybe better, for a man of 43, second oldest winner after Nicklaus at 46, after years of personal turmoil and health problems.

"Just unreal," Woods said. "Just the whole tournament has meant so much to me. Coming here in '95 for the first time, and being able to play as an amateur; winning in '97, and then come full circle, 22 years later, to be able to do it again, and just the way it all transpired today."

It was the first time Woods won a major after trailing going into the final round. He stayed close, shooting 70-68-67, and trailed, successively, by four, one and two strokes. Then, in an fairytale finish, he closed with a 70 for a 13-under 275 and won by one. The 83rd Masters was truly one for the books.

Everyone was chasing the placid Italian, Francesco Molinari, who tied for the lead in the second round and then was leading solo the rest of the way.

Faced with predictions of heavy afternoon storms, officials opted for a early start, with play to be in threesomes and splitting to start at Nos. 1 and 10.

It was a battle for second place behind Molinari until the late starters reached the water-guarded par-three 12th, the Masters' 155-yard Bermuda Triangle, where so many hopes and dreams disappear.

The toll among contenders was great. There were four double bogeys among the last two threesomes. In the next-to-last group, Ian Poulter's flickering hopes were all but snuffed out and Brooks Koepka's chances took a big hit, both on double bogeys. And in the final group, Molinari, who made just two bogeys through the first 65 holes, was leading by two when he stepped up to the 12th tee. He had played the wicked little hole in par-birdie-birdie. But this time, his tee shot pulled up short, dropped onto the bank and rolled back into the water. He double-bogeyed.

Tony Finau, who began the final round two shots off the lead, also watered his tee shot and also double-bogeyed. "I still could have made something happen down the stretch," Finau said. "But 12 was kind of a big swing."

The third man of the group, Tiger Woods, hit the green safely, 50 feet from the flag, and two-putted for par, tying Molinari for the lead. Was Molinari hit by pressure? Not likely, the pundits said, noting that he had won the 2018 Open Championship at Carnoustie, turning back Woods in the stretch, and in the 2018 Ryder Cup he went 5-0-0, including three wins against Woods.

"I was trying to hit a chippy eight iron," Molinari said. "It was probably a nine-iron yardage, but I didn't want the wind to gust and get the ball, and I just didn't hit it hard enough."

The stampede was on. Six players shared the lead at some point on the final nine, and when the final threesome was in the 15th fairway, there was a five-way tie for the lead.

"That mistake Francesco made there let a lot of guys back into the tournament — myself included," Woods said. "The leaderboard was absolutely packed. Now I know why I'm balding. This stuff is hard."

It got worse for Molinari. Negotiating a corner at the par-five 15th, he nicked a tree limb, watered the shot, and double-bogeyed again. "I think it wasn't my day today," Molinari said. "But I'm really happy of the way I felt out there. I was calm, collected, never panicked … but I'll learn from my mistakes."

The chase was intense. Koepka, after his double bogey at 12, eagled the 13th and shot 70, tying a stroke back with two — Dustin Johnson, who birdied four of five from the 13th for a 68, and Xander Schauffele who birdied five of seven from No. 8 and shot 70. Finau birdied 13, 15 and 16 for a 72 and tied for fifth with Molinari (74) and Webb Simpson (70).

Woods had his own birdie spree coming in. He birdied both par-fives, hitting an eight-iron second into 13 and a five iron from 234 yards into 15, and at the par-three 16th he hit an eight iron from 179 yards to about 18 inches.

He came to the 18th with a two-shot lead, tapped in for a bogey and a one-shot victory, and swept up his kids, son Charlie, 10, and daughter Sam, 11. Later, after the hugs, he would sign for his 70, his 13-under 275, and his sixth Masters. And his 15th major.

And was he now drawing a bead on No. 16, in pursuit of Jack Nicklaus's record 18?

"You know, I really haven't thought about that yet," Woods said. "I'm sure that I'll probably think of it going down the road. Maybe, maybe not. But right now, it's a little soon, and I'm just enjoying 15."

The final leaders: Tiger Woods 70-275, Dustin Johnson 68-276, Xander Schauffele 68-276, Brooks Koepka 70-276, Jason Day 67-277, Webb Simpson 70-277, Tony Finau 72-277, Francesco Molinari 74-277.

3. PGA Championship

With all due respect, Brooks Koepka would beg to differ.

It is generally accepted in the world of golf that the four majors — the Masters, the PGA Championship, the U.S. Open and the Open Championship — are the most difficult events to win for two principal reasons: because as the most important tournaments, they create the greatest pressure on the golfers, and because they have the strongest fields.

Not so, says Koepka. They're the easiest to win. And he had the proof at hand. In fact, he'd lived it. He won the U.S. Open in 2017 and 2018, the first to hold back-to-back Opens since Curtis Strange in 1988-89, and he won the 2018 PGA Championship — three majors in two calendar years. He was, at the moment, honing his game for a fourth in this particular week in May 2019.

Koepka had offered his revolutionary view in his news conference with the media on Tuesday at the PGA Championship at Bethpage Black. Bethpage would be a suitable site for testing his thesis. Bethpage is the very demanding public course — most classify it as a monster — on Long Island, New York, which had already held two majors, the U.S. Open in 2002 and 2009.

He offered his calculations. He wrote off half of the 156 starters immediately. "You figure at least 80 of them, I'm just going to beat," he said. "From there, you figure about half of them won't play well from there, so you're down to about 35. And then from 35, some of them just … pressure is going to get to them. It only leaves you with a few more, and you've just got to beat those guys."

As he did in the 2018 PGA at Bellerive. He had pretty much passed the rest of the field. The only guys he had to beat were — well — just Tiger Woods and Adam Scott.

"You don't have to try to go win it," Koepka said. "Just hang around. If you hang around, good things are going to happen." He said he had hurt himself in PGA Tour events by not recognizing this fact. He would press too hard to build a cushion and got ahead of himself. "In the majors," he said, "I just stay in the moment. I never think one hole ahead. I'm not thinking about tomorrow. I'm not thinking about the next shot. I'm just thinking about what I've got to do right then and there. And I kind of dummy it down and make it very simple, and I think that's what helps me."

Koepka came to the 2019 PGA and Bethpage with more than an interesting piece of logic and a deep breath. He's noted for his blunt talk, but it was clear that his theory on playing majors was not a prediction, merely a statement of intent. Much like the one he'd made on the eve of the 2018 U.S. Open. He was defending his title — someone would have to take it away from him. The same as he was feeling at Bethpage, on the eve of the 2019 PGA.

"Yeah, I mean, I have the trophy," Koepka said. "Someone has got to…" He left that one hanging. "The last time we played this championship, I won," he said. "I feel like I like my chances this week. I feel like I'm playing good. You know, if I do what I'm supposed to do, then yeah, I think I'd be tough to beat. But you never know what's going to happen. You've got to go out and play four good days. So we'll see when the gun goes off on Thursday."

FIRST ROUND

Golf found itself at Bethpage Black, that monster of a public course on Long Island, New York, for the PGA Championship in May, and not August, its date for decades. The schedule change was made largely in order to avoid complications now that golf was in the Olympic Games.

And as things unfolded, Brooks Koepka's best-laid plans were un-laid coming out of the starting gate. He'd said there was a key to handling Bethpage Black. "Take advantage of the par-fives," he said — meaning birdie them, of course — "and just try to hang on, on the rest of them." But in the first round, he merely parred both, Nos. 4 and 13.

Not that the oversight ruined his first round. He did birdie his first hole, No. 10, with a 40-foot putt, and his last from nearly 35, and between these bookend birdies was nary a bogey, and it all added up to a seven-under 63 and a one-stroke lead.

As to the par-fives: At the 13th, Koepka drove into a fairway bunker and ended up two-putting from 12 feet, and at No. 4, he drove into the native area, then caught the rough twice getting home.

"That was one of the best rounds I've played, probably, as a professional," said Koepka, 29, who needed just 25 putts. "This golf course is brutal."

He'd set the record and also became the first player to shoot a 63 in the same major twice. In winning the 2018 PGA at Bellerive, he shot 63 in the second round, where fully 47 players broke par in the first round. This time, only 16 broke par, the fewest for the opening round of a PGA since 2008 at Oakland Hills.

For all of Koepka's power — and power was invaluable on the nearly 7,500-yard course — his putter came in awfully handy. He also birdied from 13, 16 and 19 feet. And he came within a whisker of going absurdly low, missing birdies from seven feet at No. 11 and eight at No. 2.

Danny Lee, 28, a Korean-born New Zealander living in Dallas and winner of the 2015 Greenbrier Classic, was a stroke behind with a 64, his best start ever in a major. He was encouraged, but as a shorter hitter at Bethpage, he was sobered by reality. "I wasn't surprised when Brooks shot seven under this morning," he said. "When you're hitting driver, pitching wedge every hole…"

Despite Koepka's fireworks, all eyes were on Tiger Woods, just five weeks after his near-miracle comeback victory in the Masters. He had won four PGAs. Was a fifth in the offing?

It certainly didn't look that way. Woods had a remarkable front nine — in a way. He started at the 10th with a double bogey when he drove into the rough, had to hack out, wedged over the green and pitched on well past the flag. He birdied the 15th with a 15-foot putt, then double-bogeyed the par-three 17th after a tee shot into a bunker.

He was three over through the turn, then quickly got to one under with birdies at his 10th and 11th and an eagle at his 12th (No. 4) on a 31-foot putt. Then he bogeyed three of his last four, two of them on three-putts and the other on a bad chip shot at the par-three No. 8 for a two-over 72. Said Woods: "I felt like it's not that hard to make bogeys out here, but it's hard to make birdies."

The new-old Woods had the fans stirring.

"It was great that Tiger won at Augusta," Koepka said. "Everyone's going to be cheering for him, and it's going to be loud, especially if he makes a putt. You've just got to keep battling."

Koepka's 63 drew some interesting reactions from players looking at a tough job ahead.

Said Phil Mickelson, after a 69: "You just have to stay in the present. Because if you start chasing a score like that, it won't come to you, and you'll end up making big mistakes."

Said Rory McIlroy, after his one-birdie 72: "It gives me hope. It gives me hope I can go out tomorrow and shoot a low one."

"It's one day," said Rickie Fowler, who shot 69. "The tournament cannot be won on Thursday and Friday."

"Come Sunday," came the question, "how close do you think you have to be to Brooks to have a reasonable chance?" Said Fowler: "What makes you think he's going to be leading? I would say there's no lead really safe here."

The leaderboard carried a name not generally familiar — Mike Lorenzo-Vera, of France. His résumé included one win on the European Challenge Tour and one playoff loss on the European Tour, and now a 68 in the PGA.

"If I continue playing like that," Lorenzo-Vera said, "I'm going to sleep less and less, shake more and more. Yeah, I know what's waiting me the few days coming. First of all, I'm going to have a good rest, speak to my psychologist."

First-round leaders: Brooks Koepka 63, Danny Lee 64, Tommy Fleetwood 67, Mike Lorenzo-Vera 68, Chez Reavie 68, Luke List 68, Sung Kang 68, Pat Perez 68.

SECOND ROUND

Golf has an old standby remark for most every occasion, offering sympathy, instruction, wisdom or insight. "Never up, never in," for a putt left short. Or, "You can talk to a fade but a hook won't listen." For Brooks Koepka's play in this PGA Championship, one old standby seemed to fit best: "What course was he playing?"

This was Bethpage Black, the fire-breather on Long Island that handled the world's best without breaking a sweat in two U.S. Opens and that was doing fine against the field in this PGA, except for Koepka. Koepka, indeed, did seem to be playing somewhere else. After that seven-under 63 in the first round, he added a 65 in the second and was at 128, the lowest 36-hole score in any major. He was also at 12 under and leading by seven, the biggest halfway lead in a Grand Slam event in 85 years. And then he issued something of a disclaimer.

"This probably sounds bad," Koepka said, "but today was a battle. I didn't strike it that good. But the way I hung in there ... Not having your 'A' game but still being able to shoot a great score. I was very, very pleased with the way I played."

For all of Koepka's fireworks, it was still much of a Tiger Woods show, spilling over from his thrilling win at the Masters. But Woods, playing with Koepka and Francesco Molinari, ran afoul of Bethpage. He bogeyed three straight starting the back nine, missing all three fairways, shot 73, and at five-over 145 missed the cut by one stroke.

Woods' post-mortem: "Made too many mistakes and just didn't do the little things. I had a couple three-putts ... didn't hit wedges close ... didn't hit any fairways. Did a lot of little things wrong."

Koepka's scorecard didn't even hint at any real trouble. He seemed to be frolicking. He birdied three of the first four — a wedge to three feet at No. 1, a wedge to eight feet at the second, then at the par-five No. 4, a seven-iron second to 18 feet and two putts. He bogeyed the 10th, his first in 28 holes, then made more hay coming in. After a two-putt birdie at the par-five 13th (he had birdied both par-fives), he rushed to an impressive finish. At the par-four 15th, he hit a nine iron to three feet. At the par-four 16th, he wedged to five feet, and after a three-putt bogey at 17, he birdied 18, wedging out of heavy grass to 11 feet.

The next best halfway scores were five-under 135s by Jordan Spieth (66) and Adam Scott (64) — seven behind.

"I'd like to see that lead grow as large as it possibly can," Koepka said. "I still have to go out there and ... keep putting the ball in the right spot ... and I should have a good chance of winning the championship."

In the "other" PGA, as some were calling it, Spieth and Scott were trying to make a run at it. Spieth posted his fifth birdie at the 11th, then cooled with bogeys at the 15th and 16th. "If I'm able to put some good work in tomorrow, I will be in contention on Sunday," he said. Scott was on a tear with an other-worldly putter. He birdied the first three holes on putts of 25, 40 and 30 feet and added another at No. 5 from 14 feet. "Just a bizarre game sometimes," he explained.

Five players were at four-under 136 and also in contention at eight behind:

Dustin Johnson started on the back nine, bogeyed his first hole and his ninth, reeled off five birdies in between, and shot 67. "I wasn't thinking anything other than the next shot I had to hit," he said.

Daniel Berger (66): "You don't hit the fairway, you have to take your medicine. There was two shots I hit out of the rough today that were two of the worst lies I've ever had in my life."

Kelly Kraft (65): "It's just me and my caddie, and he's telling me where to hit it and I'm trying to hit it there."

Matt Wallace (67): "I missed a short one on the seventh and eighth. So, disappointed, but we're at a major. I've got to move on."

Luke List (68): "It was a grind. Just kind of pieced it together. I was pretty happy with two under."

Koepka had good reason to be optimistic with that seven-shot lead. But there was another old saying, echoing in the background, and used in all sports: "It ain't over till it's over."

Second-round leaders: Brooks Koepka 65-128, Jordan Spieth 66-135, Adam Scott 64-135, Daniel Berger 66-136, Dustin Johnson 67-136, Kelly Kraft 65-136, Matt Wallace 67-136, Luke List 68-136.

THIRD ROUND

Brooks Koepka finally came back down to earth. In the third round of the PGA Championship, it was the first time he did not break or set a scoring record. Except that he ended the day with the largest lead — seven strokes — since the PGA switched from match play to stroke play in 1958.

Luke List, one of the four players tied for second, considered all the facts and weighed the possibilities, and concluded, "I think we're all playing for second."

Koepka left the second round hoping he would increase his lead in the third, maybe put it out of sight, even. What went wrong? Or more correctly, what spectacular things didn't he do in the third round that he did in the first two, in that record carnival, when he was shooting the formidable Bethpage Black in 63-65.

With some tougher pins and some contrary breezes, he shot a par 70 that was pedestrian by his standards — three birdies, three bogeys.

"You don't hit fairways out here, you're not going to shoot under par — very simple," Koepka explained. "I didn't do a good job of that today. That's why I shot even par. It's not easy."

It looked like more domination by Koepka early on. He birdied Nos. 2 and 5 on short putts, three-putted No. 9 from 28 feet and two-putted the 10th from 18. At the par-five 13th, he came out of the rough to 16 feet and birdied, but at the par-four 16th he missed the fairway, then three-putted from long range for a bogey. Back to even.

His 70 put him at 12-under 198, and the traffic stacked up behind him, with one familiar face leading the parade — Dustin Johnson. With a wild one-under 69, Johnson inched a stroke closer, to seven behind, joining Harold Varner and Thailand's Jazz Janewattananond at 205, two new faces in the mix. Bethpage did seem to play a bit tougher. The 67s by Varner and Janewattananond were the low scores on the leaderboard after a scattering of lower ones in the first two rounds.

Varner had a largely uneventful day, posting three birdies. His take included both par-fives. He reached No. 4 in two and two-putted from 41 feet, then holed a 10-footer at the 13th. At the 18th, it was fairway-green-five footer. "I'm super-excited," Varner said. He had made his second cut in five majors and was tied for second for the first time.

Janewattananond was four under until bogeys at 14 and 17 cooled him, but he was thrilled anyway. "Arrived here on Monday, it was raining," the young Thai said. "Tuesday was raining. The course plays so tough because the rough was so long, the ball don't go anywhere. I was having a nightmare. How am I going to play this golf course? I'm not going to break 80. This exceeds my expectation already."

Johnson was three under on the front nine, then practically went through hoops for his 69 — six birdies and five bogeys. Of the bogeys, he missed the fairway on four par-four holes and missed the green on a par-three.

"Flag locations, wind — I mean, yeah, it was playing difficult," Johnson said. "Seemed like every time I got just a little bit out of position, I made bogey." But he had picked up a stroke on Koepka, now trailing by seven. What would it take in the final round? "I'm going to need some help from him," Johnson said, "and then I'm going to have to play very, very well."

Other contenders fell hard by the wayside. Kelly Kraft and Daniel Berger, tied for second after the second round — but eight behind — shot identical 78s. Phil Mickelson also fell hard. He made nine bogeys in his 76. Xander Schauffele was caught in some kind of warp. "I don't know if the tournament is just less fun because I'm 15 shots back or what," he said (actually he was nine back after his 68). "No one likes to play for second, but that's what he's doing to us."

Koepka was asked whether there was any doubt that he would win. "No," he said.

Third-round leaders: Brooks Koepka 70-198, Harold Varner 67-205, Jazz Janewattananond 67-205, Luke List 69-205, Dustin Johnson 69-205, Hideki Matsuyama 68-206, Matt Wallace 70-206, Xander Schauffele 68-207, Patrick Cantlay 68-207.

FOURTH ROUND

As the final round of the 2019 PGA Championship rolled along, with stiff winds battering Bethpage Black, some recent words had sharper meaning. Back in the first round, after Brooks Koepka had shot a stunning 63, someone asked Rickie Fowler how close he'd have to be to Koepka come the final round. Said Fowler: "What makes you think he's going to be leading? I would say there's no lead really safe here."

The other observation came from Koepka himself, after he'd finished the third round leading by seven. Was there any doubt he would win? someone wondered. Said Koepka, "No."

Luke List, one of the four players tied for second after the third round, saluting Koepka's play, had said, "I think we're all playing for second." Actually, it was for third or beyond, after Dustin Johnson got rolling and turned the PGA into a two-man battle.

Fowler was right. No lead was safe. And Koepka was wrong. There was doubt. Strong winds had come up, making a tough course even tougher. Of the 82 players who survived the cut, only 11 would break the par of 70 in the final round — two 68s and nine 69s. Koepka was not one of them.

There was Dustin Johnson, trailing by seven, on his chances of overtaking his good pal. "I'm going to need some help from him," Johnson said, "and then I'm going to have to play very, very well."

In punishing winds. "The wind was just really eating the ball up when you're hitting it into it," Johnson was to say. And said Paul Casey, after shooting one of the 69s: "There's a dog near the scoring area with a little jacket on it, says 'Emotional Support Dog,' which is what I feel like I need."

In the final round, Koepka was at even par through the front. He'd bogeyed No. 1 after missing the fairway, but birdied the par-five No. 4, hitting the fairway and two-putting from 24 feet.

Johnson, playing two groups ahead, made up ground with three birdies on the front nine, even after missing one fairway. His approaches were laser-like. He birdied on putts of four, eight and two feet.

It was like match play two groups apart.

Koepka then got his second birdie at the 10th, again hitting the fairway and then stuffing his approach with a gap wedge from 156 yards to two feet.

Johnson got just the chance he was hoping for on the final nine. He'd bogeyed the 11th, missing the fairway, but got the stroke back with a birdie at the 15th, the toughest hole on the course. Behind him, Koepka was pouring out the help in a string of bogeys, but Johnson couldn't capitalize on the gift.

"Just the last three holes is what got me," Johnson said. "Standing on 16 fairway, I'm at eight under, and hit two really good shots." His five-iron second pierced the wind and flew the green. "Hit the shot I wanted," Johnson said. "I don't know how it flew 200 yards into the wind." He bogeyed, and then bogeyed the par-three 17th, missing the green. A tee shot into the bunker at the 18th killed his hopes of a birdie there, but he parred for a 69 and a six-under 274.

"I knew, starting seven back, that it was going to be a big feat to catch Brooks," Johnson said. "I definitely gave him a run, though, so I was happy with that."

Koepka had launched a near-fatal stretch of four straight bogeys from the 11th, all on errant tee shots. He drove into a bunker at the par-four 11th and saved his bogey on a six-foot putt; drove into the right rough at the par-four 12th and two-putted from 17 feet; missed the fairway at the par-five 13th and two-putted from six feet, and missed the green at the par-three 14th and two-putted from 23 feet.

And at this point, he got the flavor of the fans. They began chanting "D.J.! D.J.!"

"It's New York," Koepka said. "What do you expect when you're half-choking it away?"

He had yet one more bogey. He hit the green at 17, but three-putted from 40 feet.

With Johnson already in and leading at six-under 274, Koepka closed with style. At the par-four 18th, he missed the fairway — again — but was on in three and holed a six-foot putt, with a great yell and a thrust of his right arm. He'd shot four-over 74 and an eight-under 272 and won by two.

"It was definitely a test," Koepka said. "I never thought about failing. Even if I would have lost, I guess you could say I choked it away. [But] I was trying my butt off. ... I tried my hardest. Sometimes that's all you've got."

It was his fourth victory in his last eight majors. "Four out of eight," Koepka said. "I like the way that sounds."

The final leaders: Brooks Koepka 74-272, Dustin Johnson 69-274, Jordan Spieth 71-278, Patrick Cantlay 71-278, Matt Wallace 72-278, Luke List 74-279.

4. U.S. Open Championship

Gary Woodland felt the way anyone would on winning the U.S. Open — thrilled and excited and beyond words. But what filled his heart that Sunday — Father's Day — was the video clip from his wife Gabby, back home, showing their little son Jaxson dragging all the pots and pans out of the cabinet.

Jaxson, almost two, born prematurely, was the twin who survived. His sister had not, to the grievous pain of her parents.

Life had been more than birdies and bogeys for Woodland. And with Gabby, expecting twins again, rooting back home in Delray Beach, Florida, and his mom and dad, Linda and Dan, with him at Pebble Beach, this U.S. Open became a classic family affair.

It was a miracle that his dad was even there. He remembered too well, 10 years earlier, when his dad had a heart attack and "coded," he said — as in died — and was revived. Woodland hugged him. "Happy Father's Day," he said.

"I love you," his dad said. "You earned it."

Dad coached him in baseball and basketball, but not in golf. And dad was something of an advocate of tough love.

"I wouldn't be where I am without my dad," Woodland said. "My dad worked nights. Growing up, I had somebody to shoot baskets with. Whatever we did, I had somebody to do that with. My dad never forced me to do anything. But if I did it, if I decided to go play catch or basketball, he was hard on me. You had to do it the right way if you were going to do it. He was hard on me. He never let me win."

Woodland was a star in Kansas high school basketball, and won all-state honors for two years and helped his team to two state championships, and startled the doctors the time he was hit by a knee in the throat and suffered a collapsed trachea. He wouldn't be playing for several weeks, the medics said. He was playing three days later and scored 20 points. Woodland, a 6-foot-1 shooting guard, had hoped to play at the University of Kansas but ended up at Division II Washburn. His mom remembered the time Washburn had a game with Kansas, a national powerhouse, and he had broken a finger in practice. But he wasn't about to miss this one. He played with two fingers taped together. "He's played through every injury ever," she said. "He never quits."

His golf career effectively started when he transferred to Kansas on a golf scholarship and he was taking the game seriously, or perhaps even earlier, when he was a little kid and would swing clubs till his little hands bled. "They didn't have gloves that small," his mom said, "and he still wanted to keep hitting balls."

Woodland's latest reward for all that work was in his hands that Sunday evening at Pebble Beach — the big, softly gleaming U.S. Open trophy. He thought back to January, at the pro-am of the Waste Management Phoenix Open. He'd invited Amy Bockerstette, a 20-year-old with Down Syndrome, to hit a shot at the famed par-three 16th. She was bunkered. He wanted to help her and hit it out. She waved him off with what became three of the most inspiring words in golf. "I've got this," she said. And she splashed it out to about 10 feet, and then holed the putt.

Said Woodland, that Sunday at Pebble: "I told myself that a million times today — 'I've got this.'"

FIRST ROUND

Graeme McDowell was something of a wet blanket. The first round of the U.S. Open at Pebble Beach had turned into a party, a free and easy birdie-fest, and here was McDowell grousing in the background, "Careful what you wish for … I think we're going to see it, come the weekend. I don't think level par wins this week." McDowell won the previous U.S. Open at Pebble in 2010 when he made only one birdie in the final round and nobody broke par for the week. This time it was a celebration of scoring, and despite his flawless two-birdie 69, he was warning everyone that Pebble would strike back.

Even the mild-mannered Justin Rose, the 2013 U.S. Open champ, was a bit subdued despite taking the first-round lead with a six-under 65. This was, after all, the celebrated Pebble Beach and 39 players had broken the par of 71, and 27 of them shot in the 60s. There were 17 eagles, the record for any U.S. Open round. Rose had come to a dramatic moment at Pebble's famed par-five 18th, as the daylight was softening. He had birdied 16 and 17 and now faced a 12-foot putt for a birdie that would give him a one-shot lead and also tie the U.S. Open record at Pebble, 65, set by Tiger Woods in his victory in 2000. The quietly resolute Rose rolled it home. His celebration was a reserved fist pump. "I wouldn't say it was exhilarating," Rose said, "because I feel like my mindset is, I am in a 72-hole tournament."

Meaning it was only the first round. And players were getting birdies in bunches. Rose was just a shot ahead of three others at 66. Xander Schauffele got a near-miracle bounce off a rock at the left side of the ocean-hugging 18th, then put his approach to 12 feet and made the eagle. Louis Oosthuizen sank his wedge approach for an eagle at his second hole, the par-four 11th, and finished his round by holing out a bunker shot for birdie at his last, No. 9. And Aaron Wise bogeyed his first hole and made six birdies the rest of the way, and offered an assessment of the course: Soft greens, gentler rough and overall "just a little bit softer than what I would imagine a normal USGA event being."

The fans were marveling at the scoring, but their eyes were on two history-seekers — Tiger Woods and two-time defending champion Brooks Koepka.

Woods was one win away from tying Sam Snead's record of 82 career tour victories, and his career-reviving win in the Masters just two months earlier, his 15th major, left him three behind Jack Nicklaus's record 18. And Woods opened his quest with one of the strangest cards of his career. From No. 4, he went birdie-double bogey-birdie-birdie and parred all the others for a one-under 70. Said Woods: "Pebble Beach — you have the first seven to get it going, and after that, it's a fight."

Koepka was going after his third straight U.S. Open, and no one had won three straight since Willie Anderson in 1903-04-05. Koepka seemed zeroed in, with four birdies through No. 6, then stumbled much of the way home to a 69. "I'm actually quite pleased," he said. "I don't know how many fairways

I hit from No. 8 on in — I didn't hit many," he said. "And didn't hit many greens. I'm pretty pleased. I didn't shoot myself out of it."

The threats came, and they went. Scott Piercy, for one, when he went to five under in four holes from No. 2, with three birdies and an eagle at No. 6. Then a double bogey at the eighth cooled him. He shot 67. "Four under the first round of the U.S. Open," Piercy said, "I'll take that every time."

Rory McIlroy, with a 68, had his first sub-70 round in a U.S. Open since he won at Congressional in 2011. "It's a very soft start to a U.S. Open," he said. "Which is a good thing."

Under the circumstances, Gary Woodland had a rather unremarkable day. He birdied Nos. 4, 5, 6 and 8, bogeyed the ninth, and parred his way home for a three-under 68, in a pack tied for eighth.

The frolic in first round averaged 72.679, nearly 2.5 strokes lower than the first round in both the 2000 and 2010 U.S. Opens at Pebble Beach. And one golfer did not have a conventional day.

Denmark's Lucas Bjerregaard, known for beating Tiger Woods in the WGC - Dell Match Play in March, was living his dream playing in the U.S. Open at Pebble Beach. He'd started at No. 10 in the first round and after three bogeys was three over coming to the 18th. He hit his first tee shot wide left into Stillwater Cove, hit his second there, too, then, overcorrecting, he hit his third wide right inland, out of bounds. He switched to his three wood, finally reached the green, and made an 11. Along the way, he hurled his driver over the cliff and into the ocean. He shot 80. Said Bjerregaard, "It's a course where you have to limit your mistakes. You can't afford to be making 11s."

First-round leaders: Justin Rose 65, Rickie Fowler 66, Louis Oosthuizen 66, Xander Schauffele 66, Aaron Wise 66, Nate Lashley 67, Scott Piercy 67.

SECOND ROUND

In the second round, surprising though it may have seemed, it was more of the same for Pebble Beach. A total of 44 players broke par, the third most in a second round in U.S. Open history. But the real stir came from a different source.

In a U.S. Open field loaded with marquee names and groaning with credentials, Gary Woodland seemed rather alone. He had won three times on the PGA Tour, which he first joined in 2009, won no majors, and in his first 27 appearances, his best finishes were ties for 12th in the 2011 PGA Championship and the 2016 Open Championship. "It's not something you're proud of," Woodland offered, almost parenthetically.

But in the 2019 U.S. Open at Pebble Beach, on a cool, overcast day, he certified that he was in the running, which he did at his final hole by muscling a tough approach from a dangerous lie to the front of the green, then holing a 50-foot putt for a birdie.

It was at the par-four No. 9 (he'd started at the 10th). The birdie was just a bonus, he said. "Hit a beautiful drive," he said. "I was in the divot [hole] ... We tried to take a little less club and hit it hard and play out safe to the right [he'd hit a seven iron from 217 yards], and it was nice to knock it in." It was for a birdie and a 65, tying the Pebble Beach Open record again, and a nine-under 133 for a two-shot lead over Justin Rose.

Said Woodland, who had made only one bogey in the first two rounds, "My ball striking was beautiful." He started by saving par from eight feet at the 10th, birdied 12 and 16, then coming home added Nos. 1, 5 and 6 before his closing heroics.

Rose, after that opening 65, wrestled his way to a three-birdie 70 and a seven-under 135. But at one point, he had a four-stroke lead. It leaked away on an errant wedge that cost him a bogey at his 10th (No. 1), and a stray approach that ended in a penalty drop from an ice plant at his 13th (No. 4). Rose was at peace with himself. It was too early to fret. "At this point, there's not a lot to worry about," he said. "If you're one ahead, one behind, it's a lot of golf to be played. But it's the perfect spot after two days."

Among other challengers, perhaps none spun a more energetic round than South Africa's Louis Oosthuizen. Oosthuizen had the ride of his life, bumping around Pebble in seven birdies, six bogeys and five pars. The most stable part of his round were the three straight pars from No. 2. Otherwise, he had back-to-back birdies twice, bogeys once. He didn't make a par on the back nine till the 18th. But it added up to a one-under 70 and a 136, one off the lead. "I'm not a big fan of bogeys," he said. "But miss these greens ... you can't control the ball."

Tiger Woods made one birdie. He holed a 10-foot putt at No. 11, his second hole, then ground out pars all the way to his last two holes, which he bogeyed for a one-over 72, finishing nine strokes out of the lead. "Yeah, I'm a little hot right now," he said. "So need a little time to cool down a little bit."

The problem, he said, was leaving the ball above the hole instead of below for the more makeable putts. "Yeah, right now I'm still in the ball game," he said. "There's so many guys with a chance to win. We've got a long way to go."

Rory McIlroy came back from the edge, shot 69, and was four behind. He'd made three birdies through the 11th. Then: "I was feeling good about myself ... and felt like I could squeeze a couple more out of the round," he said. Then he bogeyed the 13th out of bunker and rolled a wedge shot off the green at the par-five 14th and double-bogeyed. He pulled himself together and birdied 15 and 16. "Those were huge to get me back into the tournament," he said.

Brooks Koepka came out of his second 69 bubbling. After a birdie-bogey first nine (he started at the 10th), he birdied Nos. 6 and 7 to get within five of Woodland. "I feel great," Koepka said. "I'm excited — I've got a chance," he said. "That's all you can ask for. Sometimes the hole just needs to open up. If I can get off to a good start tomorrow, have that feeling where the hole's opening up, it could be a fun round."

Woodland was also bubbling, though in his own less effusive way. He'd had 10 one-putt greens and needed just 27 putts overall. Always a power hitter, he'd been working hard at his short game.

Someone noted that in his first 27 majors, he didn't have a top-10 finish, but he'd had two in his last four and now was leading the U.S. Open after 36 holes.

"Well, short game has come around," he said. "I've always been a pretty good ball-striker, I've relied on my ball-striking ... Short game and putting has been the big deal for me ... Believing in yourself. Knowing that my stroke is good. I can rely on other things and it's been working."

Second-round leaders: Gary Woodland 65-133, Justin Rose 70-135, Louis Oosthuizen 70-136, Aaron Wise 71-137, Rory McIlroy 69-137.

THIRD ROUND

The short game has come around, Gary Woodland said.

Woodland has long been known as one of the game's biggest hitters. But underneath all that power, it turns out, lies one of the game's finest understaters. That short game he'd been slaving over not only had come around. It was shimmering. There were, for example, the 10 one-putt greens in the second round and the incredible fact that he had made just two bogeys over three rounds at Pebble Beach. In addition, that short game seems to have a touch of magic to it, as well.

One of those one-putts in the second round was a 50-foot birdie. And then in the third round he performed two escape acts. At the par-three 12th he chipped in from 35 feet, and at the par-five 14th he rolled in a putt of about 40 feet, both saving pars just when it seemed he would lose some of his narrow lead. Instead, after a two-under 69, he was at 11-under 202 and leading by one going into the final round.

"I'm in a good spot," Woodland said. "You come here with intentions to play to win and give yourself a chance. And I've done that through 54 holes. We've got to get ready in the morning, have fun, come out with an attitude and see what happens."

Maybe Woodland was in a better spot than he realized. He was one ahead of Justin Rose, who shot 68, but four ahead of the next nearest challengers, a three-way tie for third among Brooks Koepka (68), Louis Oosthuizen (70) and Chez Reavie (68). Others were scattered behind — Rory McIlroy, five behind, back to a tie for ninth that included England's Danny Willett, who shot the day's low of all the contenders, a four-under 67.

Rose, after a five-birdie 68, had a different view of trailing by a stroke. "One back gives me the freedom to feel like I've got everything to gain, nothing to lose," he said. He'd been something of a wizard on Pebble's greens. He had 34 one-putt greens through 54 holes.

It seemed Woodland was going to separate himself from the field. He'd led by two starting the third round, and was up by four when Rose bogeyed No. 5 out of a bunker. Then there was the two-shot swing at the cross-water No. 8. Rose holed a 10-footer for birdie while Woodland three-putted for bogey — his first after 34 consecutive holes without one.

The duel continued at the 12th, where Rose birdied from about 10 feet, but Woodland averted another two-shot swing with the 35-foot par-saving chip. "I was trying to avoid the big number," he said. "Take your medicine and move on. Nice that went in."

Ditto for the par-five 14th, where he went from rough to deeper rough, then finally holed a 40-foot putt for par.

There was quite a scramble going on to shape up for a final push at Woodland. It fell more or less flat.

The popular favorite, Tiger Woods, went sour fast. "I got off to an awful start and clawed it around," he said. That meant three bogeys and two birdies over the first seven holes, which he considers the key to Pebble. "The first seven holes, you can get going," and then it's a fight, he'd said in the first round. He shot 71 and was at even par for the tournament, but 11 shots off the lead.

Rory McIlroy opened in a tie for fifth, shot a workaday 70, and slipped to sixth, five off the lead. He went into neutral with a birdie and a bogey and the rest pars on the first seven holes. Said McIlroy: "You can't put yourself under pressure to have a crack at those holes. You've just got to let it happen."

Dustin Johnson's promising day fizzled because of a stubborn putter. He had five chances from inside 15 feet, including an eagle try at No. 6 (he birdied) and birdie tries at the 10th and 13th (he parred). He posted a three-birdie, three-bogey par 71 and was at two-under 211.

Phil Mickelson's hopes for a career Grand Slam, very slim to begin with, disappeared beneath the waves when his tee shot at the 18th flew into the ocean. He triple-bogeyed for a 75 and was 14 off the lead.

Brooks Koepka moved up a spot, into a tie for third on a flawless 68, including a thrilling par save at the 15th, from deep rough and a 35-foot putt.

"I feel as confident as ever right now," said Koepka. "I just enjoy the pressure. I enjoy having to hit a good golf shot, making a putt when the pressure is on. If you're within three on the back nine, anything can happen. Hang around all day and see what happens."

Third-round leaders: Gary Woodland 69–202, Justin Rose 68–203, Brooks Koepka 68–206, Louis Oosthuizen 70–206, Chez Reavie 68–206, Rory McIlroy 70–207.

FOURTH ROUND

The old Gary Woodland came face-to-face with the new Gary Woodland in the fairway of Pebble Beach's brutal 14th. It's a nasty par-five dogleg-right stretching 580 yards, that has broken many hearts.

The old Woodland was the big hitter who preferred to beat a course into submission. The new one was the golfer who worked long and hard to add a soft-touch short game to all that power. And now he was faced with a decision, the 2019 U.S. Open hanging in the balance. With his playing partner, Justin Rose, having fallen away, he now led by one over the relentless Brooks Koepka, in the twosome just ahead, applying crushing pressure. Woodland was at his tee shot in the 14th fairway, facing a decision: Does he power his ball and go for the green, risking all that that entails, or does he take the safer option — finesse his way home with a layup and a wedge?

Woodland wasn't on the debate team. "The idea," he said, "was to play for the win."

Accordingly, he took his three wood and slugged it 263 yards to the green, got his birdie and a two-stroke lead.

He came to another crisis point at the par-three 17th, with its long, skinny hourglass green. His five-iron tee shot landed far to the right. The flag was 90 feet away, on the left. His problem was the skinny neck and the hump he had to go over. How to putt that one? Answer: Don't bother. He took his 64-degree wedge, delicately flipped the ball over the hump and to within three feet. "It's not one I want over," he said. He saved his par and his two-shot lead on Koepka, who couldn't squeeze another birdie out of Pebble.

Koepka, starting from four behind, blasted off on his final round, birdieing Nos. 1, 3, 4 and 5. But his last birdie was back at the 11th. And then he'd bogeyed 12 and was stuck at three under and fighting. He parred in for the three-under 69 and a 10-under 274. His bid for a historic third straight U.S. Open rested there, but not comfortably.

Woodland started the last round with a one-stroke lead on Justin Rose, birdied the second and third, then fell back to even par for the day with bogeys at the ninth and 12th. That brought him to the needed heroics at 14 and 17.

Then Woodland had another chance to demonstrate the new Woodland. At Pebble's classical par-five 18th, with the luxury of needing only a bogey to win, he restrained himself and hit a safe iron off the tee. At the 14th he had boldly gone for the green. This time, he prudently laid up with his second, then pitched safely on, 30 feet to the right. And ignoring the comfort of a big cushion, he made the 30-footer for a birdie, a 69 and a 13-under 271, taking his first major by three with the lowest 72-hole score in six U.S. Opens at Pebble Beach.

"I think from a mental standpoint, I was as good as I've ever been," Woodland said. "I never let myself get ahead of myself. I never thought about what would happen if I won, what comes with it. I wanted to execute every shot. I wanted to stay in the moment. I wanted to stay within myself."

On the clutch shot at the 14th: "It would have been pretty easy to lay up there. It was one of the better swings I made all week. That birdie there separated me a little bit from Brooks and gave me a little cushion."

On the clutch shot at the 17th: "Wasn't too many options. If I putted it, I don't think I could have got within 20 feet. Fortunately ... it came off perfectly."

Justin Rose, starting the final round just a shot behind, tied Woodland with a birdie at the first, then saw his hopes bleed away in four bogeys over an eight-hole stretch from No. 8. He shot 74 and tied for third, six behind. "I was right in the tournament," Rose said, "and then just kept missing in the wrong spot."

Koepka was trying to become only the second three-time U.S. Open winner since Willie Anderson in the early 1900s and instead became the only man to shoot in the 60s in all four rounds of the U.S. Open and not win. "I played great," Koepka said. "Nothing I could do. I gave it my all. And sometimes, no matter how good your 'good' is, it isn't there."

Woodland could classify as a surprise winner, given his lackluster play in other U.S. Opens. But he didn't surprise himself.

"We put a lot of work in this year in becoming a more complete player," he said. "People probably said the U.S. Open wouldn't suit me, because I'm a long hitter, I'm a bomber. And I went out and proved, I think to everybody else, what I always believed — that I'm pretty good."

The final leaders: Gary Woodland 69-271, Brooks Koepka 68-274, Xander Schauffele 67-277, Jon Rahm 68-277, Chez Reavie 71-277, Justin Rose 74-277.

5. The 148th Open Championship

From improbable beginnings to glorious finale, the return of the Open Championship to Royal Portrush proved truly remarkable. "It started as a joke, 'Why can't we go back?'" said Graeme McDowell. "Then the jokes turned serious."

For a young boy playing the Dunluce and Valley courses as a member of the neighboring Rathmore Golf Club, McDowell could scarcely dream of one day playing an Open in his hometown. In 2019 it became a reality and the game's oldest championship had never seen anything quite like it in its 148 stagings. Not only was the Open a sell-out for the first time in its history — with a total attendance of 237,750 behind only St. Andrews in 2000 — but the passion and energy of the gallery created an atmosphere rarely seen in golf.

In hosting its biggest ever sporting event, Northern Ireland rolled out the warmest of welcomes, albeit reserving the greatest passion for their local heroes. McDowell was the only one to make the cut. Darren Clarke hit the opening tee shot and birdied the first hole on Thursday but was distraught not to make it to the weekend. Rory McIlroy shocked himself and everyone else by hitting out of bounds with his first shot and taking an opening quadruple bogey. He also departed early, coming up one birdie short of qualifying for the last 36 holes, but not before a thrilling ride on Friday evening when he was cheered every step of the way.

Never fear, however, for there was a new champion to hail from the Republic of Ireland. Shane Lowry, 32, from Clara in County Offaly, a four-hour drive away, may have started the week "under the radar," in his words, but was borne on a wave of support so formidable that he produced the golf of his life. It resulted in a six-stroke victory over Tommy Fleetwood. The winning margin was entirely merited, the occasion never less than absorbing, so grand was it.

As Lowry came down the last couple of holes, the engraver already carving his name onto the historic Claret Jug, the cheering and chanting intensified again, echoing along the Antrim coastline seemingly forever. "I couldn't believe it was happening to me," Lowry said. "I tried to soak it in as much as I could but it was hard to do. So many people wanted me to win. It was such a surreal experience."

There has always been a romantic appeal about the big fella ever since he won the Irish Open as an amateur in 2009. As a tour player, Lowry did not win often, but his victories were always impressive, not least at the 2015 WGC – Bridgestone Invitational. Yet when he missed the cut at Carnoustie in 2018 for the fourth successive time at the Open, he sat in his car and wept. "Golf wasn't my friend at the time, I didn't like doing it. What a difference a year makes!"

Lowry lost his PGA Tour card that season and had to regroup. In September he hired a new caddie, Brian "Bo" Martin, from Ardglass, Northern Ireland. In January 2019 he won the Abu Dhabi HSBC Championship. In June he was runner-up to runaway winner McIlroy at the Canadian Open.

Still, living up to the achievements of his countrymen was not easy, not least his friend — and three-time major champion — Padraig Harrington. Along with his wife and young daughter, and his parents, Harrington and McDowell were among those to embrace Lowry when he walked off the 18th green. "I'm so happy I can add my name to our list of major champions, but I used to curse them an awful lot," he admitted. "All anybody wanted to know about in Ireland was winning majors because they were winning so many."

A long chat over coffee on the day before the Open with his coach-cum-psychologist Neil Manchip helped ease Lowry's anxieties about the scale of the occasion to come. Once on the course, it was Martin who kept him calm. "I kept telling him how nervous I was, how scared I was, how much I didn't want to mess it up," Lowry said. "He was unbelievable. He kept talking to me, kept me in the moment. He's a good friend and to share this with someone so close was very special. It helped an awful lot that people around me really believed I could do it. Neil always said I was going to win one, at least one. And look, now here I am, a major champion. I can't believe I'm saying it."

Lowry joined England's Max Faulkner from 1951 as a Champion Golfer of the Year at Royal Portrush. The Open's return to the venue was unthinkable at times. For so long the political turmoil and violence of the Troubles precluded any such notion. When Wilma Erskine, the club's secretary/manager for 35 years until she retired in triumph in 2019, first arrived overseas visitors were so rare she said, "we would go out and hug them, we were so happy."

Slowly, the visitors returned, investment in the course increased and tournaments followed. In 1993 the British Amateur was held for the first time in 33 years and two years later came the first of six Senior Open Championships. The Good Friday Agreement of 1998 was a vital step forward. But it was when Northern Irishmen started winning majors, following on from Harrington's successes, that momentum grew. McDowell, Portrush born and bred, won the 2010 U.S. Open. McIlroy, the Dunluce course record holder with a 61 aged 16, won the same major a year later. A month after that Clarke, by then a Portrush resident, won the Open at Sandwich. Peter Dawson, then chief executive of The R&A, was fielding questions constantly. "No doubt about the golf course at Portrush," he would say before raising concerns about infrastructure and commercial issues.

An attendance of 130,000 when the club hosted the 2012 Irish Open suggested the latter would not be an issue. Indeed, when tickets went on sale almost a year in advance for the 2019 Open, they sold out in weeks, with a further batch offered in April being snapped up in hours.

With the backing of the Northern Ireland government and agencies, the logistics of dealing with so many people coming to the region were arranged meticulously. That still left an issue with the Dunluce Links itself catering for the infrastructure of a modern Open Championship. The old 18th hole could not accommodate the huge grandstands, so architect Martin Ebert devised a plan to create two new holes — the seventh, a par-five, and the par-four eighth — from land used by the Valley course. That meant the old 17th and 18th holes — relatively flat and out-of-keeping with the other

16 holes — could be utilized for the tented village. "He's kept them in the character of Harry Colt and they have much more character than the holes they replaced," said Clarke.

This was not the first time Colt's 1930s masterpiece, which stretched the layout onto the dramatic sand dunes east of the town, had evolved in this way. When it became untenable to play from the original clubhouse in the town, two new holes were created out on the dunes. Ebert played the same trick with the best players in the world treated to a closing stretch that included the 236-yard par-three known as Calamity Corner as the new 16th and the old 16th, a dogleg par-four where Faulkner had played a miraculous shot on his way to victory in 1951, as the new finishing hole.

The chorus of approval from the competitors, usually a tough crowd to please, delighted McDowell. "People are saying it's the best links they've ever seen," he said. With weather conditions changing almost by the hour, it made for an exhilarating test — one that saw everything from a sad 91 from an injured David Duval on Thursday to a new course record of 63 by Lowry on Saturday. "The golf course has been phenomenal," McDowell added. "We've seen flat, calm conditions, we've seen wind directions changing all week. You could say they've seen a lot of Portrush. I'm really, really proud. We knew this was going to be a special Open. To have an Irishman at the top of the leaderboard is extra, extra special. Hopefully, we can come back soon."

FIRST ROUND

Lowry spent much of the opening day leading with a four-under-par 67. He acknowledged being "very unconfident, I'm not going to lie" on the first tee. Earlier Clarke had received an almighty ovation when he got proceedings underway. McDowell admitted to having a tear in his eye when he teed off. Clarke got to three under par early in his round and finished with a 71, level par. McDowell also started well, but a triple bogey at the last meant a 73.

McIlroy, with cries of "Go Rory" ringing in his ears, caused consternation when he pulled his iron shot at the first into the crowd and out of bounds. His next also went left but found the rough. His fourth found a bush and he had to take an unplayable. An opening eight and his Open was over before it began. He bogeyed the third, then had a stretch of 12 holes with two birdies and no dropped shots. But a double bogey at the 16th, where he casually missed a short tap-in putt, and a triple at the last meant a 79. "I didn't give a very good account of myself," he said, denying he had been more nervous than usual playing in front of his home crowd. "Maybe a bit, but I don't think it was that."

Tiger Woods, the Masters champion, parred the first hole but it was downhill from there as the 43-year-old posted a 78. His triumph in the heat at Augusta appeared a long time ago in the cool, rainy conditions here. "I'm not moving as well as I'd like and not able to shape the ball," he said. "Just Father Time." Another former champion to struggle was Duval, who had a 14 at the seventh where he lost two balls and played a wrong ball, for a two-shot penalty.

No such trials for Lowry, who birdied the third and the fifth, almost holing his tee shot at the drivable par-four, the ninth and 10th holes. He gave one back at the 11th but, at the 12th, recovered from thick rough with a good pitch to 12 feet and holed for the birdie. "I missed a few chances coming in, but I think four under is a great score on that course," he said.

Lowry hit 16 greens in regulation, more than anyone else all day, and when he did get out of position again showed his famous recovery skills. "Where my game's at now, if I hit a bad shot, I feel I can get myself out of trouble," he said. "This golf course is tricky in parts. If you miss it on the wrong side of the hole, you can get yourself into a whole lot of trouble. But if you play all right you can make some birdies as well and thankfully I did that today."

Webb Simpson, the 2012 U.S. Open champion, got to five under before bogeying the last two holes, while Jon Rahm reached the same mark before bogeys at the 15th and 18th holes. They were joined on three under par by a whole host of players, including Brooks Koepka, looking to extend a run of finishing 1-2-1-2 in majors, Sergio Garcia, Lee Westwood and Fleetwood, who did not drop a shot all day. Tony Finau and Kiradech Aphibarnrat, also went bogey-free. New Zealand's Ryan Fox, son of the All Black rugby star Grant, went out in 39 but came home in 10 strokes fewer to set a new record for the second nine at the Open, bettering Eric Brown's 30 at Royal Lytham in 1958.

J.B. Holmes dropped a shot at the first hole but birdied three of the next four holes, added two more at the 12th and 14th, and another at the last for a 66 and the first-round lead. Holing the 15-footer at the last meant he had beaten his best score in the Open by two strokes. The man from Kentucky won the Genesis Open in February but more recently had missed five cuts in a row. "My results didn't show it, but I felt confident coming in here," said the 37-year-old American. "I didn't miss too many shots and just stuck to the game plan of not getting too greedy going for pins. Try to hit the fat of the green and hopefully make some putts."

Unlike many of his competitors, Holmes had played at Portrush once before, on a trip while in college, but his memory was hazy. "We played one round here and I don't remember all the holes," he said. "Unfortunately, the caddies we had weren't used to somebody hitting 320 yards, so I got some bad lines."

First-round leaders: J.B. Holmes 66, Shane Lowry 67, Alex Noren 68, Webb Simpson 68, Sergio Garcia 68, Dylan Frittelli 68, Robert MacIntyre 68, Kiradech Aphibarnrat 68, Ryan Fox 68, Tyrrell Hatton 68, Tommy Fleetwood 68, Brooks Koepka 68, Lee Westwood 68, Tony Finau 68, Jon Rahm 68.

SECOND ROUND

Holmes, whose best result in a major was third place at the 2016 Open when the American beat everyone else left trailing in the wake of Henrik Stenson and Phil Mickelson, added a 68 on Friday to maintain his lead for much of the day. Birdies at the 12th and 13th holes had got him to nine under par but he dropped a shot at the 14th.

That left Fleetwood and Westwood only one behind after both Englishmen scored 67s with four birdies in the last seven holes. Westwood, on his 25th appearance, equaled his lowest Open score with the help of girlfriend Helen Storey on the bag. Fleetwood suffered his first two bogeys of the week but was happy enough. "That's two days in a row I've hit the ball really well and putted well," he said. Justin Rose was a stroke behind, alongside Cameron Smith and Justin Harding.

Lowry, playing later in the day, had some catching up to do. It did not take long. He birdied the first three holes, as well as the fifth, where he almost chipped in for eagle. Another birdie at the eighth took him out in a best-of-the-day 31, while his sixth of the day at the 10th hole had Lowry at 10 under par and leading by two strokes. The atmosphere by now was highly charged, the cheers getting louder as each putt was holed. "Incredible," Lowry said. "You can but laugh. There's no point shying away from it." Perhaps it startled the Clara man a bit, however, as he dropped two shots in the last seven holes, caused by a three-putt at the 14th and a "duffed" approach at the last that came up short. "There is not too many days like that on the golf course," he reflected after a 67 that tied Holmes at the top of the leaderboard. "I'm in a great position but, my God, we have got a long way to go."

The crowd was not sated for the day as now they got behind McIlroy, whose late-night charge to make the cut produced the sort of drama usually reserved for an Open Sunday. He had started at eight over par, went out in two under but was still short of the cut line at one over par. Already Clarke had missed out with a triple bogey at the last hole, while Woods added a 70 to miss his second major cut of the year.

Willed on by the fans, McIlroy birdied the 10th from 10 feet, the 11th from two feet and the 12th with a four. The wild scenes were deflated momentarily when he bogeyed the short 13th, but at the 14th he holed from 12 feet to get back to three over par. He got up and down from a bunker at the 15th before a sublime tee shot at the 16th to 10 feet brought a two, three shots better than the calamity the day before. By now the crowd was sucking his ball into the hole. Pars at the last two holes, however, left the 2014 Champion Golfer one short of staying for the weekend at his home Open.

"Today was one of the most fun rounds of golf I've ever played," McIlroy said. His 65 matched the lowest of the championship so far by Harding, Xander Schauffele and Kevin Streelman. "It's strange to say that about battling to make the cut, but I can leave with my head held high. I wanted to be here for the weekend. Selfishly, I wanted to feel that support for two more days."

Second-round leaders: J.B. Holmes 68-134, Shane Lowry 67-134, Tommy Fleetwood 67-135, Lee Westwood 67-135, Cameron Smith 66-136, Justin Harding 65-136, Justin Rose 67-136.

THIRD ROUND

That support, while not derogatory to any of the other contenders, was unequivocally and loudly behind Lowry as the Irishman took control of the 148th Open on Saturday. As he put the final touches on a new course record of 63 for the revised Dunluce Links, the grandstands at the 18th hole erupted in chants and cheering the like of which usually only grace a winning home Ryder Cup team.

Walking off the 17th tee, Lowry said to Martin, his caddie: "We might never have a day like this on the golf course again. So let's enjoy the next half-hour." And they did. "I can't believe what it was like," Lowry said. "I thought I dealt with it very well today."

In contrast to Friday's round that frizzled on the back nine, he started steadily, picked up a couple of shots at the third and fifth, and then birdied six of the last 10 holes. For much of the day, the leaderboard was relatively tightly packed. Lowry only got in front for good at the 12th. Going to the 15th he was only one in front. Suddenly he kicked clear of the field.

A 12-foot putt that curled from left-to-right give him a birdie at the 15th. Then came the shot of the day at the 16th, a magnificent four iron right on line with the hole, finishing 10 feet away. "I'm not to going to lie, I pushed it about five, 10 yards, but it was a perfect four iron," Lowry said. "To roll the putt in was really nice. Every time I had a putt today, I just wanted to hole it because I wanted to hear that roar."

A third birdie in a row came at the 17th following a pitch from 60 yards to four feet. His birdie putt at the last, to tie Branden Grace's record for a major of 62, came up just short. No matter, he was the first player from the Republic of Ireland to lead the Open after 54 holes. His total of 197 was a new record, beating Tom Lehman's 198 at Lytham in 1996, and, at 16 under par, he led by four strokes.

Fleetwood, who had been only one behind with two to play, was his nearest challenger after a 66, his second bogey-free round of the week. "It would be easy to get frustrated but you have to look at it realistically," Fleetwood said. "I had one of the best rounds of the day and I was bogey-free. Shane just played great and I'm four back. That's it. I'm happy how I played."

"But it was a very special day," added the Englishman. "A great day to be playing golf. People watching today, if they're not into golf after that … I think it was amazing for the sport. The atmosphere was just great. I loved it. For or against you, you can't help but appreciate and love what today was and what tomorrow is going to be."

Holmes, the co-leader overnight playing alongside Lowry, had led briefly after birdies at the second and third holes, but it took a birdie at the last for him to post a 69 and hang on to outright third place, six strokes behind, one ahead of Koepka and Rose. Nevertheless, Holmes reflected: "That was really cool to experience. I don't know how many times in history you get the opportunity to witness that — to have someone from the home country put up a round like that in the Open. It's something I'll never forget."

Third-round leaders: Shane Lowry 63-197, Tommy Fleetwood 66-201, J.B. Holmes 69-203, Brooks Koepka 67-204, Justin Rose 68-204.

FOURTH ROUND

At Oakmont in 2016, Lowry had led the U.S. Open by four strokes after 54 holes, but the third round did not end until early on the Sunday morning, and that afternoon the Irishman slid behind Dustin Johnson, almost more disturbed by the saga of whether the eventual champion had been panelized or not for an infraction early in the round than the man himself. Lowry was determined that the same thing would not happen again and the bad weather that arrived for the finale probably worked in his favor. A former North of Ireland Amateur champion at Portrush, the big man from County

Offaly was better prepared and more experienced at coping with an Irish storm than most.

Early in the day, conditions were relatively calm as defending champion Francesco Molinari returned a best-of-the-day 66 to finished 11th. Young left-hander Robert MacIntyre scored a 68 to become the first Scot to finish in the top 10 on debut at the Open for 60 years. He tied for sixth with Rickie Fowler, who went out of bounds at the first hole, Danny Willett and Tyrrell Hatton, who teed off two hours prior to the leaders and was the last player to break par with a 69.

Holmes followed Fowler out of bounds at the first hole on the way to an 87 that included four double bogeys and a triple. He finished 67th, beating only three other players. Rose did not fall quite as far but slumped to a surprising 79, while Koepka, whose caddie Ricky Elliott is from Portrush, uncharacteristically opened with four straight bogeys before an eagle at the fifth on the way to a 74. The PGA champion became the fourth player to finish in the top four at all four majors in one year. Tying the American for fourth was Westwood, whose 73 meant he could book trips to Augusta and Royal St. George's for 2020. Finau pipped the pair for third place, his best major result, with a quietly impressive 71, making him the only player in the last 10 pairings to match par.

Lowry made a nervy swing with a two iron from the first tee, finding the left rough but coming up short of the out-of-bounds line. His second found a bunker and he left his 40-foot putt for par eight feet short. Fleetwood, meanwhile, hit two fine shots and had a 10-footer for birdie. A three-shot swing was possible, but Fleetwood's putt dribbled wide while Lowry buried his. "That settled me an awful lot," he said.

He still led by three and it set the tone for the day. Fleetwood missed chances for birdie on the second, for par at the third, from long range at the fourth and for eagle at the fifth. "Those first few holes, when you start four back, were crucial," said the Englishman. "I didn't do a good enough job of pressing at that point."

Lowry claimed birdies at the fourth, fifth and seventh holes, so was well-cushioned when the worst of the weather hit, causing him to drop three strokes in four holes. When Fleetwood birdied the 12th he was still four back, but then he got into trouble at the 14th and took a double bogey. "That was the killer," he said. "It was pretty much over. It was brutal out there at times, but Shane controlled the tournament from the start to the end and that was very impressive."

The roar that went up when Lowry birdied the 15th allowed everyone to relax. Except, perhaps, Lowry himself, who was determined to fully realize the lesson he learnt from his U.S. Open experience. "I knew I had to fight until the bitter end today," he said. "That's where I struggled at Oakmont. I played the last five holes incredibly well today. I let myself enjoy it down 18, but before that I was really fighting."

There was plenty more time to enjoy his triumph, from the pubs of Dublin to a parade in his hometown of Clara. Both his victory and the return of the Open to the island of Ireland could be celebrated with equal zeal.

The final leaders: Shane Lowry 72-269, Tommy Fleetwood 74-275, Tony Finau 71-277, Lee Westwood 73-278, Brooks Koepka 74-278.

6. Women's Major Championships

ANA Inspiration

"I am not a robot. I'm human," said Jin Young Ko in response to a little local difficulty in the third round when a five-stroke lead was reduced to one all too quickly. Ko's golf on the demanding Dinah Shore Tournament Course was of such high quality that it may have looked pre-programmed, with victory in the ANA Inspiration the inevitable outcome, but overcoming the occasional error message made this triumph even more impressive.

"Sometimes it happens on the course," she added of finding the water at the short 14th on Saturday. "Mostly this course is really hard, so everyone can miss a shot. So okay, I'm fine. I not worry. Doesn't matter."

There was another wobble on Sunday. A second bogey in three holes at the 15th left her only one ahead. Here was the defining test for the 23-year-old from Seoul, the LPGA's most in-form player and possessor of a beautiful, ever-repeating swing.

On the hardest hole on the course, the 16th, Ko hit a nine iron to 15 feet and made a three. She almost birdied the 17th, when her closest rivals failed to find the back-left portion of the green to give themselves a chance of a two as she did. Then on the 18th, where the tee was moved up to give players the chance to go for the green in two, although those that did mostly battled for a par-five, Ko produced four perfect shots. The drive split the fairway, the lay up left her just under 90 yards over the water and the wedge finished 12 feet left of the flag.

When the putt went in, the impassive demeanor of Korea's latest champion was replaced by a very human response. Her hands flew to her face and tears of joy and relief flowed. Her first thoughts were for her grandfather, who had died almost exactly a year earlier. "I miss my grandfather," Ko said. "He would like this moment; also he will be crying, I think."

Two birdies in the last three holes had given Ko a three-stroke victory over compatriot Mi Hyang Lee. The daughter of a boxer, Ko learnt to absorb the emotional blows golf inflicts as well as deliver her own punches on the course. "I try to be the happiest golfer on the course," she said. "If the ball goes left or right, it doesn't make me happy but I still try to be happy. Focus on my swing, on the putting, that's why I won this week. But, honestly, happiest golfer. That's it. This win is just a bonus to me."

A fourth LPGA title, and a first major, took Ko into the top spot on the Rolex Rankings. This triumph had been coming. The Rookie of the Year in 2018, Ko had finished in the top three in four of her previous five events, including victory at the Founders Cup and a runner-up finish at the Kia Classic in the previous two weeks. A five-week training stint in Palm Springs — including a couple of trips to Mission Hills — at the start of the year had proved the perfect preparation.

Previously she had not enjoyed her visits to the ANA, but her caddie, Dave Brooker, believed otherwise. "My caddie always says, 'You will like this course.' I thought, How? I finish 71st and 64th the last couple years. Now I really like this course." Brooker had caddied for previous winners Grace Park and Lorena Ochoa, so made his third jump into Poppie's Pond alongside Ko's first.

Higher rainfall than usual in February led to the rough at Mission Hills being thicker than for many years. In addition, some tees were pushed back a total of 60 yards, including at the 15th where Gerald Ford Drive, just over the out-of-bounds wall on the left, threatens the tee shot. The effect on scoring was notable on a breathless first morning when the leading score was no lower than 69. Ko, with only one bogey, was among those to post that number, her first ever sub-70 score on the course. Lexi Thompson birdied the last two holes to share the early lead and the pair were joined by Hyo Joo Kim and Sweden's Linnea Strom. It was not until the final putt of the day, a five-footer for a birdie at the 18th by Ally McDonald, that a player managed to record a 68.

McDonald, who missed the cut on her debut at the ANA in 2018, collected seven birdies despite playing in the last group out and getting the worst of the conditions as the wind gusted to 15 mph late in the afternoon. "I've never found myself in this position, so it's easy to get ahead of yourself," said McDonald, who had four in a row from the seventh. "I played the par-fives really well today, which is exciting. On a major championship golf course you have to take advantage of the par-fives."

Michelle Wie also managed four birdies in a row during her round but had started five over par for the first eight holes, so ended up with a 74. Due to injuries this was only her fourth appearance since the previous August and on her last, at the HSBC Women's World Championship, she had to withdraw after 14 holes. Also on 74 was Nelly Korda, whose form was second only to Ko's entering the championship. A win and four other top-10s in her five previous events had promised much, but the younger Korda sister struggled here. Unlike Wie, she did go on to make the cut, but it was Jessica who led the Korda challenge, eventually finishing sixth.

Every time In-Kyung Kim returns to Mission Hills she must be reminded of the 14-inch putt she missed on the final green in 2012. Revenge of a sort arrived when she finally won a major at the Women's British Open in 2017, but a seven-under-par 65, the best score of the week, was a welcome tonic on Friday morning. The 30-year-old dropped only one shot and birdied the ninth, her final hole, to top the leaderboard at eight under par. Not that she was aware. "I wasn't really paying attention to the leaderboard because I'm just blessed to be here," said Kim, one of the more deeper souls to be found in professional golf. "For a long time it was one of my goals to win, but now I'm just really happy to be out here."

Australia's Katherine Kirk, with a 68 despite bogeying the last two holes, ended up her nearest challenger, three behind. Ko, after a 71 in the afternoon when the wind was at its strongest again, and McDonald, who overcame early nerves when teeing off as the leader to post a 72, were a further stroke behind. Thompson had two late bogeys in a 72 and was on three under with Danielle Kang, Charley Hull and current world No. 1 Sung Hyun Park.

Surprisingly, Park faded over the weekend and lost her No. 1 ranking, while the 2018 player of the year, Ariya Jutanugarn, never mounted a challenge at all.

Kim made a slow start on Saturday which was compounded by a double bogey at the ninth. The first of her seven shots clattered into a tree and left her merely 130 yards off the tee at the par-five. Moments later Ko birdied the 10th to turn a four-shot overnight deficit into a dramatic five-stroke lead. Although Canada's Alena Sharp returned a 67, only Ko of those pursuing Kim was able to make a move. And what a move. She birdied the second, holed a monster putt at the fourth, also birdied the fifth and sixth holes before wedging to six inches at the ninth to be out in 31.

A five at the short 14th halted the momentum and Ko also bogeyed the 15th, but a two at the 17th gave her a 68 and at eight under par she was the 54-hole leader. Kim had rallied stoically for a 73 with birdies at the 10th and 18th holes to lie just one behind, while Kang and Lee sat two shots further back. Lee also dropped three shots in two holes on the back nine but made them back with a hole-in-one at the 17th — from 181 yards with a five-hybrid, a squeal of delight when it went in — and a birdie at the last.

Lee birdied the first two holes on Sunday — five under for her last four holes — but thereafter managed only a bogey and a birdie. Her best result in a major arrived with a 70. "There were a lot of cameras and people cheering on back nine, but I still managed to control myself," she said. "I think my mental game is better than before and I am more confident."

Thompson, the 2014 champion, recovered from a 74 on Saturday with a 67 to take third place. "I knew I needed to have a low round to have any sort of chance today," said the 24-year-old. "Before I even stepped foot out on the golf course I was texting my caddie, Benji, and we said we had to just fire at every pin." Five birdies coming home put her at six under, but pars on the last two meant Ko had some breathing space. Ko was also helped by Kang dropping out of contention with a triple bogey at the third and Kim having double at the 11th when her ball got stuck up a eucalyptus tree. A 74 meant Kim shared fourth place with Carlota Ciganda. Kang was in the group in sixth place that included McDonald, after weekend scores of 74 and 70, and Jeongeun Lee$_6$, after four scores of 71.

Ko was not flawless but did what was needed in birdieing the second, fifth and 11th holes. She dropped shots at the short eighth and the 13th and 15th holes but then rebooted to clinch the victory. She had hit 12 of 14 fairways and 14 of 18 greens, while the 10- to 15-footers that needed to go in all did. A 70 left her on a 10-under-par total of 278. The situation got tight at the end but never her swing, which retained its majestic rhythm to the end — too much of a thing of beauty to be robotic.

U.S. Women's Open Championship

A Korean golfer named "Lee" won the 2019 U.S. Women's Open Championship, which was entirely predictable but not in a lazy, stereotypical, dismissive way. You only had to be paying attention to know that the new champion might be a worthy winner at the Country Club of Charleston — and the first woman to earn $1 million at a major championship.

She was the Rookie of the Year on the Korea LPGA tour in 2016 and the leading money winner in both 2017 and 2018. At the end of 2018 she won the eight-round LPGA qualifying series. In eight previous starts of her rookie season on the LPGA she had not finished lower than 26th. She was runner-up at the Mediheal Championship, losing in a playoff, and had two other top-10s. She was fifth on her debut at the U.S. Women's Open in 2017 and 17th a year later.

A pedigree game matched by a unique name. Jeongeun Lee$_6$ is so annotated because she was the sixth player of what is a common name in Korea to join the KLPGA. The fifth simply goes by "Jeong Eun Lee" in America, but Lee$_6$ always embraced her numeral. "This is really a lucky number to me," she said. Believe it. She finished sixth in her first KLPGA event as a professional. Her first win in 2017 came with three rounds of 66, six under par each day. By the end of 2018 she had six KLPGA wins. She writes "6" on her golf ball, has nicknames such as "Hot 6" and "Lucky 6," the latter being the name of her fan club in Korea. When she won the oldest prize in women's major golf, she did so by two strokes over Lexi Thompson, Angel Yin and compatriot So Yeon Ryu with a total of 278, six under par for the championship.

Adding the numeral helps Lee stand out from the crowd. So does the striking bleach-blond hair emerging from under her cap. She is an individual who comes with a unique backstory which emerged during the week. At the age of four, her father, a truck driver, was paralyzed when he fell asleep at the wheel. Her drive to succeed at golf came from wanting to provide for her family given neither of her parents work. Nor is it easy for her parents to travel, so Lee had to get used to being independent early in her golf career. "I wanted to support my family no matter what," she said.

At the trophy presentation ceremony, Lee was clearly holding back tears as she spoke in Korean, and her manager, Jennifer Kim, who was translating for the audience, became choked up with the emotion. "I'm sorry," Kim said after a moment to compose herself. "I am just really proud of her." Later, in the press room, Lee said in her native tongue: "I want to thank my family, who's in Korea right now watching me on TV and supporting me all the time. Coming to play the U.S. Women's Open is such an honor. I can't imagine winning a major tournament in the LPGA. I didn't even expect to win this fast. I think this is very lucky."

Luck may always play a part in a champion's performance, but it was her steady, consistent play across all four days that was crucial. Lee opened with a 70, had two 69s and then closed with a 70. Lee was five behind after the first day, but of the five players ahead of her on the final day the best score was a 73, two over par. That perfectly illustrated how the spectacular layout at the Country Club of Charleston, the first Seth Raynor-designed course to host a major championship, gradually increased the challenge as the week went on. With generous fairways, many elevated greens with tightly mown run-off areas, 12 of them with false fronts, and interesting bunkering, the course provided golf that was strategically interesting to play and engrossing to watch.

Mamiko Higa's 65 on the opening day was the best score of the week and the lowest by anyone on debut in the U.S. Women's Open. The 25-year-old, who had won five times on the Japan LPGA tour and is married to a sumo wrestling star, had three birdies in a row from the third hole. She added three more and did not drop a shot to become the first Japanese player to lead the first round of the U.S. Women's Open since 1993. One behind were Germany's Esther Henseleit, who had already collected six top-10s in her first seven events as a rookie on the Ladies European Tour, and Gina Kim. The 19-year-old, fresh from helping Duke win the NCAA Championship, holed an eight iron for an eagle at the eighth, her 17th, and then birdied the ninth for a 66 to tie the lowest round by an amateur in the U.S. Women's Open.

Celine Boutier, who claimed her first LPGA win at the Vic Open earlier in the season, scored a 67 on Thursday and then a 70 on Friday to be five under par, a mark reached by Jessica Korda with a second round of 68 with three birdies and 15 pars. Higa got to seven under par with an early birdie but had fallen back to four under when a thunderstorm interrupted play for two hours in the afternoon. Three birdies and only one bogey on the resumption put Higa back in the lead at six under after a 71.

Overnight a tree that had been struck by lighting during the storm had to be removed. It was located by the 18th fairway and close to the 11th green, leading to local great Beth Daniel to quip: "Not even God can hit the 11th green!" Perhaps it was some consolation to Minjee Lee after the Australian had a triple bogey at the par-three 11th, where the green slopes sharply in a "reverse Redan" manner and is bordered by deep bunkers on either side. It was the false front that did for Lee as her tee shot and two subsequent chips rolled off the front.

Minjee Lee was still only four off the lead while Jeongeun Lee$_6$ was a shot closer after a 69 that contained only two bogeys, though both at par-fives. On Saturday Jeongeun dropped only one shot in another 69 to be two off the lead, now held by Boutier, after a 69, and Yu Liu, who had a 66. Higa had another 71 to be one back, alongside Americans Thompson and Jaye Marie Green, who both scored 68s.

Thompson had adopted a claw putting grip for the week after being persuaded to change her technique by her brother Curtis on Wednesday. The putter was particularly helpful in saving par at the 11th with a long putt and holing a 30-footer for eagle at the 15th. On Sunday Thompson missed too many fairways to contend after bogeying three of the first four holes. She did birdie the last for a 73 to tie for second, her highest placing in her 13th U.S. Women's Open (she is still only 24).

Alongside Thompson on the course was Green, runner-up to Lydia Ko at the 2012 U.S. Women's Amateur. Green had missed her last four cuts and never finished better than 12th at a major. On Sunday she led briefly but came home in 38 for a 74. Tying for fifth place was her best result on the LPGA. Also on three under par were Higa, after a 74, Gerina Piller, with a 68, as well as Boutier and Liu, who both scored 75s. Two strokes further back in 12th place was leading amateur Kim, as well as Mexico's Maria Fassi, the 2019 NCAA individual champion on her professional debut. Also making her first appearance as a pro, finishing 62nd, was Jennifer Kupcho, who won the inaugural Augusta National Women's Amateur after a thrilling duel with Fassi.

Piller made a strong charge with five birdies in the first 11 holes and briefly joined a seven-way tie for the lead before bogeys at the 13th and 14th holes. Boutier and Liu, playing in the last pairing together, are friends from Duke's 2014 NCAA winning season. But neither started well. Boutier double-bogeyed the first and bogeyed the third, while Liu bogeyed three of the first five.

Both managed a couple of birdies before the turn, but it was Lee who stole into top spot early on the back nine. She got to the turn in level par and then the magic happened. She hit the flagstick at the 10th with a 70-foot chip and tapped in for a par. At the 11th, the hardest hole for the week where Lydia Ko had a hole-in-one with a six iron on Sunday, Lee hit a superb tee shot to eight feet and made a rare two. At the next, she birdied from five feet and added another from five feet at the par-five 15th to go ahead by three strokes.

The finish was still tense, however, as Lee missed the green at the 16th and 18th holes. "I was nervous starting 16, 17 and 18, and I knew that if I made all pars on those holes, I knew that I'm going to win," said Lee. "I know I made two bogeys, but I just didn't want to think about it too much. I tried the best that I can."

Yin, with a closing 68, and Ryu, the 2011 U.S. Women's Open champion who scored a 70, had both finished at four under par, two behind, but Boutier was still battling away on the course at five under. "On a scale of one to 10, today was probably a one," said the 25-year-old. "My putter was not good all day, and I just struggled to have birdie opportunities throughout the day." After six pars in a row, though the Frenchwoman was robbed of a birdie at the 16th when she lipped out from three feet, Boutier needed a birdie at the last to tie. That meant holing a bunker shot, which in fact caught a slope and ran off the green. So Boutier finished as she had started, with a double bogey. Six really must be Lee$_6$'s lucky number.

For the eighth time in 12 years, and the 10th time in all, a Korean had won the U.S. Women's Open and happened to be called "Lee". This hardly validated the "prediction" made by veteran coach Hank Haney on his PGA Tour Radio show. Haney was suspended for his belittling comments on the eve of the biggest championship in the women's game — he did not even appear to know it was happening that week.

Fittingly, Lee proved every champion has a story to be told as well as a game, and a name, to be respected.

KPMG Women's PGA Championship

Ten different champions in the last 10 women's majors and this may have been the most unexpected of all. Hannah Green entered the KPMG Women's PGA Championship ranked 114th on the Rolex Rankings. Six previous majors had brought three missed cuts and a best result of 16th. In a season and a half on the LPGA the Australian had not finished higher than third. Although she won three times on the Symetra Tour in 2017 and was runner-up to Jin Young Ko for LPGA Rookie of the Year honors in 2018, the 22-year-old from Perth had to date been overshadowed by compatriots Minjee Lee, the world No. 3, and Su Oh, a winner in Australia and a three-time runner-up on the LPGA.

No longer. Not after a command performance at Hazeltine National which saw Green secure a wire-to-wire victory with a sand save on the final hole that Karrie Webb described as "world class." For two days on the weekend playing alongside Ariya Jutanugarn, the undisputed player of 2018, Green turned from plucky newcomer into a gritty and determined champion. It was the Thai who ultimately wilted, coming home in 40 on Sunday for a 77.

Green faced her own adversity when she made three bogeys in four holes around the turn on the final day — having recorded only three over the previous three days. A fine chip to save par at the 13th stopped the rot and then she hit her best drive of the week at the 16th before holing from 20 feet for a birdie that gave her a two-shot cushion.

Still the trophy was not won. Defending champion Sung Hyun Park was the only player to score four sub-par rounds and with a last desperate, brilliant stroke — a curling putt from almost 18 feet — she birdied the 18th, the most difficult hole on the course, to get within one. Green knew immediately from the roar that she needed a par at the last, but a poor four iron up the hill was pulled into the greenside bunker. A fine recovery left a five-footer for par. Her hands were shaking, she admitted — how could they not be? — but the putt was holed.

"I was really nervous playing the last five holes," Green said. "I'm so relieved I don't have to play 18 again for a playoff." How do you explain this week, she was asked? "I have no idea. I can't believe I'm in this position right now. I've always wanted to win an event and to win a major championship as my first is crazy."

Green was engulfed on the 18th green by her supporters, including boyfriend Jarryd Felton, an Australasian Tour professional, Oh and Webb. Green was the third Australian woman to win a major after Webb and Jan Stephenson. Also present were Grace Kim and Becky Kay, two Australian junior players who as part of their Webb scholarships got to stay with Webb, Green and Oh for the week. The pair's garish outfits had given Green a smile every time she spotted them in the gallery.

Since 2008 Webb has brought promising young Australians over to the States so they can see what a major championship looks like close up. Green attended the 2015 U.S. Women's Open, her first time on site at a professional tournament. "Without a doubt getting to know Karrie," Green rated the best part of the experience. "Being able to stay in a house with her, watching everything she does in a tournament, it definitely gave me a big insight into what it was like. I'm very grateful to her and I know everyone that has had her scholarship is very grateful too."

Hazeltine National, where America beat Europe in the 2016 Ryder Cup, has thrown up the odd unexpected winner in the past — Rich Beem and Y.E. Yang (over Tiger Woods) in the PGA Championship, for example. Tony Jacklin and Payne Stewart won U.S. Opens on the layout, while Sandra Spuzich and Hollis Stacy won the U.S. Women's Open here. For Spuzich, in 1966, it was also her first LPGA victory.

At 6,807 yards, the course was the longest in the championship's history and a cool, occasionally windy, and mostly wet opening day saw only 16 players break par. Hyo Joo Kim led at lunchtime on three-under-par 69, which was matched by England's Melissa Reid and beaten only by Green's bogey-free 68. The Australian dislikes wearing waterproof trousers so soldiered on in only shorts and a not, as it turned out, very waterproof top.

Green took the lead by holing out from a bunker at the seventh, her 16th, for her fourth birdie of the day. The key to the round was actually her putting. Making up for an indifferent long game, she made 11 one-putts and had only 23 in total. "I don't think I ever had a tap-in for my par putts when I missed the green," she said. "Nearly every hole was a six-footer. I made all of them."

Jutanugarn and Park both opened with 70s. For the first time all season Jutanugarn carried a driver in her bag and used it twice, although at the 11th, her second hole, it led to a bogey-six. She dispensed with the club after the 15th and did not use it the rest of the week. Three birdies in her last four holes put the Thai in contention, while Nelly Korda and Lexi Thompson had 72s, Jeongeun Lee$_6$ a 73 and Jin Young Ko a 77.

Michelle Wie, in her first round for two months in another comeback following wrist surgery in October 2018, scored 84. Her right wrist needed icing as early as her second hole after tangling with the thick, wet rough. "I'm not entirely sure how much more I have left in me," she said, close to tears. "So even on the bad days I'm just trying to take time to enjoy it." An 82 followed the next day and Wie announced she would take the rest of the year off.

Green dropped her first shot of the week at the opening hole on Friday morning but scored a 69 to extend her lead to three at seven under par. The only other player to score in the 60s all day was Jin Young Ko with a 67, 10 better than the day before. With Reid scoring 76, the player closest to Green from her half of the draw was Park, who posted a 71 to be four back. Jutanugarn got within one of Green in the afternoon by going to the turn in 32, including an eagle at the seventh, but she came home in 38 for a 70 to lie second.

The highlight of Green's second round came at the 12th, where her second shot found the lake short-right of the green. She promptly pitched in from 54 yards for a par. "When it went in," Green said, "I just laughed because, I guess, with the hole-out on seven yesterday and with the hole-out today, it's really going my way."

Staying with a seven-time major champion has its advantages and on

Saturday morning, after Webb had read the leader's interview transcriptions, she had a word with Green. "She had some lucky breaks and that seemed to be a topic, how lucky she had been," Webb recalled, "and I just wanted to tell her that lucky breaks always happen to people that win. I said, 'Don't be embarrassed by them, enjoy them.'"

Webb also reminded the youngster that it would not just be her who was feeling nervous on the weekend. Chatting with the personable Jutanugarn during the third round helped settle Green down, as did holing from 40 feet at the fifth. The Thai went out in 32 but was three behind again after her three iron at the 16th found the reeds alongside Lake Hazeltine.

But Jutanugarn had a two at the 17th from six feet and then Green three-putted the last. A 70 put her on nine under, with Jutanugarn on eight under after a 68. Lizette Salas, also with a 68, and Korda, with a 69, were on five under, with Park on four under following a 71. On the same mark was Sei Young Kim, who holed out for an eagle at the 14th in a best-of-the-day 67.

After an Australian barbecue at the house on Saturday evening, Green birdied two of the first seven holes to go four ahead once Jutanugarn had bogeyed the eighth. However, a three-putt from Green at the ninth sparked a run of three dropped shots in four holes. Although Jutanugarn was off her game, suddenly Korda, after birdies at the fifth and seventh holes, was only one behind. But the American bogeyed the par-five 15th and had to settle for a 71 to finish on six under par in a share of third place. Reid got to the same mark with a 66, although the lowest score of the week came from 2018 runner-up Nasa Hataoka with a 65. Salas, playing with Green and Jutanugarn in the final threeball, had a 72 to share fifth place with former champion Danielle Kang.

Park was three behind Green after a bogey at the 12th, but the Korean made a birdie-four at the 15th, came close at both 16 and 17 before burying her putt at the last for a 68. That forced Green to get up and down at the last for a 72 and a one-stroke victory on a nine-under-par total of 279.

Webb, bursting with pride, was thrilled with how her compatriot had handled herself. "It's taken her 12 to 18 months to feel she belongs out here," Webb said, "and what a way to show it. The way she played for four days leading a major wire to wire, that's really impressive. And the up-and-down on the last was world class."

On the front nine, Green had been handed a note by a young girl. "I got a cute little poem saying that I had given her a ball at the ANA and also said, 'You can win this.' A couple of times on the back nine when I was feeling nervous and had some time, I actually read it to myself. I have to thank Lily for writing that. I think it really helped me."

Evian Championship

On Saturday night at the Evian Championship, as rain pounded down outside, Lorena Ochoa was honored for her work with underprivileged children in her home country of Mexico. The following morning, the former world No. 1 was introduced to Jin Young Ko. Dave Brooker, Ko's caddie, used to work for the charismatic Ochoa, who retired in 2010 after a career which saw her win two major championships. "It was really great to meet Lorena this morning," Ko said.

"She said, 'Try to make many birdies.' I said, 'So, okay, I will try.' I was happy and then I'm falling in love with Lorena." Inspired by the meeting, Ko went out and won her second major title — the second in four attempts after she triumphed at the ANA Inspiration. Since then Ko has been teaching herself English via YouTube videos and the 24-year-old from Seoul conducted all her media duties at Evian in English.

Earlier in the season, Ko had expressed her admiration for Brooks Koepka. Asked for why, she simply replied: "Everything." Then she added that "I like his poker face." She was becoming the player to beat in the women's majors in the same way Koepka has in the men's. Usually impassive to a fault, Ko dissolved into tears the moment she won the ANA, thinking of her late grandfather.

This time at Evian, Ko enjoyed the scene at the 18th to the full and the tears only came once the prize-giving ceremony reached the stage when the flag of the Republic of Korea was raised and her national anthem played. "I'm really proud of Korea," she said. "I tried never to cry again, because ANA I cried so much. So this week I try just smiling, but I heard my national anthem and then I couldn't hold it."

A delayed reaction to the emotion of the occasion may be understandable given the circumstances of her victory. Having started the final round four strokes behind Hyo Joo Kim, Ko trailed her friend and compatriot all day until the 14th hole. At the par-three, Kim, who was disturbed over her tee shot and later regretted not backing off and starting again, found a greenside bunker. This was when the trouble really started.

The ball was plugged under the lip in the wet sand after all the rain that had fallen in the previous 24 hours. A slight figure, whose accuracy is usually her strength, did not appear to have the power required to force the ball out of the trap. It caught the bank in front of her and then rolled back into her own footprints. Her second attempt at escaping only just found the fringe of the green, and from there, understandably in a state of shock, she three-putted for a six.

From being one ahead, Kim was now two behind Ko, who had safely parred the hole. Kim recovered herself to finish with a three pars and a birdie at the last to share second place with Shanshan Feng and Jennifer Kupcho. Ko, suddenly finding herself ahead, also finished strongly, holing from 25 feet for a birdie at the 17th which resulted in a two-stroke victory.

She was able to enjoy the walk down the 18th once Brooker, who had previously told her to avoid looking at the leaderboards, told Ko, as she reported: "If you three-putt, still you win. But you're a professional, so you have to make a two-putt." She did. Not since Inbee Park in 2015 had a player won multiple majors in the same season. "It's a really great honor to get a second major win of the year," Ko said. "Really, I can't believe about how can I do it?"

She did it by sticking to her usual game, as articulated by Brooker. "The things that impress most are her consistency and her ball-striking, as she showed today," he said. "She didn't miss a shot in 18 holes. Her management of distance control, because she just does not curve the ball, is phenomenal."

A closing 67, for a 15-under-par total of 269, contained five birdies and only one bogey at the 12th, where her one less-than-perfect approach ran off the green. She chipped up but the putt lipped out. She had birdied the sixth and seventh holes on the front nine and then hit her second at the 10th to a foot. A 20-footer at the 13th got her back within one of Kim, which meant she was in pole position when misfortune visited her friend. Kim closed with a 73, having been level par for the day before the triple. The all-Korean final threeball also contained Sung Hyun Park, who started as Kim's closest challenger, just one behind. But Park bogeyed the first two holes and three of the first five. A double bogey at the 11th ended her hopes and she finished with a 75 to tie for sixth place with Moriya Jutanugarn, one behind Ariya Jutanugarn, who was fifth after a 68.

Park dislikes wearing a rain jacket, but that was not an option on Sunday as the rain lasted all day, sometimes heavy, sometimes lighter. Ironically, the championship, which was celebrating its 25th anniversary since it started as the Evian Masters before being designated a major in 2013, had been moved from September back to its old July date expressly to avoid the weather that had plagued the event in its late summer date.

So the first half of the week was played in a heatwave that saw record temperatures across Europe. Paula Creamer seemed to enjoy the heat as she led the first round with a seven-under-par 64 in which she did not drop a stroke. She finished with a birdie-four at the last, which was converted to a par-five from a par-four. The 13th hole, which was a par-five, was reduced to a four, albeit a long one, but Creamer managed to birdie that anyway. Ko, after finishing with four birdies in a row, was a stroke behind on 65, along with Mi Hyang Lee, Inbee Park and Brittany Altomare. Kupcho and Mel Reid scored 66s. Lee had come to the 18th tied for the lead but a bogey dropped her into the group sharing second place.

It was the first time since she won the 2010 U.S. Women's Open that Creamer had led at a major. "It's been several years since I've felt good in my shoes," said the 32-year-old. Creamer had won the Evian Masters in 2005 and the tournament's branding also fitted with the golfer known as the Pink Panther. "I love all the pink," she said. "The first time I was here it was like it was meant for me. Then, there is the scenery. If you ever have a bad moment, you can look out at the lake."

Creamer may have taken her own advice the following afternoon, for she was philosophical in admitting she did not deal with the conditions too well. A threat of lightning interrupted play for 65 minutes, and after the resumption the wind was gusting up to 30 mph. Creamer went seven over par for five holes and ended with a 76. Instead, Lee went into the lead with a 67 to be 10 under par. The 23-year-old with two LPGA wins recovered from a double bogey at the ninth and finished the round in the worst of the weather with birdies at the 16th and 17th holes before eagling the last. "I missed a lot of greens and had a bit of luck, but just tried to take it shot by shot," Lee said.

Lee led by a stroke over Kim as well as Sung Hyun Park and Inbee Park. Kim, after an opening 69, scored a 64, along with Caroline Hedwall, the best score of the day. Kim did not drop a stroke and went five under par for the last seven holes, including an eagle at the last. Inbee Park, who won the last non-major Evian Masters in 2012, had a 68, while Sung Hyun Park added a 66 to a first round of 67. Ko had a 71, so was in sixth place, alongside Kupcho and a stroke behind Feng.

Among those missing the cut was U.S. Open champion Jeongeun Lee$_6$, by a single stroke, and Lexi Thompson, who scored 77-72. The first round had been the problem, with the American hitting only five of the fiery, sloping fairways and taking 37 putts. A social media post, subsequently deleted, suggested she was happy not to be playing on the weekend.

It was the 2014 Evian champion Kim who went low on Saturday, with a 65 that put her one ahead. After going out in 33, she had birdies at the 13th, 14th, 16th and 17th holes, but the best bit about her round was finishing just as the heavy rain began. An early morning start had ensured play finished prior to the forecasted thunderstorms. "I am very happy that I was able to finish the round before the rain started to pour really bad," Kim said. "I definitely have good memories of this tournament because of my win. I'm going to keep that going into tomorrow and forget everything else."

Sung Hyun Park had her second 66 in a row to lie second, with Ko also producing a 66 to take third place alongside Inbee Park. Ariya Jutanugarn shot up the leaderboard with a 64, while Lee had stalled with a 71 that left her in fifth place with Feng.

The Chinese golfer dropped only one stroke on Sunday in a 68 but never got closer than within a shot of the lead. Kupcho finished with a bogey-free 66, including birdies at three of the last four holes, for her best finish in eight events since turning professional. The inaugural winner of the Augusta National Women's Amateur hit the green in two at the last, one of the few to do so on the final day, and two-putted for a four, the most nervous moment of her career. "I'd definitely say over that putt on 18 I was freaking out. I had to take a couple of deep breaths as I was lining it up," she said.

A breakout performance by a potential star secured her LPGA card for 2020. Ko's victory, her third of the season, returned her to the top spot on the Rolex Rankings, a position her new idol Ochoa had once made her own.

AIG Women's British Open

Hinako Shibuno burst out laughing. A perfectly typical response usually, in this particular instant it appeared at odds with the importance of the moment. Shibuno stood over her approach shot to the final hole at the AIG Women's British Open. She needed a birdie to win and a par to force a playoff with Lizette Salas but all she could think about, as she confessed to her caddie/coach, was that "if I were to shank this second shot, it would be very embarrassing."

Fear not, it was anything but, landing safely on the green. Already nicknamed the "Smiling Cinderella" by the Japanese media, now Shibuno moved into *A Star Is Born* territory. Smile, she certainly did. Fist-bump, high-five, bow her head in respect, Shibuno interacted with the crowd all the while playing at a positively brisk pace and, ultimately, holing an 18-foot putt on the 18th green of the Marquess course at Woburn to win by one stroke.

Not only did she beat the game's best players on her debut in a major championship, but this previously unknown player won over the hearts of golf fans everywhere. "Every time I make a birdie putt or a par save, a lot of people got up their hands to high-five me, and that was a very happy feeling," Shibuno said through a translator. "We play in front of spectators, and there are many viewers that watch on TV, and I want them to enjoy watching golf."

A born entertainer, her golfing instincts could not be more finely tuned as she charged home with five birdies, including the vital one at the last. "I was looking at the board all the time, I knew where I stood. I was also thinking about if I were to make this putt, how I was going to celebrate — enough treats to feed me till I die!" For Shibuno, who closed with a 68 for an 18-under-par total of 270, there is no finer treat than Japanese sweets made from squid and seaweed.

In front of Shibuno, Salas had seen her birdie try at the last lip out from under five feet. She would come up a shot short in second place, her best major result, after a closing 65, tying the best round of the week. The American finished a stroke in front of her playing partner, Jin Young Ko, whose 66 left the world No. 1 in third place and just shy of a third major win of the season and a second in successive weeks.

It was a startling introduction on the world stage for Shibuno. This was not just her first major, but her first LPGA event and her first tournament outside Japan. The 20-year-old from Okayama only turned professional in 2018, earning her place on the Japan LPGA, where she was a rookie for 2019. Of the four-round qualifying school, she said: "It makes you want to vomit. I never want to go through it again."

A good way to avoid a return was claiming, as her maiden victory, one of the circuit's majors, the World Ladies Championship Salaponas Cup. Another win followed and she arrived in London for some sightseeing at the start of the week 46th on the Rolex Rankings. First to grab the attention was her manager, who dressed in colorful clothing as an attempt to keep her smiling. "Crazy," she said, "a little embarrassing." Her double-jointed elbows also became a fascination, though she has yet to establish if they aid or impede her swing.

At the start of the weekend, she was being followed by an ever-expanding gallery of her compatriots. By the end of the week, everyone was enthralled. When she attempted a thank-you speech in English at the trophy presentation, she laughed off the odd stumble and was rewarded with adoring cheers. Was a trophy better than Prince Charming for this Smiling Cinderella? someone wanted to know. "A trophy is a trophy, so I can't really compare to Prince Charming," she said, "but this is definitely the most valuable trophy I've ever received."

The last player to win a major on debut was Korea's Hyo Joo Kim at the 2014 Evian Championship. But the only other Japanese golfer, male or female, to win a major was Chako Higuchi at the 1977 LPGA Championship. "So I was looking online and I did see that it's been 42 years since a Japanese player has last won," Shibuno said. "I do feel that I have accomplished something great, but I really don't know the reason why I was able to accomplish it." Her timing, with the Olympics in Tokyo in 2020 a goal she definitely had in mind, was perfect.

Ashleigh Buhai opened with a seven-under-par 65 to lead on Thursday on the Marquess course that also staged the Women's British Open in 2016. On a day when 45 players broke par, the round equaled Buhai's best on the LPGA and contained three birdies in a row from the 14th. It was the first time in the 30-year-old South African's career that she had led a major. "Today was perfect golfing conditions, everything you wanted, soft greens, hardly in the wind and you could throw it at the pin," said Buhai. "I struck the ball great and I holed a lot of good putts. Everything was just coming into place."

Shibuno, in her first competitive round outside Japan, came home in 30 for a 66 to tie for second place with Danielle Kang. Woburn club member Charley Hull was a shot behind on 67 with Sung Hyun Park, Megan Khang and Moriya Jutanugarn. A high-quality trio of Ko, Ariya Jutanugarn and Jeongeun Lee$_6$ were on 68. In her mind's eye, Shibuno pictured the British Open at a traditional links course. The parkland setting of the Marquess made her feel much more at home. "It's really similar to a Japanese course, so I played relaxed and confident," she said. Her overall impression of the day was simply summed up: "Just one word — surprised."

A 67 on Friday extended Buhai's lead at 12 under par to three strokes over Shibuno, who added a 69. Buhai only made one birdie on the front nine but did not drop a shot all day and added four coming home. "My goal going out today was to get it to double figures, 10 under or better," said Buhai. "Once I got it to eight, nine and 10 under, I felt more comfortable and was able to put my foot down."

Salas, after an opening 69, started her second round with four successive birdies on the way to a 67 which put her in third place. She was a stroke ahead of Park, Hull, Caroline Masson, Bronte Law and Celine Boutier, who had a 66. Law, the latest English golfer to win on the LPGA, scored a 67 to tie Hull, while defending champion Georgia Hall was a stroke further back with Ko, who had added a 70.

At the turn on Saturday, Buhai, who went out in 34, was five ahead of the field and six ahead of her young playing partner Shibuno. But over the last seven holes there was an eight-shot swing to the Japanese player. Buhai three-putted both the 12th and 13th greens and also dropped a shot at the 16th in a 72. Meanwhile, Shibuno came home in 30 for the second time in the week, capped with a six iron to within three feet at the last. "It's definitely exceeding my expectations," she said. "I came here wanting to make the cut, so right now I feel like I'm doing something very incredible."

Shibuno was two ahead of Buhai, with Park three back and Ko, Salas and Pressel a further shot adrift. The English contingent slipped back over the weekend, while Park, as at Evian, faded in the final round, a 73 leaving her in eighth place. Pressel scored 66-67 over the weekend to take fourth place and hint at a Solheim Cup wild card selection that eventually came her way. Buhai closed with a 70 to be fifth, and although she appeared out of it after a bogey at the first hole, she was one of five players who at some point tied for the lead on a dramatic final day.

It was when Shibuno four-putted the third green for a double bogey — a long-range uphiller followed by two short misses — that the leaderboard tightened up. U.S. Open champion Lee birdied four of the first eight holes to tie but ended up with a 71 for a share of ninth place. Ko had a bogey-free day and made six birdies in nine holes to give herself a chance of back-to-back major titles but could only par the last five holes. The Korean nevertheless earned the Rolex Annika Major Award for the season after the two victories.

Salas made the best start of all with three birdies in the first four holes. Her only dropped shot came at the short sixth, but the 30-year-old Californian, with one LPGA win to her tally, birdied four of the next five holes to lead by two shots. More chances followed but only the one at the 15th, from 15 feet, fell. Over her five-footer at the last, Salas said to herself: "You got this. You're made for this."

"I put a good stroke on it," she said. "I was nervous, I'm not going to lie. I haven't been in that position in a long time. It just didn't drop, so congrats to our winner. It stings a little, but to pull off a 65 on a Sunday at a major playing alongside our No. 1 player, it's pretty awesome."

Shibuno admitted being nervous but feeling better about chasing once she fell behind than she had about leading. She responded to the double with birdies at the fifth and seventh holes before a bogey at the eighth. But just as earlier in the week, she dominated the back nine — she played the front in level for the week and the back in 18 under par. A birdie at the 10th kept her two behind Salas. Threes at the 12th and 13th holes got her level, and a four at the 15th matched the American. That left the stage set for a thrilling finish at the 18th which will be remembered not just by Shibuno but all who saw it.

The Solheim Cup

For the first time in 16 Solheim Cups, the result of the 2019 contest at Gleneagles was determined by the last putt on the 18th green of the final match on the course. Only once in the history of the Ryder Cup had a player holed such a putt to win for his team — Syd Easterbrook from three feet in 1933 at Southport and Ainsdale. It was a heart-stopping moment to lay before a record crowd for the biennial women's match — over 90,000 spectators for the week — but the circumstances to reach such a thrilling denouement were even more remarkable for two reasons.

Firstly, Europe needed to win all of the last three matches to win by a single point. In the anchor match Anna Nordqvist defeated Morgan Pressel, 4 and 3, but Bronte Law had to win three holes out of four to go from one down to a 2-and-1 victory when Ally McDonald missed for par at the 17th. Meanwhile, in match 10, Marina Alex had won the 13th and 14th holes to take her match to the 18th and missed from 10 feet above the hole to secure a third successive victory for America and Juli Inkster as captain.

Secondly, the player who faced the do-or-die putt from seven feet — miss and America would win, hole and Europe would win for only the sixth time — was Suzann Pettersen. The 38-year-old Norwegian was a controversial wild card selection by European captain Catriona Matthew as she had played only four events, missing the cut three times, since returning from maternity leave. Pettersen had been away from the game for 18 months after complications early in her pregnancy meant she could not fly. But Matthew, who played alongside Pettersen in the Dow Great Lakes pairs event in July, always wanted the veteran on her team despite Pettersen's misgivings about continuing her professional career now she was a mother to son Herman.

This was Pettersen's ninth appearance — she ended it with 21 points, fourth all-time for Europe — but injury had prevented her playing in 2017 and in 2015 her insistence on not conceding a putt to Alison Lee in the fourballs had sparked a furious American rally in the singles that secured the only previous one-point victory in the Solheim Cup.

Pettersen lost her voice on the eve of the contest at Gleneagles but enjoyed partnering the big-hitting youngster Anne van Dam to a win and a loss in the fourballs. She appeared in control of her singles against Alex, so far undefeated on debut, but was taken all the way to the 18th. Reaching the green, Pettersen was unaware of Law's match finishing on the 17th but, no matter, in went the putt. It was not just a victorious end to the match but also her career. Amid the wild celebrations with teammates — and baby Herman — Pettersen decided to retire on the spot.

"I didn't know it was for the Cup but I knew it was important," Pettersen said of her putt. "Beany [Matthew] appeared on the 18th hole and said: 'This is why I picked you.' I never thought I was going to be here four months ago. It's the perfect way to end my Solheim career and my professional career. This is it, I'm completely done. My life has completely changed in the last year. Now I know how it feels to win as a mother and I'm going to leave it like that."

"I could barely watch," said Matthew in her first experience of captaincy. "It is far harder having to watch, but you just have to trust the players out there and I always had faith in Suzann. She has been one of the trailblazers for European golf and the Solheim Cup. It was such a special moment, what a way to go out at the top."

Pettersen added: "This is the ultimate dream. To win in Scotland, for Beany in her home country, for all the fans out there, to come down to the last putt, it was the ultimate."

Europe has now won all three of the matches played in Scotland — including Dalmahoy in 1992 and Loch Lomond in 2000 — which meant a great deal to Matthew, a proud Scot who twice as a player secured the winning point for Europe. She made no immediate decision on continuing as captain, but it was farewell time for Inkster. "We had a few tears but we had a great week," Inkster said. "The Europeans played great and we're going to have a party. This will fuel us for two years' time. It's been an honor to do this three times. I'm 2 and 1 and that's good. But it's not about the wins and losses, it's about the memories and the friendships and being part of a team."

For the first time since 2011, when Europe also prevailed late in the singles, the two teams were tied at 8-8 after the first two days. Europe edged ahead in the Friday morning foursomes, but the first point came from the first pair of sisters to play together in the Solheim Cup. Annika and Charlotta Sorenstam played for Europe in 1998 but not in combination.

Jessica and Nelly Korda won four of the first five holes against Caroline Masson and Jodie Ewart Shadoff and ran out 6-and-4 winners. "That was a lot of fun," said the 21-year-old Nelly, who was making her debut. Matthew had put her top-two ranked players together at the top of the order and Carlota Ciganda, with a long birdie putt at the 17th, and Law claimed a half against Pressel and Alex. Georgia Hall and Celine Boutier then won the first of three matches together by 2 and 1 over Lexi Thompson and Brittany Altomare, Thompson's first loss since her rookie year in 2013. Charley Hull and Azahara Munoz took the anchor match over Megan Khang and Annie Park, 2 and 1, to give Europe the lead at lunch.

The afternoon fourballs proved a lost opportunity for the home side. The USA again claimed the first point via McDonald and Angel Yin, who made seven birdies in defeating the experienced Swedish combination of Nordqvist and Caroline Hedwall, 7 and 5, equaling the biggest margin of victory in fourballs. McDonald was the only one of Inkster's six rookies not to play in the morning, having only been upgraded from travelling reserve to team member on Tuesday when Stacy Lewis was ruled out with a back injury.

The top match went to the home side as Pettersen and van Dam won 4 and 2 against Danielle Kang and Lizette Salas. "When you have a superstar like this who just bombs it, you've got to be very happy," Pettersen said of her partner.

There was a chance of Europe winning the last two matches to open up a three-point margin, but the visitors fought back magnificently in each. In fact, Thompson and Jessica Korda were two up with four to play before Ciganda and Law won the next three holes, the Spaniard again birdieing the 17th. But Thompson birdied the last to force a half in a classic contest.

Even more wounding to the home side was Hull and Munoz losing a four-up lead with six to play against Altomare and Nelly Korda. The Americans birdied the 13th, then each of the last three holes. Nelly Korda almost holed in one at the 17th, with Hull lipping out from five feet for the win, while at the last Altomare holed from 25 feet before both Munoz and Hull again missed chances to take the point. "For two rookies to be four down with six holes left and to come back and tie, you can't teach that. It's just in your belly," Inkster said of Altomare and the younger Korda. "Those two half points at the end were huge."

Despite Europe leading by a point, there was no doubting the happier team were the visitors. But Matthew said: "Our objective is to try to win every session, but we would have taken a lead at the start of the day, so we're pleased."

Saturday's foursomes, played in a cold, blustery wind, also ended all-square with another American comeback in the top match. Pressel and Alex were four down after six holes to Nordqvist and van Dam. But the Americans had four birdies in a row from the ninth to go in front and produced a 2-and-1 victory. "It was a hard-fought battle," said Pressel. "The putt that Marina made on seven was really the turning point in our match."

By then there had already been another foursomes win for the Korda sisters, this time by a record-equaling 6-and-5 margin over Ciganda and Law. However, Hull and Munoz continued their unbeaten run with a 4-and-3 win over Kang and Khang, while Hall and Boutier claimed a second win together by 3 and 2 over Salas and McDonald.

It was in the afternoon fourballs that America won their first session to draw level, and that with the undefeated Korda sisters resting up for the singles. With the rain making conditions even tougher and rounds approaching six hours, it was quite a battle. Altomare and Park won at the 18th against Pettersen and van Dam, Pettersen keeping her team in touch with five birdies in six holes around the turn. Thompson and Park then produced a half against Masson and Ewart Shadoff, a pair returning for the first time since Friday morning. Masson had the chance to win at the 18th with a seven-footer which lipped out to her shock.

It was Hall and Boutier who prevented America taking the overall lead by recovering from being four down after seven holes to beat McDonald and Yin by two holes. "It was brutal out there," said Hall, the 2018 British Open champion. "When we were four down I just thought, 'enough is enough.' We both switched on and played some good golf." They were six under for the last 10 holes, with Boutier holing long putts for an eagle at the 14th and a birdie at the 16th.

Moments later, however, Salas and Kang closed out the Spaniards Ciganda and Munoz, the only two players to appear in every session. Not since 1992 had all four matches in a fourball or foursomes session gone to the 18th and that streak continued when Kang birdied the 17th for a 2-and-1 victory.

"At one point this afternoon it looked as if it could potentially go 4-0 or 3-1 against us, so we're pretty pleased," said Matthew. "That fight back from Georgia and Celine was great. Caroline is devastated she missed that putt on 18, but she hit a good putt."

In the top singles on a calmer Sunday, Ciganda left it late to gain her first win of the week as she leveled against Kang at the 16th and then won at the 18th. Hedwall led Nelly Korda three up after six holes, but the young American won five holes out of six at the start of the back nine on the way to a two-hole victory.

Thompson, who tweaked her back while warming up in the morning, nevertheless went two up on Hall early on, but the Englishwoman rallied around the turn and collected a 2-and-1 win. So did her partner of the first two days, Boutier, who beat Park by the same score as the pair collected records of four wins out of four.

Europe now led 11-9, but America took four and a half points from the next five matches. There were wins for Altomare, 5 and 4, over Ewart Shadoff, Yin over Munoz, 2 and 1, Jessica Korda, 3 and 2, over Masson, and Salas over van Dam at the 18th. That meant Jessica and Nelly Korda were America's top performers on three and a half points out of four. There was also a half for Khang over Hull, who birdied the 16th to go one up, but from 20 yards off the green at the last, took three to find the putting surface.

It looked then as if Europe would come up short by the narrowest of margins until Nordqvist, Law and Pettersen got the home team to 14½ points. "It could not have been any better," Matthew said. "To come down to Suzann was unbelievable. Everyone remembers the last putt, but we had to get there and that's down to everyone in the team. They all contributed to the victory."

7. American Tours

The year 2019 was more than the very good year of song. It was a quintessential vintage year — with the growing Rory McIlroy-Brooks Koepka rivalry (Koepka: what rivalry?), Patrick Reed's sand incident, the burst of young talent, and on and on. But it the end, it was the Year of the Tiger — again.

No golfer has ever got so much out of so little as Tiger Woods did in 2019. With just two wins, he rocked the entire golf world to its foundation. But what two wins. In a so-so year with its share of pain, Woods won the Masters, at age 43 — his fifth overall, his first in 14 years, his first major in 11 years, since the 2008 U.S. Open, and his 15th major overall.

"The rest of the tournaments I didn't really play as well as I wanted to," Woods said. He tied for 21st in the U.S. Open and missed cuts in the PGA Championship and the Open Championship. "But at the end of the day," he added, "I'm the one with the green jacket."

The second win, late in October, came in the inaugural Zozo Championship, the first PGA Tour event in Japan. It made the history books. It was Woods' 82nd tour win, tying Sam Snead's record for most wins. He'd thought his medical problems had put that out of reach. "Lo and behold," he said, "here we are tied."

Elsewhere in this vintage year:

The seeming McIlroy-Koepka rivalry perked up. For the first time in 28 years the Player of the Year awards were split. McIlroy won the PGA Tour's (in a player vote) and Koepka won the PGA of America award (in a point system). Koepka also was voted the Golf Writers Association of America Player of the Year. McIlroy capped an outstanding year with wins in The Players Championship, the RBC Canadian Open and the Tour Championship with its $15 million payout. Koepka's year was topped by great play in the majors. He won the PGA Championship (relocated to May), tied for second in the Masters, was solo second in the U.S. Open and tied for fourth in the Open Championship.

Said McIlroy: "Why do we play 25 times a year if only four weeks are important?"

Said Koepka: "Look, I love Rory ... but it's just hard to believe there's a rivalry in golf. I just don't see it."

It would take an international incident to overshadow Woods' year, and that's what the Patrick Reed Incident became. In the unofficial Hero World Challenge, a Tiger Woods benefit in the Bahamas in December, the TV camera showed Reed in a sandy waste area (not a bunker), drawing his wedge back twice, which brushed sand from behind his ball. He said it wasn't intentional. He received a two-stroke penalty for improving his lie. The incident triggered an immense media and fan storm, with accusations of cheating. The next week he was heckled by fans at the Presidents Cup in Australia.

And youth served itself. Korea's Sungjae Im, 21, with seven top-10s in 35 starts, won the tour's Rookie of the Year award (now named for Arnold Palmer). Matt Wolff, 20, won the 3M Open in just his fourth professional start, edging Collin Morikawa, 22, who won the Barracuda Championship a few weeks later. And Viktor Hovland, 22, who set the amateur scoring record at the U.S. Open, won his tour card through the Korn Ferry Tour Finals.

And one, Akshay Bhatia, turned pro and played four tour events on sponsor's exemptions, and missed all four cuts. He was 17.

U.S. PGA Tour

Sentry Tournament of Champions
Kapalua, Maui, Hawaii
Winner: Xander Schauffele

For Xander Schauffele, golf is a one-round game — the fourth round. For the first three rounds, he's just clearing his throat.

And that was tough on the hopefuls in the Sentry Tournament of Champions, that gathering of 32 winners from 2018 at the Kapalua Plantation Course to welcome the start of the 2019 schedule. It was especially tough on Gary Woodland, who started the final round leading by three but leading Schauffele by five.

"I knew what he was doing and the competitor in me knew I needed to do one better," said Woodland, "and unfortunately I didn't get it done."

He was speaking of Schauffele, who trailed through the first three rounds and was five behind going into the finale, who bogeyed his first and who then fired a whopping 11-under 62, tying the course record at the par-73 Kapalua Plantation and edging Woodland by one.

Thus Schauffele, 25, came from behind in the final round for his fourth PGA Tour win, as he had for the first three. He trailed by three in the 2017 Greenbrier, trailed by two in the 2017 Tour Championship and in the 2018 WGC - HSBC by three to tie and beat Tony Finau in a playoff. Behind by five, he was braced for this one.

"I didn't do much leaderboard watching," Schauffele said. "I knew it was going to be a birdie-fest at the end. We kept our head down and made a run for it."

With his opening 72, Schauffele was six behind Kevin Tway's 66. His 67-68 middle rounds kept him five behind Woodland each day, and in the fourth, the bogey at No. 1 left him six behind when he took off on his rampage.

Pity Woodland. After shooting 67-67-68, he was closing with another 68, bogey-free. But when they're dropping cross-country chip shots and fairway wedges on you for eagles, you know your time is running out. He totaled 270 — 22 under — and was second by a stroke.

"This one will sting," he said.

Schauffele, after his opening bogey, birdied four of five holes from No. 3, including a two-putt from 70 feet, and one-putts of four, 10 and 14 feet. At the par-five ninth, "I thought it would be kind of cool if I just chip in to spice things up," he said, and he did.

And then with a wedge at the par-four 12th, "we had about 102-ish ... take a little off that and it happened to one-hop in there." He took the lead on short birdie putts at 14 and 15. Woodland fought back with birdies at the 15th and 17th, but Schauffele birdied the 17th from nine feet and got the clincher at the par-five 18th with two putts from 12 feet for the 62 and his one-stroke win.

Schauffele revealed where the inspiration comes from when one is six behind with 17 holes to play. "You look around," he said, "and realize you have nothing to lose."

Sony Open in Hawaii
Honolulu, Hawaii
Winner: Matt Kuchar

There's that old commentary on the passing of time that says "Youth must be served," and it was clearly true in the Sony Open in Hawaii, the PGA Tour's first full-field event of 2019. Matt Kuchar was on hand, beaming with that same youthful smile but thin on top and 40 now. But he did keep faith with the old adage. He served youth memorably — with a huge helping of how-to.

"I think it's an exciting time to be part of the tour," Kuchar noted later, "to see all these young players come out and do great things."

It was a pretty fair show, as well, by a guy of 40. That was a four-shot win, and not as comfy as the margin suggested. Kuchar led from the second round, but had to rally down the final stretch to regain the lead from Andrew Putnam and do a birdie sprint to lock up the win. He whipped the par-70 Waialae course in 63-63-66-66 for a 22-under 258.

"The frustrating thing was, I felt like I was doing some good things and just not seeing results," Kuchar said. "Nice to see it turn around."

From the start, it was clear that Waialae would take a thumping. Canada's Adam Svensson, 25, a tour rookie, opened with a flawless nine-under 61 and led by one. "It was all a blur," Svensson said. "I don't even remember which holes I birdied." Putnam was second at 62 and Kuchar third at 63. And 75 of the field of 144 were below par.

Starting the second round from No. 10, Kuchar birdied four of the first five and eagled his ninth, the par-five 18th, off a 261-yard second to 16 feet, on his way to another 63. "Unexpected, but awfully excited," he said. He led Putnam (65) by one. Among the day's oddities, Chez Reavie, shooting 65, had three eagles, a record for one round, and all on hole-outs at par-four holes — No. 10 (his first hole) from 101 yards, No. 16 from 149 and No. 6 from 135. "I need to go buy a lottery ticket today, I think," Reavie said.

Kuchar inched another stroke ahead of Putnam with a flawless 66 in the third round, and then, after having made only one bogey in three rounds, he staggered early in the fourth, going bogey-birdie-bogey-bogey from No. 2. "I knew if I stayed the course ... not letting that get the best of me, that some good stuff was going to happen," Kuchar said.

Putnam led through the turn, then Kuchar took control after Putnam's bogey at the 14th. Kuchar notched three of his five back-nine birdies over the last four holes on putts of 12 feet at 15, 11 at 16 and two putts from 34 feet at 18, and it added up to a four-shot win. And a rainbow stretched across the sky.

"It was too cool," Kuchar said, "to have a rainbow appear on the 18th hole."

Desert Classic
La Quinta, California
Winner: Adam Long

Adam Long, 31, a wandering golfer since his days at Duke University, almost had the distinction of witnessing Hall-of-Famer Phil Mickelson scoring his 43rd PGA Tour victory. Instead, Long had the distinction of sidetracking Mickelson and recording his own first professional win (apart from that one on the Hooters Tour).

This he did when Mickelson, in his first competition in three months, after opening with a 12-under 60, led for three rounds but faltered just enough in the last. Long pounced and took the win with a birdie on the last hole.

"It can seem like it came out of nowhere," Long said, "but my game's been trending in the right direction for the last two years."

Long himself came out of nowhere. After graduating from Duke, he turned pro in 2010 and headed out to seek his fortune. "I've played in most tours around the world," he said. These included the Web.com (now Korn Ferry) Tour, from which in 2018 he qualified for the PGA Tour. He made one cut in five starts, tying for 63rd. And then in the Desert Classic, he caught Mickelson and Canada's Adam Hadwin and birdied the final hole to beat them by a shot.

"I didn't expect to be sitting here," Long told the media. "I just kept plugging away."

The three players were on different courses through the first three rounds.

Mickelson's opening 60 at La Quinta included an eagle-three on a five-foot putt at the sixth and a chip-in birdie at the 14th. Said Mickelson: "I didn't feel sharp heading in, and the bad shots, I got away with." Mickelson kept the lead with a 68 at the Nicklaus course and a 66 at the Stadium. Hadwin played La Quinta and the Nicklaus in 66-65. Long shot 71 on the Stadium and 63 at La Quinta.

Going into the final round at the Stadium, the final threesome were Mickelson, at 22 under, Hadwin at 20 and Long at 19.

"It was the Phil and Adam Hadwin show most of the way," Long said. "I was just in the background, plugging away."

Hadwin spread out six birdies, then bogeyed No. 13 and shot 67 for a 25-under 263. "Didn't quite have it like I did," he said.

Mickelson three-putted for bogey at No. 1, notched three birdies, then bogeyed No. 9 out of the water. He birdied the 15th and 16th for a 69 and tied Hadwin at 263. Long was grinding away. With four one-putts and two chip-ins, he birdied Nos. 1, 2, 9, 12, 14 and 15, there to be tied at 25 under.

The tournament came down to the par-four 18th. Hadwin was bunkered and parred. Mickelson also parred, two-putting from 40 feet. Long fired his six-iron second to 14 feet and holed it for his fifth one-putt birdie, a 65, a 26-under 262 and his first tour win.

"I was just trying to make a putt," Long said. "But when that thing went in, I don't know — I never felt like that in my life."

Farmers Insurance Open
San Diego, California
Winner: Justin Rose

The Farmers Insurance Open might have been the first PGA Tour tournament to start the final round on the seventh hole. That requires some explaining.

Justin Rose, ranked No. 1 in the world, led by three going into the final round, but three bogeys and one birdie in the first five holes had him muttering. Then he missed a five-foot birdie putt at No. 6. He'd had enough. He scratched a line at No. 6 on his scorecard. "All right," he said, "we build the round from this moment on." He would start the final round at No. 7.

"You're No. 1 for a reason," Rose told himself. "Just start playing like it, please."

And from the seventh on he had five birdies and no bogeys on the testing Torrey Pines South Course, scoring his 10th win, the most by any English player on the PGA Tour.

"There were times where I've had decent-sized leads and you start to throw it away and you panic," Rose said. "I just knew I couldn't do that today. I stayed calm, I stayed with it."

Rose trailed Jon Rahm by one after an opening 63 on Torrey Pines North, then went to the tougher and more famous Torrey South and reeled off 66-69-69 for a 21-under 267, the lowest in the event in 20 years. Rose won by two over Adam Scott, who kept the pressure on but couldn't quite close the gap. "As [well] as I'm playing," Scott said, "I feel like I'm a long way behind ... By the time I got it sorted out, it was a bit too late." Scott, trailing by three at the start of the final round, had a bogey-birdie exchange for a front-nine par and then a rush of four straight birdies from the 15th coming in for a 68–269.

The critical moment for Rose came at the start of the final round with the three quick bogeys, after which he drew the line at No. 6. An old trick he would play on himself, he explained.

"Sometimes I'll play match play against the golf course," he said. "Today I was three-down to the course ... it distracts you from the leaderboard and keeps you positive. You're playing more aggressive golf to try and make some shots back rather than limit the damage. Just reframes everything."

Tiger Woods was making his 2019 debut at the Farmers, on a course where he had won eight times. It was his first competition in almost two months. He shot 70-70-71-67–278, 10 under, to tie for 20th. Never in contention, he was fighting to finish in double figures under par and he did it with a flourish. He was eight under coming to his 17th, the par-three No. 8. He holed a 10-foot putt for birdie. At the par-five ninth (his 18th) he two-putted from 37 feet. The birdie-birdie finish got him in just under the wire at 10 under. "Got to have these little goals when I'm not in contention," he said. "Still something positive to end the week on."

Waste Management Phoenix Open
Scottsdale, Arizona
Winner: Rickie Fowler

Rickie Fowler had come again to the Waste Management Phoenix Open, the tournament where he had failed so famously. In 2016, hitting driver, he watered his tee shot at the short par-four 17th, blew a two-shot lead, and on the second hole of a playoff, watered his tee shot again, this time with a three wood, and lost to Hideki Matsuyama. In 2018, he led going into the final round, shot 73 and got overrun by Gary Woodland.

Come the 2019 tournament, if ever a golfer was stamped for failure, it was Fowler. Well, he ended up winning it, but he had to come through the Twilight Zone in the final round to do it. There was the double bogey at the fifth — pedestrian. But the episode at the 11th? That was unreal.

Fowler had tied for the lead in the first round, was the solo leader through the second and third, and in the final was rolling quite nicely on TPC Scottsdale on his way to his fifth PGA Tour win. He led by four starting the final round, and was up by five coming to the par-four 11th. There, in the rain, he stepped into another dimension. He'd missed the green, knocked his chip shot across and it trickled down the steep bank, grazed the bunker that would have stopped it and saved him, and tumbled into the water. He tried to drop, twice. But the ball rolled down both times. Finally, he placed the ball. It hung about 30 inches above the water. He climbed back up to the green, and while he was surveying his shot, he glanced down in time to see his ball let go and tumble into the water. He had to place another, pitched up and 17 feet past the flag and, admirably composed, he rolled in the putt — for a triple-bogey-seven. Up ahead, South Africa's Branden Grace birdied the 12th. Fowler's lead had shrunk from five to one.

"That's an interesting one," Fowler said. "We did nothing to cause it to happen, and it's a one-shot penalty."

Rotten luck, a rules official said. Fowler's ball was in play after he placed it, and under Rule 9.3, when it rolled away because of natural causes (wind, water, gravity, etc.), he would have to play it from its new position. And its new position was down in the water.

Next he bogeyed the par-three 12th out of a bunker. Grace birdied the 13th. So in the space of two holes, Fowler had gone from leading by five to trailing by one. In an earlier time, Fowler might have staggered away. But this time, he birdied the par-five 15th after reaching in two. Then the drivable par-four 17th became the clincher. Grace caught water and bunker and bogeyed it, and Fowler came along and drove it and two-putted from 60 feet for a birdie and was ahead by two. He parred the 18th, wrapping up a card of 64-65-64-74—267, 17 under, beating Grace by two.

In the media room Fowler lifted a glass of champagne. "Cheers," he said. "I finally got it done."

AT&T Pebble Beach Pro-Am
Pebble Beach, California
Winner: Phil Mickelson

Lefty, now 48, was at home at Pebble again and, as the old expression goes, in fine fettle. He came back out that Monday morning and picked up where he left off in the storm the day before, and neatly formalized his victory in the AT&T Pebble Beach Pro-Am — his fifth. And also his 44th PGA Tour victory, and it joined him with Tiger Woods as the only two players to top $90 million in career winnings.

This was the durable and determined Phil Mickelson, of course, and the win was especially sweet after he'd let the Desert Classic slip away three weeks earlier.

"It means a lot to me to play the final round as focused and as well as I did," Mickelson said. "Especially after not being my best in Palm Springs. So to finish it off and play the way I did yesterday and today means a lot."

It was his turn to come from behind this time.

Mickelson opened with a six-under 65 at Monterey Peninsula, a shot behind Brian Gay and Scott Langley. He stayed in the hunt with a 68 at Spyglass Hill when bad weather forced the finish of the second round into Saturday morning. The battle took shape in the third round. Paul Casey shot 67 at Spyglass and was at 200 while Mickelson shot 70 at Pebble Beach for a 203.

It was rain and hail at Pebble for the fourth round, and a delay and a Monday finish, and thereby hangs a little flap.

While Casey, leading by three, fell quiet with just one birdie on the front nine, Mickelson was rolling. He birdied Nos. 2, 4 and 9 — the latter spectacularly, on a 166-yard approach and a tap-in. He birdied 10, 13 and 14 comfortably while Casey bogeyed 11 and 12 and birdied 14. Mickelson was leading by three through the 16th when it became too dark to see. But Mickelson wanted to keep going. Casey noted there was no way to play the last two holes in six minutes. Mickelson relented.

"I just get in my own little bubble and I don't see the big picture," Mickelson conceded, after they returned and finished on Monday morning. Both birdied the 18th, Mickelson for a 65 and a 19-under 268, and a three-stroke win over Casey, who finished with a 71–271.

Then came the question that was as logical as it was inevitable, with the U.S. Open coming to Pebble in June: Would Mickelson have an advantage from the victory?

"I really don't think there's any carryover from here to the U.S. Open," he said. "It's a totally different golf course. The greens will be firm, the rough will be high. Here, I'm trying to hit the ball as far as I can, not worry too much about the rough ... so there's really no carryover, other than I just really enjoy this place. I seem to play some of my best golf here, and that's probably about it."

Genesis Open
Pacific Palisades, California
Winner: J.B. Holmes

The Genesis Open began on Thursday and ended on Sunday, as scheduled, and J.B. Holmes, who had had only one top-10 finish so far this year, scrambled through the final round to score his first victory in nearly three years. But for a true picture of the tournament, consider that Jordan Spieth hit his opening tee shot at 7:22 a.m. Thursday, then hit it again seven hours later, after the round was washed out by rain and restarted. Spieth went on to shoot a seven-under 64 — 12 holes of it on Thursday, the rest of it on Friday morning.

And so it went. With the tournament backed up like traffic on the freeway, note that Holmes, who had a hole-in-one on Thursday, had to play 34 holes on Sunday, when he filled in a card of 63-69-68-70 for a 14-under 270 and a one-stroke win over Justin Thomas. Holmes not only had to play 34 holes, he started the final round trailing Thomas by four shots, and the greens were getting pounded from by all that traffic, and then the wind came up.

"I knew it was going to be very difficult to shoot a low score," said Holmes, facing that four-shot deficit. "I needed some help from Justin."

Holmes got more than help from Thomas. He got a gift. As Thomas said of his stumbles down the final round, "It's always a bummer to hand him a tournament. I should have won the thing."

Shoulda-woulda — the language of golf.

Holmes and Thomas both birdied No. 1 to start the final round. And then Thomas, who had shot a powerful 65 in the third round, was betrayed by his putter. He bogeyed Nos. 2, 4 and 5. Holmes crept up with a birdie at the third, and then bogeyed No. 7. Thomas, at 15 under, was leading by one into the turn.

Holmes took his first lead of the week at the par-four 10th, where he birdied from five feet and Thomas bogeyed on three putts from 48. Thomas retook the lead at the 11th with a three-foot birdie while Holmes three-putted for a bogey. Then Thomas folded. At the par-four 13th, he three-putted from 65 feet, missing his bogey putt from three feet, and double-bogeyed. He then bogeyed the 14th, missing a five-footer for par.

Thomas rejected a comfortable alibi. "I definitely wouldn't make an excuse of being tired," he said. "I felt great out there. I think it was just more I really struggled putting in that wind out there. It was very, very difficult out there. I'm sure the scores showed that."

"It was very difficult," Holmes said. "Especially the last few holes, with all that wind. But it was a challenge just with having to get up at 4:40 the last couple days and play 27 one day and 11 holes one day, and 33 holes one day. It was a tough week. I played great all week and luckily at the end I was able to pull it out."

WGC - Mexico Championship
Mexico City, Mexico
Winner: Dustin Johnson

The high point of the World Golf Championship - Mexico Championship — for the rest of the field, at least — came in the third round, when Dustin Johnson double-bogeyed the par-fourth 10th. Johnson had gone 45 holes without a bogey, but more to the point, he had come to the 10th leading by six shots. The double bogey cut deeply into his runaway lead. Suddenly, there was hope.

Sorry. It was just an illusion. Said Rory McIlroy, who led the first round before Johnson took over: "He's arguably the best player in the world." Johnson might not have seemed so at the fractured 10th. He drove into the trees on the right, went into some bushes on hitting a branch while trying to wedge out, got a free drop from a sprinkler line, then hit a tree trunk and went into bushes again, and finally punched onto the green and two-putted from 40 feet — a brutal double-bogey-six.

Others can get badly rattled by a double bogey at a time like this. The tournament could have been thrown wide open. But Johnson doesn't and the tournament wasn't.

"I knew I was playing well, so I didn't really let it bother me," Johnson said. "I kept my focus and played really solid coming in." That is, before anyone could duck through that opening, Johnson slammed it shut with birdies at 11 and 12. He added two more at 15 and 17, shot 66 and was 16 under and leading by four over McIlroy.

Johnson, winning his second Mexico Championship in three years, formalized the finish with five birdies on the final nine to wrap up a card of 64-67-66-66, for a 21-under 263 total at the par-71 Chapultepec and a five-stroke victory. A bogey in the finale was his only other blot of the tournament. McIlroy racked up seven birdies and a closing bogey for his final-round 67–268 to finish second.

The tournament opened with some contrasting fireworks — some good, some not. McIlroy eagled the drivable No. 1 (his 10th hole) with a two iron and a six-foot putt, on his way to a 63 and a one-stroke lead. Tiger Woods, starting at No. 1, bounced his tee shot off a nearby temporary green and double-bogeyed, on his way to a par 71 and was never a factor. He finished tied for 10th but 13 shots behind. Displeased, he refused to speak to the media for the last two rounds, and instead left his parting words with a tour spokesman saying, in part, "I had never played in Mexico ... and had an unbelievable experience."

This was Johnson's 20th tour victory, his sixth WGC win, but there was even more to be pleased about.

"It's starting to feel the way it did two years ago," he said after his opening 64, meaning before he was injured in a home fall at the 2017 Masters. And after the win: "This is a big one for me," he said. "It gives me a lot of confidence for the rest of the year."

Puerto Rico Open
Rio Grande, Puerto Rico
Winner: Martin Trainer

Perhaps Martin Trainer didn't dare to dream so big, or maybe he favored lower expectations. In any event, fate found Trainer one Sunday evening in February in the Puerto Rico Open saying: "It's incredible. I never thought that I would be able to win on the PGA Tour. That's just incredible."

And thus did Trainer's doubts end. Trainer, 27, a two-time winner on the Korn Ferry Tour, making just his 11th start on the PGA Tour, trailed through the first three rounds, came from behind in the fourth and closed with a rush to take his first tour victory by three shots.

The hardest point for Trainer? "I think just teeing off on the first hole," he said.

Trainer staked his claim in the final round with birdies at the second, fourth and fifth. Then he took two quick bogeys — off a bunkered tee shot at the par-three sixth and catching rough and sand at the par-four seventh. Was his old game rearing its ugly head in this tournament played opposite the WGC - Mexico Championship?

Not quite. After carding 70-67-69 in the first three rounds, Trainer shot the last 10 holes in four under, with birdies at Nos. 9, 10, 15 and 18, blowing past the field for a 67 and a three-stroke win. His 15-under 273 left Daniel Berger (66), Roger Sloan (67), Johnson Wagner (69) and Aaron Baddeley (72) three back at 276.

But before Trainer took over in the fourth round, the tournament was completely up for grabs. Andres Romero handled Coco Beach's winds nicely for the first-round lead at six-under 66 for a one-stroke edge. Romero said he liked playing in the wind. "But of course," he said, "it is very difficult for everyone." D.J. Trahan, 38, who won twice on the PGA Tour, shot 67, and Nate Lashley, 36, a 68, to tie for the halfway lead at eight under. Said Trahan, trying to return from a back injury: "It's time to man-up and think and act positively." And said Lashley, of his two Korn Ferry Tour wins: "That experience always helps, but this is a lot bigger deal." Baddeley took a one-shot lead with a 66 in the third round. "It was pretty low stress today," said Baddeley, 37, who last won in 2016.

That opening tee shot was Trainer's nervous moment. Then there were several key moments in the final round.

- He birdied the 15th. "And so," he said, "I just assumed I'm probably either tied for the lead or up one."
- At the 16th, he saw he was leading by two. "I just wanted to lag every single putt, hit the fairways, hit the green in regulation," he said.
- At the 17th, he didn't drive into the water. "I actually hit the fairway," he said, and was leading by two. "I thought, okay, my chances are pretty good."
- And at the 18th: "I still couldn't believe that I was leading and I was going to win. I was just thinking somehow maybe I'm not going to win. I just kept going and kept hitting, and that's all you can do."

Honda Classic
Palm Beach Gardens, Florida
Winner: Keith Mitchell

If they'd held an election coming down the final round at the Honda Classic, Keith Mitchell would have won the Mr. Absolutely No Chance title in a landslide.

Consider that on the tough par-70 PGA National he had come up against the likes of Brooks Koepka and Rickie Fowler, and as to his credentials, well: He had won once on the G Pro Tour, a minitour, but otherwise, in an aggregate of 96 previous starts, his bests were a second on the Latinoamerica Tour, a third on the Korn Ferry Tour and a second on the PGA Tour, where, already in 2019, he'd missed three cuts in five starts. The immediate future held little promise for Mitchell, 27, a former University of Georgia player.

Then the next thing anyone knew in the Honda, Mitchell was saying "coming down the stretch against Rickie Fowler and Brooks ... I'm just pleased that I could prove myself against guys like that."

And with great theater. Mitchell birdied four of his final seven holes, including the last on a clutch 15-foot putt, for a one-stroke win over Koepka and Fowler.

"Everyone dreams about having that putt on the 18th to win," Mitchell said, "and I had it today."

Mitchell opened with a 68 and trailed by four, shared the lead with a 66 in the second round, trailed by one with a par 70 in the third, then closed with a flourish for a 67 and a nine-under 271 for the one-stroke win. Fowler closed with a 67 and Koepka a 66 to tie at 272.

Until that closing rush, Mitchell was getting little attention. He was four behind Jhonattan Vegas (64) in the first round, and tied Korea's Sungjae Im (64) for the halfway lead at six-under 134. Then came a formidable test and a scramble in the third. First, Wyndham Clark, 25, seeking his first tour win, took the lead with a 67 for a seven-under 203. A stroke behind were Korea's Kyoung-Hoon Lee (68), Mitchell and Vijay Singh, 56, hoping to surpass Sam Snead as the oldest winner on the tour. "I'm physically quite capable of doing it," Singh said.

The fates broke perfectly for Mitchell in the final round. Clark had increased his lead to two, then bogeyed four of six holes from No. 7. Lee could manage only a one-over 71, and Singh's bid for history sputtered out in a 70.

Mitchell did not start the final round like a winner-about-to-be. Not with those two quick bogeys. Two birdies got him even through the turn, but he bogeyed the 11th out of the rough. Then Keith Mitchell's time had come. He came home with inspired golf, mastering all putts. He birdied 12, 13, 15 and 18 on putts of 11, 17, four and 15 feet.

Someone asked him how it felt, finally, to win. Mitchell raced through the language, looking for the words to describe the feelings overwhelming him. But the words don't exist. Then he found a way to say it all. "It was awesome," he said.

Arnold Palmer Invitational
Orlando, Florida
Winner: Francesco Molinari

Francesco Molinari had just finished, having shot a tournament-low 64. And he had the clubhouse lead in the Arnold Palmer Invitational. But he'd have to wait for the rest of the field to finish before he knew whether he'd won. And thus he discovered how long that wait was. It was a lifetime. Well, actually, about two hours. But it felt like a lifetime.

"I just went to the locker room and watched the golf [on TV]," he said. "I find it a lot more nerve-racking sitting there than being out there playing."

Molinari, the unassuming Italian, thought just about anything was possible. Consider that in 2018, he won the Quicken Loans National by eight shots on July 1 and three weeks later won the Open Championship by two — his first PGA Tour victory and his first major, almost back-to-back.

Molinari had a storybook start to the Palmer — falling two behind early, then getting even with one swing. He double-bogeyed the par-five No. 4 out of a bush ("a good seven," he said), and then he aced the par-three seventh, a four iron from 203 yards. He shot 69 and trailed Rafa Cabrera Bello by four. Adding 70-73, he trailed Tommy Fleetwood and Keegan Bradley by four in the second round, and England's Matthew Fitzpatrick by five in the third.

In the final round, Molinari teed off just past noon with 10 groups — 20 players — in front of him, and on a Bay Hill course whose greens had reached the point that moved Rory McIlroy, one off the lead, to observe, "You hit it 25, 30 [feet] away, you take your two-putts, you move on, and know you're not going to lose any ground on the field."

McIlroy was just one of Molinari's problems. "I was thinking about him and the other guys at the top of the leaderboard," he said. "I thought there was a chance, yes, because ... yesterday, I saw how difficult the course was the last few holes."

It was a thrilling irony that Molinari charged to the win on the course of a legend born of the charge. Arnie would have loved this show.

In his eight-birdie finale, Molinari struck immediately at No. 1, holing a 21-foot putt. He dropped a seven-footer at the third and a 15-footer at the sixth. He chipped in from 45 feet at No. 8 and was eight under through the turn. He got to 10 under at 12 and 13, on putts of seven and 18 feet. He two-putted at the par-five 16th and was 11 under. Then came the pièce de résistance. At the par-four, water-guarded 18th, his 155-yard approach ended up 45 feet left of the cup. He read his putt, settled in and rapped it and watched. It rolled forever, then dropped for a birdie. Molinari gave a joyful punch toward the ground, a big grin, and then a gentle wave to the roaring crowd. He had shot 64, for a 12-under 276 and a two-stroke win.

"Incredible," Molinari said. "Arnie was a special player, but most of all a special person ... so to win here, it's really truly special."

The Players Championship
Ponte Vedra Beach, Florida
Winner: Rory McIlroy

Returning to March after 12 years in May, The Players Championship proved to be as iffy as a tournament can get. This iffy: In the final round, eight players either led or had at least a share of the lead.

"With so much on the line," said Rory McIlroy, "I'm thankful it was my turn this week."

His turn? Actually, McIlroy made it his turn with a desperate dash to the finish line. He shook off a crippling two-putt bogey from eight feet at the 14th, birdied 15 and 16, and found his way home for a one-stroke victory over Jim Furyk, at age 48 the unlikeliest of the challengers. Furyk, one of the last to get into the field, started the final round five shots off the lead, four behind McIlroy and 40 minutes ahead of him. Furyk eagled No. 2, keying a five-under stretch, then from the 15th finished bogey-birdie-par-birdie for a 67 and a 273, 15 under at the tough Stadium Course.

McIlroy's two principal obstacles eased themselves out of the picture. Jon Rahm, the third-round leader, finished with a 76, and Tommy Fleetwood, tied for second with McIlroy going into the final round, shot 73. Then there were England's Eddie Pepperell and Venezuela's Jhonattan Vegas, playing about an hour ahead of McIlroy, both breathtaking conquerors of the heartstopping little par-three 17th. Pepperell carved out seven birdies, Vegas six, the last for each at the 17th — Pepperrell from 50 feet, Vegas from 70. Both shot 66–274, 14 under, and shared the lead briefly, then tied for third.

Furyk, after an eagle from 10 feet at the par-five second, polished off his round with a stunning approach to three feet at the 18th for his fifth birdie and the lead at 15 under. "I feel like — a shot here, a shot there maybe could have been a little different," Furyk said. "But ultimately, left it all out there."

McIlroy had a rocky start. He double-bogeyed No. 4 out of rough and water, birdied No. 6 from four feet, but at the seventh, missed the green and bogeyed. He righted himself with three birdies in four holes from the ninth. Then came the crucial stretch. First, he bogeyed the 14th out of a greenside bunker and lost the lead, and next came to the hole of the tournament, the par-four 15th. He was bunkered off the tee, and from 177 yards put a brilliant six-iron approach to 14 feet. He birdied and was 15 under. At the par-five 16th, a 345-yard drive, 174-yard nine iron from a good lie in the rough and two putts from 19 feet gave him a birdie and put him 16 under. He slipped the snares of the island 17th again, parring with two putts from 32 feet, and parred the par-four 18th, two-putting from 15 feet for the one-stroke win. He shot 67-65-70-70, a 16-under 272 to win The Players for the first time on his 10th try.

"I almost liked today," McIlroy said, "because it was tough. I knew the guys weren't going to get away from us. And I'm just really proud of myself, the way I played the last few holes."

It was McIlroy's 15th tour win but first in a year. He had answered his critics, someone in the media noted. "I don't play golf to answer," McIlroy said. "I play golf for myself."

Valspar Championship
Palm Harbor, Florida
Winner: Paul Casey

It was Paul Casey's variation on one of golf's most cherished themes. The saying goes: "It's not how, it's how much." Said Casey, on winning his second straight Valspar Championship, but not gracefully: "It feels very different," he said, "but not any less cool."

Never mind the hiccups, he was saying. The win's the thing.

And the victory made him the first back-to-back winner in the 19 years of the tournament. For comparison purposes, Casey would note that in 2018, he came from five strokes behind and won with a closing 65, and this time he survived with a one-over 72.

Shooting Innisbrook's tough par-71 Copperhead Course in 70-66-68-72–276, eight under, Casey became the first to win there with an over-par final round. He won by one over two unexpected challengers, Jason Kokrak and Louis Oosthuizen, playing ahead of him.

"That golf course is so difficult that it's damn near impossible to have a clean round," Casey said. "I made mistakes. But then so did everyone else. I got it done, and I couldn't be happier."

It looked like an easier finish for a while. But at the par-three 17th, Casey put his tee shot 35 feet below the hole, and was five feet short with first putt, then missed the next and bogeyed. That dropped him back into a tie with Oosthuizen and Kokrak. Casey then hammered an inspired par out of the par-four 18th. He'd bunkered his tee shot, then hit a 130-yard second into the wind to an elevated green. He put it hole-high, 23 feet to the right. ("Pretty damn good," he was to say.) He just missed his birdie, and tapped in for his par and the win.

Kokrak and Oosthuizen each had a share of the lead coming in, but both bogeyed, two-putting from eight feet. Oosthuizen missed the green at the 16th — he hit only six in the round — and shot 69. "I hit four good tee shots on 16," he said, "and I bogeyed it all four days." Kokrak missed the fairway at the 18th and shot 71. "So again," he said, still hunting that first win, "another good week and another stepping stone."

The Valspar was set to end as a shootout between Casey and playing partner Dustin Johnson, No. 1 in the world, who was going for his second win in three starts. Casey had taken the lead in the second round and entered the fourth leading Johnson by one. Then Johnson had a strange round — three bogeys, but he went without a birdie in a round for the first time in 31 tournaments worldwide. He shot 74 and tied for sixth. Said Johnson: "I didn't feel like I played [badly]."

As for Casey, his battle was with Innisbrook.

"Can I rise to that test and deliver?" he said.

He birdied the first and fifth, bogeyed 3, 6 and 7. It was a standoff coming in — birdies at 11 and 14, bogeys at 13 and 17, for the one-over 72. He'd answered his own question.

WGC - Dell Technologies Match Play
Austin, Texas
Winner: Kevin Kisner

It didn't have quite the meter or gravity of Caesar's "I came, I saw, I conquered," but Kevin Kisner's statement did have a certain rhythm to it, and it did say it all: "It was a long week. I prevailed. And I'm a world champion."

To fill in the blanks: This was the World Golf Championships - Dell Technologies Match Play at Austin Country Club in March. Kisner, 35, seeded 48th in a field of 64, had reason to be poetic, and even theatrical. First, because a year earlier, he reached the final of the match play and was walloped by Bubba Watson. And more to the current point, this was his third PGA Tour win. And he was the first to win the event after losing a match in the round-robin part of the tournament, which began in 2015.

Kisner beat 23rd-seeded Matt Kuchar, 3 and 2, for the championship, and nothing about his victory was simple. Three of his matches went the full 18 holes. He played three sudden-death playoff holes to get to the weekend competition. And overall, he had to play 120 holes over five days.

"Grueling," Kisner said. "Not only from the mental side, but the physical side. A lot of golf, and a lot of stressful holes and stressful putts."

Kisner started his victory march with a 2-up loss to Ian Poulter. Then he made history, grinding the rest of the way, beating Tony Finau, 2 up; Keith Mitchell, 2 and 1; Haotong Li, 6 and 5, and then Louis Oosthuizen, 2 and 1 in the quarter-finals, and Open champion Francesco Molinari, 1 up in the semi-finals.

Kuchar's path: Defeated J.B. Holmes, 3 and 1; Si Woo Kim, 6 and 4; tied Jon Rahm; defeated Tyrrell Hatton, 4 and 3; defeated Sergio Garcia, 2 up; and in the semi-final defeated Lucas Bjerregaard, 1 up.

Kisner, thumped 7-and-6 by Bubba Watson in the 2018 final, never trailed Kuchar this time. But it was a battle. Kisner won the first hole with a birdie and Kuchar squared it with a par at No. 5. Kisner birdied the sixth to retake the lead, went 2 up on Kuchar's bogey at No. 7, then was back to 1 up through the turn when he bogeyed No. 9. Kisner went to 3 up on Kuchar's errors — a watery double bogey at the 11th and a bogey off a too-strong chip at the 15th — and he closed him out with halving birdies at the 16th.

"I gave too many holes away," Kuchar said, "and he just plodded along ... and let me make mistakes."

Said Kisner: "If you'd have told me I'd be sitting here, 10 years ago, I would probably have said you were crazy. I've had ups and downs. I've won on every tour, every level. And had tremendous downfalls on every tour and every level. So I pride myself in the way I pick myself up and keep grinding."

Corales Puntacana Resort & Club Championship
Punta Cana, Dominican Republic
Winner: Graeme McDowell

For Graeme McDowell, "big" — like beauty — is in the eye of the beholder. And from where he stood, in the winner's circle, the Corales Puntacana Resort & Club Championship was as big as they come. Well, okay, so not as big as his 2010 U.S. Open Championship — he was the first Northern Irishman to win it — but almost the next thing to it, given the circumstances.

The Corales was played in late March in the Dominican Republic, the opposite event to the WGC - Dell Technologies Match Play in Austin, Texas.

"This is big — this is big," said McDowell, 39, after wrapping up a one-stroke victory over Chris Stroud and Mackenzie Hughes. Then he noted: "Don't like calling this a second-tier event, but obviously the best players in the world are in Austin this week. Still got a great field down here."

McDowell took the final lead in the last round with a birdie at the par-three 17th on a stunning six-iron tee shot to seven feet. It proved to be the winner when his two challengers stumbled home.

Hughes, in the next-to-last grouping, started the final round four off McDowell's lead and erased his deficit with seven birdies. But then he bogeyed the par-four 18th for a 66 and a 17-under 271. Stroud, in the final grouping with McDowell, birdied four straight from No. 4, but bogeyed both the 17th and 18th for a 69 and tied Hughes for second.

And McDowell, who started the final round leading Stroud by one, had five birdies on the front nine, then ground out pars up to his birdie at the 17th, which proved to be decisive when, like Stroud and Hughes, he bogeyed the par-four 18th. The bogey, a two-putt from 30 feet, wrapped up a card of 73-64-64-69–270, 18 under, for the one-stroke win.

It was his fourth win on the PGA Tour, including the 2010 U.S. Open, and his first since late in 2015.

"This one's a pretty sweet victory," McDowell said. "This one's been coming."

"Graeme earned it," Stroud said.

There was a moment-of-truth sense to McDowell's finish.

"I was standing on 16 green," McDowell said, "and I said to myself, 'You've got to do something that's tournament-winning. The [tee] shot to 17 was tournament-winning level."

"You walked right to your bag, you didn't watch it," someone said. "Yeah," he said. "When I made contact with it and I looked up and I was like, yep, there it is."

Said someone in the media corps: "You've got three young kids at home and you're going to the U.S. Open. There's so much on the line ... Where does this win rank for you?"

"Yeah, don't make me cry," McDowell said. "Yeah, this is big, this is big ... it's been a grind. My whole family, my wife, my kids at home. It's been some rough years."

Valero Texas Open
San Antonio, Texas
Winner: Corey Conners

Winning means different things to different golfers — a windfall of money, a surge of confidence, a reward for all that hard work, and the like. For Corey Conners, 27, winning the Valero Texas Open meant something truly powerful, wonderfully liberating.

"No more Monday qualifying," said Conners, who also won $1.35 million.

And he might have added, "And a berth in the Masters." Because that's where he was heading the very next week. This for a golfer who turned pro in 2015, who did his apprenticeship on the PGA Tour Canada, the PGA Tour Latinoamerica and the Korn Ferry Tour, and who, having earned his way onto the PGA Tour, missed five cuts in seven starts before the Texas Open.

Conners shot the TPC San Antonio in 69-67-66-66–268, 20 under, and the two-stroke win came rich with irony. He had got into the tournament the hard way, through the Monday qualifier, that grueling exercise of tension and doubt for those without an established spot on the PGA Tour. This time, six hopefuls were vying for one spot. The last qualifier to go on and win a tournament was Arjun Atwal in 2010, and the one before him was 24 years earlier.

For the first three rounds, the show belonged to Korea's Si Woo Kim, the 2017 Players winner. In his 66-66-69, he aced the par-three 16th in the second round on two bounces, and almost aced it again in the third the same way, then missed a four-footer for birdie and parred. He led a pack of four by one in the first round, and was looking like a runaway when another 66 in the second put him four ahead of a crowd of six, including Jordan Spieth, Rickie Fowler and Conners. Then Conners closed the gap fast in the rainy third round, with four birdies on the front nine. Coming in, he had three more, and two bogeys, getting to within one of Kim going into the last round.

"I feel like I belong," Conners the qualifier said. "And was really excited to get into the field to start with."

Then Conners finished with an unreal flourish. In the final round, he birdied four of the first five. "And I was walking to No. 6 tee thinking, wow, this is pretty awesome," he said, "then bogeyed the next four." He made the turn and birdied three straight.

"At that point I thought, we're going to do this," Conners said. The closing stretch was a blur, he said. Actually, he birdied 14, 16 and 17.

All told, down the back nine, he had a tap-in, two one-putts inside four feet, a 34-footer, a two-putt from 65, and he closed it with a 12-footer for birdie at the 17th.

Then he was looking forward to two things: The Masters the next week, and Mondays on the tour. "It will be more of a travel day," he said. "I will not be playing in Monday qualifiers."

Masters Tournament
Winner: Tiger Woods

See Chapter 2.

RBC Heritage
Hilton Head Island, South Carolina
Winner: C.T. Pan

Taiwan's C.T. Pan would have to forgive the fates if they nailed an asterisk beside his name at the RBC Heritage, his first win on the PGA Tour. It's not every day that Dustin Johnson — in this instance, the No. 1 golfer in the world — is leading going into the final round, then gets buried under a landslide of bogeys and double bogeys.

This was one of the improbable tales of the year — of how the little known Pan, 27, whose best finish in nine previous starts in 2019 was a tie for 42nd, trailed by six in the first round, then caught fire in the final round when Johnson was stumbling and some 20 others were within four strokes of the lead.

"It's still really hard for me to believe," said Pan. "I'm so happy I finally got it done."

Pan opened with a grudging two-birdie, two-bogey 71 and trailed Shane Lowry by six. He stayed in the chase with a bogey-free 65 in the second round. The third was the formative round, if in a wild way.

Johnson had just come through a tough Masters the week before, tying for second, a shot behind the rejuvenated Tiger Woods. And he wasn't letting up in the Heritage. In brisk winds in the third round, he hit just five fairways but needed only 25 putts, and shot 68. "I didn't have my best stuff," he said, "but I made some really nice putts." He led by one over Lowry, Ian Poulter and Rory Sabbatini.

Pan was two behind after a wild 69 that was more rodeo than golf. He was only one over par through No. 10. But his card in that stretch: birdie-eagle-bogey-double bogey-birdie-birdie-bogey-bogey-par-bogey. He saved the round with birdies at 11, 13 and 17. The adventure drew an observation from Pan's wife. Said Pan: "It was too colorful for her."

There was another key to Pan's win: Johnson's astounding collapse on the final nine. He led by one starting the final round, and had a birdie-bogey par 36 on the front. Then he bogeyed 11, 12 and 13 and double-bogeyed 14 and 15 and birdied the 18th. He hit only seven of the 14 fairways, hit only half of the greens, and he had penalty drops on two holes. He shot 77 and plunged to a tie for 28th. Perhaps it was a let-down after his hard-fought tie for second in the Masters the previous week. At any rate, there went his chance for a 21st PGA Tour victory.

Pan shook off the rodeo ride of the third round and was solid in the fourth. He bogeyed just once and made five birdies on putts ranging from 18 inches at No. 5 to 10 feet at the 10th, and closed with a nine-footer at the 16th, wrapping up a card of 71-65-69-67–272, 12 under, edging Matt Kuchar by one. Patrick Cantlay (69), Scott Piercy (69) and Lowry (70) tied for third, two back.

Pan's wife was his inspiration. Just the week before, she'd told him, "Hey, I'm not patient, so you'd better get me [to Augusta]."

Zurich Classic of New Orleans
Avondale, Louisiana
Winners: Ryan Palmer and Jon Rahm

With Jordan Spieth taking the week off, Ryan Palmer found himself without a partner for the Zurich Classic of New Orleans, the only team event on the PGA Tour. And Jon Rahm's partner, Wesley Brian, was having shoulder surgery. But not only was Rahm, at 24, nearly 20 years younger, he was from Spain, so Palmer thought it was unfair to ask him to team up with both an old fogey and a foreign language. "I shot him a text, hoping he wouldn't bite," Palmer said. "But he accepted. And what an awesome week."

They spent four rounds saying "Nice shot" and "Great birdie" to one another a lot, and by Sunday evening they had themselves a three-stroke victory over Sergio Garcia and Tommy Fleetwood. The Zurich, at the TPC Louisiana, near New Orleans, was played with the first and third rounds at better ball, and the second and fourth at alternate shot. Rahm and Palmer broke from a tie starting the final round and wrapped up a card of 64-65-64-69—262, 26 under.

Drenching rains delayed play in the first round for seven hours. Only about half of the 80 teams teed off in the first round, the rest being bumped into the next day. Rory Sabbatini and Brian Gay romped to the first-round lead on an 11-under 60. Among other highlights was the play of Peter Malnati and Billy Hurley, going 36 holes Friday. They shot 63 in the morning better-ball, then 67 in the alternate shot for a 14-under 130 that was leading as darkness halted play.

"It's a long day," Malnati said, "...maybe our 28th or 29th hole, my legs were tired. I know Billy and I both, most of the guys out here ... are into our conditioning, but you're not prepared to be walking for 10 hours or more."

Rahm and Palmer played 30 holes on Saturday, completing a second-round 65 in alternate shot and then posting a 64 in better ball in the third round. And a bogey was a key. Both watered their tee shots at the par-three 17th, and Palmer held the damage to a bogey with a seven-foot putt — their first bogey in 53 holes and first of only two for the tournament. Then Rahm dropped an 18-footer for birdie at 18 to tie Scott Stallings and Trey Mullinax for the lead at 23 under. It was going to be quite a finish.

In the final round at alternate shot, Rahm's chip set up Palmer's birdie from a foot at No. 2, and they were in the lead for good. They took only their second bogey at No. 6 on Rahm's drive into the rough. Then three birdies locked it up. Rahm holed a 13-foot putt at the 10th; Rahm hit his approach to three feet at the 13th and Palmer converted, and Palmer birdied from 11 feet at the 14th. It was Palmer's fourth tour win but the first in almost 10 years.

"He's got a special art," Palmer said.

Said Rahm, about next year: "I can say to Jordan and Wesley, 'Sorry, we already have a partner.'"

Wells Fargo Championship
Charlotte, North Carolina
Winner: Max Homa

When it comes to feeling low, Max Homa figures he holds the record. What's lower than low? He was there.

"I used to say, when I hit rock bottom, I found a shovel and kept digging," said Homa, 28, for years his own poster boy for frustration and failure. "I went to some low, low places. I realized ... that my attitude was going to have to get a lot better. I'm very proud I finally found the ladder and started climbing because it was getting dark down there."

Entering the last round of the Wells Fargo Championship, Homa was tied for the lead with Jason Dufner and Joel Dahmen, and feeling the hot breath of Rory McIlroy, Justin Rose and Sergio Garcia on his neck. A 69-63-70 start got him there. Then a cool four-under 67 got him his first PGA Tour win, at 15-under 269. Dahmen, also chasing that first win, closed with a par save for a 70, three behind. "I didn't beat myself today," he said.

Rose sputtered to a one-bogey 68 and finished third. Tied for fourth: Garcia (68) with three back-nine bogeys; Rickie Fowler (68) with two; Paul Casey (69) with four bogeys on the front, and Dufner (73) with a bogey at 10 and a double bogey at 18. And McIlroy (73), the first-round co-leader, tied for eighth after dropping four strokes in six holes.

Homa staked his claim with a 63 in the second round, a gem that included two bursts of three straight birdies: From No. 8, on a tap-in and putts of 24 and 12 feet, and from the 14th on putts of three, seven and 14 feet. "My attitude is awesome nowadays," he said.

But nerves hit him hard in the final round, a round to celebrate. He birdied all three of Quail Hollow's par-fives — No. 7 with a 14-foot putt, the 10th out of a bunker to 15 feet and the 15th with two putts from 68 feet. The clincher, he said, was the par putt at the 14th, when he was leading by three. His approach had stopped just short of the water. He chipped to six feet, and a weather delay hit. He had to wait a nerve-racking hour. If he'd come back and bogeyed, he said, "all of a sudden you're standing on 15 with some negatives. I knew in the back of my mind, if I made that putt, I win this tournament." And he came back out and made it. Then he birdied 15, and made his only bogey, a harmless one, at 16. He parred the 17th and 18th, and his deflating past was forgotten. Just two years earlier, he was in his second crack at the PGA Tour and made just two cuts. Only once did he play on Sunday. And a return to qualifying school was looming just eight months earlier.

"The feeling [whether] I belonged was the worst part," Homa said. "I felt like nobody knew who I was, no one cared. It was embarrassing at times. But," he added, "it ain't embarrassing anymore. It's a cool story now."

AT&T Byron Nelson
Dallas, Texas
Winner: Sung Kang

What are those secrets caddies tell their golfers? Which club to hit? Wind, the distance, stuff like that? But down the final round of the AT&T Byron Nelson, it develops that Sung Kang's caddie was coming over to him and saying something like, "Did-ja hear the one about…?"

It all developed from the heavy storm and the six-hour delay Saturday, that left 27 holes to play on Sunday.

"I told my caddie, 27 holes is going to be long day for everyone," Kang said. "I was mentally tired. I told him, just keep telling me about the funny things and that I can laugh and forget about the golf for a while. As soon as we get to the ball, just concentrate again."

And, of course, Kang had the last laugh. He powered his way into the lead with a second-round 61 and made his way through the rain-battered tournament for his first victory in his 159th career start. Kang won by two over Matt Every and Scott Piercy, shooting the par-71 Trinity Forest in 65-61-68-67, a 23-under total of 261.

"I watched him for 72 holes," Every said. "He didn't miss. Tough to beat."

Said Piercy: "I mean he played great all day. He bounced back after a bogey, and hats off."

Kang actually came back from two bogeys, both the result of missing the green at two par-threes, Nos. 2 and 12. He also took a meaningless bogey at the 18th. It merely cut his winning margin to two.

Denny McCarthy, in his second year on the tour, opened the tournament with the lead and a round to remember. He shook off a double bogey at No. 4, and from No. 6 he played the next 12 holes in 10 under for a 63 and a one-stroke lead. His strategy: "Just play really carefree," he said.

McCarthy would finish joint 23rd, and the tournament, blossoming in low scores, turned into a duel between Kang and Every.

Kang warmed up with a two-eagle 65 in the first round, two off McCarthy's lead, then took over in the second with that blistering, no-bogey 61, matching the course record. He birdied No. 1 from nine inches, then made six straight birdies from the fifth through the 10th, and added three more at the 13th, 14th and 16th.

When the rain-delayed third round was completed Sunday morning, Kang had shot 68 and was leading at 19 under, and Every, after his 67, was three behind at 16 under.

Every turned the final round into a shootout with three consecutive birdies from the first, and Kang retook the lead for good with birdies at the 14th, 15th and 16th. The par-four 15th was the final turning point. Kang rolled in a 23-footer for birdie and Every took a three-putt bogey from 40 feet. Kang birdied the 16th, then took the meaningless closing bogey for the 67 and the two-stroke win over Every (66) and Scott Piercy (64). He had his first win.

Kang called his dad back in South Korea. "I did it," he said.

PGA Championship
Winner: Brooks Koepka

See Chapter 3.

Charles Schwab Challenge
Fort Worth, Texas
Winner: Kevin Na

To Kevin Na, the view from the first tee at Colonial was most inspiring. He was waiting to tee off in the final grouping of the final round of the Charles Schwab Challenge, and he was admiring the Wall of Champions that carries the names of those who had won at the storied Texas club made famous by Ben Hogan. He noticed, especially, just below the name of Justin Rose, the 2018 champion, the empty space awaiting the name of the 2019 champion.

"And in my head," Na said, "I engraved my name on it."

Na could dare to indulge in such fantasy. First, because he had a two-shot lead going into the final round. And second, because Colonial didn't demand power. "Fits my game," said Na. "You've got to take advantage … because there are not too many like this on tour anymore."

But the pressure was a bit heavier. Na had five hungry golfers jammed just two shots behind him — Jim Furyk, 49, who last won in 2015; struggling native son Jordan Spieth; Canadian Mackenzie Hughes, who won in 2016 on his fifth start on the PGA Tour; Taiwan's C.T. Pan, a month after he won the RBC Heritage, and big Tony Finau, 2016 Puerto Rico Open winner.

After an opening par 70, six behind Finau's lead, Na proceeded to shoot 62-69-66 for a 13-under 267 and a four-stroke win over Finau. It was his third tour win and second in two months.

Except for Jonas Blixt taking the halfway lead, the battle was pretty much confined to the few and didn't take shape till the final round.

Furyk bowed out on a difficult back nine — three bogeys and a double bogey in a 73, his only over-par round. It dropped him to joint 13th. "I'm not really looking at it as like the glass is half-empty," Furyk had said earlier, of declining chances. "The hourglass has almost run out of sand." Spieth and Hughes both scattered three bogeys and a birdie, shot 72 and tied for eighth. "But I was swinging the club better today than the entire week," Spieth said. "It's just kind of funny how the score won't show it." C.T. Pan, who took the lead briefly from Na in the third round, had an odd finale. He had bookend birdies at Nos. 1 and 18, and bogeyed No. 9 in the middle for a 69, tying for third with Andrew Putnam (66). "It wasn't my best," Pan offered, "but I somehow manage to minimize my damage."

Finau was the lone threat to Na, briefly getting within a stroke. Then Finau bogeyed 16 and Na birdied 14 behind him and led by four.

"He wasn't letting up," said Finau, who badly needed three or four birdies coming in. "I gave myself the looks to do it. Just wasn't able to make it happen."

With the four-shot win, Na also won a classic 1973 Dodge Challenger. He gave it to his caddie. But, some writer wondered, could he race his caddie? "Oh, yeah," Na said. "I got a Lamborghini at home.

Memorial Tournament
Dublin, Ohio
Winner: Patrick Cantlay

What do you say to a legend after giving his masterpiece golf course a good thumping and picking off his coveted tournament? Well, Patrick Cantlay came from four strokes behind in the final round and plucked the prestigious Memorial Tournament off Adam Scott's fingertips by virtue of a rousing eight-under 64. And as Cantlay was leaving the last green, he happened to pass by Jack Nicklaus, course and tournament creator. "I finished it," Cantlay said. And Nicklaus grinned and nodded his approval.

Earlier in the week, Nicklaus told Cantlay he had to learn how to finish. And would anyone know better? Said Nicklaus: have fun, relax, enjoy the experience. So Cantlay, after trailing all the way on his 68-69-68, had great fun with a flawless 64, the lowest final round by a winner in the 44 years of the tournament. Cantlay had learned well. He was leading the 2018 Memorial by two going into the final nine but stalled out. No more birdies. This time he kept rolling, and his longest par putt was the eight-footer at the last for a 19-under 269 and a two-stroke win. He remembered Nicklaus's advice: Have fun.

"I definitely said that to myself down the stretch today," Cantlay said. "It put me a little more at ease..."

The Memorial was looking like a rebirth for German's Martin Kaymer, the former young sensation who went cold after winning the 2010 PGA Championship and the 2014 Players Championship and U.S. Open. He led by two going into the last, but his bid sputtered with bogeys at 12, 13 and 18. He shot 72 and finished third. "You really can't make any mistakes coming down the stretch," Kaymer said. "But all credit to Patrick." Scott, who surged from six behind in the first round, still had a chance to head off Cantlay. But after three straight birdies he cooled and parred the 17th and 18th for a 68, and finished second by two. "I played really good golf," Scott said. "It just wasn't good enough."

It was Cantlay's time. Circumstances had sidetracked him. A can't-miss coming out of college, he sat out over two years with a back problem, then scored his only win late in 2017 in the Shriners Hospital for Children Open. He started the Memorial's final round four off the lead and streaked to five birdies on the front nine. He briefly caught Kaymer, the leader, with a three-wood second and a two-putt birdie from 10 feet at No. 11. Kaymer tied him with a birdie of his own there. Then as Kaymer sagged to the three bogeys coming in, Cantlay birdied the 14th from 18 feet and the par-five 15th on a long two-putt for his record 64. Then came the "I finished it" to Nicklaus.

"Being able to win on this golf course, in front of Jack, making that putt on the last hole," said Cantlay, "I can't tell you how good it feels."

RBC Canadian Open
Hamilton, Ontario, Canada
Winner: Rory McIlroy

What Rory McIlroy wanted from the RBC Canadian Open was a good tune-up for the U.S. Open the following week. What he got was not only his tune-up but also his fifth national championship — sixth if he's doing the counting — and a visit to the Twilight Zone as well.

It was an awkward situation for McIlroy. He wanted to work on his game the week before the U.S. Open, and it seemed he was insulting the Canadian national championship, using it as a tune-up. But it just happened that way after the PGA Tour, in a schedule change, moved the Canadian Open to that spot.

"I wanted my game to be in good shape for Pebble Beach," he said, "but [it] doesn't mean this tournament doesn't mean anything."

As one writer then was to note: "He turned the [national] championship into a career highlight..."

McIlroy opened with a 67-66 start that left him back in the pack on the storm-softened Hamilton Golf and Country Club. Keegan Bradley took the first-round lead with a seven-under 63. "Today I was in complete control of my ball," he said. In the second round, Brandt Snedeker blistered the course with a 60, tying for the lead at 12 under with Matt Kuchar and Scott Brown, who both shot 63. "I'm not scared about going low," Snedeker said. "More often than not, you're getting beat up."

McIlroy, five behind after 36, surfaced in the third round with a bogey-free 64, tying for the lead at 13 under with Kuchar (69) and Webb Simpson (67), who had gone 54 holes without a bogey. "I've been putting well, especially inside 10 feet," Simpson said. Snedeker then fell a stroke behind in the third round with a 69 in a difficult wind. "Hard to put the ball in the fairway," he said, "and the greens are firm and bouncing."

It all got McIlroy's appetite up. "I think the best preparation is to get into contention and feel the heat of battle," McIlroy said. "I don't think there is anything else that will give you more confidence."

And McIlroy was bristling with confidence. He started the final round with five birdies through No. 7, the longest from eight feet. He birdied four straight from the 11th and slipped into the Twilight Zone.

"By the time I got to the 14th tee, I wasn't really thinking of winning," he said. "I was thinking of trying to shoot 59. You get into stretches like this ... It's almost like you're out of your own body and looking at yourself play."

He flirted with 59. He bogeyed the par-three 16th and bounced back with an eagle at the par-five 17th, firing a seven iron from nearly 200 yards to 30 inches. But he was thwarted by the par-four 18th. He bunkered his approach and came out long and bogeyed for a 61, tying his tour low and a tournament-record 22-under 258. He won by seven over Shane Lowry and Simpson.

And so McIlroy had his fifth national open championship: the 2011 U.S. Open, 2013 Australian Open, 2014 British Open, 2016 Irish Open and the 2019 RBC Canadian Open. Or sixth, counting the 2011 Hong Kong Open, as McIlroy does.

U.S. Open Championship
Winner: Gary Woodland

See Chapter 4.

Travelers Championship
Cromwell, Connecticut
Winner: Chez Reavie

It had been such a long time for Chez Reavie, but it seems the sweet taste of success never grows old. Even so, Reavie was calm and collected when he lifted his ball from the final hole of the Travelers Championship and raised a salute to the cheering crowd at the TPC River Highlands. It had been 11 years and 250 tournaments since he last felt like this.

"I went through some injuries and some long years there in the middle," Reavie said. "But it was great because it gave me a good perspective of what life is and what golf is."

The Travelers started out as a scorekeepers' feast at the storm-softened par-70 Highlands, with a six-way tie for the lead at 64. Bronson Burgoon birdied four of his first six holes, and Ryan Armour tied his season low. Mexico's Abraham Ancer shot 30 on his back nine, and Korea's Kyoung-Hoon Lee had his low to date. Canada's Mackenzie Hughes holed an 18-footer for birdie on his last hole and Zach Sucher, No. 2,045 in the world, dropped a nine-footer for birdie in the last group on the last hole. Six others were at 65 and 12 were at 66. But the Highlands was not a feast for everyone. Phil Mickelson, Jordan Spieth and Tony Finau, among others, all missed the cut.

At the halfway point, Sucher shot 65 and was 11-under 129, and Reavie and Vermonter Keegan Bradley, a New England hero, were two behind on 66s.

Then came the stunning reversal in the third round. Reavie, after falling six behind, ended up six ahead.

Sucher, leading by two, ran off four birdies and led by six, then hit a punishing patch. He bogeyed the 10th, missing the green, and caught bunkers at 11 and 12 and double-bogeyed both and shot 71. But Reavie, his playing partner, after a bogey-birdie front, sizzled with seven birdies on the back for a 63, one on a three-foot putt, three on six-footers, and the others from 10, 11 and 24 feet. And Reavie was 16 under and leading Sucher and Bradley by six.

"Zack got some tough breaks early," Reavie said. "I kind of caught fire at the end."

In the final round, Sucher raced home with five birdies and tied for second with his 67–267, four behind. "It changes the rest of our year, it changes our plans," Sucher marveled. Bradley posted four birdies coming in, setting off the New England fans. "It felt like a Ryder Cup," he said. But he double-bogeyed the 17th, shot 67 and tied Sucher, four back.

Reavie had a muted finish. He birdied the fourth from 21 feet, bogeyed No. 8 after missing the green, holed a 14-footer for a birdie at the 17th and finished with a 69 and a 17-under 263 to win by four. He reflected on the hard years. "I enjoy every minute of every week I'm out here now," Reavie said, "and I don't think I would necessarily be that way if I didn't go through those tough times."

Rocket Mortgage Classic
Detroit, Michigan
Winner: Nate Lashley

The account of Nate Lashley scoring his first victory in the Rocket Mortgage Classic will be found in the files of the PGA Tour under the listing of "Unreal."

It's the story of Lashley scoring his first victory in his second year on the tour, leading wire-to-wire and winning by six shots, not as a crackling young prodigy but as an apprehensive 36-year-old; not as an established star but as the No. 353 player in the world; who got into the tournament at the last minute, as an alternate; and not with bright thoughts but with the memory from 2004, of his mom, dad and girlfriend flying out to watch him play in a collegiate tournament and then dying when their small plane went down in the mountains.

"Yeah," Lashley said. "I think about my parents all the time."

After graduating from the University of Arizona in 2005, Lashley was on-again-off-again in golf, then went through the Latinoamerica Tour and won his PGA Tour card in 2018, off the Web.com Tour (now Korn Ferry). In his two years on the PGA Tour, his only top-10 finish was a tie for eighth in the Puerto Rico Open in February.

In the Rocket, he took the lead in the first round and then ran away with his first victory. He shot Detroit Golf Club in 63-67-63-70 for a 25-under 263 and won by six strokes.

"It was surreal," Lashley said. "There was a lot going through my mind." It was 15 years of grief, pain and doubt.

Lashley left some heavy traffic in his wake. Dustin Johnson, No. 2 in the world, shot 71-71, and Gary Woodland, who won the U.S. Open two weeks earlier, shot 73-69, and both missed the cut by three strokes. Both had strange outings.

"I'll go home and figure it out," Johnson said. In two rounds, he made 12 birdies, but also six bogeys and two double bogeys. Woodland made 13 birdies, but 11 bogeys. "I wasn't prepared as much as I probably should have been," he said. Among the marquee names, Bubba Watson also missed the cut and Rickie Fowler made it but tied for 46th.

Said Lashley, leading by one after his opening, career-low, nine-under 63, "Hopefully … continue to play well and lock up my card."

He followed with a 67 and still led by one. "The way I'm playing," he said, "I feel like I should be out here every week."

Then another 63 lifted him to a six-shot lead on J.T. Poston. Lashley said he always thought he could play the tour. "It was just a matter of getting out here and getting comfortable," he said.

In the final round, he holed a 15-foot downhiller at No. 1, then a 10-footer at No. 3. "The birdies really calmed me down," he said. Two of his three bogeys in the tournament had him even through the turn, then he birdied

13 and 17, both from seven feet, for a 70 and his first win. And memories of his mom and dad and the crash.

"It happens all the time," Lashley said. "I think about my parents all the time ... thinking about them today, even walking up 18, even before I hit my second shot."

3M Open
Blaine, Minnesota
Winner: Matthew Wolff

When a mere sophomore wins college golf's biggest prize — the NCAA Championship — what does he do for an encore? For Matthew Wolff, so recently a sophomore star at Oklahoma State University, the answer was simple. Just go out and win one of those PGA Tour tournaments.

In July, just weeks after winning the NCAA title, Wolff was playing in only his third tournament as a pro. He had tied for 80th in the first, missed the cut in the second. This was the tour's inaugural 3M Open at the TPC Twin Cities. And "stunned disbelief" would describe what gripped the golf world when the 20-year-old neophyte, playing on a sponsor's exemption, won.

"I've been told I was born for moments like these," Wolff said. "I live for moments like these."

But actually, some wizard behind a curtain had staged this show, because this neophyte's victory was pure storybook.

Wolff started 69-67 and trailed by seven, then six strokes. He caught fire in the third round, running off nine birdies in 13 holes from No. 3 and rocketed to a nine-under 62 to tie at 15 under with another college whiz, Collin Morikawa (64), and Bryson DeChambeau (70), the former budding physicist from Southern Methodist University. Morikawa, a recent graduate of California-Berkeley, was playing in his fourth tour event. In the first three, he had tied for 14th, 35th and 36th.

The final round, with three tied for the lead at 15 under, in effect would be a three-man shootout.

"And for me," DeChambeau said, "I'm going to be aggressive tomorrow and attack."

Said Morikawa: "We're going to have to control our nerves, remember who we are..."

And said Wolff, brimming with confidence: "These guys are really good, and I know I'm really good, so it's going to be fun."

The fun started early. Morikawa quickly looked like the odd man out. He fell four behind when he bogeyed the second and third, and Wolff and DeChambeau had two early birdies. Then Morikawa birdied No. 7 and they both bogeyed No. 9. They made the turn, and from there it was a mad dash to the finish.

DeChambeau, just ahead, birdied 10, 13 and 16, then eagled the par-five 18th off a 204-yard approach to six feet. He had a 66 and was the clubhouse leader at 264, 20 under. He was the target for Wolff and Morikawa in the final pairing just behind. And this led to the decisive showdown at the 18th:

Morikawa caught fire and birdied 11, 12, 13, 15 and 16. Wolff birdied the 10th from 13 feet, 14 from nine and 15 from three. Both reached the 18th in two and were putting for eagle. Wolff was away, about 26 feet, from against the collar.

"I mean, I was shaking," Wolff said. "And as soon as it dropped, tears started coming."

Wolff had a 65 and the lead at 21-under 263. Morikawa needed an eagle to tie. But his 23-footer missed just to the left and he could only birdie for a 66 and tie DeChambeau.

Said Wolff: "And I've changed forever, I guess."

John Deere Classic
Silvis, Illinois
Winner: Dylan Frittelli

"I think," the tall, lanky golfer was saying, "I was the only one on the course who smiled after a three-putt."

This would be the friendly neighborhood masochist speaking. Who else could smile at a three-putt?

But no — this was Dylan Frittelli, 29-year-old South African. He had arrived at the John Deere Classic (1) in danger of losing his PGA Tour card, (2) of having his European Tour membership run out, and (3) of having to return to the lower-level Korn Ferry Tour. And he drove the green at the par-four 14th — and then three-putted. And he could smile?

Yes. And a short while later he surged, scoring his first tour victory, thanks ultimately to Jay Brunza, retired Navy officer, clinical psychologist and one-time caddie-psychologist to an amateur Tiger Woods. Also the man who taught Frittelli to smile at three-putts and other calamities. And then Frittelli had other, far more substantial, things to smile about. He'd just shot 66-68-65-64 for a 21-under 263 and a two-stroke win over Russell Henley. And Frittelli took just one bogey over the 72 holes.

Frittelli had seemed destined once again to labor behind the leaders. His opening 66 seemed robust enough, but Mexico's Roberto Diaz had thumped Deere Run for a nine-under 62. That had no sooner cooled off than Jhonattan Vegas took the lead with a 62 of his own. Vegas then slipped to a punishing 76, leaving the third-round lead to Cameron Tringale (65) and Andrew Landry (67) at 197.

Frittelli trailed all the way, and going into the final round he was one of a crowd of eight within two strokes of co-leaders Tringale and Langley. Frittelli then proceeded to blitz the start for three straight birdies — at No. 1, a 128-yard wedge to four feet; at No. 2, a flip wedge to two feet, and at the par-three No. 3, an 18-foot putt. He got his fourth birdie from six feet at No. 8, and at the par-five 10th, he chipped in, matching birdies with Henley, who had re-ignited his game and was on this way to a 61. Frittelli grabbed the lead for good at the 11th holing a 20-footer for birdie.

One more birdie locked it up for Frittelli. At the par-five 17th, he finessed a downhill bunker shot to 11 feet, and holed the putt, then parred the 18th uneventfully for a 64, a 21-under 263 and a two-stroke victory.

Frittelli credited the win to what he termed "mentality clarity," thanks to Brunza. "Just been carrying a lot of weight on my shoulders, what with keeping a card in Europe, a card here," he said. "So the fact that I could quiet my mind and just relax and focus on the task at hand ... plan for this week was just to be creative and have fun."

Not that it was easy, Frittelli hastened to add. "But it felt a whole lot easier than it has been the last few weeks," said the golfer who had learned to smile at three-putts.

The 148th Open Championship
Winner: Shane Lowry

See Chapter 5.

Barbasol Championship
Nicholasville, Kentucky
Winner: Jim Herman

The Barbasol Championship was a tale of the golf pro and the president — but with a reverse twist. It wasn't the pro giving the president golf tips. This time it was the pro — Jim Herman — getting advice from President Donald Trump.

And then it was Herman completing the story by lifting the Barbasol trophy in his second PGA Tour victory. But wins don't come much tighter. Herman led from the second round till Kelly Kraft took the lead midway down the final nine. Then Herman finished with three solid pars and had his victory when Kraft bogeyed the last two.

"Really proud of how I can step up on that 18th tee," Herman said, "and hit the fairway and hit the green and get out of there."

The Barbasol, played at the rain-softened par-72 Keene Trace, opposite the Open Championship, developed into a battle between two strugglers. Herman, 41, was seeking his second tour win, and Kraft, 30, his first. To this point in 2019, Herman had made three cuts in 15 previous starts, and Kraft eight in 22.

Herman's tale: He was an assistant pro and played golf with Trump at Trump National Bedminster in New Jersey some years earlier. Trump encouraged him to pursue a playing career, and he went on to win the 2016 Shell Houston Open. And recently, Trump advised him to switch to a conventional putting grip and club head. "Some great advice, so I appreciate it," Herman said.

The Barbasol became the Herman-Kraft duel in the second round. Herman shot 65-65-62-70–262, 26 under, and won by one over Kraft (65-67-61-70). Bill Haas was a threat, briefly, getting within one of Herman with a 66 in the second round.

A super-hot battle erupted in the third round. Herman shot 62, with eagles at Nos. 6 and 15 from 11 and 10 feet. Kraft shot 61, with an eagle on a 65-foot putt at the 15th.

Herman's game fell quiet in the rain-delayed final round. A birdie-bogey exchange — the bogey was his second and last in the tournament — dropped him into a halfway tie with Kraft, who had a bogey and an eagle, that from seven feet at No. 5. Kraft took the lead with birdies at 11, 14 and 15 on putts of 10, seven and six feet, and Herman trailed by one after two birdies, both two-putts from over 30 feet at the par-fives, 11 and 15. Then came Kraft's fatal bogeys. He was bunkered at the par-three 16th and two-putted from 12 feet, tying with Herman at 26 under, then dropped the decisive shot at the par-four 17th, three-putting from 48 feet.

So Herman essentially owed his second tour win to Kraft and the president of the United States.

Said Kraft: "I just didn't have my best stuff today. I just gave it to him coming down the stretch."

As to the president: "Put him on the payroll?" came the wry question to Herman. "I might have to," Herman cracked.

WGC - FedEx St. Jude Invitational
Memphis, Tennessee
Winner: Brooks Koepka

It can't be often that a golfer wins the tournament, then apologizes for spoiling the show. But that was Brooks Koepka, after leaving Rory McIlroy behind and running off with the World Golf Championships - FedEx St. Jude Invitational.

The stage had been neatly set for a shootout between two of the game's best. And they were paired together for the final round.

"That would have been incredible for the fans if it would have been us going down 18 and somebody having to make a putt on the last," Koepka said. "And I'm sure that's what everybody wanted."

Both trailed through the first two rounds and McIlroy led Koepka by one through the third. Then Koepka let all the air out of the script. While McIlroy was struggling, Koepka went on a quick birdie spree, then played catch-me-if-you-can, and closed with a flawless 65 for a 16-under 264, winning by three over Webb Simpson. McIlroy fought the TPC Southwind for a one-over 71 and tied for fourth, five behind.

A golf writer mentioned that Koepka, who shot Southwind in 68-67-64-65, seemed ill during the week.

"It doesn't affect your play," Koepka insisted. "I'm not trying to complain. Just get on with it. People go to work sick all the time."

The Koepka-McIlroy show masked the chase going on at Southwind. It started with Spain's Jon Rahm, shaking off the weariness from the Open Championship, to take the first-round lead on a 62. In the second round, England's Matthew Fitzpatrick, with a 64, took a two-shot lead almost self-consciously. "No one really wanted to watch me and Patrick [Cantlay] because they were more about watching Rory and Brooks. I'd be the same." And McIlroy finally broke free in the third. He hit 14 greens and needed only 23 putts. At the 18th, he blasted out of a fairway bunker and capped a birdie outbreak with a 27-footer for a 62 and a one-stroke lead. "I guess the pressure's off a little bit," he said.

But only until the fourth round. Then the pressure was even greater. The showdown was over before it really started. Koepka, trailing by one at the start, sprinted into the lead while McIlroy was putting too much strain on his putter. He parred the first 11 holes, but gave himself only two reasonable birdie chances, from five feet and 11. With one birdie and two bogeys, he shot 71 and tied for fourth at 269. He declined to speak to the media afterward.

Koepka was racing. He tied McIlroy with a birdie from nine feet at No. 3 and took the lead on a five-footer at No. 5. He birdied the sixth from 20 feet, the 10th from eight and the 17th from 12 for a 65 and the comfortable three-stroke win over Simpson. Simpson eagled the third, shot 64 and was never a threat. "Very happy with how the day went," he said.

Marc Leishman parred the front nine, then had five birdies and two bogeys coming in and finished third by four shots with a 67.

As for Koepka, observers wondered, was he being tongue-in-cheek?

"Rory didn't play the way he wanted to today, but still it's so much fun to watch him play," he said. "You know, it's always nice to squeak out a victory over probably the best player right now."

Barracuda Championship
Reno, Nevada
Winner: Collin Morikawa

The college kids are getting their golf degrees faster and faster.

Next, late in July, it was Collin Morikawa, just a month after getting his business degree at the University of California-Berkeley, winning the Barracuda Championship. And this in only his sixth start on the PGA Tour. It was just three weeks earlier that Matthew Wolff, after leaving Oklahoma State, won the 3M Championship in his fourth start.

Said Morikawa, in a masterpiece of youthful impatience: "It was something really special to finally get the win."

The Barracuda, at the par-72 Montreux Golf and Country Club, was played under the modified-Stableford scoring system, based on points instead of strokes: zero for a par, two for a birdie, five for an eagle, eight for a double eagle, and deducting one for a bogey and three for a double bogey and worse.

And Morikawa's finish, by whatever system, was sensational. He birdied his last three holes, closing with seven birdies against no bogeys for 14 points in the final round and a total of 47 for a three-point victory over Troy Merritt in the tournament played opposite the WGC - FedEx St. Jude Invitational.

Morikawa, never more than four points off the lead, scored 13-7-13-14 points for his 47 total. In stroke play at the par-72 Montreux, that would read 66-69-66-65–266, 22 under.

That was no rookie-type performance Morikawa put on. He made only three bogeys in the entire tournament, one in each of the first three rounds. And he posted some impressive high points in each round. In the first round, he made six birdies over the last 11 holes. In the second, three birdies in four holes from the 10th, and in the third, five over seven holes from No. 7.

And in the fourth, he made all seven over the last 13, and the last three in succession.

Morikawa was still playing catch-up in the final round. He birdied No. 6 from 17 feet, the par-five No. 8 on two putts from 21 feet and the 10th on a two-footer. The par-five 13th was deflating. He missed a birdie from five feet and the par left him three points behind Merritt. The tide started to turn at the par-four 14th. He birdied from seven feet. Then came his closing spurt. At the par-three 16th, he challenged a back pin into the wind and put his ball 10 feet away. He holed the putt. At the par-four 17th, he rolled in a 30-footer for another birdie. And at the par-five 18th, his four-iron second was just short of the green but close enough that he could putt at the pin some 30 feet away. His first went three feet by and he tapped in coming back for a third straight birdie, locking up his first win.

"I think I'm ready," the ex-college kid said. "This proves that I am ready. To get this first win off my back means a lot."

Wyndham Championship
Greensboro, North Carolina
Winner: J.T. Poston

J.T. Poston remembers having to make a couple of 10-footers to save par. Looked at another way, it means that in winning the Wyndham Championship, his first PGA Tour victory, 10 feet was the closest he came to making a bogey in the 72 holes. He was the first since Lee Trevino in 1974 to go bogey-free in a win.

Which raised a question for Poston: Which was more memorable — shooting 62 and getting his first win or going 72 holes without a bogey?

"Gosh," he said. "I'd say probably the 62 on Sunday is definitely up there. I mean, bogey-free's great. The golf course was easy enough to where if you hit fairways, you could attack some pins, and my iron play was really solid all week … and today I finally made some putts and was able to get that low one in there."

Poston, 26, in his third year on the tour, trailed by three strokes in each of the first three rounds, shooting 65-65-66 on the par-70 Sedgefield course. And he had to work his way to the top in the final round as well.

Koreans Byeong Hun An and Sungjae Im tied for the first-round lead on 62s. Im would backslide with a 67 in the second round. Webb Simpson, the 2011 Wyndham champion, moved up with a 65. Canada's Adam Svensson crashed the picture with a 61 in the second round. He got to nine under through the 13th. "I thought I would be a little more nervous than I was," he said.

But he stalled out there, shot 61 and was two behind. (A 70 in the third round thwarted him.) Jordan Spieth had a promising first round, two behind on a 64 after coolly dropping a 21-footer for bogey on the last hole. Then his miseries returned. He was cut in the third round on a 77 made up of three double bogeys and a single. And An, after tying for the opening lead, went chasing his first win with the solo lead through the second and third rounds on 65-66.

But Poston would outrun him and Simpson. From three behind, he opened his move in the final round with a birdie from three feet at No. 2, then eagled the par-five fifth from 13. Still bogey-free, he birdied Nos. 8, 10 and 13 from two, 12 and two feet, then finally took the lead at the par-five 15th with a classic birdie — his approach into a greenside bunker 42 feet from the flag, a blast out to six feet, then one cool putt for a four, a 62, and a 22-under 258 total, beating Simpson (65) by a stroke.

Said Simpson, after his 64-65-65-65: "I was too far back, unless I did something crazy."

An made only two bogeys for the tournament, both in his closing 67, and finished third, two behind Poston. "I just ran out of juice," he said.

And said Poston: "I haven't had that many bogey-free rounds this year. To do four in a row and finish it off with a 62 is pretty awesome."

PGA Tour Playoffs for the FedExCup

The Northern Trust
Jersey City, New Jersey
Winner: Patrick Reed

For Patrick Reed, success came from a kind of addition by total subtraction. The game that gave him the 2018 Masters had gone sour. He had finally decided that the best way to revive it was to quit working on it. "I was pushing too hard," he said. "My team was smart enough to tell me to shut it down and reset and get clear, because we can finish the year right."

Which he did, shooting Liberty National in 66-66-67-69 for a 16-under 268 and a one-shot victory in The Northern Trust, the opener of the three-tournament 2019 FedExCup Playoffs. "It's amazing," Reed said. "Just to be back and to feel like I've been playing some solid golf and finally having it pay off."

Troy Merritt didn't make it easy. He launched the Playoffs with a nine-under 62, tying the course record at rain-softened Liberty National. He was one up on Dustin Johnson, who made four straight, late birdies, shot 63, and went to the practice range. "Today was a really good score, but just want to make sure I keep it that way," he said.

Reed was four back on a bogey-free 66. With the scoreboard groaning with 60s, Tiger Woods found himself 13 behind at 75. "I knew I had to go get it, and I didn't," he said. He withdrew before the second round with a sore oblique muscle.

Johnson took the second-round lead with a 67-130. He made five birdies, but he missed nine others from 10 feet or less. "Don't care what position I am in the FedEx," Johnson said. "I want to win a golf tournament." Jordan Spieth (64), one behind, had just one bogey in 36 holes. "The important thing for me," he said, "is not to get ahead of myself."

Reed emerged in the third round with a 67 made up of five birdies, triggered by an 18-footer at No. 3. At 14 under, he led Mexico's Abraham Ancer by one. Could Ancer win? "I'm trying not to think about that," Ancer said.

Reed had one final test — the fourth round. First came a ragged front nine. He birdied No. 1 on a 13-foot putt, bogeyed the second (bunker) and third (rough), birdied No. 5 (seven-foot putt), bogeyed No. 6 (two bunkers), and finally birdied No. 8 on a short putt.

Spain's Jon Rahm took the lead on birdies at 12 and 13, then bogeyed the next two. Ancer threatened with birdies at 16 and 17, but missed a chance to tie when he two-putted the 18th for par from 50 feet. A 69 gave him a solo second.

Reed pulled it out dramatically down the final stretch with three crucial shots. At the 14th, it was a wedge tee shot to eight feet. He birdied. At 15, after getting out of heavy rough, a 10-foot putt to save par. And at 16, a wedge second to four feet for another birdie. Two closing pars gave him a 69, a 16-under 268 and a one-stroke win. It was Reed's seventh tour win, but first in 16 months.

"Not used to actually taking time off," Reed said. "If anything, I came back stronger."

BMW Championship
Medinah, Illinois
Winner: Justin Thomas

Justin Thomas's cakewalk was quickly turning to crumbs.

He'd entered the final round of the BMW Championship with a six-shot lead, and although no lead is ever completely safe, there is a certain sense of comfort in a cushion of that generous size. But Thomas surely felt a sense of urgency rising when in a span of only three holes around the final turn, Patrick Cantlay had beaten that six-shot cushion down to two.

"Patrick played unbelievably, put a lot of heat on me," Thomas said. "In the end, it could have been good for me. It kept me focused, kept my head down. I remembered that it's really hard to win a golf tournament."

Yes, grizzled old veteran that he was, he remembered how hard it was. All of 26, and on the PGA Tour these five years, and he'd just scored his 10th win. Of course, he'd just gone a whole year without one, thanks in large part to a wrist injury. And now he'd come to the BMW at famed Medinah as pretty much his old self, winning the second of the three-tournament FedExCup Playoffs. Thomas shared the first-round lead, then fell behind by two at the halfway point on his 65-69 start.

Then he rocketed into the six-stroke lead with an 11-under 61. He raced off with birdies on the first five holes, his shortest putt 19 inches after pitching on at the par-five fifth, and the longest from 15 feet. He took his only bogey at No. 6, then crafted the jewel of his round, an eagle at the par-five 10th, slashing a five wood from 260 yards to three feet. He also eagled the par-four 16th, holing out from 180 yards. "It's fun to watch," said Tony Finau, his playing partner. "Whenever you see a guy playing that well in a zone — really cool." The 61 gave Thomas a 21-under 195, six ahead of Cantlay and Finau, who both shot 68.

"It doesn't matter what golf course it is," Thomas said. "You give us soft, good greens and soft fairways, we're going to tear it apart. It's just how it is."

Records showed that since 1928 — 91 years ago — only seven players had lost a six-shot lead. Cantlay did his best to make it eight. After a bogey-birdie start, he sprinted to four straight birdies from No. 7. Thomas bogeyed the first, and after two birdies, bogeyed the 10th, having to hit left-handed from behind a tree, while Cantlay wedged to five feet and birdied. Cantlay had cut Thomas's lead from six to two. Thomas picked up a stroke with a birdie at the 11th, on a wedge to two feet, and both birdied 13 and 15. Then Thomas's lead went back to four when Cantlay got tangled in the rough at 16 and bogeyed. But Cantlay birdied the last two from 19 and 38 feet for a 65 and finished three behind. "When you're as far behind as you are," he said, "you kind of need everything to go right."

Hideki Matsuyama raced home with his second 63 of the tournament and finished third, five behind, and Finau fought his putter for a 69 and was fourth, seven back.

As for Thomas, the question was on his outlook for the Tour Championship the next week. "I'm going to try not to look at the leaderboards for the first couple days and just try to shoot as low as I can," he said. "I know if I shoot a lower score than anybody over 72 holes I'll be fine."

Tour Championship
Atlanta, Georgia
Winner: Rory McIlroy

Rory McIlroy would roll on to win the Tour Championship and the FedExCup that went with it, and the $15 million that went with the FedExCup, but history would note that first he had to come from five behind — and that was before the tournament had even started.

Was this the Alice-in-Wonderland Open?

Not really. It was in the first round that fans realized how different this Tour Championship would be. The scoreboard told the story. Bearing in mind that East Lake is a par 70, they noted that Xander Schauffele had shot 64, Brooks Koepka 67 and Justin Thomas a par 70, and yet all three were tied for the lead at 10 under.

Welcome to what was believed to be the first PGA Tour event played under a handicap system, one that through points awards ensures that the winner of the Tour Championship would also be the FedExCup champion, thereby focusing attention on one winner. The key was the "Starting Strokes" awarded to players based on their seeding from the season-long accrued points. The top seed was Justin Thomas, getting 10 strokes. In descending order came Patrick Cantlay eight, Brooks Koepka seven, Patrick Reed six, and Rory McIlroy five. Seeds 6-10 were at four each; 11-15 at three; 16-20 at two; 21-25 at one, and 26-30 at even par.

The players were as unsure as anyone.

"I'm sure it's going to be weird tomorrow," Thomas said.

"As long as J.T. [Justin Thomas] doesn't go out and go shoot 62s on the first two days, then I think everybody has a chance," Koepka said.

Said McIlroy: "I think it's more the psychology of it. ... starting at a different position than the rest of the field.... I think you have to play the best golf that you can."

The math in the first round: Thomas shot par 70, but had 10 starting strokes; Schauffele (64), six under plus four starting strokes, and Koepka (67), three under plus seven starting strokes. They led at 10 under. McIlroy (66), at four under plus his five starting strokes, was nine under and trailed by one.

If the tournament was a scorekeeper's scramble, it was an accountant's fantasy.

At the end, McIlroy took golf's biggest prize, $15 million, and joined Tiger Woods as the only ones to win the FedExCup twice. He shot East Lake in 66-67-68-66–267, 13 under par, but that wasn't his winning score. Under the handicap system, his scores in the rounds were 4-3-2-4, a total of 13 under, plus his five starting strokes. So his winning score was 18 under. Schauffele was second at 14 under and won $5 million; Thomas and Koepka tied for third at 13 under and won $3.5 million each. Dustin Johnson and Lucas Glover tied for last and won $400,000 each.

No matter the scoring, this Tour Championship came down to a McIlroy-Koepka shootout. Paired in the final group in the final round, both had parred the first five holes and birdied No. 6. For a reference point, McIlroy led by one in regular scoring. Then at the par-four No. 7, McIlroy rolled in a 25-foot putt for a birdie, and Koepka double-bogeyed out of the trees.

Coming in, Koepka lost his way and bogeyed three straight — the 12th from the rough and a bunker, the 13th on three putts from 19 feet, and the 14th out of the rough. McIlroy birdied 12 and 13 but bogeyed the next two. Both birdied the 17th, and McIlroy closed with a birdie at 18. Schauffele had a three-birdie, three-bogey 70 and 14 points. Thomas closed with a 68 (and 277 total) and Koepka with a 72 (and 274) and tied for third at 13 under.

"He just played better," Koepka said.

And to borrow an observation, a victory by any other means, tastes as sweet.

Said McIlroy: "I'm going to enjoy this one tonight."

Start of 2019-2020 Season

A Military Tribute at The Greenbrier
White Sulphur Springs, West Virginia
Winner: Joaquin Niemann

When that final putt dropped in West Virginia, they started partying in Chile.

Joaquin Niemann, a mere 20, became the first golfer from Chile to win on the PGA Tour, rolling to a six-stroke victory in A Military Tribute at the Greenbrier, a resort in the West Virginia mountains. "I just never thought this moment was possible," said Niemann. "I can't wait to go back home and celebrate with all my friends."

But Niemann's six-shot cushion was hard-won, built on the final backstretch. His card of 65-62-68-64–259, 21 under par on Old White TPC, was deceptive.

Niemann had convinced himself that this was his tournament. In his first visit in 2017, as an amateur on a sponsor's exemption, he tied for 29th. In 2018, as a pro, he leaped up to a tie for fifth. So… "I was just feeling like I was going to win the tournament from the first day," he said.

The Greenbrier was greeted by 21 tour rookies and other Korn Ferry Tour graduates. "I'm fired up," said Robby Shelton, who won two Korn Ferry events earlier. "I've been waiting for this moment all season." He broke from the gate to the first-round lead on an eight-under 62. Niemann, after his opening 65, shot 62 in the second round for a share of the halfway lead with Shelton (65) and Scottie Scheffler, whose 62 included birdie putts of 24, 38 and 28 feet. But everyone was upstaged by Kevin Chappell and his 11-under 59, the 11th sub-60 round in tour history. "I was trying to keep the foot on the gas and attack," said Chappell. (He would finish joint 47th.)

In the third round, Niemann took the solo lead by two with a 68. "I'm just really happy, the way I've been playing," said Niemann, who then had to rein himself in on the morning of the fourth round. "I woke up and … I just couldn't think about this moment, holding the trophy," he said. "I was [thinking], Man, take it easy. Don't think about that yet."

Niemann started the final round leading by two and was briefly tied twice. He made five birdies against one bogey through the 15th. He had taken the lead for good with a birdie at the par-four 10th, and after a par save at the 11th, he birdied 12 from nine feet and 13 from 13, then birdied the last three holes to lock it up — the 16th on a 10-foot putt; the par-five 17th, going from rough to bunker and finally holing a six-footer, and at 18, calmly rolling in a 22-footer.

Niemann's closing 64 locked up one of the tougher six-shot wins on record, and even got him fist-pumping.

"Yeah, normally I'm not really too excited any time," Niemann said. "I normally never do fist pump and those things. So just make those putts on the last three holes … I couldn't resist it. I just fist pump."

Sanderson Farms Championship
Jackson, Mississippi
Winner: Sebastian Munoz

Among the things notable at the 2019 Sanderson Farms Championship — mark the week, September 14-22 — was the presence of Akshay Bhatia. He was making his professional debut. At age 17.
"It doesn't feel much different," he said.
(Note for historians: Bhatia, from Wake Forest, North Carolina, shot the par-72 Country Club of Jackson in a five-birdie, five-bogey 70-74, for a par 144, missing the cut by three. His grade? "Probably a C at least," he said.)
In another bit of history, the Sanderson was the occasion of the first victory of Colombia's Sebastian Munoz on the PGA Tour. For Munoz, what it took was a bit of convincing, and it came from the victory of Chile's Joaquin Niemann, 20, in the Greenbrier a week earlier. "Jaco's win gave me the little extra belief I'm good enough," Munoz said. "I'm here."
And it was a classical battle. Munoz trailed through the first two rain-interrupted rounds on 70-67 and shot a flawless 63 in the third for a one-stroke edge.
The final round turned into a five-man expanded shootout.
• Kevin Streelman, teeing off 90 minutes before Munoz, gave him an alarming streak of red to look at — nine birdies, interrupted by a three-putt bogey at the 10th. ("I wish I was playing my buddies at home for money," Streelman said.) He shot 64, finishing at 16 under, eventually two short of the playoff.
• Sungjae Im went third from last and also was scary. He posted eight birdies, but bogeyed two par-threes — No. 7 (a three-putt) and No. 13 (missed green). He birdied three straight from the 14th on putts of 13, three and 13 feet, shot 66, and at 18 under was the clubhouse leader. He would be waiting nervously for Munoz to finish.
• Byeong Hun An, next-to-last at 1 p.m., went on a run but bogeyed the 13th (missing the green) and the 14th (catching water). He shot 69 and missed the playoff by one.
• Carlos Ortiz, paired with Munoz at 1:10, couldn't get rolling. (They were former North Texas University teammates. "Really good friends," Munoz said. "We don't talk to each other all day, but it's great.") Ortiz birdied Nos. 2 and 7 but bogeyed 6 and 8, and after his final birdie at the 12th, could only par in. He shot 71, two short of the playoff. "I was getting the breaks," Ortiz said. "I just couldn't get them in the hole."
Munoz knew what he had to do. But he almost couldn't do it. He birdied No. 3 from 10 feet, then the 11th from two. At the 15th, he went from rough to bunker and bogeyed. He came to the 18th desperately needing a birdie. He got it on a 15-foot putt for a 70, tying Im at 18-under 270.
In the playoff at the 18th, Im was long of the green, Munoz short. Im pitched to six feet but missed his par putt. Munoz chipped to four feet and made it for that first win.
Said Munoz: "I'm speechless."

Safeway Open
Napa, California
Winner: Cameron Champ

Golfers play with aching joints, sore backs, blisters. But how do you play with a heavy heart? Read putts with misty eyes?

"With everything going on with my family, with my grandpa, I wasn't sure if I was even going to play," Cameron Champ was saying, at the Safeway Open at Silverado. "I showed up Thursday and teed it up with no practice round, nothing. The whole week, there was nothing else on my mind."

His grandfather, Mack, battling cancer, was in a hospice not far from Silverado. The family was commuting to the Safeway from his hometown, Sacramento, some 65 miles away.

Champ took the lead in the third round and nursed it like a dying ember to a desperate birdie on the final hole for his second tour victory. He shot 67-68-67-69 for a 17-under 271, ending it with a chip-and-putt birdie at the last.

Champ, a big-hitter, started cold, but quickly made a game plan. "The par-fives are key," he said. "I feel like I have to birdie those with my length." He birdied all four in the first round, two-putting No. 5 from 80 feet, No. 9 from 15, the 16th from 16 and the 18th from 44. "Hit it extremely well, gave myself a lot of chances," Champ said. He birdied three of the four in the second round, shot 68 and was three behind Bryson DeChambeau, who rode a flawless 64 to a two-shot lead.

Champ rocketed into the lead in the third round, from three behind to three ahead, and did it without the par-fives. Strong iron play and solid putting gave him a bogey-free 67. His five birdies, all at par-fours, came on putts ranging from six feet to 16. Still, it was another heavy day. "It's still tough trying to keep my mind off…," Champ said. "He's always worrying about everyone else but himself."

A win for his grandpa? "Oh, it would be huge," he said. "It would be mind-blowing."

Champ pieced his fourth round together. On the front nine, he missed every fairway — one cost him a bogey that would haunt him — but hit key second shots and birdied the first, fifth, sixth and ninth. The birdie at the par-five No. 5 was especially pleasing — a tee shot wide into the left rough, a pitch over a tall tree to the green and two putts from 17 feet. Champ had played the back nine under par for three rounds, but now he had to work for pars, and bogeyed the 17th. Adam Hadwin, in the group ahead, had birdied the last three holes and was in at 16 under. Champ had to birdie the par-five 18th to win, and he had birdied it only once before.

This time, with grandpa still watching on TV, Champ ripped a 369-yard drive, left his second short, chipped to three feet and birdied for a 69 and a 17-under 271, and won by one. Champ hugged his dad at the green, and cried.

"The greatest moment ever in my career," he said.

Shriners Hospitals for Children Open
Las Vegas, Nevada
Winner: Kevin Na

If one were to ask Kevin Na for the key to his victory in the Shriners Hospitals for Children Open, he might be tempted to just throw a dart at the scoreboard. Perhaps his two eagles in four holes in the second round. Or maybe his 61 in the third. Or surviving his amazing hazard-free triple bogey in the fourth.

Technically, Na won with a par on the second playoff hole against Patrick Cantlay's three-putt bogey. The impetus for his win might have come from anywhere in a week when the field feasted on TPC Summerlin. But Na's secret: A magic putter that scorched the par-71 paradise. Na shot 68-62-61-70, only to be caught down the stretch by Cantlay (66-64-63-68) and tied at 23-under 261. Pat Perez finished third, two behind.

"It came down way too close," said Na, who was leading by three heading into the final nine.

Na trailed by five on his opening 68, then surfaced in a crowd in the second round with his 62, tying for the lead with Lucas Glover (63), Brian Stuard (65) and Cantlay (64). "My putter was hot," Na said, in a masterpiece of understatement. "I started with a 60-footer on the first hole." He holed from seven feet at the fifth, 17 at No. 7, and two-putted from 65 at No. 9. He eagled the two par-fives coming in, the 13th from 44 feet, the 16th from 35, then birdied the last two from 24 and 22 feet.

His explanation? "I felt confident over the putt," Na said.

Then he matched his career-low with a flawless 61 in the third round, atop six scores at 63 or better. His putter was still crackling. Three of his 10 birdies were from about eight feet, and six others ranged from 12 to 30, and there was one two-putt. Cantlay, meanwhile, was no slouch. He made six birdies on the front nine — three from six to eight feet, three from three. He shot 63 and was two behind Na, who set the tournament's 54-hole record at 22-under 191.

No. 10, a par-four of 425 yards, was the sudden equalizer. Na had already bogeyed it twice, but came to his final visit with a three-stroke lead. Then came the crash. It was a weekender's triple bogey — on in four and three putts for the seven. Cantlay bogeyed it. Then he birdied four out of five holes from the 12th, taking the lead after Na bogeyed the 16th out of the water. But Cantlay bogeyed the 17th, also out of the water, and Na caught him with a par. They parred the 18th and tied at 23 under. In the playoff at 18, they matched birdies the first time. The second, Cantlay three-putted for bogey but Na holed his four-footer for par and the win.

No sour grapes from Cantlay. But a wry observation. "I hit a lot of putts that I thought were going to go in today," he said, "and didn't."

All told, Na set a tour record, making 559 feet of putts over four rounds, then said of his putter: "I should have kissed it after I won."

Houston Open
Humble, Texas
Winner: Lanto Griffin

It had been a long time since Lanto Griffin cried like that.

Griffin holed that last six-footer, and then he slumped, his head bending into his caddie's shoulder. Then he sank into a crouch and sobbed. He had just won the Houston Open, his first victory on the PGA Tour. The tears were of joy, but also for years of struggle and doubt, the loneliness he still felt from the death of his father.

"To all those back home," he said, finally, into the camera. "We did it."

Generally, a golfer about to score his first win is ravaged by nerves. Griffin, 31, was just the opposite. "I was actually eerily calm — I don't know why," he said.

Griffin had won on the Korn Ferry Tour and the PGA Tour Latinoamerica. But this was golf's ultimate, the PGA Tour, and the treasure it offered — the precious playing card.

And so Griffin stepped right up and knocked in that six-footer.

The chase was on from the start across the Golf Club of Houston. He opened two behind with a six-under 66, but took a 74 in the rain-interrupted second round, hurt especially by the double bogey at the disagreeable par-four 18th. But he rebounded with a spirited 65 in the third — three quick birdies from No. 3, then six across eight holes from the 10th. But also a bogey at the 18th. But he had his first 54-hole lead on the PGA Tour. At 11 under, he was a stroke ahead of playing partner Mark Hubbard and three up on Scott Harrington.

And the final round was a shootout. Harrington shot a 67 that included birdies on five of 11 holes from No. 3. Hubbard eagled No. 4 and birdied Nos. 7 and 8 and had the lead till he bogeyed 15. He shot 69 and tied Harrington for second at 275, 13 under.

Griffin birdied the first and third from close and three-putted from 50 feet for a bogey at No. 4. He made the turn in three under with birdies at No. 5, from three feet, and at the par-five eighth after missing the fairway. Griffin missed the green at 11 and bogeyed, slipped behind Hubbard. Then, still in his calm world, he birdied 16 from 33 feet for the lead and arrived at his nemesis, the 18th. Leading by one, he put his second on the green, 60 feet from the flag, and finally holed a six-footer for his par, a 69, and a 14-under 274. And his first win.

And as he cried on his caddie's shoulder on winning, so had he cried on Steve Prater, then the pro at Blacksburg when his dad died young of cancer. Griffin was just 12 then and a kid from a family with little means. Prater became a second father to him. "I wouldn't be here without him," Griffin said. "He opened every door in golf that I ever had."

And he thanked others who helped him. Said Griffin: "I always felt like I owed them everything I had..."

The CJ Cup @ Nine Bridges
Jeju Island, Korea
Winner: Justin Thomas

There was this matter of a few thousand miles, to be sure, but for Justin Thomas, an American from Kentucky, it was getting to the point where a tournament in Asia was nothing but homecookin'.

Thomas won The CJ Cup in Korea in October — his fourth win in nine starts in Asia. He earlier had won the CIMB Classic in 2015 and 2016, both in Malaysia, and the 2017 and 2019 CJ Cups, both at Nine Bridges on Jeju Island, South Korea. In 2017, he shot Nine Bridges in nine-under 279, and beat Marc Leishman in a playoff. This time he shot 68-63-70-67 for a 20-under 268 and won by two over the frustrated Korean-born New Zealander Danny Lee. "I've never played exceptionally well in Korea," he said.

Thomas, on the other hand, was at a loss to understand his success in Asia. "I have no idea," he said. "It's kind of bizarre knowing that I've won four times here. I obviously like the golf courses and I feel like they fit my game well. But it must be all the beef. Maybe that's what it is. I feel comfortable over here."

The CJ, a no-cut event with a field of 78, was Thomas's 11th career win in five years and his second of the year after the BMW in August.

While the CJ was a victory-in-the-making for Thomas, defending champion Brooks Koepka stirred the contretemps between him and Rory McIlroy by denying there was one. "I'm No. 1 in the world," he said. "I'm not looking in the rearview mirror, so I don't see it as a rivalry. I've been out here for — what? — five years. Rory hasn't won a major since I've been on the PGA Tour." Koepka shot 69-75 then withdrew before the third round after aggravating the injury to his left knee when he slipped on a wet pavement Friday.

Thomas opened with a 68 and trailed homeland favorite Byeong Hun An by four in the first round, then birdied the first four holes in the second round for a flawless 63 that gave him a two-stroke lead and that amazed him for its simplicity. "It was a very easy 63 — if you can somehow say that," Thomas said.

He got caught by Lee (68–201) in the third. "Danny made it extremely difficult," Thomas said. "He really made a lot of putts, a lot of unbelievable up-and-downs, to keep me from getting all the momentum."

In the final round, Thomas took the lead on a birdie at the 14th and went ahead by two when Lee bogeyed the 15th. Lee also bogeyed the 16th, then Thomas bogeyed 17. Then both birdied the 18th, Lee for the 69 and Thomas a 67 and the two-stroke win.

"I gave my best," Lee said, "and solo second was the best I could do."

Said Thomas, with his second win in Korea: "I still haven't mastered how to write my name in Korean."

Zozo Championship
Winner: Tiger Woods

See Asia/Japan Tours chapter.

WGC - HSBC Champions
Shanghai, China
Winner: Rory McIlroy

Haotong Li had just thrilled his countrymen, shooting eight-under 64 for a one-shot lead in the first round of the World Golf Championships - HSBC Championship at red-roofed Sheshan International at Shanghai. "Obviously, it would be great joy," he said, "for Chinese golfers and Chinese golf fans to have a Chinese player winning a WGC - HSBC Champions here in China. But for the next three days, anything could happen."

Li was right. Anything did happen — "anything" being a free-wheeling no-cut battle of 78 international golfers in the fourth and final WGC event of 2019. And a battle that ended up with the surging Rory McIlroy taking his fourth win of the year on the first playoff hole over defending champion Xander Schauffele.

"Xander pushed me the whole way, or all 73 holes we played together this week," McIlroy said. "He played great. He was battling a flu all week, and so the caliber of golf he played this week, it takes some doing. He birdied the last to get into the playoff, and then I produced two of the best shots of the day when I needed it, which was really cool."

McIlroy shot Sheshan in 67-67-67-68, and Schauffele in 66-69-68-66, tying at 19-under 269. In the playoff, at the par-five 18th, McIlroy's towering tee shot split the fairway. Schauffele caught the rough and had to lay up. He reached the green and two-putted from 12 feet for a par. McIlroy's second was a four iron, rifled from 223 yards into the wind, to the green, 25 feet from the flag. He two-putted for a birdie and the win.

Schauffele was not disappointed, not considering that he spent most of the week fighting the flu. "I wasn't expecting to play this well at the beginning of the week," he said, "so I'm probably the happiest guy in the tournament."

Both had authored thrills. In the first round, McIlroy had a so-so par front nine then ran off four straight birdies from his 11th. In the second, he birdied four straight from No. 3, and eagled the 18th from three feet. He went the last 38 holes without a bogey. Schauffele bogeyed his starting hole, then birdied six of the next eight. In the second round, he had a ragged front nine, then had four birdies on the back. In the third round, he birdied the first three and the last three, and he closed with a seven-birdie, one-bogey 66 to tie McIlroy.

Louis Oosthuizen joined the hunt in the third round, launching a 65 with five straight birdies. He opened the final round with two birdies, then bogeyed twice around the turn. "You just can't give away holes," he said, shooting 69 and finishing third.

Possibly the biggest surprise of the week came from Phil Mickelson — in a decidedly un-Mickelson fashion. He shot 71-69-75-68, for a five-under 283, and tied for 28th out of the 77 finishers. But it wasn't quite enough. The figures knocked him out of the top 50 in the Official World Golf Ranking for the first time since 1993 — nearly 26 years.

"It was a good run," said Mickelson, age 49. "I'll be back."

Bermuda Championship
Southampton, Bermuda
Winner: Brendon Todd

It was the Bermuda Championship, but something of a reverse Bermuda Triangle for Brendon Todd — not where he mysteriously disappeared but where he mysteriously reappeared.

This was the former University of Georgia standout who won the 2014 Byron Nelson Championship and who later disappeared in a frightful case of the yips. Not the putting yips, but the rare full-swing yips in which the golf course becomes an alien place.

"I'm thrilled, over the moon," said Todd. He had just run off with the tournament by four strokes, shooting Port Royal in 68-63-67-62 for a 24-under 260. And just in time. "A year ago, I wasn't sure if I was going to keep playing," Todd said. By September 2018, he had missed the cut in 37 of his last 40 starts. "I would hit a four iron or a three wood 50 yards right," he said.

He found Bradley Hughes, a former tour player-turned-swing coach who focuses on ground forces and pressures.

Todd opened well back with his 68. Scottie Scheffler, 23, was out in 29. Thinking 59? "You think about it a little bit," he admitted. A par-bogey finish cost him a 60, but he had a one-stroke lead at 62. Rob Oppenheim also thought about a 59 when he birdied seven of the first eight. But his putter was "a little cold the last nine," he said, and he shot 64.

Todd rocketed into the picture in the second round, closing with four straight birdies for a 63 and in a three-way tie for the lead. He noted Port Royal's shorter length, at 6,842 yards. "It forces everyone to hit the same club off the tee," he said. "I'm hitting the same clubs into the green as everyone else, and for some reason that tends to work out well in my favor." Todd tied at 11 under with Scheffler (69) and Harry Higgs (65), the only player without a bogey through the first two rounds. He ran that clear string to 49 holes. It was broken by a bogey at the 14th in third round. But his 65 gave him a two-shot lead over Todd (67) going into the final round.

That's when Todd erupted. He parred the first, then birdied the next seven. Said Higgs, his playing partner: "I told my caddie, you become a fan — this guy might shoot 56." Todd added birdies at the 10th, 11th and 15th for the 62 and the four-stroke win.

Said Todd, signing off: "We came to a golf course that none of us have ever seen and I was able to figure it out and play spectacular golf. Always be the first Bermuda champion..."

And a history note: Local amateur Kenny Leseur, 15, qualified for the tournament, shooting 74-73–147, five over, in blustery weather. In the tournament, he shot 77-75–152, 10 over, and missed the cut by 11.

Mayakoba Golf Classic
Playa Del Carmen, Mexico
Winner: Brendon Todd

Golf's loss, pizza's gain: Would-be entry for Brendon Todd's resume.

Todd has to be the only pro ever who was going to flee golf and head for where "slice" wasn't a dirty word — the pizza business. And then, late in 2019, Todd had to be the only pro to escape the clutches of the full-body yips and win in two successive outings. It's been said golf is a funny game. Perhaps "funny" isn't quite the word.

"It is so surreal — it's just crazy, you know," Todd was saying, after winning the Mayakoba Classic in Mexico in mid-November, two weeks after he'd won his previous outing, the Bermuda Championship. And the Bermuda was his first victory after years in the clutches of the full-body yips. He had made only two cuts in 35 tournaments, in a three-year stretch that had driven him to begin talks for dropping golf and opening a nice shop somewhere.

Heavy rains on the tip of Mexico's Yucatan washed the first round into Friday, softening the par-71 El Camaleon into a shooting gallery. Of the 82 who would make the cut, 53 shot in the 60s in the first round. They were led by New Zealand's Danny Lee, who was 10 under through the 13th and thinking a forbidden thought. "It was in my mind, 59 or 58," he admitted. But he shot 62 and led by a stroke over Todd and Adam Long.

Todd, still fired up by his Bermuda win, had his goal. "Let's try and birdie every hole," he said. That amounted to a game plan of sorts, and in that frame of mind, he shot El Camaleon in 63-68-65-68 for a 20-under 264. All told, he made a tournament-best 24 birdies, had only four bogeys and won by a stroke.

And in a shootout down the final stretch. Todd, after taking the lead in the third round, came to the 14th in the final round leading Vaughn Taylor by two and Harris English by three. The picture changed abruptly. Todd bogeyed the 14th and slipped into a tie at 20 under with Taylor, who had birdied 13, and was one ahead of English, who birdied 13 and 14. At this point, play was called because of darkness, after the leaders had played 32 holes, trying to make up for the Thursday rainout. When they returned on Monday, to the 15th, Todd knocked in a 20-footer for birdie to retake the lead. Then he bogeyed the 16th, but so did Taylor, and English double-bogeyed it.

All three parred in from there: Todd for a 68 and a 20-under 264 total; Taylor also with a 68 and a stroke behind at 265, tying for second with Adam Long (66) and Carlos Ortiz (66), and English slipped to fifth with 70–267. And Todd, with the $1,296,000 first prize, went from contemplating the pizza business to back-to-back wins and $1,836,000 in winnings.

"It's just amazing how fast this game can turn," Todd said. "I'm enjoying it and I'm just going to keep grinding."

The RSM Classic
St. Simons Island, Georgia
Winner: Tyler Duncan

It was Tyler Duncan's win but it was Brendon Todd's show. For three rounds, anyway.

This was in the RSM Classic, the grand finale of the PGA Tour for 2019, and Duncan, 30, scoring his first tour victory in a playoff against Webb Simpson, put on quite a show of his own. Would he ever make a bogey? Well, yes — one.

Todd was the little known player almost driven out of golf and into pizza by the full-body yips who won two consecutive starts, the Bermuda Championship and the Mayakoba Classic. And now the world was watching: Could he get that rare straight third? Well, it was in sight. Until the final round.

Thus the RSM provided a crackling last act for the tour late in November. It was largely a three-man chase across two courses — one round at the par-72 Plantation and three at the par-70 Seaside. Duncan and Todd started in the pack in the first round — Duncan at five under (a 67 at the Plantation) and Todd at four under (66 at the Seaside). Simpson birdied seven of the Plantation's last 10 for a 65, seven under and a one-stroke lead. "My reads were better on the second nine," Simpson said.

Then a free-for-all broke out in the second round. Duncan battered the Seaside for seven birdies and a hole-out eagle at No. 8, a nine-under 61 and a two-stroke lead at 14 under. "I don't think I've ever had back-to-back rounds with no bogeys," he said. Todd shot six under (66) at the Plantation and was four behind. He wasn't thinking of three straight wins. "I'm looking at [this] as one tournament," he said. Then he leaped into the third-round lead with an eight-birdie 62 at Seaside, getting to 18 under. He led by two. "It was like a video game out there today," Todd said.

Todd's quest for that third straight win died in the final round in a double bogey out of the native area at the par-four fifth. Two pars and two bogeys on the back nine gave him a two-over 72 and dropped him to fourth at 16 under. The streak had run out of gas. "It just seemed like I couldn't summon the energy," he said.

Duncan, playing three groups earlier, gave Simpson something to shoot at. He shook off a bogey at No. 1 — his only bogey — and posted six birdies the rest of the way, with three over the last four holes: a two-putt at 15, a seven-footer at 17 and a 25-footer at 18 for a 65, five under for a 263 and a 19-under total.

"That's what great players do," said Simpson. "They birdie the last two holes." He birdied 15 on two putts and 16 from 22 feet and closed with a 67 to tie at 19 under.

Duncan's first win, then, came on a 12-foot birdie putt on the second playoff visit to the 18th. At last. And how did it feel? "Honestly, I don't even know," Duncan said. "I'm just so happy to be here playing, and to win is just unbelievable."

And thus the curtain fell on the PGA Tour for 2019.

Special Events

CVS Health Charity Classic
Barrington, Rhode Island
Winners: Brooke M. Henderson, Keegan Bradley, Billy Andrade

They'll be renaming it soon — the Keegan Bradley Member-Guest.

But for the 2019 edition, it would remain the CVS Health Charity Classic, the one-day golf exam in June at the Rhode Island Country Club for the benefit of Southern New England Charities.

New year, old story: Native sons Keegan Bradley, of the PGA Tour, and Billy Andrade, of the Champions Tour, and the LPGA Tour's Brooke M. Henderson combined for a 61-66–127, 15 under, to win by one in the best-two-balls-of-three event.

If the cast seemed familiar, it's because they won in 2018 and 2017. And when the CVS was a two-player event, Bradley teamed with Jon Curran to win it in 2015 and 2016. And thus Bradley set the PGA Tour record of winning the same event five consecutive times.

This No. 5 was a trip in the zone. "When you're in that zone," Andrade said, "you don't want to get out of it."

Henderson made six birdies on the front nine, Andrade four and Bradley chipped in for two. Bradley birdied the par-three 10th, and he and Andrade both birdied the par-five 11th, getting to 14 under. Andrade's birdie at 13 put them 15 under. They had just one threat. Kevin Kisner, Lexi Thompson and Darren Clarke got to 13 under through the 15th, but got just one more birdie, Thompson's at the 17th. They finished a stroke behind. Bradley and Andrade easily parred the 18th to lock up win number three. What was their secret?

"We're just a good team," Bradley said. "We have fun, and it's relaxing and easy to shoot low."

TaylorMade Pebble Beach Invitational
Pebble Beach, California
Winner: Kevin Sutherland

"I just really got it going," was the way Kevin Sutherland put it.

But the way the scorecard put it, Sutherland shot 30 on the front nine of his final round — making four birdies and an eagle — and went on to win the TaylorMade Pebble Beach Invitational. Sutherland had trailed by three strokes after the third round and rode that hot start into a three-stroke win over Martin Flores.

In the three-course tournament, Sutherland shot 72 at Spyglass Hill, 70 at Pebble, 67 at Spanish Bay and closed with 67 at Pebble for a 12-under 276.

Pebble Beach was sounding like Sutherland's home course. He won the event in 2000 (under a different sponsor) and finished second or tied for second four times since 2004. Sutherland estimated that he played the Invitational 25 times.

The Invitational, which began in 1972 and has had various sponsors, is played by golfers from the PGA, LPGA, Champions and Korn Ferry tours, heading teams of amateurs. The tees are adjusted for length so that the players are hitting approximately the same clubs into each green.

Flores held a hot hand, shooting the first three rounds in the 60s and going into the final round leading John Oda by one, John Mallinger and Andrew Yun by two, and Sutherland by three.

After that smoking start, Sutherland had something of a breathtaking finish. Coming in, he bogeyed three times, and closed with three straight birdies for his 67, the last from 10 feet. Flores, in the group behind, double-bogeyed the 18th and shot 73. "I won by three shots," Sutherland said, "but it was closer than the margin seems."

Mexico's Maria Fassi, dynamic LPGA rookie, opened with a 71 at Spanish Bay, then shot a six-under 66 at Spyglass Hill, leaping into a five-way tie for the lead and raising the possibility that the Pebble would have its second female champion, after Juli Inkster in 1990. Then Fassi stumbled to a 78-79 finish at Pebble and closed at six over 294. That left LPGA veteran Mina Harigae (67-71-75-71) as the leading woman golfer, tying for seventh at four-under 284.

Hero World Challenge
New Providence, Bahamas
Winner: Henrik Stenson

The Hero World Challenge — also known this trip as Captain Tiger Woods and Friends — was the story of three shots. There was the bold shot in the final round that Sweden's Henrik Stenson, the 2016 Open champion, ought to have hit, and did, and won himself a tournament and $1 million. Then there were the two practice swings Patrick Reed ought not to have taken but did anyway, and they became the practice shots heard around the world — and around and around.

The Hero, at Albany Golf Club in the Bahamas, also served as the staging event for the next week's Presidents Cup in Australia. Of the 18 in the field, 11 were on the U.S. Presidents Cup team, including Woods himself, the playing captain. The 12th member, Dustin Johnson, recovering from knee surgery, would join them later.

After sharing the lead in the first round and leading through the second, Reed had stalled out in pars through No. 10 in the third. At the par-five 11th, he was in waste area sand with a ridge of sand behind his ball. A TV replay showed Reed settling his club just behind the ball, then pulling it back, then doing it again. The ridge had been smoothed out. He would be penalized two strokes for improving his lie and shot 74. But many yelled "cheater."

They were practice swings, he said. "I wasn't intending to improve a lie or anything like that," he said. If the episode bothered Reed, it didn't show in the last round. "Honestly," he said, "I haven't been paying attention on what's been going on in the media." He notched five birdies coming in for a one-bogey 66 and finished third. Justin Thomas had three birdies and an eagle, then bogeyed 13 and double-bogeyed 18. Gary Woodland, the third-round leader, shot 73. Woods, host and captain, was four under, then couldn't chip up the slope at the 14th and bogeyed. Defending champion Jon Rahm went on a birdie-eagle-birdie sprint from 14, then stalled out.

Stenson, with Woods the oldest in the field at 43, stayed tight for three rounds (69-67-68), then was in the thick of it with three birdies and a bogey on the front. After birdies at 10 and 13, he eagled the par-five 15th, slashing a five-wood approach from 259 yards to within inches of the hole, and jumped into a one-shot lead. He parred in for his first win in over two years.

"If I can have a wish for next year," Stenson said, "that would be to put myself in the mix in a couple other majors and see if I can get another one."

PNC Father Son Challenge
Orlando, Florida
Winners: Bernhard and Jason Langer

It was a father-son golf lesson for the Langers, though not of the classical variety. This time, it was the son, Jason, 19, putting on a clinic for the dad, Bernhard, 62.

Three teams seemed set for a tough playoff in the PNC Father Son Challenge at the Ritz-Carlton Golf Club. Retief and Leo Goosen and Tom and Thomas Lehman and the Langers tied for the lead after the two rounds, were all sitting snugly in the fairway of the first extra hole, the par-five 18th. Then Jason took his three wood.

" ...270 into the wind, and he flew it all the way there," said dad, Bernhard. "It's something I don't know how to do. I don't have that in me. I could barely get a driver there."

But Jason's shot pierced the wind, cleared that front bunker and ended up 16 feet from the flag. He holed the putt for an eagle to give dad his fourth Father Son victory. Bernhard and Jason also won in 2014, and dad won the other two with son Stefan.

The three teams had tied at 24-under 120 in the scramble format. The Langers shot 60-60, the Goosens 58-62 and the Lehmans 61-59, topping a 20-team field loaded with Hall of Famers. Among them, Jack Nicklaus, 79, and grandson G.T. tied for 16th, and former LPGA star Annika Sorenstam, the first female pro ever invited, and her father Tom, 78, tied for 19th and last. "Score is kind of secondary today," Annika said.

There was also Tom Watson, playing through the pain of the recent loss of his wife, Hilary, to cancer. "My kids said, 'Dad, we think you want to play,'" Watson said. "And I really didn't want to play. But when they said I should, I told them, 'Okay, I will.'" He and son Michael tied for 13th.

The talk of the tournament ultimately returned to Jason Langer and his wondrous three wood. "I feel like I contributed a little more [this time]," Jason said.

Said Dad: "I've seen clutch shots in majors, and Ryder Cups, and all over the place. For our family, this is right up there."

The Presidents Cup
Melbourne, Australia
Winners: United States

Tiger Woods always did seem to get the better of Ernie Els on the course. So, too, when the pair made their first attempts at captaining their respective Presidents Cup teams. Except that Woods was still playing himself — the first to double up since Hale Irwin at the inaugural Presidents Cup in 1994 — and the playing captain led the USA to a narrow comeback victory 16-14 at Royal Melbourne, scene in 1998 of what remains the International team's sole win.

Woods the captain was helped immeasurably by having Woods the player leading the way, winning the first point on the first day and, America having trailed ever since, posting the first win on Sunday, when the USA won the singles for the first time since 2009. Usually, they don't need to, but from 8-10 down they won the singles 8-4 for the first ever come-from-behind victory in the Presidents Cup. Woods was the only player on either side to have a 100 percent record, winning all three of his matches. The 43-year-old gave a master class in plotting his way around the classic sand belt course, winning twice with Justin Thomas and then defeating Abraham Ancer, 3 and 2, in the singles.

Once his matches were over, Woods had to reclaim the captain's walkie-talkie from one of his assistants — Fred Couples, Zach Johnson and Steve Stricker — and catch up on the status of the other matches to which he had been oblivious while concentrating on his own game. On Saturday, Woods dropped himself from both sessions to work on the pairings and prepare for his singles.

Against the highest ever world-ranked U.S. Presidents Cup team, even after No. 1 Brooks Koepka had to withdraw due to injury, Els molded a young International team from nine countries and with seven rookies into a force that gave the visitors a mighty scare. A former winner at Royal Melbourne, Els and assistant Geoff Ogilvy, the local man, instructed their team how to handle the Alistair Mackenzie masterpiece, and the home team won the first day of fourballs 4-1. It was the first time the Internationals had led since 2005. They went 6-1 ahead during Friday's foursomes and a sweep was on the cards at one point before the USA won twice at the 18th and earned a half in the anchor match to get out of the session all square.

The Internationals edged 9-5 ahead after Saturday's fourballs, but the Americans rallied in the afternoon foursomes to get within two points. Following Woods on Sunday, wins by Dustin Johnson and Patrick Reed put the USA in front. Reed had lost all three of his previous matches while being heckled for the incident at the Hero World Challenge the previous week when he was penalized for improving his lie in a bunker. After the third session, his caddie Kessler Karain shoved a spectator and was stood down for the final day.

Sungjae Im, the 21-year-old Korean rookie, beat U.S. Open champion Gary Woodland to finish with a record of three wins, one loss and one half, the same as former Australian Open champion Ancer, whose only defeat came against Woods. There were halves for Hideki Matsuyama against Tony Finau and Adam Hadwin against Bryson DeChambeau, but then came three wins for America from Patrick Cantlay, Xander Schauffele and Webb Simpson. Cantlay and Schauffele both finished with three wins and two losses, while Thomas had three and a half points after losing to Australian rookie Cameron Smith.

An overall tie was possible when the Internationals had led in each of the last two matches, but both Matt Kuchar and Rickie Fowler rallied to earn halves. Kuchar secured the winning point in the penultimate match after coming back from three down to Louis Oosthuizen at the turn with five birdies putting him one up with one to play.

"We did it together," Woods said. "We came here as a team. I couldn't have done it without all the assistants' help and all my boys. We fought. This cup wasn't going to be given to us. We had to go earn it, and we did."

Els said of his team: "I can only give them my love. They played so hard for each other. There are a lot of young players, a lot of players that the world has never seen or heard, but you will see them a lot in the future. We're getting closer. Our team is not as deep as the U.S. team. All credit to the U.S. team. They have an absolute stacked team."

QBE Shootout
Naples, Florida
Winners: Rory Sabbatini and Kevin Tway

The way Rory Sabbatini saw it, Greg Norman's QBE Shootout is the Old Man and the Kid story, and it worked out beautifully this time — with him as the old man to the kid, Kevin Tway, Bob Tway's son.

"I'm the old guy," said Sabbatini, 43, and 12 years older than Tway. "I remember when I was the young guy, playing with John Daly, as the old guy as my partner. Now I'm the old guy, playing with the young guy as my partner. All I can say about Kevin — what a fantastic golfer, really."

Tway spoke as highly of Sabbatini after they sprinted through the third and final round to a two-stroke victory in the 12-team field at Tiburon Golf Club. "Today it was mostly Rory," Tway said. "I was just kind of hanging out. He played unbelievable … he was hot today."

Harold Varner and Ryan Palmer led the first round with a 17-under 55 in the scramble, and Sabbatini and Tway were three back at 58. In modified alternate shot in the second round, Sabbatini and Tway combined for a 67 to join a five-way tie for the lead at 125.

In the final round, at better-ball, Jason Kokrak and J.T. Poston broke out of the tie and were running away with it. They led by four through the eighth, but they cooled after a bogey at No. 9, and Sabbatini was heating up, birdieing five straight holes on his own ball from No. 6. They birdied 11, went birdie-eagle-birdie from 13, and birdied the last two for a 60 and a 31-under 185, and won by two over Kokrak and Poston.

Korn Ferry Tour

The players had just left the Lincoln Land Championship, a relatively young fixture on the Web.com Tour, and they arrived next at the Wichita Open, the third stop in June, to find themselves now playing on the Korn Ferry Tour.

The tour had a new sponsor. The move, sudden and unexpected, was another step in the evolution of the PGA Tour's developmental tour. It began as the Ben Hogan Tour in 1990 and became, in order, the Nike, the Buy.com, the Nationwide, and in 2012, the Web.com Tour. And then on June 19, 2019, it emerged as the Korn Ferry Tour, in a 10-year sponsorship by the Los Angeles-based consulting firm.

Korn Ferry couldn't have asked for a splashier introduction. The first event under the new tour name was the Wichita Open Supporting Wichita's Youth, June 20-23, and it came gift-wrapped with a steeplechase scramble, then a five-way playoff. Three players were eliminated on the first playoff hole on Sunday — Kevin Dougherty, Erik Compton and Denmark's Sebastian Cappelen. Darkness forced the survivors over to Monday morning, and then Sweden's Henrik Norlander beat Bryan Bigley on the third extra hole.

The tour's name had changed but the players were chasing the same goal — a spot at the top, the PGA Tour. At the end of the season, 50 playing cards would be awarded — 25 to the top regular-season points leaders and 25 from the final series.

Four players staked their claims as the only double winners of the year.

Scottie Scheffler, 23, former University of Texas standout, dominated the 2019 Korn Ferry Tour — in a way. In addition to his two victories, Scheffler also had eight other top-10 finishes. He swept the Player of the Year and Rookie of the Year awards, and topped the money list with $565,338, some $150,000 more than No. 2 and the third highest in tour history. He earned fully exempt status on the PGA Tour.

Scheffler broke through in the Evans Scholars Invitational at the Glen Club near Chicago. He started the final round six shots behind, shot 63 to tie Marcelo Rozo at 17-under 271, and won on a 15-foot birdie putt on the second playoff hole. "First professional win ... kind of gets the monkey off my back," he said. It had to be a young monkey. This was only his 11th start. He then took the Nationwide Children's Hospital Championship at Ohio State's Scarlet Course, winning by two with a 12-under 272. A tie for seventh in the season-ending Tour Championship sealed his spot atop the season-long points list and the Finals points list.

One good graduation deserves another:

Xinjun Zhang, second in winnings with $410,100, had graduated from the PGA Tour China Series onto the Korn Ferry Tour, and from there onto the PGA Tour with a comfortable victory in the inaugural Dormie Network Classic in April. Zhang closed with a 70 to win by five with a 26-under 262 at Briggs Ranch in San Antonio. The win, his first on the tour, gave him enough points to lock up a spot in the top 25 and on the PGA Tour. "It takes a lot of pressure off the rest of the season," he said. He took more off by winning the Lincoln Land Championship at Panther Creek, Springfield, Illinois. Zhang, 32, bogey-free over his last 41 holes, tied at 15-under 269 with Dylan Wu, 22, and won with a birdie on the third extra hole.

Robby Shelton, native son of Alabama, crowned himself king of Tennessee by sweeping both tour stops there — the Nashville Golf Open at Nashville Golf & Athletic Club, and the Knoxville Open at Fox Den. Shelton had five top-10s in all, made 14 cuts in 22 starts and finished third in winnings with $356,760.

In the Nashville's final round, Shelton squandered a three-shot lead, fought back for a 71 to tie old junior golf pal Scottie Scheffler at 15-under 273, then beat him in a playoff for his first tour win. Then in the Knoxville, Shelton recovered from another shaky spell in the final round, shot 71 for a 15-under 269 and a one-stroke win, for which he ceremonially donned the champion's jacket, and was resplendent in Tennessee orange. "Bear Bryant," Shelton said, raising the memory of the legendary University of Alabama football coach, "is probably turning over in his grave right now."

Kristoffer Ventura, of Norway, an impatient rookie, had had a number of disappointments. "It felt like, wow, the world really doesn't want me to play on tour," he said. Actually, it was nothing a little stretch of remarkable golf couldn't cure, as he proved. He'd played in only 11 events — won twice, had two top-three finishes, made seven cuts and won $336,234, fourth on the money list.

Ventura broke through in the Utah Championship, beating Joshua Creel with a par on the third playoff hole. Ventura came from three behind in the final round with 65 to tie at 270, 14 under at Oakridge. He missed two straight cuts, then won the Pinnacle Bank Championship in Omaha, outrunning Andres Gonzalez and Chad Ramsey by two with a closing 70 for a 16-under 268 at Indian Creek.

Denmark's Sebastian Cappelen had no victories but felt no less a success than the top four. Cappelen was one of the four losers in the Wichita Open playoff, but he'd still gained enough points to secure his long-coveted PGA Tour card. Said Cappelen: "It is with a smile on my face that I lose today."

Mackenzie Tour–PGA Tour Canada

There were two convenient ways to measure Paul Barjon's performance in the 2019 Mackenzie Tour–PGA Tour Canada. One was that he shot the first 28 rounds — seven tournaments — all under par. The other way — he won the tour's Player of the Year and Order of Merit awards.

And what made the tour crackle even more was the narrowness of Barjon's success. He played in all 12 events and won two of them, topping the Order of Merit with C$127,336, but led that money list by only C$2,746. That was because Canadian native son Taylor Pendrith — age 28, big (6-foot-2, 205 pounds) and big-hitting, and a graduate of Kent State University in Ohio — also won two tournaments and totaled C$124,590.

"Finishing No. 1 was the target at the beginning of the year," Barjon said. "Whether I could do it or not was definitely a question mark. You always want to be the first guy, but it's hard to put that into your mind that you can do it."

Barjon, 27, was probably the most-traveled player on the tour. He is native of New Caledonia, a Southwest Pacific island, a graduate of Texas Christian University and lives in Fort Worth, Texas.

Barjon won the Bayview Place DCBank Open in June, the second tournament on the schedule. He finished at 19 under and won by a shot. Then in mid-July, in a kind of preview of the end of the season, he won the Osprey Valley Open at 25 under. The last round turned into something of a match play finale against Pendrith. Barjon ended up winning by three, but came away impressed. "This guy is scary," he said. "He can make a lot of birdies."

A few weeks later, Pendrith showed how scary he could be. He won the 1932byBateman Open by three, after closing with a 62. And three weeks later he demolished the Mackenzie Investments Open, shooting 62-62 in the middle rounds in a 28-under 260 to win by a tour-record margin of eight.

He said after the Mackenzie win, "It was definitely the best week of tournament golf I have ever played." Pendrith, who won the Mackenzie Canadian Player of the Year award for the second time in four years, continued, "I honestly don't remember playing from the rough on the weekend…"

Barjon, with his fully exempt status as No. 1, leads the top five of the money list onto the 2020 Korn Ferry Tour. With him are the conditionally exempt Pendrith and Americans Jake Knapp, Lorens Chan and Patrick Fishburn. The others:

No. 3, Jake Knapp, 25, who won C$120,925, in the season-opening Canada Life Open, found himself trailing by five shots going into the final round. He texted his old coach: What does a guy have to do to shoot eight under? Answer: "Go shoot four under on the front and shoot four under on the back." So Knapp did, shot 64, and won by two strokes. He also won the GolfBC Championship two weeks later and had three other top-10 finishes.

No. 4, Lorens Chan, 25, won C$116,541. He was leading by one going into the final round of the HFX Pro-Am and finally solved Oakfield Golf and Country Club's par-five No. 1. "I was struggling on that hole this week," he said, "and I was just trying to two-putt." From 40 feet. And he holed the putt for an eagle and went on to win. He had seven other top-10s. "Nothing better than making a long putt to start the day," Chan said.

No. 5, Patrick Fishburn, C$81,140. Fishburn, 27, wanted to shoot 63 in the final round of the season-ending Canada Life Championship "Because I shot 66, 65, and 64, so I wanted to keep it going." But he didn't. He shot another 64 instead, and scored his first win by three. Fishburn had three other top-10s.

Other first-timer tales:

Scariest Win: The final round of the Windsor Championship opened with 26 players within two shots of the lead, and there were still 12 when Dawson Armstrong reached No. 16. Finally, Will Register, in the last group, needed a birdie at the par-four 18th to catch him, and almost made it — twice. Register's 65-yard third hit two inches from the hole, bounced forward, then burned the hole trickling back. Armstrong won with 66–284, 20 under. Six tied for second, a shot behind.

Smart Strategy: Derek Barron, on winning the Players Cup at windy Southwood: "I told myself this morning when I felt the wind that … It didn't matter if it was 20, 35, 50 or eight feet. I'd take my chances with the putter."

The Right Touch: Hayden Buckley, on taking the ATB Financial Classic: "Winning with a par in the playoff — it didn't feel like I won it. But it was good enough."

The Magic Word: After starting the season 0-for-3 on cuts, and after long rain delays in the Lethbridge Paradise Canyon Open, an anxious Alex Chiarella restrained himself on the final green and cautiously two-putted for a par, and scored his first win by a stroke. "Deep breathing, positive thoughts," Chiarella said. "Patience — that was the one word to myself this week."

PGA Tour Latinoamerica

Before calling it a year for 2019, the PGA Tour Latinoamerica statistics crew had one final task: To find whether there was any category that Augusto Nunez didn't top? What's left to say for a golfer who did just about everything?

Start with the victories — two. He was the only multiple winner, breezing to the Banco del Pacifico Open in Ecuador in October, and then most dramatically, the season-ending Shell Championship in December.

Along the way Nunez topped the Order of Merit with $148,734; authored the largest margin of victory — six strokes, in the Pacifico Open; had the lowest scoring average (68.38); the most top-10 finishes (11); the most sub-par rounds, 64 (tied with Tom Whitney); most rounds in the 60s (41); most consecutive cuts made (15); total birdies (291); most consecutive rounds, par or better, 15 (tied with Ryan Ruffels).

Nunez had already piled up a big enough money lead so that in the season-ending Shell Championship, he merely had to play 72 holes to win the Player of the Year award. Instead, he ended up winning the Shell in a battle that would go down in tour history. Nunez shot Trump National Doral in 66-66-69-70 for a 13-under 271. Jared Wolfe dogged him score for score, except for a 67 in the second round — the one stroke by which Nunez won. "It has not been easy for me to close tournaments in the past, and today I kept calm at key moments," Nunez said. "It was an amazing week."

He also had an amazing week earlier, when he entered the final round of the Banco del Pacifico Open "thinking about tying my record" [25 under in the 2016 Flor de Cana Open]. He didn't tie it, but he did get to 22 under and won by six, shooting the Quito Tennis and Golf Club in 68-67-64-67.

And thus did Nunez take the tour's fully exempt spot on the Korn Ferry Tour for 2020. Nos. 2-5 on the money list, all Americans, earned conditional exemptions.

No. 2: Tom Whitney, $86,860. In the Abierto OSDE del Centro in Argentina, Whitney came from behind and took the clubhouse lead, and on learning later he had won, said, "I like the sound of that." Whitney shot Cordoba Golf Club in 73-67-66-64–270, 14 under, winning by one. He had five other top-10 finishes, and was either No. 1 or 2 on the money list for 11 weeks.

No. 3: Jared Wolfe, $83,250. Wolfe opened and closed 2019 with crackling performances. First, he ran away with the season-opening Buenaventura Classic in Panama by five strokes, shooting Buenaventura Golf Club in 66-68-71-70–275, 13 under. Opening the season with a win "is more than I could have asked for," Wolfe said. Then in the season-ending Shell Championship, he dogged Nunez score-for-score — except for that one shot — and finished second. He also had five other top-10s.

No. 4: Evan Harmeling, $70,789. After a sluggish start, when a tie for 40th was his best finish in five events, Harmeling came to life at the BMW Jamaica Classic at Cinnamon Hill. He shot 66-66-64-71 for a 21-under 267 to edge Nunez by a stroke. "I never felt super comfortable out there,"

Harmeling said. "It was nerve-racking, especially at the end." He also had two other top-fives.

No. 5: John Somers, $69,099. Somers, a Latinoamerica rookie, took his first tour win in his third start in a spectacular finish at the Abierto de Chile. Somers trailed playing partner Alex Weiss by two starting the final round but was leading by one playing the Club de Golf Mapocho's par-five 18th. Both reached in two. But Somers holed his 45-foot putt for an eagle and won by two when Weiss two-putted from 10 for a birdie. Somers shot 68-65-67-65–265, 19 under. Said Somers, who missed the cut in his first two starts: "I just wanted something to get me started. This is more than I could have asked for." He also had three other top-10s.

There were two other remarkable finishes in 2019.

Argentina's Puma Dominguez, 34, winless on the tour, was about to give up on 2019. In three starts, with a sore wrist, he'd missed two cuts and finished 40th. But with only three tournaments left, and with a sponsor's exemption into the Neuquen Argentina Classic, he'd give it one last try. Then he birdied the final hole, forced a playoff, and beat Tom Whitney with a six-foot par putt on the first extra hole. He'd written a message to himself in his yardage book: "I am going to do it."

In the VISA Open de Argentina, a sudden scream from the gallery at the third playoff hole cost American Brandon Matthews a chance to win the tournament and take the Open Championship invitation that went with it. Colombia's Ricardo Celia had already holed a 30-footer for birdie, and Matthews had drawn back the putter for the eight-footer he needed to tie, then flinched at a scream and missed the putt. Instantly, Matthews was fuming silently. Then he learned that the scream had come from a spectator who had Down Syndrome and had lost control of his emotions. And now the man was distressed. "Take me to him," Matthews said. And he hugged him and comforted him.

"Some things," Matthews said, "are bigger than golf."

8. European Tours

Victory at the WGC-HSBC Champions gave Rory McIlroy his first European Tour title for three years. It was the 30-year-old Northern Irishman's fourth win of the year. Yet his most impressive performances came in America, where he won The Players Championship for the first time and the Tour Championship/FedExCup for the second.

McIlroy had been initially reluctant to continue his European Tour membership in 2020, played the Scottish Open instead of the Irish Open, lost a playoff at the European Masters a week after his FedEx triumph, finished nine behind Danny Willett at the BMW PGA Championship and enjoyed the Alfred Dunhill Links Championship more for the team event in which he played with his father Gerry — they were denied victory only on countback. After that event McIlroy made some remarks criticizing the quality of courses on the European Tour. He later admitted the comments were ill judged, especially at an event where the rotation of courses — the Old Course, Carnoustie and Kingsbarns — are set up with the amateurs and the autumnal weather in mind. That he also rarely plays in many of the lower profile, and even lower scoring, events on the PGA Tour might also be pertinent. Victory at Sheshan International let his golf do the talking instead, and although he arrived at the DP World Tour Championship without a chance to win the Race to Dubai, a fourth-place finish capped perhaps his most consistent season yet.

However, it was not without disappointments, the biggest coming close to home. The return of the Open Championship to Royal Portrush after 68 years was a triumph in virtually every way bar McIlroy missing the cut. Even then the shocking disaster of his opening round was almost forgotten by a thrilling charge on Friday evening in an attempt to make the weekend. The roars of approval were no less passionate for an Irish golfer from south of the border who was cheered to a six-stroke victory.

There was an almost enchanted quality to Shane Lowry's triumph as the 32-year-old from County Offaly experienced the week of his life. Tied for the lead at halfway, Lowry produced one of the great rounds of major championship golf with his 63 on Saturday. After a nervous start on Sunday, he stood firm against a battering from the Irish weather to proceed to the most joyful of celebrations down the 18th fairway. "I couldn't believe it was happening to me," he said. Tommy Fleetwood, his nearest yet distant pursuer, was the first to offer the heartiest of congratulations.

A year earlier Lowry, an obvious talent ever since winning the Irish Open as an amateur in 2009, had missed the cut at the Open for the fourth year running and sat in his car to cry. He lost his PGA Tour card, but early in 2019 he won the Abu Dhabi HSBC Championship, a sign of better days ahead.

Yet Lowry was pipped as the European Tour's Golfer of the Year by Race to Dubai winner Jon Rahm. The age of 25, and in only his third full season as a professional, Rahm became only the second Spaniard to win the Harry Vardon Trophy as Europe's No. 1. The other was six-time Order of Merit winner Seve Ballesteros.

Rahm won three times, taking his European Tour tally to six titles in only 40 tournaments, a rate of success that not even Ballesteros achieved at the start of his stellar career. Rahm was also third at the U.S. Open and finished runner-up at the Andalucia Masters and the BMW PGA Championship. He won two Rolex Series events, making four out of the six in all, as he won both the Irish Open and the DP World Tour Championship for the second time in three years and successfully defended the title at his national championship — twin victories that have revived an event that had fallen off the schedule in 2017. Between winning in Madrid and at the season-ending event Rahm had taken six week off to rest and prepare for the more important year-ending occasion of his wedding.

With a new points system introduced for the Race to Dubai, along with vastly increased first prizes for the last three tournaments of $2 million, $2.5 million and $3 million, a dramatic finale to the season ensued at Jumeirah Golf Estates. Austria's Bernd Wiesberger led the points table going into the final event thanks to victories at the Made in Denmark event and two Rolex Series events, the Scottish and Italian Opens.

This was a remarkable recovery for Wiesberger after spending seven months on the sidelines in 2018 with a wrist injury. He finished third at the penultimate event, the Nedbank Golf Challenge, when victory would have made his lead at the top of the table insurmountable. Finishing 28th the following week opened the door to his pursuers, however. Lowry and Matthew Fitzpatrick, after a season of four runner-up finishes which ended a streak of four years in a row of winning at least once, both had a chance and secured bonus place money behind Wiesberger in third.

But the No. 1 on the ranking came down to an exciting shoot-out between Rahm and Fleetwood. Rahm shared the 54-hole lead in Dubai and sprinted ahead with birdies at five of the first seven holes. Fleetwood, who won for the first time in 22 months the previous week at Sun City, was eight behind at one point but birdied five of the last seven holes to force Rahm to birdie the last hole for the title. Otherwise, there would have been a playoff for both the tournament and the Race to Dubai. With a fine bunker shot to four feet and a single putt, it was Rahm who scooped the $5 million double jackpot. "I've thought about winning the Race to Dubai all week," Rahm admitted. "It's really so hard to believe that some of the greatest champions in European golf and Spanish golf haven't been able to accomplish what I have in just three years. That's what I can't really put my mind into."

There was also a close duel for the Sir Henry Cotton Rookie of the Year award which went down to the final round of the season. Scotland's Robert MacIntyre claimed the title by finishing 11th on the Race to Dubai, three places ahead of American Kurt Kitayama. While Kitayama and another rookie, Italy's Guido Migliozzi, won twice during the 2018-19 season, MacIntyre produced consistently impressive results in some big events, finishing runner-up at the British Masters, the Made in Denmark and the European Open, as well as sixth at the Open Championship. The son of a greenkeeper from Oban, MacIntyre is familiarly known as "Bob" but is officially listed as "Robert" in deference to his mother, who still does his washing on weeks when he is back home.

While the season-ending event attracted a strong field, Keith Pelley, the chief executive of the European Tour, faced criticism that other Rolex Series events had not brought back the biggest names to the circuit as often as originally intended. Pelley replied that with around 35 tournament worldwide offering a purse of $7 million, the minimum for a Rolex Series event, there were simply too many opportunities for the game's stars to fill out their schedules of 20-odd events. One tournament that proved controversial despite the attendance of many big names was the inaugural Saudi International, won by Dustin Johnson, although Sergio Garcia also created a stir when he was disqualified for damaging a number of greens by dragging his foot in frustration.

A quest for innovation continued with the introduction of the PGA Tour of Australasia's Vic Open, where men's and women's tournaments take place alongside each other. A similar event was held on the Challenge Tour in Northern Ireland. There was also the inaugural Jordan Mixed event, where players from the Challenge Tour, the Ladies European Tour and the Staysure Tour competed against each other for one trophy using different tees. It was so successful, with the final threeball of the final round featuring a player from each tour, that the Scandinavian Mixed, hosted by Annika Sorenstam and Henrik Stenson, was introduced for 2020 with equal numbers of men and women playing in one tournament.

In a novel move, albeit in contingency rather than as planned, a playoff at the Turkish Airlines Open was concluded under floodlights, while due to a heatwave at the Alfred Dunhill Championship, the first event of the 2020 European Tour, players were allowed to wear shorts in competition, not just for practice and the pro-am. Ironically, one of the few to decline the opportunity, Pablo Larrazabal, was the winner.

European Tour

Abu Dhabi HSBC Championship
Abu Dhabi, United Arab Emirates
Winner: Shane Lowry

Back on the European Tour after losing his card on the PGA Tour, Shane Lowry started his year by equaling Henrik Stenson's Abu Dhabi course record of 62. Lowry went on to win the Abu Dhabi HSBC Championship wire-to-wire but only thanks to a birdie on the 72nd hole. Scores of 70 and 67 put the 31-year-old Irishman three ahead of Richard Sterne entering the final round, but his lead had disappeared after three holes. By the turn he was three behind and two holes later he trailed by four.

Sterne birdied four of the first five holes and went out in 31 while Lowry was out in 37. Lowry then bogeyed the 11th before birdieing the next two holes. Sterne had run out of birdies and three-putted the 14th and also bogeyed the 16th to leave the pair tied with two to play. A exquisite up-and-down by Lowry at the 17th kept the pair level before he found the green at the last in two and two-putted for a four. Sterne missed the green on the right and failed to get up and down.

"It was an emotional roller coaster today. I went out with the lead by a few and before I knew it I was four behind. I was brave out there, I ground it out well and I'm over the moon," said Lowry after his fourth European Tour victory and his first since 2015.

Lowry closed with a 71 for an 18-under-par total of 270, with Sterne adding his second 69 of the weekend. Joost Luiten, with two eagles, scored a 65 to take third place, three behind the winner. Brooks Koepka finished in the top 10, Dustin Johnson was 16th, but there was no third win in a row for Tommy Fleetwood, who was 42nd. Newly part of the Rolex Series, the purse increased to $7 million, though this was the second weakest field for the event since 2008.

Omega Dubai Desert Classic
Dubai, United Arab Emirates
Winner: Bryson DeChambeau

For three days at the Omega Dubai Desert Classic, Bryson DeChambeau was not happy with his game even though scores of 66, 66 and 68 at Emirates had him leading by one over defending champion Haotong Li. "I'm just not 100 percent with my game," DeChambeau said on Saturday evening before a long session on the practice range as night fell.

It did the trick. DeChambeau, he of the identical length irons and now, under the new Rules of Golf, putting with the flagstick in the hole, birdied the first three holes on Sunday, eagled the 10th, birdied three of the next four holes, dropped only one shot and then had a three at the short par-four 17th to score a 64. On the 30th anniversary of the first European Tour event in the Middle East, he set a new tournament record of 24-under-par 264.

"Today I was happy with my game," DeChambeau said. "I executed a lot of great shots. It was obviously a lot of fun to be able to finally hoist an international trophy, I'm so happy about that." Having won four times in America in 2017, and reaching fifth in the World Ranking, the 25-year-old from California had started the week stating his goal of winning overseas for the first time.

The victory margin was seven strokes after Matt Wallace, 68, broke a tie for second by birdieing the 18th to finish one ahead of compatriots Ian Poulter and Paul Waring, who both closed with 64s, and Spaniards Sergio Garcia and Alvaro Quiros.

Li dropped from a tie for third to a tie for 12th when he was handed a two-stroke penalty as officials judged his caddie had stood too long behind his player as Li took his stance over his putt at the 18th. It was the first such penalty for a professional under the new Rules of Golf which prohibit a caddie lining up a player.

Saudi International
King Abdullah Economic City, Saudi Arabia
Winner: Dustin Johnson

About the only routine element of the inaugural Saudi International was a two-stroke victory for Dustin Johnson. The event, a first in Saudi Arabia on the European Tour, courted controversy for merely taking place amid concerns about human rights issues in the host country and the assassination of *Washington Post* columnist Jamal Khashoggi the previous October. After winning the Farmers Insurance Open at Torrey Pines the previous Sunday, World No. 1 Justin Rose said: "I'm a pro golfer, not a politician," before making the journey to Royal Greens, on the Red Sea coast at King Abdullah Economic City. He then missed the cut.

A strong field also included Brooks Koepka, Bryson DeChambeau, Patrick Reed and Sergio Garcia. However, the Spaniard became the first player to be disqualified under new Rule 1.2a for serious misconduct. Out early in the third round, Garcia showed his displeasure for the tricky greens, laid only 18 months earlier, by inflicting a divot on the sixth green and leaving scuff marks from his golf shoes on four others. Players in the four subsequent groups alerted officials and European Tour chief executive Keith Pelley spoke to Garcia after the round. In a statement, Garcia said: "I respect the decision of my disqualification. I damaged a couple of greens, for which I apologize for, and I have informed my fellow players it will never happen again." Pelley later suggested there would be no further action taken.

Haotong Li, who suffered a two-shot penalty for his caddie standing behind his line on the final green in Dubai, scored a 62 in the third round which included four eagles, three of them at par-fours. Tied with Johnson after 54 holes, Li closed with a 69 having briefly led at the turn.

Johnson opened with a 68 and then scored his lowest ever round with a 61 on Friday. A 65 and then a 67 gave him a 19-under-par total of 261. The American was two ahead when he hit his tee shot at the short 16th into the Red Sea on the left of the green. He made a bogey but birdied the last two holes to claim his sixth European Tour title. Tom Lewis, who birdied the first five holes in a 65, was third, while Min Woo Lee, brother of Minjee Lee, had a 63 to be fourth in his second start as a professional.

ISPS Handa Vic Open
Winner: David Law

See Australasian Tour chapter.

ISPS Handa World Super 6 Perth
Winner: Ryan Fox

See Australasian Tour chapter.

Oman Open
Muscat, Oman
Winner: Kurt Kitayama

After leading on the first day at the Oman Open, on Friday morning Kurt Kitayama saw his ball blown off the third green at Al Mouj into a bunker. He got up and down for a par, but the winds increased so much that a sand storm suspended play for much of the day. It meant the third round began late on Saturday and Kitayama, now one off the lead, only had time for three holes before darkness fell. He opened with a quadruple-bogey-eight and bogeyed the next two holes. "I was like, 'Can we stop right now?'" he said. "It gave me a refresh and it was incredible coming back."

Kitayama played the last 15 holes the next morning in seven under par for a 71 that left him three off the lead. With the same groupings going straight out for the final round, Kitayama was in the final group, which allowed him to stay in touch with a crowded leaderboard. Still two behind with three to play, Kitayama got up and down for a birdie-four at the 16th and then holed from 18 feet for a three at the 17th. The 26-year-old from California, who came through all three stages of qualifying school, won for the second time in his 11 starts on the European Tour with scores of 66, 74, 71 and 70 for a seven-under-par total of 281. "This one feels good because the first win felt like it was coming, but I came in this week off three missed cuts," Kitayama said.

Four players shared second place, Jorge Campillo scoring 69, Maximilian Kieffer 72 after bogeying the 17th, Clement Sordet 70 with a bogey at the last and Fabrizio Zanotti, the 54-hole leader, 74 with three double bogeys, including a four-putt at the 16th.

Commercial Bank Qatar Masters
Doha, Qatar
Winner: Justin Harding

It took a player who has taken a liking to winning to emerge from a crowded leaderboard at the Commercial Bank Qatar Masters. A European Tour record nine players shared runner-up honors, but Justin Harding claimed a two-stroke victory thanks to three birdies in the last four holes at Doha. This was the 33-year-old South African's fifth win in nine months after two in his homeland and two in Asia in 2018 — but a first on the European Tour having started the week without full playing privileges.

Harding was three behind Oliver Wilson at the start of the final round and made three birdies in his first four holes. But he dropped two shots as early starter Jinho Choi scored a 64 to post 11 under par as the clubhouse target. Harding went five under par on the way home, starting with birdies at the 10th and 12th holes before his flying finish. With rounds of 68, 68, 73 and 66 Harding finished on 275, 13 under par.

There were still 15 players to finish before he knew whether victory would be his. Joining Choi in second place were Harding's South African compatriots George Coetzee, Christiaan Bezuidenhout and Erik van Rooyen, Spaniards Jorge Campillo and Nacho Elvira, Sweden's Anton Karlsson, Frenchman Mike Lorenzo-Vera and former Ryder Cup player Wilson.

"It feels good," said Harding. "It was nerve-racking. I didn't quite think it was enough, I thought there might be a playoff, but I'm happy to get over the line eventually. I've been knocking on the door a little recently."

Magical Kenya Open
Nairobi, Kenya
Winner: Guido Migliozzi

The Kenya Open dates back to 1967 with Seve Ballesteros and Ian Woosnam among its former winners on the old Safari Tour. From 1991 it was a Challenge Tour event with Trevor Immelman and Edoardo Molinari among the champions. In its first edition as a European Tour event, Guido Migliozzi won the Magical Kenya Open for the Italian rookie's maiden title. Migliozzi won three times on his last two seasons on the Alps Tour before earning his European Tour card at the qualifying school in November 2018. The 22-year-old has the distinction of being the first player signed by Modest Golf, a management company run by One Direction's Niall Horan.

And now the first to win after Migliozzi secured a one-stroke victory at Karen over Spain's Adri Arnaus and South Africans Louis de Jager and Justin Harding. A week after winning in Qatar, Harding set the clubhouse target at 15 under par with a closing 66. Migliozzi, the overnight leader with Arnaus, birdied the 12th to get to 16 under par and then parred in.

De Jager led by four strokes at the halfway stage, had a chance to birdie the 18th but his putt ran over the left edge of the hole. Arnaus only had a long range effort for a birdie at the last, but Migliozzi finished in style by hitting the flagstick at the 18th with his eight-iron approach. He then two-putted for a 69, while Arnaus had a 70. With earlier rounds of 67, 68 and 64, Migliozzi finished with a total of 268.

"I like this moment," he said. "I love pressure, it's like a drug, I love playing with a lot of people looking at me and a lot of cameras."

Maybank Championship
Winner: Scott Hend

See Asia/Japan Tours chapter.

Hero Indian Open
Winner: Stephen Gallacher

See Asia/Japan Tours chapter.

Trophee Hassan II
Rabat, Morocco
Winner: Jorge Campillo

"It's been a while but it was worth the wait." So said Jorge Campillo after claiming his maiden victory in his 229th event on the European Tour at the Trophee Hassan II. Campillo won by two shots on the Red course at Royal Dar Es Salam with birdies at the 16th and 17th holes to end a run of near-misses. Among 28 previous top-10 finishes, the 32-year-old Spaniard, who qualified from the Challenge Tour in 2011, had been second six times and third four times.

Two of those seconds and a third had come in his previous four starts. When he bogeyed the second and third holes of his final round, it might have been another occasion when it slipped away. However, as the leaders struggled, a birdie at the eighth and another, from eight feet, at the 11th put Campillo in a share of the lead. A fine second shot from rough to 10 feet at the 16th, the hardest hole on the closing stretch, put Campillo one ahead before he got up and down for a three at the short par-four 17th. A par at the last, after a lengthy wait on the tee, gave Campillo rounds of 72, 71, 69 and 71 for a nine-under-par total of 283 and a two-stroke win over van Rooyen, 74, Sean Crocker, 72, and Julian Suri, 71.

"It's been a long road," Campillo said. "I'm grateful, but it's been way too long. Way too many hours of work since I was a boy to today. I just love the game, I love competing. I'm just proud that I can say I'm a winner on the European Tour."

Volvo China Open
Winner: Mikko Korhonen

See Asia/Japan Tours chapter.

Betfred British Masters
Southport, England
Winner: Marcus Kinhult

Winners of the Lytham Trophy, a leading amateur tournament for over 50 years, know how to play early spring links golf, which proved an asset at the Betfred British Masters, hosted for the first time by Tommy Fleetwood at Hillside. Matthew Jordan, from Royal Liverpool, was the 2018 winner and led the first round with a nine-under-par 63 before finishing 15th, his best result in nine European Tour events.

Three years earlier then-18-year-old Marcus Kinhult led from start to finish to win by eight strokes at Lytham. Now the Swede claimed his maiden European Tour title by recovering from two late bogeys with two even later birdies to pip a trio of home players by one stroke. Kinhult battled all day with his fellow 54-hole leader Matt Wallace, who missed the chance to take the lead at the 16th, then lipped out with a short birdie putt on the 17th and saw his 15-footer at the last slip by. Kinhult, whose only bogeys of the day came inconveniently at the 15th and 16th, holed from 10 feet for a four at the 17th and then from eight feet at the last to avoid a four-way playoff. "I've been dreaming about it for such a long time and to finally do it is sort of amazing," Kinhult said. "It was so close all day between us."

Defending champion Eddie Pepperell made his sixth birdie of the day at the 17th before getting up and down at the last to post the target at 15 under par following a 66. Scotland's Robert MacIntyre, who suffered a double bogey at the second, finished brilliantly with an eagle and a birdie also to sit at 15 under par after a 68. Wallace just failed to add to his burgeoning trophy cabinet with a 71, while Kinhult had rounds of 65, 69, 68 and 70 for a 16-under-par total of 272.

Made in Denmark
Farso, Denmark
Winner: Bernd Wiesberger

After seven months out of the game with a wrist injury in 2018, Bernd Wiesberger had struggled to regain his form until he won the Made in Denmark. Wiesberger took a one-shot lead into the final day at Himmerland but was pushed all the way by Scottish left-hander Robert MacIntyre, who finished as a runner-up for the second event running.

"Winning is never easy," Wiesberger said. "I didn't expect it all, I had a rough year last year. I had so many great people helping me and getting me back to where I am right now. It's been amazing and I'm proud to pay it back that way."

After recovering from a double bogey at the fourth, Wiesberger took a two-stroke lead when he pitched in from 66 yards for an eagle at the 11th. MacIntyre leveled before Wiesberger hit his approach at the short 16th to eight feet for a birdie, only for MacIntyre to go out of bounds in trying to drive the green at the short par-four 17th.

MacIntyre saved his bogey to be two adrift going to the last, where Wiesberger saw his drive slide into the water on the right. MacIntyre could not force a birdie, and when Wiesberger secured a bogey, the 33-year-old Austrian had claimed his fifth victory and first for two years. He had rounds of 68, 69, 67 and 66 for a 14-under-par total of 270 while MacIntyre and Romain Langasque, who finished third, also closed with 66s.

"I gave it everything I had," said MacIntyre. "It was a poor shot on 17 that really cost me. It's the worst swing I've probably put on a shot in a long, long time, but I'm young, I live and I learn."

Belgian Knockout
Antwerp, Belgium
Winner: Guido Migliozzi

It was Darius van Driel's 30th birthday on the final day of the Belgian Knockout, but a maiden victory for a player whose initial plans to turn professional at 18 were delayed by a broken hand after falling off a banana boat proved just out of reach. Dutchman van Driel made it through 36 holes of stroke play qualifying and five rounds of nine-hole medal match play to reach the final at Rinkven International. However, he was unable to halt the progress of Guido Migliozzi as the 22-year-old Italian claimed his second victory of his rookie season.

In only his 20th appearance on the European Tour, Migliozzi finished fifth in his half of the draw after two days — 32 players qualified for the knockout rounds from each half of the starting field — and in the second round on Saturday defeated defending champion Adrian Otaegui. In the quarter-finals on Sunday morning he beat Made in Denmark winner Bernd Wiesberger before dismissing Scot Ewen Ferguson 32-35 in the semi-finals.

Migliozzi put his stamp on the final with a huge drive at the first hole and birdieing from 10 feet to go ahead. A bogey at the third was followed with three birdies in four holes from the fifth. Van Driel bogeyed the fifth and sixth holes and the Italian romped home by four strokes, with a three-under 32 to a one-over 36.

"I'm feeling very good," Migliozzi said. "I managed very well this afternoon, all the shots. I'm playing solid and I will try to continue this quality in the future." In the third-fourth playoff, Ferguson beat Gregory Havret also by four strokes.

GolfSixes Cascais
Cascais, Portugal
Winners: Thailand (Thongchai Jaidee and Phachara Khongwhatmai)

For the third edition of GolfSixes, the two-day 16-team event moved to Portugal and Oitavos Dunes. The sixth hole was a par-three over a swimming pool and it was the Thai pair of Thongchai Jaidee and Phachara Khongwhatmai who ended up jumping in the pool in celebration. Jaidee made a hole-in-one there on the first day to finish top of their group and eliminate defending champions Ireland (Paul Dunne and Gavin Moynihan).

Then, after beating Scotland and Spain in the knockout stages, Thailand beat England in the final in a nearest-the-pin playoff at the same hole. With the match tied playing the last in regulation, Tom Lewis missed from five feet for the victory. On the first playoff hole, Paul Waring again had the best tee shot, finishing seven feet away, but Lewis again missed the putt. When they all returned to the tee, it was Khongwhatmai — at 20, fully 29 years younger than Jaidee, and without a European Tour title to his name compared to Jaidee's eight — who finished closest to the hole, just three feet away. "I'm lucky today," said Jaidee. "We played well today but I think the teamwork was very important. Thank you to my partner, Phachara."

England beat Sweden in the quarter-finals and then Italy in the semis before falling to Thailand. "I'm gutted, I'm genuinely gutted," said Lewis. "We played so many good matches but unfortunately didn't make the putts at the end."

Two women's teams took part, Meghan MacLaren and Florentyna Parker for England finishing with only one tied match, while Germany's Esther Henseleit and Laura Fuenfstueck lost out on a quarter-final spot via a playoff against the Australian men who they had beaten earlier in the day.

BMW International Open
Munich, Germany
Winner: Andrea Pavan

Andrea Pavan led the BMW International Open with a first round of 66. The next time the Italian topped the leaderboard was after birdieing the 72nd hole at Munchen Eichenried. Middle rounds of 71 and 70 left him four strokes off the 54-hole lead, but another 66, with six birdies and no bogeys, gave Pavan the clubhouse lead on a total of 273, 15 under par. Only Matt Fitzpatrick could match that score, with a closing 69, although the Englishman was disappointed not to finish ahead after three-putting the drivable 16th, bogeying the short 17th and narrowly missing out on an eagle at the last.

Seven players finished two strokes behind, including defending champion Matt Wallace, who needed a birdie at the last to tie but twice found the water and finished with a bogey-six. Austrian Mathias Schwab had led by two with seven to play but joined the group at 13 under with Wallace, 54-hole leader Jordan Smith, who closed with a 72, Alvaro Quiros, Edoardo Molinari, Rafa Cabrera Bello and Christiaan Bezuidenhout.

Fitzpatrick had a bit of luck on the first playoff hole when his second at the 18th stayed up on the bank of the greenside lake thanks to a heavy rain shower. Both he and Pavan parred the hole, as the Englishman did at the second attempt. But Pavan hit a wedge from the left rough to two feet and holed the putt for his second European Tour victory. "I had a little pitching wedge and luckily I got a decent lie, but it just felt great, it was really close," said the 30-year-old.

Estrella Damm N.A. Andalucia Masters
Sotogrande, Spain
Winner: Christiaan Bezuidenhout

A remarkable display of ball-striking led Christiaan Bezuidenhout to his maiden victory on the European Tour. Valderrama always requires precision play and especially when the wind gets up. After an opening 66, it was a 68 on the second morning that took the 25-year-old South African four clear of the field. Rounds of 69 and 71 over the weekend resulted in a winning margin of six.

Bezuidenhout's rise in the game follows an awful childhood experience when as a two-year-old he mistakenly drank rat poison from an old Coke can. Although he recovered, he was left with a stammer and anxiety issues, for which he took beta blockers. This caused a failed drugs test at the 2014 Amateur Championship at Royal Portrush. A nine-month ban followed, but this victory sent him back to Portrush to play in the 2019 Open.

Mike Lorenzo-Vera and Adri Arnaus also qualified for the Open after sharing second place with Eduardo de la Riva, Alvaro Quiros and Jon Rahm. Sergio Garcia, tournament host and winner for the last three editions, finished seventh, his 14th top-10 in 15 appearances at Valderrama.

It was not plain sailing for Bezuidenhout on the final day, even after birdieing the first two holes to go seven clear. He bogeyed four holes out of five and Rahm was only three behind, but the Spaniard lost ground with a bogey at the 10th and a double at the 12th, while the South African rallied with three birdies in a row from the ninth.

"I'm proud of myself for hanging in there," Bezuidenhout said. "I had a tough stretch in the middle of my round. I was nervous. It's a tough golf course, anything can happen, especially those last three holes playing into the wind. To finish it off is unbelievable."

Dubai Duty Free Irish Open
Co. Clare, Republic of Ireland
Winner: Jon Rahm

After finishing third at the U.S. Open and second at the Andalucia Masters, Jon Rahm completed the progression by winning the Dubai Duty Free Irish Open for the second time in three years. The 24-year-old Spaniard has now won four times in 34 tournaments on the European Tour, three of them Rolex Series events. Having won at Portstewart in 2017, just down the road from 2019 Open venue Royal Portrush, Rahm again charged to victory at Lahinch, another classic old links selected as the venue by new host Paul McGinley.

Seven behind at the halfway stage, after rounds of 67 and 71, Rahm added a 64 on Saturday but was still five adrift. A closing 62 left him two ahead of Andy Sullivan and Bernd Wiesberger. Robert Rock, the 54-hole leader, had scored a new course record of 60 on Saturday, missing an eagle putt from just off the green at the last for a 59. He closed with a 70 to share fourth place with Rafa Cabrera Bello and Eddie Pepperell.

After five birdies in the first 10 holes, including from six feet at the blind par-three fifth, Rahm holed a 35-footer for an eagle at the 12th. A poor chip at the next cost a second bogey, but three birdies in the last five holes brought him a second Irish title. Compatriot Seve Ballesteros won the Irish Open three times in four years in 1983-1986.

"I love this tournament," Rahm said. "I love this country. I love the people and feel like I'm at home every time I come. I'm excited to repeat. My game was in great form, it just didn't show the first two days. I couldn't hole the putts and the weekend was the complete opposite. That eagle on 12 just completely got me going."

Aberdeen Standard Investments Scottish Open
North Berwick, Scotland
Winner: Bernd Wiesberger

A late finish to the Aberdeen Standard Investments Scottish Open was designed to minimize a clash with two huge sporting events in London. Given the final of the Cricket World Cup went to a "super over" after the match was tied and the Wimbledon men's final was decided for the first time by a tie-break at 12-12 in the fifth set, it was almost inevitable that extra time would also result at The Renaissance. At close to nine o'clock at night, Bernd Wiesberger defeated Benjamin Hebert at the third extra hole.

This was Wiesberger's second victory of the season after the 33-year-old Austrian won in Denmark in May following a seven-month layoff in 2018 due to a wrist injury. It was his sixth win overall and his first in a Rolex Series event. He scorched the modern links near North Berwick for a 10-under-par 61 in the second round while taking a two-shot lead to the final day.

But Hebert made nine birdies and nine pars in a 62 on Sunday to put the pressure on. Wiesberger birdied the 16th from 18 feet to go back in front by one, but dropped a shot at the 17th before holing from five feet for a par at the last. A 69 meant he tied Hebert's 22-under-par total of 262. Both men parred the 18th for the first playoff hole and bogeyed it for the second. At the third time of asking Hebert again three-putted but Wiesberger made a three-footer for the win.

"We just dug in there," Wiesberger said after going to the top of the Race to Dubai. "I would have loved to seal it off with a couple of pars coming in, but sometimes it just tests you. I'm very grateful for how it turned out."

Hebert had the consolation of qualifying for the Open at Royal Portrush, along with Andrew "Beef" Johnston, who closed with a 62 after recently articulating his battle with mental health issues over the last year, and Nino Bertasio.

Rounds of 77 and 71 gave Brendan Lawlor victory in the inaugural EDGA Scottish Open, a 36-hole event featuring 10 players from the World Rankings for Golfers with Disability held alongside the main tournament.

The 148th Open Championship
Winner: Shane Lowry

See Chapter 5.

D+D Real Czech Masters
Prague, Czech Republic
Winner: Thomas Pieters

When Thomas Pieters won his first title at the D+D Real Czech Masters in 2015 it started a whirlwind period for the Belgian. He won twice more within a year and made his debut in the Ryder Cup at Hazeltine National in 2016, scoring four points out of five. Yet he did not make the 2018 Ryder Cup team and there had been no more victories until his second at Albatross arrived by one stroke over Adri Arnaus. Rounds of 67, 67 and 66 put Pieters in front after 54 holes and he led by three with nine holes to play.

Arnaus kept the pressure up, however, and Pieters had to grind out the victory with a 69 for a 19-under-par total of 269. Arnaus also closed with a 69, that included an eagle at the 12th and birdies at two of the last three holes, to finish two ahead of Sam Horsfield and defending champion Andrea Pavan.

"I'm relieved. It's been a long time, three years since I last won," said the 27-year-old Pieters. "It feels good to win again. I never doubted myself but it's just been a long road of not feeling that great with the golf swing. It feels good to get back on track again and get another win. It's difficult when everybody says you should be winning two or three times a year. It's always nice to hear that, but it's almost a negative sometimes because I always felt like I was underachieving, but hopefully there's many more like this. I felt like I was in control today, almost the whole day, and I kind of did my own thing."

Scandinavian Invitation
Gothenburg, Sweden
Winner: Eric van Rooyen

South Africa's Eric van Rooyen collected his maiden victory on the European Tour with a birdie at the final hole at the Scandinavian Invitation. The 29-year-old had won once on the Sunshine Tour and once on the Challenge Tour but had finished second three times in the last two seasons on the main European circuit. That changed when he held off Matthew Fitzpatrick to win by one stroke after both players scored 64s on the final day at Hills Golf and Sports Club in Gothenburg.

After opening scores of 65 and 68, van Rooyen posted twin scores of 64 over the weekend for a 19-under-par total of 261. Sweden's Henrik Stenson made a hole-in-one at the sixth hole to share the lead amid wild cheering but later faded from the contest to finish in a tie for third place with Dean Burmester, the pair four adrift of Fitzpatrick.

Van Rooyen's only dropped shot of the day came at the 17th, and with Fitzpatrick birdieing the last two holes, the South African needed a birdie himself at the last. It arrived with a 15-footer for victory.

"I've been putting so well all day and to hole that one to win my first one is pretty cool," he said. "I've gone close a bunch of times and every time I'm in contention the question gets asked. I was so nervous on 18. On 17 I was fine, I just didn't hit that putt hard enough and then I asked my caddie Alex, 'what are we at?' and he told me that Matt went birdie-birdie. It's hard to describe how I feel, it's too good."

Omega European Masters
Crans Montana, Switzerland
Winner: Sebastian Soderberg

Four players had a putt on the 18th green at Crans-sur-Sierre to win the Omega European Masters. They were joined in a five-man playoff by Rory McIlroy, who followed five birdies in six holes with a sliced drive into the trees at the 18th. McIlroy had to chip out sideways before the World No. 2 hit a wedge from 122 yards to a foot.

Sebastian Soderberg, a 28-year-old from Gothenburg, who had the best chance of a winning birdie in regulation time, finished the playoff at the first extra hole with a 10-foot putt for a three. He had to watch as both Finland's Kalle Samooja and McIlroy had chances to stay alive but missed. Italy's Lorenzo Gagli, whose drive in the playoff hit a female spectator, and Andres Romero, the 54-hole leader who almost holed from long range on the 72nd hole, made up the playoff. Adri Arnaus and Mike Lorenzo-Vera both finished one back.

Soderberg, who lost his card in his rookie season on the European Tour in 2017 but regained his status by finishing fifth on the Challenge Tour in 2018, was playing in his 50th European Tour event and not sure of saving his card again. He did so in glorious fashion with five birdies in a row from the 10th while playing alongside McIlroy, who had won the FedExCup the previous Sunday. A three-putt for bogey at the 17th and a tentative attempt on the 18th might have betrayed his nerves, but he made no mistake in the playoff.

"I've dreamt of winning on the European Tour, even better doing it this way," said Soderberg. "I was more nervous in the beginning than I was towards the back nine. Just playing with Rory, there are so many people around. Playing with a guy like that adds heat to it right away. I didn't really know that I was ready to win, I was just trying to keep my card for next year. It's a surreal way to do it."

Porsche European Open
Hamburg, Germany
Winner: Paul Casey

In 1991, as a 14-year-old, Paul Casey was a standard bearer during an event that he would subsequently win as the Porsche European Open 28 years later. "I volunteered at this event at Walton Heath, which is not far from where I grew up as a kid," Casey said. "I never thought I'd be sitting here with the trophy. This is an incredibly prestigious trophy with a lot of history to it on the European Tour." Casey added that he dedicated the victory to Gordon Brand, Jr., a two-time winner of the European Open whose funeral, following his sudden death at the age of 60, was due to be held the following day.

Casey started the final round one stroke behind Germany's Bernd Ritthammer and Scotland's Robert MacIntyre. A birdie at the 13th hole, as MacIntyre bogeyed the 12th, edged Casey ahead. Two more birdies at the 16th and 17th from the veteran Ryder Cup player sealed the win at 14-under-par 274 after scores of 66, 73, 69 and 66 at Green Eagle. A three-putt for par at the last gave the overnight leaders the chance to tie, but MacIntyre, with an eagle attempt, and Ritthammer, with a birdie putt, both came up short. Their 68s left them one behind, alongside Austria's Matthias Schwab, who eagled the last for a 66. Schwab's compatriot Bernd Wiesberger was fifth after a course-record 64.

This was Casey's 14th European Tour win and his first for five years. Earlier in the season he had successfully defended his Valspar Championship title after a few years of mainly concentrating on the PGA Tour. "I'd been away from the Tour for a few years, since then I've had a couple of wins in the U.S.," Casey said. "I feel as fit at 42 as I've ever felt. I have an understanding of my golf game and a lot of enthusiasm. I love working hard for it and the quest of being as good as I can be."

KLM Open
Amsterdam, Netherlands
Winner: Sergio Garcia

Making his debut at the KLM Open on its 100th staging — first played for in 1912 — Sergio Garcia earned a hard-fought victory at The International in Amsterdam. After four birdies and three bogeys going out, the 39-year-old Spaniard produced two stunning birdies at the 15th and 16th holes, the first from the rough to two feet, the second also from the rough but additionally with his feet in a bunker to five feet. Garcia won by one stroke over 18-year-old Dane Nicolai Hojgaard, whose eagle-putt at the last only narrowly missed.

In his seventh start on the European Tour, Hojgaard closed with a 68 to keep the pressure on the former Masters champion, who claimed his 16th European Tour title with rounds of 68, 67, 66 and 69 for an 18-under-par total of 270. Matt Wallace, who broke the course record with a 63 in the third round, was also in contention until a late bogey as he finished three behind in third place. Callum Shinkwin, who shared the lead with Garcia after 54 holes, was leading until a double bogey at the 12th hole. He finished fifth after a 76, one behind countryman James Morrison.

"I played well all week under pressure," said Garcia after joining the likes of Seve Ballesteros, Jose Maria Olazabal and Miguel Angel Jimenez in winning in the Netherlands. "It wasn't easy, there were a couple of tough moments today, but I hung on. Today wasn't easy, it was quite breezy and was blowing in a different direction again, but I played nicely again. A couple of mistakes here and there, but other than that I felt like I played really well."

BMW PGA Championship
Virginia Water, Surrey, England
Winner: Danny Willett

After missing the cut in the BMW PGA Championship at Wentworth in 2018, Danny Willett had slumped to 462nd in the World Ranking. The man from Sheffield had been ranked 12th before winning the Masters in 2016, but injuries and loss of form took their toll. The 31-year-old Englishman's revival under the tutelage of coach Sean Foley led to his first victory since Augusta at the DP World Tour Championship at the end of the 2018 European Tour.

With the BMW PGA Championship moving from May to September, Willett had made steady if unspectacular progress in 2019 before winning for the first time on British soil with his seventh European Tour title. "I've watched this tournament for a lot of years," he said. "It's always nice to be able to compete on home soil. I've had a couple looks at the Open but to be able to win finally on such an iconic golf course, with I think one of the best fields they have had, is great."

Willett defeated Jon Rahm by three strokes after the pair went head-to-head over the final 36 holes. They were tied on 11 under par at the halfway stage, Willett with scores of 68 and 65, Rahm with a 66 and a 67, before both added 68s on Saturday. The Spaniard had been two ahead before finishing six-five over the pair of closing par-fives.

After three days of late summer sunshine, a rainy final round saw Willett edge ahead with birdies at the second and third holes. Rahm got one back at the fourth, but Willett birdied the eighth to go two clear again. After the pair birdied the short 10th, Willett got away with a bogey at the 11th by holing from 40 feet. A wild drive was followed by a recovery that hit a tree and ended in the heather. A full-blooded attempt for his third saw his ball dribble into a bunker two yards ahead and left a sting in his wrist.

Rahm could not capitalize, dropping shots at the long 12th and short 14th before finding water at the last. Willett birdied the last two holes — his approach at the last was good, but not quite as good as Ross Fisher's albatross on Saturday — for a 67 and a 20-under-par total of 268. Rahm finished with a 70 to be a shot ahead of Christiaan Bezuidenhout, with Americans Billy Horschel and Patrick Reed tying for fourth place.

Alfred Dunhill Links Championship
St. Andrews & Fife, Scotland
Winner: Victor Perez

Following in the footsteps of Arnaud Massy, who moved to Scotland and became the first Frenchman to win the Open Championship in 1907, Victor Perez became the first player from his country to win the Alfred Dunhill Links Championship with a one-stroke victory over Matthew Southgate. For the previous 18 months Perez was living in Dundee where his girlfriend was studying to become a dentist. "There's nothing like a win," he said. "The confidence that you get from getting it done, it's so difficult at this level to win. Being my first year, I'm obviously delighted. It wasn't easy, Matt played amazing."

The 27-year-old rookie opened with a 64 on the Old Course at St. Andrews, then had a 68 at Carnoustie and another 64 at Kingsbarns. He started the final round tied with Southgate and on a cool, windy day the pair ended up in a head-to-head duel on the Old Course. A two-shot swing at the long 14th brought the pair back level. A poor chip led to a bogey for Southgate while Perez got down in two putts from off the green.

It was at the Road Hole, as so often, that decided the affair. Perez's drive found the fairway and led to a par, while Southgate was in the rough on the left. A fine approach avoided the famous bunker and found the green, but he took three putts from long range. Perez closed with a 70 for a 22-under-par total of 266, while Southgate had a 71. Paul Waring and Joakim Lagergren shared third place another stroke back, while Tommy Fleetwood joined the tie for fifth place with a closing 64.

His score proved decisive in the team event which he won with businessman Ogden Phipps on 39 under par with a closing 62. Rory McIlroy and his dad Gerry finished on the same mark but lost on count back due to Rory finishing with a 67 despite their final round team score of 61.

Mutuactivos Open de Espana
Madrid, Spain
Winner: Jon Rahm

In the year that Max Faulkner was remembered for winning the Open at Royal Portrush in 1951 as the championship returned to Northern Ireland for the first time since then, Jon Rahm also linked his name with that of the flamboyant Englishman. Not since Faulkner in 1952 and 1953 had somebody successfully defended the title at the Mutuactivos Open de Espana, but Rahm followed his win at the Centro Nacional in 2018 with a repeat victory across Madrid at Club de Campo.

Rahm, who won the Irish Open for the second time in three years earlier in the season, cruised to a five-stroke victory over Rafa Cabrera Bello with Samuel Del Val, in third place, Adri Arnaus, who tied for fourth, and Sergio Garcia, who shared seventh place, also representing the host country at the top of the leaderboard.

A fifth victory on the European Tour arrived for the 24-year-old Rahm in his 39th start on the circuit, 10 fewer than it took Seve Ballesteros to post the same number of wins at the start of his career. After rounds of 66 and 67, Rahm went five clear of Cabrera Bello with a 63 in the third round. He then eagled the fourth hole of the final round before adding four birdies, with his only dropped shot coming at the 17th. A 66 gave Rahm a 22-under-par total of 262, while Cabrera Bello, who was unable to put any pressure on the leader in the early stages, finished with five birdies in the last six holes for his own 66.

"I'm not happy I three-putted 17, I wanted to go bogey-free, but at the end of the day, I did the important thing," Rahm said. "I was able to successfully defend it and in front of a home crowd as well. To play this weekend for them is always really fun. I can't wait to come back next year and hopefully we'll make it three times."

Italian Open
Rome, Italy
Winner: Bernd Wiesberger

Bernd Wiesberger held off celebrating his 34th birthday earlier in the week but could do so with extra gusto after winning the Italian Open for his second Rolex Series title and his third victory of the season. Wiesberger won by one stroke over Matthew Fitzpatrick after making up three shots on the final day with a bogey-free 65 at Olgiato in Rome.

"It's been a great summer for me," said the Austrian, who missed seven months due to a wrist injury in 2018. "I've made a lot of progress since coming back from last year. I've won three times and it's been the same each time, I've just enjoyed being back in contention because I know how tough it was when I had to withdraw from these great events last year."

With earlier rounds of 66, 70 and 67, Wiesberger finished on a 16-under-par total of 268 at an event where home hero Francesco Molinari and Open champion Shane Lowry both missed the cut, while Justin Rose suffered a third-round 78. Wiesberger birdied four of the last five holes on the front nine to take the lead. Two more birdies followed at the 14th and 16th holes, where his tee shot at the par-three finished five feet away, but he also made some important par saves, not least at the last where he holed from four feet after going over the back of the green with his approach.

Fitzpatrick fell back with a double bogey at the ninth, but birdies at the 13th, 15th and 17th holes got him within one. An eagle-attempt from inside 10 feet at 17 lipped out as he finished as a runner-up for the third time this year. He was three ahead of Kurt Kitayama, with Matthias Schwab, Andrew Johnston and Robert MacIntyre sharing fourth place.

Amundi Open de France
Paris, France
Winner: Nicolas Colsaerts

Nicolas Colsaerts described himself as a "man on a mission" at the Amundi Open de France. He may not have won since 2012, but the 36-year-old Belgian had finished the last nine seasons inside the top 100 on the Race to Dubai and did not want to break the streak. He arrived in Paris in 114th place to play his ninth tournament in 10 weeks. Colsaerts led by three strokes going into the final round and by five after a birdie at the first hole, but the National course, scene of the 2018 Ryder Cup, still had a dramatic finale.

When Colsaerts bogeyed the 12th hole he was two behind George Coetzee, who had collected three birdies in a row from the ninth. Colsaerts responded by birdieing the 13th and chipping in for an eagle at the 14th before finding the water at the dangerous 15th and taking a double-bogey-six. At the same hole Coetzee ended his hopes by finding the water both off the tee and with his approach for a triple-bogey-seven.

Suddenly, Joachim B. Hansen was the leader after three birdies in a row from the 13th. The Dane, who had a quintuple-bogey-nine at the 13th on Saturday, took four putts to get down from short of the 17th green — the first of which ran over the green — for a six. Hansen closed with a 68 to take second place, one ahead of Coetzee, 71, and two in front of Kurt Kitayama, who finished in the top four for the second week running.

Colsaerts calmly parred the last three holes, a broad smile erupting as he putted up stone dead at the 18th. He had scores of 67, 66, 67 and 72 for a 12-under-par total of 272. "The French Open for me is very special because I'm French-speaking," he said. "I've been coming here for I don't know how many years, it's been a long road."

Portugal Masters
Vilamoura, Portugal
Winner: Steven Brown

Ranked 150th on the Race to Dubai entering the Portugal Masters, the last full-field event of the season on the European Tour, Steven Brown needed to do something spectacular to retain his card. The 32-year-old Englishman did just that. Three behind Brandon Stone at the turn on the final day, Brown birdied the 11th and hit a five wood to four feet for an eagle at the 12th hole.

Six pars from there and Brown could cancel his plans for the qualifying school and prepare to head to Turkey for the next Rolex Series event. After scores of 69 and 67, Brown had a magical weekend of 65 and 66 for a 17-under-par total of 267 to finish one ahead of Stone, who made two late bogeys in a closing 70 after three 66s, and Justin Walters, who scored 66. An emotional Walters, at 121st on the Race to Dubai at the start of the week, had only kept playing after the death of his father in August because he needed to secure his card for 2020.

"You just never know with this game," said Brown, who played in a winning GB&I Walker Cup team in 2011 but only qualified from the Challenge

Tour in 2017. "That shot I hit into 12 was probably the best shot I've ever hit. It couldn't have come off more perfect. It's crazy to think how well I've played the last month to how bad it was the first two-thirds of the year. I never thought this was going to happen. I was just counting down the days until Tour School to get my game ready for that."

WGC - HSBC Champions
Winner: Rory McIlroy

See American Tours chapter.

Turkish Airlines Open
Antalya, Turkey
Winner: Tyrrell Hatton

Thanks goodness for the floodlights at the Montgomerie Maxx Royal that allowed the third ever six-way playoff on the European Tour to conclude at the fourth extra hole. Tyrrell Hatton was left in the spotlight as the winner at the Turkish Airlines Open after Matthias Schwab missed from four feet for a par to continue the drama. Moments earlier Hatton had been shocked to miss from a couple of feet further away for a birdie. By birdieing the 18th in regulation play and then chipping in to stay alive on the first playoff hole, Hatton more than deserved this fourth victory and second Rolex Series title.

A wrist injury that has dogged the 28-year-old Englishman for a couple of years would require surgery in the winter. "It's so surreal," Hatton said. "I actually can't believe that I've won. It's been quite a difficult year in terms of things happening off course, though, the last month, I feel like I really found my game again. I said to a few people on my team that if I was lucky enough to win again, then I would definitely savor the moment."

With a $2 million first prize, there was the little matter of $1.5 million resting on the outcome of the playoff. It was a particularly cruel defeat for Schwab. The 24-year-old Austrian, only in his second year on tour, had led from start to finish, taking a three-shot lead into the final round when he scored 70. His bogey at the fourth playoff hole was his first in 24 attempts at a par-five hole during the week.

Erik van Rooyen eagled the last to make the playoff but exited on the first extra hole along with Benjamin Hebert and Victor Perez. American Kurt Kitayama closed with a 64 and then birdied the first extra hole but dropped out when Hatton and Schwab birdied the third extra hole. Hatton had rounds of 68, 68, 65 and 67 for a 20-under-par total of 268.

Nedbank Golf Challenge
Winner: Tommy Fleetwood

See African Sunshine Tour chapter.

DP World Tour Championship, Dubai
Dubai, United Arab Emirates
Winner: Jon Rahm

Both the result of the DP World Tour Championship and the Race to Dubai came down to a bunker shot and a four-foot birdie putt at the 72nd hole on the Earth course at Jumeirah Golf Estates. After the finely judged sand shot, Jon Rahm holed the putt to collect $5 million — $3 million for winning the season-ending tournament, the largest first prize in European Tour history, and $2 million for topping the season-long points table. A par at the final hole would have meant a playoff with Tommy Fleetwood, who also had the chance to scoop the double jackpot.

Rahm and Fleetwood both had to finish first or second to win the Race to Dubai, as long as they were not beaten by the other. Bernd Wiesberger, who led the Race entering the week, finished tied for 28th and in third place, joining Shane Lowry and Matthew Fitzpatrick in benefitting from the bonus pool.

Rahm began the final round tied for the lead with Mike Lorenzo-Vera, the Frenchman having been out in front since an opening 63. Rahm birdied five of the first seven holes, helped by 30-footers at the first and sixth holes and a 20-footer at the seventh, to lead by six. Lorenzo-Vera, without a win on the European Tour, closed with a 70 to finish in third place, two behind Rahm and in front of Rory McIlroy in fourth and defending champion Danny Willett in fifth.

Fleetwood was eight behind at one point but made a late charge. The 2017 Race winner came home in 31 with birdies at the last two holes for a 65 to post the target at 18 under par. Rahm had bogeyed the eighth and ninth holes and then had two birdies and two bogeys coming home. A three-putt at the 15th meant he came to the last needing a birdie to win the tournament for the second time and became only the second Spaniard, after six-time winner Seve Ballesteros, to end the season as European No. 1. Rahm had scores of 66, 69, 66 and 68 for a 19-under-par total of 269.

Rahm had not played golf for six weeks since retaining his national Open, opting to rest up prior to his imminent wedding. "You dream of making birdies on 18 to win a tournament," said the 25-year-old. "And how I was playing early on, I was hoping not to need that, but it happened, and I came through when I needed it and really proud of myself for that."

Start of 2019-20 Season

Alfred Dunhill Championship
Winner: Pablo Larrazabal

See African Sunshine Tour chapter.

AfrAsia Bank Mauritius Open
Winner: Rasmus Hojgaard

See African Sunshine Tour chapter.

Australian PGA Championship
Winner: Adam Scotts

See Australasian Tour chapter.

Challenge Tour

Two victories in three starts earned Francesco Laporta the 2019 Road to Mallorca No. 1 spot. The Italian found form at the perfect time after finishing in a tie for seventh place at his national Open, a Rolex Series event on the European Tour. He then won his maiden title on the Challenge Tour at the Hainan Open before claiming the Grand Final itself at the new venue of Alcanada on Mallorca. In windy conditions, with rain causing a suspension on the final day, Laporta led from wire-to-wire, winning by two strokes over Sebastian Heisele and Robin Sciot-Siegrist.

"I came here just to fight for the number one spot, and I fought really hard," said Laporta. "I played some of my best golf of the year this week on a tough course under tough conditions. It feels great and I'm really happy about the week. It's just a dream. Dreams come true. To put another Italian name on the board of Challenge Tour number ones with people like Edoardo Molinari and Andrea Pavan, I'm really happy about that."

The 29-year-old spent much of his early life in South Africa, where he first played golf and later spent three years on the Sunshine Tour. He played one season on the European Tour in 2016 after coming through the qualifying school but returned to the Challenge Tour the following year.

Heisele, the German who grew up in Dubai and is a multiple club champion at Emirates, won the Open de Bretagne and finished fourth on the Ranking, but France's Sciot-Siegrist just missed out on his card. He had needed to finish second on his own at the Grand Final to dislodge Spain's Sebastian Garcia Rodriguez from 15th place on the Ranking and the last card on offer.

Scotland's Calum Hill finished runner-up to Laporta, also with two wins, at the Euram Bank Open and the Made in Denmark Challenge. Antoine Rozner was another two-time winner early in the season at the Challenge de Espana and Prague Golf Challenge.

Richard Bland returned to the European Tour at the age of 46, finishing third on the Ranking. The winner of the 2001 Grand Final had no victories but was a runner-up four times and had three other top-10s. Compatriot Matthew Jordan, who won the Italian Challenge in his seventh start on the circuit, secured his card in his rookie season as a professional, while Jack Senior also qualified.

Adrian Meronk became the first Polish player to win a European Tour-sanctioned event at the Open de Portugal and the first to secure a full card for the European Tour by finishing fifth on the Ranking. Others to earn their playing privileges for the main circuit for 2020 were France's Robin Roussel, Portugal's Ricardo Santos, Northern Ireland's Cormac Sharvin, Oliver Farr, of Wales, Netherlands' Darius van Driel, winner of the Rolex Trophy, and Scotland's Conor Syme.

Denmark's Benjamin Poke ended his rookie season on the Challenge Tour by winning the qualifying school at Lumine by six strokes over former three-time European Tour winner Gregory Havret. Poke's 18-year-old compatriot Rasmus Hojgaard also secured one of the 28 cards on offer, while his identical twin Nicolai earned a place on the Challenge Tour in 2020.

Rasmus wasted no time in bettering Nicolai's runner-up finish at the KLM Open by winning the AfrAsia Bank Mauritius Open after a playoff that included Rozner. Hojgaard became the first player born in the 21st century to win on the European Tour.

9. Asia/Japan Tours

A golfer's year can't get much better than this: Thailand's Jazz Janewattananond, 23, had two victories, seven other top-10 finishes, won a berth in the Open Championship and locked up the Asian Tour's Order of Merit title, and there were still two tournaments to go. And he won both of them, as well.

And it all started out almost as an afterthought.

(His real name is Atiwit. His father, who loved jazz, gave him the nickname.)

Janewattananond entered the Asian Tour's season-opening SMBC Singapore Open, which was co-sanctioned also by the Japan and European tours. It offered four qualifying spots for the Open Championship. "I wasn't expecting to win, actually," he said. "I was going for the Open ticket." Then he surged, came from behind in the final round, and won both.

Said Janewattananond: "When I was younger, I always say I want to be the first Thai to play on the PGA Tour and the first Thai to win a major."

He later also won the Kolon Korea Open. His two wins, along with two in earlier years, made him at the age of 23 years, six months and 27 days the youngest ever to have four wins on the Asian Tour.

Janewattananond's play put him on the world stage. In the PGA Championship at brutal Bethpage Black on Long Island, New York, he was tied for second in the third round, seven shots behind Brooks Koepka. He closed with a 77, tying for 14th at two-over 282, 10 strokes behind Koepka. But he had New York fans with him. They were trying to shout out his name — Janewattananond. "But it didn't come out right," he said. He also played in the Open Championship, missing the cut.

In December, Janewattananond won the BNI Indonesian Masters, rising to 45th in the World Ranking, the third Thai to crack the top 50 since Thongchai Jaidee in 2009 and Kiradech Aphibarnrat in 2015. The win got him into the 2020 Masters. Then the following week he won the final tournament of 2019, the Thailand Masters.

"The win in Singapore was certainly the highlight of the year for me," Janewattananond said, "because I won early in the season and that victory broke me into the world's top 100 then. It opened doors for me and I took advantage of them."

Janewattananond wasn't the only young star in Asia. There was the case of Korea's Joohyung Kim, coming from behind on the final hole to win the Panasonic Open India — at age 17 years, 149 days. (He was the tour's second youngest ever, after Thailand's Chinnarat Phadungsil at 17 years, five days.

Elsewhere on the Asian Tour:

Thailand's Sadom Kaewkanjana can be tied but can't ever be beaten on this record. Kaewkanjana, 20, was making his tour debut in the Bangabandhu Cup Golf Open in April and he won it. "I didn't expect to do so well," said Kaewkanjana, who had entered "Just to keep my [playing] card for next season."

The Hong Kong Open, scheduled for late November, was postponed because of civic unrest.

Indonesia's Rory Hie left no emotion unturned when he scored his first tour victory, taking the Classic Golf & Country Club International Championship. Said Hie: "Oh, my God! I'm finally an Asian Tour champion!"

If there were a vote for Least Likely to Succeed, Scotland's Stephen Gallacher would have won it at the Hero India Open. Gallacher, 44, tied for the lead in the first round, trailed by seven in the second, trailed by three in the third, was contending in the fourth when he quadruple-bogeyed No. 7 and was five behind at No. 8. And birdied the 17th and 18th and won.

Puzzle of the Year: Finland's Mikko Korhonen, on beating France's Benjamin Hebert and Spain's Jorge Campillo on the first playoff hole in the Volvo China Open: "I don't know how I did it."

On the Japan Tour:

Japan's Shugo Imahira and South Africa's Shaun Norris staged a repeat performance on the Japan Tour in 2019, finishing 1-2 on the money list for the second straight year at the end of a modest 25-tournament season that had 21 different winners, only six of them first-timers.

The back-to-back No. 1s of the 27-year-old Imahira put him in the exclusive company of Japan greats Isao Aoki, Masashi Ozaki, Tsuneyuki Nakajima and Shingo Katayama, the only other players who won consecutive victories in tour history. Strangely, both of Imahira's wins came in the year's two tournaments — the Bridgestone Open and Dunlop Phoenix — which were shortened because of weather problems. Otherwise, he compiled his ¥168,049,312 earnings primarily via his five runner-up and 16 top-10 finishes. He played in all 25 events. Norris made a strong run at Imahira over the last five tournaments. He placed second twice, tied for third and fourth in two other events, and suffered a fatal blow to his bid when illness forced him out of the fifth, the rich Dunlop Phoenix.

The season saw the return of two former No. 1s to victory acclaim. The highly popular Ryo Ishikawa, who only played twice before June, won an unequaled three times, including the Japan PGA Championship, his first major title, and the Nippon Series for a second time. The 2009 money leader finished third on the money list. South Korea's Kyungtae Kim, the top dog in 2010 and 2015, emerged from a fruitless spell with victory in the Casio World, his first since early 2016.

A future star may well have been born when 21-year-old Takumi Kanaya captured the long-standing Taiheiyo Masters, becoming just the fourth amateur in tour history to win a tour event. The other three — Hideki Matsuyama, Ryo Ishikawa and Masahiro Kuramoto — all went on to fine pro careers. Korean-American Chan Kim made the Japan Open Championship his fourth Japan Tour title and Mikumu Horikawa won the Tour Championship.

Asian Tour

SMBC Singapore Open
Singapore
Winner: Jazz Janewattananond

Thai whiz kid Jazz Janewattananond was actually aiming at the Open Championship when he teed off in the SMBC Singapore Open. Happily for him, he hit both.

The Singapore Open, launching the 2019 Asian Tour in January, was also co-sanctioned by the European and Japan tours, and also served as a qualifier for the Open in July. Which is what brought Janewattananond to Singapore.

"I wasn't expecting to win, actually," said Janewattananond, 23. "I was going for the Open ticket. I felt the pressure when I got to the back nine today."

Janewattananond came from behind in the final round to take the Singapore and one of the four qualifier spots available for the Open. He shot the par-71 Sentosa in 68-68-65-65–266, 18 under and two better than Japan's Yoshinori Fujimoto and England's Paul Casey. This would be Janewattananond's second Open Championship. He missed the cut in 2018. The other three qualifier spots were taken by Fujimoto, Korea's Doyeob Mun and Thailand's Prom Meesawat.

Janewattananond hung close for the first three rounds. Thailand's Poom Saksansin and Japan's Taihei Sato shared the first-round lead at six-under 65. Fujimoto led through the middle rounds with 67-66. Janewattananond stuck tight with his 68-68-65, then sprinted in the final round. A run of five birdies, at Nos. 1, 2, 4, 6 and 8, gave him an outward 31. He bogeyed the 13th, then birdied 16 and 18 for the Singapore Open and the Open Championship ticket. The win, the biggest of his career, would move him into the top 100 in the World Ranking.

"Breaking into the top 100 is a great deal for me," Janewattananond said. "When I was younger, I always say I want to be the first Thai to play on the PGA Tour and the first Thai to win a major."

Well, he had taken the first steps.

ISPS Handa World Super 6 Perth
Winner: Ryan Fox

See Australasian Tour chapter.

100th New Zealand Open
Winner: Zach Murray

See Australasian Tour chapter.

Maybank Championship
Kuala Lumpur, Malaysia
Winner: Scott Hend

Poor Nacho Elvira. Not that the Spaniard could have done anything about it, but he never got the hints — the shattering thunderclap when he was hitting at the final hole, and Scott Hend's bounce off the tree in the playoff. It was clear: The gods had stamped this Maybank Championship "Reserved for Scott Hend."

"I had the luck today, unfortunately for Nacho," the 45-year-old Australian granted. "His time will come."

Hend trailed all the way — "I'm a grinder and a fighter," he said — and was three behind Elvira starting the final round. And after he had finished, he was still some 90 minutes and three feet from winning the Asian-European Tour co-sanctioned tournament.

Hend was the leader in the clubhouse at 15-under 273 (69-70-67-67 at the par-72 Saujana Golf and Country Club). Next came the gods' first trick. Elvira, who had shot 65-72-66, needed a birdie at the par-five 18th to tie Hend. But just as he was hitting a gentle wedge to the green, a powerful thunderclap came crashing down. He flinched. His ball fizzled out 30 feet short of the cup. Then came the long wait.

Elvira then came back out and rolled that 30-footer in like a gimme for a 70 and tied Hend. "The gods did give me one back with that putt," Elvira noted.

The gods' next frolic: In the playoff, at the 18th, Elvira drove into a fairway bunker, but Hend's tee shot, rocketing for trouble, caromed off a tree and into the fairway. Hend next caught a greenside bunker, then splashed out to three feet. After Elvira settled for a par, Hend holed the three-footer for a birdie and his third European title and 10th Asian win.

"I think I played great all week," Elvira said. "I'm happy that my game has finally showed a little bit of consistency."

"Obviously I had a bit of luck on the playoff hole," said Hend. "If you don't have any luck, you won't win."

Hero Indian Open
New Delhi, India
Winner: Stephen Gallacher

One day, in all their digging and studying, etymologists might well discover that the good Scottish name "Gallacher" came from "they who see the good in things, no matter what." Or some such.

How else to explain the bright outlook of Stephen Gallacher in the face of calamity in the Hero Indian Open. Gallacher, 44, had not won in five years; had gone from a tie for the lead in the first round to trailing by seven in the second, to trailing by three in the third, and was contending in the fourth when he quadruple-bogeyed the par-four No. 7. All told, it was enough to crush the ordinary soul. But said Gallacher: "I stood on the eighth tee and saw I was only five shots behind."

Only five behind? With 11 to go? Thus fortified, Gallacher proceeded to birdie Nos. 9, 10 and 12, bogey 14, and birdie 15, 17 and 18 for a one-under 71 and a one-shot win over Japan's Masahiro Kawamura in the co-sanctioned Asian-European tour event. Along the way, Gallacher shot the DLF Golf and Country Club in 67-74-67-71–279, nine under, for his first win in India and fourth European title.

"I'm really proud of what I did out there today," Gallacher conceded. And he got some big help when American Julian Suri, leading by three, authored a quadruple-bogey-eight of his own at the 14th.

"When I birdied 15, I saw that Julian had come back," Gallacher said. "And when I got to the 16th green, I was tied for the lead. I just tried to finish as strong as I could, and I did that."

And with birdies at the 17th and 18th, which led to the question, "What's in a name?" In this case, the answer was "Winner."

Bangabandhu Cup Golf Open
Dhaka, Bangladesh
Winner: Sadom Kaewkanjana

Thailand's Sadom Kaewkanjana, a rookie of a mere 20, was making his debut on the Asian Tour in the Bangabandhu Cup Golf Open, the national championship of Bangladesh, and he figured he was aiming high. "Just to keep my [playing] card for next season," he said.

He hit even higher. He won.

"I didn't expect to do so well," said Kaewkanjana, who set a record at Kurmitola Golf Club: No qualifying school graduate ever won so fast on the Asian Tour.

With a card of 65-62-68-70, Kaewkanjana trailed Australia's Maverick Antcliff's 63 by two in the first round, then led the rest of the way, posting a 19-under 265 to win by one over India's Ajeetesh Sandhu. But it was touch-and-go in the final round.

Kaewkanjana led by two going into the final round and birdied the first two holes. Then he went sour. "My putter went cold after the first three holes," he said, "but thankfully I got it back in my closing three holes."

It was a bad time for a game to let down. Kaewkanjana parred along till he got to the par-four 13th and then posted three straight bogeys, throwing the door wide open to Sandhu, who had made three straight birdies from No. 7. The issue was resolved when Sandhu bogeyed the 17th — his first in 63 holes — while Kaewkanjana birdied 16, from 10 feet, and 17 from 20 to regain the lead, and manufactured a clutch par at the par-four 18th. He had driven behind a tree on the left, had to chip out into the fairway, then drilled his third to eight feet and holed the putt for a par, a 70 and his debut victory.

"Winning my first start on the Asian Tour — I feel very happy," Kaewkanjana said. "I will remember all the good memories here."

Volvo China Open
Shenzhen, China
Winner: Mikko Korhonen

For those who enjoy the rich smorgasbord of golf, this one was tailor-made: a Finn, a Frenchman and a Spaniard as the final principals in a tournament co-sanctioned by the Asian Tour, the European Tour and the China Golf Association, and played in China.

And for those who like a dash of suspense as well, in the final round the three were tied for the lead — standing on the 17th tee. Things don't get much tighter than that. But they did.

This was the Volvo China Open at Genzon Golf Club at Shenzhen. France's Benjamin Hebert had started the final round with a three-shot lead on Finland's Mikko Korhonen and Spain's Jorge Campillo. Then, by the turn, his lead was down to one on Campillo and two on Korhonen. Campillo, who won the Trophee Hassan II the previous week, surged ahead with three straight birdies from the 10th. Then bogeys at 14 and 15 left him with a 67 and the odd man out at 19 under. "I had the tournament in my hands, but missed a few shots in the middle of my round," said Campillo.

Korhonen birdied 10, 11, 13 and 17 for a 66 and was 20 under. Hebert had got within one of him with a birdie at 16, then drove the green at the par-four 18th and two-putted for birdie for a 69, and tied Korhonen at 268. Korhonen shot 68-69-65-66, and Hebert 67-68-64-69.

The playoff was quick. Korhonen won on the first extra hole with a chip-and-putt birdie at the 18th.

Said Hebert: "Looking at the way I played, I'm happy. I couldn't really find my rhythm."

Said Korhonen, on scoring his second win: "I don't know how I did it. It was my first time in a playoff and I had nothing to lose. I just had to make birdie. It was a battle all day."

GS Caltex Maekyung Open
Seongnam, Korea
Winner: Tae Hee Lee

Grudging matches don't come any more grudging than did the 38th GS Caltex Maekyung Open.

The Maekyung wasn't so much a 72-hole tournament as it was a 72-hole playoff. Or rather, a 75-hole playoff, given the extra holes Tae Hee Lee had to go before notching his first Asian Tour victory. It was at the third playoff hole that he finally broke away from Finland's Janne Kaske, to whom he had been attached for the last 57 of the 75 holes at Namseoul Country Club.

"Today," said Lee, nearing 27, "is the most beautiful day of my life."

Lee tied for the first-round lead at four-under 67 with Gowoong Choi, Kyeongjun Lee and Sungho Lee. Kaske, 32, a two-time winner on the Asian Developmental Tour, was at 70. Lee shot 69 in the second round, posting three birdies and a bogey coming in, and Kaske poured in six birdies against a bogey for a 66 to tie him at six-under 136. Both followed with 68s and were tied at nine under and leading by four and still tied going into the final round.

"It looked like I was going to win pretty easily at some point," Kaske said. "But I started to make stupid mistakes. I think it switched about five times in the last hour."

The fourth round was a scorekeeper's carnival. Lee birdied Nos. 1 and 4, bogeyed No. 7 and parred through the 13th. Kaske birdied No. 5, eagled No. 7 on a 120-yard hole-out, bogeyed No. 9 and birdied the 12th. Through it, Lee led by two, then one; Kaske led by two, then one, then two. At the par-five 14th, Lee birdied and Kaske bogeyed and they were tied again. In lockstep, they finished par-bogey-bogey-par, tying with 71s and at nine-under 275.

In the incredible playoff at the 18th, they tied with double bogeys on the first trip, tied with bogeys on the second, and Lee won it with a birdie from six feet on the third. "It's a moment," Lee said, "that I will treasure forever."

Asia-Pacific Diamond Cup
Winner: Yosuke Asaji

See Japan Tour section.

Kolon Korea Open
Cheonan, Korea
Winner: Jazz Janewattananond

Jazz Janewattananond, the young Thai star, had been cruising along comfortably in the Kolon Korea Open at Woo Jeong Hills. Then suddenly, it was a matter of simple, brutal arithmetic at the final hole. But he didn't realize just how simple and brutal.

"There aren't many scoreboards out there," said Janewattananond. "I told myself not to think about it."

There's always a helpful fan, however. That's how he discovered that his comforting five-shot lead had shrunk to one. "Because someone shouted," he said.

Janewattananond was more than comfortable. "I was flying," he said. He led by two strokes entering the last round and birdies at Nos. 2, 5 and 7 had him ahead by five. Then came the crash. At the par-four 11th, his approach out of rough from a downhill lie didn't carry the water. Then he three-putted. "I did feel the nerves, especially after that triple bogey," Janewattananond said. "I didn't know what was going on for a moment." His lead was down to one. But Innchoon Hwang, playing up ahead at the 13th, then missed a short par putt and bogeyed. Janewattananond, still unsettled, bogeyed the 14th on a three-putt and led by one.

As to the crisis at the final hole, a par-five: Thinking Innchoon would birdie it up ahead of him, Janewattananond opted to try for a birdie himself and not play safe for a par, and hit his driver off the tee. He caught the rough anyway, but then saw Hwang miss his birdie putt and chose to lay up and play for the par. He got it, wrapping up a card of 70-67-69-72, for a six-under 278, edging Hwang (70) by one.

"I am really proud of myself that I managed to get the job done," said Janewattananond, on taking his second victory of the season, and — at the age of 23 years, 6 months and 27 days — becoming the youngest ever to have four wins on the Asian Tour.

Sarawak Championship
Sarawak, Malaysia
Winner: Andrew Dodt

For those who like their golf unsettled, the Sarawak Championship was their piece of cake. There were nine different leaders — two three-way ties, one two-way tie and only one solo leader, and then it was only fitting that a playoff had to decide it, and that's when Australia's Andrew Dodt finally took the only lead that really mattered. It was his third Asian Tour win, but first in four years, and in his first outing since an injury in the spring. But first he had to fret in the clubhouse, sweating out Richard T. Lee's finish.

"Knowing I had to get in the playoff was hard because I probably didn't expect Richard to make eagle with a three wood in regulation," Dodt said. "But golf is a funny game and you have to expect the unexpected."

Dodt, playing in the next-to-last group, stayed close for three rounds, then closed with a flawless eight-under 64 that included five straight birdies from No. 8 for the clubhouse lead at 24-under 264. Lee, in the final grouping and needing an eagle at the par-five 18th to tie Dodt, hit a three-wood second from 275 yards to eight feet and got his 66–264. In the playoff at the 18th, both hit the fairway. Dodt laid up to about 75 yards, while Lee went for the green in two, missed to the right, then chipped to 12 feet. Lee's birdie try lipped out. Dodt, who had chipped to two feet, holed out for his birdie and the win. Mica Lauren Shin shot 65 and finished a stroke back.

"Honestly," Lee said, "losing in the playoff didn't really upset me because … to finish with that eagle, I am pretty pleased with how I performed this week."

Said Dodt: "I had a two-month injury in April. It's probably a good re-set as I gave myself a break and got the love of the game back."

Bank BRI Indonesia Open
Jakarta, Indonesia
Winner: Miguel Carballo

It's one of golf's crueler truths that one golfer's miracle very often is another's calamity. And so it was in the Bank BRI Indonesia Open.

Argentina's Miguel Carballo, veteran pro, age 40, was seeking his first win on the Asian Tour. He started the final round in second place, chasing Naraajie Emerald Ramadhanputra, an Indonesian kid of 19 and an amateur, who was leading by six strokes. It was a classic case of a pro about to be embarrassed by a precocious kid.

To tighten the drama: Naraajie was also about to become the first Indonesian in almost 30 years to win the Indonesian national championship. After starting 66-69, he thumped the par-72 Pondok Indah Course for a 63 in the third round and the six-stroke lead. This one was surely over, except for the formality of a final round. But this was golf. A puff of wind here, a crazy bounce there, and poof.

And that was precisely the fate of the unfortunate Naraajie. He started the final round at 18 under, and after an early bogey-birdie exchange was still 18 under through No. 8. Then the catastrophe: He stumbled to five bogeys over eight holes from No. 9. He caught his breath with a birdie at the 17th, then double-bogeyed the 18th for a 78 and finished fourth.

"I just kind of lost my focus on those last six holes," Naraajie said.

That was the catastrophe. So it was that while Naraajie was struggling, Carballo was on his game. He birdied Nos. 1, 4 and 6 going out, and 10 and 13 coming home, wrapping up a card of 69-69-66-67 for a 17-under 271 and a three-stroke win over Korea's Yikeun Chang (64). "I needed a solid result like this to regain my confidence," Chang said.

Said Carballo, "Unfortunately for Naraajie, he did not play well and I capitalized it."

Yeangder Tournament Players Championship
Linkou, Chinese Taipei
Winner: Yikeun Chang

It was the fourth time that was the charm — not the third — for Yikeun Chang. Three times he had almost won, only to see the win slip away, leaving him second. This included the Indonesian Open just a week ago. For his four years on the Asian Tour, he had been measuring his career in losses and near-misses. "I just couldn't get it done," Chang said.

Then came the Yeangder Tournament Players Championship at Linkou International.

"It feels really nice to get it done now," he understated.

Chang, 25, won by a comfortable three shots — the first Korean to win it — but not before this one, too, had threatened to get away. Chang was a co-leader at the halfway point with his 67-66, 11 under. Then in the third round, eight birdies lifted him to a three-stroke lead, a commanding lead until he double-bogeyed the par-five 18th. "I hit two perfect shots," Chang said, "but the second one went over like about 10 yards, right behind the tree." He shot 68 and tied for second with Shih-Chang Chan (68). Wen-Tang Lin, who started the third with five straight birdies, shot 65 and at 16 under, led by one.

But Lin cooled a bit in the final round, and his two-birdie, two-bogey par 72 opened the door. Chang stepped through. He birdied three of the first four holes and three straight from the 10th for a confident, bogey-free 66 and 21-under 267, three better over yet another whiz kid, Thailand's Kosuke Hamamoto, 20, who went the last 52 holes without a bogey. "I was quite nervous going out today," he said. "I'm just happy I got it done."

Chang found that golf can be, if not an easy game, at least a fundamental one. Said Chang: "I putted well. I hit the ball well, and I placed it in the right places."

Classic Golf & Country Club International Championship
Gurgaon, India
Winner: Rory Hie

Scoring that first win can be a pretty heady experience. Sometimes a golfer can barely find the words. But Rory Hie had no trouble. On taking the inaugural Classic Golf & Country Club International Championship, he said it all in nine words, setting the record for joy, relief, passion and brevity.

"Oh, my God!" Hie gushed. "I'm finally an Asian Tour champion!"

Then he protested: "I don't know what I did to deserve this." His scorecard told him: 64-68-67-68, for a 21-under 267 and a two-stroke victory on the par-72 Classic, a Jack Nicklaus course in northern India, site of three earlier Asian Tour events.

Hie opened the first round with five straight pars then made eight birdies over the last 13 holes for the 64 and a two-stroke lead in the first round. Gareth Paddison was crackling with a front-nine 29, but triple-bogeyed his 10th and shot 69.

Hie, the first Indonesian to win on the Asian Tour, got two of his three bogeys of the tournament in the second round, but birdied four of his last seven holes for the 68. In the third, he made three birdies on the front nine and three on the back for a 67, getting to 17 under, one ahead of India's Rashid Khan (66). Then as a golfer trying for his first win and leading by a shot, Hie came to the toughest part of the tournament — the final round.

"I was so nervous coming into today," Hie said. "I was just shaking, even on the driving range."

But he birdied No. 1, parred the next 11, and birdied 13, 14 and 15. He shot 68 for a 21-under 267 and won by two over Khan (69) and Korea's Byungjun Kim (67). And Hie dedicated his first victory to Aria Irawan, a good friend and fellow pro who passed away in April.

"I'm sure he's proud of me right now," said Hie.

Shinhan Donghae Open
Incheon, Korea
Winner: Jbe' Kruger

It may be carrying a notion too far, but Jbe' Kruger, of South Africa, said it was essentially "homecookin'" that won him the Shinhan Donghae Open in Korea. "This course is a Jack Nicklaus-design course," said Kruger, on ending his seven-year win drought on the Asian Tour. "It's the same as my own course ... the same lines, the same kind of grass. Everything is exactly the same and it almost feels like a home away from home."

This would be the Bear's Best CheongNa Golf Club at Incheon, a par-71, hosting the Shinhan, co-sanctioned by the Asian, Korean and Japan tours. Kruger didn't come to the front till the final round. Kruger opened with a

69, three off the co-leaders, Korean-American Chan Kim and Japan's Shugo Imahira, at 66. At No. 17 in the second round he made his fourth and final bogey of the tournament. He would go the final 37 holes bogey-free. He was chasing Scott Vincent, the only Zimbabwean on the Asian Tour and Rookie of the Year in 2016. Vincent led through the middle rounds with 67-68.

In the final round, as Vincent was cooling to a par-71, Kruger hit a key point at No. 7, when he notched his second birdie. "I could feel the momentum," he said. Then he birdied No. 8.

"After the 11th," he said, on his fourth birdie, "I had a good feeling it was my time again."

It was. Birdies at 15 and 16 locked it up, on a 65 for a 15-under 264 and a two-stroke win over Kim, who also shot 65. And it made for an odd record for Vincent, who finished third at 11 under. In his four straight Shinhan Opens, starting in 2016, he tied for second, tied for third, finished solo second and now solo third.

"Just tough," Vincent said. "But hey, I still haven't finished outside of the top three, so still not bad."

Panasonic Open Golf Championship
Winner: Toshinori Muto

See Japan Tour section.

Mercuries Taiwan Masters
Tamsui, Chinese Taipei
Winner: Suradit Yongcharoenchai

Come the final round of the Mercuries Taiwan Masters, and Thailand's Suradit Yongcharoenchai was following one of golf's treasured dictates: He was keeping his head down. And when he finally looked up, he had his first Asian Tour victory.

Well, there was, of course, a bit more to it than that.

Yongcharoenchai parred the final hole for a card of 71-69-68-70–278, 10 under at the Taiwan Golf and Country Club, and won by a stroke. But first there was that excruciating lifetime wait over the next half hour. Others still had a clear shot at him.

There was Brazil's Adilson Da Silva, four off the final-round lead. "Cheeky," he said, of his target score. He posted four birdies through the 13th but bogeyed the 14th, shot 68 and fell short, tying for second at 279. "Overall," he said, "I was happy with myself."

India's Ajeetesh Sandhu, starting as co-leader at nine under with the Philippines' Miguel Tabuena, birded 13, double-bogeyed the par-four 16th, then birdied 18 for a 72. He also tied for second. "I made two wrong decisions on 16...," he said, "and that really cost me the tournament."

Then Tabuena: After four birdies and two bogeys, he was two under through the 16th. Then he bogeyed 17 and 18 for a 72 and a tie. "I really struggled with the greens," said Tabuena. "A bit too slow. But that's not an excuse."

Yongcharoenchai, starting the final round a stroke behind, birdied No. 3 but took a sobering double bogey at No. 4. "At that point," he said, "I was just telling myself to play my own game." Regrouping, he birdied Nos. 6, 7 and 9, and added the 13th coming in. A bogey at the 14th slowed him. He shot 70 for his 278.

"I'm an Asian Tour winner now," Yongcharoenchai said. "All these years and I'm glad I've been finally rewarded."

Thailand Open
Chachoengsao, Thailand
Winner: John Catlin

For John Catlin, of Sacramento, California — some 8,000 miles away — the Thailand Open was a home game, with all the warm feelings that go with that notion. "It means a lot to me, winning in Thailand," Catlin said. "I've lived here for three years … this place is starting to feel like a second home. To win the national open here means the world to me."

This Catlin did with a superbly crafted birdie on the first hole of a playoff against India's Shiv Kapur and a real native son, Pavit Tangkamolprasert. It was Catlin's fourth Asian Tour win. He'd won the first three in 2018.

Catlin, who shot Thai Country Club in 67-70-69-67, for an 11-under 273 total, narrowly missed winning in regulation when his chip shot at the 18th slid by an inch from the hole. "I really thought it was going in," Catlin said. "I was pretty nervous going into the playoff."

Kapur charged to the finish with a sizzling final nine, getting birdies at 10 and 11 and, after a bogey at the 12th, going birdie-eagle-birdie-birdie from the 13th for a 65 to tie Catlin. "I started thinking," said Kapur, "oh, now I have a chance to go for the title."

Tangkamolprasert surprised himself. "I didn't expect to play so good and give myself a chance to win," he said. He closed with a bogey-free 65.

In the playoff at the 466-yard, par-four 18th, Kapur drove into the left rough, Tangkamolprasert into the right rough, and Catlin hit to the left side of the fairway. Kapur's bold approach through the trees ended up 80 feet from the flag. Tangkamolprasert's second caught a bunker, leaving him a 35-yard shot. His sand shot left him 12 feet from the cup.

Catlin had put his 200-yard approach comfortably on and he holed the birdie putt for the win. In a playoff, he said, "You got to play like your back's against the wall."

Panasonic Open India
Gurgaon, India
Winner: Joohyung Kim

A rip of birdies, a spot of luck, a boyish grin, and the kid was a winner on the Asian Tour.

That was a landmark victory for Korea's Joohyung Kim in the Panasonic Open India, considering that he trailed all the way and came from behind at the final hole; that he was playing against seasoned pros, and that he was making just his third start on the Asian Tour. And also considering that he was 17 years old.

"I'm really speechless," said Kim, the second youngest ever to win on the tour, at 17 years and 149 days. Thailand's Chinnarat Phadungsil was the youngest, at 17 years, five days, when he won the Double A International Open in 2005.

Kim shot 70-68-65 to win by one at 13-under 203. (The tournament was reduced to three rounds because of smog.)

"It's been a dream of mine to play on the Asian Tour ever since I was young," Kim said. "And it's really wonderful to be in contention and win. I cannot describe the feeling now."

He was already having a strong year. He'd won three times on the Asian Development Tour, gaining his Asian Tour playing card. Then he showed the game and poise of a veteran in his first two starts, finishing a solo third at 13 under in the Indonesia Open and tying for sixth at nine under in the Thailand Open.

He was deep in the hunt from the beginning in the Panasonic at the par-72 Classic Golf and Country Club. His 70-68 opening had him just four behind a three-way tie of veterans — Shiv Kapur (67-67), Terry Pilkadaris (66-68) and Adam Blyth (71-63). Kapur, who tied for second in the Thailand Open the previous week, led by one coming to the par-five 18th. But he drove out of bounds, double-bogeyed, shot 70 and tied for second with India's Chikkarangappa S., one behind Kim.

Kim was blazing through the final round, birdieing seven of the first 10 holes. Then a pinch of nerves hit. "I kind of struggled in my back nine, knowing I was in contention," Kim said. "But I managed ... and now I'm a winner."

Sabah Masters
Sabah, Malaysia
Winner: Pavit Tangkamolprasert

It was all a matter of timing for Thailand's Pavit Tangkamolprasert in the inaugural Sabah Masters. Just in time, that is. Tangkamolprasert was packed and about to leave for the airport when an official caught up with him to say there was going to be a playoff — and that he was in it.

"I really didn't expect this," Tangkamolprasert said. "It's really incredible."

It became even more incredible. Tangkamolprasert, 30, quickly changed back into his golf clothes, went out and chipped in for birdie on the second extra hole to take his second Asian Tour title. He shot Sutera Harbor Golf and Country Club in 73-66-67-65 to join the tie at 13-under 271.

The Sabah was up for grabs all the way, starting with a four-way traffic jam in the first round. Thailand's Phachara Khongwatmai, Indonesia's Joshua Andrew Wirawan and Australians Aaron Wilkin and David Gleeson tied at five-under 66.

Khongwatmai, 20, completed his rain-interrupted second round on Saturday morning for a 67 and a two-stroke lead, then trailed Gleeson, who took a one-stroke lead with a 68 in the third. Things just got more tangled in the fourth, ending up in a four-way tie at 13-under 271. India's Aman Raj came from five off the lead with a 63 to join the crowd. With him were Khongwatmai, 67, Gleeson, 68, and Tangkamolprasert, who shot 65 then packed his bags, figuring he was out of it.

"This is golf," Tangkamolprasert was to say. "You never know what will happen until the last minute."

Granted. What did happen was that Raj left the playoff with a bogey on the first hole. At the second, also at No. 18, all three missed the green. Khongwatmai and Gleeson missed their chips. And Tangkamolprasert didn't, from 15 yards.

"In golf, you just got to keep trying," he said. "You don't know when it will come, so you need to keep trying."

AfrAsia Bank Mauritius Open
Winner: Rasmus Hojgaard

See African Sunshine Tour chapter.

BNI Indonesian Masters
Jakarta, Indonesia
Winner: Jazz Janewattananond

The BNI Indonesian Masters, the next-to-last event on the 2019 Asian Tour, was expected to be a showcase for Joohyung Kim, the Korean sensation who won his first pro event a month earlier, at age 17. Instead, it was a command performance by Thai whiz Jazz Janewattananond, 24, whose magic number was 45.

When the Official World Golf Ranking came out on December 15, after his romp in this Indonesian Masters, there he was — 45th in the world. He was the third Thai to crack the top 50 in the World Ranking, after Thongchai Jaidee in 2009 and Kiradech Aphibarnrat in 2015.

And Janewattananond announced his arrival with a breezy five-stroke win.

Janewattananond got off to a 68-70 start, encouraging but not exceptional at the par-72 Royale Jakarta. Then he got exceptional in the third round, rocketing to a 10-under 62 and a one-stroke lead. It was fueled by a searing seven-under rampage across seven holes from No. 8 — birdie-eagle-birdie-par-eagle-par-birdie. And the 62 included a bogey.

"I put in a new putter today," Janewattananond cracked. "Maybe I'll stick with it tomorrow."

He cooled to a 65 in the final round. He birdied three of four from No. 6, then pulled ahead by four with another eagle at the par-five 12th, sticking his approach to three feet. He birdied three of the last five, and a bogey at 16 merely reduced his winning margin to five. He had shot the last two rounds in 17 under.

It was his third victory of 2019 and the fifth after he won his first in 2017, which was his fifth year on the Asian Tour.

The prize money would put him at $968,524, adding to his stature. He'd already been declared the Order of Merit winner weeks earlier, on December 3, because he could not be overtaken. He also won a spot in the 2020 Masters.

And his next goal? Said Janewattananond: "Maybe ... top 40?"

Thailand Masters
Pattaya, Thailand
Winner: Jazz Janewattananond

Jazz Janewattananond was absolutely bushed. He'd just come from the BNI Indonesian Masters, which he'd won by five shots, the kind of effort that takes a lot out of a fellow. "I was really tired," Janewattananond said. "But I guess it was about survival ... I don't think I was actually cruising towards another win ... I was really tired and made some silly mistakes."

Which had to be of no great comfort to the rest of the field at Phoenix Gold Golf and Country Club, in the Asian Tour's 2019 finale, because mistakes and all, it was all Janewattananond could do to win by — well, five shots again.

This one was in doubt early, however. Janewattananond, 24, opened with 69-67, first trailing Belgium's Thomas Detry (63), then Thailand's Phachara Khongwatmai (64–130) by six each round. Then Janewattananond vaulted the field with a stunning 11-under 60 in the third round, tying the tour's record low and taking a one-shot lead at 196. The 60 was a stunner to watch unfold — a birdie at No. 2, seven straight from No. 6, and three more from the 15th.

"I didn't even know my score until I walked into the score recording area," Janewattananond said. "I was wondering why everyone was asking me if I had birdied the last hole until I realized I was just one shot away from a 59. To be honest, my mind was pretty blank ... I'm really tired."

In the final round, Janewattananond hammered out eight more birdies, but also bogeyed twice for a 65 and a 23-under 261. He one-putted 13 times and needed only 24 putts. All told, he made 27 birdies and four bogeys to become — after countryman Thaworn Wiratchant in 2005 — only the second player to win four times in a year.

"It's a huge honor to win on home soil," Janewattananond said. But one question went unanswered: What were the silly mistakes?

China Tours

A point of information for those charting the growth of Chinese golf: Of the four amateurs in the Hainan Open, co-sanctioned by both the China Golf Association Tour and the European Challenge Tour, only one made the cut — China's Enhua Liu, who went on to tie for 52nd at Sanya Luhuitou Golf Club. With his 71-73–144 start, he became the youngest ever to make the cut on the Challenge Tour. He was age 13 years, 10 months, 24 days.

With golf in China in the formative stage, the game in 2019 centered on an American, Max McGreevy, who dominated the PGA Tour Series-China (under the U.S. PGA Tour), and an Australian, Maverick Antcliff, who did likewise on the domestic China Golf Association Tour. Both took their place on the world stage.

If McGreevy was looking for someone to thank for his success on the PGA Series China, it would be his former University of Oklahoma teammate Charlie Saxon, who told him, "Go west, young man." And McGreevy did — all the way west till he was in China.

In 13 PGA Series China starts, McGreevy won once, had eight other top-10 finishes, never missed a cut, won Player of the Year honors and topped the Order of Merit, leading four others into membership on the 2020 Korn Ferry Tour. McGreevy was fully exempt, and Americans Trevor Sluman and David Kocher, France's Cyril Bouniol and Korea's Luke Kwon were conditionally exempt.

"I'm super-happy with the season," said McGreevy, former Oklahoma star. "The way I played in China is a good springboard for me."

McGreevy topped the Order of Merit with some $137,842. He finally scored that first victory but it wasn't as fulfilling as he'd hoped because continuing bad weather forced officials to cut the Guangzhou Open, in July, to two rounds.

"I'm a little upset that we didn't get to get more rounds in," he said, "but it ended up how it is and I can't do anything about it." McGreevy shot 62-67–129, nine under at Nansha Golf Club, to beat American Trevor Sluman by two. Said the tour's account: "Although considered an unofficial victory, the prize money is very much real." It lifted him to the top of the Order of Merit.

Sluman, No. 2 on the money list, broke through in the Sanya Championship and finished with $111,482. The Sanya was shortened to three rounds out of respect for the death of a golfer, Malaysia's Arie Irawan. Sluman shot Yalong Bay in 67-65-66, and won by two over McGreevy, Matt Gilchrest and Michael Perras. His 66 was fueled by a "miraculous" shot at the ninth, where he had to stand outside the bunker to swing at a plugged lie, yet got the ball to within a foot and made birdie. Sluman also finished second at the Suzhou and Guangzhou Opens.

American David Kocher, No. 3 with $109,144, wasted no time in getting his first victory. After finishing third and tying for 18th in the first two events, he shot Sunac Golf Club in 68-75-69-66, 10-under 278, to win the

Haikou Championship, beating Japan's Yuwa Kosaihira with a 10-foot birdie putt on the first extra hole. Said Kocher, "No more Monday qualifiers."

France's Cyril Bouniol became the tour's first European winner when he holed a 20-foot par putt the final hole to edge Sluman in the Suzhou Open. "That definitely wasn't the easy way to win," said Bouniol, who shot Jinji Lake in 69-66-66-69, finishing at 18 under. Bouniol also had four other top-five finishes, capped by a solo fourth in the season-finale Macau Championship that lifted him to No. 4 on the list with $95,507.

Korea's Luke Kwon won the Qinhuangdao Championship the hard way. He started the final round four strokes off the lead, went eight under through the 13th, bogeyed 14 and double-bogeyed 16, then birdied 17 from 30 feet and 18 from seven, wrapping up a card of 67-67-71-65, 18-under 270 at Qinhuangdao Poly Golf Club. "I was feeling the nerves coming down the stretch," Kwon said, "but I couldn't be happier with the finish." With five other top-10s, he finished fifth on the Order with $94,572.

Zhengkai "Bobby" Bai, 22, had a career year in his rookie season. He won the Huangshan Championship in only his third start, shooting 69-68-67–204, taking the storm-shortened event by two shots. He also was a runner-up in the Haikou Classic, tied for 10th in the Guangzhou Open, and tied for ninth in the season-ending Macau Championship, finishing seventh on the Order of Merit and earning a spot in the final stage of the Korn Ferry Tour qualifying tournament. Bai also won the China Golf Association's Foshan Open.

Also with strong showings: Hong Kong's Motin Yeung, 26, a Beijing native, rallied with a final-round 67 for a one-shot win in the Zhuzhou Classic. Zecheng Dou, with his 22-under 262, was the runner-up to Canada's Justin Shin in the season-ending Macau Championship.

The outside world came to golf in a sobering way. Civil unrest in Hong Kong forced the cancellation of the Clearwater Bay Open, October 17-20, and the Hong Kong Open, November 28-December 1.

On the China Golf Association Tour, there was the surprising Maverick Antcliff, 26, who laid the foundation of his game at Augusta (Georgia) University, turned pro in 2016 and began competing on the PGA Tour of Australasia and in China. He exploded onto the China Tour in 2019. He won three events — the first two, then the fifth, had four other top-five finishes, played in all 12 events and didn't miss a cut. He breezed to the top of the money list with RMB 710,369 (about $101,000).

Antcliff began his run with the tour opener, the Bo Ao Open at the BFA Course. He solved Hainan's tricky April winds and led Bowen Xiao by one going into the final round. And when Xiao slipped to a 75, Antcliff scored his first win in China by six, shooting 66-69-69-68–272, 16 under.

In the Shenzhou Peninsula Open, the second tournament, he surged on bursts of low scoring — four straight birdies in the second round, four straight in the third, and the killer stretch for the field in the final round. In seven holes from No. 6, he had five birdies, an eagle and a par. He shot the Dunes Golf Club in 71-69-66-66–272, 16 under, and won by four.

Three starts later, the Beijing Open, Antcliff's third win was possibly the finest performance of his young career. He shot Fragrant Hills International in 69-65-72-67, and in order, was tied for 32nd and four strokes behind in the first round; in the second, tied for third and still four behind; in the third, solo third and one behind, and then he won by four at 15-under 273. And early in the final round, 14 players were within two strokes of the lead until Antcliff broke away with an eagle at No. 3.

Shun Yat Hak became the first Chinese winner of the season when he took the Lushan Open, the fourth stop on the schedule, by three strokes. Hak led for the last three rounds and shot Lushan International in 67-71-66-67–271, 13 under, for his first win since 2017.

Zhengkai "Bobby" Bai (he got the nickname from his college days in the United States) crashed the history books when he raced down the final nine to a four-stroke win in the Foshan Open — the first Chinese to win on the European Challenge Tour. The tournament, played at Foshan Golf Club, was co-sanctioned by both the China Tour and the Challenge Tour. Bai shot 71-63-66-65–265, 23 under, playing the last eight holes in six under, including birdies on the last four. "It feels amazing," he said. "I'm honored to become the first Chinese player to win on the Challenge Tour."

The Wuhan Optics Valley Open had two distinctions. For one, Korea's Woojin Jung, 21, scored his first win as a pro, shooting Yishan Golf Club in 65-71-71-67–274, 14 under, to win by four. The other: Australia's Kade McBride, 22, tied for fourth after closing on a 12-under 60, a tour record. Said McBride: "Unbelievable."

Huilin Zhang, who turned pro eight years ago and who had gone winless for three years, had a surprise waiting for him at the final green when he wrapped up the Hunan Taohuayuan Open at Changde Taohuayuan Golf Club. His parents had come to the club and watched from a distance, and then when the winning putt dropped, they went onto the green and hugged him. Zhang shot 69-68-66-69 for a 16-under 272 to win by four.

It would seem fanciful to think a golfer found a certain segment of a course much to his liking, but the case could be made for Haimeng Chao and the final five holes (Nos. 5-9) of the front nine at the Fuchun Resort. Over the last three rounds of the Hangzhou International Championship, Chao played the stretch in an aggregate of seven under and won by a stroke, shooting 68-67-69-70–274, six under. In the second round, he played it in three birdies and a bogey; in the third, three birdies and a bogey, and in the fourth, three birdies and no bogeys. It was Chao's second win, his first since 2015.

Japan Tour

SMBC Singapore Open
Winner: Jazz Janewattananond
See Asian Tour section.

Token Homemate Cup
Nagoya, Mie
Winner: Brendan Jones

Memories of his earlier victory in the Token Homemate Cup tournament kindled a final-round surge and another win in the season-opening event on the Japan Tour for veteran Australian Brendan Jones, who has collected more money than any other overseas player ever on the Japanese circuit.

After a shaky third-round finish at Token Tado Country Club, the disappointed 44-year-old "remembered back in 2012 when I last won [the Token]. I had a fantastic final round, so I thought if I could get off to a great start [Sunday] I could do that again."

That's just what he did. He nailed five birdies and an eagle as he rolled to a brilliant seven-under-par 64. His final 269 was just enough to hold off fellow Aussie Matthew Griffin, who birdied four of the last five holes for 65–270 in a futile bid for his first victory in Japan. Jones, on the other hand, won his 15th, spread over 17 seasons in the country.

"When we turn up to play at Token at the start of the year, everybody has the ambition to win the tournament," Jones observed. "To be standing here again, having won seven years ago, is an amazing feeling."

Jones trailed by two strokes after 54 holes as David Oh, the 38-year-old American who won the 2014 Taiheiyo Masters, opened with a sizzling 63 and shared the lead for three days, with Akio Sadakata the first day and with Koumei Oda, the 2014 leading money winner, Friday and Saturday. Oh managed only a par round Sunday as Jones, despite two of the birdies and the eagle on the first six holes, slipped a shot behind yet another Aussie, Won Joon Lee, who birdied four of the first five holes. Jones then went in front to stay with the other three birdies early on the back nine, outlasting Griffin.

The Crowns
Togo, Aichi
Winner: Katsumasa Miyamoto

First, it looked as though there might be two consecutive victories by Australians to open the domestic Japan Tour season. Then it was a South African newcomer playing under the Greek flag who took over the driver's seat in the venerable Crowns tournament. In the end, though, the title wound up the hands of Katsumasa Miyamoto, one of Japan's own stalwarts exhibiting remarkable winning longevity.

Playing in his 22nd season at age 46, Miyamoto edged Shugo Imahira, 2018's leading money winner, by a single stroke and Matthew Griffin, the Aussie who led after 36 holes, by two shots for his 12th tour victory, a string of wins that includes two Tour Championships and dates back to 1998, when he won his first two titles as a 25-year-old.

Griffin, who finished second behind countryman Brendan Jones the week before in the Token Homemate Cup in quest of his first win in Japan, had fired a blistering, eight-under-par 62 in the second round to race into a first-place tie at 134 with Daijiro Izumida.

They yielded the lead Saturday to Peter Karmis, a native South African with seven victories, six on the Sunshine Tour, who just joined the Japan Tour the previous week. The 37-year-old Karmis, who has dual citizenship and is using the Greek identity in hopes of representing that country in the Olympics and World Cup, shot 65–201 on Nagoya Country Club's Wago course and sat a stroke ahead of Miyamoto (67–202).

Katsumasa, who was never more than a shot off the lead all week, closed with 69–271 to take the title as Karmis shot 73 and dropped into a tie for fifth. Imahira posted 66–272, and Griffin, who bogeyed the last hole, 68–273.

Asia-Pacific Diamond Cup
Chiba
Winner: Yosuke Asaji

Yosuke Asaji went from Monday qualifier to the top of the Japan Tour's money list in a single week at the Asia-Pacific Diamond Cup and wrapped up a long-sought victory with his mother in his gallery on Mother's Day.

The 25-year-old Asaji, who had never finished higher than 56th in the rankings in his eight previous seasons, finally snared his first title, barely hanging on to win by a stroke in the tournament co-sanctioned by the Japan and Asian tours. In fact, he was currently 56th when he landed one of just three spots in the Asia-Pacific field at Sobu Country Club in Chiba.

His strong play in the qualifier carried over to the tournament proper. His opening, two-under-par 69 set him two shots behind leader Danthai Boonma and one back of Token Homemate winner Brendan Jones and Tomoyo Ikemura. He slipped another stroke behind Friday, his 72 putting him three off the pace of Asian Tour winner Micah Lauren Shin of the United States (71-67–138), before taking over first place the third day with his 68 and 209 total.

His margin was only a stroke over Shin and Denzel Ieremia and his closing 72 and three-under-par 281 was just enough to edge Shin (72–282) and Japanese amateur Ren Yonezawa (68–282). "It was such a tough battle out there," Asaji said. "I was also lucky some of them did not manage to catch me," a reference particularly to Shin, who took three bogeys on the final nine. "I'm happy ... to deliver the best gift to my mother on this special day."

The victory not only vaulted Asaji into the No. 1 slot but also earned him an invitation to the Open Championship at Royal Portrush in Northern Ireland.

Kansai Open
Nara
Winner: Tomoharu Otsuki

Tomoharu Otsuki ended 10 years of winless competition on the Japan Tour with his victory in the Kansai Open and it didn't come easily for the 29-year-old journeyman pro, who stood 270th in the Official World Golf Ranking at the time. He entered the final round at Koma Country Club, Nara Prefecture, three strokes behind the leader, Seungau Han, who climbed into first place with middle rounds of 63-67 after a 71 start.

Han supplanted Hyunwoo Ryu, who was on top the first two days with his 66-67–133 start, sharing the first-round lead with Shugo Imahira and Hiroyuki Fujita, both former No. 1s in past seasons, and holding it alone after the Friday round.

The last day Otsuki needed a 10-foot birdie putt on the 18th green for 65–269 just to gain entry into a playoff against 23-year-old Rikuya Hoshino, who came from five shots back with a blazing 63 for his 269. Han dropped into a fourth-place tie with Angelo Que with his final-round 72–273.

The two playoff opponents matched pars on three extra holes before Otsuki made birdie on the fourth go-around for the win. Otsuki was the second straight first-time victor on the circuit, following Yosuke Asaji's win the previous Sunday in the Asia-Pacific Diamond Cup.

Gateway to The Open Mizuno Open
Hokota, Ibaraki
Winner: Yuta Ikeda

It came as no surprise when Yuta Ikeda picked off the Gateway to The Open Mizuno Open title in early June. As regular as clockwork, Ikeda has won at least once every year since his first full season on the Japan Tour in 2009, the latest running his total to 21 and inserting him into the race for a second money-list championship.

The 33-year-old, who was 2016's No. 1, had been conspicuously missing from contention in the 2019 campaign before arriving for the Mizuno Open at the Royal Golf Club at Hokota, Ibaraki Prefecture, the longest course on the Japan Tour at 8,016 yards from its tips. His only strong finish had been a tie for eighth in the season-opening Token Homemate Cup and he had missed cuts in his previous two starts.

Ikeda hadn't done much the first two days at Royal Golf Club either, sitting eight strokes behind leader Shugo Imahira (69-67), the 2018 No. 1, with his 70-74 start. But, he came alive Saturday, firing a six-under-par 66 despite a double bogey, bogey finish. His 210 gave him a one-shot lead over Chan Kim, the 29-year-old, Korea-born American from Hawaii who won twice on the 2017 tour. Imahira surprisingly faded with a 77.

Sunday's round turned into a duel between Ikeda and Kim, Ikeda building a three-shot lead with a four-birdie, two-bogey front nine. He carried that margin until he bogeyed the last hole, losing two shots to a Kim birdie. Both players closed with 71s, Ikeda's for the winning 281.

They, along with third-place finishers Sanghyun Park and Gunn Charoenkul, earned the tournament bonus — invitations to the Open Championship in July at Royal Portrush in Northern Ireland.

Japan Golf Tour Championship
Kasama, Ibaraki
Winner: Mikumu Horikawa

Mikumu Horikawa wasn't going to let it happen again. Four times during his five seasons on the Japan Tour, he played in the final group in the last round of a tournament and failed to come out on top at the end of the day. Most recently it happened at the rich and prestigious Dunlop Phoenix the previous season when he bogeyed the last hole and lost to Kodai Ichihara by a shot.

This time in another prized tournament — the Japan Golf Tour Championship — the 26-year-old Horikawa took a three-stroke lead into the final round after leading from the start and rolled to a four-shot victory, his first on the circuit. He was the third first-time winner of the young season.

After showing potential with a 19th-place finish on the previous year's money list, Horikawa led up to the Tour Championship with three finishes in the 20s range, then got off to a fast start with a five-under-par 66 at Shishido Hills Country Club in Ibaraki. Last year's No. 1 Shugo Imahira, three-time winner Shaun Norris of South Africa and little-known Taichi Nabatani were all a shot back. Horikawa widened his margin to two with a Friday 67 for 133 as Thailand's Gunn Charoenkul took over second place with his 70-65–135. The lead went to three in the third round as Horikawa shot 68–201 and Charoenkul (69–204) held on to second place.

No threat appeared Sunday. Horikawa put up another 68 with five birdies and a pair of bogeys for his final 15-under-par 269. He climbed into third place on the money list behind Jazz Janewattananond and Imahira, who also shot 68 Sunday and finished second.

Dunlop Srixon Fukushima Open
Nishigo, Fukushima
Winner: Rikuya Hoshino

Rikuya Hoshino took advantage of the Japan Tour's first fourth-round washout since late 2017 to register his second career win, making up for his playoff defeat a month earlier in the Kansai Open.

The 23-year-old's triumph came at the expense of Hiroshi Iwata, who played brilliant golf the first two days at Grandee Nasushirakawa in Nishigo, Fukushima Prefecture. Iwata, 37, four years beyond his most recent of two tour victories, had opened with a nine-birdie 63 and retained the lead Friday with a follow-up 65, when he birdied four of the last five holes of his round. At 128 he led by three strokes over Hoshino, who conjured up a 64 by finishing his day with an eagle-deuce at the 16th hole and an eagle-three at the 18th.

Iwata ran out of birdies the third day and only managed a par round as Hoshino raced in front with a 65, starting with a bogey, then running out the round with eight birdies. Shota Akiyoshi, the defending champion, climbed into second place two shots behind Hoshino and his 196 as he reeled off 10 birdies to go with a lone bogey for 63-198.

A relentless rain set in early Sunday, rendering the course unplayable and forcing cancellation of the final round, giving the young pro the title and his sixth 2019 finish of 24th-place or better. Jazz Janewattananond, the Thai money leader, tied for third with Iwata at 200, strengthening his hold on the No. 1 position.

Japan PGA Championship
Kagoshima
Winner: Ryo Ishikawa

Long the darling of golf fans in Japan, Ryo Ishikawa had been short on achievement in recent years, both in his homeland and during his foray on the PGA Tour in America. His three-year victory drought came to an end in sensational fashion when the 27-year-old crowd favorite came from behind to score a playoff victory in the Japan PGA Championship.

"I still can't believe this. It feels like a dream," said teary-eyed Ishikawa after winning his 15th Japan Tour tournament and first since the RIZAP KBC Augusta in August of 2016. "It took so long to get here. I think many of the fans believed in me more than I did myself ... but now I am back."

The championship, staged at Ibusuki Golf Club in Kagoshima, which hosted the Casio World Open until 2004, got off to a late start when bad weather and threatening hazardous conditions forced officials to cancel Thursday play ahead of time and schedule a 36-hole Sunday finish. Though devoid of practice rounds, Ishikawa, frequent adversary Jung-Gon Hwang and 50-year-old Hiroyuki Fujita shot 65s to share the first-round lead. Ishikawa and Hwang matched scores again Saturday, their 65-67s keeping them atop the standings along with Koichi Kitamura, who posted a pair of 66s.

Ishikawa nearly took himself out of contention in the first of Sunday's two rounds. Only a three-birdie finish salvaged an even-par 71 after he suffered through a pair of double bogeys and three bogeys on the first 12 holes. That left him four strokes behind new leader Ryuko Tokimatsu (65-199) with Hwang (68) at 200 and three others, including Rikuya Hoshino, the previous week's winner, in between.

Hwang, who won the Mizuno, his first of three tour victories, when he was 19, had the upper hand through most of the afternoon round as Ishikawa again got off to a shaky start. He trailed Hwang by two shots before the South Korean's tee shot on the par-three 17th hole trickled into water, costing him a double bogey. They both missed eagle putts and birdied the 18th for 269s and returned to that tee in the playoff. Again, with both men on the par-five green in two, Ishikawa holed a 17-footer for the winning eagle after Hwang's missed from longer range.

Shigeo Nagashima Invitational
Chitose, Hokkaido
Winner: Ryo Ishikawa

Ryo Ishikawa's victory in the Shigeo Nagashima Invitational Sega Sammy Cup came with strong bittersweet overtones. The Japanese star gave serious thought to not playing when his beloved mother-in-law succumbed the Thursday of tournament week after a year-long battle with cancer, but he decided to go ahead at the urging of his wife.

"When I got to the tee box [Thursday], I felt calm and I told myself that mother-in-law will be looking over me," Ishikawa related. "Then suddenly I was focused." He was so focused that he led the tournament from start to finish, following up on his victory in the immediately preceding Japan PGA Championship.

With 67 he shared the lead that first round at the North Country Golf Club in Hokkaido with Prom Meesawat, 35, twice a winner on the Asian Tour. He moved two strokes ahead of the Thailand veteran Friday with a seven-birdie, one-bogey 66 for 133 and expanded the lead Saturday with another 67, this one bogey-free. At 200 he was three in front of Mikumu Horikawa (67) and Chan Kim (64), 29, the Korean-American who took the Sega Sammy Cup during his three-win 2017 season.

Ishikawa jumped two more strokes ahead with an opening birdie Sunday as both Horikawa and Chan bogeyed the first hole. He breezed to a 68 with three more birdies and a bogey, finishing at 20-under-par 268, four strokes ahead of Juvic Pagunsan of the Philippines, 41, another Asian Tour winner, who shot 67 for his 272.

As he wrapped up his 16th victory on the Japan Tour, replaced Jazz Janewatttananond atop the money list and became the season's first multiple winner, Ishikawa looked skyward in a meaningful gesture acknowledging his departed mother-in-law.

RIZAP KBC Augusta
Itoshima, Fukuoka
Winner: Kazuki Higa

A little man made a big move when Kazuki Higa, standing just five feet, three inches or 158 centimeters tall, rolled to a five-stroke victory and tournament record in the RIZAP KBC Augusta tournament.

Years ago acknowledging his lack of height as a handicap, the 24-year-old Higa was determined and took steps to overcome it. Practicing every day, working hard. As he explained: "It's like brushing your teeth. Must do every day. If you have a handicap like me being short, [you] must practice more. I [wanted to] show the people with some handicaps like me that there is a chance if you work hard enough."

Higa certainly showed them.

After veteran winner Yuta Ikeda shot a sparkling, nine-under-par 64 to lead after the first round at Keya Golf Club at Itoshima, Fukuoka Prefecture, the tournament was all Higa's. He birdied six of the last eight holes and posted a nine-birdie 63 the second day for 129, taking a three-stroke lead over Jung-Gon Hwang, Koumei Oda and 2018 money leader Shugo Imahira.

Higa maintained the three-shot margin with 67–196 Saturday, Imahira also shooting 67 and New Zealand's Michael Hendry joining him in second place with 67-66-66 rounds, then put it away with his Sunday 66–262. At one point that last day his lead shrank to two shots, but Higa closed with an explanation-point birdie-eagle finish, five shots in front of runner-up Rikuya Hoshino's 65–267. It locked up his first win in his third season on the Japan Tour.

Fujisankei Classic
Fujikawaguchiko, Yamanashi
Winner: Sanghyun Park

Sanghyun Park, sitting four strokes behind a pair of co-leaders in the Fujisankei Classic entering the final round, had a feeling. "I thought if Chan Kim and Hosung Choi get heated up against each other, I might have the chance to close in without being noticed."

Park did more than "close in." He shot a six-under-par 65 for 269 and a two-stroke victory, the second on the Japan Tour for the 36-year-old, playing a full schedule in Japan after finishing second on the Asian Tour in 2018. He also won a race against a typhoon, the early bands of heavy rain hitting Fujizakura Country Club just as the tournament concluded.

Chan Kim, who had so far endured a feast-or-famine season with four top-11s mixed in with seven missed cuts, seized the first-round lead with a 65. The 27-year-old Korean-American bomber, who won three times on the Japan Tour in 2017, repeated the 65 Friday but was overtaken by Hosung Choi, he of the funky swing, who came up with a 10 birdie-one bogey 62 for his 130. Park was then in a fourth-place tie but seven strokes back.

Choi and Kim both shot 70s the third day, taking the four-shot lead into the final round before falling victim to faulty play and Park's surge. Maintaining a bogey-free run that began on the 14th hole in the first round, Park grabbed the lead for good Sunday when he ran off the last three of six birdies at 13-14-15. He finished two shots in front of Choi (71–271) and Hiroshi Iwata, who closed with an eagle-led 64 for his 271. Chan shot 72–272 and took fourth place.

ANA Open
Sapporo, Hokkaido
Winner: Yosuke Asaji

Things had not gone particularly well for Yosuke Asaji after his long-sought-after first win on the Japan Tour in the early weeks of the season in the

Asia-Pacific Diamond Cup. He had had only two respectable finishes before teeing it up in the ANA Open.

"I suddenly got nervous of the fact that I was ranking top of the money list … got too tight and couldn't fight the pressure," he explained. "Eventually my play got worse and I plunged in the rankings. But with this win I got my second chance, so from now on I will play as if I was aiming for my first win again."

The second victory for the eight-season veteran did not come easily in a tournament that had a never-before finish. With rounds of 73-68-66–207, the 26-year-old was five strokes and 10 players behind Ryuko Tokimatsu (66-67-69–202), the leader or co-leader all three days, and South Africa's Peter Karmis (68-68-66–202) after 54 holes on Sapporo Golf Club's Wattsu course in Hokkaido.

Asaji and another South African, Shaun Norris, also starting the day five back, posted leading 65–272s and watched as Terumichi Kakazu (67), then Seungsu Han (68) and finally Tokimatsu (72) joined them with their 16-under-par totals, bringing about the first-ever five-man playoff in Japan Tour history. Norris had a seven-birdie, one-bogey round. Kakazu birdied the last four holes. Asaji had a bogey-free round and cut short what could have been a marathon playoff when he sank a four-footer for the only birdie on the first extra hole. It jumped him into second place behind Ryo Ishikawa on the money list.

The defeat was a particular jolt to Tokimatsu, who also lost in a playoff to Yuta Ikeda the last time the ANA Open was played in 2017. An earthquake forced cancellation of the 2018 tournament.

Shinhan Donghae Open
Winner: Jbe' Kruger

See Asian Tour section

Panasonic Open
Hyogo
Winner: Toshinori Muto

Although Japanese great Toru Taniguchi finished near the bottom of the tournament's standings and never was a contender that week, he had an influential role in Toshinori Muto's Panasonic Open victory. Before the 41-year-old Muto had victory securely in hand Sunday afternoon, he was concerned. "I was afraid that, if I messed up, I would get scolded by my mentor, Toru Taniguchi."

Muto, whose sixth victory during his 19 seasons on the Japan Tour had come more than four years earlier, had his hands full at Higashi Hirono Golf Club in the final stages of the tournament co-sanctioned by the Japan and Asian Tours. He entered the last round with a slim lead despite just shooting a seven-under-par 64. His 199 gave him a one-shot lead on Shugo Imahira, the 2018 money king; two on Thailand's Jazz Janewattananond and three on Ryo Ishikawa, the current money leader, whose second-round 62 had pulled him within a shot of India's Rahil Gangjee, the 36-hole leader at 133, who then collapsed the last two days.

Even though he birdied the first two holes Sunday, Muto still had only the one-stroke lead on Imahira after five and admitted to having the negative thoughts until his veteran caddie got on his case. "He said, 'Hey, are you going for the pin or not? What do you want to do?' Those words waken me up," Muto recalled. He birdied five of the next nine holes and breezed to a 64–263, a four-stroke margin over Imahira and a victory water shower. Among the celebrants — Taniguchi, who waited some four hours after finishing his round to help salute his protégé. (Taniguchi had won on the Japan Senior Tour eight days earlier.)

It was the third second-place finish of the season for Imahira, who surprisingly was still without a 2019 victory. Ishikawa, twice a winner earlier in the year, came in third at 268.

Tokai Classic
Miyoshi, Aichi
Winner: Shaun Norris

South African Shaun Norris ran the gamut of emotions in his two most recent victories on the Japan Tour. He was all smiles the previous November when he won the Heiwa PGM tournament, his third in Japan, just days after returning from home where his wife gave birth to their baby. Eleven months later, he crouched, covered his face and cried uncontrollably after eking out a one-stroke triumph in the Tokai Classic. The win came three months after the death of his 75-year-old father, a golf professional himself who had led his three sons into the game.

"I dedicate this victory to my father," the sobbing victor declared after sinking a short putt for 72 and the nine-under-par 275 that gave him his fourth win in Japan. "He always told us, 'If you keep on believing, the chance will come,'" he said.

"I told you that Dad will be watching from heaven above," added Kyle Norris, his younger brother and caddie.

With Kyle on the bag, Shaun had strung together top-10 finishes in the three tournaments prior to the Tokai and his strong play continued on Myoshi Country Club's West course. He was just a stroke behind the 67s of co-leaders Kazui Higa and Mikumu Horikawa after the first round and the second-day 136s of Horikawa and Shugo Imahira, 2018's No. 1, who once again challenged for his initial win of the season before a weak 74 finish.

Norris came up with a seven-birdie, two-bogey 66 Saturday, his 203 giving him the lead by stroke over Higa and two over Horikawa, both winners earlier in the season. He built the lead to four shots when he birdied the first two holes Sunday, but "careless mistakes" cost him two bogeys and a double bogey over the next four. He righted the ship with pars and a lone birdie the rest of the way to secure the one-shot victory over Shota Akiyoshi and Ryuko Tokimatsu. It was his seventh career win.

Bridgestone Open
Chiba
Winner: Shugo Imahira

With Typhoon Hagibis bearing down on the area and Saturday's third round already cancelled, Shugo Imahira knew what to do as he played the par-five 18th hole in the second round of the Bridgestone Open. "If the damage of the typhoon is really bad, there will be no more holes to play, so I told myself to make birdie so that I could finish as the sole leader," surmised Imahira.

That's the way things played out. He made a tap-in birdie for 67–131 and a one-stroke lead over a quartet of hot second-day shooters — Akio Sadakata with 63 and Seungsu Han, Hiroyuki Fujita and Tomoharu Otsuki with 64s. Sunday's round was subsequently scratched and the 2018 money leader finally had the first 2019 victory he had been seeking all season.

Imahira had done just about everything except win during the previous months, finishing second three times and in the top 10 seven other times. The 27-year-old put himself in prime position again in the opening round of the Bridgestone Open. Defending the title that was also his first win of the 2018 season, he fired a seven-under-par 64 at Sodegaura Country Club, taking a one-shot lead over Thailand's Gunn Charoenkul, runner-up the previous week in the Tokai Classic, and two ahead of Ryuko Tokimatsu and amateur Kosuke Sunagawa.

Imahira reached nine under with two early birdies Sunday, but when he made nothing but pars on 10 straight holes, he found himself after 16 holes in a five-way tie with the four eventual runners-up who all had made impressive birdie runs. Imahira's birdie at the 17th made the difference as all five players birdied the final hole.

Besides taking over the lead from Ryo Ishikawa in the current money race, Imahira headed a group of 10 players, including Ishikawa, who qualified for the PGA Tour co-sponsored Zozo Championship played two weeks later.

Japan Open Championship
Fukuoka
Winner: Chan Kim

Chan Kim was the last man standing.

The 29-year-old, Korea-born Hawaiian started the final round of the Japan Open Championship eight strokes in back of the leader and behind 15 other players with his 74-69-75 scores. One by one, that pack of contenders faded on the difficult Koga Golf Club course, most notably Koki Shiomi, who began the day with a four-stroke lead and still had that margin at the turn.

Kim, a triple winner in 2017, closed out an erratic back nine well ahead of him with his last two of eight birdies, posted a four-under-par 67 for a one-over 285 and waited as player after player fell short and Shiomi fell apart. A non-winner who began the week 67th on the money list and led for two days with his 138 and 210 scores, Shiomi's downfall began with a double bogey on the 14th hole, followed by triple bogeys at the 15th and 17th and a bogey at the 18th.

When Mikumu Horikawa, the last player who could win bogeyed the last two holes, Kim had the prestigious major title and moved up into the No. 1 spot on the money list, supplanting Shugo Imahira. Horikawa, with 72 the last day, shared second place with South Africa's Shaun Norris, the Tokai Classic winner two weeks earlier, who closed with a 71 for his 286.

"I did aim to play aggressive the last two days and I think that paid off," said a tearful Kim, who played on several tours around the world before joining the Japan Tour in 2015 and had experienced an up-and-down season leading up to the Open victory with two runner-up finishes and three other top-fives against eight missed cuts. "I am really happy that I achieved the best major of this tour."

Zozo Championship
Chiba
Winner: Tiger Woods

Tiger Woods arrived in Japan in late October — six months after winning the Masters, two months after yet another knee surgery and after six starts of some of the most humdrum, deflated golf of his career. And he had a date with history.

He had come to Accordia Golf Narashino Country Club for the new Zozo Championship, the first PGA Tour event ever played in Japan. That made golf history, and did it in a tale straight from Hollywood — with Woods at his most brilliant, with a biblical storm, a rainout, an empty course and a punishing marathon finish. At the end, Woods had tied the legendary Sam Snead's once-unreachable record of 82 victories.

First, when it comes to giving the competition the edge, Tiger Woods turned Santa Claus for the entire field. At the Indianapolis 500, it would have been a 50-mile head start. Or for a stroll up Everest, maybe a 3,000-foot climb. Woods spotted the other 77 starters three shots by bogeying the first three holes — a ragged start by a golfer with a date with history waiting for him.

"The start I got off to wasn't very good," Woods said. "I hit bad shot after bad shot after bad shot and next thing you know, things aren't looking very good."

Dismal, actually. He steadied himself with a par at No. 13, his fourth hole, and then raced through the remaining 14 holes with nine birdies, shooting six under and launching a card of 64-64-66-67 for a 19-under 261. He led wire-to-wire, finishing three ahead of Hideki Matsuyama and six ahead of Rory McIlroy and Korea's Sungjae Im, who tied for third. It was his 82nd victory, coming 23 years after he won his first at the 1996 Las Vegas Invitational at age 20.

"To have won this tournament in Japan, it's just so ironic," Woods said, "because I've always been a global player ... and to tie the record outside the United States is pretty cool."

Woods' first-round 64 was a rocket and tied him with Gary Woodland. His start of three bogeys and a par left him four shots behind Woodland and five behind Matsuyama. "It was ugly early and it was nice to be able to flip it," Woods said. "Now I'm in a position … that hopefully I can keep it going."

A torrential storm that would kill nine people in the region hit on Friday, forcing the second round into Saturday. Woods shot another 64, but in eerie and strange silence. Fans were not admitted to the soaked course. "When you make a putt and you put your hand up," he said, "you're like, hmmm — don't really need to put your hand up because there's no one clapping." He was 12 under and leading Woodland (66) by two. Then came the race to get as much of the final 36 holes played as possible on Sunday.

Sunday became a very long moment of truth for Woods. With his newly repaired knee, he had to play 29 holes. He shot 66 for the third round and led Matsuyama (65) by three, then played 11 holes of the fourth round in two under before darkness fell, still leading Matsuyama by three.

Woods resumed his final round Monday at the 12th. Matsuyama, one group ahead, twice got within two strokes, first on Woods' bogey at 12, then on his own birdie at the 16th. Woods then birdied the 18th for a 67, the three-stroke win and the history.

Woods recalled once playing with Sam Snead at an exhibition, just the last two holes. Woods bogeyed both. "With Sam Snead," he said, "I was two down through two." Woods was six at the time.

"It's an honor to be tied with Sam Snead for most wins in PGA Tour history," Woods said. "Thanks mom and pop and everyone who helped make this possible … I'll never forget. It's been an awesome year."

Mynavi ABC Championship
Kato, Hyogo
Winner: Junggon Hwang

Shugo Imahira elected to remain in Japan to play in the Mynavi ABC Championship rather that compete in the rich and prestigious World Golf Championship - HSBC Champions in Shanghai the same week. He wanted the opportunity to take over the No. 1 position on the Japan Tour money list.

He achieved that goal, although he lost by a stroke to poker-faced Junggon Hwang, the 27-year-old South Korean nicknamed Stone Buddha, in a duel that climaxed spectacularly with both men making eagles on the final hole. The win, his fourth in Japan, evoked a smile from Hwang, who noted: "It's been four years since I have won [2015 Casio World Open]. I am so happy." It also soothed memories that had plagued him "from the way I lost at the Japan PGA," where he double-bogeyed the 71st hole and was defeated by Ryo Ishikawa in the subsequent playoff.

Imahira, who won the 2018 money title despite only winning once and had only one win so far in 2019, took a one-stroke lead over Hwang into Mynavi's final round at ABC Golf Club, shooting a flawless eight-under-par 64–201 Saturday with an eagle at the 18th. Hwang shot 66–202, also having an eagle, but three bogeys in a wild round.

Imahira was still one stroke ahead through 14 holes in Sunday's final round before making a fatal mistake at the par-five 15th after his drive ended up in the rough. "I made a terrible decision to lay up," he explained afterward.

He hooked and lost the chosen eight-iron shot into trees, had to take a lost-ball penalty and wound up holing a 15-foot bogey putt. Another bogey at the 16th dropped him a stroke behind Hwang, and his 13-foot eagle putt at the last hole wasn't enough to force a playoff when Hwang topped it from seven feet. Still, the ¥15 million for his fourth second-place finish of the season jumped Imahira past Chan Kim into the money lead by ¥12 million.

Heiwa PGM Championship
Okinawa
Winner: Hosung Choi

Whatever it takes. A superstitious Hosung Choi, "wanting to keep the good luck to play well again on Sunday," washed the shirt he wore in taking the third-round lead in the Heiwa PGM Championship, donned it Sunday and went on to a two-stroke victory over leading money winner Shugo Imahira.

The 46-year-old South Korean, whose unique "fisherman's golf swing" and animated, dancing gestures on the putting greens brought him international attention via the internet and exhausting, back-stressing world travel after his 2018 win in the Casio World Open, had struggled in the early months of the season, suffering through three withdrawals and three missed cuts. Things turned around in September and the man they call "Tora-san" (meaning Tiger) climbed to 26th on the money list in the weeks prior to the Heiwa PGM tournament.

Then, wearing the lucky shirt, Choi shot his third straight round in the 60s on a windy Saturday at Okinawa's PGM Golf Resort, supplanting midway leader Zimbabwean Scott Vincent. With his 203, Choi took a one-stroke lead on Imahira, who had put himself into contention once again with a seven-under-par 64 Friday.

Two bogeys on the back nine cost Imahira Sunday after taking the lead with an outgoing 32. Choi meanwhile was bogey-free and broke from a tie with Imahira at the 17th hole with his third and final birdie to Imahira's second bogey. Choi dedicated the win, his third on the Japan Tour and fifth of his career, to his ailing father: "I really wanted to win and give him the good news."

Imahira fattened his money lead over Chan Kim to more than ¥30 million with his fourth second-place finish of the season.

Mitsui Sumitomo VISA Taiheiyo Masters
Gotemba, Shizuoka
Winner: Takumi Kanaya

Past history pointed to a bright future for Takumi Kanaya after his dramatic victory in the Mitsui Sumitomo VISA Taiheiyo Masters.

When the 21-year-old college student, sitting in the No. 1 spot in the World Amateur Golf Rankings, rolled in a winning, 23-foot eagle putt on the final hole at the Taiheiyo Club in mid-November, he joined Masahiro Kuramoto (1980), Ryo Ishikawa (2007) and Hideki Matsuyama (2011), three of his country's most successful professionals, as the only amateurs to have won titles on the Japan Tour.

Kanaya, who idolizes Matsuyama, "was so glad that I could report to him the great news." How soon he would follow Matsuyama into the pro ranks remained to be seen. He remained noncommittal about it when asked by JTO President Isao Aoki after the win.

The victory came at the expense of Shaun Norris, who was having a career season, and with the first-place money of ¥40 million he received for his low-professional, runner-up finish, he moved within ¥7.2 million of money leader Shugo Imahira. "Shugo, I will not let you run away," he remarked boldly afterward.

After early rounds of 73-66, Kanaya took the lead away from second-round leader Y.E. Yang Saturday when he blistered the Gotemba course with a seven-under-par 63 for 202, a shot in front of Yang and Norris. The South African, who had a win and two seconds on his 2019 record, took a one-stroke lead over Kanaya onto the back nine Sunday. Yang dropped back. Norris matched birdies with Kanaya at the 15th and 16th holes and fell back into a tie when he bogeyed the 17th before the budding star sank the winning eagle putt on the par-five 18th for his closing 65–267. Norris also shot 65 as he came up one shot shy.

Dunlop Phoenix
Miyazaki
Winner: Shugo Imahira

The weather worked again in favor of Shugo Imahira when a heavy Sunday storm washed out the final round of the venerable Dunlop Phoenix tournament with him sitting on the 54-hole lead. A similar thing happened a month earlier when a typhoon forced the shortening of the Bridgestone Open to 36 holes with Imahira in the top spot at the end.

While happy with those two victories, his third and fourth on the Japan Tour, Imahira had a bit of a guilty feeling about them. "Winning by not playing four days seems to be not really a victory to me," he pointed out. "I would like to win by playing four rounds next time."

The ¥30 million first prize fattened his money race lead measurably as Shaun Norris, his primary rival, took ill and withdrew after the first round at Phoenix Country Club.

Only an opening-round 64 by unheralded Dongkyu Jang prevented Imahira from occupying first place from start to finish in the field that attracted its usual handful of players off the U.S. PGA Tour, including much-admired Hideki Matsuyama. Imahira shot 65 and followed that with a one-over-par 72. That was good enough on the rain-swept Friday to put him in a tie for the lead with veteran Yuta Ikeda (67-70) at 137. Matsuyama was a casualty that day, taking a career-high nine on the first hole.

Imahira moved two strokes in front on a windy but dry Saturday, shooting a seven-birdie, two-bogey 66–203. Ikeda managed only a 71 and Junggon Hwang, who nipped Imahira by a stroke in the Mynavi ABC three weeks earlier, took over second place with 67–205. That turned out to be the end of things as Imahira added his name to the roster of distinguished Dunlop Phoenix winners over its 47-year history.

Casio World Open
Geisei, Kochi
Winner: Kyungtae Kim

Things had gone from bad to worse for Kyungtae Kim, who was twice No. 1 on the Japan Tour (2010 and 2015). Not only had he not won since early in the 2016 season and dropped far down the money list in 2018, but his game had declined so much in the current year that he missed seven straight cuts from July until the start of October.

"Everything was falling apart and going the wrong way. I was mentally stressed," the 33-year-old Kim explained amid a flood of tears after he had righted the ship with some mental care help and scored a come-from-behind victory, his 14th, in the Casio World Open, the season's final full-field tournament. "I never have cried this much, even becoming speechless," he professed. "I am overwhelmed."

A third-round 66 at Geisei's Kochi Kuroshio Country Club had elevated Kim into a third-place tie with Seungsu Han at 204, three behind young Australian Anthony Quayle, playing the Japan Tour in just his second season as a pro. Quayle had birdied his last five holes for his second straight 65 Saturday. His 201 moved him two strokes in front of Shintaro Kobayashi, the second-round leader.

The Aussie maintained his lead through his first 10 holes Sunday, getting to 19 under before he ran out of birdies, absorbed bogeys at 14 and 18 and finished third behind Kim and Shaun Norris, who both shot 64s with 32s on the incoming nine ahead of him. Kim edged Norris by a shot with his 20-under 268.

The second-place money put Norris back within striking distance of Shugo Imahira for the year's No. 1 position as Imahira's game took a rare week off. He tied for 39th place. Going into the next week's Japan Series finale, the South African, whose chances had dimmed when he was forced out of the previous week's Dunlop Phoenix by illness, was a little over ¥18 million behind Imahira, who was shooting for his second straight money title.

Golf Nippon Series JT Cup
Inagi, Tokyo
Winner: Ryo Ishikawa

It was almost as though the 2018 Golf Nippon Series had been repeated when the top performers of 2019 ended the season again at Tokyo's Yomiuri Country Club with: Another playoff involving Ryo Ishikawa, although this time Ishikawa was the overtime winner; and another tight finish from the same two men in the season's Order of Merit money race with Shaun Norris challenging, but finishing second to Shugo Imahira for the second consecutive year.

All three were in the midst of the final action in the season finale. Rikuya Hoshino, the Fukushima Open winner, had led for two days before Ryuko Tokimatsu and Junggon Hwang, the Mynavi ABC victor, went in front Saturday with 204 scores. Norris was only a shot back, Ishikawa and Imahira another stroke further behind.

The South African never mustered a strong showing Sunday and had to settle for a tie-for-fourth finish with a par-70 round. Ishikawa and Imahira kept pace with each other all day, and first Imahira then, one group later, Ishikawa came to the 18th hole at nine under par. Forty-five-year-old Australian Brad Kennedy, a three-time winner in Japan over the years, was already finished at eight under (65-272). Surprisingly, both leaders faltered on the par-three. Imahira three-putted for a double bogey and Ishikawa missed the green and bogeyed, dropping into a tie with Kennedy with his 66-272.

The playoff went three holes before Ishikawa ran in the winning eight-foot birdie putt on that same 18th hole but with the pin in a new position and claimed the JT Cup.

Imahira's final total of ¥168,049,312 gave him a ¥23 million margin over Norris and, as a fellow back-to-back Order of Merit champion, he joined tour greats Isao Aoki, Masashi Ozaki, Tsuneyuki Nakajima and Shingo Katayama. Ishikawa, who finished third on the money list despite only beginning to play regularly in June, topped the ¥10 billion mark in career earnings with the ¥40 million first-place check.

10. ISPS Handa PGA Tour of Australasia

At the age of 39, Adam Scott reestablished himself as the leading Australian player, but until the last tournament of the year he was still without a win — something also suffered by Marc Leishman, Jason Day and Cameron Smith. That was put right at the Australian PGA Championship at RACV Royal Pines when Scott won by two strokes over New Zealand's Michael Hendry. It was an early Christmas present for the Queenslander's daughter. "She's asked all year for a trophy, and I had not been able to deliver," Scott said. "So that will be fun for me tonight, see if that makes her happy."

Scott had not won anywhere since he claimed the WGC - Cadillac Championship in March 2016. And he had not won in Australia since his first PGA title in 2013 was followed a week later with victory at the Australian Masters. It had been a win at the end of 2012 that set up his magical 2013 season in which he became the first Australian to win that other Masters at Augusta National.

"It's big for the confidence," Scott said of his 2019 PGA win. "I've seen what it's done for me in the past — a win, you feel like you're just never going to lose again, so you want to run with that while the confidence is up. At the end of 2012, I won the Masters in Melbourne, off some good golf where I didn't win, and what that kicked me on to in '13 and on. It's nice to have reassurance and the belief of winning."

Scott twice finished runner-up in the States, at the Farmers Insurance Open and the Memorial, and had seven other top-10s during the year, including seventh at the U.S. Open at Pebble Beach and eighth at the PGA Championship at Bethpage. When the Presidents Cup returned to Royal Melbourne for the third time, Scott was the leading home star on show. He was joined by Leishman and Smith but Day had to withdraw due to injury.

There was no repeat of the International team's only victory, which came in Melbourne in 1998, but the 2019 match certainly breathed much needed life into a contest which had proved a snooze-fest with the Americans' runaway win in New York two years earlier. A combination of a classic course and large, enthusiastic galleries — many of whom heeded Scott's request not to cheer the mere presence of Tiger Woods, megastar and the visitors' playing captain — produced an enthralling spectacle for four days.

On his captaincy debut, Ernie Els, the course record holder and a winner at Royal Melbourne, along with his assistant Geoff Ogilvy, a local resident, and Scott, delivered strict guidelines on how to play Royal Melbourne to his mainly young and inexperienced International team. They listened well, taking a 4-1 lead after the first day of fourballs. It was the first time the Internationals had led since 2005. Scott, playing all five matches, won his first two but only added a half after that. Leishman was also an ever-present, winning only once but gaining a crucial half on Saturday afternoon as he and Abraham Ancer rallied from five down with eight to play against Justin Thomas and Rickie Fowler. The end of that foursomes session was compelling. The Americans looked like sweeping to tie the overall score, but twice the Internationals fought back for a half to keep themselves two points ahead.

On Sunday the overall strength of the American team shown through — they were the highest-ever ranked Presidents Cup side — but Smith beat Thomas, 2 and 1, one of only two wins for the Internationals in singles, the other coming from Sungjae Im, a rising star from Korea who earned three and a half points in all. "There are a lot of young players, a lot of players that the world has never seen or heard, but you will see them a lot in the future," Els said of his team. "They played so hard for each other."

Matt Jones' victory at the Emirates Australian Open came too late to put him in contention for the Presidents Cup, but he became only the second player after Jack Nicklaus to win at least two Opens at The Australian Golf Club. Jones followed up his victory at his home club from 2015 with another impressive performance. At times during the tournament, as at the NSW Open the previous week, smoke from bushfires outside Sydney made for an eerie atmosphere and poor air quality.

Ryan Fox won the World Super 6 Perth, a co-sanctioned event with the European and Asian tours, to claimed the 2019 ISPS Handa Order of Merit title. With the accolade came a spot in the 2020 Open Championship at Sandwich for the New Zealander, who in 2019 at Royal Portrush set a new Open record for the second nine holes of a round of 29. He had made the turn in 39 and may have been concerned his streak of missing cuts in Europe and America was about to be extended to eight.

With Fox already exempt for the European Tour, a full card for the circuit was passed down to Josh Murray, the runner-up on the PGA Tour of Australasia Order of Merit. Murray followed his win as an amateur at the 2018 WA Open with another at the 100th New Zealand Open in only his seventh start as a professional. He was the first player to win wire-to-wire at the event since Sir Bob Charles in 1954.

Continuing the run of amateurs winning on the PGA Tour of Australasia, 17-year-old Kazuma Kobori triumphed at the SEC New Zealand PGA Championship at his home club of Pegasus. He had pre-qualified on the Monday of the event, while the Monday afterwards he was back playing in a school tournament.

Perhaps the most impressive newcomer, however, was Min Woo Lee, the brother of leading women's star Minjee. Lee, the 2016 U.S. Junior champion, finished fourth on his second start as a professional at the Saudi International on the European Tour and then fifth at the World Super 6. He narrowly missed a full card on the European Tour by two spots on the Race to Dubai but ended the year with third-place finishes at both the NSW Open and the Australian PGA Championship.

Overseas, Jason Scrivener finished as the leading Australian on the Race to Dubai in 32nd place, while Scott Hend, who won the Maybank Championship on the European and Asian tours, finished runner-up on the Asian Tour Order of Merit for the third time, a title he claimed in 2016. Brendan Jones finished 16th on the Japanese money list after winning the Token Homemate Cup, with Brad Kennedy 18th.

ISPS Handa Vic Open
Geelong, Victoria
Winner: David Law

A winter that might have seen David Law working for one of his sponsors as a sales agent for gym equipment instead brought the 27-year-old Scot his maiden victory on the European Tour by one stroke at the ISPS Handa Vic Open. Law was three behind when he birdied the 16th hole on the Beach course and still two behind when he hit a hybrid to eight feet at the 18th.

He holed the putt for an eagle, only for overnight leader Wade Ormsby, who had not dropped a stroke all day, to miss left of the green at the par-three 17th. Ormsby failed to find the green from down the bank and ended up with a double bogey. The 38-year-old two-putted from the fringe at the last for a birdie to tie for second with Brad Kennedy but leave Law, who came home in 31, as the champion.

Law, who came through the Paul Lawrie Foundation and is mentored by the former Open champion, had called a one-shot penalty on himself for accidentally causing his ball to move at the ninth hole. He closed with a 66, after scores of 67, 66 and 71, for a total of 270, 18 under par. Kennedy, who went out in 30, closed with a 67 and Ormsby with a 70. South African Justin Harding took fourth place with a 68.

"I never thought it would have happened at the start of today, but I dug in on the back nine," said Law, whose winter's employment status changed after he won the Scottish Hydro on the Challenge Tour the previous summer. "Standing on the 18th fairway we knew making eagle would put pressure on. Had a great shot in. It was a nice putt."

For the first time the European Tour co-sanctioned the Vic Open. In the first round, James Nitties equaled the world record of nine successive birdies.

ISPS Handa World Super 6 Perth
Perth, Western Australia
Winner: Ryan Fox

Having not won in three years and with his wedding set for early March, when it came to his speech Ryan Fox had planned to joke that he was not used to giving a winner's speech. Scrap that line. The 32-year-old New Zealander got some practice in by winning the ISPS Handa World Super 6 Perth at Lake Karrinyup. It was his third win on the Australasian Tour but his first on either the European or Asian circuits, coming seven months after he lost a playoff at the Irish Open.

Fox, son of the All Black rugby legend Grant, qualified for the knockout stages by scoring eight under par for 54 holes, two off the lead. By finishing in the top eight he earned a bye into the second round of Sunday's six-hole knockout matches. In 25 holes over four matches he never lost a hole and had only one bogey.

"I've been close a couple of times and it was certainly nice to get one over the line today in a place I hold pretty special," Fox said of his first European title. His first Australasian title also came in Perth.

However, Fox would have departed in the second round had Jazz Janewattananond holed from two feet at the second extra hole. Instead, Fox survived to win at the third playing of the 90-yard shootout hole. He then beat Kristoffer Reitan by one hole and, in the semi-finals, Paul Dunne also by one hole.

In the final he faced Adrian Otaegui, who lived up to his reputation for head-to-head golf after winning the Paul Lawrie Matchplay (18 holes) and the Belgian Knockout (nine holes). The Spaniard defeated Daniel Gale by two holes, then 54-hole medalist Per Langfors, 2 and 1. In the quarter-finals he beat Perth newcomer Min Woo Lee, and then Scott Vincent, 3 and 2, in the semis. But his long run of matchplay scalps came to an end in the final with Fox, thanks to a par and two birdies, winning the first three holes and the match 3 and 2.

Coca-Cola Queensland PGA Championship
Toowoomba, Queensland
Winner: Daniel Nisbet

A week before defending his maiden title at the New Zealand Open, Daniel Nisbet completed a third victory in a year at the Coca-Cola Queensland PGA Championship. "It's good to finally get one in my home state," he said. "I've been trying for a while, so it is great. Finally my family got to see me win an event."

At City Golf Club Toowoomba, Nisbet won by six strokes over Deyen Lawson and Harrison Endycott. An opening 66 followed by two 63s put Nisbet two ahead of Lawson before three birdies going out and an eagle at the 10th put him well clear of the field. A double bogey two holes later was recovered with birdies at the 13th, 14th and 17th holes as he closed with a 64 for a 24-under-par total of 256. Endycott, playing ahead of the leaders, also finished with a 64 helped by five birdies coming home, four of them in a row from the 10th. Lawson went out in one over par but eagled the 10th and birdied the 17th for a 68. The two runners-up finished three ahead of Andrew Evans, Cameron John, Jarryd Felton and Lincoln Tighe.

"It's a big confidence boost before heading to the New Zealand Open," Nisbet added. "I'm hitting the ball well and putting well, so for me those are the two key aspects of my game."

100th New Zealand Open
Arrowtown, New Zealand
Winner: Zach Murray

At the age of 82, Sir Bob Charles made the 11th hole-in-one of his career in the Champions' par-three event prior to the 100th New Zealand Open. "Still lucky," Charles said. "That's all I've got to be in this game, a little bit of talent and a lot of luck."

Charles won the first of four NZ Open titles in 1954 and it was thought no player had won wire-to-wire until Zach Murray in 2019. The 21-year-old

Australian, who won the Western Australia Open as an amateur in 2018, won his second ISPS Handa Tour title at The Hills with scores of 63, 65, 70 and 68 for a 22-under-par total of 266. Compatriot Ashley Hall and New Zealand's own Josh Geary shared runner-up honors, two strokes behind.

Murray was five ahead at the halfway stage but was pegged back to one in front by Geary after 54 holes. The final round was a tight affair until Murray eagled the 13th and then birdied the next two holes. Geary closed with a 69 and Hall a 65, while Jazz Janewattananond had two eagles coming home in a 64 to take fourth place.

"Starting my career like this is so huge, and to win the 100th New Zealand Open, I don't really think words can describe that," said Murray. "I've etched my name in history a little bit and I'll come back and support this tournament as long as I'm a professional. I was speaking to Sir Bob just now, I'd never met him before, he's an amazing man and I reckon if I could have a 10th of the career that he had I'll die a happy man."

SEC New Zealand PGA Championship
Pegasus, New Zealand
Winner: Kazuma Kobori

A day after winning his maiden title at the SEC New Zealand PGA Championship, 17-year-old amateur Kazuma Kobori was back playing in a school golf tournament. The previous Monday he had pre-qualified to play at his home course at Pegasus. The nerves hit home in the third round when he took the lead, but did not seem to bother him on the final day as he claimed a four-stroke victory over veteran countryman David Smails, with Australian Cameron Johns a further stroke back.

Kobori collected two birdies on each nine and his bogey at the 17th was only his second dropped shot of the week, an incredible consistency for such an inexperienced player. Smails said: "My son is playing a lot with Kazuma, so I've seen plenty of his play and enough to know he's a real talent. He's done fantastic this week, so it's good for the future." Kobori jumped from 2017th on the World Ranking to 764th.

Rounds of 67, 65, 66 and 69 gave the youngster a 21-under-par total of 267. "It feels incredible," said Kobori. "It hasn't actually sunk in yet but I think it will later on. I saw the leaderboard on 14, I didn't know it was there, I just accidentally looked at it, saw that I had a four-shot lead at that point and I thought that was pretty sweet. I just kept playing my own game and then it was all good. I think my ability to keep calm and not get too angry has helped this week."

SP PNG Golf Open
Port Moresby, Papua New Guinea
Winner: Peter Cooke

Five years after finishing runner-up at the Western Australia PGA in 2014, Peter Cooke finally secured his maiden victory with a two-stroke win at the SP PNG Golf Open at Royal Port Moresby. After an opening round of 71, it was middle rounds of 65 and 64 that put Cooke at the top of the leaderboard, and a closing 70 gave him an 18-under-par total of 270. An eagle at the eighth hole helped maintain his advantage and it was only bogeys at the last two holes that narrowed his advantage over Jack Wilson, who also closed with a 70. Kade McBride and Jordan Mullaney shared third place, two strokes further back.

"It's awesome," Cooke said. "I've obviously waited a long time. It's what I live for, I love golf and I've always wanted to be a pro. This justifies a lot of hard work that I've put into the game, so it's so satisfying and such a great feeling.

"I didn't watch any scores through the whole round today, so I didn't really have any idea where I was at when playing the last few holes. Obviously we had the scoreboard for our group, but I kind of had to wait until I'd holed the last putt and judge by the reaction of everyone and ask a few officials. Once I got the okay and all clear, it was awesome, I'm stoked."

Tailor-made Building Services NT PGA Championship
Palmerston, Northern Territory
Winner: Brett Rankin

Brett Rankin finally made the step up from winning on the pro-am circuit to a maiden victory on the PGA Tour of Australasia by claiming the Tailor-made Building Services Northern Territory PGA Championship at Palmerston. The 32-year-old from Queensland was one of five players to share second place with a round to go, three behind Andrew Martin. Rankin made the perfect start with birdies at the first and third holes sandwiching an eagle at the second. He added another birdie at the eighth and responded to his only dropped shot at the 12th with four birdies in the next five holes.

His closing round of 63 equaled the course record and, following scores of 65, 68 and 68, gave him a 20-under-par total of 264. He won by three shots over Taylor Macdonald, who grabbed his highest finish with a 66, with amateur Lawry Flynn a stroke further back. Martin, after three 66s, finished with a one-over-par 72 to be sixth.

"I was so hungry for the win," Rankin said. "It was the win I have been chasing for so long. Today was a dream. I just played so well. I feel like I've been playing really well the past couple of years and not really getting as much as I would like out of the game. I've always been known as a pro-am player and never getting it done on the Tour scenes. It's just so good to get it done."

TX Civil & Logistics WA PGA Championship
Kalgoorlie, Western Australia
Winner: Darren Beck

It took a homeward run of 30 strokes for Darren Beck to win the TX Civil & Logistics Western Australia PGA Championship at Kalgoorlie. A double bogey and a bogey in the first five holes in an outward 39 had dropped the 41-year-old Beck three behind Jarryd Felton, but while the Western Australian dropped shots at the 12th and 13th holes, Beck thanked a hot putter as he raced to the title with a run capped by birdieing the last three holes.

This was Beck's first victory in Australia since he won the 2008 Queensland PGA, while the South African-born player, who moved to Australia at the age of seven, had won the Brunei Open on the Asian Tour in 2009. Rounds of 68, 67, 68 and 69 gave Beck a 16-under-par total of 272 and a two-stroke win over Felton, who closed with a 70. Michael Sim took third place with a 67 to be two shots further back.

"It was a little nerve-racking five or six holes in," Beck said. "There was a big change in scores. I birdied the 12th hole and Felts bogeyed, so it quickly turned round. I thought I was playing for second for a while there. It just feels good to keep it together and finish the way I did. The putter was just unbelievable, so I can't explain how good that felt."

Victorian PGA Championship
Cape Schanck, Victoria
Winner: Campbell Rawson

Eight years after giving up on making his mark on the Australian Football League, Campbell Rawson achieved his maiden victory on the PGA Tour of Australasia at the Victorian PGA Championship. The New Zealander moved to Adelaide to pursue a career in the Aussie Rules code but conceded he did not have the attributes to succeed after missing out on his senior debut by breaking his ankle playing netball. Aged 23, Rawson turned to the financial sector, but three years later decided to return to his sporting dream by turning professional at golf.

Now aged 31, Rawson had not previously finished in the top 10 on tour and almost missed the cut at RACV Cape Schanck when he opened with rounds of 71 and 70. But a weekend of 65-64 saw him finish one ahead of Marcus Fraser on a 10-under-par total of 270. It was an eagle at the second that propelled Rawson into contention and a sixth birdie of the day at the 16th secured the victory. Fraser also finished with a 64 to finish three ahead of Michael Sim, with Blake Collyer, who pre-qualified to make his tour debut after turning professional at the start of the week, finishing in fourth place. Collyer had led at halfway after a second round of 61.

"To be frank, I got sick of sitting behind the desk and felt I needed to have a crack at golf," Rawson said. "At the time I wasn't world class, but knew I had a lot of ability. I'm an over-thinker, so all day I've told myself not to try not to think. It was just a matter of getting out of my own way, not over-complicate it. I'm overwhelmed to win."

Gippsland Super 6
Yallourn Heights, Victoria
Winner: Tom Power Horan

Frequent rain delays that left greens flooded at Yallourn meant the inaugural Gippsland Super 6 was reduced to 54 holes of stroke play with the scheduled knockout rounds of six-hole matches that were due to follow cancelled. The second round only finished on Sunday morning and the third was played as a shotgun start at 4 p.m. that afternoon with players hurrying to complete the round as the sun set. It all worked out well for Tom Power Horan, who claimed his maiden title with a one-stroke win over Brady Watt.

Power Horan led with an opening 66, but a second-round 70 left him one behind Watt. The 26-year-old turned the tables with a closing 69 for an 11-under-par total of 205. Watt eagled the fifth hole at the start of a tight duel between the two, but Power Horan birdied the 15th and the 17th, with a putt from 25 feet, to go two clear, which meant his bogey at the last did not deny him the win.

"I'm really relieved," said Power Horan, who stared 2019 without a full tour card. "I really didn't think we were going to get it done today. I didn't think we were going to play at all, but we did and everything was managed really well to finish in the end. I was a bit nervous to start with, but it was okay in the end."

AVJennings NSW Open
Luddenham, New South Wales
Winner: Josh Younger

Victoria's Josh Younger claimed his maiden victory at the AV Jennings NSW Open despite a double-bogey-six at the final hole. Younger, 35, hooked his drive into the water, but when he was given a reprieve and returned to the same hole for a playoff against Travis Smyth, he found the fairway both times. On the second occasion, Younger then hit his approach shot to six feet and holed the putt for a long-awaited win.

"It's a relief. I've been a professional for 10 years. I got pipped in a playoff in the New Zealand PGA in 2016, finished runner-up at the Australian Masters," Younger said. "It's just so hard to win, that's the reality of it. There's 150 blokes each week, competition is just that good now and the cards have got to fall your way."

Younger had rounds of 63, 70, 67 and 71 for a 17-under-par total of 271. While Andrew Dodt, who finished fifth, scored a course-record 61 in the second round, Sunday saw warm winds bake the Twin Creeks course in west Sydney. Local New South Welshman Smyth bogeyed the 17th and parred the last for a 71 for join the playoff, while Min Woo Lee missed a birdie chance at the last in his 73 to finish one back, and fourth-placed Justin Warren found the water with his second at the last for a double bogey and 74.

Emirates Australian Open
Rosebery, New South Wales
Winner: Matt Jones

Matt Jones joined The Australian Golf Club as a teenager and it remains his home club despite long since having been based in America, where he won the 2014 Houston Open. The following year Jones won the Emirates Australian Open at the historic venue and the special homecomings have kept coming. In 2017 he was runner-up to Cameron Davis and in 2019 the 39-year-old won his national championship for the second time. Jack Nicklaus, with three victories at the course he has twice redesigned, is the only other player to have won multiple Australian Opens at The Australian. "To be able to do it twice is very special and something that I'll be able to look back on later in life and be very proud of," Jones said. "Something like this has been coming, but when it's your national Open that's pretty unbelievable."

Jones took the lead at the halfway stage with rounds of 67 and 65 — at times playing in smoke and sepia-toned light from bush fires on the outskirts of Sydney — before adding a 68 to go three ahead after 54 holes. He held the lead throughout the final round of 69, for a 15-under-par total of 269, but Louis Oosthuizen finished only one behind after an eagle at the final hole. Jones had holed from 40 feet for a birdie at the 17th which appeared to seal the victory, but Oosthuizen hit a hybrid over the water at the last to 12 feet and holed the putt for a 66.

Erroneously informed that the South African had made a par, Jones thought he could make a bogey and still win. His drive finished in a bunker and his next hit a tree and fell down onto pine needles. His third missed the green but he chipped to four feet and made the putt. Japanese amateur Takumi Kanaya shared third place with Aaron Pike, five behind Oosthuizen, with Paul Casey and Cameron Tringale among those a further stroke back.

The Presidents Cup
Winner: United States

See American Tours chapter.

Australian PGA Championship
Gold Coast, Queensland
Winner: Adam Scott

Adam Scott, famously, won the Masters with a long putter. When the anchoring ban came in from 2016, he switched back to a traditional putter and won back-to-back in March that year, including the WGC - Cadillac Championship. Since then nothing. Having returned to the long putter, just not anchoring now, Scott finally won again at the Australian PGA Championship at RACV Royal Pines. The 39-year-old Queenslander had not won in his homeland since he first raised the Joe Kirkwood Cup and added the Australian Masters title the following week at the end of his magical 2013 season.

"It's been a long time between drinks for me and maybe only once or twice did the thought cross my mind that I'll never win again," Scott said. "It's very difficult to win. I'm on the wrong side of this age thing now, where these young guys are really good. Just being all right doesn't really get you in, you've got to be pretty much sensational."

Scott's ball-striking has always been that, as demonstrated once again by an eagle at the 15th hole from six feet which put him clear of the field. But the putter also needs to co-operate and a par-save at the 12th and a birdie at the 14th were also crucial. Scott bogeyed the last for a 69 to win by two over Michael Hendry.

The Kiwi was struggling with a rib injury and did not know, when he teed off, whether he would be able to complete the round. While Scott found the water at the eighth, Hendry, two behind overnight, led by one after birdies at the eighth, ninth and 10th holes. Despite bogeys at the last two holes, Hendry closed with a 69 to finish one ahead of Nick Flanagan, Cameron Davis, Min Woo Lee, Wade Ormsby and China's Yechun Yuan. Scott led by one after 54 holes after rounds of 70, 67 and 69 before finishing on a 13-under-par total of 275.

11. African Sunshine Tour

When Ernie Els accepted the captaincy of the International team at the Presidents Cup, following in the footsteps of Gary Player and Nick Price, he might have expected a number of his compatriots to be playing for him. In fact, only Louis Oosthuizen made the trip to Royal Melbourne. Never before had only one player from southern Africa contributed to the International team — and only once had there been as few as two, also at Royal Melbourne in 1998 when Els and Price were part of that famous winning effort. History was not to be repeated, and although Oosthuizen won his first two matches, Els' team came up just short when his compatriot could only earn a half with Matt Kuchar in the singles.

Just six years ago, in 2013, half the side had been made up of representatives from the African continent, including Els, Oosthuizen, Branden Grace and Charl Schwartzel. Oosthuizen and Grace were regulars at the last three Presidents Cups, Schwartzel the last four, dating back to 2011, the year of his Masters victory. But a wrist injury hampered his appearances in 2019 as he fell out of the world's top 200 for the first time in a decade and a half.

At least there was an encouraging third place on his return at the Alfred Dunhill Championship. He missed out on adding to his four wins and four runner-up finishes at Leopard Creek, but it was his first event since April, so a definite positive. Grace also tied for third that week, but it had been a long and unfulfilling season since he was a runner-up at the Waste Management Open in Phoenix. He missed the cut 11 times, more than in the previous three years put together.

Oosthuizen, who won the South African Open at the end of 2018, did not add to his victory tally in 2019, but he was a runner-up at the Valspar Championship in March and the Emirates Australian Open in December, an eagle at the final hole putting the pressure on home winner Matt Jones. Oosthuizen was also third at the WGC - HSBC Champions and seventh at the U.S. Open at Pebble Beach, the best performance by a South African in a major championship in 2019.

Talent from the Sunshine Tour continued to shine on the international stage, however, with Justin Harding, Christiaan Bezuidenhout and Eric van Rooyen all claiming their maiden victories on the European Tour. Harding could not keep up the strike rate of his 2018 campaign, when he won twice in Africa and twice in Asia, but he did win the Commercial Bank Qatar Masters, following it up with a second place at the Magical Kenya Open the next week.

Bezuidenhout, who wrote on the European Tour website about the long-term effects of mistakenly drinking rat poison as a child, was a runner-up in Qatar, as well as being third at the BMW International and the BMW PGA Championship, finishing just behind Danny Willett and Jon Rahm at Wentworth, but the highlight of his year was an outstanding ball-striking performance at Valderrama in the Andalucia Masters where he won by six strokes against a strong field that included Rahm and Sergio Garcia.

Van Rooyen's win came at the Scandinavian Invitation, as he edged out

Matt Fitzpatrick by one stroke. It was a victory that had been coming and he ended the year with three runner-up finishes, including in a playoff at the Turkish Airlines Open. He was also eighth at the PGA Championship at Bethpage Black.

Meanwhile, an emotional Shaun Norris finished runner-up on the Japanese Order of Merit to Shugo Imahira for the second year running. It was a remarkable effort following the death of his father in July. With his younger brother by his side as caddie, Norris finished in the top 10 in nine of his last 13 events, winning the Top Cup Tokai Classic and having four runner-up results, including at the Japan Open, the Visa Taiheiyo Masters and the Casio World Open. He needed to win the last event, the Golf Nippon Series JT Cup, to overhaul Imahira but came up just short in fourth. "So many things happened this season, so I must be happy with my position," Norris said.

"I did my best, so I have no regrets. I can't help getting emotional when I think about my father. I really miss him, but I know he would be proud of me fighting hard after such a big loss. It would have been great if I became the Order of Merit champion, but I still have next year to challenge."

On the domestic front, Zander Lombard won the Sunshine Tour Order of Merit for 2018-19 after a strong showing late in 2018. By finishing runner-up at the RAM Cape Town Open, he was able to secure the No. 1 spot before the final event, the Tour Championship, which went to Jean-Paul Strydom, one of nine maiden winners during 2019. Another was his namesake Ockie Strydom, whose first win came after 11 second places.

J.C. Ritchie won three times early in 2019 including at the Team Championship with Jaco Prinsloo and then the following week at the Limpopo Championship, as well as at the Zanaco Masters the first week of April. Jaco Ahlers won twice later in the year, the King's Cup and the Selborne Vodacom Origins event, but Daniel von Tonder, helped by winning the Zambia Open, was leading the 2019-20 Order of Merit at the end of the calendar year. George Coetzee returned from Europe to win the Vodacom Origins of Golf Final, while Jean Hugo claimed his 19th Sunshine Tour victory after a four-year wait, and Hennie Otto, after years of back issues, won for the first time at home since the 2011 South Africa Open.

Eye of Africa PGA Championship
Johannesburg, South Africa
Winner: Louis de Jager

Rarely are thunderstorms a welcome interruption at a golf tournament, but the near two-hour delay during a playoff at the Eye of Africa PGA Championship was particularly ill-timed. After driving off on the 18th, Louis de Jager and Trevor Fisher, Jr. had plenty of time to contemplate their approach shots. Eventually, returning to the course, de Jager managed to secure a par while Fisher could only make a bogey.

This was de Jager's fifth victory on the Sunshine Tour and the biggest of his career. A third playoff win in three attempts gave the 31-year-old a second victory on the 2018-19 season after the Sibaya Challenge. "It's a big trophy to have your name on. I'm really honored. It's been one of my goals and it feels great to have achieved it," de Jager said. "I'm glad to keep my playoff record up, and I'm proud of that," said de Jager. "During the delay, I knew what I had to do, so even though there was a lot of pressure, I was able to hit it really close to the hole and I could just tap it in."

De Jager scored 68, 70, 67 and 71 for a 12-under-par total of 276 on the Eye of Africa Signature course. Daniel Greene, who bogeyed three of the last four holes, finished one behind in third place. De Jager birdied the 13th and 14th holes, but a bogey-six at the 17th meant he tied with Fisher, who closed with a 69.

RAM Cape Town Open
Cape Town, South Africa
Winner: Benjamin Follett-Smith

Six strokes behind the leader after 54 holes, even before bogeying the first hole of his final round of the RAM Cape Town Open, Benjamin Follett-Smith set his sights on a top-10 finish to avoid having to pre-qualify for the Dimension Data Pro-Am. When the 24-year-old from Zimbabwe came home in 30 at Royal Cape he achieved even more — a maiden title during his rookie season. Follett-Smith won by two strokes over Jean-Paul Strydom, the 54-hole leader, and Zander Lombard.

With the wind playing havoc with the leaders, Follett-Smith posted the lowest round of the day with a 66 to finish on a 13-under-par total of 275 following earlier scores of 68, 69 and 72. He was still level par for the day until he got up and down for a birdie-four at the 11th. It was the start of a run of six birdies in seven holes, with pars at the 14th and the last.

"I played the back nine so well," he said. "My putter was hot, I could read the lines and everything was just going well for me. I am happy to be able to show that I can win and am worthy of being here."

Lombard closed with a 73 after bogeying the final two holes and Strydom a 74, while Peter Karmis took fourth place after a 72.

Dimension Data Pro-Am
George, South Africa
Winner: Philip Eriksson

A season on the Sunshine Tour proved worthwhile for Sweden's Philip Eriksson as the 27-year-old claimed his first professional victory at the Dimension Data Pro-Am at Fancourt. After starting the final round tied with Jaco van Zyl, Eriksson ended up wining by three strokes over Justin Walters and equaling the tournament record of 21 under par with a total of 268.

Consistency over the three courses at Fancourt was the key to Eriksson's win. Missing the cut the previous week helped in giving him an extra day to scout the layouts. He opened with a 66 on Montagu, followed that with a 67 on Outeniqua and a 67 on The Links before finishing with a 68 back on Montagu.

Still tied with nine holes to play, Eriksson birdied the 11th and then three of the last four holes. His only dropped shot came at the 17th when he was already three ahead. Van Zyl made four bogeys coming home and ended with a 73 to finish fourth, one behind Dean Burmester. Walters closed with a 67 to take runner-up honors.

"It feels like a dream come true," Eriksson said. "I've heard so much about this tournament though the years, even in Sweden. And even though it's not a European Tour event or anything, it's such a big event that a lot of people come here just to play this tournament. So playing here for the first time and winning feels unbelievable."

Team Championship
Johannesburg, South Africa
Winners: Jaco Prinsloo and J.C. Ritchie

An eagle at the 18th hole vaulted Jaco Prinsloo and J.C. Ritchie to victory at the Team Championship at Dainfern. Trailing Jacques Blaauw and Merrick Bremner by one playing the last hole, both Prinsloo and Ritchie produced remarkable approaches at the par-five. From the rough, Ritchie faded his second shot around the trees to 15 feet. Prinsloo then hit his nine iron to a foot to guarantee a tap-in eagle. With Blaauw and Bremner both missing the green with their second shots, a par was the best the pair could do.

"The eagle on 18 was a very special shot," said Prinsloo. "It was made easier for me by J.C.'s approach. He hit a magnificent shot. People won't talk about that one, but he made my shot so much easier. He freed me up and let me go straight at the flag."

Prinsloo and Ritchie, who missed the cut in the inaugural event in 2018, opened with a fourball score of 61 before posting a 66 in the second round of foursomes. Back to fourballs for the final round, they closed with a 62 for a 27-under-par total of 189. Prinsloo provided all three of the eagles they made on the last day, leaving Ritchie to comment: "I need to organize him a back massage pretty soon because he carried me pretty much the whole week."

Blaauw and Bremner scored 62, 65, 63 to finish one behind, with Tyrone Ferreira and Anton Haig birdieing the last two holes to take third place on 24 under par.

Limpopo Championship
Modimolle, South Africa
Winner: J.C. Ritchie

A week after sharing victory at the Team Championship, J.C. Ritchie claimed his third official tour title at the inaugural Limpopo Championship. Ritchie, 25, who won earlier in the 2018-19 season at the Sun Carnival City Challenge, mounted a desperate late charge which ended up with him beating Steve Surry at the first extra hole.

Englishman Surry had led after 36 and 54 holes before going out in 32 in the final round at Euphoria. But after eight pars on the back nine, he needed to birdie the last to tie Ritchie, which he did for a closing 67. Ritchie was only one under par for the day at the turn but then sprinted home with an eagle and four birdies, including at the last two holes. Scores of 66, 69, 70 and 65 gave him an 18-under-par total of 270. Hennie du Plessis, despite a pair of 65s on the weekend, came up one stroke short of the playoff.

Ritchie missed from five feet for eagle at the 18th in regulation but made no mistake in the playoff after hitting a four iron to three and a half feet. "I feel like I have to feel sorry for Steve because he played so solidly the whole week," Ritchie said. "He played beautifully today and did everything he could. This win is huge for me, not only for the win itself but my Order of Merit position."

Sunshine Tour Championship
Kempton Park, South Africa
Winner: Jean-Paul Strydom

Following two runner-up finishes in the previous 13 months, most recently at the Cape Town Open, Jean-Paul Strydom secured his maiden victory at the Sunshine Tour Championship at Serengeti Estates. The 27-year-old started the final round five strokes off the lead but burst out of a crowded leaderboard to win by one shot from Jean Hugo, Jake Roos, Thriston Lawrence and namesake Ockie Strydom. The last three all had birdie chances at the last hole to tie that slipped by, while Hugo three-putted from 45 feet after sending his birdie try eight feet past the hole.

Strydom's winning run started with a 40-footer at the ninth for the first of three birdies in a row. He holed from five feet at the next and missed from the same distance at the 11th for an eagle. But two more birdies followed at the 13th and 17th holes as he set an insurmountable target of 274, 14 under par, following rounds of 69, 67, 72 and 66. "It's an amazing feeling," Strydom said. "I've been close a couple of times now. I've been playing well and I'm just glad I could pull one off. Somehow, I found something and here we are."

With Justin Harding not teeing up ahead of the following week's WGC - Dell Matchplay, Zander Lombard was confirmed as the winner of the 2018-19 Order of Merit even before finishing down the field.

Start of 2019-2020 Season

Mopani Redpath Greendoor Logistics Zambia Open
Kitwe, Zambia
Winner: Daniel van Tonder

Almost five years after the second of his two wins in 2014, Daniel van Tonder at last tasted victory again by winning the Mopani Redpath Greendoor Logistics Zambia Open at Nkana. On a tight course that was yielding few low scores, van Tonder's ability to keep his driver in play proved a key asset as the 28-year-old won by one stroke over Callum Mowat. Two ahead overnight, three birdies in the first four holes gave van Tonder a cushion, only for three bogey around the turn to bring him back to the field.

Birdies at the 12th and 16th holes sealed the long-awaited victory as he scored 72, 73, 68 and 70 for a total of 283, five under par. Mowat closed with a pair of 68s on the weekend, with Neil Schietekat and Jacques Blaauw, three behind second place, the only other players to finish under par for the week.

"I've been playing well for a while but it hasn't been showing in my scores, but finally, something came," said van Tonder, whose wife Abigail was acting as his caddie. "I enjoy playing adventurous golf. I can hit the ball far if I want to, but this week I didn't need to. Shape a draw or fade, that's fine with me. I love the course here. It's tight and I love that. Not everyone is as accurate as I am with the driver, so I take advantage of that."

Zanaco Masters
Lusaka, Zambia
Winner: J.C. Ritchie

A month after winning the penultimate event on the 2018-19 Sunshine Tour, J.C. Ritchie continued his fine form with victory in the second tournament of the new season at the Zanaco Masters at Lusaka Golf Club. Ritchie won at the first extra hole of a sudden-death playoff against Wales' Rhys Enoch, but despite starting the final day with a two-stroke lead, it proved an unlikely fourth career victory.

He ended the front nine with three bogeys in four holes, then had five birdies in six holes before catching a gust of wind at the short 16th and finding the water for a double bogey. Needing an eagle to tie at the last, he hit a hard nine iron to a flag tucked behind a bunker and made the three. Then his second shot at the 18th in the playoff found a hospitality tent, but the 25-year-old got up and down for a four by holing from nine feet. After that he could only watch as Enoch, seemingly in control of the playoff, three-putted to hand victory to Ritchie.

"After putting it in the tent, I just tried to give myself a chance because I'm putting really well," Ritchie said. "I feel for Rhys three-putting the last, because that's not the way you want to win it, but that's the way it goes. Today was the weirdest round of golf I've played in a while."

Ritchie had rounds of 70, 68, 66 and 70 for an 18-under-par total of 274, while Enoch closed with a 66 to finish two ahead of Garrick Higgo and England's Chris Cannon.

Investec Royal Swazi Open
Mbabane, Swaziland
Winner: Martin Rohwer

Within three years of turning professional Martin Rohwer completed his maiden victory in dominating fashion at the Investec Royal Swazi Classic. Under the modified-Stableford scoring system, Rohwer led from start to finish in winning by 12 points over Steve Surry and Jake Roos. The 25-year-old from Durban, with five previous top-10 finishes on the Sunshine Tour, opened with 18 points to share the lead with James Allan but then went ahead on his own with 12 points on day two.

Another 18 points in the third round, including two eagles, put him six clear of Roos, who only added five points in the final round while Rohwer added 11 for a total of 59. Surry also closed with 11 points to share second place, while Stephen Ferreira and Jean Hugo shared fourth place on 47.

"It feels unbelievable to be honest," Rohwer said. "For me, the key was keeping the ball in play," he said, "and hitting a lot of good irons. I never, really, got short-sided or I didn't really look like making a bogey. I kept things stress-free from that point of view. But I played well the whole week. I stayed patient, I had a game plan and I stuck to it and I'm glad it paid off."

Lombard Insurance Classic
Mbabane, Swaziland
Winner: Jake Redman

After earlier free-wheeling rounds of 65 and 64 at Royal Swazi, Jake Redman came under pressure during the final round but eventually sealed his maiden win on the Sunshine Tour at the Lombard Insurance Classic by one stroke.

Redman, two ahead overnight, went out in 32 but then had a run of pars before bogeying the 13th and momentarily losing his outright lead. Birdies at the 15th and 17th holes gave the 32-year-old, a runner-up in the event in 2014, a closing 67 and a 20-under-par total of 196. He pipped Toto Thimba and Thriston Lawrence who both scored 65s — Lawrence coming home in 31 — while Ruan Conradie was fourth after a 66.

"I made a silly bogey on 13, and I thought to myself that I needed to get it to 20 under coming in to have a good chance," Redman said. "It's taken a hell of a long time. I've had a few seconds along the way, a few heartache moments, and to eventually come out and win really feels great. There's been a lot of hard work, endless support from my wife and my mom and dad. It's unbelievable what I've gone through. I almost gave up, and now I got a win."

Sun City Challenge
Sun City, South Africa
Winner: Garrick Higgo

Three months after graduating from the qualifying school, Garrick Higgo sealed his maiden victory over more experienced contenders at the Sun City Challenge. The 20-year-old from Stellenbosch, who turned professional earlier in the year after a stint at the University of Nevada at Las Vegas, beat Ockie Strydom by one stroke and Jaco van Zyl by three.

A third place at the Zanaco Masters, plus a win on the Big Easy tour, prepared Higgo for a stern test at the Gary Player Country Club where rounds of 69, 71 and 69 gave him a seven-under-par total of 209. Two behind van Zyl heading into the final round, Higgo made seven birdies and four bogeys with the gains at the 14th and 15th holes proving crucial. Strydom set the target at six under par after a 67, while van Zyl slipped to a 74 to finish a shot ahead of Kyle Barker and J.C. Ritchie.

"I'm still stressed but I'm sure it will sink in a bit later," Higgo said. "I'm very happy my family was here to witness it. It was a difficult three days, but I got it done. I was in contention in Zambia and I remember on one hole I kind of threw it away because I thought I was out of it, but for the whole day today I knew that whether I win or not, I will be up there."

KCB Karen Masters
Nairobi, Kenya
Winner: Toto Thimba

An eagle and nine birdies helped Stephen Ferreira to a five-stroke lead with a 62 on the first day at the KCB Karen Masters. But in Kenya, as anywhere else in golf, 72 holes is a marathon not a sprint, although it was only on the final day that Toto Thimba caught the frontrunner to record his maiden title.

After an opening 68, 10 birdies on Friday was the foundation of a 63 that left him trailing Ferreira by three strokes. A 66 on Saturday cut that deficit to one, and then two eagles plus three birdies in a row from the 15th propelled Thimba to a 65 and a three-shot win on 262, 26 under par. Ferreira finished with rounds of 66, 68 and 69 to be second, six ahead of Keith Horne.

On Friday the normally modest Thimba speculated that he would win by 10 strokes. The margin did not work out, but his aggressive approach, hitting driver whenever he could off the tee, did earn him the blue jacket.

"To be honest, I'm really impressed with the way I played this week," said the 33-year-old, the first member of the Gary Player Class, the Sunshine Tour's development program which started in 2016, to win. "I knew I was going to win. "This one is for the Gary Player Class. They are my brothers and we work hard together. I hope it can open some doors for all of us."

Royal Swazi Spa Challenge
Mbabane, Swaziland
Winner: Ruan Conradie

Ruan Conradie went on the attack to win his maiden title at the Royal Swazi Spa Challenge. Only one of his seven previous rounds at Royal Swazi, where he was fourth in the Lombard Insurance Classic in May, had been higher than 69, but he started here with a 61, containing 11 birdies, an eagle and two bogeys. A quiet 71 followed to put the 23-year-old a shot behind Deon Germishuys.

However, on the final day, Conradie went back on the offensive with four birdies in a row from the fourth. Another at the ninth put him out in 31, and after two more birdies coming home he could afford a bogey at the last for a 66 and an 18-under-par total of 198. He won by one stroke over Paul Boshoff, Anthony Michael and Jaco van Zyl, who were all hot on his heels with rounds of 63, 64 and 65 respectively.

"It's definitely been a dream of mine since I was a kid. I'm just happy to be chasing the dream," said Conradie. "That birdie on nine was like a final push that got me to where I wanted to go. From there, it was smooth sailing up until the last couple of holes when I realized I was ahead and I needed to know what I was doing. I just felt that playing defensive golf was a lot harder than attacking."

Vodacom Origins of Golf - Sishen
Kathu, South Africa
Winner: Ockie Strydom

"I've been knocking on the door for a while now," said Ockie Strydom, which as a summary of 11 runner-up finishes on the Sunshine Tour was something of an understatement. A maiden victory finally arrived in the grand manner with a six-stroke win for the 34-year-old at the Vodacom Origins of Golf event at Sishen. Strydom, who turned professional in 2009 and finished third at the South Africa Open as long ago as 2011, started the final round with a three-shot lead and relentlessly kept focused until a sixth birdie of the day arrived from six feet at the 18th hole.

His closing 66 was the best round of the day and, added to earlier scores of 69 and 65, gave him a 16-under-par total of 200. He had two bogeys on the opening day but then avoided dropping a shot over the last two rounds. Thriston Lawrence, who shared the first-round lead on 68, started the last day five behind and dropped a shot at the last for a 67 to take second place, two ahead of Riekus Nortje, Michael Palmer, Luke Jerling and Chris Swanepoel.

"I kept myself calm throughout the week," Strydom said. "When I walked towards the green on 18, I was still in the mode of getting the job finished. I started getting goose bumps. I just told myself to take deep breaths, read the putt and see if I could make it — and it went in."

King's Cup
Mbabane, Swaziland
Winner: Jaco Ahlers

Jaco Ahlers dominated the par-fives at Royal Swazi Spa in winning the King's Cup by three strokes. The 36-year-old South African claimed birdie-fours 11 times out of 12 in the three rounds and dropped only one stroke — amply compensating with eight birdies in a 65 on the second day — as he closed as he had opened with a bogey-free 66. Ahlers' total of 197 was 19 under par with a birdie at the 17th taking the pressure off his final tee shot at the par-three 18th. Daniel Greene finished with two rounds of 66 to take second place on 200, one ahead of Alex Haindl and Estiaan Conradie.

This was an eighth Sunshine Tour victory but his first since February 2018 and came after two months at home to reflect on his game. "It's been a tough few months," he said. "I took some time off to reflect on a few things and start working on them. It's nice to see the work come off. It's great to get some form going. I did enjoy the day out there, but I made it a bit more difficult than I wanted. I had to make up and down a few times, which I didn't have to do on the first few days and that made it a bit more stressful."

Vodacom Origins of Golf - Humewood
Port Elizabeth, South Africa
Winner: Merrick Bremner

Merrick Bremner did not drop a shot in winning for the first time on the coast at the Vodacom Origins of Golf event at Humewood. A first win for three years, and a sixth in all, arrived for the 33-year-old with rounds of 65, 65 and 67 for a 19-under-par total of 197. He won by five strokes over Ruan Conradie, who closed with a 63, Clinton Grobler, 66, and Jonathan Agren, 67.

"My first-ever South African Open was here at Humewood," Bremner said, "when Ernie Els won by a country mile. I led the SA Open after three holes and then failed dismally. But I'm happy to get the win at a coastal course. It was the first time ever for me that I was bogey-free in a tournament. I'm really pleased with how I performed this week — mentally, I was really good and this win means a lot."

Setting out for the final round five ahead, Bremner had two birdies going out and then three in a row from the 15th, where the wind switched to behind as he teed off. "And then on 17, the wind switched again and it played downwind, which is unbelievable. I hit the two iron of my life and hit a seven iron to about 10 feet. I just missed the eagle putt and made birdie there, and that was it."

Major Champions

Tiger Woods claimed his 15th major title, and a first for 11 years, at the Masters Tournament.

Brooks Koepka repeated as PGA Champion.

Shane Lowry was Champion Golfer of the Year.

A first U.S. Open victory for Gary Woodland.

Masters Tournament

A fifth green jacket, 14 years after his last, for an emotional Woods at Augusta National.

Dustin Johnson birdied four of the last six holes to tie for second place, his best Masters finish.

Koepka (left) rallied after finding the water at the 12th to tie Johnson and Xander Schauffele (right).

PGA Championship

Defending his title at Bethpage, Koepka almost let a huge lead slip before winning by two.

Johnson put pressure on Koepka before settling for runner-up honors.

Both Patrick Cantlay (top right) and Matt Wallace (right) had their best major results, sharing third place with Jordan Spieth (left).

U.S. Open

Woodland celebrated a three-shot victory at Pebble Beach after holing from 30 feet for a closing birdie.

Trying for a third successive U.S. Open, Koepka was the first to have four rounds in the 60s and not win.

Those in third included Jon Rahm (middle), Chez Reavie (left) and Schauffele, who closed with a 67.

The Open Championship

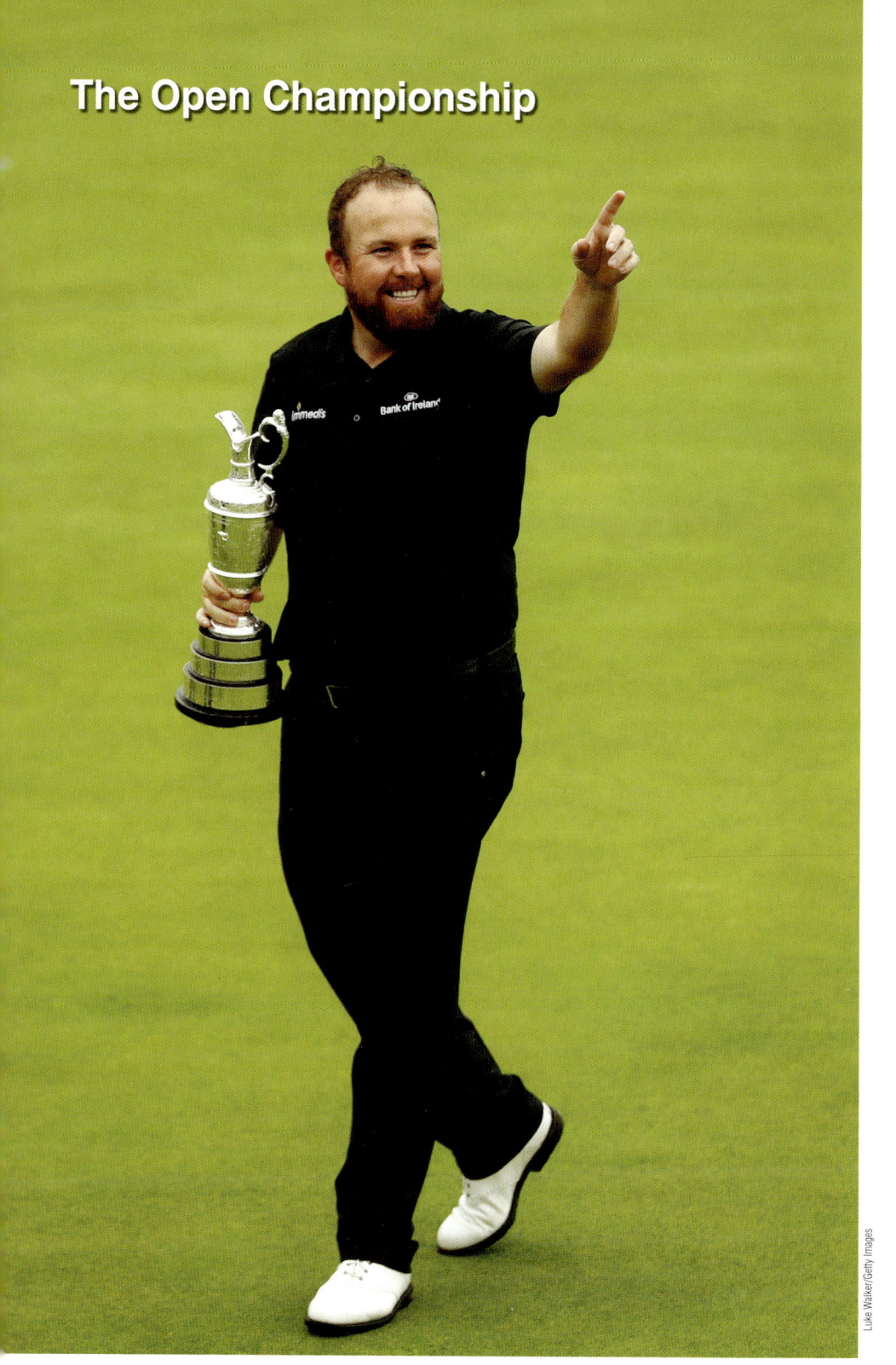

Irishman Lowry was a popular winner of the first Open at Royal Portrush for 68 years.

Tommy Fleetwood had chances early on the last day but held on for second place, six strokes behind.

Third place for the impressive Tony Finau.

An evergreen Lee Westwood tied fourth.

The Presidents Cup

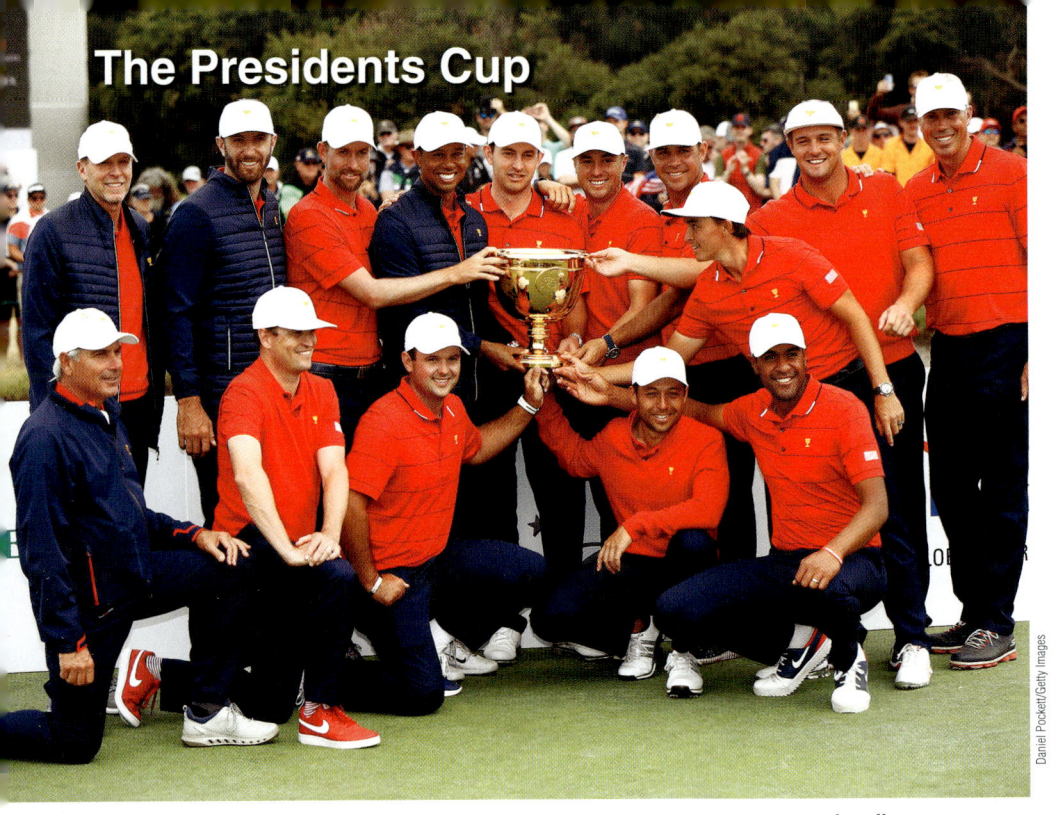

Playing-captain Tiger Woods led the USA team to a tense 16-14 victory at Royal Melbourne.

Woods beat Abraham Ancer in the singles.

International captain Ernie Els.

Two wins and a half for Adam Scott.

Matt Kuchar sealed America's victory.

Cantlay and Schauffele won twice together.

Three wins and a half for Justin Thomas.

Ancer and Sungjae Im were Els' top scorers.

Woods won all three of his matches.

Around The World

Twin triumphs for Rory McIlroy at the Players and the Tour Championship to claim the FedExCup.

Rahm won the DP World Tour Championship to top the Race to Dubai on the European Tour.

A first World Golf Championship title for Koepka at the FedEx St. Jude Invitational.

A playoff win for Fleetwood at the Nedbank Challenge.

Schauffele won the Sentry Tournament of Champions.

Thomas claimed the BMW Championship.

Six birdies in the last 10 holes gave Kuchar victory at the Sony Open, his ninth PGA Tour title.

Victory in Germany for Paul Casey.

Cantlay won the Memorial with a 64.

Four runner-up finishes for Webb Simpson.

For the first time in eight attempts, Woodland converted a 54-hole lead at the U.S. Open for his first major.

Johnson won in Mexico by five over McIlroy.

Four wins in Asia for Jazz Janewattananond.

Bernd Wiesberger won three times in Europe.

Victory at Torrey Pines for Justin Rose.

Eight top-10s in a consistent season for Finau.

Three victories in Japan for Ryo Ishikawa.

Vodacom Origins of Golf - Stellenbosch
Stellenbosch, South Africa
Winner: Thriston Lawrence

After three runner-up finishes during the year, Thriston Lawrence completed his maiden victory on the Sunshine Tour at the Vodacom Origins of Golf event at Stellenbosch. Lawrence came from five strokes behind to win by one over Riekus Nortje, J.J. Senekal, Jean-Paul Strydom and Deon Germishuys on a 15-under-par total of 201. The 22-year-old from Nelspruit, in his third season on tour, had two rounds of 68 and then closed with a 65 that included one bogey, four birdies and eagles at the eighth and 14th holes. Germishuys and Strydom were the overnight leaders who both closed with 71, while Nortje and Senekal had 67s.

"I was five shots back but I knew I was playing solidly all day. So, to get my first win is special," said Lawrence, who moved to the top of the Order of Merit. "This win means a lot to me because not everybody wins, and to get that breakthrough is special. I've been knocking on the door for quite a long time now. But it's all down to staying patient. I knew this is not a sprint but a marathon, there's a lot of events and I'm playing well, so I stayed patient and got it done."

Sun Wild Coast Sun Challenge
Port Edward, South Africa
Winner: Jean Hugo

It took four years to arrive but a 19th victory at the Sun Wild Coast Sun Challenge proved Jean Hugo had not lost the winning touch on the Sunshine Tour. The 43-year-old had enjoyed only one top-10 finish so far on the season but opened with a 60 at the Wild Coast Sun Country Club with eight birdies and an eagle followed by a 65 to take a five-stroke lead into the last round.

Hugo had only one bogey in the first 36 holes, but on a windy final day when the course lived up to its name, three arrived in the first six holes and there were five in all during a closing 74. There was a birdie at the seventh as his 11-under-par total of 199 gave Hugo a four-shot win over Clinton Grobler, the rookie who also finished as a runner-up a fortnight earlier, Hennie du Plessis and Ruan de Smidt, who suffered a double bogey at the last.

Hugo used all his experience to par the last five holes and seal a sweet success. "This feels just as special as the first one," Hugo said. "I'll remember this for a long time. It was the first one for a long while, and it was the toughest, actually. I could have played better today, but it's a step in the right direction for me."

Vodacom Origins of Golf - Selborne
Pennington, South Africa
Winner: Jaco Ahlers

After fading while in contention at the Wild Coast Sun the previous week, Jaco Ahlers impressively converted another chance to win at the Vodacom Origins of Golf event at Selborne. It was his second win of the season having won the King's Cup in September. With J.C. Ritchie, the 36-hole leader, slipping down the standings with a closing 80, Ahlers birdied the first three holes to take command of the tournament.

However, his grip on proceedings could have been loosened by a double bogey at the seventh but for a calm response. Ahlers birdied the eighth and got up and down from 100 yards for a par at the ninth. An eagle at the 12th followed by six pars brought the 36-year-old his ninth Sunshine Tour title by two strokes. Rounds of 64, 70 and 67 gave him a 15-under-par total of 201. Ockie Strydom closed with a 64 to finish second, two ahead of James Hart du Preez and Jacques Blaauw.

"I've been in this position a few times," Ahlers said. "I've been on tour for 14 years, and it's nice to know that I can finish it off, and I can perform under the gun. It was a tough 18 months after winning at Di Data — I lost a bit of game, and off the course wasn't great — and then winning in Swaziland at the beginning of September was nice, and justifying it with a second one is great."

Sibaya Challenge
Durban, South Africa
Winner: Hennie Otto

A brilliant final round of 62, with eight birdies and no bogeys, enabled Hennie Otto to overcome a six-shot deficit to win the Sibaya Challenge at The Woods at Mount Edgecombe. This was Otto's 13th victory on the Sunshine Tour but his first since the 2011 South African Open. The eight-year gap included four runner-up finishes as he ploughed his trade around the globe — the third of his three European Tour wins came at the 2014 Italian Open — but also time out for a litany of back injuries.

"It is just my second full season back after surgery," Otto said. "It's a long road. It takes longer than you think. It has been coming. I've been playing really nicely. The scoring didn't show that the last couple of weeks. If I can break 30 putts average for a round then I can be up there and today showed it — 26 putts with a chip-in. I said this morning if I could shoot eight under, I'd have a chance."

Otto, after earlier rounds of 69 and 66, finished on a 13-under-par total of 197 to win by one over James Hart du Preez, who birdied five of the last six holes to add a second place to his third of the previous week. Daniel van Tonder, helped by a hole-in-one at the 12th hole, tied for third place with Anthony Michael and Malcolm Mitchell.

Vodacom Origins of Golf Final
Knysna, South Africa
Winner: George Coetzee

After a solid run of golf in Europe, including a third place at the Open de France, George Coetzee returned to South Africa to enjoy a little evening fishing at Knysna and, even more, his 10th Sunshine Tour victory at the Vodacom Origins of Golf Final at Simola.

Coetzee led from start to finish after opening with a 61 that included two eagles. A 69 in the second round was followed by a closing 66, his second bogey-free round of the week, for a 20-under-par total of 196 and a three-stroke victory over M.J. Viljoen. His own 66 meant Viljoen finished two ahead of Martin Rowher, who closed with a 64, and Keenan Davidse, who scored 65.

"I had a couple of goals I wanted to achieve this year and going wire-to-wire was one of them," Coetzee, 33, revealed after his first win since the Tshwane Open in 2018, one of four victories that also count for the European Tour. "I wasn't going to say it. But I don't think I've gone wire-to-wire in my career and it was one of my goals at the start of the year and I'm happy to have done it just before the end of the year."

Nedbank Golf Challenge
Sun City, South Africa
Winner: Tommy Fleetwood

Not even three eagles in his final round were enough for Tommy Fleetwood to win the Nedbank Golf Challenge. The 28-year-old still had to win a sudden-death playoff against Marcus Kinhult to claim his first victory since the Abu Dhabi HSBC Championship early in 2018. One extra hole was all that was needed for Fleetwood to collect the highest ever winner's prize on the European Tour — until the following week's finale — of $2.5 million. The victory moved the 2019 Open Championship runner-up into second place on the Race to Dubai.

Fleetwood, after rounds of 69, 69 and 73, started the final round six strokes off the lead, but his closing 65, for a 12-under-par total of 276, was the lowest of the day by three strokes. He chipped in at the ninth hole for his first eagle to go out in 31 and then holed from 15 feet at the 10th for a second successive eagle. Dropped shots followed at the next two holes, but at the 14th Fleetwood hit a five wood to 10 feet for his third eagle in six holes. He birdied the 15th but dropped a shot at the short 16th which allowed Kinhult to tie with a birdie at the 15th.

Kinhult, whose maiden victory came in May at the British Masters hosted by Fleetwood, hit a tree on the left of the 18th fairway in the playoff and had to chip out sideways. The Swede could do no better than a five while Fleetwood, whose second hit the grandstand on the right of the green, got up and down for a par. "It has been a long time coming, and I'm not one to complain, but I really did want to win something," Fleetwood said.

"Winning is just such a good feeling and it's great to have a chance to win the Race to Dubai in the last event." Leader Bernd Wiesberger would have secured the No. 1 spot with a tournament to spare with a victory but finished tied for third, four strokes behind, with Thomas Detry and Jason Scrivener. Louis Oosthuizen was leading when he hit into a ravine at the 11th for a double bogey that presaged a back nine of 40.

Alfred Dunhill Championship
Malelane, South Africa
Winner: Pablo Larrazabal

With temperatures over 100°F (40°C) at Leopard Creek, the European and Sunshine tours sanctioned the wearing of shorts during the Alfred Dunhill Championship. One of the few players to stick with long trousers was Pablo Larrazabal, who said shorts were for "pro-ams and practice rounds." By Sunday, despite a three-stroke lead, the 36-year-old Spaniard had bigger problems, namely blisters. "I woke up this morning and I didn't think I was going to play," said Larrazabal. "I couldn't put my shoe on, I couldn't walk to the buggy. I really struggled on the back nine, I have a big blister on my right toe and I said to myself, 'If Tiger can win a U.S. Open with a broken leg...' and I just fought hard."

With his swing severely affected, with many hooks and pulls, Larrazabal went out in 41 and carded six bogeys and a double before birdieing three of the last four holes to win by one over Sweden's Joel Sjoholm. Laying up at the last, Larrazabal hit a pitch shot over the water to two feet for a winning birdie. Dutchman Wil Besseling also shared the lead playing the last but saw his second shot finish on the rocks above the water behind the green and he took a bogey-six to fall into a tie for third place with locals Branden Grace and Charl Schwartzel. Four-time winner Schwartzel was playing for the first time since April due to a wrist injury.

Larrazabal, who had rounds of 66, 69, 70 and 75 for an eight-under-par total of 280, had not won since his fourth European Tour victory at the BMW International in 2015. "It's been a long road the last few years and this is where I want to be. Being a winner again means so much. This is a place that I really love and I will come back until I cannot play anymore."

AfrAsia Bank Mauritius Open
Bel Ombre, Mauritius
Winner: Rasmus Hojgaard

Rasmus Hojgaard became the first player born in the 21st century to win on the European Tour with a spectacular playoff victory at the AfrAsia Bank Mauritius Open. The 18-year-old Dane, whose twin Nicolai finished runner-up to Sergio Garcia at the KLM Open, was playing in only his fifth European Tour event, and second as a professional, after earning his card for the 2020 season from the qualifying school.

On the third extra hole, Hojgaard's brilliant second shot set up an eagle from 12 feet at Heritage's 18th as he defeated 2019 Challenge Tour graduate

Antoine Rozner of France. Hojgaard had birdied the 18th hole in regulation and then twice previously in the playoff, missing from a similar distance on the first extra hole, when Italy's Renato Paratore dropped.

Hojgaard had rounds of 66, 69, 66 and 68 for a 19-under-par total of 269, which was matched by Rozner with a closing 69 and Paratore with a 67. On a day when a congested leaderboard left the result in doubt throughout, four players finished a stroke behind: Louis de Jager with a 64; Thomas Detry, 70; Grant Forrest, 66, and Benjamin Hebert, 66.

A member of the winning Danish Eisenhower Trophy team with Nicola in 2018, Hojgaard became the third youngest winner on the European Tour after Matteo Manassero and Danny Lee. "I'm lost for words," he said. "It's amazing, a dream come true for me. I just kept telling myself to believe in yourself. I was obviously nervous, but I was confident especially with my shots coming in. It was pretty cool to close out the 18th hole today and to win so early in my career."

12. Women's Tours

As an indication of how the women's game continues to move on, neither Ariya Jutanugarn, who started the year as the undisputed No. 1, nor Lydia Ko, another dominant force of recent vintage, won on the LPGA in 2019. Instead it was the latter's namesake, Jin Young Ko, who matched Jutanugarn's feat from 2018 of sweeping the main end-of-year awards. The 24-year-old South Korean was the Rolex Player of the Year, won the money list, topped the scoring average table, with a mark of 60.052 that had only ever been bettered by Annika Sorenstam, and claimed the Rolex Annika Major Award.

Ko's two major titles came at the ANA Inspiration and the Evian Championship. At Mission Hills, Ko won by three strokes over Mi Hyang Lee by playing relentlessly steady golf, the result of a sweet swing with an enviably natural tempo. But there were moments of adversity along the way, including a blip on Saturday afternoon when she hit into the water at the short 14th and within a couple of holes found a five-stroke lead reduced to one. "I am not a robot. I'm human, sometimes it happens," said a golfer who started the year with the goal not of winning tournaments — there were five worldwide — but simply aiming "to be happy."

At Evian, Ko rallied from four behind Hyo Joo Kim with an almost flawless final round in difficult conditions. Her two major victories were bookended by wins at the Founders Cup and CP Women's Open, while she returned to Korea to win one of her home circuit's majors, the Hite Jinro Championship.

About the only thing she did not win on the LPGA Tour was the CME Group Tour Championship. She did top the Race to the season-ending event, ahead of Brooke M. Henderson and Minjee Lee, but the Tour Championship was then "winner takes all" with a record first prize of $1.5 million — another sign of the advancement of the women's game — going to Sei Young Kim. While Ko was hampered by an ankle injury, Kim picked up her third win of the season by holing a curling 25-footer on the final green.

Succeeding Ko as Rookie of the Year was another recent graduate of the KLPGA, Jeongeun Lee$_6$, who made a name of her number by winning the U.S. Women's Open with a superbly impressive performance at the Country Club of Charleston. Lee was one of three first-time major winners, with the other two somewhat more of a surprise. Australian Hannah Green entered the KPMG Women's PGA Championship 114th on the Rolex Rankings but led from start to finish at Hazeltine National, ultimately getting up and down from a bunker at the final hole to join her mentor Karrie Webb and Jan Stephenson as a major winner from Down Under.

While Green, who went on to win a second time at the Cambia Portland Open, had at least come to attention outside her homeland by finishing runner-up in the rookie stakes to Ko in 2018, Hinako Shibuno was unknown outside Japan before winning the AIG Women's British Open at Woburn. In her rookie season, Shibuno had already won twice on the JLPGA, and would do so twice more before the end of the season, but this was her first tournament overseas, let alone in an LPGA major.

Yet her golf was as fearless, a birdie at the final hole sealing the unlikely triumph, as her charisma was infectious. She played quickly, was even swifter to smile and celebrated holed putts by high-fiving with members of the gallery. It was *A Star Is Born* moment as she became only the second Japanese player to win a major after Chako Higuchi in 1977. Aged just 20, Shibuno decided at the end of the season that she would continue to base herself in Japan in 2020 rather than take up LPGA membership, but her emergence was perfectly timed with the Olympics about to return to her country.

The single most thrilling moment of the year came at Gleneagles when the Solheim Cup rested on the final putt of the week, an seven-footer holed by Suzann Pettersen, the 38-year-old Norwegian who was a surprise wild card selection after being out of the game for 18 months after becoming a mother. She promptly retired on the spot, the ultimate walk-off putt. "It's the perfect way to end my Solheim career and my professional career," Pettersen said. "This is it, I'm completely done."

A third victory for Europe in Scotland, and only the sixth in all, was also a triumph for Catriona Mathew as captain. Georgia Hall and Celine Boutier both recorded four wins out of four, but the win would not have been possible without late singles wins for Bronte Law and Anna Nordqvist, as well as Pettersen. For the Americans, who lost for the first time in three matches under the captaincy of Juli Inkster, the Korda sisters, Jessica and Nelly, led the way. Nelly Korda ended the year as the leading American after two LPGA wins, in Australia and Taiwan, as well as in France on the Ladies European Tour.

Victory at Gleneagles for Europe became even more important for the LET, in a year when yet another chief executive left the organization, when the membership later accepted an offer from Mike Whan of the LPGA of a joint venture partnership. On the course, Germany's Esther Henseleit, with a victory at the Magical Kenya Open in December following four runner-up finishes, became the third player after Laura Davies and Carlota Ciganda to win both the Order of Merit and the Rookie of the Year award in the same season.

In Korea, Hye Jin Choi, who finished runner-up at the 2017 U.S. Women's Open as an amateur, won five times to top the money list in only her second full year as a professional. Ha Na Jang finished second on the money list with two wins, including the LPGA co-sanctioned BMW Ladies Championship, her first KLPGA win for two years.

Meanwhile, in Japan, even Shibuno was outshone by Ai Suzuki, who won seven times in all, including the Toto Japan Classic co-sponsored by the LPGA Tour. Despite playing in only 25 of those events, many of the absences because of injury, the 25-year-old Suzuki captured her second money title in three seasons and might well have had three in a row were it not for a wrist injury in 2018 that sidelined her for eight weeks. She won seven times and had eight other top-10s among those 2019 starts, just the third person with seven or more victories in a single season in the modern era. She rode a three-tournament winning streak late in the season to the money title, again only the third lady to do so and the first since Mi-Jeong Jeon in 2007.

Otherwise, center stage belonged to what was dubbed the "Golden Generation" much of the season. Ten different players between the ages of 19 and 21 scored victories in 2019, two of them — Shibuno and fellow 20-year-old

Nasa Hataoka — multiple winners. Six others were among the season's 10 first-time winners.

Shibuno, the "Smiling Cinderella" who startled and charmed the golfing scene with her aforementioned victory in the Women's British Open in August, surrounded that win with four in Japan, including the World Ladies Championship. Hataoka, taking five weeks off the LPGA Tour to play in Japan, won twice, both majors. Besides the Japan LPGA Championship, Hataoka won the Japan Women's Open Championship for the third time in four years, the first when she was a 17-year-old amateur. Another amateur — 19-year-old Ayaka Furue — was one of the other eight young winners. She turned pro after landing the Fujitsu Ladies in October and tied for second with Shibuno in the season-finale Tour Championship.

The year ended in particular disappointment for veteran Jiyai Shin. The 31-year-old South Korean, once World No. 1 and winner of 57 titles around the globe, 24 of them in Japan, led the money list for much of the season but again came up short in her bid for the top spot in Japan, finishing third behind Suzuki and Shibuno.

U.S. LPGA Tour

Diamond Resorts Tournament of Champions
Lake Buena Vista, Florida
Winner: Eun-Hee Ji

Resurrecting a winners-only event for the first time since 2007 and combining it with an existing celebrity competition proved a hit at the Diamond Resorts Tournament of Champions. Eun-Hee Ji certainly enjoyed sharing the stage with stars of sport and entertainment as the 32-year-old Korean registered her fifth LPGA victory by two strokes over compatriot Mirim Lee. Alongside Ji in the final group, former baseball pitching legend John Smoltz sealed a three-point victory over fellow pitcher Mark Mulder in the celebrity event (played with a modified-Stableford format).

The season-opening event saw 26 winners from the previous two seasons tee up alongside 49 celebrities and 10 amateurs in front of large galleries at the Tranquilo course at the Four Seasons Golf and Country Club in Orlando. The relaxed atmosphere included music being played on the range and the 18th tee. "I love this tournament," said Ji. "Actually, with celebrities, they're really funny, and they make me laugh every hole." Smoltz said of the LPGA players: "Their skill set is extraordinary."

Ji started the final round tied with Lydia Ko and overcame bogeys at the first two holes to return a 70 in cold and windy conditions. With earlier rounds of 65, 69 and 66, she finished on 270, 14 under par. Lee closed with a 68 to finish one ahead of Nelly Korda, with Shanshan Feng and Moriya Jutanugarn in fourth. Stacy Lewis tied for sixth in her first event since giving birth to daughter Chesnee in October. Ko lost a ball at the 13th as she fell to eighth after playing the last six holes in five over.

ISPS Handa Vic Open
Barwon Heads, Victoria, Australia
Winner: Celine Boutier

Starting her third season on the LPGA, Celine Boutier claimed her maiden title at the ISPS Handa Vic Open. The event, with equal purses for the men's and women's sections, was on the LPGA schedule for the first time, but the former NCAA player of the year had enjoyed success Down Under in 2018 with one of her two LET wins coming at the Australian Ladies Classic. The 25-year-old of Thai descent became the fourth Frenchwoman to win on the LPGA after Catherine Lacoste, Patricia Meunier-Lebouc and Anne-Marie Palli. "It's been something I've been working toward since I turned pro," Boutier said. "I'm super excited with the way I handled myself."

American Kim Kaufman led the way with two rounds of 66 over each of the Beach and Creek courses but then struggled on the weekend on the

Beach layout. In winds of up to 30 mph on Saturday, Kaufman scored 75 but maintained a two-stroke advantage over Boutier, who had returned rounds of 69, 71 and 69. Kaufman birdied the first hole on Sunday but then went bogey-bogey-double from the third and ended up with a 78 to drop into a tie for eighth place.

Boutier holed from 30 feet for a birdie on the 15th to go ahead by two strokes and then made important up-and-downs at the next two holes. She ended on eight-under-par 281 after a 72, with Sarah Kemp, Charlotte Thomas and Su Oh sharing second place. Kemp had started the final round 11 shots behind and double-bogeyed the first before responding with five birdies in a row from the fourth. Her 65 set an early clubhouse target that only the calm Boutier could better. Oh closed with a 74 while England's Thomas moved up with a 69.

ISPS Handa Women's Australian Open
Grange, South Australia
Winner: Nelly Korda

Nelly Korda knew precisely what she needed to do to, as she put it on social media, #KeepingUpWithTheKordashians. A two-stroke victory at the ISPS Handa Women's Australian Open achieved what she craved most. "Welcome to the club," sister Jessica said via FaceTime moments after Korda had putted out at The Grange. The exclusive family club has its origins in father Petr winning his only tennis grand slam at the Australian Open in 1998. Elder sister Jessica won the Australian Open on the LPGA in 2012 and then younger brother Sebastian won the junior event at the tennis version in 2018. Each of the siblings has now celebrated a triumph Down Under with a scissor kick, their father's trademark.

"I think there's something in the air here," said Korda. "I'm just happy to finally be a part of the club. I kind of felt left out. I was playing all day for my parents, and I'm really proud of that." The 20-year-old opened with a 71, then added a 66 and two weekend 67s to finish on a 17-under-par total of 271. She was three ahead after the third round and five birdies in six holes around the turn on Sunday helped move her six clear.

But defending champion Jin Young Ko posted the best round of the week, a 64 with eight birdies and no bogeys, to put the pressure on in the closing stages. When Korda bogeyed the 15th she was only two ahead, but a birdie at the 17th effectively put her out of reach. "I felt Jin Young was coming in close," said Korda. "It was actually just one bad hole that I had today. But I bounced back on 17."

Honda LPGA Thailand
Chonburi, Thailand
Winner: Amy Yang

Amy Yang continued her streak of winning in alternate years on the LPGA with her third victory at the Honda LPGA Thailand. The 29-year-old's first win came at the KEB Hana Bank Championship in 2013 and since then she has triumphed on the Pattaya Old Course at Siam Country Club in 2015, 2017 and now 2019. "This is a special tournament for me," Yang said. "I love coming to Thailand. I love to play Honda. Just enjoying it so much, I think that's helpful to play better." But why she only wins in odd-numbered years, she had no answer. "I don't know. Even my friends ask me, too, and I really don't know."

Yang was sharing the lead with Minjee Lee ahead of the final round in which she had five birdies in a row on the outward half. She led by three at the turn when there was a one-hour delay due to lightning. However, although she had nine birdies on the day, there were also two bogeys, and with three holes to play she was level with Lee and Carlota Ciganda, who had two eagles in a closing 63.

A long putt for a birdie at the 16th was the key for Yang, who then two-putted for a birdie at the last. She had rounds of 69, 66, 66 and 65 for a 22-under-par total of 266. Lee had a putt from 14 feet on the last for an eagle to tie, but it just missed. The Australian did not drop a shot in a closing 66 that left her one behind Yang and one ahead of Ciganda.

A "backstopping" controversy erupted at the 18th on Friday when Amy Olson's chip hit Ariya Jutanugarn's ball on the green, but both players were cleared of a breach of Rule 15.3a.

HSBC Women's World Championship
Singapore
Winner: Sung Hyun Park

Among Sung Hyun Park's many nicknames is "Dak Gong," which translates as "Shut up and attack." On a hot and humid day at Sentosa, with an umbrella pulled down over her head so she could only see the ground and the sweat dripping off her nose, the always impassive Park did just that. A closing round of 64, the best score of the week on the New Tanjong course, gave the 25-year-old Korean a two-stroke victory in the HSBC Women's World Championship.

Park started four behind Ariya Jutanugarn, who closed with a 75 to fall into a tie for eighth place. Minjee Lee finished second for the second week running with a 69 putting the Australian two ahead of Jin Young Ko and Azahara Munoz.

Lee only had one lapse, pulling her drive at the short par-four 14th into a tongue of rough by a bunker and taking four to get down for her only bogey of the day.

When Park notched her ninth birdie of the day at the 16th, she was out of reach. Five birdies came on the front nine, her only bogey a three-putt at the eighth, after which she added birdies at 10, 13 and 14, as well as 16.

After claiming her sixth LPGA win, which returned her to the Rolex Rankings No. 1 spot ahead of Jutanugarn, Park revealed she had been inspired by a surprise meeting with Tiger Woods at a recent photoshoot for their equipment company. At the press conference, she said: "If Tiger is watching this interview, then I would want to say that because we met, you gave me such a good energy, that made me win this tournament." Another of Park's nicknames is, inevitably, "Tiger."

Bank of Hope Founders Cup
Phoenix, Arizona
Winner: Jin Young Ko

With the LPGA returning to America for its West Coast swing, Jin Young Ko capitalized on her recent good form to claim her first victory in the States at the Bank of Hope Founders Cup. It was the 23-year-old Korean's third LPGA win and followed her runner-up finish at the Australian Open and a third place in the HSBC Women's World Championship. Ko finished one stroke ahead of not one but two Kordas, Nelly and Jessica, as well as Carlota Ciganda and Yu Liu at Wildfire.

In a low-scoring week in Phoenix that produced a crowded leaderboard, Ko scored a bogey-free 65 on the final day, after rounds of 65, 72 and 64, for a 22-under-par total of 266. Four birdies in the first 11 holes merely kept Ko in touch with the leaders, but it was only after three in a row from the 14th that she went ahead for the first time as she walked off the 16th green.

Jessica Korda, in her first event of the season due to a forearm injury that had prevented her from defending her Honda Thailand title, came home in 30 with eagles at the 11th and 15th holes to get to 21 under par after a 64. Nelly Korda, playing alongside Ko, matched her elder sister with a second 66 of the weekend but saw her birdie chance at the last to tie Ko lip out. Ciganda closed with a 69, while China's Liu, the leader after 36 and 54 holes, had a steady 70 in which her one dropped shot came at the last when she failed to get up and down.

Marilyn Smith, an LPGA founder who was in her usual position behind the 18th green talking to players as they finished their rounds, died on April 9 at the age of 89.

Kia Classic
Carlsbad, California
Winner: Nasa Hataoka

It ended up tight at the Kia Classic, except for one player. Five players shared second place and a further five were tied for seventh, one shot further back. The runners-up included World No. 1 Sung Hyun Park, overnight leader Inbee Park, another major winner in Danielle Kang, plus Azahara Munoz and Jin Young Ko, the previous week's winner. Like Kang, Ko closed with a

65 at Avaria, the Korean adding a fourth top-three finish of a young season to head the Race to the CME Globe going into the first major championship of the year.

Yet Nasa Hataoka outpaced them all. The 20-year-old from Japan had scored a 64 in the third round, after opening up with scores of 69 and 70, to sit one off Inbee Park's lead. On Sunday she birdied three of the first five holes to go two clear at the turn and added two more at the 10th and 15th holes to be three ahead. She gave the chasing pack a flicker of hope by finding the water at the 16th for a bogey but bounced back with her final birdie of the day at the next. A 67 put her three ahead of the pack on an 18-under-par total of 270.

This was Hataoka's third LPGA win after two in 2018 but her first in a 72-hole event, one of her aims starting the season. "The goal for me this year was to win a four-day tournament as well as a major. So I'm happy that I accomplished one of them," she said. "I'm still in my third year on the LPGA and I'm only 20 years old. I don't really have much to be afraid of. I also feel like I'm always a challenger out here, just taking one shot at a time."

ANA Inspiration
Winner: Jin Young Ko

See Chapter 6.

Lotte Championship
Kapolei, Oahu, Hawaii
Winner: Brooke M. Henderson

By winning for the eighth time in her career, Brooke M. Henderson tied an important landmark for Canadian golfers. A four-stroke victory at the Lotte Championship put Henderson, still only 21 years of age, alongside Sandra Post on the LPGA, as well as Mike Weir and George Knudson on the PGA Tour, with eight wins. "It's really amazing to even be mentioned in the same sentence as Mike, George, and Sandra," Henderson said.

"When I was younger it was just a goal to be on the LPGA Tour, to win my first event. When that happened and then I won my first major, things kind of just started to fall into place. I knew the record was eight and this year it's been on the back of my mind every week that I tee it up."

For the second time in her short career Henderson successfully defended a title, having also won at Ko Olina in 2018. As the year before, Henderson handled the strong winds better than anyone else. Of the top six on the 54-hole leaderboard, she was the only player to break par with a 70, which following scores of 65, 68 and 69, gave her a 16-under-par total of 272. Her co-leader overnight, Nelly Korda, who opened the week with a 63, closed with a 77. Eun-Hee Ji, who won the opening event of the season, took second place, while Ariya Jutanugarn claimed her best result of the season to date by sharing third place with Minjee Lee.

Henderson recovered from a bogey at the opening hole to post three birdies and 14 pars in an accomplished act of front-running. "I always love coming to Hawaii," she said. "I knew it was going to be a tough task with the wind blowing as strong as it was."

Hugel-Air Premia LA Open
Los Angeles, California
Winner: Minjee Lee

It was perhaps inevitable that a victory would arrive for Minjee Lee and it happened at the Hugel-Air Premia LA Open. The Australian's fifth LPGA title arrived following second places in Thailand and Singapore earlier in the season and a third place in Hawaii the previous week. Only Karrie Webb, her mentor, Jan Stephenson and Rachel Hetherington, of her compatriots, have won more on the LPGA than the 22-year-old whose win took her to a career-best second place on the Rolex Rankings.

"The two seconds that I had, Thailand, Singapore, I didn't really feel like I lost — the two people who won, they just outplayed me on the day. I didn't feel like I played badly. And the same in Hawaii. I knew I was close to probably winning out here."

Patience was the key at Wilshire, the famous Los Angeles club celebrating its 100th year. Lee took the lead at halfway with scores of 66 and 69 before recovering from a triple bogey at the third hole of her third round to maintain her lead with a round to play. On Sunday she cruised to the turn in two under par and found her one-stroke lead extended to five. Nanna Koerstz Madsen, her nearest rival, fell back to 13th with a 76, but Sei Young Kim came from six behind to within two with three birdies in a row from the 13th.

Kim made her only bogey of a closing 66 at the last, while Lee produced one of only three birdies on the day at the par-three 18th for a 68 and a 14-under-par total of 270. She won by four over Kim, with Annie Park, a University of South California graduate, and Morgan Pressel sharing third place.

LPGA Mediheal Championship
Daly City, California
Winner: Sei Young Kim

When Sei Young Kim claimed the LPGA scoring record at the Thornberry Classic in 2018, the work she had done to improve her swing appeared to be paying off. But when that new swing started causing her lower back problems in 2019, she knew she had to make further adjustments. The result was a second place at the LA Open followed by Kim's eighth LPGA title at the Mediheal Championship.

Not that it came easily in cold temperatures at Lake Merced. A three-shot overnight lead disappeared with a double bogey and a bogey on the first two holes. Out in 40, she birdied the 15th before dropping another shot at the 17th. Only a birdie at the par-five 18th got Kim into a playoff, which, like the previous three on the LPGA, she won — defeating Bronte Law and Jeungeon Lee$_6$ at the first extra hole with another birdie at the 18th.

It was England's Law who set the final round aflutter by matching the low round of the week with a 65. She made five birdies in six holes from the seventh and then hit a three wood to four feet for an eagle at the 15th. Her total of 281 was posted two hours prior to the leaders finishing. First Lee$_6$, known to all simply as "Six," finished eagle-birdie-par-birdie for a 67 to tie Law. Kim almost holed a long eagle putt at the last and was left with a tap-in to make the playoff. "I got a lot of nerves and my heart almost came out," Kim said.

The 25-year-old added: "I think this win is very hardest to win in my life, ever, because last seven wins, I played really well final round. But today I wasn't good."

Pure Silk Championship
Williamsburg, Virginia
Winner: Bronte Law

Three weeks after losing a playoff at the Mediheal Championship, Bronte Law claimed her maiden victory in her very next tournament at the Pure Silk Championship at Kingsmill. Law, a 24-year-old from England in her third season on tour, shared the lead on the first three days and then won by two strokes over Nasa Hataoka, Brooke M. Henderson and Madelene Sagstrom.

Four birdies in the first eight holes put Law in front before she started struggling with her driving. However, she only dropped a shot at the ninth, and after six pars to start the back nine, Law rolled in a birdie putt from 15 feet at the 16th accompanied by her customary fist punch.

Sagstrom made five birdies in 15 holes to get within one, but then missed a short putt at the 17th and saw her approach at the last hit the flagstick and rebound 40 feet away. Her bogey-free 66 brought her level with Henderson, after a 68, and Hataoka, who shared the 54-hole lead with Law and closed with a 69. Law, after rounds of 65, 68 and 67, closed with another 67 for a 17-under-par total of 267.

"I guess after San Fran it really gave me perspective that I can compete at the top," said Law, a two-time English Amateur champion and a multiple winner in college at UCLA. "I came in this week with the sole intention of getting that one better. I believe in hard work and determination. I really stayed so focused out there today. It feels really good."

U.S. Women's Open Championship
Winner: Jeongeun Lee$_6$

See Chapter 6.

ShopRite LPGA Classic
Galloway, New Jersey
Winner: Lexi Thompson

Nine years after making her professional debut at Seaview, Lexi Thompson's dramatic eagle at the final hole brought an 11th LPGA victory for the 24-year-old. Thompson's heroics also denied Jeongeun Lee$_6$ becoming the fifth player to win the tournament after becoming the U.S. Women's Open champion and the first since Meg Mallon in 2004.

Lee continued her form from Charleston with an opening 63 to share the lead with Pornanong Phatlum and then added a 69 to go one ahead of Mariah Stackhouse. On the final day the Korean birdied the 11th to go two ahead of Thompson but saw her approach at the 13th trickle off the back of the green and it prompted three bogeys in a row.

Thompson, after 64 and 70 on the first two days, holed from three feet at the 16th, which Lee matched from long range. At the par-five 18th, Thompson hit a three wood, as she had all day to keep the ball lower in the wind, and then hit a pitching wedge from 190 yards from light rough to 15 feet. "It's crazy to think about the numbers, but with a jumper lie and the wind, it landed 50 yards short and rolled up there."

Having adopted a claw grip for her putting the previous week, and despite a four-putt double bogey at the first hole on the second day, Thompson made the putt for a 67 and a 12-under-par total of 201. "I got chills," Thompson said, "like my hair on my arms was sticking up once I made that putt."

Lee finished one behind after two-putting from 50 feet at the last for a closing 70. Ally McDonald and two-time ShopRite winner Anna Nordqvist shared third place.

Meijer LPGA Classic for Simply Give
Grand Rapids, Michigan
Winner: Brooke M. Henderson

Lexi Thompson eagled the final hole for the second week running but had to settle for a share of second place at the Meijer LPGA Classic for Simply Give. Brooke M. Henderson was not to be denied at Blythefield as the 21-year-old Canadian became the most successful golfer from her nation with a ninth LPGA victory. Her tally surpassed Sandra Post's eight wins, as well as the eight PGA Tour wins by Mike Weir and George Knudson. "That's so special and so incredible," said Henderson. "Earlier this year to get my eighth win was a huge deal for myself and, I felt, the whole country as well, and to break that record now is really exciting. I just look forward to the rest of the summer and hopefully a lot more wins in the future."

This was Henderson's fourth consecutive season with multiple wins and she was also the first player to win the Meijer Classic for a second time. After a rain delay on Thursday morning, Henderson played 30 holes on Friday as she posted twin rounds of 64 to lead by three strokes. Thompson equaled the course record with a 62 on Saturday, but Henderson birdied the last three holes to lead by two over Annie Park. Three birdies in the first 13 holes of the final round kept the Canadian ahead, but a dropped shot at the 16th meant a couple of pars were required to secure a one-stroke win over a group of four players: Thompson, after a 68, and Nasa Hataoka, who also eagled the last for a 65, Su Oh with a 66, and Brittany Altomare thanks to a 68.

"I looked at the leaderboard and it was getting packed," Henderson said. "I'm glad I only needed a par at the last because I was really shaking over those last couple of putts."

KPMG Women's PGA Championship
Winner: Hannah Green

See Chapter 6.

Walmart NW Arkansas Championship
Rogers, Arkansas
Winner: Sung Hyun Park

Sung Hyun Park, calm as ever under pressure, birdied the final hole to win the Walmart NW Arkansas Championship and return to the top of the Rolex Rankings. It was her fourth stint as the World No. 1 and the first person to congratulate her was compatriot Jin Young Ko, the former No. 1.

After rounds of 66 and 63 at Pinnacle, Park dropped only one stroke on Sunday, coming home in four under par for another 66 and an 18-under-par total of 195. And she was pushed all the way by a trio of contenders whose hopes of a playoff were dashed when Park found the final green in two and two-putted from 30 feet. Hyo Joo Kim went out in 30, Danielle Kang played the last five holes in five under — an eagle at the 14th and birdies at the last three — and Inbee Park, who opened with a 62, did not drop a shot as all three ended with 65s.

"I knew I needed to make a birdie on either 17 or 18 to win," Park said. "To be honest, my round today didn't go as well as I thought it would. On the front nine there were a lot of opportunities that I missed. But I talked with my caddie, and we both said there's still a lot of hope left, and we waited. Every single shot was really important."

This was Park's second win of the season after victory at the HSBC Women's World Championship and her seventh in three years on the LPGA. "There was a lot of pressure when I was the World No. 1, but it will be nice to be back on top again," she added.

Thornberry Creek LPGA Classic
Oneida, Wisconsin
Winner: Shanshan Feng

With eight birdies in her final round, including tap-ins at the 14th and 16th holes after brilliant eight-iron approaches, Shanshan Feng thought she had done enough to win for the first time in two years. Fortunately, for someone who does not routinely look at scoreboards, she saw the one at the last and knew the four-foot putt, after another fine eight iron, had to be holed. "Oh, no, I had to make that one," was Feng's reaction. "So actually the last putt was under a lot of pressure. But I was like, you know what, you've been doing really well this week. Just make another good putt. That's what I did."

Feng won for the 10th time on the LPGA with a closing nine-birdie 63 for a 29-under-par total of 259. She won by one over Ariya Jutanugarn, who capped a 64 by birdieing the last from two feet. Two eagles in a front nine of 30 helped the Thai to a three-shot lead after birdies at the 12th and 13th holes, but a bogey at the par-five 15th proved the lapse that helped Feng to victory.

The 29-year-old from China had struggled recently. "I haven't been having a good year so far. I missed all three cuts at the first three majors, so I was a little lost," said Feng. "But starting last week I felt like my iron game kind of came back. This week I think I got everything together."

Sung Hyun Park, the World No. 1, led at halfway after a 62 on Friday but finished tied for sixth, alongside 17-year-old Monday qualifier Yealimi Noh. Patty Tavatanakit scored a final round of 61 in her fourth event as a professional to finish 15th.

Marathon Classic
Sylvania, Ohio
Winner: Sei Young Kim

A burst of five birdies in a row from the seventh hole on the final day propelled Sei Young Kim to her second victory of the year at the Marathon Classic. Even though Lexi Thompson eagled the 18th for the second day running, Kim held firm to win by two strokes over the American.

Kim scored 67, 64, 66 and 65 for a 22-under-par total of 262, one stroke outside the tournament record set by Korean great Se Ri Pak, who won the event five times. "I'm very honored my name alongside Se Ri Pak," Kim said. "Since I was young she is one of my idols. I really wanted another win because the last two weeks I played really bad." Having won at the Mediheal Championship earlier in the season, Kim here notched her ninth LPGA victory, although the tally comes with an unwanted tag given no one has won as many without winning a major.

"She played some amazing golf today," Thompson, who closed with a 66, said of Kim. "She went through a stretch where she stuck every shot. Had it under five feet about four times in a row, so it was a very well deserved win by her. I tried to catch her, made a run. Too late, but it's okay."

Stacy Lewis also scored 66 to finish in third place, her first top-10 finish since returning to the tour as a mother. Augusta Amateur winner Jennifer Kupcho finished in a tie for fifth behind U.S. Open winner Jeongeun Lee$_6$ in fourth.

Dow Great Lakes Bay Invitational
Midland, Michigan
Winners: Jasmine Suwannapura and Cydney Clanton

Jasmine Suwannapura and Cydney Clanton, or "Team All In" as they styled themselves for the Dow Great Lakes Bay Invitational, combined to hold off some of the best golfers in the world and win the LPGA's first official team event at Midland Country Club. The pairing of a 26-year-old from Thailand and a 30-year-old from North Carolina won by six strokes over Jin Young Ko and Minjee Lee, the World Nos. 2 and 4.

Suwannapura and Clanton opened with a 67 in foursomes and then added a 64 in fourballs, but it was the 63 back as a foursome in round three that spurted them five ahead of four pairs, including the Jutanugarn sisters, Ariya and Moriya. A bogey at the first hole on Sunday as a fourball was recovered at the next and then five birdies came in a row from the fifth. They closed with a 59 after making 12 birdies. Ko and Lee also managed 12 birdies in a 58, with Lee scoring an estimated 62 on her own ball. The Jutanugarns had a 61 to share third place with Jenny Shin and Na Yeon Choi.

"I couldn't ask for a better partner at all," said Suwannapura. This was the Thai's second LPGA title after she won the Marathon Classic in 2018, itself a remarkable recovery from breaking her back in 2016 and requiring surgery and six months of intensive physiotherapy.

Clanton had failed to get her full LPGA card for 2019 by $8 but picked up her second win on the Symetra Tour before posting a maiden LPGA title which booked her into two major championships in the following two weeks. "This is 100 percent a God plan," said Clanton. "I couldn't even dream up to have won a Symetra event earlier this year and then to come out and win with Jasmine."

Evian Championship
Winner: Jin Young Ko

See Chapter 6.

AIG Women's British Open
Winner: Hinako Shibuno

See Chapter 6.

Aberdeen Standard Investments Ladies Scottish Open
Winner: Mi Jung Hur

See Ladies European Tour section.

CP Women's Open
Aurora, Ontario, Canada
Winner: Jin Young Ko

Jin Young Ko became the first player for four years to win on the LPGA without making a bogey during the tournament with her five-stroke victory at the CP Women's Open at Magna Golf Club. Ko's closing 64, during which she ran away from her rivals with a homeward nine of 30, came while playing alongside the home fans' favorite Brooke M. Henderson, who was attempting to defend her title from the previous year.

Henderson had the crowd roaring at full volume on Saturday when she played the last 11 holes in nine under par for a 65, but the Canadian closed with a 69 to share third place with Lizette Salas, who scored 64. Nicole Broch Larsen, who improved her LPGA best of third at the same event in 2017, pipped the pair for second place with a 69.

Ko, who had scores of 66, 67 and 65 in the first three rounds for a new tournament record total of 262, 26 under par, matched Inbee Park's feat of going bogey-free from the 2015 HSBC Women's World Championship. Park had a run of 93 holes without a dropping a shot that year, the longest since the LPGA kept such records. Ko's last bogey came at the second hole of the third round of the AIG Women's British Open, making her streak to 106 by the end of the week. "That's so cool," Ko said. "It's my first time bogey-free for 72 holes. It was incredible with the crowd, playing with Brooke in Canada, it was more than fun but there were lots of Koreans, too."

Brittany Altomare, Angel Yin and Annie Park claimed the remaining places on the U.S. Solheim Cup team, while captain Juli Inkster added Morgan Pressel and Stacy Lewis as wild cards.

Cambia Portland Classic
Portland, Oregon
Winner: Hannah Green

When Hannah Green started with rounds of 64 and 63 to lead by five strokes at the Cambia Portland Classic, another wire-to-wire victory appeared on the cards for the KPMG Women's PGA champion. However, a 73 in the third round left the 22-year-old Australian trailing Yealimi Noh by three going into the last day at Columbia Edgewater. That was still the deficit with four holes to play until Green birdied the 15th and 17th holes, and Noh, an 18-year-old Monday qualifier, bogeyed the 16th and 18th holes.

Tied playing the last hole, both players went over the green, but while Noh chipped 10 feet past and missed the putt back, Green holed from five feet for her second victory following her breakthrough in July. "Yesterday I was more nervous than I was today because I pretty much knew it was mine to lose, having a five-stroke lead," Green admitted.

"Today I can definitely say that having that KPMG experience helped me, especially the last five holes — grinding it out and making sure that I stayed patient."

Green closed with a 67 for a 21-under-par total of 267, while Noh had a

71 to finish three ahead of Brittany Altomare. "It was all going good till 16 I think, just the last two bogeys on 16 and 18 really hurts, because I was playing okay up until that," said Noh, who finished sixth at the Thornberry Creek Classic. "I really thought I could hang in there, but just made a couple mistakes."

Jin Young Ko extended her record run of holes without a bogey to 114 before she three-putted at the ninth in the first round. The best run on the PGA Tour was 110 holes by Tiger Woods in 2000.

The Solheim Cup
Winners: Europe

See Chapter 6.

Indy Women in Tech Championship
Indianapolis, Indiana
Winner: Mi Jung Hur

After winning twice in her first 10 years on the LPGA, Mi Jung Hur collected her second victory in four events at the Indy Women in Tech Championship. Hur won at the Scottish Open and the common denominator was her husband Kevin Wang caddieing for her. A year and a half of marriage was paying off for the 29-year-old Korean.

"My married life makes me more comfortable," said Hur. "If I hit a bad shot, it's just a bad shot as a human, but before I get married I'm like, if I had a miss shot, how dare you, MJ, that was so stupid. But right now I'm just trying to enjoy my game. I'm so happy to win."

A lot of hard practice had also gone into her good form which saw her race to the top of the grid with an opening 63. It turned into a wire-to-wire victory as she added rounds of 70, 66 and 68 for a 21-under-par total of 267. In the last staging of the event at Brickyard Crossing, at the Indianapolis Motor Speedway, Hur ended up lapping the field to win by five strokes over Nanna Koerstz Madsen, whose 67 left her two ahead of American Solheim Cup player Marina Alex.

Hur did not drop a stroke on Sunday, which started in rainy conditions, making four birdies as she left the rest behind in her rearview mirror. "My game is working really well," Hur said. "Every day's not too much stress."

Volunteers of America Classic
The Colony, Texas
Winner: Cheyenne Knight

In a three-way battle of Americans looking for their maiden LPGA victory, Cheyenne Knight emerged as the winner at the Volunteers of America Classic at Old American. The 22-year-old rookie, who was in danger of losing her caddie coming into the week at a tournament just 60 miles from home, won by one stroke over Brittany Altomare and Jaye Marie Green. Knight was swamped in celebration by family and friends at the conclusion but also raised her arms to the sky to salute her late brother Brandon Burgett, who 11 years earlier was killed when his truck was hit by a drunk driver on the wrong side of the road. Of her faith, which she credited with helping her through good times and bad alike, Knight said: "I think I had a second caddie out there."

The title turned Knight's way when she chipped in at both the ninth and 10th holes. "You have to laugh about that. I mean, two chip-ins in a row?" she said. A closing 66, after scores of 66, 67 and 67, gave Knight an 18-under-par total of 266. Altomare, a runner-up for the second time this season, bogeyed the last hole, only her third dropped shot of the week, in a 67, while Green had a 69, following a 64 that had given her the 54-hole lead, to secure her best finish on tour. Jane Park and England's Georgia Hall tied for fourth place.

"I've always dreamt of a putt to win an LPGA event," Knight said. "I said when I got my card that this was the event I was most looking forward to and who would have thought this helped me secure my card. I was planning on going back to q-school."

Buick LPGA Shanghai
Shanghai, China
Winner: Danielle Kang

For the second year running Danielle Kang celebrated her birthday at the Buick LPGA Shanghai by taking the title. Her successful defense at Qizhong Garden was completed on her 27th birthday with a one-stroke victory over Jessica Korda after a head-to-head duel.

After Korda led by one overnight, a two-shot swing at the first hole put Kang in front. While Korda had three bogeys and three birdies in a 72, Kang did not drop a shot, crediting work on her chipping with her brother Alex in Las Vegas the previous week with helping her on numerous occasions in the final round. She also had a few birdie chances that went begging until she holed from 10 feet at the 15th to lead by two.

Korda cut her deficit with a four at the par-five 17th, but Kang held on at the last, although her first putt came up three feet short. "It was a really stressful day," Kang said of battling her Solheim Cup teammate. "I definitely played well out there. It was really tough because you're definitely watching what Jessica is shooting and scoring, and always just trying to keep in my own game. I've never been more nervous than the last putt, for some reason, but I made it."

Kang won for the third time on the LPGA and had previously won successive U.S. Amateur titles in 2010-11. She had rounds of 69, 67, 66 and 70 for a 16-under-par total of 272. Two strokes behind Korda were Yu Liu, the leading home player who closed with a 65, Nasa Hataoka and Kristen Gillman. Megan Khang tied for seventh place after a 64 that included a hole-in-one at the 11th.

BMW Ladies Championship
Busan, Korea
Winner: Ha Na Jang

A day after her victory in Shanghai, Danielle Kang was given honorary citizenship of Busan, where the San Francisco-born golfer spent much of her childhood when her late father's work took the family back to his hometown. Kang only fell short of ending the week of the inaugural BMW Ladies Championship at the newly renamed LPGA International Busan in the perfect fashion when she lost at the third extra hole of a sudden-death playoff to Ha Na Jang.

Kang made a superb run for the title on the final day with an eight-under-par 64, the lowest score of the week, that included four birdies in a row around the turn. But she was caught on a 19-under-par total of 269 by Jang, who followed scores of 69, 67 and 68 with a closing 65. An eagle at the 11th helped Jang to believe she could win, and while Kang parred the last five holes, Jang birdied the 15th and 17th holes to force the playoff.

Twice the pair parred the 18th, with Jang holing a par-save from 12 feet on the first extra hole and Kang lipping out from eight feet for a birdie at the second. Moving to the 10th hole, Jang hit her approach to three feet and secured the winning birdie.

Jang, who won on the KLPGA circuit three weeks earlier, had not won on the LPGA tour since 2017. The 27-year-old returned home later that year due to her mother's ill health. "After the 11th hole, I felt that I could really win this event," said Jang. "I played to the level of this game which is the best. I'm also happy that I went into a playoff with one of my closest friends, Danielle Kang."

Taiwan Swinging Skirts LPGA
New Taipei City, Chinese Taipei
Winner: Nelly Korda

Despite battling a misfiring putter down the stretch at the Taiwan Swinging Skirts LPGA, Nelly Korda successfully defended her title at Miramar. The 21-year-old American again displayed the quality of her long game to win a three-way playoff at the first extra hole against Caroline Masson and Minjee Lee. On an 18th hole with water down the left-hand side, Korda not only bombed her drive but was the only one of the three to find the fairway. From almost 190 yards she then hit a five-hybrid to within five feet of the hole.

This stunning shot was not quite matched by her tentative eagle putt, which came up short, but her birdie could not be matched by either Masson or Lee. It was Korda's fifth birdie of the week at the hole, but over the previous hour her three-stroke lead had disappeared as she three-putted three holes out of four.

Korda, who had posted rounds of 66, 67 and 68, not dropping a shot on Friday or Saturday, closed with a 72 that saw five bogeys on a day of tricky winds. Masson, whose 68 was the best score of the final threeball, was four behind with five to play, yet took a one-shot lead to the 18th hole. A par, after the German missed from 10 feet for the victory, meant she was caught by the birdies of Korda, who almost chipped in for an eagle, and Lee, who scored 69. Brooke M. Henderson, Sei Young Lee and Mi Jung Hur all tied for fourth place, four strokes behind.

Korda thanked her caddie, Jason McDede, who is engaged to Masson. "Jason gave me a little pep talk going from 17 to 18, win or get into a playoff, so he was definitely great today," Korda said. "I kept telling myself, 'from the heart, from the heart, from the heart.' I was very nervous because it was my first playoff."

CME Group Tour Championship
Naples, Florida
Winner: Sei Young Kim

Unaware that she had to hole it to avoid a playoff, Sei Young Kim made a curling, left-to-right 25-footer for a birdie on the final green at Tiberon to claim the largest first prize in women's golf of $1.5 million. Kim not only won the CME Group Tour Championship but the Race to the CME Globe. All 60 players who qualified for the season-ending tournament had the chance to win the Globe by simply winning the tournament in a change from previous years.

There was nothing simple about it as Kim did it the hard way, leading wire-to-wire with rounds of 65, 67, 68 and 70 for an 18-under-par total of 270 and a one-stroke victory over Charley Hull. While Nelly Korda, Kim's nearest challenger overnight, finished with a 71 to tie for third place with Danielle Kang, Kim did not know that she was tied with Hull as she played the last hole.

Kang went out in 31 and then had an eagle at the 17th in her 65. But the American missed from 12 feet at the 18th hole and was pipped by Hull, winner of the event in 2016, when the English newlywed posted her second 66 of the weekend. She came home in 31 with birdies on the last three holes, including from 10 feet at the last.

Kim, whose nerves had shown when missing a par putt at the 14th and a birdie putt at the 17th, raised her putter in triumph as her ball tracked towards the hole. "Last putt, I just tried to make two-putt because I didn't see the leaderboard. I didn't know that if I made a two-putt it could be go to playoff," said Kim after her third win of the season and 10th LPGA title. "I just try and make the right distance — made it. It's unbelievable. I was so emotional, almost crying."

Ladies European Tour

Fatima Bint Mubarak Ladies Open
Abu Dhabi, United Arab Emirates
Winner: Charley Hull

Charley Hull may have been overtaken as the British No. 1 in 2018 by her friend, and Women's British Open champion, Georgia Hall, but there was plenty of good news as well. Over Christmas her fiancé Ozzie Smith proposed with a diamond ring, while he was in attendance as Hull won her first event of 2019 at the Fatima Bint Mubarak Open.

Hull led from start to finish at Saadiyat Beach in Abu Dhabi with rounds of 67, 72 and 69, for an eight-under-par total of 208, to win by one stroke over Marianne Skarpnord. The Norwegian had set the clubhouse target of seven under with a closing 68 to finish one ahead of Caroline Hedwall, Anne van Dam, Nicole Broch Larsen, Luna Sobron and Jodi Ewart Shadoff. An eagle at the 11th, thanks to a six iron to 15 feet, and three birdies meant Hull came to the last one ahead but had to play a delicate recovery shot from a bunker at the last, to three feet, to ensure her second Ladies European Tour victory and her first anywhere since winning the 2016 CME Group Tour Championship on the LPGA.

The 22-year-old year Englishwoman collected the trophy from course designer Gary Player, who would have approved of her off-season preparation. "I've practiced really, really hard over the winter and it feels great to win back on the LET, especially since I had my first pro win in Morocco five years ago," Hull said. "Today the wind got up in the end and it was a tricky finish. I had a 35-yard bunker shot and I stiffed it, made the putt, so it feels really good to be back in the winner's circle again."

Pacific Bay Resort Australian Ladies Classic
Bonville, New South Wales, Australia
Winner: Marianne Skarpnord

Norway's Marianne Skarpnord, who speaks English with a heavy Australian twang, won her first LET title in six years, and a fourth in all, at the Pacific Bay Resort Australian Ladies Classic at Bonville. Skarpnord shares a winter residence with partner Richard Green at 13th Beach Links, where she won the Vic Open on the ALPG in 2015, but admitted doubts about continuing her career. "Do I want to put myself through all this misery and pain? Somehow I pulled through that, because a lot of times I've been thinking that I've had enough and I'm going to get a proper job and be at home," she said. "There's something in me and I can't give up. This is what I love doing."

Skarpnord started the year as a runner-up at the Fatima Bint Mubarak Open in Abu Dhabi and then won by two strokes at Bonville thanks to birdies on the last two holes. A tee shot to 12 feet set up a two at the 17th before she had a four at the last, her long eagle putt rolling over the edge of the hole.

Skarpnord scored 70, 72, 69, 69 for an eight-under-par total of 280, while Australia's Hannah Green and Spain's Nuria Iturrios shared second place. Sydney amateur Doey Choi, who led the first day with a 66, suffered a double bogey at the 14th and a bogey at the 17th to fall into a tie for fourth with Daniela Holmqvist.

ActewAGL Canberra Classic
Canberra, ACT, Australia
Winner: Anne van Dam

Anne van Dam earned her third title inside six months with a powerful finish to win the ActewAGL Canberra Classic. An eagle at the 15th hole at Royal Canberra followed by birdies at the 16th and 18th holes gave the 23-year-old from the Netherlands a three-stroke victory over Slovenia's Katja Pogacar.

Korea's Jiyai Shin, the defending champion, was attempting to win for the third time at Royal Canberra in three starts — she won the Australian Open here in 2013 — and drew level twice on the back nine but could not keep pace with van Dam. Shin finished in third place after a 67, two ahead of Carly Booth, and one behind Pogacar, whose 68 gave her a best-ever finish on the LET.

After an opening 68, van Dam shared the 36-hole lead with Pogacar after a 63 which contained seven birdies in the first 10 holes and eight in all. On the last day she had to be patient, picking up two shots on the front nine, before accelerating away to victory over the last four holes. "It gave me so much confidence that I knew I could birdie every hole here," van Dam said of her second-round performance. "I just had to stay patient today, trust my long game and I was really happy with the way I putted."

Worrells NSW Women's Open
Queanbeyan, New South Wales, Australia
Winner: Meghan MacLaren

To prove she was no one-win wonder, Meghan MacLaren claimed her second LET title by successfully defending at the Worrells New South Wales Women's Open. MacLaren made her breakthrough at Coffs Harbour in 2018, but at Queanbeyan she won by three strokes over Munchin Keh and Lynn Carlsson after a tense finish.

MacLaren shared the lead with Swede Carlsson going into the final round and was one ahead when she turned in level par. But the 24-year-old Englishwoman dropped a shot at the 13th, and when Keh eagled the 16th, the 26-year-old from New Zealand, who had started five behind, led by two.

MacLaren matched Keh at the 16th by slicing a three wood around the trees to six feet. Keh then got into trouble at the 18th, seeing her second shot hit a tree and rebound onto the eighth fairway, and took a double bogey, her only dropped shots in a closing 67. MacLaren hit an eight iron to 12 feet at the same hole for a closing birdie. Her scores of 70, 66, 67 and 69 gave her a 12-under-par total of 272. Carlsson closed with a 72 to tie for second, two ahead of Christine Wolf.

"I wish I could play all of my golf in New South Wales," said MacLaren. "My first win was a big deal, but you don't want to be a one-win wonder. There was a bit more pressure this week and at the end I needed something, and found it, it's always going to be special for me."

Investec South African Women's Open
Cape Town, South Africa
Winner: Diksha Dagar

Defeating Lee-Anne Pace, attempting to win her national championship for the fourth time in front of a vocal home support, is the least of the issues India's Diksha Dagar has faced in life. The 19-year-old from New Delhi is hearing impaired and wears a cochlear implant. In only her fourth start as a professional, having left the amateur ranks after earning her card at the LET qualifying school the previous December, the former World Deaf champion overcame Pace and the rest of the field to win the Investec South African Women's Open.

On a windy first day at Westlake in Cape Town, Dagar started with two double bogeys in the first three holes. She had only one more bogey in an opening 76 and none at all in the last two rounds of 66 and 69. With a five-under-par total of 211, she beat Pace by one stroke, with fellow rookie Esther Henseleit, of Germany, sharing third place with Scotland's Michele Thomson.

Pace led with rounds of 72 and 68 before going three ahead with six to play in the final round. But she bogeyed the 13th before Dagar holed a long putt for birdie at the 15th and then chipped in at the 16th. With Pace bogeying the 17th for a 72, Dagar parred the last for victory.

"I really didn't expect to win, but it happened and I am very happy," Dagar said. "I got two lucky breaks towards the end. With the chip on 16, I had a feeling I could do it and it went in."

Jordan Mixed Open
Aqaba, Jordan
Winner: Daan Huizing

A new tournament featuring men and women competing against each other in the same competition ended with an intriguing duel between Daan Huizing and Meghan MacLaren. After two rounds of 65 at Alya, MacLaren led by two strokes, and after a fast start to the final round was three ahead at the turn. But Huizing, helped by MacLaren dropping three shots at the 10th and 11th holes, completed a five-stroke swing in four holes with birdies at the 12th and 13th to become the inaugural winner of the Jordan Mixed Open.

A starting field of 123 included 40 players from each of the Ladies European Tour, the European Challenge Tour and the over-50s Staysure Tour, plus three amateurs. The different tees used meant the women playing off 6,139 yards, the seniors from 6,601 and the Challenge Tour players from 7,100. Of those making the cut there were 20 from the LET, 21 from the Staysure and 25 from the Challenge Tour. The final group contained MacLaren, Huizing and Paul Streeter, who fell to ninth and was overtaken as low senior by Jose Coceres, who tied for fourth. Martin Simonsen took third place with a closing 64, while the second-ranked woman was Laura Fuenfstueck in 16th.

Huizing had rounds of 64, 68 and 68 for a 16-under-par total of 200, with MacLaren ending with a 72. "I'm obviously pretty disappointed not to win," she said, "but it was still an honor to represent women's golf alongside two other great tours. It was pretty tight coming down the last few holes, so I think it was great entertainment for everybody watching."

Huizing added: "I think it's a great initiative. It was great fun playing in a final group, it was a great battle, a different vibe and very special to be the first winner. I hope it's something that can continue in the future."

Lalla Meryem Cup
Rabat, Morocco
Winner: Nuria Iturrios

Even with extensive renovations to the Blue course at Royal Dar Es Salam, Nuria Iturrios felt just as at home. In 2016 as a rookie she won her maiden LET title at the Lalla Meryem Cup by six strokes. Three years later, and with all the greens and tees re-laid plus changes to the layout and bunkering, the 23-year-old from Palma de Mallorca re-claimed the title by seven strokes.

Iturrios was the only player to record four sub-par scores as rounds of 68, 71, 70 and 70 gave her a 13-under-par total of 279. Sweden's Lina Boqvist shared the lead with the Spaniard after 54 holes and was only two behind at the turn, but came home in 41 for a 77 to fall into a share of second place with compatriot Caroline Hedwall, who closed with a 70.

Iturrios birdied three of the first eight holes and did not drop a shot all day, making a spectacular save at the ninth after hitting a tree off the tee and threading her second through a small gap in the branches before getting up and down from off the green. "It's amazing for me to win again here," Iturrios said.

At the joint prize giving for the Trophee Hassan II, played on the Red course, and the Lalla Meryem Cup, Iturrios shared the stage with fellow Spaniard Jorge Campillo.

Omega Dubai Moonlight Classic
Dubai, United Arab Emirates
Winner: Nuria Iturrios

Just five days after winning in Morocco, Nuria Iturrios claimed back-to-back titles by capturing the inaugural Omega Dubai Moonlight Classic where each day's play finished under the floodlights of the Faldo course at Emirates. In the first professional tournament of its type, the day-night event saw players experience nine holes under lights on one of the first two days before Iturrios sealed victory under the illuminations by one stroke over the German pair of Olivia Cowen and Esther Henseleit.

Scores of 67, 68 and 71 gave Iturrios a 10-under-par total of 206 with the 23-year-old Spaniard recovering from a double bogey at the seventh when she hit into the water. Cowan also closed with a 71, while rookie Henseleit went out in 41 with a triple bogey at the eighth before coming home in 31. Another German, Karolin Lampert, was fourth, while Leona Maguire, who set the course record of 64 in the first round, was fifth with Caroline Hedwall.

"It's amazing to win again and I'm so excited," said Iturrios, who became the first player to win back-to-back since Aditi Ashok at the Indian and Qatar Opens in 2016. "It was so cool. I loved playing in the first day-night tournament and I hope to come back next year."

La Reserva de Sotogrande Invitational
Sotogrande, Spain
Winner: Celine Herbin

Two birdies in the last two holes gave Celine Herbin victory in the inaugural La Reserva de Sotogrande Invitational in windy conditions high above the Costa del Sol. In the final round, Herbin led by three strokes at the turn but made only one par coming home. That was a three-putt at the 16th where she lost the lead to Esther Henseleit as the 20-year-old German rookie claimed her second birdie of the inward half.

Henseleit, who finished as runner-up for the second tournament running and had finished outside the top 10 only once in her seven tournaments to date, got up and down for pars at the last two holes in a closing 70 but could not stop Herbin sweeping past her. The 36-year-old Frenchwoman, who only turned professional aged 29 following a career as a biomedical engineer, hit her tee shot to four feet at the short 17th and then struck her approach at the last over the flagstick to 10 feet. A closing 69, along with scores of 70, 70 and 73, gave her a six-under-par total of 282.

While delighted to be presented with the trophy by tournament host Annika Sorenstam, Herbin was most pleased with winning in Spain, where she practices often with her coach Vicente Ballesteros, brother of the late Seve. "I really wanted to do well here in Spain, so definitely a special win," she said. "It was also emotional to win in front of my parents."

Jabra Ladies Open
Evian-les-Bains, France
Winner: Annabel Dimmock

A steady nerve helped England's Annabel Dimmock overcome local amateur star Pauline Roussin Bouchard to win the Jabra Ladies Open by one stroke for her maiden title. Both players earned spots in the Evian Championship, having separated themselves from the field, with Meghan MacLaren taking third place, four strokes adrift of the runner-up.

Dimmock, 22, who turned professional in 2015, had scores of 69, 69 and 68 for a seven-under-par total of 206. Roussin Bouchard had shared the first-round lead with MacLaren on 68 and then held the solo lead after a 69 in round two before closing with a 70.

Roussin Bouchard first played in competitions at Evian aged 10 and has been a member of the club since she was 14. The now 18-year-old from Toulon had already won amateur tournaments in France, Portugal and Italy in 2019, but trailed after Dimmock produced four birdies in five holes from the third. Birdies at the 14th and 15th holes put the Frenchwoman ahead only for her to find the water at the short 16th for the first of two double bogeys in a row.

"It was quite a battle out there and I was disappointed about the bogey on 17, because I didn't want to make any mistakes, but it turned out well in the end," Dimmock said. "I've wanted to do this for so long and I'm so relieved I've finally won. I've been struggling a bit over the last few years since I first turned pro, so to finally get a win is really special."

Ladies European Thailand Championship
Pattaya, Thailand
Winner: Atthaya Thitikul

Thai amateur Atthaya Thitikul won the Ladies European Thailand Championship for the second time in three years — at the age of only 16. In fact, the 2018 Asia-Pacific Amateur champion ran away with the title to finish five strokes ahead of Esther Henseleit. Not even a three-hour delay due to a storm on the final day could disturb the young star.

Two off the lead after an opening 69 at Phoenix Gold, Thitikul went two ahead with a 67 on Friday before accelerating away from her opposition. A course record of 63 in the third round consisted of an eagle and seven birdies, five of them in a row from the 10th. She did not drop a stroke over the weekend and closed out with a 67 for a 22-under-par total of 266.

That her eight-stroke 54-hole lead was cut to five was solely due to a 64 from Henseleit, the German rookie who claimed her third runner-up finish of the season a week after earning her maiden professional victory on the Access Series the previous week. Third-placed Olivia Cowan finished six shots behind Henseleit and 11 behind the winner.

"It's unreal," said Thitikul. "I'm really pleased with all the things I've done in this tournament. I just put the ball where I wanted it. Since I won two years ago I've kept working hard and I've grown in confidence."

Evian Championship
Winner: Jin Young Ko

See Chapter 6.

AIG Women's British Open
Winner: Hinako Shibuno

See Chapter 6.

Aberdeen Standard Investments Ladies Scottish Open
North Berwick, Scotland
Winner: Mi Jung Hur

Mi Jung Hur won her first LPGA title in 2009 and her second in 2014. That five-year cycle continued when, 112 starts after her last victory, Hur won the Aberdeen Standard Investments Ladies Scottish Open. It was the 29-year-old Korean's first win since getting married in 2018 and her husband was on hand to drench her in champagne after she secured a four-stroke victory over Moriya Jutanugarn and Jeongeun Lee$_6$.

Despite the heavy rain at the Renaissance Club, Hur said: "Actually, I don't like links courses, but after this week, I love them." She was a stroke behind Jutanugarn after 54 holes, but the Thai lost her ball in thick rough just off the second fairway and took a double bogey.

Hur three-putted the third, at which point her Scottish caddie, Gary Marshall, repeated something he had told his player on the first day when Hur started birdie-bogey-bogey: "Come on MJ, you can win this." She did so with six birdies in the last 10 holes. While there was briefly a four-way tie for the lead around the turn, also including Mi Hyang Lee who finished fourth in the end, Hur stretched away with four birdies in a row from the ninth followed by two in the last three holes. She closed with a 66, tying the best of the day, following scores of 66, 62 and 70 for a 20-under-par total of 264. Lee$_6$ had a 70 and Jutanugarn a 71, while younger sister Ariya Jutanugarn was fifth.

Minjee Lee finished tied for sixth, the highest ranked player who came through the late-early half of the draw for the first two days which averaged six strokes worse. Wind and rain made conditions extremely difficult on Friday morning with a 68 from 55-year-old Dame Laura Davies, as she made the cut for the first time all year, a remarkable performance. She had a hole-in-one and thought it among the best rounds of her career.

Tipsport Czech Ladies Open
Belec, Czech Republic
Winner: Carly Booth

After victories at the Scottish and Swiss Opens in 2012, it took seven years for Carly Booth, now 27, to win again at the Tipsport Czech Ladies Open. Booth did not know the scores until she asked walking off the 18th green and burst into tears of joy at hearing that she had won. "Have I just played golf, or been at Alton Towers?" Booth said to her caddie. "I never want to go on a rollercoaster again."

Booth, sharing the lead with a round to play, drove out of bounds from the first tee and bogeyed three of the first four holes. Birdies at five of the next nine holes put the Scot back into the lead, but then she bogeyed the 14th and 15th holes. Salvation came in birdies at the next two before a par at the last. With scores of 68, 69 and 70 for a nine-under-par total of 207, Booth won by one stroke over Charlotte Thompson, Hayley Davis, Anais Meyssonier and Sanna Nuutinen, the Finn who closed with a 71 after sharing the lead with Booth after 36 holes.

"It was probably just as well I didn't know what the situation was," said Booth. "I'm a little bit flabbergasted by the whole day. I played good golf and I really had to dig deep in the final round. I'm overwhelmed with happiness. It's been seven years, so it's a bit of a shock."

The Solheim Cup
Winners: Europe

See Chapter 6.

Lacoste Ladies Open de France
Le Pian-Medoc, France
Winner: Nelly Korda

A week after making her debut in the Solheim Cup in a losing cause at Gleneagles, Nelly Korda cruised to victory at the Lacoste Ladies Open de France at Golf de Medoc near Bordeaux. Korda, the daughter of two tennis players from the Czech Republic, won for the first time on the Ladies European Tour and for the third time around the world in less than a year. The 21-year-old from Florida won in Taiwan late in 2018 and at the Australian Open early in 2019 for her two LPGA titles. "It feels great to win in Europe and hopefully I'll win one day in Czech."

Korda opened with a 68 and then added a 64 with six birdies, an eagle and one bogey on Friday to lead by six strokes. That advantage was cut to one in the third round as she scored a 70 and Joanna Klatten returned a 65. But Klatten was eight over par for her first six holes on Sunday as a 76 dropped the Frenchwoman into a tie for third place with Caroline Hedwall. Celine Boutier, one of the stars of the European Solheim Cup team, took second place, eight strokes behind Korda, who closed with a 67 for a 15-under-par total of 269.

"Conditions were tough, but I tried to stay level-headed and I tried to keep my head down and make as many birdies as possible," said Korda. "I played really well last week and unfortunately we didn't get the win, but I've been playing really solidly."

Estrella Damm Mediterranean Ladies Open
Sitges, Spain
Winner: Carlota Ciganda

In 2017 Carlota Ciganda saw her putt from three feet to win the Estrella Damm Mediterranean Ladies Open lip out and she ending up losing in a playoff at Terramar. A similar length effort at the final hole found the cup this time as the 29-year-old from Pamplona won her first LET title on Spanish soil. She won by one over Esther Henseleit, who recorded the fourth runner-up finish of her rookie season.

After rounds of 72 and 68, it was a 65 in the third round that put Ciganda, who two weeks earlier was part of Europe's winning Solheim Cup team, within two strokes of longtime leader Laura Fuenfstueck. But the German collapsed on Sunday, starting with two double bogeys and suffering another on the way to a 79. Conditions were difficult in the wind, with Fuenfstueck still finishing tied for fourth place with Ursula Wikstrom and Christine Wolf, while Sanna Nuutinen took third place.

Henseleit, taking up the German challenge, produced the best score of the final groups with a 68 that included five birdies in seven holes from the seventh. Experience prevailed for Ciganda with a 71 leaving her on an eight-under-par total of 276. A bogey at the 13th left her just one ahead, but five pars to finish sealed a fourth LET win but her first for six years.

"I'm very happy to win in Spain, with all the people here," Ciganda said. "My family is here and playing in Spain is always very special. It was a tough day with some crazy gusts on the course."

Hero Women's Indian Open
Gurgaon, India
Winner: Christine Wolf

A year earlier, Christine Wolf had suffered a quadruple-bogey-nine at the 18th hole in the third round at DLF Golf and Country Club and a double bogey in the final round and still managed to finish second. By getting her revenge on the par-five final hole, Wolf returned to claim the Hero Women's Indian Open and a maiden title on the Ladies European Tour. This time Wolf birdied the hole in the third round to take a one-shot lead into the last day, when she hit her third shot into a bunker behind the green. An exquisite recovery shot to little more than an inch from the hole secured a par and a three-shot victory for the 30-year-old Austrian over Marianne Skarpnord. Meghan MacLaren finished a further stroke back.

Wolf, from Igls near Innsbruck, had scores of 73, 68, 67 and 69 for an 11-under-par total of 277 and did not drop a shot over the final 44 holes. She became the second Austrian to win on the LET after Nicole Gergely in 2009.

"I'm very relieved. I was looking forward to coming back here. I didn't think, in my wildest dreams, that I would actually pull through," Wolf said. "I am super happy, obviously, to post my first victory but also because I did it here. I love the course and I already knew that coming into this week.

Everyone knew about the drama that went on last year. When I left last year, I was ready to be back, play the course and get some revenge on the 18th."

Andalucia Costa del Sol Open de Espana
Marbella, Spain
Winner: Anne van Dam

Anne van Dam won for the third time in Spain, and the fifth time in all, when she defended her title at the Andalucia Costa del Sol Open de Espana. On the tight Aloha course, the big-hitting Solheim Cup player did not hit her driver all week. Three behind starting the final round, the 24-year-old from the Netherlands was still one behind Nanna Koerstz Madsen playing the last.

While Madsen pulled her drive into a lake on the left as the wind strengthened, van Dam hit the fairway with a four iron before finding the green and two-putting from long range for a par. Madsen three-putted for a double-bogey-six to fall into a tie for second place with Aditi Ashok. It was one of three double bogeys for Madsen in a closing 74 that also included an eagle at the ninth when she holed her approach shot. Van Dam did not drop a shot in a final round of 70 for a total of 13-under-par 275 after earlier scores of 68, 69 and 68.

"It was a crazy day," said van Dam. "If you would have told me at the beginning of the day that two under was enough to win, I would have said, okay, I'll take it! It was a different day with harder conditions, a little bit of wind and it got really cold towards the end. Nanna is a good friend of mine and I would have loved to have beaten her in a playoff; that would have been a better feeling for me, but that's golf."

Magical Kenya Ladies Open
Kilifi County, Kenya
Winner: Esther Henseleit

To pass Marianne Skarpnord and win the Order of Merit at the last event of the year, Esther Henseleit had to win the inaugural Magical Kenya Ladies Open. With a round to play she was tied for second place but seven strokes behind Julia Engstrom, the 18-year-old Swede who had led for three days with scores of 67, 66 and 70. It took a brilliant new course record of 64 for the Baobab course at Vipingo Ridge to become the third player, after Laura Davies in 1985 and Carlota Ciganda in 2012, to win the Rookie of the Year award and finish as the European No. 1 in in the same season.

The first German to win the LET Order of Merit, Henseleit, 20 from Hamburg, turned professional in January with a handicap of +7.1. Although she won on the LET Access Series, she had finished runner-up four times on the main circuit. Previous scores of 69, 70 and 71 helped her to a 14-under-par total of 274 and a one-stroke victory over India's Aditi Ashok, whose 65 included a triple bogey at the short eighth hole.

"To close the season with a win is the best feeling I could imagine,"

Henseleit said. "I definitely tried to win, although I knew it would be really hard. After nine holes, I saw I was two shots back and I knew it was possible. I hit some great iron shots and gave myself many short birdie putts."

Henseleit made five birdies to turn in 31 as the pressure grew on Engstrom, the 2018 Rookie of the Year, who was out in level par and then three-putted the 10th. Henseleit swept past her with further birdies at the 11th, 13th and 15th holes. Engstrom also dropped a shot at the 13th but rallied with a birdie at the 15th before hitting a superb second at the 16th to little more than a foot from the hole but missing the putt. A 74 left her in third place, five ahead of Cheyenne Woods.

Japan LPGA Tour

Daikin Orchid Ladies
Nanjo, Okinawa
Winner: Mamiko Higa

Fourteen years after working as a fifth-grade volunteer at the Daikin Orchid Ladies tournament, Mamiko Higa made her childhood dreams come true when she won the traditional season opener on the Japan LPGA Tour in her native Okinawa.

The 25-year-old, who was on the fringes of the 2018 race for the tour's No. 1 position and finished fourth, landed her fifth title despite a final-round 76 amid weekend rains that played havoc with the field in one of the circuit's more-frequent 72-hole events.

"I felt like I was drifting between a dream and reality," the relieved Higa said after her birdie-par finish secured a three-stroke victory at five-under-par 283 and made her the first Okinawan to win the Daikin Orchid since Ai Miyazato, the island's long-time star who had recently retired, did it in 2004.

Higa took the lead with a second-round 66, the low score of the week at Ryukyu Golf Club, her 136 two shots better than the 138 of Sakura Koiwai. Her margin rose to seven over four damp players — Rei Matsuda, Jiyai Shin, Erina Hara and Koiwai — when the rains set in Saturday. Higa shot 71, the only sub-par score of the day for 207, and that big lead served her well as rain revisited Sunday.

Her early 10-under-par status dissolved amid two double bogeys and three bogeys, leaving her with only a two-stroke lead before she came up with a clutch birdie on the wind-blown 17th and parred the 18th to finish three strokes ahead of runners-up Hina Arakaki, Lala Anai and Eimi Koga.

Yokohama Tire PRGR Ladies Cup
Konan, Kochi
Winner: Ai Suzuki

Ai Suzuki was well on her way to a second consecutive money-winning championship in the middle of the 2018 Japan LPGA Tour season when a serious wrist injury sidelined the young star for eight weeks. The then-24-year-old had won four times by the middle of June and built a ¥34 million lead in the race for No. 1 when the injury occurred.

Though she had four top-10s after returning to action in September, Suzuki was unable to overcome the strong, late-season surge of Sun-Ju Ahn and finished third on the final money list. She resumed her strong play in the new season, rolling to a four-stroke victory in the Yokohama Tire PRGR Ladies Cup the week after missing the cut by a shot in the season-opening Daikin Orchid tournament.

A strong finish and the dual collapse of the second-round leaders did the trick for Suzuki at Tosa Country Club in Konan, Kochi Prefecture. Satsuki Oshiro and Seonwoo Bae, two unlikely leaders, had taken the 36-hole lead with matching rounds of 68-69–137 after Rumi Yoshiba topped the field the first day with her 67. Suzuki was tied for third with Min-Young Lee, both posting 69-70 scores through 36 holes.

Suzuki's 68 Sunday, matching the day's low score, gave her a nine-under-par 207 and brought home her 10th title as both Oshiro and Bae stumbled to 76s. Yoshiba shot 71 and finished second at 211. Ahn, the defending champion, was never a contender and tied for 22nd place.

T-Point Eneos Ladies
Osaka
Winner: Momoko Ueda

Momoko Ueda has never been able to replicate her brilliant 2007 season on the Japan LPGA Tour when, at age 21, she racked up five wins and led the final money list, but she keeps adding titles to her excellent record.

The most recent, the 13th of her career, was the T-Point Eneos Ladies in Osaka, when she strung together three 69s for a two-stroke victory at Ibaraki Kokusai Golf Club.

Ueda, now 32, might well have a gaudier total had she not chosen to spend most of six seasons on the big-stage LPGA Tour in the United States after gaining eligibility via her victory in the Mizuno Classic, the Japanese stop on the LPGA's international schedule. Playing full-time in her homeland since 2014, Ueda has been a consistent money winner, placing 10th or better in three seasons, but hadn't won since late 2017.

Jiyai Shin, who, like Ueda, abandoned the U.S. tour several years back, opened a bid for a 22nd win in Japan with a three-under-par 68, a stroke ahead of Ueda, S. Langkul and Ai Suzuki, the previous week's victor in Yokohama, and stayed in front by a shot Saturday with 69–137. Ueda's second 69 kept her just a stroke off the pace, tied then with Langkul and Sakura Koiwai (70-68).

Ueda took the top prize Sunday with the third 69 and 207 as Shin slipped to 72 and 20-year-old Minami Katsu joined her at 209 with a closing 67, the day's low round.

AXA Ladies
Miyazaki
Winner: Yui Kawamoto

Another neophyte entered the winner's circle as young players dominated the AXA Ladies tournament at the end of March. Though not still a teenager as were Nasa Hataoka and Minami Katsu when they captured their titles on the Japan LPGA Tour in recent years, Yui Kawamoto was just 20 years old when she rolled to a five-stroke victory at UMK Country Club in Miyazaki Prefecture.

Kawamoto was early into her first full season on the main tour after making her mark by topping the money list on the secondary Step-Up Tour in 2018 and playing in eight events after moving up late in the season. She had posted three top-20 finishes in 11 starts before the triumph in the AXA Ladies.

Strong showings the first two days set up Kawamoto's decisive win. With an opening 66, she trailed only Hana Wakimoto, another tour newcomer who had won money in each of the year's first three tournaments. Wakimoto shot 65 Friday, but 70 on Saturday as Kawamoto surged into a four-stroke lead with a 65 of her own. Wakimoto shared the runner-up spot with Reika Usui (68-67), yet another rookie making her first start.

A two-under-par 70 was all Kawamoto needed Sunday to polish off her initial Japan LPGA Tour victory. Four strokes behind her 201 and sharing the runner-up position were Chae-Young Yoon, who closed with a 66, and Thailand's S. Langkul (short for Saranporn Langkulgasettrin). Langkul, who was an early contender the previous week and, at age 19, fit into the youthful tenor of the tournament, matched Kawamoto's 70 for her 206.

Yamaha Ladies Open
Fukuroi, Shizuoka
Winner: Misuzu Narita

...and the beat goes on for Misuzu Narita.

As high as fifth and no lower than 27th on the final money lists while piling up 11 victories in her previous seven seasons on the Japan LPGA Tour, Narita added the 12th in the Yamaha Ladies Open in early April. The 26-year-old model of consistency, with at least one win in all but one season since her maiden victory in her rookie 2012 year, came from four strokes off the pace the last day to edge South Korean star Sun-Ju Ahn.

Coming off two top-20 finishes, Narita started slowly on the Yamana course of Katsuragi Golf Club with a 73 as Ah-Reum Hwang led with a three-under-par round on a tough day when her 69 was the only score in the 60s.

Scoring wasn't much better in the second round as Lala Anai (73-69) and Shina Kanazawa (71-71) took the lead, a shot ahead of Hwang (74) and five others, including Ahn.

Narita drifted five shots off the lead with a 74 and only gained a stroke Saturday with a 69 as Ahn also had a three-under round and went three in front of Kanazawa (73). Ahn managed only a par round Sunday, while Narita generated the week's lowest score of 67 to land No. 12 by a stroke and move to third place on the money list. Her 283 was one of only four sub-par 72-hole totals.

Studio Alice Ladies Open
Miki, Hyogo
Winner: Jiyai Shin

Jiyai Shin continues to reap dividends from a decision she made in 2014 to abandon the LPGA Tour in America to get close to her South Korea home by rejoining the Japan LPGA Tour on a full-time basis.

Her victory in the 2019 Studio Alice tournament was her 17th during that span, when she did everything except capture the season No. 1 position on the tour's money list. Coming off a four-win 2018, when she finished in second place, the 30-year-old standout had posted ties for second, fifth and sixth in her 2019 starts before her one-stroke win at Hanayashiki Golf Club vaulted her atop the money list. Over the four-season period starting in 2014, Shin finished fourth, third, second and fifth on the money lists before trailing only compatriot Sun-Ju Ahn in 2018.

Studio Alice was her 22nd triumph in Japan and 55th of her international career that includes wins on the U.S., European and Korean Tours and possession of the World No. 1 position for much of her 2010 campaign in America.

Shin nearly led all the way on Hanayashiki's Yokawa course in early April. She shared the lead the first day at 68 with lightly regarded Eri Fukuyama, then slipped a stroke off the pace with 70–138, as another unheralded player, Eimi Koga, shot 65, the week's lowest round, to go ahead with 137. Shin wrapped up the win with a 69 Sunday for a nine-under-par 207, a shot in front of Erika Kikuchi, who closed with a 66, and Saki Takeo, who finished with a 68 for her 208.

Vantelin Ladies Open KKT Cup
Kikuyo, Kumamoto
Winner: Ji-Hee Lee

Ji-Hee Lee, at 40 the senior member of a South Korean quintet of active 20-plus winners on the Japan LPGA Tour, emerged from a lengthy dry spell and claimed her 22nd title in the KKT Cup Vantelin Open.

It came with little forewarning. Lee, a former Open and PGA champion who twice finished second in the annual money races during her 18 seasons in Japan, had suffered through a feeble start to the 2019 season, entering the

Vantelin off a 52nd-place finish in the previous week's Studio Alice tournament. At Kumamoto Kuko Country Club, though, she rode three solid but unspectacular rounds to the one-stroke victory.

Her opening, two-under-par 70 stationed Lee in a sixth-place tie, three off the 67 of pace-setting Miki Sakai, who had gone nearly five years since scoring her lone tour victory. Saturday's 69 moved Lee just a stroke off the lead, tied then with Sakai (72) behind Solar Lee and Aoi Ohnishi, both having shot 68-70 rounds.

Lee repeated the 69 Sunday for her 208 total, edging Hikaru Yoshimoto (68) by a shot as Solar Lee managed only a 74 and Ohnishi skied to an 80. Mamiko Higa, who tied for fourth place, squeezed into the top spot on the money list, displacing the idle Jiyai Shin by ¥4 million.

Fujisankei Ladies Classic
Ito, Shizuoka
Winner: Jiyai Shin

Jiyai Shin gave herself a wonderful present on her 31st birthday.

Living up to her nickname — "Final-Round Queen" — with a dazzling 63 on the last day of the Fujisankei Ladies Classic, Shin grabbed her second victory of the current Japan LPGA Tour season. It continued a year in which she had been so dominant that the only time she wasn't winning or contending was when she wasn't in the field.

Besides the two wins, she tied for second and twice for sixth in the five events she entered among the first eight on the schedule, regaining the No. 1 position on the money list, a spot she would like to add to her glorious career record at season's end. It was her 23rd win in Japan and 56th of her brilliant international career.

Coming into the Fujisankei on the Fuji course of the Kawana Hotel Golf Club following her Studio Alice victory and absence from the previous week's Vantelin Open, Shin meandered seven strokes off the pace after 36 holes as Ritsuko Ryu led the first day with a 67 and Hikaru Yoshimoto the second day with 69-66–135.

Then she flashed her reputed finishing form Sunday. After a modest 34 on the front side, Shin cut loose with seven birdies and a pair of pars coming in for a 29 and the winning 63. She finished two strokes ahead of Ai Suzuki, Hinako Shibuno and Yoshimoto.

Panasonic Open Ladies
Ichihara, Chiba
Winner: Minami Katsu

Minami Katsu, a golfing sensation when she won the 2014 Vantelin Open as a 15-year-old high schooler, seems to have settled into a role in the uppermost echelon of players on the Japan LPGA Tour.

Coming off her initial victory at the end of her first full pro season in 2018, Katsu tallied four top-eight finishes in her first six starts in 2019, then picked off the Panasonic Open title the next time out, defeating veteran Mi-Jeong Jeon in the year's first playoff.

After two days, it appeared that Ai Suzuki, the 2017 money leader, might become the season's initial multiple winner. The 25-year-old Suzuki, the Yokohama Tire victor in March, opened on top with a seven-under-par 65 and remained in first place with a following 70 in Saturday's round, tied with Min-Young Lee, 27, who had a reverse 70-65 for her 135. Katsu entered the final round at Hamano Golf Club, Chiba, two behind after 69-68 scores, Jeon another stroke back after 71-67.

When Lee shot 71 and Suzuki 73 Sunday, Katsu and Jeon took advantage of the opportunity. Jeon shot 66 and Katsu 67 to forge a 204 deadlock and force the playoff, which Katsu won with a birdie on the first extra hole. That evened her playoff record at 1-1, while Jeon's fell to 3-7. Money leader Jiyai Shin tied for 10th. Katsu moved into third place in the standings.

World Ladies Championship Salonpas Cup
Ibaraki
Winner: Hinako Shibuno

A second 20-year-old joined the ranks of winners on the Japan LPGA Tour when Hinako Shibuno won a final-round battle with another circuit newcomer in the World Ladies Championship Salonpas Cup, the season's first major.

Like 20-year-old Yui Kawamoto, whose first win came in the AXA Ladies in March, Shibuno was playing in her first full season when she became the year's second maiden victor with her one-stroke win on the tough East course of Ibaraki Golf Club.

South Korean Seonwoo Bae, on the tour for the first time through the pre-season qualifier, turned out to be Shibuno's only serious impediment along the way. In fact, the 25-year-old led the tournament for two days with a 68-70 start that put her a stroke ahead of Shibuno and Yuri Yoshida with rounds of 71-68 and Ritsuko Ryu, who shot 69-70.

Shibuno, a second-place finisher a month earlier in the Fujisankei Ladies, caught Bae in the third round, producing a 66, the week's low score, to Bae's 67 for the 205s. Their nearest competitor, Yoshida, was then four back with her 70–209. Only Sakura Koiwai, well off the pace, broke 70 Sunday with a 69 as Shibuno and Bae matched strokes, Shibuno finally prevailing with 71–276 over Bae's 72–277. Lala Anai finished a distant third at 281.

The ¥24 million first prize jumped Shibuno into second place on the year's money list behind Jiyai Shin, who tied for 16th after a 69 start.

Hoken no Madoguchi Ladies
Fukuoka
Winner: Min-Young Lee

While playing a bit in the shadow of her more prominent South Korean compatriots, Min-Young Lee continued to make waves on the Japan LPGA Tour. Lee posted her fourth victory in the front end of her third season in

Japan, a one-stroke win in the Hoken no Madoguchi Ladies tournament in Fukuoka.

Her third had come in the Daikin Orchid opener at the start of what turned out to be a moderately successful 2018 season — 18th on the final money list. In the early stages of the 2019 campaign, things looked more promising for the 27-year-old, who beat kidney cancer in 2015. She finished in the top 10 in five of her eight starts prior to the Hoken No Madoguchi triumph.

Riding that momentum on the Wajiro course of Fukuoka Country Club, Lee opened with a 67 that tied her for second place with Minami Katsu, a stroke off the leading pace of Shina Kanazawa. With a 70 the second day, she moved into a first-place tie with Satsuki Oshiro (69-68), a shot ahead of Kanazawa (66-72) and money leader Jiyai Shin (69-69). She matched 69s with Shin Sunday and her 10-under-par 206 also held off Momoko Ueda (68–207) to secure the victory. Kanazawa slipped back into a tie for sixth with a closing 71.

Sun-Ju Ahn, the three-time and reigning No. 1, returned to action after being sidelined with a neck injury for five weeks, but missed the cut. The ¥21.6 million first prize jumped Lee into second place on the money list as second money widened Shin's lead to ¥13 million.

Chukyo TV Bridgestone Ladies Open
Toyota, Aichi
Winner: Minami Katsu

How often can one expect to see two 20-year-old golfers, both already current winners, finish one-two in a professional tour tournament?

Such a rarity occurred in the Chukyo TV Bridgestone Ladies Open in May when Minami Katsu won her fourth title on the circuit and Yui Kawamoto, the AXA Ladies champion, closed in to finish in second place. It was the second victory of the season for Katsu, who astonished the golfing world when she won the 2015 Vantelin Open when she was 15 years old. It moved her into second place on the money list within breathing distance of leader Jiyai Shin, the only other two-time 2019 victor, who was one of several top names who skipped the tournament on the Ishino course of Chukyo Golf Club in Aichi Prefecture.

Kawamoto joined Seonwoo Bae and Saki Asai atop the leaderboard with first-round, five-under-par 67s. But they and the rest of the field fell well behind Katsu Saturday as she put together a dazzling 62 for a 130 total, three ahead of runner-up Rei Matsuda and a massive six shots in front of third-placed Kawamoto (69), Hikaru Yoshimoto (68-68) and Hina Arakaki (72-64).

When Matsuda could not mount a challenge and finished with a par 72, Katsu was able to ease to victory Sunday despite a closing 72 of her own. Her 202 gave her a two-stroke victory over Kawamoto, who shot 68 the last day for her 204.

Resort Trust Ladies
Shizuoka
Winner: Erika Hara

The "Golden Generation" struck again at the Resort Trust Ladies tournament.

Following in the winning 2019 footsteps of Yui Kawamoto, Minami Katsu and Hinako Shibuno, all among eight successful players on the Japan LPGA Tour who were born just before the turn of the century, 20-year-old Erika Hara made off with her first circuit title, defeating South Korean Seonwoo Bae on the second hole of a playoff at the tournament's new site — Grandy Hamanako Golf Club in Shizuoka.

Hara, who carried a pair of fourth-place finishes into the tournament in her second season, started and finished with six-under-par 66s. The first one gave her a one-stroke lead over Kawamoto, who was coming off her victory the previous Sunday in the Chukyo TV Bridgestone tournament. Hara yielded first place the second day to amateur Ayaka Furue (69-65–134), who had made three strong showings earlier in the season. Hara shot 70, sitting in third place with Shibuno at 136 behind Furue and Kawamoto (67-68–135).

Bae, three back after 36 holes, shot 65 Sunday for her 202 to tie with Hara and bring about the playoff as Furue shot 70 and tied for third place with Kawamoto. Hara and Bae parred the first extra hole (No. 18), then Hara birdied No. 15, the next extra hole, and became the third first-time winner of the season — all members of the "Golden Generation."

Yonex Ladies
Nagaoka, Niigata
Winner: Momoko Ueda

Momoko Ueda joined Jiyai Shin and Minami Katsu as multiple winners in a tightly knitted cluster atop the Japan LPGA Tour money list when she romped to a six-stroke victory in the Yonex Ladies tournament in early June. All three players then had a pair of 2019 victories and stood 1-2-3 in the cash standings with only ¥3 million separating leader Shin and third-placed Katsu with Ueda in the middle.

With 14 victories blanketing her 13-year career on the circuit, Ueda blew away the field after entering the final round of the Yonex a stroke behind surprise co-leaders Rio Ishii (70-67) and Hyo-Joo Kim (67-70). The 32-year-old had rounds of 70-68 at Yonex Country Club in Nagaoka, Niigata Prefecture, before running away with the title Sunday with the week's best score, a 65, and the winning, 13-under-par 203. Kim shot 72 and Ishii 79 Sunday.

Ueda's six-stroke margin over tri-runners-up Yuki Ichinose, Rumi Yoshiba and Kim was the widest up to then in the season. The tournament field was slightly depleted with only four of the previous week's top 10 in action. Most of the absentees played in the U.S. Women's Open in America the preceding week.

Ai Miyazato Suntory Ladies Open
Kobe, Hyogo
Winner: Ai Suzuki

Back on the Japan LPGA Tour after a three-week absence while playing in the U.S. Women's Open, Ai Suzuki resumed her quest for a second money title with a narrow victory in the first Suntory Ladies Open dedicated to Ai Miyazato, one of the country's highly admired all-time stars, who had recently retired from active tournament golf.

The 25-year-old Suzuki, the 2017 No. 1 whose 2018 chances were crippled by a lengthy injury recuperation, bagged her second win of the season and 11th of her career, finishing with a 12-under-par 276 at Rokko Kokusai Golf Club in Kobe, Hyogo Prefecture, in mid-June. She edged Mamiko Higa, the Daikin Orchid winner in March, by a stroke and joined Jiyai Shin, Minami Katsu and Momoko Ueda as a two-time 2019 winner.

Min-Young Lee, another leading player gunning for her second win of the season, led the Suntory the first two days. She opened with a seven-under-par 65, a stroke ahead of Hina Arakaki and two in front of Suzuki, Shina Kanazawa, Miyuki Takeuchi and Bo-Mee Lee, the 2016 and 2017 leading money winner, and followed with a 68 for 133. Suzuki took over second place Friday with her 67-68–135.

A 71 was enough for Suzuki to move into the lead the third day at 206, a shot better than Yui Kawamoto, the AXA Ladies winner in March who recorded three straight 69s, as Min-Young Lee faltered with a 75. Higa, who was on the edge of contention all week, mounted the biggest challenge to Suzuki Sunday. Her closing 67 fell a stroke short as Suzuki shot 70 for the winning 276.

Injuries sidelined both Jiyai Shin, No. 1 on the current money list, and Sun-Ju Ahn, the four-time No. 1. Ahn entered the tournament but did not start because of a recurrent neck ailment. Shin injured her right hand and withdrew after a 70-72 start.

Nichirei Ladies
Chiba
Winner: Ai Suzuki

Ai Suzuki returned to a familiar spot in the Japan LPGA Tour standings when she made it back-to-back wins with her second straight victory in the Nichirei Ladies tournament. It vaulted her atop the money list for the first time since mid-summer of 2018 when a wrist injury forced her out of action for eight weeks and probably cost her a second straight No. 1 season.

The third 2019 victory and career 12th did not come easily in her title defense on Sodegaura Country Club's Shinsode course in Chiba Prefecture. She had to go an extra hole to overcome the bid of Sayaka Takahashi, yet another up-and-coming young Japanese player seeking her first professional win, after the two finished in a tie at nine-under-par 207.

Takahashi had led the tournament for two days. The 20-year-old, who joined the tour in mid-2018, had been playing well for the previous six weeks after making only one cut in her first nine 2019 starts. Placing no worse than 32nd since the World Championship in mid-May, she jumped off Friday with a 67, tied for first place with Asako Fujimoto. A 68 in the second round moved her alone at the top, a stroke ahead of Mamiko Higa (71-65) and two in front of Suzuki (70-67) and Eri Fukuyama (68-69).

Takahashi managed just a par round Sunday, enabling Suzuki to overtake her with her 70 and defeat her in the subsequent playoff with a birdie on the 18th, the first overtime hole. Suzuki supplanted Jiyai Shin as the money leader. Shin had held the No. 1 slot through the previous eight tournaments.

Earth Mondahmin Cup
Chiba
Winner: Jiyai Shin

Jiyai Shin wasted little time reclaiming the No. 1 position of the Japan LPGA Tour's money list. Just seven days after Ai Suzuki slipped past her into the top spot, Shin rebounded far in front of her younger rival with a lucrative, wire-to-wire victory in the Earth Mondahmin Cup tournament. The ¥36 million first prize, by far the biggest that far into the 2019 season, gave the veteran South Korean star a ¥25 million lead.

The solid performance continued an outstanding season for Shin. In her 11 starts, she won three times, had four other top-sixes and did not finish any worse than 16th place. The three-stroke Earth Mondahmin Cup win was her 24th in Japan and 57th worldwide.

Shin began the run to her latest victory in a three-way tie for the lead as she, Erika Hara and Nana Suganuma shot 67s before she took full command of the proceedings. Her second-round 66 moved her a stroke ahead of Satsuki Oshiro (69-65), and her 68–201 on a rainy Saturday gave her a three-shot cushion over Hara (69), the Resort Trust winner, and six ahead of third-placed Miya Miyazoto. Shin had only one bogey through the first three rounds.

Rain and blustery winds greeted the field Sunday. Only seven players broke par and Shin's 72 carried her to the three-stroke win. Hara (72) and Miyazato (69) finished second at 276.

Shiseido Anessa Ladies Open
Kanagawa
Winner: Hinako Shibuno

It happened again. For a fifth consecutive week on the Japan LPGA Tour, a player with at least one 2019 win already on her record added another as Hinako Shibuno, dubbed the "Smiling Cinderella" in recognition of her pleasant on-course demeanor, pulled off a playoff victory in the damp inaugural Shiseido Anessa Ladies Open.

The 20-year-old Shibuno, a member of Japan's so-called "Golden Generation" of young standouts, who had broken the ice two months earlier in the major World Ladies Championship, managed one of just two sub-par rounds recorded in a rain-swept final round to extend the tournament into extra holes.

Her one-under-par 71 enabled her to overtake South Korea's Min-Young Lee, another lady with a current-season win under her belt. Lee had taken the lead the third day from compatriot Hee-Kyung Bae, who held first place for 36 holes with a 66-68 start. Lee's Saturday 67–203 gave her a two-stroke margin over Shibuno, who tacked a bogey-free 66 on to her earlier 71-68 scores.

A double bogey by Lee at the 15th hole Sunday opened the door for Shibuno, who birded three of the last six holes for her 71–276 and forged the tie as Lee, making only one birdie all day in the wet weather, shot 73 for her 276. Another double bogey cost her on the first playoff hole, Shibuno winning with a par. The ¥21.6 million first prize moved her back into second place behind Jiyai Shin on the money list.

Nippon Ham Ladies Classic
Hokuto, Hokkaido
Winner: S. Langkul

The parade of young winners continued at the Nippon Ham Classic. The only difference was that on that occasion it wasn't a member of the Japanese "Golden Generation" of young stars. Instead, it was a 19-year-old from Thailand whose full name — Saranporn Langkulgasettrin — she conveniently shortened to S. Langkul for playing purposes.

The teenager spent two seasons on China's LPGA Tour before tackling the stronger Japan LPGA Tour in 2019 and playing reasonably well through her first four months, missing only three cuts and finishing as high as a second-place tie in the AXA Ladies in March.

Then, after barely making the cut in the previous two events, Langkul's game jelled at Katsura Golf Club in Hokkaido. She took the lead away from Yui Kawamoto (66), one of those young winners, shooting a second-round 65–134. Then, she gave it back to Kawamoto and Eri Okayama Saturday with her par–206 to Kawamoto's 69–205 and Okayama's 68–205.

Langkul pulled away to a three-stroke victory Sunday, fashioning a five-birdie, bogey-free 67 for 15-under-par 273 to become the season's fourth first-time winner. Kawamoto shot 71 and shared second place with Mone Inami, who closed with a 70 for her 276. Money leader Jiyai Shin withdrew after a first-round 70.

Samantha Thavasa Girls Collection Ladies
Ami, Ibaraki
Winner: Sakura Koiwai

The remarkable display of young talent on the Japan LPGA Tour added another name to the list of 2019 winners with Sakura Koiwai's victory in the Samantha Thavasa Girls Collection Ladies tournament in mid-July.

Seven of the season's first 20 titles were claimed by players either 19 or

20 years old and Koiwai was only three months beyond her 21st birthday when she posted the lowest 54-hole winning score of the season at Eagle Point Golf Club at Ami, Ibaraki Prefecture. Her 17-under-par 199 produced a one-stroke victory, her first, as she played in every one of the first 20 tournaments and finished 12th or better in four of the five events preceding the Samantha Thavasa. She had three second-place finishes, including a playoff loss, in her 2018 maiden season on the tour.

Things were tight the first two days at Eagle Point. Koiwai jumped off in front Friday with a 66, but only led Min-Young Lee, Kana Mikashima and Mone Inami by a shot and seven others by two. Lee, a four-time winner, moved two strokes ahead of Koiwai Saturday with 65-132 as Koiwai shot 68-134 with eight others within five strokes of the lead.

Koiwai then matched Lee's 65 in the final round and claimed the victory when the 25-year-old South Korean fell a shot short with her 68-200. The Hokkaido native, who has been playing golf since she was eight years old, set a new tournament record with the 199.

Century 21 Ladies
Saitama
Winner: Mone Inami

It was probably overstating the case, but it had come to a point that, if a player was much beyond her 21st birthday, she could forget about winning when she teed it up in mid-season in one of the Japan LPGA Tour's tournaments. For the fourth consecutive week and eighth time during the 21-event season, the person accepting the winner's trophy was 19, 20 or barely 21 years old when the Century 21 Ladies tournament concluded in late July.

This time it was Mone Inami, who was just a day short of her 20th birthday when she finished up a nice run of showings with a one-stroke victory at Ishizawa Golf Club. The win was not a big surprise. Inami had been one of Japan's leading amateurs before turning pro in 2018, but was not eligible to enter quite a few of the 2019 tournaments in her first full season until a reshuffle of standings elevated her status at the end of June. Still, in those early months, she had three top-10s and in July she had two more, including a runner-up two weeks before becoming 2019's sixth first-time winner.

Inami took permanent possession of the lead the second day after starting with a four-under-par 68, tied for second place with Eriko Kobashi a stroke behind Erika Hara, the 20-year-old Resort Trust victor in June. Inami's second-round 69-137 thrust her two shots in front of Hara (67-72) and three ahead of five others. She closed out her win with a 70 and 207 total, just enough to edge Na-Ri Lee (67-208) and Serena Aoki (67-208). Hara shot 72 Sunday.

Daito Kentaku Eheyanet Ladies
Narusawa, Yamanashi
Winner: Misuzu Narita

Misuzu Narita became the sixth multiple winner of the season when she landed the title in the Daito Kentaku Eheyanet Ladies tournament in early August.

The 26-year-old Narita, who has won at least once in every season save one since she picked up her first title in her rookie 2012 season, came from two strokes off the pace to eke out a one-shot victory to go with her April triumph in the Yamaha Ladies Open.

She improved her position in the standings every day at Narusawa Golf Club in Yamanashi Prefecture. She started in 13th place with a 70, four strokes behind first-win-seeking Mayu Hamada, who followed up her 66 with a 67 Friday to build a four-shot lead over Chie Arimura, Ah-Reum Hwang and Saiki Fujita. Narita (70 again) was then in an 11th-place tie seven strokes off the pace.

The bubble burst for Hamada on the weekend. She shot 73 Saturday and yielded the lead to Arimura, 31, who had a 68–205 as she sought her 14th career victory. Narita, with 67–207, advanced into a four-way tie for third place with Hwang, Fujita and amateur Ayaka Furue. Narita polished off her 13th tour victory Sunday. Her 70–277 was just enough to edge Arimura (73) and South Korea's Seonwoo Bae (69), who finished second for a third time in 2019, including a playoff loss to Erika Hara in the Resort Trust tournament. With a 77, Hamada dropped into a massive, eighth-place tie at 283.

Hokkaido Meiji Cup
Kitahiroshima, Hokkaido
Winner: Seonwoo Bae

Seonwoo Bae had been knocking vigorously on the victory door time and again during the 2019 season. It finally opened in early August when she scored a playoff win in the Hokkaido Meiji Cup as she joined six others in the ranks of this year's first-time winners.

A rookie on the tour, the 25-year-old South Korean was coming off her third second-place finish of the season, an earlier one a playoff loss to Erika Hara in the Resort Trust tournament, and had placed third in two other events. Battling against several of the tour's most successful players, she didn't let her latest chance escape.

Money leader Jiyai Shin, making her first start in a month, grabbed the first-round lead with a five-under-par 67 on Sapporo International Country Club's Shimamatsu course. Bae was just a stroke back, tied with veteran winners Sun-Ju Ahn, Ai Suzuki and Teresa Lu, and she assumed the top spot the second day with her 67–133. Lu, Ahn and Suzuki shot 69s and trailed by two shots.

Suzuki faded Sunday, but Lu and Ahn overtook Bae on the front nine with 32s to her 34. Birdies, though, were rare on the final side. Lu birdied the 11th, Bae the 12th and that was it. The three parred every other hole on the back nine, putting Lu (67) and Bae (69) into a deadlock at 204 and Ahn (68), the four-time No. 1, a stroke out of the year's fifth playoff.

Taiwan's Lu was seeking her first win since her four-victory 2017 season, but succumbed to Bae's birdie on the first extra hole.

NEC Karuizawa 72
Karuizawa, Nagano
Winner: Lala Anai

In this day and age, most professional golfers, male and female, believe it necessary to take a week or two away from the tour every now and then to keep their games fresh.

Not Lala Anai.

The veteran Japanese pro plays every tournament and it paid off at the NEC Karuizawa 72 in mid-August as she racked up her third victory in her 10th season on the Japan LPGA Tour.

The win in a playoff against South Korea's Min-Young Lee capped a strong record the grinder had compiled earlier in the season. She started the year with a second-place finish in the Daikin Orchid tournament and subsequently posted five other top-fives and eight top-10s before the triumph on the North course of Karuizawa 72 Golf in Nagano.

The 31-year-old lingered a few strokes behind Mayu Hamada the first two days. Hamada, winless on the tour, started off with a bang (64) with 10 birdies and two bogeys. She led 2018's No. 1 Sun-Ju Ahn by a shot and maintained first place Saturday, shooting 70–134 and leading Erika Hara and Hinako Shibuno (67-68s) by a shot, Lee (67-69) by two and Anai (67-70) by three.

Anai and Lee were brilliant on the final nine Sunday in forging the deadlock. Anai birdied four of the last seven holes for 65–202 and Lee matched it by birdieing 16, 17 and 18 for 66 and her 14-under-par total. Hamada had a bogey-free 69, but fell a stroke short, tied for second with Shinobu (68).

Anai joined a flock of serious contenders for the money title when she won the playoff with a par on the first extra hole to Lee's bogey. It was the second playoff defeat of the year for Lee, who did win the Hoken No Madoguchi. Anai rose to fourth on the money list.

CAT Ladies
Hakone, Kanagawa
Winner: Saki Asai

Saki Asai joined the party.

The 21-year-old became the eighth winner her age or younger — seven for the first time — during the first six months of the season when she commanded the CAT Ladies tournament from the first hole to the final putt.

Asai's victory was a bit surprising since, although she had missed only one cut in her previous 15 starts, she had posted only one top-10 finish earlier in her first full season on the main circuit after spending most of her previous two years on the secondary Step Up Tour.

But she got off to a great start when she eagled the par-five first hole at the par-73 Daihakone Country Club course in Kanagawa Prefecture and went on to a five-under-par 68, the only score under 70 in the opening round. She followed with 69–137, establishing a three-stroke lead over Serena Aoki (72-68) and four atop Lala Anai, the previous Sunday's winner who bounced back from an opening 75 with 66, the best score of the week.

Anai mounted the biggest challenge Sunday, shooting a 69–210, as Aoki skied to 78 and a tie for 17th. Asai had just enough cushion that her bogey at the last hole still gave her the title by a single stroke with her 72–209.

Nitori Ladies
Otaru, Hokkaido
Winner: Ai Suzuki

Ai Suzuki finished atop a star-spangled leaderboard at the Nitori Ladies tournament, stashing away her fourth victory of the season.

Suzuki, the 2017 money leader on the Japan LPGA Tour, closed out the win, her 13th, two shots in front of current No. 1 Jiyai Shin and Sun-Ju Ahn, who won her fourth season title in 2018 when the Nitori Ladies was one of her five victories. The two have 49 wins between them on their Japan LPGA Tour records. Another star, popular newcomer Hinako Shibuno, the two-time victor in Japan who also won the Women's British Open Championship, finished fifth. Despite being the first player to bag four 2019 titles, the 25-year-old Suzuki still trailed Shin and Shibuno in the tight money race.

The cream came to the top in Friday's second round after lightly regarded Moeno Tan led the first round at Otaru Country Club in Hokkaido with a five-under-par 67 only to flameout the rest of the way. Suzuki and Ahn with 70-67 rounds and Sayaka Takahashi with 69-68 took over first place Friday, two shots ahead of Shibuno and amateur Yuka Yasuda (71-68s).

Suzuki and Ahn remained ahead Saturday when they matched 71s for 208s, as Shin recovered from a Friday 76 that included a triple bogey, shooting a seven-birdie 65, the week's low score. Yusuda (70) was a shot off the lead. Shibuno (71) and Karis Davidson (70) were two behind.

Suzuki moved two shots in front with four birdies on the first 10 holes Sunday, then closed it out after two bogeys with a final birdie on the 18th hole for 69–277. Pairs of back-nine bogeys blunted the chances of Ahn and Shin, scores of 71 and 68 putting them into the runners-up deadlock at 279.

Golf 5 Ladies
Ibaraki
Winner: Min-Young Lee

Min-Young Lee, one of the most consistent contenders on the Japan LPGA Tour, joined the title race with a hard-fought, one-stroke victory in the Golf 5 Ladies tournament.

Lee's second win of the season and fifth overall carried her into third place in the money standings behind leader Jiyai Shin, the Golf 5 defending champion who finished second to the 27-year-old South Korean for a second time in the season, and right on the heels of runner-up Hinako Shibuno, who was not in the field. Besides the victories, Lee's previous 2019 record included, among seven other top-five showings, three second-place finishes, two of them playoff losses.

The Golf 5 victory evolved from a tournament-long battle with Shin and Saki Asai, the CAT Ladies winner in August, who opened with a 10-birdie, one-bogey 63 on the Golf 5 Club Sunnyfield to lead Lee and Shin by a stroke. The runners-up became co-leaders Saturday, both shooting 68s to move a stroke ahead of Asai (70).

Nothing changed on the front nine the last day as all three players went out in 34. Lee dropped back into a first-place tie with Asai when she bogeyed the par-three 12th hole, matched birdies with her on the 13th and went in front to stay with another birdie at No. 16. Shin birdied the last hole for 69 to join Asai (68) in second place a shot behind Lee's 68–200, and extended her first-place margin on the money list to nearly ¥20 million.

Japan LPGA Championship Konica Minolta Cup
Hyogo
Winner: Nasa Hataoka

Of all the young Japanese players who were enjoying winning ways in recent years, the exploits of 20-year-old Nasa Hataoka stood head and shoulders above the rest. During the four years after she won the Japan Women's Open as a 17-year-old amateur, she turned pro and picked up six more victories. Two came in America on the U.S. LPGA Tour, on which she spent most of that time, and four others in Japan, including another Women's Open and in mid-September a third major, the Japan LPGA Championship Konica Minolta Cup.

That last one was the most decisive. She ran away from the field in the final round of the rich (¥200 million) tournament, winning by eight strokes, the biggest margin of the season.

Hataoka, one back with a 69 the first day at Cherry Hills Golf Club in Hyogo Prefecture, took a one-stroke lead Friday with her first of three consecutive, five-under-par 67s and was only two shots up on Hikaru Yoshimoto with her 203 after three rounds. Chinese star Shanshan Feng shot 63 Saturday to threaten at 206. Both of those closest pursuers went in the wrong direction Sunday, Yoshimoto collapsing to an 80 and Feng managing just a par round.

On the other hand, Hataoka started the day with a pair of birdies and, still two under par for the day after two more birdies and two bogeys through 14 holes, ended any doubts when she holed out for an eagle on the par-four 15th en route to the final 67–270, a new tournament record. Feng and Aoi Ohnishi tied for second at 278.

Descente Ladies Tokai Classic
Mihama, Aichi
Winner: Hinako Shibuno

Hinako Shibuno had already dazzled the world of women's golf with two victories on the Japan LPGA Tour and her monumental triumph over the female game's best in the British Women's Open in England in her first foray outside her native Japan. All at age 20 in her first full season on tour. She added another spectacular performance in September in the Descente Ladies Tokai Classic, racing from eight strokes off the pace with a final-round, eight-under-par 64 for 203 to make off with her fourth title of the year.

Five players finished in second place, but the one who was there most surprisingly was Jiyai Shin, the veteran star and current leader on the tour's money list. Shin, owner of 24 tour victories and 57 worldwide seeking her first No. 1 season title, had led the field the first two days at Shin Minami Aichi Country Club in Aichi Prefecture. She and Ji-Hee Lee, her South Korean compatriot, had brilliant opening rounds themselves — 63s — Shin with 11 birdies and two bogeys, Lee with an eagle, eight birdies and a bogey.

Shin took command Saturday with 68–131, jumping into a three-stroke lead over Min-Young Lee, another South Korean standout. Shibuno was nowhere in sight at that point after rounds of 69-70–139, but she was flawless Sunday. She rang up four birdies on each side for the 64, finishing early and watching as, in order, Momoko Ueda (65), Mayu Hamada (68), Lee and Teresa Lu (70s) and, in the final grouping, Shin came up two strokes short at 205, Shin astonishingly shooting 74 with two bogeys and nary a birdie.

Shin still retained the top spot on the money list at ¥116,521,332, some ¥10 million ahead of runner-up Shibuno.

Miyagi TV Cup Dunlop Ladies Open
Rifu, Miyagi
Winner: Asuka Kashiwabara

Asuka Kashiwabara had enjoyed moderate success in her six years as a professional, but had yet to win on the Japan LPGA Tour and had her doubts that it might ever happen. Sitting just two strokes off the lead going into the final round of the Miyagi TV Cup Dunlop Ladies Open in late September, "I decided to fight that feeling. I [felt I] had to be bullish, especially with my putting."

The result of that change of attitude was a Sunday 68 and a two-stroke victory as Kashiwabara, who had finished among the top 50 money winners in each of the previous four seasons and had posted three top-10s in 2019, became the ninth first-time winner on the circuit.

The lead had changed hands in the first two rounds at Rifu Golf Club in Miyagi Prefecture. Seonwoo Bae, the Hokkaido Meiji Cup winner in August, had it with her first-round 66, then yielded it Saturday when she shot 75. Mamiko Higa, who won the season-opening Daikin Orchid tournament in March, and lesser-known Rie Tsuji took over with matching 68-68 rounds. Kashiwabara had shot 68-70 rounds and was tied for fourth place with Mao Nozawa.

Her aggressive resolve paid off in spades Sunday as she ran off a four-birdie, one-bogey front nine to become the frontrunner. Three more birdies offsetting a pair of bogeys coming home established the winning 68–206. Bae rebounded with a 67 to land in second place at 208. Higa slipped into a four-way tie for third with a 74, and Jiyai Shin added a bit to her season money lead with her tie for seventh.

Japan Women's Open Championship
Hakusan Village, Mie
Winner: Nasa Hataoka

Nasa Hataoka took a brief absence from the LPGA Tour in America to return home and play in three tournaments, two of them major championships. The talented 20-year-old added both of those majors to her already gaudy record, the Japan LPGA Championship by eight strokes in mid-September and the Japan Women's Open by a mere four shots three weeks later.

As impressive as her other achievements at home and abroad had been, her record in the Women's Open is perhaps unprecedented in the realm of major championships worldwide. The latest victory was her third in that major event in four years, beginning with her win in 2016 when she was a 17-year-old schoolgirl. Furthermore, she finished second to international star So Yeon Ryu in the one she didn't win in 2018.

Things did not start well for Hataoka this time. She bogeyed her first two holes on the Hakusan Village Golf Club course, Mie Prefecture, but still shot 67, sitting three strokes off the lead of Hee-Kyung Bae and Eri Okayama the first day. She was two back after Friday's round with another 67 as Bae shot 68–132, then joined Momoko Osato (68–201) in first place the third day with a third 67, defending champion Ryu lurking two back in third place.

Hataoka had to shake off another slow start Sunday, bogeying the third and fourth holes and yielded the lead to Ryu. "At that time, my caddie told me not to think too much," she recalled. "Finally, I felt calm." So calm that she birdied three of the next five holes and rolled on to a 69 and the winning, 18-under-par 270. Ryu finished in the four-back, second-place slot with Okayama and Osato. It was Hataoka's fifth win in Japan, plus two victories on the U.S. LPGA Tour.

Stanley Ladies
Susano, Shizuoka
Winner: Ah-Reum Hwang

Ah-Reum Hwang's career record will carry a winning score — 100 — that is unlikely to ever be matched in the annals of golf. This happened because the disruption caused by a destructive storm resulted in the Stanley Ladies tournament winding up a 27-hole event. The arrival of Typhoon Hagibis in Shizuoka Prefecture not only wiped out Saturday's second round but led to the decision to just play nine holes on the back nine of Tomei Country Club in eerie solitude Sunday. For safety's sake, no gallery was admitted.

Hwang, three times a winner in 2018, made the most of the unfortunate situation, posting her unique, eight-under-par score and her fifth Japan LPGA Tour victory. The 31-year-old veteran, three times a winner in 2018, carried a two-stroke lead into that unusual half-round. Her game rejuvenated after skipping a tournament two weeks earlier, she rang up eight birdies against a lone bogey Friday. Two shots back of her 65 were Erika Kikuchi and Maria Shinohara and three others trailed by just two.

"I was nervous in the [Sunday] morning," admitted Hwang. "I [knew I] couldn't make a single mistake." She didn't, although she needed several par saves before making her lone birdie from seven feet at the 15th hole. She then parred in for 35 and the 100. Four players tied for second at 102, Hinano Hoshikawa and Saki Takeo with 34s and Kikuchi and Shinohara with 35s.

Fujitsu Ladies
Chiba
Winner: Ayaka Furue

The parade of young winners on the Japan LPGA Tour continued at the Fujitsu Ladies tournament, but this time with a twist. Ayaka Furue, a 19-year-old amateur, made off with the title, joining nine others no more than 21 years of age with 2019 victories to their credit.

Furue's win was not overly surprising. Playing in 10 previous events on sponsor invitations, she had three top-10 finishes and missed only two cuts before the life-changing victory. Immediately afterward, she turned professional and applied for LPGA of Japan membership.

She was in the thick of things from the start at Fujitsu's Tokyu Seven Hundred course, joining a six-way tie for third place as one of those other youthful winners, Mone Inami (Century 21), opened with a nine-birdie 63. Furue followed with a 65 Saturday, her 132 moving her into solo second place a stroke behind Kana Mikashima (65-66) and one ahead of Inami (70) and Sayaka Takahashi (67-67).

Pointing out that "I was able to concentrate without being nervous," Furue overtook Mikashima with her second birdie at the seventh hole in the final round. She took command of the lead and "felt something different" when she paired birdies at the 13th and 14th holes, added another at the 16th and took her only bogey of the tournament at the final hole. That gave her a 67, a 199 total and a two-stroke margin over Inami (68) and Mikashima (70), who split first and second prize money, each getting ¥10.8 million.

Furue became the 10th first-time winner of the season and seventh amateur to win in Japan LPGA Tour history, four of the others coming since 2012.

Nobuta Group Masters Golf Club Ladies
Miki, Hyogo
Winner: Asuka Kashiwabara

It took Asuka Kashiwabara six years before landing her first victory on the Japan LPGA Tour, but only a month more to get her second one, which, as she remarked later, "is said to be the most difficult." Actually, it wasn't easy.

Kashiwabara, still only 23 years old, came from six strokes off the lead in the 72-hole Nobuta Group Masters Golf Club Ladies tournament, taking advantage of an uncharacteristic collapse of Taiwan star Teresa Lu to win by a single stroke at Masters Golf Club in Miki, Hyogo Prefecture.

Lu, the winner of 16 tournaments in Japan but without a victory since her four-title 2017 season, had blazed into a three-stroke lead in the third round, racking up nine birdies and a closing bogey for 64–202. Mone Inami, the Century 21 winner in July, had led the first two days with 67-68 rounds. Kashiwabara was at 208 but tied for fourth place with money leader Jiyai Shin.

Lu started adequately Sunday until she bogeyed the seventh hole. Then three more followed on the next five holes as she faded to a final 75. Meanwhile, Kashiwabara was cruising up the leaderboard. She termed her fifth birdie at the par-five 15th hole the turning point and added a final one at the par-three 17th — "I struggled with this hole every year" — for 66–274 and the one-stroke victory over Bo-Mee Lee, who had encountered hard times since her back-to-back No. 1 title seasons in 2015 and 2016.

Mitsubishi Electric/Hisako Higuchi Ladies
Hanno, Saitama
Winner: Ai Suzuki

Ai Suzuki took a realistic approach to her incongruous position on the Japan LPGA Tour money list: "[I'll] have to win one or two more. You can't give up."

She said this after winning her fifth tournament of the season and still sitting a fairly distant third on the money list behind leader Jiyai Shin, whom she edged by a stroke in a down-to-the-wire finish in the Mitsubishi Electric/Hisako Higuchi Ladies tournament in early November.

As was the case in 2018 when she led the race for much of the season, an injury was a major factor inhibiting the 25-year-old's bid for a second No. 1 season finish. The 2017 champion missed four weeks earlier in the fall while nursing an injured left hand as the consistent Shin continued to add to her earnings with a run of high finishes.

Suzuki never trailed in the Mitsubishi at Musashigaoka Golf Club in Saitama Prefecture, sharing the first-round lead at 66 with Minami Hiruta and, with 68-134, taking a one-stroke lead on Shin (69-66–135) the second day. Suzuki pulled away with three early birdies in the Sunday round only to have Shin close the gap to one stroke with her fourth back-nine birdie at the 15th hole when Suzuki took her lone bogey. Both players birdied the next hole and parred in, Suzuki notching her 14th tour victory with her 68-202 and Shin finishing second (68-203) for the sixth time in 2019.

Toto Japan Classic
Shiga
Winner: Ai Suzuki

The Toto Japan Classic is clearly a level well above the other tournaments on the Japan LPGA Tour and an admittedly nervous Ai Suzuki knew it as she carried a three-stroke lead into the final round of the event co-sanctioned with the U.S.-based LPGA Tour.

"One of my dreams has been to win this tournament. If I can only play [today] like I am playing on the Japan LPGA Tour," thought Suzuki, who was coming off her fifth win of the season.

She already had, making a lone bogey while co-leading (with Hannah Green) after the first round and leading alone by three strokes over Gaby Lopez after 36 holes with rounds of 67 and 65.

Suzuki was never threatened Sunday. She ran off four birdies on the first seven holes of the North Course of Seta Golf Club in Shiga and capped the bogey-free round with a fifth birdie on the final hole. It gave her another 67 and 199, 17 under par and three strokes ahead of runner-up Hyo-Joo Kim, an LPGA regular who birdied the last three holes for 66-202.

With the victory, her 15th in six full seasons, Suzuki advanced to second place on the Japan LPGA Tour money list within shouting distance of the leader, Jiyai Shin, who finished in a 40th-place tie. It also presented her with a decision to make. The win qualified her for playing privileges on the U.S. Tour, which she admitted "has always been my dream. But the first thing I want is to win the money title."

(Suzuki was No. 1 in 2017 and was far ahead in 2018 before being sidelined for eight weeks with a wrist injury.)

Itoen Ladies
Chonan, Chiba
Winner: Ai Suzuki

Ai Suzuki achieved what few before her ever accomplished as she vaulted into first place in her quest for a second money title on the Japan LPGA Tour with her victory in the Itoen Ladies tournament.

For one thing the one-stroke triumph was Suzuki's third in a row, a run that hadn't been accomplished since Mi-Jeong Jeon did it in 2007 and only Akiko Fukushima before then in 1997.

For another it was her seventh win of the season, a total that had only been reached by two other players — Bo-Mee Lee in 2015 and the great Yuri Fudoh twice, seven in 2004 and 10, the record, in 2003.

The Itoen victory did not come easily for Suzuki. The red-hot 25-year-old trailed Jiyai Shin (69-65), the money leader she was chasing, and Kaori Ohe (68-66) by a stroke after her rounds of 68-67 put her amid a cluster of contenders after 36 holes at the Great Island Club in Chiba. However, neither leader stayed in the picture Sunday, Shin surprisingly shooting 72 and Ohe 73. Instead, Suzuki had to battle 42-year-old Shiho Oyama, winner of 18 tournaments over the years, and Seonwoo Bae, the Hokkaido Meiji Cup champion, most of the way.

The three were tied at 13 under par when Oyama birdied the 15th hole. Then Bae dropped back when she bogeyed the 17th, and Suzuki wrapped up the victory with her fifth birdie at the last hole for 67 and 202. Matching 67s gave Oyama 203 and Bae 204.

The ¥18 million purse jumped Suzuki's season earnings to ¥144 million, nearly ¥8 million ahead of Shin, who had led the race since bypassing Suzuki in late June.

Daio Paper Elleair Ladies Open
Matsuyama, Ehime
Winner: Hinako Shibuno

A classic cast crowded the top of the standings going into the final round of the Daio Paper Elleair Ladies Open. The top five players on the money list were there among the eight top contenders, seven of them 2019 winners in pursuit of Haruka Morita, who had dominated during the first 54 holes.

Eighteen holes later, the ever-smiling Hinako Shibuno emerged from a battle down the stretch with money leader Ai Suzuki with a fourth tour victory that elevated her into position to challenge for the "Prize Queen" title in the following week's finale Tour Championship. On the other hand, the outcome prevented Suzuki from winning an unprecedented fourth straight victory. It was her 14th top-10 finish.

Morita, the 23-year-old daughter of Chinese parents who was born in Japan, led the first and third rounds with her 65-69-67 cards and maintained her lead over the first 11 holes Sunday at Elleair Golf Club, one ahead of Shibuno and two up on Suzuki. Then she fell out of contention with three bogeys over the final holes, as did Jiyai Shin, the other valid contender for the money title, who tumbled with a 74 final round.

Shibuno's sixth birdie on the 15th hole inched her a shot ahead of Suzuki, and the lead held up when Suzuki finished bogey-birdie for 67–270, one behind Shibuno's bogey-free 66–269. Going into the Tour Championship, Suzuki maintained her sizeable lead over Shin on the money list as Shibuno, although in third place, moved herself within range of the top spot.

Japan LPGA Tour Championship Ricoh Cup
Miyazaki
Winner: Seonwoo Bae

The season-concluding Japan LPGA Tour Championship had colorful overtones to it, thanks to Seonwoo Bae and Ai Suzuki.

Bae donned her favorite color — red — for the final round and picked off the major title by four strokes with a closing, five-under-par 67. "Red is a birdie color," the 25-year-old explained, giving no indication that she was emulating Tiger Woods' last-day pattern. The win, her second of 2019, capped an exceptional first-year season for the South Korean, who also had four seconds and three thirds among her 13 top-10 finishes.

Suzuki wore an all-white outfit — "I play with a pure white feeling" — as she wrapped up the "Prize Queen" money title, the check for her tie-for-fifth finish giving her a ¥160,189,665 total and a ¥7.5 million edge over Hinako Shibuno, who jumped Jiyai Shin into the runner-up with her second-place finish at Miyazaki Country Club. It was the second money title in three years for Suzuki, who had seven victories and said she would have been "embarrassed" by any other outcome. Shin, who led the money list for much of the season, killed her chances with an opening 75. She tied for fifth place.

The outcome was a big disappointment for Bo-Mee Lee, whose game showed signs of life in the late months of 2019 after she went through two meager seasons on the heels of her consecutive money titles in 2015 and 2016. With rounds of 71-68-69, Lee had taken a one-stroke lead over Bae into the final round, but suffered a five-bogey string on the front nine Sunday and fell into fifth place with a closing 74.

Bae was one over par before a 20-foot birdie putt at No. 8 ignited a run of five more over the remaining 10 holes that carried her to a four-stroke victory with her 277 total. Shibuno, also concluding a brilliant season, shared second place with 19-year-old Ayaka Furue, who turned pro after winning the Fujitsu Ladies in October.

Korea LPGA Tour

After World No. 1 Jin Young Ko, a two-time major champion in 2019, and U.S. Women's Open winner Jeongeun Lee$_6$ became the latest stars of the Korea LPGA to find global success at the very top of the game, attention in their homeland turned to who might be next to follow in their footsteps. One clear answer was Hye Jin Choi, who won the KLPGA money list, the points list and the stroke average table.

The 20-year-old, who grew up playing golf in Busan, had already signaled her talent by finishing as runner-up to Sung Hyun Park at the 2017 U.S. Women's Open as an amateur. She also won twice on the KLPGA that year before turning professional and two more wins in the 2018 season made her the Rookie of the Year.

In 2019 Choi won five times to extend her tally of titles to nine. She also finished as a runner-up twice and made the cut in all 27 of her events. Her steady game produced a greens-in-regulation percentage of 82 percent, the best on the circuit.

Choi won her first domestic major title in April at the CreaS F&C KLPGA Championship in a playoff over So Yeon Park, then beat Ha Na Jang by three strokes at the NH Investment & Securities Championship. She then won the S-Oil Championship in June, an event shortened to 36 holes, before adding the McCol Yongpyong Resort Open the same month. In another of the majors in October at the Hite Jinro Championship, she finished a stroke behind the returning World No. 1 Ko, who won for the fifth time worldwide, before Choi won for the fifth time herself at the SK Networks Seokyung Ladies Classic a month later.

Da Yeon Lee, 22, won the Kia Motors Korea Women's Open by two strokes at Bear's Best CheongNa, with a 65 in the third round matching the best score of the week. Lee, who finished third on the 2019 money list, won twice more during the year, the last of them in December counting as the first event on the 2020 schedule. The other majors were won by Chae Yoon Park at the Hanwha Classic, where Nelly Korda was among the runners-up, and Hee Jeong Lim at the KB Financial Group Star Championship, her third win in two months. The 17-year-old was just pipped for Rookie of the Year honors by 19-year-old Ayeon Cho, who won twice.

Jang, as well as being a runner-up three times in the season and finishing second on the money list to Choi, won two events with the biggest purses. After victory at the Hana Financial Group Championship, formerly a tournament co-sanctioned with the LPGA, Jang also claimed the BMW Ladies Championship, the new LPGA co-sanctioned event at the newly renamed LPGA International Busan. It was a 12th KLPGA win for the 27-year-old and her fifth LPGA title, but a first since 2017 when Jang returned to the Korean circuit full-time. It was a dramatic victory with a best-of-the-week 64 in the final round putting her in a playoff with American Danielle Kang, who spent part of her childhood in her father's hometown of Busan. Jang won with a birdie at the third extra hole.

At the end of the year, the KLPGA team defeated the LPGA for only the second time in the five-year history of the Orange Life Champions Trophy hosted by Inbee Park. Although Jin Young Ko defeated Hye Jin Choi, 5 and 3, in their head-to-head on the final day, and Lee$_6$ beat Cho, 5 and 4, the KLPGA won seven and halved one of the 12 singles to win 15-9. Among the KLPGA winners were Da Yeon Lee and Hee Jeong Lim, while Jang beat Kang, 2 and 1.

Australian Ladies Tour

Hannah Green provided the highlight of the year for Australian Women's golf by winning her maiden major title at the KPMG Women's PGA Championship. The 22-year-old from Perth was in only her second season on the LPGA, where she had yet to win, and entered the week at Hazeltine National ranked 114th in the world. But she led from start to finish, surviving a weekend in the spotlight playing in the final group each day to par the last hole, getting up and down from a bunker, to win by one stroke over Sung Hyun Park.

"I've always wanted to win an event and to win a major championship as my first is crazy," said Green, whose support group included mentor Karrie Webb. "The up-and-down on the last was world class," said Webb. "It's taken her 12 to 18 months to feel she belongs out here and what a way to show it."

Green also won the Cambia Portland Classic five events later and finished the year 12th on the LPGA money list, four places behind Minjee Lee, who won the Hugel-Air LA Open and had six other top-three finishes. But it was Green who scooped the Greg Norman Medal as the leading Australian professional of the year, a second woman to win the award following Lee in 2018.

All the main ALPG tournaments at home were won by overseas players. American Nelly Korda added to a remarkable family success story Down Under by winning the ISPS Handa Women's Australian Open at The Grange in Adelaide. Elder sister Jessica won the event in 2012, while in the tennis version of the Australian Open, father Petr won his only grand slam title in 1998 while younger brother Sebastian won the junior event in 2018. "I think there's something in the air here," said Korda, who would win twice more during the year in France and Taiwan. "I'm just happy to finally be a part of the club."

Celine Boutier claimed her first LPGA title at the ISPS Handa Vic Open, while in the events co-sanctioned with the Ladies European Tour there were wins for Marianne Skarpnord at the Pacific Bay Resort Australian Classic,

Anne van Dam at the Canberra Classic and Meghan MacLaren, defending her title, at the NSW Women's Open.

Sarah Kemp won the ALPG Order of Merit for the first time thanks to her tied-second finish at the Vic Open, where she closed with a 65, followed by a top-10 finish at the Australian Open the next week. Those results meant the 33-year-old regained her status on the LPGA for 2020, but Kemp also claimed a 12th ALPG pro-am title at the Aoyuan International Moss Vale Pro-Am.

Tanhia Ravnjak won the ClubCar Series with victories at the Ballarat Icons Pro-Am and the Findex Yamba Pro-Am, where she defeated Whitney Hillier, winner of the Brisbane Invitational, in a playoff. Both players could have scooped the A$9,500 bonus for winning the Series by winning the event, but it was the 25-year-old Ravnjak, from Wollongong, who prevailed by holing from six feet at the second extra hole.

China's Weiwei Zhang won the Trust Golf Thailand LPGA Masters at Panya Indra by two strokes over local Patcharajutar Kongkraphan. Zhang, 22, from Hainan Island, became the first player to win four times in one season at the China LPGA circuit which also sanctioned the event along with the ALPG, for which this was the opening event of the 2019-20 season, and the Thailand LPGA. Having won by seven strokes the previous week, Zhang led from wire-to-wire with scores of 65, 70 and 69 for a 12-under-par total of 204. Eagles at the first and sixth holes in the final round helped Zhang outlast Kongkraphan, who also closed with a 69. China's Du Mohan took third place, while the leading ALPG performer was Hanee Song of New Zealand in sixth place.

At the end of 2019 it was announced that the ALPG and the PGA of America had agreed to align their organizations but would retain separate identities.

13. Senior Tours

The big names on the Champions Tour in 2019 were McCarron, Kelly and Goosen, but perhaps the year would be better known for the name that was missing.

This was the year that most reports from the tour didn't begin with the name Bernhard Langer. Langer didn't dominate the tour and didn't win the Player of the Year award, to which he'd all but developed a proprietary relationship. He first won it in 2008, and for 11 years missed winning it only three times — 2011, 2012 and 2013. And he'd won it the past five years.

Had time finally taken its toll? Langer was 62, already past the age when most senior careers begin to fade. But he was still a phenomenon. Had the marvelous skills of strength and timing weakened? Or had the competition gotten keener? Not long ago, he seemed to be winning every other week. A mirage, of course. Those weren't exactly amateurs he was playing against. But in 2019, he won only twice — the Oasis Championship in February and the Senior British Open in July. The year was a downer compared to, say, 2017, when he won seven times. Langer also had 10 top-10 finishes and won over $1.8 million, finishing the year with 40 Champions Tour career victories, just five behind Hale Irwin's record 45. (Langer did also team with his son Jason to win the unofficial Father Son Challenge in December.)

Down year or not, Langer was in excellent company. Only two players won more, and both were three-time tour winners — Scott McCarron and Jerry Kelly. And they provided the real heat on the tour, along with rookie Retief Goosen.

McCarron won the Jack Nicklaus Player of the Year Award for the first time, and with an unusual performance. He took the Mitsubishi Electric Classic in April, the Insperity Invitational in May and the Mastercard Japan Championship in June, and then became the target for the rest of the tour. McCarron, who led the Charles Schwab Cup standings for 21 consecutive weeks, also was runner-up three times, had 14 top-10 finishes and topped the money list with $2.5 million.

"This is like a new lease on life for me," said McCarron, 54, on his first win, the Mitsubishi. "But I know that there's an end in sight … I'm putting everything I can into these, whatever — 10, 15 years."

Jerry Kelly was second in winnings at over $2.3 million, followed by Goosen at $1.8 million and Langer. The million-dollar winners went 17 deep, to Steve Flesch, at $1,029,288. There were four others with two victories — Kirk Triplett, Steve Stricker, Miguel Angel Jimenez and Kevin Sutherland. Stricker continued to split time between the Champions Tour and PGA Tour and was the 2020 U.S. Ryder Cup captain.

South Africa's Retief Goosen, a member of the World Golf Hall of Fame, won the Rookie of the Year award on a record highlighted by one win, the Bridgestone Senior Players Championship, two seconds and 12 top-10s.

The 2019 Champions Tour became the Catch Scottie chase, led by the good-natured Kelly, who if he had a coat of arms, it wouldn't have a lightning bolt or a sword, it would have a goatee and a big grin. Ironically, it was the week after McCarron posted the last of his three victories that Kelly won the first of his three, the American Family Insurance Championship in mid-June. He added the Ally Challenge in September and the SAS Championship in October, and uttered a heartfelt victory message. Said Kelly: "I'm very happy to be healthy, very happy to be playing well at this time."

In senior golf outside the United States, Phillip Price made off with the John Jacobs Trophy as the Staysure Tour's No. 1 player at the end of a season without a truly standout performer. The 53-year-old Welshman led the Order of Merit with only a single victory — albeit the major Staysure PGA Seniors Championship — and season-long consistency, posting 12 top-10 finishes in his 15 starts in the 17 European events on the schedule.

Only four titles went to first-time winners and South Africa's James Kingston was not among them, despite finishing second to Price on the Order of Merit standings. He placed second four times during the season. Only three players had multiple victories, Barry Lane, David Shacklady and Jose Coceres each picking up two wins.

No surprise that Bernhard Langer captured the Senior Open at Royal Lytham & St. Annes in the only one of the five U.S. majors also on the Staysure Tour schedule that is played in Britain. It was the brilliant German's fourth victory in that event.

Once again, a Thailand player led the final standings of the Japan Senior Tour, but this time it wasn't Prayad Marksaeng. Instead, compatriot Thaworn Wiratchant nosed him out for the top spot, breaking Marksaeng's string of season No. 1s at three in a row. Wiratchant got the edge when Marksaeng elected not to play in the final two of the year's 18 tournaments. Both had two victories, as did Eiji Mizoguchi and Shinichi Akiba, the only other multiple winners.

Long-time star Toru Taniguchi, still active on the regular Japan Tour, played in just two events, winning the Japan Senior Open after losing to Masahiro Kuramoto in a playoff in the Starts Senior earlier in the season. He was one of the season's six first-time winners. Hidezumi Shirakata took the Japan Senior PGA Championship, the other major, finishing three shots ahead of runners-up Marksaeng, Wiratchant and Kuramoto.

Champions Tour

Mitsubishi Electric Championship
Kailua-Kona, Hawaii
Winner: Tom Lehman

Tom Lehman wanted to win as badly as the next guy. But there's winning, and then there's, well, winning.

Lehman, 59, a sensitive and thoughtful man, plucked the restricted-field Mitsubishi Electric Championship out of the hands of David Toms, co-leader in the first round and solo leader of the second, who lost on a bogey on the final hole.

Said Lehman: "As a competitor, you don't want to win that way. You would rather make a putt than have somebody miss a putt. So I felt bad for him, because I thought he played extremely well."

Toms, chasing his second victory in three years on the Champions Tour, shot 65-65 in the first two rounds, tying Joe Durant for the lead in the first, then leading Durant and Lehman by four through the second. "I just have to go out and shoot another low round," Toms said. He was okay — for 17 more holes.

Toms bogeyed the first hole of the final round, then posted four birdies through the 10th, getting to 17 under and holding off Jerry Kelly and Bernhard Langer. They closed with 67s and tied for third, three back.

Lehman, four behind entering the final round, was relentless. Four birdies on the front got him to within two of Toms, then he caught him with birdies at 13, 14 and 16, completing his 69-65-65–199, 17 under. Toms came to the decisive par-four 18th. He had a 70-foot putt for birdie, knocked it seven feet past and missed the return for his par. He bogeyed for a 70–200.

"Hate to end up that way on the last hole," Toms said.

Lehman had his 12th tour win. "I wouldn't say I deserve it," Lehman said, "but I feel like I've earned a win. I'm not going to give the trophy back."

Oasis Championship
Boca Raton, Florida
Winner: Bernhard Langer

"The key this week was not making many bogeys," Bernhard Langer told the media group. "I think I made two bogeys all week. Would that be correct?"

"One," came a voice.

So in the Oasis Championship in February, the first full-field event on the 2019 Champions Tour, Langer made only one bogey on the par-72 Old Course at Broken Sound — practically his home course — to take his 39th tour victory by five strokes over Marco Dawson. "It means a great deal to win in front of your home crowd," Langer said, and one other thing made it even more so. "My first win with my daughter Jackie, who's only caddied three times for me." And the $255,000 first prize gave him the tour career record of $27,196,504.

Gary Nicklaus, 50, son of Jack, and two-time U.S. Open champion Retief Goosen, were making their tour debuts. Said Nicklaus: "I was ... kind of shaking like a leaf, which I didn't expect." He shot 67-77-73–217, one over, and tied for 51st. Said Goosen: "I feel like I'm playing okay, but you've got to go out and make the scores." He shot 69-69-72–210, six under, and tied for 24th.

Langer would shoot Broken Sound in 64-68-65, a 19-under 197, but first he had to contend with free-spirited Jesper Parnevik, who figured he went through probably 40 putters and 50 strokes trying to solve his putting problems. Things worked best, he said, when he felt the most uncomfortable. "Man, I'm mostly shocked right now," he said. He led the first round with a 63. His solution didn't last.

Langer surged in the wind-whipped second round, with eagles at the 11th and 18th, both par-fives, in a 68. Then Langer ran away in the final round, riding five birdies over the first seven holes to a 65.

"When I came out on this tour, I was trying to be one of the better players," Langer said. "It worked out better than I had hoped for."

Chubb Classic
Naples, Florida
Winner: Miguel Angel Jimenez

As golf tournaments go, the Chubb Classic gave a pretty fair imitation of a grand steeplechase. Consider that down the final round nine players shared the lead at one time or another. And Spain's free-spirited Miguel Angel Jimenez — who trailed by five strokes after the first round and three after the second — didn't tie until the last hole of regulation, and didn't taste the solo lead until his par putt on the first playoff hole made him the winner.

"I go to any competition, I want to win," Jimenez said. "I'm working for that, no?"

Yes, and this time against the formidable Bernhard Langer and former U.S. Senior Open champion Olin Browne, on the verge of his third Champions Tour victory.

Browne led by two coming to the final hole, Lely Resort's par-four 18th. There, he double-bogeyed off a poor drive, shot 66 and a 13-under 200. He was paired in the sixth-from-last grouping with Jimenez, who shot the day's only bogey-free round, a five-under 66 to tie Browne. Then they had a nervous wait as Langer, in the next-to-last group, parred in for a 68 and tied them.

They left wreckage in their wake. Kevin Sutherland rallied for two closing birdies for a 69 and tied for fourth, a shot back with Woody Austin (69). Stephen Ames had a double bogey and two singles coming in, shot 71 and tied for sixth. Glen Day and Ken Tanigawa each bogeyed twice coming in, shot 72 and tied for 11th. And Marco Dawson bogeyed five of 11 holes from No. 6, shot 72 and tied for 25th.

Jimenez, shooting 68-66-66, never led and finally tied at 13-under 200. In the playoff, at the 18th, Browne and Langer missed the green and bogeyed, and Jimenez two-putted from 30 feet for a par and his seventh tour win.

His secret? "I'm working hard and I practice and go to the gym," Jimenez said, "apart from smoking and drinking."

Cologuard Classic
Tucson, Arizona
Winner: Mark O'Meara

Is seven under good enough? To any golfer worth his calluses, the answer is no way. Case in point: Mark O'Meara, in the first round of the Cologuard Classic. "Anytime you shoot seven under, you can't be too disappointed," O'Meara conceded, "but certainly when you're eight under after nine holes, you would like to do a little better."

He'd had a remarkable day on the par-73 Tucson National, shooting a seven-under 66. But he figured he should have done one or two better. He parred No. 1, then ran off eight straight birdies, tying a Champions Tour record, parred the next eight holes from the 10th, then bogeyed the 18th. He'd had an excellent day. But, he noted, you just can't ever get too many birdies on this tour.

"I've had 15 or 16 seconds, so that's been pretty disappointing," said O'Meara, 62, who had won twice on the tour but not in over eight years. "You just can't take your foot off the pedal. Because somebody's going to come up from behind you."

Like, for example, Kenny Perry, who opened with a 65, leaving O'Meara second. O'Meara took over from there. He shot a five-birdie 70 in the windy second round and led by one over Willie Wood (71), Kirk Triplett (69) and Scott McCarron (70). In the final round, O'Meara notched five birdies on the front nine, three more and a bogey on the back, and shot 66 for a four-stroke victory on 17-under 202.

"So, you know, I'm a lucky guy," O'Meara said. "I'm glad to have finally got another win under my belt."

O'Meara had to share the stage with baseball Hall of Fame pitcher John Smoltz, 51, making his Champions debut. Smoltz, playing on a sponsor's invitation, shot 73-74-73, tying for 53rd at one-over 220. "It's much easier closing baseball games," said Smoltz, "than it's been closing out the golf tournaments."

Hoag Classic
Newport Brach, California
Winner: Kirk Triplett

The Hoag Classic, at Newport Beach Country Club, turned out to be the tournament everybody grabbed for but nobody could get a grip on. Not, that is, until Kirk Triplett became the third player in Champions Tour history to win a playoff with an eagle.

Before that, there were some pretty good threats. Fran Quinn, 53, trying for his first tour win, led by three going into the final round. But it slipped away from him. Six others were within a shot of each other. David McKenzie, David Toms and Esteban Toledo all dropped from the picture. Jeff Maggert rocketed from a 76 in the first round and finished within one.

It all left Triplett and Woody Austin to slug it out in a playoff. Triplett ended it with a 12-foot eagle putt on the second extra hole.

"If anybody made two or three birdies on the back nine, they would have taken control," Triplett said.

Quinn had birdied seven of his first 11 holes in the first round and three of the last four in the second, shot 64-67, and led by three. Then in the final round he hit one fairway bunker and missed three fairways, made four bogeys and shot 74 to tie for fifth. "I didn't miss a shot for two days, and today I looked like an eight-handicap," Quinn said.

Triplett (70-65) and Austin (68-67) started the final round four behind. They closed with 68s, Austin getting an eagle and a birdie and Triplett two bogeys and five birdies, and tied at 10-under 203. In the playoff at the par-five 18th, they tied with pars in the first visit, and in the second, Austin missed the green with his second and Triplett reached in two and rolled in his 12-footer for an eagle and the win.

Said Austin: "He hit three quality shots there to win, but I gave him the chance."

Said Triplett: "I feel pretty lucky to have just had a chance to be in the playoff."

Rapiscan Systems Classic
Biloxi, Mississippi
Winner: Kevin Sutherland

It's not often a golfer can forgive himself overnight for missing a two-foot putt for the win. But so it was for Kevin Sutherland, in the Rapiscan Systems Classic. Thereby hangs another great golf tale.

Sutherland, 54, had one win in his five years on the Champions Tour, and now he was grinding out his second at Fallen Oak. In the first round, after six birdies and an eagle, a bogey at the par-three 17th — "really a good two-putt," he said — cooled him to a seven-under 65 and a tie for the lead with Marco Dawson. He shot 69 in the windy second — "I was really very fortunate," he noted — for an encouraging three-shot lead. Then the surging Scott Parel, who had opened with 68-72, supplied the discouraging.

Parel, a huge six strokes behind starting the cold, rainy, windy final round, stood still with two birdies and two bogeys on the front. Three birdies coming in, the last from 18 feet at the 18th, gave him a 69 and a seven-under 209. Parel needed help, and he got it from Sutherland, whose game stalled out in the blustery weather to a three-bogey 75 and a tie with Parel. Billy Andrade, after leading briefly, bogeyed two of the last three holes, shot 71 and missed the playoff by a stroke.

The playoff was a seven-hole grind over two days. Sutherland and Parel tied five times — four pars and a bogey — before darkness ended play Sunday.

But first, Sutherland knew the pain of victory flitting from his fingertips. All he needed was that two-foot putt for par at the second extra hole. But he missed. The next morning, they parred the sixth extra hole. At the seventh, both were putting for birdies. Parel missed from 20 feet, but Sutherland holed his 15-footer for the win. The agony was over.

"Last night, I didn't sleep well," Sutherland said. "I was constantly thinking about that putt I missed. But I got a second chance. It's all good now."

Mitsubishi Electric Classic
Duluth, Georgia
Winner: Scott McCarron

For Scott McCarron, there was a lot to love about TPC Sugarloaf. Namely, his three victories there, the latest being the 2019 edition of the Mitsubishi Electric Classic in April. He led wire-to-wire in the bad weather, stumbled early in the final round, regained his feet, and held off a pack of hounds for a two-shot victory.

"Obviously," McCarron said, "it's a golf course I like." He spoke of an earlier time, when he played it with architect Greg Norman and learned the nuances and necessaries of the course, and then went on to win the 1997 and 2001 BellSouth Classics on the PGA Tour. He posted his ninth Champions Tour victory on 68-70-71–209, seven under, for a two-stroke win over Jerry Kelly (67), Joe Durant (69), Kirk Triplett (69) and Kent Jones (69).

As to when McCarron won:

"I would say I won the tournament, really, the first day," McCarron said. If that sounded high-handed, his explanation filled in the blanks. "Because," he said, "I played so well, shot four under in such difficult conditions ... that's [what] probably led me to victory."

Foul weather Friday forced first-round play into Saturday. McCarron, who finished his opening 68 on Saturday, and Bob May, at 69, were the only two players in the 60s in the first round. McCarron (68-70–138) led by three going into the final round, when he ran into a shaky spell. He started bogey-birdie-double bogey. Then he settled down and birdied the fourth.

Durant birdied four of the first six, led briefly, but bogeyed No. 9 and parred in. "Had my chances," he said, "but just didn't capitalize." McCarron drove the green of the par-four 13th and birdied to retake the lead, then birdied the 15th to set up his two-shot win.

"This," he said, of playing on the Champions Tour, "is like a new lease on life for me. But I know that there's an end in sight ... I'm putting everything I can into these, whatever — 10, 15 years."

Bass Pro Shops Legends of Golf at Big Cedar Lodge
Ridgedale, Missouri
Winners: Scott Hoch and Tom Pernice, Jr.

If the rest of the field needed something to shoot at going into the final round, Tom Pernice, Jr. certainly gave it to them. Pernice, teamed with Scott

Hoch in the Bass Pro Shops Legends of Golf at Big Cedar Lodge, opened the final round 1-2. As in ace-birdie.

And they rolled from there to a wire-to-wire victory in the event generally acknowledged to be the foundation of the Senior PGA (now Champions) Tour.

"My game plan today — we were 15 [under]," he said. "I thought if we could get it to 22, we would have a good chance. We needed to get to 22 as quickly as we could."

Said Hoch: "He was trying to get there in the first two holes."

This was on the Top of the Rock, the par-three course. Pernice and Hoch closed with an eight-under 46, playing the front nine at modified alternate shot and the back nine at better-ball. They shot 48 in the second round with the same format, after opening with a nine-under 62 in better ball at the 18-hole Ozarks National.

Pernice and Hoch totaled 23-under 156 for a five-stroke win over the teams of Paul Broadhurst and Kirk Triplett and Vijay Singh and Carlos Franco. And they had a simple strategy. "I told him early, 'Hey, I'll get the front, you get the back,' and that's kind of what happened," Hoch said.

With the win, Hoch, at 63 years, five months and four days, became the oldest winner ever on the Champions Tour. But he rejected the distinction. "It's a team event," Hoch said. "It's great that I won, but I don't think you can compare that to an individual win."

Insperity Invitational
The Woodlands, Texas
Winner: Scott McCarron

Sometimes there's nothing like a nice sore neck to get a guy's mind off his game.

"I woke up this morning," Scott McCarron was saying, "and I went to dry my hair and my neck just tightened up. I knew I was going to have to play a lot of holes today ... I went in the fitness trailer and they kind of loosened it up a little bit, but it was bothering me all day. But I think I was more just thinking about keeping it loose and wasn't really thinking too much about score. And lo and behold, I played pretty [well]."

Which is to say that he won the Insperity Invitational without much friction, posting his 10th Champions Tour victory, matching Arnold Palmer and Jack Nicklaus, just two weeks after taking the Mitsubishi Electric Classic.

It was a tough outing for all. Heavy weather rolled in over Woodlands Country Club, delaying play. McCarron, starting at No. 10 in the first round, made a three-putt bogey and was halfway through his second hole when play was suspended. Thus on Friday he played 34½ holes with a sore neck, shot 67-65 for a 12-under 132, and went into the final round leading by three over Paul Goydos (68-67) and Scott Parel (67-68).

"If he goes out and shoots five or six under like he did today," Goydos said, "kind of a moot point."

Said Parel: "If I hit the ball like I did today, and make a few more putts, then I might have a chance."

Both were right. Parel closed with the day-low 66, getting within a stroke once, and finished second. Goydos shot 70 and tied for fourth.

McCarron locked it up with birdies at 13, 14 and 16 for a 67, a 17-under 199 and a two-shot margin in his second win in three weeks. "I'm not done yet," he said. "I want to win a lot more."

Regions Tradition
Birmingham, Alabama
Winner: Steve Stricker

This was Steve Stricker, whooping it up after winning the Regions Tradition, his first major, senior or otherwise: A wild celebration? Not quite. A fist pump, a hug for his caddie, a hug for playing partner Bernhard Langer, and then a little cry. "This is special," Stricker said. "I get emotional. I hate this part."

The understated Stricker, 52, captain of the U.S. team for the 2020 Ryder Cup, was in his second season on the Champions Tour and had just scored his fourth victory in 18 total starts. And he made just one bogey in the 72 holes.

"It was finally good to get a major win out here on the Champions Tour," Stricker said. "Never was able to do that on the regular tour [which he continues to play], so this is the next best thing."

And Stricker did it with authority, a thumping six-stroke victory. He shot the par-72 Greystone's Founders Course in an 18-under-par 270, posting a card of 68-64-70-68. Billy Andrade (72), Paul Goydos (70) and David Toms (72) tied at 276.

The tough part was the 4:30 a.m. wakeup call on Friday, to complete the lightning-interrupted first round in 68, four behind Glen Day's leading 64, then going into the second. Under preferred lies, he posted eight birdies on the soaked course for his own 64. "The ball isn't rolling," Stricker said. "It's plugging where you're hitting it, so I was able to get the ball in hand, get it cleaned up."

Stricker led by two heading into the final round and survived some intermittent pressure. Toms tied him through the 15th in the third round, but through the next 10 holes went four over to Stricker's three under. Toms closed with a 72 and tied for a distant second. Andrade sputtered to a three-birdie, three-bogey 72 for his best finish in a Champions major. And Goydos, after going 46 holes without a bogey, made three in his closing 70. "I never looked like I was going to win," he said, "but I had a good week."

Stricker made only one bogey in the four rounds, and he made hay on the five par-fives, going bogey-free and getting 10 of his 19 birdies. An anticipated duel with Bernhard Langer never developed. Langer started the final round two behind, then stumbled to a 75 and tied for sixth.

"He didn't have his best stuff," Stricker said. "I wanted to win and I wanted to beat him and I wanted to beat everybody."

KitchenAid Senior PGA Championship
Rochester, New York
Winner: Ken Tanigawa

Ken Tanigawa had dreamed of being a career amateur, but he kept breaking the spell by showing there was a real pro in there. For example, a Champions Tour rookie winning the 2018 PURE Insurance Championship with an eagle on the last hole of the last round at Pebble Beach. Then, in the 2019 KitchenAid Senior PGA Championship at Oak Hill, with a masterpiece par on the final hole of the final round for his first major. Thus ends an amateur dream.

"To hold this trophy...," Tanigawa said. "It's unbelievable."

Tanigawa trailed from the start, shooting the first three rounds in 67-74-66, and was three behind defending champion Paul Broadhurst going into the fourth. Broadhurst stumbled, bogeying three of the first 10 holes then, after a birdie at 11, he doubled-bogeyed 16 from the rough and bogeyed the 18th, shot 75 and finished third. Scott McCarron, the tour money leader and an old friend of Tanigawa, bogeyed three of five from No. 3, shot 70 and finished second by a stroke.

"I told him once he got out here he would be a top-10 player," McCarron said. "And he is certainly proving that."

Tanigawa, playing just ahead of Broadhurst, bogeyed No. 3, next bogeyed the 10th. But he was only two behind the struggling Broadhurst. Then Tanigawa hit the key to his round. He birdied the par-three 11th, birdied the par-three 15th, dropping a six-foot putt, and next birdied the par-four 16th with a 20-footer and was tied when Broadhurst double-bogeyed it from the rough. "I'm really pleased for him," Broadhurst was to say.

A bogey at the 17th cut Tanigawa's lead to one and he needed at least a par at the par-four 18th. But that became almost fatally iffy when he drove into a fairway bunker, close to the front lip. He could get out, but couldn't go for the green. So on his third, from 123 yards, he hit to the back slope and the ball rolled back down, leaving him a 10-foot uphill putt. McCarron flashed him a thumbs-up. "[If] that flies another foot and he's in the rough and dead," McCarron said, "and he loses the tournament and I win. That was really cool of him."

Tanigawa — a wreck inside, he said — made the putt and had the championship when Broadhurst missed his 50-foot birdie try minutes later.

"...numbed ... thrilled ... magical," Tanigawa said. "Tomorrow morning, I'll probably wake up in hysterics."

Pro hysterics, of course.

Principal Charity Classic
Des Moines, Iowa
Winner: Kevin Sutherland

Those baffled by the outcome of the Principal Charity Classic are referred to the words of noted baseball philosopher Lawrence Peter "Yogi" Berra, who said, "It ain't over till it's over."

Thus does Berra explain how Kevin Sutherland, trailing by eight strokes going into the final round, won the Principal.

Clearly, the tournament belonged to Scot Parel. He tied the Wakonda Club record with a 63 in the first round and led by two over Chris DiMarco, then shot 66 in the second, breaking the tournament record with a 15-under 129 and led by five over Marco Dawson and Jerry Kelly. Which is rather the point: Sutherland shot 72-65 and at 137 was eight shots off the lead going into the final round. That is, out of the running.

Parel was hit by a bolt of prescience. "You know, somebody back there probably's going to shoot seven to nine under," he said. "I doubt that 15 under's going to win this tournament."

Said Sutherland later: "Leading wasn't in my consideration. But I knew if I shot a great round, you never know. It just worked out well for me."

It worked out sensationally. In the last round, after a two-birdie front nine, and in one of the great performances in Champions Tour history, Sutherland birdied six straight from the 10th, parred the 16th, then birdied 17 and 18 for a 28 and a 10-under 62. Parel shot two-under 70, and they tied at 17-under 199. Sutherland birdied the second playoff hole for his second win of the season. Ironically, in the first he beat Parel in the Rapiscan Systems Classic in March — in a seven-hole playoff.

"I feel bad for Scott," Sutherland said. "He deserved to win this tournament." And of his birdie rampage, Sutherland noted: "Sometimes when you're rolling like that you get hungry. The birdies come easy."

So Sutherland proved again that it ain't over till it's over. So eight behind wasn't far enough back this time. What number would be safe from him?

Well, nine behind might be it. For now, anyway.

Mastercard Japan Championship
Narita, Chiba, Japan
Winner: Scott McCarron

Scott McCarron wasn't about to let this one get away. The first one got away, two years ago, but not this one. And so with the guys trying to turn up the heat behind him, he turned it up himself even more down the stretch and took the Mastercard Japan Championship by three strokes for his third win of the young 2019 season.

Unfinished business? "It always is when you finish second," McCarron said, recalling the Champions Tour's first visit to Japan, the 2017 Japan Airlines Championship. He seemed to be in good shape in the final round and then got overrun when Colin Montgomerie's putter caught fire down the final nine. "I felt I certainly was playing well enough to win," said McCarron, tying for second. "So we've got a little unfinished business."

After a year's absence, the tour returned in June 2019, and McCarron completed that unfinished business. He opened 69-67 and carried a one-stroke lead into the final round. As Billy Andrade was to say, after tying for second with Kirk Triplett three strokes behind, "It would have been nice if all of us that were up there could have put some pressure on him — but we didn't."

McCarron proved to be pressure-proof. Andrade tried, but faltered with a bogey, and Triplett had three birdies on the back nine. But McCarron responded with birdies at Nos. 8, 12, 14 and 17 for a closing 67 and a 203 total, 13 under and good for a three-stroke win over Andrade (68) and Triplett (69). McCarron made no secret of his ambition.

"I'm doing everything I can to win the Charles Schwab Cup," said McCarron, of the tour's season-long points-based competition for the bonus $1 million annuity. "I've got to win as many tournaments as possible, and so that's what I'm trying to do. That's my goal."

American Family Insurance Championship
Madison, Wisconsin
Winner: Jerry Kelly

Much to the delight of fans in Madison, Wisconsin, the American Family Insurance Championship was almost guaranteed to end as a hometown-boy-makes-good tale. That is, two-thirds of a three-man playoff were hometown boys — Jerry Kelly and Steve Stricker, with South Africa's Retief Goosen providing the suspense.

After Stricker bowed out with a three-putt bogey on the first playoff hole, it was Kelly, finally, who triggered the roars at University Ridge with a six-foot birdie putt on the third extra hole that obediently bent into the cup to beat Goosen, Champions Tour rookie.

"It really is truly awesome," said Kelly, who let out a roar of his own when that putt dropped. "It's about friends and family — this is pretty sweet."

The script for this one came out of Hollywood. The suspense and drama built until well into the final round, when the two local boys became real factors.

Kelly, grinning and greeting fans along the way, shot 65-70-66, led the first round, slipped behind in the second and returned in the third to finish at 15-under 201. Stricker, with three consecutive 67s, didn't lead till the tie at the end. Goosen, on 69-66-66, trailed by four in the first round, then two, and finally tied.

The logjam was created at the 18th in regulation. Kelly three-putted for bogey, and Goosen missed an eight-foot birdie putt, and Stricker, in the final group, also missed a birdie from eight feet.

Then Stricker exited the playoff on the first extra hole, the 18th. Kelly and Goosen both parred it, and parred it again on the second try. At the third extra hole, the par-four 15th, Goosen parred and Kelly calmly holed that bender for his fourth tour win.

"The chills were flying up and down," Kelly said. "My dad was there. I haven't won since my dad passed, and I was talking to him all the time. I was like, 'Hey, hey, Dad, how are you?' It was kind of surreal."

U.S. Senior Open Championship
Notre Dame, Indiana
Winner: Steve Stricker

Steve Stricker might've been a guy playing for the national championship in his mind. There wasn't much he didn't do in his fantasy: He went 57 holes without making a bogey; he made just two over the four rounds, the record fewest by a winner in the event; shot a record 19 under par; made 19 birdies; tied for the lead in the first round, then raced away and won by six shots. Then came the next real part, where the old dream comes true: They presented him with the U.S. Senior Open trophy.

"I was never able to win a USGA event in my career, whether it was in the amateur ranks or when I turned pro," Stricker said. "Had some good U.S. Open finishes, but this is it." It was his second senior major victory, after the Regions Tradition in May.

It was a tussle for one round, when Stricker and David Toms, the defending champion, tied at 62, eight under at Notre Dame's rain-softened Warren Course. They led by two over Jerry Kelly, Stricker's fellow Wisconsite and longtime friend, and Kirk Triplett. Said Kelly: "It's competition and support and friendship."

Toms made a tournament-record 10 birdies. Stricker made the first of his two bogeys at the par-four sixth, and after a burst of five birdies over six holes from No. 8, he eagled the par-five 17th with a 30-foot putt. But he was still miffed at not winning the American Family Insurance tournament the week before, missing the winning birdie putt on the final hole, then losing to Kelly in a playoff. "It was eating at me ... not winning," he said.

But Stricker rolled this time. He added a 64, setting the Senior Open record for two rounds at 14-under 126 and maintaining a two-stroke edge on Kelly, who shot a second 64. Then Stricker broke away in the third round, rolling to another flawless day, a four-birdie 66, an 18 under — another record — 192 total and a six-stroke lead.

"Much the same as it was the first two days — just driving it in the fairway," Stricker said. "Just didn't get into too many problems." More to the point: Stricker had hit 35 of 42 fairways and 45 of the 54 greens and needed just 83 putts. And he was four under for the most demanding part of the course, Nos. 3-5.

The final round was almost anticlimax. "I played defensive ... trying not to make a mistake," Stricker said. He birdied the first, made his second and last bogey at No. 10, then chipped in for birdie from 46 feet at the par-three 12th. He parred in for a 69 and a 19-under 261 and the six-stroke win over Kelly (69) and Toms (68).

Stricker won $720,000, and someone wondered how much his caddie — his wife Nicki — would be paid.

"She gets," Stricker noted, "whatever she wants."

Bridgestone Senior Players Championship
Akron, Ohio
Winner: Retief Goosen

For Retief Goosen, two-time U.S. Open champion and the very soul of patience, it seemed an eternity and he still hadn't won on the Champions Tour. Finally — in July 2019 — his patience was rewarded at the Bridgestone Senior Players Championship, all of his 10th start on the tour.

And quite a show it was on long, demanding Firestone South. He scrambled through three rounds, led in one, then birdied the last two holes and won by two.

It wasn't just his first Champions win. "It's been 10 years since I last won a tournament," said Goosen, going back to the 2009 Transitions, his seventh and last win on the PGA Tour. And it felt like old times. "I wasn't like really shaking or anything," Goosen said.

He shot the par-70 Firestone, former home of the World Golf Championships, in 69-62-75-68–274, six under, for the two-stroke win over Jay Haas (67) and Tim Petrovic (68).

Goosen opened five behind the storm-delayed 64 posted by Steve Stricker, who just the week before won his second senior major of the year, the U.S. Senior Open. Then, in an abrupt reversal, Goosen caught fire in the second round, getting an eagle at the par-five second and six birdies, the last at the monster 16th for an eight-under 62 and a three-stroke lead on Stricker (70) and Brandt Jobe (65). Goosen had a dismal five-over 75 in the third ("just let the course get to me," he said), falling one behind Scott Parel (67) and setting the stage for a scrambled finish.

In the fourth round, Parel bogeyed 15 and double-bogeyed 16, shot 73 and tied for fourth. Stricker's bid for a third major, hurt by a third-round 73, was stifled by three bogeys in five holes from the 13th. He shot 72 and finished sixth. And rallies by Jay Haas (67) and Tim Petrovic (68) fell short and they tied for second at 276, two behind.

Goosen had a jagged finale. He started bogey-eagle and double-bogeyed the 11th. He birdied 12 and 13, bogeyed 14, then took the lead at 17 with a 15-foot birdie putt. He got a cushion with a birdie from 10 feet at the 18th for his 68.

"You know," said the man who finally won again, "you've just got to put yourself in a position to get used to it again, and that's what I've done and it finally paid off this week."

The Senior Open Championship presented by Rolex
Winner: Bernhard Langer

See Staysure Tour section.

Dick's Sporting Goods Open
Endicott, New York
Winner: Doug Barron

Cracking that Monday qualifier was just the beginning of Doug Barron's problems. Good ones, that is. That qualifier got him into the Dick's Sporting Goods Open. Three rounds later, he was a winner and it changed his life.

"I've got a place to play now," said Barron, who had been playing in some off-tour places. "I've got to reset my goals a little bit. It's not the Emerald Coast Tour anymore."

Barron, 50, winless in 238 starts on the PGA Tour, had hit the big time of senior golf. He took the Dick's, his second Champions Tour tournament, with a wire-to-wire 65-68-66 for a 17-under 199 total at the par-72 En-Joie Golf Club, beating Fred Couples by two, Woody Austin by four, and Scott McCarron and Colin Montgomerie by five.

Barron, who tied for fifth in the Senior British Open in his Champions Tour debut, was familiar with En-Joie. He had played the former B.C. Open on the PGA Tour there seven times. "It fits my eye," he said. So comfortably, in fact, that he tied Spain's formidable Miguel Angel Jimenez for the first-round lead at 65. From there, even a lightning storm delay in the second round failed to distract him. He was 10 under and leading by one when the storm stopped him at the 15th. Resuming play on Sunday, he birdied the 16th and shot 68, taking a two-stroke lead on McCarron (66) and Scott Parel (69).

Couples, 59, finished with a tournament-low 63 and was the leader in the clubhouse at 201, with Barron still playing. "Doug's brand-new out here — he just played well at the British Senior," Couples said. "I haven't won in a while and I felt a little gun-shy out there."

Barron, meantime, never faltered, and wrapped up the tournament with a flawless 66.

"I had fun," he said. "I enjoyed every minute of it. When you're competing and you can bring out your best at the end, that's cool stuff."

Boeing Classic
Snoqualmie, Washington
Winner: Brandt Jobe

The Boeing Classic was shaping up as a rousing homecoming for native son Fred Couples. He was one round from scoring his first professional victory in front of the Seattle fans. And he was about as safe as a golfer can get — 18 under and leading by five. He'd shot the first two rounds in 65-63, and the 63 included a hole-in-one at the 203-yard, par-three No. 9.

It's golf: Couples' game turned sour, and while he was closing with a 76, Brandt Jobe, who had trailed with 69-66, was sizzling with a 63 of his own and took the tournament, his second Champions Tour victory.

Jobe wasn't trying to trash Couples' homecoming party. He was just going about his game. "I thought we were going to be playing for second," said Jobe, trailing by a whopping seven strokes going into the final round. "I've birdied the first five holes and thought, well at least that's making a little noise."

Couples started the final round with a birdie, and it turned out to be his last one. He had gone the first 41 holes without a bogey, through No. 5 in the last round, then he made five over the last 13. "At the end," Couples said, "it was like, let me just finish and get the hell out of here."

Jobe was getting up steam, fighting a seven-shot deficit. He started the final round hot, with five straight birdies. He took his fourth and final bogey at No. 6, then closed strong with birdies at 14 (where he took the lead), 17 and 18 for a 63 and an 18-under 198, three better than Tom Pernice (65–201). Couples closed with 76 and tied for third with Jerry Kelly (69).

The day was great fun, Jobe said. "When you can go out there and do what you're trying to do and it happens," he said. "It's really gratifying."

Shaw Charity Classic
Calgary, Alberta, Canada
Winner: Wes Short, Jr.

Not that Michael Bradley was going to give it back or anything, but on opening the Shaw Charity Classic with a superhot round, he offered: "I've got no business shooting 61. I'm just being honest."

It was a plaintive call. The gods heard Bradley's disclaimer and allowed him to escape from his discomfort zone. (He would add 72-75 and tie for 36th.)

Then the Shaw Charity Classic, at the par-70 Canyon Meadows, could be pretty well summed up by the great break Wes Short, Jr. got at the final hole, when his approach bounced off a rock and up onto the green. He got the winning birdie. He was battling Scott McCarron, who had pretty much taken over as the Champions Tour's dominant player. McCarron had won three times already this season, and he won the previous two Shaws. Playing ahead of Short, McCarron was rolling with five birdies through the 14th. Then McCarron made a huge stumble and bogeyed 16 and 17. But not out of it, McCarron, at the par-five 18th, hit an excellent second to the green, 39 feet from the flag. He holed the putt for eagle, a 65 and a 12-under 198. Then he stepped aside to watch Short come in with the final grouping — and author his own sensational finish. Short hit the fairway, and then his troubles started with his three-wood second.

"When I saw it in the air — I caught it just a hair thin," he said, "I was thinking, I hope it carries the water, because I know it's not getting to the green. Then it hit a rock … then I saw it land on the green and roll to the left, and I was thinking, that's a good break." Short's eagle try was three feet short, but he holed that for his birdie, a 66, a 13-under 197 and his second win.

"All the hard work you put into this stupid game," Short said, "comes to the top."

Ally Challenge
Grand Blanc, Michigan
Winner: Jerry Kelly

True, Jerry Kelly did make just one bogey in the Ally Challenge, at No. 9 in the first round. But if a tournament can come down to one fine point, then for Kelly it would have been his second shot at Warwick Hills' 10th, just when the final round was getting tighter. He had driven into the left rough and faced a shot that was both tough and critical.

"Well, I'm glad it was a hook instead of a fade," he said. "That's my go-to." His problem: Keep the ball low, scoot it up, avoid getting short-sided in the bunker, and get it on the left side of the green. "It came out just perfect and spun and still released up there just pin high," he said. He got the birdie.

Kelly, winner of the American Family Insurance Championship in June, was challenged but not seriously threatened. Trailing only in the first round, he shot 67-65-68–200, 16 under, and won by two.

The final round began as a three-way shootout, with Kelly leading at 12 under, and Woody Austin and Scott McCarron a stroke behind. McCarron left the chase with four bogeys in five holes from No. 9. He shot 75 and tied for 15th. Austin briefly tied Kelly with a birdie at No. 3. Kelly kept rolling, notching birdies at the sixth and seventh. Then came Kelly's inspired birdie at the 10th, and after Austin bogeyed the 15th, Kelly got his final bird at the par-three 17th and led by three. Austin's birdie at the last left Kelly with the two-stroke win.

"Any time you have a chance to win, it's a good week," Austin said. "It just wasn't my day."

For Kelly, it was some relief from knee and elbow injuries. "So I'd like to think I'm going to be healthy for the long haul now," he said.

Sanford International
Sioux Falls, South Dakota
Winner: Rocco Mediate

For Rocco Mediate, golf's greatest joy came through a simple exercise in arithmetic with his scorecard. "When I added them up, I went, 'Holy [mackerel] — 64!'" And thus did Mediate greet his victory in the Sanford International, his fourth win on the Champions Tour and first since 2016. But for all of his excellent play he still needed help, and he got it in the form of a weird catastrophe that sank Ken Duke at the final hole.

Mediate shot 69-68 in the first two rounds and entered the final round trailing co-leaders Duke and Kirk Triplett by three. Mediate birdied twice going out, then whipped Minnehaha Country Club's back nine for birdies at the 12th, 14th, 17th and then, critically, the 18th for the 64. Playing 40 minutes ahead of the leaders, Mediate walked off with a nine-under 201 total and the clubhouse lead.

Triplett, solo leader in the first round and tied with Duke at six under through the second, stalled out, scattering three bogeys through the 15th. He shot 71 and tied for seventh. Duke had two birdies and a bogey on the front, then birdied Nos. 8, 12 and 16, the last getting him to nine under. Then came his downfall. At the par-four 18th, his tee shot jumped into a bad lie in the right rough and he double-bogeyed, shot 69, and tied for second at 203 with the strong-closing Bob Estes (67) and Colin Montgomerie (67).

"It was probably one of the worst lies I ever had," Duke said. "Not that I hit bad shots, I just got some bad breaks and that's part of golf. We all know that, right?"

Said Mediate: "It was just one of those days when everything went really good. I hit a lot of greens, kept my head together and here we are."

PURE Insurance Championship
Monterey Peninsula, California
Winner: Kirk Triplett

Maybe it's the beauty of Pebble Beach, maybe the infectious spirit of the First Tee kids. Whatever it was, Kirk Triplett is making a career out of winning the PURE Insurance Championship. Triplett came from behind to win the 2019 edition, beating Billy Andrade in a playoff. It was Triplett's third win in the event — in 2012 and 2013 — and his second of the year. He won the Hoag Classic in March, also played on the California coast, at Newport Beach, and also in a playoff.

"I was really more focused on my junior today," said Triplett, partnering Sam Sommerhauser, of Sacramento, California. The event pairs tour pros with First Tee program youths. "I was just playing more to help him," he said. "The leaders were at 10 [under] and I was at six or seven. Boy, the guys came back a little bit and I made some birdies."

The scoreboard had a traffic problem. With the tournament being played at the par-72 Pebble Beach and at nearby par-71 Poppy Hills, the scores were listed in relation to par. Joey Sindelar and Rod Pampling, making his Champions debut, shared the first-round lead with 67s, five under at Pebble Beach. Triplett was three back with a 70 at Pebble. Steve Flesch took the second-round lead at eight under with a 67 at Poppy Hills. Triplett was four behind at four under after a 69 at Poppy.

In the final round, at Pebble, Triplett birdied three of the last five holes for a no-bogey 67, five under. Andrade made three birdies on the front but coming in had three birdies and three bogeys for a 69, three under. They tied at nine under. Andrade missed his birdie try on the first playoff hole, the 18th, and Triplett dropped an eight-footer for his third win at Pebble.

What was the magic? "I think it's just that I embrace it," Triplett said.

SAS Championship
Cary, North Carolina
Winner: Jerry Kelly

Time sure flies when you're having fun, and so do the birdies, as Jerry Kelly discovered at the SAS Championship. Before he knew it, he had his third win of the year.

"When the guys are so close and you're bunched up … it's 'I have to make another birdie,'" he said. "It kind of shocked me to see I was three, four shots clear."

Kelly trailed Doug Barron and Woody Austin by a stroke starting the final round, and after a birdie at No. 2, he blitzed Prestonwood Golf Club for five straight from No. 5, then added the 15th and 17th. The bogey at 18 merely cut his winning margin to one. Kelly shot 68-67-65–200, 16 under, beating winless David McKenzie.

The SAS, in mid-October, was the last event of the Champions Tour season before the Charles Schwab Cup Playoffs, and had its share of hard-luck stories. Barron's might have been the toughest. In the first round, he had bolted to nine under through his 14th, then bogeyed three of the last four and his lead was down to one on a 66. In the second, he got to five under with an eagle at 12, then bogeyed 13 for a 68 and was tied by Woody Austin (67) at 10 under, sharing a one-shot lead. "This isn't life-or-death stuff for me," Barron said. His hopes finally sputtered out in the last round on a triple bogey at No. 6. He shot 71 and tied for third, five behind. McKenzie finished with a 63 and had that first win at his fingertips until Kelly nipped him by one. Sandy Lyle was about to take the 72nd and final Playoffs spot until Mike Goodes nudged him out by $323.

And said Kelly, who made 19 birdies and just three bogeys in the tournament: "I'm very happy to be healthy, very happy to be playing well at this time."

Dominion Energy Charity Classic
Richmond, Virginia
Winner: Miguel Angel Jimenez

It's not often that a golfer, answering a routine question, can pack so much into so little. For example: Miguel Angel Jimenez had just come from behind for his second win of the year in the Dominion Energy Classic, the first of the three-tournament Charles Schwab Cup Playoffs. Came the question: "What worked for you today?"

"Everything," Jimenez said.

Uh-huh. And then from the sweeping elegance of that one-word response, he expanded. "Even if I missed some fairways on the edge," he offered, "my irons are amazing to the flag."

And, of course, there was the putting. And so Jimenez, after starting the final round three behind, won with a bogey-free, nine-under 63. He trailed through the first two rounds with 67-68, then finished with an 18-under 198 at the Country Club of Virginia's James River Course and won by two over Tommy Tolles.

Tolles — thwarted again. Newly 53, Tolles was looking for that first win in his three years. He led through the first round and was co-leader with Scott Parel in the second. Then Tolles' putter got cranky just when Jimenez got hot. Tolles eagled the last hole for a 68 to leap over Colin Montgomerie. "It's been a long time since I've been in this position and I'm happy with the way it turned out," said Tolles. "Most of it anyway."

Others had their disappointments. Montgomerie (68) finished third and Woody Austin (65), Bernhard Langer (68) and Scott Parel (71) tied for fourth. Schwab points leader Scott McCarron tied for 17th at 209, 11 behind.

A total of 67 of the 72 Cup-eligible golfers teed it up in this first Playoff. The top 54 finishers would advance to the second two weeks' later, the Invesco QQQ Championship at Thousand Oaks, California.

Jimenez, who would lift a glass and light a cigar, already had a game plan. "Hole by hole, shot for shot," he said, "and I would do my best."

Invesco QQQ Championship
Thousand Oaks, California
Winner: Colin Montgomerie

"How often does that happen with Bernhard?" Colin Montgomerie was asking in disbelief. He had just seen Bernhard Langer self-destruct in a bunker.

This was the stunning end of the Invesco QQQ Championship at Sherwood Country Club, the second of the three tournaments in the Champions Tour's Charles Schwab Cup Playoffs. Neither had led until the end, when they tied. And this was, itself, at the first hole of the Invesco playoff.

Montgomerie had shot 69-70 and was five behind Retief Goosen going into the final round. Langer, a five-time Schwab Cup winner, had shot 70-65 and started only one behind. Both had bogey-free final rounds. Montgomerie, playing five groups ahead of Langer, sprinted to seven birdies and an eagle at the par-five 11th, and he closed with a flourish, holing a 40-foot putt for a birdie at the par-four 18th for a tournament-record, nine-under 63. Langer had made five birdies and had to settle for pars on the last four holes for a 67, tying Montgomerie at 14-under 202.

In the playoff, at the 18th, both hit the fairway. Langer's second, from 191 yards, ended up in an awkward lie in the left greenside bunker. "It was a downhill lie with a big lip in front," Langer said. "It's hell down there. You just can't go down there." Langer eventually made six. Montgomerie, from 174 yards, put his approach to 20 feet and two-putted comfortably for his seventh tour win.

Schwab points leader Scott McCarron was five off the lead, then shot 77 and tied for 43rd. Jerry Kelly, No. 2, shot 66 and tied for 10th. Overall, the top 36 in points would advance to the season-ending Schwab Cup Championship the following week. That would include, of course, the disappointed Langer.

"I made one bad shot and paid the price," Langer said. But, he added, "It's been a good week."

For Montgomerie, the win was a surprise. "When you wake up five behind, you look at who's ahead of you...," he said. "No, I didn't think of winning, to be honest. But to be four under after five — four under after five — yeah, it was good."

Charles Schwab Cup Championship
Phoenix, Arizona
Winner: Jeff Maggert

As the November dusk was falling on the Charles Schwab Cup Championship, there was one more golf swing — and suddenly two winners. Jeff Maggert and Scott McCarron were celebrating and carrying on.

That was Jeff Maggert in the fairway, thrusting his arms heavenward and doing a 55-year-old's version of leaping and running. His 123-yard wedge approach at the third playoff hole dropped and beat Retief Goosen, whose beckoning birdie try abruptly became meaningless. "I've seen it happen," Maggert said. "I never, ever thought it would happen to me."

The other winner was Scott McCarron, one of several who could win the $1 million, points-based Charles Schwab Cup. He led in points for the last 20 weeks after three early wins. He tied for 27th in the 34-man field. He was in the clubhouse when Maggert's shot dropped. "Are you kidding me?" he was yelling.

Maggert won $440,000, McCarron a $1 million annuity.

Coming to the Schwab finale, at Phoenix Country Club, Maggert was among the least likely to win. His fifth and last victory was in 2015, and he was also having a so-so 2019, and he was well back in the first two Cup Playoffs.

Then he shot the Cup Championship in 63-65-69-66–263, 21 under. Goosen shot 66-67-66-64, birdieing three of the last four holes for his 263 in the next-to-last group, forcing Maggert to make a miracle escape from the trees at the 18th. He had to lay up, then wedged to eight feet and birdied for the 66 and the tie.

In the first playoff hole at the 18th, Maggert missed a birdie from eight feet, then Goosen missed the win by missing a four-footer. Next, again at 18, Maggert got a great break when his stray approach bounced off a fan and back into the fairway. Both chipped beautifully. Maggert birdied from three feet, Goosen from two.

Then the playoff moved to the par-four 17th. Goosen drove into a fairway bunker but recovered brilliantly to eight feet, a real threat to Maggert in the fairway from 123 yards.

"I was just trying to hit it close and make a putt up there," Maggert said. His shot hit just a few feet from the hole and bounced and rolled right in, sending Maggert dancing.

Goosen came over wearing a huge grin. "I had my chances," he would say. "What can I do?"

Said Maggert: "It's nice to be back in the winner's circle."

Said McCarron: "Jeff Maggert is my favorite player."

Staysure Tour

Jordan Mixed Open
Winner: Daan Huizing

See Ladies European Tour section

KitchenAid Senior PGA Championship
Winner: Ken Tanigawa

See Champions Tour section

Senior Italian Open
Fagagna, Italy
Winner: Barry Lane

Instead of overthinking everything, Barry Lane decided to "just play golf" at the Senior Italian Open and it paid off with his seventh victory on the Staysure Tour as the circuit began its domestic season in Europe.

"When I practice really hard and work on something, I can't get it out of my mind [when] I go out on the golf course," said the 58-year-old Englishman about his "poor" play in previous weeks. "[I decided] all I'm going to do is just play golf and that's exactly what I did."

To land the win, though, he had to birdie the 54th hole and overcome his winless playoff record with another birdie on the second extra hole to defeat Frenchman Marc Farry. Lane had lost all four of his previous playoff opportunities on the Staysure and European Tours.

He never led until he rolled in an eight-foot putt for the win, but had remained in close touch with the lead all weekend at the rain-soaked Villaverde Resort at Fagagna, Italy. His opening three-under-par 69 put him just a stroke behind the four leaders — Gary Wolstenholme, Gary Orr, Gary Evans and Markus Brier. However, with 72 he slipped three shots off the pace when Farry, who had opened with a 72, got a 66 round going with an eagle-deuce early. His 138 jumped Farry into a first-place tie with Argentina's Jose Coceres (71-67), who was off to strong start on the 2019 season in quest of his first Staysure Tour title.

Lane's final-hole birdie Sunday gave him a 67 and 208 total that Farry matched with a 70 and forced the overtime work. Coceres shot 71 and joined three others — Miguel Angel Martin, Jean-Francois Remesy and David Shacklady — just a stroke back.

Senior Open Hauts de France
Anzin-Saint-Aubin, France
Winner: Peter Baker

Comfortable playing in the country where he had won three lesser events in earlier years, Peter Baker captured his first title on the Staysure Tour going away with a five-stroke victory in the Senior Open Hauts de France, a new event hosted by Jean van de Velde, the prominent national golfer who played in the tournament.

"France has really been kind to me," the 51-year-old Englishman said afterward. "I like playing over here and it's great to get my first win under my belt. No matter which tour you play on, it's always hard to win."

Baker never trailed after sharing the first-round lead with Miguel Angel Martin at six-under-par 66. He moved a stroke in front the second day with a rain-interrupted 70 on the demanding Arras Golf Resort course in Anzin-Saint-Aubin. Closest behind were rookie qualifying school graduate American Dan Olsen (68-69–137) and Spain's Martin, who followed his 66 with 73 for 139.

Baker turned things into a runaway in the final round, overcoming a second-hole bogey with four birdies on the next five holes. Two more birdies on the back nine increased his lead to five strokes through 16 holes. He parred in for 67 and his winning 203, five ahead of South Africa's James Kingston, who closed with 66–208, a shot ahead of Austria's Markus Brier. Olsen shot 73 and Martin 71 the last day.

The season's initial first-time winner became just the 11th man to have posted victories on the Challenge, European and Staysure Tours, his last of three wins on the main circuit coming in 1993.

Farmfoods European Legends Links Championship
Padstow, England
Winner: Jean-Francois Remesy

Jean-Francois Remesy achieved a long-time goal when he captured the Farmfoods European Legends Links Championship at Trevose Golf and Country Club in Padstow, England.

"It was my dream to win in England," said the 55-year-old Frenchman, whose four previous tour victories — three on the European Tour and the 2018 Swiss Seniors Open on the Staysure Tour — all came on the Continent. "After 40 years I finally managed to do it. I'm very delighted with this moment."

Remesy emerged from a three-man battle the last day with a one-stroke victory over Order of Merit leader Barry Lane, closing with a five-under-par 67 for a final 206. He had entered the final round tied for the lead with Sweden's Jarmo Sandelin at 139, his 71 one of only two sub-par rounds on a blustery Saturday. They were a shot ahead of Lane (67-73). Sandelin had opened the tournament with a leading 66.

Remesy took control of things in the final round when he sank long putts on the 10th hole for an eagle and the 11th for a birdie. Lane made a late charge and matched Remesy's 67, but Remesy clung to the lead with a tough par at the 17th and another at the 18th. Sandelin slipped to a fourth-place tie at 210 with a closing 71.

U. S. Senior Open Championship
Winner: Steve Stricker

See Champions Tour section

Swiss Seniors Open
Bad Ragaz, Switzerland
Winner: Jose Coceres

Argentina's Jose Coceres added another circuit to his victory record when he scored a come-from-behind triumph in the Swiss Seniors Open stop on the Staysure Tour in early July.

"We won in Spain and we won in Dubai and I've also won on the PGA Tour in America, so I'm very happy to have won on this tour, too," proclaimed the 55-year-old South American, who finished two strokes in front of five other contenders with his final-round 66 and 11-under-par 199. "I played for about 20 years on the European Tour and I'm really happy to be back here."

Coceres sat just off the pace the first two days at Golf Club Bad Ragaz. Opening 65s put him and Welshman Mark Mouland a shot behind American Clark Dennis, the 2017 Order of Merit champion who was gunning for his fifth Staysure title. Australian Peter O'Malley, winless since a victory in his homeland in 2010, took over first place Saturday. His 65-131 gave O'Malley a one-stroke edge on Scot Andrew Oldcorn and two on four other pursuers — Coceres (68), Dennis (69) and Englishman Peter Baker and Welshman Phillip Price (66-67s).

First O'Malley, then Oldcorn yielded the lead to Coceres Sunday. The Argentine nailed his third and fourth birdies to take command on the back nine and close two strokes ahead of O'Malley (70), Baker and Price (68s), Chris Williams (66) and Jean-Francois Remesy (64).

"Chino Fernandez, my coach, has helped me every day to improve and I am really happy that our work has paid off," Coceres concluded.

Bridgestone Senior Players Championship
Winner: Retief Goosen

See Champions Tour section

European Tour Destinations Senior Classic
Girona, Spain
Winner: Jose Manuel Carriles

Determination paid off for Jose Manuel Carriles with victory in the European Tour Destinations Classic.

Back on the Staysure Tour for the 2019 season after a third trip to the qualifying school in January, the 56-year-old Spaniard, who lives in Pedrena, the hometown of the late, great Seve Ballesteros, picked up his first win on the senior circuit in his native land at the Catalunya Resort.

Carriles outplayed South African Chris Williams, 60, a two-time Staysure winner, in the final round after the two men shot six-under-par 66s the second day to replace first-round leader David Shacklady (67). Williams, with 136, finished the day a shot ahead of Carriles, who eagled the seventh and 12th holes during his round.

The Spaniard went ahead for good Sunday when he nailed his third birdie of the day on the 12th hole. He closed out the victory with a birdie at the 18th, set up by a brilliant fairway bunker shot. His 203 gave him a three-shot win over Williams.

"To have to go back to qualifying school and then come out and get my first win means a lot," said Carriles, the immediate benefit being a spot in the Senior Open, which came up two weeks later. "To win in front of my friends and local supporters is really special."

WINSTONgolf Senior Open
Vorbeck, Germany
Winner: Clark Dennis

Clark Dennis, one of the very few Americans who have enjoyed success in senior golf in Europe, already had four victories to his credit, two of which made him the Order of Merit winner in 2017, but none of his accomplishments could stack up to his astonishing triumph in the WINSTONgolf Senior Open in mid-July.

Six strokes out of first place and trailing six players, including Hall of Famers Jose Maria Olazabal, the leader, and Bernhard Langer, the 53-year-old Texan birdied five of the last six holes, shot 63, the Staysure Tour season's lowest score, and secured the WINSTONgolf title by a single stroke.

"I played fantastic today," Dennis remarked afterward. "Aside from hitting it in the water and making par on the first hole, the round could not have been any better. Olazabal and Langer are the best of all time. They are incredible players. To be able to compete against them is great, but to beat them is even better."

Olazabal, 53, playing in just his second event of the season, seized first place after Saturday's second round from Mexico's Esteban Toledo, who opened with an eight-under-par 64 on the WINSTONopen course in Vorbeck, Germany. The two-time Masters champion paired 66s and took a three-stroke lead into Sunday's finale in his bid for his initial senior victory. Dennis posted 70-68 rounds the first two days and "figured I was playing for second place."

Even though he birdied three of the first five holes, he still trailed the Spaniard by six shots at the turn. He picked up a stroke at the 11th, then ran off five straight birdies starting at the 13th and signed for the 63–201. Olazabal, playing behind him, bogeyed the 16th and failed to make a tying birdie on the last two holes, shooting 70–202.

The Senior Open Championship presented by Rolex
Lytham, England
Winner: Bernhard Langer

If you think Bernhard Langer doesn't "own" the Senior Open Championship presented by Rolex, think again. When the 61-year-old German great carved out a splendid victory in the 2019 edition at Royal Lytham & St. Annes, he established the following remarkable achievements:
• Won a record fourth Senior Open Championship, surpassing the three each of Gary Player and Tom Watson.
• Extended his record number of senior major championships to 11, two more than Player's career total.
• Embellished his Senior Open history to four wins, two seconds and 11 top-10s in 12 starts. He tied for 12th in the other one.
• Became the oldest winner of the Senior Open.
• Scored his 41st victory in international senior golf.

Langer's triumph at Royal Lytham & St. Annes was particularly impressive. Coming to England off a stretch of, for him, mediocre play on the U.S. Champions Tour, he maneuvered his way through miserable rain-swept conditions to convert a three-stroke deficit into a two-stroke victory with a closing, four-under-par 66–274.

The lead had changed hands each day. Four players — Americans Scott Dunlap, Wes Short, Jr. and Scott Parel and England's Paul Broadhurst, a two-time senior-major winner — shared the first-round lead with 67s. Dunlap went in front Friday with his 68–135, leading fellow Americans Ken Duke, Doug Barron and Short by two.

Broadhurst, 53, who won the 2016 Senior Open at Carnoustie and the 2017 KitchenAid Senior PGA in the U.S., reclaimed first place Saturday in difficult weather with 67–205, a shot ahead of American Woody Austin, two in front of Duke and Short. Langer was then in a four-way tie for fifth, three behind Broadhurst after rounds of 71-67-70 for 208.

Undaunted by heavy rainfall that delayed action for more than five hours, Langer played masterfully Sunday, forging into the lead with his fourth front-nine birdie at the ninth hole, building the margin to three shots through 13 and, for all intents and purposes, wrapping up the title when he ran in a 50-foot birdie putt at 14. Bogeys at 15 and 17 only reduced his margin of victory.

"It's always special to walk down 18 in a major, but especially over here," Langer remarked afterward. "The people are so knowledgeable about golf ... It's tremendous how they even came out in these conditions and cheered us on in the rain."

Staysure PGA Seniors Championship
Ash, Kent, England
Winner: Phillip Price

It had been a season of "close but no cigar" for Phillip Price on the Staysure Tour.

"I've been playing quite well all year with a lot of top-10 finishes, but without a win," said Price after his two-stroke victory in the Staysure PGA Seniors Championship, "so this was quite a relief for me." Actually, the 52-year-old Welshman had finished ninth or better in all of his six starts before a mediocre showing the previous week in the Senior Open Championship.

"This win is a little nicer than the first [and only other] one," he observed, referring to his WINSTONgolf Senior Open victory in his rookie 2017 season. "I had my wife and two children here with me and the children had never seen me win anything, so that made it special."

Price and Australian Peter Lonard had let the lead get away from them in Saturday's third round as another Aussie, David McKenzie, the first-round leader with 65, surged back in front with a four-under-par 68 for 202. Price and Lonard, the 36-hole leaders at 133, shot 71s and slipped two strokes behind McKenzie and a stroke in back of South Africa's James Kingston.

Price birdied three of his first six holes Sunday, moved in front to stay with an eagle at No. 11 and established the final, two-shot margin with his last birdie at the 16th to secure his final-round 67 and winning 271. New Zealand's Michael Campbell, the 2005 U.S. Open champion returning to tournament competition at age 50 after a six-year absence, closed with a matching 67 and tied for second at 273 with Lonard (68) and Kingston (70). McKenzie dropped to fifth place with 72–274.

Scottish Senior Open
Craigielaw, Scotland
Winner: Paul Lawrie

There's no place like home in the opinion of Scotsman Paul Lawrie after he carved out his first victory in the Scottish Senior Open in his initial season on the Staysure Tour.

"I think a lot of players struggle to play in their own country, but I've always felt comfortable playing in front of Scottish people," observed Lawrie, who did it 20 years earlier in the Open Championship at Carnoustie. "That is my fourth win in my home country and I'm very proud of that."

Lawrie overcame strong, gusty winds and a two-stroke deficit Sunday to shoot a par 71 and post the only sub-par final score, his 211 giving him a two-stroke victory over Australia's Peter Fowler, a six-time senior winner, and England's Peter Baker, the Arras Open victor in France in June.

The weather was rugged from the start at Craigielaw Golf Club in East Lothian. Lawrie, who won eight times on the European Tour, was one of only three players to break 70 Friday, his 68 one better than the rounds of Spaniard Jose Manuel Carriles, the European Tour Destinations Classic titlist, and American Tim Thelen, who has won five Staysure tournaments.

Fowler, the 2011 Order of Merit leader who began the tournament with a triple bogey and a 72, rebounded with a 66, the week's best score, and moved in front, two ahead of Lawrie and three over Englishman Paul Eales and Austrian Markus Brier. An outgoing 33 enabled Lawrie to recapture the lead Sunday on his way to his winning 71-211. Fowler slipped to a 75 and into the second-place tie with Baker (70).

The Sinclair Invitational
Ware, Hertfordshire, England
Winner: David Shacklady

David Shacklady will take a victory any way he can get it.

In the case of his second win on the Staysure Tour, Shacklady thought a missed short birdie putt on the final green had cost him the victory until he learned that Phillip Price, the leader, had taken a triple bogey on the 71st hole. Instead, Shacklady's six-under-par 66 and 205 gave him a one-stroke triumph over Austria's Markus Brier.

"It is horrible that it's gone that way," sympathized Shacklady, "but he [Price] will be the first one to come and shake my hand." As for his own play, he said: "I felt as calm as I did in Russia [his initial victory in 2018]. It's nice to be able to repeat it."

The 52-year-old Englishman was four strokes off the lead after 36 holes at Hanbury Manor Marriott Hotel and Country Club with 68-71 rounds. Fellow Englishman Gary Evans led the first day with 66, then yielded first place to Sweden's Magnus P. Atlevi and Price, who was seeking his second victory of the season to go with his Senior PGA Championship in early August. Price shot a bogey-free 68 and Atlevi started with an eagle and finished with a birdie for 67 for his 135. They were a just a shot ahead of Evans, Stephen Dodd and Paul Streeter.

Shacklady made up the four-stroke deficit with his bogey-free 66 Sunday and garnered the win thanks to Price's misfortune. Despite dropping into fourth place, though, Price took over the top spot on the money list, bypassing the absent Paul Broadhurst and Bernhard Langer, both playing in American on the PGA Tour Champions.

Paris Legends Championship
Paris, France
Winner: David Shacklady

A player with no previous experience on the world's tours pops up every now and then as a multiple winner in senior golf. Such is the case of David Shacklady, who won for a third time in the Paris Legends Championship.

Playing in only his second season on the Staysure Tour, the 52-year-old Englishman, who gained Staysure Tour privileges via the qualifying school, put the Paris Legends title back to back with his victory in the Sinclair Invitational, the immediately preceding tournament, but it didn't come easily.

He had to go overtime against home-country favorite Jean-Francois Remesy, who had to settle for second place for a second year in a row at the Racing Club de France la Boulie.

"It's not easy to win on this tour, as there are some great players out here, so to win twice is beyond my wildest dreams," summed up Shacklady, who had his other victory in the Russian Open in his rookie season.

With rounds of 69-66–135 he entered the final day tied with South Africa's James Kingston (68-67–135), a stroke ahead of Remesy (70-66–136) and three ahead of another Frenchman, Thomas Levet (67-71–138), the first-round leader who once shot a nine-hole 27 at the Racing Club, then his home course.

Remesy proved to be the one to beat for Shacklady Sunday. They were tied at the turn, and when they reached the 18th green, the Frenchman, who won the European Legends in June, missed a 10-foot eagle putt. The birdie for 67 tied him at 203, 13 under par, with Shacklady, whose tap-in par gave him a 68 and his 203. Remesy's tee shot on the first extra hole went awry and the Englishman won with a two-putt par.

Murhof Legends – Austrian Senior Open
Frohnleiten, Austria
Winner: Jose Coceres

Low scores have served as the ticket to success for Jose Coceres on the 2019 Staysure Tour. His winning score of 199 in the Swiss Senior Open ranked as the season's lowest until he bested it by two strokes in capturing his second Staysure title with a 19-under-par 197 in the Murhof Legends – Austrian Senior Open at the end of September.

The engine for the victory for the 56-year-old Argentinean was his spotless 10-under-par 62 in the second round at Golfclub Murhof, as Austria became the 45th country to host a European senior event. He called the bogey-free performance "one of the best rounds of my life. Today was special. It was nearly perfect."

The 66-62–128 staked Coceres to a six-stroke lead over France's Thomas Levet, Wales' Phillip Price and fellow Argentinean Rafael Gomez, but it was former Open champion Paul Lawrie, a winner already in his first senior season, who caused what little trouble Coceres encountered in the final round.

Entering the last day eight strokes off the pace, Lawrie got off to an eagle-deuce, birdie start, and bogeys by Coceres on the fourth and sixth holes enabled the Scotsman to climb within three strokes of the lead. But that was as close as he came. He eventually shot 65 and finished second as Coceres finished birdie-birdie, holing a 25-footer for 69 and the 197 that gave him a four-stroke victory.

"It's special to have my son here caddying for me. When we work together it really helps me to play my best," explained Coceres, who moved into second place behind Price on the tour's Order of Merit listing.

Farmfoods European Senior Masters
Coventry, England
Winner: Thomas Levet

Thomas Levet made an albatross (double-eagle) the week before in the Austrian Open and won a big bottle of wine, which he passed along to his friend, Markus Brier. He made a much more lucrative win seven days later in the Farmfoods European Senior Masters, his first victory on the Staysure Tour, nosing out Brier by a shot. No gifts this time.

"Maybe that's why I won the tournament," he joked afterward. "I gave him something last week and I wasn't going to give him a playoff today."

The 51-year-old Frenchman, winding up his first full season on the senior circuit, emerged from a crowd vying for the title in the final event before the long break to the three-week finale along the Indian Ocean in December.

Paul Broadhurst, the 2016 and 2018 Order of Merit winner playing in his first Staysure Tour event of the year after spending the season in the United States on the PGA Tour Champions, replaced tournament host Peter Baker — 66 the first day — atop the standings after 36 holes.

Broadhurst's 69-68–137, though, only gave him a one-stroke lead over seven players, including Levet, who shot a pair of 69s, and Brier (68-70).

Also at 138 were major champions Ian Woosnam and Paul Lawrie, Peter Fowler, Mauricio Molina and Gary Evans. Stephen Dodd, Jarmo Sandelin and two-time 2019 winner David Shacklady were just another shot back.

Levet moved into the lead Sunday with four birdies on the front nine of the course at Forest of Arden Hotel and Country Club and was never caught. Still, he needed the par he made at the difficult 18th for the 68 that gave him his winning, 10-under-par 206. "The last hole [is] 218 yards into the wind," Levet pointed out. "I managed to hold my nerve and make par there. I finally made some putts this week."

MCB Tour Championship – Madagascar
Andakana, Madagascar
Winner: Barry Lane

Barry Lane kept his wits about him as he came from behind to win the first leg of the three-tournament MCB Tour Championship in Madagascar, the new addition to the unique finish of the Staysure Tour season along the Indian Ocean coast.

"This week was all about mental ability. Whatever happened you had to accept it and try to do the best you could," explained Lane after scoring his second win of the season and eighth overall on the senior circuit. "It's such a difficult golf course because it's quite bouncy."

His winning 210 was just three under par at International Golf Club Du Rova and he was only two under with the closing 69 as he came from four strokes off the pace. American Clark Dennis, a five-time Staysure winner who won the WINSTONgolf Senior Open earlier in the season in spectacular fashion, took a three-stroke lead over Paul Streeter the second day with another brilliant showing, shooting 65, the week's low round.

Streeter collapsed Sunday (79), but Lane played steadily until Dennis fell apart, losing six strokes in a seven-hole stretch on the back nine. Lane moved into the lead with birdies at the 13th and 15th, parring in for the 210 that gave him a one-stroke victory over Juan Quiros and Jean-Francois Remesy.

"It's great that at 59 years old I am still winning," enthused Lane. "May it continue for another few years."

MCB Tour Championship – Seychelles
Praslin, Seychelles
Winner: Peter Fowler

Peter Fowler struck another blow for the older cast with his seventh victory on the Staysure Tour in the Seychelles segment of the MCB Tour Championship, the 60-year-old Australian following up the win of 59-year-old Barry Lane the previous week in the first leg in Madagascar.

"The golf ball doesn't know how old you are," quipped Fowler. "I've said that I still need to work hard. I've proved over the last 10 years that your fitness is key to success."

Fowler won in blazing-hot weather at Constance Lemuria in the Seychelles in much the same fashion as Lane did seven days earlier. He made up four strokes in the final round to squeeze past James Kingston, nipping the South African by a stroke with his four-under-par 204. Winless as a senior, Kingston, 54, had taken the lead away from Gary Orr the second day by birdieing the last four holes for 66–135.

Fowler, with his 70-69, was tied for fifth place, but cut into his deficit quickly the last day. He birdied the first two holes, picked up another at the sixth and, after his lone bogey at No. 7, ran off eight straight pars. His final birdie at No. 16 gave him the one-stroke margin he needed to edge Kingston, who fell behind with three bogeys in a four-hole stretch. Fowler had 67–206 while Kingston wound up with a two-over-par 72 for 207. It was his third second-place finish of the season. Phillip Price fattened his lead in the Order of Merit race with a tie-for-third posting.

MCB Tour Championship – Mauritius
Poste de Flacq, Mauritius
Winner: Jarmo Sandelin

The season-ending MCB Tour Championship - Mauritius had several consequences, to wit:
- Jarmo Sandelin gained his first victory on the Staysure Tour.
- Phillip Price finished atop the year's Order of Merit point standings and was awarded the coveted John Jacobs Trophy.
- James Kingston was crowned King of the Swing for the best overall record in the three-tournament, year-concluding MCB Tour Championship series on the Indian Ocean.
- Paul Lawrie took Rookie of the Year honors, finishing 11th in the Order of Merit rankings.

Sandelin fired a sizzling, seven-under-par 65 in the final round at Mauritius' Constance Belle Mare Plage course, coming from four strokes behind and winning by three over South Africa's Kingston, the second-round co-leader who also was gunning for his initial victory on the circuit. Strikingly, all three winners of the MCB events made up four-shot deficits in the final round.

"It's been a long time since I last won," exclaimed the 52-year-old Swede. "There has been a lot of practice balls, a lot of tears and a lot of hard work in the gym. Now I know that my game is good enough to win tournaments."

Rounds of 69 and 70 had put Sandelin in a three-way tie for sixth place, four back of Kingston (68-67) and Frenchman Jean-Francois Remesy, the first-round leader, after 36 holes. He got away fast Sunday with birdies on four of the first six holes. Undaunted by the double bogey he incurred when he found water at the ninth, Sandelin poured in five consecutive birdies starting at the 11th; a 10th at the 18th for the 65 and the 204 total that stood up for the victory as Kingston followed him in with 72–207 and Remesy with 73–208. It was the second straight and fourth 2019 runner-up finish for Kingston, who also led after 36 holes the previous week in Seychelles.

Welshman Price tied for third with Remesy and American Clark Dennis in winning the John Jacobs Trophy. "To be No. 1 is really important to me. I wanted to be No. l, not No. 2 or 3," said Price, who was Order of Merit runner-up to Paul Broadhurst in 2018.

Japan PGA Senior Tour

Kanehide Senior Okinawa Open
Kise, Okinawa
Winner: Taichi Teshima

Taichi Teshima wasted no time carrying on his winning ways on the Japan Senior Tour. Playing in his first event after turning 50, Teshima picked off the title in the season-opening Kanehide Senior Okinawa Open.

It hadn't been that long since, as a 46-year-old, he scored his eighth victory in the 2015 Mizuno Open on the regular Japan Tour. At Okinawa's Kane Kise Country Club in April, he won by a stroke in the 36-hole event.

The first day belonged to 63-year-old Masahiro (Massy) Kuramoto, one of the stars in the Japan Tour's early seasons who had won his seventh Senior Tour title in 2016. He shot a six-under-par 66 to take a one-shot lead over Teshima and Akio Nishizawa and two over Masayuki Kawamura and Thailand's Thaworn Wiratchant.

Kuramoto managed only a par 72 the second day as Teshima rode a three-shot swing on the last two holes to edge Kawamura by a stroke. Teshima closed birdie-par for 68-135 while Kawamura bogeyed the last two holes for 68-136.

Nojima Champion Cup Hakone Senior
Kanagawa
Winner: Shinichi Akiba

Shinichi Akiba's chances of winning the Nojima Hakone's Champion Cup for a second time in four years seemed quite dim after the first round of the 36-hole tournament at Hakone Country Club.

Masami Ito, at 63 winless in his previous 13 seasons on the Japan Senior Tour, shot his age plus one below it and took a five-stroke lead the first day. He birdied nine of the last 12 holes in shooting a record 32-30-62. That left Akiba and four others six strokes off the pace despite respectable, four-under-par 68s. Katsunori Kuwabara, Jong-Duck Kim and Hiroo Okamo shared second place with 67s.

Ito's hopes for that long-sought victory vanished the next day as he struggled to a 78 and a tie-for-sixth finish. That opened the door for Akiba, who shot 67-135 and edged Kuwabara (69) by a stroke to register his third Senior Tour victory. Defending champion Gregory Meyer, Shoichi Kuwabara and Kim finished two back, Meyer and Kuwabara with 68s and Kim with a closing 70 for his 137.

Fubon Yeangder Senior Cup
Chinese Taipei
Winner: Eiji Mizoguchi

In an astonishing turn of events, Eiji Mizoguchi captured his first title on the Japan Senior Tour in the weather-shortened Fubon Yeangder Senior Cup in Chinese Taipei.

It looked like another decisive victory was in the cards for Prayad Marksaeng when the dominating Thai star, winner of 13 tournaments in his three previous seasons in Japan, racked up nine birdies and a bogey on his way to an opening 64 and a three-stroke lead at Linkou International Golf Club.

Instead, Marksaeng stunningly tumbled to a 76 the second day, eventually finishing eighth, as Mizoguchi and Takeshi Sakiyama, a seven-time senior winner, took over the lead. Mizoguchi, 54, a former Asian Tour player who had been nursing an aching back since early in the year, piled up eight birdies en route to a 66, while Sakiyama, who was in second place behind Marksaeng Friday, shot 71 for his 136.

When heavy weather rolled in Sunday morning, officials decided to cancel the final round and, despite conditions, ordered a playoff. The two men each bogeyed the first extra hole and Mizoguchi won with a par on the second one, observing afterward about his five previous fruitless seasons on the senior tour: "Although the hard times lasted for many years, winning was a great experience."

Sumaiida Cup
Tochigi
Winner: Masayoshi Yamazoe

Another four-stroke, final-round rally brought Masayoshi Yamazoe his second victory on the Japan Senior Tour in the Sumaiida Cup Senior tournament the first of June.

Little more than a year earlier in the Kanehide Okinawa Open just months after turning 50, Yamazoe came from four back to forge a tie and score his first career tour win in the subsequent playoff. In the Sumaiida Cup, he was again four shots off the lead entering the last round. This time he closed with a seven-under-par 65 to bypass the nine players ahead of him and win by a stroke over Suk Joug Yul with his 202 total.

Among those who started the Sunday round in front of him, Yamazoe victimized the second round's one-two leaders — Hawaiian David Ishii (67-66–133) and Masahiro (Massy) Kuramoto (69-65–134), both standouts on the Japan Tour in their younger days, and Prayad Marksaeng (71-64–135) and Katsunari Takahashi (69-66–135), two of the top career winners on the circuit with 13 apiece. Yamazoe posted 68-69 rounds before his powerful finish. Yul closed with 67 to nab second place.

Starts Senior
Ibaraki
Winner: Masahiro Kuramoto

Masahiro (Massy) Kuramoto prevailed in a battle of golfing heavyweights on the Japan Senior Tour at the Starts Senior tournament in mid-June.

Kuramoto, a Japan Tour star with 30 victories on his fine record, defeated Toru Taniguchi, a 20-win standout in more recent years on the Japan Tour, in a sudden-death playoff for the title. It was the eighth senior title for the 63-year-old, who has played worldwide since turning 50, picking up two titles on the Staysure (European Senior) Tour.

To reach the playoff, those two stars had to contend with Thailand's Prayad Marksaeng, the dominant figure on the circuit with 13 wins in the previous three seasons. Marksaeng opened his bid for a third straight Starts Senior title with a sparkling, seven-under-par 65, taking a two-stroke lead on Taniguchi, 51, playing in just his second Japan Senior Tour tournament and first of the current season.

Taniguchi, with 70–137, cut the margin to one as Marksaeng shot 71 the second day. At that point, Kuramoto was in sixth place, five shots off the lead with his 70-71–141, but he turned on the power Sunday, racking up an eagle and six birdies. His 64–205 stood up as the lead until Taniguchi finished with 68 for the tie. Marksaeng managed only 70 and missed the playoff by a shot, deadlocking for third at 206 with Chien-Soon Lu, the 2017 Senior PGA champion.

Kuramoto ended the playoff quickly with a birdie to Taniguchi's par on the first extra hole.

Kumamoto Aso Senior Open
Kumamoto
Winner: Gregory Meyer

Gregory Meyer, the only American regular on the Japan Senior Tour, picked up his third victory in the Kumamoto Aso Senior Open, all three wins occurring in 36-hole tournaments.

The 57-year-old pro, whose earlier victories came in the 2004 Maruhan Cup Taiheiyo Club and 2018 Nojima Hakone Senior tournaments, jumped off to a big lead the first day at the Kosgi Resort's Aso Highland course with a blistering, eight-under-par 64. He was three strokes ahead of runners-up Jong-Duck Kim and Masahiro (Massy) Kuramoto, veteran victors on the circuit, and winless Suk Joug Yul.

Meyer's Sunday 68 and 132 total barely held off the second-round runs of Yul (66) and Hidezumi Shirakata (65), who shared second place at 133, a shot better than Kim (67) and the defending champion, Kiyoshi Murota (66), the ever-present career wins leader (20) who was just three weeks shy of his 64th birthday. Kuramoto tumbled into a 25th-place tie with his 73–140.

Fancl Classic
Susono, Shizuoka
Winner: Prayad Marksaeng

It took a little longer in his fourth season on the Japan Senior Tour for Prayad Marksaeng to continue his winning ways, but he did so by successfully defending his Fancl Classic championship the hard way.

The 53-year-old Thailand standout made up a two-stroke deficit on the final three holes at Susono Country Club in Shizuoka Prefecture and prevailed in the subsequent three-man playoff for his 14th victory on the circuit.

Seeking to win two in a row, American Gregory Meyer, the Kumamoto Aso winner earlier in August, got off to a fast start on a rainy Friday, sharing the first-round lead with Toshimitzu Izawa and Hidesumi Shirakata at five-under-par 67. Just one stroke back the first day, Marksaeng moved a shot in front of Izawa (69–136) and South Korean senior rookie Suk Joug Yul (66–136) Saturday, shooting 67–135. (Yul had a wild round ranging from a hole-in-one to a double bogey.)

Marksaeng fell two shots behind Yul through 15 holes Sunday, but overtook him when Yul bogeyed the 16th hole and Marksaeng birdied the 18th as the Korean three-putted for a par on the par-five finishing hole. The two were joined in the playoff by Naoyuki Tamura, the 2016 Fuji Film winner, who had finished well ahead of them with a 66 for his 207.

The playoff action was repeated three times on the 18th, Yul going out the first time with a par to a pair of birdies. Marksaeng and Tamura both birdied again on the second go-around before Marksaeng birdied the hole for a fourth straight time for the victory when Tamura only managed a par. It was a second straight second-place finish for Yul.

Hiroshima Senior
Hiroshima
Winner: Shinsuke Yanagisawa

Shinsuke Yanagisawa reprised his earlier first victory on the Japan Senior Tour when he added the 36-hole Hiroshima Senior tournament to his record in late August.

Just as when he won the ISPS Handa Cup Philanthropy at the end of the 2017 season, Yanagisawa came from two strokes back to score a one-stroke victory on the Saijo course at Hiroshima Country Club. His 65-132 edged Chien-Soon Lu, whose matching 65 gave him the second-place slot by a shot over Wen-Teh Lu (64) and Seiki Okuda (65).

Veteran senior Kiyoshi Murota, the all-time senior winner (20), and two others — Mitsutaka Kusakabe and Toru Suzuki — shared the first-round lead with 65s as the 53-year-old Yanagisawa opened in a five-way tie for fifth at 67. Yanagisawa raced into the lead the second day with three birdies on the first four holes and remained in front the rest of the way, posting four more birdies against a single bogey to land the title.

Maruhan Cup Taiheiyo Club Senior
Hyogo
Winner: Prayad Marksaeng

Normally, it's rare for a tour player to successfully defend a championship. Such does not seem to be the case for Prayad Marksaeng, the domineering shotmaker on the Japan Senior Tour. Two weeks after repeating victory in the Fancl Classic, the Thailander won the Maruhan Cup Taiheiyo Club tournament for the second year in a row and the third time in four seasons.

Marksaeng entered the final round a stroke behind Nobuo Serizawa, whose leading 67 the first day at the Pacific Club Rokko course included a hole-in-one at No. 3 along with four birdies and a bogey. But he fell back to a 74 the second day as Marksaeng dueled for the title down the stretch with Hidezumi Shirakata, who was shooting for his first senior win.

Shirakata's bogey at the 15th hole, the lone bogey between the two, proved decisive. It briefly gave Marksaeng a one-stroke lead and he countered Shirakata's birdie at the next hole with the winning one at the 17th. Both shot 66s Sunday, Marksaeng for 134 and the victory, his 15th in his four years on the circuit.

Komatsu Open
Komatsu, Ishikawa
Winner: Thaworn Wiratchant

Thaworn Wiratchant prevailed in a rare matchup of long-time friends and top players from another country when he beat Prayad Marksaeng, his fellow Thailander, in what for most of the final afternoon seemed a highly unlikely playoff for the Komatsu Open title.

Marksaeng, already a two-time winner earlier in the season and the dominant figure on the Japan Senior Tour since 2016, was breezing toward his 16th victory on the circuit that September Sunday when he knocked first a tee shot and then a wedge out of bounds and absorbed a shocking, quadruple-bogey-eight on the next-to-last hole at Komatsu Country Club. Impressively, he rallied with his eighth birdie of the day on the 18th for 68-202 to salvage a tie.

Wiratchant, who had started the day at 69-68-137, four strokes behind and four groups ahead of second-round leader Chien-Soon Lu (68-65-133), was "cleaning up in the locker room" when he got word of Marksaeng's disaster. He had rung up an eight-birdie, one-bogey 65 for his 202 and the clubhouse lead, but had never thought it would hold up. Instead, it put him in the playoff, which he won on the first extra hole against his friend of 38 years with a 10-foot birdie putt. Marksaeng missed his five-footer to extend the overtime.

"I'm glad my friend won," said Marksaeng graciously at the award ceremony.

"I'm happy to be with you. I didn't expect to catch up," replied Wiratchant, whose previous win in Japan came in the 2018 Seven Hills KBC tournament.

Japan Senior Open Championship
Saitama
Winner: Toru Taniguchi

Toru Taniguchi was certainly living up to his long-established reputation as one of Japan's all-time great golfers during his few ventures onto the Japan Senior Tour.

Although he became eligible 19 months earlier, Taniguchi was making just his third appearance when he teed it up in the Japan Senior Open Championship on Hidaka Country Club's East-West course in late September. In his two previous tournaments, he had finished second to Prayad Marksaeng in the 2018 Open and lost in a playoff to Masahiro Kuramoto earlier in the current season in the Starts Senior.

This time Taniguchi came out on top, leading all the way in a close battle with Thailand's Thaworn Wiratchant, who was coming off his victory the previous weekend in the Komatsu Senior Open.

Taniguchi got off to fast start with a bogey-free 66, leading Yoichi Shimizu by a stroke and Wiratchant and Boo Won Park by two. His margin grew to three over Wiratchant the second day as he shot 70-136. He still led Wiratchant by two Saturday after three back-nine bogeys, settling for a par 72 and 208 to Wiratchant's 71. A two-stroke swing in the middle of the closing stretch Sunday gave Taniguchi a three-shot edge and he needed it when Wiratchant birdied and he bogeyed the final hole. He finished with 72 and an eight-under-par 280. Wiratchant shot 71-281.

"It seems the journey to win a championship took longer than I expected," reflected the man who won 20 tournaments during his Japan Tour career. "The Senior Tour is fun."

Seven Hills Cup KBC Senior Open
Saga
Winner: Akira Teranishi

Akira Teranishi made his annual visit to the Japan Senior Tour's winner's circle at the Seven Hills Cup KBC Senior Open in late September. This time the 53-year-old pro took a different approach. When he won his two previous titles — the Iwasaki Shiratsuyu in 2017 and the ISPS Handa Cup Philanthropy in 2018 — he carried a lead into the final round.

At Seven Hills Golf Club in 2019, he trailed by four strokes after the first round of the 36-hole event as Suk Joug Yul opened with a 10-birdie 62 to the 66 Teranishi and four others shot that first day. Yul led runners-up Jong-Duck Kim, Hiroo Okama and Seiki Okuda by two strokes.

Even with a nine-birdie, one-bogey 64 and the early clubhouse lead Sunday, Teranishi did not feel comfortable until the last group finished and Okuda three-putted the last green after birdies at the 16th and 17th. The bogey dropped Okuda into a tie for second with Okama, who matched his 67, and Kazuo Seike, who duplicated Teranishi's 64.

"I wouldn't have won if I hadn't been lucky," Akira observed, noting Okuda's three-putt.

Japan PGA Senior Championship
Ibaraki
Winner: Hidezumi Shirakata

It took Hidezumi Shirakata eight seasons to land a victory on the Japan Tour. He did it in three on the Japan Senior Tour when he captured the Japan PGA Senior Championship at the end of a typhoon-interrupted weekend in Ibaraki Prefecture.

The 53-year-old pro never trailed as he rolled to a three-stroke triumph at Summit Golf Club, outplaying three of the tour's strongest shotmakers and overcoming a scare in the final round that prevented him from breezing down the stretch to the major title.

Shirakata was one of the five leaders who shot 67s the first day, sharing the top spot with Gregory Meyer, Masayoshi Yamazoe, Prayad Marksaeng and Shinsuke Yanagisawa. With the third round already cancelled because of the impending arrival of Typhoon Hagibis, Shirakata put himself in excellent position atop the standings after Friday's play in case Sunday's play had to be cancelled too. He shot 65–132, making the last two of nine birdies on the final holes to wind up two strokes ahead of senior rookie Yoshinobu Tsukada and three ahead of Thaworn Wiratchant, who finished birdie-eagle. Both had 66s.

The course was playable and the weather sunny Sunday. Shirakata was sailing nicely 14 under par with no threats at hand when he staggered to a triple bogey at the 15th hole. "My head turned white. Why did I do this?" he admitted later after shaking off the setback, birdieing the 17th hole and posting a par 72 for a 12-under 204 and three-stroke margin over Masahiro Kuramoto and Marksaeng (70s), Wiratchant (72) and Tsukada (73).

Trust Group Cup Sasebo Senior Open
Nagasaki
Winner: Shinichi Akiba

Shinichi Akiba only had to make up half as much ground to win his second tournament of the 2019 Japan Senior Tour season as he did in landing his first one, when he came from six strokes back to take the Hakone title in April. In mid-October, he overcame a three-shot deficit and claimed his fifth senior victory in the Trust Group Cup Sasebo Senior Open.

Circumstances differed, though. The 54-year-old had nobody to catch except winless leader Masami Ito at Hakone, but was behind eight players after the first round of the 36-hole event at wind-swept Sasebo Country Club. Besides, the leader was seasoned veteran Masahiro (Massy) Kuramoto, who had won his eighth senior title in the Starts Senior earlier in the season.

Kuramoto had opened with an erratic 69 — the product of seven birdies, two bogeys and a double bogey — finishing a stroke ahead of three players at 70 and four at 71. He opened the door to the field early in Sunday's round with two bogeys and a double bogey on the first four holes, and Akiba, who had started with 72, took the greatest advantage. He shot a flawless, five-under-par 67, just enough with his 139 total to edge Kuramoto, who rallied to finish second with two late birdies for 71-140, as Akiba become the season's second multiple winner.

Fukuoka Senior Open
Higashi-ku, Fukuoka
Winner: Toshimitsu Izawa

It seemed it was only a matter of time before Toshimitsu Izawa joined the ranks of winners on the Japan Senior Tour. Izawa came aboard in 2018 sporting an illustrious Japan Tour record — 16 victories, twice the leading money winner (2001, 2003) — but had a mediocre season that carried over well into 2019.

The also-ran tag ended in October in the Fukuoka Senior Open. The 51-year-old came from two strokes off the pace and scored a single-stroke victory with his eight-under-par 136, sharing it with his 17-year-old son Joichiro, who caddied for his father for the first time in his life.

Hidezumi Shirakata, the Japan Senior PGA winner two weeks earlier, launched another victory bid the first day on Fukuoka Kantree Club's Waijiro Course, piling up an eagle and six birdies against a lone bogey, his 65 giving him a one-stroke lead over tour-dominating Prayad Marksaeng and Yoshikatsu Saito.

Marksaeng, seeking his 16th title on the senior circuit, took a brief lead in the final round Sunday when he birdied and Shirakata double-bogeyed the first hole on his way to a 77. Izawa caught the Thailand star with birdies at the sixth and seventh holes and went ahead to stay with two more at the 12th and 13th. He bogeyed the last hole, shooting 69, just enough to edge Yoshinobu Tsukada, who closed with 67-137.

Fujifilm Senior Championship
Ibaraki
Winner: Thaworn Wiratchant

An all-Thailand run to the finishing wire of the Japan Senior Tour's money race developed with Thaworn Wiratchant's decisive victory in the late-season Fujifilm Championship.

Wielding a driver that he just picked up at a used-club shop and a change of putters, the 52-year-old Thai romped to a six-stroke triumph and moved within a narrow ¥500,000 of his friend and countryman Prayad Marksaeng with just two tournaments remaining on the schedule.

"I was lucky. If the driver was bad, the putter was good. If the putter was bad, the driver was good," said Wiratchant in appraising his second win of the season and third on the circuit.

The key to the victory was the eight-birdie 64 he shot the second day at Edosaki Country Club in Ibaraki Prefecture. His 12-under-par 132 lifted him four strokes into the lead over Suk Joug Yul and he coasted home unchallenged with a 68 (five birdies and a bogey) for the winning 200, a Fujifilm tournament record low.

Toru Suzuki grabbed second place with his 66–206 and Marksaeng made the money margin a little wider with a fourth-place tie in his bid for a fourth straight No. 1 season.

Elite Grip Senior Open
Hyogo
Winner: Eiji Mizoguchi

Oddly enough, Eiji Mizoguchi wasn't particularly happy when he made a hole-in-one in the first round of the Elite Grip Senior Open.

"You can't win if you achieve a hole-in-one," Mizoguchi explained that day although he was only a stroke out of the lead, citing a jinx many in the golf world believe. "I didn't think I could win."

But he did, making up the narrow deficit to score his second win of the season, the earlier one in the Fubon Yeangder Cup in a playoff that ended five winless seasons on the Japan Senior Tour for the 54-year-old.

Three former senior winners — Kazuhiro Takami, Yoshinori Mizumaki and 62-year-old Tsukasa Watanabe — led after the first round with three-under-par 67s at Naruto Golf Club in Hyogo with Mizoguchi at 68 with Chien-Soon Lu, Masahiro Kuramoto and Gregory Meyer.

Mizoguchi took over first place on the front nine on the Saturday final round with an outgoing 33, but Suk Joug Yul and Akira Teranishi caught him at the 11th, all three standing at four under par. Mizoguchi and Yul matched birdies on the next two holes, and Yul went in front when Mizoguchi bogeyed the 15th. But all Mizoguchi needed were his three closing pars and his 67–135 as Yul bogeyed the last three holes and dropped into a four-way tie for second with Norio Shinozaki, Masayuki Kawamura and Teranishi at 137.

ISPS Handa Cup Philanthropy Senior
Saitama
Winner: Suk Joug Yul

Plagued by four second-place finishes in his quest for victory on the Japan Senior Tour, South Korea's Suk Joug Yul finally broke through in the season's final tournament in a dramatic 18th-hole climax against Kiyoshi Murota, the circuit's all-time victory king.

Yul, who had opened the ISPS Handa Cup Philanthropy tournament with a six-birdie 66 and a two-stroke lead over six players, including Murota, battled him neck-and-neck in the final round of the 36-hole event at Hatoyama Country Club in Saitama Prefecture, but trailed him by a stroke at the tee on the par-five 18th. Murota, gunning for his 21st win on the tour, caught the pond in front of the green with his second shot, took a bogey for 68–136 and lost by a stroke when Yul birdied for 69–135. The win came just four days after a three-bogey finish cost Yul victory in the Elite Grip Open. Katsumi Kubo birdied four of the last seven holes for 67 to share the runner-up slot with Murota.

Thaworn Wiratchant, who shot 72 in the first round despite a hole-in-one, produced a 67 the next day to finish in a tie for fifth, its ¥760,000 check boosting him past fellow Thai Prayad Marksaeng into first place on the final money list. Wiratchant, who won twice in 2019, compiled ¥47,388,525 to ¥46,978,478 for Marksaeng, who also won twice, his 14th and 15th, but did not play in the last two events.

APPENDIXES

American Tours

Sentry Tournament of Champions

Plantation Course at Kapalua, Maui, Hawaii
Par 36-37–73; 7,518 yards

January 3-6
purse, $6,500,000

	SCORES				TOTAL	MONEY
Xander Schauffele	72	67	68	62	269	$1,300,000
Gary Woodland	67	67	68	68	270	759,000
Justin Thomas	67	72	70	65	274	475,000
Dustin Johnson	67	74	69	67	277	305,333.34
Marc Leishman	68	70	68	71	277	305,333.33
Rory McIlroy	69	68	68	72	277	305,333.33
Bryson DeChambeau	69	68	70	71	278	218,000
Patton Kizzire	69	71	71	68	279	191,000
Jon Rahm	70	71	69	69	279	191,000
Webb Simpson	70	72	72	65	279	191,000
Cameron Champ	71	68	74	67	280	162,500
Kevin Tway	66	71	72	71	280	162,500
Jason Day	69	71	75	66	281	147,000
Charles Howell	74	70	69	69	282	132,000
Andrew Putnam	69	73	70	70	282	132,000
Paul Casey	73	71	68	71	283	113,000
Troy Merritt	73	71	69	70	283	113,000
Ian Poulter	71	69	73	71	284	102,000
Brice Garnett	73	72	73	68	286	92,333.34
Matt Kuchar	72	73	72	69	286	92,333.33
Scott Piercy	76	72	69	69	286	92,333.33
Andrew Landry	69	75	71	72	287	82,500
Brandt Snedeker	75	69	71	72	287	82,500
Brooks Koepka	76	70	73	69	288	78,000
Billy Horschel	72	75	71	72	290	74,000
Patrick Reed	70	75	72	73	290	74,000
Keegan Bradley	77	69	72	73	291	68,250
Francesco Molinari	73	71	73	74	291	68,250
Ted Potter, Jr.	75	73	71	72	291	68,250
Aaron Wise	74	71	73	73	291	68,250
Bubba Watson	70	79	74	69	292	65,000
Michael Kim	71	72	80	73	296	63,500
Satoshi Kodaira	77	76	73	70	296	63,500

Sony Open in Hawaii

Waialae Country Club, Honolulu, Hawaii
Par 35-35–70; 7,044 yards

January 10-13
purse, $6,400,000

	SCORES				TOTAL	MONEY
Matt Kuchar	63	63	66	66	258	$1,152,000
Andrew Putnam	62	65	67	68	262	691,200
Corey Conners	68	67	64	64	263	307,200
Marc Leishman	67	64	68	64	263	307,200
Chez Reavie	65	65	66	67	263	307,200
Hudson Swafford	65	67	67	64	263	307,200
Davis Love	67	68	64	65	264	214,400
Charles Howell	69	66	64	66	265	192,000

	SCORES				TOTAL	MONEY
Brian Stuard	66	69	64	66	265	192,000
Bryson DeChambeau	69	67	63	67	266	160,000
Sung Kang	70	67	65	64	266	160,000
Sebastian Munoz	68	65	68	65	266	160,000
Patrick Reed	68	66	68	65	267	123,733.34
Patton Kizzire	67	68	67	65	267	123,733.33
Ted Potter, Jr.	66	65	68	68	267	123,733.33
Sungjae Im	71	64	65	68	268	99,200
Keith Mitchell	68	65	63	72	268	99,200
Brandt Snedeker	66	69	65	68	268	99,200
Justin Thomas	67	68	67	66	268	99,200
Stewart Cink	68	62	70	69	269	80,000
J.T. Poston	68	66	69	66	269	80,000
Ryan Armour	72	64	68	66	270	57,691.43
Joel Dahmen	67	70	66	67	270	57,691.43
Harris English	68	68	67	67	270	57,691.43
Brian Gay	67	69	68	66	270	57,691.43
Cameron Smith	66	68	69	67	270	57,691.43
Kyle Stanley	73	64	68	65	270	57,691.43
Emiliano Grillo	70	68	63	69	270	57,691.42
Abraham Ancer	68	66	68	69	271	42,560
Keegan Bradley	68	65	70	68	271	42,560
Matt Jones	67	69	67	68	271	42,560
Carlos Ortiz	68	69	70	64	271	42,560
Dominic Bozzelli	71	64	64	73	272	31,040
Scott Brown	68	66	70	68	272	31,040
Brice Garnett	70	68	68	66	272	31,040
Shugo Imahira	65	67	71	69	272	31,040
Scott Piercy	71	66	66	69	272	31,040
Ian Poulter	69	69	66	68	272	31,040
Rory Sabbatini	68	67	68	69	272	31,040
Sam Saunders	68	69	68	67	272	31,040
Roger Sloan	69	65	66	72	272	31,040
Y.E. Yang	68	68	70	66	272	31,040
Julian Etulain	67	67	68	71	273	19,488
Jim Herman	69	68	69	67	273	19,488
Stephan Jaeger	69	69	65	70	273	19,488
Russell Knox	68	67	69	69	273	19,488
Anirban Lahiri	68	68	71	66	273	19,488
Scott Langley	70	67	66	70	273	19,488
Hank Lebioda	70	67	68	68	273	19,488
Adam Svensson	61	74	70	68	273	19,488
Dylan Frittelli	67	69	67	71	274	15,061.34
Alex Prugh	73	65	65	71	274	15,061.34
Brandon Harkins	71	66	70	67	274	15,061.33
Jim Knous	66	69	69	70	274	15,061.33
Hideki Matsuyama	69	67	65	73	274	15,061.33
Jimmy Walker	69	69	67	69	274	15,061.33
Tyler Duncan	72	66	66	71	275	14,080
Fabian Gomez	70	67	69	69	275	14,080
Adam Hadwin	73	65	70	67	275	14,080
Trey Mullinax	68	70	70	67	275	14,080
Wes Roach	67	68	70	70	275	14,080
Jose de Jesus Rodriguez	66	70	70	69	275	14,080
Chase Wright	69	68	67	71	275	14,080
Ryan Blaum	68	66	71	71	276	13,504
Yuki Inamori	69	68	71	68	276	13,504
Russell Henley	68	69	71	69	277	13,312
Rikuya Hoshino	66	72	69	71	278	13,120
Johnson Wagner	68	69	70	71	278	13,120
Kevin Kisner	69	69	68	73	279	12,864
Michael Thompson	66	69	70	74	279	12,864
Danny Lee	70	66	70	74	280	12,672

	SCORES				TOTAL	MONEY
Eric Dugas	67	71	71		209	12,544
Cameron Champ	69	68	73		210	12,224
Jason Dufner	66	72	72		210	12,224
Steve Stricker	71	67	72		210	12,224
Martin Trainer	69	68	73		210	12,224
Mackenzie Hughes	70	68	73		211	11,840
Sean O'Hair	69	68	74		211	11,840
Brady Schnell	71	67	74		212	11,648
Gary Woodland	71	66	76		213	11,520
Joey Garber	71	67	76		214	11,392

Desert Classic

Stadium Course: Par 36-36-72; 7,113 yards
La Quinta CC: Par 36-36-72; 7,060 yards
Nicklaus Tournament Course: Par 36-36-72; 7,159 yards
La Quinta, California

January 17-20
purse, $5,900,000

	SCORES				TOTAL	MONEY
Adam Long	63	71	63	65	262	$1,062,000
Adam Hadwin	65	66	65	67	263	519,200
Phil Mickelson	60	68	66	69	263	519,200
Talor Gooch	67	67	66	64	264	283,200
Dominic Bozzelli	67	69	64	66	266	236,000
Jon Rahm	66	66	68	67	267	212,400
J.T. Poston	68	68	64	69	269	190,275
Vaughn Taylor	68	66	69	66	269	190,275
Patrick Cantlay	67	66	66	71	270	159,300
Sean O'Hair	66	67	68	69	270	159,300
Michael Thompson	68	66	65	71	270	159,300
Daniel Berger	67	67	69	68	271	112,100
Lucas Glover	68	68	68	67	271	112,100
Sungjae Im	71	65	64	71	271	112,100
Scott Langley	70	65	66	70	271	112,100
Nate Lashley	72	68	66	65	271	112,100
Roger Sloan	70	68	68	65	271	112,100
Abraham Ancer	66	67	73	66	272	64,723
Aaron Baddeley	71	68	68	65	272	64,723
Sam Burns	68	66	68	70	272	64,723
Wyndham Clark	65	67	72	68	272	64,723
Russell Knox	73	66	64	69	272	64,723
Jason Kokrak	71	65	66	70	272	64,723
Peter Malnati	70	65	68	69	272	64,723
Steve Marino	66	65	67	74	272	64,723
Adam Svensson	66	68	69	69	272	64,723
Harold Varner	68	67	68	69	272	64,723
Cameron Davis	67	70	67	69	273	39,235
Dylan Frittelli	72	67	64	70	273	39,235
Zach Johnson	71	68	64	70	273	39,235
Andrew Landry	68	67	69	69	273	39,235
Chez Reavie	67	68	69	69	273	39,235
Jose de Jesus Rodriguez	67	70	69	67	273	39,235
Anders Albertson	68	69	70	67	274	29,795
Charles Howell	67	69	68	70	274	29,795
Trey Mullinax	65	71	67	71	274	29,795
Andrew Putnam	70	69	67	68	274	29,795
Justin Rose	68	68	68	70	274	29,795
Kevin Streelman	70	66	68	70	274	29,795
Cody Gribble	70	67	68	70	275	19,663.10
Roberto Castro	71	67	69	68	275	19,663.09

	SCORES				TOTAL	MONEY
Alex Cejka	66	68	68	73	275	19,663.09
Julian Etulain	71	66	69	69	275	19,663.09
Kramer Hickok	67	72	68	68	275	19,663.09
Si Woo Kim	70	70	67	68	275	19,663.09
Sam Ryder	72	66	66	71	275	19,663.09
Robert Streb	66	70	68	71	275	19,663.09
Brian Stuard	70	68	68	69	275	19,663.09
Nick Taylor	70	66	67	72	275	19,663.09
Josh Teater	68	69	67	71	275	19,663.09
Tyler Duncan	73	66	66	71	276	13,884.67
C.T. Pan	66	70	70	70	276	13,884.67
J.J. Spaun	69	67	68	72	276	13,884.67
Nick Watney	68	70	68	70	276	13,884.67
Harris English	70	70	67	69	276	13,884.66
Cameron Tringale	70	71	66	69	276	13,884.66
Jonathan Byrd	71	68	66	72	277	12,921
Chad Collins	69	70	68	70	277	12,921
Joey Garber	68	64	69	76	277	12,921
James Hahn	70	70	67	70	277	12,921
Kevin Kisner	69	68	69	71	277	12,921
Scott Piercy	72	65	70	70	277	12,921
Rory Sabbatini	68	70	66	73	277	12,921
Brendan Steele	69	69	67	72	277	12,921
Carlos Ortiz	72	62	68	76	278	12,331
Hudson Swafford	71	71	65	71	278	12,331
John Catlin	69	69	69	72	279	12,095
Adam Schenk	66	71	69	73	279	12,095
Jhonattan Vegas	66	73	68	73	280	11,918
John Huh	68	72	67	74	281	11,741
Curtis Luck	64	66	76	75	281	11,741
Ollie Schniederjans	71	68	68	75	282	11,564
Ryan Blaum	67	73	67	78	285	11,446

Farmers Insurance Open

Torrey Pines, San Diego, California
South Course: Par 36-36–72; 7,698 yards
North Course: Par 36-36–72; 7,258 yards

January 24-27
purse, $7,100,000

	SCORES				TOTAL	MONEY
Justin Rose	63	66	69	69	267	$1,278,000
Adam Scott	70	66	65	68	269	766,800
Talor Gooch	69	68	67	68	272	411,800
Hideki Matsuyama	66	66	73	67	272	411,800
Jason Day	67	71	69	67	274	259,150
Rory McIlroy	71	65	69	69	274	259,150
Jon Rahm	62	72	68	72	274	259,150
Billy Horschel	66	68	71	70	275	220,100
Scott Brown	70	68	68	70	276	184,600
Joel Dahmen	68	67	70	71	276	184,600
Cameron Smith	71	69	71	65	276	184,600
Gary Woodland	71	70	69	66	276	184,600
Bud Cauley	66	70	74	67	277	121,714.29
Matt Jones	67	74	69	67	277	121,714.29
Ryan Palmer	67	67	75	68	277	121,714.29
Sepp Straka	69	67	71	70	277	121,714.29
Tony Finau	69	69	69	70	277	121,714.28
Patrick Reed	69	69	69	70	277	121,714.28
Michael Thompson	68	69	69	71	277	121,714.28
Doug Ghim	63	73	67	75	278	79,804

	SCORES				TOTAL	MONEY
Charles Howell	66	70	75	67	278	79,804
Sung Kang	71	70	66	71	278	79,804
Jason Kokrak	71	69	69	69	278	79,804
Tiger Woods	70	70	71	67	278	79,804
John Huh	68	68	71	72	279	56,622.50
Trey Mullinax	70	71	68	70	279	56,622.50
Xander Schauffele	69	70	70	70	279	56,622.50
Danny Willett	71	68	70	70	279	56,622.50
Jonas Blixt	68	69	74	69	280	45,144.17
Mackenzie Hughes	70	70	70	70	280	45,144.17
Si Woo Kim	67	68	73	72	280	45,144.17
Robert Streb	69	68	72	71	280	45,144.17
Jim Knous	70	71	70	69	280	45,144.16
Hank Lebioda	70	67	68	75	280	45,144.16
Sangmoon Bae	68	67	71	75	281	35,003
Keegan Bradley	68	71	69	73	281	35,003
Wyndham Clark	69	67	70	75	281	35,003
Jordan Spieth	65	72	72	72	281	35,003
Adam Svensson	70	67	69	75	281	35,003
Sam Burns	70	66	74	72	282	29,110
Luke List	70	69	71	72	282	29,110
J.T. Poston	72	68	69	73	282	29,110
Julian Etulain	71	67	71	74	283	21,158
Russell Knox	67	70	73	73	283	21,158
Martin Laird	73	66	69	75	283	21,158
Marc Leishman	68	73	70	72	283	21,158
Nicholas Lindheim	71	69	70	73	283	21,158
Sam Ryder	69	69	72	73	283	21,158
Scott Stallings	69	71	71	72	283	21,158
Nick Taylor	71	68	72	72	283	21,158
Kevin Tway	70	71	72	70	283	21,158
Emiliano Grillo	67	74	70	73	284	16,557.20
Sungjae Im	72	68	72	72	284	16,557.20
Chris Stroud	66	71	74	73	284	16,557.20
Chris Thompson	74	66	70	74	284	16,557.20
Braden Thornberry	71	67	72	74	284	16,557.20
Cameron Davis	72	69	72	72	285	15,762
Bill Haas	67	72	70	76	285	15,762
Beau Hossler	67	70	74	74	285	15,762
Adam Schenk	72	69	74	70	285	15,762
John Senden	68	73	72	72	285	15,762
Grayson Murray	68	72	71	75	286	15,123
Ben Silverman	68	71	72	75	286	15,123
Brandt Snedeker	68	73	71	74	286	15,123
Shawn Stefani	67	74	70	75	286	15,123
Rickie Fowler	73	66	74	74	287	14,555
Brandon Hagy	66	71	74	76	287	14,555
Stephan Jaeger	70	71	72	74	287	14,555
C.T. Pan	64	75	71	77	287	14,555
Ryan Blaum	71	70	75	72	288	14,129
Rory Sabbatini	72	68	76	72	288	14,129
John Chin	66	71	77	75	289	13,703
Sebastian Munoz	68	72	75	74	289	13,703
Joaquin Niemann	66	73	70	80	289	13,703
Nick Watney	72	68	74	75	289	13,703
Sean O'Hair	71	69	77	73	290	13,348
Morgan Hoffmann	70	70	79	72	291	13,206

Waste Management Phoenix Open

TPC Scottsdale, Scottsdale, Arizona
Par 35-36–71; 7,261 yards

January 31-February 3
purse, $7,100,000

	SCORES				TOTAL	MONEY
Rickie Fowler	64	65	64	74	267	$1,278,000
Branden Grace	67	64	69	69	269	766,800
Justin Thomas	64	66	68	72	270	482,800
Chez Reavie	71	69	64	68	272	293,466.67
Bubba Watson	66	67	68	71	272	293,466.67
Matt Kuchar	67	65	65	75	272	293,466.66
Chris Stroud	71	66	67	69	273	221,283.34
Sungjae Im	69	68	67	69	273	221,283.33
Gary Woodland	68	67	66	72	273	221,283.33
Russell Knox	71	66	69	68	274	163,300
Jon Rahm	67	68	70	69	274	163,300
Xander Schauffele	67	72	67	68	274	163,300
Harold Varner	64	71	68	71	274	163,300
Jhonattan Vegas	70	69	66	69	274	163,300
Tyrrell Hatton	66	71	70	68	275	113,600
Russell Henley	68	68	69	70	275	113,600
Hideki Matsuyama	68	69	69	69	275	113,600
Trey Mullinax	67	64	72	72	275	113,600
Cameron Smith	67	65	71	72	275	113,600
Chesson Hadley	71	65	70	70	276	76,916.67
Charley Hoffman	66	68	70	72	276	76,916.67
Scott Piercy	66	71	71	68	276	76,916.67
Webb Simpson	67	69	70	70	276	76,916.67
Byeong Hun An	66	68	66	76	276	76,916.66
Jason Kokrak	73	66	65	72	276	76,916.66
Bud Cauley	68	72	66	71	277	50,410
Brandon Harkins	70	66	69	72	277	50,410
J.B. Holmes	69	68	68	72	277	50,410
Max Homa	70	68	71	68	277	50,410
Kevin Kisner	70	69	70	68	277	50,410
Martin Laird	65	68	70	74	277	50,410
J.T. Poston	65	74	68	70	277	50,410
Kiradech Aphibarnrat	69	70	71	68	278	37,511.67
Emiliano Grillo	67	73	67	71	278	37,511.67
David Hearn	67	68	71	72	278	37,511.67
Hunter Mahan	70	68	69	71	278	37,511.67
Denny McCarthy	69	65	71	73	278	37,511.66
Ollie Schniederjans	67	69	69	73	278	37,511.66
Brian Harman	69	72	69	69	279	29,110
Billy Horschel	71	68	73	67	279	29,110
Beau Hossler	70	71	66	72	279	29,110
Zach Johnson	71	67	69	72	279	29,110
Nick Watney	67	69	69	74	279	29,110
John Catlin	70	71	68	71	280	21,465.67
Adam Hadwin	72	67	69	72	280	21,465.67
Danny Lee	72	68	67	73	280	21,465.67
Jimmy Walker	72	69	66	73	280	21,465.67
Tom Hoge	67	68	69	76	280	21,465.66
Alex Noren	69	72	69	70	280	21,465.66
Stewart Cink	69	70	70	72	281	17,288.50
Chris Kirk	71	70	69	71	281	17,288.50
J.J. Spaun	69	69	72	71	281	17,288.50
Kevin Streelman	71	67	70	73	281	17,288.50
Matthew Wolff[A]	67	70	72	72	281	
Brian Gay	67	73	72	70	282	16,259
Adam Schenk	70	71	71	70	282	16,259
Brandt Snedeker	69	70	72	71	282	16,259

	SCORES				TOTAL	MONEY
Brian Stuard	71	69	71	71	282	16,259
Grayson Murray	68	72	70	73	283	15,904
Andrew Landry	67	68	74	75	284	15,336
Kevin Na	68	72	74	70	284	15,336
Carlos Ortiz	70	68	70	76	284	15,336
Ryan Palmer	68	71	71	74	284	15,336
C.T. Pan	73	68	72	71	284	15,336
Sam Ryder	72	67	71	74	284	15,336
Richy Werenski	69	69	73	73	284	15,336
Keegan Bradley	68	69	75	73	285	14,626
Cameron Champ	70	69	71	75	285	14,626
James Hahn	68	72	70	75	285	14,626
John Huh	67	73	69	77	286	14,271
Freddie Jacobson	68	72	72	74	286	14,271
Satoshi Kodaira	71	70	72	75	288	14,058
Keith Mitchell	74	67	74	74	289	13,916

AT&T Pebble Beach Pro-Am

Pebble Beach GL: Par 36-36–72; 6,816 yards
Spyglass Hill GC: Par 36-36–72; 6,960 yards
Monterey Peninsula CC: Par 34-37–71; 6,958 yards
Pebble Beach, California
(Tournament completed on Monday—darkness.)

February 7-11
purse, $7,600,000

	SCORES				TOTAL	MONEY
Phil Mickelson	65	68	70	65	268	$1,368,000
Paul Casey	69	64	67	71	271	820,800
Scott Stallings	67	70	69	66	272	516,800
Jason Day	65	69	72	68	274	334,400
Si Woo Kim	66	71	69	68	274	334,400
Scott Langley	64	69	73	69	275	273,600
Kevin Streelman	70	70	71	65	276	236,867
Brian Gay	64	72	69	71	276	236,867
Lucas Glover	68	66	70	72	276	236,867
Max Homa	73	69	68	67	277	182,400
Michael Thompson	70	72	69	66	277	182,400
Chris Stroud	69	71	67	70	277	182,400
Scott Piercy	70	65	69	73	277	182,400
Jim Furyk	72	68	68	70	278	133,000
Sung Kang	69	69	69	71	278	133,000
Russell Knox	68	70	68	72	278	133,000
Matt Every	65	71	69	73	278	133,000
Roberto Diaz	69	69	71	70	279	102,600
Graeme McDowell	68	70	70	71	279	102,600
Adam Hadwin	72	70	65	72	279	102,600
D.J. Trahan	68	72	72	67	279	102,600
Matt Kuchar	67	73	70	70	280	70,553
Tyler Duncan	71	68	70	71	280	70,553
Patrick Reed	68	70	73	69	280	70,553
Trey Mullinax	71	68	73	68	280	70,553
Rafael Cabrera Bello	69	68	69	74	280	70,553
Jonathan Byrd	69	69	68	74	280	70,553
Nick Taylor	69	70	71	71	281	46,360
Ernie Els	69	68	73	71	281	46,360
Kevin Kisner	65	71	74	71	281	46,360
Brandon Harkins	69	73	67	72	281	46,360
Curtis Luck	70	67	73	71	281	46,360
Martin Trainer	69	73	66	73	281	46,360
Brady Schnell	67	72	72	70	281	46,360

	SCORES				TOTAL	MONEY
Branden Grace	67	69	71	74	281	46,360
Cameron Champ	73	69	70	69	281	46,360
Tom Lovelady	72	70	70	69	281	46,360
Hank Lebioda	71	69	71	71	282	31,160
Andrew Putnam	75	70	66	71	282	31,160
Chez Reavie	68	70	71	73	282	31,160
Sam Saunders	69	70	72	71	282	31,160
Julian Etulain	71	72	69	70	282	31,160
Tony Finau	69	73	70	70	282	31,160
Jonas Blixt	67	69	76	70	282	31,160
Benjamin Silverman	70	71	69	73	283	20,919
Adam Schenk	70	72	67	74	283	20,919
Jordan Spieth	66	68	74	75	283	20,919
Josh Teater	70	70	71	72	283	20,919
Nate Lashley	67	71	73	72	283	20,919
Dustin Johnson	66	73	73	71	283	20,919
Tommy Fleetwood	73	68	71	71	283	20,919
Brian Stuard	69	70	73	71	283	20,919
Roberto Castro	68	70	72	74	284	17,594
Alex Prugh	69	72	68	75	284	17,594
Cameron Tringale	71	68	72	73	284	17,594
Matt Jones	71	71	70	72	284	17,594
Johnson Wagner	67	73	71	74	285	17,176
John Rollins	73	69	70	74	286	17,024
Cody Gribble	66	73	73	78	290	16,796
Cameron Davis	72	68	72	78	290	16,796
Charley Hoffman	69	72	72		213	15,732
Martin Laird	68	74	71		213	15,732
Sang-Moon Bae	69	71	73		213	15,732
John Senden	72	72	69		213	15,732
Austin Cook	66	74	73		213	15,732
Adam Scott	70	72	71		213	15,732
Fabian Gomez	67	71	75		213	15,732
Steve Stricker	68	75	70		213	15,732
Dominic Bozzelli	72	73	68		213	15,732
Wyndham Clark	73	69	71		213	15,732

Genesis Open

Riviera Country Club, Pacific Palisades, California
Par 35-36–71; 7,322 yards

February 14-17
purse, $7,400,000

	SCORES				TOTAL	MONEY
J.B. Holmes	63	69	68	70	270	$1,332,000
Justin Thomas	66	65	65	75	271	799,200
Si Woo Kim	68	70	68	66	272	503,200
Marc Leishman	69	69	67	68	273	325,600
Rory McIlroy	72	63	69	69	273	325,600
Charles Howell	69	69	68	69	275	266,400
Adam Scott	66	65	69	76	276	238,650
Michael Thompson	69	64	73	70	276	238,650
Dustin Johnson	73	66	69	69	277	177,600
Kelly Kraft	69	68	69	71	277	177,600
Hideki Matsuyama	71	69	70	67	277	177,600
Carlos Ortiz	67	72	69	69	277	177,600
Jon Rahm	67	70	69	71	277	177,600
Vaughn Taylor	67	69	74	67	277	177,600
Jonas Blixt	71	68	66	73	278	100,788
Patrick Cantlay	68	71	70	69	278	100,788
Bryson DeChambeau	70	68	69	71	278	100,788

		SCORES			TOTAL	MONEY
Tony Finau	66	68	72	72	278	100,788
Beau Hossler	68	69	70	71	278	100,788
Luke List	71	66	73	68	278	100,788
Patrick Rodgers	66	67	73	72	278	100,788
Xander Schauffele	74	68	67	69	278	100,788
Bubba Watson	70	66	69	73	278	100,788
Tiger Woods	70	71	65	72	278	100,788
Rafa Cabrera Bello	68	71	69	71	279	60,433.34
Paul Casey	70	66	71	72	279	60,433.33
Kyoung-Hoon Lee	72	69	68	70	279	60,433.33
Tommy Fleetwood	70	69	70	71	280	50,320
Dylan Frittelli	68	72	72	68	280	50,320
Matt Kuchar	68	72	69	71	280	50,320
Ryan Moore	68	72	73	67	280	50,320
J.T. Poston	67	70	70	73	280	50,320
Kyle Jones	68	67	70	76	281	40,885
Kevin Na	70	70	69	72	281	40,885
Nick Taylor	70	71	68	72	281	40,885
Danny Willett	71	71	69	70	281	40,885
Scott Brown	70	71	69	72	282	31,820
Jim Furyk	67	73	70	72	282	31,820
Sergio Garcia	75	67	69	71	282	31,820
Max Homa	69	70	74	69	282	31,820
Jason Kokrak	69	73	68	72	282	31,820
Scott Langley	69	70	70	73	282	31,820
Phil Mickelson	72	69	71	70	282	31,820
Abraham Ancer	69	71	70	73	283	22,999.20
Russell Henley	69	73	66	75	283	22,999.20
Peter Malnati	72	69	70	72	283	22,999.20
Joaquin Niemann	71	66	72	74	283	22,999.20
C.T. Pan	69	73	69	72	283	22,999.20
Aaron Baddeley	69	71	71	73	284	18,944
Cameron Smith	72	69	69	74	284	18,944
Keegan Bradley	66	74	75	70	285	17,523.20
Alex Cejka	70	70	73	72	285	17,523.20
Bill Haas	67	72	71	75	285	17,523.20
Brian Harman	69	71	75	70	285	17,523.20
Jordan Spieth	64	70	70	81	285	17,523.20
Ernie Els	71	71	71	73	286	16,650
Freddie Jacobson	70	71	68	77	286	16,650
Pat Perez	69	73	68	76	286	16,650
Sam Ryder	69	71	75	71	286	16,650
Brian Gay	71	69	71	76	287	16,058
Martin Kaymer	71	69	75	72	287	16,058
Brian Stuard	69	70	73	75	287	16,058
Peter Uihlein	69	73	68	77	287	16,058
Robert Garrigus	69	71	73	76	289	15,318
Kramer Hickok	66	74	71	78	289	15,318
Sung Kang	69	72	78	70	289	15,318
Ted Potter, Jr.	70	69	77	73	289	15,318
Seamus Power	70	72	75	72	289	15,318
Shawn Stefani	72	70	73	74	289	15,318
Stephan Jaeger	71	71	72	76	290	14,652
Tae Hee Lee	68	74	75	73	290	14,652
Davis Love	69	71	74	76	290	14,652
Richard Lee	70	71	74	76	291	14,356
Jimmy Walker	67	75	75	75	292	14,208
Adam Hadwin	68	72	77	77	294	14,060
Cody Gribble	71	70	79	76	296	13,912

WGC - Mexico Championship

Club de Golf Chapultepec, Mexico City, Mexico
Par 35-36–71; 7,345 yards

February 21-24
purse, $10,250,000

		SCORES			TOTAL	MONEY
Dustin Johnson	64	67	66	66	263	$1,745,000
Rory McIlroy	63	70	68	67	268	1,095,000
Kiradech Aphibarnrat	68	69	68	68	273	472,000
Paul Casey	71	72	65	65	273	472,000
Ian Poulter	68	68	69	68	273	472,000
Patrick Cantlay	72	67	65	70	274	261,666.67
Sergio Garcia	69	66	69	70	274	261,666.67
Cameron Smith	69	67	68	70	274	261,666.66
Justin Thomas	66	73	74	62	275	201,000
Keegan Bradley	69	73	69	65	276	161,500
David Lipsky	68	71	68	69	276	161,500
Joost Luiten	71	67	74	64	276	161,500
Tiger Woods	71	66	70	69	276	161,500
Charles Howell	69	68	73	67	277	128,000
Patrick Reed	72	68	64	73	277	128,000
Xander Schauffele	69	73	66	69	277	128,000
Francesco Molinari	71	67	70	70	278	115,500
Gary Woodland	71	71	67	69	278	115,500
Rafa Cabrera Bello	76	69	66	68	279	103,750
Tommy Fleetwood	70	65	72	72	279	103,750
Tyrrell Hatton	67	70	72	70	279	103,750
Haotong Li	69	72	71	67	279	103,750
Hideki Matsuyama	72	70	67	70	279	103,750
Aaron Wise	73	68	71	67	279	103,750
Tony Finau	73	69	69	69	280	93,250
Louis Oosthuizen	72	66	69	73	280	93,250
Matthew Fitzpatrick	72	71	68	70	281	85,000
Kevin Kisner	73	67	70	71	281	85,000
Patton Kizzire	69	73	70	69	281	85,000
Brooks Koepka	73	70	69	69	281	85,000
Bubba Watson	70	75	66	70	281	85,000
Danny Willett	71	69	70	71	281	85,000
Branden Grace	71	71	69	71	282	78,000
Matt Wallace	74	71	70	67	282	78,000
Lee Westwood	73	71	65	73	282	78,000
Rickie Fowler	71	73	68	71	283	75,000
Kevin Na	72	75	66	70	283	75,000
Erik van Rooyen	72	68	74	69	283	75,000
Abraham Ancer	71	72	71	70	284	70,500
Alexander Bjork	75	70	72	67	284	70,500
Shugo Imahira	73	67	73	71	284	70,500
Russell Knox	72	72	70	70	284	70,500
Phil Mickelson	79	65	72	68	284	70,500
Webb Simpson	73	72	68	71	284	70,500
Byeong Hun An	77	74	64	70	285	65,000
Billy Horschel	68	76	70	71	285	65,000
Jake McLeod	70	69	76	70	285	65,000
Thorbjorn Olesen	72	74	68	71	285	65,000
Jon Rahm	72	72	72	69	285	65,000
Matt Kuchar	66	67	79	74	286	62,000
Satoshi Kodaira	75	72	76	64	287	60,000
Aaron Rai	70	74	71	72	287	60,000
Richard Sterne	69	68	74	76	287	60,000
Jordan Spieth	75	69	75	69	288	57,500
Henrik Stenson	72	73	71	72	288	57,500
George Coetzee	67	74	74	75	290	55,500
Bryson DeChambeau	75	73	73	69	290	55,500

	SCORES				TOTAL	MONEY
Emiliano Grillo	76	73	69	73	291	53,500
Kyle Stanley	73	72	72	74	291	53,500
Adrian Otaegui	77	74	71	70	292	51,750
Shubhankar Sharma	70	77	70	75	292	51,750
Marc Leishman	77	75	69	72	293	50,500
Shane Lowry	70	76	72	75	293	50,500
Alex Noren	71	74	74	74	293	50,500
Tom Lewis	74	73	77	70	294	49,625
Chez Reavie	75	76	72	71	294	49,625
Ryan Fox	72	72	75	76	295	49,125
Eddie Pepperell	77	70	73	75	295	49,125
Lucas Bjerregaard	76	76	72	73	297	48,750
Matthew Millar	74	82	74	71	301	48,500
Shaun Norris	79	80	73	72	304	48,250

Puerto Rico Open

Coco Beach Golf & Country Club, Rio Grande, Puerto Rico
Par 36-36–72; 7,506 yards

February 21-24
purse, $3,000,000

	SCORES			TOTAL	MONEY
Martin Trainer	70	67	69	67	273	$540,000
Aaron Baddeley	70	68	66	72	276	198,000
Daniel Berger	70	71	69	66	276	198,000
Roger Sloan	70	67	72	67	276	198,000
Johnson Wagner	69	69	69	69	276	198,000
Charl Schwartzel	71	68	72	66	277	104,250
Shawn Stefani	70	71	71	65	277	104,250
Ben Crane	68	69	71	70	278	90,000
Nate Lashley	68	68	69	73	278	90,000
Scott Brown	71	71	69	68	279	66,500
Wyndham Clark	70	68	69	72	279	66,500
Roberto Diaz	68	68	72	71	279	66,500
Joey Garber	68	74	65	72	279	66,500
J.J. Henry	74	69	67	69	279	66,500
Austen Truslow	70	71	72	66	279	66,500
Cameron Davis	73	71	67	69	280	45,000
Matt Every	72	70	68	70	280	45,000
Adam Schenk	75	69	69	67	280	45,000
Sepp Straka	67	73	71	69	280	45,000
D.J. Trahan	69	67	71	73	280	45,000
Jonathan Byrd	71	67	70	73	281	32,400
John Chin	74	70	70	67	281	32,400
Derek Fathauer	72	71	71	67	281	32,400
Martin Flores	69	73	69	70	281	32,400
Dominic Bozzelli	71	71	70	70	282	21,015
Roberto Castro	68	72	68	74	282	21,015
Fabian Gomez	72	72	70	68	282	21,015
David Hearn	68	73	70	71	282	21,015
Curtis Luck	70	68	73	71	282	21,015
Sebastian Munoz	74	71	67	70	282	21,015
Martin Piller	68	73	66	75	282	21,015
Andres Romero	66	73	69	74	282	21,015
Brendon Todd	70	73	70	69	282	21,015
Cameron Tringale	71	73	69	69	282	21,015
Julian Etulain	72	70	70	71	283	14,164.29
Kramer Hickok	69	71	70	73	283	14,164.29
Alex Kang	68	75	70	70	283	14,164.29
Parker McLachlin	72	70	69	72	283	14,164.29
Kyoung-Hoon Lee	70	71	69	73	283	14,164.28

	SCORES				TOTAL	MONEY
Jose de Jesus Rodriguez	71	69	70	73	283	14,164.28
Boo Weekley	72	73	65	73	283	14,164.28
Chad Campbell	70	74	72	68	284	10,500
Brian Davis	69	74	68	73	284	10,500
Tim Herron	71	71	72	70	284	10,500
Graeme McDowell	70	72	73	69	284	10,500
D.A. Points	71	72	72	69	284	10,500
Tom Lovelady	70	73	72	70	285	8,700
Bryson Nimmer [A]	69	75	72	69	285	
Robert Allenby	72	73	73	68	286	7,540
Stuart Appleby	71	74	69	72	286	7,540
Rafael Campos	73	68	74	71	286	7,540
Ben Griffin	74	71	69	72	286	7,540
David Lingmerth	69	75	71	71	286	7,540
Ollie Schniederjans	68	77	73	68	286	7,540
Ryan Blaum	70	70	72	75	287	6,870
Tom Hoge	70	72	75	70	287	6,870
Matt Jones	72	72	74	69	287	6,870
Jim Knous	71	70	74	72	287	6,870
Zac Blair	71	73	70	74	288	6,660
Trevor Immelman	72	71	72	73	288	6,660
Robert Streb	75	69	69	75	288	6,660
Ken Duke	71	72	70	76	289	6,450
Tyler Duncan	71	73	74	71	289	6,450
Billy Hurley	74	69	73	73	289	6,450
John Senden	74	69	74	72	289	6,450
Chris Couch	70	75	73	73	291	6,240
Derek Ernst	72	70	76	73	291	6,240
Peter Uihlein	71	73	74	73	291	6,240
Chris Thompson	74	71	73	74	292	6,120
Arjun Atwal	72	73	74	75	294	6,060
Chad Collins	71	74	76	74	295	5,910
Jonathan Kaye	73	72	73	77	295	5,910
Whee Kim	71	74	75	75	295	5,910
Charlie Wi	74	71	73	77	295	5,910
Wes Roach	74	71	76	75	296	5,760

Honda Classic

PGA National, Champion Course, Palm Beach Gardens, Florida
Par 35-35–70; 7,125 yards

February 28-March 3
purse, $6,800,000

	SCORES				TOTAL	MONEY
Keith Mitchell	68	66	70	67	271	$1,224,000
Rickie Fowler	67	72	66	67	272	598,400
Brooks Koepka	67	69	70	66	272	598,400
Lucas Glover	66	69	72	66	273	299,200
Ryan Palmer	70	71	69	63	273	299,200
Vijay Singh	70	69	65	70	274	244,800
Wyndham Clark	69	67	67	72	275	219,300
Kyoung-Hoon Lee	67	69	68	71	275	219,300
Jim Furyk	69	72	68	67	276	183,600
Sergio Garcia	67	70	70	69	276	183,600
Jason Kokrak	69	71	68	68	276	183,600
Ryan Armour	68	68	70	71	277	137,700
Lucas Bjerregaard	70	68	72	67	277	137,700
Bud Cauley	67	71	71	68	277	137,700
Harris English	70	71	68	68	277	137,700
Billy Horschel	67	71	73	67	278	105,400
Charl Schwartzel	67	70	72	69	278	105,400

356 / AMERICAN TOURS

		SCORES			TOTAL	MONEY
Michael Thompson	71	69	66	72	278	105,400
Jhonattan Vegas	64	73	69	72	278	105,400
Scott Brown	70	70	70	69	279	64,736
Roberto Castro	67	70	69	73	279	64,736
Ernie Els	66	73	71	69	279	64,736
Brian Gay	71	70	70	68	279	64,736
Talor Gooch	71	68	72	68	279	64,736
Chesson Hadley	68	70	73	68	279	64,736
Russell Henley	69	72	70	68	279	64,736
Max Homa	69	71	70	69	279	64,736
Brian Stuard	69	70	72	68	279	64,736
Matt Wallace	71	68	72	68	279	64,736
Kramer Hickok	69	72	66	73	280	41,310
Patrick Rodgers	68	71	72	69	280	41,310
Adam Schenk	67	71	68	74	280	41,310
Roger Sloan	71	71	66	72	280	41,310
Nick Taylor	72	66	70	72	280	41,310
Justin Thomas	68	74	67	71	280	41,310
Byeong Hun An	74	68	70	69	281	25,345.87
Daniel Berger	72	67	70	72	281	25,345.87
Jonas Blixt	70	72	70	69	281	25,345.87
Julian Etulain	67	70	74	70	281	25,345.87
Danny Lee	69	67	75	70	281	25,345.87
Sebastian Munoz	69	70	71	71	281	25,345.87
J.T. Poston	73	68	69	71	281	25,345.87
Sam Saunders	68	72	70	71	281	25,345.87
Ben Silverman	66	71	75	69	281	25,345.87
Webb Simpson	72	69	71	69	281	25,345.87
Matt Jones	69	69	69	74	281	25,345.86
Peter Malnati	69	68	71	73	281	25,345.86
Rory Sabbatini	67	74	67	73	281	25,345.86
Cameron Tringale	69	68	70	74	281	25,345.86
Gary Woodland	72	70	66	73	281	25,345.86
Bill Haas	69	70	69	74	282	15,827
Sungjae Im	70	64	77	71	282	15,827
Sung Kang	68	68	71	75	282	15,827
Russell Knox	69	72	71	70	282	15,827
Trey Mullinax	70	72	68	72	282	15,827
Harold Varner	72	69	67	74	282	15,827
Nick Watney	71	67	71	73	282	15,827
Chase Wright	72	68	72	70	282	15,827
Bronson Burgoon	67	71	73	72	283	14,620
Cameron Davis	70	72	68	73	283	14,620
John Huh	70	72	67	74	283	14,620
Zach Johnson	66	72	71	74	283	14,620
Anirban Lahiri	67	70	71	75	283	14,620
Joaquin Niemann	71	70	71	71	283	14,620
Adam Svensson	72	64	72	75	283	14,620
Vaughn Taylor	70	68	69	76	283	14,620
Martin Kaymer	71	70	68	75	284	14,008
Freddie Jacobson	69	67	74	75	285	13,804
Grayson Murray	71	68	71	75	285	13,804
Hank Lebioda	67	74	70	76	287	13,600
Tyler Duncan	69	71	73		213	13,396
Kevin Streelman	72	70	71		213	13,396
Sam Burns	70	71	73		214	13,124
Hudson Swafford	70	72	72		214	13,124
Stewart Cink	71	71	73		215	12,784
Austin Cook	74	67	74		215	12,784
Jason Dufner	73	69	73		215	12,784
Ryan Blaum	69	73	74		216	12,308
Stephan Jaeger	68	72	76		216	12,308
Jim Knous	71	71	74		216	12,308

	SCORES	TOTAL	MONEY
Richy Werenski	71 71 74	216	12,308
Graeme McDowell	72 70 76	218	11,968
Drew Nesbitt	71 71 77	219	11,832

Arnold Palmer Invitational

Bay Hill Club & Lodge, Orlando, Florida
Par 36-36–72; 7,454 yards

March 7-10
purse, $9,100,000

	SCORES	TOTAL	MONEY
Francesco Molinari	69 70 73 64	276	$1,638,000
Matthew Fitzpatrick	70 70 67 71	278	982,800
Rafa Cabrera Bello	65 75 70 69	279	473,200
Tommy Fleetwood	69 66 76 68	279	473,200
Sungjae Im	71 69 71 68	279	473,200
Sung Kang	69 72 71 68	280	294,612.50
Rory McIlroy	72 70 66 72	280	294,612.50
Keith Mitchell	71 68 75 66	280	294,612.50
Matt Wallace	71 69 69 71	280	294,612.50
Byeong Hun An	72 72 69 68	281	209,300
Lucas Glover	70 71 71 69	281	209,300
Jason Kokrak	70 73 68 70	281	209,300
Luke List	70 72 68 71	281	209,300
Adam Long	74 71 69 67	281	209,300
Charles Howell	74 67 69 72	282	159,250
Chris Kirk	71 73 66 72	282	159,250
Ryan Blaum	73 72 70 68	283	123,153.34
Brendan Steele	70 71 72 70	283	123,153.34
Aaron Baddeley	70 70 69 74	283	123,153.33
Chesson Hadley	71 71 71 70	283	123,153.33
Henrik Stenson	77 66 69 71	283	123,153.33
Bubba Watson	68 72 71 72	283	123,153.33
Kiradech Aphibarnrat	71 70 72 71	284	78,715
Kevin Kisner	70 69 70 75	284	78,715
Marc Leishman	72 70 72 70	284	78,715
Ian Poulter	73 68 73 70	284	78,715
Roger Sloan	70 69 74 71	284	78,715
Jhonattan Vegas	69 70 75 70	284	78,715
Tyrrell Hatton	70 75 66 74	285	60,515
Carlos Ortiz	72 71 70 72	285	60,515
Adam Schenk	70 73 71 71	285	60,515
Hudson Swafford	70 74 73 68	285	60,515
Adam Hadwin	70 75 68 73	286	47,060
Sam Horsfield	74 69 74 69	286	47,060
Martin Kaymer	72 69 70 75	286	47,060
Hideki Matsuyama	72 70 71 73	286	47,060
Ryan Moore	71 72 73 70	286	47,060
Sam Ryder	74 69 74 69	286	47,060
Johnson Wagner	71 72 72 71	286	47,060
Rickie Fowler	74 71 71 71	287	35,490
Zach Johnson	70 71 76 70	287	35,490
Hunter Mahan	76 69 74 68	287	35,490
Scott Stallings	69 74 73 71	287	35,490
Aaron Wise	72 70 74 71	287	35,490
Viktor Hovland (A)	74 70 73 70	287	
Keegan Bradley	67 68 75 78	288	27,391
Bryson DeChambeau	75 70 74 69	288	27,391
Joaquin Niemann	71 71 76 70	288	27,391
Patrick Rodgers	68 73 73 74	288	27,391
Billy Horschel	68 71 73 77	289	22,704.50

358 / AMERICAN TOURS

	SCORES				TOTAL	MONEY
Pat Perez	69	73	72	75	289	22,704.50
Patrick Reed	70	70	76	73	289	22,704.50
Brandt Snedeker	73	71	74	71	289	22,704.50
Sam Burns	76	69	73	72	290	21,172.67
Scott Piercy	74	70	70	76	290	21,172.67
Graeme McDowell	68	75	69	78	290	21,172.66
Eddie Pepperell	72	68	79	72	291	20,748
Beau Hossler	76	66	73	77	292	20,202
D.A. Points	72	71	74	75	292	20,202
Kevin Streelman	70	72	71	79	292	20,202
Steve Stricker	75	69	76	72	292	20,202
Jimmy Walker	70	71	81	70	292	20,202
Justin Rose	71	70	77	75	293	19,474
Sam Saunders	73	68	74	78	293	19,474
J.J. Spaun	71	70	75	77	293	19,474
J.T. Poston	71	72	73	78	294	19,019
Martin Trainer	70	71	79	74	294	19,019
Harris English	76	69	72	78	295	18,746
Tim Herron	72	70	76	78	296	18,473
Anirban Lahiri	74	69	80	73	296	18,473

The Players Championship

TPC Sawgrass, Ponte Vedra Beach, Florida
Par 36-36–72; 7,189 yards

March 14-17
purse, $12,500,000

	SCORES				TOTAL	MONEY
Rory McIlroy	67	65	70	70	272	$2,250,000
Jim Furyk	71	64	71	67	273	1,350,000
Eddie Pepperell	72	68	68	66	274	725,000
Jhonattan Vegas	72	69	67	66	274	725,000
Tommy Fleetwood	65	67	70	73	275	456,250
Dustin Johnson	69	68	69	69	275	456,250
Brandt Snedeker	69	72	65	69	275	456,250
Jason Day	70	66	68	72	276	350,000
Brian Harman	66	69	71	70	276	350,000
Hideki Matsuyama	71	72	66	67	276	350,000
Justin Rose	74	66	68	68	276	350,000
Abraham Ancer	69	66	70	72	277	253,125
Joel Dahmen	69	71	67	70	277	253,125
Jon Rahm	69	68	64	76	277	253,125
Adam Scott	70	69	68	70	277	253,125
Keegan Bradley	65	73	68	72	278	193,750
Ollie Schniederjans	71	70	65	72	278	193,750
Webb Simpson	70	70	70	68	278	193,750
Nick Taylor	73	69	69	67	278	193,750
Bryson DeChambeau	70	69	69	71	279	156,250
Ryan Moore	67	74	69	69	279	156,250
Tony Finau	69	71	68	72	280	125,000
Sergio Garcia	69	70	74	67	280	125,000
Kevin Kisner	68	68	71	73	280	125,000
J.T. Poston	68	69	73	70	280	125,000
Byeong Hun An	66	71	73	71	281	94,375
Emiliano Grillo	70	72	73	66	281	94,375
Billy Horschel	69	70	73	69	281	94,375
Matt Kuchar	69	70	72	70	281	94,375
Lucas Bjerregaard	70	70	70	72	282	77,625
Tom Hoge	69	71	70	72	282	77,625
Matt Wallace	69	73	70	70	282	77,625
Gary Woodland	72	69	73	68	282	77,625

	SCORES				TOTAL	MONEY
Tiger Woods	70	71	72	69	282	77,625
Brice Garnett	71	69	73	70	283	60,312.50
Charles Howell	69	70	75	69	283	60,312.50
Russell Knox	70	68	73	72	283	60,312.50
Seamus Power	74	67	73	69	283	60,312.50
Rory Sabbatini	68	69	74	72	283	60,312.50
Justin Thomas	71	72	70	70	283	60,312.50
Corey Conners	72	70	68	74	284	45,000
Matthew Fitzpatrick	70	71	72	71	284	45,000
Denny McCarthy	69	72	72	71	284	45,000
Thorbjorn Olesen	70	69	76	69	284	45,000
Vaughn Taylor	67	70	71	76	284	45,000
Martin Trainer	73	69	72	70	284	45,000
Bud Cauley	69	70	76	70	285	31,388.89
Rickie Fowler	74	67	68	76	285	31,388.89
Sung Kang	73	66	74	72	285	31,388.89
Jason Kokrak	73	68	74	70	285	31,388.89
Kelly Kraft	73	70	71	71	285	31,388.89
Andrew Landry	73	68	73	71	285	31,388.89
Keith Mitchell	71	65	75	74	285	31,388.89
Richy Werenski	72	71	68	74	285	31,388.89
Patrick Reed	69	69	69	78	285	31,388.88
Brian Gay	76	67	68	75	286	27,250
Si Woo Kim	73	68	72	73	286	27,250
Chris Kirk	74	69	72	71	286	27,250
Brooks Koepka	72	71	73	70	286	27,250
Luke List	69	68	75	74	286	27,250
Francesco Molinari	72	70	72	72	286	27,250
Louis Oosthuizen	73	70	73	70	286	27,250
Scott Piercy	74	68	72	72	286	27,250
Ian Poulter	69	66	75	76	286	27,250
Cameron Smith	72	70	73	71	286	27,250
Bubba Watson	72	71	70	73	286	27,250
Daniel Berger	75	68	70	74	287	25,500
Scott Langley	69	72	75	71	287	25,500
Jimmy Walker	75	68	73	71	287	25,500
Michael Thompson	69	71	72	76	288	25,000
Martin Kaymer	71	69	73	78	291	24,750
Branden Grace	73	70	72	77	292	24,375
C.T. Pan	72	70	74	76	292	24,375
Jason Dufner	70	73	74		217	23,750
Tyler Duncan	70	71	76		217	23,750
Anirban Lahiri	70	71	76		217	23,750
Patrick Rodgers	72	70	76		218	23,250
Kevin Na	71	70	78		219	23,000
Patton Kizzire	71	70	79		220	22,625
Adam Long	71	72	77		220	22,625

Valspar Championship

Innisbrook Resort, Copperhead Course, Palm Harbor, Florida
Par 36-35–71; 7,340 yards

March 21-24
purse, $6,700,000

	SCORES				TOTAL	MONEY
Paul Casey	70	66	68	72	276	$1,206,000
Jason Kokrak	69	71	66	71	277	589,600
Louis Oosthuizen	70	72	66	69	277	589,600
Sungjae Im	70	67	71	70	278	294,800
Bubba Watson	69	71	70	68	278	294,800
Ryan Armour	70	72	68	69	279	224,450

	SCORES				TOTAL	MONEY
Dustin Johnson	69	69	67	74	279	224,450
Jon Rahm	71	68	72	68	279	224,450
Austin Cook	69	67	72	72	280	174,200
Luke Donald	67	70	70	73	280	174,200
Denny McCarthy	68	74	69	69	280	174,200
Scott Stallings	69	68	70	73	280	174,200
Lucas Glover	72	67	72	70	281	121,940
Bill Haas	72	70	69	70	281	121,940
Mackenzie Hughes	70	72	68	71	281	121,940
Matt Jones	73	68	68	72	281	121,940
Curtis Luck	70	68	70	73	281	121,940
Jim Furyk	69	71	68	74	282	84,420
Charley Hoffman	69	74	69	70	282	84,420
Sung Kang	71	71	72	68	282	84,420
Rory Sabbatini	70	69	73	70	282	84,420
Brian Stuard	68	72	69	73	282	84,420
Vaughn Taylor	74	69	71	68	282	84,420
Julian Etulain	69	73	71	70	283	54,270
Zach Johnson	71	72	70	70	283	54,270
Kevin Kisner	67	75	72	69	283	54,270
Russell Knox	67	76	67	73	283	54,270
Henrik Stenson	70	73	69	71	283	54,270
Nick Taylor	71	70	67	75	283	54,270
Joel Dahmen	66	72	76	70	284	39,817.15
Anirban Lahiri	70	71	75	68	284	39,817.15
Sam Burns	69	74	67	74	284	39,817.14
Rafa Cabrera Bello	71	71	71	71	284	39,817.14
Billy Hurley	74	69	71	70	284	39,817.14
Brandt Snedeker	70	70	73	71	284	39,817.14
Shawn Stefani	68	71	73	72	284	39,817.14
Wyndham Clark	71	70	72	72	285	30,150
Dylan Frittelli	72	71	67	75	285	30,150
Satoshi Kodaira	70	71	72	72	285	30,150
Joaquin Niemann	69	73	70	73	285	30,150
Nick Watney	71	72	69	73	285	30,150
Jonas Blixt	74	69	72	71	286	24,120
Russell Henley	69	72	71	74	286	24,120
C.T. Pan	71	70	71	74	286	24,120
Danny Willett	69	71	74	72	286	24,120
Brian Gay	73	69	69	76	287	17,654.50
Kramer Hickok	71	68	73	75	287	17,654.50
Kelly Kraft	69	72	75	71	287	17,654.50
Andrew Landry	72	71	76	68	287	17,654.50
Hank Lebioda	69	73	74	71	287	17,654.50
Graeme McDowell	71	72	70	74	287	17,654.50
Sam Saunders	71	69	73	74	287	17,654.50
Sepp Straka	66	76	69	76	287	17,654.50
Ryan Blaum	73	67	76	72	288	15,209
Roberto Diaz	69	72	74	73	288	15,209
Harris English	75	68	67	78	288	15,209
Sergio Garcia	71	72	72	73	288	15,209
Danny Lee	72	71	73	72	288	15,209
Trey Mullinax	71	72	77	68	288	15,209
Alex Cejka	71	70	77	71	289	14,472
Brandon Harkins	73	69	74	73	289	14,472
Patton Kizzire	70	71	76	72	289	14,472
Peter Malnati	69	74	72	74	289	14,472
Roger Sloan	70	72	70	77	289	14,472
Chesson Hadley	74	69	70	77	290	13,936
Peter Uihlein	72	71	73	74	290	13,936
Harold Varner	69	74	75	72	290	13,936
Roberto Castro	68	71	73	81	293	13,601
Chris Stroud	72	71	74	76	293	13,601
Morgan Hoffmann	73	70	77	75	295	13,400

WGC - Dell Technologies Match Play

Austin Country Club, Austin, Texas
Par 35-36–71; 7,108 yards

March 27-31
purse, $10,250,000

FIRST ROUND

Tommy Fleetwood defeated Byeong Hun An, 3 and 2.
Kyle Stanley defeated Louis Oosthuizen, 3 and 2.
Bryson DeChambeau defeated Russell Knox, 3 and 1.
Marc Leishman defeated Kiradech Aphibarnrat, 2 up.
Tony Finau defeated Keith Mitchell, 2 and 1.
Ian Poulter defeated Kevin Kisner, 2 up.
Brooks Koepka halved with Tom Lewis.
Haotong Li defeated Alex Noren, 5 and 4.
Paul Casey defeated Abraham Ancer, 5 and 3.
Charles Howell defeated Cameron Smith, 2 and 1.
Francesco Molinari defeated Satoshi Kodaira, 5 and 4.
Thorbjorn Olesen defeated Webb Simpson, 2 and 1.
Kevin Na defeated Bubba Watson, 1 up.
Jordan Spieth halved with Billy Horschel.
Justin Rose defeated Emiliano Grillo, 2 and 1.
Gary Woodland defeated Eddie Pepperell, 2 and 1.
Jim Furyk defeated Jason Day, 2 up.
Henrik Stenson defeated Phil Mickelson, 2 and 1.
Lucas Bjerregaard defeated Justin Thomas, 3 and 2.
Matt Wallace defeated Keegan Bradley, 1 up.
Tiger Woods defeated Aaron Wise, 3 and 1.
Patrick Cantlay halved with Brandt Snedeker.
Rory McIlroy defeated Luke List, 5 and 4.
Justin Harding defeated Matthew Fitzpatrick, 1 up.
Xander Schauffele defeated Lee Westwood, 1 up.
Tyrrell Hatton defeated Rafa Cabrera Bello, 4 and 3.
Jon Rahm defeated Si Woo Kim, 7 and 5.
Matt Kuchar defeated J.B. Holmes, 3 and 1.
Andrew Putnam defeated Patrick Reed, 3 and 2.
Sergio Garcia defeated Shane Lowry, 4 and 2.
Dustin Johnson defeated Chez Reavie, 4 and 3.
Branden Grace defeated Hideki Matsuyama, 4 and 3.

SECOND ROUND

Casey halved with Howell.
Ancer defeated Smith, 3 and 2.
Molinari defeated Olesen, 4 and 3.
Simpson halved with Kodaira.
Horschel defeated Watson, 2 and 1.
Spieth defeated Na, 3 and 2.
Rose halved with Pepperell.
Woodland defeated Grillo, 1 up.
Stenson defeated Day, 4 and 3.
Furyk defeated Mickelson, 1 up.
Thomas defeated Wallace, 3 and 1.
Bradley halved with Bjerregaard.
Snedeker defeated Woods, 2 and 1.
Patrick Cantlay defeated Wise, 4 and 2.
McIlroy defeated Harding, 3 and 2.
List defeated Fitzpatrick, 2 and 1.
Schauffele halved with Hatton.
Cabrera Bello halved with Westwood.
Holmes defeated Rahm, 2 and 1.
Kuchar defeated Kim, 6 and 4.
Reed halved with Lowry.
Garcia defeated Putnam, 5 and 4.
Grace defeated Johnson, 1 up.

Matsuyama halved with Reavie.
Fleetwood halved with Stanley.
Oosthuizen defeated An, 1 up.
Aphibarnrat defeated DeChambeau, 2 and 1.
Leishman defeated Knox, 2 up.
Kisner defeated Finau, 2 up.
Mitchell defeated Poulter, 1 up.
Li defeated Koepka, 1 up.
Noren defeated Lewis, 4 and 2.

THIRD ROUND

Mickelson (1-2-0) defeated Day (0-3-0), 2 up.
Stenson (3-0-0) defeated Furyk (2-1-0), 5 and 4.
Thomas (1-1-1) halved with Bradley (0-1-2).
Bjerregaard (2-0-1) defeated Wallace (1-2-0), 1 up.
Woods (2-1-0) defeated Cantlay (1-1-1), 4 and 2.
Aaron Wise (1-2-0) defeated Snedeker (1-1-1), 6 and 4.
McIlroy (3-0-0) defeated Fitzpatrick (0-3-0), 4 and 2.
Harding (2-1-0) defeated List (1-2-0), 2 up.
Cabrera Bello (1-1-1) defeated Schauffele (1-1-1), 1 up.
Hatton (2-0-1) defeated Westwood (0-2-1), 3 and 1.
Rahm (1-1-1) halved with Kuchar (2-0-1).
Holmes (2-1-0) defeated Kim (0-3-0), 6 and 4.
Reed (1-1-1) defeated Garcia (2-1-0), 2 and 1.
Lowry (1-1-1) defeated Putnam (1-2-0), 3 and 2.
Matsuyama (1-1-1) defeated Johnson (1-2-0), 3 and 2.
Grace (3-0-0) defeated Reavie (0-2-1), 2 and 1.
Oosthuizen (2-1-0) defeated Fleetwood (1-1-1), 4 and 3.
An (1-2-0) defeated Stanley (1-1-1), 6 and 5.
Leishman (3-0-0) defeated DeChambeau (1-2-0), 5 and 4.
Knox (1-2-0) defeated Aphibarnrat (1-2-0), 2 up.
Poulter (2-1-0) defeated Finau (1-2-0), 1 up.
Kisner (2-1-0) defeated Mitchell (1-2-0), 2 and 1. (Kisner advanced via playoff with Poulter.)
Noren (2-1-0) defeated Koepka (0-2-1), 3 and 2.
Lewis (1-1-1) defeated Li (2-1-0), 1 up. (Li advanced via playoff with Noren.)
Casey (2-0-1) defeated Smith (0-3-0), 4 and 3.
Ancer (2-1-0) defeated Howell (1-1-1), 5 and 3.
Molinari (3-0-0) defeated Simpson (0-2-1), 2 and 1.
Kodaira (1-1-1) defeated Olesen (1-2-0), 3 and 1.
Watson (1-2-0) defeated Spieth (1-1-1), 1 up.
Na (2-1-0) defeated Horschel (1-1-1), 3 and 1.
Rose (2-0-1) defeated Woodland (2-1-0), 1 up.
Grillo (1-2-0) defeated Pepperell (0-2-1), 4 and 3.

(Players with 2 points received $108,429; players with 1½ points received $81,313; players with 1 point received $62,500; players with ½ point received $53,000; players with 0 points received $50,750.)

ROUND OF 16

Bjerregaard defeated Stenson, 3 and 2.
Woods defeated McIlroy, 2 and 1.
Kuchar defeated Hatton, 4 and 3.
Garcia defeated Grace, 1 up.
Oosthuizen defeated Leishman, 2 and 1.
Kisner defeated Li, 6 and 5.
Molinari defeated Casey, 5 and 4.
Na defeated Rose, 2 up.

(Losing players received $167,000.)

QUARTER-FINALS

Bjerregaard defeated Woods, 1 up.
Kuchar defeated Garcia, 2 up.
Kisner defeated Oosthuizen, 2 and 1.
Molinari defeated Na, 6 and 5.

(Losing players received $315,000.)

SEMI-FINALS

Kuchar defeated Bjerregaard, 1 up.
Kisner defeated Molinari, 1 up.

PLAYOFF FOR THIRD-FOURTH PLACE

Molinari defeated Bjerregaard, 4 and 2.
(Molinari received $712,000; Bjerregaard received $574,000.)

FINAL

Kisner defeated Kuchar, 3 and 2.

(Kisner received $1,745,000; Kuchar received $1,095,000.)

Corales Puntacana Resort & Club Championship

Corales Golf Club, Punta Cana, Dominican Republic
Par 36-36–72; 7,670 yards

March 28-31
purse, $3,000,000

	SCORES				TOTAL	MONEY
Graeme McDowell	73	64	64	69	270	$540,000
Mackenzie Hughes	69	70	66	66	271	264,000
Chris Stroud	70	68	64	69	271	264,000
Jonathan Byrd	68	67	71	66	272	144,000
Kelly Kraft	70	67	68	68	273	114,000
Chip McDaniel	72	67	71	63	273	114,000
Aaron Baddeley	68	67	68	71	274	93,500
Sungjae Im	67	67	69	71	274	93,500
George McNeill	70	65	71	68	274	93,500
Kramer Hickok	71	68	69	67	275	78,000
D.J. Trahan	69	72	68	66	275	78,000
Sam Burns	68	74	68	66	276	57,000
Joel Dahmen	66	71	72	67	276	57,000
Paul Dunne	66	69	70	71	276	57,000
Grayson Murray	69	69	70	68	276	57,000
Brady Schnell	68	70	69	69	276	57,000
Ben Silverman	70	68	69	69	276	57,000
Dylan Frittelli	71	67	72	67	277	40,500
David Hearn	72	70	66	69	277	40,500
Matt Jones	66	71	73	67	277	40,500
Seth Reeves	69	71	68	69	277	40,500
Jonas Blixt	71	65	70	72	278	30,000
Jim Knous	70	68	70	70	278	30,000
David Lipsky	71	71	66	70	278	30,000
Peter Uihlein	73	68	67	70	278	30,000
Julian Etulain	72	69	66	72	279	21,300
Seungsu Han	71	68	69	71	279	21,300
Stephan Jaeger	69	69	72	69	279	21,300
Kyoung-Hoon Lee	71	68	67	73	279	21,300
Denny McCarthy	69	69	71	70	279	21,300
Sepp Straka	68	70	67	74	279	21,300
Jhonattan Vegas	69	69	69	72	279	21,300
Daniel Chopra	73	68	70	69	280	15,850

364 / AMERICAN TOURS

	SCORES				TOTAL	MONEY
Ben Crane	70	69	68	73	280	15,850
Thomas Detry	72	66	72	70	280	15,850
Freddie Jacobson	72	67	73	68	280	15,850
Alex Prugh	69	73	68	70	280	15,850
Adam Schenk	71	68	70	71	280	15,850
Dominic Bozzelli	74	67	71	69	281	12,300
Brice Garnett	71	69	71	70	281	12,300
Carlos Ortiz	70	68	73	70	281	12,300
Rory Sabbatini	69	73	70	69	281	12,300
Brendon Todd	70	71	68	72	281	12,300
Charlie Beljan	70	69	72	71	282	8,670
Roberto Díaz	68	74	67	73	282	8,670
Brandon Harkins	73	69	69	71	282	8,670
Martin Piller	70	72	67	73	282	8,670
Seamus Power	72	68	72	70	282	8,670
Wes Roach	71	71	68	72	282	8,670
Shawn Stefani	74	67	70	71	282	8,670
Tyrone Van Aswegen	70	68	75	69	282	8,670
Max Homa	70	70	71	72	283	6,925.72
John Merrick	72	68	71	72	283	6,925.72
Cameron Tringale	72	69	70	72	283	6,925.72
Chris Couch	70	72	70	71	283	6,925.71
Joey Garber	71	71	70	71	283	6,925.71
Curtis Luck	71	71	72	69	283	6,925.71
Hunter Mahan	74	68	72	69	283	6,925.71
Sangmoon Bae	70	68	72	74	284	6,630
Tyler Duncan	71	71	70	72	284	6,630
Jim Herman	69	70	76	70	285	6,450
Hank Lebioda	71	71	71	72	285	6,450
Trey Mullinax	71	70	69	75	285	6,450
Charl Schwartzel	71	71	72	71	285	6,450
Harris English	71	70	75	70	286	6,270
Parker McLachlin	69	70	71	76	286	6,270
John Chin	71	71	70	75	287	6,150
John Senden	73	68	75	71	287	6,150
Jason Bohn	76	65	77	72	290	5,970
Derek Fathauer	73	66	74	77	290	5,970
Julio Santos	72	70	73	75	290	5,970
Ryan Vermeer	72	70	77	71	290	5,970
Chad Campbell	73	69	76	75	293	5,820
Omar Uresti	73	69	79	77	298	5,760

Valero Texas Open

TPC San Antonio, AT&T Oaks Course, San Antonio, Texas
Par 36-36–72; 7,435 yards

April 4-7
purse, $7,500,000

	SCORES				TOTAL	MONEY
Corey Conners	69	67	66	66	268	$1,350,000
Charley Hoffman	71	68	64	67	270	810,000
Ryan Moore	68	70	69	64	271	510,000
Si Woo Kim	66	66	69	72	273	330,000
Brian Stuard	67	70	70	66	273	330,000
Kevin Streelman	72	69	69	64	274	270,000
Byeong Hun An	69	68	73	66	276	203,035.72
Jason Kokrak	70	73	65	68	276	203,035.72
Graeme McDowell	69	69	72	66	276	203,035.72
Scott Brown	71	67	67	71	276	203,035.71
Matt Kuchar	69	71	67	69	276	203,035.71
Danny Lee	68	72	66	70	276	203,035.71

	SCORES				TOTAL	MONEY
Adam Schenk	70	66	70	70	276	203,035.71
Zack Fischer	71	69	71	66	277	135,000
Lucas Glover	72	70	66	69	277	135,000
Kyoung-Hoon Lee	69	67	69	72	277	135,000
Rickie Fowler	68	68	73	69	278	112,500
Hank Lebioda	68	70	70	70	278	112,500
Cameron Tringale	69	74	68	67	278	112,500
Wyndham Clark	69	73	70	67	279	90,500
Sungjae Im	73	69	68	69	279	90,500
Scottie Scheffler	71	68	70	70	279	90,500
Jim Furyk	70	72	68	70	280	63,214.29
Fabian Gomez	73	67	70	70	280	63,214.29
Scott Stallings	68	69	73	70	280	63,214.29
Harold Varner	70	66	73	71	280	63,214.29
Sam Burns	72	69	73	66	280	63,214.28
Peter Malnati	71	68	70	71	280	63,214.28
Jose de Jesus Rodriguez	71	70	68	71	280	63,214.28
Aaron Baddeley	71	70	69	71	281	45,562.50
Jonas Blixt	72	70	69	70	281	45,562.50
Matt Jones	69	68	74	70	281	45,562.50
Jordan Spieth	68	68	73	72	281	45,562.50
Jhonattan Vegas	67	71	67	76	281	45,562.50
Jimmy Walker	70	69	69	73	281	45,562.50
Beau Hossler	69	70	71	72	282	34,562.50
Martin Laird	74	68	68	72	282	34,562.50
Andrew Putnam	72	70	68	72	282	34,562.50
Rory Sabbatini	69	68	72	73	282	34,562.50
Ollie Schniederjans	70	71	69	72	282	34,562.50
Kristoffer Ventura	71	72	70	69	282	34,562.50
Abraham Ancer	67	72	71	73	283	23,040
Dylan Frittelli	71	72	69	71	283	23,040
Max Homa	68	74	68	73	283	23,040
Mackenzie Hughes	70	71	69	73	283	23,040
Sung Kang	70	73	71	69	283	23,040
Martin Kaymer	72	71	70	70	283	23,040
Sam Ryder	73	66	73	71	283	23,040
Sam Saunders	72	71	71	69	283	23,040
Brendan Steele	70	72	67	74	283	23,040
Adam Svensson	73	69	71	70	283	23,040
Russell Henley	71	72	70	71	284	17,490
Kyle Jones	76	67	71	70	284	17,490
Haotong Li	70	70	73	71	284	17,490
Kyle Stanley	70	70	74	70	284	17,490
Nick Taylor	69	72	71	72	284	17,490
Ryan Armour	69	71	75	70	285	16,725
Roberto Diaz	68	71	75	71	285	16,725
Ernie Els	71	69	74	71	285	16,725
Josh Teater	69	68	75	73	285	16,725
Tony Finau	72	71	70	73	286	16,275
Richy Werenski	72	71	69	74	286	16,275
Jim Knous	70	67	74	76	287	15,900
Joost Luiten	72	69	70	76	287	15,900
Robert Streb	72	70	73	72	287	15,900
Martin Trainer	73	70	72	73	288	15,600
Morgan Hoffmann	68	75	72	74	289	15,375
J.T. Poston	67	74	74	74	289	15,375
K.J. Choi	73	69	72	76	290	15,075
Joel Dahmen	70	73	67	80	290	15,075
Padraig Harrington	72	71	73		216	14,550
J.B. Holmes	69	73	74		216	14,550
Hunter Mahan	70	71	75		216	14,550
Chip McDaniel	74	69	73		216	14,550
Vaughn Taylor	70	73	73		216	14,550

	SCORES			TOTAL	MONEY
Trey Mullinax	71	72	74	217	14,100
Anders Albertson	73	70	76	219	13,800
Brian Gay	71	72	76	219	13,800
Ted Potter, Jr.	68	73	78	219	13,800
Curtis Luck	73	68	81	222	13,500

Masters Tournament

Augusta National Golf Club, Augusta, Georgia
Par 36-36–72; 7,475 yards

April 11-14
purse, $11,500,000

	SCORES				TOTAL	MONEY
Tiger Woods	70	68	67	70	275	$2,070,000
Dustin Johnson	68	70	70	68	276	858,667
Brooks Koepka	66	71	69	70	276	858,667
Xander Schauffele	73	65	70	68	276	858,667
Jason Day	70	67	73	67	277	403,938
Tony Finau	71	70	64	72	277	403,938
Francesco Molinari	70	67	66	74	277	403,938
Webb Simpson	72	71	64	70	277	403,938
Patrick Cantlay	73	73	64	68	278	310,500
Rickie Fowler	70	71	68	69	278	310,500
Jon Rahm	69	70	71	68	278	310,500
Justin Harding	69	69	70	72	280	225,400
Matt Kuchar	71	69	68	72	280	225,400
Ian Poulter	68	71	68	73	280	225,400
Justin Thomas	73	68	69	70	280	225,400
Bubba Watson	72	72	67	69	280	225,400
Aaron Wise	75	71	68	67	281	184,000
Patton Kizzire	70	70	73	69	282	161,000
Phil Mickelson	67	73	70	72	282	161,000
Adam Scott	69	68	72	73	282	161,000
Lucas Bjerregaard	70	72	69	72	283	107,956
Matthew Fitzpatrick	78	67	68	70	283	107,956
Si Woo Kim	72	72	70	69	283	107,956
Kevin Kisner	69	73	72	69	283	107,956
Rory McIlroy	73	71	71	68	283	107,956
Thorbjorn Olesen	71	71	68	73	283	107,956
Jordan Spieth	75	68	69	71	283	107,956
Kyle Stanley	72	72	70	69	283	107,956
Bryson DeChambeau	66	75	73	70	284	78,200
Charley Hoffman	71	71	72	70	284	78,200
Louis Oosthuizen	71	66	71	76	284	78,200
Charles Howell	73	67	76	69	285	68,042
Hideki Matsuyama	75	70	68	72	285	68,042
Gary Woodland	70	71	74	70	285	68,042
Viktor Hovland [A]	72	71	71	71	285	
Rafa Cabrera Bello	73	70	75	68	286	55,488
Tommy Fleetwood	71	71	70	74	286	55,488
Patrick Reed	73	70	74	69	286	55,488
Henrik Stenson	74	72	67	73	286	55,488
Kevin Tway	72	71	70	73	286	55,488
Jimmy Walker	72	72	72	70	286	55,488
Alvaro Ortiz Becerra [A]	73	71	73	69	286	
Keegan Bradley	76	68	71	72	287	44,850
Haotong Li	72	74	73	68	287	44,850
Keith Mitchell	72	74	72	69	287	44,850
Corey Conners	70	71	71	76	288	37,950
Andrew Landry	72	73	73	70	288	37,950
Kevin Na	71	73	73	71	288	37,950

	SCORES				TOTAL	MONEY
Kiradech Aphibarnrat	69	72	75	73	289	32,430
Marc Leishman	72	72	70	75	289	32,430
Trevor Immelman	74	72	75	69	290	28,693
Martin Kaymer	73	74	72	71	290	28,693
Eddie Pepperell	74	73	72	71	290	28,693
Cameron Smith	70	74	69	77	290	28,693
Devon Bling [A]	74	73	71	73	291	
Tyrrell Hatton	73	73	72	74	292	26,910
Billy Horschel	72	75	74	71	292	26,910
Branden Grace	72	75	72	74	293	26,335
Zach Johnson	74	73	73	73	293	26,335
Takumi Kanaya [A]	73	74	68	78	293	
Satoshi Kodaira	75	70	73	76	294	25,990
Emiliano Grillo	72	75	73	76	296	25,415
J.B. Holmes	70	72	74	80	296	25,415
Bernhard Langer	71	72	75	78	296	25,415
Alex Noren	75	72	75	74	296	25,415

Out of Final 36 Holes

Stewart Cink	76	72	148	Shugo Imahira	76	74	150
Sergio Garcia	73	75	148	Shane Lowry	78	73	151
Sandy Lyle	73	75	148	Larry Mize	77	74	151
Kevin O'Connell	77	71	148	Jovan Rebula	73	79	152
Justin Rose	75	73	148	Matt Wallace	75	77	152
Mike Weir	72	76	148	Paul Casey	81	73	154
Danny Willett	75	73	148	Michael Kim	76	78	154
Fred Couples	78	71	149	Vijay Singh	80	76	156
Adam Long	75	74	149	Ian Woosnam	80	76	156
Charl Schwartzel	77	72	149	Angel Cabrera	82	75	157
Brandt Snedeker	75	74	149	Jose Maria Olazabal	78	79	157

(All professionals not completing 72 holes earned $10,000.)

RBC Heritage

Harbour Town Golf Links, Hilton Head Island, South Carolina
Par 36-35–71; 7,099 yards

April 18-21
purse, $6,900,000

	SCORES				TOTAL	MONEY
C.T. Pan	71	65	69	67	272	$1,242,000
Matt Kuchar	69	69	68	67	273	745,200
Patrick Cantlay	67	72	66	69	274	358,800
Shane Lowry	65	68	71	70	274	358,800
Scott Piercy	67	70	68	69	274	358,800
J.T. Poston	71	71	67	66	275	231,150
Seamus Power	68	72	68	67	275	231,150
Kevin Streelman	69	69	69	68	275	231,150
Sam Burns	67	70	69	70	276	200,100
K.J. Choi	70	66	69	72	277	152,950
Troy Merritt	69	67	72	69	277	152,950
Kevin Na	67	72	71	67	277	152,950
Ian Poulter	70	67	67	73	277	152,950
Rory Sabbatini	67	69	68	73	277	152,950
Michael Thompson	68	71	69	69	277	152,950
Rafa Cabrera Bello	68	69	70	71	278	90,620
Joel Dahmen	70	68	71	69	278	90,620
Zach Johnson	69	69	72	68	278	90,620
Jason Kokrak	69	68	72	69	278	90,620
Peter Malnati	67	72	69	70	278	90,620

	SCORES				TOTAL	MONEY
Trey Mullinax	66	68	71	73	278	90,620
Eddie Pepperell	71	69	68	70	278	90,620
Webb Simpson	69	73	65	71	278	90,620
Brian Stuard	68	70	72	68	278	90,620
Harris English	72	69	69	69	279	56,350
Tommy Fleetwood	71	68	70	70	279	56,350
Boo Weekley	69	70	70	70	279	56,350
Dustin Johnson	68	67	68	77	280	46,920
Alex Noren	67	74	67	72	280	46,920
Ryan Palmer	66	71	74	69	280	46,920
Chez Reavie	68	71	68	73	280	46,920
J.J. Spaun	70	69	68	73	280	46,920
Daniel Berger	66	69	72	74	281	36,455
Luke Donald	70	70	69	72	281	36,455
Emiliano Grillo	68	67	70	76	281	36,455
Andrew Landry	69	71	73	68	281	36,455
Denny McCarthy	70	68	70	73	281	36,455
Hudson Swafford	68	74	71	68	281	36,455
Bud Cauley	69	72	72	69	282	30,360
Matthew Fitzpatrick	71	71	68	72	282	30,360
Kevin Kisner	71	68	72	72	283	26,220
Danny Lee	72	69	70	72	283	26,220
Luke List	66	73	73	71	283	26,220
Ryan Moore	66	74	72	71	283	26,220
Charley Hoffman	68	69	70	77	284	21,390
Billy Horschel	67	70	72	75	284	21,390
Patton Kizzire	72	69	71	72	284	21,390
Jonathan Byrd	68	73	73	71	285	17,342
Adam Hadwin	71	69	74	71	285	17,342
Kyoung-Hoon Lee	70	69	74	72	285	17,342
Graeme McDowell	68	71	73	73	285	17,342
Brandt Snedeker	71	71	69	74	285	17,342
Scott Stallings	70	69	71	75	285	17,342
Wyndham Clark	70	69	78	69	286	15,801
Brian Gay	71	68	71	76	286	15,801
Brandon Harkins	71	67	74	74	286	15,801
Jordan Spieth	71	66	74	75	286	15,801
Marc Leishman	70	69	77	71	287	15,318
Nick Taylor	72	70	68	77	287	15,318
Richy Werenski	74	68	74	71	287	15,318
Branden Grace	70	72	75	71	288	14,973
Scott Langley	68	74	75	71	288	14,973
Ryan Armour	72	69	74	74	289	14,559
Jason Dufner	73	69	71	76	289	14,559
Mackenzie Hughes	70	70	72	77	289	14,559
Xander Schauffele	71	70	73	75	289	14,559
Cody Gribble	72	69	73	77	291	14,076
Ted Potter, Jr.	73	69	77	72	291	14,076
Ben Silverman	73	68	76	74	291	14,076
Satoshi Kodaira	73	68	77	82	300	13,800

Zurich Classic of New Orleans

TPC Louisiana, Avondale, Louisiana
Par 36-36–72; 7,425 yards

April 25-28
purse, $7,300,000

	SCORES				TOTAL	MONEY (Each)
Ryan Palmer/Jon Rahm	64	65	64	69	262	$1,051,200
Tommy Fleetwood/Sergio Garcia	65	68	64	68	265	423,400
Brian Gay/Rory Sabbatini	60	70	66	71	267	256,412.50

	SCORES				TOTAL	MONEY (Each)
Matt Every/Kyoung-Hoon Lee	65	69	65	68	267	256,412.50
Hank Lebioda/Curtis Luck	67	66	64	71	268	163,337.50
David Hearn/Seamus Power	68	68	64	68	268	163,337.50
Roberto Castro/Cameron Tringale	65	69	66	68	268	163,337.50
Scott Brown/Kevin Kisner	62	69	68	69	268	163,337.50
Billy Hurley/Peter Malnati	63	67	66	73	269	92,345
Martin Laird/Nick Taylor	62	74	64	69	269	92,345
Charley Hoffman/Nick Watney	65	70	63	71	269	92,345
Sam Horsfield/Ian Poulter	67	69	66	67	269	92,345
Kelly Kraft/Kevin Tway	63	72	64	71	270	51,136.50
Billy Horschel/Scott Piercy	66	68	66	70	270	51,136.50
Alex Cejka/Alex Prugh	63	71	64	72	270	51,136.50
Trey Mullinax/Scott Stallings	61	70	62	77	270	51,136.50
Adam Hadwin/Jim Knous	66	68	65	71	270	51,136.50
Joel Dahmen/Brandon Harkins	63	71	63	74	271	33,716.87
Lucas Glover/Chez Reavie	62	70	68	71	271	33,716.87
Ryan Blaum/Russell Henley	65	67	65	74	271	33,716.87
Graeme McDowell/Henrik Stenson	65	67	66	73	271	33,716.87
Troy Merritt/Robert Streb	66	68	66	72	272	19,609.62
Jason Kokrak/Chris Stroud	65	69	68	70	272	19,609.62
Austin Cook/Andrew Landry	65	70	62	75	272	19,609.62
Russell Knox/Brian Stuard	62	69	66	75	272	19,609.62
Stephan Jaeger/J.T. Poston	62	70	67	73	272	19,609.62
Anirban Lahiri/Shubhankar Sharma	67	69	65	71	272	19,609.62
Brooks Koepka/Chase Koepka	67	68	63	74	272	19,609.62
Matt Jones/J.J. Spaun	67	69	64	72	272	19,609.62
Corey Conners/Mackenzie Hughes	67	68	68	70	273	15,987
Bill Haas/Shawn Stefani	65	69	68	71	273	15,987
Andres Romero/Julian Etulain	64	69	65	73	271	15,403
Branden Grace/Justin Harding	65	68	61	80	274	15,403
J.B. Holmes/Bubba Watson	64	70	66	75	275	14,819
J.J. Henry/Tom Hoge	67	68	66	74	275	14,819
Keegan Bradley/Jon Curran	64	71	69	75	279	14,381
Sungjae Im/Whee Kim	64	72	73	73	282	13,797
Roberto Diaz/Denny McCarthy	63	73	70	76	282	13,797
Joey Garber/Cody Gribble	61	75	76	70	282	13,797

Wells Fargo Championship

Quail Hollow Club, Charlotte, North Carolina
Par 35-36–71; 7,554 yards

May 2-5
purse, $7,900,000

	SCORES			TOTAL	MONEY
Max Homa	69	63	70	67	269	$1,422,000
Joel Dahmen	66	66	70	70	272	853,200
Justin Rose	70	67	68	68	273	537,200
Paul Casey	69	71	66	69	275	311,062.50
Jason Dufner	68	63	71	73	275	311,062.50
Rickie Fowler	71	70	66	68	275	311,062.50
Sergio Garcia	69	73	65	68	275	311,062.50
Rory McIlroy	66	70	68	73	277	213,300
Keith Mitchell	68	74	66	69	277	213,300
Pat Perez	69	68	66	74	277	213,300
Kyle Stanley	69	69	71	68	277	213,300
Jhonattan Vegas	72	67	69	69	277	213,300
Jim Knous	68	72	70	68	278	143,780
Seamus Power	69	68	69	72	278	143,780
Adam Schenk	67	74	67	70	278	143,780
Shawn Stefani	76	65	70	67	278	143,780

	SCORES				TOTAL	MONEY
Vaughn Taylor	68	71	68	71	278	143,780
Chez Reavie	70	71	70	68	279	99,540
Doc Redman	70	70	67	72	279	99,540
Rory Sabbatini	76	66	67	70	279	99,540
Webb Simpson	69	73	69	68	279	99,540
Brendon Todd	68	70	73	68	279	99,540
Aaron Wise	69	70	69	71	279	99,540
Bud Cauley	73	70	68	69	280	67,347.50
Jason Day	68	69	74	69	280	67,347.50
Dylan Frittelli	67	74	70	69	280	67,347.50
Brian Harman	68	75	69	68	280	67,347.50
Patrick Reed	67	69	71	74	281	56,090
Ollie Schniederjans	74	69	68	70	281	56,090
Henrik Stenson	74	67	70	70	281	56,090
Lucas Glover	70	69	72	71	282	44,804.29
Hideki Matsuyama	73	70	70	69	282	44,804.29
Alex Prugh	73	68	71	70	282	44,804.29
Nick Watney	70	72	72	68	282	44,804.29
Cody Gribble	71	72	68	71	282	44,804.28
Sungjae Im	70	69	71	72	282	44,804.28
Martin Laird	67	71	71	73	282	44,804.28
Adam Hadwin	73	69	68	73	283	32,390
Matt Jones	70	70	72	71	283	32,390
Colt Knost	73	68	67	75	283	32,390
Sebastian Munoz	68	70	73	72	283	32,390
Joaquin Niemann	73	70	69	71	283	32,390
Richy Werenski	70	69	73	71	283	32,390
Chase Wright	71	72	69	71	283	32,390
Ryan Blaum	71	72	68	73	284	23,131.20
Nate Lashley	71	70	69	74	284	23,131.20
Adam Long	70	71	73	70	284	23,131.20
Kevin Streelman	71	69	70	74	284	23,131.20
Jimmy Walker	71	70	72	71	284	23,131.20
Bill Haas	69	72	71	73	285	19,236.50
Hank Lebioda	71	72	74	68	285	19,236.50
Trey Mullinax	72	69	73	71	285	19,236.50
Zack Sucher	72	71	73	69	285	19,236.50
Daniel Berger	73	69	70	74	286	17,933
Roberto Diaz	70	72	71	73	286	17,933
Harris English	71	71	72	72	286	17,933
John Senden	68	73	69	76	286	17,933
Brendan Steele	72	70	75	69	286	17,933
Nick Taylor	67	75	72	72	286	17,933
Tony Finau	72	69	72	74	287	17,064
Brice Garnett	70	71	70	76	287	17,064
J.J. Henry	70	72	72	73	287	17,064
Kramer Hickok	72	69	72	74	287	17,064
Kyoung-Hoon Lee	72	70	70	75	287	17,064
Brandon Harkins	73	69	71	76	289	16,432
Tom Hoge	70	70	75	74	289	16,432
Luke List	75	68	71	75	289	16,432
Julian Etulain	73	70	70	77	290	16,116
Jason Kokrak	70	70	74	78	292	15,958
Wes Roach	70	71	74	78	293	15,721
Matthew Short	76	67	74	76	293	15,721
Fabian Gomez	70	69	80	77	296	15,484
Beau Hossler	69	72	76	80	297	15,326

AT&T Byron Nelson

Trinity Forest Golf Club, Dallas, Texas
Par 36-35–71; 7,371 yards

May 9-12
purse, $7,900,000

	SCORES				TOTAL	MONEY
Sung Kang	65	61	68	67	261	$1,422,000
Matt Every	65	65	67	66	263	695,200
Scott Piercy	67	69	63	64	263	695,200
Brooks Koepka	65	66	68	65	264	379,200
Kiradech Aphibarnrat	69	68	66	64	267	267,810
Tyler Duncan	64	66	70	67	267	267,810
Matt Jones	65	70	65	67	267	267,810
Rory Sabbatini	67	65	68	67	267	267,810
Peter Uihlein	69	71	63	64	267	267,810
Justin Harding	66	73	64	65	268	205,400
Sebastian Munoz	69	66	65	68	268	205,400
Doug Ghim	69	66	66	68	269	154,840
Padraig Harrington	69	69	66	65	269	154,840
Nicholas Lindheim	70	69	62	68	269	154,840
Carlos Ortiz	69	69	66	65	269	154,840
Pat Perez	67	71	67	64	269	154,840
Kramer Hickok	65	73	66	66	270	118,500
Stephan Jaeger	69	66	67	68	270	118,500
Vaughn Taylor	69	67	68	66	270	118,500
Jonas Blixt	65	70	70	66	271	95,326.67
Henrik Stenson	67	69	66	69	271	95,326.67
Shawn Stefani	65	72	64	70	271	95,326.66
Daniel Berger	66	72	66	68	272	68,335
Hideki Matsuyama	67	70	68	67	272	68,335
Denny McCarthy	63	77	65	67	272	68,335
Thomas Pieters	70	66	69	67	272	68,335
Brady Schnell	72	67	64	69	272	68,335
Cameron Tringale	69	69	69	65	272	68,335
Joey Garber	68	69	66	70	273	50,230.84
Morgan Hoffmann	70	68	65	70	273	50,230.84
Nate Lashley	67	73	67	66	273	50,230.83
Davis Riley	68	69	66	70	273	50,230.83
Jordan Spieth	68	67	67	71	273	50,230.83
Sepp Straka	69	71	68	65	273	50,230.83
Kevin Na	69	68	67	70	274	36,488.13
Alex Noren	70	68	67	69	274	36,488.13
C.T. Pan	66	70	69	69	274	36,488.13
Scottie Scheffler	67	69	69	69	274	36,488.13
Cameron Davis	67	69	70	68	274	36,488.12
Russell Henley	71	67	69	67	274	36,488.12
Martin Laird	67	66	70	71	274	36,488.12
Zack Sucher	67	68	68	71	274	36,488.12
Bud Cauley	70	69	64	72	275	23,083.80
Roberto Diaz	66	67	69	73	275	23,083.80
Harris English	68	71	68	68	275	23,083.80
Beau Hossler	67	66	70	72	275	23,083.80
Russell Knox	68	69	68	70	275	23,083.80
David Lingmerth	71	68	65	71	275	23,083.80
Curtis Luck	71	67	66	71	275	23,083.80
Ryan Palmer	68	69	71	67	275	23,083.80
Johnson Wagner	72	68	67	68	275	23,083.80
Aaron Wise	69	69	66	71	275	23,083.80
Michael Thompson	66	68	71	71	276	18,117.34
Kevin Tway	70	66	70	70	276	18,117.34
Rafa Cabrera Bello	70	70	67	69	276	18,117.33
Bill Haas	68	70	69	69	276	18,117.33
Brandon Harkins	68	72	69	67	276	18,117.33

372 / AMERICAN TOURS

	SCORES				TOTAL	MONEY
Troy Merritt	65	74	68	69	276	18,117.33
Abraham Ancer	69	71	69	68	277	17,301
Keith Mitchell	66	73	66	72	277	17,301
J.J. Spaun	66	70	72	69	277	17,301
Brian Stuard	67	72	70	68	277	17,301
Daniel Chopra	72	67	69	70	278	16,669
Branden Grace	69	70	66	73	278	16,669
Patrick Reed	70	68	67	73	278	16,669
Seth Reeves	66	70	70	72	278	16,669
Dylan Frittelli	68	72	69	70	279	16,195
Tom Hoge	64	75	70	70	279	16,195
Brian Gay	68	72	69	71	280	15,800
Ryan Moore	69	70	68	73	280	15,800
Ollie Schniederjans	68	69	70	73	280	15,800
Sam Burns	66	72	72		210	15,010
Chad Campbell	65	73	72		210	15,010
Ben Crane	68	72	70		210	15,010
Kyoung-Hoon Lee	68	72	70		210	15,010
Peter Malnati	70	69	71		210	15,010
Wes Roach	70	70	70		210	15,010
Chase Wright	68	72	70		210	15,010
Chad Collins	68	72	71		211	14,141
Seamus Power	72	67	72		211	14,141
Alex Prugh	68	71	72		211	14,141
Roger Sloan	72	68	71		211	14,141
Sungjae Im	71	69	73		213	13,746

PGA Championship

Bethpage State Park Black Course, Farmingdale, New York
Par 35-35–70; 7,459 yards

May 16-19
purse, $11,000,000

	SCORES				TOTAL	MONEY
Brooks Koepka	63	65	70	74	272	$1,980,000
Dustin Johnson	69	67	69	69	274	1,188,000
Patrick Cantlay	69	70	68	71	278	575,500
Jordan Spieth	69	66	72	71	278	575,500
Matt Wallace	69	67	70	72	278	575,500
Luke List	68	68	69	74	279	380,000
Sung Kang	68	70	70	72	280	343,650
Matt Kuchar	70	70	72	69	281	264,395
Shane Lowry	75	69	68	69	281	264,395
Rory McIlroy	72	71	69	69	281	264,395
Erik van Rooyen	70	68	70	73	281	264,395
Adam Scott	71	64	72	74	281	264,395
Gary Woodland	70	70	73	68	281	264,395
Jazz Janewattananond	70	68	67	77	282	191,665
Chez Reavie	68	71	71	72	282	191,665
Abraham Ancer	73	70	69	71	283	143,100
Lucas Bjerregaard	71	69	70	73	283	143,100
Lucas Glover	72	69	69	73	283	143,100
Mike Lorenzo-Vera	68	71	75	69	283	143,100
Hideki Matsuyama	70	68	68	77	283	143,100
Xander Schauffele	70	69	68	76	283	143,100
Brandt Snedeker	74	67	73	69	283	143,100
Jason Day	69	74	69	72	284	91,000
Emiliano Grillo	76	67	70	71	284	91,000
Billy Horschel	70	72	71	71	284	91,000
Jason Kokrak	73	70	71	70	284	91,000
Thomas Pieters	74	70	71	69	284	91,000

		SCORES			TOTAL	MONEY
Jimmy Walker	70	70	71	73	284	91,000
Keegan Bradley	70	70	73	72	285	65,000
Sam Burns	70	72	69	74	285	65,000
Paul Casey	70	71	75	69	285	65,000
Adam Hadwin	72	70	70	73	285	65,000
Graeme McDowell	70	72	73	70	285	65,000
Justin Rose	70	67	73	75	285	65,000
Webb Simpson	72	69	72	72	285	65,000
Rickie Fowler	69	69	71	77	286	48,200
Beau Hossler	72	69	77	68	286	48,200
Danny Lee	64	74	71	77	286	48,200
Haotong Li	73	69	70	74	286	48,200
Harold Varner	71	67	67	81	286	48,200
Kiradech Aphibarnrat	76	68	68	75	287	36,035.71
Matthew Fitzpatrick	75	65	76	71	287	36,035.71
Charles Howell	72	67	73	75	287	36,035.71
Adam Long	73	70	69	75	287	36,035.71
Scott Piercy	72	67	72	76	287	36,035.71
Danny Willett	71	70	69	77	287	36,035.71
Aaron Wise	70	71	71	75	287	36,035.71
Bronson Burgoon	73	66	74	75	288	26,250
Tommy Fleetwood	67	71	72	78	288	26,250
Tyrrell Hatton	71	69	72	76	288	26,250
Kelly Kraft	71	65	78	74	288	26,250
Francesco Molinari	72	68	73	75	288	26,250
Henrik Stenson	74	68	75	71	288	26,250
Cameron Champ	72	71	73	73	289	22,850
Justin Harding	74	70	73	72	289	22,850
Charley Hoffman	73	69	75	72	289	22,850
Zach Johnson	71	69	73	76	289	22,850
Alex Noren	73	69	74	73	289	22,850
J.J. Spaun	72	72	70	75	289	22,850
Ross Fisher	74	67	77	72	290	21,300
Rob Labritz	75	69	74	72	290	21,300
Louis Oosthuizen	70	68	73	79	290	21,300
J.T. Poston	77	67	71	75	290	21,300
Corey Conners	72	72	76	71	291	20,200
Tony Finau	70	73	69	79	291	20,200
Max Homa	70	71	79	71	291	20,200
Kurt Kitayama	74	68	77	72	291	20,200
Joost Luiten	72	72	77	70	291	20,200
Thorbjorn Olesen	73	70	71	77	291	20,200
Cameron Smith	73	70	74	74	291	20,200
Daniel Berger	70	66	78	78	292	19,250
Rafa Cabrera Bello	75	69	74	74	292	19,250
Joel Dahmen	70	72	71	79	292	19,250
Lucas Herbert	74	70	73	75	292	19,250
David Lipsky	70	74	77	71	292	19,250
Phil Mickelson	69	71	76	76	292	19,250
Kevin Tway	73	70	76	74	293	18,900
Pat Perez	68	73	76	77	294	18,750
Andrew Putnam	74	70	75	75	294	18,750
Rich Beem	75	69	82	69	295	18,550
Ryan Vermeer	70	74	72	79	295	18,550
Marty Jertson	72	69	79	79	299	18,400

Out of Final 36 Holes

Ryan Armour	74	71	145
Dylan Frittelli	77	68	145
Jim Furyk	73	72	145
Sergio Garcia	74	71	145
Tyler Hall	72	73	145

J.B. Holmes	71	77	148
Mikko Korhonen	74	74	148
Marc Leishman	74	74	148
Richard Sterne	75	73	148
Jason Caron	70	79	149

Sungjae Im	71	74	145
Martin Kaymer	74	71	145
Michael Kim	74	71	145
Patton Kizzire	70	75	145
Russell Knox	72	73	145
Keith Mitchell	74	71	145
Kevin Na	72	73	145
Adrian Otaegui	73	72	145
Jon Rahm	70	75	145
Kyle Stanley	71	74	145
Steve Stricker	73	72	145
Julian Suri	72	73	145
Martin Trainer	75	70	145
Bubba Watson	76	69	145
Tiger Woods	72	73	145
Bryson DeChambeau	72	74	146
Branden Grace	73	73	146
Si Woo Kim	69	77	146
Joaquin Niemann	75	71	146
Ian Poulter	72	74	146
Patrick Reed	74	72	146
Richy Werenski	72	74	146
Ben Cook	74	73	147
Shugo Imahira	74	73	147
Tom Lewis	76	71	147
Brian Mackey	74	73	147
Troy Merritt	72	75	147
Shaun Norris	73	74	147
Lee Westwood	75	72	147
Byeong Hun An	74	74	148
Jason Dufner	76	72	148
Ryan Fox	78	70	148
Chesson Hadley	72	77	149
Satoshi Kodaira	73	76	149
C.T. Pan	78	71	149
Michael Thompson	77	72	149
Justin Bertsch	77	73	150
Jorge Campillo	77	73	150
Ryan Moore	73	77	150
Casey Russell	77	73	150
Rich Berberian, Jr.	76	75	151
John Daly	75	76	151
Eddie Pepperell	76	75	151
Y.E. Yang	76	75	151
Alex Beach	77	75	152
Padraig Harrington	75	77	152
Ryan Palmer	77	75	152
Brandon Stone	79	73	152
Craig Bowden	78	75	153
Kevin Kisner	77	76	153
Jhonattan Vegas	76	77	153
Brian Harman	77	77	154
Shaun Micheel	77	77	154
Rod Perry	77	77	154
Daniel Balin	78	77	155
Alexander Bjork	80	75	155
Brendan Jones	78	77	155
John O'Leary	79	78	157
Stuart Deane	82	76	158
Craig Hocknull	82	77	159
Jeff Schmid	81	78	159
Cory Schneider	74	85	159
Andrew Filbert	84	82	166
Brian Gay	81		WD

Charles Schwab Challenge

Colonial Country Club, Fort Worth, Texas
Par 35-35–70; 7,209 yards

May 23-26
purse, $7,300,000

	SCORES				TOTAL	MONEY
Kevin Na	70	62	69	66	267	$1,314,000
Tony Finau	64	68	71	68	271	788,400
C.T. Pan	68	67	68	69	272	423,400
Andrew Putnam	69	70	67	66	272	423,400
Jonas Blixt	67	64	74	68	273	292,000
Ryan Palmer	68	69	68	69	274	253,675
Rory Sabbatini	68	66	73	67	274	253,675
Tyrrell Hatton	71	66	69	69	275	197,100
Mackenzie Hughes	68	70	65	72	275	197,100
Russell Knox	71	68	71	65	275	197,100
Jordan Spieth	65	70	68	72	275	197,100
Nick Watney	67	68	70	70	275	197,100
Jim Furyk	69	66	68	73	276	136,875
Brian Gay	69	71	67	69	276	136,875
Charley Hoffman	70	71	63	72	276	136,875
Peter Uihlein	67	73	67	69	276	136,875
Matt Every	70	69	69	69	277	113,150
Josh Teater	68	70	71	68	277	113,150
Austin Cook	72	67	65	74	278	79,387.50
Emiliano Grillo	69	70	68	71	278	79,387.50
Billy Horschel	72	69	69	68	278	79,387.50
Adam Long	70	69	71	68	278	79,387.50
Scott Piercy	70	68	68	72	278	79,387.50

	SCORES				TOTAL	MONEY
Brandt Snedeker	74	67	68	69	278	79,387.50
Kevin Tway	68	70	69	71	278	79,387.50
Jimmy Walker	67	74	70	67	278	79,387.50
J.J. Henry	67	73	69	70	279	55,115
Max Homa	70	68	73	68	279	55,115
Talor Gooch	72	70	71	67	280	50,735
Tyrone Van Aswegen	69	71	71	69	280	50,735
Corey Conners	69	73	71	68	281	39,663.34
Brian Harman	70	69	72	70	281	39,663.34
Jhonattan Vegas	74	67	73	67	281	39,663.34
Sam Burns	69	72	70	70	281	39,663.33
Chesson Hadley	67	72	71	71	281	39,663.33
Joaquin Niemann	71	70	70	70	281	39,663.33
Roger Sloan	65	72	70	74	281	39,663.33
Kevin Streelman	69	71	69	72	281	39,663.33
David Toms	71	68	70	72	281	39,663.33
Jason Dufner	67	68	72	75	282	26,280
Brice Garnett	73	66	73	70	282	26,280
Tom Hoge	70	69	71	72	282	26,280
Beau Hossler	70	71	72	69	282	26,280
Martin Kaymer	73	65	71	73	282	26,280
Peter Malnati	74	67	72	69	282	26,280
Trey Mullinax	67	69	75	71	282	26,280
Ben Silverman	69	71	72	70	282	26,280
Aaron Baddeley	73	69	71	70	283	18,571.20
Scott Brown	67	73	72	71	283	18,571.20
Bill Haas	69	71	72	71	283	18,571.20
Danny Lee	69	71	71	72	283	18,571.20
Chris Stroud	72	70	71	70	283	18,571.20
Daniel Berger	71	67	71	75	284	16,819.20
Branden Grace	71	71	72	70	284	16,819.20
Anirban Lahiri	68	71	72	73	284	16,819.20
Martin Laird	72	69	68	75	284	16,819.20
Francesco Molinari	71	70	70	73	284	16,819.20
Abraham Ancer	68	72	75	70	285	15,987
Cameron Champ	70	72	72	71	285	15,987
Ted Potter, Jr.	70	72	72	71	285	15,987
Justin Rose	74	67	74	70	285	15,987
Vaughn Taylor	74	67	70	74	285	15,987
Mike Weir	71	71	72	71	285	15,987
Ben Crane	75	67	71	73	286	15,257
Matthew Fitzpatrick	69	71	75	71	286	15,257
Kyoung-Hoon Lee	72	69	71	74	286	15,257
Brian Stuard	70	72	73	71	286	15,257
Byeong Hun An	69	72	77	69	287	14,892
Nate Lashley	69	71	75	73	288	14,746
Dominic Bozzelli	73	69	68	79	289	14,527
Ian Poulter	73	69	72	75	289	14,527
Tim Herron	72	68	77	74	291	14,308
Graeme McDowell	71	71	78	72	292	14,162

Memorial Tournament

Muirfield Village Golf Club, Dublin, Ohio
Par 36-36–72; 7,392 yards

May 30-June 2
purse, $9,100,000

	SCORES				TOTAL	MONEY
Patrick Cantlay	68	69	68	64	269	$1,638,000
Adam Scott	71	66	66	68	271	982,800
Martin Kaymer	67	68	66	72	273	618,800
Kevin Streelman	72	68	69	66	275	436,800
Marc Leishman	67	71	69	69	276	364,000
Hideki Matsuyama	71	70	64	72	277	327,600
Jason Dufner	72	69	68	69	278	293,475
Jordan Spieth	66	70	69	73	278	293,475
Bud Cauley	67	70	70	72	279	236,600
Emiliano Grillo	69	68	71	71	279	236,600
Billy Horschel	71	70	70	68	279	236,600
Tiger Woods	70	72	70	67	279	236,600
Justin Rose	75	63	71	71	280	191,100
Rickie Fowler	69	68	72	72	281	163,800
Xander Schauffele	69	70	72	70	281	163,800
Michael Thompson	71	71	71	68	281	163,800
Byeong Hun An	72	72	70	68	282	127,400
Kiradech Aphibarnrat	70	71	71	70	282	127,400
Peter Malnati	72	72	69	69	282	127,400
Troy Merritt	69	66	74	73	282	127,400
Andrew Putnam	68	70	74	70	282	127,400
Ryan Armour	71	71	71	70	283	87,360
Aaron Baddeley	72	70	68	73	283	87,360
Bryson DeChambeau	74	70	73	66	283	87,360
Steve Stricker	69	76	67	71	283	87,360
Nick Watney	74	68	69	72	283	87,360
Austin Cook	71	67	76	70	284	63,245
Brian Harman	71	69	71	73	284	63,245
Russell Knox	68	73	72	71	284	63,245
Joaquin Niemann	72	71	68	73	284	63,245
Rory Sabbatini	73	71	70	70	284	63,245
Danny Willett	69	69	72	74	284	63,245
Jim Furyk	72	69	75	69	285	50,277.50
Tyrrell Hatton	71	72	72	70	285	50,277.50
Ryan Moore	65	75	75	70	285	50,277.50
Brian Stuard	78	65	71	71	285	50,277.50
Max Homa	70	72	74	70	286	41,860
Kyoung-Hoon Lee	68	67	72	79	286	41,860
Haotong Li	69	72	74	71	286	41,860
Henrik Stenson	70	70	75	71	286	41,860
Rafa Cabrera Bello	72	71	74	70	287	31,850
Matt Jones	75	67	69	76	287	31,850
Si Woo Kim	69	70	76	72	287	31,850
Kevin Kisner	75	67	73	72	287	31,850
David Lingmerth	71	74	71	71	287	31,850
Alex Noren	73	70	69	75	287	31,850
Brendan Steele	71	73	75	68	287	31,850
David Lipsky	70	70	76	72	288	23,478
Keith Mitchell	73	69	70	76	288	23,478
Scott Stallings	69	74	73	72	288	23,478
Vaughn Taylor	67	72	72	77	288	23,478
Lucas Glover	72	72	69	76	289	21,221.20
Adam Hadwin	72	73	73	71	289	21,221.20
Anirban Lahiri	67	76	75	71	289	21,221.20
J.T. Poston	72	73	71	73	289	21,221.20
Gary Woodland	69	71	74	75	289	21,221.20
Luke Donald	72	73	65	80	290	20,202

	SCORES				TOTAL	MONEY
Sungjae Im	72	70	75	73	290	20,202
Louis Oosthuizen	73	70	71	76	290	20,202
Pat Perez	75	70	71	74	290	20,202
Sam Ryder	69	71	74	76	290	20,202
Jason Kokrak	71	73	72	75	291	19,474
Joost Luiten	73	71	74	73	291	19,474
Shubhankar Sharma	73	71	69	78	291	19,474
Abraham Ancer	72	71	75	74	292	18,928
Corey Conners	72	69	74	77	292	18,928
Adam Schenk	71	74	72	75	292	18,928
Joel Dahmen	72	70	77	74	293	18,382
Matthew Fitzpatrick	73	71	74	75	293	18,382
Norman Xiong	72	73	76	72	293	18,382
K.J. Choi	76	67	77	77	297	17,927
Boo Weekley	74	71	79	73	297	17,927
Ted Potter, Jr.	70	73	77	80	300	17,654

RBC Canadian Open

Hamilton Golf & Country Club, Hamilton, Ontario, Canada
Par 35-35–70; 6,967 yards

June 6-9
purse, $6,600,000

	SCORES				TOTAL	MONEY
Rory McIlroy	67	66	64	61	258	$1,368,000
Shane Lowry	64	68	66	67	265	668,800
Webb Simpson	66	64	67	68	265	668,800
Matt Kuchar	65	63	69	70	267	334,400
Brandt Snedeker	69	60	69	69	267	334,400
Adam Hadwin	65	66	67	70	268	273,600
Sungjae Im	64	68	73	64	269	254,600
Graeme McDowell	65	67	70	68	270	220,400
Henrik Stenson	66	66	68	70	270	220,400
Danny Willett	66	68	69	67	270	220,400
Sebastian Munoz	65	72	70	64	271	174,800
Wes Roach	68	68	69	66	271	174,800
Cameron Tringale	68	68	69	66	271	174,800
Jonathan Byrd	67	71	64	70	272	125,400
Mackenzie Hughes	66	66	69	71	272	125,400
Stephan Jaeger	71	64	71	66	272	125,400
Hank Lebioda	67	67	71	67	272	125,400
Collin Morikawa	70	66	69	67	272	125,400
Jose de Jesus Rodriguez	67	66	71	68	272	125,400
Paul Barjon	68	70	67	68	273	79,257.15
Ben Silverman	71	61	72	69	273	79,257.15
Harris English	66	69	69	69	273	79,257.14
Dustin Johnson	71	65	68	69	273	79,257.14
Danny Lee	65	72	67	69	273	79,257.14
Justin Thomas	70	65	69	69	273	79,257.14
Erik van Rooyen	64	70	68	71	273	79,257.14
Sangmoon Bae	69	68	70	67	274	55,100
Jim Furyk	69	67	67	71	274	55,100
Joey Garber	68	70	70	66	274	55,100
Nick Taylor	64	65	73	72	274	55,100
Scott Brown	65	63	75	72	275	46,075
Peter Malnati	66	68	69	72	275	46,075
Joaquin Niemann	67	70	68	70	275	46,075
Chris Thompson	69	66	71	69	275	46,075
Talor Gooch	66	70	71	69	276	34,326.67
Zach Johnson	71	67	70	68	276	34,326.67
Ryan Palmer	68	69	72	67	276	34,326.67

	SCORES				TOTAL	MONEY
Rod Pampling	69	69	69	69	276	34,326.67
Harold Varner	68	70	71	67	276	34,326.67
Jimmy Walker	65	72	71	68	276	34,326.67
Daniel Berger	67	71	69	69	276	34,326.66
Roberto Castro	64	71	69	72	276	34,326.66
Robert Streb	67	69	69	71	276	34,326.66
Keegan Bradley	63	71	72	71	277	22,977.34
Kevin Tway	67	70	74	66	277	22,977.34
Jonas Blixt	67	67	70	73	277	22,977.33
Ben Crane	69	65	71	72	277	22,977.33
J.J. Spaun	67	70	69	71	277	22,977.33
Peter Uihlein	67	71	67	72	277	22,977.33
Cody Gribble	69	68	72	69	278	18,189.34
Martin Laird	69	69	72	68	278	18,189.34
Brian Harman	69	65	71	73	278	18,189.33
Colt Knost	67	71	69	71	278	18,189.33
Brooks Koepka	70	66	72	70	278	18,189.33
Scott Langley	67	68	70	73	278	18,189.33
Jim Knous	68	69	71	71	279	17,176
Adam Schenk	66	68	73	72	279	17,176
Roger Sloan	68	70	68	73	279	17,176
Dylan Frittelli	67	68	75	70	280	16,872
Tyler Duncan	69	68	74	70	281	16,568
George McNeill	69	68	72	72	281	16,568
Sepp Straka	68	65	72	76	281	16,568
Brian Gay	72	66	73	71	282	15,960
Alex Noren	67	71	73	71	282	15,960
Josh Teater	68	68	72	74	282	15,960
D.J. Trahan	67	68	75	72	282	15,960
Bubba Watson	71	67	73	71	282	15,960
Dominic Bozzelli	69	69	77	69	284	15,504
Richard Jung	67	69	75	74	285	15,352
Jake Knapp	69	69	75	74	287	15,200
Kelly Kraft	68	70	76	76	290	15,048

U.S. Open Championship

Pebble Beach Golf Links, Pebble Beach, California
Par 35-36–71; 7,075 yards

June 13-16
purse, $12,500,000

	SCORES				TOTAL	MONEY
Gary Woodland	68	65	69	69	271	$2,250,000
Brooks Koepka	69	69	68	68	274	1,350,000
Jon Rahm	69	70	70	68	277	581,872
Chez Reavie	68	70	68	71	277	581,872
Justin Rose	65	70	68	74	277	581,872
Xander Schauffele	66	73	71	67	277	581,872
Louis Oosthuizen	66	70	70	72	278	367,387
Adam Scott	70	69	71	68	278	367,387
Chesson Hadley	68	70	70	71	279	288,715
Rory McIlroy	68	69	70	72	279	288,715
Henrik Stenson	68	71	70	70	279	288,715
Matthew Fitzpatrick	69	71	72	68	280	226,609
Matt Wallace	70	68	71	71	280	226,609
Danny Willett	71	71	67	71	280	226,609
Viktor Hovland [A]	69	73	71	67	280	
Byeong Hun An	70	72	68	71	281	172,455
Matt Kuchar	69	69	70	73	281	172,455
Graeme McDowell	69	70	70	72	281	172,455
Francesco Molinari	68	72	71	70	281	172,455

	SCORES				TOTAL	MONEY
Webb Simpson	74	68	73	66	281	172,455
Patrick Cantlay	73	71	68	70	282	117,598
Paul Casey	70	72	73	67	282	117,598
Jason Day	70	73	70	69	282	117,598
Tyrrell Hatton	70	74	69	69	282	117,598
Hideki Matsuyama	69	73	70	70	282	117,598
Alex Prugh	75	69	70	68	282	117,598
Tiger Woods	70	72	71	69	282	117,598
Jim Furyk	73	67	72	71	283	86,071
Nate Lashley	67	74	70	72	283	86,071
Shane Lowry	75	69	70	69	283	86,071
Sepp Straka	68	72	76	67	283	86,071
Billy Horschel	73	70	71	70	284	72,928
Marcus Kinhult	74	70	74	66	284	72,928
Patrick Reed	71	73	72	68	284	72,928
Bryson DeChambeau	69	74	73	69	285	57,853
Jason Dufner	70	71	73	71	285	57,853
Dustin Johnson	71	69	71	74	285	57,853
Martin Kaymer	69	75	71	70	285	57,853
Marc Leishman	69	74	70	72	285	57,853
Collin Morikawa	71	73	72	69	285	57,853
Aaron Wise	66	71	79	69	285	57,853
Brandon Wu [A]	71	69	71	74	285	
Rickie Fowler	66	77	71	72	286	41,500
Tom Hoge	71	73	71	71	286	41,500
Andrew Putnam	73	71	73	69	286	41,500
Rory Sabbatini	72	71	73	70	286	41,500
Nick Taylor	74	70	70	72	286	41,500
Erik van Rooyen	71	73	72	70	286	41,500
Abraham Ancer	74	68	69	76	287	31,385
Daniel Berger	73	70	74	70	287	31,385
Kevin Kisner	73	70	75	69	287	31,385
Sergio Garcia	69	70	75	74	288	27,181
Charles Howell	72	70	74	72	288	27,181
Haotong Li	71	70	72	75	288	27,181
Phil Mickelson	72	69	75	72	288	27,181
Carlos Ortiz	70	70	75	73	288	27,181
Scott Piercy	67	72	72	77	288	27,181
Adri Arnaus	69	75	73	72	289	25,350
Charlie Danielson	72	70	77	70	289	25,350
Harris English	71	69	76	73	289	25,350
Emiliano Grillo	68	74	74	73	289	25,350
Zach Johnson	70	69	79	71	289	25,350
Andy Pope	72	71	75	71	289	25,350
Chandler Eaton [A]	72	70	73	74	289	
Rafa Cabrera Bello	70	74	74	72	290	23,851
Tommy Fleetwood	71	73	73	73	290	23,851
Jordan Spieth	72	69	73	76	290	23,851
Kyle Stanley	71	73	75	71	290	23,851
Brian Stuard	71	73	74	72	290	23,851
Justin Walters	72	72	77	69	290	23,851
Rhys Enoch	78	66	71	76	291	22,977
Luke Donald	72	70	77	73	292	22,353
Billy Hurley	73	70	73	76	292	22,353
Cameron Smith	71	72	77	72	292	22,353
Clement Sordet	76	68	74	74	292	22,353
Bernd Wiesberger	71	73	78	72	294	21,728
Brandt Snedeker	75	69	74	77	295	21,478
Chip McDaniel	71	73	76	77	297	21,224
Michael Thorbjornsen [A]	71	73	84	76	304	

Out of Final 36 Holes

Joseph Bramlett	73	72	145	Keegan Bradley	73	76	149
Lucas Glover	73	72	145	Luis Gagne	71	78	149
Nick Hardy	73	72	145	Stewart Hagestad	74	75	149
Matt Jones	74	71	145	Daniel Hillier	76	73	149
Rob Oppenheim	73	72	145	J.B. Holmes	72	77	149
Ollie Schniederjans	75	70	145	Sam Horsfield	75	74	149
Lee Slattery	73	72	145	Kevin Na	72	77	149
Spencer Tibbits	74	71	145	Renato Paratore	75	74	149
Julian Etulain	76	70	146	Mito Pereira	77	72	149
Tony Finau	74	72	146	Jhonattan Vegas	72	77	149
Branden Grace	75	71	146	Connor Arendell	77	73	150
Justin Harding	73	73	146	Luke Guthrie	75	75	150
Luke List	74	72	146	Shugo Imahira	75	75	150
Keith Mitchell	76	70	146	Si Woo Kim	76	74	150
Ian Poulter	73	73	146	Kyoung-Hoon Lee	76	74	150
Jovan Rebula	70	76	146	Richard Lee	72	78	150
Scottie Scheffler	72	74	146	Kevin O'Connell	76	74	150
Hayden Shieh	77	69	146	Bubba Watson	75	75	150
Justin Thomas	73	73	146	Brian Davis	75	76	151
Brendon Todd	72	74	146	Anirban Lahiri	74	77	151
David Toms	72	74	146	Matt Parziale	74	77	151
Jimmy Walker	75	71	146	Cameron Young	75	76	151
Aaron Baddeley	72	75	147	Marcus Fraser	73	79	152
Dean Burmester	76	71	147	Chan Kim	77	75	152
Joel Dahmen	75	72	147	Thomas Pieters	76	76	152
Austin Eckroat	72	75	147	Ryan Sullivan	73	79	152
Ryan Fox	74	73	147	Brett Drewitt	77	76	153
Patton Kizzire	80	67	147	Matthew Naumec	74	79	153
Alex Noren	75	72	147	C.T. Pan	80	73	153
Matthieu Pavon	73	74	147	Kodai Ichihara	80	74	154
Sam Saunders	72	75	147	Lucas Bjerregaard	80	75	155
Chun-An Yu	74	73	147	Zac Blair	83	72	155
Ernie Els	75	73	148	Roberto Castro	78	77	155
Cody Gribble	74	74	148	Noah Norton	80	75	155
Mikumu Horikawa	73	75	148	Andreas Halvorsen	74	82	156
Thorbjorn Olesen	71	77	148	Merrick Bremner	79	79	158
Callum Tarren	73	75	148	Eric Dietrich	83	75	158
Mike Weir	74	74	148	Devon Bling	82	80	162
Kiradech Aphibarnrat	75	74	149				

Travelers Championship

TPC River Highlands, Cromwell, Connecticut
Par 35-35–70; 6,841 yards

June 20-23
purse, $7,200,000

	SCORES			TOTAL	MONEY
Chez Reavie	65 66 63 69			263	$1,296,000
Keegan Bradley	65 66 69 67			267	633,600
Zack Sucher	64 65 71 67			267	633,600
Vaughn Taylor	68 66 69 65			268	345,600
Paul Casey	65 68 71 65			269	262,800
Joaquin Niemann	69 65 69 66			269	262,800
Kevin Tway	68 68 66 67			269	262,800
Abraham Ancer	64 73 70 63			270	194,400
Jason Day	70 63 68 69			270	194,400
Bryson DeChambeau	68 70 64 68			270	194,400
Roberto Diaz	69 65 67 69			270	194,400
Brian Harman	72 66 66 66			270	194,400
Tommy Fleetwood	66 69 67 69			271	144,000
Kyoung-Hoon Lee	64 72 67 68			271	144,000

	SCORES				TOTAL	MONEY
Patrick Cantlay	66	72	65	69	272	115,200
Wyndham Clark	68	67	68	69	272	115,200
Kevin Kisner	69	65	71	67	272	115,200
Ryan Moore	68	64	72	68	272	115,200
Kevin Streelman	67	67	69	69	272	115,200
Alex Prugh	68	68	68	69	273	93,600
Cody Gribble	69	69	67	69	274	65,760
Sungjae Im	68	69	71	66	274	65,760
Russell Knox	69	69	71	65	274	65,760
Martin Laird	67	67	68	72	274	65,760
Marc Leishman	66	70	70	68	274	65,760
Adam Long	66	67	70	71	274	65,760
Brendan Steele	71	67	68	68	274	65,760
Robert Streb	65	68	71	70	274	65,760
Harold Varner	69	66	72	67	274	65,760
Freddie Jacobson	70	65	72	68	275	43,740
Stephan Jaeger	70	68	70	67	275	43,740
Peter Malnati	66	70	69	70	275	43,740
Patrick Reed	68	66	70	71	275	43,740
J.J. Spaun	68	69	66	72	275	43,740
Nick Watney	66	69	69	71	275	43,740
Collin Morikawa	66	67	75	68	276	32,451.43
Louis Oosthuizen	66	68	74	68	276	32,451.43
C.T. Pan	67	70	71	68	276	32,451.43
Kyle Stanley	67	68	73	68	276	32,451.43
Josh Teater	68	68	69	71	276	32,451.43
Justin Thomas	68	68	70	70	276	32,451.43
Ryan Blaum	67	67	69	73	276	32,451.42
Sangmoon Bae	68	70	69	70	277	21,924
Sam Burns	67	69	72	69	277	21,924
Joel Dahmen	70	68	69	70	277	21,924
Cameron Davis	70	68	69	70	277	21,924
Tyler Duncan	67	70	71	69	277	21,924
Andrew Landry	67	71	65	74	277	21,924
Chip McDaniel	69	68	68	72	277	21,924
Brandt Snedeker	68	69	71	69	277	21,924
Mackenzie Hughes	64	74	69	71	278	17,328
Hank Lebioda	69	65	74	70	278	17,328
Sam Ryder	67	67	74	70	278	17,328
Ryan Armour	64	71	71	73	279	16,560
Viktor Hovland	67	71	68	73	279	16,560
Bubba Watson	69	66	73	71	279	16,560
Brooks Koepka	71	66	72	71	280	16,128
Francesco Molinari	69	69	71	71	280	16,128
Andrew Putnam	66	67	71	76	280	16,128
Scott Brown	67	67	70	77	281	15,480
Bronson Burgoon	64	68	75	74	281	15,480
Emiliano Grillo	67	71	71	72	281	15,480
Brandon Harkins	66	72	70	73	281	15,480
Kramer Hickok	70	68	69	74	281	15,480
Richy Werenski	67	69	72	73	281	15,480
Scott Langley	65	73	68	76	282	14,904
Seamus Power	66	70	71	75	282	14,904
Brady Schnell	65	68	75	75	283	14,688
Seth Reeves	68	70	70	77	285	14,544
Sam Saunders	67	67	72	80	286	14,400
Harris English	72	66	72		210	13,824
Jim Herman	67	70	73		210	13,824
Matt Jones	69	69	72		210	13,824
Troy Merritt	70	65	75		210	13,824
Shawn Stefani	68	69	73		210	13,824
Nick Taylor	69	69	72		210	13,824
Cameron Tringale	66	69	75		210	13,824

	SCORES			TOTAL	MONEY
Beau Hossler	69	69	73	211	13,176
Sung Kang	68	70	73	211	13,176
Tom Hoge	67	69	76	212	12,888
Matthew Wolff	70	68	74	212	12,888
Alex Cejka	69	69	75	213	12,672

Rocket Mortgage Classic

Detroit Golf Club, Detroit, Michigan
Par 36-36–72; 7,340 yards

June 27-30
purse, $7,300,000

	SCORES				TOTAL	MONEY
Nate Lashley	63	67	63	70	263	$1,314,000
Doc Redman	68	67	67	67	269	788,400
Wes Roach	67	68	67	68	270	423,400
Rory Sabbatini	65	69	68	68	270	423,400
Joaquin Niemann	68	66	69	68	271	239,075
Ted Potter, Jr.	68	67	68	68	271	239,075
Patrick Reed	68	68	65	70	271	239,075
Brandt Snedeker	70	69	65	67	271	239,075
Brian Stuard	66	72	65	68	271	239,075
Cameron Tringale	68	67	65	71	271	239,075
J.T. Poston	70	63	66	73	272	175,200
Sepp Straka	68	67	70	67	272	175,200
Byeong Hun An	68	66	69	70	273	136,875
Viktor Hovland	70	69	70	64	273	136,875
Hideki Matsuyama	68	67	68	70	273	136,875
J.J. Spaun	66	73	68	66	273	136,875
Wyndham Clark	68	70	68	68	274	105,850
Brice Garnett	69	67	71	67	274	105,850
Talor Gooch	65	72	67	70	274	105,850
Billy Horschel	69	70	71	64	274	105,850
J.B. Holmes	67	68	70	70	275	68,528.75
Mackenzie Hughes	66	70	72	67	275	68,528.75
Sungjae Im	69	68	66	72	275	68,528.75
Danny Lee	66	71	69	69	275	68,528.75
Denny McCarthy	69	68	69	69	275	68,528.75
Roger Sloan	70	68	69	68	275	68,528.75
Kyle Stanley	69	69	70	67	275	68,528.75
Jimmy Walker	68	71	70	66	275	68,528.75
Jonas Blixt	67	68	72	69	276	46,415.84
Cameron Smith	70	68	71	67	276	46,415.84
Joey Garber	67	72	68	69	276	46,415.83
Jason Kokrak	66	71	68	71	276	46,415.83
Peter Malnati	68	66	68	74	276	46,415.83
Martin Piller	66	69	71	70	276	46,415.83
Bronson Burgoon	66	70	72	69	277	34,466.43
Shawn Stefani	69	70	68	70	277	34,466.43
Kevin Streelman	66	70	68	73	277	34,466.43
Nick Taylor	68	70	69	70	277	34,466.43
Josh Teater	68	69	73	67	277	34,466.43
Aaron Wise	69	69	67	72	277	34,466.43
Charles Howell	65	67	71	74	277	34,466.42
Sam Burns	70	67	71	70	278	26,280
Max Homa	68	69	71	70	278	26,280
Anirban Lahiri	69	68	72	69	278	26,280
Adam Schenk	65	71	71	71	278	26,280
Ryan Armour	64	69	74	72	279	18,980
Cameron Champ	66	65	75	73	279	18,980
Luke Donald	67	69	72	71	279	18,980

	SCORES				TOTAL	MONEY
Rickie Fowler	68	68	72	71	279	18,980
Dylan Frittelli	66	70	72	71	279	18,980
Kevin Kisner	66	70	72	71	279	18,980
Vaughn Taylor	70	69	69	71	279	18,980
Nick Watney	64	72	69	74	279	18,980
Chase Wright	65	70	73	71	279	18,980
Harris English	66	68	71	75	280	16,571
Carlos Ortiz	67	70	74	69	280	16,571
Seth Reeves	68	71	71	70	280	16,571
Brendan Steele	68	70	71	71	280	16,571
Dominic Bozzelli	69	69	75	68	281	15,914
Roberto Castro	70	69	72	70	281	15,914
Bud Cauley	69	69	72	71	281	15,914
Colt Knost	70	68	72	71	281	15,914
Andrew Landry	71	67	70	73	281	15,914
Anders Albertson	69	67	76	70	282	15,184
Chad Collins	67	72	70	73	282	15,184
Tom Hoge	67	70	73	72	282	15,184
Wes Homan	71	68	71	72	282	15,184
Scott Stallings	66	72	70	74	282	15,184
Kyle Jones	70	69	74	70	283	14,746
Stewart Cink	65	73	72	74	284	14,600
Smylie Kaufman	69	70	80	69	288	14,454

3M Open

TPC Twin Cities, Blaine, Minnesota
Par 35-36–71; 7,468 yards

July 4-7
purse, $6,400,000

	SCORES				TOTAL	MONEY
Matthew Wolff	69	67	62	65	263	$1,152,000
Bryson DeChambeau	66	62	70	66	264	563,200
Collin Morikawa	68	66	64	66	264	563,200
Adam Hadwin	64	66	69	67	266	307,200
Wyndham Clark	66	69	64	68	267	243,200
Carlos Ortiz	67	67	69	64	267	243,200
Sam Burns	66	66	72	64	268	179,733.34
Lucas Glover	67	72	67	62	268	179,733.34
Joey Garber	73	65	65	65	268	179,733.33
Brian Harman	65	67	71	65	268	179,733.33
Hideki Matsuyama	64	70	66	68	268	179,733.33
Troy Merritt	70	64	66	68	268	179,733.33
Fabian Gomez	68	68	68	65	269	128,000
Viktor Hovland	69	66	69	65	269	128,000
Daniel Berger	68	66	69	67	270	92,960
Scott Brown	68	65	68	69	270	92,960
Charlie Danielson	73	66	64	67	270	92,960
Sungjae Im	65	70	68	67	270	92,960
Scott Piercy	62	70	69	69	270	92,960
Roger Sloan	67	67	67	69	270	92,960
Shawn Stefani	69	66	68	67	270	92,960
Adam Svensson	70	64	69	67	270	92,960
Brice Garnett	67	71	67	66	271	49,105.46
Tom Hoge	68	71	65	67	271	49,105.46
Denny McCarthy	66	68	70	67	271	49,105.46
Sam Saunders	65	67	72	67	271	49,105.46
Chase Wright	69	66	69	67	271	49,105.46
Arjun Atwal	65	68	68	70	271	49,105.45
Tony Finau	66	68	69	68	271	49,105.45
Charles Howell	68	66	66	71	271	49,105.45

	SCORES				TOTAL	MONEY
Joaquin Niemann	73	63	65	70	271	49,105.45
Patrick Reed	69	67	68	67	271	49,105.45
Johnson Wagner	69	69	64	69	271	49,105.45
Bronson Burgoon	73	64	67	68	272	30,960
Bud Cauley	71	67	68	66	272	30,960
Beau Hossler	68	71	65	68	272	30,960
Patton Kizzire	65	74	67	66	272	30,960
Hank Lebioda	69	68	67	68	272	30,960
Sam Ryder	69	66	71	66	272	30,960
Robert Streb	68	70	67	67	272	30,960
Kevin Streelman	68	65	69	70	272	30,960
Ryan Armour	66	71	69	67	273	23,040
Kramer Hickok	68	69	68	68	273	23,040
Martin Laird	70	67	71	65	273	23,040
Cameron Tringale	66	71	67	69	273	23,040
Keegan Bradley	70	68	69	67	274	17,115.43
Roberto Castro	69	69	67	69	274	17,115.43
Corey Conners	70	64	70	70	274	17,115.43
Peter Malnati	67	70	70	67	274	17,115.43
Nick Taylor	67	69	70	68	274	17,115.43
Richy Werenski	71	67	70	66	274	17,115.43
Dylan Frittelli	66	69	66	73	274	17,115.42
Brendan Steele	66	68	73	68	275	14,890.67
Tyrone Van Aswegen	69	70	69	67	275	14,890.67
Pat Perez	67	72	67	69	275	14,890.66
Brian Gay	67	72	68	69	276	14,528
Rod Pampling	70	69	68	69	276	14,528
David Hearn	70	67	69	71	277	13,952
Kyle Jones	70	69	69	69	277	13,952
Satoshi Kodaira	70	67	70	70	277	13,952
Tom Lehman	67	69	68	73	277	13,952
Curtis Luck	68	65	73	71	277	13,952
Zack Sucher	68	71	68	70	277	13,952
Justin Suh	67	68	73	69	277	13,952
Brooks Koepka	67	72	67	72	278	13,440
Jason Day	69	70	69	71	279	12,992
Jason Dufner	70	65	70	74	279	12,992
Mackenzie Hughes	67	68	72	72	279	12,992
Stephan Jaeger	69	68	69	73	279	12,992
Keith Mitchell	69	66	69	75	279	12,992
J.J. Spaun	68	70	69	72	279	12,992
Sebastian Munoz	70	66	67	77	280	12,544
Talor Gooch	69	70	67	75	281	12,416
Ryan Blaum	68	67	74		209	12,032
Robert Garrigus	71	67	71		209	12,032
Bill Haas	70	68	71		209	12,032
Scott Stallings	70	66	73		209	12,032
Jimmy Walker	69	70	70		209	12,032
Roberto Diaz	67	71	72		210	11,520
Matt Every	73	64	73		210	11,520
Max Homa	68	69	73		210	11,520
Anders Albertson	72	67	72		211	11,264
Tyler Duncan	70	68	74		212	11,136
Anirban Lahiri	71	67	75		213	11,008
Michael Thompson	71	67	76		214	10,880

John Deere Classic

TPC Deere Run, Silvis, Illinois
Par 35-36–71; 7,268 yards

July 11-14
purse, $6,000,000

	SCORES				TOTAL	MONEY
Dylan Frittelli	66	68	65	64	263	$1,080,000
Russell Henley	64	68	72	61	265	648,000
Andrew Landry	65	65	67	69	266	408,000
Collin Morikawa	70	66	65	66	267	264,000
Chris Stroud	68	66	66	67	267	264,000
Charles Howell	68	70	65	65	268	194,250
Adam Schenk	67	65	66	70	268	194,250
Vaughn Taylor	65	68	66	69	268	194,250
Nick Watney	68	67	64	69	268	194,250
Lucas Glover	67	64	69	69	269	133,000
Bill Haas	66	68	64	71	269	133,000
Joaquin Niemann	66	69	69	65	269	133,000
Wes Roach	69	67	66	67	269	133,000
Sam Saunders	68	69	67	65	269	133,000
Roger Sloan	68	65	67	69	269	133,000
Viktor Hovland	69	69	68	64	270	99,000
Cameron Tringale	66	66	65	73	270	99,000
Bud Cauley	67	67	68	69	271	70,500
Ryan Moore	67	67	65	72	271	70,500
Ryan Palmer	65	71	68	67	271	70,500
Sam Ryder	67	67	69	68	271	70,500
Scott Stallings	69	67	66	69	271	70,500
Kyle Stanley	68	66	68	69	271	70,500
Adam Svensson	70	65	68	68	271	70,500
Brendon Todd	66	71	67	67	271	70,500
Roberto Castro	68	68	69	67	272	42,600
Tyler Duncan	69	69	71	63	272	42,600
Brian Harman	67	67	71	67	272	42,600
Beau Hossler	67	68	70	67	272	42,600
Sungjae Im	68	67	67	70	272	42,600
Nate Lashley	67	71	65	69	272	42,600
Sepp Straka	70	67	64	71	272	42,600
Daniel Berger	66	66	72	69	273	33,150
Freddie Jacobson	67	70	69	67	273	33,150
Shawn Stefani	70	69	67	67	273	33,150
Nick Taylor	67	69	66	71	273	33,150
Brice Garnett	67	67	70	70	274	24,000
Zach Johnson	72	67	69	66	274	24,000
Martin Laird	65	69	70	70	274	24,000
Sebastian Munoz	70	68	64	72	274	24,000
Pat Perez	69	69	68	68	274	24,000
Doc Redman	69	65	72	68	274	24,000
Michael Thompson	71	67	68	68	274	24,000
Jhonattan Vegas	67	62	76	69	274	24,000
Johnson Wagner	68	68	73	65	274	24,000
Matthew Wolff	67	71	67	69	274	24,000
Sangmoon Bae	67	71	67	70	275	15,620
Bronson Burgoon	69	65	73	68	275	15,620
Brandon Harkins	67	70	70	68	275	15,620
Anirban Lahiri	74	65	68	68	275	15,620
Ollie Schniederjans	67	70	70	68	275	15,620
Richy Werenski	69	69	68	69	275	15,620
Cameron Davis	66	70	70	70	276	13,960
Adam Long	64	73	72	67	276	13,960
Harold Varner	67	65	76	68	276	13,960
Ryan Blaum	65	73	69	70	277	13,440
Luke Donald	68	68	70	71	277	13,440

	SCORES				TOTAL	MONEY
Tom Lovelady	71	68	70	68	277	13,440
Peter Malnati	67	68	71	71	277	13,440
Zack Sucher	65	74	70	68	277	13,440
J.J. Henry	69	68	71	70	278	13,020
Seamus Power	69	65	75	69	278	13,020
Stewart Cink	68	66	73	72	279	12,720
Billy Hurley	72	67	67	73	279	12,720
Whee Kim	68	70	70	71	279	12,720
Kelly Kraft	70	67	71	72	280	12,480
Austin Cook	66	72	71	72	281	12,240
Derek Fathauer	70	69	70	72	281	12,240
Josh Teater	70	69	70	72	281	12,240
John Senden	67	71	71	74	283	12,000
Wyndham Clark	68	71	71		210	11,760
Martin Piller	70	69	71		210	11,760
Ted Potter, Jr.	66	71	73		210	11,760
Roberto Diaz	62	73	76		211	11,280
Joey Garber	69	70	72		211	11,280
Talor Gooch	69	69	73		211	11,280
Dicky Pride	71	68	72		211	11,280
Seth Reeves	71	68	72		211	11,280
Anders Albertson	72	66	74		212	10,920
Chad Campbell	67	72	74		213	10,800

The 148th Open Championship

See European Tours chapter.

Barbasol Championship

Keene Trace Golf Club, Nicholasville, Kentucky
Par 36-36–72; 7,328 yards

July 18-21
purse, $3,500,000

	SCORES				TOTAL	MONEY
Jim Herman	65	65	62	70	262	$630,000
Kelly Kraft	65	67	61	70	263	378,000
Sepp Straka	68	68	63	66	265	238,000
Austin Cook	67	66	63	70	266	154,000
Matt Jones	66	70	67	63	266	154,000
Martin Laird	68	66	70	63	267	117,250
Josh Teater	65	70	64	68	267	117,250
D.J. Trahan	65	67	69	66	267	117,250
Dominic Bozzelli	67	68	65	68	268	98,000
Sebastian Munoz	65	68	66	69	268	98,000
Cameron Davis	67	69	69	64	269	77,000
Bill Haas	65	66	65	73	269	77,000
Denny McCarthy	67	69	67	66	269	77,000
Jose de Jesus Rodriguez	68	65	69	67	269	77,000
Ryan Blaum	68	70	65	67	270	59,500
Kyle Jones	67	71	65	67	270	59,500
Nick Taylor	63	72	69	66	270	59,500
Anders Albertson	66	70	67	68	271	47,250
Jason Dufner	67	70	68	66	271	47,250
Brice Garnett	69	67	68	67	271	47,250
Adam Schenk	70	66	70	65	271	47,250
Roberto Castro	65	69	70	68	272	37,800
Stephan Jaeger	68	70	65	69	272	37,800
Kramer Hickok	65	67	70	71	273	29,050
Billy Hurley	68	67	67	71	273	29,050

	SCORES				TOTAL	MONEY
Ted Potter, Jr.	71	68	69	65	273	29,050
Zack Sucher	70	65	69	69	273	29,050
Richy Werenski	69	67	70	67	273	29,050
Harris English	72	66	68	68	274	21,775
Cody Gribble	68	66	70	70	274	21,775
Scott Langley	69	68	68	69	274	21,775
J.T. Poston	62	73	69	70	274	21,775
Alex Prugh	68	69	66	71	274	21,775
David Toms	68	64	73	69	274	21,775
Chase Wright	67	67	72	68	274	21,775
Fabian Gomez	71	68	70	66	275	17,208.34
Tom Hoge	67	69	68	71	275	17,208.33
Tom Lovelady	69	65	68	73	275	17,208.33
John Chin	73	66	67	70	276	14,000
Chris Couch	70	69	69	68	276	14,000
Tommy Gainey	72	68	65	71	276	14,000
Ben Silverman	70	68	65	73	276	14,000
Shawn Stefani	69	70	65	72	276	14,000
Tyrone Van Aswegen	70	66	72	68	276	14,000
Ricky Barnes	66	70	72	69	277	9,633.75
Charlie Beljan	68	66	72	71	277	9,633.75
Case Cochran	71	64	68	74	277	9,633.75
David Hearn	69	69	68	71	277	9,633.75
Whee Kim	69	70	68	70	277	9,633.75
Hunter Mahan	70	70	69	68	277	9,633.75
Wes Roach	64	69	75	69	277	9,633.75
Stephen Stallings, Jr.	70	68	69	70	277	9,633.75
Ryan Armour	70	67	72	69	278	7,882
Daniel Chopra	67	73	68	70	278	7,882
Brandon Harkins	68	72	68	70	278	7,882
Satoshi Kodaira	67	72	71	68	278	7,882
Nicholas Lindheim	69	70	69	70	278	7,882
George McNeill	71	67	73	67	278	7,882
Rod Pampling	68	71	68	71	278	7,882
Seamus Power	69	69	72	68	278	7,882
Brendon Todd	70	70	71	67	278	7,882
Peter Uihlein	69	69	71	69	278	7,882
Cullan Brown [A]	72	68	67	71	278	
Jonathan Byrd	73	66	68	72	279	7,385
Julian Etulain	69	70	72	68	279	7,385
Robert Garrigus	70	65	72	72	279	7,385
Jhonattan Vegas	69	69	70	71	279	7,385
Chip McDaniel	71	67	72	70	280	7,210
Boo Weekley	68	72	71	71	282	7,140
Freddie Jacobson	67	68	72	76	283	7,035
Hank Lebioda	70	64	76	73	283	7,035
Arjun Atwal	71	69	70	76	286	6,930
Peter Malnati	70	68	74		212	6,825
Charlie Wi	71	69	72		212	6,825
John Merrick	69	67	77		213	6,685
Heath Slocum	71	69	73		213	6,685
Sam Saunders	70	70	74		214	6,580
Will MacKenzie	67	69	79		215	6,510
Johnson Wagner	69	71	77		217	6,440

WGC - FedEx St. Jude Invitational

TPC Southwind, Memphis, Tennessee
Par 35-35–70; 7,237 yards

July 25-28
purse, $10,250,000

	SCORES				TOTAL	MONEY
Brooks Koepka	68	67	64	65	264	$1,745,000
Webb Simpson	69	66	68	64	267	1,095,000
Marc Leishman	69	69	63	67	268	602,000
Tommy Fleetwood	68	70	65	66	269	384,333.34
Matthew Fitzpatrick	67	64	69	69	269	384,333.33
Rory McIlroy	69	67	62	71	269	384,333.33
Jon Rahm	62	71	68	69	270	273,000
Ian Poulter	66	69	67	69	271	242,000
Billy Horschel	67	66	69	70	272	205,000
Bubba Watson	65	70	68	69	272	205,000
Justin Rose	67	68	70	68	273	183,000
Rafa Cabrera Bello	70	71	67	66	274	143,625
Patrick Cantlay	65	68	73	68	274	143,625
Alex Noren	66	69	66	73	274	143,625
Aaron Rai	72	69	66	67	274	143,625
Patrick Reed	73	66	67	68	274	143,625
Cameron Smith	65	68	73	68	274	143,625
Jordan Spieth	70	70	66	68	274	143,625
Justin Thomas	68	69	66	71	274	143,625
Dustin Johnson	69	69	69	68	275	113,500
Nate Lashley	66	70	71	68	275	113,500
Haotong Li	69	69	67	70	275	113,500
Louis Oosthuizen	73	69	66	67	275	113,500
Adam Long	71	70	67	68	276	103,000
Andrew Putnam	66	71	72	67	276	103,000
Matthew Wolff	72	70	65	69	276	103,000
Paul Casey	70	71	69	67	277	86,250
Corey Conners	67	71	70	69	277	86,250
Tony Finau	70	71	68	68	277	86,250
Jim Furyk	74	65	70	68	277	86,250
Shugo Imahira	65	69	71	72	277	86,250
Kevin Kisner	77	67	66	67	277	86,250
Thorbjorn Olesen	66	71	65	75	277	86,250
Chez Reavie	68	70	68	71	277	86,250
Xander Schauffele	69	70	69	69	277	86,250
Brandt Snedeker	69	73	69	66	277	86,250
Henrik Stenson	69	67	72	69	277	86,250
Matt Wallace	70	69	65	73	277	86,250
Keith Mitchell	73	70	71	64	278	76,000
Jason Day	72	69	68	70	279	74,000
Sergio Garcia	69	71	70	69	279	74,000
Adam Scott	70	68	74	67	279	74,000
Justin Harding	72	70	64	74	280	70,000
Tyrrell Hatton	66	71	69	74	280	70,000
Matt Kuchar	70	70	71	69	280	70,000
Hideki Matsuyama	65	71	72	72	280	70,000
Kevin Na	70	66	70	74	280	70,000
Bryson DeChambeau	67	74	72	68	281	66,000
C.T. Pan	72	70	70	69	281	66,000
Danny Willett	69	72	70	70	281	66,000
Lucas Bjerregaard	69	74	72	69	284	63,000
Philip Eriksson	73	72	72	67	284	63,000
Eddie Pepperell	70	74	66	74	284	63,000
J.B. Holmes	76	71	68	70	285	61,000
Kodai Ichihara	71	70	75	70	286	59,500
Gary Woodland	73	71	70	72	286	59,500
Phil Mickelson	68	73	73	74	288	58,000

	SCORES				TOTAL	MONEY
Mikumu Horikawa	75	77	66	72	290	56,500
Poom Saksansin	68	73	75	74	290	56,500
Sung Kang	69	75	73	74	291	55,000
Keegan Bradley	74	78	65	75	292	53,500
Max Homa	74	73	77	68	292	53,500
Kevin Tway	76	77	74	70	297	52,000

Barracuda Championship

Montreux Golf & Country Club, Reno, Nevada
Par 36-36–72; 7,472 yards

July 25-28
purse, $3,500,000

	POINTS				TOTAL	MONEY
Collin Morikawa	13	7	13	14	47	$630,000
Troy Merritt	7	12	18	7	44	378,000
John Chin	9	11	11	9	40	203,000
Robert Streb	13	12	10	5	40	203,000
Bronson Burgoon	12	2	10	15	39	140,000
Tom Hoge	13	8	7	10	38	126,000
Charlie Danielson	5	12	10	10	37	105,437.50
Martin Laird	5	12	11	9	37	105,437.50
Ryan Palmer	8	7	14	8	37	105,437.50
Roger Sloan	10	11	9	7	37	105,437.50
Sebastian Munoz	4	8	9	15	36	87,500
Sepp Straka	1	14	7	13	35	80,500
George McNeill	6	16	2	10	34	70,000
Josh Teater	10	5	10	9	34	70,000
Jonathan Byrd	10	7	12	4	33	59,500
Russell Henley	3	9	9	12	33	59,500
Chris Stroud	10	8	8	7	33	59,500
Alex Cejka	6	9	13	4	32	42,600
Roberto Diaz	5	3	8	16	32	42,600
Emiliano Grillo	8	8	10	6	32	42,600
Kyle Jones	5	6	7	14	32	42,600
Cameron Tringale	7	7	15	3	32	42,600
Peter Uihlein	3	13	9	7	32	42,600
Chase Wright	7	4	8	13	32	42,600
Dominic Bozzelli	9	-1	11	12	31	26,716.67
Billy Hurley	0	11	7	13	31	26,716.67
Andrea Pavan	4	9	11	7	31	26,716.66
Seamus Power	11	4	11	5	31	26,716.66
Brendon Todd	8	11	1	11	31	26,716.67
Johnson Wagner	4	4	13	10	31	26,716.67
Will Gordon	11	7	11	1	30	21,218.75
Martin Kaymer	3	7	11	9	30	21,218.75
Kyoung-Hoon Lee	8	7	11	4	30	21,218.75
Tom Lovelady	9	5	9	7	30	21,218.75
Brandon Harkins	3	11	14	1	29	18,025
Beau Hossler	8	12	3	6	29	18,025
Denny McCarthy	5	12	8	4	29	18,025
Matt Every	5	9	8	6	28	16,450
John Rollins	7	4	4	12	27	15,400
Brendan Steele	2	13	0	12	27	15,400
Nicholas Lindheim	8	1	15	2	26	13,300
D.J. Trahan	1	12	12	1	26	13,300
Tyrone Van Aswegen	13	-1	13	1	26	13,300
Richy Werenski	10	7	4	5	26	13,300
Sam Ryder	3	7	6	9	25	11,550
Wes Roach	7	4	0	13	24	10,500
J.J. Spaun	3	12	4	5	24	10,500

	POINTS				TOTAL	MONEY
Jonas Blixt	4	7	7	5	23	9,170
David Lingmerth	18	2	-3	6	23	9,170
Seth Reeves	9	7	0	7	23	9,170
Sangmoon Bae	5	7	5	5	22	8,423.33
Jim Herman	5	5	5	7	22	8,423.33
Andres Romero	5	3	1	13	22	8,423.34
Ryan Blaum	5	7	7	2	21	8,015
David Hearn	3	7	9	2	21	8,015
Zack Sucher	1	14	1	5	21	8,015
Y.E. Yang	12	1	3	5	21	8,015
Daniel Berger	1	8	-2	13	20	7,840
Patrick Rodgers	7	3	5	4	19	7,735
Sam Saunders	5	10	5	-1	19	7,735
Tommy Gainey	9	8	5	-4	18	7,560
Bill Haas	4	4	6	4	18	7,560
Pat Perez	4	7	1	6	18	7,560
Tyler Duncan	-2	11	0	8	17	7,420
Adam Svensson	6	3	3	2	14	7,350
Alistair Docherty	5	9	5	-6	13	7,280
Robert Allenby	5	7	-2	2	12	7,175
Harris English	0	8	2	2	12	7,175
John Daly	-2	12	4	-4	10	7,070
Cody Gribble	6	3	-5	4	8	7,000
Trent Phillips [A]	3	6	0	-4	5	
Omar Uresti	2	6	0	-3	5	6,930
Chip McDaniel	-3	12	-4	-3	2	6,860

Wyndham Championship

Sedgefield Country Club, Greensboro, North Carolina
Par 35-35–70; 7,127 yards

August 1-4
purse, $6,200,000

	SCORES				TOTAL	MONEY
J.T. Poston	65	65	66	62	258	$1,116,000
Webb Simpson	64	65	65	65	259	669,600
Byeong Hun An	62	65	66	67	260	421,600
Viktor Hovland	66	66	64	65	261	297,600
Si Woo Kim	66	65	68	64	263	248,000
Josh Teater	64	65	71	64	264	181,128.58
Brice Garnett	64	64	66	70	264	181,128.57
Brian Harman	67	65	66	66	264	181,128.57
Billy Horschel	68	67	65	64	264	181,128.57
Sungjae Im	62	67	70	65	264	181,128.57
Jason Kokrak	70	64	64	66	264	181,128.57
Rory Sabbatini	63	68	66	67	264	181,128.57
Joaquin Niemann	67	66	69	63	265	109,533.34
Kyle Stanley	65	69	67	64	265	109,533.34
Paul Casey	65	65	66	69	265	109,533.33
Fabian Gomez	67	64	66	68	265	109,533.33
Patton Kizzire	65	64	69	67	265	109,533.33
Johnson Wagner	63	69	67	66	265	109,533.33
Roberto Diaz	67	68	65	66	266	80,600
Andrew Landry	65	68	65	68	266	80,600
Matthew Wolff	65	67	67	67	266	80,600
Bud Cauley	65	66	69	67	267	53,044.45
Cameron Davis	66	67	69	65	267	53,044.45
Denny McCarthy	65	69	68	65	267	53,044.45
Patrick Reed	68	66	70	63	267	53,044.45
Ryan Armour	64	66	65	72	267	53,044.44
Corey Conners	69	66	65	67	267	53,044.44

	SCORES				TOTAL	MONEY
Charles Howell	66	65	68	68	267	53,044.44
Mackenzie Hughes	63	66	69	69	267	53,044.44
Shawn Stefani	66	66	67	68	267	53,044.44
Russell Henley	69	64	67	68	268	36,766
Collin Morikawa	66	67	70	65	268	36,766
Scott Stallings	69	64	67	68	268	36,766
Brian Stuard	66	66	67	69	268	36,766
Adam Svensson	68	61	70	69	268	36,766
Paul Peterson	68	66	68	67	269	30,483.34
Brandon Harkins	68	64	69	68	269	30,483.33
Scott Piercy	69	66	66	68	269	30,483.33
Daniel Berger	69	67	67	67	270	22,940
Tyler Duncan	68	67	69	66	270	22,940
Harris English	68	68	70	64	270	22,940
Carlos Ortiz	69	64	66	71	270	22,940
Roger Sloan	69	66	70	65	270	22,940
Brandt Snedeker	64	70	68	68	270	22,940
Sepp Straka	65	66	67	72	270	22,940
Vaughn Taylor	68	66	68	68	270	22,940
Richy Werenski	68	68	68	66	270	22,940
Branden Grace	67	68	70	66	271	15,772.80
Russell Knox	67	68	69	67	271	15,772.80
Sebastian Munoz	69	66	68	68	271	15,772.80
Chez Reavie	66	67	68	70	271	15,772.80
Aaron Wise	71	64	65	71	271	15,772.80
Roberto Castro	66	68	69	69	272	14,153.72
Joel Dahmen	65	68	72	67	272	14,153.72
Zach Johnson	68	68	70	66	272	14,153.72
Bill Haas	66	68	69	69	272	14,153.71
Chesson Hadley	69	64	69	70	272	14,153.71
Anirban Lahiri	67	67	68	70	272	14,153.71
Wes Roach	67	68	68	69	272	14,153.71
Kiradech Aphibarnrat	64	72	69	68	273	13,144
Scott Brown	67	68	68	70	273	13,144
Alex Cejka	69	67	69	68	273	13,144
Alex Noren	69	67	69	68	273	13,144
Ted Potter, Jr.	64	70	71	68	273	13,144
Seamus Power	64	69	71	69	273	13,144
Jose de Jesus Rodriguez	67	67	70	69	273	13,144
Sam Ryder	68	68	70	67	273	13,144
Harold Varner	66	66	71	70	273	13,144
John Chin	67	67	70	70	274	12,400
J.J. Spaun	67	69	70	68	274	12,400
Boo Weekley	67	67	69	71	274	12,400
Austin Cook	66	68	66	75	275	12,028
Lucas Glover	67	68	71	69	275	12,028
Peter Uihlein	68	68	70	69	275	12,028
Michael Thompson	69	67	70	70	276	11,780
Mike Weir	67	69	68	74	278	11,656
Tom Hoge	66	69	72		207	11,532
Kyle Jones	67	69	72		208	11,284
Hank Lebioda	71	65	72		208	11,284
Jordan Spieth	64	67	77		208	11,284
Wyndham Clark	68	68	73		209	10,912
Alex Prugh	66	70	73		209	10,912
Patrick Rodgers	63	72	74		209	10,912

PGA Tour Playoffs for the FedExCup

The Northern Trust

Liberty National Golf Club, Jersey City, New Jersey
Par 36-35–71; 7,370 yards

August 8-11
purse, $9,250,000

	SCORES				TOTAL	MONEY
Patrick Reed	66	66	67	69	268	$1,665,000
Abraham Ancer	67	65	68	69	269	999,000
Jon Rahm	64	68	69	69	270	536,500
Harold Varner	67	67	68	68	270	536,500
Adam Scott	68	69	69	65	271	370,000
Rory McIlroy	65	68	70	69	272	299,468.75
Louis Oosthuizen	68	65	70	69	272	299,468.75
Brandt Snedeker	71	67	63	71	272	299,468.75
Jordan Spieth	67	64	74	67	272	299,468.75
Ian Poulter	68	66	71	68	273	240,500
Justin Rose	65	68	69	71	273	240,500
Patrick Cantlay	70	67	70	67	274	175,750
Kevin Kisner	64	70	72	68	274	175,750
Jason Kokrak	68	70	70	66	274	175,750
Troy Merritt	62	70	72	70	274	175,750
Andrew Putnam	69	64	74	67	274	175,750
Justin Thomas	67	68	71	68	274	175,750
Wyndham Clark	67	66	73	69	275	129,500
Ryan Moore	68	72	67	68	275	129,500
Webb Simpson	65	73	67	70	275	129,500
Cameron Champ	71	70	66	69	276	103,600
Corey Conners	66	71	70	69	276	103,600
Billy Horschel	72	67	67	70	276	103,600
Bryson DeChambeau	68	68	71	70	277	74,925
Dustin Johnson	63	67	74	73	277	74,925
C.T. Pan	68	67	72	70	277	74,925
Adam Schenk	67	72	71	67	277	74,925
Kevin Tway	68	73	71	65	277	74,925
Danny Willett	66	70	66	75	277	74,925
Branden Grace	68	73	71	66	278	53,765.63
Andrew Landry	68	67	73	70	278	53,765.63
Joaquin Niemann	70	71	71	66	278	53,765.63
Vaughn Taylor	69	68	73	68	278	53,765.63
Tony Finau	65	73	70	70	278	53,765.62
Matt Jones	67	71	68	72	278	53,765.62
Brooks Koepka	70	69	69	70	278	53,765.62
Hideki Matsuyama	68	68	70	72	278	53,765.62
Byeong Hun An	73	66	68	72	279	39,775
Max Homa	66	71	67	75	279	39,775
Sungjae Im	67	68	76	68	279	39,775
Chez Reavie	66	74	69	70	279	39,775
Jhonattan Vegas	72	69	71	67	279	39,775
Ryan Armour	70	68	70	72	280	27,565
Tommy Fleetwood	69	72	69	70	280	27,565
Dylan Frittelli	69	67	75	69	280	27,565
Lucas Glover	71	68	72	69	280	27,565
Chesson Hadley	66	72	73	69	280	27,565
Adam Hadwin	67	71	73	69	280	27,565
Sebastian Munoz	70	69	68	73	280	27,565
Rory Sabbatini	68	73	71	68	280	27,565
Aaron Wise	68	73	71	68	280	27,565
Brian Harman	68	71	70	72	281	21,354.29
J.B. Holmes	70	71	69	71	281	21,354.29

	SCORES				TOTAL	MONEY
Collin Morikawa	71	70	72	68	281	21,354.29
Gary Woodland	73	68	71	69	281	21,354.29
Jim Furyk	72	66	69	74	281	21,354.28
Shane Lowry	69	67	72	73	281	21,354.28
Brian Stuard	66	69	70	76	281	21,354.28
Tyrrell Hatton	69	69	72	72	282	20,165
Russell Henley	69	70	70	73	282	20,165
J.T. Poston	67	70	70	75	282	20,165
Cameron Smith	67	74	70	71	282	20,165
Nick Watney	71	69	71	71	282	20,165
Keegan Bradley	70	69	72	72	283	19,425
Keith Mitchell	70	70	71	72	283	19,425
Roger Sloan	68	70	71	74	283	19,425
Joel Dahmen	67	69	75	73	284	18,777.50
Mackenzie Hughes	73	68	70	73	284	18,777.50
Carlos Ortiz	67	74	73	70	284	18,777.50
Scott Piercy	71	70	71	72	284	18,777.50
Kiradech Aphibarnrat	67	73	76	69	285	17,945
Talor Gooch	74	67	72	72	285	17,945
Phil Mickelson	72	66	75	72	285	17,945
Kyle Stanley	69	70	72	74	285	17,945
Matthew Wolff	69	71	72	73	285	17,945
Scott Brown	70	69	77	71	287	17,390
Charley Hoffman	74	67	75	72	288	16,927.50
Luke List	69	70	76	73	288	16,927.50
Kevin Na	69	67	72	80	288	16,927.50
Ryan Palmer	70	67	78	73	288	16,927.50
Danny Lee	70	69	73	77	289	16,465
Francesco Molinari	69	72	75	74	290	16,280
Martin Laird	71	70	75	75	291	16,095
Si Woo Kim	70	71	76	76	293	15,910

BMW Championship

Medinah Country Club, No. 3, Medinah, Illinois
Par 36-36–72; 7,613 yards

August 15-18
purse, $9,250,000

	SCORES				TOTAL	MONEY
Justin Thomas	65	69	61	68	263	$1,665,000
Patrick Cantlay	66	67	68	65	266	999,000
Hideki Matsuyama	69	63	73	63	268	629,000
Tony Finau	67	66	68	69	270	444,000
Jon Rahm	68	69	66	69	272	351,500
Brandt Snedeker	66	71	67	68	272	351,500
Corey Conners	69	66	69	69	273	298,312.50
Lucas Glover	66	69	69	69	273	298,312.50
Kevin Kisner	68	68	69	69	274	259,000
Adam Scott	67	71	69	67	274	259,000
Tommy Fleetwood	70	66	70	69	275	196,100
Rickie Fowler	67	70	68	70	275	196,100
Sungjae Im	70	72	66	67	275	196,100
Louis Oosthuizen	70	69	68	68	275	196,100
Kevin Tway	69	67	70	69	275	196,100
J.T. Poston	68	74	66	68	276	148,000
Rory Sabbatini	67	68	67	74	276	148,000
Vaughn Taylor	73	70	67	66	276	148,000
Jason Kokrak	65	73	70	69	277	112,110
Marc Leishman	72	71	67	67	277	112,110
Rory McIlroy	69	67	70	71	277	112,110
Patrick Reed	68	71	68	70	277	112,110

	SCORES				TOTAL	MONEY
Xander Schauffele	67	68	70	72	277	112,110
Paul Casey	70	70	67	71	278	78,856.25
Joel Dahmen	66	71	69	72	278	78,856.25
Brooks Koepka	68	71	72	67	278	78,856.25
Webb Simpson	70	72	67	69	278	78,856.25
Byeong Hun An	71	70	69	69	279	65,675
Abraham Ancer	68	72	69	70	279	65,675
Si Woo Kim	70	67	71	71	279	65,675
Wyndham Clark	69	73	65	73	280	53,650
Emiliano Grillo	72	70	68	70	280	53,650
Joaquin Niemann	74	65	69	72	280	53,650
C.T. Pan	71	67	70	72	280	53,650
Ian Poulter	70	70	71	69	280	53,650
Gary Woodland	70	73	64	73	280	53,650
Billy Horschel	71	73	69	68	281	40,700
Charles Howell	70	69	73	69	281	40,700
Ryan Moore	71	69	69	72	281	40,700
Scott Piercy	67	73	70	71	281	40,700
Jordan Spieth	70	71	70	70	281	40,700
Tiger Woods	71	71	67	72	281	40,700
Keegan Bradley	69	74	68	71	282	30,525
Adam Hadwin	67	68	71	76	282	30,525
Troy Merritt	69	76	71	66	282	30,525
Ryan Palmer	68	72	70	72	282	30,525
Andrew Putnam	71	69	73	69	282	30,525
Bryson DeChambeau	71	71	71	70	283	23,865
Shane Lowry	72	74	68	69	283	23,865
Phil Mickelson	70	73	69	71	283	23,865
Collin Morikawa	67	73	72	71	283	23,865
Jason Day	70	71	69	74	284	21,571
Dylan Frittelli	72	69	71	72	284	21,571
Matt Kuchar	71	70	73	70	284	21,571
Keith Mitchell	72	74	67	71	284	21,571
Justin Rose	68	73	73	70	284	21,571
Jim Furyk	66	72	75	72	285	20,627.50
Dustin Johnson	70	72	72	71	285	20,627.50
Graeme McDowell	69	72	73	71	285	20,627.50
Chez Reavie	67	68	74	76	285	20,627.50
Max Homa	70	67	71	78	286	20,072.50
Francesco Molinari	72	73	68	73	286	20,072.50
Rafa Cabrera Bello	69	72	74	72	287	19,702.50
Sung Kang	69	73	73	72	287	19,702.50
Cameron Champ	71	68	78	71	288	19,240
J.B. Holmes	69	71	76	72	288	19,240
Adam Long	72	70	71	75	288	19,240
Harold Varner	72	74	71	72	289	18,870
Nate Lashley	72	73	70	76	291	18,685

Tour Championship

East Lake Golf Club, Atlanta, Georgia
Par 35-35–70; 7,346 yards

August 22-25
purse, $60,000,000

	SCORES				FEDEXCUP TOTAL	MONEY
Rory McIlroy	66	67	68	66	-18	$15,000,000
Xander Schauffele	64	69	67	70	-14	5,000,000
Brooks Koepka	67	67	68	72	-13	3,500,000
Justin Thomas	70	68	71	68	-13	3,500,000
Paul Casey	66	67	68	72	-9	2,500,000

	SCORES				FEDEXCUP TOTAL	MONEY
Adam Scott	68	70	71	66	-8	1,900,000
Tony Finau	70	69	70	67	-7	1,300,000
Chez Reavie	71	64	70	70	-6	1,100,000
Kevin Kisner	71	70	68	68	-5	843,333
Hideki Matsuyama	66	75	66	71	-5	843,333
Patrick Reed	70	70	73	68	-5	843,333
Bryson DeChambeau	68	71	67	70	-4	682,500
Jon Rahm	68	72	68	72	-4	682,500
Jason Kokrak	71	67	72	67	-3	620,000
Gary Woodland	68	73	69	71	-2	595,000
Tommy Fleetwood	69	70	71	70	-1	551,667
Matt Kuchar	66	72	71	74	-1	551,667
Webb Simpson	74	70	68	71	-1	551,667
Sungjae Im	67	71	73	70	E	512,500
Rickie Fowler	71	71	70	70	E	512,500
Louis Oosthuizen	70	71	70	70	1	478,000
Abraham Ancer	72	69	72	72	1	478,000
Patrick Cantlay	70	71	75	73	1	478,000
Marc Leishman	71	73	72	67	2	450,500
Brandt Snedeker	73	72	67	72	2	450,500
Corey Conners	68	71	71	74	3	430,000
Justin Rose	68	74	71	72	3	430,000
Charles Howell	68	73	71	72	4	415,000
Lucas Glover	73	75	70	72	10	400,000
Dustin Johnson	73	72	75	73	10	400,000

Start of 2019-2020 Season

A Military Tribute at The Greenbrier

The Old White TPC, White Sulphur Springs, West Virginia
Par 34-36–70; 7,292 yards

September 12-15
purse, $7,500,000

	SCORES				TOTAL	MONEY
Joaquin Niemann	65	62	68	64	259	$1,350,000
Tom Hoge	68	65	67	65	265	817,500
Harris English	66	65	68	67	266	366,093.75
Brian Harman	65	66	70	65	266	366,093.75
Nate Lashley	68	64	65	69	266	366,093.75
Richy Werenski	67	65	65	69	266	366,093.75
Sebastian Munoz	69	66	66	66	267	235,625
Scottie Scheffler	65	62	71	69	267	235,625
Robby Shelton	62	65	70	70	267	235,625
Viktor Hovland	68	68	68	64	268	189,375
Mark Hubbard	64	70	67	67	268	189,375
Matt Jones	68	66	68	66	268	189,375
Lanto Griffin	64	68	70	67	269	159,375
Joseph Bramlett	67	67	65	71	270	129,375
Bud Cauley	69	67	67	67	270	129,375
Austin Cook	66	68	68	68	270	129,375
Adam Long	66	62	70	72	270	129,375
Kevin Na	64	70	68	68	270	129,375
Bronson Burgoon	65	68	69	69	271	92,175
Harry Higgs	67	66	69	69	271	92,175
Sungjae Im	66	67	67	71	271	92,175

	SCORES				TOTAL	MONEY
Scott Piercy	69	65	69	68	271	92,175
Harold Varner	65	66	72	68	271	92,175
Rob Oppenheim	65	68	72	67	272	59,732.15
Nick Taylor	70	65	72	65	272	59,732.15
Keegan Bradley	67	68	67	70	272	59,732.14
Scott Harrington	64	69	69	70	272	59,732.14
Doc Redman	69	67	68	68	272	59,732.14
Cameron Smith	67	64	72	69	272	59,732.14
Zack Sucher	64	69	70	69	272	59,732.14
Scott Brown	66	70	66	71	273	44,850
Doug Ghim	65	71	68	69	273	44,850
Morgan Hoffmann	66	65	71	71	273	44,850
Denny McCarthy	72	61	73	67	273	44,850
Sam Ryder	65	66	71	71	273	44,850
Danny Lee	70	66	72	66	274	31,159.10
Mark Anderson	68	66	67	73	274	31,159.09
Joel Dahmen	69	65	71	69	274	31,159.09
Brice Garnett	68	68	71	67	274	31,159.09
Hank Lebioda	67	67	72	68	274	31,159.09
Grayson Murray	66	67	69	72	274	31,159.09
Andrew Novak	66	69	68	71	274	31,159.09
Brendan Steele	69	67	70	68	274	31,159.09
D.J. Trahan	67	67	70	70	274	31,159.09
Cameron Tringale	66	69	71	68	274	31,159.09
Peter Uihlein	68	68	71	67	274	31,159.09
Byeong Hun An	67	67	69	72	275	19,035
Dominic Bozzelli	67	69	68	71	275	19,035
Jonathan Byrd	71	65	72	67	275	19,035
Kevin Chappell	71	59	73	72	275	19,035
Vince Covello	67	67	70	71	275	19,035
Sung Kang	65	71	69	70	275	19,035
Martin Laird	66	68	72	69	275	19,035
Tyler McCumber	70	66	67	72	275	19,035
Patrick Rodgers	68	66	66	75	275	19,035
Bubba Watson	69	67	69	70	275	19,035
Roberto Castro	67	68	70	71	276	16,950
Jason Dufner	67	66	69	74	276	16,950
Rhein Gibson	71	65	69	71	276	16,950
David Hearn	67	69	70	70	276	16,950
Russell Henley	68	68	67	73	276	16,950
J.J. Spaun	66	70	69	71	276	16,950
Cameron Percy	67	67	73	70	277	16,425
Sebastian Cappelen	69	67	70	72	278	16,200
Johnson Wagner	70	66	71	71	278	16,200
Robert Streb	69	65	77	70	281	15,975
Beau Hossler	69	67	71	78	285	15,825

Sanderson Farms Championship

Country Club of Jackson, Jackson, Mississippi
Par 36-36–72; 7,460 yards

September 19-22
purse, $6,600,000

	SCORES				TOTAL	MONEY
Sebastian Munoz	70	67	63	70	270	$1,188,000
Sungjae Im	68	69	67	66	270	719,400
(Munoz defeated Im on first playoff hole.)						
Byeong Hun An	66	66	70	69	271	455,400
Carlos Ortiz	65	71	65	71	272	297,000
Kevin Streelman	72	67	69	64	272	297,000
Dominic Bozzelli	70	67	67	69	273	208,230

		SCORES			TOTAL	MONEY
Bronson Burgoon	69	69	70	65	273	208,230
Harris English	65	71	68	69	273	208,230
Dylan Frittelli	71	69	67	66	273	208,230
George McNeill	67	67	70	69	273	208,230
Lanto Griffin	71	67	70	66	274	153,450
Cameron Percy	65	70	68	71	274	153,450
J.T. Poston	64	70	70	70	274	153,450
Brian Harman	71	69	68	67	275	123,750
Zach Johnson	67	71	68	69	275	123,750
Scottie Scheffler	68	66	72	70	276	110,550
Cameron Tringale	70	68	69	69	276	110,550
Fabian Gomez	72	66	69	70	277	87,450
Denny McCarthy	69	71	69	68	277	87,450
Garrett Osborn	70	67	71	69	277	87,450
Zack Sucher	69	69	70	69	277	87,450
Richy Werenski	69	68	70	70	277	87,450
David Hearn	68	73	67	70	278	59,070
Charley Hoffman	73	64	70	71	278	59,070
Adam Long	68	70	71	69	278	59,070
Robert Streb	65	72	69	72	278	59,070
Peter Uihlein	71	69	69	69	278	59,070
Mark Anderson	67	71	71	70	279	42,363.75
Cameron Champ	68	72	69	70	279	42,363.75
Stewart Cink	72	66	71	70	279	42,363.75
Cameron Davis	68	70	72	69	279	42,363.75
Robby Shelton	73	67	71	68	279	42,363.75
Scott Stallings	66	72	71	70	279	42,363.75
Shawn Stefani	72	65	73	69	279	42,363.75
Brian Stuard	71	70	70	68	279	42,363.75
Tommy Gainey	72	67	71	70	280	32,780
Adam Schenk	69	70	72	69	280	32,780
J.J. Spaun	71	70	68	71	280	32,780
Scott Brown	72	68	69	72	281	26,730
Michael Gellerman	68	73	68	72	281	26,730
Emiliano Grillo	67	71	73	70	281	26,730
Tom Hoge	64	70	75	72	281	26,730
Davis Riley	69	72	71	69	281	26,730
Aaron Wise	70	69	73	69	281	26,730
Sam Burns	75	64	74	69	282	18,828.86
Ben Crane	70	71	72	69	282	18,828.86
Anirban Lahiri	69	70	74	69	282	18,828.86
Jamie Lovemark	69	69	72	72	282	18,828.86
Peter Malnati	70	70	70	72	282	18,828.86
Brandt Snedeker	69	69	71	73	282	18,828.85
Vincent Whaley	69	71	70	72	282	18,828.85
Roberto Castro	72	69	72	70	283	16,038
Doc Redman	70	71	74	68	283	16,038
Jonathan Byrd	69	71	72	72	284	15,312
Sebastian Cappelen	70	68	75	71	284	15,312
Bill Haas	70	71	70	73	284	15,312
Russell Henley	70	70	69	75	284	15,312
Bo Hoag	73	66	75	70	284	15,312
Joaquin Niemann	68	73	73	70	284	15,312
Xinjun Zhang	71	69	72	73	285	14,850
Rafael Campos	72	67	76	71	286	14,520
Alex Cejka	68	70	75	73	286	14,520
Si Woo Kim	69	68	75	74	286	14,520
Patrick Rodgers	69	72	72	73	286	14,520
Brian Gay	69	72	70	76	287	14,124
Chase Seiffert	69	69	75	74	287	14,124
Ricky Barnes	72	69	75	74	290	13,926
Daniel Chopra	69	71	74	80	294	13,794

Safeway Open

Silverado Resort & Spa, North Course, Napa, California
Par 36-36—72; 7,166 yards

September 26-29
purse, $6,600,000

	SCORES				TOTAL	MONEY
Cameron Champ	67	68	67	69	271	$1,188,000
Adam Hadwin	68	70	67	67	272	719,400
Marc Leishman	70	72	67	65	274	455,400
Zac Blair	75	66	66	68	275	277,750
Charles Howell	73	65	69	68	275	277,750
Justin Thomas	71	64	71	69	275	277,750
Dylan Frittelli	70	65	75	66	276	207,350
Cameron Percy	70	69	70	67	276	207,350
Xinjun Zhang	69	68	70	69	276	207,350
Collin Morikawa	72	64	70	71	277	166,650
Nick Taylor	69	66	70	72	277	166,650
Nick Watney	69	65	72	71	277	166,650
Corey Conners	68	73	72	65	278	125,400
Bryson DeChambeau	68	64	76	70	278	125,400
Mark Hubbard	71	71	67	69	278	125,400
Roger Sloan	70	69	69	70	278	125,400
Jim Furyk	71	67	71	70	279	90,750
Lanto Griffin	69	73	67	70	279	90,750
Adam Scott	65	73	73	68	279	90,750
Brandt Snedeker	73	67	69	70	279	90,750
Brian Stuard	70	70	70	69	279	90,750
Harold Varner	72	69	67	71	279	90,750
Daniel Berger	73	69	66	72	280	52,140
Brice Garnett	70	70	72	68	280	52,140
Brian Gay	70	67	70	73	280	52,140
Chesson Hadley	72	69	68	71	280	52,140
Scott Harrington	72	70	70	68	280	52,140
Harry Higgs	71	69	71	69	280	52,140
Andrew Landry	65	74	69	72	280	52,140
Adam Long	67	68	77	68	280	52,140
Francesco Molinari	66	71	72	71	280	52,140
Michael Thompson	71	68	68	73	280	52,140
Aaron Baddeley	69	70	71	71	281	34,461.43
Rafael Campos	71	71	73	66	281	34,461.43
Harris English	70	68	72	71	281	34,461.43
Rhein Gibson	74	68	66	73	281	34,461.43
Chez Reavie	69	68	69	75	281	34,461.43
Isaiah Salinda	72	70	71	68	281	34,461.43
Sebastian Munoz	71	67	67	76	281	34,461.42
Patrick Cantlay	69	71	70	72	282	26,730
Kevin Chappell	72	70	71	69	282	26,730
John Oda	70	66	77	69	282	26,730
Carlos Ortiz	72	69	72	69	282	26,730
Bud Cauley	69	72	66	76	283	20,842.80
Bo Hoag	71	70	70	72	283	20,842.80
Hank Lebioda	71	70	72	70	283	20,842.80
Patrick Rodgers	70	71	70	72	283	20,842.80
Cameron Tringale	68	74	69	72	283	20,842.80
Michael Gligic	72	69	71	72	284	17,006
Sungjae Im	70	72	71	71	284	17,006
Si Woo Kim	69	70	75	70	284	17,006
David Hearn	71	70	72	72	285	15,807
Maverick McNealy	70	71	72	72	285	15,807
Rob Oppenheim	68	74	74	69	285	15,807
Robby Shelton	70	67	74	74	285	15,807
Tyler Duncan	68	74	71	73	286	15,180
Fabian Gomez	71	70	71	74	286	15,180

		SCORES			TOTAL	MONEY
Talor Gooch	69	69	72	76	286	15,180
Jhonattan Vegas	70	71	67	78	286	15,180
Brendan Steele	74	68	72	73	287	14,784
Vaughn Taylor	73	69	72	73	287	14,784
Ricky Barnes	72	70	72	74	288	14,388
Max Homa	70	70	76	72	288	14,388
Bo Van Pelt	72	70	72	74	288	14,388
Kristoffer Ventura	72	70	71	75	288	14,388
Tyler McCumber	74	68	75	75	292	14,058
Scott Piercy	70	72	80	71	293	13,926

Shriners Hospitals for Children Open

TPC Summerlin, Las Vegas, Nevada
Par 35-36–71; 7,255 yards

October 3-6
purse, $7,000,000

		SCORES			TOTAL	MONEY
Kevin Na	68	62	61	70	261	$1,260,000
Patrick Cantlay	66	64	63	68	261	763,000
(Na defeated Cantlay on second playoff hole.)						
Pat Perez	69	64	62	68	263	483,000
Bryson DeChambeau	66	68	67	63	264	294,583.34
Adam Hadwin	67	66	68	63	264	294,583.33
Brian Stuard	65	65	67	67	264	294,583.33
Brian Gay	65	69	64	67	265	227,500
Webb Simpson	67	66	64	68	265	227,500
Joel Dahmen	70	64	67	65	266	183,750
Tony Finau	68	68	62	68	266	183,750
Lucas Glover	67	63	66	70	266	183,750
Denny McCarthy	69	66	63	68	266	183,750
Cameron Smith	69	64	69	65	267	137,083.34
Luke List	70	66	63	68	267	137,083.33
Ryan Moore	69	64	65	69	267	137,083.33
Hideki Matsuyama	68	67	68	65	268	117,250
Xinjun Zhang	70	65	67	66	268	117,250
Chesson Hadley	68	66	69	66	269	75,377.28
Brian Harman	64	71	68	66	269	75,377.28
Matthew Wolff	67	69	68	65	269	75,377.28
Daniel Berger	66	67	69	67	269	75,377.27
Matt Every	70	66	67	66	269	75,377.27
Lanto Griffin	67	65	67	70	269	75,377.27
Matthew NeSmith	67	68	65	69	269	75,377.27
Andrew Putnam	68	66	67	68	269	75,377.27
Sam Ryder	65	67	64	73	269	75,377.27
Adam Schenk	66	69	65	69	269	75,377.27
Kristoffer Ventura	69	66	65	69	269	75,377.27
Beau Hossler	67	65	71	67	270	43,900
Matt Jones	68	63	69	70	270	43,900
Sung Kang	71	63	68	68	270	43,900
Brendan Steele	68	69	68	65	270	43,900
Ben Taylor	67	67	69	67	270	43,900
Nick Taylor	63	69	69	69	270	43,900
Kevin Tway	68	69	67	66	270	43,900
Jack Trent	67	69	66	68	270	
Aaron Baddeley	67	69	65	70	271	33,320
Russell Henley	68	68	66	69	271	33,320
Maverick McNealy	65	69	69	68	271	33,320
Carlos Ortiz	70	65	67	69	271	33,320
Ryan Palmer	70	66	67	68	271	33,320
Mark Hubbard	68	69	66	69	272	25,550

400 / AMERICAN TOURS

	SCORES				TOTAL	MONEY
Patton Kizzire	66	67	70	69	272	25,550
Collin Morikawa	67	66	67	72	272	25,550
Doc Redman	70	67	65	70	272	25,550
Adam Scott	66	67	65	74	272	25,550
Robby Shelton	69	68	67	68	272	25,550
John Huh	66	71	68	68	273	18,330
Russell Knox	68	67	65	73	273	18,330
Martin Laird	68	65	71	69	273	18,330
Brandt Snedeker	67	70	68	68	273	18,330
Kyle Stanley	71	66	66	70	273	18,330
Chris Stroud	67	68	67	71	273	18,330
Harold Varner	68	67	66	72	273	18,330
Bronson Burgoon	66	68	69	71	274	16,240
Jim Furyk	68	66	70	70	274	16,240
Fabian Gomez	69	67	68	70	274	16,240
Si Woo Kim	71	64	70	69	274	16,240
Scott Stallings	67	65	72	70	274	16,240
Gary Woodland	69	65	71	69	274	16,240
Phil Mickelson	65	69	74	67	275	15,750
Nate Lashley	67	68	70	71	276	15,610
Jason Kokrak	70	67	73	67	277	15,260
Troy Merritt	66	68	68	75	277	15,260
John Oda	69	66	74	68	277	15,260
Peter Uihlein	68	69	70	70	277	15,260
Chase Koepka	66	69	75	68	278	14,910
James Hahn	67	69	71	72	279	14,700
Charles Howell	69	68	66	76	279	14,700
Keegan Bradley	69	68	69	74	280	14,490
Talor Gooch	71	66	73	71	281	14,280
Danny Lee	69	68	71	73	281	14,280
Bo Hoag	67	70	70	75	282	14,070
Charley Hoffman	70	67	67	79	283	13,860
Scottie Scheffler	67	67	74	75	283	13,860
Isaiah Salinda	69	68	72	79	288	13,650

Houston Open

Golf Club of Houston, Humble, Texas
Par 36-36–72; 7,441 yards

October 10-13
purse, $7,500,000

	SCORES				TOTAL	MONEY
Lanto Griffin	66	74	65	69	274	$1,350,000
Scott Harrington	69	67	72	67	275	667,500
Mark Hubbard	68	69	69	69	275	667,500
Harris English	70	72	69	66	277	286,875
Talor Gooch	64	72	72	69	277	286,875
Carlos Ortiz	70	67	71	69	277	286,875
Sepp Straka	65	71	72	69	277	286,875
Xinjun Zhang	67	76	68	66	277	286,875
Chad Campbell	70	72	68	68	278	196,875
Bud Cauley	72	69	70	67	278	196,875
Stewart Cink	70	68	71	69	278	196,875
Denny McCarthy	71	72	66	69	278	196,875
Bronson Burgoon	69	73	71	66	279	142,500
Beau Hossler	70	69	68	72	279	142,500
Doc Redman	71	72	69	67	279	142,500
Cameron Tringale	68	71	68	72	279	142,500
Austin Cook	64	74	70	72	280	110,625
Peter Malnati	69	65	73	73	280	110,625
Maverick McNealy	68	74	73	65	280	110,625

	SCORES				TOTAL	MONEY
Brandon Wu	69	70	69	72	280	110,625
Kyle Stanley	70	71	70	70	281	88,125
Boo Weekley	70	73	71	67	281	88,125
Ryan Armour	70	74	67	71	282	67,125
Cameron Champ	69	75	71	67	282	67,125
James Hahn	69	73	72	68	282	67,125
Kramer Hickok	68	73	69	72	282	67,125
Andy Zhang	68	73	73	68	282	67,125
Ricky Barnes	71	73	73	66	283	42,482.15
Zac Blair	68	76	72	67	283	42,482.15
Luke List	71	73	73	66	283	42,482.15
Brendon Todd	76	67	74	66	283	42,482.15
Matt Every	70	72	70	71	283	42,482.14
Michael Gligic	67	75	74	67	283	42,482.14
Russell Knox	71	70	71	71	283	42,482.14
Tyler McCumber	66	74	73	70	283	42,482.14
Sebastian Munoz	70	74	72	67	283	42,482.14
Wes Roach	69	68	72	74	283	42,482.14
Sam Ryder	70	69	72	72	283	42,482.14
Scottie Scheffler	69	74	69	71	283	42,482.14
Robert Streb	72	68	72	71	283	42,482.14
Nick Watney	67	73	74	69	283	42,482.14
Brice Garnett	71	72	70	71	284	28,125
Brian Gay	69	74	69	72	284	28,125
Martin Laird	70	73	74	67	284	28,125
Lucas Bjerregaard	70	73	70	72	285	21,825
Ryan Brehm	72	72	71	70	285	21,825
Roberto Castro	73	69	72	71	285	21,825
Henrik Norlander	68	76	69	72	285	21,825
Rob Oppenheim	71	73	72	69	285	21,825
D.J. Trahan	73	70	71	71	285	21,825
Braden Bailey	67	74	72	73	286	18,262.50
Michael Gellerman	72	72	71	71	286	18,262.50
Bo Hoag	72	71	70	73	286	18,262.50
Patrick Rodgers	69	70	76	71	286	18,262.50
Rich Beem	69	71	76	71	287	17,400
Mackenzie Hughes	68	71	74	74	287	17,400
John Huh	67	72	74	74	287	17,400
Ben Taylor	71	73	70	73	287	17,400
Dominic Bozzelli	75	69	74	70	288	16,950
Rafael Campos	69	74	72	73	288	16,950
Russell Henley	66	77	77	69	289	16,500
J.J. Henry	74	67	73	75	289	16,500
Seamus Power	67	76	74	72	289	16,500
Chris Stroud	73	70	72	74	289	16,500
Cole Hammer [A]	67	77	72	73	289	
Sebastian Cappelen	74	68	75	73	290	15,900
Jeremy Gandon	68	76	73	73	290	15,900
George McNeill	72	72	72	74	290	15,900
Shawn Stefani	72	72	73	73	290	15,900
Graham DeLaet	73	71	77	70	291	15,375
Robert Garrigus	70	73	73	75	291	15,375
Chandler Phillips	73	71	71	76	291	15,375
J.J. Spaun	70	74	78	72	294	15,075
Joseph Bramlett	69	74	79	73	295	14,850
Nelson Ledesma	71	69	80	75	295	14,850
Rhein Gibson	73	68	77	78	296	14,625
Jim Herman	73	71	77	76	297	14,475
Bill Haas	72	71	77	78	298	14,325

The CJ Cup @ Nine Bridges

Nine Bridges, Jeju Island, Korea
Par 36-36–72; 7,241 yards

October 17-20
purse, $9,750,000

	SCORES				TOTAL	MONEY
Justin Thomas	68	63	70	67	268	$1,755,000
Danny Lee	67	66	68	69	270	1,053,000
Hideki Matsuyama	69	70	69	65	273	507,000
Cameron Smith	67	69	68	69	273	507,000
Gary Woodland	71	71	65	66	273	507,000
Byeong Hun An	64	69	73	69	275	338,812.50
Tyrrell Hatton	69	68	70	68	275	338,812.50
Kiradech Aphibarnrat	69	69	69	69	276	273,000
Wyndham Clark	71	67	67	71	276	273,000
Ryan Moore	69	67	72	68	276	273,000
Jordan Spieth	70	65	70	71	276	273,000
Corey Conners	70	72	69	66	277	197,047.50
Joaquin Niemann	65	73	71	68	277	197,047.50
Ryan Palmer	70	69	70	68	277	197,047.50
Kevin Streelman	69	69	69	70	277	197,047.50
K.J. Choi	69	74	68	67	278	148,785
Graeme McDowell	68	71	68	71	278	148,785
Ian Poulter	69	72	66	71	278	148,785
Jhonattan Vegas	73	70	72	63	278	148,785
Tommy Fleetwood	71	70	71	67	279	103,285
Charles Howell	67	70	72	70	279	103,285
Matt Jones	72	70	72	65	279	103,285
Nate Lashley	72	69	70	68	279	103,285
Kevin Na	72	68	70	69	279	103,285
Andrew Putnam	70	70	71	68	279	103,285
Rafa Cabrera Bello	68	74	68	70	280	69,810
Emiliano Grillo	69	66	72	73	280	69,810
Sung Kang	72	72	68	68	280	69,810
Si Woo Kim	69	68	74	69	280	69,810
Harold Varner	71	71	68	70	280	69,810
Jason Day	66	73	71	71	281	55,477.50
Viktor Hovland	69	69	74	69	281	55,477.50
Phil Mickelson	70	72	71	68	281	55,477.50
Pat Perez	73	69	70	69	281	55,477.50
Rory Sabbatini	71	69	69	72	281	55,477.50
Charley Hoffman	67	72	73	70	282	45,597.50
Junggon Hwang	67	71	74	70	282	45,597.50
Collin Morikawa	69	73	65	75	282	45,597.50
Lucas Glover	74	69	71	69	283	38,610
Sungjae Im	68	73	70	72	283	38,610
Kyoung-Hoon Lee	69	67	72	75	283	38,610
Soomin Lee	68	72	73	70	283	38,610
Joel Dahmen	74	71	70	69	284	31,785
Dylan Frittelli	70	70	71	73	284	31,785
Marc Leishman	72	69	72	71	284	31,785
Branden Grace	71	71	70	73	285	22,717.50
Chase Koepka	70	72	73	70	285	22,717.50
Hyungjoon Lee	71	71	71	72	285	22,717.50
Adam Long	73	72	70	70	285	22,717.50
Keith Mitchell	74	72	68	71	285	22,717.50
Kyongjun Moon	76	72	71	66	285	22,717.50
Chez Reavie	68	77	70	70	285	22,717.50
Adam Schenk	71	74	67	73	285	22,717.50
Kevin Tway	70	72	71	72	285	22,717.50
Danny Willett	76	71	70	68	285	22,717.50
C.T. Pan	74	69	72	71	286	19,890
Abraham Ancer	73	74	71	69	287	19,500

	SCORES				TOTAL	MONEY
Luke List	70	75	71	71	287	19,500
Troy Merritt	74	72	70	71	287	19,500
Sergio Garcia	73	70	72	73	288	18,915
Sanghyun Park	74	68	74	72	288	18,915
Vaughn Taylor	74	71	71	72	288	18,915
Chesson Hadley	75	76	72	66	289	18,525
Billy Horschel	71	74	76	69	290	18,330
Max Homa	69	82	69	71	291	18,037.50
Jazz Janewattananond	74	74	70	73	291	18,037.50
Jeongwoo Ham	74	72	73	74	293	17,647.50
Won Joon Lee	74	73	79	67	293	17,647.50
Michael Kim	76	72	71	75	294	17,257.50
Whee Kim	76	75	70	73	294	17,257.50
Yongjun Bae [A]	78	72	73	71	294	
Yikeun Chang	73	73	80	70	296	16,867.50
Brian Stuard	72	76	75	73	296	16,867.50
Matthew Wolff	73	78	78	70	299	16,575
Scott Piercy	72	72	79	78	301	16,380
Tae Hee Lee	74	77	77	79	307	16,185

Zozo Championship

See Asia/Japan Tours chapter.

WGC - HSBC Champions

Sheshan International Golf Club, Shanghai, China
Par 36-36–72; 7,264 yards

October 31-November 3
purse, $10,250,000

	SCORES				TOTAL	MONEY
Rory McIlroy	67	67	67	68	269	$1,745,000
Xander Schauffele	66	69	68	66	269	1,095,000
(McIlroy defeated Schauffele on first playoff hole.)						
Louis Oosthuizen	68	69	65	69	271	602,000
Abraham Ancer	68	71	67	67	273	370,000
Victor Perez	65	71	71	66	273	370,000
Matthias Schwab	67	71	69	66	273	370,000
Matthew Fitzpatrick	66	67	70	71	274	256,000
Patrick Reed	72	69	69	66	276	200,333.34
Jason Kokrak	69	70	66	71	276	200,333.33
Paul Waring	73	65	66	72	276	200,333.33
Sungjae Im	66	69	70	72	277	155,000
Hideki Matsuyama	75	67	68	67	277	155,000
Adam Scott	66	69	75	67	277	155,000
Byeong Hun An	69	71	69	69	278	127,000
Tyrrell Hatton	72	73	68	65	278	127,000
Jazz Janewattananond	70	69	69	70	278	127,000
Christiaan Bezuidenhout	69	72	66	72	279	111,000
Robert MacIntyre	70	69	73	67	279	111,000
Carl Yuan	69	70	74	66	279	111,000
Corey Conners	67	73	74	66	280	99,000
Henrik Stenson	70	70	70	70	280	99,000
Masahiro Kawamura	72	74	66	69	281	92,500
Francesco Molinari	74	67	71	69	281	92,500
Keegan Bradley	73	72	71	66	282	85,000
Billy Horschel	69	71	73	69	282	85,000
Haotong Li	64	72	74	72	282	85,000
J.T. Poston	69	73	72	68	282	85,000
Scott Hend	75	69	70	69	283	76,666.67

	SCORES				TOTAL	MONEY
Kurt Kitayama	70	72	73	68	283	76,666.67
Phil Mickelson	71	69	75	68	283	76,666.67
Bubba Watson	70	69	72	72	283	76,666.67
Kevin Kisner	72	67	67	77	283	76,666.66
Justin Rose	69	70	71	73	283	76,666.66
Jorge Campillo	73	69	70	72	284	72,500
Joost Luiten	70	74	72	68	284	72,500
Charles Howell	74	73	67	71	285	70,500
Andrew Putnam	71	71	73	70	285	70,500
Yosuke Asaji	70	75	76	65	286	67,000
Paul Casey	75	71	71	69	286	67,000
Mike Lorenzo-Vera	70	74	72	70	286	67,000
Erik van Rooyen	73	71	71	71	286	67,000
Xinjun Zhang	68	73	73	72	286	67,000
Bryce Easton	70	73	74	70	287	63,000
Shane Lowry	72	72	72	71	287	63,000
Jordan Spieth	70	73	74	70	287	63,000
Adam Hadwin	74	77	69	68	288	60,000
Chan Kim	71	70	75	72	288	60,000
Romain Langasque	75	68	69	76	288	60,000
Lucas Glover	73	70	74	72	289	56,500
Mikumu Horikawa	74	68	77	70	289	56,500
Andrea Pavan	71	70	75	73	289	56,500
Bernd Wiesberger	70	73	71	75	289	56,500
Tony Finau	69	70	75	76	290	52,875
Tommy Fleetwood	74	76	73	67	290	52,875
Sergio Garcia	72	68	75	75	290	52,875
Justin Harding	75	74	71	70	290	52,875
Rafa Cabrera Bello	73	72	69	77	291	51,000
Jake McLeod	70	73	79	69	291	51,000
Neil Schietekat	70	72	74	75	291	51,000
Jbe' Kruger	71	71	75	75	292	49,150
Chez Reavie	69	74	75	74	292	49,150
Cameron Smith	70	72	74	76	292	49,150
Kevin Tway	71	72	72	77	292	49,150
Matt Wallace	69	84	70	69	292	49,150
Benjamin Hebert	70	74	77	73	294	48,125
Tae Hee Lee	75	73	73	73	294	48,125
Zecheng Dou	71	80	72	72	295	47,500
Ryo Ishikawa	69	79	74	73	295	47,500
Matthew Millar	69	73	74	79	295	47,500
Zhengkai Bai	73	76	74	73	296	46,875
Richard Sterne	72	75	74	75	296	46,875
Zander Lombard	73	73	74	78	298	46,500
Ashun Wu	80	71	72	76	299	46,000
Wenchong Liang	74	74	75	76	299	46,000
Danny Willett	68	77	78	76	299	46,000
Yikeun Chang	76	75	75	78	304	45,500
Daniel Nisbet	77	80	79	73	309	45,250
Ian Poulter	73	74			147	

Bermuda Championship

Port Royal Golf Club, Southampton, Bermuda
Par 36-35–71; 6,828 yards

October 31-November 3
purse, $3,000,000

	SCORES				TOTAL	MONEY
Brendon Todd	68	63	67	62	260	$540,000
Harry Higgs	66	65	65	68	264	327,000
Brian Gay	69	65	65	67	266	146,437.50
Hank Lebioda	66	70	67	63	266	146,437.50
Scottie Scheffler	62	69	69	66	266	146,437.50
Aaron Wise	67	65	69	65	266	146,437.50
Fabian Gomez	67	69	66	65	267	101,250
Ryan Armour	70	66	65	68	269	87,750
David Hearn	67	68	68	66	269	87,750
Wes Roach	63	69	69	68	269	87,750
Bo Hoag	64	71	64	71	270	66,750
Russell Knox	64	69	68	69	270	66,750
Shawn Stefani	69	66	67	68	270	66,750
Josh Teater	72	67	67	64	270	66,750
Kramer Hickok	68	69	66	68	271	51,750
Denny McCarthy	67	71	65	68	271	51,750
Alex Noren	69	67	68	67	271	51,750
Rafael Campos	66	70	69	67	272	38,350
Ben Crane	68	67	68	69	272	38,350
Tyler Duncan	70	68	67	67	272	38,350
Lanto Griffin	71	66	68	67	272	38,350
Scott Stallings	66	70	69	67	272	38,350
Boo Weekley	66	66	74	66	272	38,350
Beau Hossler	66	68	74	65	273	25,725
John Merrick	67	69	70	67	273	25,725
Rob Oppenheim	64	70	73	66	273	25,725
D.J. Trahan	71	68	66	68	273	25,725
Nelson Ledesma	67	69	72	66	274	21,450
Henrik Norlander	68	69	70	67	274	21,450
Ben Taylor	70	68	70	66	274	21,450
Chris Baker	66	68	71	70	275	18,337.50
Joseph Bramlett	67	70	70	68	275	18,337.50
Rod Pampling	70	69	65	71	275	18,337.50
Seamus Power	70	67	72	66	275	18,337.50
Dominic Bozzelli	69	71	68	68	276	14,625
Sebastian Cappelen	68	69	73	66	276	14,625
Rhein Gibson	68	69	67	72	276	14,625
Maverick McNealy	71	66	70	69	276	14,625
Doc Redman	69	70	66	71	276	14,625
Robert Streb	68	70	68	70	276	14,625
Arjun Atwal	69	69	69	70	277	10,650
Patrick Fishburn	66	71	71	69	277	10,650
Mark Hubbard	70	67	68	72	277	10,650
Tyler McCumber	69	68	68	72	277	10,650
Chip McDaniel	70	67	69	71	277	10,650
Roger Sloan	69	70	71	67	277	10,650
Kristoffer Ventura	70	70	70	67	277	10,650
Roberto Díaz	70	70	71	67	278	8,010
Cameron Percy	69	70	70	69	278	8,010
Tim Wilkinson	69	69	70	70	278	8,010
Ryan Brehm	68	68	71	72	279	7,440
Brian Stuard	70	70	70	69	279	7,440
Ricky Barnes	69	71	70	70	280	7,095
Derek Ernst	71	69	71	69	280	7,095
Michael Gligic	71	66	72	71	280	7,095
Scott Harrington	73	67	70	70	280	7,095
Zac Blair	70	68	70	73	281	6,930

406 / AMERICAN TOURS

	SCORES				TOTAL	MONEY
Sangmoon Bae	69	67	75	71	282	6,780
Alex Cejka	68	70	72	72	282	6,780
Kyoung-Hoon Lee	69	69	75	69	282	6,780
Ted Purdy	69	71	73	69	282	6,780
Chase Seiffert	67	73	70	73	283	6,600
John Senden	65	71	73	74	283	6,600
Robert Garrigus	69	69	73	73	284	6,510
Parker McLachlin	72	67	74	73	286	6,450
Carlos Franco	67	72	75	74	288	6,390

Mayakoba Golf Classic

El Camaleon Golf Club, Playa del Carmen, Mexico, November 14-18
Par 36-35–71; 7,017 yards purse, $7,200,000
(Tournament completed on Monday—rain.)

	SCORES				TOTAL	MONEY
Brendon Todd	63	68	65	68	264	$1,296,000
Adam Long	63	69	67	66	265	544,800
Carlos Ortiz	69	65	65	66	265	544,800
Vaughn Taylor	64	66	67	68	265	544,800
Harris English	65	64	68	70	267	295,200
Joel Dahmen	69	69	66	65	269	252,000
Robby Shelton	66	66	72	65	269	252,000
Abraham Ancer	66	72	65	67	270	210,600
Billy Horschel	65	71	66	68	270	210,600
Pat Perez	68	65	68	69	270	210,600
Dylan Frittelli	66	69	71	65	271	167,400
Brice Garnett	71	67	69	64	271	167,400
C.T. Pan	68	70	66	67	271	167,400
Zac Blair	67	73	65	67	272	127,800
Brian Gay	66	72	69	65	272	127,800
Matt Kuchar	69	68	73	62	272	127,800
Robert Streb	71	64	67	70	272	127,800
Scottie Scheffler	66	69	70	68	273	106,200
Chris Stroud	66	70	70	67	273	106,200
Bo Hoag	66	69	71	68	274	88,200
Charles Howell	70	71	67	66	274	88,200
Ben Martin	67	69	66	72	274	88,200
Zach Johnson	64	70	72	69	275	69,480
Graeme McDowell	66	71	71	67	275	69,480
Brian Stuard	69	72	64	70	275	69,480
Aaron Baddeley	70	67	72	67	276	51,480
Chris Baker	64	69	74	69	276	51,480
Danny Lee	62	70	70	74	276	51,480
Maverick McNealy	71	69	71	65	276	51,480
Scott Piercy	70	66	68	72	276	51,480
Chez Reavie	66	70	68	72	276	51,480
Nick Taylor	67	70	70	69	276	51,480
Ryan Armour	68	70	69	70	277	36,810
Bronson Burgoon	66	73	69	69	277	36,810
Cameron Champ	70	69	70	68	277	36,810
Harry Higgs	70	68	71	68	277	36,810
Matt Jones	71	69	70	67	277	36,810
Chris Kirk	70	69	67	71	277	36,810
Russell Knox	69	72	69	67	277	36,810
Rory Sabbatini	69	72	68	68	277	36,810
Emiliano Grillo	70	67	70	71	278	25,560
David Hearn	69	70	71	68	278	25,560
Beau Hossler	70	71	69	68	278	25,560

	SCORES				TOTAL	MONEY
Henrik Norlander	67	71	74	66	278	25,560
J.T. Poston	68	71	74	65	278	25,560
Chase Seiffert	68	69	73	68	278	25,560
Brendan Steele	68	72	72	66	278	25,560
Denny McCarthy	69	71	72	67	279	18,257.15
Matthew NeSmith	67	71	70	71	279	18,257.15
Tyler Duncan	73	67	66	73	279	18,257.14
Calum Hill	69	66	71	73	279	18,257.14
Alvaro Ortiz	66	67	68	78	279	18,257.14
Scott Stallings	70	71	69	69	279	18,257.14
Xinjun Zhang	70	71	68	70	279	18,257.14
Talor Gooch	71	69	71	70	281	16,776
Will Gordon	70	70	70	71	281	16,776
Brandon Wu	68	69	70	74	281	16,776
Kevin Chappell	70	71	73	68	282	15,984
Graham DeLaet	68	71	72	71	282	15,984
James Hahn	68	73	68	73	282	15,984
Mark Hubbard	64	71	73	74	282	15,984
Patton Kizzire	67	71	71	73	282	15,984
Peter Malnati	72	69	71	70	282	15,984
Patrick Rodgers	68	71	71	72	282	15,984
Harold Varner	68	69	73	72	282	15,984
Rafael Campos	71	70	72	70	283	14,976
Sebastian Cappelen	71	70	71	71	283	14,976
Wes Roach	70	69	73	71	283	14,976
Sam Ryder	66	75	70	72	283	14,976
Hudson Swafford	69	70	69	75	283	14,976
Cameron Tringale	69	71	71	72	283	14,976
Ryan Brehm	71	69	68	76	284	14,256
Luke Donald	66	72	73	73	284	14,256
Brian Harman	71	70	74	69	284	14,256
Scott Harrington	69	69	75	71	284	14,256
Scott Brown	72	69	71	73	285	13,752
Lanto Griffin	71	68	74	72	285	13,752
Kevin Kisner	70	71	70	74	285	13,752
Shawn Stefani	69	72	72	73	286	13,464
Jim Herman	70	71	73	73	287	13,176
Satoshi Kodaira	70	71	74	72	287	13,176
J.J. Spaun	69	72	77	69	287	13,176

The RSM Classic

Sea Island Resort, Sea Island, Georgia
Seaside Course: Par 35-35–70; 7,005 yards
Plantation Course: Par 36-36–72; 7,060 yards

November 21-24
purse, $6,600,000

	SCORES				TOTAL	MONEY
Tyler Duncan	67	61	70	65	263	$1,188,000
Webb Simpson	65	68	63	67	263	719,400
(Duncan defeated Simpson on second playoff hole.)						
Sebastian Munoz	67	63	66	68	264	455,400
Brendon Todd	66	66	62	72	266	323,400
Kyoung-Hoon Lee	64	68	66	69	267	244,200
Henrik Norlander	67	65	67	68	267	244,200
Scottie Scheffler	70	66	63	68	267	244,200
Denny McCarthy	71	62	68	67	268	199,650
D.J. Trahan	67	63	67	71	268	199,650
Will Gordon	68	65	70	66	269	160,050
Alex Noren	68	65	67	69	269	160,050
Brian Stuard	70	66	66	67	269	160,050

	SCORES				TOTAL	MONEY
Vaughn Taylor	68	67	65	69	269	160,050
Scott Brown	65	67	68	70	270	110,550
Brian Harman	67	66	66	71	270	110,550
Keith Mitchell	70	66	66	68	270	110,550
Matthew NeSmith	68	67	68	67	270	110,550
J.T. Poston	66	70	68	66	270	110,550
Nick Watney	67	67	66	70	270	110,550
Ricky Barnes	68	63	67	73	271	80,850
Russell Knox	71	67	64	69	271	80,850
Cameron Tringale	64	71	71	65	271	80,850
Ryan Armour	70	65	68	69	272	57,420
Jim Furyk	69	69	68	66	272	57,420
Fabian Gomez	68	63	69	72	272	57,420
Talor Gooch	69	68	65	70	272	57,420
Doc Redman	66	67	66	73	272	57,420
Chase Seiffert	68	69	66	69	272	57,420
Davis Thompson [A]	68	70	68	66	272	
David Hearn	66	69	69	69	273	43,230
Hank Lebioda	67	68	67	71	273	43,230
Troy Merritt	68	68	66	71	273	43,230
Kyle Stanley	69	64	70	70	273	43,230
Tim Wilkinson	68	66	67	72	273	43,230
Alex Cejka	67	67	69	71	274	32,257.50
Dylan Frittelli	68	67	68	71	274	32,257.50
Bill Haas	68	68	67	71	274	32,257.50
Brandon Hagy	71	66	66	71	274	32,257.50
Jim Herman	72	65	67	70	274	32,257.50
Harry Higgs	70	67	67	70	274	32,257.50
Adam Long	71	66	67	70	274	32,257.50
Scott Stallings	67	70	69	68	274	32,257.50
Mark Anderson	66	68	70	71	275	22,147.72
Stewart Cink	69	67	68	71	275	22,147.72
David Lingmerth	69	67	67	72	275	22,147.72
Luke Donald	70	68	69	68	275	22,147.71
Rhein Gibson	66	64	74	71	275	22,147.71
Scott Harrington	65	73	64	73	275	22,147.71
Kyle Reifers	71	63	68	73	275	22,147.71
Ryan Brehm	68	69	67	72	276	17,006
Chesson Hadley	71	65	67	73	276	17,006
Anirban Lahiri	71	67	66	72	276	17,006
Tim Herron	70	64	73	70	277	15,493.50
Kramer Hickok	68	70	67	72	277	15,493.50
Mark Hubbard	68	67	69	73	277	15,493.50
Luke List	67	69	68	73	277	15,493.50
Tyler McCumber	70	68	70	69	277	15,493.50
Maverick McNealy	71	66	68	72	277	15,493.50
Rob Oppenheim	69	69	71	68	277	15,493.50
Rory Sabbatini	67	70	70	70	277	15,493.50
Austin Cook	71	66	68	73	278	14,652
Ben Crane	68	70	66	74	278	14,652
Zach Johnson	69	69	68	72	278	14,652
Wes Roach	72	66	65	75	278	14,652
Doug Ghim	68	70	70	71	279	14,190
Mackenzie Hughes	66	70	69	74	279	14,190
Vincent Whaley	67	71	71	70	279	14,190
Adam Hadwin	71	67	74	68	280	13,728
Patton Kizzire	69	69	67	75	280	13,728
Shawn Stefani	71	64	69	76	280	13,728
Michael Thompson	71	65	70	74	280	13,728
Matt Jones	70	66	72	73	281	13,332
Peter Uihlein	69	68	70	74	281	13,332
Satoshi Kodaira	68	70	72	72	282	13,134
Bo Hoag	68	70	73	72	283	13,002
Davis Riley	68	67	71	78	284	12,870

The Presidents Cup

See Special Events section.

Special Events

CVS Health Charity Classic

Rhode Island Country Club, Barrington, Rhode Island
Par 36-35–71; 6,716 yards

June 24
purse $1,500,000

	SCORES		TOTAL	MONEY (Each)
Brooke Henderson/Keegan Bradley/Billy Andrade	61	66	127	$140,000
Lexi Thompson/Kevin Kisner/Darren Clarke	65	63	128	110,000
Morgan Pressel/Keith Mitchell/Colin Montgomerie	65	66	131	70,000
Paula Creamer/Billy Horschel/Mark O'Meara	65	66	131	70,000
So Yeon Ryu/Max Homa/Brad Faxon	66	65	131	70,000
Lydia Ko/Sam Saunders/Rocco Mediate	68	71	139	40,000

TaylorMade Pebble Beach Invitational

Pebble Beach GL: Par 36-36–72; 6,828 yards
Spyglass Hill GC: Par 36-36–72; 6,960 yards
Links at Spanish Bay: Par 35-37–72; 6,821 yards
Pebble Beach, California

November 21-24
purse, $300,000

	SCORES				TOTAL	MONEY
Kevin Sutherland	72	70	67	67	276	$60,000
Martin Flores	68	69	69	73	279	
John Mallinger	67	70	71	72	280	
Andrew Yun	68	69	71	73	281	
Justin Suh	71	70	72	70	283	
Kevin Dougherty	69	72	69	73	283	
Kirk Triplett	72	73	70	69	284	
Mina Harigae	67	71	75	71	284	
Duffy Waldorf	73	68	70	73	284	
Brandon Harkins	71	70	67	76	284	
Scott Langley	72	71	69	73	285	
Charlie Wi	70	70	72	74	286	
Brittany Lincicome	69	70	71	76	286	
Dylan Wu	70	70	70	76	286	
Parker McLachlin	69	75	70	73	287	
Tom Pernice, Jr.	74	68	72	73	287	
Daniel Summerhays	77	66	71	74	288	
Cameron Beckman	73	72	68	75	288	
Angela Stanford	73	68	71	76	288	
John Oda	68	70	69	81	288	

	SCORES				TOTAL
Matt Bettencourt	68	69	75	77	289
Daniel Chopra	69	71	72	77	289
Jordan Niebrugge	68	73	75	74	290
John Greco	75	68	72	75	290
Linnea Strom	75	70	69	76	290
Theo Humphrey	69	71	76	75	291
Ollie Schniederjans	71	73	72	75	291
Kyle Thompson	77	68	71	75	291
Jeff Gove	75	64	74	78	291
Lee Janzen	73	70	70	78	291
Jason Bohn	76	69	71	76	292
Smylie Kaufman	74	70	72	76	292
Dawie van der Walt	74	73	69	76	292
Brian Mogg	73	69	73	78	293
Maria Fassi	71	66	78	79	294
Sam Triplett	73	74	67	81	295
Chad Ramey	70	71	70	84	295
Brandel Chamblee	72	71	73	82	298
Steve Wheatcroft	68	73	73	84	298
Paul Stankowski	71	71	71	85	298
Tommy Armour	72	69	68	WD	WD

Hero World Challenge

Albany, New Providence, Bahamas
Par 36-36–72; 7,309 yards

December 4-7
purse, $3,500,000

	SCORES				TOTAL	MONEY
Henrik Stenson	69	67	68	66	270	$1,000,000
Jon Rahm	70	66	69	66	271	400,000
Patrick Reed	66	66	74	66	272	250,000
Tiger Woods	72	66	67	69	274	175,000
Justin Rose	69	70	71	65	275	147,500
Justin Thomas	69	69	67	70	275	147,500
Kevin Kisner	71	70	70	65	276	137,500
Gary Woodland	66	69	68	73	276	137,500
Rickie Fowler	69	69	72	68	278	125,000
Tony Finau	79	68	69	65	281	115,000
Xander Schauffele	73	70	70	68	281	115,000
Webb Simpson	73	68	71	69	281	115,000
Chez Reavie	68	73	69	73	283	109,000
Matt Kuchar	71	70	70	73	284	108,000
Bryson DeChambeau	76	71	70	68	285	107,000
Jordan Spieth	75	70	69	72	286	106,000
Patrick Cantlay	74	72	71	71	288	105,000
Bubba Watson	72	73	71	73	289	100,000

PNC Father Son Challenge

Ritz-Carlton Golf Club, Orlando, Florida
Par 36-36–72; 6,853 yards

December 15-16
purse, $1,085,000

	SCORES		TOTAL	MONEY
				(Money to professional)
Bernhard Langer/Jason Langer	60	60	120	$200,000
Tom Lehman/Thomas A. Lehman	61	59	120	68,625
Retief Goosen/Leo Goosen	58	62	120	68,625

(Team Langer defeated Team Lehman and Team Goosen on first playoff hole.)

David Duval/Brady Duval	60	63	123	50,000
John Daly/Little John Daly	64	60	124	49,000
Vijay Singh/Qass Singh	63	62	125	47,500
Lee Trevino/Daniel Trevino	63	62	125	47,500
Hale Irwin/Steve Irwin	65	61	126	46,000
Gary Player/James Throssell	65	62	127	44,750
Darren Clarke/Tyrone Clarke	63	64	127	44,750
Tom Kite/David Kite	63	65	128	43,750
Jim Furyk/Mike Furyk	62	66	128	43,750
Tom Watson/Michael Watson	64	65	129	42,500
Lee Janzen/Connor Janzen	64	65	129	42,500
Padraig Harrington/Paddy Harrington	64	65	129	42,500
Jack Nicklaus/G.T. Nicklaus	67	65	132	41,000
Nick Price/Greg Price	66	66	132	41,000
Mark O'Meara/Shaun O'Meara	63	69	132	41,000
Jerry Pate/Jenni Pate	69	68	137	40,125
Annika Sorenstam/Tom Sorenstam	66	71	137	40,125

The Presidents Cup

Royal Melbourne Golf Club, Melbourne, Australia
Par 35-36–71; 7,047 yards

December 12-15

FIRST DAY
Fourball

Tiger Woods and Justin Thomas (US) defeated Joaquin Niemann and Marc Leishman, 4 and 3.
Sungjae Im and Adam Hadwin (Int) defeated Patrick Cantlay and Xander Schauffele, 1 up.
Byeong Hun An and Adam Scott (Int) defeated Tony Finau and Bryson DeChambeau, 2 and 1.
C.T. Pan and Hideki Matsuyama (Int) defeated Patrick Reed and Webb Simpson, 1 up.
Louis Oosthuizen and Abraham Ancer (Int) defeated Gary Woodland and Dustin Johnson, 4 and 3.

POINTS: United States 1, International 4

SECOND DAY
Foursomes

Scott and Oosthuizen (Int) defeated Matt Kuchar and Johnson, 3 and 2.
Cantlay and Schauffele (US) defeated Niemann and Hadwin, 1 up.
Ancer and Leishman (Int) defeated Reed and Simpson, 3 and 2.
Woods and Thomas (US) defeated Matsuyama and An, 1 up.
Cameron Smith and Im (Int) halved with Rickie Fowler and Woodland.

POINTS: United States 3½, International 6½

THIRD DAY
Morning Fourball

Fowler and Thomas (US) defeated Li and Leishman, 3 and 2.
Ancer and Im (Int) defeated Cantlay and Schauffele, 3 and 2.
Pan and Matsuyama (Int) defeated Simpson and Reed, 5 and 3.
An and Scott (Int) halved with Finau and Kuchar.

POINTS: United States 5, International 9

Afternoon Foursomes

Woodland and Johnson (US) defeated Scott and Oosthuizen, 2 and 1.
Ancer and Leishman (Int) halved with Fowler and Thomas.
Cantlay and Schauffele (US) defeated Im and Smith, 2 and 1.
Niemann and An (Int) halved with Finau and Kuchar.

POINTS: United States 8, International 10

FOURTH DAY
Singles

Woods (US) defeated Ancer, 3 and 2.
Matsuyama (Int) halved with Finau.
Reed (US) defeated Pan, 4 and 2.
Johnson (US) defeated Li, 4 and 3.
Hadwin (Int) halved with DeChambeau.
Im (Int) defeated Woodland, 4 and 3.
Cantlay (US) defeated Niemann, 3 and 2.
Schauffele (US) defeated Scott, 2 and 1.
Simpson (US) defeated An, 2 and 1.
Smith (Int) defeated Thomas, 2 and 1.
Oosthuizen (Int) halved with Kuchar.
Leishman (Int) halved with Fowler.

FINAL POINTS: United States 16, International 14

QBE Shootout

Tiburon Golf Course, Naples, Florida
Par 36-36–72; 7,362 yards

December 13-15
purse, $3,500,000

	SCORES			TOTAL	MONEY (Each)
Kevin Tway/Rory Sabbatini	58	67	60	185	$435,000
J.T. Poston/Jason Kokrak	57	68	62	187	272,500
Harold Varner/Ryan Palmer	55	70	63	188	147,750
Brendon Todd/Billy Horschel	59	66	63	188	147,750
Ian Poulter/Graeme McDowell	61	65	63	189	114,500
Matthew Wolff/Viktor Hovland	65	65	60	190	97,500
Andrew Putnam/Corey Conners	61	66	63	190	97,500
Kevin Kisner/Charley Hoffman	58	69	65	192	91,250
Bubba Watson/Charles Howell	59	66	67	192	91,250
Chez Reavie/Kevin Chappell	60	67	68	195	87,500
Patton Kizzire/Brian Harman	62	72	62	196	85,000
Lexi Thompson/Sean O'Hair	64	74	70	208	82,500

AMERICAN TOURS / 413

Korn Ferry Tour

Bahamas Great Exuma Classic

Sandals Emerald Bay Golf Course, Great Exuma, Bahamas
Par 36-36–72; 7,001 yards

January 13-16
purse, $600,000

	SCORES				TOTAL	MONEY
Zecheng Dou	67	66	67	70	270	$108,000
Ben Kohles	73	67	68	64	272	52,800
Steve LeBrun	76	65	66	65	272	52,800
Steven Alker	72	69	66	66	273	23,625
John Oda	63	68	72	70	273	23,625
Rob Oppenheim	70	68	67	68	273	23,625
Willy Wilcox	66	69	69	69	273	23,625
Zac Blair	71	66	72	65	274	18,600
Matthew NeSmith	71	68	72	65	276	16,200
Austin Smotherman	67	68	72	69	276	16,200
Brett Stegmaier	71	69	68	68	276	16,200
Billy Kennerly	68	70	66	73	277	13,200
Callum Tarren	71	72	67	67	277	13,200
Casey Wittenberg	72	71	70	65	278	11,100
Carl Yuan	73	68	68	69	278	11,100
Albin Choi	72	70	69	68	279	9,300
Bo Hoag	70	68	69	72	279	9,300
Lee Hodges	70	71	69	69	279	9,300
Cameron Percy	71	72	68	68	279	9,300
Michael Gligic	69	71	71	69	280	6,990
Chad Ramey	70	72	68	70	280	6,990
Ben Taylor	70	69	69	72	280	6,990
Drew Weaver	71	71	70	68	280	6,990
Brett Drewitt	70	70	70	71	281	4,712.25
Scott Gutschewski	72	72	68	69	281	4,712.25
Paul Haley	71	70	70	70	281	4,712.25
Michael Hebert	71	73	69	68	281	4,712.25
Morgan Hoffmann	74	70	69	68	281	4,712.25
Jack Maguire	74	69	70	68	281	4,712.25
Andrew Novak	73	69	66	73	281	4,712.25
Conrad Shindler	70	73	72	66	281	4,712.25

Bahamas Great Abaco Classic

Abaco Club on Winding Bay, Great Abaco, Bahamas
Par 36-36–72; 7,141 yards

January 20-23
purse, $600,000

	SCORES				TOTAL	MONEY
Rafael Campos	70	69	72	70	281	$108,000
Vincent Whaley	73	68	69	72	282	64,800
Paul Imondi	69	71	73	70	283	40,800
Tyler McCumber	70	65	76	73	284	24,800
John Oda	68	70	70	76	284	24,800
Willy Wilcox	69	70	69	76	284	24,800
Scottie Scheffler	69	69	75	72	285	20,100
Brad Hopfinger	67	70	76	73	286	18,600

414 / AMERICAN TOURS

	SCORES				TOTAL	MONEY
Wade Binfield	68	76	71	72	287	16,800
Brett Stegmaier	71	68	75	73	287	16,800
Brett Coletta	71	74	71	72	288	13,200
Vince Covello	68	72	76	72	288	13,200
Cameron Percy	73	66	72	77	288	13,200
Ryan Yip	74	68	74	72	288	13,200
Kevin Dougherty	72	69	75	73	289	10,500
Maverick McNealy	69	73	75	72	289	10,500
Steven Alker	75	69	76	70	290	7,590
Jamie Arnold	75	68	74	73	290	7,590
Albin Choi	71	72	75	72	290	7,590
Rhein Gibson	73	70	73	74	290	7,590
Harry Higgs	70	69	75	76	290	7,590
Billy Kennerly	73	71	71	75	290	7,590
Max Rottluff	70	66	80	74	290	7,590
Steve Wheatcroft	74	70	72	74	290	7,590
Mark Anderson	72	69	73	77	291	4,468.50
Blayne Barber	73	70	74	74	291	4,468.50
Oliver Bekker	70	68	81	72	291	4,468.50
Erik Compton	69	65	74	83	291	4,468.50
Justin Lower	75	71	76	69	291	4,468.50
Byron Meth	70	73	74	74	291	4,468.50
Jimmy Stanger	71	72	72	76	291	4,468.50
Carl Yuan	71	69	75	76	291	4,468.50

Country Club de Bogota Championship

Country Club de Bogota-Lagos, Bogota, Colombia
Par 35-36–71; 7,237 yards

January 31-February 3
purse, $700,000

	SCORES				TOTAL	MONEY
Mark Anderson	62	71	66	67	266	$126,000
Drew Weaver	69	69	65	67	270	75,600
Doug Ghim	74	61	68	68	271	40,600
Tyler McCumber	72	63	66	70	271	40,600
Derek Fathauer	72	66	70	64	272	25,550
Andrew Novak	71	62	71	68	272	25,550
Scottie Scheffler	63	69	73	67	272	25,550
Rhein Gibson	70	64	69	70	273	20,300
Tim Wilkinson	69	66	70	68	273	20,300
Ryan Yip	70	65	70	68	273	20,300
Matt Every	64	69	69	72	274	16,800
Andres Gallegos	70	67	69	68	274	16,800
Joseph Bramlett	71	66	68	70	275	12,740
Bo Hoag	71	65	71	68	275	12,740
Sebastian Munoz	64	71	71	69	275	12,740
Ben Polland	70	69	67	69	275	12,740
Andrew Svoboda	66	71	70	68	275	12,740
Connor Arendell	67	69	70	70	276	8,520
Max Greyserman	71	67	68	70	276	8,520
Steven Ihm	68	69	67	72	276	8,520
Steve Marino	67	71	67	71	276	8,520
Davis Riley	67	71	70	68	276	8,520
David Skinns	65	74	69	68	276	8,520
Ben Taylor	69	67	71	69	276	8,520
Rafael Campos	68	68	71	70	277	5,108.45
Ricardo Celia	63	69	75	70	277	5,108.45
Nelson Ledesma	68	67	72	70	277	5,108.45
Byron Meth	66	73	70	68	277	5,108.45
Todd Baek	69	68	73	67	277	5,108.44

	SCORES				TOTAL	MONEY
Justin Hueber	71	66	70	70	277	5,108.44
Ben Kohles	69	67	71	70	277	5,108.44
Jordan Niebrugge	72	65	70	70	277	5,108.44
Casey Wittenberg	75	64	67	71	277	5,108.44

Panama Championship

Panama Golf Club, Panama City, Panama
Par 35-35–70; 7,194 yards

February 7-10
purse, $625,000

	SCORES				TOTAL	MONEY
Michael Gligic	70	70	67	65	272	$112,500
Xinjun Zhang	66	70	71	66	273	67,500
Carl Yuan	69	68	68	69	274	42,500
Ben Taylor	70	65	69	71	275	30,000
Rhein Gibson	68	70	71	68	277	23,750
Cameron Percy	68	73	65	71	277	23,750
Chris Baker	67	69	73	69	278	18,187.50
Mickey DeMorat	69	68	69	72	278	18,187.50
Nicolas Echavarria	68	68	71	71	278	18,187.50
Derek Ernst	69	69	68	72	278	18,187.50
Tyler McCumber	72	67	67	72	278	18,187.50
Brett Coletta	66	74	71	68	279	13,125
Oscar Fraustro	72	68	70	69	279	13,125
Steve LeBrun	71	69	68	71	279	13,125
Mark Anderson	70	68	73	69	280	10,312.50
Brian Campbell	67	72	69	72	280	10,312.50
Steve Marino	68	68	73	71	280	10,312.50
John Oda	68	70	72	70	280	10,312.50
Brad Fritsch	72	70	72	67	281	6,420.63
Michael Hebert	71	68	73	69	281	6,420.63
Mark Hubbard	70	72	71	68	281	6,420.63
Maverick McNealy	73	69	70	69	281	6,420.63
Brett Stegmaier	68	71	73	69	281	6,420.63
Steven Ihm	69	72	69	71	281	6,420.62
Edward Loar	67	75	66	73	281	6,420.62
Andrew Novak	74	69	68	70	281	6,420.62
Steve Wheatcroft	70	72	68	71	281	6,420.62
Tim Wilkinson	65	73	72	71	281	6,420.62

LECOM Suncoast Classic

Lakewood National Golf Club, Lakewood Ranch, Florida
Par 36-36–72; 7,184 yards

February 14-17
purse, $550,000

	SCORES				TOTAL	MONEY
Mark Hubbard	65	66	64	67	262	$99,000
Maverick McNealy	64	64	69	67	264	59,400
Rick Lamb	68	67	66	64	265	31,900
Jimmy Stanger	66	66	65	68	265	31,900
J.T. Griffin	63	65	71	69	268	22,000
Billy Kennerly	69	68	67	66	270	19,800
Chris Baker	66	64	71	71	272	16,005
Max Greyserman	71	64	67	70	272	16,005
Nelson Ledesma	68	68	67	69	272	16,005
Vincent Whaley	67	68	67	70	272	16,005
Motin Yeung	67	68	68	69	272	16,005

	SCORES				TOTAL	MONEY
Chase Seiffert	66	66	68	73	273	12,100
Xinjun Zhang	66	69	68	70	273	12,100
Wade Binfield	65	66	72	71	274	9,900
Tyler McCumber	66	69	72	67	274	9,900
Robby Shelton	68	66	72	68	274	9,900
Ricky Barnes	67	71	68	69	275	6,957.50
Derek Fathauer	66	68	69	72	275	6,957.50
Vince India	67	69	69	70	275	6,957.50
Michael Johnson	67	69	73	66	275	6,957.50
Steve LeBrun	66	70	69	70	275	6,957.50
Taylor Moore	70	69	65	71	275	6,957.50
Charlie Saxon	68	70	68	69	275	6,957.50
Steve Wheatcroft	69	70	65	71	275	6,957.50
Joseph Bramlett	72	67	69	68	276	4,182.36
Lanto Griffin	68	69	68	71	276	4,182.36
Harry Higgs	69	70	70	67	276	4,182.36
David Lingmerth	69	70	69	68	276	4,182.36
Zach Wright	73	66	70	67	276	4,182.36
Chris Naegel	67	70	67	72	276	4,182.35
Ben Taylor	71	64	69	72	276	4,182.35

Chitimacha Louisiana Open

Le Triomphe Golf & Country Club, Broussard, Louisiana
Par 36-35–71; 7,067 yards

March 21-24
purse, $550,000

		SCORES			TOTAL	MONEY
Vince Covello	63	67	67	68	265	$99,000
Justin Lower	68	63	64	70	265	59,400
(Covello defeated Lower on third playoff hole.)						
Fabian Gomez	68	65	71	62	266	28,600
Steve Marino	68	67	66	65	266	28,600
Xinjun Zhang	66	64	68	68	266	28,600
Erik Barnes	68	67	66	66	267	18,425
Scott Harrington	66	66	69	66	267	18,425
Michael Johnson	71	64	64	68	267	18,425
Greg Yates	64	67	68	69	268	15,950
Joshua Creel	68	70	65	66	269	13,750
Josh Teater	67	67	65	70	269	13,750
Boo Weekley	69	63	72	65	269	13,750
Jamie Arnold	68	63	69	70	270	9,716.67
Rafael Campos	64	68	67	71	270	9,716.67
Max Greyserman	68	67	69	66	270	9,716.67
Timothy Madigan	67	67	69	67	270	9,716.67
Michael Gellerman	70	66	64	70	270	9,716.66
Ben Kohles	66	65	66	73	270	9,716.66
Joseph Bramlett	66	69	68	68	271	6,666
Sebastian Cappelen	69	66	68	68	271	6,666
Doug Ghim	72	63	67	69	271	6,666
Andre Metzger	67	69	68	67	271	6,666
Matthew NeSmith	67	69	69	66	271	6,666
Austin Smotherman	69	70	66	67	272	4,319.57
Jimmy Stanger	71	67	68	66	272	4,319.57
Erik Compton	67	68	69	68	272	4,319.56
Andrew Novak	67	69	69	67	272	4,319.56
Chase Seiffert	68	68	69	67	272	4,319.56
Robby Shelton	71	67	66	68	272	4,319.56
Ben Taylor	65	71	68	68	272	4,319.56
Casey Wittenberg	66	66	72	68	272	4,319.56

Savannah Golf Championship

Landings Club, Deer Creek Golf Course, Savannah, Georgia
Par 36-36–72; 7,128 yards

March 24-27
purse, $550,000

	SCORES				TOTAL	MONEY
Dan McCarthy	65	67	71	69	272	$99,000
Scottie Scheffler	71	65	67	70	273	59,400
Brian Campbell	69	67	69	69	274	28,600
Brett Coletta	66	70	68	70	274	28,600
Kevin Lucas	66	67	73	68	274	28,600
Cameron Percy	67	72	69	67	275	19,800
Joseph Bramlett	67	70	70	69	276	17,737.50
Timothy Madigan	68	68	67	73	276	17,737.50
Jamie Arnold	69	71	73	65	278	14,850
Wade Binfield	69	68	68	73	278	14,850
Brett Stegmaier	71	69	68	70	278	14,850
Joshua Creel	69	71	69	70	279	8,690
George Cunningham	72	70	68	69	279	8,690
Rico Hoey	68	69	71	71	279	8,690
Justin Lower	71	71	69	68	279	8,690
Tyler McCumber	70	66	75	68	279	8,690
Rob Oppenheim	67	70	71	71	279	8,690
Kyle Reifers	74	68	68	69	279	8,690
Max Rottluff	72	67	70	70	279	8,690
Andrew Svoboda	71	66	70	72	279	8,690
Nicholas Thompson	67	75	66	71	279	8,690
T.J. Vogel	70	64	73	72	279	8,690
Will Zalatoris	69	69	70	71	279	8,690
Oscar Fraustro	71	70	70	69	280	4,521.92
Michael Gligic	73	69	70	68	280	4,521.92
Harry Higgs	72	70	68	70	280	4,521.92
Andrew Novak	69	71	73	67	280	4,521.92
Corey Pereira	73	68	68	71	280	4,521.91
Patrick Sullivan	69	71	67	73	280	4,521.91

Robert Trent Jones Golf Trail Championship

The Senator Course, Prattville, Alabama
Par 36-36–72; 7,654 yards

April 18-21
purse, $550,000

	SCORES				TOTAL	MONEY
Lanto Griffin	68	68	69	68	273	$99,000
Robby Shelton	65	67	72	69	273	59,400
(Griffin defeated Shelton on fourth playoff hole.)
Tyler McCumber	68	69	72	67	276	31,900
Austin Smotherman	66	75	67	68	276	31,900
Scottie Scheffler	68	72	70	67	277	22,000
Zac Blair	67	74	68	69	278	19,112.50
Xinjun Zhang	69	71	65	73	278	19,112.50
Jonathan Randolph	68	70	68	73	279	16,500
Jimmy Stanger	67	71	70	71	279	16,500
Oliver Bekker	71	69	73	67	280	12,191.67
Martin Flores	71	73	71	65	280	12,191.67
Chris Thompson	70	71	69	70	280	12,191.67
Tim Wilkinson	71	69	72	68	280	12,191.67
Charlie Saxon	75	68	68	69	280	12,191.66
Will Zalatoris	72	71	66	71	280	12,191.66
Bo Hoag	72	72	70	67	281	9,075
Callum Tarren	71	71	73	66	281	9,075

	SCORES				TOTAL	MONEY
Matt Atkins	70	74	70	68	282	6,462.50
George Cunningham	69	71	72	70	282	6,462.50
Brad Hopfinger	68	76	67	71	282	6,462.50
Henrik Norlander	67	74	72	69	282	6,462.50
Brett Stegmaier	70	72	67	73	282	6,462.50
Ben Taylor	68	71	70	73	282	6,462.50
Casey Wittenberg	71	71	71	69	282	6,462.50
Norman Xiong	70	71	72	69	282	6,462.50

Dormie Network Classic

Briggs Ranch Golf Club, San Antonio, Texas
Par 36-36–72; 7,247 yards

April 25-28
purse, $550,000

	SCORES				TOTAL	MONEY
Xinjun Zhang	63	64	65	70	262	$99,000
Lanto Griffin	67	65	65	70	267	48,400
Chase Seiffert	66	67	68	66	267	48,400
Zack Sucher	65	70	68	65	268	22,733.34
Steven Alker	65	64	69	70	268	22,733.33
Robby Shelton	69	68	65	66	268	22,733.33
Nelson Ledesma	65	67	70	69	271	17,737.50
Scottie Scheffler	69	67	66	69	271	17,737.50
Ryan Brehm	68	65	66	73	272	14,300
Max Greyserman	68	69	69	66	272	14,300
Harry Higgs	65	71	68	68	272	14,300
T.J. Vogel	72	67	69	64	272	14,300
Erik Compton	68	69	70	66	273	10,633.34
Sebastian Cappelen	69	66	71	67	273	10,633.33
Scott Harrington	69	70	66	68	273	10,633.33
Kevin Dougherty	68	64	71	71	274	8,800
Scott Gutschewski	68	67	67	72	274	8,800
Bo Hoag	70	67	70	67	274	8,800
Ricky Barnes	69	70	65	71	275	5,650.15
Brandon Crick	66	69	69	71	275	5,650.15
George Cunningham	72	67	69	67	275	5,650.15
Brett Drewitt	68	66	67	74	275	5,650.15
Grant Hirschman	67	69	71	68	275	5,650.15
Rico Hoey	70	67	68	70	275	5,650.15
Justin Lower	65	72	70	68	275	5,650.15
Brian Richey	63	70	71	71	275	5,650.15
Charlie Saxon	65	66	70	74	275	5,650.15
Callum Tarren	71	68	69	67	275	5,650.15

Nashville Golf Open

Nashville Golf & Athletic Club, Nashville, Tennessee
Par 36-36–72; 7,600 yards

May 2-5
purse, $550,000

	SCORES				TOTAL	MONEY
Robby Shelton	64	73	65	71	273	$99,000
Scottie Scheffler	68	67	74	64	273	59,400
(Shelton defeated Scheffler on first playoff hole.)
Henrik Norlander	71	68	66	69	274	37,400
Chris Baker	69	67	70	69	275	24,200
Chase Seiffert	68	67	70	70	275	24,200
Ryan Brehm	70	65	71	70	276	18,425

	SCORES				TOTAL	MONEY
Brian Campbell	71	67	67	71	276	18,425
Matthew NeSmith	68	69	71	68	276	18,425
Drew Weaver	69	72	66	70	277	15,950
Jamie Arnold	73	67	67	71	278	13,200
John Merrick	71	69	68	70	278	13,200
Garrett Osborn	67	73	70	68	278	13,200
Andy Zhang	72	65	69	72	278	13,200
Lanto Griffin	70	69	68	72	279	9,625
Mark Hubbard	70	66	73	70	279	9,625
Horacio Leon	69	68	69	73	279	9,625
David Lingmerth	71	71	69	68	279	9,625
Mark Anderson	72	70	70	68	280	7,172
Corey Pereira	71	69	74	66	280	7,172
Jimmy Stanger	71	72	69	68	280	7,172
Vincent Whaley	71	70	69	70	280	7,172
Xinjun Zhang	71	68	67	74	280	7,172
Wade Binfield	70	74	67	70	281	5,105.38
Lee Hodges	71	69	71	70	281	5,105.38
M.J. Daffue	69	69	72	71	281	5,105.37
Michael McGowan	73	68	74	66	281	5,105.37

KC Golf Classic

Blue Hills Country Club, Kansas City, Missouri
Par 36-36–72; 7,347 yards

May 9-12
purse, $675,000

	SCORES				TOTAL	MONEY
Michael Gellerman	71	67	70	69	277	$121,500
Harry Higgs	73	67	70	68	278	59,400
Nelson Ledesma	72	68	65	73	278	59,400
Paul Haley	72	73	67	67	279	29,700
Henrik Norlander	69	72	71	67	279	29,700
Luke Guthrie	69	67	72	72	280	21,853.13
Max Rottluff	73	71	68	68	280	21,853.13
Jack Maguire	71	68	69	72	280	21,853.12
Kyle Reifers	74	66	67	73	280	21,853.12
Lee Hodges	72	72	68	69	281	16,200
Chris Naegel	71	69	71	70	281	16,200
David Skinns	72	70	68	71	281	16,200
Tim Wilkinson	71	67	72	71	281	16,200
Jamie Arnold	71	72	69	70	282	10,462.50
Wade Binfield	72	71	71	68	282	10,462.50
Joseph Bramlett	73	70	70	69	282	10,462.50
Erik Compton	70	72	71	69	282	10,462.50
Austin Smotherman	72	67	72	71	282	10,462.50
Nick Voke	72	69	71	70	282	10,462.50
Steve Wheatcroft	67	75	71	69	282	10,462.50
Xinjun Zhang	74	71	67	70	282	10,462.50
Albin Choi	73	71	68	71	283	6,750
George Cunningham	71	70	75	67	283	6,750
Lanto Griffin	73	71	71	68	283	6,750
Edward Loar	72	73	69	69	283	6,750

Knoxville Open

Fox Den Country Club, Knoxville, Tennessee
Par 35-36–71; 7,088 yards

May 16-19
purse, $550,000

		SCORES			TOTAL	MONEY
Robby Shelton	67	65	66	71	269	$99,000
Mark Anderson	67	66	69	68	270	59,400
Mark Hubbard	65	65	70	71	271	28,600
Tim Wilkinson	66	67	68	70	271	28,600
Xinjun Zhang	68	65	68	70	271	28,600
Billy Kennerly	65	66	69	72	272	19,800
George Cunningham	70	68	68	67	273	17,141.67
Brian Richey	67	71	67	68	273	17,141.67
Chase Seiffert	69	65	68	71	273	17,141.66
Wes Roach	71	67	71	65	274	13,750
Ben Taylor	68	68	64	74	274	13,750
Greg Yates	70	69	66	69	274	13,750
Joseph Bramlett	71	66	67	71	275	10,010
Ryan Brehm	64	68	73	70	275	10,010
Chad Campbell	67	67	69	72	275	10,010
Talor Gooch	67	68	71	69	275	10,010
Henrik Norlander	68	68	70	69	275	10,010
Michael Arnaud	72	67	71	66	276	6,253.50
Chris Baker	69	67	69	71	276	6,253.50
Will Cannon	74	64	67	71	276	6,253.50
Michael Gligic	70	68	69	69	276	6,253.50
Brock Mackenzie	70	66	72	68	276	6,253.50
John Merrick	72	67	66	71	276	6,253.50
Chad Ramey	71	67	71	67	276	6,253.50
Jonathan Randolph	68	70	72	66	276	6,253.50
Vincent Whaley	73	64	69	70	276	6,253.50

Evans Scholars Invitational

The Glen Club, Glenview, Illinois
Par 36-36–72; 7,225 yards

May 23-26
purse, $550,000

		SCORES			TOTAL	MONEY
Scottie Scheffler	68	70	70	63	271	$99,000
Marcelo Rozo	67	68	67	69	271	59,400
(Scheffler defeated Rozo on second playoff hole.)						
Nicolas Echavarria	71	68	70	63	272	37,400
Vince Covello	68	65	70	70	273	24,200
Luke Guthrie	68	68	69	68	273	24,200
Lanto Griffin	71	66	70	67	274	16,638
Blayne Barber	72	69	70	63	274	16,638
Mark Hubbard	71	70	68	65	274	16,638
Jimmy Stanger	69	69	71	65	274	16,638
Nicholas Thompson	70	70	70	64	274	16,638
George Cunningham	68	69	68	69	274	16,638
Tag Ridings	71	70	68	66	275	12,100
Michael Gligic	73	65	66	71	275	12,100
Brett Drewitt	70	69	72	65	276	9,350
Jordan Niebrugge	71	70	71	64	276	9,350
Sebastian Cappelen	70	70	71	65	276	9,350
Erik Compton	69	69	71	67	276	9,350
Paul D. Haley	69	69	73	65	276	9,350
Chase Seiffert	73	69	71	64	277	6,004
Kevin Dougherty	73	65	73	66	277	6,004

	SCORES				TOTAL	MONEY
Steve Marino	71	66	71	69	277	6,004
Tyler McCumber	65	72	67	73	277	6,004
Bo Hoag	72	69	67	69	277	6,004
Rob Oppenheim	67	65	76	69	277	6,004
Corey Pereira	70	71	70	66	277	6,004
Vince India	67	70	71	69	277	6,004

Rex Hospital Open

The Country Club at Wakefield Plantation, Raleigh, North Carolina   May 30-June 2
Par 36-35–71; 7,257 yards   purse, $650,000

	SCORES				TOTAL	MONEY
Sebastian Cappelen	65	65	69	64	263	$117,000
Grayson Murray	70	67	68	61	266	57,200
Zack Sucher	68	69	62	67	266	57,200
Chris Baker	67	60	68	72	267	28,600
Rhein Gibson	65	71	65	66	267	28,600
Luke Guthrie	69	62	68	69	268	23,400
Davis Riley	69	66	68	66	269	20,258.34
Horacio Leon	65	69	65	70	269	20,258.33
Sebastian Munoz	68	67	65	69	269	20,258.33
Martin Flores	67	66	70	67	270	16,900
Doug Ghim	72	65	65	68	270	16,900
Marcelo Rozo	65	68	70	68	271	14,950
Ryan Brehm	68	69	70	65	272	12,187.50
Bo Hoag	66	68	72	66	272	12,187.50
Andrew Novak	69	69	65	69	272	12,187.50
Chase Seiffert	68	69	69	66	272	12,187.50
Erik Barnes	68	66	66	73	273	9,425
Timothy Madigan	68	69	70	66	273	9,425
Cameron Percy	69	69	68	67	273	9,425
Ben Taylor	67	68	72	66	273	9,425
Harry Higgs	68	65	70	71	274	6,760
Henrik Norlander	67	69	70	68	274	6,760
Kyle Reifers	68	70	69	67	274	6,760
Brian Richey	69	68	68	69	274	6,760
Jose de Jesus Rodriguez	70	66	68	70	274	6,760

BMW Charity Pro-Am

Thornblade Club: Par 35-36–71; 7,024 yards   June 6-9
Cliffs Valley: Par 36-36–72; 7,029 yards   purse, $700,000
Greer, South Carolina
(Tournament reduced to 54 holes—rain.)

	SCORES			TOTAL	MONEY
Rhein Gibson	66	64	63	193	$126,000
Michael Miller	65	63	68	196	75,600
Brian Campbell	67	67	64	198	36,400
Jonathan Randolph	67	65	66	198	36,400
Kristoffer Ventura	67	62	69	198	36,400
Chris Baker	65	64	70	199	23,450
Ryan Brehm	68	65	66	199	23,450
Brian Richey	68	65	66	199	23,450
Michael Arnaud	67	65	68	200	16,800
Scott Gutschewski	72	65	63	200	16,800

422 / AMERICAN TOURS

	SCORES			TOTAL	MONEY
Scott Harrington	69	67	64	200	16,800
Harry Higgs	67	66	67	200	16,800
T.J. Vogel	67	67	66	200	16,800
Will Zalatoris	67	66	67	200	16,800
Erik Barnes	71	64	66	201	9,846.67
Thomas Bass	70	65	66	201	9,846.67
Mark Hubbard	69	67	65	201	9,846.67
Davis Riley	69	66	66	201	9,846.67
Drew Weaver	69	65	67	201	9,846.67
Greg Yates	68	65	68	201	9,846.67
Lanto Griffin	70	67	64	201	9,846.66
Steve LeBrun	66	66	69	201	9,846.66
Maverick McNealy	66	66	69	201	9,846.66
Jimmy Beck	68	69	65	202	5,059.25
Vince Covello	63	71	68	202	5,059.25
Derek Ernst	68	69	65	202	5,059.25
Brad Fritsch	66	68	68	202	5,059.25
J.T. Griffin	70	65	67	202	5,059.25
Matt Harmon	64	71	67	202	5,059.25
William Harrold	67	70	65	202	5,059.25
Steve Marino	67	66	69	202	5,059.25
Andrew Novak	67	66	69	202	5,059.25
John Oda	67	66	69	202	5,059.25
Rob Oppenheim	73	64	65	202	5,059.25
Conrad Shindler	68	65	69	202	5,059.25

Lincoln Land Championship

Panther Creek Country Club, Springfield, Illinois
Par 35-36–71; 7,244 yards

June 13-16
purse, $550,000

	SCORES				TOTAL	MONEY
Xinjun Zhang	68	72	63	66	269	$99,000
Dylan Wu	68	73	65	63	269	59,400
(Zhang defeated Wu on third playoff hole.)						
Nelson Ledesma	74	66	65	65	270	31,900
Vincent Whaley	68	68	68	66	270	31,900
James Driscoll	71	72	63	65	271	20,075
Chase Seiffert	70	68	67	66	271	20,075
Braden Thornberry	68	70	67	66	271	20,075
Steven Alker	70	68	65	69	272	15,950
Robby Shelton	69	71	63	69	272	15,950
Eric Steger	70	66	69	67	272	15,950
Matthew Campbell	66	71	68	68	273	12,100
Michael Gligic	69	69	66	69	273	12,100
Bo Hoag	68	70	67	68	273	12,100
Tag Ridings	69	71	68	65	273	12,100
Brad Hopfinger	67	71	67	69	274	8,525
Mark Hubbard	72	67	68	67	274	8,525
Matthew NeSmith	70	71	68	65	274	8,525
Jonathan Randolph	70	67	69	68	274	8,525
Davis Riley	70	71	64	69	274	8,525
Steve Wheatcroft	72	69	65	68	274	8,525
Nicolas Echavarria	71	70	66	68	275	5,940
Kyle Jones	74	67	67	67	275	5,940
Ben Kohles	75	68	66	66	275	5,940
Kyle Reifers	70	70	66	69	275	5,940
Thomas Bass	73	69	66	68	276	4,013.78
Joshua Creel	72	69	67	68	276	4,013.78
Rick Lamb	69	68	69	70	276	4,013.78

	SCORES				TOTAL	MONEY
Edward Loar	69	72	67	68	276	4,013.78
Lee McCoy	71	71	65	69	276	4,013.78
Conrad Shindler	69	74	65	68	276	4,013.78
Ethan Tracy	72	69	69	66	276	4,013.78
Martin Flores	70	71	64	71	276	4,013.77
Rico Hoey	69	69	68	70	276	4,013.77

Wichita Open Supporting Wichita's Youth

Crestview Country Club, Wichita, Kansas
Par 35-35–70; 6,910 yards
(Tournament completed on Monday—darkness.)

June 20-24
purse, $625,000

	SCORES				TOTAL	MONEY
Henrik Norlander	63	68	68	66	265	$112,500
Bryan Bigley	67	64	68	66	265	41,250
Sebastian Cappelen	66	71	63	65	265	41,250
Erik Compton	64	67	67	67	265	41,250
Kevin Dougherty	64	69	66	66	265	41,250

(Norlander won on third playoff hole.)

Danny Walker	69	66	65	66	266	22,500
Doug Ghim	69	67	65	66	267	19,479.17
Scottie Scheffler	66	64	70	67	267	19,479.17
Chad Ramey	66	68	65	68	267	19,479.16
Chris Baker	68	68	66	66	268	15,000
Vince Covello	67	68	69	64	268	15,000
Oscar Fraustro	66	71	67	64	268	15,000
Taylor Moore	63	71	67	67	268	15,000
Tyson Alexander	66	64	73	66	269	9,687.50
Ryan Baca	66	73	67	63	269	9,687.50
Tommy Gainey	65	72	66	66	269	9,687.50
Rhein Gibson	67	69	66	67	269	9,687.50
Paul Haley	66	68	67	68	269	9,687.50
Matthew NeSmith	67	69	65	68	269	9,687.50
Tag Ridings	70	68	63	68	269	9,687.50
Joseph Winslow	71	66	66	66	269	9,687.50
Andres Gallegos	67	66	70	67	270	5,690.18
Jordan Niebrugge	69	68	68	65	270	5,690.18
Marcelo Rozo	67	70	68	65	270	5,690.18
Charlie Saxon	67	68	68	67	270	5,690.18
Ethan Tracy	67	71	66	66	270	5,690.18
Tim Wilkinson	71	66	67	66	270	5,690.18
Rafael Campos	67	66	69	68	270	5,690.17

Utah Championship

Oakridge Country Club, Farmington, Utah
Par 36-35–71; 7,045 yards

June 27-30
purse, $725,000

	SCORES				TOTAL	MONEY
Kristoffer Ventura	69	70	66	65	270	$130,500
Joshua Creel	68	66	69	67	270	78,300

(Ventura defeated Creel on third playoff hole.)

Ryan Brehm	69	69	67	66	271	37,700
Kevin Dougherty	69	68	66	68	271	37,700
Charlie Saxon	66	73	64	68	271	37,700
Daniel Summerhays	66	68	68	70	272	26,100

	SCORES				TOTAL	MONEY
Tyson Alexander	69	71	68	65	273	21,840.63
Jimmy Gunn	69	71	67	66	273	21,840.63
David Hearn	69	69	68	67	273	21,840.62
Rob Oppenheim	68	68	67	70	273	21,840.62
Zac Blair	69	67	71	67	274	16,675
Harry Higgs	69	70	69	66	274	16,675
Dawie van der Walt	71	67	67	69	274	16,675
Joseph Bramlett	68	71	66	70	275	11,962.50
Trevor Cone	73	64	69	69	275	11,962.50
Lanto Griffin	72	64	68	71	275	11,962.50
Byron Meth	71	70	67	67	275	11,962.50
Chad Ramey	67	71	71	66	275	11,962.50
Tyrone Van Aswegen	68	65	74	68	275	11,962.50
Brian Campbell	69	69	67	71	276	8,149
Andres Gallegos	69	69	70	68	276	8,149
Robert Garrigus	64	73	67	72	276	8,149
Luke Guthrie	67	69	69	71	276	8,149
Davis Riley	70	72	65	69	276	8,149
Jonathan Randolph	74	68	67	68	277	6,048.92
Kyle Westmoreland	69	67	72	69	277	6,048.92
Matthew Campbell	66	72	68	71	277	6,048.91

LECOM Health Challenge

Peek'n Peak Resort, Upper Course, Findley Lake, New York
Par 36-36–72; 7,088 yards

July 4-7
purse, $600,000

	SCORES				TOTAL	MONEY
Ryan Brehm	70	66	64	68	268	$108,000
Tim Wilkinson	65	67	67	69	268	64,800
(Brehm defeated Wilkinson on first playoff hole.)						
Blayne Barber	69	67	66	67	269	31,200
Chase Seiffert	67	70	69	63	269	31,200
Will Zalatoris	65	68	68	68	269	31,200
Jamie Arnold	66	68	66	70	270	20,100
Byron Meth	67	67	67	69	270	20,100
Greg Yates	72	66	67	65	270	20,100
Oliver Bekker	71	65	71	64	271	15,600
Zac Blair	69	67	67	68	271	15,600
Will Cannon	67	65	70	69	271	15,600
Maverick McNealy	66	68	68	69	271	15,600
Matthew Campbell	64	69	69	70	272	10,920
Nelson Ledesma	67	67	71	67	272	10,920
Henrik Norlander	69	68	66	69	272	10,920
Robby Shelton	68	66	70	68	272	10,920
Zach Wright	69	67	65	71	272	10,920
Tyson Alexander	69	69	67	68	273	7,302.86
Oscar Fraustro	74	63	69	67	273	7,302.86
William Kropp	69	67	70	67	273	7,302.86
Charlie Saxon	72	67	67	67	273	7,302.86
Dawie van der Walt	66	68	72	67	273	7,302.86
Andres Gonzales	68	68	69	68	273	7,302.85
Lanto Griffin	67	66	70	70	273	7,302.85
Chris Baker	74	64	69	67	274	4,879.50
Sebastian Cappelen	72	66	68	68	274	4,879.50
Martin Flores	70	67	71	66	274	4,879.50
Jimmy Gunn	65	69	74	66	274	4,879.50

TPC Colorado Championship at Heron Lakes

TPC Colorado, Berthoud, Colorado
Par 36-36–72; 7,991 yards

July 11-14
purse, $600,000

	SCORES				TOTAL	MONEY
Nelson Ledesma	65	69	69	70	273	$108,000
Brett Coletta	68	70	65	71	274	64,800
Michael Gellerman	74	66	64	71	275	28,800
Scott Harrington	71	68	71	65	275	28,800
Harry Higgs	71	68	68	68	275	28,800
Dawie van der Walt	73	66	69	67	275	28,800
Erik Barnes	71	69	67	69	276	18,700
Zecheng Dou	72	69	69	66	276	18,700
Braden Thornberry	70	70	70	66	276	18,700
Michael Gligic	69	69	67	72	277	15,000
Joseph Winslow	68	68	71	70	277	15,000
Xinjun Zhang	71	68	68	70	277	15,000
Lee Hodges	69	68	70	71	278	12,600
John Oda	69	67	68	75	279	11,100
T.J. Vogel	69	70	70	70	279	11,100
Joseph Bramlett	76	67	69	68	280	9,600
Rhein Gibson	71	71	67	71	280	9,600
Zach Wright	69	73	68	70	280	9,600
Tyson Alexander	74	69	69	69	281	6,163.80
Jamie Arnold	68	71	69	73	281	6,163.80
Doug Ghim	70	69	70	72	281	6,163.80
William Harrold	72	70	68	71	281	6,163.80
Grant Hirschman	70	71	68	72	281	6,163.80
Rico Hoey	67	70	71	73	281	6,163.80
Ben Kohles	71	70	69	71	281	6,163.80
Rick Lamb	69	72	72	68	281	6,163.80
Taylor Moore	70	71	68	72	281	6,163.80
Callum Tarren	69	70	69	73	281	6,163.80
Kevin Dougherty	71	68	69	74	282	4,057.50
Scottie Scheffler	75	68	70	69	282	4,057.50
Chase Seiffert	71	70	71	70	282	4,057.50
Daniel Summerhays	72	70	68	72	282	4,057.50

Pinnacle Bank Championship

The Club at Indian Creek, Omaha, Nebraska
Par 36-35–71; 7,581 yards

July 18-21
purse, $600,000

	SCORES				TOTAL	MONEY
Kristoffer Ventura	67	64	67	70	268	$108,000
Andres Gonzales	67	67	69	67	270	52,800
Chad Ramey	66	67	70	67	270	52,800
Jamie Arnold	68	69	68	68	273	22,620
Joseph Bramlett	69	67	71	66	273	22,620
Brett Coletta	70	65	72	66	273	22,620
Lanto Griffin	67	68	64	74	273	22,620
Ethan Tracy	70	68	69	66	273	22,620
Zac Blair	70	66	72	67	275	13,885.72
Brian Campbell	70	65	74	66	275	13,885.72
Scott Gutschewski	70	65	73	67	275	13,885.72
Tyson Alexander	66	66	70	73	275	13,885.71
Steven Ihm	70	68	70	67	275	13,885.71
Edward Loar	67	70	70	68	275	13,885.71
Byron Meth	64	70	69	72	275	13,885.71

	SCORES				TOTAL	MONEY
M.J. Daffue	67	72	68	69	276	9,900
Jonathan Randolph	70	70	68	68	276	9,900
Brett Drewitt	71	69	70	68	278	8,100
John Oda	69	65	69	75	278	8,100
Callum Tarren	68	69	72	69	278	8,100
Nicholas Thompson	73	68	69	68	278	8,100
Harry Higgs	74	68	66	71	279	5,799.60
Bo Hoag	69	72	67	71	279	5,799.60
Mark Hubbard	69	69	73	68	279	5,799.60
Denzel Ieremia	69	69	69	72	279	5,799.60
Zach Wright	73	64	70	72	279	5,799.60

Price Cutter Charity Championship

Highland Springs Country Club, Springfield, Missouri
Par 36-36–72; 7,115 yards

July 25-28
purse, $700,000

	SCORES				TOTAL	MONEY
Harry Higgs	66	68	65	67	266	$126,000
Andrew Svoboda	68	67	65	68	268	61,600
Steve Wheatcroft	66	66	69	67	268	61,600
Martin Flores	66	67	70	67	270	28,933.34
Grant Hirschman	63	68	67	72	270	28,933.33
Conrad Shindler	63	67	72	68	270	28,933.33
Rafael Campos	69	68	67	67	271	21,816.67
Andres Gallegos	64	70	69	68	271	21,816.67
Jonathan Randolph	64	66	69	72	271	21,816.66
Steven Alker	67	71	64	70	272	18,200
Zac Blair	70	68	66	68	272	18,200
Erik Compton	70	68	68	67	273	14,700
Henrik Norlander	69	68	68	68	273	14,700
Zach Wright	67	68	69	69	273	14,700
Wade Binfield	69	66	69	70	274	11,900
Will Cannon	68	65	73	68	274	11,900
M.J. Daffue	64	70	70	70	274	11,900
Bryan Bigley	69	70	65	71	275	9,128
Brad Hopfinger	67	69	72	67	275	9,128
D.H. Lee	69	68	71	67	275	9,128
Taylor Moore	67	72	69	67	275	9,128
Braden Thornberry	72	67	68	68	275	9,128
Trevor Cone	70	67	69	70	276	6,304.20
Denzel Ieremia	67	72	69	68	276	6,304.20
William Kropp	68	68	69	71	276	6,304.20
Chad Ramey	66	70	70	70	276	6,304.20
Dawie van der Walt	65	70	66	75	276	6,304.20

Ellie Mae Classic

TPC Stonebrae, Hayward, California
Par 35-35–70; 7,024 yards

August 1-4
purse, $600,000

	SCORES				TOTAL	MONEY
Zac Blair	66	65	65	67	263	$108,000
Brandon Crick	67	67	62	68	264	64,800
Maverick McNealy	65	63	68	69	265	40,800
Tyson Alexander	69	63	65	69	266	23,625
Todd Baek	64	68	68	66	266	23,625

	SCORES				TOTAL	MONEY
Joshua Creel	71	64	66	65	266	23,625
Ethan Tracy	68	64	66	68	266	23,625
Grant Hirschman	70	63	65	69	267	17,400
Kevin Lucas	70	63	66	68	267	17,400
Matthew NeSmith	63	63	69	72	267	17,400
David Gazzolo	69	66	67	66	268	13,800
Scott Harrington	65	66	68	69	268	13,800
T.J. Vogel	66	69	65	68	268	13,800
Scott Gutschewski	68	61	68	72	269	9,600
Bo Hoag	68	67	67	67	269	9,600
Mark Hubbard	64	72	68	65	269	9,600
Billy Kennerly	66	64	71	68	269	9,600
Danny Walker	68	64	66	71	269	9,600
Dylan Wu	68	69	64	68	269	9,600
Carl Yuan	70	63	67	69	269	9,600
Blayne Barber	69	66	65	70	270	6,960
Michael Hebert	64	70	66	70	270	6,960
Matt Atkins	62	74	67	68	271	5,119.72
Albin Choi	74	63	65	69	271	5,119.72
Rob Oppenheim	66	68	69	68	271	5,119.72
Joseph Bramlett	66	66	67	72	271	5,119.71
Matthew Campbell	72	64	67	68	271	5,119.71
Horacio Leon	69	68	63	71	271	5,119.71
Justin Suh	66	69	68	68	271	5,119.71

WinCo Foods Portland Open

Pumpkin Ridge Golf Club, Witch Hollow Course, North Plains, Oregon
Par 36-35–71; 7,109 yards

August 8-11
purse, $800,000

	SCORES				TOTAL	MONEY
Bo Hoag	66	68	63	65	262	$144,000
Scott Harrington	67	63	65	69	264	86,400
Kristoffer Ventura	68	63	65	69	265	54,400
Chris Naegel	65	67	70	64	266	38,400
Vince India	64	65	68	70	267	32,000
Rob Oppenheim	67	67	65	69	268	28,800
James Driscoll	68	67	68	66	269	24,100
Fabian Gomez	69	68	66	66	269	24,100
Lee Hodges	70	65	67	67	269	24,100
Edward Loar	67	67	67	68	269	24,100
Rafael Campos	69	65	67	69	270	17,600
Rhein Gibson	70	67	66	67	270	17,600
Robby Shelton	61	70	68	71	270	17,600
Dawie van der Walt	67	70	66	67	270	17,600
Brandon Crick	71	65	69	66	271	13,600
David Lingmerth	64	68	73	66	271	13,600
Charlie Saxon	66	67	69	69	271	13,600
Wade Binfield	67	66	69	70	272	10,080
Ryan Brehm	67	67	71	67	272	10,080
Brett Drewitt	70	66	69	67	272	10,080
Grant Hirschman	67	71	66	68	272	10,080
Mark Hubbard	66	67	69	70	272	10,080
Tyler McCumber	70	67	69	66	272	10,080
Zac Blair	66	68	69	70	273	6,283
Nicolas Echavarria	65	67	72	69	273	6,283
William Harrold	70	65	69	69	273	6,283
Billy Kennerly	67	71	65	70	273	6,283
Max Rottluff	68	67	68	70	273	6,283
Brett Stegmaier	66	70	67	70	273	6,283

428 / AMERICAN TOURS

	SCORES				TOTAL	MONEY
Nicholas Thompson	68	70	69	66	273	6,283
Will Zalatoris	66	69	69	69	273	6,283

Korn Ferry Tour Finals

Nationwide Children's Hospital Championship

The OSU Golf Club, Scarlet Course, Columbus, Ohio
Par 36-35–71; 7,444 yards

August 15-18
purse, $1,000,000

	SCORES				TOTAL	MONEY
Scottie Scheffler	70	68	67	67	272	$180,000
Beau Hossler	69	69	68	68	274	74,666.67
Brendon Todd	72	64	71	67	274	74,666.67
Ben Taylor	68	69	69	68	274	74,666.66
Brandon Hagy	68	67	69	71	275	38,000
Robert Streb	67	71	71	66	275	38,000
Justin Harding	69	70	69	68	276	30,125
Tom Hoge	73	68	68	67	276	30,125
Anirban Lahiri	67	71	68	70	276	30,125
Curtis Luck	72	67	70	67	276	30,125
Jamie Arnold	71	69	66	71	277	23,000
Viktor Hovland	64	73	69	71	277	23,000
Cameron Percy	64	74	71	68	277	23,000
Harris English	75	68	67	68	278	17,000
Scott Harrington	70	67	68	73	278	17,000
Ben Martin	67	70	68	73	278	17,000
T.J. Vogel	69	74	66	69	278	17,000
Johnson Wagner	71	69	69	69	278	17,000
Ryan Brehm	68	74	68	69	279	12,550
Bronson Burgoon	68	70	71	70	279	12,550
Kramer Hickok	70	68	71	70	279	12,550
Chase Seiffert	71	71	68	69	279	12,550
Dominic Bozzelli	73	70	69	68	280	8,136.67
Harry Higgs	68	75	68	69	280	8,136.67
Billy Hurley	68	73	69	70	280	8,136.67
Grayson Murray	72	71	70	67	280	8,136.67
Henrik Norlander	69	74	70	67	280	8,136.67
Adam Svensson	69	73	70	68	280	8,136.67
Joseph Bramlett	73	68	69	70	280	8,136.66
Doug Ghim	65	73	70	72	280	8,136.66
Vincent Whaley	72	69	67	72	280	8,136.66

Albertsons Boise Open

Hillcrest Country Club, Boise, Idaho
Par 36-35–71; 6,880 yards

August 22-25
purse, $1,000,000

	SCORES				TOTAL	MONEY
Matthew NeSmith	70	64	67	64	265	$180,000
Brandon Hagy	70	67	65	64	266	88,000
Viktor Hovland	67	67	64	68	266	88,000
Mark Hubbard	67	69	65	66	267	48,000

		SCORES			TOTAL	MONEY
Ryan Brehm	67	63	70	68	268	35,125
Bronson Burgoon	68	65	66	69	268	35,125
Kramer Hickok	67	68	66	67	268	35,125
Anirban Lahiri	68	65	69	66	268	35,125
Zac Blair	66	66	72	66	270	28,000
Rob Oppenheim	68	70	61	71	270	28,000
Kevin Dougherty	72	63	67	69	271	18,666.67
Joey Garber	70	66	69	66	271	18,666.67
Harry Higgs	69	69	68	65	271	18,666.67
Grayson Murray	64	68	69	70	271	18,666.67
Scottie Scheffler	71	68	67	65	271	18,666.67
Dawie van der Walt	70	67	69	65	271	18,666.67
Hank Lebioda	65	70	65	71	271	18,666.66
Cameron Percy	69	69	64	69	271	18,666.66
Charlie Saxon	64	67	70	70	271	18,666.66
Jonathan Byrd	72	65	65	70	272	11,240
Tom Hoge	65	69	71	67	272	11,240
Scott Langley	70	68	67	67	272	11,240
Jose de Jesus Rodriguez	68	65	73	66	272	11,240
Brendon Todd	66	67	73	66	272	11,240
Joseph Bramlett	70	69	68	66	273	7,946
Cameron Davis	67	70	66	70	273	7,946
Beau Hossler	71	66	70	66	273	7,946
Kyle Jones	66	70	69	68	273	7,946
Justin Lower	68	71	66	68	273	7,946

Korn Ferry Tour Championship

Victoria National Golf Club, Newburgh, Indiana
Par 36-36–72; 7,242 yards

August 30-September 2
purse, $1,000,000

		SCORES			TOTAL	MONEY
Tom Lewis	68	66	66	65	265	$180,000
Fabian Gomez	69	69	66	66	270	108,000
Kramer Hickok	69	66	72	65	272	68,000
Tyler Duncan	67	71	71	66	275	41,333.34
Chris Baker	63	69	73	70	275	41,333.33
David Hearn	70	69	70	66	275	41,333.33
D.J. Trahan	71	67	68	70	276	28,083.34
Richy Werenski	72	66	69	69	276	28,083.34
Lanto Griffin	69	65	68	74	276	28,083.33
Grayson Murray	73	66	65	72	276	28,083.33
Henrik Norlander	68	69	68	71	276	28,083.33
Scottie Scheffler	71	65	68	72	276	28,083.33
Blayne Barber	71	68	68	70	277	20,000
Cameron Davis	68	73	69	67	277	20,000
Lee Hodges	72	69	68	69	278	16,500
Adam Svensson	70	68	72	68	278	16,500
Peter Uihlein	70	72	66	70	278	16,500
Will Zalatoris	72	68	71	67	278	16,500
Brandon Crick	67	73	68	71	279	13,000
Doug Ghim	71	70	66	72	279	13,000
Hank Lebioda	71	68	69	71	279	13,000
Ben Crane	70	68	72	70	280	10,000
Joshua Creel	72	71	68	69	280	10,000
Billy Hurley	70	69	69	72	280	10,000
Vincent Whaley	70	72	67	71	280	10,000

Mackenzie Tour–PGA Tour Canada

Canada Life Open

Point Grey Golf & Country Club, Vancouver, British Columbia
Par 36-36–72; 6,801 yards

May 23-26
purse, C$200,000

	SCORES				TOTAL	MONEY
Jake Knapp	65	68	70	64	267	C$36,000
James Allenby	68	63	67	71	269	17,600
Brian Carlson	63	71	69	66	269	17,600
Lorens Chan	69	69	69	63	270	8,800
Dylan Wu	69	68	67	66	270	8,800
Paul Barjon	71	64	69	68	272	7,200
Chris O'Neill	71	68	67	67	273	6,450
Eric Ricard	70	65	70	68	273	6,450
Dawson Armstrong	68	69	64	73	274	5,000
Hayden Buckley	68	70	68	68	274	5,000
Charlie Danielson	68	69	69	68	274	5,000
Gerardo Ruiz	68	68	66	72	274	5,000
Hunter Stewart	69	67	70	68	274	5,000
Tyler Weworski	65	70	68	72	275	3,700
Zach Zaback	69	67	72	67	275	3,700
Derek Bayley	71	68	68	69	276	3,200
Case Cochran	67	67	70	72	276	3,200
Mark Silvers	69	71	68	68	276	3,200
Jared Bettcher	69	68	71	69	277	2,510
Jeremy Gandon	72	66	72	67	277	2,510
Joseph Harrison	69	69	69	70	277	2,510
Doc Redman	68	69	72	68	277	2,510

Bayview Place DCBank Open

Uplands Golf Club, Victoria, British Columbia
Par 35-35–70; 6,420 yards

May 30-June 2
purse, C$200,000

	SCORES				TOTAL	MONEY
Paul Barjon	69	64	63	65	261	C$36,000
Doc Redman	64	65	65	68	262	21,600
Patrick Fishburn	66	68	66	66	266	13,600
Ian Holt	67	66	67	68	268	8,800
Cole Miller	65	68	67	68	268	8,800
Zach Cabra	66	63	68	72	269	6,475
Charlie Danielson	69	68	68	64	269	6,475
Andrew Dorn	69	64	68	68	269	6,475
Travis Trace	70	65	62	72	269	6,475
Lorens Chan	69	71	65	65	270	5,000
Chris O'Neill	65	70	68	67	270	5,000
Taylor Pendrith	67	70	66	67	270	5,000
Greyson Sigg	70	64	68	69	271	4,200
Bryson Nimmer	72	65	70	65	272	3,600
Ryan Snouffer	68	68	67	69	272	3,600
Peyton White	69	66	68	69	272	3,600
Theo Humphrey	67	72	62	72	273	3,200

	SCORES				TOTAL	MONEY
Derek Barron	72	68	66	68	274	2,608
Carter Jenkins	67	69	69	69	274	2,608
Andrew McCain	68	71	68	67	274	2,608
Yannik Paul	68	69	66	71	274	2,608
Carr Vernon	70	70	65	69	274	2,608

GolfBC Championship

Gallagher's Canyon Golf & Country Club, Kelowna, British Columbia June 13-16
Par 36-36–72; 6,802 yards purse, C$200,000

	SCORES				TOTAL	MONEY
Jake Knapp	64	67	70	63	264	C$36,000
Jonathan Garrick	67	64	70	64	265	21,600
Greyson Sigg	71	67	70	59	267	13,600
Lorens Chan	68	65	67	68	268	9,600
Kyler Dunkle	68	67	66	68	269	8,000
Paul Barjon	70	67	65	69	271	6,700
Greg Eason	72	66	66	67	271	6,700
William Register	72	67	64	68	271	6,700
Dawson Armstrong	68	68	69	67	272	4,800
Kolton Crawford	71	68	65	68	272	4,800
Jon Curran	69	71	63	69	272	4,800
Lee Detmer	67	70	68	67	272	4,800
Tain Lee	70	68	67	67	272	4,800
Drew McCullough	66	74	66	66	272	4,800
Stephen Franken	68	66	71	68	273	3,400
Will Gordon	72	66	66	69	273	3,400
Brad Miller	72	66	68	67	273	3,400
Ian Holt	74	67	62	71	274	2,700
Philip Knowles	69	66	69	70	274	2,700
S.M. Lee	71	68	66	69	274	2,700
Jeremy Paul	70	68	68	68	274	2,700

Lethbridge Paradise Canyon Open

Paradise Canyon Golf Resort, Lethbridge, Alberta June 20-23
Par 36-35–71; 6,810 yards purse, C$200,000

	SCORES				TOTAL	MONEY
Alex Chiarella	64	67	65	68	264	C$36,000
Travis Trace	63	65	70	67	265	21,600
Hayden Buckley	64	71	65	66	266	9,600
Justin Doeden	68	62	68	68	266	9,600
Jake Johnson	66	69	67	64	266	9,600
Andrew Yun	66	70	63	67	266	9,600
Lorens Chan	64	67	69	68	268	6,450
Theo Humphrey	70	66	64	68	268	6,450
Bryson Nimmer	68	70	68	63	269	5,600
Zane Thomas	62	70	70	67	269	5,600
Dawson Armstrong	64	71	67	68	270	3,850
Derek Bayley	65	73	68	64	270	3,850
Sebastian Crampton	67	69	69	65	270	3,850
Jared du Toit	66	68	68	68	270	3,850
Jake Knapp	66	71	64	69	270	3,850
Drew McCullough	68	68	68	66	270	3,850
David Pastore	67	65	69	69	270	3,850

	SCORES				TOTAL	MONEY
Andrew Paysse	67	69	67	67	270	3,850
Patrick Martin	68	70	68	65	271	2,600
Andrew McCain	67	71	68	65	271	2,600
Brad Miller	68	68	68	67	271	2,600

Windsor Championship

Ambassador Golf Club, Windsor, Ontario
Par 35-36–71; 7,033 yards

July 4-7
purse, C$200,000

	SCORES				TOTAL	MONEY
Dawson Armstrong	68	63	67	66	264	C$36,000
Paul Barjon	65	67	66	67	265	11,116.67
Patrick Fishburn	67	68	65	65	265	11,116.67
Anthony Maccaglia	64	66	70	65	265	11,116.67
Ryan Ruffels	69	63	67	66	265	11,116.67
Jonathan Garrick	65	65	66	69	265	11,116.66
William Register	66	66	66	67	265	11,116.66
Grady Brame	64	68	68	66	266	5,600
Hayden Buckley	68	64	66	68	266	5,600
Paul McConnell	68	67	66	65	266	5,600
Riley Wheeldon	64	67	67	68	266	5,600
Matt Gilchrest	63	68	73	63	267	4,050
Tain Lee	70	67	64	66	267	4,050
Eric McCardle	64	65	69	69	267	4,050
Charles Wang	63	73	67	64	267	4,050
Nathan Jeansonne	62	70	68	68	268	3,100
Bryson Nimmer	69	67	61	71	268	3,100
Taylor Pendrith	67	68	66	67	268	3,100
David Wicks	65	67	68	68	268	3,100
James Allenby	69	65	67	68	269	2,035
Zach Cabra	66	68	66	69	269	2,035
Joseph Harrison	66	66	71	66	269	2,035
Matt Marshall	66	70	66	67	269	2,035
Cooper Musselman	69	66	69	65	269	2,035
Sean Walsh	69	67	65	68	269	2,035
Dalton Ward	69	68	67	65	269	2,035
Peyton White	64	72	66	67	269	2,035

Osprey Valley Open

TPC Toronto at Osprey Valley, Caledon, Ontario
Par 36-36–72; 7,151 yards

July 11-14
purse, C$200,000

	SCORES				TOTAL	MONEY
Paul Barjon	64	66	66	67	263	C$36,000
Taylor Pendrith	63	68	67	68	266	21,600
Jake Knapp	69	65	66	67	267	13,600
David Pastore	68	67	64	69	268	9,600
Hayden Buckley	67	69	65	68	269	7,600
Jared Wolfe	67	66	69	67	269	7,600
Justin Doeden	68	67	66	69	270	6,025
Elliott Paylor	67	67	70	66	270	6,025
Greyson Sigg	70	65	67	68	270	6,025
Sean Walsh	65	66	68	71	270	6,025
Stephen Franken	67	68	67	69	271	4,240
Jeremy Gandon	64	70	66	71	271	4,240

	SCORES				TOTAL	MONEY
Bryson Nimmer	67	65	69	70	271	4,240
Yannik Paul	68	66	71	66	271	4,240
Ashton Van Horne	63	72	71	65	271	4,240
Brian Carlson	68	68	69	67	272	3,200
Jorge Garcia	67	70	66	69	272	3,200
Tain Lee	68	64	70	70	272	3,200
Grady Brame	68	69	68	68	273	2,510
Lorens Chan	71	64	72	66	273	2,510
Brent Grant	67	66	71	69	273	2,510
Brad Miller	67	68	66	72	273	2,510

HFX Pro-Am

Oakfield Golf & Country Club, Halifax, Nova Scotia
Par 36-36–72; 6,747 yards

July 18-21
purse, C$200,000

	SCORES				TOTAL	MONEY
Lorens Chan	66	63	68	67	264	C$36,000
Jake Knapp	66	67	66	67	266	21,600
Taylor Pendrith	65	66	68	69	268	10,400
Blake Sattler	67	71	64	66	268	10,400
Hayden Shieh	65	65	68	70	268	10,400
Patrick Fishburn	68	66	69	66	269	6,950
Jared Wolfe	62	70	68	69	269	6,950
Kyle Mueller	65	68	69	68	270	6,200
Paul Barjon	68	64	71	68	271	5,600
Ian Holt	65	68	67	71	271	5,600
Hayden Buckley	67	68	70	67	272	4,240
Lee Detmer	69	62	70	71	272	4,240
Greg Eason	70	66	67	69	272	4,240
Cole Miller	69	69	67	67	272	4,240
Greyson Sigg	68	69	68	67	272	4,240
Jorge Garcia	68	69	70	66	273	2,805.72
Brent Grant	65	69	71	68	273	2,805.72
Riley Wheeldon	70	66	70	67	273	2,805.72
Mark Anguiano	65	71	74	63	273	2,805.71
Jared Bettcher	68	67	73	65	273	2,805.71
Stoney Crouch	64	65	69	75	273	2,805.71
Anthony Maccaglia	67	69	66	71	273	2,805.71

1932byBateman Open

Edmonton Country Club, Edmonton, Alberta
Par 36-35–71; 6,963 yards

August 1-4
purse, C$200,000

	SCORES				TOTAL	MONEY
Taylor Pendrith	69	67	69	62	267	C$36,000
Lorens Chan	69	70	66	65	270	21,600
Will Gordon	64	64	73	70	271	10,400
Ian Holt	65	67	71	68	271	10,400
Ryan Ruffels	66	67	70	68	271	10,400
Zach Cabra	65	67	71	69	272	6,475
Stoney Crouch	67	65	71	69	272	6,475
Jorge Garcia	70	66	69	67	272	6,475
David Pastore	66	68	71	67	272	6,475
Derek Barron	69	69	67	68	273	4,800
Wil Bateman	67	70	69	67	273	4,800

434 / AMERICAN TOURS

	SCORES				TOTAL	MONEY
Brinson Paolini	68	69	68	68	273	4,800
Greyson Sigg	70	68	70	65	273	4,800
Brian Carlson	71	67	67	69	274	3,200
Myles Creighton	67	70	68	69	274	3,200
Jeremy Paul	67	70	67	70	274	3,200
Yannik Paul	73	65	70	66	274	3,200
Christopher Petefish	67	69	72	66	274	3,200
David Wicks	69	69	68	68	274	3,200
Andrew Yun	66	69	69	70	274	3,200

ATB Financial Classic

Country Hills Golf Club, Talons Course, Calgary, Alberta
Par 36-36–72; 7,209 yards

August 8-11
purse, C$200,000

	SCORES				TOTAL	MONEY
Hayden Buckley	66	66	64	70	266	C$36,000
Sam Fidone	64	67	68	67	266	21,600
(Buckley defeated Fidone on first playoff hole.)						
Lorens Chan	66	69	66	68	269	13,600
Paul Barjon	66	67	70	67	270	9,600
Andrew Yun	70	67	69	65	271	6,328.58
Stoney Crouch	63	67	72	69	271	6,328.57
Carter Jenkins	67	70	67	67	271	6,328.57
Jeremy Paul	68	68	69	66	271	6,328.57
Taylor Pendrith	62	69	71	69	271	6,328.57
Christopher Petefish	64	70	70	67	271	6,328.57
Zach Zaback	64	69	67	71	271	6,328.57
James Love	71	65	68	68	272	4,400
Cole Miller	69	65	71	67	272	4,400
Wes Heffernan	66	68	70	69	273	3,500
David Pastore	67	69	68	69	273	3,500
Yannik Paul	66	67	75	65	273	3,500
Travis Trace	65	69	69	70	273	3,500
James Allenby	71	66	68	69	274	2,608
Will Gordon	67	68	70	69	274	2,608
Evan Harmeling	69	69	68	68	274	2,608
Stuart Macdonald	63	71	69	71	274	2,608
Jared Wolfe	70	69	70	65	274	2,608

Players Cup

Southwood Golf & Country Club, Winnipeg, Manitoba
Par 36-36–72; 7,311 yards

August 15-18
purse, C$200,000

	SCORES				TOTAL	MONEY
Derek Barron	70	68	64	72	274	C$36,000
Kyler Dunkle	67	69	69	70	275	17,600
Ryan Snouffer	69	65	70	71	275	17,600
Paul Barjon	73	68	70	65	276	8,266.67
Will Gordon	73	61	75	67	276	8,266.67
Jared Wolfe	68	71	66	71	276	8,266.66
Ian Holt	69	69	68	71	277	6,025
Jake Knapp	69	68	68	72	277	6,025
Richard Lee	72	66	69	70	277	6,025
Kyle Mueller	71	67	69	70	277	6,025
Derek Chang	64	68	76	70	278	4,100

		SCORES			TOTAL	MONEY
Sebastian Crampton	68	68	72	70	278	4,100
Eric McCardle	72	69	71	66	278	4,100
Cooper Musselman	69	71	69	69	278	4,100
Ryan Ruffels	67	68	76	67	278	4,100
Daniel Stringfellow	70	63	74	71	278	4,100
Hayden Buckley	69	69	64	77	279	2,900
Myles Creighton	71	67	73	68	279	2,900
Michael Schoolcraft	71	65	72	71	279	2,900
Zach Zaback	68	67	73	71	279	2,900

Mackenzie Investments Open

Elm Ridge Country Club, North Course, Montreal, Quebec
Par 36-36–72; 6,996 yards

September 5-8
purse, C$200,000

		SCORES			TOTAL	MONEY
Taylor Pendrith	69	62	62	67	260	C$36,000
Kyle Mueller	64	67	67	70	268	21,600
David Pastore	69	69	64	67	269	13,600
Greyson Sigg	70	65	66	69	270	9,600
Sam Fidone	65	68	68	70	271	7,600
Hayden Shieh	69	66	66	70	271	7,600
James Allenby	70	68	69	65	272	5,616.67
Hayden Buckley	69	68	69	66	272	5,616.67
Eric Dietrich	68	66	71	67	272	5,616.67
Matthew Naumec	66	71	69	66	272	5,616.67
Lorens Chan	69	69	65	69	272	5,616.66
Theo Humphrey	67	70	65	70	272	5,616.66
Ian Holt	67	67	72	67	273	3,640
Philip Knowles	70	68	70	65	273	3,640
Richard Lee	72	69	64	68	273	3,640
Ryan Ruffels	67	67	71	68	273	3,640
Billy Walthouse	67	68	67	71	273	3,640
Paul Barjon	70	71	69	64	274	2,700
Grady Brame	68	71	65	70	274	2,700
S.M. Lee	67	70	70	67	274	2,700
Cooper Musselman	70	68	68	68	274	2,700

Canada Life Championship

Highland Country Club, London, Ontario
Par 36-36–72; 6,584 yards

September 12-15
purse, C$225,000

		SCORES			TOTAL	MONEY
Patrick Fishburn	66	65	64	64	259	C$40,500
David Pastore	68	66	65	63	262	24,300
Eric McCardle	65	66	68	65	264	15,300
Jonathan Garrick	69	62	69	66	266	10,800
Brad Miller	67	67	67	66	267	9,000
Brian Carlson	68	60	72	68	268	7,537.50
Jeremy Paul	70	61	66	71	268	7,537.50
Blake Sattler	71	66	66	65	268	7,537.50
Chris O'Neill	72	64	63	70	269	6,300
Travis Trace	65	69	67	68	269	6,300
James Allenby	68	70	70	62	270	4,331.25
Lorens Chan	70	67	66	67	270	4,331.25
Ian Holt	71	68	62	69	270	4,331.25

	SCORES				TOTAL	MONEY
Theo Humphrey	69	64	68	69	270	4,331.25
Cooper Musselman	69	67	68	66	270	4,331.25
Taylor Pendrith	66	63	72	69	270	4,331.25
Greyson Sigg	69	65	71	65	270	4,331.25
Riley Wheeldon	71	67	64	68	270	4,331.25
Jorge Garcia	66	73	64	68	271	3,150
Alex Chiarella	70	66	67	69	272	2,621.25
Andrew McCain	69	66	67	70	272	2,621.25
Kyle Mueller	71	69	68	64	272	2,621.25
Sean Walsh	69	67	69	67	272	2,621.25

PGA Tour Latinoamerica

Buenaventura Classic

Buenaventura Golf Club, Rio Hato, Panama
Par 36-36–72; 7,383 yards

March 27-30
purse, $175,000

	SCORES				TOTAL	MONEY
Jared Wolfe	66	68	71	70	275	$31,500
Mitchell Meissner	74	69	67	70	280	13,066.67
Ryan Ruffels	66	75	68	71	280	13,066.67
Mito Pereira	69	69	69	73	280	13,066.66
Michael Davan	67	70	75	71	283	7,000
Charlie Bull	74	68	75	67	284	5,665.63
Brian Hughes	73	71	71	69	284	5,665.63
Rafael Becker	73	72	68	71	284	5,665.62
Jose Toledo	74	69	71	70	284	5,665.62
Santiago Gomez	73	69	71	72	285	4,550
Tom Whitney	74	73	70	68	285	4,550
Cristobal Del Solar	73	73	71	69	286	3,850
Harrison Endycott	72	71	75	68	286	3,850
Will Collins	71	75	72	69	287	3,062.50
Patrick Flavin	74	73	69	71	287	3,062.50
Augusto Nunez	72	75	74	66	287	3,062.50
Sulman Raza	73	72	67	75	287	3,062.50
Clodomiro Carranza	74	71	75	68	288	2,210.84
Cristian DiMarco	73	72	73	70	288	2,210.84
Jacob Bergeron	71	73	73	71	288	2,210.83
Edward Figueroa	73	73	70	72	288	2,210.83
Andreas Halvorsen	77	71	69	71	288	2,210.83
Curtis Reed	73	71	73	71	288	2,210.83

Molino Canuelas Championship

Canuelas Golf Club, Buenos Aires, Argentina
Par 36-36–72; 7,267 yards

April 11-14
purse, US$175,000

	SCORES				TOTAL	MONEY
Andres Echavarria	68	68	72	66	274	$31,500
Ryan Ruffels	69	71	67	67	274	18,900
(Echavarria defeated Ruffels on second playoff hole.)						
Andreas Halvorsen	70	68	68	69	275	11,900
Rafael Becker	69	71	69	67	276	8,400
Cesar Costilla	70	68	69	70	277	6,387.50
Victor Lange	68	70	69	70	277	6,387.50
Patrick Newcomb	73	67	70	67	277	6,387.50
Ryan Baca	69	68	72	69	278	4,725
Jose Coceres	72	67	72	67	278	4,725
Mario Galiano Aguilar	71	71	68	68	278	4,725
Augusto Nunez	74	67	70	67	278	4,725
Alexandre Rocha	69	71	68	70	278	4,725
Curtis Yonke	73	68	71	67	279	3,383.34
Clodomiro Carranza	71	66	70	72	279	3,383.33
Tom Whitney	73	67	69	70	279	3,383.33
Seth Fair	71	67	71	71	280	2,625
Chase Johnson	70	70	68	72	280	2,625
Leandro Marelli	73	67	70	70	280	2,625
Paulo Pinto	73	68	71	68	280	2,625
Dalan Refioglu	69	70	74	67	280	2,625

Abierto de Chile

Club de Golf Mapocho, Santiago, Chile
Par 35-36–71; 7,276 yards

April 18-21
purse, US$175,000

	SCORES				TOTAL	MONEY
John Somers	68	65	67	65	265	$31,500
Alex Weiss	63	69	66	69	267	18,900
Joaquin Niemann	64	67	71	66	268	11,900
Alexandre Rocha	65	67	71	67	270	8,400
Augusto Nunez	68	67	67	69	271	6,387.50
Mito Pereira	70	66	67	68	271	6,387.50
Matt Ryan	67	70	65	69	271	6,387.50
Jared Wolfe	64	70	70	68	272	5,425
Joshua Lee	69	68	67	69	273	4,900
Shad Tuten	69	68	68	68	273	4,900
Derek Bayley	69	69	67	69	274	4,375
Cesar Costilla	69	67	70	69	275	3,543.75
Harrison Endycott	68	70	68	69	275	3,543.75
Brian Hughes	69	69	68	69	275	3,543.75
Franck Medale	69	70	67	69	275	3,543.75
Isidro Benitez	68	67	70	71	276	2,380
Jorge Fernandez-Valdes	68	70	71	67	276	2,380
Patrick Flavin	67	71	67	71	276	2,380
Maximiliano Godoy	72	67	72	65	276	2,380
Ricardo Gonzalez	66	68	71	71	276	2,380
Toni Hakula	68	67	67	74	276	2,380
Victor Lange	67	70	69	70	276	2,380
Mark Tullo	68	71	70	67	276	2,380

Abierto OSDE del Centro

Cordoba Golf Club, Cordoba, Argentina
Par 35-37–72; 6,768 yards

April 25-28
purse, US$175,000

	SCORES				TOTAL	MONEY
Tom Whitney	73	67	66	64	270	$31,500
Nicolo Galletti	73	64	67	67	271	18,900
Santiago Gomez	75	65	67	65	272	11,900
Russell Budd	71	66	65	72	274	7,700
Maximiliano Godoy	74	67	65	68	274	7,700
John Somers	69	71	65	70	275	6,300
Tommy Cocha	69	69	67	73	278	5,092.50
Greg Eason	74	68	69	67	278	5,092.50
Mito Pereira	72	69	67	70	278	5,092.50
Paulo Pinto	64	67	74	73	278	5,092.50
Manav Shah	70	71	68	69	278	5,092.50
German Tagle [A]	71	67	70	70	278	
Isidro Benitez	73	71	69	67	280	3,543.75
Jorge Fernandez-Valdes	70	70	70	70	280	3,543.75
Andreas Halvorsen	72	70	71	67	280	3,543.75
Ignacio Marino	74	69	68	69	280	3,543.75
Clodomiro Carranza	76	67	70	68	281	2,887.50
Seth Fair	73	67	73	68	281	2,887.50
Steven Fox	72	69	67	74	282	2,362.50
Augusto Nunez	70	74	70	68	282	2,362.50
Matt Ryan	74	65	70	73	282	2,362.50
Alejandro Tosti	74	69	70	69	282	2,362.50

Puerto Plata Open

Playa Dorada Golf Course, Puerto Plata, Dominican Republic
Par 36-35–72; 6,990 yards

May 2-5
purse, US$175,000

	SCORES				TOTAL	MONEY
Cristobal Del Solar	66	66	69	69	270	$31,500
Scott Wolfes	68	66	68	69	271	18,900
Willy Pumarol	71	65	64	74	274	10,150
Alexandre Rocha	71	66	68	69	274	10,150
Blake Cannon	66	71	68	70	275	5,932.50
Harrison Endycott	68	72	67	68	275	5,932.50
Seth Fair	68	69	71	67	275	5,932.50
Augusto Nunez	69	68	71	67	275	5,932.50
Mito Pereira	67	70	72	66	275	5,932.50
Tommy Cocha	68	68	72	68	276	4,375
Chase Hanna	68	74	69	65	276	4,375
Nicholas Maruri	70	69	74	63	276	4,375
Luis Fernando Barco	69	73	67	68	277	3,091.67
Jacob Bergeron	70	70	70	67	277	3,091.67
Santiago Gomez	71	67	73	66	277	3,091.67
Patrick Newcomb	70	71	71	65	277	3,091.67
Clodomiro Carranza	67	72	67	71	277	3,091.66
Jason Thresher	74	64	67	72	277	3,091.66
Russell Budd	66	67	73	72	278	2,198.44
Ben Corfee	69	71	71	67	278	2,198.44
Andreas Halvorsen	66	73	70	69	278	2,198.44
Shad Tuten	70	67	69	72	278	2,198.43

BMW Jamaica Classic

Cinnamon Hill Golf Club, Montego Bay, Jamaica May 16-19
Par 36-36–72; 6,828 yards purse, US$175,000

	SCORES				TOTAL	MONEY
Evan Harmeling	66	66	64	71	267	US$31,500
Augusto Nunez	66	67	66	69	268	18,900
Leandro Marelli	68	68	68	65	269	11,900
Tom Whitney	65	69	66	70	270	8,400
Mito Pereira	66	68	65	72	271	7,000
Camilo Aguado	67	72	67	66	272	6,081.25
Ryan Ruffels	67	69	69	67	272	6,081.25
Dawson Armstrong	69	64	67	73	273	4,725
Mario Beltran	66	70	71	66	273	4,725
Rowin Caron	69	68	71	65	273	4,725
Juan Pablo Luna	67	67	67	72	273	4,725
Jose Toledo	69	64	70	70	273	4,725
Jorge Fernandez-Valdes	72	63	69	70	274	3,185
Santiago Gomez	67	71	67	69	274	3,185
Carson Jacobs	71	65	69	69	274	3,185
Barrett Kelpin	67	67	68	72	274	3,185
Matt Ryan	69	67	71	67	274	3,185
Steven Fox	70	70	68	67	275	2,283.75
Mario Galiano	66	69	69	71	275	2,283.75
Andreas Halvorsen	68	68	68	71	275	2,283.75
Rodrigo Lee	70	70	68	67	275	2,283.75
Samuel Stevens	68	70	67	70	275	2,283.75

Abierto Mexicano de Golf

Club Campestre Tijuana, Tijuana, Mexico March 23-26
Par 36-36–72; 6,834 yards purse, US$175,000

	SCORES				TOTAL	MONEY
Drew Nesbitt	64	69	68	62	263	US$31,500
Andreas Halvorsen	67	70	66	62	265	15,400
Gustavo Silva	68	67	61	69	265	15,400
Matthew Pinizzotto	63	69	70	64	266	6,890.63
Sulman Raza	67	68	66	65	266	6,890.63
Rodrigo Lee	68	69	63	66	266	6,890.62
Matt Ryan	68	62	66	70	266	6,890.62
Shad Tuten	66	68	68	65	267	5,425
Ryan Baca	67	67	69	65	268	4,050
Will Collins	66	68	67	67	268	4,050
Harrison Endycott	66	71	65	66	268	4,050
Carson Jacobs	65	71	65	67	268	4,050
Mito Pereira	65	65	72	66	268	4,050
Sebastian Vazquez	69	67	69	63	268	4,050
Michael Weaver	69	66	66	67	268	4,050
Jared Wolfe	70	65	66	68	269	2,975
Ryan Ruffels	67	66	67	70	270	2,712.50
Jose Toledo	69	69	68	64	270	2,712.50
Blake Abercrombie	69	69	66	67	271	1,944.69
Fernando Cruz Valle	67	70	67	67	271	1,944.69
Greg Eason	70	68	68	65	271	1,944.69
Raul Pereda	67	68	69	67	271	1,944.69
Dalan Refioglu	68	68	66	69	271	1,944.69
Tom Whitney	68	66	68	69	271	1,944.69
Augusto Nunez	65	67	68	71	271	1,944.68
Sebastian Szirmak	70	64	66	71	271	1,944.68

Bupa Match Play

Playa Paraiso Golf Club, Playa del Carmen, Mexico, May 30-June 2
Par 36-36–72; 6,800 yards purse, US$125,000

ROUND OF 16

Harrison Endycott defeated Tom Whitney, 1 up.
Tommy Cocha defeated Willy Pumarol, 4 and 3.
Leandro Marelli defeated Jared Wolfe, 20 holes.
Patrick Flavin defeated Edward Figueroa, 3 and 1.
Rodrigo Lee defeated Alex Weiss, 1 up.
Chase Hanna defeated John Somers, 6 and 5.
Camilo Aguado defeated Patrick Newcomb, 1 up.
Alexandre Rocha defeated Jacob Bergeron, 3 and 1.

(Each losing player received $1,500.)

QUARTER-FINALS

Cocha defeated Endycott, 19 holes.
Flavin defeated Marelli, 2 up.
Lee defeated Hanna, 2 up.
Rocha defeated Aguado, 19 holes.

(Each losing player received $4,000.)

SEMI-FINALS

Flavin defeated Cocha, 19 holes.
Lee defeated Rocha, 1 up.

(Each losing player received $10,000.)

FINAL

Flavin defeated Lee, 1 up.

(Flavin received $30,000; Lee received $15,000.)

Sao Paulo Golf Club Championship

Sao Paulo Golf Club, Sao Paulo, Brazil September 19-22
Par 35-36–71; 6,574 yards purse, US$175,000

	SCORES				TOTAL	MONEY
Chandler Blanchet	69	61	67	69	266	US$31,500
Augusto Nunez	68	63	67	69	267	18,900
Evan Harmeling	71	67	65	67	270	10,150
Eric Steger	70	67	69	64	270	10,150
Rowin Caron	69	65	69	68	271	6,650
Jorge Fernandez-Valdes	68	64	69	70	271	6,650
Vince India	70	68	67	67	272	5,271.88
Michael Weaver	67	68	70	67	272	5,271.88
Brad Hopfinger	68	69	67	68	272	5,271.87
Leandro Marelli	72	66	66	68	272	5,271.87
Drew Nesbitt	69	66	72	66	273	4,025
Paulo Pinto	70	67	68	68	273	4,025
Sebastian Szirmak	68	69	66	70	273	4,025
Otto Black	71	66	67	70	274	2,800
Michael Buttacavoli	67	68	67	72	274	2,800
Clodomiro Carranza	69	65	69	71	274	2,800
Seth Fair	67	67	75	65	274	2,800
Dalan Refioglu	67	67	66	74	274	2,800
Shad Tuten	66	70	67	71	274	2,800
Jared Wolfe	70	66	68	70	274	2,800

JHSF Aberto do Brasil

Fazenda Boa Vista, Porto Feliz, Brazil
Par 35-36–71; 7,284 yards

September 26-29
purse, US$175,000

	SCORES				TOTAL	MONEY
Shad Tuten	67	65	64	67	263	US$31,500
Patrick Flavin	63	68	65	69	265	15,400
Patrick Newcomb	64	66	65	70	265	15,400
Jorge Fernandez-Valdes	66	70	69	61	266	7,700
Sam Stevens	65	69	69	63	266	7,700
Matt Ryan	65	67	71	64	267	6,300
Andres Gallegos	67	69	65	67	268	5,454.17
Rodrigo Lee	65	65	68	70	268	5,454.17
Augusto Nunez	61	72	65	70	268	5,454.16
Steven Fox	67	65	69	68	269	4,025
Tano Goya	66	65	70	68	269	4,025
M.J. Maguire	71	64	68	66	269	4,025
Jose Toledo	68	64	64	73	269	4,025
Jared Wolfe	70	66	65	68	269	4,025
Tom Whitney	65	68	69	68	270	3,150
Chase Hanna	73	64	67	67	271	2,712.50
Evan Harmeling	65	71	70	65	271	2,712.50
Mito Pereira	67	67	71	66	271	2,712.50
Alex Weiss	70	64	67	70	271	2,712.50
Clodomiro Carranza	69	69	70	65	273	2,047.50
Tommy Cocha	64	68	75	66	273	2,047.50
Felipe Navarro	65	68	69	71	273	2,047.50
Juan Carlos Serrano	67	70	71	65	273	2,047.50

Banco del Pacifico Open

Quito Tennis y Golf Club, Quito, Ecuador
Par 36-36–72; 7,356 yards

October 3-6
purse, US$175,000

	SCORES				TOTAL	MONEY
Augusto Nunez	68	67	64	67	266	US$31,500
Clodomiro Carranza	63	66	72	71	272	18,900
Evan Harmeling	69	69	68	68	274	11,900
Camilo Aguado	73	67	72	63	275	7,233.34
Ricardo Celia	69	65	70	71	275	7,233.33
Tommy Cocha	65	70	71	69	275	7,233.33
Alex Weiss	68	70	72	67	277	5,454.17
Tom Whitney	69	70	69	69	277	5,454.17
Shad Tuten	69	69	67	72	277	5,454.16
Andreas Halvorsen	68	65	76	69	278	4,550
Vince India	69	68	69	72	278	4,550
Rowin Caron	69	71	70	69	279	3,675
Ryan Ruffels	69	71	70	69	279	3,675
Manav Shah	66	72	73	68	279	3,675
Chandler Blanchet	70	69	64	77	280	3,150
Ryan Baca	69	73	70	69	281	2,800
Russell Budd	68	74	70	69	281	2,800
Matt Ryan	67	69	76	69	281	2,800
Sam Stevens	73	70	70	69	282	2,063.55
Jorge Fernandez-Valdes	71	71	68	72	282	2,063.54
Chris Korte	72	69	71	70	282	2,063.54
Marcos Montenegro	70	73	69	70	282	2,063.54
Mito Pereira	71	69	70	72	282	2,063.54
Jose Toledo	67	70	71	74	282	2,063.54

Diners Club Peru Open

Los Inkas Golf Club, Lima, Peru
Par 36-36–72; 6,914 yards

October 17-20
purse, US$175,000

	SCORES				TOTAL	MONEY
Leandro Marelli	66	68	68	67	269	US$31,500
John Somers	69	67	65	69	270	18,900
Andres Gallegos	67	64	67	73	271	11,900
Nicolas Echavarria	67	72	65	68	272	6,890.63
Santiago Gomez	72	68	67	65	272	6,890.63
Russell Budd	69	68	64	71	272	6,890.62
Justin Suh	66	63	68	75	272	6,890.62
Evan Harmeling	69	71	68	65	273	5,250
Matt Ryan	64	69	69	71	273	5,250
Thomas Baik	70	67	66	71	274	4,025
Toni Hakula	68	67	72	67	274	4,025
Augusto Nunez	67	67	70	70	274	4,025
Hunter Richardson	69	69	66	70	274	4,025
Jose Toledo	72	68	66	68	274	4,025
John Coultas	66	70	69	70	275	2,800
Carson Jacobs	67	70	70	68	275	2,800
Felipe Navarro	67	70	70	68	275	2,800
Raul Pereda	68	70	71	66	275	2,800
Sebastian Szirmak	69	70	64	72	275	2,800
Will Collins	68	71	68	69	276	1,986.25
Steven Fox	71	68	68	69	276	1,986.25
Matt Hutchins	68	70	69	69	276	1,986.25
Jose Luis Montano	71	66	70	69	276	1,986.25
Marcelo Rozo	68	70	71	67	276	1,986.25

Termas de Rio Hondo Invitational

Rio Hondo Golf Club, Rio Hondo, Argentina
Par 36-35–71; 6,370 yards

October 31-November 3
purse, US$175,000

	SCORES				TOTAL	MONEY
Alejandro Tosti	68	69	68	64	269	US$31,500
Mario Beltran	70	70	69	61	270	15,400
Justin Suh	69	67	68	66	270	15,400
Blair Hamilton	70	66	73	62	271	7,233.34
Camilo Aguado	65	66	70	70	271	7,233.33
Cameron Young	71	71	62	67	271	7,233.33
Clodomiro Carranza	70	69	66	67	272	5,271.88
Andreas Halvorsen	67	68	69	68	272	5,271.88
Augusto Nunez	69	69	65	69	272	5,271.87
Dalan Refioglu	66	71	65	70	272	5,271.87
Michael Davan	69	66	68	70	273	4,375
Isidro Benitez	72	67	67	68	274	4,025
Rowin Caron	72	66	67	70	275	3,000
Matt Hutchins	66	71	69	69	275	3,000
Joshua Lee	71	68	68	68	275	3,000
Jose Luis Montano	70	67	68	70	275	3,000
Ryan Ruffels	70	68	67	70	275	3,000
John Somers	71	68	64	72	275	3,000
Shad Tuten	68	71	71	65	275	3,000
Brian Mogg	67	69	68	72	276	2,275

Neuquen Argentina Classic

Chapelco Golf Club, Neuquen, Argentina
Par 36-36–72; 7,163 yards

November 7-10
purse, US$175,000

	SCORES				TOTAL	MONEY
Puma Dominguez	72	65	68	67	272	US$31,500
Tom Whitney	71	71	64	66	272	18,900
(Dominguez defeated Whitney on first playoff hole.)						
Andres Gallegos	70	66	69	69	274	11,900
Tano Goya	71	68	70	66	275	8,400
Jorge Fernandez-Valdes	70	67	69	70	276	6,650
Brandon Matthews	72	69	65	70	276	6,650
Ryan Baca	73	64	70	70	277	5,454.17
Jason Thresher	69	67	72	69	277	5,454.17
Otto Black	65	68	69	75	277	5,454.16
Camilo Aguado	73	67	69	69	278	3,879.17
Ricardo Gonzalez	69	69	75	65	278	3,879.17
Justin Suh	77	65	68	68	278	3,879.17
Alejandro Tosti	72	69	71	66	278	3,879.17
M.J. Maguire	69	69	68	72	278	3,879.16
Nicholas Maruri	70	67	68	73	278	3,879.16
Ricardo Celia	73	69	70	67	279	2,625
Raul Cortes	73	67	73	66	279	2,625
Ignacio Marino	72	65	69	73	279	2,625
Augusto Nunez	66	72	71	70	279	2,625
Mito Pereira	70	63	69	77	279	2,625

VISA Open de Argentina

Jockey Club Buenos Aires, Buenos Aires, Argentina
Par 34-36–70; 6,569 yards

November 14-17
purse, US$175,000

	SCORES				TOTAL	MONEY
Ricardo Celia	67	68	68	66	269	US$31,500
Brandon Matthews	69	68	65	67	269	18,900
(Cella defeated Matthews on third playoff hole.)						
Jared Wolfe	65	63	72	70	270	11,900
Tommy Cocha	70	69	69	65	273	7,233.34
Jonathan Garrick	65	68	67	73	273	7,233.33
Ryan Ruffels	68	69	70	66	273	7,233.33
Augusto Nunez	69	67	63	75	274	5,643.75
Justin Suh	70	68	71	65	274	5,643.75
Will Collins	70	69	67	69	275	4,550
Taylor Pendrith	71	64	73	67	275	4,550
Paulo Pinto	69	68	70	68	275	4,550
Alexandre Rocha	66	72	67	70	275	4,550
Rafael Becker	71	66	69	70	276	3,185
Kent Bulle	69	71	65	71	276	3,185
Clodomiro Carranza	71	65	66	74	276	3,185
Jose Toledo	72	69	71	64	276	3,185
Tom Whitney	68	74	66	68	276	3,185
Isidro Benitez	71	69	64	73	277	2,362.50
Toni Hakula	67	68	73	69	277	2,362.50
Jaime Lopez Rivarola	69	73	66	69	277	2,362.50
Joseph Winslow	69	67	70	71	277	2,362.50

Shell Championship

Trump National Doral Golden Palm, Miami, Florida
Par 36-35–71; 6,991 yards

December 5-8
purse, US$175,000

	SCORES				TOTAL	MONEY
Augusto Nunez	66	66	69	70	271	US$31,500
Jared Wolfe	66	67	69	70	272	18,900
Patrick Flavin	69	69	68	67	273	11,900
M.J. Maguire	67	70	70	68	275	8,400
Jose Toledo	68	69	67	72	276	7,000
Andres Gallegos	73	63	69	72	277	6,300
Rowin Caron	69	72	68	70	279	5,454.17
Seth Fair	73	66	69	71	279	5,454.17
Ryan Ruffels	69	68	70	72	279	5,454.16
Chandler Blanchet	68	68	74	70	280	4,200
Tommy Cocha	74	67	71	68	280	4,200
Jorge Fernandez-Valdes	71	68	70	71	280	4,200
Drew Nesbitt	70	72	69	69	280	4,200
Puma Dominguez	73	67	67	74	281	3,062.50
Chase Hanna	69	72	68	72	281	3,062.50
Evan Harmeling	70	70	73	68	281	3,062.50
Matt Ryan	69	70	69	73	281	3,062.50
Steven Fox	69	72	71	70	282	2,210.84
Willy Pumarol	73	67	72	70	282	2,210.84
Santiago Gomez	74	68	69	71	282	2,210.83
Tano Goya	71	70	68	73	282	2,210.83
Sulman Raza	71	68	68	75	282	2,210.83
John Somers	68	74	69	71	282	2,210.83

European Tours

Abu Dhabi HSBC Championship

Abu Dhabi Golf Club, Abu Dhabi, United Arab Emirates
Par 36-36–72; 7,583 yards

January 16-19
purse, US$7,000,000

	SCORES				TOTAL	MONEY
Shane Lowry	62	70	67	71	270	€1,024,194.58
Richard Sterne	65	68	69	69	271	682,793.46
Joost Luiten	69	68	71	65	273	384,689.68
Louis Oosthuizen	65	68	75	66	274	307,260.13
Soren Kjeldsen	66	69	71	69	275	260,556.59
Pablo Larrazabal	65	72	68	71	276	184,356.08
Ian Poulter	66	69	69	72	276	184,356.08
Paul Waring	70	67	70	69	276	184,356.08
Brooks Koepka	67	70	70	70	277	130,278.29
Tom Lewis	68	67	75	67	277	130,278.29
Dominic Foos	68	68	72	70	278	100,412.61
Rafa Cabrera Bello	68	71	72	67	278	100,412.61
Scott Jamieson	69	66	71	72	278	100,412.61
David Horsey	71	66	71	70	278	100,412.61
Jordan Smith	72	66	70	70	278	100,412.61
Lee Westwood	66	68	73	72	279	78,351.33
Thomas Pieters	67	70	69	73	279	78,351.33
David Lipsky	68	73	69	69	279	78,351.33
Dustin Johnson	69	71	72	67	279	78,351.33
Matt Wallace	70	68	71	70	279	78,351.33
Jason Scrivener	72	65	74	68	279	78,351.33
Martin Kaymer	66	72	74	68	280	65,753.67
Maximilian Kieffer	68	71	67	74	280	65,753.67
Adri Arnaus	69	68	72	71	280	65,753.67
Matthias Schwab	70	68	72	70	280	65,753.67
Thomas Bjorn	70	71	69	70	280	65,753.67
Benjamin Hebert	68	71	69	73	281	56,535.86
Ryan Fox	69	70	70	72	281	56,535.86
Branden Grace	70	69	71	71	281	56,535.86
Gaganjeet Bhullar	70	70	69	72	281	56,535.86
Scott Hend	71	68	75	67	281	56,535.86
Mike Lorenzo-Vera	65	76	73	68	282	44,429.81
Alexander Bjork	66	71	72	73	282	44,429.81
Fabrizio Zanotti	67	73	70	72	282	44,429.81
Gavin Green	69	67	73	73	282	44,429.81
Jack Singh Brar	69	68	73	72	282	44,429.81
James Morrison	69	69	75	69	282	44,429.81
Sam Horsfield	69	71	74	68	282	44,429.81
Andy Sullivan	69	72	70	71	282	44,429.81
Erik van Rooyen	70	69	73	70	282	44,429.81
Darren Fichardt	73	68	69	72	282	44,429.81
Nicolas Colsaerts	69	72	72	70	283	33,798.61
Tommy Fleetwood	69	72	72	70	283	33,798.61
Bernd Wiesberger	70	68	73	72	283	33,798.61
Sam Brazel	70	69	72	72	283	33,798.61
Justin Walters	70	69	72	72	283	33,798.61
Matthew Southgate	70	71	71	71	283	33,798.61
Grant Forrest	71	65	72	75	283	33,798.61
Eddie Pepperell	70	68	72	74	284	26,424.37
Andres Romero	70	70	73	71	284	26,424.37
Edoardo Molinari	71	68	75	70	284	26,424.37

	SCORES	TOTAL	MONEY
Dean Burmester	71 69 73 71	284	26,424.37
Lucas Bjerregaard	71 70 72 71	284	26,424.37
Aaron Rai	68 70 76 71	285	18,845.29
Joachim B. Hansen	69 71 74 71	285	18,845.29
Ross Fisher	69 72 73 71	285	18,845.29
Bradley Dredge	70 68 74 73	285	18,845.29
Lucas Herbert	71 65 76 73	285	18,845.29
Callum Shinkwin	71 68 73 73	285	18,845.29
Jorge Campillo	71 69 72 73	285	18,845.29
Renato Paratore	71 70 72 72	285	18,845.29
Victor Perez	75 66 75 69	285	18,845.29
Robert MacIntyre	70 71 72 73	286	15,055.75
Raphael Jacquelin	71 70 71 74	286	15,055.75
Thomas Detry	72 67 76 72	287	13,826.71
Alvaro Quiros	72 69 71 75	287	13,826.71
Alexander Levy	69 71 74 75	289	12,597.67
Kurt Kitayama	72 69 75 73	289	12,597.67
Richie Ramsay	70 70 74 76	290	11,675.88
Zander Lombard	70 70 80 71	291	11,210.61
Nino Bertasio	69 70 79 74	292	9,218

Omega Dubai Desert Classic

Emirates Golf Club, Dubai, United Arab Emirates
Par 35-37–72; 7,328 yards

January 24-27
purse, US$3,250,000

	SCORES	TOTAL	MONEY
Bryson DeChambeau	66 66 68 64	264	€476,394.03
Matt Wallace	70 64 69 68	271	317,598.95
Sergio Garcia	66 70 70 66	272	135,773.97
Paul Waring	67 70 71 64	272	135,773.97
Ian Poulter	67 71 70 64	272	135,773.97
Alvaro Quiros	69 64 71 68	272	135,773.97
Jason Scrivener	67 67 71 68	273	66,200.53
Lee Westwood	67 70 69 67	273	66,200.53
Lucas Herbert	69 63 72 69	273	66,200.53
Thorbjorn Olesen	69 67 68 69	273	66,200.53
Justin Harding	70 68 72 63	273	66,200.53
Haotong Li	67 67 67 73	274	45,234.17
Ernie Els	68 65 70 71	274	45,234.17
Shane Lowry	69 67 71 67	274	45,234.17
Byeong Hun An	70 68 68 68	274	45,234.17
Matthew Fitzpatrick	65 70 70 70	275	37,802.33
Kalle Samooja	66 70 68 71	275	37,802.33
Tommy Fleetwood	68 70 68 69	275	37,802.33
Romain Wattel	68 70 70 67	275	37,802.33
Romain Langasque	66 70 74 66	276	32,800.13
Alexander Bjork	68 70 72 66	276	32,800.13
Tapio Pulkkanen	68 73 69 66	276	32,800.13
Pablo Larrazabal	72 66 74 64	276	32,800.13
Matthieu Pavon	66 68 72 71	277	28,869.83
Bradley Dredge	68 68 71 70	277	28,869.83
Ross Fisher	69 69 69 70	277	28,869.83
Martin Kaymer	71 67 72 67	277	28,869.83
Andrew Johnston	72 69 65 71	277	28,869.83
Jordan Smith	68 68 69 73	278	23,057.76
Adri Arnaus	68 68 72 70	278	23,057.76
Fabrizio Zanotti	69 66 72 71	278	23,057.76
Aaron Rai	70 68 72 68	278	23,057.76
Victor Perez	70 70 67 71	278	23,057.76

	SCORES				TOTAL	MONEY
Shubhankar Sharma	71	69	70	68	278	23,057.76
Lucas Bjerregaard	72	68	67	71	278	23,057.76
Thomas Bjorn	72	68	69	69	278	23,057.76
Thomas Pieters	72	69	68	69	278	23,057.76
Kim Koivu	67	68	72	72	279	17,436.24
Tyrrell Hatton	69	70	71	69	279	17,436.24
George Coetzee	70	65	71	73	279	17,436.24
Mikko Korhonen	71	67	70	71	279	17,436.24
Ashun Wu	71	68	69	71	279	17,436.24
Victor Dubuisson	71	70	69	69	279	17,436.24
Gaganjeet Bhullar	71	70	69	69	279	17,436.24
Eddie Pepperell	72	67	69	71	279	17,436.24
Robert Karlsson	75	65	71	68	279	17,436.24
Thongchai Jaidee	66	71	74	69	280	14,577.84
Scott Hend	66	70	75	70	281	12,291.12
Thomas Detry	68	68	74	71	281	12,291.12
Tom Lewis	68	72	71	70	281	12,291.12
Haydn Porteous	69	72	72	68	281	12,291.12
Dean Burmester	70	69	73	69	281	12,291.12
Jens Dantorp	70	70	71	70	281	12,291.12
Nicolas Colsaerts	74	67	67	73	281	12,291.12
Thomas Aiken	71	68	73	70	282	10,004.40
Callum Shinkwin	66	68	75	74	283	8,632.37
Jorge Campillo	69	67	75	72	283	8,632.37
Richie Ramsay	69	72	67	75	283	8,632.37
Sam Brazel	71	70	74	68	283	8,632.37
Chris Paisley	73	68	72	70	283	8,632.37
Raphael Jacquelin	69	72	73	70	284	7,431.84
Shaun Norris	72	69	72	71	284	7,431.84
Joachim B. Hansen	73	66	71	74	284	7,431.84
Wade Ormsby	67	69	77	72	285	6,574.32
Hideto Tanihara	67	74	71	73	285	6,574.32
Matthias Schwab	69	72	69	75	285	6,574.32
Stephen Gallacher	68	72	76	70	286	5,859.72
Ashley Chesters	72	69	72	73	286	5,859.72
Christiaan Bezuidenhout	67	74	75	71	287	5,323.22
Matthew Southgate	71	70	77	69	287	5,323.22
Marc Warren	70	71	76	72	289	4,286.50
Kurt Kitayama	71	69	75	74	289	4,286.50
Nino Bertasio	68	71	78	74	291	4,282

Saudi International

Royal Greens Golf & Country Club,
King Abdullah Economic City, Saudi Arabia
Par 35-35–70; 7,010 yards

January 31-February 3
purse, US$3,500,000

	SCORES				TOTAL	MONEY
Dustin Johnson	68	61	65	67	261	€508,260.02
Haotong Li	67	65	62	69	263	338,834.20
Tom Lewis	71	66	62	65	264	190,903.55
Min Woo Lee	69	70	63	63	265	152,478.88
Alexander Levy	69	65	67	65	266	129,302.09
Joost Luiten	66	71	69	63	269	80,752.81
Ryan Fox	67	67	67	68	269	80,752.81
Ian Poulter	68	67	68	66	269	80,752.81
Bryson DeChambeau	68	68	68	65	269	80,752.81
Scott Hend	70	63	69	67	269	80,752.81
Justin Harding	65	72	70	63	270	54,282.48
Gavin Green	68	68	67	67	270	54,282.48

		SCORES			TOTAL	MONEY
Ross Fisher	65	72	65	69	271	44,950.77
Richard Sterne	66	68	70	67	271	44,950.77
Victor Perez	66	70	71	64	271	44,950.77
Bradley Dredge	67	70	72	62	271	44,950.77
Mike Lorenzo-Vera	69	71	63	68	271	44,950.77
Zander Lombard	65	67	70	70	272	37,281.09
Renato Paratore	65	74	65	68	272	37,281.09
Marcus Kinhult	67	71	67	67	272	37,281.09
Victor Dubuisson	72	65	69	66	272	37,281.09
Thomas Pieters	63	74	69	67	273	34,002.79
Yusaku Miyazato	71	65	70	67	273	34,002.79
Chris Paisley	66	68	70	70	274	30,343.30
Fabrizio Zanotti	67	66	71	70	274	30,343.30
Joachim B. Hansen	67	70	65	72	274	30,343.30
Adrian Otaegui	69	68	69	68	274	30,343.30
Matthias Schwab	69	69	70	66	274	30,343.30
David Lipsky	71	67	69	67	274	30,343.30
Shaun Norris	66	73	64	72	275	25,768.93
Niklas Lemke	68	72	69	66	275	25,768.93
Liam Johnston	70	66	70	69	275	25,768.93
Nino Bertasio	70	70	64	71	275	25,768.93
Jake McLeod	65	70	73	68	276	21,347.04
Sam Horsfield	68	70	69	69	276	21,347.04
Gaganjeet Bhullar	68	72	66	70	276	21,347.04
Robert Rock	69	69	69	69	276	21,347.04
Aaron Rai	69	70	66	71	276	21,347.04
Edoardo Molinari	69	71	70	66	276	21,347.04
Andrea Pavan	71	67	69	69	276	21,347.04
Matthew Jordan	73	65	67	71	276	21,347.04
Jorge Campillo	66	72	68	71	277	18,297.47
Thomas Detry	68	70	66	73	277	18,297.47
Justin Walters	66	70	69	73	278	15,552.85
Lorenzo Gagli	67	70	69	72	278	15,552.85
Romain Langasque	67	70	71	70	278	15,552.85
Robert Karlsson	68	69	72	69	278	15,552.85
Mikko Korhonen	68	69	68	73	278	15,552.85
Gonzalo Fernandez-Castano	68	70	69	71	278	15,552.85
Robert MacIntyre	69	70	71	68	278	15,552.85
Matthew Southgate	67	71	71	70	279	12,503.27
Paul Dunne	68	69	70	72	279	12,503.27
Haydn Porteous	68	70	70	71	279	12,503.27
Paul Waring	69	70	73	68	280	10,978.48
Jordan Smith	69	71	70	70	280	10,978.48
Patrick Reed	67	71	72	71	281	10,063.61
Jens Dantorp	69	68	76	69	282	8,996.25
Maximilian Kieffer	69	69	72	72	282	8,996.25
Brooks Koepka	69	70	74	69	282	8,996.25
Trevor Immelman	72	67	71	72	282	8,996.25
Alfie Plant	65	74	72	73	284	7,928.90
Nicolas Colsaerts	70	70	74	70	284	7,928.90
Clement Sordet	71	69	73	71	284	7,928.90
Pablo Larrazabal	67	73	76	69	285	7,166.51
Stuart Manley	73	66	72	74	285	7,166.51

ISPS Handa Vic Open

See Australasian Tour chapter.

ISPS Handa World Super 6 Perth

See Australasian Tour chapter.

Oman Open

Al Mouj Golf, Muscat, Oman
Par 36-36–72; 7,365 yards

February 28-March 3
purse, US$1,750,000

	SCORES				TOTAL	MONEY
Kurt Kitayama	66	74	71	70	281	€256,246.70
Maximilian Kieffer	69	70	71	72	282	102,286.50
Jorge Campillo	69	78	66	69	282	102,286.50
Fabrizio Zanotti	71	69	68	74	282	102,286.50
Clement Sordet	71	71	70	70	282	102,286.50
Thomas Pieters	68	75	69	71	283	46,125.46
Joachim B. Hansen	70	69	71	73	283	46,125.46
Peter Hanson	71	73	66	73	283	46,125.46
Scott Jamieson	67	76	66	75	284	31,160.31
Chris Paisley	71	72	69	72	284	31,160.31
Ashley Chesters	73	74	68	69	284	31,160.31
David Horsey	68	76	70	72	286	23,293.36
Gavin Moynihan	69	73	71	73	286	23,293.36
Joost Luiten	69	77	68	72	286	23,293.36
Jordan Smith	71	76	70	69	286	23,293.36
Victor Dubuisson	72	70	72	72	286	23,293.36
Jeff Winther	73	73	69	71	286	23,293.36
Benjamin Hebert	70	72	71	74	287	19,116.44
Thongchai Jaidee	71	72	75	69	287	19,116.44
Sean Crocker	72	72	70	73	287	19,116.44
Hugo Leon	71	71	72	74	288	17,604.55
Sebastian Soderberg	72	72	68	76	288	17,604.55
Hideto Tanihara	70	72	70	77	289	16,220.79
David Drysdale	70	76	70	73	289	16,220.79
Louis de Jager	71	77	70	71	289	16,220.79
David Borda	72	74	74	69	289	16,220.79
Mike Lorenzo-Vera	70	75	75	70	290	14,375.77
Gaganjeet Bhullar	71	69	72	78	290	14,375.77
Max Schmitt	71	73	72	74	290	14,375.77
Deyen Lawson	72	72	73	73	290	14,375.77
Adrien Saddier	68	76	72	75	291	11,633.87
Brandon Stone	70	70	80	71	291	11,633.87
Mikko Korhonen	70	78	71	72	291	11,633.87
Andrea Pavan	71	75	76	69	291	11,633.87
Richard McEvoy	72	74	72	73	291	11,633.87
Nick Cullen	72	76	70	73	291	11,633.87
Justin Walters	73	73	72	73	291	11,633.87
Scott Hend	73	74	71	73	291	11,633.87
Thomas Aiken	75	73	69	74	291	11,633.87
Thomas Detry	70	73	76	73	292	9,378.84
Filippo Bergamaschi	72	74	72	74	292	9,378.84
Nicolas Colsaerts	72	76	71	73	292	9,378.84
Jinho Choi	73	73	74	72	292	9,378.84
Darren Fichardt	75	73	70	74	292	9,378.84
Raphael Jacquelin	68	79	72	74	293	6,918.82
Matthew Baldwin	70	75	71	77	293	6,918.82
Adri Arnaus	70	78	70	75	293	6,918.82
Robert MacIntyre	71	74	70	78	293	6,918.82
Espen Kofstad	72	70	71	80	293	6,918.82
Nino Bertasio	72	73	72	76	293	6,918.82
Zander Lombard	72	75	71	75	293	6,918.82
Romain Langasque	72	75	71	75	293	6,918.82
Matteo Manassero	72	76	73	72	293	6,918.82
Bradley Dredge	74	72	74	73	293	6,918.82
Jeunghun Wang	77	71	72	73	293	6,918.82
Oliver Wilson	72	74	73	75	294	4,920.05
Masahiro Kawamura	73	71	74	76	294	4,920.05

	SCORES				TOTAL	MONEY
Pedro Figueiredo	71	77	76	71	295	4,458.79
Paul Dunne	74	74	74	73	295	4,458.79
John Catlin	76	72	73	74	295	4,458.79
Victor Perez	73	75	73	75	296	4,074.42
Jaco van Zyl	75	73	74	74	296	4,074.42
Yusaku Miyazato	67	79	75	77	298	3,613.16
Scott Vincent	68	80	71	79	298	3,613.16
Guido Migliozzi	73	73	73	79	298	3,613.16
Matthew Southgate	75	70	78	75	298	3,613.16
Christiaan Bezuidenhout	70	78	75	76	299	3,075.03
Shubhankar Sharma	72	74	75	78	299	3,075.03
Ashun Wu	76	71	79	73	299	3,075.03
Andy Sullivan	72	75	75	79	301	2,811.46
James Morrison	72	76	75	79	302	2,306

Commercial Bank Qatar Masters

Doha Golf Club, Doha, Qatar
Par 36-36–72; 7,400 yards

March 7-10
purse, US$1,750,000

	SCORES				TOTAL	MONEY
Justin Harding	68	68	73	66	275	€259,668.79
Mike Lorenzo-Vera	68	68	71	70	277	68,988.40
George Coetzee	68	68	73	68	277	68,988.40
Oliver Wilson	69	68	69	71	277	68,988.40
Erik van Rooyen	69	68	70	70	277	68,988.40
Nacho Elvira	71	67	69	70	277	68,988.40
Anton Karlsson	72	66	70	69	277	68,988.40
Jorge Campillo	72	69	68	68	277	68,988.40
Jinho Choi	72	69	72	64	277	68,988.40
Christiaan Bezuidenhout	72	71	66	68	277	68,988.40
Thomas Detry	70	68	70	70	278	26,850.37
Andy Sullivan	70	71	69	68	278	26,850.37
Fabrizio Zanotti	72	68	70	68	278	26,850.37
Adri Arnaus	67	70	72	70	279	22,435.90
Nick Cullen	69	70	68	72	279	22,435.90
Maximilian Kieffer	69	71	72	67	279	22,435.90
Jeff Winther	70	70	72	67	279	22,435.90
Bradley Dredge	68	71	70	71	280	19,709.31
Mikko Korhonen	72	70	68	70	280	19,709.31
Masahiro Kawamura	69	68	73	71	281	17,160.79
Kurt Kitayama	69	70	70	72	281	17,160.79
Jens Dantorp	72	68	70	71	281	17,160.79
Sebastian Soderberg	72	68	72	69	281	17,160.79
Jake McLeod	72	70	66	73	281	17,160.79
Min Woo Lee	75	66	67	73	281	17,160.79
Darren Fichardt	76	64	71	70	281	17,160.79
Justin Walters	67	73	71	71	282	14,567.75
Nicolas Colsaerts	68	70	72	72	282	14,567.75
Adrien Saddier	72	69	70	71	282	14,567.75
Pablo Larrazabal	74	69	73	66	282	14,567.75
Gaganjeet Bhullar	69	71	75	68	283	12,130.52
Robert MacIntyre	69	72	72	70	283	12,130.52
Lee Slattery	69	74	68	72	283	12,130.52
Niclas Johansson	70	72	68	73	283	12,130.52
Gavin Green	71	69	72	71	283	12,130.52
Matthias Schwab	72	69	72	70	283	12,130.52
Oliver Fisher	73	67	70	73	283	12,130.52
Jacques Kruyswijk	71	67	73	73	284	10,283.12
Adrian Otaegui	71	72	69	72	284	10,283.12

	SCORES				TOTAL	MONEY
Liam Johnston	72	71	69	72	284	10,283.12
Scott Jamieson	73	69	68	74	284	10,283.12
Hugo Leon	68	72	74	71	285	8,725.07
Matthew Southgate	72	70	72	71	285	8,725.07
Thomas Bjorn	72	71	72	70	285	8,725.07
Tapio Pulkkanen	72	71	70	72	285	8,725.07
Tom Murray	73	68	71	73	285	8,725.07
Louis de Jager	74	67	72	72	285	8,725.07
Yusaku Miyazato	69	71	73	73	286	6,855.41
Lucas Herbert	69	73	70	74	286	6,855.41
Thomas Aiken	71	69	73	73	286	6,855.41
Kalle Samooja	71	70	74	71	286	6,855.41
Alexander Bjork	73	70	69	74	286	6,855.41
Chris Paisley	74	69	70	73	286	6,855.41
Wilco Nienaber [A]	75	68	70	73	286	
Paul Waring	69	70	74	74	287	4,963.50
Ross Fisher	69	74	70	74	287	4,963.50
Deyen Lawson	70	68	76	73	287	4,963.50
Alejandro Canizares	71	68	78	70	287	4,963.50
Robert Rock	72	69	72	74	287	4,963.50
Bernd Wiesberger	72	71	72	72	287	4,963.50
Pedro Figueiredo	73	70	74	70	287	4,963.50
Robert Karlsson	69	73	81	65	288	3,817.22
Stuart Manley	69	73	74	72	288	3,817.22
Ashley Chesters	70	70	75	73	288	3,817.22
Kristoffer Broberg	71	67	72	78	288	3,817.22
Jordan Smith	71	68	74	75	288	3,817.22
Kim Koivu	73	70	72	73	288	3,817.22
Filippo Bergamaschi	74	68	76	71	289	3,271.90
Richie Ramsay	68	70	76	76	290	2,975.13
Grant Forrest	69	72	75	74	290	2,975.13
Brandon Stone	71	72	76	71	290	2,975.13
Thongchai Jaidee	71	70	77	73	291	2,335.50
David Horsey	71	71	75	74	291	2,335.50

Magical Kenya Open

Karen Golf Club, Nairobi, Kenya
Par 35-36–71; 6,922 yards

March 14-17
purse, €1,100,000

	SCORES				TOTAL	MONEY
Guido Migliozzi	67	68	64	69	268	€183,330
Louis de Jager	64	66	70	69	269	82,026.67
Adri Arnaus	66	68	65	70	269	82,026.67
Justin Harding	70	65	68	66	269	82,026.67
Gaganjeet Bhullar	65	70	66	69	270	46,640
Romain Langasque	67	70	69	65	271	35,750
Kalle Samooja	70	67	64	70	271	35,750
Liam Johnston	67	69	67	71	274	27,500
Josh Geary	67	73	67	68	275	22,293.33
Christiaan Bezuidenhout	67	73	66	69	275	22,293.33
Anton Karlsson	69	70	68	68	275	22,293.33
Jack Singh Brar	64	70	69	73	276	17,028
Haydn Porteous	69	73	68	66	276	17,028
Thomas Bjorn	70	70	70	66	276	17,028
Niklas Lemke	72	69	71	64	276	17,028
Sean Crocker	72	71	68	65	276	17,028
Michael Hoey	66	74	69	68	277	13,310
Cormac Sharvin	69	71	65	72	277	13,310
Chikkarangappa S.	70	69	69	69	277	13,310

452 / EUROPEAN TOURS

		SCORES			TOTAL	MONEY
Robert MacIntyre	71	73	70	63	277	13,310
George Coetzee	72	66	67	72	277	13,310
Adrien Saddier	72	72	68	65	277	13,310
Johannes Veerman	76	65	68	68	277	13,310
Matthew Nixon	69	71	73	65	278	11,770
Simon Ngige Mburu	68	72	70	69	279	10,615
Sebastian Soderberg	70	72	70	67	279	10,615
Lasse Jensen	71	67	72	69	279	10,615
Tom Murray	72	68	70	69	279	10,615
Ben Stow	75	67	69	68	279	10,615
Jose-Filipe Lima	75	68	70	66	279	10,615
Filippo Bergamaschi	67	75	70	68	280	8,965
Max Schmitt	69	70	73	68	280	8,965
Marcel Schneider	70	69	70	71	280	8,965
Ewen Ferguson	73	69	71	67	280	8,965
Hyowon Park	69	70	76	66	281	7,260
Ivan Cantero Gutierrez	71	68	73	69	281	7,260
Connor Syme	71	70	70	70	281	7,260
Pedro Figueiredo	72	68	71	70	281	7,260
Khalin H. Joshi	72	69	69	71	281	7,260
Pep Angles	73	70	69	69	281	7,260
Ricardo Gouveia	74	66	72	69	281	7,260
Oscar Lengden	74	70	72	65	281	7,260
Renato Paratore	74	70	68	69	281	7,260
Mathieu Fenasse	75	69	68	69	281	7,260
Christofer Blomstrand	70	72	66	74	282	5,390
Stuart Manley	71	65	76	70	282	5,390
Gonzalo Fernandez-Castano	71	66	73	72	282	5,390
Bryce Easton	72	70	71	69	282	5,390
Steven Tiley	73	70	69	70	282	5,390
Martin Simonsen	73	71	71	67	282	5,390
Ross McGowan	74	68	70	70	282	5,390
Clement Sordet	70	73	71	69	283	4,400
Oliver Wilson	72	70	67	74	283	4,400
Kim Koivu	70	69	72	73	284	3,850
Nick Cullen	72	70	73	69	284	3,850
Nick McCarthy	73	71	70	70	284	3,850
Aaron Cockerill	69	68	70	78	285	3,190
Bernd Ritthammer	71	73	67	74	285	3,190
Ben Evans	72	72	72	69	285	3,190
Kristoffer Reitan	73	68	69	75	285	3,190
Simon Forsstrom	74	70	70	71	285	3,190
Jack Senior	69	72	70	75	286	2,695
David Boote	69	75	71	71	286	2,695
Maarten Lafeber	72	70	72	72	286	2,695
Nico Geyger	76	67	73	70	286	2,695
John Catlin	71	71	71	74	287	2,365
Calum Hill	71	71	72	73	287	2,365
Hugo Leon	67	72	77	72	288	1,987.50
David Cooke	70	71	69	78	288	1,987.50
Henric Sturehed	73	69	73	73	288	1,987.50
Jeff Winther	80	64	72	72	288	1,987.50
Hugues Joannes	70	73	68	78	289	1,644
Jastus Madoya	71	71	72	75	289	1,644
Joel Girrbach	72	71	71	75	289	1,644
Borja Virto	75	68	74		217	1,638
Oliver Farr	70	74	74		218	1,633.50
Joseph Dean	75	68	75		218	1,633.50
Max Orrin	74	70	76		220	1,629
Darius van Driel	71	73	80		224	1,626

Maybank Championship
See Asia/Japan Tours chapter.

Hero Indian Open
See Asia/Japan Tours chapter.

Trophee Hassan II

Royal Golf Dar Es Salam, Rabat, Morocco
Par 36-37–73; 7,632 yards

April 25-28
purse, €2,500,000

	SCORES				TOTAL	MONEY
Jorge Campillo	72	71	69	71	283	€416,660
Sean Crocker	67	74	72	72	285	186,423.33
Julian Suri	71	71	72	71	285	186,423.33
Erik van Rooyen	74	69	68	74	285	186,423.33
David Lipsky	71	70	74	72	287	106,000
Masahiro Kawamura	75	69	71	73	288	81,250
Grant Forrest	75	70	69	74	288	81,250
Tapio Pulkkanen	75	74	67	73	289	62,500
Matthias Schwab	70	73	74	73	290	47,050
Richard Sterne	71	76	69	74	290	47,050
Thongchai Jaidee	73	72	73	72	290	47,050
Thomas Detry	73	76	69	72	290	47,050
Alexander Bjork	74	71	73	72	290	47,050
Jordan Smith	66	76	73	76	291	33,892.86
Kristoffer Reitan	70	73	78	70	291	33,892.86
Kurt Kitayama	73	74	72	72	291	33,892.86
Wade Ormsby	74	70	70	77	291	33,892.86
David Law	75	71	73	72	291	33,892.86
Christiaan Bezuidenhout	75	71	73	72	291	33,892.86
Clement Sordet	76	70	74	71	291	33,892.86
Dimitrios Papadatos	70	72	78	72	292	27,875
Andrea Pavan	72	74	73	73	292	27,875
Tom Lewis	72	75	71	74	292	27,875
Andy Sullivan	74	73	73	72	292	27,875
Guido Migliozzi	72	71	77	73	293	24,500
Joost Luiten	73	75	71	74	293	24,500
Adrian Otaegui	73	77	72	71	293	24,500
Paul Waring	73	77	72	71	293	24,500
Jeff Winther	74	72	72	75	293	24,500
Mikko Korhonen	72	76	71	75	294	21,125
Jake McLeod	72	78	67	77	294	21,125
Victor Dubuisson	75	70	76	73	294	21,125
Ricardo Gouveia	75	74	73	72	294	21,125
Alejandro Canizares	67	76	78	74	295	18,500
Lee Slattery	70	72	72	81	295	18,500
Mike Lorenzo-Vera	73	76	70	76	295	18,500
Michael Hoey	74	73	74	74	295	18,500
Jack Senior	70	77	75	74	296	14,750
Pablo Larrazabal	70	79	76	71	296	14,750
Ashley Chesters	72	73	74	77	296	14,750
Kalle Samooja	72	76	68	80	296	14,750
Peter Hanson	72	78	72	74	296	14,750
Benjamin Hebert	73	74	74	75	296	14,750
Paul Dunne	73	75	77	71	296	14,750
Romain Langasque	74	75	73	74	296	14,750
Chris Paisley	75	72	73	76	296	14,750
Joachim B. Hansen	75	74	73	74	296	14,750
Steven Brown	76	74	75	71	296	14,750

454 / EUROPEAN TOURS

	SCORES				TOTAL	MONEY
Matthieu Pavon	68	78	78	73	297	10,750
Maximilian Kieffer	72	78	74	73	297	10,750
Lasse Jensen	73	76	74	74	297	10,750
Marcel Siem	74	73	76	74	297	10,750
Kim Koivu	74	76	73	74	297	10,750
James Morrison	72	75	72	79	298	8,750
Justin Walters	74	72	76	76	298	8,750
Oliver Wilson	74	75	74	75	298	8,750
Stephen Gallacher	68	82	77	72	299	7,500
Sebastian Soderberg	72	78	75	74	299	7,500
Richie Ramsay	77	72	78	72	299	7,500
Raphael Jacquelin	72	74	80	74	300	6,750
David Horsey	73	75	76	76	300	6,750
Callum Shinkwin	74	76	72	78	300	6,750
Edoardo Molinari	69	78	75	79	301	5,875
Fabrizio Zanotti	74	70	75	82	301	5,875
Gavin Moynihan	74	74	71	82	301	5,875
Hyowon Park	75	74	75	77	301	5,875
Joel Girrbach	74	75	76	77	302	5,250
Marc Warren	72	73	79	80	304	4,875
Tom Murray	77	69	80	78	304	4,875
Alvaro Quiros	73	77	73	82	305	4,570
Hideto Tanihara	76	74	80	78	308	3,750

Volvo China Open

See Asia/Japan Tours chapter.

Betfred British Masters

Hillside Golf Club, Southport, England
Par 36-36–72; 6,953 yards

May 9-12
purse, £3,000,000

	SCORES				TOTAL	MONEY
Marcus Kinhult	65	69	68	70	272	€579,550.03
Matt Wallace	65	67	70	71	273	259,302.27
Robert MacIntyre	68	69	68	68	273	259,302.27
Eddie Pepperell	70	67	70	66	273	259,302.27
Richie Ramsay	66	67	71	72	276	147,437.53
Jordan Smith	68	74	67	68	277	113,012.26
Paul Waring	72	70	68	67	277	113,012.26
Tommy Fleetwood	68	69	68	73	278	66,764.16
Martin Kaymer	68	71	73	66	278	66,764.16
Niklas Lemke	69	64	75	70	278	66,764.16
Joost Luiten	70	71	68	69	278	66,764.16
Pablo Larrazabal	71	71	70	66	278	66,764.16
Oliver Wilson	71	71	67	69	278	66,764.16
Renato Paratore	73	67	72	66	278	66,764.16
Matthew Jordan	63	72	73	71	279	44,552.91
Thomas Detry	66	67	73	73	279	44,552.91
Ross Fisher	68	65	75	71	279	44,552.91
Soren Kjeldsen	69	69	72	69	279	44,552.91
Dimitrios Papadatos	69	70	69	71	279	44,552.91
Victor Perez	71	70	72	66	279	44,552.91
Andrea Pavan	71	71	68	69	279	44,552.91
Gavin Green	74	67	68	70	279	44,552.91
Victor Dubuisson	69	67	72	72	280	37,728.71
Nino Bertasio	73	68	70	69	280	37,728.71
Robert Rock	69	69	76	67	281	34,077.54

	SCORES				TOTAL	MONEY
Haydn Porteous	70	69	69	73	281	34,077.54
Gonzalo Fernandez-Castano	72	68	69	72	281	34,077.54
Gaganjeet Bhullar	72	68	71	70	281	34,077.54
Gregory Bourdy	72	69	70	70	281	34,077.54
Lasse Jensen	68	71	76	67	282	28,861.59
Michael Hoey	68	71	73	70	282	28,861.59
Hugo Leon	72	68	69	73	282	28,861.59
David Horsey	72	70	68	72	282	28,861.59
Edoardo Molinari	72	70	71	69	282	28,861.59
Lee Westwood	66	70	74	73	283	23,993.37
Scott Hend	68	69	73	73	283	23,993.37
Guido Migliozzi	70	67	76	70	283	23,993.37
Tyrrell Hatton	70	70	70	73	283	23,993.37
Lucas Herbert	72	68	74	69	283	23,993.37
Oliver Fisher	73	68	73	69	283	23,993.37
Thongchai Jaidee	74	68	74	67	283	23,993.37
Sean Crocker	67	71	72	74	284	17,734.23
Ashley Chesters	68	69	74	73	284	17,734.23
Andrew Johnston	68	71	73	72	284	17,734.23
Nacho Elvira	70	68	71	75	284	17,734.23
Jaco van Zyl	70	69	74	71	284	17,734.23
Liam Johnston	71	68	71	74	284	17,734.23
Matthias Schwab	71	70	74	69	284	17,734.23
Dean Burmester	71	71	73	69	284	17,734.23
Connor Syme	72	68	73	71	284	17,734.23
David Howell	72	70	71	71	284	17,734.23
Nicolas Colsaerts	73	68	70	73	284	17,734.23
Jack Singh Brar	67	71	74	73	285	12,170.55
Tom Lewis	70	69	75	71	285	12,170.55
David Law	71	71	71	72	285	12,170.55
Fabrizio Zanotti	73	69	71	72	285	12,170.55
Richard McEvoy	75	67	67	76	285	12,170.55
Robert Karlsson	66	73	76	71	286	8,867.12
Maximilian Kieffer	69	67	76	74	286	8,867.12
Scott Jamieson	69	70	73	74	286	8,867.12
Richard Sterne	70	68	78	70	286	8,867.12
Pedro Figueiredo	71	69	75	71	286	8,867.12
Stuart Manley	71	70	71	74	286	8,867.12
Steven Brown	72	68	70	76	286	8,867.12
Jack Senior	72	69	72	73	286	8,867.12
Jason Scrivener	72	70	70	74	286	8,867.12
Jens Dantorp	74	67	73	72	286	8,867.12
Oliver Farr	71	70	75	71	287	6,780.74
Grant Forrest	73	68	72	74	287	6,780.74
Bernd Wiesberger	69	72	71	76	288	5,589.76
Paul Dunne	71	69	78	70	288	5,589.76
Matthew Baldwin	71	70	73	74	288	5,589.76
Jamie Donaldson	72	68	77	72	289	5,210
Sam Horsfield	69	73	74	74	290	5,207
Lorenzo Gagli	69	71	75	76	291	5,204
Raphael Jacquelin	71	71	76	74	292	5,201

Made in Denmark

Himmerland Golf & Spa Resort, Farso, Denmark
Par 36-35-71; 6,749 yards

May 23-26
purse, €3,000,000

	SCORES				TOTAL	MONEY
Bernd Wiesberger	68	69	67	66	270	€500,000
Robert MacIntyre	67	70	68	66	271	333,330
Romain Langasque	69	66	72	66	273	187,800
Paul Dunne	68	70	70	67	275	109,440
Max Schmitt	68	70	68	69	275	109,440
Chris Paisley	68	71	71	65	275	109,440
Oliver Wilson	68	71	68	68	275	109,440
Pablo Larrazabal	68	71	68	68	275	109,440
Alejandro Canizares	66	69	73	68	276	60,800
Matthew Southgate	66	73	69	68	276	60,800
Matthias Schwab	68	66	72	70	276	60,800
John Catlin	67	74	70	66	277	47,475
Espen Kofstad	68	72	69	68	277	47,475
Tapio Pulkkanen	70	70	70	67	277	47,475
Richie Ramsay	72	69	68	68	277	47,475
Adrian Otaegui	71	72	68	67	278	41,400
Gavin Moynihan	74	68	70	66	278	41,400
Paul Waring	66	75	69	69	279	35,100
Alvaro Quiros	70	67	74	68	279	35,100
S.S.P. Chawrasia	70	71	73	65	279	35,100
Lee Westwood	70	73	66	70	279	35,100
Gonzalo Fernandez-Castano	71	72	67	69	279	35,100
Jeff Winther	73	67	73	66	279	35,100
Aaron Rai	74	68	70	67	279	35,100
Alexander Bjork	68	70	74	68	280	28,050
Oliver Fisher	68	71	74	67	280	28,050
Andrew Johnston	68	74	71	67	280	28,050
Louis de Jager	68	75	68	69	280	28,050
Jason Scrivener	69	74	67	70	280	28,050
Grant Forrest	70	71	70	69	280	28,050
Darren Fichardt	70	73	70	67	280	28,050
Andrea Pavan	74	68	71	67	280	28,050
Guido Migliozzi	70	71	73	67	281	21,637.50
Thomas Pieters	70	71	72	68	281	21,637.50
Wade Ormsby	71	70	70	70	281	21,637.50
Thongchai Jaidee	71	71	73	66	281	21,637.50
Thomas Detry	72	69	71	69	281	21,637.50
Lasse Jensen	72	69	69	71	281	21,637.50
Richard McEvoy	72	71	67	71	281	21,637.50
Andy Sullivan	73	68	72	68	281	21,637.50
Edoardo Molinari	66	73	71	72	282	17,400
Matt Wallace	67	73	74	68	282	17,400
Michael Hoey	68	73	74	67	282	17,400
Stuart Manley	69	70	72	71	282	17,400
Adrien Saddier	70	68	76	68	282	17,400
Scott Jamieson	70	70	69	73	282	17,400
Joakim Lagergren	67	74	73	69	283	14,700
Haydn Porteous	69	72	73	69	283	14,700
Christofer Blomstrand	70	72	72	69	283	14,700
James Morrison	69	71	75	69	284	13,500
Benjamin Hebert	67	72	72	74	285	12,300
Niklas Lemke	69	72	77	67	285	12,300
Kim Koivu	70	72	71	72	285	12,300
Victor Dubuisson	68	71	75	72	286	11,100
Pelle Edberg	67	75	74	71	287	9,480
Mathias Gladbjerg	69	72	76	70	287	9,480
David Horsey	69	73	73	72	287	9,480

	SCORES				TOTAL	MONEY
Joel Girrbach	71	69	76	71	287	9,480
Marcus Kinhult	72	71	73	71	287	9,480
Kristian Krogh Johannessen	68	72	76	72	288	8,250
Morten Orum Madsen	72	71	74	71	288	8,250
Robert Rock	70	72	73	74	289	7,350
Gaganjeet Bhullar	70	73	71	75	289	7,350
Jamie Donaldson	71	70	74	74	289	7,350
Ben Evans	75	67	76	71	289	7,350
Martin Simonsen	71	68	74	77	290	6,014
Jinho Choi	71	71	76	72	290	6,014
Kurt Kitayama	72	68	78	72	290	6,014
Nick Cullen	73	69	71	77	290	6,014
David Law	74	69	76	71	290	6,014
Tom Murray	66	75	73	77	291	4,500
David Drysdale	68	73	73	78	292	4,497
Shubhankar Sharma	72	70	77	74	293	4,492.50
Ivan Cantero Gutierrez	73	70	75	75	293	4,492.50

Belgian Knockout

Rinkven International Golf Club, Antwerp, Belgium
Par 36-36–72; 6,924 yards

May 30-June 2
purse, €1,000,000

QUALIFYING ROUNDS

	SCORES		TOTAL	MONEY
Guido Migliozzi	70	66	136	€166,660
Darius van Driel	69	65	134	111,110
Ewen Ferguson	70	67	137	62,600
Gregory Havret	69	69	138	50,000
Gavin Green	69	66	135	42,400
Matthew Southgate	70	68	138	32,500
Marcel Siem	71	67	138	32,500
Bernd Wiesberger	76	64	140	25,000
Dean Burmester	65	71	136	21,200
Hugo Leon	69	67	136	21,200
Jeff Winther	67	70	137	18,400
Nacho Elvira	70	68	138	17,200
Thomas Detry	67	72	139	15,366.67
Antoine Rozner	69	70	139	15,366.67
David Law	71	68	139	15,366.67
Daniel Gavins	71	70	141	14,100
Chris Paisley	65	65	130	13,500
Anton Karlsson	63	68	131	12,900
Espen Kofstad	66	67	133	12,400
Gonzalo Fernandez-Castano	65	69	134	12,000
Sebastian Soderberg	67	69	136	11,450
Kristoffer Reitan	69	67	136	11,450
Alexander Levy	70	67	137	11,000
Louis de Jager	70	68	138	10,550
Anders Hansen	71	67	138	10,550
J.C. Ritchie	66	73	139	9,800
Adrian Otaegui	67	72	139	9,800
Edoardo Molinari	71	68	139	9,800
Rikard Karlberg	69	71	140	8,750
Renato Paratore	70	70	140	8,750
Wade Ormsby	70	70	140	8,750
Oscar Lengden	71	69	140	8,750
Justin Walters	66	67	133	8,000
David Horsey	66	69	135	7,500
Robert MacIntyre	66	69	135	7,500
Oliver Wilson	67	68	135	7,500

	SCORES		TOTAL	MONEY
Ashley Chesters	68	68	136	7,100
Sihwan Kim	67	70	137	6,600
Adrien Saddier	67	70	137	6,600
Oliver Fisher	68	69	137	6,600
Kevin Hesbois	68	69	137	6,600
Jake McLeod	69	69	138	5,700
Jens Dantorp	69	69	138	5,700
Richie Ramsay	70	68	138	5,700
Ben Evans	70	68	138	5,700
Richard McEvoy	71	67	138	5,700
Lorenzo Gagli	66	73	139	4,700
Gavin Moynihan	70	69	139	4,700
Benjamin Hebert	70	69	139	4,700
Joakim Lagergren	72	67	139	4,700
Tom Murray	73	66	139	4,700
Kristian Krogh Johannessen	68	72	140	3,366.67
Stanislav Matus	69	71	140	3,366.67
Pedro Oriol	70	70	140	3,366.67
Daan Huizing	70	70	140	3,366.67
Jack Singh Brar	71	69	140	3,366.67
Haydn Porteous	71	69	140	3,366.67
Grant Forrest	71	69	140	3,366.67
Matthias Schwab	72	68	140	3,366.67
Filippo Bergamaschi	72	68	140	3,366.67
Soren Kjeldsen	70	71	141	2,550
Sam Horsfield	70	71	141	2,550
Steven Brown	73	68	141	2,550
Nino Bertasio	74	67	141	2,550

ROUND OF 64

David Law defeated Ben Evans, -4 to -3.
Edoardo Molinari defeated Richie Ramsay, -2 to par.
Darius van Driel defeated Nino Bertasio, -3 to 2.
Gonzalo Fernandez-Castano tied with Kristian Krogh Johannessen, par to par. Fernandez-Castano advanced via seeding.
Bernd Wiesberger defeated Oliver Fisher, -4 to -2.
J.C. Ritchie defeated Kevin Hesbois, -2 to par.
Hugo Leon defeated Haydn Porteous, -3 to -2.
Oscar Lengden defeated Ashley Chesters, -2 to par.
Anders Hansen defeated Benjamin Hebert, -2 to par.
Kristoffer Reitan defeated Daan Huizing, -3 to par.
Jeff Winther defeated Lorenzo Gagli, -2 to 1.
Gavin Green defeated Stanislav Matus, par to 2.
Daniel Gavins defeated Justin Walters, par to 1.
Alexander Levy defeated Filippo Bergamaschi, -2 to -1.
Dean Burmester tied with Grant Forrest, -2 to -2. Burmester advanced via seeding.
Louis de Jager defeated Tom Murray, par to 3.
Guido Migliozzi defeated Pedro Oriol, -3 to par.
Marcel Siem defeated Gavin Moynihan, 1 to 3.
Rikard Karlberg defeated Oliver Wilson, -3 to 1.
Adrian Otaegui defeated Sihwan Kim, -2 to -1.
Ewen Ferguson defeated Matthias Schwab, -2 to 1.
Espen Kofstad defeated Steven Brown, -5 to -2.
Matthew Southgate defeated Joakim Lagergren, -3 to 1.
Sebastian Soderberg tied with Jack Singh Brar, -1 to -1. Soderberg advanced via seeding.
Wade Ormsby defeated David Horsey, -2 to par.
Renato Paratore defeated Robert MacIntyre, -4 to par.
Antoine Rozner defeated Richard McEvoy, -2 to par.
Thomas Detry defeated Adrien Saddier, -1 to 1.
Anton Karlsson defeated Soren Kjeldsen, -3 to -2.
Chris Paisley defeated Sam Horsfield, -3 to 1.
Gregory Havret defeated Jake McLeod, -1 to par.
Nacho Elvira defeated Jens Dantorp, -3 to -2.

ROUND OF 32

Van Driel defeated Molinari, -3 to -2.
Law defeated Fernandez-Castano, par to 1.
Wiesberger defeated Lengden, -2 to 2.
Leon defeated Ritchie, par to 1.
Winther defeated Reitan, -3 to -1.
Green defeated Hansen, -3 to par.
Gavins defeated de Jager, -3 to par.
Burmester defeated Levy, -1 to par.
Siem defeated Karlberg, -3 to 4.
Migliozzi defeated Otaegui, -3 to 3.
Ferguson defeated Soderberg, -4 to par.
Southgate defeated Kofstad, -1 to 1.
Rozner defeated Paratore, -3 to -2.
Detry defeated Ormsby, -3 to -2.
Elvira defeated Karlsson, -3 to -1.
Havret defeated Paisley, -2 to 1.

ROUND OF 16

Van Driel defeated Winther, par to 1.
Wiesberger defeated Gavins, -3 to -2.
Migliozzi defeated Law, -1 to par.
Southgate defeated Leon, par to 1.
Siem defeated Rozner, -3 to -1.
Green defeated Detry, -3 to -2.
Havret defeated Burmester, 1 to 4.
Ferguson defeated Elvira, -2 to par.

QUARTER-FINALS

Van Driel defeated Southgate, -2 to -1.
Havret defeated Siem, -3 to 2.
Migliozzi defeated Wiesberger, -2 to -1.
Ferguson defeated Green, -1 to par.

SEMI-FINALS

Van Driel defeated Havret, -1 to 1.
Migliozzi defeated Ferguson, -3 to par.

PLAYOFF FOR THIRD-FOURTH PLACE

Ferguson defeated Havret, -3 to 1.

(Ferguson received €62,600; Havret received €50,000.)

FINAL

Migliozzi defeated van Driel, -3 to 1.

(Migliozzi received €166,660; van Driel received €111,110.)

GolfSixes Cascais

Oitavos Dunes, Cascais, Portugal
Par 24; 1,960 yards

June 7-8
purse, €1,000,000

Group A

England Men (Tom Lewis and Paul Waring) defeated Portugal (Ricardo Gouveia and Pedro Figueiredo), 3-1.
Scotland (Stephen Gallacher and David Law) defeated India (S.S.P. Chawrasia and Gaganjeet Bhullar), 2-1.

India defeated England Men, 2-1.
Scotland defeated Portugal, 2-1.

England Men defeated Scotland, 2-1.
Portugal defeated India, 2-1.

Group B

Ireland (Paul Dunne and Gavin Moynihan) defeated England Women (Meghan MacLaren and Florentyna Parker), 1-0.
Sweden (Alexander Bjork and Joakim Lagergren) tied with Thailand (Thongchai Jaidee and Phachara Khongwhatmai), 1-1.

Ireland tied with Sweden, 0-0.
Thailand tied with England Women, 1-1.

Thailand defeated Ireland, 3-1.
Sweden defeated England Women, 3-0.

Group C

Australia (Scott Hend and Wade Ormsby) defeated Wales (Jamie Donaldson and Stuart Manley), 3-1.
Germany Women (Esther Henseleit and Laura Fuenfstueck) tied with France (Victor Perez and Roman Wattell), 2-2.

Germany Women defeated Australia, 2-0.
France defeated Wales, 2-1.

Australia tied with France, 1-1.
Wales defeated Germany Women, 2-0.

Group D

Spain (Jorge Campillo and Nacho Elvira) defeated South Africa (Brandon Stone and George Coetzee), 3-1.
Italy (Lorenzo Gagli and Edoardo Molinari) defeated Denmark (Joachim B. Hansen and Jeff Winther), 2-1.

South Africa defeated Denmark, 2-1.
Italy tied with Spain, 2-2.

South Africa tied with Italy, 0-0.
Spain defeated Denmark, 3-1.

(Portugal, Ireland, Germany Women, South Africa team members received €20,000 each; India, Wales, Denmark, England Women team members received €15,000 each.)

KNOCKOUT STAGE
Quarter-Finals

England Men defeated Sweden, 2-1.
Italy defeated France, 2-1.
Thailand defeated Scotland, 3-1
Spain defeated Australia, 2-1.
(Losing team members received €25,000 each.)

Semi-Finals

England Men defeated Italy, 3-0.
Thailand defeated Spain, 1-0.

Playoff for Third-Fourth Place

Spain defeated Italy, 3-0.
(Spain team members received €50,000 each; Italy team members received €35,000 each.)

Final

Thailand defeated England Men, 2-1 (playoff).
(Thailand team members received €100,000 each; England Men team members received €75,000 each.)

BMW International Open

Golfclub Munchen Eichenried, Munich, Germany
Par 36-36–72; 7,284 yards

June 20-23
purse, €2,000,000

	SCORES				TOTAL	MONEY
Andrea Pavan	66	71	70	66	273	€333,330
Matthew Fitzpatrick	73	66	65	69	273	222,220
(Pavan defeated Fitzpatrick on second playoff hole.)						
Alvaro Quiros	69	68	72	66	275	76,400
Matt Wallace	69	68	68	70	275	76,400
Christiaan Bezuidenhout	70	65	70	70	275	76,400
Jordan Smith	70	67	66	72	275	76,400
Edoardo Molinari	70	67	71	67	275	76,400
Matthias Schwab	70	69	65	71	275	76,400
Rafa Cabrera Bello	70	69	70	66	275	76,400
Lee Westwood	68	69	69	70	276	35,850
Callum Shinkwin	69	69	70	68	276	35,850
Matthieu Pavon	70	70	66	70	276	35,850
Thorbjorn Olesen	71	68	72	65	276	35,850
Sebastian Soderberg	69	67	70	71	277	30,000
Filippo Bergamaschi	70	69	68	70	277	30,000
Martin Kaymer	67	66	75	70	278	26,450
Kim Koivu	70	66	74	68	278	26,450
Erik van Rooyen	71	69	71	67	278	26,450
Bernd Wiesberger	72	70	71	65	278	26,450
Joachim B. Hansen	70	70	68	71	279	24,000
Joakim Lagergren	69	70	72	69	280	22,000
Ashley Chesters	70	70	69	71	280	22,000
Kurt Kitayama	71	68	72	69	280	22,000
Sam Horsfield	72	67	71	70	280	22,000
Sihwan Kim	73	69	72	66	280	22,000
Oliver Wilson	67	74	71	69	281	18,100
Haydn Porteous	69	71	71	70	281	18,100
Alex Noren	69	71	71	70	281	18,100
Andy Sullivan	69	72	69	71	281	18,100

	SCORES				TOTAL	MONEY
Espen Kofstad	71	71	68	71	281	18,100
Jason Scrivener	73	68	72	68	281	18,100
David Horsey	74	66	72	69	281	18,100
David Lipsky	74	68	70	69	281	18,100
Jeff Winther	68	72	72	70	282	15,000
Andrew Johnston	70	69	72	71	282	15,000
Steven Brown	71	71	71	69	282	15,000
Gavin Green	69	72	71	71	283	13,200
Robert Rock	70	71	72	70	283	13,200
Ashun Wu	71	69	68	75	283	13,200
Jens Dantorp	71	71	73	68	283	13,200
Maximilian Kieffer	73	67	70	73	283	13,200
David Law	74	67	73	69	283	13,200
Adam Bland	70	70	73	71	284	11,800
Masahiro Kawamura	70	71	74	70	285	10,600
Ricardo Gouveia	70	72	74	69	285	10,600
Jaco van Zyl	72	70	74	69	285	10,600
David Howell	72	70	72	71	285	10,600
John Catlin	73	66	74	72	285	10,600
Andres Romero	71	71	71	73	286	8,800
Lucas Herbert	72	70	71	73	286	8,800
Paul Peterson	73	69	73	71	286	8,800
Robert MacIntyre	74	68	73	71	286	8,800
Max Schmitt	69	68	74	76	287	6,685.71
Joel Girrbach	70	71	72	74	287	6,685.71
Hugo Leon	71	71	73	72	287	6,685.71
Dominic Foos	72	70	72	73	287	6,685.71
Anton Karlsson	72	70	74	71	287	6,685.71
Niklas Lemke	72	70	73	72	287	6,685.71
S.S.P. Chawrasia	73	68	73	73	287	6,685.71
Marcel Schneider	73	69	74	72	288	5,500
Fabrizio Zanotti	75	66	77	70	288	5,500
Gaganjeet Bhullar	69	71	75	74	289	4,900
Darius van Driel	69	73	74	73	289	4,900
Richard McEvoy	69	73	72	75	289	4,900
Luis Gagne	71	68	77	73	289	4,900
David Drysdale	74	67	76	73	290	4,400
Pablo Larrazabal	72	66	76	78	292	4,200
Renato Paratore	74	68	76	75	293	4,000

Estrella Damm N.A. Andalucia Masters

Real Club Valderrama, Sotogrande, Spain
Par 35-36–71; 7,001 yards

June 27-30
purse, €3,000,000

	SCORES				TOTAL	MONEY
Christiaan Bezuidenhout	66	68	69	71	274	€500,000
Adri Arnaus	68	70	73	69	280	180,666
Mike Lorenzo-Vera	68	72	72	68	280	180,666
Jon Rahm	69	72	67	72	280	180,666
Alvaro Quiros	70	68	76	66	280	180,666
Eduardo De La Riva	71	71	69	69	280	180,666
Sergio Garcia	66	72	73	70	281	90,000
Gavin Green	66	74	73	69	282	61,800
Hideto Tanihara	70	70	68	74	282	61,800
Bernd Ritthammer	71	72	69	70	282	61,800
Thomas Bjorn	71	73	67	71	282	61,800
Thomas Detry	74	68	68	72	282	61,800
Gaganjeet Bhullar	68	71	72	72	283	47,100
Andy Sullivan	71	71	70	71	283	47,100

	SCORES				TOTAL	MONEY
Julian Suri	67	73	75	69	284	40,560
Scott Jamieson	68	71	74	71	284	40,560
Steven Brown	70	72	69	73	284	40,560
Jack Singh Brar	72	71	71	70	284	40,560
Jorge Campillo	73	71	68	72	284	40,560
Joost Luiten	68	75	72	70	285	34,900
Victor Dubuisson	69	73	69	74	285	34,900
Nicolas Colsaerts	73	67	70	75	285	34,900
Matthieu Pavon	67	73	71	75	286	32,100
Kristoffer Reitan	73	71	71	71	286	32,100
Min Woo Lee	75	67	74	70	286	32,100
Victor Perez	65	74	74	74	287	25,881.82
Sihwan Kim	66	77	70	74	287	25,881.82
Pablo Larrazabal	68	72	71	76	287	25,881.82
Fabrizio Zanotti	69	71	77	70	287	25,881.82
David Horsey	69	73	70	75	287	25,881.82
George Coetzee	70	69	73	75	287	25,881.82
Justin Walters	70	70	76	71	287	25,881.82
Jason Scrivener	71	72	73	71	287	25,881.82
Edoardo Molinari	71	72	73	71	287	25,881.82
Richard Sterne	72	71	75	69	287	25,881.82
Sean Crocker	72	72	70	73	287	25,881.82
Chris Paisley	69	71	73	75	288	21,000
Grant Forrest	72	72	69	75	288	21,000
Masahiro Kawamura	67	73	76	73	289	18,300
Mikko Korhonen	70	69	78	72	289	18,300
Andres Romero	70	72	72	75	289	18,300
David Law	70	72	76	71	289	18,300
Soren Kjeldsen	71	70	73	75	289	18,300
Dean Burmester	71	73	69	76	289	18,300
Hugo Leon	73	69	71	76	289	18,300
Anton Karlsson	66	76	77	71	290	14,100
Tapio Pulkkanen	70	74	70	76	290	14,100
Daniel Gavins	70	74	68	78	290	14,100
Jeunghun Wang	71	71	75	73	290	14,100
Ashley Chesters	71	73	76	70	290	14,100
Paul Peterson	72	71	73	74	290	14,100
Stuart Manley	72	72	72	74	290	14,100
David Lipsky	70	72	75	74	291	11,100
Alejandro Canizares	71	73	72	75	291	11,100
Nino Bertasio	73	70	72	76	291	11,100
Bradley Dredge	67	71	76	78	292	9,400
Wade Ormsby	73	71	72	76	292	9,400
Shiv Kapur	74	70	76	72	292	9,400
Andrew Johnston	70	73	74	76	293	8,100
Joakim Lagergren	70	74	77	72	293	8,100
Samuel Del Val	71	70	73	79	293	8,100
Kim Koivu	72	70	76	75	293	8,100
Adrien Saddier	73	70	77	73	293	8,100
Niklas Lemke	68	75	71	80	294	6,900
Espen Kofstad	70	70	81	73	294	6,900
Christofer Blomstrand	75	69	75	75	294	6,900
Filippo Bergamaschi	69	74	81	72	296	6,150
Thongchai Jaidee	73	70	72	81	296	6,150
Lorenzo Gagli	71	73	75	78	297	5,700
Oliver Wilson	69	73	79	81	302	5,470
Hyowon Park	73	71	78	83	305	4,500

Dubai Duty Free Irish Open

Lahinch Golf Club, Co. Clare, Republic of Ireland
Par 34-36–70; 7,036 yards

July 4-7
purse, US$7,000,000

	SCORES				TOTAL	MONEY
Jon Rahm	67	71	64	62	264	€1,034,477.58
Andy Sullivan	68	66	66	66	266	539,100.38
Bernd Wiesberger	69	66	65	66	266	539,100.38
Eddie Pepperell	65	67	66	69	267	263,586.39
Robert Rock	67	70	60	70	267	263,586.39
Rafa Cabrera Bello	68	67	63	69	267	263,586.39
Paul Waring	67	68	67	66	268	170,689.77
Jorge Campillo	69	64	69	66	268	170,689.77
Zander Lombard	64	67	68	70	269	116,813.88
Mike Lorenzo-Vera	65	70	66	68	269	116,813.88
Martin Kaymer	66	70	68	65	269	116,813.88
Gavin Green	66	72	65	66	269	116,813.88
Edoardo Molinari	68	68	67	66	269	116,813.88
Grant Forrest	71	66	65	68	270	94,965.58
Thorbjorn Olesen	65	69	69	68	271	85,655.23
Cormac Sharvin	66	69	66	70	271	85,655.23
Haotong Li	68	68	69	66	271	85,655.23
Adri Arnaus	68	68	70	65	271	85,655.23
Wade Ormsby	65	69	69	69	272	73,396.60
Abraham Ancer	66	67	71	68	272	73,396.60
Oliver Wilson	66	69	67	70	272	73,396.60
Gonzalo Fernandez-Castano	69	70	69	64	272	73,396.60
Lee Westwood	66	67	71	69	273	65,482.80
Tommy Fleetwood	67	69	70	67	273	65,482.80
Andres Romero	68	70	68	67	273	65,482.80
Thomas Detry	70	68	69	66	273	65,482.80
Lee Slattery	65	74	70	65	274	58,034.52
Robert Karlsson	68	70	69	67	274	58,034.52
Robin Dawson	68	71	64	71	274	58,034.52
Nino Bertasio	70	68	69	67	274	58,034.52
Russell Knox	67	68	70	70	275	51,517.28
Joakim Lagergren	67	71	67	70	275	51,517.28
Alejandro Canizares	68	69	70	68	275	51,517.28
Shane Lowry	66	72	70	68	276	44,069
Brandon Stone	67	67	69	73	276	44,069
Oliver Fisher	67	69	69	71	276	44,069
Jacques Kruyswijk	67	72	72	65	276	44,069
Niklas Lemke	68	66	69	73	276	44,069
George Coetzee	70	67	66	73	276	44,069
Richard Sterne	72	67	70	67	276	44,069
Chris Paisley	65	72	70	70	277	36,620.72
Robert MacIntyre	66	69	72	70	277	36,620.72
Ian Poulter	66	73	69	69	277	36,620.72
Sebastian Soderberg	67	68	72	70	277	36,620.72
Max Schmitt	70	68	69	70	277	36,620.72
Hyowon Park	65	69	72	72	278	31,034.50
Anton Karlsson	67	72	69	70	278	31,034.50
Masahiro Kawamura	69	68	71	70	278	31,034.50
Louis Oosthuizen	71	67	70	70	278	31,034.50
Padraig Harrington	63	73	73	70	279	25,448.29
Sam Brazel	68	71	70	70	279	25,448.29
Jack Singh Brar	70	69	72	68	279	25,448.29
Bradley Dredge	72	67	69	71	279	25,448.29
Alexander Bjork	72	67	72	68	279	25,448.29
Matt Wallace	68	68	73	71	280	19,613.81
Lorenzo Gagli	68	70	70	72	280	19,613.81
Lucas Herbert	70	68	77	65	280	19,613.81

	SCORES				TOTAL	MONEY
Benjamin Hebert	71	67	71	71	280	19,613.81
Clement Sordet	71	68	70	71	280	19,613.81
Seamus Power	70	66	73	72	281	17,379.32
Marcus Kinhult	67	70	77	68	282	16,137.94
Tom Lewis	68	68	76	70	282	16,137.94
Victor Perez	70	68	73	71	282	16,137.94
Liam Johnston	68	70	76	71	285	14,275.87
Richard McEvoy	71	68	69	77	285	14,275.87
Jeff Winther	72	67	73	73	285	14,275.87

Aberdeen Standard Investments Scottish Open

The Renaissance Club, North Berwick, Scotland
Par 35-36–71; 7,136 yards

July 11-14
purse, US$7,000,000

	SCORES				TOTAL	MONEY
Bernd Wiesberger	67	61	65	69	262	€1,035,098.93
Benjamin Hebert	67	67	66	62	262	690,062.99
(Wiesberger defeated Hebert on third playoff hole.)						
Romain Langasque	65	67	65	67	264	388,785.38
Nino Bertasio	63	67	67	68	265	226,563.75
Henrik Stenson	65	65	69	66	265	226,563.75
Andrea Pavan	68	69	62	66	265	226,563.75
Andrew Johnston	69	65	69	62	265	226,563.75
Andrew Putnam	69	67	65	64	265	226,563.75
Lee Slattery	64	64	70	68	266	116,884.04
Jamie Donaldson	64	69	65	68	266	116,884.04
Rafa Cabrera Bello	66	67	67	66	266	116,884.04
Justin Thomas	67	64	70	65	266	116,884.04
George Coetzee	68	68	64	66	266	116,884.04
Erik van Rooyen	64	64	67	72	267	85,810.19
Ian Poulter	65	67	69	66	267	85,810.19
Matthew Fitzpatrick	67	65	67	68	267	85,810.19
Lorenzo Gagli	68	63	67	69	267	85,810.19
Matt Wallace	68	66	64	69	267	85,810.19
Tyrrell Hatton	70	66	64	67	267	85,810.19
Matt Kuchar	63	70	67	68	268	69,352.02
Romain Wattel	63	71	68	66	268	69,352.02
Kalle Samooja	64	67	69	68	268	69,352.02
Thomas Pieters	64	68	68	68	268	69,352.02
Adrian Otaegui	67	64	67	70	268	69,352.02
Martin Kaymer	68	69	66	65	268	69,352.02
Calum Hill	68	64	71	66	269	61,795.76
Scott Jamieson	70	64	69	66	269	61,795.76
Andy Sullivan	64	69	68	69	270	54,343
Guido Migliozzi	66	65	71	68	270	54,343
Jeff Winther	66	69	68	67	270	54,343
Renato Paratore	67	65	68	70	270	54,343
Mike Lorenzo-Vera	68	67	66	69	270	54,343
Victor Perez	68	68	68	66	270	54,343
Edoardo Molinari	63	69	69	70	271	42,853.34
Chris Paisley	65	70	66	70	271	42,853.34
Richie Ramsay	65	70	69	67	271	42,853.34
David Horsey	67	66	68	70	271	42,853.34
Rory McIlroy	67	67	68	69	271	42,853.34
Brandon Stone	68	64	70	69	271	42,853.34
Haydn Porteous	68	68	68	67	271	42,853.34
Christiaan Bezuidenhout	70	67	65	69	271	42,853.34
Shubhankar Sharma	71	66	67	67	271	42,853.34
Eddie Pepperell	67	67	69	69	272	34,158.46

466 / EUROPEAN TOURS

	SCORES				TOTAL	MONEY
Grant Forrest	67	68	70	67	272	34,158.46
Tom Lewis	67	69	70	66	272	34,158.46
Kurt Kitayama	68	68	65	71	272	34,158.46
Thomas Detry	69	65	70	68	272	34,158.46
Darren Fichardt	66	67	68	72	273	26,705.71
Mikko Korhonen	66	70	70	67	273	26,705.71
Oliver Fisher	67	70	66	70	273	26,705.71
Max Schmitt	68	65	70	70	273	26,705.71
Nacho Elvira	68	68	68	69	273	26,705.71
Paul Waring	69	67	69	68	273	26,705.71
Marcus Kinhult	71	66	67	69	273	26,705.71
Thomas Aiken	64	71	69	70	274	18,898.06
Sean Crocker	66	66	70	72	274	18,898.06
Stuart Manley	67	69	69	69	274	18,898.06
Masahiro Kawamura	67	70	66	71	274	18,898.06
Julian Suri	68	66	69	71	274	18,898.06
Fabrizio Zanotti	69	66	71	68	274	18,898.06
Lee Westwood	70	67	67	70	274	18,898.06
Alexander Bjork	66	69	68	72	275	14,594.98
Lucas Herbert	67	66	72	70	275	14,594.98
Hideto Tanihara	67	67	71	70	275	14,594.98
Jack Singh Brar	69	68	67	71	275	14,594.98
Ben Evans	71	66	69	69	275	14,594.98
Bradley Dredge	73	63	69	70	275	14,594.98
Louis de Jager	70	65	71	70	276	12,421.26
Oliver Wilson	65	68	69	75	277	10,815.39
Nicolas Colsaerts	69	67	69	72	277	10,815.39
Jens Dantorp	70	66	67	74	277	10,815.39
Pablo Larrazabal	67	66	73	75	281	9,313
Gonzalo Fernandez-Castano	66	68	73		207	9,308.50
Jorge Campillo	69	68	70		207	9,308.50
Trevor Immelman	66	71	71		208	9,301
Dean Burmester	69	67	72		208	9,301
Hyowon Park	73	64	71		208	9,301
Ashley Chesters	67	70	72		209	9,293.50
David Drysdale	68	69	72		209	9,293.50
Kiradech Aphibarnrat	71	66	75		212	9,289

The 148th Open Championship

Royal Portrush Golf Club, Portrush, County Antrim, Northern Ireland July 18-21
Par 36-35–71; 7,344 yards purse, US$10,750,000

	SCORES				TOTAL	MONEY
Shane Lowry	67	67	63	72	269	€1,718,319.87
Tommy Fleetwood	68	67	66	74	275	994,583.07
Tony Finau	68	70	68	71	277	637,598.79
Lee Westwood	68	67	70	73	278	447,118.37
Brooks Koepka	68	69	67	74	278	447,118.37
Tyrrell Hatton	68	71	71	69	279	277,950.45
Robert MacIntyre	68	72	71	68	279	277,950.45
Rickie Fowler	70	69	66	74	279	277,950.45
Danny Willett	74	67	65	73	279	277,950.45
Patrick Reed	71	67	71	71	280	198,028.59
Jon Rahm	68	70	68	75	281	152,473.14
Alex Noren	68	71	68	74	281	152,473.14
Justin Thomas	71	70	68	72	281	152,473.14
Francesco Molinari	74	69	72	66	281	152,473.14
Tom Lewis	75	68	68	70	281	152,473.14
Ryan Fox	68	75	70	69	282	112,168.10

		SCORES			TOTAL	MONEY
Sanghyun Park	69	72	68	73	282	112,168.10
Lucas Bjerregaard	70	68	74	70	282	112,168.10
Rory Sabbatini	70	70	71	71	282	112,168.10
Justin Rose	69	67	68	79	283	81,120.68
Cameron Smith	70	66	71	76	283	81,120.68
Jordan Spieth	70	67	69	77	283	81,120.68
Erik van Rooyen	70	68	72	73	283	81,120.68
Henrik Stenson	70	69	68	76	283	81,120.68
Louis Oosthuizen	70	72	72	69	283	81,120.68
Matthew Fitzpatrick	71	69	70	73	283	81,120.68
Doc Redman	71	71	71	70	283	81,120.68
Lucas Glover	72	69	71	71	283	81,120.68
Stewart Cink	74	68	71	70	283	81,120.68
Webb Simpson	68	71	71	74	284	62,050.44
Kevin Kisner	70	71	70	73	284	62,050.44
Dylan Frittelli	68	69	70	78	285	49,975.83
Kiradech Aphibarnrat	68	73	77	67	285	49,975.83
Andrew Putnam	70	67	70	78	285	49,975.83
Bernd Wiesberger	70	71	74	70	285	49,975.83
Ernie Els	71	69	72	73	285	49,975.83
Byeong Hun An	73	67	70	75	285	49,975.83
Joost Luiten	73	69	71	72	285	49,975.83
Jason Kokrak	74	69	74	68	285	49,975.83
Andrew Wilson	76	67	71	71	285	49,975.83
Matt Kuchar	70	68	69	79	286	32,790.16
Patrick Cantlay	70	71	71	74	286	32,790.16
Callum Shinkwin	70	71	75	70	286	32,790.16
Russell Knox	70	71	68	77	286	32,790.16
Justin Harding	71	65	74	76	286	32,790.16
Aaron Wise	72	69	71	74	286	32,790.16
Innchoon Hwang	72	71	70	73	286	32,790.16
Benjamin Hebert	73	69	73	71	286	32,790.16
Xander Schauffele	74	65	69	78	286	32,790.16
Kyle Stanley	75	67	73	71	286	32,790.16
Branden Grace	70	71	75	71	287	25,145.78
Shubhankar Sharma	70	72	77	68	287	25,145.78
Charley Hoffman	70	73	70	74	287	25,145.78
Dustin Johnson	72	67	72	76	287	25,145.78
Bubba Watson	72	71	73	71	287	25,145.78
Matt Wallace	73	70	72	72	287	25,145.78
Ashton Turner	69	74	77	68	288	23,502.95
Thorbjorn Olesen	72	68	77	71	288	23,502.95
Paul Casey	72	70	73	73	288	23,502.95
Graeme McDowell	73	70	68	77	288	23,502.95
Adam Hadwin	74	69	72	73	288	23,502.95
Kevin Streelman	77	65	74	72	288	23,502.95
Romain Langasque	69	72	70	78	289	22,910.93
Mikko Korhonen	72	69	71	77	289	22,910.93
Jim Furyk	73	68	75	73	289	22,910.93
Paul Waring	75	68	75	71	289	22,910.93
J.B. Holmes	66	68	69	87	290	22,278.22
Sergio Garcia	68	73	71	78	290	22,278.22
Thomas Pieters	72	68	74	76	290	22,278.22
Yosuke Asaji	72	71	71	76	290	22,278.22
Eddie Pepperell	70	72	76	74	292	21,867.51
Yuki Inamori	70	73	70	80	293	21,701
Nino Bertasio	72	71	75	75	293	21,701

Out of Final 36 Holes

Jason Day	70	74			144	6,660.15
James Sugrue [A]	71	73			144	
Brian Harman	72	72			144	6,660.15

	SCORES		TOTAL	MONEY
Connor Syme	72	72	144	6,660.15
Abraham Ancer	72	72	144	6,660.15
Andrew Johnston	73	71	144	6,660.15
Alexander Levy	73	71	144	6,660.15
Takumi Kanaya [A]	73	71	144	
Keegan Bradley	73	71	144	6,660.15
Brandt Snedeker	74	70	144	6,660.15
Nate Lashley	75	69	144	6,660.15
Keith Mitchell	75	69	144	6,660.15
Rory McIlroy	79	65	144	6,660.15
Si Woo Kim	70	75	145	5,328.12
Hideki Matsuyama	71	74	145	5,328.12
Darren Clarke	71	74	145	5,328.12
Adrian Otaegui	73	72	145	5,328.12
Chez Reavie	73	72	145	5,328.12
Chris Wood	73	72	145	5,328.12
Kurt Kitayama	74	71	145	5,328.12
Christiaan Bezuidenhout	74	71	145	5,328.12
Gary Woodland	74	71	145	5,328.12
Padraig Harrington	75	70	145	5,328.12
Dongkyu Jang	76	69	145	5,328.12
Patton Kizzire	73	73	146	5,328.12
Zach Johnson	74	72	146	5,328.12
Doyeob Mun	74	72	146	5,328.12
Sunghoon Kang	74	72	146	5,328.12
Haotong Li	74	72	146	5,328.12
David Lipsky	74	72	146	5,328.12
Jack Senior	75	71	146	5,328.12
Yoshinori Fujimoto	75	71	146	5,328.12
Matthew Baldwin	78	68	146	5,328.12
Mikumu Horikawa	71	76	147	4,440.10
Brandon Stone	72	75	147	4,440.10
Bryson DeChambeau	74	73	147	4,440.10
Jazz Janewattananond	74	73	147	4,440.10
Paul Lawrie	75	72	147	4,440.10
Isidro Benitez	75	72	147	4,440.10
Matthias Schmid [A]	76	71	147	
Joaquin Niemann	76	71	147	4,440.10
Jake McLeod	76	71	147	4,440.10
Robert Rock	76	71	147	4,440.10
Billy Horschel	76	71	147	4,440.10
Alexander Bjork	77	70	147	4,440.10
Zander Lombard	71	77	148	4,440.10
Gunn Charoenkul	72	76	148	4,440.10
Corey Conners	72	76	148	4,440.10
Oliver Wilson	73	75	148	4,440.10
Rafa Cabrera Bello	73	75	148	4,440.10
Jimmy Walker	74	74	148	4,440.10
Joel Dahmen	76	72	148	4,440.10
Tiger Woods	78	70	148	4,440.10
Shaun Norris	73	76	149	4,440.10
Brandon Wu [A]	73	76	149	
Andrea Pavan	73	76	149	4,440.10
Luke List	73	76	149	4,440.10
Ryan Palmer	74	75	149	4,440.10
Chan Kim	75	74	149	4,440.10
Ian Poulter	75	74	149	4,440.10
Jorge Campillo	76	73	149	4,440.10
Adri Arnaus	75	75	150	4,440.10
Phil Mickelson	76	74	150	4,440.10
Mike Lorenzo-Vera	77	73	150	4,440.10
Marc Leishman	78	72	150	4,440.10
Sungjae Im	71	80	151	4,440.10

	SCORES		TOTAL	MONEY
Curtis Knipes [A]	72	79	151	
Andy Sullivan	76	75	151	4,440.10
Yuta Ikeda	76	75	151	4,440.10
C.T. Pan	77	74	151	4,440.10
Richard Sterne	78	73	151	4,440.10
Adam Scott	78	73	151	4,440.10
Emiliano Grillo	73	79	152	4,440.10
Sam Locke	75	77	152	4,440.10
Garrick Porteous	79	73	152	4,440.10
Shugo Imahira	83	69	152	4,440.10
Prom Meesawat	73	81	154	4,440.10
Austin Connelly	75	79	154	4,440.10
Tom Lehman	78	76	154	4,440.10
Miguel Angel Jimenez	82	73	155	4,440.10
Dimitrios Papadatos	83	72	155	4,440.10
Thomas Thurloway [A]	83	73	156	
David Duval	91	78	169	4,440.10

D+D Real Czech Masters

Albatross Golf Resort, Prague, Czech Republic
Par 36-36–72; 7,467 yards

August 15-18
purse, €1,000,000

	SCORES				TOTAL	MONEY
Thomas Pieters	67	67	66	69	269	€166,660
Adri Arnaus	71	65	65	69	270	111,110
Andrea Pavan	68	68	71	65	272	56,300
Sam Horsfield	69	66	69	68	272	56,300
Erik van Rooyen	65	72	66	71	274	30,960
Hugo Leon	66	69	67	72	274	30,960
Liam Johnston	67	69	68	70	274	30,960
Rikard Karlberg	69	67	66	72	274	30,960
Matthias Schwab	70	65	69	70	274	30,960
Robert Karlsson	67	68	67	73	275	20,000
Kim Koivu	66	72	70	68	276	17,233.33
Zander Lombard	68	70	73	65	276	17,233.33
Haydn Porteous	69	70	69	68	276	17,233.33
Edoardo Molinari	66	66	70	75	277	14,400
Kristoffer Reitan	66	71	66	74	277	14,400
Romain Wattel	68	71	69	69	277	14,400
Jack Singh Brar	69	68	67	73	277	14,400
Ashley Chesters	70	68	71	69	278	12,040
Alexander Levy	70	70	70	68	278	12,040
Daniel Gavins	71	67	68	72	278	12,040
Masahiro Kawamura	72	68	65	73	278	12,040
Ben Evans	72	69	68	69	278	12,040
Jacques Kruyswijk	69	67	71	72	279	10,100
Robert MacIntyre	69	72	68	70	279	10,100
Berry Henson	70	68	72	69	279	10,100
Gonzalo Fernandez-Castano	70	70	67	72	279	10,100
Paul Dunne	70	71	69	69	279	10,100
Ivan Cantero Gutierrez	71	67	72	69	279	10,100
Alexander Bjork	71	68	69	71	279	10,100
Joachim B. Hansen	66	70	72	72	280	7,811.11
Bernd Wiesberger	67	70	71	72	280	7,811.11
Jason Scrivener	67	71	70	72	280	7,811.11
Darren Fichardt	67	74	72	67	280	7,811.11
David Howell	69	71	70	70	280	7,811.11
John Catlin	70	69	72	69	280	7,811.11
Matthew Southgate	70	70	69	71	280	7,811.11

470 / EUROPEAN TOURS

	SCORES				TOTAL	MONEY
Paul Waring	70	71	70	69	280	7,811.11
James Morrison	73	68	68	71	280	7,811.11
Lee Slattery	65	71	71	74	281	5,900
Tapio Pulkkanen	69	69	71	72	281	5,900
Mikko Korhonen	70	67	67	77	281	5,900
Victor Dubuisson	70	67	74	70	281	5,900
Bradley Dredge	70	71	68	72	281	5,900
Renato Paratore	71	68	71	71	281	5,900
Dimitrios Papadatos	71	69	71	70	281	5,900
Scott Jamieson	72	67	70	72	281	5,900
Aaron Rai	72	69	69	71	281	5,900
J.C. Ritchie	70	67	68	77	282	4,700
Ricardo Gouveia	70	71	70	71	282	4,700
Espen Kofstad	74	67	71	70	282	4,700
Kalle Samooja	68	70	69	76	283	3,700
Bryce Easton	68	73	73	69	283	3,700
Wilco Nienaber	69	68	73	73	283	3,700
Oliver Fisher	69	72	69	73	283	3,700
Sihwan Kim	70	68	73	72	283	3,700
Tom Murray	70	69	72	72	283	3,700
Mathiam Keyser	71	70	71	71	283	3,700
Gavin Green	64	75	70	75	284	2,600
Chris Hanson	69	70	68	77	284	2,600
Matthew Nixon	70	67	77	70	284	2,600
Dean Burmester	70	69	72	73	284	2,600
Nicolas Colsaerts	70	69	71	74	284	2,600
Richie Ramsay	70	71	71	72	284	2,600
Thomas Bjorn	70	71	69	74	284	2,600
Justin Walters	72	69	72	71	284	2,600
Padraig Harrington	73	68	73	70	284	2,600
Stuart Manley	71	70	72	72	285	2,100
Chris Lloyd	70	70	72	74	286	2,000
Liam Robinson	70	71	70	77	288	1,900
Jeff Winther	69	72	79	77	297	1,830

Scandinavian Invitation

Hills Golf & Sports Club, Gothenburg, Sweden
Par 36-34–70; 6,865 yards

August 22-25
purse, €1,500,000

	SCORES			TOTAL	MONEY
Erik van Rooyen	65	68	64	64	261	€250,000
Matthew Fitzpatrick	64	65	69	64	262	166,660
Dean Burmester	66	72	62	66	266	84,450
Henrik Stenson	69	62	69	66	266	84,450
Wade Ormsby	62	71	65	69	267	46,440
Alexander Levy	63	71	66	67	267	46,440
Sihwan Kim	66	68	68	65	267	46,440
Sebastian Soderberg	67	69	68	63	267	46,440
Jamie Donaldson	69	68	63	67	267	46,440
Joakim Lagergren	63	69	71	65	268	25,425
Matthew Southgate	65	72	64	67	268	25,425
Victor Perez	68	65	69	66	268	25,425
Sam Horsfield	69	70	67	62	268	25,425
Andrew Johnston	70	70	63	65	268	25,425
Matthieu Pavon	74	66	64	64	268	25,425
Gavin Green	66	67	71	65	269	19,837.50
Zander Lombard	70	68	64	67	269	19,837.50
Joachim B. Hansen	70	69	66	64	269	19,837.50
Andrea Pavan	74	64	67	64	269	19,837.50

		SCORES			TOTAL	MONEY
Ashun Wu	67	64	67	72	270	16,066.67
Alexander Bjork	67	67	72	64	270	16,066.67
Paul Waring	68	71	66	65	270	16,066.67
Jason Scrivener	69	63	70	68	270	16,066.67
Marcus Kinhult	69	71	66	64	270	16,066.67
Niklas Lemke	70	69	64	67	270	16,066.67
Thomas Detry	72	66	63	69	270	16,066.67
Renato Paratore	72	67	67	64	270	16,066.67
Andy Sullivan	74	65	66	65	270	16,066.67
James Morrison	66	68	71	66	271	12,281.25
John Catlin	66	69	66	70	271	12,281.25
Soren Kjeldsen	68	68	69	66	271	12,281.25
Haydn Porteous	70	66	69	66	271	12,281.25
Joost Luiten	70	67	67	67	271	12,281.25
Matthew Nixon	70	69	66	66	271	12,281.25
Aaron Rai	70	70	66	65	271	12,281.25
Ryan Evans	71	68	69	63	271	12,281.25
Borja Virto	69	70	66	67	272	10,350
Jack Singh Brar	71	68	66	67	272	10,350
Jeff Winther	73	65	68	66	272	10,350
Masahiro Kawamura	67	70	69	67	273	8,850
Kristian Krogh Johannessen	68	69	70	66	273	8,850
Alejandro Canizares	68	72	65	68	273	8,850
Lorenzo Gagli	69	69	66	69	273	8,850
Lee Slattery	69	70	67	67	273	8,850
Jens Dantorp	70	67	70	66	273	8,850
Alex Noren	72	67	67	67	273	8,850
Kalle Samooja	67	68	72	67	274	7,050
David Nyfjall [A]	67	72	67	68	274	
Austin Connelly	67	73	64	70	274	7,050
Bradley Dredge	68	70	67	69	274	7,050
Gavin Moynihan	69	67	64	74	274	7,050
Stephen Gallacher	70	67	67	70	274	7,050
Nicolas Colsaerts	67	71	68	69	275	5,400
Rikard Karlberg	68	71	65	71	275	5,400
Per Langfors	69	69	67	70	275	5,400
Gaganjeet Bhullar	71	69	69	66	275	5,400
Deyen Lawson	72	67	70	66	275	5,400
Chris Wood	72	68	66	69	275	5,400
Ivan Cantero Gutierrez	69	66	68	73	276	4,050
Tom Lewis	69	71	68	68	276	4,050
Bernd Ritthammer	69	71	68	68	276	4,050
Paul Peterson	70	67	69	70	276	4,050
Gonzalo Fernandez-Castano	70	70	68	68	276	4,050
Justin Walters	71	68	70	67	276	4,050
Henric Sturehed	72	67	68	69	276	4,050
Hyowon Park	67	71	70	69	277	3,375
Ben Evans	73	67	68	69	277	3,375
Christiaan Bezuidenhout	67	70	69	72	278	3,075
Zheng-Kai Bai	73	64	69	72	278	3,075
Robert Rock	68	66	69	76	279	2,795
Max Orrin	71	69	69	70	279	2,795
Max Schmitt	69	69	71	71	280	2,250
Brett Rumford	70	68	70	73	281	2,247
Adrien Saddier	67	73	69	75	284	2,244
Adam Bland	70	69	71		210	2,238
Edoardo Molinari	70	70	70		210	2,238
Brandon Stone	73	67	70		210	2,238
Johan Edfors	70	70	71		211	2,229
Anton Karlsson	71	68	72		211	2,229
Jeunghun Wang	72	68	71		211	2,229
Ricardo Gouveia	68	70	74		212	2,223
Nick Cullen	71	67	75		213	2,220

	SCORES			TOTAL	MONEY
Min Woo Lee	67	72	75	214	2,217
Oliver Wilson	71	69	77	217	2,214

Omega European Masters

Crans-sur-Sierre Golf Club, Crans Montana, Switzerland
Par 35-35–70; 6,848 yards

August 29-September 1
purse, €2,500,000

	SCORES				TOTAL	MONEY
Sebastian Soderberg	64	70	66	66	266	€416,660
Lorenzo Gagli	64	68	67	67	266	166,317.50
Kalle Samooja	66	71	62	67	266	166,317.50
Rory McIlroy	67	63	69	67	266	166,317.50
Andres Romero	69	61	66	70	266	166,317.50
(Soderberg won on first playoff hole.)						
Mike Lorenzo-Vera	63	72	67	65	267	81,250
Adri Arnaus	66	67	70	64	267	81,250
Matthias Schwab	63	67	70	68	268	53,625
Tommy Fleetwood	65	65	68	70	268	53,625
Wade Ormsby	66	64	67	71	268	53,625
Lucas Herbert	70	67	67	64	268	53,625
Gavin Green	65	64	69	71	269	36,312.50
Erik van Rooyen	65	69	68	67	269	36,312.50
Renato Paratore	67	66	67	69	269	36,312.50
Thomas Pieters	67	67	70	65	269	36,312.50
Christiaan Bezuidenhout	67	67	65	70	269	36,312.50
Marcus Kinhult	67	72	65	65	269	36,312.50
Scott Jamieson	70	65	67	67	269	36,312.50
Andrea Pavan	70	68	66	65	269	36,312.50
Hideto Tanihara	66	66	71	67	270	29,083.33
Nino Bertasio	66	70	65	69	270	29,083.33
Thomas Detry	68	71	65	66	270	29,083.33
David Drysdale	65	70	70	66	271	26,000
Sergio Garcia	66	68	66	71	271	26,000
Miguel Angel Jimenez	67	66	69	69	271	26,000
Joost Luiten	69	68	68	66	271	26,000
Andrew Johnston	69	69	66	67	271	26,000
Lucas Bjerregaard	66	68	70	68	272	22,250
James Morrison	67	67	70	68	272	22,250
Alexander Bjork	67	68	67	70	272	22,250
Lee Westwood	67	72	64	69	272	22,250
Sean Crocker	68	67	68	69	272	22,250
Guido Migliozzi	65	72	70	66	273	19,625
Jack Singh Brar	69	68	67	69	273	19,625
Mikko Korhonen	64	70	75	65	274	17,000
Jamie Donaldson	65	74	69	66	274	17,000
Lee Slattery	66	70	68	70	274	17,000
Troy Merritt	67	71	70	66	274	17,000
Ross Fisher	68	70	65	71	274	17,000
Pedro Figueiredo	68	71	67	68	274	17,000
Haydn Porteous	70	65	72	67	274	17,000
Eddie Pepperell	70	66	67	71	274	17,000
Darren Fichardt	66	69	69	71	275	13,750
Sam Horsfield	68	69	70	68	275	13,750
David Horsey	69	67	66	73	275	13,750
Victor Dubuisson	69	69	64	73	275	13,750
Joachim B. Hansen	73	66	69	67	275	13,750
Alvaro Quiros	67	70	70	69	276	10,000
Yusaku Miyazato	67	70	72	67	276	10,000
Max Schmitt	68	68	75	65	276	10,000

	SCORES				TOTAL	MONEY
Oliver Wilson	68	69	68	71	276	10,000
Eduardo De La Riva	68	71	68	69	276	10,000
Richard Sterne	69	70	67	70	276	10,000
Jens Dantorp	69	70	67	70	276	10,000
Chris Paisley	70	69	68	69	276	10,000
Romain Langasque	72	67	65	72	276	10,000
Daniel Gavins	72	67	69	68	276	10,000
Sam Brazel	67	69	73	68	277	7,250
Grant Forrest	69	68	74	66	277	7,250
Richie Ramsay	70	69	67	71	277	7,250
Bradley Dredge	66	69	69	74	278	6,625
Liam Johnston	69	69	68	72	278	6,625
Robert Karlsson	68	71	71	69	279	5,750
David Howell	69	70	71	69	279	5,750
Jaco van Zyl	70	67	70	72	279	5,750
Nick Cullen	70	69	70	70	279	5,750
Giovanni Manzoni[A]	70	69	71	69	279	
Rory Sabbatini	71	65	68	75	279	5,750
Chris Wood	67	71	72	70	280	4,773.33
Matthew Fitzpatrick	69	69	73	69	280	4,773.33
Deyen Lawson	69	70	72	69	280	4,773.33
Ashley Chesters	70	67	69	75	281	3,747
Zander Lombard	71	67	70	73	281	3,747
Wilco Nienaber	72	63	73	73	281	3,747
Clement Sordet	68	70	77	70	285	3,741
Stuart Manley	70	69	75	79	293	3,738

Porsche European Open

Green Eagle Golf Courses, Hamburg, Germany
Par 34-38–72; 6,898 yards

September 5-8
purse, €2,000,000

	SCORES				TOTAL	MONEY
Paul Casey	66	73	69	66	274	€333,330
Matthias Schwab	67	72	70	66	275	149,140
Robert MacIntyre	68	65	74	68	275	149,140
Bernd Ritthammer	71	66	70	68	275	149,140
Bernd Wiesberger	71	69	72	64	276	84,800
Romain Wattel	72	74	67	64	277	70,000
Pablo Larrazabal	70	71	68	69	278	55,000
Guido Migliozzi	71	68	72	67	278	55,000
Ashley Chesters	71	71	70	67	279	42,400
Niklas Lemke	71	73	68	67	279	42,400
Jeff Winther	72	69	70	70	281	36,800
Padraig Harrington	71	74	68	69	282	33,300
Louis de Jager	72	69	71	70	282	33,300
Ben Evans	69	73	68	73	283	29,400
Dominic Foos	74	67	75	67	283	29,400
Sam Horsfield	75	68	71	69	283	29,400
Sihwan Kim	72	74	69	69	284	25,866.67
Hugo Leon	73	72	72	67	284	25,866.67
Jaco van Zyl	78	69	71	66	284	25,866.67
Thomas Pieters	70	72	74	69	285	23,600
Joakim Lagergren	77	69	69	70	285	23,600
Alexander Bjork	69	71	73	73	286	21,100
Lucas Herbert	69	75	73	69	286	21,100
Stuart Manley	72	75	70	69	286	21,100
Oliver Fisher	73	70	76	67	286	21,100
Richard Sterne	75	69	69	73	286	21,100
Daniel Gavins	76	70	71	69	286	21,100

	SCORES				TOTAL	MONEY
Max Rottluff	68	75	72	72	287	17,800
Per Langfors	72	73	70	72	287	17,800
Scott Gregory	73	72	68	74	287	17,800
Paul Waring	74	72	72	69	287	17,800
Adrien Saddier	77	68	71	71	287	17,800
Pedro Figueiredo	70	71	74	73	288	15,466.67
Lasse Jensen	71	73	73	71	288	15,466.67
Jorge Campillo	74	71	72	71	288	15,466.67
Nacho Elvira	71	74	71	73	289	12,800
Ricardo Gouveia	72	70	71	76	289	12,800
Zander Lombard	72	75	72	70	289	12,800
Scott Hend	73	71	73	72	289	12,800
Min Woo Lee	73	72	69	75	289	12,800
Andy Sullivan	74	70	75	70	289	12,800
Patrick Reed	74	72	71	72	289	12,800
Kurt Kitayama	74	72	74	69	289	12,800
Johannes Veerman	76	69	76	68	289	12,800
Ashun Wu	77	70	74	68	289	12,800
Kristian Krogh Johannessen	70	71	71	78	290	9,000
Ross Fisher	72	75	71	72	290	9,000
Marc Hammer [A]	72	75	73	70	290	
Xander Schauffele	73	69	76	72	290	9,000
Alvaro Quiros	73	73	72	72	290	9,000
Rikard Karlberg	74	71	71	74	290	9,000
Matthew Southgate	74	71	76	69	290	9,000
Clement Sordet	75	72	76	67	290	9,000
Troy Merritt	77	70	74	69	290	9,000
Rory Sabbatini	78	69	73	70	290	9,000
Darren Fichardt	73	69	75	74	291	6,600
Hideto Tanihara	74	72	72	73	291	6,600
Gavin Moynihan	74	72	71	74	291	6,600
Max Orrin	72	75	73	72	292	6,000
Dimitrios Papadatos	74	72	74	73	293	5,600
Ryan Fox	76	71	75	71	293	5,600
Alexander Knappe	77	67	75	74	293	5,600
Jake McLeod	72	74	75	73	294	5,200
Harrison Endycott	72	71	78	74	295	4,900
Jack Singh Brar	74	73	75	73	295	4,900
Ben Stow	68	75	78	76	297	4,200
Adam Bland	71	76	74	76	297	4,200
Ivan Cantero Gutierrez	72	74	76	75	297	4,200
Michael Hoey	74	71	75	77	297	4,200
Jacques Kruyswijk	75	70	76	76	297	4,200

KLM Open

The International, Amsterdam, Netherlands
Par 36-36—72; 7,039 yards

September 12-15
purse, €2,000,000

	SCORES				TOTAL	MONEY
Sergio Garcia	68	67	66	69	270	€333,330
Nicolai Hojgaard	67	69	67	68	271	222,220
Matt Wallace	75	67	63	68	273	125,200
James Morrison	68	67	69	70	274	100,000
Callum Shinkwin	66	69	66	74	275	84,800
Rikard Karlberg	70	68	70	68	276	70,000
Hugo Leon	70	69	68	70	277	51,600
Joakim Lagergren	71	66	69	71	277	51,600
Wil Besseling	72	66	69	70	277	51,600
Matthew Southgate	67	68	70	73	278	34,800

	SCORES				TOTAL	MONEY
Joost Luiten	69	69	70	70	278	34,800
Thomas Pieters	71	66	70	71	278	34,800
Bradley Dredge	72	65	72	69	278	34,800
Mike Lorenzo-Vera	72	69	67	70	278	34,800
Steven Brown	69	68	68	74	279	26,533.33
Liam Johnston	70	68	72	69	279	26,533.33
Ashley Chesters	71	68	69	71	279	26,533.33
George Coetzee	71	69	67	72	279	26,533.33
Padraig Harrington	71	71	68	69	279	26,533.33
Patrick Reed	72	69	70	68	279	26,533.33
Scott Jamieson	68	65	76	71	280	21,700
Kurt Kitayama	69	70	70	71	280	21,700
Antoine Rozner	70	67	71	72	280	21,700
Andres Romero	70	69	70	71	280	21,700
Edoardo Molinari	70	71	69	70	280	21,700
Brandon Stone	70	72	70	68	280	21,700
Chris Paisley	67	73	71	70	281	17,222.22
Rowin Caron	68	69	71	73	281	17,222.22
Romain Langasque	68	71	70	72	281	17,222.22
Maximilian Kieffer	69	68	73	71	281	17,222.22
Hideto Tanihara	69	71	70	71	281	17,222.22
Jake McLeod	70	68	73	70	281	17,222.22
Jamie Donaldson	70	70	70	71	281	17,222.22
Paul Dunne	71	69	73	68	281	17,222.22
Jeunghun Wang	72	68	70	71	281	17,222.22
Max Orrin	68	69	74	71	282	14,000
Sean Crocker	70	72	66	74	282	14,000
Jeff Winther	71	69	67	75	282	14,000
Thomas Detry	71	70	70	71	282	14,000
Gavin Green	67	73	72	71	283	11,600
Eduardo De La Riva	69	68	70	76	283	11,600
Johannes Veerman	69	73	72	69	283	11,600
Shubhankar Sharma	70	68	70	75	283	11,600
Euan Walker	72	69	69	73	283	11,600
Espen Kofstad	72	70	67	74	283	11,600
Chris Wood	72	70	70	71	283	11,600
Lee Slattery	74	67	71	71	283	11,600
Troy Merritt	73	65	75	71	284	9,800
Sam Horsfield	67	69	74	75	285	8,400
Pedro Figueiredo	70	70	71	74	285	8,400
Daniel Gavins	70	71	72	72	285	8,400
Nino Bertasio	71	68	77	69	285	8,400
Yusaku Miyazato	74	65	71	75	285	8,400
Nick McCarthy	74	68	72	71	285	8,400
Haydn Porteous	68	72	73	73	286	6,320
Ashun Wu	69	72	73	72	286	6,320
Soren Kjeldsen	70	70	72	74	286	6,320
Stuart Manley	73	69	75	69	286	6,320
Richie Ramsay	73	69	72	72	286	6,320
Koen Kouwenaar [A]	68	70	75	74	287	
Gaganjeet Bhullar	72	69	76	70	287	5,400
David Law	72	70	73	72	287	5,400
Trevor Immelman	73	69	73	72	287	5,400
Gavin Moynihan	70	71	68	79	288	5,000
Marc Warren	67	74	70	78	289	4,700
Mikko Korhonen	70	69	76	74	289	4,700
Reinier Saxton	69	73	71	77	290	4,200
Anton Karlsson	70	69	78	73	290	4,200
Niklas Lemke	73	69	72	76	290	4,200
Per Langfors	67	73	75	76	291	3,725
Sebastian Soderberg	75	67	74	75	291	3,725
Sven Maurits	71	71	76	76	294	2,998.50
Christofer Blomstrand	74	67	74	79	294	2,998.50

BMW PGA Championship

Wentworth Club, Virginia Water, Surrey, England
Par 35-37–72; 7,284 yards

September 19-22
purse, US$7,000,000

	SCORES				TOTAL	MONEY
Danny Willett	68	65	68	67	268	€1,056,661.54
Jon Rahm	66	67	68	70	271	704,438.01
Christiaan Bezuidenhout	68	67	69	68	272	396,884.34
Patrick Reed	70	70	67	66	273	292,908.25
Billy Horschel	72	65	71	65	273	292,908.25
Rafa Cabrera Bello	69	70	67	69	275	206,050.18
Richie Ramsay	71	68	67	69	275	206,050.18
Justin Rose	67	68	69	72	276	158,500.14
Andrew Johnston	69	70	69	69	277	134,408.12
Rory McIlroy	76	69	65	67	277	134,408.12
Paul Casey	68	69	71	70	278	109,259.43
Viktor Hovland	69	69	70	70	278	109,259.43
Shane Lowry	72	71	69	66	278	109,259.43
Francesco Molinari	69	70	69	71	279	93,198.08
Erik van Rooyen	70	74	67	68	279	93,198.08
Kurt Kitayama	71	71	68	69	279	93,198.08
Henrik Stenson	66	69	74	71	280	80,518.07
Romain Langasque	69	74	70	67	280	80,518.07
Shubhankar Sharma	71	67	66	76	280	80,518.07
Bernd Wiesberger	74	67	69	70	280	80,518.07
Paul Waring	70	71	68	72	281	71,642.06
Ashley Chesters	70	73	68	70	281	71,642.06
Andrew Putnam	71	67	70	73	281	71,642.06
Jordan Smith	69	71	70	72	282	66,887.06
Joakim Lagergren	70	71	71	70	282	66,887.06
Aaron Rai	71	70	72	70	283	63,083.05
Tapio Pulkkanen	71	73	69	70	283	63,083.05
Robert MacIntyre	69	72	70	73	284	58,328.05
Alex Noren	69	72	69	74	284	58,328.05
Matthias Schwab	70	75	70	69	284	58,328.05
Joost Luiten	68	72	73	72	285	50,086.04
Miguel Angel Jimenez	69	74	74	68	285	50,086.04
Ross Fisher	70	73	66	76	285	50,086.04
Sam Horsfield	71	71	70	73	285	50,086.04
Richard Sterne	71	71	70	73	285	50,086.04
Julian Suri	71	74	69	71	285	50,086.04
Mike Lorenzo-Vera	70	70	75	71	286	43,112.04
Mikko Korhonen	71	69	71	75	286	43,112.04
Benjamin Hebert	72	72	69	73	286	43,112.04
Thomas Pieters	73	71	70	72	286	43,112.04
Matt Wallace	65	76	72	74	287	37,406.03
Gonzalo Fernandez-Castano	70	73	70	74	287	37,406.03
Renato Paratore	71	71	71	74	287	37,406.03
Ashun Wu	72	73	68	74	287	37,406.03
Soren Kjeldsen	73	71	73	70	287	37,406.03
Andrea Pavan	68	76	75	69	288	31,066.03
Russell Knox	69	71	76	72	288	31,066.03
Marcus Kinhult	70	72	75	71	288	31,066.03
Matthew Fitzpatrick	73	71	74	70	288	31,066.03
Padraig Harrington	73	72	75	68	288	31,066.03
Tony Finau	70	68	77	74	289	24,092.02
Chris Wood	70	75	71	73	289	24,092.02
Yusaku Miyazato	71	72	71	75	289	24,092.02
Haotong Li	71	72	70	76	289	24,092.02
Kiradech Aphibarnrat	73	72	71	73	289	24,092.02
Alexander Bjork	76	69	76	68	289	24,092.02
Scott Jamieson	68	77	75	70	290	19,020.02

		SCORES			TOTAL	MONEY
Martin Kaymer	70	74	73	73	290	19,020.02
Nicolas Colsaerts	73	66	78	73	290	19,020.02
Julien Guerrier	69	76	77	69	291	16,801.01
Tommy Fleetwood	70	75	70	76	291	16,801.01
Branden Grace	72	72	68	79	291	16,801.01
Ian Poulter	73	70	77	71	291	16,801.01
Ernie Els	68	76	76	72	292	13,948.01
Sebastian Soderberg	68	77	76	71	292	13,948.01
Steven Brown	69	75	74	74	292	13,948.01
Alvaro Quiros	69	75	76	72	292	13,948.01
Edoardo Molinari	71	74	75	72	292	13,948.01
Trevor Immelman	71	74	73	76	294	11,806
Robert Coles	71	74	76	73	294	11,806
George Coetzee	68	72	79	77	296	9,510
Gavin Green	72	73	72	80	297	9,505.50
David Law	75	69	78	75	297	9,505.50
Andy Sullivan	71	74	76	81	302	9,501

Alfred Dunhill Links Championship

St. Andrews Old Course: Par 36-36–72; 7,318 yards
Carnoustie Championship Course: Par 36-36–72; 7,394 yards
Kingsbarns Golf Links: Par 36-36–72; 7,227 yards
St. Andrews & Fife, Scotland

September 26-29
purse, US$5,000,000

		SCORES			TOTAL	MONEY
Victor Perez	64	68	64	70	266	€732,265.40
Matthew Southgate	65	66	65	71	267	488,173.90
Paul Waring	65	68	65	70	268	247,359.30
Joakim Lagergren	69	62	68	69	268	247,359.30
Jordan Smith	64	68	68	69	269	136,025.60
Matthew Jordan	66	64	71	68	269	136,025.60
Tommy Fleetwood	66	69	70	64	269	136,025.60
Jeunghun Wang	70	65	66	68	269	136,025.60
Tom Lewis	70	70	65	64	269	136,025.60
Richie Ramsay	65	67	70	68	270	76,448.52
Tony Finau	67	66	66	71	270	76,448.52
Andrea Pavan	68	65	67	70	270	76,448.52
Luke Donald	68	68	64	70	270	76,448.52
Callum Shinkwin	72	68	63	67	270	76,448.52
Russell Knox	66	66	70	69	271	56,292.91
Tyrrell Hatton	66	68	67	70	271	56,292.91
Mike Lorenzo-Vera	68	65	72	66	271	56,292.91
Alex Noren	69	66	68	68	271	56,292.91
Eddie Pepperell	70	66	68	67	271	56,292.91
Harry Hall	70	68	68	65	271	56,292.91
Matt Wallace	70	68	68	65	271	56,292.91
Shane Lowry	73	66	64	68	271	56,292.91
Lucas Bjerregaard	67	68	66	71	272	47,011.44
Haotong Li	71	68	64	69	272	47,011.44
Thomas Detry	72	69	63	68	272	47,011.44
Calum Hill	66	65	70	72	273	39,762.02
Zander Lombard	67	68	71	67	273	39,762.02
Victor Dubuisson	68	67	70	68	273	39,762.02
Matthew Fitzpatrick	69	67	67	70	273	39,762.02
Padraig Harrington	69	68	66	70	273	39,762.02
Rory McIlroy	70	66	70	67	273	39,762.02
Robert MacIntyre	71	66	66	70	273	39,762.02
Danny Willett	72	66	66	69	273	39,762.02
Robert Karlsson	67	70	67	70	274	31,633.87

	SCORES				TOTAL	MONEY
Justin Rose	68	64	70	72	274	31,633.87
Sebastian Soderberg	71	64	69	70	274	31,633.87
Sam Horsfield	72	67	68	67	274	31,633.87
Oliver Wilson	72	67	68	67	274	31,633.87
Dean Burmester	73	68	66	67	274	31,633.87
Tapio Pulkkanen	65	68	74	68	275	26,361.56
Marcus Kinhult	66	70	70	69	275	26,361.56
Oliver Fisher	68	69	70	68	275	26,361.56
Joost Luiten	69	67	71	68	275	26,361.56
Ricardo Gouveia	70	67	67	71	275	26,361.56
John Catlin	72	65	69	69	275	26,361.56
Fabrizio Zanotti	66	71	70	69	276	21,089.24
Wil Besseling	68	67	71	70	276	21,089.24
David Horsey	68	67	72	69	276	21,089.24
Matthieu Pavon	68	71	68	69	276	21,089.24
Scott Jamieson	69	66	72	69	276	21,089.24
Benjamin Hebert	73	64	67	72	276	21,089.24
Lee Slattery	68	66	72	71	277	17,574.37
Johannes Veerman	72	63	70	72	277	17,574.37
Ryan Fox	64	68	73	73	278	15,816.93
Aaron Rai	68	66	69	75	278	15,816.93
Julien Guerrier	69	69	69	74	281	14,059.50
Grant Forrest	72	70	65	74	281	14,059.50
Rikard Karlberg	69	68	68	77	282	12,961.10
Alvaro Quiros	70	70	66	76	282	12,961.10
Raphael Jacquelin	69	69	67	79	284	12,302.06
Justin Walters	63	71	74		208	8,950.11
George Coetzee	66	72	70		208	8,950.11
Euan Walker	68	70	70		208	8,950.11
David Law	68	72	68		208	8,950.11
Renato Paratore	69	66	73		208	8,950.11
Neil Schietekat	69	67	72		208	8,950.11
Liam Johnston	69	69	70		208	8,950.11
Rafa Cabrera Bello	69	69	70		208	8,950.11
Nacho Elvira	70	67	71		208	8,950.11
Matthias Schwab	70	70	68		208	8,950.11
Richard Sterne	70	73	65		208	8,950.11
Wade Ormsby	71	68	69		208	8,950.11
Jason Scrivener	71	69	68		208	8,950.11
Wilco Nienaber	75	65	68		208	8,950.11

Mutuactivos Open de Espana

Club de Campo Villa de Madrid, Madrid, Spain
Par 36-35–712; 7,112 yards

October 3-6
purse, €1,500,000

	SCORES				TOTAL	MONEY
Jon Rahm	66	67	63	66	262	€250,000
Rafa Cabrera Bello	66	65	70	66	267	166,660
Samuel Del Val	67	65	69	68	269	93,900
Adri Arnaus	65	66	72	68	271	63,700
Joachim B. Hansen	69	69	67	66	271	63,700
Jeff Winther	70	69	69	63	271	63,700
Zander Lombard	67	67	69	69	272	34,740
Jason Scrivener	67	68	68	69	272	34,740
Sergio Garcia	69	69	69	65	272	34,740
Justin Harding	69	72	64	67	272	34,740
Masahiro Kawamura	70	67	68	67	272	34,740
Andrea Pavan	66	75	67	65	273	24,300
Jens Dantorp	67	70	65	71	273	24,300

	SCORES				TOTAL	MONEY
Fabrizio Zanotti	71	69	65	68	273	24,300
Alexander Levy	70	69	67	68	274	21,600
James Morrison	70	70	69	65	274	21,600
Nicolas Colsaerts	67	73	71	64	275	18,425
Ross Fisher	69	68	70	68	275	18,425
Calum Hill	69	72	65	69	275	18,425
Mikko Korhonen	70	65	72	68	275	18,425
Nick McCarthy	70	68	71	66	275	18,425
Alejandro Canizares	72	69	68	66	275	18,425
Jamie Donaldson	66	71	69	70	276	15,150
Jack Singh Brar	68	69	70	69	276	15,150
Nino Bertasio	69	67	71	69	276	15,150
Edoardo Molinari	69	69	69	69	276	15,150
Yusaku Miyazato	70	70	69	67	276	15,150
Dimitrios Papadatos	70	71	65	70	276	15,150
Thomas Aiken	72	68	70	66	276	15,150
Ashun Wu	68	71	70	68	277	12,900
Chris Hanson	68	74	66	69	277	12,900
Brett Rumford	70	71	66	70	277	12,900
Miguel Angel Jimenez	68	73	70	67	278	11,437.50
Rikard Karlberg	70	68	68	72	278	11,437.50
Pablo Larrazabal	70	69	70	69	278	11,437.50
Pedro Figueiredo	71	68	70	69	278	11,437.50
Dean Burmester	66	71	72	70	279	9,600
Sihwan Kim	67	74	67	71	279	9,600
Per Langfors	68	68	72	71	279	9,600
Steven Brown	68	68	70	73	279	9,600
Eduardo De La Riva	68	73	70	68	279	9,600
Lee Slattery	69	73	67	70	279	9,600
Ben Evans	71	68	73	67	279	9,600
Nacho Elvira	73	66	70	70	279	9,600
Ryan Lumsden	70	70	71	69	280	7,800
David Horsey	71	70	68	71	280	7,800
Johannes Veerman	71	71	69	69	280	7,800
Andres Romero	76	66	69	69	280	7,800
Jake McLeod	68	70	75	68	281	6,900
Maximilian Kieffer	72	70	65	74	281	6,900
Kristian Krogh Johannessen	63	73	76	70	282	6,000
David Lipsky	68	73	70	71	282	6,000
Bernd Ritthammer	70	69	73	70	282	6,000
Alfredo Garcia-Heredia	70	69	73	70	282	6,000
Deyen Lawson	68	71	72	72	283	4,650
Borja Virto	70	69	73	71	283	4,650
S.S.P. Chawrasia	70	71	73	69	283	4,650
Julian Suri	72	70	70	71	283	4,650
Joel Girrbach	73	67	68	75	283	4,650
Clement Sordet	74	68	67	74	283	4,650
Adrian Otaegui	67	69	73	75	284	3,975
Grant Forrest	73	69	71	71	284	3,975
Marcel Siem	66	69	76	74	285	3,525
David Drysdale	69	72	75	69	285	3,525
Anton Karlsson	70	71	73	71	285	3,525
John Catlin	71	71	69	74	285	3,525
Matthew Nixon	67	75	70	74	286	3,150
Justin Walters	69	72	74	75	290	3,000

Italian Open

Olgiata Golf Club, Rome, Italy
Par 35-36–71; 7,523 yards

October 10-13
purse, US$7,000,000

	SCORES				TOTAL	MONEY
Bernd Wiesberger	66	70	67	65	268	€1,059,540.49
Matthew Fitzpatrick	67	65	68	69	269	706,357.30
Kurt Kitayama	66	70	65	71	272	397,965.68
Andrew Johnston	67	68	70	68	273	269,972.46
Matthias Schwab	68	69	70	66	273	269,972.46
Robert MacIntyre	69	69	64	71	273	269,972.46
Shubhankar Sharma	66	69	72	68	275	164,017.81
Matt Wallace	69	67	67	72	275	164,017.81
Francesco Laporta	69	70	68	68	275	164,017.81
Rory Sabbatini	65	70	75	66	276	110,616.66
Erik van Rooyen	68	68	70	70	276	110,616.66
Andrea Pavan	69	67	70	70	276	110,616.66
Justin Walters	70	71	70	65	276	110,616.66
Jeunghun Wang	72	69	64	71	276	110,616.66
Justin Rose	66	69	78	64	277	89,637.64
Graeme McDowell	69	66	71	71	277	89,637.64
Richard Sterne	72	69	68	68	277	89,637.64
Tyrrell Hatton	68	69	71	70	278	75,439.71
Danny Willett	68	70	69	71	278	75,439.71
Aaron Rai	69	67	69	73	278	75,439.71
Julian Suri	70	69	69	70	278	75,439.71
Ryan Fox	70	71	69	68	278	75,439.71
Marcus Kinhult	72	67	70	69	278	75,439.71
Jordan Smith	69	70	72	68	279	68,022.89
Joost Luiten	66	72	71	71	280	58,486.97
Joachim B. Hansen	67	66	74	73	280	58,486.97
Soren Kjeldsen	68	70	66	76	280	58,486.97
Ross Fisher	68	71	69	72	280	58,486.97
Mikko Korhonen	69	67	75	69	280	58,486.97
Paul Waring	70	67	73	70	280	58,486.97
Stephen Gallacher	70	71	69	70	280	58,486.97
Jacques Kruyswijk	70	72	70	68	280	58,486.97
Sebastian Soderberg	74	68	70	68	280	58,486.97
Sam Horsfield	68	71	73	69	281	45,772.41
Thongchai Jaidee	69	70	71	71	281	45,772.41
David Horsey	69	70	72	70	281	45,772.41
Nino Bertasio	72	69	72	68	281	45,772.41
Alex Noren	72	70	70	69	281	45,772.41
Lucas Herbert	74	65	69	73	281	45,772.41
Tapio Pulkkanen	64	72	72	74	282	36,872.22
Chris Paisley	68	71	71	72	282	36,872.22
Julien Guerrier	69	67	74	72	282	36,872.22
Kalle Samooja	70	69	77	66	282	36,872.22
Edoardo Molinari	70	70	72	70	282	36,872.22
Dean Burmester	70	72	70	70	282	36,872.22
Mike Lorenzo-Vera	71	65	73	73	282	36,872.22
Wade Ormsby	71	70	68	73	282	36,872.22
Alexander Levy	69	71	70	73	283	27,336.30
George Coetzee	69	73	70	71	283	27,336.30
Adri Arnaus	70	68	73	72	283	27,336.30
Eddie Pepperell	70	72	71	70	283	27,336.30
Renato Paratore	71	70	72	70	283	27,336.30
Guido Migliozzi	72	66	75	70	283	27,336.30
Gonzalo Fernandez-Castano	72	69	70	72	283	27,336.30
Jason Scrivener	71	70	72	71	284	21,614.75
Oliver Fisher	71	70	72	71	284	21,614.75
Justin Harding	72	69	73	71	285	19,071.84

Women's Tours

Rolex Rankings No. 1 Jin Young Ko added the Evian Championship to her earlier ANA Inspiration title.

U.S. Open champion Jeongeun Lee$_6$.

Hinako Shibuno, the "Smiling Cinderella".

Hannah Green won the KPMG Women's PGA.   A $1.5 million putt for Sei Young Kim at the CME.

Sung Hyun Park, the world No. 2, won twice, including at the HSBC Women's World Championship.

Nelly Korda won in Australia, France and Taiwan.

A world-best seven wins for Japan's Ai Suzuki.

Hye Jin Choi won the KLPGA Championship and five times in all to top the Korean money list.

Brooke Henderson's two LPGA wins made her the most successful Canadian with nine victories.

Japan Open champion Nasa Hataoka.

Minjee Lee was a star in Los Angeles.

Catriona Matthew's European team won the Solheim Cup thanks to Suzann Pettersen's last putt.

Korea's Jiyai Shin won three times in Japan.

Lexi Thompson's eagle won the ShopRite.

Senior Tours

Steve Stricker won the U.S. Senior Open on his championship debut, as well as the Regions Tradition.

A fourth Senior Open title, and 11th Senior major, for Bernhard Langer at Royal Lytham.

Jeff Maggert won the Schwab Cup Championship.

Retief Goosen was the Senior Players champion.

Scott McCarron won the season-long Schwab Cup.

Kirk Triplett was a two-time winner.

Three victories for Jerry Kelly.

Senior PGA champion Ken Tanigawa.

Miguel Angel Jimenez earned two wins.

Phillip Price, Staysure PGA Seniors winner.

	SCORES				TOTAL	MONEY
S.S.P. Chawrasia	74	68	75	68	285	19,071.84
Victor Perez	74	68	72	71	285	19,071.84
Adrian Otaegui	68	70	73	75	286	16,846.79
Lee Westwood	69	72	73	72	286	16,846.79
Joakim Lagergren	71	71	75	69	286	16,846.79
James Morrison	72	68	73	73	286	16,846.79
Nacho Elvira	72	68	74	73	287	14,939.61
Nicolas Colsaerts	72	69	70	76	287	14,939.61
Ashun Wu	70	70	76	74	290	13,668.15
Ashley Chesters	71	71	77	71	290	13,668.15
Thomas Pieters	71	71	79	71	292	12,714.56
David Lipsky	72	70	76	76	294	12,078.83

Amundi Open de France

Le Golf National, Paris, France
Par 36-35–71; 7,245 yards

October 17-20
purse, €1,600,000

	SCORES				TOTAL	MONEY
Nicolas Colsaerts	67	66	67	72	272	€266,660
Joachim B. Hansen	68	68	69	68	273	177,770
George Coetzee	65	68	70	71	274	100,160
Kurt Kitayama	66	68	70	71	275	80,000
Richie Ramsay	66	69	70	71	276	57,280
Martin Kaymer	68	69	69	70	276	57,280
Gavin Moynihan	68	69	68	71	276	57,280
Hugo Leon	68	72	70	67	277	35,946.67
Chris Paisley	68	74	68	67	277	35,946.67
Thomas Detry	71	68	70	68	277	35,946.67
Marcus Kinhult	69	71	69	69	278	27,573.33
Joost Luiten	69	76	65	68	278	27,573.33
Steven Brown	71	68	69	70	278	27,573.33
Sam Horsfield	70	72	65	72	279	24,000
Lucas Herbert	71	73	65	70	279	24,000
Benjamin Hebert	66	71	69	74	280	22,080
Victor Perez	67	71	69	73	280	22,080
Ryan Fox	65	74	71	71	281	19,264
Kalle Samooja	67	72	71	71	281	19,264
Romain Langasque	68	73	70	70	281	19,264
Kristoffer Reitan	68	74	69	70	281	19,264
Alex Noren	72	72	71	66	281	19,264
Andy Sullivan	70	71	68	73	282	17,120
Jamie Donaldson	71	67	66	78	282	17,120
Trevor Immelman	73	70	68	71	282	17,120
Brandon Stone	68	69	69	77	283	15,680
Jason Scrivener	69	73	71	70	283	15,680
Thomas Pieters	74	69	69	71	283	15,680
Gregory Bourdy	70	72	70	72	284	14,240
David Lipsky	71	72	69	72	284	14,240
Hudson Swafford	74	65	69	76	284	14,240
Jaco van Zyl	67	70	73	75	285	11,900
Jerome Lando Casanova	69	72	69	75	285	11,900
Stephen Gallacher	70	72	70	73	285	11,900
David Horsey	70	72	69	74	285	11,900
Lee Slattery	71	68	75	71	285	11,900
Lorenzo Gagli	71	74	70	70	285	11,900
Niklas Lemke	73	67	74	71	285	11,900
Adrien Saddier	73	72	68	72	285	11,900
Deyen Lawson	68	72	72	74	286	9,280
Renato Paratore	69	72	73	72	286	9,280

	SCORES				TOTAL	MONEY
Charlie Saxon	70	71	72	73	286	9,280
Ben Evans	71	73	69	73	286	9,280
Romain Wattel	72	70	71	73	286	9,280
Shubhankar Sharma	72	71	70	73	286	9,280
Frederic Lacroix	72	72	66	76	286	9,280
Alejandro Canizares	75	70	70	71	286	9,280
Bradley Dredge	69	73	72	73	287	7,040
S.S.P. Chawrasia	70	69	72	76	287	7,040
Stewart Cink	70	70	74	73	287	7,040
Callum Shinkwin	70	74	70	73	287	7,040
Gavin Green	73	68	71	75	287	7,040
Jeunghun Wang	74	69	72	72	287	7,040
Jordan Smith	68	74	70	76	288	5,600
Ashley Chesters	70	73	71	74	288	5,600
Yusaku Miyazato	72	73	72	71	288	5,600
James Morrison	71	73	72	73	289	4,800
Haydn Porteous	72	73	72	72	289	4,800
Jeong Weon Ko [A]	73	69	70	77	289	
Matthieu Pavon	73	72	70	74	289	4,800
Justin Walters	67	77	75	71	290	4,240
Liam Johnston	68	76	69	77	290	4,240
Gonzalo Fernandez-Castano	69	73	73	75	290	4,240
Victor Dubuisson	69	76	73	72	290	4,240
Tapio Pulkkanen	76	69	77	69	291	3,840
Nicolai Hojgaard	67	76	73	76	292	3,520
Darren Fichardt	67	77	75	73	292	3,520
Richard McEvoy	69	75	74	74	292	3,520
Ricardo Gouveia	71	74	71	77	293	3,120
Max Schmitt	72	72	76	73	293	3,120
Jake McLeod	73	69	73	79	294	2,930
Oliver Fisher	70	72	75	79	296	2,400
Ashun Wu	70	74	76	78	298	2,397
Charles Larcelet [A]	71	71	76	80	298	
Marc Warren	71	72	80	76	299	2,394
Julien Quesne	70	72	78	80	300	2,391

Portugal Masters

Dom Pedro Victoria Golf Course, Vilamoura, Portugal
Par 35-36–71; 7,191 yards

October 24-27
purse, €1,500,000

	SCORES			TOTAL	MONEY
Steven Brown	69	67	65	66	267	€250,000
Justin Walters	65	66	71	66	268	130,280
Brandon Stone	66	66	66	70	268	130,280
Adrien Saddier	67	68	68	66	269	75,000
Chris Paisley	69	69	68	64	270	63,600
Jeunghun Wang	66	65	71	69	271	48,750
Eddie Pepperell	67	66	70	68	271	48,750
Oliver Fisher	65	65	70	72	272	29,775
Jake McLeod	65	72	72	63	272	29,775
Jack Singh Brar	67	68	71	66	272	29,775
Matt Wallace	67	70	66	69	272	29,775
Andy Sullivan	68	72	66	66	272	29,775
Tom Lewis	69	66	68	69	272	29,775
Louis de Jager	63	72	70	68	273	20,335.71
George Coetzee	69	65	68	71	273	20,335.71
Joakim Lagergren	69	71	66	67	273	20,335.71
Dean Burmester	70	65	65	73	273	20,335.71
Pablo Larrazabal	70	66	68	69	273	20,335.71

	SCORES				TOTAL	MONEY
Guido Migliozzi	71	68	69	65	273	20,335.71
Bradley Dredge	71	68	67	67	273	20,335.71
Renato Paratore	66	70	67	71	274	16,275
Martin Kaymer	67	70	72	65	274	16,275
Shubhankar Sharma	67	71	68	68	274	16,275
Kalle Samooja	68	70	68	68	274	16,275
Hugo Leon	69	69	68	68	274	16,275
Kristoffer Reitan	73	67	67	67	274	16,275
Ricardo Gouveia	70	68	70	68	276	14,025
Matthieu Pavon	72	67	68	69	276	14,025
Tomas Santos Silva	72	68	66	70	276	14,025
Bernd Ritthammer	72	69	72	63	276	14,025
Matthew Southgate	66	73	74	64	277	11,350
Ashley Chesters	67	70	70	70	277	11,350
Jamie Donaldson	68	67	73	69	277	11,350
Jordan Smith	69	68	70	70	277	11,350
Kristian Krogh Johannessen	70	69	67	71	277	11,350
David Borda	71	68	69	69	277	11,350
Thomas Aiken	71	69	70	67	277	11,350
Mikko Korhonen	72	67	73	65	277	11,350
Ryan Fox	72	67	71	67	277	11,350
Darren Fichardt	66	67	71	74	278	8,700
Haydn Porteous	68	65	69	76	278	8,700
Tapio Pulkkanen	68	69	69	72	278	8,700
Adri Arnaus	68	69	72	69	278	8,700
Robert Rock	68	69	72	69	278	8,700
Tiago Cruz	69	66	73	70	278	8,700
Nick Cullen	70	70	67	71	278	8,700
Liam Johnston	70	70	69	69	278	8,700
David Horsey	66	73	73	67	279	7,350
Sam Horsfield	67	71	75	67	280	6,150
Gonzalo Fernandez-Castano	68	69	72	71	280	6,150
Alexander Bjork	68	71	70	71	280	6,150
Jacques Kruyswijk	69	72	69	70	280	6,150
Richard McEvoy	70	69	73	68	280	6,150
Ross Fisher	70	69	72	69	280	6,150
Adrian Otaegui	70	69	72	69	280	6,150
Lee Westwood	68	72	71	70	281	4,530
Niklas Lemke	69	72	70	70	281	4,530
Oliver Wilson	70	69	72	70	281	4,530
Marc Warren	71	68	69	73	281	4,530
Paul Lawrie	72	69	72	68	281	4,530
Sihwan Kim	66	73	72	71	282	3,975
Joachim B. Hansen	69	68	74	71	282	3,975
Romain Wattel	68	72	69	74	283	3,450
Anton Karlsson	68	72	70	73	283	3,450
Tom Murray	69	71	70	73	283	3,450
Trevor Immelman	70	71	71	71	283	3,450
Min Woo Lee	72	69	69	73	283	3,450
Chris Wood	69	72	77	68	286	3,000
Robert Karlsson	68	73	71	75	287	2,795
Nicolai Hojgaard	70	70	70	77	287	2,795

WGC - HSBC Champions

See American Tours chapter.

Turkish Airlines Open

Montgomerie Maxx Royal, Antalya, Turkey
Par 35-37–72; 7,133 yards

November 7-10
purse, US$7,000,000

	SCORES				TOTAL	MONEY
Tyrrell Hatton	68	68	65	67	268	€1,809,627.27
Matthias Schwab	65	67	66	70	268	389,603.69
Benjamin Hebert	67	70	64	67	268	389,603.69
Victor Perez	68	69	66	65	268	389,603.69
Kurt Kitayama	69	68	67	64	268	389,603.69
Erik van Rooyen	70	67	66	65	268	389,603.69

(Hatton won on fourth playoff hole.)

Robert MacIntyre	71	63	67	69	270	146,217.88
Shubhankar Sharma	71	64	71	64	270	146,217.88
Romain Langasque	70	66	70	65	271	112,739.77
Scott Jamieson	67	68	68	69	272	81,863.01
Joachim B. Hansen	68	68	68	68	272	81,863.01
Ross Fisher	69	64	68	71	272	81,863.01
Patrick Reed	71	65	65	71	272	81,863.01
Lee Westwood	71	65	68	68	272	81,863.01
Guido Migliozzi	72	67	68	65	272	81,863.01
Paul Waring	70	67	68	68	273	65,915.67
Thomas Pieters	66	70	71	67	274	59,355.77
Marcus Kinhult	70	68	68	68	274	59,355.77
Kalle Samooja	71	68	69	66	274	59,355.77
Zander Lombard	73	67	66	68	274	59,355.77
Justin Rose	67	67	73	68	275	51,777.96
Jason Scrivener	68	66	73	68	275	51,777.96
Matthew Southgate	68	71	69	67	275	51,777.96
Ryan Fox	73	65	69	68	275	51,777.96
Joost Luiten	67	69	71	69	276	46,914.59
Justin Harding	69	65	70	72	276	46,914.59
Sean Crocker	71	67	72	66	276	46,914.59
Alex Noren	66	67	74	70	277	42,164.31
Jorge Campillo	68	68	71	70	277	42,164.31
Andrea Pavan	68	69	69	71	277	42,164.31
Nino Bertasio	70	69	70	68	277	42,164.31
Tom Lewis	65	70	71	72	278	36,735.43
David Lipsky	66	68	73	71	278	36,735.43
Thomas Detry	67	66	73	72	278	36,735.43
Richie Ramsay	68	73	64	73	278	36,735.43
Scott Hend	69	68	72	70	279	33,342.38
Renato Paratore	73	68	69	69	279	33,342.38
Danny Willett	67	66	74	73	280	29,723.13
Edoardo Molinari	68	68	74	70	280	29,723.13
Fabrizio Zanotti	69	67	68	76	280	29,723.13
Martin Kaymer	70	72	69	69	280	29,723.13
Nicolas Colsaerts	71	68	67	74	280	29,723.13
Wade Ormsby	72	68	69	71	280	29,723.13
Aaron Rai	68	67	75	71	281	26,103.87
Francesco Molinari	71	70	66	74	281	26,103.87
Jordan Smith	71	71	71	69	282	23,841.84
Haotong Li	73	71	70	68	282	23,841.84
Masahiro Kawamura	75	67	66	74	282	23,841.84
Bernd Wiesberger	71	72	70	70	283	22,032.21
Richard Sterne	70	72	72	70	284	20,222.58
Gavin Green	73	69	67	75	284	20,222.58
Matt Wallace	74	67	69	74	284	20,222.58
Sebastian Soderberg	72	70	69	74	285	17,508.14
Joakim Lagergren	73	68	73	71	285	17,508.14
Sam Horsfield	74	73	70	68	285	17,508.14
Adrian Otaegui	69	72	72	73	286	14,039.69

	SCORES				TOTAL	MONEY
Oliver Wilson	71	74	72	69	286	14,039.69
Christiaan Bezuidenhout	71	75	70	70	286	14,039.69
Kiradech Aphibarnrat	72	67	70	77	286	14,039.69
C.T. Pan	73	70	71	72	286	14,039.69
Alvaro Quiros	76	71	71	68	286	14,039.69
Shane Lowry	72	65	75	75	287	11,853.06
Chris Paisley	73	72	68	74	287	11,853.06
Padraig Harrington	75	66	74	72	287	11,853.06
Adri Arnaus	75	67	70	76	288	10,948.24
George Coetzee	71	71	77	70	289	10,495.84
Nacho Elvira	71	67	71	81	290	9,817.23
Justin Walters	75	73	68	74	290	9,817.23
Pablo Larrazabal	72	70	75	74	291	9,138.62
Hideto Tanihara	70	73	72	77	292	8,460.01
Steven Brown	74	75	71	72	292	8,460.01
Lucas Bjerregaard	71	75	76	71	293	7,781.40
David Drysdale	72	72	76	76	296	7,328.99
Taner Yamac [A]	72	72	79	75	298	
Eddie Pepperell	70	72			DQ	

Nedbank Golf Challenge
See African Sunshine Tour chapter.

DP World Tour Championship, Dubai

Jumeirah Golf Estates, Dubai, United Arab Emirates
Par 36-36–72; 7,677 yards

November 21-24
purse, US$8,000,000

	SCORES				TOTAL	MONEY
Jon Rahm	66	69	66	68	269	€2,712,722.67
Tommy Fleetwood	67	68	70	65	270	803,418.03
Mike Lorenzo-Vera	63	69	69	70	271	535,762.73
Rory McIlroy	64	74	65	73	276	302,468.58
Danny Willett	69	72	67	69	277	240,980.20
Tom Lewis	67	70	73	68	278	172,710.01
Thomas Pieters	70	68	68	72	278	172,710.01
Sergio Garcia	71	73	67	67	278	172,710.01
Matthew Fitzpatrick	71	71	68	69	279	120,716.16
Andy Sullivan	70	74	67	69	280	102,631.34
Jason Scrivener	71	72	72	65	280	102,631.34
Christiaan Bezuidenhout	71	67	70	73	281	86,355.01
Shane Lowry	73	68	70	70	281	86,355.01
Robert MacIntyre	71	74	68	69	282	76,408.36
Paul Waring	71	77	68	66	282	76,408.36
Marcus Kinhult	68	71	68	76	283	69,174.43
Guido Migliozzi	73	70	68	72	283	69,174.43
Jorge Campillo	73	72	69	70	284	63,748.98
Paul Casey	73	73	66	72	284	63,748.98
Rafa Cabrera Bello	68	73	74	70	285	53,689.30
Justin Rose	69	70	73	73	285	53,689.30
Matthias Schwab	69	73	70	73	285	53,689.30
Louis Oosthuizen	70	70	73	72	285	53,689.30
Richard Sterne	71	72	71	71	285	53,689.30
David Lipsky	72	71	71	71	285	53,689.30
Victor Perez	73	73	72	67	285	53,689.30
Joost Luiten	74	71	68	72	285	53,689.30
Thomas Detry	69	71	71	75	286	42,273.26
Adri Arnaus	70	70	72	74	286	42,273.26

Bernd Wiesberger	70	71	73	72	286	42,273.26
Matt Wallace	70	74	69	73	286	42,273.26
Erik van Rooyen	71	72	73	70	286	42,273.26
Mikko Korhonen	72	76	70	68	286	42,273.26
Patrick Reed	74	68	72	72	286	42,273.26
Matthew Southgate	75	71	70	70	286	42,273.26
Justin Harding	73	73	70	71	287	35,491.45
Joachim B. Hansen	74	73	68	72	287	35,491.45
Benjamin Hebert	70	74	73	71	288	33,004.79
Lee Westwood	73	70	74	71	288	33,004.79
Francesco Molinari	69	76	71	73	289	30,744.19
Romain Langasque	71	74	71	73	289	30,744.19
Aaron Rai	75	69	76	69	289	30,744.19
Haotong Li	69	77	74	70	290	28,935.71
Henrik Stenson	74	70	77	70	291	27,579.35
Ian Poulter	74	76	70	71	291	27,579.35
Tyrrell Hatton	73	79	69	71	292	26,222.99
Jordan Smith	74	73	70	76	293	25,318.74
Kurt Kitayama	71	75	77	73	296	24,414.50
Scott Hend	76	75	73	73	297	23,058.14
Andrea Pavan	77	74	71	75	297	23,058.14

Start of 2019-2020 Season

Alfred Dunhill Championship
See African Sunshine Tour chapter.

AfrAsia Bank Mauritius Open
See African Sunshine Tour chapter.

Australian PGA Championship
See Australian Tour chapter.

Challenge Tour

Jordan Mixed Open

See LET section of Women's Tours chapter.

Turkish Airlines Challenge

Samsun Golf Club, Atakum, Samsun, Turkey
Par 36-36–72; 6,710 yards

April 25-28
purse, €200,000

		SCORES			TOTAL	MONEY
Connor Syme	65	67	66	67	265	€32,000
Francesco Laporta	62	70	66	67	265	22,000
(Syme defeated Laporta on first playoff hole.)						
Darius van Driel	64	69	66	67	266	13,000
Wil Besseling	66	68	67	65	266	13,000
Mark Flindt Haastrup	67	61	68	71	267	9,000
Gregory Havret	68	70	62	67	267	9,000
Gary Boyd	67	66	68	67	268	5,600
Matthew Jordan	68	62	67	71	268	5,600
Adrian Meronk	68	62	65	73	268	5,600
Toby Tree	65	67	68	69	269	4,066.67
Robin Roussel	67	65	69	68	269	4,066.67
Emilio Cuartero Blanco	68	70	66	65	269	4,066.67
Niclas Johansson	65	71	64	70	270	3,300
Ruaidhri McGee	66	66	67	71	270	3,300
Oliver Lindell	68	67	68	67	270	3,300
Antoine Schwartz	69	65	69	67	270	3,300
Moritz Lampert	67	71	65	68	271	2,343.33
Julien Brun	68	65	67	71	271	2,343.33
Ben Stow	70	64	63	74	271	2,343.33
Santiago Tarrio Ben	70	66	64	71	271	2,343.33
Marcus Helligkilde	70	67	67	67	271	2,343.33
Nicolai Hojgaard	70	68	65	68	271	2,343.33
Mathieu Fenasse	70	67	66	69	272	1,900
Chris Lloyd	71	64	66	71	272	1,900
Clement Berardo	70	69	66	68	273	1,800
Magnus A. Carlsson	71	67	66	69	273	1,800
Matt Ford	71	67	66	69	273	1,800

Challenge de Espana

Izki Golf, Urturi, Alava, Spain
Par 36-36–72; 7,181 yards

May 2-5
purse, €200,000

		SCORES			TOTAL	MONEY
Antoine Rozner	69	73	67	66	275	€32,000
Sebastian Garcia Rodriguez	68	70	68	73	279	13,200
Martin Simonsen	69	69	70	71	279	13,200
Joel Sjoholm	70	69	71	69	279	13,200
Antti Ahokas	70	71	69	69	279	13,200
Rasmus Hojgaard	71	67	71	70	279	13,200

	SCORES				TOTAL	MONEY
Adrian Meronk	71	69	74	66	280	6,000
Robin Roussel	72	70	70	68	280	6,000
Ben Stow	68	72	68	73	281	4,250
Henric Sturehed	70	71	72	68	281	4,250
Calum Hill	72	69	71	69	281	4,250
Laurie Canter	73	70	70	68	281	4,250
Ewen Ferguson	68	74	69	71	282	3,000
Matthew Baldwin	69	74	71	68	282	3,000
Jacopo Vecchi Fossa	69	74	69	70	282	3,000
Marcus Armitage	70	68	74	70	282	3,000
Simon Forsstrom	70	70	69	73	282	3,000
Joseph Dean	71	71	68	72	282	3,000
Lukas Nemecz	74	70	66	72	282	3,000
Matthew Jordan	70	71	70	72	283	2,086.67
Alexander Knappe	72	70	72	69	283	2,086.67
Duncan Stewart	72	71	69	71	283	2,086.67
Martin Wiegele	67	73	73	71	284	1,860
Thomas Linard	69	74	71	70	284	1,860
Christopher Mivis	71	70	72	71	284	1,860
Richard Bland	71	73	69	71	284	1,860

Prague Golf Challenge

Prague City Golf, Prague, Czech Republic
Par 36-36–72; 7,156 yards

May 9-12
purse, €200,000

	SCORES				TOTAL	MONEY
Antoine Rozner	70	65	68	68	271	€32,000
Richard Bland	65	72	70	71	278	14,500
Mathieu Fenasse	67	66	71	74	278	14,500
Martin Simonsen	68	72	69	69	278	14,500
Mark Flindt Haastrup	68	72	67	71	278	14,500
Robin Roussel	68	69	70	72	279	7,200
Fredrik Nilehn	69	71	68	71	279	7,200
Jonas Kolbing	65	69	70	76	280	4,700
Cormac Sharvin	69	69	67	75	280	4,700
Sebastien Gros	71	69	67	73	280	4,700
Felipe Aguilar	71	71	70	68	280	4,700
Wil Besseling	65	70	71	75	281	3,000
Ewen Ferguson	65	77	68	71	281	3,000
Benjamin Poke	66	72	72	71	281	3,000
Toby Tree	68	72	71	70	281	3,000
Gregory Havret	69	71	65	76	281	3,000
Robin Dawson	69	73	70	69	281	3,000
Rhys Enoch	70	69	67	75	281	3,000
Dave Coupland	70	74	67	70	281	3,000
James Erkenbeck	71	69	71	70	281	3,000
Ricardo Santos	68	72	71	71	282	1,965
Chris Lloyd	69	71	68	74	282	1,965
Rasmus Hojgaard	69	72	67	74	282	1,965
Jordan Wrisdale	73	68	69	72	282	1,965
Laurie Canter	67	70	71	75	283	1,780
Borja Virto	70	71	68	74	283	1,780
Pep Angles	71	73	71	68	283	1,780
Pedro Oriol	72	71	67	73	283	1,780

D+D Real Czech Challenge

Kaskada Golf Resort, Brno, Czech Republic
Par 36-35–71; 7,053 yards

May 23-26
purse, €200,000

		SCORES			TOTAL	MONEY
Ross McGowan	66	66	66	68	266	€32,000
Ricardo Santos	70	67	65	68	270	22,000
Adrian Meronk	70	69	64	68	271	14,000
Cormac Sharvin	72	65	69	66	272	12,000
Alvaro Arizabaleta	67	69	68	69	273	7,500
Scott Fernandez	67	70	70	66	273	7,500
Marcel Schneider	68	68	68	69	273	7,500
Borja Virto	70	66	68	69	273	7,500
Rasmus Hojgaard	69	66	70	69	274	4,400
Damien Perrier	70	72	68	64	274	4,400
Daan Huizing	71	66	63	74	274	4,400
Robin Roussel	66	68	70	71	275	3,700
Victor Riu	71	71	65	68	275	3,700
Stanislav Matus	71	70	67	68	276	3,400
Darius van Driel	68	72	69	68	277	2,700
Emilio Cuartero Blanco	68	74	66	69	277	2,700
Richard Bland	70	69	69	69	277	2,700
Sebastian Heisele	71	65	70	71	277	2,700
Chris Hanson	71	69	66	71	277	2,700
Ben Stow	71	71	70	65	277	2,700
Josh Geary	68	68	71	71	278	1,965
Jerome Lando Casanova	69	69	74	66	278	1,965
Ewen Ferguson	71	70	66	71	278	1,965
Lukas Nemecz	72	67	70	69	278	1,965
David Boote	69	68	72	70	279	1,800
Calum Hill	70	68	73	68	279	1,800
Robin Dawson	72	70	68	69	279	1,800

Swiss Challenge

Golf Sempach, Lucerne, Switzerland
Par 36-35–71; 7,179 yards

June 6-9
purse, €185,000

		SCORES			TOTAL	MONEY
Ricardo Santos	65	68	71	65	269	€29,600
Moritz Lampert	66	68	71	65	270	16,650
Richard Bland	69	65	70	66	270	16,650
Mathieu Fenasse	67	68	69	67	271	11,100
Christofer Blomstrand	66	64	72	70	272	7,523.33
Ben Stow	68	68	69	67	272	7,523.33
Oliver Farr	71	68	66	67	272	7,523.33
Connor Syme	67	70	66	70	273	4,810
Julien Quesne	70	64	68	71	273	4,810
Ewen Ferguson	72	67	69	66	274	4,070
Oliver Lindell	66	69	67	73	275	3,607.50
Dave Coupland	66	71	69	69	275	3,607.50
Lars van Meijel	68	65	74	69	276	3,145
Marcel Schneider	68	70	67	71	276	3,145
Nicolai Tinning	72	68	69	67	276	3,145
Antoine Rozner	67	72	72	66	277	2,590
Robin Sciot-Siegrist	67	72	66	72	277	2,590
Cormac Sharvin	71	69	68	69	277	2,590
Calum Hill	69	66	69	74	278	2,127.50
Daan Huizing	69	72	68	69	278	2,127.50

	SCORES				TOTAL	MONEY
Minkyu Kim	63	74	73	69	279	1,817.63
Thomas Linard	67	74	68	70	279	1,817.63
Matthew Jordan	69	70	73	67	279	1,817.63
David Boote	70	71	68	70	279	1,817.63
Duncan Stewart	66	69	72	73	280	1,572.50
Alvaro Arizabaleta	67	72	74	67	280	1,572.50
Rasmus Hojgaard	67	74	70	69	280	1,572.50
Emilio Cuartero Blanco	68	70	74	68	280	1,572.50
Benjamin Rusch	68	71	70	71	280	1,572.50
Nicolai Von Dellingshausen	70	71	69	70	280	1,572.50
Laurie Canter	72	66	71	71	280	1,572.50
Benjamin Poke	75	65	71	69	280	1,572.50

Hauts de France - Pas de Calais Golf Open

Aa Saint-Omer Golf Club, Lumbres, France
Par 36-35–71; 6,840 yards

June 13-16
purse, €190,000

	SCORES				TOTAL	MONEY
Robin Roussel	70	68	67	66	271	€30,400
Richard Bland	72	70	64	67	273	20,900
Cormac Sharvin	69	71	69	68	277	13,300
Daan Huizing	67	67	70	74	278	11,400
Ben Stow	68	71	71	69	279	8,550
Ricardo Santos	70	69	72	68	279	8,550
Calum Hill	74	70	72	64	280	6,080
Ruaidhri McGee	71	71	67	72	281	4,940
Pep Angles	73	71	68	69	281	4,940
David Boote	68	72	67	75	282	3,752.50
Matthew Jordan	71	70	70	71	282	3,752.50
Scott Henry	72	68	72	70	282	3,752.50
Franck Daux	72	70	72	68	282	3,752.50
Thomas Linard	69	71	73	70	283	2,850
Gregory Havret	71	73	72	67	283	2,850
Nicolai Hojgaard	74	64	74	71	283	2,850
Simon Forsstrom	74	68	70	71	283	2,850
Marcel Schneider	74	70	66	73	283	2,850
Jacob Glennemo	71	66	74	73	284	2,010.20
James Heath	71	68	75	70	284	2,010.20
Bryce Easton	72	70	70	72	284	2,010.20
Lars van Meijel	73	69	70	72	284	2,010.20
Robert Dinwiddie	75	69	71	69	284	2,010.20
Nicolai Von Dellingshausen	69	71	72	73	285	1,691
Aaron Cockerill	71	69	72	73	285	1,691
Martin Simonsen	71	70	70	74	285	1,691
Sebastian Heisele	71	74	71	69	285	1,691
Jonathan Thomson	72	71	70	72	285	1,691
Ivan Cantero Gutierrez	72	72	72	69	285	1,691

Andalucia - Costa del Sol Match Play 9

Valle Romano Golf, Estepona, Malaga, Spain
Par 35-36–71; 6,781 yards

June 20-23
purse, €200,000

ROUND OF 32
Sebastian Garcia Rodriguez defeated Ruaidhri McGee, 1 up.
Ricardo Santos defeated Matt Ford, 10 holes.
Carlos Pigem defeated Garrick Porteous, 3 and 1.
Ugo Coussaud defeated Gary King, 10 holes.
Thomas Linard defeated Simon Forsstrom, 3 and 2.
Robin Sciot-Siegrist defeated Nick McCarthy, 10 holes.
Dave Coupland defeated Jerome Lando Casanova, 11 holes.
Chris Hanson defeated Adrian Meronk, 12 holes.
Rasmus Hojgaard defeated Gregory Havret, 10 holes.
Connor Syme defeated Alfredo Garcia-Heredia, 10 holes.
Antoine Schwartz defeated Christian Gloet, 1 up.
Chris Robb defeated Mark Flindt Haastrup, 3 and 1.
Matthew Jordan defeated Nicolai Hojgaard, 1 up.
Jordan Zunic defeated Manuel Elvira, 4 and 3.
Eirik Tage Johansen defeated Francesco Laporta, 1 up.
Benjamin Poke defeated Dale Whitnell, 1 up.

ROUND OF 16
Coussaud defeated Garcia Rodriguez, 12 holes.
Pigem defeated Santos, 1 up.
Hanson defeated Linard, 2 and 1.
Sciot-Siegrist defeated Coupland, 2 and 1.
Hojgaard defeated Robb, 2 and 1.
Syme defeated Schwartz, 2 and 1.
Poke defeated Jordan, 3 and 1.
Johansen defeated Zunic, 1 up.

QUARTER-FINALS
Johansen defeated Syme, 2 and 1.
Sciot-Siegrist defeated Pigem, 2 and 1.
Poke defeated Hojgaard, 2 and 1.
Coussaud defeated Hanson, 2 and 1.

SEMI-FINALS
Johansen defeated Sciot-Siegrist, 10 holes.
Coussaud defeated Poke, 3 and 2.

PLAYOFF FOR THIRD-FOURTH PLACE
Sciot-Siegrist defeated Poke, 1 up.

(Sciot-Siegrist received €14,000; Poke received €12,000.)

FINAL
Johansen defeated Coussaud, 2 and 1.

(Johansen received €32,000; Coussaud received €22,000.)

Italian Challenge Open Eneos Motor Oil

Terre Dei Consoli Golf Club, Monterosi, Italy
Par 35-37–72; 7,305 yards

June 27-30
purse, €300,000

		SCORES			TOTAL	MONEY
Matthew Jordan	69	67	69	66	271	€48,000
Lorenzo Scalise	67	71	68	65	271	33,000
(Jordan defeated Scalise on first playoff hole.)						
Carlos Pigem	66	70	71	65	272	21,000
Antoine Rozner	68	66	67	72	273	15,000
Oliver Farr	68	70	66	69	273	15,000
Raphael De Sousa	70	70	65	68	273	15,000
Connor Syme	68	70	68	68	274	9,000
Lars van Meijel	69	69	69	67	274	9,000
Rasmus Hojgaard	71	70	71	63	275	7,200
Jacob Glennemo	68	72	67	69	276	6,100
Mathieu Fenasse	69	69	71	67	276	6,100
Gregory Havret	71	68	66	71	276	6,100
Nicolai Hojgaard	67	69	70	71	277	4,650
Seve Benson	71	68	70	68	277	4,650
Mateusz Gradecki	71	71	68	67	277	4,650
Christopher Mivis	72	70	68	67	277	4,650
Ryan Evans	73	68	66	70	277	4,650
Ewen Ferguson	75	67	65	70	277	4,650
Ben Eccles	68	68	69	73	278	3,450
Robin Sciot-Siegrist	70	71	69	68	278	3,450
Filip Mruzek	71	69	70	69	279	3,045
Oscar Lengden	71	69	68	71	279	3,045
Bryce Easton	66	70	71	73	280	2,760
Francesco Laporta	71	72	69	68	280	2,760
Marcel Schneider	73	69	72	66	280	2,760
Ben Stow	74	68	68	70	280	2,760
Dominic Foos	75	66	72	67	280	2,760

D+D Real Slovakia Challenge

Penati Golf Resort, Senica, Slovakia
Par 36-36–72; 7,115 yards

July 4-7
purse, €200,000

		SCORES			TOTAL	MONEY
Rhys Enoch	68	69	65	68	270	€32,000
Josh Geary	68	68	69	66	271	22,000
Lars van Meijel	68	69	66	70	273	13,000
Dale Whitnell	71	69	67	66	273	13,000
Robin Roussel	67	71	72	65	275	8,133.33
Joel Sjoholm	68	73	66	68	275	8,133.33
Garrick Porteous	74	65	67	69	275	8,133.33
Darius van Driel	64	69	67	76	276	5,200
Ivan Cantero Gutierrez	67	68	74	67	276	5,200
Jack Senior	66	70	71	70	277	3,525
Nicolai Von Dellingshausen	68	67	72	70	277	3,525
Bryce Easton	68	69	72	68	277	3,525
Sebastian Garcia Rodriguez	69	67	68	73	277	3,525
Rasmus Hojgaard	70	68	67	72	277	3,525
Johan Carlsson	71	65	73	68	277	3,525
Adrian Meronk	72	68	70	67	277	3,525
Santiago Tarrio Ben	73	68	68	68	277	3,525
Stanislav Matus	69	70	69	70	278	2,600
Scott Fernandez	67	68	71	73	279	2,076.67

	SCORES				TOTAL	MONEY
Chase Koepka	69	67	68	75	279	2,076.67
Carlos Pigem	70	68	70	71	279	2,076.67
Toby Tree	71	70	68	70	279	2,076.67
Nick McCarthy	71	70	68	70	279	2,076.67
Jan Cafourek	72	70	71	66	279	2,076.67
Samuel Del Val	66	74	69	71	280	1,780
Lukas Nemecz	68	72	67	73	280	1,780
Julien Quesne	68	74	69	69	280	1,780
Minkyu Kim	69	69	69	73	280	1,780

Le Vaudreuil Golf Challenge

Golf PGA France du Vaudreuil, Le Vaudreuil, France
Par 35-36–71; 6,888 yards

July 11-14
purse, €210,000

	SCORES				TOTAL	MONEY
Steven Tiley	64	68	69	72	273	€33,600
Richard Bland	70	66	70	68	274	23,100
Gregory Havret	66	70	69	70	275	14,700
Nicolai Von Dellingshausen	67	72	72	65	276	12,600
Cormac Sharvin	72	71	65	69	277	10,500
Robin Sciot-Siegrist	64	73	70	71	278	6,132
Dave Coupland	67	68	69	74	278	6,132
Matt Ford	69	66	70	73	278	6,132
Sebastian Garcia Rodriguez	69	73	65	71	278	6,132
Wil Besseling	69	74	65	70	278	6,132
Wilco Nienaber	67	73	70	69	279	3,675
Bryce Easton	68	67	71	73	279	3,675
Santiago Tarrio Ben	68	67	76	68	279	3,675
Martin Wiegele	68	70	75	66	279	3,675
Matthew Jordan	71	71	68	69	279	3,675
Thomas Linard	72	66	68	73	279	3,675
Gregory Bourdy	65	73	69	73	280	2,397
Josh Geary	67	75	70	68	280	2,397
Darius van Driel	68	68	68	76	280	2,397
Jerome Lando Casanova	68	70	75	67	280	2,397
Marcus Helligkilde	69	67	73	71	280	2,397
Duncan Stewart	70	72	65	73	280	2,397
Max Orrin	71	70	68	71	280	2,397
Benjamin Poke	72	71	69	69	281	1,911
Ricardo Santos	72	71	69	69	281	1,911
Oliver Farr	74	68	68	71	281	1,911
Borja Virto	74	69	73	65	281	1,911

Euram Bank Open

Golf Club Adamstal, Ramsau, Austria
Par 36-34–70; 6,476 yards

July 18-21
purse, €185,000

	SCORES				TOTAL	MONEY
Calum Hill	65	64	67	66	262	€29,600
Jose-Filipe Lima	67	69	65	65	266	16,650
Ewen Ferguson	68	67	67	64	266	16,650
Oliver Lindell	66	66	68	67	267	8,417.50
Matt Ford	67	65	67	68	267	8,417.50
Rikard Karlberg	67	68	66	66	267	8,417.50
Gregory Havret	70	64	69	64	267	8,417.50

	SCORES				TOTAL	MONEY
Ugo Coussaud	65	69	68	66	268	4,810
Adrian Meronk	68	66	68	66	268	4,810
Lorenzo Scalise	65	69	68	67	269	3,653.75
Joel Stalter	68	65	68	68	269	3,653.75
Benjamin Rusch	68	71	67	63	269	3,653.75
Edouard Dubois	70	63	68	68	269	3,653.75
Marcel Schneider	62	69	70	69	270	2,960
Mikael Salminen	69	65	69	67	270	2,960
Alessandro Tadini	69	66	66	69	270	2,960
Evan Holmes	69	66	69	67	271	2,497.50
Darius van Driel	70	68	70	63	271	2,497.50
Felipe Aguilar	65	67	72	68	272	1,920.92
Nicolai Von Dellingshausen	66	67	69	70	272	1,920.92
Steven Tiley	67	68	71	66	272	1,920.92
Matthew Jordan	68	68	70	66	272	1,920.92
Julien Quesne	68	71	72	61	272	1,920.92
Mathieu Fenasse	69	67	66	70	272	1,920.92
Pontus Widegren	67	71	62	73	273	1,628
Marcus Armitage	70	65	65	73	273	1,628
Stanislav Matus	70	67	69	67	273	1,628
Paul McBride	70	68	66	69	273	1,628
Nick McCarthy	70	68	68	67	273	1,628

Vierumaki Finnish Challenge

Vierumaki Resort, Vierumaki, Finland
Par 36-36–72; 7,010 yards

August 1-4
purse, €200,000

	SCORES				TOTAL	MONEY
Jose-Filipe Lima	68	70	70	66	274	€32,000
Bryce Easton	66	72	66	71	275	22,000
Joel Stalter	69	67	71	69	276	12,000
Calum Hill	69	71	66	70	276	12,000
Roope Kakko	71	68	66	71	276	12,000
Rikard Karlberg	66	69	68	74	277	5,840
Clement Berardo	67	69	72	69	277	5,840
Matthew Baldwin	68	71	68	70	277	5,840
Cormac Sharvin	70	69	71	67	277	5,840
Christian Braeunig	70	70	67	70	277	5,840
Gavin Moynihan	68	70	71	69	278	3,600
Jack Senior	69	68	69	72	278	3,600
Federico Maccario	69	71	68	70	278	3,600
Oliver Lindell	70	69	70	69	278	3,600
Robin Dawson	70	72	66	70	278	3,600
Dominic Foos	67	72	70	70	279	2,437.14
Antoine Rozner	68	71	70	70	279	2,437.14
Jerome Lando Casanova	69	69	72	69	279	2,437.14
Richard Bland	69	70	69	71	279	2,437.14
Daan Huizing	70	69	70	70	279	2,437.14
Mark Young	71	65	69	74	279	2,437.14
Max Schmitt	74	66	71	68	279	2,437.14
Darius van Driel	63	73	73	71	280	1,900
Ricardo Santos	71	67	68	74	280	1,900
Rasmus Hojgaard	70	70	68	73	281	1,800
Garrick Porteous	70	71	71	69	281	1,800
Jacob Glennemo	71	69	69	72	281	1,800

Made in Denmark Challenge

Silkeborg Ry Golf Club, Skanderborg, Denmark
Par 36-36–72; 6,933 yards

August 7-10
purse, €200,000

	SCORES				TOTAL	MONEY
Calum Hill	67	68	64	67	266	€32,000
Joel Sjoholm	65	69	65	68	267	22,000
Benjamin Poke	64	70	67	67	268	13,000
Daan Huizing	71	66	64	67	268	13,000
Matthew Jordan	65	68	66	70	269	7,500
John Axelsen [A]	68	67	67	67	269	
Nicolai Von Dellingshausen	68	68	65	68	269	7,500
Francesco Laporta	70	66	67	66	269	7,500
Antoine Rozner	70	68	64	67	269	7,500
Roope Kakko	65	66	68	71	270	4,800
Richard Bland	66	72	61	72	271	3,628.57
Pep Angles	67	64	70	70	271	3,628.57
Wil Besseling	67	68	67	69	271	3,628.57
Rhys Enoch	67	70	67	67	271	3,628.57
Mario Galiano Aguilar	68	65	67	71	271	3,628.57
Oliver Farr	68	65	70	68	271	3,628.57
Dominic Foos	70	68	65	68	271	3,628.57
Moritz Lampert	65	69	68	70	272	2,150
Christofer Blomstrand	65	70	68	69	272	2,150
Borja Virto	66	71	66	69	272	2,150
Gregory Bourdy	67	67	70	68	272	2,150
Robin Dawson	67	68	66	71	272	2,150
Chris Hanson	68	65	68	71	272	2,150
Lars Van Meijel	68	67	69	68	272	2,150
Oscar Lengden	69	64	67	72	272	2,150
Hugo Leon	70	65	67	70	272	2,150
Ryan Evans	70	67	67	68	272	2,150

ISPS Handa World Invitational

Galgorm Spa & Golf Resort, Ballymena, Northern Ireland
Par 34-36–70; 7,078 yards

August 15-18
purse, US$250,000

	SCORES				TOTAL	MONEY
Jack Senior	68	68	66	67	269	€36,029.54
Matthew Baldwin	67	70	68	64	269	24,770.31
(Senior defeated Baldwin on second playoff hole.)						
Todd Clements	67	66	68	70	271	15,762.92
Damien Perrier	66	69	66	71	272	13,511.08
Francesco Laporta	68	66	68	72	274	10,133.31
Oscar Lengden	72	65	68	69	274	10,133.31
Calum Hill	66	68	71	70	275	6,305.17
Rowin Caron	67	69	69	70	275	6,305.17
Moritz Lampert	72	67	66	70	275	6,305.17
Richard Mansell	65	75	67	69	276	4,447.40
Connor Syme	67	69	70	70	276	4,447.40
Dave Coupland	69	70	69	68	276	4,447.40
Darius van Driel	70	68	67	71	276	4,447.40
Sebastian Garcia Rodriguez	67	67	74	69	277	3,152.59
Jordan Wrisdale	67	70	67	73	277	3,152.59
Garrick Porteous	68	73	65	71	277	3,152.59
Laurie Canter	69	65	74	69	277	3,152.59
Jacob Glennemo	69	72	64	72	277	3,152.59
Ben Stow	70	67	72	68	277	3,152.59

	SCORES				TOTAL	MONEY
Minkyu Kim	71	70	66	70	277	3,152.59
Cormac Sharvin	68	71	70	69	278	2,244.34
Ricardo Santos	70	69	71	68	278	2,244.34
Victor Riu	71	69	68	70	278	2,244.34
Christopher Mivis	70	69	71	69	279	2,094.22
Rasmus Hojgaard	71	66	70	72	279	2,094.22

Rolex Trophy

Golf Club de Geneve, Geneva, Switzerland
Par 36-36–72; 6,821 yards

August 21-24
purse, €290,000

	SCORES				TOTAL	MONEY
Darius van Driel	68	70	63	64	265	€35,000
Cormac Sharvin	68	66	68	64	266	26,000
Calum Hill	67	66	68	67	268	13,600
Ricardo Santos	67	66	64	71	268	13,600
Daan Huizing	69	66	67	66	268	13,600
Richard Bland	69	68	65	66	268	13,600
Nicolai Von Dellingshausen	69	62	74	64	269	9,500
Eirik Tage Johansen	68	68	69	66	271	8,400
Ben Stow	66	68	70	68	272	7,700
Ewen Ferguson	70	69	67	67	273	7,000
Adrian Meronk	66	67	71	70	274	5,925
Carlos Pigem	67	69	67	71	274	5,925
Josh Geary	70	71	66	67	274	5,925
Bryce Easton	71	64	72	67	274	5,925
Jack Senior	68	68	71	69	276	4,471.67
Robin Roussel	70	73	67	66	276	4,471.67
Oliver Farr	72	64	70	70	276	4,471.67
Ugo Coussaud	73	62	72	69	276	4,471.67
Wil Besseling	73	70	65	68	276	4,471.67
Mathieu Fenasse	75	68	67	66	276	4,471.67
Jose-Filipe Lima	69	68	70	70	277	3,760
Antoine Rozner	67	70	70	71	278	3,449.29
Robin Sciot-Siegrist	68	71	68	71	278	3,449.29
Rasmus Hojgaard	69	69	71	69	278	3,449.29
Ross McGowan	70	68	74	66	278	3,449.29
Matthew Baldwin	71	68	66	73	278	3,449.29
Connor Syme	71	70	68	69	278	3,449.29
Marcel Schneider	72	69	66	71	278	3,449.29

KPMG Trophy

Millennium Golf, Paal, Beringen, Belgium
Par 35-36–71; 6,797 yards

August 29-September 1
purse, €185,000

	SCORES				TOTAL	MONEY
Dale Whitnell	70	64	64	63	261	€29,600
Laurie Canter	65	67	63	66	261	20,350
(Whitnell defeated Canter on second playoff hole.)						
Jack Senior	63	66	67	66	262	12,025
Christofer Blomstrand	64	68	67	63	262	12,025
Richard Mansell	66	65	64	68	263	8,325
Jonas Kolbing	66	68	66	63	263	8,325
Julian Kunzenbacher	67	65	66	66	264	5,920
Ross McGowan	64	66	65	70	265	4,810

	SCORES				TOTAL	MONEY
Bryce Easton	64	67	65	69	265	4,810
Ben Stow	64	67	70	65	266	3,761.67
Benjamin Poke	68	67	66	65	266	3,761.67
Martin Simonsen	69	65	68	64	266	3,761.67
Sebastian Heisele	61	69	69	68	267	3,237.50
Tomas Santos Silva	69	66	67	65	267	3,237.50
Robin Roussel	62	73	65	68	268	2,497.50
Sebastian Garcia Rodriguez	64	69	64	71	268	2,497.50
Daan Huizing	65	69	66	68	268	2,497.50
Frederic Lacroix	67	66	69	66	268	2,497.50
Christopher Mivis	67	67	68	66	268	2,497.50
Garrick Higgo	72	65	65	66	268	2,497.50
Scott Henry	66	69	68	66	269	1,752.21
Aksel Olsen	67	67	71	64	269	1,752.21
Peter Launer Baek	67	69	64	69	269	1,752.21
Seve Benson	67	70	67	65	269	1,752.21
Samuel Del Val	68	66	68	67	269	1,752.21
Clement Berardo	68	68	65	68	269	1,752.21
Stanislav Matus	68	68	68	65	269	1,752.21

Open de Bretagne

Golf Blue Green de Pleneuf Val Andre, Pleneuf, France
Par 35-35–70; 6,454 yards

September 5-8
purse, €230,000

	SCORES				TOTAL	MONEY
Sebastian Heisele	73	64	65	65	267	€32,000
Josh Geary	68	67	70	64	269	22,000
Jonathan Thomson	73	67	66	65	271	14,000
Damien Perrier	69	68	68	67	272	9,100
Santiago Tarrio Ben	70	67	71	64	272	9,100
Martin Wiegele	70	67	68	67	272	9,100
Robin Sciot-Siegrist	71	68	66	67	272	9,100
Dale Whitnell	68	71	64	70	273	5,200
Scott Henry	69	69	67	68	273	5,200
Darius van Driel	71	71	66	66	274	4,066.67
Jordan Wrisdale	72	67	66	69	274	4,066.67
Rowin Caron	75	66	67	66	274	4,066.67
Robert Dinwiddie	66	72	69	69	276	3,000
Gudmundur Kristjansson	67	72	69	68	276	3,000
Raphael De Sousa	70	67	69	70	276	3,000
Antoine Rozner	70	69	66	71	276	3,000
Craig Ross	71	71	70	64	276	3,000
Richard Mansell	73	64	68	71	276	3,000
James Ruth	74	69	67	66	276	3,000
Marcus Armitage	69	70	69	69	277	2,012
Toby Tree	70	71	71	65	277	2,012
Oscar Lengden	73	70	67	67	277	2,012
Felipe Aguilar	74	68	67	68	277	2,012
Matt Ford	76	64	67	70	277	2,012
Minkyu Kim	69	69	72	68	278	1,760
Gregory Bourdy	71	70	71	66	278	1,760
Matthew Jordan	72	65	73	68	278	1,760
Daan Huizing	74	66	71	67	278	1,760
Marcel Schneider	76	65	64	73	278	1,760

Open de Portugal

Morgado Golf & Country Club, Portimao, Portugal
Par 36-36–72; 7,317 yards

September 12-15
purse, €200,000

	SCORES				TOTAL	MONEY
Adrian Meronk	67	72	68	66	273	€32,000
Sebastian Garcia Rodriguez	73	64	69	69	275	22,000
Martin Wiegele	69	70	69	69	277	13,000
Francesco Laporta	71	69	67	70	277	13,000
Henric Sturehed	66	75	65	72	278	7,500
Rhys Enoch	69	66	72	71	278	7,500
Cormac Sharvin	70	67	69	72	278	7,500
Jack Senior	71	72	64	71	278	7,500
Joel Sjoholm	68	71	70	70	279	4,120
Mathieu Fenasse	69	68	70	72	279	4,120
Bryce Easton	69	68	71	71	279	4,120
Benjamin Poke	71	70	69	69	279	4,120
Marcel Schneider	73	68	72	66	279	4,120
Philipp Mejow	68	71	73	68	280	3,200
Chris Robb	71	72	70	67	280	3,200
Jose-Filipe Lima	72	70	69	69	280	3,200
Aaron Cockerill	67	71	71	72	281	2,500
Richard Bland	68	68	70	75	281	2,500
Simon Forsstrom	68	73	71	69	281	2,500
Ben Stow	73	70	72	66	281	2,500
Bradley Neil	73	71	67	71	282	2,030
Sebastian Heisele	76	68	72	66	282	2,030
Carlos Pigem	70	71	71	71	283	1,900
Eirik Tage Johansen	71	72	72	68	283	1,900
Ruaidhri McGee	68	72	71	73	284	1,740
Stefano Mazzoli	71	72	71	70	284	1,740
Matthew Baldwin	72	69	72	71	284	1,740
Matthew Jordan	72	70	72	70	284	1,740
Ryan Evans	72	71	68	73	284	1,740
Oliver Farr	72	73	68	71	284	1,740

Hopps Open de Provence

Golf International de Pont Royal, Mallemort, France
Par 36-36–72; 6,920 yards

September 26-29
purse, €200,000

	SCORES				TOTAL	MONEY
Lars van Meijel	69	67	69	67	272	€32,000
Sebastian Heisele	69	65	74	65	273	22,000
Francesco Laporta	67	71	70	66	274	13,000
Sebastian Garcia Rodriguez	71	68	67	68	274	13,000
Aaron Cockerill	66	70	69	70	275	8,133.33
Robin Roussel	70	67	69	69	275	8,133.33
Adrian Meronk	74	69	65	67	275	8,133.33
Steven Tiley	70	70	71	65	276	5,600
Oliver Farr	69	69	74	65	277	4,600
Antoine Rozner	71	68	66	72	277	4,600
Roope Kakko	68	70	70	70	278	3,900
Eirik Tage Johansen	71	67	70	70	278	3,900
Connor Syme	67	71	70	71	279	3,200
Henric Sturehed	69	68	71	71	279	3,200
David Boote	69	72	67	71	279	3,200
Damien Perrier	71	70	69	69	279	3,200
David Borda	75	68	69	67	279	3,200

	SCORES				TOTAL	MONEY
Jeong Weon Ko [A]	64	70	74	72	280	
Samuel Del Val	67	72	71	70	280	2,252
Bradley Neil	69	69	74	68	280	2,252
Jeppe Pape Huldahl	70	72	69	69	280	2,252
Mathieu Fenasse	71	70	70	69	280	2,252
Jack Senior	74	69	68	69	280	2,252
Raphael De Sousa	70	74	67	70	281	1,840
Reinier Saxton	71	71	68	71	281	1,840
Clement Berardo	71	72	67	71	281	1,840
Cormac Sharvin	72	69	74	66	281	1,840
Gregory Havret	72	71	70	68	281	1,840
Charles Larcelet [A]	73	67	69	72	281	

Lalla Aicha Challenge Tour

Royal Golf Dar Es Salam, Rabat, Morocco   October 3-6
Par 36-36–72; 7,002 yards   purse, €200,000

	SCORES				TOTAL	MONEY
Oliver Farr	69	71	70	63	273	€32,000
Jack Senior	65	73	68	70	276	22,000
Oliver Hundeboll	69	70	72	66	277	14,000
Ewen Ferguson	67	72	70	69	278	10,000
Joel Sjoholm	69	66	71	72	278	10,000
Rasmus Hojgaard	69	71	67	71	278	10,000
Craig Ross	69	72	68	70	279	6,000
Aaron Cockerill	71	74	65	69	279	6,000
Sebastien Gros	71	69	72	69	281	4,600
Connor Syme	71	71	67	72	281	4,600
Oscar Lengden	66	73	73	70	282	3,600
Christopher Mivis	70	73	69	70	282	3,600
Gregory Havret	70	73	68	71	282	3,600
Alexander Knappe	70	74	67	71	282	3,600
Robin Roussel	72	71	71	68	282	3,600
Santiago Tarrio Ben	67	70	72	74	283	2,600
David Boote	67	72	72	72	283	2,600
Garrick Porteous	71	70	68	74	283	2,600
Enrico Di Nitto	72	70	72	69	283	2,600
Wil Besseling	75	70	63	75	283	2,600
Todd Clements	68	71	73	72	284	1,916.67
Richard Mansell	68	76	72	68	284	1,916.67
Antoine Rozner	69	65	74	76	284	1,916.67
Lukas Nemecz	70	70	72	72	284	1,916.67
Steven Tiley	72	72	69	71	284	1,916.67
Bryce Easton	73	68	71	72	284	1,916.67

Stone Irish Challenge

Headfort Golf Club, Kells, County Meath, Ireland
Par 36-36–72; 7,092 yards
(Fourth round cancelled—rain.)

October 10-13
purse, €200,000

	SCORES			TOTAL	MONEY
Emilio Cuartero Blanco	67	68	70	205	€32,000
Oscar Lengden	69	67	69	205	22,000
(Cuartero Blanco defeated Lengden on third playoff hole.)
Todd Clements	72	67	67	206	14,000
Bradley Neil	68	70	69	207	12,000
Aaron Cockerill	67	70	71	208	7,500
Daan Huizing	67	71	70	208	7,500
Cormac Sharvin	69	69	70	208	7,500
Henric Sturehed	72	67	69	208	7,500
Gudmundur Kristjansson	70	67	72	209	4,800
Gavin Moynihan	70	67	73	210	3,950
Daniel Hillier	70	71	69	210	3,950
Richard Mansell	71	71	68	210	3,950
Darius van Driel	72	70	68	210	3,950
Oscar Stark	68	74	69	211	3,300
J.R. Galbraith	71	71	69	211	3,300
Clement Berardo	69	72	71	212	2,700
Damien Perrier	70	69	73	212	2,700
Sebastien Gros	70	71	71	212	2,700
Max Orrin	71	68	73	212	2,700
Laurie Canter	67	74	72	213	1,983.33
Mathieu Decottignies-Lafon	68	71	74	213	1,983.33
Marcus Helligkilde	70	73	70	213	1,983.33
Magnus A. Carlsson	71	72	70	213	1,983.33
Jordan Wrisdale	74	67	72	213	1,983.33
Sebastian Garcia Rodriguez	74	69	70	213	1,983.33

Hainan Open

See Asia/Japan Tours chapter.

Foshan Open

See Asia/Japan Tours chapter.

Challenge Tour Grand Final

Club de Golf Alcanada, Port d'Alcudia, Mallorca, Spain
Par 36-35–71; 7,108 yards

November 7-10
purse, €420,000

	SCORES				TOTAL	MONEY
Francesco Laporta	68	69	70	71	278	€72,000
Robin Sciot-Siegrist	71	68	70	71	280	37,500
Sebastian Heisele	71	69	67	73	280	37,500
Matthew Jordan	70	70	69	72	281	20,250
Jack Senior	70	73	66	72	281	20,250
Oliver Farr	72	72	68	71	283	15,666.67
Marcel Schneider	73	72	67	71	283	15,666.67
Bryce Easton	74	70	68	71	283	15,666.67
Adrian Meronk	72	71	69	72	284	13,000
Darius van Driel	74	72	67	71	284	13,000

	SCORES				TOTAL	MONEY
Wil Besseling	72	71	71	71	285	11,000
Jose-Filipe Lima	75	75	69	66	285	11,000
Rasmus Hojgaard	74	74	67	71	286	9,000
Damien Perrier	75	72	71	68	286	9,000
Rhys Enoch	69	73	69	76	287	5,981.67
Ewen Ferguson	71	71	74	71	287	5,981.67
Connor Syme	73	71	70	73	287	5,981.67
Oscar Lengden	73	71	70	73	287	5,981.67
Ben Stow	74	71	68	74	287	5,981.67
Richard Bland	74	72	72	69	287	5,981.67
Daan Huizing	73	71	69	75	288	4,475
Ross McGowan	75	66	73	74	288	4,475
Carlos Pigem	75	71	71	71	288	4,475
Ricardo Santos	75	73	65	75	288	4,475
Joel Sjoholm	72	71	74	72	289	4,030
Lars van Meijel	74	71	72	72	289	4,030

Asian Tour

SMBC Singapore Open

Sentosa Golf Club, Serapong Course, Singapore
Par 36-35–71; 7,398 yards

January 17-20
purse, US$1,000,000

	SCORES				TOTAL	MONEY
Jazz Janewattananond	68	68	65	65	266	US$180,000
Paul Casey	68	67	68	65	268	86,500
Yoshinori Fujimoto	67	67	66	68	268	86,500
Matthew Fitzpatrick	68	67	66	69	270	50,000
Prom Meesawat	69	69	69	68	275	37,150
Doyeob Mun	71	65	67	72	275	37,150
Sergio Garcia	69	68	71	68	276	26,500
Gunn Charoenkul	68	71	67	70	276	26,500
Panuphol Pittayarat	71	70	70	66	277	19,316.67
Jarin Todd	69	69	70	69	277	19,316.67
Davis Love	69	68	70	70	277	19,316.67
Masahiro Kawamura	68	72	70	68	278	14,266.67
Berry Henson	70	70	71	67	278	14,266.67
Yikeun Chang	69	68	71	70	278	14,266.67
Dru Love	73	67	73	65	278	14,266.67
Kazuki Higa	69	71	68	70	278	14,266.67
Hosung Choi	69	69	69	71	278	14,266.67
Jake Higginbottom	70	70	70	69	279	11,091.67
Won Joon Lee	70	69	71	69	279	11,091.67
Miguel Tabuena	67	74	68	70	279	11,091.67
Dongkyu Jang	71	66	71	71	279	11,091.67
Phachara Khongwatmai	67	73	68	71	279	11,091.67
Chapchai Nirat	67	70	66	76	279	11,091.67
Johannes Veerman	70	69	71	70	280	8,720
Suradit Yongcharoenchai	69	71	71	69	280	8,720
Angelo Que	68	72	70	70	280	8,720
Nicholas Fung	68	68	73	71	280	8,720
Keith Horne	70	71	70	69	280	8,720
S. Chikkarangappa	71	66	72	71	280	8,720
Travis Smyth	68	69	71	72	280	8,720
Scott Vincent	71	69	68	72	280	8,720
Shaun Norris	69	68	70	73	280	8,720
Poom Saksansin	65	70	69	76	280	8,720

ISPS Handa World Super 6 Perth

See Australasian Tour chapter.

100th New Zealand Open

See Australasian Tour chapter.

Maybank Championship

Saujana Golf & Country Club, Kuala Lumpur, Malaysia
Par 36-36–72; 7,135 yards

March 21-24
purse, US$3,000,000

	SCORES				TOTAL	MONEY
Scott Hend	69	70	67	67	273	US$500,000
Nacho Elvira	65	72	66	70	273	333,330
(Hend defeated Elvira on first playoff hole.)						
Jazz Janewattananond	66	72	68	69	275	187,800
Johannes Veerman	72	69	69	66	276	150,000
Oliver Fisher	70	70	68	69	277	116,100
Max Kieffer	71	67	68	71	277	116,100
Jordan Smith	74	68	71	65	278	66,500
Darren Fichardt	76	65	71	66	278	66,500
Fabrizio Zanotti	72	72	66	68	278	66,500
Andy Sullivan	72	70	67	69	278	66,500
Ernie Els	68	70	69	71	278	66,500
Benjamin Hebert	69	73	65	71	278	66,500
Ross Fisher	72	71	66	70	279	47,100
David Lipsky	72	66	67	74	279	47,100
Masahiro Kawamura	69	70	73	68	280	40,560
Erik van Rooyen	71	69	72	68	280	40,560
Dean Burmester	68	70	73	69	280	40,560
Nicholas Fung	68	73	69	70	280	40,560
Siddikur Rahman	70	71	68	71	280	40,560
Julian Suri	69	71	73	68	281	33,960
Jorge Campillo	70	73	70	68	281	33,960
S. Chikkarangappa	75	69	68	69	281	33,960
Matthew Southgate	74	69	68	70	281	33,960
Louis de Jager	71	69	69	72	281	33,960
Thongchai Jaidee	72	71	70	69	282	29,400
Terry Pilkadaris	69	75	68	70	282	29,400
Lucas Herbert	69	69	73	71	282	29,400
Angelo Que	66	77	73	66	282	29,400
Robert Karlsson	71	73	74	64	282	29,400
Shubhankar Sharma	71	68	74	70	283	24,500
Gavin Green	74	70	69	70	283	24,500
Padraig Harrington	70	73	71	69	283	24,500
Shaun Norris	71	71	72	69	283	24,500
Paul Peterson	70	68	73	72	283	24,500
Matthias Schwab	66	75	70	72	283	24,500
Danny Masrin	69	68	76	71	284	20,700
Christiaan Bezuidenhout	69	74	70	71	284	20,700
Ryan Fox	71	73	70	70	284	20,700
Matthieu Pavon	73	69	72	70	284	20,700
Kristoffer Broberg	72	70	71	71	284	20,700
Thomas Pieters	67	69	78	71	285	17,100
Kurt Kitayama	70	71	72	72	285	17,100
S.S.P. Chawrasia	69	74	70	72	285	17,100
Guido Migliozzi	71	68	73	73	285	17,100
Zach Murray	68	71	73	73	285	17,100
Hyunwoo Ryu	74	70	73	68	285	17,100
Renato Paratore	73	71	73	68	285	17,100
Marcus Fraser	65	77	72	72	286	12,900
George Coetzee	72	71	72	71	286	12,900
Mike Lorenzo-Vera	72	72	72	70	286	12,900
Viraj Madappa	70	72	70	74	286	12,900
Prom Meesawat	68	71	72	75	286	12,900
Ashun Wu	71	73	73	69	286	12,900
Gaganjeet Bhullar	68	75	75	68	286	12,900
Robert Rock	73	71	72	71	287	10,200
Thomas Detry	70	71	76	70	287	10,200

	SCORES				TOTAL	MONEY
Chris Paisley	71	71	74	72	288	9,000
Min Woo Lee	73	71	73	71	288	9,000
Minchel Choi	71	73	74	70	288	9,000
Andrea Pavan	69	71	73	76	289	7,650
Jarin Todd	73	71	71	74	289	7,650
Lee Slattery	72	71	73	73	289	7,650
Scott Vincent	70	72	74	73	289	7,650
W.T. Lin	73	70	74	72	289	7,650
Poom Saksansin	68	74	76	71	289	7,650
Ajeetesh Sandhu	72	72	72	74	290	6,150
Brandon Stone	68	74	74	74	290	6,150
Richard McEvoy	70	74	73	73	290	6,150
Nicolas Colsaerts	70	74	78	68	290	6,150
Pavit Tangkamolprasert	72	69	74	76	291	4,984.92
Ricardo Gouveia	69	73	74	75	291	4,984.92
David Law	73	71	74	74	292	4,496.42
Keith Horne	71	73	78	72	294	4,493
Micah Lauren Shin	74	70	77	74	295	4,489.59

Hero Indian Open

DLF Golf & Country Club, New Delhi, India
Par 36-36–72; 7,379 yards

March 28-31
purse, US$1,750,000

	SCORES				TOTAL	MONEY
Stephen Gallacher	67	74	67	71	279	US$291,660
Masahiro Kawamura	69	70	68	73	280	194,440
Jorge Campillo	70	73	71	67	281	109,550
Christiaan Bezuidenhout	68	76	70	68	282	80,850
Julian Suri	67	67	71	77	282	80,850
Nacho Elvira	72	69	72	70	283	49,175
Erik van Rooyen	69	73	69	72	283	49,175
George Coetzee	70	66	74	73	283	49,175
Callum Shinkwin	72	65	68	78	283	49,175
Keith Horne	73	73	70	68	284	28,284.38
Adrian Otaegui	70	72	73	69	284	28,284.38
Rashid Khan	72	70	72	70	284	28,284.38
Jarin Todd	73	69	72	70	284	28,284.38
Victor Dubuisson	71	72	70	71	284	28,284.38
Sihwan Kim	76	68	67	73	284	28,284.38
Mikko Korhonen	71	69	70	74	284	28,284.38
S. Chikkarangappa	74	70	66	74	284	28,284.38
Nino Bertasio	70	75	73	67	285	21,070
Robert Rock	70	70	75	70	285	21,070
Kalle Samooja	75	71	69	70	285	21,070
Matthias Schwab	72	68	70	75	285	21,070
James Morrison	70	71	69	75	285	21,070
Prayad Marksaeng	69	69	78	70	286	18,987.50
Bernd Wiesberger	71	70	75	70	286	18,987.50
Panuphol Pittayarat	71	70	74	72	287	17,937.50
Ashley Chesters	69	73	71	74	287	17,937.50
Jake Higginbottom	73	70	77	68	288	16,100
Haydn Porteous	73	73	70	72	288	16,100
Andrea Pavan	75	68	72	73	288	16,100
Lorenzo Gagli	76	65	72	75	288	16,100
Shubhankar Sharma	69	73	71	75	288	16,100
Ben Campbell	72	71	73	73	289	14,000
Aaron Rai	74	69	73	73	289	14,000
Raphael Jacquelin	70	74	70	75	289	14,000
Marcus Fraser	71	71	74	74	290	12,600

		SCORES			TOTAL	MONEY
Scott Vincent	72	72	72	74	290	12,600
Poom Saksansin	69	75	71	75	290	12,600
Scott Hend	69	68	74	79	290	12,600
Berry Henson	70	72	79	70	291	10,850
Gaganjeet Bhullar	72	74	74	71	291	10,850
Wenchong Liang	72	73	74	72	291	10,850
Jack Singh Brar	72	70	75	74	291	10,850
Pablo Larrazabal	68	76	73	74	291	10,850
Joachim Hansen	73	72	70	76	291	10,850
Justin Walters	74	71	78	69	292	8,225
Rattanon Wannasrichan	73	73	74	72	292	8,225
N. Thangaraja	71	70	77	74	292	8,225
John Catlin	71	75	72	74	292	8,225
S.S.P. Chawrasia	74	72	71	75	292	8,225
Sam Brazel	73	69	73	77	292	8,225
Hideto Tanihara	71	73	71	77	292	8,225
Prom Meesawat	68	74	71	79	292	8,225
Robert Karlsson	68	68	73	83	292	8,225
Ajeetesh Sandhu	74	71	73	75	293	5,950
Steven Brown	73	70	74	76	293	5,950
Daniel Nisbet	70	73	73	77	293	5,950
Richie Ramsay	69	71	75	78	293	5,950
Jbe' Kruger	73	71	75	75	294	4,987.50
Jeunghun Wang	73	69	76	76	294	4,987.50
David Horsey	72	73	70	79	294	4,987.50
Gavin Green	72	71	71	80	294	4,987.50
Jens Dantorp	70	72	70	83	295	4,550
Terry Pilkadaris	75	70	76	75	296	4,375
Daisuke Kataoka	76	69	74	78	297	4,025
Adilson da Silva	71	73	73	80	297	4,025
Dean Burmester	71	73	73	80	297	4,025
Tirawat Kaewsiribandit	71	75	71	81	298	3,675
Soren Kjeldsen	71	75	77	77	300	3,500
Rahil Gangjee	70	74	77	80	301	3,262.50
Gaurav Pratap Singh	73	73	73	82	301	3,262.50

Bangabandhu Cup Golf Open

Kurmitola Golf Club, Dhaka, Bangladesh
Par 35-36–71; 6,642 yards

April 3-6
purse, US$350,000

		SCORES			TOTAL	MONEY
Sadom Kaewkanjana	65	62	68	70	265	US$63,000
Ajeetesh Sandhu	70	66	65	65	266	38,500
Rashid Khan	66	64	67	70	267	22,050
Maverick Antcliff	63	70	69	70	272	17,500
Wei-Lun Wang	65	72	71	65	273	11,993.33
Jazz Janewattananond	65	71	68	69	273	11,993.33
Jack Harrison	68	67	68	70	273	11,993.33
Trevor Simsby	66	70	71	67	274	8,032.50
Berry Henson	68	67	69	70	274	8,032.50
Md. Zamal Hossain Mollah	72	66	72	65	275	6,396.50
Mikumu Horikawa	67	67	74	67	275	6,396.50
Suttijet Kooratanapisan	68	73	69	66	276	5,349.67
Karandeep Kochhar	69	67	70	70	276	5,349.67
Siddikur Rahman	66	68	68	74	276	5,349.67
Itthipat Buranatanyarat	71	70	71	65	277	4,435
Daniel Fox	69	67	73	68	277	4,435
Poom Pattaropong	67	69	72	69	277	4,435
Md. Sajib Ali	66	70	72	69	277	4,435

506 / ASIA/JAPAN TOURS

	SCORES				TOTAL	MONEY
Akbar Hossain	67	68	69	73	277	4,435
Prayad Marksaeng	68	70	73	67	278	3,706.60
Terry Pilkadaris	72	69	70	67	278	3,706.60
Pawin Ingkhapradit	69	69	72	68	278	3,706.60
Danny Masrin	68	69	72	69	278	3,706.60
Phachara Khongwatmai	73	68	68	69	278	3,706.60
Veer Ahlawat	67	71	74	67	279	3,132.50
Soomin Lee	67	74	72	66	279	3,132.50
Md. Nazim	67	69	74	69	279	3,132.50
Tomoharu Otsuki	72	67	70	70	279	3,132.50
Udayan Mane	70	69	70	70	279	3,132.50
Settee Prakongvech	65	70	72	72	279	3,132.50

Volvo China Open

Genzon Golf Club, Shenzhen, China
Par 36-36–72; 7,145 yards

May 2-5
purse, CN¥20,000,000

	SCORES				TOTAL	MONEY
Mikko Korhonen	68	69	65	66	268	US$485,625
Benjamin Hebert	67	68	64	69	268	323,750
(Korhonen defeated Hebert on first playoff hole.)
Jorge Campillo	65	69	68	67	269	182,400.93
Haotong Li	67	73	66	66	272	145,687.65
Mike Lorenzo-Vera	67	71	71	64	273	90,209.79
David Lipsky	65	72	70	66	273	90,209.79
Romain Langasque	67	69	70	67	273	90,209.79
Jordan Smith	67	70	69	67	273	90,209.79
Ashun Wu	66	65	72	70	273	90,209.79
Sean Crocker	68	68	72	66	274	58,275.06
Jacques Kruyswijk	70	67	70	68	275	50,213.67
Yuta Ikeda	68	71	68	68	275	50,213.67
Victor Dubuisson	68	68	68	71	275	50,213.67
Richie Ramsay	69	71	70	66	276	41,083.92
Bernd Wiesberger	69	71	68	68	276	41,083.92
Minwoo Lee	69	67	70	70	276	41,083.92
Adilson da Silva	72	69	65	70	276	41,083.92
Tapio Pulkkanen	65	68	72	71	276	41,083.92
Alexander Bjork	70	70	69	68	277	31,701.63
Julian Suri	69	72	68	68	277	31,701.63
Panuphol Pittayarat	70	71	68	68	277	31,701.63
John Catlin	66	76	68	67	277	31,701.63
Sam Brazel	68	71	72	66	277	31,701.63
Berry Henson	70	70	71	66	277	31,701.63
Marcel Siem	71	67	69	70	277	31,701.63
Gavin Green	67	72	68	70	277	31,701.63
Jazz Janewattananond	70	71	66	70	277	31,701.63
Miguel Tabuena	67	75	65	70	277	31,701.63
Enqi Liang [A]	70	72	66	70	278	
Adri Arnaus	75	65	71	67	278	26,369.47
Erik van Rooyen	68	68	70	72	278	26,369.47
Jason Scrivener	70	66	73	70	279	22,363.06
Haydn Porteous	69	73	67	70	279	22,363.06
Yechun Yuan	68	71	72	68	279	22,363.06
Sam Horsfield	70	69	69	71	279	22,363.06
Paul Peterson	69	72	67	71	279	22,363.06
Joachim Hansen	69	73	69	68	279	22,363.06
Guido Migliozzi	73	68	71	67	279	22,363.06
Nacho Elvira	68	69	68	74	279	22,363.06
Jack Singh Brar	68	73	70	69	280	18,939.39

	SCORES				TOTAL	MONEY
Jin Cheng	69	69	69	73	280	18,939.39
Matthieu Pavon	68	69	75	68	280	18,939.39
Nicolas Colsaerts	68	72	69	72	281	16,317.02
Wenchong Liang	71	70	69	71	281	16,317.02
James Morrison	71	69	71	70	281	16,317.02
Fabrizio Zanotti	68	72	72	69	281	16,317.02
Tirawat Kaewsiribandit	68	74	65	74	281	16,317.02
Jianfeng Ye	72	68	73	68	281	16,317.02
Richard T. Lee	70	69	69	74	282	13,986.02
Aaron Rai	71	70	71	70	282	13,986.02
Scott Jamieson	68	69	72	74	283	12,237.77
Ajeetesh Sandhu	74	67	69	73	283	12,237.77
Louis de Jager	72	68	68	75	283	12,237.77
Daniel van Tonder	73	69	72	69	283	12,237.77
Kuang Yang [A]	71	71	69	73	284	
Hongfu Wu	68	73	71	72	284	9,906.76
Stuart Manley	68	70	76	70	284	9,906.76
Kalle Samooja	71	71	72	70	284	9,906.76
Romain Wattel	70	72	74	68	284	9,906.76
Zach Murray	70	71	68	76	285	8,304.20
Micah Lauren Shin	69	70	71	75	285	8,304.20
Wade Ormsby	72	70	70	73	285	8,304.20
Malcolm Kokocinski	69	73	72	71	285	8,304.20
Khalin Joshi	69	70	78	70	287	7,575.76
S.S.P. Chawrasia	71	71	72	74	288	7,138.70
Scott Hend	68	70	80	70	288	7,138.70
Scott Vincent	70	72	78	71	291	6,701.63
Chen Guxin [A]	70	72	77	76	295	

GS Caltex Maekyung Open

Namseoul Country Club, Seongnam, Korea
Par 36-35–71; 7,039 yards

May 2-5
purse, KRW1,200,000,000

	SCORES				TOTAL	MONEY
Tae Hee Lee	67	69	68	71	275	US$266,797.81
Janne Kaske	70	66	68	71	275	106,719.13
(Lee defeated Kaske on third playoff hole.)						
Daehyun Kim	72	67	72	65	276	66,699.45
Sanghyun Park	72	68	69	69	278	46,244.95
Hyungjoon Lee	70	69	69	71	279	35,128.38
Junwon Park	69	68	72	70	279	35,128.38
Prom Meesawat	72	71	69	68	280	30,237.09
Jeongmin Park	70	73	70	68	281	25,568.13
Phachara Khongwatmai	70	68	70	73	281	25,568.13
Dongha Lee #562	70	72	74	66	282	18,616.56
Hyungseok Seo	71	71	70	70	282	18,616.56
Jeonghyeob Hyun	73	70	67	72	282	18,616.56
Dongseop Maeng	71	72	71	69	283	12,699.58
Bio Kim	73	68	71	71	283	12,699.58
Jiho Jung	73	71	68	71	283	12,699.58
Jinho Choi	72	67	71	73	283	12,699.58
Innchoon Hwang	70	71	68	74	283	12,699.58
Ben Leong	72	74	69	70	285	9,960.45
Bongsub Kim	72	69	72	72	285	9,960.45
Seungtaek Lee	74	70	74	67	285	9,960.45
Poom Pattaropong	70	73	68	74	285	9,960.45
Sungho Yun	70	70	71	74	285	9,960.45
Jake Higginbottom	74	71	70	71	286	8,181.80
Han Lee	71	71	73	71	286	8,181.80

	SCORES	TOTAL	MONEY
Danthai Boonma	74 70 73 69	286	8,181.80
Jason Norris	73 71 74 68	286	8,181.80
Yoseop Seo	68 69 75 74	286	8,181.80

Asia-Pacific Diamond Cup

See Japan Tour section.

Kolon Korea Open

Woo Jeong Hills Country Club, Cheonan, Korea
Par 36-35–71; 7,328 yards

June 20-23
purse, KRW1,200,000,000

	SCORES	TOTAL	MONEY
Jazz Janewattananond	70 67 69 72	278	US$266,797.81
Innchoon Hwang	67 69 73 70	279	106,719.13
Chan Kim	72 70 70 68	280	66,699.45
Minjun Kim	71 70 72 68	281	41,798.32
Dongkyu Jang	68 72 69 72	281	41,798.32
Kevin Na	68 72 71 71	282	32,905.06
Songgyu Yoo	71 68 69 75	283	30,237.09
Kyongjun Moon	67 73 70 74	284	25,568.13
Berry Henson	74 67 69 74	284	25,568.13
Scott Vincent	73 72 72 68	285	17,819.87
Richard T. Lee	72 68 72 73	285	17,819.87
Prom Meesawat	71 68 71 75	285	17,819.87
Soomin Lee	69 70 71 75	285	17,819.87
Doyeob Mun	70 74 72 70	286	11,531.60
Sanghyun Park	73 71 70 72	286	11,531.60
Bio Kim	73 72 67 74	286	11,531.60
Jeongwoo Ham	70 74 71 72	287	9,462.43
Kyungtae Kim	70 70 74 73	287	9,462.43
Jaemin Hwang	71 71 70 75	287	9,462.43
Seungsu Han	72 70 73 73	288	8,324.09
Jiho Yang	70 73 72 73	288	8,324.09
Tirawat Kaewsiribandit	70 71 71 76	288	8,324.09
Taehoon Kim	69 71 73 75	288	8,324.09
Jihoon Lee	73 72 73 71	289	7,225.14
Zach Murray	70 73 74 72	289	7,225.14
Sungho Yun	72 73 72 72	289	7,225.14
Hanbyeol Kim	72 70 74 73	289	7,225.14
Tae Hee Lee	72 68 75 74	289	7,225.14
Junggon Hwang	65 75 74 75	289	7,225.14
Johannes Veerman	70 73 72 74	289	7,225.14

Sarawak Championship

Damai Golf & Country Club, Sarawak, Malaysia
Par 36-36–72; 6,970 yards

August 15-18
purse, US$300,000

	SCORES	TOTAL	MONEY
Andrew Dodt	66 64 70 64	264	US$54,000
Richard T. Lee	66 68 64 66	264	33,000
(Dodt defeated Lee on first playoff hole.)			
Micah Lauren Shin	69 65 66 65	265	18,900
Chien-Yao Hung	64 66 68 68	266	15,000

	SCORES				TOTAL	MONEY
Miguel Tabuena	65	65	71	66	267	12,300
Scott Vincent	68	66	72	62	268	7,608
Terry Pilkadaris	66	68	71	63	268	7,608
Itthipat Buranatanyarat	68	67	69	64	268	7,608
Justin Quiban	64	71	67	66	268	7,608
Jazz Janewattananond	65	64	70	69	268	7,608
Danthai Boonma	67	66	68	68	269	5,055
Sadom Kaewkanjana	66	67	67	69	269	5,055
Pavit Tangkamolprasert	68	65	65	72	270	4,545
Jack Harrison	67	69	68	67	271	4,245
Yanwei Liu	67	70	67	67	271	4,245
Jesse Yap	67	68	73	64	272	3,639
Mardan Mamat	68	66	70	68	272	3,639
Travis Smyth	71	66	66	69	272	3,639
Lloyd Jefferson Go	69	65	68	70	272	3,639
Kosuke Hamamoto	68	71	62	71	272	3,639
Danny Masrin	67	68	71	67	273	3,180
Shiv Kapur	70	69	70	64	273	3,180
Natipong Srithong	67	71	68	67	273	3,180
Ben Leong	64	72	70	68	274	2,820
Han Lee	71	67	68	68	274	2,820
Chikkarangappa S.	69	68	69	68	274	2,820
Prom Meesawat	68	67	70	69	274	2,820
Tomoharu Otsuki	67	68	68	71	274	2,820

Bank BRI Indonesia Open

Pondok Indah Golf Course, Jakarta, Indonesia
Par 36-36–72; 7,243 yards

August 29-September 1
purse, US$500,000

	SCORES				TOTAL	MONEY
Miguel Carballo	69	69	66	67	271	US$90,000
Yikeun Chang	67	75	68	64	274	55,000
Joohyung Kim	69	71	67	68	275	31,500
Naraajie E. Ramadhanputra [A]	66	69	63	78	276	
Naoki Sekito	68	70	70	69	277	25,000
Pavit Tangkamolprasert	69	69	71	69	278	15,912.50
Daniel Fox	70	68	70	70	278	15,912.50
Kwanchai Tannin	69	67	71	71	278	15,912.50
Jazz Janewattananond	67	71	69	71	278	15,912.50
Jarryd Felton	70	72	69	68	279	8,650
Natipong Srithong	71	69	70	69	279	8,650
J.C. Ritchie	69	66	74	70	279	8,650
Shiv Kapur	68	70	71	70	279	8,650
Daniel Van Tonder	67	73	69	70	279	8,650
Kosuke Hamamoto	66	74	68	71	279	8,650
Philip Eriksson	68	72	71	69	280	6,208.33
Sadom Kaewkanjana	67	71	72	70	280	6,208.33
Rashid Khan	68	72	70	70	280	6,208.33
Adilson da Silva	69	70	70	71	280	6,208.33
Siddikur Rahman	70	70	69	71	280	6,208.33
Doyeob Mun	72	67	69	72	280	6,208.33
Jake Higginbottom	68	68	75	70	281	5,000
Viraj Madappa	65	74	73	69	281	5,000
Chiragh Kumar	71	71	70	69	281	5,000
Ajeetesh Sandhu	66	72	75	68	281	5,000
Zach Murray	70	66	71	74	281	5,000
Rory Hie	67	72	68	74	281	5,000
Itthipat Buranatanyarat	65	69	71	76	281	5,000

Yeangder Tournament Players Championship

Linkou International Golf & Country Club, Chinese Taipei
Par 36-36–72; 7,108 yards

September 5-8
purse, US$500,000

	SCORES				TOTAL	MONEY
Yikeun Chang	67	66	68	66	267	US$90,000
Kosuke Hamamoto	66	69	68	67	270	55,000
Shih-Chang Chan	69	64	68	70	271	31,500
Wen-Tang Lin	67	68	65	72	272	25,000
Richard T. Lee	70	66	72	65	273	18,575
Casey O'Toole	68	67	71	67	273	18,575
Danny Masrin	67	71	68	68	274	14,250
Suradit Yongcharoenchai	69	67	70	70	276	11,475
Phachara Khongwatmai	71	68	65	72	276	11,475
Malcolm Kokocinski	69	67	73	68	277	8,493.75
Kwanchai Tannin	70	67	72	68	277	8,493.75
Karandeep Kochhar	67	71	69	70	277	8,493.75
Doyeob Mun	67	66	72	72	277	8,493.75
Siddikur Rahman	71	71	70	66	278	6,925
Wei-Lun Wang	72	67	72	67	278	6,925
Prom Meesawat	69	70	69	70	278	6,925
Miguel Tabuena	71	68	74	66	279	5,925
Chapchai Nirat	68	73	69	69	279	5,925
Shiv Kapur	69	70	70	70	279	5,925
Ben Leong	70	70	67	72	279	5,925
Tomoharu Otsuki	71	67	72	70	280	5,225
Pawin Ingkhapradit	71	70	69	70	280	5,225
Tirawat Kaewsiribandit	69	71	75	65	280	5,225
Aman Raj	71	67	70	72	280	5,225
Jarin Todd	69	73	69	70	281	4,414.29
Minchel Choi	67	70	73	71	281	4,414.29
Viraj Madappa	72	65	72	72	281	4,414.29
Masahiro Kawamura	68	74	73	66	281	4,414.29
Pavit Tangkamolprasert	69	74	66	72	281	4,414.29
Sadom Kaewkanjana	72	71	72	66	281	4,414.29
Wei-Hsuan Wang	68	70	70	73	281	4,414.29

Classic Golf & Country Club International Championship

Classic Golf & Country Club, Gurgaon, India
Par 36-36–72; 7,114 yards

September 12-15
purse, $300,000

	SCORES				TOTAL	MONEY
Rory Hie	64	68	67	68	267	US$54,000
Byungjun Kim	69	66	67	67	269	25,950
Rashid Khan	68	66	66	69	269	25,950
Aadil Bedi	67	68	69	66	270	15,000
Aman Raj	67	67	72	66	272	9,547.50
Kwanchai Tannin	66	72	68	66	272	9,547.50
Suttijet Kooratanapisan	70	72	63	67	272	9,547.50
Abhijit Chadha	68	65	68	71	272	9,547.50
Masahiro Kawamura	70	67	70	66	273	6,420
Suradit Yongcharoenchai	66	69	74	65	274	5,482.50
Mathiam Keyser	70	68	68	68	274	5,482.50
Kosuke Hamamoto	69	65	70	71	275	4,875
Pawin Ingkhapradit	72	66	73	65	276	4,252.50
Settee Prakongvech	72	71	67	66	276	4,252.50
Veer Ahlawat	71	67	72	66	276	4,252.50
Karan Pratap Singh	72	71	66	67	276	4,252.50

	SCORES				TOTAL	MONEY
Kshitij Naveed Kaul	69	70	71	67	277	3,555
Karandeep Kochhar	72	66	71	68	277	3,555
Shivendra Singh Sisodia	71	70	68	68	277	3,555
Viraj Madappa	69	71	68	69	277	3,555
Travis Smyth	72	67	72	67	278	3,045
Sattaya Supupramai	66	74	72	66	278	3,045
Sachin Baisoya	73	70	69	66	278	3,045
Chikkarangappa S.	70	67	71	70	278	3,045
Daniel Fox	68	70	70	70	278	3,045
Abhinav Lohan	69	68	70	71	278	3,045

Shinhan Donghae Open

Bear's Best Golf Club, CheongNa, Incheon, Korea
Par 36-35–71; 7,252 yards

September 19-22
purse, KRW1,200,000,000

	SCORES				TOTAL	MONEY
Jbe' Kruger	69	67	68	65	269	US$192,094.43
Chan Kim	66	71	69	65	271	117,391.04
Scott Vincent	67	67	68	71	273	67,233.05
Sunghoon Kang	69	70	65	70	274	53,359.56
Rikuya Hoshino	74	67	66	68	275	43,754.84
Shugo Imahira	66	70	68	72	276	35,537.47
Jeongwoo Ham	68	69	71	69	277	28,280.57
Matthew Griffin	70	72	65	70	277	28,280.57
Shaun Norris	74	69	67	68	278	20,614.58
Sang-Hee Lee	69	73	66	70	278	20,614.58
Hyungjoon Lee	70	66	70	72	278	20,614.58
Sadom Kaewkanjana	68	70	72	69	279	15,225.26
Travis Smyth	70	71	69	69	279	15,225.26
Paul Peterson	68	68	73	70	279	15,225.26
Viraj Madappa	73	69	67	70	279	15,225.26
Yosuke Tsukada	71	70	72	66	279	15,225.26
Jiho Jung	70	70	68	71	279	15,225.26
Andrew Dodt	72	71	67	70	280	11,341.87
Bongsub Kim	74	67	70	69	280	11,341.87
Rahil Gangjee	70	71	70	69	280	11,341.87
Woohyun Kim	68	70	72	70	280	11,341.87
Mikumu Horikawa	71	72	68	69	280	11,341.87
Doyeob Mun	71	71	68	70	280	11,341.87
Yosuke Asaji	72	69	72	67	280	11,341.87
Zach Murray	69	71	69	71	280	11,341.87
Panuphol Pittayarat	73	70	70	67	280	11,341.87

Panasonic Open Golf Championship

See Japan Tour section.

Mercuries Taiwan Masters

Taiwan Golf & Country Club, Chinese Taipei
Par 36-36–72; 6,923 yards

October 3-6
purse, US$900,000

	SCORES				TOTAL	MONEY
Suradit Yongcharoenchai	71	69	68	70	278	US$180,000
Adilson da Silva	72	71	68	68	279	72,000
Ajeetesh Sandhu	68	69	70	72	279	72,000
Miguel Tabuena	67	72	68	72	279	72,000
Rashid Khan	72	71	74	67	284	29,250
Mardan Mamat	73	73	69	69	284	29,250
Wen-Tang Lin	71	71	70	72	284	29,250
Siddikur Rahman	70	71	68	75	284	29,250
Keith Horne	67	74	76	68	285	16,500
Nicholas Fung	67	76	68	74	285	16,500
Viraj Madappa	72	72	65	76	285	16,500
Danthai Boonma	69	74	72	71	286	13,050
Andrew Dodt	75	70	70	71	286	13,050
Yikeun Chang	74	68	72	72	286	13,050
Wei-Chih Lu	74	72	68	72	286	13,050
Prom Meesawat	71	70	77	69	287	11,250
Wen-Teh Lu	71	71	77	69	288	10,575
Shih-Chang Chan	74	72	70	72	288	10,575
Scott Vincent	72	74	72	71	289	9,427.50
Khalin Joshi	71	73	73	72	289	9,427.50
Kosuke Hamamoto	73	72	72	72	289	9,427.50
Miguel Carballo	72	66	78	73	289	9,427.50
Jake Higginbottom	74	71	73	72	290	8,460
Wei-Tze Yeh	70	75	73	72	290	8,460
Chien-Yao Hung	74	72	71	73	290	8,460
Sadom Kaewkanjana	71	72	73	74	290	8,460
Ben Leong	72	74	67	77	290	8,460

Thailand Open

Thai Country Club, Chachoengsao, Thailand
Par 35-36–71; 7,198 yards

November 7-10
purse, US$300,000

	SCORES				TOTAL	MONEY
John Catlin	67	70	69	67	273	US$54,000
Shiv Kapur	74	63	71	65	273	25,950
Pavit Tangkamolprasert	70	70	68	65	273	25,950

(Catlin defeated Kapur and Tangkamolprasert on first playoff hole.)

Wei-Lun Wang	70	67	70	67	274	13,650
Andrew Martin	67	68	68	71	274	13,650
Ben Leong	71	67	71	66	275	8,077.50
Joohyung Kim	68	71	68	68	275	8,077.50
Phachara Khongwatmai	65	72	69	69	275	8,077.50
Natthaphat Harnchokchaiskul [A]	64	70	70	71	275	
S.S.P. Chawrasia	68	67	68	72	275	8,077.50
Taewoo Kim	69	70	71	67	277	5,280
Ajeetesh Sandhu	68	67	73	69	277	5,280
Suradit Yongcharoenchai	68	68	70	71	277	5,280
Danthai Boonma	73	69	69	67	278	4,161
Jake Higginbottom	70	69	71	68	278	4,161
Jyoti Randhawa	71	72	67	68	278	4,161
Miguel Tabuena	70	70	69	69	278	4,161
Nicholas Latimer	69	71	68	70	278	4,161
Shinichi Mizuno	68	72	70	69	279	3,540

	SCORES				TOTAL	MONEY
Soomin Lee	66	72	71	70	279	3,540
Malcolm Kokocinski	71	71	72	66	280	3,043.13
Pawin Ingkhapradit	69	71	72	68	280	3,043.13
Viraj Madappa	70	71	70	69	280	3,043.13
Poom Saksansin	71	70	70	69	280	3,043.13
Prom Meesawat	68	67	75	70	280	3,043.13
Poom Pattaropong	69	65	75	71	280	3,043.13
Peradol Panyathanasedh	69	68	71	72	280	3,043.13
Chinnarat Phadungsil	72	70	65	73	280	3,043.13

Panasonic Open India

Classic Golf & Country Club, Gurgaon, India
Par 36-36–72; 7,114 yards
(Tournament reduced to 54 holes—smog.)

November 14-17
purse, US$400,000

	SCORES			TOTAL	MONEY
Joohyung Kim	70	68	65	203	US$72,000
Chikkarangappa S.	69	68	67	204	34,600
Shiv Kapur	67	67	70	204	34,600
Terry Pilkadaris	66	68	71	205	20,000
Rory Hie	70	68	68	206	13,706.67
Vikrant Chopra	67	70	69	206	13,706.67
Chien-Yao Hung	67	69	70	206	13,706.67
Settee Prakongvech	70	69	69	208	8,666.67
Veer Ahlawat	69	69	70	208	8,666.67
Siddikur Rahman	69	67	72	208	8,666.67
Arjun Prasad	67	74	68	209	6,513.33
M. Dharma	67	73	69	209	6,513.33
Teemu Putkonen	70	67	72	209	6,513.33
Danthai Boonma	70	71	69	210	4,908.89
Pavit Tangkamolprasert	70	71	69	210	4,908.89
Om Prakash Chouhan	70	70	70	210	4,908.89
Itthipat Buranatanyarat	64	75	71	210	4,908.89
Karandeep Kochhar	67	72	71	210	4,908.89
Mathiam Keyser	69	69	72	210	4,908.89
Khalin Joshi	67	71	72	210	4,908.89
Travis Smyth	69	69	72	210	4,908.89
Rashid Khan	67	70	73	210	4,908.89
Miguel Tabuena	69	72	70	211	3,760
Jesse Yap	68	73	70	211	3,760
Suttijet Kooratanapisan	73	67	71	211	3,760
Kshitij Naveed Kaul	67	72	72	211	3,760
Anura Rohana	68	70	73	211	3,760
N. Thangaraja	69	68	74	211	3,760
Adam Blyth	71	63	77	211	3,760

514 / ASIA/JAPAN TOURS

Sabah Masters

Sutera Harbour Golf & Country Club, Sabah, Malaysia
Par 36-35–71; 6,932 yards

November 21-24
purse, US$300,000

	SCORES				TOTAL	MONEY
Pavit Tangkamolprasert	73	66	67	65	271	US$54,000
Aman Raj	68	70	70	63	271	22,300
David Gleeson	66	69	68	68	271	22,300
Phachara Khongwatmai	66	67	71	67	271	22,300
(Tangkamolprasert won on second playoff hole.)
Yikeun Chang	70	68	70	66	274	10,280
Rashid Khan	67	70	69	68	274	10,280
Wei-Lun Wang	67	68	70	69	274	10,280
Daniel Fox	71	68	68	68	275	6,183.75
Jakraphan Premsirigorn	68	71	66	70	275	6,183.75
Danthai Boonma	73	66	71	65	275	6,183.75
Sungho Lee	67	68	71	69	275	6,183.75
Suttijet Kooratanapisan	68	71	69	68	276	4,377
Rory Hie	73	69	65	69	276	4,377
Aaron Wilkin	66	71	71	68	276	4,377
Joohyung Kim	67	70	71	68	276	4,377
Udayan Mane	68	68	69	71	276	4,377
Sattaya Supupramai	70	70	67	70	277	3,795
Ben Geyer	71	69	69	69	278	3,475
Travis Smyth	70	71	68	69	278	3,475
Mardan Mamat	70	71	68	69	278	3,475
Aadil Bedi	70	70	70	69	279	3,000
Josh Younger	69	71	70	69	279	3,000
Kosuke Hamamoto	69	72	72	66	279	3,000
Brian Jung	73	66	71	69	279	3,000
Taewoo Kim	72	70	69	68	279	3,000
Siddikur Rahman	68	69	71	71	279	3,000
Soonsang Hong	70	67	69	73	279	3,000

AfrAsia Bank Mauritius Open

See African Sunshine Tour chapter.

BNI Indonesian Masters

Royale Jakarta Golf Club, Jakarta, Indonesia
Par 36-36–72; 7,361 yards

December 12-15
purse, US$750,000

	SCORES				TOTAL	MONEY
Jazz Janewattananond	68	70	62	65	265	US$135,000
Gunn Charoenkul	68	65	68	69	270	82,500
Taewoo Kim	73	65	68	65	271	42,375
Josh Younger	66	65	74	66	271	42,375
Danny Masrin	68	71	68	66	273	25,700
Phachara Khongwatmai	73	67	66	67	273	25,700
Alex Cejka	68	66	70	69	273	25,700
Jeunghun Wang	70	71	66	68	275	17,212.50
Shiv Kapur	70	65	71	69	275	17,212.50
Micah Lauren Shin	71	67	73	66	277	12,741
Rashid Khan	73	65	71	68	277	12,741
Jinho Choi	70	70	67	70	277	12,741
Sihwan Kim	69	66	70	72	277	12,741
Yosuke Asaji	70	68	70	70	278	10,838

	SCORES				TOTAL	MONEY
Jyoti Randhawa	71	69	72	67	279	9,313
Shohei Hasegawa	70	69	72	68	279	9,313
Prom Meesawat	67	68	75	69	279	9,313
Taehee Lee	69	71	70	69	279	9,313
Panuphol Pittayarat	72	68	68	71	279	9,313
Keith Horne	65	67	71	76	279	9,313
Sadom Kaewkanjana	72	70	69	69	280	7,725
Wolmer Murillo	70	71	70	69	280	7,725
Ajeetesh Sandhu	69	67	74	70	280	7,725
Joohyung Kim	69	73	72	66	280	7,725
John Catlin	71	67	71	71	280	7,725

Thailand Masters

Phoenix Gold Golf & Country Club, Pattaya, Thailand
Par 36-35–71; 6,889 yards

December 19-22
purse, US$500,000

	SCORES				TOTAL	MONEY
Jazz Janewattananond	69	67	60	65	261	US$90,000.00
Suradit Yongcharoenchai	67	70	67	62	266	37,166.67
Phachara Khongwatmai	66	64	69	67	266	37,166.67
Thomas Detry	63	68	66	69	266	37,166.67
Gunn Charoenkul	65	68	68	66	267	20,500.00
Jarin Todd	67	69	67	65	268	16,650.00
Berry Henson	65	69	70	65	269	11,687.50
Nicolas Colsaerts	68	71	64	66	269	11,687.50
Suteepat Prateeptienchai	69	67	65	68	269	11,687.50
Miguel Tabuena	68	68	65	68	269	11,687.50
Ajeetesh Sandhu	67	66	70	67	270	8,725.00
Settee Prakongvech	64	73	69	65	271	7,133.33
Kyongjun Moon	68	66	71	66	271	7,133.33
Tanapat Pichaikool [A]	68	68	68	67	271	
Kosuke Hamamoto	68	64	71	68	271	7,133.33
Wei-Hsuan Wang	66	67	70	68	271	7,133.33
Scott Hend	68	66	68	69	271	7,133.33
Panuphol Pittayarat	67	66	68	70	271	7,133.33
Sangchai Kaewcharoen	71	66	66	69	272	6,025.00
Sattaya Supupramai	67	71	69	66	273	5,225.00
Danny Masrin	69	69	68	67	273	5,225.00
Wei-Lun Wang	68	68	69	68	273	5,225.00
Sadom Kaewkanjana	67	69	69	68	273	5,225.00
Chinnarat Phadungsil	69	66	69	69	273	5,225.00
Haydn Porteous	68	66	69	70	273	5,225.00
Seungtaek Lee	68	67	67	71	273	5,225.00
Sihwan Kim	69	65	66	73	273	5,225.00

PGA Tour Series–China

Chongqing Championship

Poly Golf Club, Chongqing
Par 36-37–73; 7,236 yards

March 28-31
purse, CN¥1,600,000

	SCORES				TOTAL	MONEY
Taihei Sato	66	67	68	73	274	CN¥288,000
Yanwei Liu	67	72	66	69	274	172,800
(Sato defeated Liu on third playoff hole.)						
David Kocher	70	66	68	71	275	108,800
Max McGreevy	68	69	72	67	276	76,800
Trevor Sluman	69	66	71	71	277	60,800
Stephen Lewton	70	68	69	70	277	60,800
Benjamin Lein	73	70	70	65	278	44,933
Charlie Dann	69	73	69	67	278	44,933
Luke Kwon	67	72	72	67	278	44,933
Jin Zhang	70	70	71	67	278	44,933
Christopher Wood	71	68	71	68	278	44,933
Wenyi Huang	72	63	72	71	278	44,933
Enqi Liang [A]	68	68	75	68	279	
Bryden Macpherson	71	68	71	69	279	32,000
Chiehpo Lee	68	68	73	70	279	32,000
Linqiang Li [A]	70	69	74	67	280	
Taewoo Kim	75	66	70	69	280	28,000
Chengyao Ma	71	67	71	71	280	28,000
Kenta Endo	73	67	72	69	281	19,306
Max McCardle	68	67	74	72	281	19,306
Yinong Yang	70	66	73	72	281	19,306

Sanya Championship

Yalong Bay Golf Club, Sanya
Par 36-36–72; 7,189 yards
(Final round cancelled.)

April 4-7
purse, CN¥1,600,000

	SCORES			TOTAL	MONEY
Trevor Sluman	67	65	66	198	CN¥288,000
Matt Gilchrest	64	68	68	200	119,466
Max McGreevy	66	67	67	200	119,466
Michael Perras	69	63	68	200	119,466
Daejin Jeong	66	68	67	201	58,400
Christopher Hickman	68	65	68	201	58,400
Yuwa Kosaihira	68	64	69	201	58,400
Samuel Del Val	67	68	67	202	49,600
Gunn Charoenkul	67	71	66	204	44,800
Shotaro Ban	69	71	64	204	44,800
Jin Cheng	72	66	68	206	31,771
Corey Hale	69	69	68	206	31,771
Ryann Ree	67	71	68	206	31,771
Kevin Techakanokboon	73	65	68	206	31,771
Patrick Cover	70	70	66	206	31,771
Taihei Sato	70	66	70	206	31,771

	SCORES			TOTAL	MONEY
Michael Skelton	65	69	72	206	31,771
Woojin Jung	67	71	69	207	21,600
Charlie Dann	67	69	71	207	21,600
David Kocher	68	68	71	207	21,600
Stuart Macdonald	71	70	66	207	21,600

Haikou Championship

3 Km Golf Club, Sunac, Haikou
Par 36-36–72; 7,095 yards

April 11-14
purse, CN¥1,600,000

	SCORES				TOTAL	MONEY
David Kocher	68	75	69	66	278	CN¥288,000
Yuwa Kosaihira	72	70	70	66	278	172,800
(Kocher defeated Kosaihira on first playoff hole.)
Quincy Quek	66	73	72	68	279	108,800
Justin Hicks	72	74	69	65	280	76,800
James Marchesani	69	70	70	72	281	64,000
Kevin Techakanokboon	74	72	66	70	282	53,600
Kenta Endo	70	71	70	71	282	53,600
Velten Meyer	72	69	72	69	282	53,600
Jared Howard	75	66	74	68	283	46,400
Lloyd Jefferson Go	71	74	69	70	284	34,285
Shunyat Hak	72	74	69	69	284	34,285
Trevor Sluman	73	69	73	69	284	34,285
Corey Shaun	72	69	75	68	284	34,285
Michael Perras	72	70	71	71	284	34,285
Gunn Charoenkul	67	74	74	69	284	34,285
Zheng Ouyang	73	68	67	76	284	34,285
Hongfu Wu	71	74	72	68	285	24,800
Bryden Macpherson	73	73	70	69	285	24,800
Abdul Hadi	71	74	72	69	286	18,057
Douglas Quinones	72	71	74	69	286	18,057
Max McCardle	70	73	72	71	286	18,057
Max McGreevy	74	69	69	74	286	18,057
Matt Gilchrest	75	67	75	69	286	18,057
Huilin Zhang	71	76	70	69	286	18,057
Charlie Netzel	70	71	71	74	286	18,057

Beijing Championship

Topwin Golf & Country Club, Huairou, Beijing
Par 36-36–72; 7,126 yards

May 9-12
purse, CN¥1,600,000

	SCORES				TOTAL	MONEY
Richard Jung	66	70	65	68	269	CN¥288,000
Ryann Ree	70	64	68	69	271	172,800
Chiehpo Lee	69	69	68	66	272	92,800
Max McGreevy	70	64	67	71	272	92,800
Kevin Yuan	68	65	71	69	273	64,000
Gunn Charoenkul	66	72	68	68	274	57,600
John Young Kim	68	69	70	68	275	53,600
Patrick Cover	72	67	66	71	276	49,600
Brad Gehl	71	68	68	70	277	41,600
Xuewen Luo	70	67	68	72	277	41,600
Huilin Zhang	68	68	67	74	277	41,600
Myles Creighton	68	67	68	74	277	41,600

518 / ASIA/JAPAN TOURS

	SCORES				TOTAL	MONEY
Shunyat Hak	74	65	72	67	278	29,120
Charlie Netzel	70	65	74	69	278	29,120
Tuxuan Wu	70	68	68	72	278	29,120
Taihei Sato	71	68	67	72	278	29,120
Cyril Bouniol	68	69	67	74	278	29,120
Joseph Lane	72	69	67	71	279	24,000
Wenyi Huang	71	66	73	70	280	18,720
Max McCardle	71	67	73	69	280	18,720
Gyungsik Yoon	67	69	73	71	280	18,720
Weihsuan Wang	74	64	71	71	280	18,720
Stephen Lewton	67	69	70	74	280	18,720
Benjamin Lein	70	70	66	74	280	18,720

Qinhuangdao Championship

Qinhuangdao Poly Golf Club, Qinhuangdao, Hebei
Par 36-36–72; 7,424 yards

May 16-19
purse, CN¥1,600,000

	SCORES				TOTAL	MONEY
Luke Kwon	67	67	71	65	270	CN¥288,000
Myles Creighton	66	71	65	69	271	172,800
Suteepat Prateeptienchai	71	66	68	67	272	92,800
Matthew Negri	71	64	67	70	272	92,800
Weihsuan Wang	69	66	66	72	273	64,000
Huilin Zhang	70	71	69	65	275	51,800
Patrick Cover	70	67	72	66	275	51,800
Kevin Techakanokboon	71	69	68	67	275	51,800
Stephen Lewton	69	67	71	68	275	51,800
Christopher Wood	69	71	68	69	277	41,600
Justin Hicks	70	68	67	72	277	41,600
Tim Stewart	73	70	68	67	278	32,400
Simon Griffiths	68	70	71	69	278	32,400
Max McGreevy	68	71	70	69	278	32,400
Ryann Ree	67	74	68	69	278	32,400
Cyril Bouniol	71	69	73	66	279	25,600
Stuart Macdonald	71	70	70	68	279	25,600
John Young Kim	72	66	69	72	279	25,600
Samuel Del Val	71	71	70	68	280	18,057
Berni Reiter	68	69	74	69	280	18,057
Yuwa Kosaihira	71	71	72	66	280	18,057
Hongfu Wu	67	72	72	69	280	18,057
Dylan Healey	68	70	71	71	280	18,057
Lloyd Jefferson Go	69	67	72	72	280	18,057
Yanwei Liu	72	67	70	71	280	18,057

Nantong Championship

Nantong Yangtze River Golf Club, Nantong, Jiangsu
Par 36-36–72; 7,349 yards

May 23-26
purse, CN¥1,600,000

	SCORES				TOTAL	MONEY
Kevin Techakanokboon	66	73	65	67	271	CN¥288,000
Stephen Lewton	66	71	68	66	271	172,800

(Techakanokboon defeated Lewton on second playoff hole.)

	SCORES				TOTAL	MONEY
Max McGreevy	67	67	69	69	272	108,800
Michael Perras	70	68	68	70	276	70,400
Brad Gehl	64	73	69	70	276	70,400

	SCORES				TOTAL	MONEY
Andrew Hudson	69	71	70	69	279	48,400
Woojin Jung	67	69	72	71	279	48,400
Jaewon Lee	68	73	67	71	279	48,400
Lloyd Jefferson Go	73	67	67	72	279	48,400
Luke Kwon	71	67	69	72	279	48,400
Samuel Del Val	66	70	70	73	279	48,400
Christopher Hickman	70	72	70	68	280	33,600
Taeyoung Kang	69	71	69	71	280	33,600
Matthew Negri	69	69	69	73	280	33,600
John Young Kim	70	68	72	71	281	28,000
Christopher Wood	69	70	70	72	281	28,000
Guozhen Xu	70	68	70	74	282	25,600
Charlie Netzel	72	68	67	76	283	24,000
Henry Westmoreland	67	72	72	73	284	21,600
Toks Pedro	69	72	69	74	284	21,600

Suzhou Open

Jinji Lake Golf Club, Suzhou, Jiangsu
Par 36-36–72; 7,291 yards

June 13-16
purse, CN¥1,600,000

	SCORES				TOTAL	MONEY
Cyril Bouniol	69	66	66	69	270	CN¥288,000
Trevor Sluman	73	67	66	65	271	172,800
Kenta Endo	63	71	70	69	273	92,800
Niall Turner	70	65	69	69	273	92,800
Michael Perras	70	71	68	65	274	58,400
Stephen Lewton	70	68	69	67	274	58,400
Matt Gilchrest	67	66	69	72	274	58,400
Max McGreevy	67	73	70	65	275	44,800
Gunn Charoenkul	69	72	68	66	275	44,800
John Young Kim	70	67	70	68	275	44,800
Myles Creighton	67	70	67	71	275	44,800
Peter Campbell	73	70	67	66	276	33,600
Frederick Wedel	70	69	70	67	276	33,600
Patrick Cover	72	68	66	70	276	33,600
Corey Shaun	69	75	66	67	277	27,200
Charlie Netzel	68	68	69	72	277	27,200
Daewon Kim	72	69	63	73	277	27,200
Huilin Zhang	73	68	69	68	278	22,400
Joey Lane	74	65	70	69	278	22,400
Enqi Liang [A]	68	72	68	70	278	
Samuel Del Val	70	67	67	74	278	22,400

Huangshan Championship

Hidden Tiger Golf Club, Huangsham, Anhui
Par 36-36–72; 7,288 yards
(Tournament reduced to 54 holes—rain.)

June 20-23
purse, CN¥1,600,000

	SCORES			TOTAL	MONEY
Zhengkai Bai	69	68	67	204	CN¥288,000
David Kocher	65	68	73	206	172,800
Guxin Chen [A]	68	69	70	207	
Sejun Yoon	68	71	70	209	83,200
Max McGreevy	69	68	72	209	83,200
Luke Kwon	69	67	73	209	83,200

520 / ASIA/JAPAN TOURS

	SCORES			TOTAL	MONEY
Joey Lane	75	69	66	210	55,600
Gunn Charoenkul	69	74	67	210	55,600
Bowen Xiao	73	70	68	211	41,600
Ryann Ree	72	71	68	211	41,600
Koki Ishihara	74	68	69	211	41,600
Brad Gehl	68	70	73	211	41,600
Woojin Jung	67	70	74	211	41,600
Dinggen Chen	67	70	74	211	41,600
Corey Shaun	73	69	70	212	29,600
Tuxuan Wu	69	71	72	212	29,600
Guozhen Xu	73	68	72	213	26,400
Douglas Quinones	66	73	74	213	26,400
James Marchesani	73	71	70	214	21,600
Abdul Hadi	73	72	69	214	21,600
Suzuchiyo Ishida	72	70	72	214	21,600
Stuart Macdonald	72	70	72	214	21,600

Guangzhou Open

Nansha Golf Club, Guangdong
Par 35-34–69; 6,573 yards
(Tournament reduced to 36 holes—rain.)

July 18-21
purse, CN¥1,600,000

	SCORES		TOTAL	MONEY
Max McGreevy	62	67	129	CN¥288,000
Trevor Sluman	64	67	131	172,800
David Kocher	66	66	132	68,400
Brad Gehl	64	68	132	68,400
Cyril Bouniol	64	68	132	68,400
Kenta Endo	66	66	132	68,400
Cheng Jin	68	64	132	68,400
Aaron Wilkin	64	68	132	68,400
Jeffrey Kang	67	66	133	46,400
John Young Kim	68	66	134	34,285
Zhengkai Bai	67	67	134	34,285
Nick Latimer	69	65	134	34,285
Matt Gilchrest	67	67	134	34,285
Frederick Wedel	67	67	134	34,285
Woojin Jung	67	67	134	34,285
Charlie Netzel	70	64	134	34,285
Aaron Du [A]	66	68	134	34,285
Aron Zemmer	68	67	135	24,000
Yinong Yang	68	67	135	24,000
Weihsuan Wang	67	68	135	24,000

Dongguan Open

Mission Hills Dongguan Golf Club, Norman Course, Dongguan
Par 36-36–72; 7,228 yards
(Tournament reduced to 36 holes—rain.)

July 35-28
purse, CN¥1,600,000

	SCORES		TOTAL	MONEY
Joey Lane	62	68	130	CN¥288,000
Yuwa Kosaihira	67	66	133	172,800
Richard Jung	66	68	134	92,800
Masamichi Uehira	67	67	134	92,800
Charlie Netzel	70	65	135	60,800

	SCORES	TOTAL	MONEY
Cyril Bouniol	68 67	135	60,800
Stuart Macdonald	67 69	136	48,200
Chiehpo Lee	69 67	136	48,200
David Kocher	68 68	136	48,200
Wenyi Huang	70 66	136	48,200
Martin Kim	71 66	137	30,800
Enqi Liang [A]	71 66	137	
Taeyoung Kang	70 67	137	30,800
Benjamin Lein	70 67	137	30,800
Jaeil Kim	69 68	137	30,800
Quincy Quek	66 71	137	30,800
Samuel Del Val	70 67	137	30,800
Gunn Charoenkul	71 66	137	30,800
Luke Kwon	66 71	137	30,800
John Young Kim	70 68	138	20,080
Douglas Quinones	68 70	138	20,080
Matt Gilchrest	70 68	138	20,080
Kevin Techakanokboon	69 69	138	20,080
Wocheng Ye [A]	67 71	138	

Haikou Classic

Mission Hills, Sandbelt Trails Course, Haikou, Hainan
Par 35-36–71; 7,146 yards

September 12-15
purse, CN¥1,600,000

	SCORES	TOTAL	MONEY
Quincy Quek	65 67 63 73	268	CN¥288,000
Zhengkai Bai	72 66 66 66	270	172,800
Weihsuan Wang	66 71 68 66	271	83,200
James Marchesani	69 66 68 68	271	83,200
Brad Gehl	68 66 68 69	271	83,200
William Harrold	74 66 66 66	272	51,800
Suteepat Prateeptienchai	68 73 62 69	272	51,800
Charlie Dann	70 68 65 69	272	51,800
Chiehpo Lee	67 66 68 71	272	51,800
Max McGreevy	70 72 67 64	273	40,000
Charlie Netzel	72 64 68 69	273	40,000
Ryan Siegler	68 66 69 70	273	40,000
Christopher Wood	67 67 71 69	274	33,600
Ryann Ree	70 68 68 69	275	28,800
Yuwa Kosaihira	71 69 66 69	275	28,800
Bryden Macpherson	71 67 68 69	275	28,800
Kenta Endo	74 69 66 67	276	23,200
Jaeil Kim	69 71 69 67	276	23,200
Richard Jung	71 69 67 69	276	23,200
Kevin Techakanokboon	71 70 71 64	276	23,200

Zhuzhou Classic

Xiangshui Bay Golf Club, Zhuzhou, China
Par 36-36–72; 7,193 yards

September 19-22
purse, CN¥1,600,000

	SCORES	TOTAL	MONEY
Motin Yeung	67 69 71 67	274	CN¥288,000
Peter Campbell	74 66 70 65	275	140,800
Keisuke Otawa	69 69 69 68	275	140,800
Matthew Cheung	66 72 68 71	277	76,800

	SCORES				TOTAL	MONEY
Frederick Wedel	70	69	74	65	278	60,800
Cyril Bouniol	70	70	69	69	278	60,800
Max McGreevy	69	67	70	73	279	53,600
Richard Jung	71	66	72	71	280	49,600
Luke Kwon	68	70	75	68	281	40,000
Callum Tarren	70	69	72	70	281	40,000
Samuel Del Val	69	72	69	71	281	40,000
John Young Kim	68	70	71	72	281	40,000
Aaron Wilkin	68	70	70	73	281	40,000
Stuart Macdonald	71	72	69	70	282	28,800
Joey Lane	75	68	67	72	282	28,800
Yuwa Kosaihira	65	71	69	77	282	28,800
Zhengkai Bai	73	69	71	70	283	23,200
Guozhen Xu	72	68	72	71	283	23,200
Suteepat Prateeptienchai	64	72	75	72	283	23,200
Trevor Sluman	71	73	71	68	283	23,200

Macau Championship

Caesar's Golf Club Macau, Macao
Par 36-35–71; 6,913 yards

October 10-13
purse, CN¥2,100,000

	SCORES				TOTAL	MONEY
Justin Shin	63	62	66	68	259	CN¥378,000
Zecheng Dou	69	66	62	65	262	226,800
Richard Jung	65	67	66	67	265	142,800
Cyril Bouniol	66	66	67	68	267	100,800
Suteepat Prateeptienchai	65	72	67	64	268	73,762
Luke Kwon	66	71	66	65	268	73,762
Shotaro Ban	65	71	66	66	268	73,762
Aaron Wilkin	66	67	67	68	268	73,762
Zhengkai Bai	67	67	69	66	269	56,700
Velten Meyer	70	65	67	67	269	56,700
Charlie Netzel	67	63	70	69	269	56,700
Benjamin Lein	67	67	71	65	270	46,200
Yanwei Liu	67	68	66	69	270	46,200
Stuart Macdonald	69	67	67	68	271	37,800
Yechun Yuan	69	69	65	68	271	37,800
Myles Creighton	73	65	65	68	271	37,800
Brad Gehl	68	66	72	66	272	26,565
Weihsuan Wang	68	74	64	66	272	26,565
Kevin Yuan	70	68	68	66	272	26,565
Max McCardle	70	70	65	67	272	26,565
Corey Shaun	67	66	72	67	272	26,565
Ryan Siegler	68	69	68	67	272	26,565
Ryann Ree	70	68	71	63	272	26,565
Tim Stewart	67	66	70	69	272	26,565

China Golf Association Tour

Bo Ao Open

Dongyu Island, BFA Course, Bo'ao, Hainan
Par 36-36–72

April 18-21
purse, CN¥700,000

	SCORES				TOTAL	MONEY
Maverick Antcliff	66	69	69	68	272	CN¥126,000
Yung-Lung Lin	74	69	69	66	278	75,600
K.P. Lin	71	73	64	71	279	36,400
Matthew Negri	71	69	72	67	279	36,400
Yechun Yuan	73	70	67	69	279	36,400
Bowen Xiao	67	67	71	75	280	23,450
Yanwei Liu	68	72	67	73	280	23,450
Chieh-Po Lee	73	69	72	66	280	23,450
Bryden Macpherson	71	72	69	69	281	20,300
Wenyi Huang	69	71	70	73	283	18,200
Lawrence Ting	72	70	74	67	283	18,200
Yuxin Lin [A]	75	70	66	73	284	
Andreas Gronkvist	72	70	73	69	284	16,100
Guozhen Xu	71	74	71	69	285	14,000
Kieran Muir	70	77	71	67	285	14,000
Daxing Jin	71	71	71	73	286	11,900
Huilin Zhang	72	67	75	72	286	11,900
Yu-Chen Yeh	69	71	74	72	286	11,900
Chinnarat Phadungsil	68	72	72	75	287	8,520
Zihao Chen	71	72	71	73	287	8,520
Hongfu Wu	69	70	71	77	287	8,520
Cristiano Terragni	72	66	77	72	287	8,520
Shun Yat Hak	70	69	70	78	287	8,520
Wei Lin	69	75	72	71	287	8,520
Nicolas Paez	69	75	70	73	287	8,520

Shenzhou Peninsula Open

The Dunes Golf Club, Wanning, Hainan
Par 34-38–72

April 25-28
purse, CN¥700,000

	SCORES			TOTAL	MONEY
Maverick Antcliff	71	69	66	66	272	CN¥126,000
K.P. Lin	69	68	76	63	276	52,266.67
Cheng Jin	69	73	65	69	276	52,266.67
Kieran Muir	72	67	67	70	276	52,266.67
Bryden Macpherson	74	71	64	70	279	28,000
Zeming He	72	67	70	71	280	24,325
Jackson Dick	65	69	71	75	280	24,325
Linqiang Li [A]	74	72	69	66	281	
Zihao Chen	71	69	69	73	282	18,900
Xuefeng Yao	74	68	71	69	282	18,900
Xuewen Luo	72	75	67	68	282	18,900
Kevin Yuan	71	68	69	74	282	18,900
Kade McBride	70	71	71	70	282	18,900
Daxing Jin	72	69	70	72	283	13,533.33
Teng Kao	76	70	69	68	283	13,533.33

	SCORES				TOTAL	MONEY
Guozhen Xu	76	72	68	67	283	13,533.33
Zheng Ouyang	75	71	69	69	284	10,850
Alex Belt	74	74	69	67	284	10,850
Cory Crawford	75	69	68	72	284	10,850
Di Wu	72	72	67	73	284	10,850

Wuhan Optics Valley Open

Wuhan Yishan Golf Club, Wuhan, Hubei
Par 36-36–72

May 29-June 1
purse, CN¥700,000

	SCORES				TOTAL	MONEY
Woojin Jung	65	71	71	67	274	CN¥126,000
Sam Chien	71	70	68	69	278	75,600
Maverick Antcliff	71	73	70	65	279	47,600
Huilin Zhang	69	71	68	73	281	30,800
Kade McBride	69	76	76	60	281	30,800
K.P. Lin	72	70	70	70	282	25,200
Lloyd Jefferson Go	74	70	71	68	283	23,450
Yanwei Liu	75	73	68	68	284	21,700
Aron Zemmer	70	72	71	72	285	20,300
Zihan She	72	70	73	71	286	18,200
Troy Moses	69	75	77	65	286	18,200
Guxin Chen [A]	69	72	73	73	287	
Yung-Lung Lin	71	69	78	70	288	14,175
Zehao Liu	73	68	75	72	288	14,175
Linqiang Li [A]	75	70	70	73	288	
Cory Oride	72	75	72	69	288	14,175
Yu-Chen Yeh	75	70	76	67	288	14,175
Bowen Xiao	70	73	74	72	289	10,850
Cheng Jin	74	76	65	74	289	10,850
Yuxin Lin [A]	76	71	67	75	289	
Jaewon Lee	76	69	71	73	289	10,850
Nicolas Paez	75	70	69	75	289	10,850

Lushan Open

Lushan International Golf Club, Jiujiang City, Jiangxi
Par 36-35–71

June 6-9
purse, CN¥700,000

	SCORES				TOTAL	MONEY
Shun Yat Hak	67	71	66	67	271	CN¥126,000
Huilin Zhang	72	72	64	66	274	75,600
Guxin Chen [A]	71	68	70	66	275	
Linqiang Li [A]	69	72	69	66	276	
Hongfu Wu	69	72	67	69	277	40,600
Nicolas Paez	69	75	67	66	277	40,600
Yung-Lung Lin	70	69	69	71	279	26,600
Chi Huang	73	66	71	69	279	26,600
Maverick Antcliff	71	70	70	69	280	23,450
Yanwei Liu	70	74	69	68	281	21,000
Zihao Chen	69	69	76	67	281	21,000
Sam Chien	70	76	69	67	282	16,800
K.P. Lin	69	73	68	72	282	16,800
Bowen Xiao	74	71	71	66	282	16,800
Shaocai He	72	67	72	71	282	16,800
Jia Zhang	72	69	72	70	283	12,600

	SCORES				TOTAL	MONEY
Yilong Chen	68	74	72	69	283	12,600
Enqi Liang (A)	70	73	68	72	283	
Di Wu	66	75	71	71	283	12,600
Wenyi Huang	75	66	69	74	284	10,500
Aron Zemmer	71	71	70	72	284	10,500
Kade McBride	72	71	69	72	284	10,500

Beijing Open

Beijing Fragrant Hills International Golf Club, Beijing
Par 36-36–72

June 27-30
purse, CN¥700,000

	SCORES				TOTAL	MONEY
Maverick Antcliff	69	65	72	67	273	CN¥126,000
Bryden Macpherson	67	70	72	68	277	46,200
Guowu Zhou	65	70	72	70	277	46,200
Cheng Jin	71	69	70	67	277	46,200
Andreas Gronkvist	68	68	69	72	277	46,200
Zihong Zhang	66	74	69	69	278	23,450
Kade McBride	73	70	67	68	278	23,450
Yushi Ito	70	67	71	70	278	23,450
Shaocai He	66	71	70	72	279	18,200
Xuefeng Yao	72	67	69	71	279	18,200
Oliver Roberts	67	67	75	70	279	18,200
Yu-Chen Yeh	68	67	74	70	279	18,200
Hongfu Wu	66	64	75	75	280	14,700
Sam Chien	67	71	70	73	281	11,200
Wenyi Huang	69	67	77	68	281	11,200
Jin Zhang	68	65	74	74	281	11,200
Yan Sun	70	66	73	72	281	11,200
Chieh-Po Lee	66	69	72	74	281	11,200
Chi Huang	73	71	69	68	281	11,200
Nicolas Paez	72	70	69	70	281	11,200

Tianjin Binhai Forest Open

Tianjin Binhai Forest Golf Club, Tianjin
Par 36-36–72

July 4-7
purse, CN¥700,000

	SCORES				TOTAL	MONEY
Nicolas Paez	66	69	70	66	271	CN¥126,000
Guowu Zhou	71	63	70	72	276	61,600
Yanwei Liu	68	68	69	71	276	61,600
Suteepat Prateeptienchai	69	72	68	68	277	33,600
Haimeng Chao	67	73	72	70	282	25,550
Kevin Yuan	73	66	69	74	282	25,550
Woojin Jung	66	72	76	68	282	25,550
Cheng Jin	72	73	70	68	283	21,700
Yuxin Lin (A)	68	71	75	69	283	
Chinnarat Phadungsil	67	74	72	71	284	18,900
Zihong Zhang	70	70	72	72	284	18,900
Linqiang Li (A)	71	71	70	72	284	
Cory Crawford	70	70	72	72	284	18,900
Changlei Zhang	78	70	71	66	285	14,700
Yilong Chen	68	72	76	69	285	14,700
Beomsoo Kim	68	70	73	74	285	14,700
Maverick Antcliff	75	71	68	72	286	11,900

526 / ASIA/JAPAN TOURS

	SCORES				TOTAL	MONEY
Kieran Muir	68	73	74	71	286	11,900
Miki Yamaji	66	74	70	76	286	11,900
Bowen Xiao	71	72	75	69	287	8,520
Daxing Jin	77	68	72	70	287	8,520
Jin Zhang	71	72	71	73	287	8,520
Xuefeng Yao	69	71	76	71	287	8,520
Yinong Yang	74	72	73	68	287	8,520
Shang Zhi	69	72	73	73	287	8,520
Enqi Liang [A]	76	72	69	70	287	
Fraser Wilkin	70	71	77	69	287	8,520

Huangshan Open

Huangshan Golf, Huangshan, Anhui
Par 36-36–72; 7,182 yards

August 22-25
purse, CN¥700,000

	SCORES				TOTAL	MONEY
Kieran Muir	70	70	67	72	279	CN¥126,000
Maverick Antcliff	68	72	72	68	280	75,600
Yang Kuang [A]	71	69	70	70	280	
Yongxuan Yin	73	65	72	71	281	47,600
Guxin Chen [A]	72	70	70	70	282	
Linqiang Li [A]	69	70	69	74	282	
Lloyd Jefferson Go	66	69	72	75	282	30,800
Suteepat Prateeptienchai	69	76	65	72	282	30,800
Andreas Gronkvist	72	69	71	71	283	25,200
Teng Kao	72	74	67	71	284	21,816.67
Aron Zemmer	73	72	69	70	284	21,816.67
Beomsoo Kim	71	72	71	70	284	21,816.67
Yanwei Liu	68	74	67	76	285	18,900
Bo Peng [A]	70	68	71	76	285	
Enqi Liang [A]	69	77	66	74	286	
Hsiang-Hao Huang	67	73	72	74	286	16,800
Yushi Ito	70	74	67	75	286	16,800
Zheng Ouyang	71	73	75	69	288	14,000
Kevin Yuan	75	73	70	70	288	14,000
Chinnarat Phadungsil	71	71	73	74	289	11,550
Hongfu Wu	73	74	69	73	289	11,550
Miki Yamaji	73	73	74	69	289	11,550
Ter-Chang Wang	71	70	68	80	289	11,550

Hangzhou International Championship

Fuchun Resort, Zhejiang, Hangzhou
Par 35-35–70

August 22-25
purse, CN¥700,000

	SCORES				TOTAL	MONEY
Haimeng Chao	68	67	69	70	274	CN¥126,000
Suteepat Prateeptienchai	69	73	67	66	275	75,600
Chieh-Po Lee	72	67	65	73	277	47,600
Huilin Zhang	67	73	70	68	278	27,562.50
Kevin Yuan	68	73	69	68	278	27,562.50
Cory Crawford	72	72	66	68	278	27,562.50
Kento Nakai	70	70	67	71	278	27,562.50
Zheng Ouyang	68	63	74	74	279	20,300
Andreas Gronkvist	69	71	66	73	279	20,300
Maverick Antcliff	74	69	71	65	279	20,300

	SCORES			TOTAL	MONEY
Guxin Chen [A]	70	69	71	70	280	
Kade McBride	69	70	73	68	280	16,800
Yushi Ito	68	65	76	71	280	16,800
Yang Kuang [A]	71	69	70	70	280	
Zihan She	70	66	76	69	281	14,700
Daxing Jin	72	72	68	70	282	11,900
Zihao Chen	74	67	74	67	282	11,900
Yung-Lung Lin	70	68	70	74	282	11,900
Jaewon Lee	71	68	71	72	282	11,900
Nicolas Paez	72	65	76	69	282	11,900

Hunan Taohuayuan Open

Taohuayuan International Golf Club, Changde, Hunan
Par 36-36–72

September 5-8
purse, CN¥700,000

	SCORES			TOTAL	MONEY
Huilin Zhang	69	68	66	69	272	CN¥126,000
Yung-Lung Lin	68	70	70	68	276	75,600
Kevin Yuan	73	70	70	66	279	47,600
Aron Zemmer	69	73	71	67	280	27,562.5
Maverick Antcliff	66	75	69	70	280	27,562.5
Woojin Jung	74	67	70	69	280	27,562.5
Kade McBride	67	70	72	71	280	27,562.5
Hongfu Wu	69	73	68	71	281	21,700
Guxin Chen [A]	71	73	71	66	281	
Zeming He	72	70	68	72	282	18,900
Lawrence Ting	73	66	73	70	282	18,900
Kieran Muir	70	69	75	68	282	18,900
Haimeng Chao	70	71	73	69	283	16,100
Jin Zhang	74	71	72	67	284	14,000
Fraser Wilkin	71	72	72	69	284	14,000
Zihao Chen	71	72	68	74	285	11,900
Yongxuan Yin	72	73	68	72	285	11,900
Minsu Jung	74	71	70	70	285	11,900
Dianchao Wu [A]	72	68	72	73	285	
Bryden Macpherson	70	68	71	77	286	9,128
Zheng Ouyang	70	71	76	69	286	9,128
Tian Yuan	68	73	73	72	286	9,128
Yinong Yang	73	70	72	71	286	9,128
Joya Kimbara	76	76	68	66	286	9,128

Hainan Open

Sanya Luhuitou Golf Club, Sanya, Hainan
Par 36-36–72; 7,166 yards

October 17-20
purse, US$350,000

	SCORES			TOTAL	MONEY
Francesco Laporta	69	71	64	70	274	CN¥395,810.83
Robin Roussel	69	68	70	68	275	272,119.95
Sebastian Heisele	70	70	68	68	276	160,798.19
Wil Besseling	70	67	69	70	276	160,798.19
Yanwei Liu	71	66	72	69	278	111,321.84
Adrian Meronk	72	71	65	70	278	111,321.84
Bowen Xiao	69	68	74	68	279	62,340.19
Antoine Rozner	65	75	71	68	279	62,340.19
Ben Stow	69	73	66	71	279	62,340.19

	SCORES				TOTAL	MONEY
Richard Bland	70	67	71	71	279	62,340.19
Rasmus Hojgaard	73	70	70	66	279	62,340.19
Nicolai Von Dellingshausen	70	72	71	67	280	47,002.58
Oscar Lengden	72	72	69	68	281	43,291.79
Pep Angles	72	70	71	68	281	43,291.79
Bryden Macpherson	72	67	75	68	282	32,336.34
Cheng Jin	70	72	73	67	282	32,336.34
Maverick Antcliff	71	71	71	69	282	32,336.34
Ricardo Santos	73	69	68	72	282	32,336.34
Jack Senior	72	71	72	67	282	32,336.34
Calum Hill	71	70	73	68	282	32,336.34
Jaewoong Eom	69	68	77	68	282	32,336.34
Zhengkai Bai	70	68	76	69	283	24,243.39
Aron Zemmer	70	71	70	73	284	23,501.25
Fraser Wilkin	73	70	68	73	284	23,501.25
Matthew Baldwin	71	74	71	69	285	21,769.61
Oliver Lindell	70	72	71	72	285	21,769.61
Yu-Chen Yeh	70	68	72	75	285	21,769.61
Damien Perrier	68	70	76	71	285	21,769.61
Dave Coupland	71	73	72	69	285	21,769.61

Foshan Open

Foshan Golf Club, Shishan, Foshan
Par 36-36–72; 7,117 yards

October 24-27
purse, US$500,000

	SCORES				TOTAL	MONEY
Zhengkai Bai	71	63	66	65	265	CN¥565,681.86
Zecheng Dou	71	67	64	67	269	388,906.24
Calum Hill	68	66	68	68	270	247,485.77
Alexander Knappe	65	65	71	70	271	194,453.12
Richard Bland	68	66	69	68	271	194,453.12
Adrian Meronk	68	66	69	69	272	117,850.39
Ben Stow	64	69	69	70	272	117,850.39
Benjamin Poke	70	70	65	67	272	117,850.39
Christofer Blomstrand	71	65	69	68	273	77,781.25
Ricardo Santos	67	66	67	73	273	77,781.25
Matthew Jordan	66	67	73	67	273	77,781.25
Cory Crawford	66	65	73	70	274	65,406.95
Lorenzo Scalise	68	70	67	69	274	65,406.95
Yanwei Liu	67	70	69	69	275	56,568.2
Francesco Laporta	73	65	68	69	275	56,568.2
Roope Kakko	66	71	68	70	275	56,568.2
K.P. Lin	70	70	71	65	276	40,355.3
Bowen Xiao	72	64	70	70	276	40,355.3
Kevin Yuan	68	73	67	68	276	40,355.3
Guxin Chen [A]	69	72	66	69	276	
Sebastian Heisele	69	68	70	69	276	40,355.3
Ewen Ferguson	69	70	67	70	276	40,355.3
Sebastian Garcia Rodriguez	68	71	68	69	276	40,355.3
Connor Syme	70	69	68	69	276	40,355.3
Aron Zemmer	66	72	65	74	277	32,173.17
Garrick Porteous	72	66	69	70	277	32,173.17
Rhys Enoch	75	66	68	68	277	32,173.17
Bryce Easton	68	73	68	68	277	32,173.17

China Tour Championship

Kingrun Nanshan Golf Club, Chongqing
Par 36-36–72; 7,281 yards

November 28-December 1
purse, CN¥1,200,000

	SCORES				TOTAL	MONEY
Suteepat Prateeptienchai	65	71	68	68	272	CN¥216,000
Haotong Li	70	68	66	68	272	129,600
(Prateeptienchai defeated Li on second playoff hole.)						
Maverick Antcliff	71	66	67	73	277	81,600
Cheng Jin	71	71	68	69	279	52,800
Huilin Zhang	71	70	69	69	279	52,800
Yu-Chen Yeh	68	68	71	73	280	43,200
K.P. Lin	68	71	73	69	281	40,200
Sam Chien	65	74	70	73	282	37,200
Yechun Yuan	71	71	71	70	283	33,600
Ashun Wu	71	72	69	71	283	33,600
Wenyi Huang	71	71	73	69	284	24,600
Zihao Chen	75	68	71	70	284	24,600
Teng Kao	71	71	70	72	284	24,600
Zihong Zhang	73	68	71	72	284	24,600
Han Xue	72	72	70	70	284	24,600
Guxin Chen	75	68	72	69	284	24,600
Haimeng Chao	68	71	70	76	285	18,600
Jianfeng Ye	72	73	68	72	285	18,600
Yanwei Liu	74	69	71	72	286	15,060
Changlei Zhang	72	71	68	75	286	15,060
Woojin Jung	73	73	72	68	286	15,060
Di Wu	70	71	69	76	286	15,060

Japan Tour

SMBC Singapore Open

See Asian Tour section.

Token Homemate Cup

Token Tado Country Club, Nagoya, Mie
Par 35-36–71; 7,081 yards

April 18-21
purse, ¥130,000,000

	SCORES				TOTAL	MONEY
Brendan Jones	65	69	71	64	269	¥26,000,000
Matthew Griffin	70	68	67	65	270	13,000,000
Koumei Oda	65	67	71	68	271	8,840,000
Akio Sadakata	63	71	72	66	272	5,373,333
Sanghyun Park	68	69	68	67	272	5,373,333
Kazuki Higa	69	67	69	67	272	5,373,333
Won Joon Lee	68	68	70	67	273	4,290,000
Yoshinori Fujimoto	67	70	72	65	274	3,413,800
Yuta Ikeda	65	70	73	66	274	3,413,800
Seung-Hyuk Kim	67	70	70	67	274	3,413,800
Dylan Perry	66	68	72	68	274	3,413,800
David Oh	63	69	71	71	274	3,413,800
Naoto Nakanishi	66	73	70	66	275	2,262,000
Gunn Charoenkul	69	69	70	67	275	2,262,000
Rikuya Hoshino	65	68	74	68	275	2,262,000
Ryuko Tokimatsu	70	68	69	68	275	2,262,000
David Bransdon	72	67	68	68	275	2,262,000
Shunya Takeyasu	69	70	71	67	277	1,373,272
Michael Hendry	72	68	69	68	277	1,373,272
Brad Kennedy	68	73	69	67	277	1,373,272
Shaun Norris	72	69	69	67	277	1,373,272
Paul Peterson	69	69	71	68	277	1,373,272
Shugo Imahira	69	71	71	66	277	1,373,272
Seungsu Han	69	67	71	70	277	1,373,272
Wenchong Liang	68	69	70	70	277	1,373,272
Kyungtae Kim	70	68	68	71	277	1,373,272
Sung-Joon Park	66	73	66	72	277	1,373,272
Daijiro Izumida	67	67	70	73	277	1,373,272

The Crowns

Nagoya Golf Club, Wago Course, Togo, Aichi
Par 35-35–70; 6,557 yards

May 2-5
purse, ¥120,000,000

	SCORES				TOTAL	MONEY
Katsumasa Miyamoto	66	69	67	69	271	¥24,000,000
Shugo Imahira	70	65	71	66	272	12,000,000
Matthew Griffin	72	62	71	68	273	6,960,000
Junggon Hwang	72	63	68	70	273	6,960,000
Rikuya Hoshino	67	69	72	66	274	3,878,000
Shingo Katayama	68	71	68	67	274	3,878,000

	SCORES				TOTAL	MONEY
Anthony Quayle	67	69	70	68	274	3,878,000
Hiroyuki Fujita	69	71	67	67	274	3,878,000
Peter Karmis	66	70	65	73	274	3,878,000
Akio Sadakata	66	70	67	71	274	3,878,000
Shota Akiyoshi	72	67	68	68	275	2,664,000
Chan Kim	72	66	68	69	275	2,664,000
Atomu Shigenaga	69	66	69	71	275	2,664,000
Takumi Kanaya [A]	70	66	71	69	276	
Won Joon Lee	69	70	70	68	277	2,064,000
Daijiro Izumida	68	66	73	70	277	2,064,000
Gunn Charoenkul	71	69	66	71	277	2,064,000
Hiroshi Iwata	71	74	67	66	278	1,764,000
Brad Kennedy	70	65	69	74	278	1,764,000
Juvic Pagunsan	74	69	70	66	279	1,368,000
Seungsu Han	71	67	72	69	279	1,368,000
Taihei Sato	68	72	70	69	279	1,368,000
Mikumu Horikawa	76	69	65	69	279	1,368,000
Tomoharu Otsuki	71	67	71	70	279	1,368,000
Kazuki Higa	67	69	72	71	279	1,368,000

Asia-Pacific Diamond Cup

Sobu Country Club, Sobu Course, Chiba
Par 35-36–71; 7,333 yards

May 9-12
purse, ¥150,000,000

	SCORES				TOTAL	MONEY
Yosuke Asaji	69	72	68	72	281	¥30,000,000
Ren Yonezawa [A]	69	74	71	68	282	
Micah Lauren Shin	71	67	72	72	282	16,500,000
Y.E. Yang	69	71	72	71	283	9,525,000
Denzel Ieremia	76	68	66	73	283	9,525,000
Dongkyu Jang	72	69	73	70	284	5,775,000
Scott Vincent	71	73	68	72	284	5,775,000
Hosung Choi	73	72	71	69	285	3,435,000
Tomoyo Ikemura	68	72	73	72	285	3,435,000
Prayad Marksaeng	70	72	71	72	285	3,435,000
Wei-Chih Lu	71	71	71	72	285	3,435,000
Jinichiro Kozuma	74	67	71	73	285	3,435,000
Sihwan Kim	72	74	71	69	286	2,105,000
Sadom Kaewkanjana	71	74	71	70	286	2,105,000
Kunihiro Kamii	76	68	71	71	286	2,105,000
Sanghyun Park	72	73	71	71	287	1,584,000
Jack Harrison	72	74	73	68	287	1,584,000
Shunya Takeyasu	75	70	71	71	287	1,584,000
Matthew Griffin	73	71	70	73	287	1,584,000
Ryuko Tokimatsu	72	72	69	74	287	1,584,000
Shugo Imahira	70	72	77	69	288	1,350,000
Shingo Katayama	73	69	74	73	289	1,233,000
Siddikur Rahman	74	72	72	71	289	1,233,000
Won Joon Lee	72	72	74	71	289	1,233,000
Jbe' Kruger	72	72	69	76	289	1,233,000
Shota Akiyoshi	73	72	68	76	289	1,233,000

Kansai Open

Koma Country Club, Nara
Par 36-36–72; 7,043 yards

May 23-26
purse, ¥70,000,000

	SCORES				TOTAL	MONEY
Tomoharu Otsuki	73	65	66	65	269	¥14,000,000
Rikuya Hoshino	67	69	70	63	269	7,000,000
(Otsuki defeated Hoshino on fourth playoff hole.)						
Hyunwoo Ryu	66	67	69	70	272	4,760,000
Angelo Que	70	69	69	65	273	3,080,000
Seungsu Han	71	63	67	72	273	3,080,000
Gunn Charoenkul	70	70	66	68	274	2,520,000
Koumei Oda	72	69	69	65	275	2,063,250
Anthony Quayle	76	66	68	65	275	2,063,250
Ryutaro Nagano	70	72	67	66	275	2,063,250
Shugo Imahira	66	69	71	69	275	2,063,250
Takaya Onoda	70	71	71	64	276	1,554,000
Terumichi Kakazu	71	71	66	68	276	1,554,000
Naoto Nakanishi	69	66	68	73	276	1,554,000
Kunihiro Kamii	70	69	71	67	277	1,239,000
Ryuko Tokimatsu	71	70	66	70	277	1,239,000
Junggon Hwang	70	70	73	65	278	1,002,400
Panuphol Pittayarat	74	70	68	66	278	1,002,400
David Bransdon	71	70	69	68	278	1,002,400
Matthew Griffin	72	69	69	68	278	1,002,400
Daisuke Matsubara	68	68	73	69	278	1,002,400
Young-Woong Kim	71	71	70	67	279	742,000
Takashi Ogiso	73	69	74	63	279	742,000
Tomohiro Umeyama	70	70	69	70	279	742,000
Tomoyo Ikemura	69	68	70	72	279	742,000
Takanori Konishi	70	73	69	68	280	588,000
Mikumu Horikawa	70	71	71	68	280	588,000
Hiroyuki Fujita	66	76	68	70	280	588,000
Jazz Janewattananond	70	70	69	71	280	588,000

Gateway to The Open Mizuno Open

Royal Golf Club, Hokota, Ibaraki
Par 36-36–72; 8,016 yards

May 30-June 2
purse, ¥100,000,000

	SCORES				TOTAL	MONEY
Yuta Ikeda	70	74	66	71	281	¥20,000,000
Chan Kim	69	73	69	71	282	10,000,000
Sanghyun Park	74	71	72	67	284	5,800,000
Gunn Charoenkul	69	73	74	68	284	5,800,000
Young-Woong Kim	70	68	79	69	286	3,487,500
Jazz Janewattananond	73	73	69	71	286	3,487,500
Ryosuke Kinoshita	69	73	72	72	286	3,487,500
Kyungtae Kim	67	73	72	74	286	3,487,500
Y.E. Yang	69	73	78	67	287	2,620,000
Ryutaro Nagano	69	70	74	74	287	2,620,000
Shugo Imahira	69	67	77	74	287	2,620,000
Scott Vincent	71	73	75	69	288	2,120,000
Konosuke Nakazato	70	72	76	70	288	2,120,000
Seong-Hyeon Kim	72	74	73	70	289	1,485,000
Tatsuya Kodai	70	72	76	71	289	1,485,000
Toshinori Muto	74	70	73	72	289	1,485,000
Yuki Inamori	71	74	71	73	289	1,485,000
Kazuki Higa	72	70	73	74	289	1,485,000

	SCORES	TOTAL	MONEY
Poom Saksansin	73 71 71 74	289	1,485,000
Dylan Perry	67 73 73 76	289	1,485,000
Won Joon Lee	70 70 72 77	289	1,485,000
Brad Kennedy	74 70 75 72	291	1,060,000
Mikumu Horikawa	74 72 71 74	291	1,060,000
Hiroshi Iwata	71 72 77 72	292	800,000
Tatsunori Nukaga	73 72 76 71	292	800,000
Ryosuke Narimatsu	75 69 76 72	292	800,000
Anthony Quayle	71 72 75 74	292	800,000
Hyung-Sung Kim	72 75 75 70	292	800,000
Yoseop Seo	72 72 74 74	292	800,000
Shaun Norris	74 72 72 74	292	800,000
Rikuya Hoshino	73 73 72 74	292	800,000

Japan Golf Tour Championship

Shishido Hills Country Club, Kasama, Ibaraki
Par 36-35–71; 7,387 yards

June 6-9
purse, ¥150,000,000

	SCORES	TOTAL	MONEY
Mikumu Horikawa	66 67 68 68	269	¥30,000,000
Shugo Imahira	67 69 69 68	273	15,000,000
Chan Kim	68 73 71 62	274	8,700,000
Jazz Janewattananond	73 70 64 67	274	8,700,000
Junggon Hwang	76 68 68 64	276	6,000,000
Takashi Iwamoto	70 71 69 67	277	5,175,000
Hyunwoo Ryu	69 68 71 69	277	5,175,000
Koumei Oda	69 69 70 70	278	4,402,500
Gunn Charoenkul	70 65 69 74	278	4,402,500
Ryosuke Kinoshita	73 69 66 71	279	3,780,000
Tomoyo Ikemura	71 69 67 72	279	3,780,000
Mikiya Akutsu	72 71 67 70	280	3,180,000
Brad Kennedy	69 67 72 72	280	3,180,000
Jay Choi	69 70 72 70	281	2,655,000
Shingo Katayama	72 69 69 71	281	2,655,000
Ryuko Tokimatsu	69 72 71 70	282	2,212,500
Kodai Ichihara	70 72 70 70	282	2,212,500
Yuta Ikeda	68 71 72 71	282	2,212,500
Matthew Griffin	72 70 68 72	282	2,212,500
Ryo Ishikawa	73 72 68 70	283	1,770,000
Koki Shiomi	70 75 68 70	283	1,770,000
Rikuya Hoshino	69 69 69 76	283	1,770,000
Taihei Sato	73 70 70 71	284	1,430,000
Brendan Jones	70 73 69 72	284	1,430,000
Tomohiro Umeyama	76 66 69 73	284	1,430,000

Dunlop Srixon Fukushima Open

Grandee Nasushirakawa Golf Club, Nishigo, Fukushima
Par 36-36–72; 6,961 yards
(Fourth round cancelled—rain.)

June 27-30
purse, ¥50,000,000

	SCORES	TOTAL	MONEY
Rikuya Hoshino	67 64 65	196	¥7,500,000
Shota Akiyoshi	70 65 63	198	3,750,000
Jazz Janewattananond	67 66 67	200	2,175,000
Hiroshi Iwata	63 65 72	200	2,175,000

	SCORES			TOTAL	MONEY
Richard Jung	66	70	65	201	1,425,000
Shugo Imahira	67	66	68	201	1,425,000
Toshinori Muto	67	70	65	202	1,065,750
Ryosuke Kinoshita	69	67	66	202	1,065,750
Masaru Takahashi	71	65	66	202	1,065,750
Tomoharu Otsuki	67	68	67	202	1,065,750
Yuki Inamori	65	67	70	202	1,065,750
Naoto Nakanishi	68	68	67	203	729,375
Yosuke Asaji	69	67	67	203	729,375
Mikiya Akutsu	69	66	68	203	729,375
Ren Yonezawa (A)	69	65	69	203	
Ryuji Masaoka	65	67	71	203	729,375
Thanyakon Khrongpha	70	68	66	204	537,000
Arnond Vongvanij	69	68	67	204	537,000
Shunya Takeyasu	68	69	67	204	537,000
I.J. Jang	69	71	64	204	537,000
Shaun Norris	72	63	69	204	537,000
Mikumu Horikawa	69	69	67	205	365,357
Kazuki Higa	69	70	66	205	365,357
Chan Kim	70	68	67	205	365,357
Michael Hendry	70	69	66	205	365,357
Masashi Nishimura	67	69	69	205	365,357
Sushi Ishigaki	68	67	70	205	365,357
Scott Vincent	68	67	70	205	365,357

Japan PGA Championship

Ibusuki Golf Club, Kagoshima
Par 35-35–70; 7,150 yards

July 4-7
purse, ¥150,000,000

	SCORES				TOTAL	MONEY
Ryo Ishikawa	65	67	71	66	269	¥30,000,000
Junggon Hwang	65	67	68	69	269	15,000,000
(Ishikawa defeated Hwang on first playoff hole.)						
Rikuya Hoshino	67	67	67	70	271	10,200,000
Hiroyuki Fujita	65	70	69	68	272	6,200,000
Ryuko Tokimatsu	66	68	65	73	272	6,200,000
Shaun Norris	68	65	69	70	272	6,200,000
Kazuki Higa	71	68	68	66	273	4,421,250
Min-Gyu Cho	67	69	70	67	273	4,421,250
David Bransdon	66	70	68	69	273	4,421,250
Shugo Imahira	66	69	68	70	273	4,421,250
Masanori Kobayashi	71	69	65	69	274	3,480,000
Mikiya Akutsu	70	71	69	64	274	3,480,000
Tatsuya Kodai	67	72	67	69	275	2,880,000
Daisuke Matsubara	66	68	66	75	275	2,880,000
Katsumasa Miyamoto	70	69	70	67	276	2,355,000
Hyung-Sung Kim	67	70	72	67	276	2,355,000
Toru Taniguchi	72	65	68	71	276	2,355,000
Naoto Nakanishi	68	67	69	72	276	2,355,000
Yoshinori Fujimoto	70	69	67	71	277	1,658,571
Yuki Kitagawa	68	70	69	70	277	1,658,571
Mikumu Horikawa	68	69	68	72	277	1,658,571
Ryuji Masaoka	70	66	72	69	277	1,658,571
Shunya Takeyasu	67	68	71	71	277	1,658,571
Atomu Shigenaga	70	64	74	69	277	1,658,571
Koichi Kitamura	66	66	73	72	277	1,658,571

Shigeo Nagashima Invitational

North Country Golf Club, Chitose, Hokkaido
Par 36-36–72; 7,178 yards

August 22-25
purse, ¥150,000,000

	SCORES				TOTAL	MONEY
Ryo Ishikawa	67	66	67	68	268	¥30,000,000
Juvic Pagunsan	69	69	67	67	272	15,000,000
Takahiro Hataji	69	69	70	65	273	8,700,000
Chan Kim	70	69	64	70	273	8,700,000
Yuta Ikeda	70	68	67	69	274	6,000,000
Anthony Quayle	73	67	69	66	275	4,975,000
Junggon Hwang	73	66	68	68	275	4,975,000
Mikumu Horikawa	69	69	65	72	275	4,975,000
Sanghyun Park	71	69	68	68	276	4,230,000
Ryutaro Nagano	72	71	66	68	277	3,330,000
Gunn Charoenkul	73	67	67	70	277	3,330,000
Bio Kim	72	65	69	71	277	3,330,000
Tatsuya Kodai	74	68	65	70	277	3,330,000
Tomoharu Otsuki	71	71	64	71	277	3,330,000
Scott Vincent	71	71	69	67	278	2,355,000
Sang-Hee Lee	73	69	67	69	278	2,355,000
Prom Meesawat	67	68	73	70	278	2,355,000
Shota Akiyoshi	70	68	68	72	278	2,355,000
Yoshinori Fujimoto	71	70	70	68	279	1,658,571
Jinichiro Kozuma	72	72	68	67	279	1,658,571
Angelo Que	72	72	65	70	279	1,658,571
Seong-Hyeon Kim	74	68	67	70	279	1,658,571
Shugo Imahira	74	67	72	66	279	1,658,571
Seungsu Han	72	68	68	71	279	1,658,571
Azuma Yano	74	69	71	65	279	1,658,571

RIZAP KBC Augusta

Keya Golf Club, Itoshima, Fukuoka
Par 36-36–72; 7,103 yards

August 29-September 1
purse, ¥100,000,000

	SCORES				TOTAL	MONEY
Kazuki Higa	66	63	67	66	262	¥20,000,000
Rikuya Hoshino	71	66	65	65	267	10,000,000
Junggon Hwang	65	67	70	66	268	6,800,000
Gunn Charoenkul	68	65	69	67	269	4,400,000
Ryuko Tokimatsu	69	65	66	69	269	4,400,000
Sang-Hee Lee	67	68	72	63	270	3,316,666
Scott Vincent	72	66	64	68	270	3,316,666
Michael Hendry	67	66	66	71	270	3,316,666
Nicholas Fung	65	69	71	67	272	2,520,000
Akio Sadakata	69	67	69	67	272	2,520,000
Ryosuke Kinoshita	68	67	68	69	272	2,520,000
Juvic Pagunsan	69	70	66	67	272	2,520,000
Yosuke Asaji	66	70	69	68	273	1,853,333
Ryo Ishikawa	67	67	69	70	273	1,853,333
Shugo Imahira	66	66	67	74	273	1,853,333
Hyunwoo Ryu	67	68	71	68	274	1,570,000
Brad Kennedy	69	66	70	69	274	1,570,000
Angelo Que	72	64	70	69	275	1,380,000
Hiroshi Iwata	65	68	67	75	275	1,380,000
Danthai Boonma	69	70	68	69	276	1,220,000
Katsumasa Miyamoto	68	66	72	70	276	1,220,000
Tomoyo Ikemura	68	68	71	70	277	1,060,000

	SCORES				TOTAL	MONEY
Dongkyu Jang	69	68	69	71	277	1,060,000
Taichiro Ideriha (A)	71	67	71	69	278	
Todd Baek	68	68	71	71	278	860,000
Brendan Jones	68	71	68	71	278	860,000
Jeong-Woo Ham	70	71	69	68	278	860,000
Taichi Nabetani	69	72	65	72	278	860,000
Satoshi Kodaira	66	71	68	73	278	860,000

Fujisankei Classic

Fujizakura Country Club, Fujikawaguchiko, Yamanashi
Par 35-36–71; 7,566 yards

September 5-8
purse, ¥110,000,000

	SCORES				TOTAL	MONEY
Sanghyun Park	68	69	67	65	269	¥22,000,000
Hiroshi Iwata	72	66	69	64	271	9,240,000
Hosung Choi	68	62	70	71	271	9,240,000
Chan Kim	65	65	70	72	272	5,280,000
Ryo Ishikawa	68	72	69	64	273	4,400,000
Shugo Imahira	68	69	70	70	277	3,795,000
Gunn Charoenkul	68	66	70	73	277	3,795,000
Sang-Hee Lee	73	70	66	69	278	3,228,500
Seungsu Han	74	68	66	70	278	3,228,500
Kodai Ichihara	67	71	73	68	279	2,442,000
Rahil Gangjee	75	68	68	68	279	2,442,000
Konosuke Nakazato	69	70	71	69	279	2,442,000
Todd Baek	67	72	69	71	279	2,442,000
Jinichiro Kozuma	68	70	69	72	279	2,442,000
Peter Karmis	70	67	73	70	280	1,727,000
Yoshinori Fujimoto	68	71	70	71	280	1,727,000
Takaya Onoda	70	70	68	72	280	1,727,000
Angelo Que	66	72	68	74	280	1,727,000
Satoshi Kodaira	71	70	71	69	281	1,298,000
Ryuko Tokimatsu	71	70	73	67	281	1,298,000
Kunihiro Kamii	68	75	68	70	281	1,298,000
Seong-Hyeon Kim	70	71	68	72	281	1,298,000
Katsumasa Miyamoto	72	69	68	72	281	1,298,000
Junggon Hwang	69	71	73	69	282	968,000
Dylan Perry	71	68	74	69	282	968,000
Hiroyuki Fujita	70	72	69	71	282	968,000
Tomoyo Ikemura	71	69	69	73	282	968,000

ANA Open

Sapporo Golf Club, Wattsu Course, Sapporo, Hokkaido
Par 36-36–72; 7,063 yards

September 12-15
purse, ¥110,000,000

	SCORES				TOTAL	MONEY
Yosuke Asaji	73	68	66	65	272	¥22,000,000
Shaun Norris	67	69	71	65	272	7,040,000
Terumichi Kakazu	70	67	68	67	272	7,040,000
Seungsu Han	71	66	67	68	272	7,040,000
Ryuko Tokimatsu	66	67	69	70	272	7,040,000
(Asaji won on first playoff hole.)						
Wenchong Liang	69	67	72	66	274	3,648,333
Ryo Ishikawa	72	64	71	67	274	3,648,333
Gunn Charoenkul	71	67	66	70	274	3,648,333

	SCORES				TOTAL	MONEY
Tomoyo Ikemura	72	66	71	66	275	2,662,000
Han Lee	68	67	71	69	275	2,662,000
Shugo Imahira	66	70	69	70	275	2,662,000
Yoshitaka Takeya	72	66	67	70	275	2,662,000
Ryuji Masaoka	71	69	64	71	275	2,662,000
Brendan Jones	73	66	71	66	276	2,002,000
Jinichiro Kozuma	72	68	68	69	277	1,727,000
Toshinori Muto	70	68	70	69	277	1,727,000
Y.E. Yang	69	69	69	70	277	1,727,000
Tomohiro Kondo	72	67	68	70	277	1,727,000
Yuta Ikeda	70	71	70	67	278	1,216,285
Hosung Choi	71	67	71	69	278	1,216,285
Ryosuke Kinoshita	70	68	71	69	278	1,216,285
Jay Choi	72	67	70	69	278	1,216,285
Junggon Hwang	71	69	68	70	278	1,216,285
Konosuke Nakazato	74	69	70	65	278	1,216,285
Peter Karmis	68	68	66	76	278	1,216,285

Shinhan Donghae Open

See Asian Tour section.

Panasonic Open

Higashi Hirono Golf Club, Hyogo
Par 35-36–71; 7,058 yards

September 26-29
purse, ¥150,000,000

	SCORES				TOTAL	MONEY
Toshinori Muto	65	70	64	64	263	¥30,000,000
Shugo Imahira	65	69	66	67	267	15,000,000
Ryo Ishikawa	72	62	68	66	268	10,200,000
Jazz Janewattananond	66	69	66	70	271	7,200,000
Jbe' Kruger	71	66	69	66	272	5,231,250
Hosung Choi	68	68	69	67	272	5,231,250
Hiroyuki Fujita	70	70	66	66	272	5,231,250
Katsumasa Miyamoto	73	66	66	67	272	5,231,250
Brendan Jones	67	70	66	70	273	4,230,000
Shaun Norris	68	71	69	66	274	3,780,000
Shingo Katayama	70	67	69	68	274	3,780,000
Yoshitaka Takeya	73	68	66	68	275	3,030,000
Sanghyun Park	69	70	67	69	275	3,030,000
Miguel Carballo	67	68	66	74	275	3,030,000
Masanori Kobayashi	69	70	70	67	276	2,430,000
Taihei Sato	69	68	70	69	276	2,430,000
Koki Shiomi	71	70	66	69	276	2,430,000
Young-Woong Kim	69	70	71	67	277	1,890,000
Suradit Yongcharoenchai	68	72	70	67	277	1,890,000
Danthai Boonma	70	71	69	67	277	1,890,000
Yikeun Chang	66	70	72	69	277	1,890,000
Sang-Hee Lee	67	67	72	71	277	1,890,000
Rikuya Hoshino	72	69	70	67	278	1,430,000
Adilson da Silva	70	67	71	70	278	1,430,000
Yuta Kinoshita	68	72	68	70	278	1,430,000

Tokai Classic

Miyoshi Country Club, West Course, Miyoshi, Aichi
Par 36-36–72; 7,295 yards

October 3-6
purse, ¥110,000,000

	SCORES				TOTAL	MONEY
Shaun Norris	68	69	66	72	275	¥22,000,000
Shota Akiyoshi	73	66	67	70	276	9,240,000
Ryuko Tokimatsu	71	68	69	68	276	9,240,000
Jazz Janewattananond	71	71	69	67	278	4,546,666
Taihei Sato	73	69	68	68	278	4,546,666
Kazuki Higa	67	71	66	74	278	4,546,666
Han Lee	72	68	70	70	280	3,362,333
Tomoharu Otsuki	71	68	70	71	280	3,362,333
Shugo Imahira	68	68	70	74	280	3,362,333
Richard Jung	73	70	68	70	281	2,772,000
Mikumu Horikawa	67	69	69	76	281	2,772,000
Takahiro Hataji	74	67	72	69	282	2,139,500
Taichi Kimura [A]	69	73	71	69	282	
Paul Peterson	69	72	71	70	282	2,139,500
Seung-Hyuk Kim	68	73	69	72	282	2,139,500
Jbe' Kruger	77	67	66	72	282	2,139,500
Sang-Hee Lee	73	68	71	71	283	1,727,000
Angelo Que	72	70	70	71	283	1,727,000
Keisuke Otawa	70	75	70	69	284	1,430,000
Koumei Oda	74	71	68	71	284	1,430,000
Kyung-Nam Kang	72	71	69	72	284	1,430,000
Chan Kim	76	70	72	66	284	1,430,000
Ryosuke Kinoshita	72	71	72	70	285	1,089,000
Tomoyo Ikemura	73	73	67	72	285	1,089,000
Jinichiro Kozuma	74	70	72	69	285	1,089,000
Rikuya Hoshino	70	74	69	72	285	1,089,000

Bridgestone Open

Sodegaura Country Club, Chiba
Par 35-36–71; 7,119 yards
(Tournament reduced to 36 holes—typhoon.)

October 10-13
purse, ¥150,000,000

	SCORES		TOTAL	MONEY
Shugo Imahira	64	67	131	¥15,000,000
Seungsu Han	68	64	132	4,800,000
Akio Sadakata	69	63	132	4,800,000
Hiroyuki Fujita	68	64	132	4,800,000
Tomoharu Otsuki	68	64	132	4,800,000
Taisei Shimizu [A]	68	66	134	
Paul Peterson	67	67	134	2,394,375
Ryosuke Kinoshita	67	67	134	2,394,375
Brad Kennedy	68	66	134	2,394,375
Shota Akiyoshi	69	65	134	2,394,375
Kosuke Sunagawa [A]	66	68	134	
Panuphol Pittayarat	70	65	135	1,448,333
Juvic Pagunsan	71	64	135	1,448,333
David Bransdon	68	67	135	1,448,333
Brendan Jones	71	64	135	1,448,333
Kazuki Higa	70	65	135	1,448,333
Adam Bland	70	65	135	1,448,333
Ryuko Tokimatsu	66	69	135	1,448,333
Michael Hendry	67	68	135	1,448,333
Gunn Charoenkul	65	70	135	1,448,333

	SCORES				TOTAL	MONEY
Tsubasa Ukita [A]	67	69			136	
Matthew Griffin	69	67			136	915,000
Koumei Oda	69	67			136	915,000
Shingo Katayama	69	67			136	915,000
Yosuke Asaji	70	66			136	915,000

Japan Open Championship

Koga Golf Club, Fukuoka
Par 36-35–71; 6,817 yards

October 17-20
purse, ¥210,000,000

	SCORES				TOTAL	MONEY
Chan Kim	74	69	75	67	285	¥42,000,000
Shaun Norris	71	72	72	71	286	19,635,000
Mikumu Horikawa	72	71	71	72	286	19,635,000
Scott Vincent	71	73	70	73	287	10,500,000
Brad Kennedy	74	73	70	71	288	6,510,000
In-Hoi Hur	74	73	71	70	288	6,510,000
Adam Scott	76	69	74	69	288	6,510,000
Brendan Jones	68	75	73	72	288	6,510,000
Kazuki Higa	70	72	72	74	288	6,510,000
Rikuya Hoshino	69	75	72	73	289	3,832,500
Koki Shiomi	71	67	72	79	289	3,832,500
Hiroyuki Fujita	71	75	70	74	290	2,639,000
Atomu Shigenaga	75	74	74	67	290	2,639,000
Ryo Ishikawa	76	74	69	71	290	2,639,000
Seung-Hyuk Kim	73	77	72	68	290	2,639,000
Shugo Imahira	71	71	73	75	290	2,639,000
Kyung-Nam Kang	71	70	75	74	290	2,639,000
Ryuji Masaoka	74	75	73	69	291	1,953,000
Dongkyu Jang	71	74	71	75	291	1,953,000
Jinichiro Kozuma	72	72	71	76	291	1,953,000
Kodai Ichihara	74	70	71	76	291	1,953,000
Takanori Konishi	74	73	72	73	292	1,764,000
Masahiro Kawamura	73	75	73	72	293	1,680,000
Jack Thompson [A]	76	73	72	72	293	
Tomohiro Ishizaka [A]	72	74	71	76	293	
Yuto Katsuragawa [A]	72	74	76	71	293	
Satoshi Kodaira	75	75	72	71	293	1,680,000
Ryutaro Nagano	74	76	71	72	293	1,680,000

Zozo Championship

Accordia Golf Narashino Country Club, Chiba, Japan
Par 34-36–70; 7,041 yards
(Tournament completed on Monday.)

October 24-28
purse, US$9,750,000

	SCORES				TOTAL	MONEY
Tiger Woods	64	64	66	67	261	¥94,348,800
Hideki Matsuyama	65	67	65	67	264	56,609,280
Rory McIlroy	72	65	63	67	267	30,401,280
Sungjae Im	71	64	67	65	267	30,401,280
Gary Woodland	64	66	68	70	268	20,966,400
Billy Horschel	68	67	64	70	269	18,214,560
Corey Conners	69	64	66	70	269	18,214,560
Byeong Hun An	70	68	66	66	270	15,724,800
Charles Howell	70	65	66	69	270	15,724,800

ASIA/JAPAN TOURS

	SCORES				TOTAL	MONEY
Danny Lee	70	65	68	68	271	13,104,000
Ryan Palmer	67	68	69	67	271	13,104,000
Xander Schauffele	68	66	65	72	271	13,104,000
Shane Lowry	71	69	67	65	272	9,775,584
Ian Poulter	71	71	64	66	272	9,775,584
Matthew Wolff	69	65	67	71	272	9,775,584
Keegan Bradley	69	63	71	69	272	9,775,584
Patrick Reed	72	68	65	68	273	7,212,441
Justin Thomas	70	69	69	65	273	7,212,441
Paul Casey	69	69	68	67	273	7,212,441
Sunghoon Kang	67	69	70	67	273	7,212,441
Daniel Berger	67	66	70	70	273	7,212,441
Jason Day	73	66	67	68	274	4,906,137
Dylan Frittelli	71	69	67	67	274	4,906,137
Tommy Fleetwood	71	69	67	67	274	4,906,137
Adam Schenk	69	67	68	70	274	4,906,137
Collin Morikawa	71	64	69	70	274	4,906,137
Harold Varner	72	70	69	64	275	3,752,985
Keith Mitchell	69	68	71	67	275	3,752,985
J.T. Poston	70	65	72	68	275	3,752,985
Rafa Cabrera Bello	73	66	70	67	276	3,281,241
Troy Merritt	71	68	70	67	276	3,281,241
Emiliano Grillo	69	69	68	70	276	3,281,241
Adam Scott	73	67	66	71	277	2,770,185
Rory Sabbatini	71	68	68	70	277	2,770,185
Sergio Garcia	70	71	67	69	277	2,770,185
Joaquin Niemann	68	68	67	74	277	2,770,185
Kevin Tway	69	72	71	66	278	2,285,337
Lucas Glover	72	69	68	69	278	2,285,337
Si Woo Kim	76	67	66	69	278	2,285,337
Satoshi Kodaira	69	66	69	74	278	2,285,337
Chan Kim	71	69	72	67	279	1,813,593
Adam Hadwin	71	69	71	68	279	1,813,593
Viktor Hovland	75	65	67	72	279	1,813,593
Abraham Ancer	74	68	68	69	279	1,813,593
Vaughn Taylor	70	73	71	65	279	1,813,593
Max Homa	71	68	66	75	280	1,327,173
Kevin Na	71	70	68	71	280	1,327,173
Tomoharu Otsuki	70	68	67	75	280	1,327,173
Louis Oosthuizen	69	69	71	71	280	1,327,173
Wyndham Clark	74	68	70	68	280	1,327,173
Shaun Norris	73	67	72	69	281	1,107,724
Rikuya Hoshino	68	71	72	70	281	1,107,724
Adam Long	71	70	74	66	281	1,107,724
Bubba Watson	69	69	68	75	281	1,107,724
Pat Perez	72	70	69	70	281	1,107,724
Ryo Ishikawa	68	68	70	75	281	1,107,724
Jazz Janewattananond	74	67	71	70	282	1,053,561
Jinichiro Kozuma	75	69	71	67	282	1,053,561
Andrew Putnam	68	72	73	70	283	1,022,111
Tony Finau	72	69	69	73	283	1,022,111
C.T. Pan	68	75	71	69	283	1,022,111
Shugo Imahira	74	69	72	68	283	1,022,111
Yosuke Asaji	72	67	70	75	284	985,420
Sanghyun Park	71	70	74	69	284	985,420
Seungsu Han	72	69	68	75	284	985,420
Kevin Kisner	75	70	68	72	285	953,971
Jordan Spieth	74	71	69	71	285	953,971
Scott Piercy	78	68	68	71	285	953,971
Marc Leishman	76	70	69	71	286	933,004
Chez Reavie	77	70	66	74	287	922,521
Jason Kokrak	74	70	70	74	288	912,038
Ryan Moore	72	69	72	76	289	896,313

	SCORES				TOTAL	MONEY
Mikumu Horikawa	72	75	68	74	289	896,313
Kevin Streelman	78	69	72	72	291	880,588
Matthew Fitzpatrick	75	71	74	72	292	870,105
Joel Dahmen	72	76	72	78	298	859,622

Mynavi ABC Championship

ABC Golf Club, Kato, Hyogo
Par 36-36–72; 7,200 yards

October 31-November 3
purse, ¥150,000,000

	SCORES				TOTAL	MONEY
Junggon Hwang	66	70	66	67	269	¥30,000,000
Shugo Imahira	69	68	64	69	270	15,000,000
Satoshi Kodaira	71	70	62	69	272	10,200,000
Richard Jung	68	70	69	67	274	6,200,000
Hiroshi Iwata	65	69	70	70	274	6,200,000
Hiroyuki Fujita	72	67	65	70	274	6,200,000
Sang-Hee Lee	69	70	69	67	275	4,107,500
Brendan Jones	69	70	69	67	275	4,107,500
Sanghyun Park	69	69	69	68	275	4,107,500
Kyung-Nam Kang	66	71	69	69	275	4,107,500
Gunn Charoenkul	68	70	67	70	275	4,107,500
Todd Baek	68	70	67	70	275	4,107,500
Shota Akiyoshi	69	69	71	67	276	2,692,500
Shingo Katayama	68	72	69	67	276	2,692,500
David Bransdon	67	69	72	68	276	2,692,500
Dongkyu Jang	69	68	70	69	276	2,692,500
Scott Vincent	71	68	72	66	277	2,016,000
Toshinori Muto	70	71	70	66	277	2,016,000
Rikuya Hoshino	70	68	70	69	277	2,016,000
Daijiro Izumida	68	69	70	70	277	2,016,000
Min-Gyu Cho	69	65	71	72	277	2,016,000
Taihei Sato	71	69	70	68	278	1,530,000
Jinichiro Kozuma	67	71	69	71	278	1,530,000
Won Joon Lee	65	74	68	71	278	1,530,000
Shaun Norris	73	69	71	66	279	1,320,000
Mikiya Akutsu	68	69	68	74	279	1,320,000

Heiwa PGM Championship

PGM Golf Resort, Okinawa
Par 36-35–71; 7,226 yards

November 7-10
purse, ¥200,000,000

	SCORES				TOTAL	MONEY
Hosung Choi	68	67	68	67	270	¥40,000,000
Shugo Imahira	71	64	69	68	272	20,000,000
Shaun Norris	69	69	70	65	273	11,600,000
Dylan Perry	67	70	70	66	273	11,600,000
Brad Kennedy	66	69	72	67	274	7,600,000
Scott Vincent	67	65	74	68	274	7,600,000
Richard Jung	70	70	66	69	275	6,600,000
Ryuko Tokimatsu	71	71	69	65	276	6,100,000
Angelo Que	66	74	70	67	277	5,240,000
Seong-Hyeon Kim	68	70	71	68	277	5,240,000
Todd Baek	67	72	70	68	277	5,240,000
Wenchong Liang	69	72	70	67	278	3,890,000
Ryuji Masaoka	71	71	69	67	278	3,890,000

	SCORES				TOTAL	MONEY
Yuta Ikeda	67	71	71	69	278	3,890,000
Rattanon Wannasrichan	69	74	66	69	278	3,890,000
Han Lee	68	72	72	67	279	3,240,000
Kyungtae Kim	73	71	69	67	280	2,445,000
Dongkyu Jang	70	70	73	67	280	2,445,000
Kyung-Nam Kang	74	70	70	66	280	2,445,000
Shih-Chang Chan	68	73	70	69	280	2,445,000
Gunn Charoenkul	67	76	68	69	280	2,445,000
Seungsu Han	66	71	73	70	280	2,445,000
Katsumasa Miyamoto	66	68	75	71	280	2,445,000
Ryosuke Kinoshita	67	71	71	71	280	2,445,000
Jinichiro Kozuma	72	70	72	67	281	1,680,000
Junggon Hwang	72	72	69	68	281	1,680,000
Shota Akiyoshi	73	69	73	66	281	1,680,000
Hiroshi Iwata	72	68	71	70	281	1,680,000

Mitsui Sumitomo VISA Taiheiyo Masters

Taiheiyo Club, Gotemba Course, Gotemba, Shizuoka
Par 35-35–70; 7,262 yards

November 14-17
purse, ¥200,000,000

	SCORES				TOTAL	MONEY
Takumi Kanaya (A)	73	66	63	65	267	
Shaun Norris	71	65	67	65	268	¥40,000,000
Y.E. Yang	66	68	69	69	272	20,000,000
Mikumu Horikawa	74	69	66	65	274	13,600,000
Kyungtae Kim	71	68	70	66	275	7,850,000
Shota Akiyoshi	73	65	69	68	275	7,850,000
Shingo Katayama	71	67	67	70	275	7,850,000
Ryuji Masaoka	66	68	71	70	275	7,850,000
Yuta Ikeda	70	68	66	72	276	6,100,000
Jazz Janewattananond	70	68	72	67	277	5,240,000
Sang-Hyun Park	65	71	72	69	277	5,240,000
Ryuko Tokimatsu	68	68	69	72	277	5,240,000
Matthew Griffin	72	67	71	68	278	3,890,000
Yosuke Tsukada	71	70	68	69	278	3,890,000
Kazuki Higa	70	71	68	69	278	3,890,000
Ren Yonezawa (A)	70	73	66	69	278	
Brad Kennedy	71	69	68	70	278	3,890,000
Anthony Quayle	69	73	70	67	279	2,864,000
Takanori Konishi	74	70	71	64	279	2,864,000
Yuki Inamori	71	69	69	70	279	2,864,000
Keita Nakajima (A)	72	71	73	63	279	
Kyung-Nam Kang	70	71	66	72	279	2,864,000
Daijiro Izumida	72	69	65	73	279	2,864,000
Paul Peterson	72	68	71	69	280	2,120,000
Michael Hendry	71	69	71	69	280	2,120,000
David Bransdon	68	75	66	71	280	2,120,000
Tomoyo Ikemura	70	69	69	72	280	2,120,000

Dunlop Phoenix

Phoenix Country Club, Miyazaki
Par 36-35–71; 7,027 yards
(Tournament reduced to 54 holes—rain.)

November 21-24
purse, ¥200,000,000

	SCORES			TOTAL	MONEY
Shugo Imahira	65	72	66	203	¥30,000,000
Junggon Hwang	71	67	67	205	15,000,000
Daijiro Izumida	72	70	64	206	8,700,000
Scott Vincent	71	69	66	206	8,700,000
Max Homa	69	72	66	207	5,450,000
Seungsu Han	69	71	67	207	5,450,000
Collin Morikawa	71	67	69	207	5,450,000
Hideki Matsuyama	66	75	67	208	3,939,000
Brad Kennedy	70	71	67	208	3,939,000
Cameron Champ	73	67	68	208	3,939,000
Ryosuke Kinoshita	68	71	69	208	3,939,000
Yuta Ikeda	67	70	71	208	3,939,000
Jinichiro Kozuma	70	72	67	209	2,530,000
Kyung-Nam Kang	74	68	67	209	2,530,000
Yoshinori Fujimoto	73	68	68	209	2,530,000
Hiroyuki Fujita	73	68	68	209	2,530,000
Kazuki Higa	70	71	68	209	2,530,000
Kodai Ichihara	68	71	70	209	2,530,000
Rikuya Hoshino	69	71	70	210	2,010,000
Hideto Tanihara	68	75	68	211	1,600,000
Anthony Quayle	73	70	68	211	1,600,000
Atomu Shigenaga	70	72	69	211	1,600,000
Gary Woodland	70	71	70	211	1,600,000
Jazz Janewattananond	69	72	70	211	1,600,000
Prayad Marksaeng	69	70	72	211	1,600,000

Casio World Open

Kochi Kuroshio Country Club, Geisei, Kochi
Par 36-36–72; 7,335 yards

November 28-December 1
purse, ¥200,000,000

	SCORES				TOTAL	MONEY
Kyungtae Kim	70	68	66	64	268	¥40,000,000
Shaun Norris	69	69	68	64	270	20,000,000
Anthony Quayle	71	65	65	70	271	13,600,000
Seungsu Han	69	69	66	68	272	9,600,000
Chan Kim	72	68	67	66	273	7,600,000
Katsumasa Miyamoto	66	71	68	68	273	7,600,000
Toshinori Muto	68	73	68	65	274	6,113,333
Kyung-Nam Kang	71	69	67	67	274	6,113,333
Masahiro Kawamura	67	72	67	68	274	6,113,333
Tatsunori Nukaga	69	68	70	68	275	4,640,000
Ryo Ishikawa	69	70	67	69	275	4,640,000
Koumei Oda	71	66	68	70	275	4,640,000
Shintaro Kobayashi	67	67	69	72	275	4,640,000
Daisuke Kataoka	72	70	69	65	276	3,340,000
Sang-Hee Lee	70	70	69	67	276	3,340,000
Yosuke Asaji	69	71	66	70	276	3,340,000
Atomu Shigenaga	70	70	66	70	276	3,340,000
Dylan Perry	71	71	69	66	277	2,520,000
Naoto Nakanishi	68	70	70	69	277	2,520,000
Yuwa Kosaihira	73	70	70	64	277	2,520,000
Yosuke Tsukada	69	71	68	69	277	2,520,000

	SCORES				TOTAL	MONEY
Ryuko Tokimatsu	72	68	68	69	277	2,520,000
Scott Vincent	70	72	69	67	278	1,773,333
Min-Gyu Cho	73	69	68	68	278	1,773,333
Rahil Gangjee	68	71	72	67	278	1,773,333
Daisuke Matsubara	68	69	71	70	278	1,773,333
Tomoharu Otsuki	73	68	72	65	278	1,773,333
Jinichiro Kozuma	67	70	70	71	278	1,773,333

Golf Nippon Series JT Cup

Tokyo Yomiuri Country Club, Inagi, Tokyo
Par 35-35–70; 7,023 yards

December 5-8
purse, ¥130,000,000

	SCORES				TOTAL	MONEY
Ryo Ishikawa	68	70	68	66	272	¥40,000,000
Brad Kennedy	66	70	71	65	272	15,000,000
(Ishikawa defeated Kennedy on third playoff hole.)						
Shugo Imahira	67	70	69	67	273	10,000,000
Kyungtae Kim	68	68	71	68	275	5,074,093
Gunn Charoenkul	70	69	68	68	275	5,074,093
Brendan Jones	69	72	65	69	275	5,074,093
Shaun Norris	66	69	70	70	275	5,074,093
Rikuya Hoshino	65	69	75	68	277	3,385,392
Satoshi Kodaira	70	69	69	69	277	3,385,392
Mikumu Horikawa	68	72	68	69	277	3,385,392
Ryuko Tokimatsu	68	70	66	73	277	3,385,392
Junggon Hwang	69	67	68	73	277	3,385,392
Y.E. Yang	69	70	70	70	279	2,597,593
Anthony Quayle	68	68	79	65	280	2,207,593
Toshinori Muto	69	70	70	71	280	2,207,593
Chan Kim	69	69	67	75	280	2,207,593
Hosung Choi	70	76	69	66	281	1,882,593
Scott Vincent	71	68	69	73	281	1,882,593
Matthew Griffin	67	75	69	71	282	1,713,593
Hiroyuki Fujita	67	74	73	69	283	1,557,592
Jazz Janewattananond	71	71	71	70	283	1,557,592
Tomoharu Otsuki	69	73	72	70	284	1,349,592
Kazuki Higa	68	71	72	73	284	1,349,592
Yosuke Asaji	72	70	75	68	285	1,167,592
Katsumasa Miyamoto	67	75	72	71	285	1,167,592
Shota Akiyoshi	70	76	71	69	286	1,089,592
Seungsu Han	75	69	71	72	287	1,011,592
Yuta Ikeda	77	69	68	73	287	1,011,592
Sang-Hyun Park	72	75	70	71	288	933,592
Jbe' Kruger	70	75	75	72	292	881,592

ISPS Handa PGA Tour of Australasia

ISPS Handa Vic Open

13th Beach Golf Links, Geelong, Victoria
Par 36-36–72; 6,796 yards

February 7-10
purse, A$1,500,000

	SCORES				TOTAL	MONEY
David Law	67	66	71	66	270	A$237,500
Brad Kennedy	67	65	72	67	271	123,766
Wade Ormsby	65	66	70	70	271	123,766
Justin Harding	67	71	66	68	272	71,250
Jason Scrivener	64	66	76	67	273	51,015
David Drysdale	66	69	71	67	273	51,015
David Bransdon	69	69	67	68	273	51,015
Clement Sordet	69	64	74	67	274	33,772.50
Nicolas Colsaerts	66	71	68	69	274	33,772.50
Nick Flanagan	62	68	76	69	275	27,360
Callum Shinkwin	64	73	66	72	275	27,360
Ashley Chesters	68	67	73	69	277	22,550.63
Anton Karlsson	65	69	73	70	277	22,550.63
Jarryd Felton	71	68	68	70	277	22,550.63
Blake Windred [A]	70	67	69	71	277	
Aaron Townsend	69	69	68	71	277	22,550.63
Michael Hoey	66	68	75	69	278	18,496.50
Marcus Fraser	70	66	73	69	278	18,496.50
Aaron Rai	67	69	73	69	278	18,496.50
Paul Dunne	69	66	70	73	278	18,496.50
Matthew Stieger	71	67	65	75	278	18,496.50
Jason Norris	66	71	72	70	279	16,316.25
Grant Forrest	65	69	72	73	279	16,316.25
Terry Pilkadaris	71	68	70	71	280	15,247.50
Thomas Aiken	69	70	70	71	280	15,247.50
Nick Cullen	66	67	75	72	280	15,247.50
Gavin Moynihan	67	72	70	72	281	13,965
Daniel Gavins	68	68	71	74	281	13,965
Jazz Janewattananond	68	70	68	75	281	13,965
David Micheluzzi [A]	67	68	74	73	282	
Matthew Nixon	71	68	70	73	282	12,896.25
Steven Jeffress	69	69	71	73	282	12,896.25
Matthew Griffin	65	69	75	75	284	12,041.25
Daniel Nisbet	68	70	70	76	284	12,041.25
Geoff Ogilvy	66	72	71	76	285	11,400
James Anstiss	64	71	74	83	292	10,972.50
Dylan Perry	68	71	71		210	9,120
Peter Lonard	66	72	72		210	9,120
Scott Vincent	68	70	72		210	9,120
Adam Burdett	72	67	71		210	9,120
Sihwan Kim	71	68	71		210	9,120
Stuart Manley	66	71	73		210	9,120
Andrew Evans	68	67	75		210	9,120
Lucas Herbert	65	69	76		210	9,120
Ryan Fox	66	68	76		210	9,120
Michael Sim	66	70	74		210	9,120
Hugo Leon	64	72	74		210	9,120
Yuta Ikeda	66	71	73		210	9,120
Andrew Dodt	67	71	73		211	6,412.50
Connor Syme	71	67	73		211	6,412.50
Masahiro Kawamura	68	70	73		211	6,412.50

	SCORES			TOTAL	MONEY
Richard Green	72	66	73	211	6,412.50
Austin Connelly	70	68	73	211	6,412.50
Kristoffer Reitan	72	67	72	211	6,412.50
Darren Beck	67	70	74	211	6,412.50
Sam Brazel	69	69	74	212	4,631.25
Kim Koivu	66	72	74	212	4,631.25
Louis de Jager	67	69	76	212	4,631.25
Espen Kofstad	71	65	76	212	4,631.25
James Morrison	68	69	75	212	4,631.25
Robert MacIntyre	67	70	75	212	4,631.25
James Nitties	64	74	75	213	3,633.75
Michael Long	66	73	74	213	3,633.75
Adrian Otaegui	70	69	74	213	3,633.75
Dale Williamson	68	71	74	213	3,633.75
Michael Hendry	68	66	79	213	3,633.75
Matt Jager	66	66	81	213	3,633.75
Taylor Macdonald	68	70	76	214	2,921.25
Maverick Antcliff	67	71	76	214	2,921.25
Andrew Martin	68	71	75	214	2,921.25
Ashley Hall	71	66	77	214	2,921.25
Max McCardle	68	71	76	215	2,290.89
Scott Hend	69	67	79	215	2,290.89
Aaron Pike	66	70	79	215	2,290.89
Andre Lautee (A)	65	72	78	215	
Kurt Kitayama	64	74	78	216	2,128
Jordan Mullaney	67	69	81	217	2,123.44
Stephen Leaney	69	70	79	218	2,116.60
Peter Cooke	65	71	82	218	2,116.60

ISPS Handa World Super 6 Perth

Lake Karrinyup Country Club, Perth, Western Australia
Par 36-36–72; 7,162 yards

February 14-17
purse, A$1,600,000

FIRST ROUND OF 16

Panuphol Pittayarat defeated Ben Evans, second shootout hole.
Jazz Janewattananond defeated Steven Jeffress, 1 up.
Connor Syme defeated Robert MacIntyre, 1 up.
Matt Jager defeated Andrew Martin, first shootout hole.
Scott Vincent defeated Wade Ormsby, 3 and 2.
Benjamin Campbell defeated Clement Sordet, first shootout hole.
Min Woo Lee defeated Gregory Bourdy, third shootout hole.
Adrian Otaegui defeated Daniel Gale, 2 up.

SECOND ROUND OF 16

Kristoffer Reitan defeated Pittayarat, 1 up.
Ryan Fox defeated Janewattananond, third shootout hole.
Gareth Paddison defeated Syme, 1 up.
Paul Dunne defeated Jager, second shootout hole.
Vincent defeated Yuta Ikeda, 2 up.
Lee defeated Thomas Pieters, 1 up.
Campbell defeated Brad Kennedy, 1 up.
Otaegui defeated Per Langfors, 2 and 1.

QUARTER-FINALS

Fox defeated Reitan, 1 up.
Dunne defeated Paddison, 1 up.
Vincent defeated Campbell, second shootout hole.
Otaegui defeated Lee, 2 up.

(Losing players received €32,318.11.)

SEMI-FINALS

Fox defeated Dunne, 1 up.
Otaegui defeated Vincent, 3 and 2.

PLAYOFF FOR THIRD-FOURTH PLACE

Dunne defeated Vincent, first shootout hole.
(Dunne received €61,121.26; Vincent received €48,818.90.)

FINAL

Fox defeated Otaegui, 3 and 2.
(Fox received €162,728; Otaegui received €108,485.)

Coca-Cola Queensland PGA Championship

City Golf Club, Toowoomba, Queensland
Par 33-37–70; 6,562 yards

February 21-24
purse, A$150,000

	SCORES				TOTAL	MONEY
Daniel Nisbet	66	63	63	64	256	A$22,500
Harrison Endycott	63	71	64	64	262	12,375
Deyen Lawson	68	63	63	68	262	12,375
Andrew Evans	64	69	66	66	265	5,906.25
Cameron John	67	68	64	66	265	5,906.25
Jarryd Felton	66	69	63	67	265	5,906.25
Lincoln Tighe	64	63	70	68	265	5,906.25
Nathan Green	63	69	70	65	267	3,937.50
Max McCardle	65	67	66	69	267	3,937.50
Daniel Pearce	67	64	68	69	268	3,300
James Nitties	68	64	69	68	269	2,850
Michael Sim	68	67	66	68	269	2,850
Peter Wilson	69	64	67	70	270	2,400
Daniel Fox	67	71	68	65	271	1,980
Brad Moules	66	71	68	66	271	1,980
Daniel Gale	65	70	69	67	271	1,980
Blake Proverbs	68	68	66	69	271	1,980
Denzel Ieremia	66	66	67	72	271	1,980
David Bransdon	66	73	66	67	272	1,612.50
Darren Beck	70	65	70	67	272	1,612.50
Andrew Martin	66	68	69	69	272	1,612.50
Marco Zirov	65	71	67	69	272	1,612.50
James Marchesani	69	63	70	70	272	1,612.50
Damien Jordan	69	69	64	70	272	1,612.50
Brett Rankin	74	64	69	66	273	1,425
Rick Kulacz	66	70	70	67	273	1,425
Peter Cooke	68	66	71	68	273	1,425
Ryan Lynch	62	73	70	68	273	1,425
Chris Crabtree [A]	65	71	67	70	273	
Scott Arnold	67	68	67	71	273	1,425
Josh Younger	70	64	67	72	273	1,425

100th New Zealand Open

The Hills, Arrowtown, New Zealand
Par 36-36–72; 7,135 yards

February 28-March 3
purse, NZ$1,250,000

	SCORES				TOTAL	MONEY
Zach Murray	63	65	70	68	266	A$211,724.85
Ashley Hall	67	69	67	65	268	99,687.12
Josh Geary	67	69	63	69	268	99,687.12
Jazz Janewattananond	69	70	66	64	269	56,459.96
Brad Kennedy	71	63	69	67	270	42,344.97
Rikuya Hoshino	71	68	63	68	270	42,344.97
Ryuko Tokimatsu	64	69	68	69	270	42,344.97
Steven Alker	68	69	69	65	271	31,758.73
Kodai Ichihara	66	68	67	70	271	31,758.73
Harry Bateman	64	70	67	70	271	31,758.73
Won Joon Lee	70	70	66	66	272	24,701.23
Ryan Fox	68	66	71	67	272	24,701.23
Andrew Dodt	72	67	68	67	274	19,231.68
Paul Peterson	69	68	68	69	274	19,231.68
Travis Smyth	67	71	67	69	274	19,231.68
Matthew Griffin	71	69	64	70	274	19,231.68
Geoff Ogilvy	73	65	71	66	275	13,262.21
Harrison Endycott	69	70	68	68	275	13,262.21
Adilson da Silva	68	69	69	69	275	13,262.21
K.J. Choi	69	70	67	69	275	13,262.21
Adam Bland	68	72	66	69	275	13,262.21
Aaron Pike	71	66	65	73	275	13,262.21
Ajeetesh Sandhu	69	71	70	66	276	10,562.72
Daniel Gale	67	70	70	69	276	10,562.72
Daisuke Kataoka	69	68	69	70	276	10,562.72
Jang Hyun Lee [A]	67	72	67	70	276	
Poom Saksansin	68	68	69	71	276	10,562.72
Dimitrios Papadatos	68	66	68	74	276	10,562.72

SEC New Zealand PGA Championship

Pegasus Golf & Sports Club, Pegasus, New Zealand
Par 36-36–72; 6,916 yards

March 7-10
purse, NZ$125,000

	SCORES				TOTAL	MONEY
Kazuma Kobori [A]	67	65	66	69	267	
David Smail	68	66	70	67	271	17,555.85
Cameron John	71	64	67	70	272	11,118.71
Blake Proverbs	66	69	72	66	273	6,281.09
Mark Purser	71	68	68	66	273	6,281.09
Anthony Quayle	69	70	67	67	273	6,281.09
Ben Eccles	69	68	70	67	274	3,481.91
Denzel Ieremia	67	69	69	69	274	3,481.91
Josh Geary	63	69	72	70	274	3,481.91
Daniel Fox	66	67	70	71	274	3,481.91
James Anstiss	70	69	73	63	275	2,340.78
Nick Flanagan	66	70	68	71	275	2,340.78
Damien Jordan	69	70	64	72	275	2,340.78
Jack Wilson	68	64	73	71	276	1,755.59
Michael Hendry	70	66	68	72	276	1,755.59
Josh Younger	71	66	67	72	276	1,755.59
Hayden Webb	71	69	69	68	277	1,474.70
Jarryd Felton	68	70	69	70	277	1,474.70
Jordan Zunic	74	68	68	68	278	1,357.65

AUSTRALASIAN TOUR / 549

	SCORES				TOTAL	MONEY
Harry Bateman	71	72	64	71	278	1,357.65
Oscar Cadenhead	72	69	68	70	279	1,281.58
Maverick Antcliff	69	72	65	73	279	1,281.58
Brad Kennedy	70	72	67	71	280	1,193.80
Pieter Zwart	67	71	69	73	280	1,193.80
Ashley Hall	69	72	73	66	280	1,193.80
Frazer Droop	72	68	67	73	280	1,193.80
Matthew Millar	69	66	71	74	280	1,193.80

SP PNG Golf Open

Royal Port Moresby Golf Club, Port Moresby, Papua New Guinea
Par 37-35–72; 6,854 yards

March 9-12
purse, A$150,000

	SCORES				TOTAL	MONEY
Peter Cooke	71	65	64	70	270	A$22,500
Jack Wilson	71	65	66	70	272	14,250
Kade McBride	69	68	70	67	274	9,000
Jordan Mullaney	67	66	70	71	274	9,000
Dale Brandt-Richards	69	67	70	69	275	5,375
Brady Watt	67	71	68	69	275	5,375
Blake Proverbs	70	69	66	70	275	5,375
Charlie Dann	69	70	69	68	276	3,375
Tim Hart	71	68	68	69	276	3,375
Josh Geary	72	69	65	70	276	3,375
Daniel Fox	65	70	69	72	276	3,375
Steven Jeffress	68	65	69	74	276	3,375
Adam Burdett	68	71	69	69	277	2,325
Douglas Klein	67	70	68	72	277	2,325
Peter Wilson	73	71	67	67	278	1,912.50
Jacob Boyce	68	73	72	65	278	1,912.50
Andrew Campbell	68	66	73	71	278	1,912.50
Lincoln Tighe	72	68	64	74	278	1,912.50
Damien Jordan	72	71	69	68	280	1,665
Andrew Schonewille	69	70	72	69	280	1,665
Brett Rankin	69	72	72	67	280	1,665
Kieran Muir	68	68	75	70	281	1,545
James Grierson	67	71	72	71	281	1,545
Josh Younger	70	70	67	74	281	1,545
James Anstiss	68	67	70	76	281	1,545

Tailor-made Building Services NT PGA Championship

Palmerston Golf Course, Palmerston, Northern Territory
Par 35-36–71; 6,554 yards

August 22-25
purse, A$150,000

	SCORES				TOTAL	MONEY
Brett Rankin	65	68	68	63	264	A$22,500
Taylor Macdonald	66	69	66	66	267	14,250
Lawry Flynn [A]	68	66	67	67	268	
Kade McBride	65	70	67	67	269	9,000
Adam Burdett	66	68	67	68	269	9,000
Andrew Martin	66	66	66	72	270	6,150
Scott Strange	68	71	66	66	271	5,250
Matt Jager	70	68	69	65	272	4,462.50
Peter Wilson	70	64	67	71	272	4,462.50
James Anstiss	72	66	69	66	273	3,487.50

	SCORES				TOTAL	MONEY
Andrew Dodt	70	68	66	69	273	3,487.50
James Marchesani	70	68	70	66	274	2,318.57
Shae Wools-Cobb	71	68	68	67	274	2,318.57
Damien Jordan	68	69	69	68	274	2,318.57
Jacob Boyce	72	70	63	69	274	2,318.57
Ryan Chisnall	68	65	71	70	274	2,318.57
Aaron Pike	66	67	70	71	274	2,318.57
Jordan Mullaney	68	67	68	71	274	2,318.57
Charlie Dann	72	68	68	67	275	1,691.25
Daniel Nisbet	74	68	65	68	275	1,691.25
Tim Hart	65	71	71	68	275	1,691.25
Steven Jeffress	67	68	68	72	275	1,691.25
Christopher Wood	69	68	71	68	276	1,560
Aaron Wilkin	68	73	66	69	276	1,560
Jake Higginbottom	67	69	70	70	276	1,560

TX Civil & Logistics WA PGA Championship

Kalgoorlie Golf Course, Kalgoorlie, Western Australia
Par 36-36–72; 7,399 yards

October 10-13
purse, A$137,500

	SCORES				TOTAL	MONEY
Darren Beck	68	67	68	69	272	A$20,625
Jarryd Felton	65	67	72	70	274	13,062.50
Michael Sim	71	69	69	67	276	9,625
Robert Hogan	68	69	70	70	277	6,875
Blake Proverbs	69	71	72	66	278	5,637.50
Jordan Zunic	65	72	71	71	279	4,812.50
Stephen Dartnall	73	65	68	74	280	4,331.25
Blake Windred	72	69	74	66	281	3,414.58
Daniel Fox	69	71	73	68	281	3,414.58
Matt Jager	66	74	71	70	281	3,414.58
Robbie Morrison	72	73	68	69	282	2,475
Douglas Klein	74	65	77	66	282	2,475
David Micheluzzi	67	74	70	71	282	2,475
Daniel Nisbet	69	72	75	67	283	1,706.72
Benjamin Stowe	71	74	68	70	283	1,706.72
Peter Lonard	70	68	75	70	283	1,706.72
Taylor Macdonald	68	70	74	71	283	1,706.72
Chang Gi Lee	73	71	73	66	283	1,706.72
Cameron John	71	71	69	72	283	1,706.72
Justin Warren	68	68	73	74	283	1,706.72
Jordan Mullaney	73	71	70	70	284	1,388.75
Andrew Campbell	76	65	73	70	284	1,388.75
Adam Burdett	70	70	76	68	284	1,388.75
James Anstiss	72	72	69	71	284	1,388.75
Brad Moules	73	70	70	71	284	1,388.75
Lawry Flynn [A]	68	72	72	72	284	

Victorian PGA Championship

RACV Cape Schanck, Cape Schanck, Victoria
Par 35-35–70; 6,138 yards

October 24-27
purse, A$25,000

	SCORES				TOTAL	MONEY
Campbell Rawson	71	70	65	64	270	A$18,750
Marcus Fraser	72	67	68	64	271	11,875
Michael Sim	67	71	66	70	274	8,750
Blake Collyer	69	61	76	69	275	6,250
Mark Brown	69	70	69	68	276	4,750
Andrew Dodt	69	64	72	71	276	4,750
James Anstiss	70	71	71	65	277	2,857.14
Jordan Mullaney	70	67	75	65	277	2,857.14
Andrew Martin	72	67	72	66	277	2,857.14
Blake Windred	71	64	74	68	277	2,857.14
Jarryd Felton	67	69	73	68	277	2,857.14
Aaron Wilkin	67	69	71	70	277	2,857.14
David Micheluzzi	69	66	69	73	277	2,857.14
Matias Sanchez	69	70	75	64	278	1,693.75
Jake Higginbottom	69	70	70	69	278	1,693.75
Braden Becker	69	70	69	70	278	1,693.75
Taylor Macdonald	68	65	73	72	278	1,693.75
Jason Norris	67	67	78	67	279	1,377.08
Brett Rankin	74	64	74	67	279	1,377.08
Tom Power Horan	69	67	75	68	279	1,377.08
Daniel Gale	68	66	76	69	279	1,377.08
Nick O'Hern	72	68	70	69	279	1,377.08
Brady Watt	64	69	74	72	279	1,377.08
Michael Wright	67	71	74	68	280	1,275
Terry Pilkadaris	73	68	71	69	281	1,225
Josh Younger	71	68	75	67	281	1,225
Shae Wools-Cobb	71	67	70	73	281	1,225

Gippsland Super 6

Yallourn Golf Club, Yallourn Heights, Victoria
Par 36-36–72; 6,564 yards
(Tournament reduced to 54 holes strokeplay—rain.)

November 7-10
purse, A$125,000

	SCORES			TOTAL	MONEY
Tom Power Horan	66	70	69	205	A$18,750
Brady Watt	68	67	71	206	11,875
Ryan Chisnall	72	66	70	208	8,750
James Marchesani	73	68	68	209	6,250
Taylor Macdonald	73	72	65	210	5,125
Matthew Millar	72	71	69	212	3,718.75
Marcus Fraser	71	72	69	212	3,718.75
Campbell Rawson	71	73	68	212	3,718.75
Maverick Antcliff	73	71	68	212	3,718.75
Dale Brandt-Richards	71	73	69	213	2,750
Hayden Hopewel [A]	72	73	68	213	
D.J. Loypur	69	73	72	214	2,250
Aaron Townsend	74	69	71	214	2,250
Andrew Schonewille	77	69	68	214	2,250
Peter Martin	74	70	71	215	1,812.50
Robert Hogan	73	72	70	215	1,812.50
Matias Sanchez	72	70	74	216	1,512.50
Aaron Wilkin	74	70	72	216	1,512.50
Rick Kulacz	72	73	71	216	1,512.50

	SCORES	TOTAL	MONEY
Ashley Hall	73 73 70	216	1,512.50
Aiden Didone [A]	71 74 72	217	
Christopher Wood	71 74 72	217	1,354.17
Robbie Morrison	72 74 71	217	1,354.17
Jarrod Stirling	72 76 69	217	1,354.17
Darren Beck	76 69 73	218	1,237.50
Max McCardle	73 72 73	218	1,237.50
Andre Lautee [A]	70 76 72	218	
Anthony Choat	72 74 72	218	1,237.50
Ben Murphy	74 72 72	218	1,237.50
Blake Proverbs	74 73 71	218	1,237.50
Benjamin Stowe	77 71 70	218	1,237.50

AVJennings NSW Open

Twin Creeks Golf & Country Club, Luddenham, NSW
Par 36-36–72; 7,047 yards

November 28–December 1
purse, A$400,000

	SCORES	TOTAL	MONEY
Josh Younger	63 70 67 71	271	A$72,000
Travis Smyth	65 69 66 71	271	40,800
(Younger defeated Smyth on second playoff hole.)			
Min Woo Lee	64 67 68 73	272	27,000
Justin Warren	64 71 64 74	273	19,200
Andrew Dodt	69 61 72 73	275	16,000
Denzel Ieremia	74 66 67 69	276	14,400
Andrew Martin	69 72 69 67	277	11,733.33
James Marchesani	69 68 71 69	277	11,733.33
Jake Higginbottom	71 66 68 72	277	11,733.33
Ben Eccles	69 73 71 65	278	8,160
Brody Martin	69 70 73 66	278	8,160
Peter Lonard	68 73 71 66	278	8,160
Christopher Wood	69 68 71 70	278	8,160
Max McCardle	70 70 66 72	278	8,160
Matthew Millar	72 68 70 69	279	5,332
Jordan Zunic	71 70 68 70	279	5,332
Peter Wilson	70 71 68 70	279	5,332
Darren Beck	70 71 68 70	279	5,332
Marcus Fraser	70 72 66 71	279	5,332
Jason Norris	70 69 73 68	280	3,720
Mark Hensby	72 68 71 69	280	3,720
Aaron Wilkin	71 72 68 69	280	3,720
Jordan Mullaney	70 70 70 70	280	3,720
Aaron Townsend	71 69 70 70	280	3,720
Nick Voke	72 68 69 71	280	3,720
Simon Hawkes	70 70 68 72	280	3,720
Douglas Klein	73 70 65 72	280	3,720
Brett Rankin	71 69 66 74	280	3,720

Emirates Australian Open

The Australian Golf Club, Rosebery, New South Wales
Par 35-36–71; 7,179 yards

December 5-8
purse, A$1,500,000

	SCORES				TOTAL	MONEY
Matt Jones	67	65	68	69	269	A$270,000
Louis Oosthuizen	68	66	70	66	270	153,000
Aaron Pike	71	66	69	69	275	101,250
Takumi Kanaya [A]	65	69	70	71	275	
Chun-An Yu [A]	65	70	74	67	276	
Greg Chalmers	71	68	70	67	276	58,500
Denzel Ieremia	69	65	71	71	276	58,500
Paul Casey	68	65	71	72	276	58,500
Cameron Tringale	69	65	69	73	276	58,500
Deyen Lawson	72	65	74	66	277	40,500
Marc Leishman	69	67	70	71	277	40,500
Jamie Arnold	70	71	64	72	277	40,500
Jason Scrivener	68	71	68	71	278	31,500
Richard Green	72	67	68	71	278	31,500
Shae Wools-Cobb	69	65	72	73	279	27,000
Stephen Allan	70	68	72	70	280	21,720
Cory Crawford	71	69	69	71	280	21,720
Dimitrios Papadatos	67	66	75	72	280	21,720
David Bransdon	71	66	70	73	280	21,720
Blake Windred	68	68	70	74	280	21,720
Maverick Antcliff	71	70	73	67	281	15,795
James Marchesani	68	73	71	69	281	15,795
Ryan Fox	71	68	72	70	281	15,795
Darren Beck	71	69	71	70	281	15,795
Lukas Michel [A]	68	67	74	72	281	
K.J. Choi	69	71	69	72	281	15,795

The Presidents Cup

See American Tours chapter.

Australian PGA Championship

RACV Royal Pines Resort, Gold Coast, Queensland
Par 36-36–72; 7,346 yards

December 19-22
purse, A$1,500,000

	SCORES				TOTAL	MONEY
Adam Scott	70	67	69	69	275	A$250,000
Michael Hendry	70	68	70	69	277	166,660
Cameron Davis	72	70	69	67	278	66,000
Yechun Yuan	70	65	73	70	278	66,000
Min Woo Lee	68	72	68	70	278	66,000
Nick Flanagan	72	73	63	70	278	66,000
Wade Ormsby	68	69	70	71	278	66,000
Andrew Dodt	69	72	70	68	279	37,500
Minkyu Kim	72	69	72	67	280	33,600
Johannes Veerman	70	71	73	67	281	26,100
Denzel Ieremia	77	67	69	68	281	26,100
Brett Rankin	67	73	72	69	281	26,100
Cameron Smith	74	65	72	70	281	26,100
Bryce Easton	71	68	71	71	281	26,100
Brett Rumford	72	69	72	69	282	20,700
Travis Smyth	68	72	72	70	282	20,700

554 / AUSTRALASIAN TOUR

	SCORES				TOTAL	MONEY
Greg Chalmers	74	69	68	71	282	20,700
Nick Cullen	68	73	68	73	282	20,700
Damien Perrier	70	72	73	68	283	18,000
Brad Kennedy	71	72	71	69	283	18,000
Anthony Quayle	70	66	75	72	283	18,000
Tom Power Horan	72	66	75	71	284	16,050
Steven Jeffress	71	70	72	71	284	16,050
Stewart Cink	70	72	71	71	284	16,050
Jamie Arnold	73	72	67	72	284	16,050
Brady Watt	72	70	69	73	284	16,050
Josh Geary	73	69	73	70	285	13,575
Matthew Stieger	74	70	70	71	285	13,575
Stephen Allan	70	75	69	71	285	13,575
Ryan Fox	69	72	72	72	285	13,575
Cameron Champ	71	70	71	73	285	13,575
Aaron Cockerill	70	71	69	75	285	13,575
Jack Senior	70	74	70	72	286	11,600
Romain Wattel	73	70	67	76	286	11,600
Alejandro Canizares	73	72	64	77	286	11,600
Zach Murray	71	73	74	69	287	10,350
Ashley Hall	72	73	72	70	287	10,350
Daniel Hillier	74	71	71	71	287	10,350
Harry Bateman	69	71	75	72	287	10,350
Blake Windred	72	70	73	72	287	10,350
Daniel Nisbet	73	72	74	69	288	9,150.
Louis de Jager	74	71	73	70	288	9,150.
Mark Brown	72	71	74	71	288	9,150.
Harrison Endycott	73	72	75	69	289	7,950
Mikumu Horikawa	72	68	77	72	289	7,950
Ryan Chisnall	68	72	77	72	289	7,950
Nick Voke	69	71	76	73	289	7,950
Maverick Antcliff	73	71	71	74	289	7,950
Daniel Pearce	72	72	75	71	290	6,750
Rhein Gibson	71	69	76	74	290	6,750
Simon Hawkes	72	70	70	78	290	6,750
Jason Norris	69	75	76	71	291	6,000
Daniel Gale	72	71	70	78	291	6,000
Pedro Figueiredo	72	72	77	71	292	5,250
Peter Fowler	72	72	76	72	292	5,250
Terry Pilkadaris	70	75	75	72	292	5,250
Dylan Perry	73	72	75	73	293	4,425
Ross McGowan	73	72	75	73	293	4,425
James Anstiss	76	68	75	74	293	4,425
Janne Kaske	74	71	72	76	293	4,425
Richard Green	71	73	76	74	294	3,900
Michael Wright	69	75	73	77	294	3,900
Troy Moses	75	68	73	78	294	3,900
Lucas Herbert	67	77	78	73	295	3,375
Dimitrios Papadatos	72	73	77	73	295	3,375
Dale Whitnell	71	73	77	74	295	3,375
Sami Valimaki	72	73	73	77	295	3,375
Calum Hill	70	72	76	78	296	2,863.33
Rod Pampling	70	73	75	78	296	2,863.33
Michael Sim	73	70	75	78	296	2,863.33
Taylor Macdonald	73	71	75	81	300	2,249.60
Fraser MacLachlan	72	72	82	78	304	2,244.80

African Sunshine Tour

Eye of Africa PGA Championship

Eye of Africa Signature Golf Estate, Johannesburg, South Africa
Par 36-36—72; 7,826 yards

January 31-February 3
purse, R2,000,000

	SCORES				TOTAL	MONEY
Louis de Jager	68	70	67	71	276	R317,000
Trevor Fisher, Jr.	66	68	73	69	276	221,000
(De Jager defeated Fisher on first playoff hole.)
Daniel Greene	67	69	70	71	277	139,800
Thriston Lawrence	69	68	70	71	278	84,000
Bennie van der Merwe	68	69	72	70	279	60,000
Steve Surry	67	71	72	70	280	52,500
Hennie du Plessis	71	68	71	70	280	52,500
Keenan Davidse	68	72	70	71	281	42,500
Jaco Ahlers	70	69	68	74	281	42,500
Jacques Blaauw	68	67	71	76	282	35,000
Neil Schietekat	69	72	72	70	283	28,700
Clinton Grobler	70	72	70	71	283	28,700
Matias Calderon	69	69	73	72	283	28,700
Michael Palmer	72	67	70	74	283	28,700
Teaghan Gauche	71	66	71	75	283	28,700
Victor Lange	65	73	68	77	283	28,700
Anthony Michael	69	72	74	69	284	25,400
Ruan Conradie	74	68	73	69	284	25,400
Benjamin Follett-Smith	73	70	71	70	284	25,400
Jean-Paul Strydom	71	73	69	71	284	25,400
J.C. Ritchie	65	75	71	73	284	25,400
Kyle Pilgrim	69	73	71	72	285	22,750
M.J. Viljoen	72	69	76	68	285	22,750
Andre Nel	68	72	72	73	285	22,750
Neil O'Briain	72	72	73	68	285	22,750

RAM Cape Town Open

Royal Cape Golf Club, Cape Town, South Africa
Par 36-36—72; 6,843 yards

February 7-10
purse, R2,000,000

	SCORES				TOTAL	MONEY
Benjamin Follett-Smith	68	69	72	66	275	R317,000
Zander Lombard	68	67	69	73	277	180,400
Jean-Paul Strydom	62	72	69	74	277	180,400
Peter Karmis	63	66	77	72	278	84,000
Hennie Otto	71	64	76	68	279	55,000
Jack Harrison	71	70	68	70	279	55,000
Jaco Ahlers	70	71	68	70	279	55,000
Jacques P. de Villiers	73	64	76	67	280	33,885.71
Adilson da Silva	71	63	75	71	280	33,885.71
Herman Loubser	71	71	67	71	280	33,885.71
Jacques Kruyswijk	67	72	69	72	280	33,885.71
Andrew Curlewis	67	64	76	73	280	33,885.71
Thriston Lawrence	66	68	72	74	280	33,885.71
Madalitso Muthiya	67	69	70	74	280	33,885.71
Victor Lange	71	70	70	70	281	27,200

	SCORES				TOTAL	MONEY
Daniel Greene	67	71	72	71	281	27,200
Justin Walters	66	69	73	73	281	27,200
Richard Bland	66	69	73	74	282	26,000
Dawie van der Walt	71	67	76	69	283	25,100
Keith Horne	69	71	70	73	283	25,100
Rhys Enoch	67	73	76	68	284	23,040
Scott Campbell	67	70	76	71	284	23,040
Tyrone Ryan	70	70	72	72	284	23,040
Jbe' Kruger	69	67	75	73	284	23,040
Lyle Rowe	67	71	70	76	284	23,040

Dimension Data Pro-Am

Montagu Golf Course, Fancourt, George, South Africa
Par 36-36–72; 7,342 yards

February 14-17
purse, R5,050,000

	SCORES				TOTAL	MONEY
Philip Eriksson	66	67	67	68	268	R752,875
Justin Walters	64	69	71	67	271	524,875
Dean Burmester	68	67	68	69	272	332,025
Jaco van Zyl	65	66	69	73	273	199,500
Merrick Bremner	70	74	65	65	274	130,625
Jaco Ahlers	68	67	71	68	274	130,625
Jbe' Kruger	66	68	68	72	274	130,625
Bradley Neil	73	68	68	66	275	100,937.50
Jeff Winther	70	69	66	70	275	100,937.50
Fredrik From	69	67	73	67	276	77,425
Jaco Prinsloo	71	67	68	70	276	77,425
Thriston Lawrence	73	71	69	64	277	69,587.50
Daniel van Tonder	73	71	65	68	277	69,587.50
Bryce Easton	70	73	66	69	278	66,025
Laurie Canter	68	71	68	71	278	66,025
Anthony Michael	67	71	73	67	278	66,025
Peter Karmis	78	68	68	65	279	58,900
Garth Mulroy	72	71	68	68	279	58,900
Wallie Coetsee	73	68	70	68	279	58,900
Darren Fichardt	70	74	66	69	279	58,900
Herman Loubser	75	68	67	69	279	58,900
Steve Surry	67	68	71	73	279	58,900
Riekus Nortje	63	72	68	76	279	58,900
Michael Palmer	68	73	72	67	280	50,350
Keith Horne	73	66	70	71	280	50,350
Jacques P. de Villiers	69	69	71	71	280	50,350
Christiaan Bezuidenhout	68	70	70	72	280	50,350
Neil O'Briain	67	72	68	73	280	50,350
Daniel Greene	70	71	69	70	280	50,350
Martin Rohwer	70	67	73	70	280	50,350

Team Championship

Dainfern Country Club, Johannesburg, South Africa
Par 36-36–72; 7,294 yards

February 28-March 2
purse, R1,500,000

	SCORES			TOTAL	MONEY (Each)
Jaco Prinsloo/J.C. Ritchie	61	66	62	189	R105,000
Jacques Blaauw/Merrick Bremner	62	65	63	190	86,250
Tyrone Ferreira/Anton Haig	63	66	63	192	61,200
Christiaan Basson/Jake Roos	63	67	63	193	43,875
Ruan de Smidt/Wynand Dingle	63	71	60	194	37,650
Ockie Strydom/M.J. Viljoen	63	71	61	195	28,750
Daniel Greene/Jake Redman	59	72	64	195	28,750
Jade Buitendag/Philip Geerts	64	65	66	195	28,750
Toby Tree/Daniel van Tonder	66	68	62	196	20,381.25
Jean-Paul Strydom/Rourke van der Spuy	62	70	64	196	20,381.25
Aubrey Beckley/Kyle McClatchie	64	68	64	196	20,381.25
Stephen Ferreira/Benjamin Follett-Smith	64	66	66	196	20,381.25
Luke Jerling/Andrew van der Knaap	62	71	64	197	16,605
Anthony Michael/Ryan Tipping	63	70	64	197	16,605
Michael Palmer/Tyrone Ryan	63	69	65	197	16,605
Jacques P. de Villiers/Allan Versfeld	64	67	66	197	16,605
Hennie du Plessis/Jean Hugo	58	73	66	197	16,605
Breyten Meyer/Callum Mowat	67	68	63	198	14,925
Pieter Moolman/Riekus Nortje	66	70	63	199	14,400
Doug McGuigan/Hennie Otto	65	69	65	199	14,400
Matthew Carvell/Toto Thimba	65	71	65	201	13,800
Jason Smith/Wayne Stroebel	64	69	68	201	13,800
Jaco Ahlers/Vaughn Groenewald	62	69	70	201	13,800
Coert Groenewald/Dayne Moore	64	71	69	204	13,350

Limpopo Championship

Euphoria Golf & Lifestyle Estate, Modimolle, South Africa
Par 36-36–72; 7,699 yards

March 7-10
purse, R1,500,000

	SCORES				TOTAL	MONEY
J.C. Ritchie	66	69	70	65	270	R237,750
Steve Surry	68	67	68	67	270	165,750
(Ritchie defeated Surry on first playoff hole.)						
Hennie du Plessis	73	68	65	65	271	104,850
Ross McGowan	68	74	67	64	273	49,750
Jaco Ahlers	67	71	68	67	273	49,750
Andrew van der Knaap	68	70	66	69	273	49,750
Andre Nel	69	69	69	67	274	37,500
Christiaan Basson	70	66	68	71	275	33,750
Anthony Michael	69	70	70	67	276	25,275
Luke Jerling	68	71	67	70	276	25,275
Lyle Rowe	68	67	70	71	276	25,275
Neil Schietekat	68	68	69	71	276	25,275
Keenan Davidse	71	66	72	68	277	21,750
Daniel van Tonder	70	68	72	68	278	21,300
Thriston Lawrence	71	68	69	71	279	20,625
Jade Buitendag	70	67	70	72	279	20,625
Merrick Bremner	68	74	71	67	280	19,050
Philip Eriksson	73	68	71	68	280	19,050
Matias Calderon	70	72	70	68	280	19,050
Fredrik From	71	68	70	71	280	19,050
Ruan Conradie	71	71	66	72	280	19,050

	SCORES			TOTAL	MONEY
Martin Rohwer	74	69 69 69		281	17,250
Chris Cannon	73	71 68 69		281	17,250
Jason Smith	69	71 68 73		281	17,250
Jason Viljoen	74	70 69 69		282	15,600
Ulrich van den Berg	69	75 69 69		282	15,600
Rhys Enoch	72	72 70 68		282	15,600
Madalitso Muthiya	70	69 72 71		282	15,600
Louis Albertse	68	72 69 73		282	15,600
Bryce Easton	74	65 69 74		282	15,600
Riekus Nortje	67	72 67 76		282	15,600

Sunshine Tour Championship

Serengeti Estates, Kempton Park, South Africa
Par 36-36–72; 7,761 yards

March 21-24
purse, R1,500,000

		SCORES			TOTAL	MONEY
Jean-Paul Strydom	69	67	72	66	274	R240,000
Jean Hugo	67	68	70	70	275	107,837.50
Jake Roos	71	67	67	70	275	107,837.50
Ockie Strydom	74	65	65	71	275	107,837.50
Thriston Lawrence	69	69	65	72	275	107,837.50
Keenan Davidse	67	70	70	70	277	57,850
Philip Eriksson	68	69	72	69	278	48,700
Jaco Ahlers	72	68	70	69	279	41,050
Martin Rohwer	70	75	68	68	281	32,575
Bryce Easton	73	71	68	69	281	32,575
J.J. Senekal	68	70	72	71	281	32,575
J.C. Ritchie	68	71	70	72	281	32,575
Merrick Bremner	70	69	74	69	282	27,100
Trevor Fisher, Jr.	74	72	67	69	282	27,100
Daniel van Tonder	77	68	70	68	283	24,130
Daniel Greene	71	74	69	69	283	24,130
Jaco van Zyl	72	71	69	71	283	24,130
Lyle Rowe	71	70	70	72	283	24,130
Michael Palmer	72	71	68	72	283	24,130
Hennie Otto	70	71	69	74	284	22,150
Steve Surry	73	70	70	72	285	21,325
Jaco Prinsloo	72	69	71	73	285	21,325
Doug McGuigan	75	71	70	70	286	20,200
Anthony Michael	74	68	72	72	286	20,200
Vaughn Groenewald	72	70	67	77	286	20,200

Start of 2019-2020 Season

Mopani Redpath Greendoor Logistics Zambia Open

Nkana Golf Club, Kitwe, Zambia
Par 36-36–72; 7,195 yards

March 28-31
purse, R2,500,000

	SCORES				TOTAL	MONEY
Daniel van Tonder	72	73	68	70	283	R396,250
Callum Mowat	73	75	68	68	284	276,250
Neil Schietekat	71	72	74	70	287	139,875
Jacques Blaauw	69	75	71	72	287	139,875
Rhys Enoch	71	74	72	71	288	75,000
Ross McGowan	77	69	76	67	289	59,375
Christiaan Basson	73	72	75	69	289	59,375
Jaco Ahlers	73	74	72	70	289	59,375
J.J. Senekal	73	73	69	74	289	59,375
Jacques P. de Villiers	73	71	77	69	290	38,687.50
Doug McGuigan	74	70	75	71	290	38,687.50
Jaco Prinsloo	72	72	74	72	290	38,687.50
Lyle Rowe	73	72	73	72	290	38,687.50
Pieter Moolman	73	77	72	69	291	34,375
Jonathan Agren	77	70	74	70	291	34,375
Merrick Bremner	73	72	73	73	291	34,375
Steve Surry	73	73	70	75	291	34,375
Ruan Conradie	78	71	72	71	292	32,500
Hennie Otto	74	74	73	72	293	31,375
Kyle Pilgrim	71	74	75	73	293	31,375
Daniel Greene	75	69	80	70	294	28,800
Anthony Michael	74	75	74	71	294	28,800
Fredrik From	72	74	75	73	294	28,800
Juran Dreyer	71	71	76	76	294	28,800
Thriston Lawrence	71	75	71	77	294	28,800

Zanaco Masters

Lusaka Golf Club, Lusaka, Zambia
Par 35-38–73; 7,225 yards

April 4-7
purse, R2,000,000

	SCORES				TOTAL	MONEY
J.C. Ritchie	70	68	66	70	274	R317,000
Rhys Enoch	68	65	75	66	274	221,000

(Ritchie defeated Enoch on first playoff hole.)

Garrick Higgo	71	69	67	69	276	111,900
Chris Cannon	70	71	65	70	276	111,900
Luke Jerling	68	71	68	70	277	60,000
Daniel van Tonder	72	69	67	70	278	55,000
Pieter Moolman	71	70	72	66	279	50,000
Ryan Cairns	69	74	68	69	280	37,550
Adilson da Silva	71	69	70	70	280	37,550
Merrick Bremner	73	68	68	71	280	37,550
Michael Palmer	71	72	65	72	280	37,550
Ruan de Smidt	72	70	70	69	281	28,700
Jaco Prinsloo	65	74	71	71	281	28,700
Thriston Lawrence	72	67	71	71	281	28,700
Ross McGowan	70	68	68	75	281	28,700
Trevor Fisher, Jr.	71	72	71	68	282	26,600

560 / AFRICAN SUNSHINE TOUR

	SCORES				TOTAL	MONEY
J.J. Senekal	69	70	71	72	282	26,600
Jaco Ahlers	68	66	72	76	282	26,600
Rhys West	70	69	72	72	283	25,400
Vaughn Groenewald	72	74	68	70	284	24,200
Sean Bradley	70	72	69	73	284	24,200
Tristen Strydom	69	70	70	75	284	24,200
Jbe' Kruger	73	70	72	70	285	22,250
Luke Joy	74	72	69	70	285	22,250
Rourke van der Spuy	67	70	77	71	285	22,250
Anthony Michael	72	69	71	73	285	22,250
Jean Hugo	72	70	71	73	286	21,000
Keith Horne	69	73	70	74	286	21,000

Investec Royal Swazi Open

Royal Swazi Spa Country Club, Mbabane, Swaziland
Par 36-36–72; 6,715 yards

May 1-4
purse, R1,500,000

	POINTS				TOTAL	MONEY
Martin Rohwer	18	12	18	11	59	R237,750
Steve Surry	14	9	13	11	47	137,925
Jake Roos	8	20	14	5	47	137,925
Stephen Ferreira	15	9	8	13	45	71,550
Jean Hugo	9	11	6	19	45	71,550
Thriston Lawrence	13	9	11	11	44	49,875
Jaco Prinsloo	9	17	11	7	44	49,875
Vaughn Groenewald	7	10	17	9	43	37,650
Derick Petersen	5	10	13	14	42	30,250
Estiaan Conradie	11	14	6	11	42	30,250
Daniel Greene	15	11	14	2	42	30,250
M.J. Viljoen	17	10	7	7	41	25,950
Keenan Davidse	11	11	11	7	40	24,450
Neil Schietekat	12	12	9	6	39	22,575
Merrick Bremner	11	7	8	13	39	22,575
J.C. Ritchie	6	11	8	13	38	20,700
Michael Palmer	12	7	12	7	38	20,700
Ruan Conradie	13	8	16	1	38	20,700
Ockie Strydom	9	6	12	10	37	18,750
Christiaan Basson	9	12	6	10	37	18,750
Titch Moore	10	14	11	2	37	18,750
Toto Thimba	7	8	7	14	36	17,475
Jacques Blaauw	7	9	11	9	36	17,475
Musiwalo Nethunzwi	7	11	2	14	34	16,125
Andre Nel	9	9	6	10	34	16,125
Luke Jerling	12	2	10	10	34	16,125
Fredrik From	11	8	14	1	34	16,125

Lombard Insurance Classic

Royal Swazi Spa Country Club, Mbabane, Swaziland
Par 36-36–72; 6,715 yards

May 17-19
purse, R1,000,000

	SCORES			TOTAL	MONEY
Jake Redman	65	64	67	196	R158,500
Toto Thimba	65	67	65	197	97,500
Thriston Lawrence	63	69	65	197	97,500
Ruan Conradie	65	67	66	198	63,000

	SCORES			TOTAL	MONEY
Keenan Davidse	69	67	63	199	47,000
Jaco Ahlers	64	69	67	200	34,750
Doug McGuigan	67	64	69	200	34,750
Titch Moore	70	64	67	201	27,500
Jake Roos	70	68	64	202	23,500
Ruan de Smidt	68	68	66	202	23,500
Daniel van Tonder	69	70	64	203	19,500
Hennie Otto	66	68	69	203	19,500
Jacques Blaauw	63	71	69	203	19,500
Keith Horne	68	64	71	203	19,500
C.J. du Plessis	69	70	65	204	15,775
Vaughn Groenewald	69	67	68	204	15,775
Franklin Manchest	67	68	69	204	15,775
Clinton Grobler	65	67	72	204	15,775
Lyle Rowe	69	71	65	205	13,950
Fredrik From	68	67	70	205	13,950
Jaco Prinsloo	69	70	67	206	12,450
Pieter Moolman	68	69	69	206	12,450
Heinrich Bruiners	67	70	69	206	12,450
Neil Schietekat	68	67	71	206	12,450
Combrinck Smit	71	67	69	207	10,950
Aubrey Beckley	64	69	74	207	10,950

Sun City Challenge

Gary Player Country Club, Sun City, South Africa
Par 36-36–72; 7,831 yards

June 5-7
purse, R1,000,000

	SCORES			TOTAL	MONEY
Garrick Higgo	69	71	69	209	R158,500
Ockie Strydom	72	71	67	210	115,000
Jaco van Zyl	70	68	74	212	80,000
Kyle Barker	66	75	72	213	55,000
J.C. Ritchie	68	72	73	213	55,000
Keith Horne	73	70	71	214	28,800
Jaco Ahlers	68	75	71	214	28,800
Ryan Cairns	71	71	72	214	28,800
Rhys West	70	72	72	214	28,800
Neil Schietekat	70	69	75	214	28,800
Callum Mowat	73	72	70	215	20,000
Jacquin Hess	74	70	71	215	20,000
Keenan Davidse	71	72	72	215	20,000
Jacques P. de Villiers	68	77	71	216	17,033.33
Christiaan Basson	72	72	72	216	17,033.33
James Allan	70	73	73	216	17,033.33
Titch Moore	68	76	73	217	14,733.33
Thriston Lawrence	74	69	74	217	14,733.33
Jacques Blaauw	70	72	75	217	14,733.33
Jbe' Kruger	73	73	72	218	12,700
Jake Roos	74	72	72	218	12,700
Michael Palmer	73	72	73	218	12,700
Wallie Coetsee	73	71	74	218	12,700
Wynand Dingle	73	71	74	218	12,700
Christiaan Bezuidenhout	75	72	72	219	10,440
Bennie van der Merwe	75	71	73	219	10,440
Louis de Jager	73	73	73	219	10,440
Ruan de Smidt	72	74	73	219	10,440
Ryan Tipping	73	70	76	219	10,440

KCB Karen Masters

Karen Country Club, Nairobi, Kenya
Par 36-36–72; 7,022 yards

June 27-30
purse, R2,200,000

	SCORES				TOTAL	MONEY
Toto Thimba	68	63	66	65	262	R348,700
Stephen Ferreira	62	66	68	69	265	243,100
Keith Horne	70	69	67	65	271	153,780
J.C. Ritchie	69	64	69	70	272	92,400
Garrick Higgo	67	67	69	71	274	66,000
M.J. Viljoen	69	69	67	70	275	60,500
Thriston Lawrence	73	69	68	67	277	52,250
Greg Snow	67	74	66	70	277	52,250
Merrick Bremner	70	68	71	69	278	38,573.33
Estiaan Conradie	69	72	67	70	278	38,573.33
Steve Surry	71	70	66	71	278	38,573.33
Daniel van Tonder	73	71	68	67	279	31,900
Jaco Prinsloo	70	72	69	68	279	31,900
Keenan Davidse	71	71	68	69	279	31,900
Rhys West	71	71	73	65	280	28,600
Keelan van Wyk	70	72	71	67	280	28,600
Jack Harrison	73	70	69	68	280	28,600
Ockie Strydom	71	70	69	70	280	28,600
Deon Germishuys	71	67	71	71	280	28,600
Kyle McClatchie	74	67	68	71	280	28,600
Michael Palmer	69	67	72	72	280	28,600
Chris Swanepoel	70	69	73	69	281	24,772
Heinrich Bruiners	68	73	71	69	281	24,772
Jean Hugo	72	71	69	69	281	24,772
Andrew Odoh	69	70	71	71	281	24,772
C.J. du Plessis	69	67	70	75	281	24,772

Royal Swazi Spa Challenge

Royal Swazi Spa Country Club, Mbabane, Swaziland
Par 36-36–72; 6,715 yards

July 31-August 2
purse, R1,000,000

	SCORES			TOTAL	MONEY
Ruan Conradie	61	71	66	198	R158,500
Paul Boshoff	66	70	63	199	86,000
Anthony Michael	67	68	64	199	86,000
Jaco van Zyl	71	63	65	199	86,000
J.C. Ritchie	66	68	66	200	38,833.33
Michael Palmer	68	64	68	200	38,833.33
Madalitso Muthiya	64	68	68	200	38,833.33
Deon Germishuys	64	67	70	201	27,500
Combrinck Smit	69	67	66	202	22,000
Hayden Griffiths	69	67	66	202	22,000
Haydn Porteous	67	68	67	202	22,000
Christiaan Basson	68	65	69	202	22,000
Luke Jerling	73	65	65	203	18,500
Thriston Lawrence	68	67	68	203	18,500
Neil Schietekat	66	71	67	204	16,133.33
Wynand Dingle	69	66	69	204	16,133.33
Jacques Blaauw	68	66	70	204	16,133.33
Jean Hugo	71	67	67	205	13,200
Ruan de Smidt	68	68	69	205	13,200
C.J. du Plessis	71	65	69	205	13,200
Louis de Jager	70	65	70	205	13,200

	SCORES	TOTAL	MONEY
Jacques P. de Villiers	67 67 71	205	13,200
Allister de Kock	68 66 71	205	13,200
Rhys West	66 67 72	205	13,200
Kyle Barker	67 71 68	206	10,600
M.J. Viljoen	73 64 69	206	10,600
Jake Roos	69 67 70	206	10,600
Titch Moore	69 67 70	206	10,600

Vodacom Origins of Golf - Sishen

Sishen Golf Club, Kathu, South Africa
Par 36-36–72; 7,171 yards

August 22-24
purse, R1,000,000

	SCORES	TOTAL	MONEY
Ockie Strydom	69 65 66	200	R158,500
Thriston Lawrence	68 71 67	206	115,000
Riekus Nortje	71 69 68	208	57,000
Michael Palmer	70 70 68	208	57,000
Luke Jerling	70 69 69	208	57,000
Chris Swanepoel	69 68 71	208	57,000
Neil Schietekat	73 67 69	209	31,500
Estiaan Conradie	71 73 66	210	26,000
Hennie Otto	71 70 69	210	26,000
Stefan Wears-Taylor	70 73 68	211	20,625
Herman Loubser	69 72 70	211	20,625
Philip Geerts	73 67 71	211	20,625
Trevor Fisher, Jr.	71 67 73	211	20,625
Rhys West	72 72 68	212	15,571.43
Jared Harvey	75 69 68	212	15,571.43
Hendrikus Stoop	72 71 69	212	15,571.43
Michael Hollick	68 74 70	212	15,571.43
Yubin Jung	71 70 71	212	15,571.43
Alex Haindl	72 69 71	212	15,571.43
Daniel van Tonder	70 70 72	212	15,571.43
Keenan Davidse	69 75 69	213	11,950
Dylan Naidoo	74 70 69	213	11,950
Erhard Lambrechts	71 72 70	213	11,950
Jacques Blaauw	72 71 70	213	11,950
Louis Albertse	69 73 71	213	11,950
Victor Lange	71 67 75	213	11,950

King's Cup

Royal Swazi Spa Country Club, Mbabane, Swaziland
Par 36-36–72; 6,715 yards

September 5-7
purse, R1,000,000

	SCORES	TOTAL	MONEY
Jaco Ahlers	66 65 66	197	R158,500
Daniel Greene	68 66 66	200	115,000
Alex Haindl	66 68 67	201	71,500
Estiaan Conradie	65 67 69	201	71,500
Jaco Prinsloo	69 67 66	202	36,000
Neil Schietekat	70 66 66	202	36,000
Philip Geerts	67 67 68	202	36,000
Peetie van der Merwe	67 67 68	202	36,000
Jacques Blaauw	70 70 64	204	22,000
James Hart du Preez	69 67 68	204	22,000

	SCORES			TOTAL	MONEY
Andre Nel	68	66	70	204	22,000
Ruan de Smidt	66	68	70	204	22,000
Ruan Conradie	68	71	66	205	18,500
Titch Moore	65	69	71	205	18,500
Christiaan Basson	67	72	67	206	15,775
Rhys West	71	67	68	206	15,775
Hennie Otto	71	67	68	206	15,775
Martin Rohwer	67	67	72	206	15,775
Thriston Lawrence	69	71	67	207	12,950
Clinton Grobler	68	69	70	207	12,950
Jacques P. de Villiers	65	71	71	207	12,950
Benjamin Follett-Smith	64	72	71	207	12,950
Fredrik From	67	69	71	207	12,950
Toto Thimba	66	68	73	207	12,950
Riekus Nortje	70	70	68	208	10,440
Doug McGuigan	68	71	69	208	10,440
Callum Mowat	68	71	69	208	10,440
Theunis Bezuidenhout	69	68	71	208	10,440
Wynand Dingle	67	67	74	208	10,440

Vodacom Origins of Golf - Humewood

Humewood Golf Club, Port Elizabeth, South Africa
Par 35-37–72; 4,936 yards

September 26-29
purse, R1,000,000

	SCORES			TOTAL	MONEY
Merrick Bremner	65	65	67	197	R158,500
Ruan Conradie	69	70	63	202	86,000
Clinton Grobler	70	66	66	202	86,000
Jonathan Agren	71	64	67	202	86,000
Ruan de Smidt	69	67	67	203	47,000
Daniel Greene	70	71	64	205	28,800
Daniel van Tonder	70	70	65	205	28,800
Doug McGuigan	71	69	65	205	28,800
Andrew Curlewis	72	67	66	205	28,800
Steve Surry	68	70	67	205	28,800
Martin Rohwer	72	68	66	206	21,000
Fredrik From	75	66	66	207	19,000
Benjamin Follett-Smith	73	67	67	207	19,000
Ryan Tipping	72	67	68	207	19,000
Allister de Kock	69	72	67	208	15,775
Jacques Blaauw	71	69	68	208	15,775
Christiaan Basson	70	70	68	208	15,775
Philip Geerts	70	67	71	208	15,775
Breyten Meyer	74	69	66	209	12,950
Jaco Prinsloo	71	71	67	209	12,950
Garrick Higgo	74	68	67	209	12,950
J.J. Senekal	69	72	68	209	12,950
Wallie Coetsee	70	71	68	209	12,950
Lyle Rowe	71	68	70	209	12,950
Jean-Paul Strydom	72	71	67	210	10,600
James Hart du Preez	69	72	69	210	10,600
Luke Jerling	71	69	70	210	10,600
M.J. Viljoen	71	67	72	210	10,600

Vodacom Origins of Golf - Stellenbosch

Stellenbosch Golf Club, Stellenbosch, South Africa
Par 36-36–72; 6,987 yards

October 3-5
purse, R1,000,000

	SCORES			TOTAL	MONEY
Thriston Lawrence	68	68	65	201	R158,500
Riekus Nortje	66	69	67	202	76,250
J.J. Senekal	65	70	67	202	76,250
Jean-Paul Strydom	63	68	71	202	76,250
Deon Germishuys	66	65	71	202	76,250
Garrick Higgo	71	67	66	204	34,750
Stefan Wears-Taylor	65	69	70	204	34,750
Chris Cannon	69	69	67	205	26,000
Hennie Otto	68	66	71	205	26,000
Keenan Davidse	66	73	67	206	20,625
Estiaan Conradie	70	68	68	206	20,625
Erhard Lambrechts	69	67	70	206	20,625
Jonathan Agren	69	67	70	206	20,625
Andrew van der Knaap	66	73	68	207	18,000
Duane Keun	70	71	67	208	15,166.67
Toto Thimba	74	67	67	208	15,166.67
Garth Mulroy	72	67	69	208	15,166.67
Jake Roos	71	68	69	208	15,166.67
Philip Geerts	67	69	72	208	15,166.67
Martin Rohwer	67	67	74	208	15,166.67
Ruan Conradie	68	73	68	209	11,728.57
Oliver Bekker	72	68	69	209	11,728.57
Jaco Ahlers	70	70	69	209	11,728.57
Trevor Fisher, Jr.	67	73	69	209	11,728.57
Louis Albertse	69	68	72	209	11,728.57
Hendrikus Stoop	73	64	72	209	11,728.57
Aubrey Beckley	70	66	73	209	11,728.57

Sun Wild Coast Sun Challenge

Wild Coast Sun Country Club, Port Edward, South Africa
Par 35-35–70; 6,351 yards

October 9-11
purse, R1,000,000

	SCORES			TOTAL	MONEY
Jean Hugo	60	65	74	199	R158,500
Clinton Grobler	68	67	68	203	86,000
Hennie du Plessis	64	71	68	203	86,000
Ruan de Smidt	65	65	73	203	86,000
Titch Moore	68	69	67	204	36,000
Estiaan Conradie	68	67	69	204	36,000
Luke Jerling	67	66	71	204	36,000
Jaco Ahlers	63	69	72	204	36,000
Neil Schietekat	65	73	67	205	22,000
Jonathan Agren	69	69	67	205	22,000
Jacques Blaauw	67	71	67	205	22,000
Merrick Bremner	68	68	69	205	22,000
Louis Albertse	69	68	69	206	19,000
Jean-Paul Strydom	71	69	67	207	17,033.33
Divan van den Heever	67	71	69	207	17,033.33
Keenan Davidse	68	68	71	207	17,033.33
Hennie Otto	70	70	68	208	14,220
Oliver Bekker	69	70	69	208	14,220
Scott Campbell	68	70	70	208	14,220
Anton Haig	71	67	70	208	14,220

	SCORES			TOTAL	MONEY
Ruan Conradie	70	64	74	208	14,220
Ruan Korb	69	71	69	209	12,200
C.J. du Plessis	67	69	73	209	12,200
Chris Cannon	67	67	75	209	12,200
Teaghan Gauche	65	75	70	210	10,950
Roberto Lupini	65	74	71	210	10,950

Vodacom Origins of Golf - Selborne

Selborne Park Golf Club, Pennington, South Africa
Par 36-36–72; 6,509 yards

October 17-19
purse, R1,000,000

	SCORES			TOTAL	MONEY
Jaco Ahlers	64	70	67	201	R158,500
Ockie Strydom	69	70	64	203	115,000
James Hart du Preez	69	70	66	205	71,500
Jacques Blaauw	70	66	69	205	71,500
Allister de Kock	68	68	70	206	42,500
Thriston Lawrence	68	66	72	206	42,500
Rhys West	71	71	65	207	25,400
Dylan Kok	72	68	67	207	25,400
Steve Surry	67	70	70	207	25,400
Trevor Fisher, Jr.	70	66	71	207	25,400
Heinrich Bruiners	68	67	72	207	25,400
David McIntyre	71	73	65	209	18,500
Keith Horne	73	69	67	209	18,500
J.J. Senekal	69	70	70	209	18,500
Ruan Conradie	67	71	71	209	18,500
Breyten Meyer	72	71	67	210	15,366.67
Fredrik From	73	68	69	210	15,366.67
Neil Schietekat	71	68	71	210	15,366.67
Luke Jerling	75	69	67	211	13,950
Hennie Otto	72	69	70	211	13,950
D.K. Kim	71	73	68	212	11,525
Oliver Bekker	75	69	68	212	11,525
Jean Hugo	72	71	69	212	11,525
Anton Haig	74	68	70	212	11,525
Christiaan Basson	74	68	70	212	11,525
Madalitso Muthiya	70	71	71	212	11,525
Adilson da Silva	71	70	71	212	11,525
Lyle Rowe	66	71	75	212	11,525

Sibaya Challenge

The Woods at Mount Edgecombe, Durban, South Africa
Par 35-35–70; 6,435 yards

October 23-25
purse, R1,000,000

	SCORES			TOTAL	MONEY
Hennie Otto	69	66	62	197	R158,500
James Hart du Preez	68	63	67	198	115,000
Daniel van Tonder	68	68	63	199	63,333.33
Anthony Michael	64	70	65	199	63,333.33
Malcolm Mitchell	64	68	67	199	63,333.33
Steve Surry	68	66	66	200	32,333.33
Oliver Bekker	67	67	66	200	32,333.33
Neil Schietekat	68	62	70	200	32,333.33
Luke Mayo	68	68	65	201	22,000

	SCORES			TOTAL	MONEY
Kyle Barker	71	65	65	201	22,000
Chris Cannon	68	67	66	201	22,000
Dylan Naidoo	66	69	66	201	22,000
Jake Redman	68	69	65	202	16,683.33
Martin Rohwer	67	69	66	202	16,683.33
Christiaan Basson	69	66	67	202	16,683.33
Titch Moore	64	71	67	202	16,683.33
Jacques P. de Villiers	69	64	69	202	16,683.33
Andre Nel	68	65	69	202	16,683.33
Ryan Cairns	71	67	65	203	13,450
J.C. Ritchie	69	68	66	203	13,450
Andrew van der Knaap	67	70	66	203	13,450
Toto Thimba	68	68	67	203	13,450
Heinrich Bruiners	71	67	66	204	11,450
Clinton Grobler	69	69	66	204	11,450
Jaco Prinsloo	73	64	67	204	11,450
Mark Williams	70	66	68	204	11,450

Vodacom Origins of Golf Final

Simola Golf & Country Estate, Knysna, South Africa
Par 36-36–72; 6,965 yards

October 31-November 2
purse, R1,000,000

	SCORES			TOTAL	MONEY
George Coetzee	61	69	66	196	R158,500
M.J. Viljoen	67	66	66	199	115,000
Martin Rohwer	67	70	64	201	71,500
Keenan Davidse	67	69	65	201	71,500
Jake Roos	72	68	62	202	38,833.33
Andre De Decker	68	67	67	202	38,833.33
Deon Germishuys	71	64	67	202	38,833.33
Luke Jerling	69	69	65	203	26,000
Daniel van Tonder	68	67	68	203	26,000
Fredrik From	67	66	71	204	20,625
Malcolm Mitchell	69	68	67	204	20,625
Hennie du Plessis	69	70	65	204	20,625
Jean Hugo	66	69	69	204	20,625
Anton Haig	69	68	68	205	17,500
Garrick Higgo	71	65	69	205	17,500
Doug McGuigan	69	68	69	206	15,075
Franklin Manchest	68	71	67	206	15,075
Hennie Otto	70	68	68	206	15,075
Combrinck Smit	68	70	68	206	15,075
Breyten Meyer	67	73	67	207	12,700
Stefan Wears-Taylor	70	70	67	207	12,700
Jade Buitendag	71	68	68	207	12,700
James Hart du Preez	70	69	68	207	12,700
Jake Redman	64	71	72	207	12,700
Hayden Griffiths	72	68	68	208	10,766.67
C.J. du Plessis	68	72	68	208	10,766.67
Jaco Ahlers	71	68	69	208	10,766.67

Nedbank Golf Challenge

Gary Player Country Club, Sun City, South Africa
Par 36-36–72; 7,847 yards

November 14-17
purse, US$7,500,000

	SCORES				TOTAL	MONEY
Tommy Fleetwood	69	69	73	65	276	€2,268,190.89
Marcus Kinhult	69	69	70	68	276	766,648.52
(Fleetwood defeated Kinhult on first playoff hole.)						
Thomas Detry	66	71	69	74	280	343,555.31
Jason Scrivener	69	70	71	70	280	343,555.31
Bernd Wiesberger	71	69	70	70	280	343,555.31
Louis Oosthuizen	63	72	71	75	281	178,052.98
Lee Westwood	68	73	69	71	281	178,052.98
Zander Lombard	68	65	72	77	282	126,905.28
Robert Macintyre	73	76	65	68	282	126,905.28
Matthew Fitzpatrick	71	69	73	71	284	93,751.89
Joost Luiten	72	70	69	73	284	93,751.89
Kalle Samooja	72	71	72	69	284	93,751.89
Jorge Campillo	69	72	74	70	285	73,205.86
Aaron Rai	70	69	71	75	285	73,205.86
Nacho Elvira	70	70	71	74	285	73,205.86
Tom Lewis	71	73	69	72	285	73,205.86
Joachim B. Hansen	69	70	71	76	286	62,602.07
Rafa Cabrera Bello	74	70	69	73	286	62,602.07
Henrik Stenson	74	71	69	72	286	62,602.07
Padraig Harrington	71	72	73	71	287	57,158.41
Guido Migliozzi	67	73	72	76	288	53,680.52
Martin Kaymer	70	72	72	74	288	53,680.52
Gavin Green	74	70	73	71	288	53,680.52
Paul Waring	69	71	78	71	289	47,405.19
Alvaro Quiros	70	70	72	77	289	47,405.19
Mikko Korhonen	70	70	70	79	289	47,405.19
Benjamin Hebert	72	73	72	72	289	47,405.19
Christiaan Bezuidenhout	74	70	71	74	289	47,405.19
Kiradech Aphibarnrat	76	73	71	69	289	47,405.19
Oliver Wilson	69	72	67	82	290	37,349.54
Sebastian Soderberg	69	72	73	76	290	37,349.54
George Coetzee	69	73	73	75	290	37,349.54
Kurt Kitayama	70	72	73	75	290	37,349.54
Erik van Rooyen	70	73	70	77	290	37,349.54
Nicolas Colsaerts	72	73	74	71	290	37,349.54
Romain Langasque	73	74	72	71	290	37,349.54
Thomas Pieters	73	76	72	69	290	37,349.54
Adri Arnaus	74	73	72	71	290	37,349.54
Joakim Lagergren	73	75	71	72	291	30,847.40
Ian Poulter	74	71	73	73	291	30,847.40
Branden Grace	74	75	72	70	291	30,847.40
Richie Ramsay	72	78	70	72	292	28,579.21
Steven Brown	73	75	69	75	292	28,579.21
Alex Noren	73	69	73	78	293	25,857.38
Scott Jamieson	73	71	72	77	293	25,857.38
Matt Wallace	73	74	71	75	293	25,857.38
Chris Paisley	75	74	72	72	293	25,857.38
Jordan Smith	73	74	72	75	294	22,228.27
Justin Harding	73	78	69	74	294	22,228.27
Pablo Larrazabal	76	72	72	74	294	22,228.27
Scott Hend	77	73	70	74	294	22,228.27
Ernie Els	68	81	72	74	295	18,599.17
Mike Lorenzo-Vera	72	71	72	80	295	18,599.17
Matthew Southgate	72	79	70	74	295	18,599.17
Haotong Li	73	76	71	75	295	18,599.17
Shubhankar Sharma	70	74	78	74	296	16,330.97

	SCORES				TOTAL	MONEY
Ryan Fox	74	75	74	74	297	15,423.70
David Lipsky	72	74	77	75	298	14,516.42
Masahiro Kawamura	72	75	76	76	299	14,062.78
Richard Sterne	69	79	77	75	300	13,609.15
Andy Sullivan	75	73	74	80	302	13,155.51
Andrea Pavan	77	74	80	72	303	12,701.87
Lucas Bjerregaard	81	75	75	80	311	12,248.23

Alfred Dunhill Championship

Leopard Creek Country Club, Malelane, South Africa
Par 35-37–72; 7,249 yards

November 28-December 1
purse, €1,500,000

	SCORES				TOTAL	MONEY
Pablo Larrazabal	66	69	70	75	280	€237,750
Joel Sjoholm	70	74	68	69	281	165,000
Wil Besseling	65	73	70	74	282	82,300
Branden Grace	68	70	71	73	282	82,300
Charl Schwartzel	70	72	70	70	282	82,300
Daniel van Tonder	68	75	73	68	284	53,100
Justin Harding	70	73	71	71	285	35,737.50
Zander Lombard	72	70	69	74	285	35,737.50
M.J. Viljoen	72	71	69	73	285	35,737.50
Johannes Veerman	72	71	70	72	285	35,737.50
Garrick Porteous	66	75	75	70	286	25,800
Connor Syme	69	75	73	69	286	25,800
Calum Hill	73	73	71	70	287	23,550
Robin Roussel	68	75	74	71	288	20,550
Jaco van Zyl	69	72	75	72	288	20,550
Richard Sterne	70	74	72	72	288	20,550
Laurie Canter	71	73	70	74	288	20,550
Jonathan Caldwell	74	69	74	71	288	20,550
Eddie Pepperell	71	73	72	73	289	17,700
Christiaan Basson	71	74	77	67	289	17,700
Renato Paratore	74	71	75	69	289	17,700
Alex Haindl	71	72	76	71	290	16,425
Dylan Naidoo	71	72	76	71	290	16,425
Keith Horne	66	79	72	74	291	14,000
Alejandro Canizares	67	77	74	73	291	14,000
Jack Harrison	71	72	78	70	291	14,000
Jaco Ahlers	72	72	72	75	291	14,000
Daniel Greene	72	73	72	74	291	14,000
Wilco Nienaber	72	73	72	74	291	14,000
Clement Sordet	72	75	71	73	291	14,000
George Coetzee	73	71	72	75	291	14,000
Lars van Meijel	74	70	76	71	291	14,000
Thomas Aiken	68	72	78	74	292	11,850
Adrian Otaegui	69	72	71	80	292	11,850
Edoardo Molinari	74	73	72	73	292	11,850
Jack Singh Brar	68	72	75	78	293	10,500
David Drysdale	68	77	70	78	293	10,500
Adrien Saddier	71	73	78	71	293	10,500
Benjamin Poke	73	72	72	76	293	10,500
Jacques Blaauw	73	73	74	73	293	10,500
Antoine Rozner	74	67	78	74	293	10,500
Adrian Meronk	69	76	70	79	294	8,700
Marcus Armitage	70	70	71	83	294	8,700
Matthieu Pavon	71	72	78	73	294	8,700
Pedro Figueiredo	72	74	77	71	294	8,700
Jayden Trey Schaper [A]	73	73	70	78	294	

	SCORES				TOTAL	MONEY
Lorenzo Gagli	74	70	80	70	294	8,700
Richard Bland	76	71	69	78	294	8,700
Matthew Jordan	69	74	80	72	295	6,900
Rasmus Hojgaard	72	70	78	75	295	6,900
Gregory Havret	72	72	70	81	295	6,900
Jeff Winther	75	72	72	76	295	6,900
Thriston Lawrence	77	68	79	71	295	6,900
Hennie Otto	78	68	74	75	295	6,900
Grant Forrest	68	79	73	76	296	5,400
J.C. Ritchie	72	71	79	74	296	5,400
James Morrison	72	71	78	75	296	5,400
Haydn Porteous	73	71	75	77	296	5,400
Brandon Stone	72	75	78	72	297	4,725
David Law	72	75	76	74	297	4,725
Martin Rohwer	69	75	76	78	298	4,350
Adilson da Silva	70	76	75	77	298	4,350
Oliver Wilson	73	73	77	75	298	4,350
Toby Tree	70	73	81	75	299	3,825
Lee Slattery	72	75	73	79	299	3,825
Ernie Els	74	73	75	77	299	3,825
Keenan Davidse	76	71	76	76	299	3,825
Carlos Pigem	74	71	81	76	302	3,450
Niklas Lemke	72	73	88	74	307	3,225
Ross Fisher	74	73	81	79	307	3,225
Oliver Bekker	73	71	80	84	308	3,000

AfrAsia Bank Mauritius Open

Heritage Golf Club, Bel Ombre, Mauritius
Par 36-36–72; 7,113 yards

December 5-8
purse, €1,000,000

	SCORES				TOTAL	MONEY
Rasmus Hojgaard	66	69	66	68	269	€158,500
Antoine Rozner	67	67	66	69	269	92,100
Renato Paratore	69	67	66	67	269	92,100
(Hojgaard defeated Paratore on first and Rozner on third playoff hole.)						
Benjamin Hebert	66	68	70	66	270	38,825
Grant Forrest	66	71	67	66	270	38,825
Thomas Detry	67	66	67	70	270	38,825
Louis de Jager	72	65	69	64	270	38,825
Robin Sciot-Siegrist	73	68	65	65	271	24,600
Sihwan Kim	67	67	67	71	272	18,900
Connor Syme	68	66	69	69	272	18,900
Oliver Bekker	69	70	66	67	272	18,900
Julien Guerrier	71	67	68	66	272	18,900
Brandon Stone	66	67	69	71	273	14,575
Soren Kjeldsen	68	67	69	69	273	14,575
Ashun Wu	71	65	68	69	273	14,575
Thomas Pieters	74	66	67	66	273	14,575
Matthieu Pavon	67	66	75	66	274	12,475
Calum Hill	68	64	68	74	274	12,475
Thriston Lawrence	69	70	66	69	274	12,475
Jyoti Randhawa	70	69	70	65	274	12,475
Christiaan Bezuidenhout	67	68	68	72	275	10,950
Garrick Higgo	70	67	71	67	275	10,950
Johannes Veerman	70	71	67	67	275	10,950
George Coetzee	71	70	66	68	275	10,950
Marcel Siem	69	71	69	67	276	10,200
Romain Langasque	66	74	71	66	277	9,042.86
Zander Lombard	67	71	73	66	277	9,042.86

		SCORES			TOTAL	MONEY
Haydn Porteous	69	69	70	69	277	9,042.86
Yanwei Liu	70	70	68	69	277	9,042.86
Joel Sjoholm	71	66	75	65	277	9,042.86
Lorenzo Gagli	71	67	70	69	277	9,042.86
Ashley Chesters	71	67	71	68	277	9,042.86
Jaco Ahlers	67	72	69	70	278	7,700
Travis Smyth	70	66	71	71	278	7,700
Daniel van Tonder	70	71	67	70	278	7,700
Thomas Linard	72	68	67	71	278	7,700
Justin Walters	74	67	69	68	278	7,700
Ockie Strydom	68	72	72	67	279	6,700
Jean-Paul Strydom	69	69	70	71	279	6,700
Jack Singh Brar	69	71	68	71	279	6,700
Neil Schietekat	70	68	71	70	279	6,700
Rhys Enoch	70	70	71	68	279	6,700
David Law	68	71	71	70	280	5,600
John Catlin	70	69	72	69	280	5,600
Lee Slattery	70	70	66	74	280	5,600
Gonzalo Fernandez-Castano	70	71	71	68	280	5,600
Bryce Easton	72	64	75	69	280	5,600
Trevor Fisher, Jr.	72	68	70	70	280	5,600
Sebastian Garcia Rodriguez	70	67	72	72	281	4,700
Paul Lawrie	71	69	68	73	281	4,700
Carlos Pigem	72	65	73	71	281	4,700
J.C. Ritchie	70	68	71	73	282	4,200
Seungjae Maeng	72	69	72	69	282	4,200
Keith Horne	67	71	74	71	283	3,450
Abhijit Singh Chadha	69	70	71	73	283	3,450
Hennie Otto	70	68	73	72	283	3,450
Jake Higginbottom	70	70	72	71	283	3,450
Gregory Havret	70	71	70	72	283	3,450
Udayan Mane	73	68	74	68	283	3,450
Darren Fichardt	68	69	73	74	284	2,900
Jack Senior	69	71	72	72	284	2,900
Richard Bland	70	71	69	74	284	2,900
Keenan Davidse	70	71	74	70	285	2,650
Oliver Farr	72	68	73	72	285	2,650
Ricardo Santos	67	74	74	71	286	2,450
Christiaan Basson	71	70	73	72	286	2,450
Suttijet Kooratanapisan	71	70	75	73	289	2,250
Settee Prakongvech	74	67	74	74	289	2,250
Doug McGuigan	73	68	74	75	290	2,050
Anthony Michael	74	64	75	77	290	2,050
Viraj Madappa	71	70	75	75	291	1,600
Estiaan Conradie	69	69	79	75	292	1,597

Women's Tours

Diamond Resorts Tournament of Champions

Four Season Golf & Sports Club Orlando, Lake Buena Vista, Florida January 17-20
Par 34-37–71; 6,645 yards purse, $1,200,000

	SCORES				TOTAL	MONEY
Eun-Hee Ji	65	69	66	70	270	$180,000
Mirim Lee	67	68	69	68	272	147,962
Nelly Korda	70	67	65	71	273	107,336
Moriya Jutanugarn	71	67	67	69	274	74,933
Shanshan Feng	71	67	66	70	274	74,933
Stacy Lewis	66	74	66	70	276	50,225
Brooke M. Henderson	65	67	69	75	276	50,225
Lydia Ko	66	68	66	77	277	40,100
Georgia Hall	73	66	69	70	278	36,049
Lexi Thompson	67	69	73	70	279	31,593
Gaby Lopez	69	68	69	73	279	31,593
In Gee Chun	70	71	71	69	281	27,461
Annie Park	68	70	73	70	281	27,461
Amy Yang	75	69	69	69	282	24,221
Cristie Kerr	72	72	67	71	282	24,221
Nasa Hataoka	73	72	71	67	283	21,629
Marina Alex	69	67	72	75	283	21,629
Danielle Kang	68	74	70	72	284	19,334
Ariya Jutanugarn	67	67	75	75	284	19,334
Mi Hyang Lee	68	71	69	76	284	19,334
Anna Nordqvist	71	74	69	71	285	17,984
Katherine Kirk	73	72	71	70	286	17,012
Brittany Lincicome	71	72	70	73	286	17,012
Pernilla Lindberg	77	70	68	72	287	16,040
Sei Young Kim	69	69	73	77	288	15,473
Thidapa Suwannapura	68	69	79	76	292	14,906

ISPS Handa Vic Open

See Australian Ladies Tour section.

ISPS Handa Women's Australian Open

See Australian Ladies Tour section.

Honda LPGA Thailand

Siam Country Club, Pattaya Old Course, Chonburi, Thailand February 21-24
Par 36-36–72; 6,576 yards purse, $1,600,000

	SCORES				TOTAL	MONEY
Amy Yang	69	66	66	65	266	$240,000
Minjee Lee	65	69	67	66	267	149,659
Carlota Ciganda	70	67	68	63	268	108,567
Jenny Shin	65	68	70	68	271	83,985
Eun-Hee Ji	63	71	70	68	272	67,599
Brooke M. Henderson	66	73	66	68	273	55,308

	SCORES				TOTAL	MONEY
Nelly Korda	69	69	66	70	274	46,295
Megan Khang	70	69	70	66	275	40,559
Danielle Kang	65	71	69	71	276	36,462
Cristie Kerr	75	67	66	69	277	29,866
Moriya Jutanugarn	69	68	71	69	277	29,866
Yu Liu	68	70	67	72	277	29,866
Austin Ernst	69	66	69	73	277	29,866
Ariya Jutanugarn	68	72	68	70	278	25,236
Sandra Gal	69	73	72	65	279	21,959
Bronte Law	68	72	72	67	279	21,959
Sei Young Kim	71	71	67	70	279	21,959
Shanshan Feng	71	71	66	71	279	21,959
Lydia Ko	73	67	71	69	280	19,173
Katherine Kirk	66	71	71	72	280	19,173
Sung Hyun Park	69	72	72	68	281	17,862
Charley Hull	69	71	73	68	281	17,862
Marina Alex	69	76	68	69	282	15,377
Mi Hyang Lee	71	73	69	69	282	15,377
Angel Yin	70	72	68	72	282	15,377
Michelle Wie	68	72	68	74	282	15,377
Amy Olson	68	67	72	75	282	15,377
Lizette Salas	66	68	71	77	282	15,377
Beatriz Recari	74	73	73	63	283	11,444
Jin Young Ko	72	73	70	68	283	11,444
Ally McDonald	69	72	74	68	283	11,444
So Yeon Ryu	74	71	69	69	283	11,444
Pannarat Thanapolboonyaras	72	71	71	69	283	11,444
Gaby Lopez	71	72	71	69	283	11,444
Brittany Altomare	69	75	69	70	283	11,444
Jodi Ewart Shadoff	70	72	69	72	283	11,444
Jennifer Song	66	75	70	72	283	11,444

HSBC Women's World Championship

Sentosa Golf Club, Tanjong Course, Singapore
Par 36-36–72; 6,718 yards

February 28-March 3
purse, $1,500,000

	SCORES			TOTAL	MONEY
Sung Hyun Park	69	71	69	64	273	$225,000
Minjee Lee	68	71	67	69	275	143,696
Jin Young Ko	69	73	66	69	277	92,440
Azahara Munoz	71	68	69	69	277	92,440
Hyo Joo Kim	70	71	67	70	278	59,005
Amy Olson	68	69	71	70	278	59,005
Eun-Hee Ji	71	71	67	70	279	44,450
Jodi Ewart Shadoff	69	70	68	73	280	36,977
Ariya Jutanugarn	68	71	66	75	280	36,977
Nelly Korda	74	70	69	69	282	31,862
Jeongeun Lee$_6$	70	74	73	66	283	27,613
Brittany Altomare	74	71	68	70	283	27,613
Lydia Ko	72	70	69	72	283	27,613
Inbee Park	70	69	72	73	284	24,231
In Gee Chun	70	71	75	69	285	21,084
Mi Hyang Lee	74	73	67	71	285	21,084
Brooke M. Henderson	75	71	67	72	285	21,084
Carlota Ciganda	69	71	72	73	285	21,084
Thidapa Suwannapura	74	76	67	69	286	17,780
Caroline Masson	73	71	71	71	286	17,780
Jeong Eun Lee	74	70	70	72	286	17,780
Nasa Hataoka	69	72	73	72	286	17,780

	SCORES	TOTAL	MONEY
Bronte Law	73 74 68 72	287	15,604
Celine Boutier	68 75 72 72	287	15,604
Moriya Jutanugarn	69 71 72 75	287	15,604
Lexi Thompson	72 74 75 67	288	13,138
Pornanong Phatlum	74 74 72 68	288	13,138
Anna Nordqvist	76 69 73 70	288	13,138
Gaby Lopez	72 75 70 71	288	13,138
So Yeon Ryu	75 74 67 72	288	13,138
Shanshan Feng	69 76 68 75	288	13,138

Bank of Hope Founders Cup

Wildfire Golf Club at JW Marriott Phoenix Desert Ridge Resort & Spa,
Phoenix, Arizona
Par 36-36—72; 6,656 yards

March 21-24
purse, $1,500,000

	SCORES	TOTAL	MONEY
Jin Young Ko	65 72 64 65	266	$225,000
Jessica Korda	69 67 67 64	267	92,317
Nelly Korda	68 67 66 66	267	92,317
Carlota Ciganda	66 69 63 69	267	92,317
Yu Liu	68 64 65 70	267	92,317
Shanshan Feng	70 69 64 66	269	45,776
Charlotte Thomas	65 71 67 66	269	45,776
Brooke M. Henderson	67 68 69 66	270	34,701
Lydia Ko	67 67 67 69	270	34,701
Cristie Kerr	69 67 68 67	271	27,810
Sei Young Kim	69 67 67 68	271	27,810
Hyo Joo Kim	69 68 64 70	271	27,810
Mi Jung Hur	68 66 69 69	272	24,216
Jeongeun Lee$_6$	70 65 72 66	273	20,894
Pornanong Phatlum	66 70 70 67	273	20,894
Amy Yang	68 66 71 68	273	20,894
Sung Hyun Park	66 66 69 72	273	20,894
Su Oh	69 72 69 64	274	16,123
Emma Talley	73 69 66 66	274	16,123
Caroline Masson	71 69 67 67	274	16,123
Ariya Jutanugarn	70 70 67 67	274	16,123
Hee Young Park	71 67 69 67	274	16,123
Sarah Schmelzel	67 70 68 69	274	16,123
Linnea Strom	69 65 70 70	274	16,123
Bronte Law	69 69 65 71	274	16,123
Nanna Koerstz Madsen	65 69 72 69	275	13,586
Brittany Lincicome	74 65 70 67	276	11,623
Annie Park	71 68 69 68	276	11,623
Jodi Ewart Shadoff	70 69 69 68	276	11,623
Haru Nomura	70 71 66 69	276	11,623
Na Yeon Choi	65 71 69 71	276	11,623
Azahara Munoz	70 71 63 72	276	11,623
Angel Yin	67 67 66 76	276	11,623

Kia Classic

Aviara Golf Club, Carlsbad, California
Par 36-36–72; 6,609 yards

March 28-31
purse, $1,800,000

	SCORES				TOTAL	MONEY
Nasa Hataoka	69	70	64	67	270	$270,000
Danielle Kang	72	70	66	65	273	102,114
Jin Young Ko	68	73	67	65	273	102,114
Azahara Munoz	70	68	68	67	273	102,114
Sung Hyun Park	68	66	71	68	273	102,114
Inbee Park	68	67	67	71	273	102,114
Hyo Joo Kim	70	72	70	62	274	41,105
Chella Choi	65	70	72	67	274	41,105
Gaby Lopez	68	70	68	68	274	41,105
Mi Jung Hur	74	69	62	69	274	41,105
Thidapa Suwannapura	68	66	70	70	274	41,105
Stacy Lewis	71	68	69	67	275	31,480
Katherine Kirk	72	69	70	65	276	27,762
Jing Yan	68	73	66	69	276	27,762
Lydia Ko	71	69	67	69	276	27,762
Jeongeun Lee[6]	73	67	69	68	277	24,015
Mariajo Uribe	68	69	69	71	277	24,015
Jenny Shin	71	71	68	68	278	22,306
Moriya Jutanugarn	71	71	71	67	280	20,327
Shanshan Feng	70	72	69	69	280	20,327
Xiyu Lin	71	68	72	69	280	20,327
In-Kyung Kim	70	70	70	70	280	20,327
Eun-Hee Ji	69	70	74	68	281	17,198
Kristen Gillman	71	70	71	69	281	17,198
Pernilla Lindberg	73	70	68	70	281	17,198
Jodi Ewart Shadoff	72	70	69	70	281	17,198
Haru Nomura	68	74	68	71	281	17,198
Jane Park	72	70	73	67	282	13,334
Anne van Dam	73	72	69	68	282	13,334
Ariya Jutanugarn	68	72	74	68	282	13,334
Caroline Masson	72	73	68	69	282	13,334
Nicole Broch Larsen	70	71	72	69	282	13,334
Mi Hyang Lee	71	69	70	72	282	13,334
Celine Boutier	69	70	70	73	282	13,334
Minjee Lee	68	69	72	73	282	13,334

ANA Inspiration

Mission Hills Country Club, Dinah Shore Tournament Course,
Rancho Mirage, California
Par 36-36–72; 6,763 yards

April 4-7
purse, $3,000,000

	SCORES				TOTAL	MONEY
Jin Young Ko	69	71	68	70	278	$450,000
Mi Hyang Lee	70	73	68	70	281	275,721
Lexi Thompson	69	72	74	67	282	200,016
Carlota Ciganda	72	72	71	68	283	139,634
In-Kyung Kim	71	65	73	74	283	139,634
Kristen Gillman	74	71	73	66	284	74,472
Hyo Joo Kim	69	76	70	69	284	74,472
Jessica Korda	70	73	71	70	284	74,472
Ally McDonald	68	72	74	70	284	74,472
Jeongeun Lee[6]	71	71	71	71	284	74,472
Danielle Kang	72	69	70	73	284	74,472

	SCORES				TOTAL	MONEY
Moriya Jutanugarn	74	73	71	67	285	46,795
Jaye Marie Green	74	71	72	68	285	46,795
Jenny Shin	72	71	72	70	285	46,795
Charley Hull	72	69	74	70	285	46,795
Jing Yan	70	71	74	70	285	46,795
Lizette Salas	70	73	73	70	286	36,833
Brooke M. Henderson	71	72	71	72	286	36,833
Alena Sharp	76	70	67	73	286	36,833
Katherine Kirk	71	68	74	73	286	36,833
Jiyai Shin	75	74	69	69	287	31,127
Minjee Lee	73	74	69	71	287	31,127
Yu Liu	73	73	70	71	287	31,127
Anna Nordqvist	73	71	72	71	287	31,127
Mo Martin	71	73	71	72	287	31,127
Pornanong Phatlum	77	71	72	68	288	24,266
Patty Tavatanakit [A]	75	73	72	68	288	
Eun-Hee Ji	72	73	74	69	288	24,266
Jennifer Song	73	71	74	70	288	24,266
Megan Khang	71	75	71	71	288	24,266
Linnea Strom	69	76	72	71	288	24,266
Ayako Uehara	75	72	68	73	288	24,266
Amy Yang	70	72	73	73	288	24,266
Stacy Lewis	71	73	70	74	288	24,266
Jacqui Concolino	74	75	69	71	289	18,945
Chella Choi	72	73	73	71	289	18,945
Gaby Lopez	71	74	72	72	289	18,945
Xiyu Lin	70	74	70	75	289	18,945
So Yeon Ryu	75	74	73	68	290	15,730
Jodi Ewart Shadoff	73	70	77	70	290	15,730
Sakura Yokomine	76	73	69	72	290	15,730
Nasa Hataoka	73	72	73	72	290	15,730
Angel Yin	71	74	69	76	290	15,730
Mi Jung Hur	72	75	75	69	291	12,170
Brittany Altomare	76	71	73	71	291	12,170
Morgan Pressel	76	70	73	72	291	12,170
Lydia Ko	70	75	74	72	291	12,170
Ryann O'Toole	73	74	71	73	291	12,170
Lauren Stephenson	70	74	73	74	291	12,170
Sandra Gal	74	73	69	75	291	12,170
Alison Lee	71	72	72	76	291	12,170
Nelly Korda	74	75	74	69	292	9,057
Cristie Kerr	70	78	74	70	292	9,057
Haeji Kang	74	75	72	71	292	9,057
Amy Olson	76	71	74	71	292	9,057
Caroline Masson	73	74	73	72	292	9,057
Madelene Sagstrom	72	75	71	74	292	9,057
Hee Young Park	71	74	72	75	292	9,057
Brittany Lincicome	75	69	71	77	292	9,057
Sung Hyun Park	71	70	73	78	292	9,057
Jane Park	70	79	78	66	293	7,246
Wei-Ling Hsu	73	76	71	73	293	7,246
Mariajo Uribe	72	74	74	73	293	7,246
Ariya Jutanugarn	75	70	75	73	293	7,246
Georgia Hall	74	70	76	73	293	7,246
Nanna Koerstz Madsen	74	75	75	70	294	6,792
Albane Valenzuela [A]	75	72	74	73	294	
Azahara Munoz	72	77	76	70	295	6,491
Marissa Steen	72	75	77	71	295	6,491
Inbee Park	73	72	76	74	295	6,491
Marina Alex	75	71	76	74	296	6,114
Austin Ernst	71	78	72	75	296	6,114
Beatriz Recari	72	74	76	76	298	5,964
Sarah Jane Smith	74	75	76	76	301	5,886

	SCORES				TOTAL	MONEY
Ashleigh Buhai	73	76	82	73	304	5,774
Sarah Schmelzel	76	73	79	76	304	5,774
Mariah Stackhouse	75	74	79	79	307	5,667

Lotte Championship

Ko Olina Golf Club, Kapolei, Oahu, Hawaii
Par 36-36–72; 6,397 yards

April 17-20
purse, $2,000,000

	SCORES				TOTAL	MONEY
Brooke M. Henderson	65	68	69	70	272	$300,000
Eun-Hee Ji	64	65	74	73	276	180,553
Ariya Jutanugarn	67	71	66	73	277	116,150
Minjee Lee	67	66	70	74	277	116,150
Gaby Lopez	72	69	70	67	278	68,043
Danielle Kang	67	73	69	69	278	68,043
Hyejin Choi	65	71	70	72	278	68,043
Nelly Korda	63	68	71	77	279	48,932
Haru Nomura	67	72	73	68	280	40,364
So Yeon Ryu	66	72	73	69	280	40,364
Moriya Jutanugarn	67	67	75	71	280	40,364
Nicole Broch Larsen	68	69	80	64	281	30,643
Hyo Joo Kim	70	69	72	70	281	30,643
Jeongeun Lee$_6$	75	67	68	71	281	30,643
Brittany Altomare	68	73	69	71	281	30,643
Pajaree Anannarukarn	68	71	69	73	281	30,643
Sakura Yokomine	74	70	70	68	282	22,849
Chella Choi	67	71	74	70	282	22,849
Emma Talley	69	68	74	71	282	22,849
Minami Katsu	70	70	70	72	282	22,849
Carlota Ciganda	68	73	67	74	282	22,849
Jin Young Ko	69	69	70	74	282	22,849
Azahara Munoz	68	66	73	75	282	22,849
Inbee Park	71	71	72	69	283	18,881
P.K. Kongkraphan	67	73	71	72	283	18,881
Jing Yan	69	70	72	72	283	18,881
Ayako Uehara	74	67	74	69	284	16,172
In Gee Chun	67	72	74	71	284	16,172
Hannah Green	66	74	71	73	284	16,172
Lizette Salas	71	70	69	74	284	16,172
Giulia Molinaro	70	68	71	75	284	16,172

Hugel-Air Premia LA Open

Wilshire Country Club, Los Angeles, California
Par 35-36–71; 6,450 yards

April 25-28
purse, $1,500,000

	SCORES				TOTAL	MONEY
Minjee Lee	66	69	67	68	270	$225,000
Sei Young Kim	70	70	68	66	274	139,217
Annie Park	70	72	66	67	275	89,559
Morgan Pressel	71	66	70	68	275	89,559
Amy Yang	71	71	70	64	276	45,809
Gaby Lopez	69	68	73	66	276	45,809
Megan Khang	72	72	64	68	276	45,809
Jin Young Ko	70	70	67	69	276	45,809
Inbee Park	68	70	68	70	276	45,809

	SCORES				TOTAL	MONEY
Brooke M. Henderson	68	73	69	68	278	28,709
Stacy Lewis	65	73	71	69	278	28,709
Danielle Kang	72	66	70	70	278	28,709
Nanna Koerstz Madsen	69	67	67	76	279	25,000
Daniela Holmqvist	70	69	74	67	280	21,037
Chella Choi	71	73	67	69	280	21,037
Mariajo Uribe	71	72	68	69	280	21,037
Lizette Salas	68	71	71	70	280	21,037
Hannah Green	65	73	71	71	280	21,037
Mi Jung Hur	74	66	75	66	281	16,322
So Yeon Ryu	70	69	74	68	281	16,322
Mirim Lee	71	74	67	69	281	16,322
Carlota Ciganda	73	68	71	69	281	16,322
Azahara Munoz	71	70	71	69	281	16,322
Ashleigh Buhai	70	71	70	70	281	16,322
Ally McDonald	71	69	70	71	281	16,322
Sarah Schmelzel	72	72	71	67	282	13,224
Christina Kim	70	71	72	69	282	13,224
Jenny Shin	71	71	70	70	282	13,224
Kristen Gillman	69	74	67	72	282	13,224
Gemma Dryburgh	72	73	71	67	283	10,627
In-Kyung Kim	71	73	69	70	283	10,627
Angela Stanford	70	73	70	70	283	10,627
Aditi Ashok	70	71	71	71	283	10,627
Haeji Kang	71	71	69	72	283	10,627
Pajaree Anannarukarn	70	70	71	72	283	10,627
Jing Yan	68	71	71	73	283	10,627

LPGA Mediheal Championship

Lake Merced Golf Club, Daly City, California
Par 36-36–72; 6,551 yards

May 2-5
purse, $1,800,000

	SCORES				TOTAL	MONEY
Sei Young Kim	72	66	68	75	281	$270,000
Bronte Law	73	68	75	65	281	142,055
Jeongeun Lee$_6$	74	69	71	67	281	142,055
Lexi Thompson	73	70	69	71	283	69,641
Amy Yang	68	74	70	71	283	69,641
Eun-Hee Ji	67	72	73	71	283	69,641
Charley Hull	69	70	70	74	283	69,641
Marina Alex	74	72	70	68	284	38,765
Yu Liu	76	66	72	70	284	38,765
Azahara Munoz	69	73	72	70	284	38,765
Minjee Lee	76	69	67	72	284	38,765
Jenny Shin	71	73	72	69	285	29,629
Ryann O'Toole	73	65	77	70	285	29,629
Kristen Gillman	71	74	69	71	285	29,629
Jing Yan	73	73	71	69	286	24,761
Shanshan Feng	73	67	75	71	286	24,761
Maria Torres	69	71	71	75	286	24,761
Celine Boutier	68	76	74	69	287	20,771
Megan Khang	75	66	75	71	287	20,771
Lizette Salas	74	71	70	72	287	20,771
Danielle Kang	73	71	71	72	287	20,771
Louise Ridderstrom	71	69	72	75	287	20,771
Inbee Park	70	69	80	69	288	17,557
Cristie Kerr	72	73	71	72	288	17,557
In Gee Chun	69	71	76	72	288	17,557
Angela Stanford	71	72	72	73	288	17,557

	SCORES				TOTAL	MONEY
Morgan Pressel	70	76	74	69	289	13,917
Haeji Kang	73	71	76	69	289	13,917
Austin Ernst	72	73	74	70	289	13,917
Alena Sharp	76	71	70	72	289	13,917
Caroline Masson	76	70	71	72	289	13,917
Amy Olson	70	73	74	72	289	13,917
Nanna Koerstz Madsen	73	71	72	73	289	13,917
So Yeon Ryu	67	70	79	73	289	13,917

Pure Silk Championship

Kingsmill Resort, River Course, Williamsburg, Virginia
Par 36-35–71; 6,445 yards

May 23-26
purse, $1,300,000

	SCORES				TOTAL	MONEY
Bronte Law	65	68	67	67	267	$195,000
Madelene Sagstrom	68	66	69	66	269	90,853
Brooke M. Henderson	66	71	64	68	269	90,853
Nasa Hataoka	68	67	65	69	269	90,853
Wei-Ling Hsu	72	67	65	66	270	53,840
Azahara Munoz	71	69	67	64	271	40,461
Carlota Ciganda	69	65	68	69	271	40,461
Jennifer Song	65	68	68	71	272	32,304
Cristie Kerr	70	70	70	63	273	27,736
Katherine Perry	66	73	66	68	273	27,736
Caroline Masson	69	69	67	69	274	23,656
Ashleigh Buhai	68	67	70	69	274	23,656
Shanshan Feng	75	67	69	64	275	17,751
Hee Young Park	68	73	68	66	275	17,751
Minjee Lee	68	73	67	67	275	17,751
Amy Olson	70	68	70	67	275	17,751
Jessica Korda	69	68	71	67	275	17,751
Gaby Lopez	68	72	67	68	275	17,751
Mi Jung Hur	68	71	68	68	275	17,751
Charley Hull	68	69	69	69	275	17,751
Gemma Dryburgh	66	75	70	65	276	13,457
Hannah Green	70	69	70	67	276	13,457
Jin Young Ko	71	68	69	68	276	13,457
Austin Ernst	68	70	70	68	276	13,457
Haru Nomura	69	67	71	69	276	13,457
Lauren Kim	71	70	69	67	277	10,693
Lindy Duncan	70	71	67	69	277	10,693
Jeongeun Lee6	68	68	72	69	277	10,693
Morgan Pressel	71	69	67	70	277	10,693
Kendall Dye	70	70	67	70	277	10,693
Brittany Lincicome	68	69	70	70	277	10,693
Jasmine Suwannapura	66	71	70	70	277	10,693

U.S. Women's Open Championship

Country Club of Charleston, Charleston, South Carolina
Par 36-35-71; 6,732 yards

May 30-June 2
purse, $5,500,000

	SCORES				TOTAL	MONEY
Jeongeun Lee[6]	70	69	69	70	278	$1,000,000
Angel Yin	72	68	72	68	280	412,168
So Yeon Ryu	71	68	71	70	280	412,168
Lexi Thompson	70	69	68	73	280	412,168
Gerina Piller	70	70	73	68	281	178,633
Jaye Marie Green	71	68	68	74	281	178,633
Mamiko Higa	65	71	71	74	281	178,633
Yu Liu	69	71	66	75	281	178,633
Celine Boutier	67	70	69	75	281	178,633
Ally McDonald	72	72	67	71	282	125,518
Jessica Korda	69	68	72	73	282	125,518
Maria Fassi	72	73	68	70	283	103,065
Sung Hyun Park	71	69	71	72	283	103,065
Gina Kim [(A)]	66	72	73	72	283	
Minjee Lee	71	69	70	73	283	103,065
Inbee Park	70	70	75	69	284	76,124
Pornanong Phatlum	73	71	70	70	284	76,124
Charley Hull	72	70	70	72	284	76,124
Jin Young Ko	72	70	69	73	284	76,124
Sei Young Kim	68	71	72	73	284	76,124
Nanna Koerstz Madsen	73	71	66	74	284	76,124
Jing Yan	73	72	69	71	285	54,935
Minami Katsu	72	70	72	71	285	54,935
Carlota Ciganda	69	74	69	73	285	54,935
Ai Suzuki	73	70	68	74	285	54,935
Lindy Duncan	72	73	72	69	286	42,951
Lizette Salas	71	71	73	71	286	42,951
Ariya Jutanugarn	72	73	69	72	286	42,951
Chella Choi	72	72	69	73	286	42,951
Mi Hyang Lee	71	73	73	70	287	35,724
Esther Henseleit	66	77	71	73	287	35,724
Caroline Masson	70	71	71	75	287	35,724
Gaby Lopez	72	70	67	78	287	35,724
Hannah Green	76	68	77	67	288	28,751
Patty Tavatanakit	74	71	72	71	288	28,751
Katherine Kirk	73	72	70	73	288	28,751
Hina Arakaki	72	71	71	74	288	28,751
Jeong Eun Lee	74	71	68	75	288	28,751
Eri Okayama	72	72	77	68	289	19,492
Anna Nordqvist	75	70	73	71	289	19,492
Lydia Ko	72	73	73	71	289	19,492
Megan Khang	72	71	75	71	289	19,492
Aditi Ashok	72	71	75	71	289	19,492
Jenny Shin	69	74	73	73	289	19,492
Eun-Hee Ji	72	72	71	74	289	19,492
Wei-Ling Hsu	72	71	72	74	289	19,492
Brooke M. Henderson	72	73	69	75	289	19,492
Ryann O'Toole	70	72	72	75	289	19,492
Nelly Korda	69	71	73	76	289	19,492
Peiyun Chien	75	66	77	72	290	12,757
Morgan Pressel	70	72	75	73	290	12,757
Moriya Jutanugarn	71	70	76	73	290	12,757
Wichanee Meechai	74	71	71	74	290	12,757
Austin Ernst	71	73	72	74	290	12,757
Brittany Altomare	70	75	76	70	291	11,870
Rose Zhang [(A)]	75	70	72	74	291	
Ashleigh Buhai	74	71	72	74	291	11,870

	SCORES				TOTAL	MONEY
Haeji Kang	73	72	70	76	291	11,870
Azahara Munoz	68	72	75	76	291	11,870
Andrea Lee [A]	69	72	79	72	292	
Maria Torres	72	73	72	75	292	11,589
Jiwon Jeon [A]	74	71	74	74	293	
Jennifer Kupcho	71	72	76	74	293	11,303
Tiffany Chan	75	70	73	75	293	11,303
Misuzu Narita	69	75	74	75	293	11,303
Jennifer Chang [A]	75	70	72	76	293	
Dottie Ardina	71	70	76	76	293	11,303
Jodi Ewart Shadoff	73	72	78	71	294	10,962
Brittany Lang	76	69	74	75	294	10,962
Jasmine Suwannapura	71	73	74	77	295	10,791

ShopRite LPGA Classic

Seaview Hotel & Golf Club, Bay Course, Galloway, New Jersey June 7-9
Par 37-34–71; 6,217 yards purse, $1,750,000

	SCORES			TOTAL	MONEY
Lexi Thompson	64	70	67	201	$262,500
Jeongeun Lee6	63	69	70	202	161,223
Ally McDonald	67	67	70	204	116,956
Anna Nordqvist	68	69	69	206	90,474
Ariya Jutanugarn	72	67	68	207	60,758
Yu Liu	66	69	72	207	60,758
Mariah Stackhouse	66	67	74	207	60,758
Jodi Ewart Shadoff	68	72	68	208	39,574
Paula Creamer	67	70	71	208	39,574
Marina Alex	70	66	72	208	39,574
Anne-Catherine Tanguay	69	73	67	209	25,606
Dana Finkelstein	69	73	67	209	25,606
Brooke M. Henderson	68	73	68	209	25,606
Tiffany Joh	67	72	70	209	25,606
Amy Yang	69	69	71	209	25,606
Morgan Pressel	68	70	71	209	25,606
Mina Harigae	68	69	72	209	25,606
Stacy Lewis	67	70	72	209	25,606
Sandra Gal	67	68	74	209	25,606
Nanna Koerstz Madsen	66	68	75	209	25,606
Pornanong Phatlum	63	77	70	210	18,201
Bronte Law	69	70	71	210	18,201
Jacqui Concolino	67	71	72	210	18,201
Alena Sharp	67	71	72	210	18,201
Kristen Gillman	64	73	73	210	18,201
Caroline Masson	69	73	69	211	14,189
Katherine Perry	72	69	70	211	14,189
Nicole Broch Larsen	71	68	72	211	14,189
Lee-Anne Pace	70	69	72	211	14,189
Sakura Yokomine	69	69	73	211	14,189
Gerina Piller	68	70	73	211	14,189
Pajaree Anannarukarn	67	71	73	211	14,189
Anne van Dam	66	70	75	211	14,189

Meijer LPGA Classic for Simply Give

Blythefield Country Club, Grand Rapids, Michigan
Par 36-36–72; 6,638 yards

June 13-16
purse, $2,000,000

	SCORES				TOTAL	MONEY
Brooke M. Henderson	64	64	69	70	267	$300,000
Nasa Hataoka	68	68	67	65	268	123,864
Su Oh	69	69	64	66	268	123,864
Lexi Thompson	70	68	62	68	268	123,864
Brittany Altomare	66	65	69	68	268	123,864
Morgan Pressel	67	70	65	70	272	66,866
Nelly Korda	68	69	69	67	273	52,503
Annie Park	69	65	65	74	273	52,503
Shanshan Feng	68	70	70	67	275	35,393
Kristen Gillman	71	70	66	68	275	35,393
So Yeon Ryu	69	68	70	68	275	35,393
Danielle Kang	69	68	68	70	275	35,393
Moriya Jutanugarn	69	67	69	70	275	35,393
Alena Sharp	67	72	64	72	275	35,393
Madelene Sagstrom	67	70	65	73	275	35,393
Jessica Korda	76	67	67	66	276	23,860
Inbee Park	70	70	67	69	276	23,860
Lydia Ko	72	67	68	69	276	23,860
Sakura Yokomine	69	70	68	69	276	23,860
Minjee Lee	71	69	66	70	276	23,860
Mariah Stackhouse	70	69	67	70	276	23,860
Lauren Stephenson	69	70	66	71	276	23,860
Laura Gonzalez Escallon	68	73	70	66	277	18,242
Azahara Munoz	72	70	68	67	277	18,242
Jin Young Ko	68	69	70	70	277	18,242
Angela Stanford	68	68	71	70	277	18,242
In Gee Chun	70	70	66	71	277	18,242
Megan Khang	70	66	70	71	277	18,242
Jennifer Kupcho	67	67	67	76	277	18,242
Katherine Kirk	72	68	70	68	278	14,958
Gemma Dryburgh	73	64	70	71	278	14,958
Chella Choi	70	68	67	73	278	14,958

KPMG Women's PGA Championship

Hazeltine National Golf Club, Chaska, Minnesota
Par 36-36–72; 6,807 yards

June 20-23
purse, $3,850,000

	SCORES				TOTAL	MONEY
Hannah Green	68	69	70	72	279	$577,500
Sung Hyun Park	70	71	71	68	280	349,817
Mel Reid	69	76	71	66	282	225,038
Nelly Korda	72	70	69	71	282	225,038
Danielle Kang	75	70	68	70	283	143,642
Lizette Salas	72	71	68	72	283	143,642
Mirim Lee	71	74	70	69	284	96,081
Hyo Joo Kim	69	74	71	70	284	96,081
Inbee Park	72	73	68	71	284	96,081
So Yeon Ryu	71	75	71	68	285	69,809
Lydia Ko	71	70	76	68	285	69,809
Megan Khang	74	72	69	70	285	69,809
Ariya Jutanugarn	70	70	68	77	285	69,809
Nasa Hataoka	76	72	73	65	286	51,647
Sarah Schmelzel	75	71	69	71	286	51,647
Pajaree Anannarukarn	74	70	71	71	286	51,647

	SCORES				TOTAL	MONEY
Pornanong Phatlum	72	72	71	71	286	51,647
In-Kyung Kim	70	74	71	71	286	51,647
Jin Young Ko	77	67	70	72	286	51,647
Sei Young Kim	73	72	67	75	287	44,049
Jessica Korda	74	70	73	71	288	39,492
Brittany Lang	73	71	71	73	288	39,492
Lauren Stephenson	72	73	68	75	288	39,492
Amy Yang	70	74	69	75	288	39,492
Angel Yin	71	71	71	75	288	39,492
Brittany Altomare	76	71	71	71	289	33,229
Georgia Hall	76	70	70	73	289	33,229
Lexi Thompson	72	71	72	74	289	33,229
Moriya Jutanugarn	71	72	71	75	289	33,229
Jeongeun Lee$_6$	73	75	74	68	290	26,703
Daniela Darquea	75	73	73	69	290	26,703
Brooke M. Henderson	76	73	71	70	290	26,703
Minjee Lee	74	74	71	71	290	26,703
Chella Choi	71	75	73	71	290	26,703
In Gee Chun	74	70	73	73	290	26,703
Annie Park	70	75	71	74	290	26,703
Wei-Ling Hsu	73	73	76	69	291	20,397
Marina Alex	76	70	74	71	291	20,397
Azahara Munoz	73	75	70	73	291	20,397
Jenny Shin	72	76	70	73	291	20,397
Pavarisa Yoktuan	73	74	71	73	291	20,397
Haeji Kang	72	74	71	74	291	20,397
Yu Liu	72	73	77	70	292	16,317
Mariah Stackhouse	78	70	71	73	292	16,317
Caroline Masson	72	72	75	73	292	16,317
Gemma Dryburgh	75	70	73	74	292	16,317
Xiyu Lin	70	73	74	75	292	16,317
Jeong Eun Lee	75	73	75	70	293	13,521
Maria Fassi	73	76	73	71	293	13,521
Madelene Sagstrom	76	72	74	71	293	13,521
Mariajo Uribe	75	70	77	71	293	13,521
Carlota Ciganda	71	75	73	74	293	13,521
Su Oh	74	75	73	72	294	11,108
Alena Sharp	77	70	75	72	294	11,108
Kendall Dye	72	75	74	73	294	11,108
Celine Boutier	73	76	71	74	294	11,108
Nuria Iturrioz	73	70	77	74	294	11,108
Tiffany Joh	73	74	72	75	294	11,108
Caroline Hedwall	72	71	74	77	294	11,108
Cristie Kerr	76	73	74	72	295	9,097
Sakura Yokomine	75	74	74	72	295	9,097
Peiyun Chien	74	73	73	75	295	9,097
Pernilla Lindberg	72	71	77	75	295	9,097
Kristen Gillman	74	74	71	76	295	9,097
Jennifer Song	74	70	75	76	295	9,097
Jaye Marie Green	75	74	73	74	296	8,140
Wichanee Meechai	72	76	73	75	296	8,140
Sandra Gal	74	74	72	76	296	8,140
Angela Stanford	74	73	73	76	296	8,140
Jane Park	77	72	72	76	297	7,662
Mi Hyang Lee	74	75	78	71	298	7,469
Na Yeon Choi	76	73	73	76	298	7,469
Anne van Dam	76	73	72	77	298	7,469
Ryann O'Toole	76	72	78	73	299	7,189
Karine Icher	75	74	76	74	299	7,189
Katherine Perry	76	73	73	77	299	7,189
Marissa Steen	75	74	76	76	301	7,009
Sarah Burnham	78	71	76	78	303	6,875
Jimin Kang	73	70	80	80	303	6,875
Kris Tamulis	74	73	80	80	307	6,743

Walmart NW Arkansas Championship

Pinnacle Country Club, Rogers, Arkansas
Par 36-35–71; 6,331 yards

June 28-30
purse, $2,000,000

	SCORES			TOTAL	MONEY
Sung Hyun Park	66	63	66	195	$300,000
Danielle Kang	68	63	65	196	141,128
Hyo Joo Kim	67	64	65	196	141,128
Inbee Park	62	69	65	196	141,128
Brittany Altomare	66	65	66	197	83,633
Ryann O'Toole	69	65	64	198	55,249
Mi Jung Hur	68	66	64	198	55,249
Daniela Darquea	66	65	67	198	55,249
Carlota Ciganda	63	66	69	198	55,249
Nicole Broch Larsen	69	66	64	199	38,183
Amy Yang	68	66	65	199	38,183
Jenny Shin	65	68	66	199	38,183
Tiffany Chan	69	66	65	200	29,601
Gaby Lopez	67	67	66	200	29,601
Lauren Kim	66	68	66	200	29,601
Paula Creamer	63	70	67	200	29,601
Linnea Strom	66	65	69	200	29,601
Jessica Korda	69	67	65	201	20,994
Mirim Lee	68	68	65	201	20,994
Jeong Eun Lee	70	65	66	201	20,994
Katherine Kirk	68	67	66	201	20,994
Minjee Lee	68	67	66	201	20,994
Austin Ernst	68	67	66	201	20,994
Annie Park	64	71	66	201	20,994
Lizette Salas	67	67	67	201	20,994
Azahara Munoz	70	63	68	201	20,994
Aditi Ashok	66	67	68	201	20,994
Jin Young Ko	65	66	70	201	20,994
Cheyenne Knight	69	67	66	202	15,611
Giulia Molinaro	67	68	67	202	15,611
So Yeon Ryu	68	66	68	202	15,611
In Gee Chun	68	66	68	202	15,611

Thornberry Creek LPGA Classic

Thornberry Creek, Oneida, Wisconsin
Par 36-36–72; 6,646 yards

July 4-7
purse, $2,000,000

	SCORES				TOTAL	MONEY
Shanshan Feng	64	67	65	63	259	$300,000
Ariya Jutanugarn	65	64	67	64	260	186,096
Amy Yang	64	70	64	65	263	119,716
Tiffany Joh	64	66	66	67	263	119,716
Hyo Joo Kim	71	63	66	64	264	84,057
Yealimi Noh	63	65	69	68	265	63,170
Sung Hyun Park	65	62	69	69	265	63,170
Jing Yan	68	68	63	67	266	50,434
Marina Alex	69	67	68	63	267	37,545
Alana Uriell	68	67	69	63	267	37,545
Kristen Gillman	69	63	71	64	267	37,545
Celine Boutier	66	69	67	65	267	37,545
Eun-Hee Ji	68	67	66	66	267	37,545
Mina Harigae	67	63	68	69	267	37,545
Patty Tavatanakit	68	70	69	61	268	25,166

	SCORES				TOTAL	MONEY
Ally McDonald	65	70	70	63	268	25,166
Giulia Molinaro	69	67	67	65	268	25,166
Carlota Ciganda	65	69	69	65	268	25,166
Anne van Dam	69	68	65	66	268	25,166
Chella Choi	70	66	66	66	268	25,166
Dottie Ardina	68	67	67	66	268	25,166
Gaby Lopez	66	67	68	67	268	25,166
Pornanong Phatlum	67	69	69	64	269	20,208
Tiffany Chan	64	71	67	67	269	20,208
Alison Lee	65	68	67	69	269	20,208
Jeong Eun Lee	63	73	70	64	270	17,341
Elizabeth Szokol	69	68	68	65	270	17,341
Megan Khang	66	70	69	65	270	17,341
Caroline Masson	66	68	69	67	270	17,341
Yu Liu	62	69	71	68	270	17,341

Marathon Classic

Highland Meadows Golf Club, Sylvania, Ohio
Par 34-37–71; 6,550 yards

July 11-14
purse, $1,750,000

	SCORES				TOTAL	MONEY
Sei Young Kim	67	64	66	65	262	$262,500
Lexi Thompson	66	67	65	66	264	160,458
Stacy Lewis	65	68	69	66	268	116,401
Jeongeun Lee6	66	66	69	69	270	90,045
Linnea Strom	67	71	70	65	273	52,798
Tiffany Joh	70	67	69	67	273	52,798
Caroline Masson	65	70	70	68	273	52,798
Pavarisa Yoktuan	68	70	66	69	273	52,798
Jennifer Kupcho	67	66	69	71	273	52,798
Jing Yan	70	68	70	66	274	35,579
Brittany Altomare	69	69	72	65	275	26,717
Ruixin Liu	68	70	70	67	275	26,717
Stephanie Meadow	71	66	71	67	275	26,717
Emma Talley	70	68	69	68	275	26,717
Mariajo Uribe	72	69	65	69	275	26,717
Dana Finkelstein	70	69	66	70	275	26,717
Youngin Chun	64	70	71	70	275	26,717
Brooke M. Henderson	67	70	67	71	275	26,717
Giulia Molinaro	68	74	68	66	276	18,156
Xiyu Lin	71	69	70	66	276	18,156
Wichanee Meechai	70	69	71	66	276	18,156
Annie Park	71	69	68	68	276	18,156
Jodi Ewart Shadoff	67	71	70	68	276	18,156
Paula Creamer	69	71	67	69	276	18,156
Su Oh	69	69	69	69	276	18,156
Christina Kim	68	68	71	69	276	18,156
Minjee Lee	69	72	65	70	276	18,156
Charlotte Thomas	70	71	68	68	277	14,627
Azahara Munoz	65	70	74	68	277	14,627
Gemma Dryburgh	72	69	70	67	278	12,738
Sarah Schmelzel	72	71	67	68	278	12,738
Sandra Changkija	69	70	70	69	278	12,738
Jaye Marie Green	68	73	66	71	278	12,738
Ashleigh Buhai	67	69	71	71	278	12,738

Dow Great Lakes Bay Invitational

Midland Country Club, Midland, Michigan
Par 35-35–70; 6,256 yards

July 17-20
purse, $2,000,000

	SCORES				TOTAL	MONEY (Each)
Cydney Clanton/Jasmine Suwannapura	67	64	63	59	253	$241,269
Jin Young Ko/Minjee Lee	67	66	68	58	259	117,427
Ariya Jutanugarn/Moriya Jutanugarn	70	65	64	61	260	63,961
Na Yeon Choi/Jenny Shin	68	64	67	61	260	63,961
Brooke M. Henderson/Alena Sharp	65	66	69	61	261	42,474
Megan Khang/Annie Park	72	62	67	61	262	28,992
Kim Kaufman/Kris Tamulis	69	62	70	61	262	28,992
In Gee Chun/Lydia Ko	69	63	68	62	262	28,992
Eun-Hee Ji/Hyo Joo Kim	68	64	68	62	262	28,992
Paula Creamer/Morgan Pressel	66	64	69	63	262	28,992
Stephanie Meadow/Giulia Molinaro	69	61	71	62	263	21,787
Danielle Kang/Lizette Salas	71	62	71	61	265	15,591
Jessica Korda/Nelly Korda	68	67	68	62	265	15,591
Hee Young Park/Jennifer Song	72	61	69	63	265	15,591
P. Anannarukarn/P. Thanapolboonyaras	68	63	71	63	265	15,591
Lauren Kim/Sarah Schmelzel	69	67	65	64	265	15,591
Caroline Hedwall/Anna Nordqvist	72	61	68	64	265	15,591
Celine Boutier/Karine Icher	68	62	70	65	265	15,591
Simin Feng/Ruixin Liu	70	62	67	66	265	15,591
Brittany Altomare/Elizabeth Szokol	70	63	70	63	266	9,794
Mirim Lee/Amy Yang	67	64	71	64	266	9,794
Tiffany Chan/Peiyun Chien	69	62	69	66	266	9,794
Jaye Marie Green/Daniela Holmqvist	72	64	67	64	267	8,345
Youngin Chun/Alana Uriell	71	65	70	63	269	7,196
Aditi Ashok/Louise Stahle	72	64	70	63	269	7,196
Lindy Duncan/Ally McDonald	72	64	67	66	269	7,196
Yu Liu/Angel Yin	69	65	73	63	270	5,380
Clariss Guce/Maddie McCrary	71	65	71	63	270	5,380
Muni He/P.K. Kongkraphan	71	64	72	63	270	5,380
Celine Herbin/Joanna Klatten	73	60	73	64	270	5,380
S. Santiwiwatthanaphong/Marissa Steen	71	64	69	66	270	5,380
Mariajo Uribe/Karrie Webb	70	65	69	66	270	5,380

Evian Championship

See Ladies European Tour.

AIG Women's British Open

See Ladies European Tour.

Aberdeen Standard Investments Ladies Scottish Open

See Ladies European Tour.

CP Women's Open

Magna Golf Club, Aurora, Ontario, Canada
Par 36-36–72; 6,709 yards

August 22-25
purse, $2,250,000

	SCORES				TOTAL	MONEY
Jin Young Ko	66	67	65	64	262	$337,500
Nicole Broch Larsen	66	66	66	69	267	208,304
Lizette Salas	73	67	65	64	269	134,002
Brooke M. Henderson	66	69	65	69	269	134,002
Carlota Ciganda	73	67	65	67	272	85,534
Nasa Hataoka	69	69	66	68	272	85,534
Caroline Masson	71	69	66	67	273	60,444
Amy Olson	68	68	68	69	273	60,444
Ariya Jutanugarn	73	66	66	69	274	50,751
Yu Liu	68	67	71	69	275	42,956
Jessica Korda	69	70	66	70	275	42,956
Angel Yin	69	68	68	70	275	42,956
Jane Park	71	71	68	66	276	31,704
Danielle Kang	70	72	66	68	276	31,704
Xiyu Lin	70	68	70	68	276	31,704
Brittany Altomare	71	66	71	68	276	31,704
Aditi Ashok	70	69	66	71	276	31,704
Megan Khang	67	71	67	71	276	31,704
Pajaree Anannarukarn	66	69	69	72	276	31,704
Sung Hyun Park	69	73	68	67	277	24,406
Lexi Thompson	72	69	68	68	277	24,406
Sakura Yokomine	70	69	69	69	277	24,406
Mi Jung Hur	71	66	71	69	277	24,406
Nelly Korda	69	70	68	70	277	24,406
Celine Boutier	71	72	67	68	278	19,806
Katherine Kirk	71	69	69	69	278	19,806
Minjee Lee	69	68	72	69	278	19,806
Jasmine Suwannapura	72	67	68	71	278	19,806
Su Oh	68	71	68	71	278	19,806
Wei-Ling Hsu	69	69	65	75	278	19,806

Cambia Portland Classic

Columbia Edgewater Country Club, Portland, Oregon
Par 36-36–72; 6,478 yards

August 29-September 1
purse, $1,300,000

	SCORES				TOTAL	MONEY
Hannah Green	64	63	73	67	267	$195,000
Yealimi Noh	65	68	64	71	268	119,765
Brittany Altomare	69	65	68	69	271	86,881
Nasa Hataoka	66	71	70	66	273	60,653
Brooke M. Henderson	67	68	67	71	273	60,653
Sarah Schmelzel	72	62	69	71	274	44,260
Jane Park	65	70	74	66	275	34,753
Marina Alex	70	65	73	67	275	34,753
Alena Sharp	67	70	70	69	276	24,163
Jeongeun Lee6	66	68	72	70	276	24,163
Sei Young Kim	71	61	73	71	276	24,163
Sarah Burnham	69	66	69	72	276	24,163
Peiyun Chien	69	67	67	73	276	24,163
Mi Jung Hur	64	70	69	73	276	24,163
Azahara Munoz	69	70	71	67	277	17,180
Su Oh	70	67	72	68	277	17,180
Lydia Ko	67	70	72	68	277	17,180

	SCORES				TOTAL	MONEY
Jeong Eun Lee	72	69	66	70	277	17,180
Dana Finkelstein	66	69	68	74	277	17,180
Jin Young Ko	68	69	72	69	278	13,781
Giulia Molinaro	67	68	74	69	278	13,781
Gerina Piller	71	67	69	71	278	13,781
Amy Yang	74	66	66	72	278	13,781
Wei-Ling Hsu	66	69	71	72	278	13,781
Sung Hyun Park	67	65	73	73	278	13,781
Anne van Dam	70	69	74	66	279	11,377
Tiffany Chan	69	71	70	69	279	11,377
Celine Boutier	69	68	72	70	279	11,377
Mi Hyang Lee	68	71	68	72	279	11,377
Elizabeth Szokol	72	67	74	67	280	8,967
Cydney Clanton	69	72	70	69	280	8,967
Austin Ernst	68	71	72	69	280	8,967
Ariya Jutanugarn	70	68	71	71	280	8,967
Charlotte Thomas	67	69	73	71	280	8,967
Xiyu Lin	67	68	73	72	280	8,967
Isi Gabsa	70	64	74	72	280	8,967
Carlota Ciganda	68	72	66	74	280	8,967

The Solheim Cup

See Ladies European Tour section.

Indy Women in Tech Championship

Brickyard Crossing Golf Club, Indianapolis, Indiana
Par 36-36–72; 6,456 yards

September 26-29
purse, $2,000,000

	SCORES				TOTAL	MONEY
Mi Jung Hur	63	70	66	68	267	$300,000
Nanna Koerstz Madsen	65	75	64	67	271	186,577
Marina Alex	66	71	64	72	273	135,349
Megan Khang	69	70	68	68	275	78,911
Sakura Yokomine	65	70	72	68	275	78,911
Bronte Law	65	75	65	70	275	78,911
Maria Torres	69	68	66	72	275	78,911
Hyo Joo Kim	70	73	67	67	277	50,565
Georgia Hall	69	71	68	70	278	41,711
Caroline Masson	69	70	68	71	278	41,711
Chella Choi	67	72	67	72	278	41,711
Brittany Altomare	71	73	68	67	279	33,573
Alison Lee	70	72	68	69	279	33,573
Clariss Guce	71	68	69	71	279	33,573
Angel Yin	69	74	70	67	280	26,763
Su Oh	74	70	68	68	280	26,763
Sarah Kemp	71	71	69	69	280	26,763
Tiffany Chan	73	65	72	70	280	26,763
Amy Yang	71	70	67	72	280	26,763
Ruixin Liu	70	72	70	69	281	21,860
Brooke M. Henderson	69	72	70	70	281	21,860
Christina Kim	72	69	69	71	281	21,860
Inbee Park	69	71	70	71	281	21,860
Ryann O'Toole	68	72	70	71	281	21,860
Austin Ernst	72	71	72	67	282	17,740
Jasmine Suwannapura	69	73	73	67	282	17,740
Xiyu Lin	71	71	72	68	282	17,740
Gemma Dryburgh	71	70	72	69	282	17,740

	SCORES				TOTAL	MONEY
Brittany Lang	68	73	71	70	282	17,740
Ally McDonald	67	72	73	70	282	17,740

Volunteers of America Classic

Old American Golf Club, The Colony, Texas
Par 35-36–71; 6,475 yards

October 3-6
purse, $1,300,000

	SCORES				TOTAL	MONEY
Cheyenne Knight	66	67	67	66	266	$195,000
Brittany Altomare	67	66	68	67	268	102,834
Jaye Marie Green	67	68	64	69	268	102,834
Georgia Hall	68	68	71	66	273	60,365
Jane Park	69	67	69	68	273	60,365
Stephanie Meadow	63	71	73	67	274	40,461
Katherine Perry	67	68	66	73	274	40,461
Gerina Piller	69	71	67	68	275	28,062
Inbee Park	67	70	70	68	275	28,062
Jeongeun Lee$_6$	67	70	68	70	275	28,062
Sei Young Kim	68	69	67	71	275	28,062
Hyo Joo Kim	70	68	69	69	276	22,123
Caroline Hedwall	69	67	69	71	276	22,123
Pornanong Phatlum	68	70	69	70	277	19,512
Alena Sharp	68	65	72	72	277	19,512
Brittany Lang	70	73	68	68	279	16,315
Brooke M. Henderson	71	67	72	69	279	16,315
Gaby Lopez	67	74	67	71	279	16,315
Nanna Koerstz Madsen	74	66	68	71	279	16,315
Amy Olson	65	73	70	71	279	16,315
Sung Hyun Park	69	71	71	69	280	14,227
Kristen Gillman	67	71	71	71	280	14,227
Ariya Jutanugarn	68	68	72	73	281	13,444
Na Yeon Choi	71	73	71	67	282	11,347
Cydney Clanton	69	75	69	69	282	11,347
Mi Jung Hur	68	75	70	69	282	11,347
In-Kyung Kim	70	71	72	69	282	11,347
Peiyun Chien	68	73	71	70	282	11,347
Sarah Schmelzel	71	71	68	72	282	11,347
Wei-Ling Hsu	68	68	73	73	282	11,347
In Gee Chun	68	69	71	74	282	11,347

Buick LPGA Shanghai

Qizhong Garden Golf Club, Shanghai, China
Par 36-36–72; 6,691 yards

October 17-20
purse, $2,100,000

	SCORES				TOTAL	MONEY
Danielle Kang	69	67	66	70	272	$315,000
Jessica Korda	68	67	66	72	273	192,103
Yu Liu	76	66	68	65	275	111,310
Nasa Hataoka	67	73	67	68	275	111,310
Kristen Gillman	73	66	68	68	275	111,310
Sei Young Kim	73	67	68	68	276	70,993
Megan Khang	74	71	69	64	278	55,743
Ariya Jutanugarn	73	69	69	67	278	55,743
Nelly Korda	71	72	68	68	279	42,947
Jin Young Ko	72	70	68	69	279	42,947

	SCORES				TOTAL	MONEY
Brooke M. Henderson	69	64	73	73	279	42,947
Nanna Koerstz Madsen	71	69	72	68	280	35,653
Jodi Ewart Shadoff	69	72	69	70	280	35,653
Shanshan Feng	70	71	72	68	281	30,570
Georgia Hall	71	69	72	69	281	30,570
Angel Yin	68	71	69	73	281	30,570
Marina Alex	71	67	74	70	282	27,346
Jing Yan	74	70	71	68	283	25,558
Caroline Masson	72	73	69	69	283	25,558
Nicole Broch Larsen	72	73	72	67	284	22,928
Alena Sharp	72	72	71	69	284	22,928
Jeongeun Lee$_6$	72	68	75	69	284	22,928
Brittany Altomare	70	69	74	71	284	22,928
Annie Park	71	72	72	70	285	20,089
Hyo Joo Kim	73	74	67	71	285	20,089
Amy Yang	67	71	75	72	285	20,089
Jennifer Kupcho	69	75	71	71	286	18,615
Jasmine Suwannapura	74	71	73	69	287	16,533
Gerina Piller	70	78	69	70	287	16,533
Carlota Ciganda	72	73	70	72	287	16,533
Lydia Ko	69	74	70	74	287	16,533
Na Yeon Choi	70	71	71	75	287	16,533

BMW Ladies Championship

See Korea LPGA section.

Taiwan Swinging Skirts LPGA

Miramar Golf Country Club, New Taipei City, Chinese Taipei October 31-November 3
Par 36-36–72; 6,437 yards purse, $2,200,000

	SCORES				TOTAL	MONEY
Nelly Korda	66	67	65	72	270	$330,000
Caroline Masson	68	68	66	68	270	174,437
Minjee Lee	67	67	67	69	270	174,437
(Korda defeated Masson and Lee on first playoff hole.)						
Brooke M. Henderson	71	64	71	68	274	93,173
Sei Young Kim	71	68	66	69	274	93,173
Mi Jung Hur	66	66	71	71	274	93,173
Hyo Joo Kim	69	67	69	70	275	62,546
Morgan Pressel	70	67	71	69	277	49,631
Su Oh	68	67	70	72	277	49,631
In-Kyung Kim	69	65	70	73	277	49,631
Ariya Jutanugarn	75	68	69	66	278	37,665
Charley Hull	73	68	70	67	278	37,665
Jessica Korda	69	69	73	67	278	37,665
Azahara Munoz	69	73	64	72	278	37,665
Brittany Altomare	75	69	68	67	279	29,668
Chella Choi	73	69	70	67	279	29,668
Sung Hyun Park	73	69	70	67	279	29,668
Inbee Park	72	69	69	69	279	29,668
Na Yeon Choi	74	71	70	65	280	25,018
Celine Boutier	71	72	71	66	280	25,018
Gaby Lopez	73	69	70	68	280	25,018
Wei-Ling Hsu	73	69	70	68	280	25,018
Ssu-Chia Cheng	73	72	69	67	281	21,559
So Yeon Ryu	70	70	71	70	281	21,559
Kristen Gillman	71	70	69	71	281	21,559

	SCORES				TOTAL	MONEY
Anna Nordqvist	71	71	67	72	281	21,559
Jenny Shin	71	69	73	69	282	18,459
Ally McDonald	69	72	71	70	282	18,459
Jeongeun Lee6	73	66	72	71	282	18,459
Amy Yang	70	70	69	73	282	18,459

Toto Japan Classic

See Japan LPGA Tour section.

CME Group Tour Championship

Tiburon Golf Club, Naples, Florida
Par 36-36–72; 6,556 yards

November 19-22
purse, $5,000,000

	SCORES				TOTAL	MONEY
Sei Young Kim	65	67	68	70	270	$1,500,000
Charley Hull	72	67	66	66	271	480,000
Danielle Kang	69	70	68	65	272	269,637
Nelly Korda	67	68	66	71	272	269,637
Brooke M. Henderson	68	67	71	67	273	176,570
Lexi Thompson	70	67	70	68	275	119,683
Jessica Korda	70	67	69	69	275	119,683
Su Oh	69	67	70	69	275	119,683
Brittany Altomare	69	72	69	66	276	82,790
So Yeon Ryu	67	72	68	69	276	82,790
Ally McDonald	74	66	70	67	277	59,613
Marina Alex	68	70	72	67	277	59,613
Georgia Hall	67	71	71	68	277	59,613
Ariya Jutanugarn	76	66	66	69	277	59,613
Jeongeun Lee6	72	67	69	69	277	59,613
Jin Young Ko	71	69	66	71	277	59,613
Caroline Masson	68	66	70	73	277	59,613
Katherine Kirk	72	69	70	67	278	46,289
Bronte Law	69	70	68	71	278	46,289
Inbee Park	72	73	66	68	279	42,234
Mi Jung Hur	70	68	69	72	279	42,234
Yu Liu	71	66	70	72	279	42,234
Megan Khang	70	71	74	65	280	39,529
Hyo Joo Kim	73	71	67	70	281	38,179
Shanshan Feng	71	71	72	68	282	35,052
Nasa Hataoka	70	68	73	71	282	35,052
Carlota Ciganda	73	67	70	72	282	35,052
Amy Yang	71	68	68	75	282	35,052
Eun-Hee Ji	73	73	71	66	283	30,447
Alena Sharp	71	71	69	72	283	30,447
Lizette Salas	68	71	72	72	283	30,447
Nanna Koerstz Madsen	68	70	70	75	283	30,447

Ladies European Tour

Fatima Bint Mubarak Ladies Open

Saadiyat Beach Golf Club, Abu Dhabi, United Arab Emirates
Par 36-36–72; 6,337 yards

January 10-12
purse, US$300,000

	SCORES			TOTAL	MONEY
Charley Hull	67	72	69	208	€38,115.60
Marianne Skarpnord	71	70	68	209	22,869.36
Caroline Hedwall	71	75	67	213	10,164.16
Anne van Dam	72	73	68	213	10,164.16
Nicole Broch Larsen	69	73	71	213	10,164.16
Luna Sobron	69	72	72	213	10,164.16
Jodi Ewart Shadoff	70	70	73	213	10,164.16
Aditi Ashok	76	72	66	214	6,132.38
Jenny Haglund	71	74	69	214	6,132.38
Nanna Koerstz Madsen	72	70	72	214	6,132.38
Noora Komulainen	75	72	68	215	5,259.95
Marta Sanz Barrio	75	71	69	215	5,259.95
Laura Fuenfstueck	71	74	70	215	5,259.95
Amy Boulden	73	71	71	215	5,259.95
Cheyenne Woods	74	75	67	216	4,624.69
Stacy Lee Bregman	73	75	70	218	4,307.07
Sarah Kemp	72	70	76	218	4,307.07
Catriona Matthew	73	74	72	219	3,695.40
Camilla Lennarth	74	73	72	219	3,695.40
Lydia Hall	76	71	72	219	3,695.40
Gabriella Cowley	74	71	74	219	3,695.40
Ursula Wikstrom	72	73	74	219	3,695.40
Rebecca Artis	70	73	76	219	3,695.40
Cajsa Persson	70	71	78	219	3,695.40

Pacific Bay Resort Australian Ladies Classic
See Australian Ladies Tour section.

ActewAGL Canberra Classic
See Australian Ladies Tour section.

Worrells NSW Women's Open
See Australian Ladies Tour section.

Investec South African Women's Open

Westlake Golf Club, Cape Town, South Africa
Par 36-36–72; 6,298 yards

March 14-16
purse, R2,000,000

	SCORES			TOTAL	MONEY
Diksha Dagar	76	66	69	211	€19,347.46
Lee-Anne Pace	72	68	72	212	13,427.26
Michele Thomson	73	72	68	213	7,745.09
Esther Henseleit	76	67	70	213	7,745.09
Carly Booth	74	71	69	214	4,803.30
Lydia Hall	73	71	70	214	4,803.30
Julia Engstrom	72	73	70	215	3,686.39
Laura Fuenfstueck	82	67	68	217	2,612.21
Carrie Park	77	71	69	217	2,612.21
Ashleigh Buhai	75	72	70	217	2,612.21
Meghan MacLaren	76	69	72	217	2,612.21
Noemi Jimenez Martin	73	75	70	218	1,989.68
Stacy Lee Bregman	74	74	70	218	1,989.68
Silvia Banon	72	74	72	218	1,989.68
Karolin Lampert	79	72	68	219	1,745.54
Sofie Bringner	78	69	72	219	1,745.54
Astrid Vayson de Pradenne	73	71	75	219	1,745.54
Camille Chevalier	80	71	69	220	1,550.24
Kelsey MacDonald	73	77	70	220	1,550.24
Emma Westin	74	74	72	220	1,550.24
Annabel Dimmock	74	73	73	220	1,550.24

Jordan Mixed Open

Ayla Golf Club, Aqaba, Jordan
Par 36-36–72; 7,100 yards

April 4-6
purse, US$393,000

	SCORES			TOTAL	MONEY
Daan Huizing	64	68	68	200	€53,847.18
Meghan MacLaren	65	65	72	202	36,481.43
Martin Simonsen	69	71	64	204	24,312.05
Jack Senior	65	71	69	205	16,797.28
Oliver Farr	68	68	69	205	16,797.28
Jose Coceres	70	69	66	205	16,797.28
Peter Fowler	68	71	67	206	11,109.18
Oscar Lengden	70	68	68	206	11,109.18
Paul Streeter	66	70	71	207	8,677.53
Phillip Price	70	69	68	207	8,677.53
Pep Angles	67	72	69	208	6,699.80
Francesco Laporta	69	68	71	208	6,699.80
Ben Stow	70	68	70	208	6,699.80
Scott Henry	71	67	70	208	6,699.80
Calum Hill	74	69	65	208	6,699.80
Wil Besseling	70	69	70	209	5,380.71
Laura Fuenfstueck	73	70	66	209	5,380.71
Matt Ford	66	73	71	210	4,105.70
Stacy Lee Bregman	68	70	72	210	4,105.70
Cormac Sharvin	68	70	72	210	4,105.70
Martin Wiegele	69	72	69	210	4,105.70
Michael Hoey	69	73	68	210	4,105.70
Dan Olsen	70	70	70	210	4,105.70
Borja Virto	71	67	72	210	4,105.70
Rafael Gomez	67	76	68	211	3,191.20
Marianne Skarpnord	69	72	70	211	3,191.20

	SCORES			TOTAL	MONEY
Caroline Hedwall	72	70	69	211	3,191.20
Emily Kristine Pedersen	74	67	70	211	3,191.20
Ursula Wikstrom	74	69	68	211	3,191.20

Lalla Meryem Cup

Royal Golf Dar Es Salam, Blue Course, Rabat, Morocco
Par 37-36–73; 6,480 yards

April 25-28
purse, €450,000

	SCORES				TOTAL	MONEY
Nuria Iturrios	68	71	70	70	279	€67,500
Caroline Hedwall	74	74	68	70	286	33,750
Lina Boqvist	66	74	69	77	286	33,750
Esther Henseleit	75	73	72	67	287	15,750
Marianne Skarpnord	74	72	71	70	287	15,750
Laura Fuenfstueck	71	74	71	71	287	15,750
Hannah Burke	72	74	70	71	287	15,750
Jenny Haglund	75	75	75	64	289	10,575
Charlotte Thompson	74	74	72	69	289	10,575
Sarah Kemp	73	76	71	69	289	10,575
Sian Evans	75	73	70	71	289	10,575
Annabel Dimmock	73	77	71	69	290	9,450
Karolin Lampert	77	74	70	70	291	8,325
Jade Schaeffer-Calmels	72	77	70	72	291	8,325
Sarah Schober	76	74	69	72	291	8,325
Camilla Lennarth	68	76	73	74	291	8,325
Emily Kristine Pedersen	75	77	71	69	292	7,087.50
Diksha Dagar	69	75	75	73	292	7,087.50
Maria Hernandez	74	72	72	74	292	7,087.50
Christine Wolf	75	72	71	74	292	7,087.50

Omega Dubai Moonlight Classic

Emirates Golf Club, Faldo Course, Dubai, United Arab Emirates
Par 36-36–72; 6,289 yards

May 1-3
purse, US$285,000

	SCORES			TOTAL	MONEY
Nuria Iturrios	67	68	71	206	€38,193.30
Olivia Cowan	66	70	71	207	19,096.65
Esther Henseleit	69	66	72	207	19,096.65
Karolin Lampert	68	70	70	208	11,457.99
Caroline Hedwall	68	72	69	209	8,529.84
Leona Maguire	64	75	70	209	8,529.84
Carly Booth	68	75	67	210	7,129.42
Gabriella Cowley	73	72	66	211	6,263.70
Sarah Kemp	69	74	68	211	6,263.70
Marianne Skarpnord	69	72	71	212	5,779.92
Noora Komulainen	70	70	72	212	5,779.92
Hannah Burke	72	69	72	213	5,397.99
Katja Pogacar	74	72	69	215	4,481.35
Trish Johnson	73	72	70	215	4,481.35
Christine Wolf	74	70	71	215	4,481.35
Lynn Carlsson	71	73	71	215	4,481.35
Ursula Wikstrom	73	71	71	215	4,481.35
Liz Young	71	72	72	215	4,481.35
Kanyalak Preedasuttijit	71	69	75	215	4,481.35
Laura Fuenfstueck	73	72	71	216	3,730.22
Linda Wessberg	74	70	72	216	3,730.22

La Reserva de Sotogrande Invitational

La Reserva Club de Sotogrande, Sotogrande, Spain
Par 36-36–72; 6,427 yards

May 16-19
purse, €300,000

	SCORES				TOTAL	MONEY
Celine Herbin	70	70	73	69	282	€45,000
Esther Henseleit	67	72	74	70	283	27,000
Charlotte Thompson	66	73	78	69	286	14,100
Camille Chevalier	70	70	74	72	286	14,100
Caroline Hedwall	72	70	70	74	286	14,100
Kelsey MacDonald	72	76	72	67	287	8,100
Carmen Alonso	72	70	74	71	287	8,100
Daniela Holmqvist	70	75	71	71	287	8,100
Maria Parra	68	74	72	73	287	8,100
Tonje Daffinrud	74	77	71	67	289	6,600
Marianne Skarpnord	70	77	73	69	289	6,600
Lee-Anne Pace	73	76	71	69	289	6,600
Sofie Bringner	76	74	74	67	291	5,137.50
Katja Pogacar	71	74	75	71	291	5,137.50
Luna Sobron	72	78	69	72	291	5,137.50
Liz Young	72	75	72	72	291	5,137.50
Carly Booth	71	77	71	72	291	5,137.50
Maria Hernandez	71	73	74	73	291	5,137.50
Olivia Cowan	68	73	75	75	291	5,137.50
Eleanor Givens	73	73	69	76	291	5,137.50

Jabra Ladies Open

Evian Resort Golf Club, Evian-les-Bains, France
Par 35-36–71; 6,481 yards

May 23-25
purse, €150,000

	SCORES			TOTAL	MONEY
Annabel Dimmock	69	69	68	206	€24,000
Pauline Roussin Bouchard [A]	68	69	70	207	
Meghan MacLaren	68	74	69	211	15,655.80
Camilla Lennarth	74	70	68	212	6,875.80
Hannah Burke	71	70	71	212	6,875.80
Olivia Cowan	71	69	72	212	6,875.80
Marianne Skarpnord	75	68	70	213	3,955.80
Gabriella Cowley	71	71	71	213	3,955.80
Lejan Lewthwaite	72	71	71	214	3,655.80
Natalia Escuriola Martinez	73	73	69	215	3,370.80
Kylie Henry	74	68	73	215	3,370.80
Esther Henseleit	74	74	68	216	2,840.80
Filippa Moork	69	73	74	216	2,840.80
Emma Grechi	70	71	75	216	2,840.80
Karolin Lampert	74	73	70	217	2,570.80
Tonje Daffinrud	74	73	70	217	2,570.80
Johanna Gustavsson	71	77	69	217	2,570.80
Valentine Derrey	71	76	71	218	2,320.80
Noora Komulainen	72	74	72	218	2,320.80
Charlotte Thompson	72	73	73	218	2,320.80
Astrid Vayson de Pradenne	70	74	74	218	2,320.80

Ladies European Thailand Championship

Phoenix Gold Golf & Country Club, Pattaya, Thailand
Par 36-36–72; 6,217 yards

June 20-23
purse, €300,000

	SCORES				TOTAL	MONEY
Atthaya Thitikul [A]	69	67	63	67	266	
Esther Henseleit	70	68	69	64	271	€45,000
Olivia Cowan	68	72	67	70	277	27,000
Tonje Daffinrud	71	70	69	69	279	15,750
Marianne Skarpnord	73	69	68	69	279	15,750
Hannah Burke	75	69	70	66	280	9,500
Nattagate Nimitpongkul	75	70	67	68	280	9,500
Beth Allen	69	71	70	70	280	9,500
Carmen Alonso	71	69	73	70	283	7,350
Chorphaka Jaengkit	75	71	66	71	283	7,350
Parinda Phokan	71	74	71	68	284	6,750
Chonlada Chayanun	73	71	70	70	284	6,750
Diksha Dagar	72	72	72	69	285	5,700
Felicity Johnson	69	73	73	70	285	5,700
Lina Boqvist	67	74	72	72	285	5,700
Christine Wolf	72	71	70	72	285	5,700
Kanyalak Preedasuttijit	69	74	70	72	285	5,700
Maha Haddioui	76	72	68	70	286	4,800
Pannapa Polnamin	71	74	70	71	286	4,800
Camilla Lennarth	73	70	71	72	286	4,800

Evian Championship

Evian Resort Golf Club, Evian-les-Bains, France
Par 35-36–71; 6,527 yards

July 25-28
purse, US$4,100,000

	SCORES				TOTAL	MONEY
Jin Young Ko	65	71	66	67	269	€551,961
Hyo Joo Kim	69	64	65	73	271	264,172.07
Shanshan Feng	69	66	68	68	271	264,172.07
Jennifer Kupcho	66	70	69	66	271	264,172.07
Ariya Jutanugarn	70	71	64	68	273	157,853.38
Moriya Jutanugarn	68	72	66	68	274	119,423.75
Sung Hyun Park	67	66	66	75	274	119,423.75
Inbee Park	65	68	69	73	275	91,306.10
Megan Khang	68	70	67	70	275	91,306.10
Carlota Ciganda	70	69	67	70	276	79,120.23
In-Kyung Kim	74	66	68	69	277	71,151.55
Ally McDonald	71	68	69	69	277	71,151.55
Mirim Lee	71	68	70	69	278	61,060.61
Mi Jung Hur	68	71	67	72	278	61,060.61
Lizette Salas	74	67	69	68	278	61,060.61
Marina Alex	71	67	70	71	279	54,562.22
Sei Young Kim	68	68	70	74	280	48,115
Jessica Korda	70	70	70	70	280	48,115
Caroline Hedwall	72	64	68	76	280	48,115
Mi Hyang Lee	65	67	71	77	280	48,115
Brooke M. Henderson	72	70	68	70	280	48,115
Chella Choi	67	70	68	76	281	41,816.30
Bronte Law	72	69	66	74	281	41,816.30
Brittany Altomare	65	73	71	72	281	41,816.30
So Yeon Ryu	72	71	67	72	282	36,379.91
Austin Ernst	67	74	72	69	282	36,379.91
Eun-Hee Ji	71	70	72	69	282	36,379.91

	SCORES				TOTAL	MONEY
Nelly Korda	73	70	69	70	282	36,379.91
Pajaree Anannarukarn	68	68	72	74	282	36,379.91
Katherine Kirk	70	71	72	70	283	29,336.30
Jing Yan	70	70	71	72	283	29,336.30
Charley Hull	68	70	72	73	283	29,336.30
Amy Olson	70	66	73	74	283	29,336.30
Hannah Green	72	72	69	70	283	29,336.30
Yu Liu	70	73	70	70	283	29,336.30
Annie Park	68	71	70	74	283	29,336.30
Ashleigh Buhai	70	73	70	71	284	23,557.74
Mel Reid	66	72	72	74	284	23,557.74
Xiyu Lin	69	73	68	74	284	23,557.74
Georgia Hall	69	73	73	69	284	23,557.74
Albane Valenzuela [A]	72	66	71	75	284	
Wei-Ling Hsu	71	70	70	73	284	23,557.74
Yuka Yasuda [A]	70	70	69	75	284	
Amy Yang	71	69	72	73	285	19,808.47
Gerina Piller	74	67	70	74	285	19,808.47
Su Oh	74	69	71	71	285	19,808.47
Pavarisa Yoktuan	73	71	68	73	285	19,808.47
Yealimi Noh	71	72	70	72	285	19,808.47
Jeong Eun Lee	73	70	72	71	286	17,445.80
In Gee Chun	73	71	72	70	286	17,445.80
Hye Jin Choi	73	70	70	73	286	17,445.80
Stacy Lewis	69	74	71	73	287	15,946.94
Sakura Yokomine	71	73	72	71	287	15,946.94
Anne van Dam	72	71	69	75	287	15,946.94
Brittany Lang	72	70	74	72	288	14,259.32
Caroline Masson	73	70	70	75	288	14,259.32
Mariajo Uribe	71	73	70	74	288	14,259.32
Paula Creamer	64	76	73	75	288	14,259.32
Alena Sharp	71	70	79	68	288	14,259.32
Ai Suzuki	74	70	73	71	288	14,259.32
Gaby Lopez	71	72	73	73	289	12,949.21
Sarah Kemp	72	69	78	72	291	12,198.17
Haeji Kang	71	73	75	72	291	12,198.17
Celine Herbin	69	72	77	73	291	12,198.17
Ryann O'Toole	72	71	76	72	291	12,198.17
Nicole Broch Larsen	74	69	74	74	291	12,198.17
Celine Boutier	71	72	78	71	292	11,541.01
Shi Hyun Ahn	70	72	75	75	292	11,541.01
Aditi Ashok	73	71	76	73	293	11,261.60
Tiffany Joh	71	72	76	75	294	10,978.47
Nuria Iturrioz	74	69	75	76	294	10,978.47
Nanna Koerstz Madsen	72	72	81	72	297	10,699.06

AIG Women's British Open

Woburn Golf Club, Milton Keynes, England
Par 36-36–72; 6,756 yards

August 1-4
purse, US$4,500,000

	SCORES				TOTAL	MONEY
Hinako Shibuno	66	69	67	68	270	€610,443
Lizette Salas	69	67	70	65	271	399,401.31
Jin Young Ko	68	70	68	66	272	289,737.28
Morgan Pressel	69	71	66	67	273	224,134.42
Ashleigh Buhai	65	67	72	70	274	180,403.52
Celine Boutier	71	66	73	66	276	147,602.09
Carlota Ciganda	69	69	69	70	277	123,548.58
Sung Hyun Park	67	70	68	73	278	108,242.98

	SCORES				TOTAL	MONEY
Nelly Korda	70	69	72	68	279	92,935.22
Jeongeun Lee6	68	71	69	71	279	92,935.22
Minjee Lee	71	68	72	69	280	72,203.13
Moriya Jutanugarn	67	74	70	69	280	72,203.13
Ariya Jutanugarn	68	70	72	70	280	72,203.13
Caroline Masson	69	68	72	71	280	72,203.13
Anna Nordqvist	71	70	68	71	280	72,203.13
Lexi Thompson	71	70	73	67	281	54,667.31
Teresa Lu	73	70	69	69	281	54,667.31
Hannah Green	73	71	68	69	281	54,667.31
Marina Alex	69	70	72	70	281	54,667.31
Jing Yan	71	70	67	73	281	54,667.31
Su Oh	72	72	72	66	282	46,796.07
Ayako Uehara	70	74	70	68	282	46,796.07
Ally McDonald	72	70	71	69	282	46,796.07
Maria Torres	72	71	73	67	283	40,235.20
Hyo-Joo Kim	71	70	71	71	283	40,235.20
Sei Young Kim	70	73	68	72	283	40,235.20
Sakura Yokomine	70	73	67	73	283	40,235.20
Charley Hull	67	70	70	76	283	40,235.20
Yu Liu	72	71	71	70	284	33,018.72
Angela Stanford	73	72	69	70	284	33,018.72
Olivia Cowan	73	67	73	71	284	33,018.72
Atthaya Thitikul [A]	73	68	70	73	284	
Brittany Altomare	73	71	67	73	284	33,018.72
Pavarisa Yoktuan	73	67	70	74	284	33,018.72
Angel Yin	74	70	71	70	285	26,349.50
In Gee Chun	70	75	70	70	285	26,349.50
Minami Katsu	70	74	70	71	285	26,349.50
Georgia Hall	69	69	74	73	285	26,349.50
Kristen Gillman	71	74	66	74	285	26,349.50
Bronte Law	70	67	70	78	285	26,349.50
Azahara Munoz	73	71	72	70	286	21,867.62
Brooke M. Henderson	69	71	74	72	286	21,867.62
Danielle Kang	66	72	75	73	286	21,867.62
Caroline Hedwall	74	68	74	71	287	17,961.45
Anne van Dam	72	72	72	71	287	17,961.45
Megan Khang	67	74	73	73	287	17,961.45
Mirim Lee	72	71	71	73	287	17,961.45
Pornanong Phatlum	73	72	69	73	287	17,961.45
Jessica Korda	72	72	69	74	287	17,961.45
Jeong Eun Lee	70	71	70	76	287	17,961.45
Sarah Schmelzel	73	72	73	70	288	14,213.37
In-Kyung Kim	69	71	76	72	288	14,213.37
Xiyu Lin	74	69	73	72	288	14,213.37
Momoko Ueda	75	69	72	72	288	14,213.37
Cheyenne Knight	73	71	72	72	288	14,213.37
Jenny Shin	69	73	70	76	288	14,213.37
Jasmine Suwannapura	72	72	72	73	289	12,463.51
Annie Park	73	70	72	74	289	12,463.51
Jodi Ewart Shadoff	73	70	75	72	290	11,807.30
Yuka Yasuda [A]	73	70	70	77	290	
Austin Ernst	76	68	74	73	291	11,007.69
Brittany Lang	71	72	72	76	291	11,007.69
Karolin Lampert	73	71	70	77	291	11,007.69
Charlotte Thomas	72	73	74	73	292	10,277.61
Mi Jung Hur	71	73	74	74	292	10,277.61
Linnea Strom	70	74	74	74	292	10,277.61
Mariajo Uribe	73	72	75	73	293	9,730.05
Nicole Broch Larsen	72	70	74	77	293	9,730.05
Annabel Dimmock	75	70	75	74	294	9,404.12
Gerina Piller	71	72	77	75	295	9,073.85
Sarah Kemp	72	70	75	78	295	9,073.85
Felicity Johnson	76	69	79	75	299	8,747.92

Aberdeen Standard Investments Ladies Scottish Open

The Renaissance Club, North Berwick, Scotland
Par 35-36–71; 6,427 yards

August 8-11
purse, US$1,500,000

	SCORES				TOTAL	MONEY
Mi Jung Hur	66	62	70	66	264	US$200,832
Jeongeun Lee[6]	67	65	66	70	268	100,416
Moriya Jutanugarn	64	66	67	71	268	100,416
Mi Hyang Lee	63	70	68	68	269	60,249.60
Ariya Jutanugarn	68	67	68	68	271	48,199.68
Minjee Lee	69	73	64	67	273	37,488.64
Elizabeth Szokol	67	69	68	69	273	37,488.64
Anne van Dam	63	69	71	70	273	37,488.64
Karolin Lampert	68	70	68	68	274	30,124.80
Xiyu Lin	68	68	68	70	274	30,124.80
Jane Park	63	71	69	71	274	30,124.80
Carly Booth	70	67	66	71	274	30,124.80
Hyo-Joo Kim	66	72	69	68	275	24,936.64
Anna Nordqvist	67	69	69	70	275	24,936.64
Yu Liu	70	67	67	71	275	24,936.64
Su Oh	65	73	66	71	275	24,936.64
Madelene Sagstrom	67	70	72	67	276	22,091.52
Wichanee Meechai	69	67	69	71	276	22,091.52
Chella Choi	65	70	68	73	276	22,091.52
Annie Park	71	71	69	67	278	19,346.82
Amy Olson	70	69	70	69	278	19,346.82
Ursula Wikstrom	69	69	70	70	278	19,346.82
Na Yeon Choi	72	64	71	71	278	19,346.82
Louise Ridderstrom	68	74	70	67	279	13,267.08
Bronte Law	70	72	70	67	279	13,267.08
Laura Davies	72	68	71	68	279	13,267.08
Celine Boutier	70	69	71	69	279	13,267.08
Charley Hull	69	72	68	70	279	13,267.08
Christine Wolf	70	69	70	70	279	13,267.08
Georgia Hall	69	68	71	71	279	13,267.08
Luna Sobron	69	68	69	73	279	13,267.08
Linnea Strom	69	69	68	73	279	13,267.08
Nanna Koerstz Madsen	69	70	67	73	279	13,267.08
Gaby Lopez	69	68	68	74	279	13,267.08

Tipsport Czech Ladies Open

Golf Course Karlstejn, Belec, Czech Republic
Par 36-36–72; 6,125 yards

August 23-25
purse, €120,000

	SCORES			TOTAL	MONEY
Carly Booth	68	69	70	207	€19,200
Charlotte Thompson	69	71	68	208	7,224
Anais Meyssonnier	68	70	70	208	7,224
Hayley Davis	68	70	70	208	7,224
Sanna Nuutinen	67	70	71	208	7,224
Olivia Cowan	69	70	71	210	3,252
Laura Murray	70	71	70	211	2,728.80
Laura Fuenfstueck	70	75	66	211	2,728.80
Karolin Lampert	68	72	71	211	2,728.80
Agathe Sauzon	66	73	72	211	2,728.80
Kylie Henry	68	70	73	211	2,728.80
Nina Pegova	73	70	69	212	2,140
Eleanor Givens	69	71	72	212	2,140

	SCORES			TOTAL	MONEY
Ursula Wikstrom	70	70	72	212	2,140
Patricie Mackova [A]	66	73	73	212	
Isabella Deilert	70	71	72	213	1,980
Emma Nilsson	71	69	73	213	1,980
My Leander	74	71	69	214	1,896
Whitney Hillier	74	71	69	214	1,896
Noora Komulainen	70	73	72	215	1,614.55
Chloe Williams	70	74	71	215	1,614.55
Caroline Rominger	71	72	72	215	1,614.55
Johanna Gustavsson	66	76	73	215	1,614.55
Tonje Daffinrud	75	67	73	215	1,614.55
Christine Wolf	71	73	71	215	1,614.55
Lydia Hall	74	68	73	215	1,614.55
Lynn Carlsson	70	75	70	215	1,614.55
Carmen Alonso	70	72	73	215	1,614.55
Linda Wessberg	73	72	70	215	1,614.55
Esther Henseleit	74	72	69	215	1,614.55

The Solheim Cup

Gleneagles Hotel, PGA Centenary Course, **Perthshire, Scotland** September 12-15
Par 36-36–72; 6,434 yards

FIRST DAY
Morning Foursomes

Carlota Ciganda and Bronte Law (Eur) halved with Morgan Pressel and Marina Alex.
Georgia Hall and Celine Boutier (Eur) defeated Lexi Thompson and Brittany Altomare, 2 and 1.
Jessica Korda and Nelly Korda (US) defeated Caroline Masson and Jodi Ewart Shadoff, 6 and 4.
Charley Hull and Azahara Munoz (Eur) defeated Megan Khang and Annie Park, 2 and 1.

POINTS: Europe 2½, United States 1½

Afternoon Fourball

Suzann Pettersen and Anne van Dam (Eur) defeated Danielle Kang and Lizette Salas, 4 and 2.
Ally McDonald and Angel Yin (US) defeated Anna Nordqvist and Caroline Hedwall, 7 and 5.
Hull and Munoz (Eur) halved with Nelly Korda and Altomare.
Ciganda and Law (Eur) halved with Jessica Korda and Thompson.

POINTS: Europe 4½, United States 3½

SECOND DAY
Morning Foursomes

Pressel and Alex (US) defeated van Dam and Nordqvist, 2 and 1.
Hall and Boutier (Eur) defeated Salas and McDonald, 3 and 2.
Hull and Munoz (Eur) defeated Khang and Kang, 4 and 3.
Jessica Korda and Nelly Korda (US) defeated Ciganda and Law, 6 and 5.

POINTS: Europe 6½, United States 5½

Afternoon Fourball

Altomare and Park (US) defeated Pettersen and van Dam, 1 up.
Ewart Shadoff and Masson (Eur) halved with Thompson and Alex.
Hall and Boutier (Eur) defeated McDonald and Yin, 2 up.
Salas and Kang (US) defeated Ciganda and Munoz, 2 and 1.

POINTS: Europe 8, United States 8

THIRD DAY
Singles

Ciganda (Eur) defeated Kang, 1 up.
Nelly Korda (US) defeated Hedwall, 2 up.
Hall (Eur) defeated Thompson, 2 and 1.
Boutier (Eur) defeated Park, 2 and 1.
Yin (US) defeated Munoz, 2 and 1.
Hull (Eur) halved with Khang.
Salas (US) defeated van Dam, 1 up.
Jessica Korda (US) defeated Masson, 3 and 2.
Altomare (US) defeated Ewart Shadoff, 5 and 4.
Pettersen (Eur) defeated Alex, 1 up.
Law (Eur) defeated McDonald, 2 and 1.
Nordqvist (Eur) defeated Pressel, 4 and 3.

TOTAL POINTS: Europe 14½, United States 13½

Lacoste Ladies Open de France

Golf de Medoc, Chateaux Course, Le Pian-Medoc, France September 19-22
Par 36-35–71; 6,296 yards purse, €325,000

	SCORES				TOTAL	MONEY
Nelly Korda	68	64	70	67	269	€48,750
Celine Boutier	70	69	67	71	277	29,250
Caroline Hedwall	72	70	67	70	279	17,062.50
Joanna Klatten	68	70	65	76	279	17,062.50
Laura Fuenfstueck	72	70	72	67	281	9,360
Julia Engstrom	76	71	66	68	281	9,360
Azahara Munoz	66	72	74	69	281	9,360
Olivia Cowan	69	72	69	71	281	9,360
Manon De Roey	70	72	67	72	281	9,360
Jessica Karlsson	69	73	72	68	282	7,312.50
Charlotte Thompson	68	70	69	75	282	7,312.50
Jenny Haglund	70	69	74	70	283	6,500
Esther Henseleit	69	72	72	70	283	6,500
Nobuhle Dlamini	70	69	71	73	283	6,500
Linnea Strom	68	72	74	70	284	5,850
Kelsey MacDonald	72	71	75	67	285	5,362.50
Emily Kristine Pedersen	74	67	78	66	285	5,362.50
Luna Sobron	73	70	70	72	285	5,362.50
Celine Herbin	72	70	74	70	286	4,793.75
Tonje Daffinrud	72	71	73	70	286	4,793.75
Madelene Sagstrom	66	73	76	71	286	4,793.75
Valdis Thora Jonsdottir	79	66	70	71	286	4,793.75

Estrella Damm Mediterranean Ladies Open

Club de Golf Terramar, Sitges, Spain September 26-29
Par 36-35–71; 6,214 yards purse, €300,000

	SCORES				TOTAL	MONEY
Carlota Ciganda	72	68	65	71	276	€45,000
Esther Henseleit	70	71	68	68	277	27,000
Sanna Nuutinen	71	70	67	73	281	18,000
Ursula Wikstrom	75	71	66	70	282	11,200
Christine Wolf	75	68	68	71	282	11,200
Laura Fuenfstueck	68	68	67	79	282	11,200

	SCORES				TOTAL	MONEY
Whitney Hillier	75	66	72	70	283	8,400
Aditi Ashok	74	67	71	72	284	7,500
Marianne Skarpnord	70	74	70	71	285	7,200
Emma Nilsson	74	66	76	70	286	6,300
Beatriz Recari	70	70	75	71	286	6,300
Krista Bakker	70	75	70	71	286	6,300
Lydia Hall	73	68	72	73	286	6,300
Kelsey MacDonald	73	71	69	73	286	6,300
Olivia Cowan	70	69	76	72	287	5,250
Nobuhle Dlamini	72	70	68	77	287	5,250
Elina Nummenpaa	71	72	75	70	288	4,650
Liz Young	75	69	74	70	288	4,650
Magdalena Simmermacher	73	70	75	70	288	4,650
Emily Kristine Pedersen	73	73	70	72	288	4,650
Charlotte Thompson	74	71	76	67	288	4,650

Hero Women's Indian Open

DLF Golf & Country Club, Gurgaon, India
Par 36-36–72; 6,111 yards

October 3-6
purse, US$500,000

	SCORES				TOTAL	MONEY
Christine Wolf	73	68	67	69	277	€68,392.50
Marianne Skarpnord	68	71	71	70	280	41,035.50
Meghan MacLaren	67	73	69	72	281	27,357
Whitney Hillier	67	71	72	72	282	20,517.75
Anika Varma [A]	76	72	67	70	285	
Tvesa Malik	72	72	71	72	287	14,438.42
Cloe Frankish	73	73	69	72	287	14,438.42
Emma Nilsson	70	73	71	73	287	14,438.42
Kelsey MacDonald	76	72	70	70	288	10,942.80
Lydia Hall	72	69	75	72	288	10,942.80
Manon De Roey	71	74	69	74	288	10,942.80
Charlotte Thompson	74	67	79	69	289	8,695.62
Stacy Lee Bregman	71	73	73	72	289	8,695.62
Linda Wessberg	69	71	76	73	289	8,695.62
Noora Komulainen	74	69	73	73	289	8,695.62
Laura Fuenfstueck	72	72	72	73	289	8,695.62
Johanna Gustavsson	75	74	67	73	289	8,695.62
Trichat Cheenglab	73	71	68	77	289	8,695.62
Astha Madan	73	75	72	70	290	7,181.22
Tonje Daffinrud	73	70	68	79	290	7,181.22

Andalucia Costa del Sol Open de Espana

Aloha Golf Club, Marbella, Spain
Par 36-36–72; 6,393 yards

November 28-December 1
purse, €300,000

	SCORES				TOTAL	MONEY
Anne van Dam	68	69	68	70	275	€45,000
Aditi Ashok	70	67	69	70	276	22,500
Nanna Koerstz Madsen	71	66	65	74	276	22,500
Azahara Munoz	71	70	67	71	279	11,200
Olivia Cowan	65	73	69	72	279	11,200
Julia Engstrom	69	71	64	75	279	11,200
Cheyenne Woods	68	70	72	70	280	7,700
Christina Kim	67	71	70	72	280	7,700

	SCORES				TOTAL	MONEY
Marianne Skarpnord	66	71	70	73	280	7,700
Sanna Nuutinen	74	69	72	67	282	6,600
Nuria Iturrioz	70	74	70	68	282	6,600
Sarah Kemp	71	75	68	68	282	6,600
Whitney Hillier	74	71	71	68	284	5,700
Leona Maguire	73	74	68	69	284	5,700
Karolin Lampert	68	68	73	75	284	5,700
Klara Spilkova	74	73	69	69	285	4,875
Liz Young	72	69	73	71	285	4,875
Christine Wolf	75	72	67	71	285	4,875
Maha Haddioui	69	72	70	74	285	4,875
Beatriz Recari	71	72	74	69	286	4,350
Luna Sobron	73	75	68	70	286	4,350
Jessica Karlsson	74	70	70	72	286	4,350

Magical Kenya Ladies Open

Vipingo Ridge, Kilifi County, Kenya
Par 36-36–72; 6,478 yards

December 5-8
purse, €300,000

	SCORES				TOTAL	MONEY
Esther Henseleit	69	70	71	64	274	€45,000
Aditi Ashok	73	70	67	65	275	27,000
Julia Engstrom	67	66	70	74	277	18,000
Cheyenne Woods	70	70	74	68	282	13,500
Astrid Vayson de Pradenne	69	74	67	73	283	10,800
Christine Wolf	73	71	66	74	284	9,300
Laura Fuenfstueck	78	68	69	70	285	7,950
Gemma Dryburgh	74	73	68	70	285	7,950
Beth Allen	73	72	75	67	287	6,900
Olivia Cowan	79	70	68	70	287	6,900
Manon De Roey	72	73	71	71	287	6,900
Maria Hernandez	75	72	72	69	288	5,850
Elia Folch	74	70	71	73	288	5,850
Ursula Wikstrom	71	68	75	74	288	5,850
Kylie Henry	73	71	70	74	288	5,850
Lakareber Abe	73	75	73	68	289	4,725
Diksha Dagar	77	73	70	69	289	4,725
Liz Young	68	76	74	71	289	4,725
Noemi Jimenez Martin	78	73	66	72	289	4,725
Michele Thomson	72	68	75	74	289	4,725
Sanna Nuutinen	72	68	71	78	289	4,725

Japan LPGA Tour

Daikin Orchid Ladies

Ryukyu Golf Club, Nanjo, Okinawa
Par 36-36–72; 6,514 yards

March 7-10
purse, ¥120,000,000

	SCORES				TOTAL	MONEY
Mamiko Higa	70	66	71	76	283	¥21,600,000
Hina Arakaki	72	74	72	68	286	8,720,000
Lala Anai	74	70	73	69	286	8,720,000
Eimi Koga	71	72	72	71	286	8,720,000
Mami Fukuda	75	67	73	72	287	5,000,000
Rei Matsuda	69	72	73	73	287	5,000,000
Jiyai Shin	71	70	73	73	287	5,000,000
Mika Miyazato	73	71	74	71	289	3,000,000
Teresa Lu	74	69	73	73	289	3,000,000
Erina Hara	71	69	74	75	289	3,000,000
S. Langkul	72	71	76	71	290	2,172,000
Asuka Kashiwabara	73	68	77	72	290	2,172,000
Ayako Uehara	72	73	76	70	291	1,812,000
Misuzu Narita	73	73	74	71	291	1,812,000
Sakura Yokomine	73	70	76	72	291	1,812,000
Momoko Ueda	72	71	74	74	291	1,812,000
Saiki Fujita	74	71	76	71	292	1,234,285
Miki Saiki	73	73	73	73	292	1,234,285
Saki Nagamine	71	71	77	73	292	1,234,285
Maria Shinohara	73	71	74	74	292	1,234,285
Akira Yamaji	72	72	74	74	292	1,234,285
Nasa Hataoka	73	71	73	75	292	1,234,285
Sakura Koiwai	71	67	76	78	292	1,234,285

Yokohama Tire PRGR Ladies Cup

Tosa Country Club, Konan, Kochi
Par 36-36–72; 6,228 yards

March 15-17
purse, ¥80,000,000

	SCORES			TOTAL	MONEY
Ai Suzuki	69	70	68	207	¥14,400,000
Rumi Yoshiba	67	73	71	211	7,040,000
Eri Okayama	70	74	68	212	4,800,000
Mami Fukuda	74	70	68	212	4,800,000
Min-Young Lee	69	70	73	212	4,800,000
Minami Katsu	69	74	70	213	2,246,666
Jiyai Shin	72	71	70	213	2,246,666
Momoko Ueda	68	72	73	213	2,246,666
Hinako Shibuno	71	69	73	213	2,246,666
Satsuki Oshiro	68	69	76	213	2,246,666
Seonwoo Bae	68	69	76	213	2,246,666
Shiho Oyama	72	68	74	214	1,400,000
Kana Nagai	71	73	71	215	1,160,000
Rei Matsuda	75	69	71	215	1,160,000
Teresa Lu	69	75	71	215	1,160,000
Kumiko Kaneda	73	73	69	215	1,160,000

	SCORES			TOTAL	MONEY
Ah-Reum Hwang	69	73	73	215	1,160,000
Yui Kawamoto	70	72	74	216	816,000
Lala Anai	73	69	74	216	816,000
Hina Arakaki	70	71	75	216	816,000
Phoebe Yao	73	68	75	216	816,000

T-Point Eneos Ladies

Ibaraki Kokusai Golf Club, Osaka
Par 36-35–71; 6,219 yards

March 22-24
purse, ¥100,000,000

	SCORES			TOTAL	MONEY
Momoko Ueda	69	69	69	207	¥18,000,000
Minami Katsu	71	71	67	209	7,900,000
Jiyai Shin	68	69	72	209	7,900,000
Hikaru Yoshimoto	75	67	68	210	4,300,000
Mi-Jeong Jeon	73	69	68	210	4,300,000
Rei Matsuda	72	69	69	210	4,300,000
Minami Hiruta	74	67	69	210	4,300,000
Sakura Koiwai	70	68	72	210	4,300,000
Mamiko Higa	72	70	69	211	2,010,000
Ai Suzuki	69	71	71	211	2,010,000
Ah-Reum Hwang	72	67	72	211	2,010,000
Mone Inami	72	67	72	211	2,010,000
Ritsuko Ryu	74	68	70	212	1,620,000
Yukiko Nishiki	72	73	68	213	1,420,000
Miki Sakai	72	71	70	213	1,420,000
S. Langkul	69	69	75	213	1,420,000
Ha-Neul Kim	75	71	68	214	1,120,000
Chie Arimura	72	72	70	214	1,120,000
Hee-Kyung Bae	71	70	73	214	1,120,000
Misuzu Narita	71	74	70	215	870,000
Mayu Hamada	72	73	70	215	870,000
Eimi Koga	71	74	70	215	870,000
Mami Fukuda	73	73	69	215	870,000
Kumiko Kaneda	73	74	68	215	870,000
Teresa Lu	75	72	68	215	870,000

AXA Ladies

UMK Country Club, Miyazaki
Par 36-36–72; 6,525 yards

March 29-31
purse, ¥80,000,000

	SCORES			TOTAL	MONEY
Yui Kawamoto	66	65	70	201	¥14,400,000
Chae-Young Yoon	67	73	66	206	6,320,000
S. Langkul	67	69	70	206	6,320,000
Hee-Kyung Bae	70	66	71	207	4,400,000
Hana Wakimoto	65	70	72	207	4,400,000
Hikaru Yoshimoto	68	70	70	208	2,800,000
Mi-Jeong Jeon	70	67	71	208	2,800,000
Reika Usui	68	67	73	208	2,800,000
Erika Kikuchi	72	68	69	209	1,636,000
Min-Young Lee	71	68	70	209	1,636,000
Miki Saiki	71	68	70	209	1,636,000
Teresa Lu	68	70	71	209	1,636,000
Seonwoo Bae	69	69	72	210	1,352,000

	SCORES	TOTAL	MONEY
Ah-Reum Hwang	71 70 70	211	1,152,000
Sakura Koiwai	72 68 71	211	1,152,000
Misuzu Narita	70 69 72	211	1,152,000
Momoko Ueda	69 68 74	211	1,152,000
Nayeon Eum	72 70 70	212	816,000
Mao Nozawa	74 68 70	212	816,000
Ji-Hee Lee	70 72 70	212	816,000
Phoebe Yao	70 69 73	212	816,000
Hinako Yamauchi	71 68 73	212	816,000
Eri Okayama	72 67 73	212	816,000

Yamaha Ladies Open

Katsuragi Golf Club, Yamana Course, Fukuroi, Shizuoka April 4-7
Par 36-36–72; 6,564 yards purse, ¥100,000,000

	SCORES	TOTAL	MONEY
Misuzu Narita	73 74 69 67	283	¥18,000,000
Sun-Ju Ahn	70 73 69 72	284	8,800,000
Hina Arakaki	73 75 71 68	287	6,500,000
Seonwoo Bae	74 69 73 71	287	6,500,000
Eri Okayama	71 74 73 70	288	4,166,666
Min-Young Lee	73 73 72 70	288	4,166,666
Ah-Reum Hwang	69 74 73 72	288	4,166,666
Minami Katsu	75 74 70 71	290	2,750,000
Shiho Oyama	75 68 73 74	290	2,750,000
Mika Miyazato	75 76 71 69	291	1,766,666
Chie Arimura	73 74 73 71	291	1,766,666
Lala Anai	73 69 74 75	291	1,766,666
Teresa Lu	73 72 76 71	292	1,500,000
Miki Sakai	73 74 75 71	293	1,150,000
Ai Suzuki	73 70 77 73	293	1,150,000
Ayano Yasuda	74 73 73 73	293	1,150,000
Mi-Jeong Jeon	75 74 71 73	293	1,150,000
Mizuki Ooide	77 68 74 74	293	1,150,000
Shina Kanazawa	71 71 73 78	293	1,150,000
Eriko Kobashi	71 74 77 72	294	790,000
Hee-Kyung Bae	72 74 73 75	294	790,000

Studio Alice Ladies Open

Hanayashiki Golf Club, Yokawa Course, Miki, Hyogo April 12-14
Par 36-36–72; 6,316 yards purse, ¥60,000,000

	SCORES	TOTAL	MONEY
Jiyai Shin	68 70 69	207	¥10,800,000
Erika Kikuchi	69 73 66	208	4,740,000
Saki Takeo	73 67 68	208	4,740,000
Ai Suzuki	71 69 70	210	3,300,000
Kaho Kumagai	72 68 70	210	3,300,000
Miki Sakai	70 73 70	213	1,950,000
Haruka Morita	72 71 70	213	1,950,000
Kana Nagai	70 70 73	213	1,950,000
Hikaru Yoshimoto	70 68 75	213	1,950,000
Mamiko Higa	71 71 72	214	1,132,000
Ayaka Furue (A)	72 69 73	214	
Eri Fukuyama	68 72 74	214	1,132,000

	SCORES			TOTAL	MONEY
Eimi Koga	72	65	77	214	1,132,000
Maaya Suzuki	75	69	71	215	978,000
Eriko Kobashi	69	74	72	215	978,000
Min-Young Lee	73	72	71	216	768,000
Hiromu Ono	71	72	73	216	768,000
Hinako Shibuno	76	71	69	216	768,000
Mayu Hirota	70	71	75	216	768,000
Minami Hiruta	71	70	75	216	768,000

Vantelin Ladies Open KKT Cup

Kumamoto Kuko Country Club, Kikuyo, Kumamoto
Par 36-36–72; 6,428 yards
April 19-21
purse, ¥100,000,000

	SCORES			TOTAL	MONEY
Ji-Hee Lee	70	69	69	208	¥18,000,000
Hikaru Yoshimoto	73	68	68	209	8,800,000
Ah-Reum Hwang	70	71	69	210	7,000,000
Lala Anai	73	71	67	211	4,625,000
Mamiko Higa	72	69	70	211	4,625,000
Erika Hara	72	68	71	211	4,625,000
Miki Sakai	67	72	72	211	4,625,000
Momoko Ueda	73	70	69	212	2,322,500
Hina Arakaki	72	70	70	212	2,322,500
Hiroko Azuma	70	70	72	212	2,322,500
Solar Lee	68	70	74	212	2,322,500
Serena Aoki	72	72	69	213	1,590,000
Rumi Yoshiba	72	71	70	213	1,590,000
Seonwoo Bae	70	71	72	213	1,590,000
Mi-Jeong Jeon	72	73	69	214	1,190,000
Hee-Kyung Bae	73	72	69	214	1,190,000
Asuka Kashiwabara	72	72	70	214	1,190,000
Eri Okayama	75	71	68	214	1,190,000
Chie Arimura	70	72	72	214	1,190,000
Kaho Kumagai	73	72	70	215	850,000
Ritsuko Ryu	73	71	71	215	850,000
Hinako Shibuno	81	66	68	215	850,000
Sakura Koiwai	71	70	74	215	850,000
Erika Kikuchi	71	70	74	215	850,000

Fujisankei Ladies Classic

Kawana Hotel Golf Club, Fuji Course, Ito, Shizuoka
Par 36-35–71; 6,376 yards
April 26-28
purse, ¥80,000,000

	SCORES			TOTAL	MONEY
Jiyai Shin	70	72	63	205	¥14,400,000
Hinako Shibuno	71	69	67	207	5,813,333
Ai Suzuki	72	68	67	207	5,813,333
Hikaru Yoshimoto	69	66	72	207	5,813,333
Yukiko Nishiki	71	70	67	208	2,666,666
Misuzu Narita	69	71	68	208	2,666,666
Hina Arakaki	69	71	68	208	2,666,666
Minami Katsu	69	70	69	208	2,666,666
Hikari Fujita	71	68	69	208	2,666,666
Kaori Ohe	69	68	71	208	2,666,666
Mamiko Higa	71	72	66	209	1,352,000

	SCORES			TOTAL	MONEY
Rei Matsuda	70	72	67	209	1,352,000
Moeno Tan	70	71	68	209	1,352,000
Yumiko Yoshida	69	71	69	209	1,352,000
Momoko Ueda	70	67	72	209	1,352,000
Kana Nagai	72	70	68	210	1,072,000
Ah-Reum Hwang	69	72	69	210	1,072,000
Mizuki Tanaka	69	73	69	211	872,000
Karis Davidson	73	69	69	211	872,000
Saki Nagamine	70	71	70	211	872,000

Panasonic Open Ladies

Hamano Golf Club, Ichihara, Chiba
Par 36-36–72; 6,566 yards

May 3-5
purse, ¥80,000,000

	SCORES			TOTAL	MONEY
Minami Katsu	69	68	67	204	¥14,400,000
Mi-Jeong Jeon	71	67	66	204	7,040,000
(Katsu defeated Jeon on first playoff hole.)					
Kana Nagai	67	69	69	205	5,200,000
Ah-Reum Hwang	68	68	69	205	5,200,000
Hina Arakaki	70	68	68	206	3,333,333
Mone Inami	66	70	70	206	3,333,333
Min-Young Lee	70	65	71	206	3,333,333
Mika Miyazato	68	71	68	207	2,200,000
Satsuki Oshiro	68	68	71	207	2,200,000
Jiyai Shin	71	71	66	208	1,498,666
Rei Matsuda	68	72	68	208	1,498,666
Ai Suzuki	65	70	73	208	1,498,666
Eri Okayama	68	72	69	209	1,128,000
Hinako Shibuno	68	71	70	209	1,128,000
Yui Kawamoto	71	68	70	209	1,128,000
Sakura Yokomine	68	70	71	209	1,128,000
Sakura Koiwai	69	69	71	209	1,128,000
Erina Hara	70	68	71	209	1,128,000
Megumi Kido	68	73	69	210	754,666
Akira Yamaji	71	69	70	210	754,666
Saki Takeo	69	70	71	210	754,666
Chae-Young Yoon	68	70	72	210	754,666
Nana Suganuma	68	70	72	210	754,666
Sakura Kito	70	68	72	210	754,666

World Ladies Championship Salonpas Cup

Ibaraki Golf Club, East Course, Ibaraki
Par 36-36–72; 6,560 yards

May 9-12
purse, ¥120,000,000

	SCORES				TOTAL	MONEY
Hinako Shibuno	71	68	66	71	276	¥24,000,000
Seonwoo Bae	68	70	67	72	277	12,000,000
Lala Anai	72	68	70	71	281	9,000,000
Ritsuko Ryu	69	70	73	71	283	7,200,000
Yuri Yoshida [A]	71	68	70	74	283	
Hee-Kyung Bae	71	72	71	70	284	4,880,000
Kana Nagai	74	70	70	70	284	4,880,000
Karis Davidson	71	70	72	71	284	4,880,000
Rei Matsuda	72	71	72	70	285	2,640,000

	SCORES				TOTAL	MONEY
Min-Young Lee	73	69	71	72	285	2,640,000
Asuka Kashiwabara	69	72	71	73	285	2,640,000
Sakura Koiwai	73	71	73	69	286	2,100,000
Hiroko Azuma	71	71	73	72	287	1,860,000
Sayaka Takahashi	73	70	72	72	287	1,860,000
Serena Aoki	70	74	71	72	287	1,860,000
Ah-Reum Hwang	73	70	74	71	288	1,250,000
Momoko Osato	74	67	75	72	288	1,250,000
Jae-Eun Chung	74	73	69	72	288	1,250,000
Yui Kawamoto	76	71	68	73	288	1,250,000
Jiyai Shin	69	72	73	74	288	1,250,000
Ji Hyun Oh	74	69	69	76	288	1,250,000

Hoken no Madoguchi Ladies

Fukuoka Country Club, Wajiro Course, Fukuoka
Par 36-36–72; 6,292 yards

May 17-19
purse, ¥120,000,000

	SCORES			TOTAL	MONEY
Min-Young Lee	67	70	69	206	¥21,600,000
Momoko Ueda	72	67	68	207	9,480,000
Jiyai Shin	69	69	69	207	9,480,000
Erika Hara	72	68	68	208	6,600,000
Minami Katsu	67	72	69	208	6,600,000
Ji-Hee Lee	73	69	67	209	3,900,000
Erika Kikuchi	70	70	69	209	3,900,000
Yui Kawamoto	72	68	69	209	3,900,000
Shina Kanazawa	66	72	71	209	3,900,000
S. Langkul	72	72	66	210	2,193,000
Phoebe Yao	72	69	69	210	2,193,000
Asako Fujimoto	68	72	70	210	2,193,000
Hee-Kyung Bae	71	69	70	210	2,193,000
Karis Davidson	73	70	68	211	1,704,000
Eri Okayama	70	70	71	211	1,704,000
Ai Suzuki	76	64	71	211	1,704,000
Yumiko Yoshida	69	70	72	211	1,704,000
Mi-Jeong Jeon	71	72	69	212	1,344,000
Hiroko Azuma	72	73	67	212	1,344,000
Serena Aoki	70	72	71	213	1,116,000
Lala Anai	72	70	71	213	1,116,000
Ha-Neul Kim	70	71	72	213	1,116,000
Ah-Reum Hwang	71	68	74	213	1,116,000
Satsuki Oshiro	69	68	76	213	1,116,000

Chukyo TV Bridgestone Ladies Open

Chukyo Golf Club, Ishino Course, Toyota, Aichi
Par 36-36–72; 6,482 yards

May 24-26
purse, ¥70,000,000

	SCORES			TOTAL	MONEY
Minami Katsu	68	62	72	202	¥12,600,000
Yui Kawamoto	67	69	68	204	6,300,000
Seonwoo Bae	67	71	67	205	4,200,000
Mone Inami	71	66	68	205	4,200,000
Rei Matsuda	67	66	72	205	4,200,000
Karis Davidson	72	68	66	206	2,940,000
Shina Kanazawa	73	66	68	207	2,100,000

	SCORES			TOTAL	MONEY
Nana Suganuma	72	66	69	207	2,100,000
Hikaru Yoshimoto	68	68	71	207	2,100,000
Saiki Fujita	70	71	67	208	1,305,500
Erina Hara	70	69	69	208	1,305,500
Sakura Koiwai	69	68	71	208	1,305,500
Yumiko Yoshida	70	67	71	208	1,305,500
Ritsuko Ryu	70	72	67	209	1,134,000
Ayaka Furue [A]	71	73	65	209	
Maria Shinohara	71	70	69	210	959,000
Chie Arimura	68	71	71	210	959,000
Ah-Reum Hwang	69	70	71	210	959,000
Kana Mikashima	72	67	71	210	959,000
Na-Ri Lee	69	72	70	211	702,333
Serena Aoki	69	71	71	211	702,333
Momoko Ueda	70	73	68	211	702,333
Chae-Young Yoon	68	71	72	211	702,333
Moeno Tan	72	67	72	211	702,333
Hina Arakaki	72	64	75	211	702,333

Resort Trust Ladies

Grandy Hamanako Golf Club, Shizuoka
Par 36-36–72; 6,560 yards

May 31-June 2
purse, ¥80,000,000

	SCORES			TOTAL	MONEY
Erika Hara	66	70	66	202	¥14,400,000
Seonwoo Bae	69	68	65	202	7,040,000
(Hara defeated Bae on second playoff hole.)					
Yui Kawamoto	67	68	69	204	5,600,000
Ayaka Furue [A]	69	65	70	204	
Lala Anai	69	69	68	206	4,400,000
Sakura Koiwai	70	68	68	206	4,400,000
Saki Asai	71	68	68	207	2,800,000
Moeno Tan	70	68	69	207	2,800,000
Ritsuko Ryu	71	66	70	207	2,800,000
Sae Ogura [A]	74	69	66	209	
Mi-Jeong Jeon	69	72	68	209	1,616,000
Maaya Suzuki	70	70	69	209	1,616,000
Teresa Lu	69	70	70	209	1,616,000
Hinako Shibuno	67	69	73	209	1,616,000
Rei Matsuda	74	70	66	210	1,192,000
Hikaru Yoshimoto	72	68	70	210	1,192,000
Ulala Onuki	68	71	71	210	1,192,000
Momoko Osato	70	69	71	210	1,192,000
Min-Young Lee	71	72	68	211	844,800
Misae Yanagisawa	70	71	70	211	844,800
Megumi Kido	69	71	71	211	844,800
Asuka Kashiwabara	71	73	67	211	844,800
Naruha Miyata	76	68	67	211	844,800

Yonex Ladies

Yonex Country Club, Nagaoka, Niigata
Par 36-36–72; 6,456 yards

June 7-9
purse, ¥70,000,000

	SCORES			TOTAL	MONEY
Momoko Ueda	70	68	65	203	¥12,600,000
Yuki Ichinose	70	72	67	209	5,086,666
Rumi Yoshiba	69	71	69	209	5,086,666
Hyo Joo Kim	67	70	72	209	5,086,666
Asako Fujimoto	68	74	68	210	3,150,000
Yumiko Yoshida	70	72	68	210	3,150,000
Sun-Ju Ahn	71	71	69	211	2,100,000
Momoko Osato	70	71	70	211	2,100,000
Kana Mikashima	71	69	71	211	2,100,000
Sara Ota [A]	69	70	72	211	
Ritsuko Ryu	70	73	69	212	1,289,750
Lala Anai	68	76	68	212	1,289,750
Mi-Jeong Jeon	70	71	71	212	1,289,750
Hee-Kyung Bae	71	69	72	212	1,289,750
Min-Young Lee	69	70	74	213	1,113,000
Solar Lee	69	74	71	214	938,000
Seonwoo Bae	69	73	72	214	938,000
Karen Gondo	70	74	70	214	938,000
Kokone Yoshimoto	66	75	73	214	938,000
Miki Saiki	69	74	72	215	711,666
Reika Usui	70	71	74	215	711,666
Serena Aoki	68	72	75	215	711,666

Ai Miyazato Suntory Ladies Open

Rokko Kokusai Golf Club, Kobe, Hyogo
Par 36-36–72; 6,511 yards

June 13-16
purse, ¥100,000,000

	SCORES				TOTAL	MONEY
Ai Suzuki	67	68	71	70	276	¥18,000,000
Mamiko Higa	68	71	71	67	277	8,800,000
Lala Anai	70	68	70	70	278	6,000,000
Yui Kawamoto	69	69	69	71	278	6,000,000
Hina Arakaki	66	71	74	67	278	6,000,000
Min-Young Lee	65	68	75	71	279	4,000,000
Yuka Saso [A]	69	72	76	63	280	
Hee-Kyung Bae	72	72	69	67	280	3,500,000
Mika Miyazato	68	72	69	72	281	3,000,000
Sayaka Takahashi	68	77	69	68	282	2,250,000
Rei Matsuda	70	67	74	71	282	2,250,000
Yaeeun Hong [A]	68	73	74	68	283	
Ah-Reum Hwang	72	69	70	72	283	1,620,000
Momoko Osato	69	71	72	71	283	1,620,000
Sakura Koiwai	72	67	76	68	283	1,620,000
Eri Okayama	76	69	68	70	283	1,620,000
Chae-Young Yoon	70	69	70	74	283	1,620,000
Erika Hara	71	69	74	70	284	1,170,000
Yumiko Yoshida	69	70	74	71	284	1,170,000
Momoko Ueda	70	75	68	71	284	1,170,000
Saki Nagamine	71	66	73	74	284	1,170,000

Nichirei Ladies

Sodegaura Country Club, Shinsode Course, Chiba
Par 36-36–72; 6,548 yards

June 21-23
purse, ¥80,000,000

	SCORES			TOTAL	MONEY
Ai Suzuki	70	67	70	207	¥14,400,000
Sayaka Takahashi	67	68	72	207	7,040,000
(Suzuki defeated Takahashi on first playoff hole.)					
Sakura Koiwai	70	71	68	209	4,400,000
Yui Kawamoto	72	68	69	209	4,400,000
Kana Mikashima	71	68	70	209	4,400,000
Mamiko Higa	71	65	73	209	4,400,000
Megumi Shimokawa	69	73	68	210	2,400,000
Hinako Shibuno	70	72	68	210	2,400,000
Eri Fukuyama	68	69	73	210	2,400,000
Erika Hara	73	67	71	211	1,556,000
Ah-Reum Hwang	69	70	72	211	1,556,000
Eimi Koga	68	75	69	212	1,232,000
Rumi Yoshiba	70	74	68	212	1,232,000
Saki Asai	73	69	70	212	1,232,000
Jiyai Shin	71	74	67	212	1,232,000
Mio Kotaki	70	71	71	212	1,232,000
Asako Fujimoto	67	73	72	212	1,232,000
Akira Yamaji	71	72	70	213	848,000
Eri Okayama	72	71	70	213	848,000
S. Langkul	69	73	71	213	848,000
Maria Shinohara	70	69	74	213	848,000

Earth Mondahmin Cup

Camellia Hills Country Club, Chiba
Par 36-36–72; 6,622 yards

June 27-30
purse, ¥200,000,000

	SCORES				TOTAL	MONEY
Jiyai Shin	67	66	68	72	273	¥36,000,000
Mika Miyazato	69	67	71	69	276	15,800,000
Erika Hara	67	68	69	72	276	15,800,000
Hinako Shibuno	72	67	69	72	280	12,000,000
Sun-Ju Ahn	72	71	66	72	281	9,000,000
Nana Suganuma	67	72	68	74	281	9,000,000
Lala Anai	73	69	70	70	282	7,000,000
Satsuki Oshiro	69	65	73	76	283	6,000,000
Ah-Reum Hwang	75	67	70	72	284	3,420,000
Miki Sakai	73	65	73	73	284	3,420,000
Min-Young Lee	70	69	72	73	284	3,420,000
Chae-Young Yoon	72	68	71	73	284	3,420,000
Sakura Koiwai	72	70	68	74	284	3,420,000
Misuzu Narita	69	68	72	75	284	3,420,000
Asuka Kashiwabara	73	70	71	71	285	1,880,000
Mao Nozawa	70	70	72	73	285	1,880,000
Mi-Jeong Jeon	76	69	71	69	285	1,880,000
Ji-Hee Lee	70	71	70	74	285	1,880,000
Aoi Ohnishi	71	70	69	75	285	1,880,000
Eimi Koga	73	65	70	77	285	1,880,000

Shiseido Anessa Ladies Open

Totsuka Country Club, Kanagawa
Par 36-36–72; 6,513 yards

July 4-7
purse, ¥120,000,000

	SCORES				TOTAL	MONEY
Hinako Shibuno	71	68	66	71	276	¥21,600,000
Min-Young Lee	69	67	67	73	276	10,560,000
(Shibuno defeated Lee on first playoff hole.)						
Eri Okayama	71	67	68	74	280	8,400,000
Mi-Jeong Jeon	72	67	68	74	281	7,200,000
Sakura Koiwai	74	68	70	70	282	4,650,000
Hee-Kyung Bae	66	68	74	74	282	4,650,000
Yui Kawamoto	71	67	70	74	282	4,650,000
Bo-Mee Lee	70	70	68	74	282	4,650,000
Hikari Fujita	71	68	71	73	283	2,246,400
Mami Fukuda	72	71	67	73	283	2,246,400
Ah-Reum Hwang	71	72	67	73	283	2,246,400
Mone Inami	67	70	70	76	283	2,246,400
Kana Nagai	71	65	70	77	283	2,246,400
Asuka Kashiwabara	69	71	70	74	284	1,464,000
Karis Davidson	70	71	69	74	284	1,464,000
Reika Usui	72	71	67	74	284	1,464,000
Jiyai Shin	73	66	69	76	284	1,464,000
Rei Matsuda	70	70	68	76	284	1,464,000
Hana Wakimoto	72	68	71	74	285	1,104,000
Erika Hara	71	69	72	74	286	924,000
Ritsuko Ryu	72	69	71	74	286	924,000
Eimi Koga	69	73	70	74	286	924,000
Mizuki Tanaka	71	71	70	74	286	924,000
Chie Arimura	75	70	66	75	286	924,000
Ha-Neul Kim	67	69	73	77	286	924,000

Nippon Ham Ladies Classic

Katsura Golf Club, Hokuto, Hokkaido
Par 36-36–72; 6,602 yards

July 11-14
purse, ¥100,000,000

	SCORES				TOTAL	MONEY
S. Langkul	69	65	72	67	273	¥18,000,000
Mone Inami	70	67	69	70	276	7,900,000
Yui Kawamoto	66	69	70	71	276	7,900,000
Ritsuko Ryu	68	70	72	67	277	5,000,000
Jae-Eun Chung	70	68	68	71	277	5,000,000
Eri Okayama	68	69	68	72	277	5,000,000
Hinako Shibuno	70	69	72	67	278	3,500,000
Kana Mikashima	74	69	70	66	279	2,500,000
Saki Nagamine	69	71	70	69	279	2,500,000
Bo-Mee Lee	67	70	70	72	279	2,500,000
Yukari Nishiyama	68	73	71	68	280	1,760,000
Teresa Lu	68	68	70	74	280	1,760,000
Shin-Ae Ahn	70	71	71	69	281	1,510,000
Momoko Osato	76	68	68	69	281	1,510,000
Asuka Kashiwabara	72	71	68	70	281	1,510,000
Akira Yamaji	72	71	74	65	282	1,073,333
Momoko Ueda	71	69	74	68	282	1,073,333
Reika Usui	74	68	72	68	282	1,073,333
Shina Kanazawa	71	70	72	69	282	1,073,333
Haruka Morita	72	71	70	69	282	1,073,333
Rei Matsuda	70	70	70	72	282	1,073,333

Samantha Thavasa Girls Collection Ladies

Eagle Point Golf Club, Ami, Ibaraki
Par 36-36–72; 6,601 yards

July 19-21
purse, ¥60,000,000

	SCORES			TOTAL	MONEY
Sakura Koiwai	66	68	65	199	¥10,800,000
Min-Young Lee	67	65	68	200	5,280,000
Kana Mikashima	67	70	69	206	3,900,000
Misuzu Narita	68	68	70	206	3,900,000
Eriko Kobashi	70	69	68	207	2,325,000
Lala Anai	73	66	68	207	2,325,000
Momoko Ueda	71	66	70	207	2,325,000
Megumi Kido	71	66	70	207	2,325,000
Erika Kikuchi	69	71	68	208	1,224,000
Asuka Kashiwabara	68	71	69	208	1,224,000
Miki Sakai	68	70	70	208	1,224,000
Serena Aoki	68	68	72	208	1,224,000
Hikaru Yoshimoto	70	69	70	209	948,000
Satsuki Oshiro	70	73	66	209	948,000
Sara Ota [A]	70	68	71	209	
Haruka Kudo	68	67	74	209	948,000
Shina Kanazawa	69	72	69	210	654,000
Miyuki Takeuchi	70	71	69	210	654,000
Ritsuko Ryu	71	70	69	210	654,000
Minami Hiruta	69	71	70	210	654,000
Kokone Yoshimoto	70	70	70	210	654,000
Mizuki Ooide	71	71	68	210	654,000
Aoi Ohnishi	71	69	70	210	654,000
Ayako Kimura	68	74	68	210	654,000

Century 21 Ladies

Ishizaka Golf Club, Saitama
Par 36-36–72; 6,470 yards

July 26-28
purse, ¥80,000,000

	SCORES			TOTAL	MONEY
Mone Inami	68	69	70	207	¥14,400,000
Na-Ri Lee	71	70	67	208	6,320,000
Serena Aoki	69	71	68	208	6,320,000
Ritsuko Ryu	72	70	67	209	4,400,000
Reika Usui	69	71	69	209	4,400,000
Rumi Yoshiba	70	72	68	210	3,200,000
Hee-Kyung Bae	71	73	67	211	2,060,800
Hikaru Yoshimoto	70	72	69	211	2,060,800
Sakura Koiwai	70	75	66	211	2,060,800
Miki Sakai	70	71	70	211	2,060,800
Erika Hara	67	72	72	211	2,060,800
Saki Asai	72	72	68	212	1,304,000
Jae-Eun Chung	74	70	68	212	1,304,000
Hana Wakimoto	69	74	69	212	1,304,000
Eri Okayama	71	70	71	212	1,304,000
Eri Fukuyama	70	74	69	213	840,000
Chie Arimura	73	72	68	213	840,000
Hiromu Ono	71	72	70	213	840,000
Satsuki Oshiro	71	72	70	213	840,000
Rei Matsuda	73	72	68	213	840,000
Minami Hiruta	74	69	70	213	840,000
Minami Katsu	71	71	71	213	840,000
Eriko Kobashi	68	72	73	213	840,000

	SCORES			TOTAL	MONEY
Mao Nozawa	70	70	73	213	840,000
Mami Fukuda	71	69	73	213	840,000

Daito Kentaku Eheyanet Ladies

Narusawa Golf Club, Narusawa, Yamanishi
Par 35-37–72; 6,605 yards

August 1-4
purse, ¥120,000,000

	SCORES				TOTAL	MONEY
Misuzu Narita	70	70	67	70	277	¥21,600,000
Seonwoo Bae	72	68	69	69	278	9,480,000
Chie Arimura	69	68	68	73	278	9,480,000
Ah-Reum Hwang	70	67	70	72	279	7,200,000
Min-Young Lee	71	67	72	71	281	5,400,000
Saiki Fujita	72	65	70	74	281	5,400,000
Hiromu Ono	71	70	69	72	282	4,200,000
Yuna Nishimura [A]	74	68	72	69	283	
Na-Ri Lee	74	70	69	70	283	2,538,000
Bo-Mee Lee	72	66	73	72	283	2,538,000
Ha-Neul Kim	71	70	70	72	283	2,538,000
Megumi Kido	73	68	70	72	283	2,538,000
Shina Kanazawa	69	73	68	73	283	2,538,000
Ayaka Furue [A]	70	70	67	76	283	
Mayu Hamada	66	67	73	77	283	2,538,000
Erika Kikuchi	67	75	70	72	284	1,836,000
Asako Fujimoto	73	70	71	71	285	1,416,000
Fumie Jo	71	68	74	72	285	1,416,000
Saki Nagamine	71	70	72	72	285	1,416,000
Satsuki Oshiro	70	70	72	73	285	1,416,000
Chae-Young Yoon	69	72	69	75	285	1,416,000
Saki Asai	71	71	68	75	285	1,416,000

Hokkaido Meiji Cup

Sapporo International Country Club, Shimamatsu Course,
Kitahiroshima, Hokkaido
Par 36-36–72; 6,531 yards

August 9-11
purse, ¥90,000,000

	SCORES			TOTAL	MONEY
Seonwoo Bae	68	67	69	204	¥16,200,000
Teresa Lu	68	69	67	204	7,920,000
(Bae defeated Lu on first playoff hole.)					
Sun-Ju Ahn	68	69	68	205	6,300,000
Erika Hara	72	69	66	207	5,400,000
Jiyai Shin	67	73	68	208	4,050,000
Sakura Koiwai	69	71	68	208	4,050,000
Lala Anai	69	72	68	209	2,700,000
Mone Inami	69	70	70	209	2,700,000
Hee-Kyung Bae	72	67	70	209	2,700,000
Eimi Koga	70	73	67	210	1,750,500
Ai Suzuki	68	69	73	210	1,750,500
Yui Kawamoto	70	69	72	211	1,611,000
Shina Kanazawa	71	72	69	212	1,386,000
Yuki Ichinose	70	72	70	212	1,386,000
Mi-Jeong Jeon	71	71	70	212	1,386,000
Hinako Shibuno	70	70	72	212	1,386,000
Hana Wakimoto	74	70	69	213	1,071,000

	SCORES			TOTAL	MONEY
Kumiko Kaneda	72	70	71	213	1,071,000
Mayu Hamada	70	69	74	213	1,071,000
Saki Asai	70	74	70	214	855,000
Momoka Miura	70	72	72	214	855,000
Momoko Ueda	71	71	72	214	855,000
Miki Sakai	72	69	73	214	855,000
Ha-Neul Kim	75	70	69	214	855,000

NEC Karuizawa 72

Karuizawa 72 Golf Club, North Course, Karuizawa, Nagano
Par 36-36–72; 6,705 yards

August 16-18
purse, ¥80,000,000

	SCORES			TOTAL	MONEY
Lala Anai	67	70	65	202	¥14,400,000
Min-Young Lee	67	69	66	202	7,200,000
(Anai defeated Lee on first playoff hole.)					
Hinako Shibuno	67	68	68	203	5,200,000
Mayu Hamada	64	70	69	203	5,200,000
Jiyai Shin	68	72	65	205	3,600,000
Momoko Ueda	68	71	66	205	3,600,000
Sakura Koiwai	69	70	67	206	2,600,000
Seonwoo Bae	68	69	69	206	2,600,000
Minami Hiruta	69	69	69	207	1,588,800
Miki Saiki	71	67	69	207	1,588,800
Ah-Reum Hwang	69	67	71	207	1,588,800
Minami Katsu	70	66	71	207	1,588,800
Erika Hara	67	68	72	207	1,588,800
Megumi Shimokawa	69	72	67	208	1,168,000
Yuka Yasuda [A]	70	69	69	208	
Ayako Kimura	66	72	70	208	1,168,000
Ritsuko Ryu	67	70	71	208	1,168,000
Mamiko Higa	69	67	72	208	1,168,000
Ha-Neul Kim	68	71	70	209	928,000
Saki Asai	66	71	72	209	928,000

CAT Ladies

Daihakone Country Club, Hakone, Kanagawa
Par 37-36–73; 6,704 yards

August 23-25
purse, ¥60,000,000

	SCORES			TOTAL	MONEY
Saki Asai	68	69	72	209	¥10,800,000
Lala Anai	75	66	69	210	5,280,000
Bo-Mee Lee	71	71	69	211	4,200,000
Minami Hiruta	74	72	66	212	3,300,000
Asuka Kashiwabara	73	69	70	212	3,300,000
Momoko Ueda	70	72	71	213	2,400,000
Kumiko Kaneda	73	72	69	214	1,800,000
Eimi Koga	73	71	70	214	1,800,000
Minami Katsu	74	69	71	214	1,800,000
Erika Hara	72	70	73	215	1,164,000
Rumi Yoshiba	73	69	73	215	1,164,000
Teresa Lu	75	74	68	217	948,000
Hana Wakimoto	72	74	71	217	948,000
Mamiko Higa	74	72	71	217	948,000
Hee-Kyung Bae	70	73	74	217	948,000

	SCORES	TOTAL	MONEY
Saiki Fujita	72 71 74	217	948,000
Ai Suzuki	74 74 70	218	678,000
Mone Inami	72 75 71	218	678,000
Kaori Ohe	74 71 73	218	678,000
Serena Aoki	72 68 78	218	678,000

Nitori Ladies

Otaru Country Club, Otaru, Hokkaido
Par 36-36–72; 6,650 yards

August 29-September 1
purse, ¥100,000,000

	SCORES	TOTAL	MONEY
Ai Suzuki	70 67 71 69	277	¥18,000,000
Jiyai Shin	70 76 65 68	279	7,900,000
Sun-Ju Ahn	70 67 71 71	279	7,900,000
Yuka Yasuda [A]	71 68 70 71	280	
Hinako Shibuno	71 68 71 71	281	6,000,000
Erika Hara	73 70 70 69	282	5,000,000
Teresa Lu	71 70 72 70	283	3,750,000
Hana Wakimoto	71 71 71 70	283	3,750,000
Karis Davidson	70 70 70 74	284	3,000,000
Mayu Wakui [A]	71 71 73 70	285	
Mika Miyazato	73 67 74 71	285	2,500,000
Ayako Kimura	71 74 66 75	286	2,000,000
Saki Nagamine	70 71 75 71	287	1,590,000
Mamiko Higa	69 75 72 71	287	1,590,000
Sayaka Takahashi	69 68 77 73	287	1,590,000
Yuki Ichinose	73 69 72 73	287	1,590,000
Solar Lee	71 73 69 74	287	1,590,000
S. Langkul	70 70 72 75	287	1,590,000
Erika Kikuchi	73 73 70 72	288	1,030,000
Mi-Jeong Jeon	72 73 71 72	288	1,030,000
Serena Aoki	74 71 73 70	288	1,030,000
Nanoko Hayashi	71 73 72 72	288	1,030,000
Minami Hiruta	70 71 73 74	288	1,030,000
Lala Anai	70 70 72 76	288	1,030,000

Golf 5 Ladies

Golf 5 Club, Sunnyfield Course, Ibaraki
Par 36-36–72; 6,380 yards

September 6-8
purse, ¥60,000,000

	SCORES	TOTAL	MONEY
Min-Young Lee	64 68 68	200	¥10,800,000
Saki Asai	63 70 68	201	4,740,000
Jiyai Shin	64 68 69	201	4,740,000
Sayaka Takahashi	70 65 67	202	3,600,000
Eri Okayama	67 69 67	203	2,700,000
Na-Ri Lee	67 67 69	203	2,700,000
Saki Takeo	67 73 65	205	1,650,000
Haruka Morita	69 69 67	205	1,650,000
Ah-Reum Hwang	66 71 68	205	1,650,000
Sun-Ju Ahn	68 68 69	205	1,650,000
Hiromu Ono	67 70 69	206	1,098,000
Miyuki Takeuchi	68 68 70	206	1,098,000
Lala Anai	70 71 66	207	948,000
Saki Nagamine	67 71 69	207	948,000

	SCORES	TOTAL	MONEY
Haruka Kudo	69 68 70	207	948,000
Mizuki Seto	67 72 69	208	768,000
Kana Mikashima	68 71 69	208	768,000
Mi-Jeong Jeon	71 67 70	208	768,000
Miki Saiki	68 72 69	209	594,000
Ayako Kimura	69 71 69	209	594,000
Naruha Miyata	72 68 69	209	594,000
Rei Matsuda	72 66 71	209	594,000

Japan LPGA Championship Konica Minolta Cup

Cherry Hills Golf Club, Hyogo
Par 36-36–72; 6,425 yards

September 12-15
purse, ¥200,000,000

	SCORES	TOTAL	MONEY
Nasa Hataoka	69 67 67 67	270	¥36,000,000
Aoi Ohnishi	72 73 64 69	278	15,800,000
Shanshan Feng	72 71 63 72	278	15,800,000
Sun-Ju Ahn	69 74 69 68	280	8,600,000
Serena Aoki	71 71 68 70	280	8,600,000
Yui Kawamoto	73 67 69 71	280	8,600,000
Maria Shinohara	76 65 68 71	280	8,600,000
Kana Mikashima	70 67 70 73	280	8,600,000
Inbee Park	68 72 71 70	281	5,000,000
Erina Hara	71 70 70 71	282	4,000,000
Bo-Mee Lee	71 71 71 70	283	2,880,000
Ha-Neul Kim	72 70 70 71	283	2,880,000
Sayaka Takahashi	68 71 72 72	283	2,880,000
Miki Saiki	72 71 68 72	283	2,880,000
Mi-Jeong Jeon	69 72 69 73	283	2,880,000
Satsuki Oshiro	71 71 68 73	283	2,880,000
Miki Sakai	70 72 68 73	283	2,880,000
Shina Kanazawa	72 67 68 76	283	2,880,000
Chie Arimura	74 70 69 71	284	1,800,000
Hiroko Azuma	71 73 69 71	284	1,800,000
Karen Gondo	71 73 69 71	284	1,800,000
Min-Young Lee	69 75 68 72	284	1,800,000

Descente Ladies Tokai Classic

Shin Minami Aichi Country Club, Mihama, Aichi
Par 36-36–72; 6,437 yards

September 20-22
purse, ¥80,000,000

	SCORES	TOTAL	MONEY
Hinako Shibuno	69 70 64	203	¥14,400,000
Momoko Ueda	70 70 65	205	4,960,000
Mayu Hamada	71 66 68	205	4,960,000
Ji-Hee Lee	63 72 70	205	4,960,000
Teresa Lu	70 65 70	205	4,960,000
Jiyai Shin	63 68 74	205	4,960,000
Mao Nozawa	69 67 70	206	2,600,000
Min-Young Lee	69 65 72	206	2,600,000
Rie Tsuji	72 69 66	207	1,538,666
Eriko Kobashi	70 68 69	207	1,538,666
Eri Okayama	70 68 69	207	1,538,666
Hiroko Azuma	71 67 69	207	1,538,666
Kana Mikashima	68 69 70	207	1,538,666

	SCORES			TOTAL	MONEY
Ai Suzuki	69	66	72	207	1,538,666
Yuka Yasuda [A]	71	68	69	208	
Saiki Fujita	71	70	67	208	1,168,000
Phoebe Yao	72	67	69	208	1,168,000
Eimi Koga	70	70	69	209	928,000
Shiho Oyama	73	67	69	209	928,000
Nana Suganuma	73	68	68	209	928,000
Mone Inami	72	66	71	209	928,000

Miyagi TV Cup Dunlop Ladies Open

Rifu Golf Club, Rifu, Miyagi
Par 36-36–72; 6,505 yards

September 27-29
purse, ¥70,000,000

	SCORES			TOTAL	MONEY
Asuka Kashiwabara	68	70	68	206	¥12,600,000
Seonwoo Bae	66	75	67	208	6,300,000
Kana Nagai	76	68	66	210	3,850,000
Minami Katsu	71	71	68	210	3,850,000
Erika Kikuchi	71	69	70	210	3,850,000
Mamiko Higa	68	68	74	210	3,850,000
Jiyai Shin	73	72	66	211	1,807,400
Aoi Ohnishi	71	70	70	211	1,807,400
Yui Kawamoto	69	71	71	211	1,807,400
Nasa Hataoka	69	68	74	211	1,807,400
Rie Tsuji	68	68	75	211	1,807,400
Hina Arakaki	70	71	71	212	1,267,000
Eri Okayama	73	71	69	213	1,092,000
Miki Sakai	69	73	71	213	1,092,000
Ayako Kimura	74	66	73	213	1,092,000
Mao Nozawa	71	67	75	213	1,092,000
Akira Yamaji	73	71	70	214	847,000
Ayaka Matsumori	75	68	71	214	847,000
Megumi Kido	73	73	68	214	847,000
Miyu Yamato	68	76	71	215	700,000
Eriko Kobashi	75	67	73	215	700,000

Japan Women's Open Championship

Hakusan Village Golf Club, Hakusan Village, Mie
Par 36-36–72; 6,479 yards

October 3-6
purse, ¥150,000,000

	SCORES				TOTAL	MONEY
Nasa Hataoka	67	67	67	69	270	¥30,000,000
Eri Okayama	64	71	69	70	274	11,850,000
So Yeon Ryu	68	66	69	71	274	11,850,000
Momoko Osato	66	67	68	73	274	11,850,000
Sayaka Takahashi	67	72	71	68	278	5,775,000
Hee-Kyung Bae	64	68	73	73	278	5,775,000
Hinako Shibuno	67	70	70	72	279	4,500,000
Teresa Lu	68	68	74	71	281	3,900,000
Mizuki Tanaka	71	70	70	71	282	3,075,000
Rei Matsuda	69	70	71	72	282	3,075,000
Tsubasa Kajitani [A]	70	69	69	74	282	
Ha-Neul Kim	65	72	77	69	283	2,625,000
Lala Anai	69	70	75	70	284	1,830,000
Serena Aoki	72	69	72	71	284	1,830,000

	SCORES				TOTAL	MONEY
Min-Young Lee	69	70	73	72	284	1,830,000
Eimi Koga	69	71	71	73	284	1,830,000
Minami Katsu	73	67	71	73	284	1,830,000
Aoi Ohnishi	70	70	70	74	284	1,830,000
Jiyai Shin	68	68	73	75	284	1,830,000
Seonwoo Bae	65	73	72	75	285	1,387,500
Kana Nagai	70	69	71	75	285	1,387,500

Stanley Ladies

Tomei Country Club, Susano, Shizuoka
Par 36-36–72; 6,572 yards
(Tournament reduced to 27 holes—typhoon.)

October 11-13
purse, ¥100,000,000

	SCORES		TOTAL	MONEY
Ah-Reum Hwang	65	35	100	¥13,500,000
Hinano Hoshikawa (A)	68	34	102	
Saki Takeo	68	34	102	5,450,000
Maria Shinohara	67	35	102	5,450,000
Erika Kikuchi	67	35	102	5,450,000
Hinako Shibuno	71	32	103	2,500,000
Mone Inami	70	33	103	2,500,000
Bo-Mee Lee	70	33	103	2,500,000
Mi-Jeong Jeon	70	33	103	2,500,000
Ritsuko Ryu	70	33	103	2,500,000
Haruka Morita	68	35	103	2,500,000
Akira Yamaji	69	35	104	1,372,500
Na-Ri Lee	71	34	105	1,147,500
Mamiko Higa	71	34	105	1,147,500
Sayaka Takahashi	70	35	105	1,147,500
Momoka Miura	70	35	105	1,147,500
Hiroko Azuma	69	36	105	1,147,500
Sora Kamiya (A)	69	36	105	
Hinako Yamauchi	72	34	106	735,000
Hina Arakaki	71	35	106	735,000
Miki Saiki	71	35	106	735,000
Miki Sakai	70	36	106	735,000
Erina Hara	70	36	106	735,000
Rumi Yoshiba	70	36	106	735,000
Mayu Hirota	69	37	106	735,000
Misuzu Narita	69	37	106	735,000

Fujitsu Ladies

Tokyu Seven Hundred Club, Chiba
Par 36-36–72; 6,675 yards

October 18-20
purse, ¥90,000,000

	SCORES			TOTAL	MONEY
Ayaka Furue (A)	67	65	67	199	
Mone Inami	63	70	68	201	¥10,800,000
Kana Mikashima	65	66	70	201	10,800,000
Sayaka Takahashi	67	66	70	203	5,600,000
Natsuki Hatano	70	68	67	205	4,800,000
Hee-Kyung Bae	67	69	70	206	3,220,000
Minami Hiruta	68	68	70	206	3,220,000
Erika Kikuchi	68	68	70	206	3,220,000
Rie Tsuji	70	66	70	206	3,220,000

	SCORES			TOTAL	MONEY
Reika Usui	67	69	71	207	2,000,000
Yuna Nishimura [A]	68	68	71	207	
Minami Katsu	72	68	68	208	1,541,333
Akira Yamaji	67	71	70	208	1,541,333
Sakura Koiwai	70	68	70	208	1,541,333
Solar Lee	71	69	69	209	1,352,000
Momoko Ueda	68	69	72	209	1,352,000
Shoko Sasaki	67	72	71	210	1,032,000
Karen Gondo	69	72	69	210	1,032,000
Kana Nagai	70	69	71	210	1,032,000
Hikaru Yoshimoto	72	67	71	210	1,032,000
Mamiko Higa	70	68	72	210	1,032,000
Misuzu Narita	70	67	73	210	1,032,000

Nobuta Group Masters Golf Club Ladies

Masters Golf Club, Miki, Hyogo
Par 36-36–72; 6,510 yards

October 24-27
purse, ¥200,000,000

	SCORES				TOTAL	MONEY
Asuka Kashiwabara	70	70	68	66	274	¥36,000,000
Bo-Mee Lee	68	70	69	68	275	18,000,000
Sakura Koiwai	73	70	66	67	276	13,000,000
Mone Inami	67	68	70	71	276	13,000,000
Teresa Lu	68	70	64	75	277	10,000,000
Sayaka Takahashi	71	69	71	68	279	7,700,000
Chie Arimura	71	69	70	69	279	7,700,000
Saki Nagamine	70	70	69	71	280	5,500,000
Jiyai Shin	68	69	71	72	280	5,500,000
Kana Mikashima	70	70	71	70	281	3,920,000
Momoko Ueda	71	68	71	71	281	3,920,000
Seonwoo Bae	71	72	69	70	282	3,340,000
Misuzu Narita	72	72	67	71	282	3,340,000
Hinako Shibuno	73	66	71	72	282	3,340,000
Lala Anai	69	73	67	73	282	3,340,000
Mao Nozawa	70	70	74	69	283	2,740,000
Mami Fukuda	70	70	72	71	283	2,740,000
Minami Katsu	72	70	72	70	284	2,180,000
Saiki Fujita	75	68	71	70	284	2,180,000
Chae-Young Yoon	69	71	73	71	284	2,180,000
Nana Suganuma	72	70	70	72	284	2,180,000

Mitsubishi Electric/Hisako Higuchi Ladies

Musashigaoka Golf Club, Hanno, Saitama
Par 36-36–72; 6,585 yards

November 1-3
purse, ¥80,000,000

	SCORES			TOTAL	MONEY
Ai Suzuki	66	68	68	202	¥14,400,000
Jiyai Shin	69	66	68	203	7,040,000
Sakura Koiwai	68	67	69	204	5,600,000
Eri Okayama	67	68	70	205	4,800,000
Seonwoo Bae	68	69	70	207	4,000,000
Minami Katsu	67	71	70	208	3,000,000
Sayaka Takahashi	70	68	70	208	3,000,000
Hina Arakaki	70	73	67	210	2,200,000
Rumi Yoshiba	69	72	69	210	2,200,000

	SCORES			TOTAL	MONEY
Eri Fukuyama	69	74	68	211	1,504,000
Phoebe Yao	72	70	69	211	1,504,000
Maria Shinohara	69	70	72	211	1,504,000
Saki Takeo	72	71	69	212	1,216,000
Shiho Oyama	69	72	71	212	1,216,000
Erika Hara	69	72	71	212	1,216,000
Kaori Ohe	68	69	75	212	1,216,000
Chae-Young Yoon	70	73	70	213	848,000
Mio Kotaki	71	72	70	213	848,000
Eriko Kobashi	72	71	70	213	848,000
Hikaru Yoshimoto	71	71	71	213	848,000
Sun-Ju Ahn	71	70	72	213	848,000
Ha-Neul Kim	69	68	76	213	848,000

Toto Japan Classic

Seta Golf Club, North Course, Shiga
Par 36-36–72; 6,659 yards

November 8-10
purse, ¥165,000,000

	SCORES			TOTAL	MONEY
Ai Suzuki	67	65	67	199	¥24,340,500
Hyo-Joo Kim	68	68	66	202	14,810,166
Minjee Lee	68	69	68	205	10,743,788
Jing Yan	69	69	68	206	7,500,335
Jennifer Kupcho	68	70	68	206	7,500,335
Sakura Koiwai	70	69	68	207	4,419,153
Erika Kikuchi	70	68	69	207	4,419,153
Shanshan Feng	70	67	70	207	4,419,153
Gaby Lopez	68	67	72	207	4,419,153
Azahara Munoz	70	71	67	208	3,054,137
Morgan Pressel	70	71	67	208	3,054,137
Hannah Green	67	69	72	208	3,054,137
Hinako Shibuno	69	69	71	209	2,502,744
Ah-Reum Hwang	72	66	71	209	2,502,744
Chella Choi	70	68	71	209	2,502,744
Yui Kawamoto	71	71	68	210	2,165,006
Sun-Ju Ahn	70	71	69	210	2,165,006
Seonwoo Bae	69	72	70	211	1,970,390
Nicole Larsen	70	71	70	211	1,970,390
Erika Hara	73	70	69	212	1,767,661
Eri Okayama	70	72	70	212	1,767,661
Mel Reid	73	69	70	212	1,767,661
Ariya Jutanugarn	73	68	71	212	1,767,661
So Yeon Ryu	74	69	70	213	1,409,909
Kana Mikashima	69	73	71	213	1,409,909
Pornanong Phatlum	74	69	70	213	1,409,909
Momoko Ueda	72	70	71	213	1,409,909
Jeongeun Lee$_6$	70	74	69	213	1,409,909
Lexi Thompson	74	68	71	213	1,409,909
Saki Asai	74	71	68	213	1,409,909
Yu Liu	69	71	73	213	1,409,909

Itoen Ladies

Great Island Club, Chonan, Chiba
Par 36-36–72; 6,741 yards

November 15-17
purse, ¥100,000,000

	SCORES			TOTAL	MONEY
Ai Suzuki	68	67	67	202	¥18,000,000
Shiho Oyama	69	67	67	203	9,000,000
Seonwoo Bae	69	68	67	204	7,000,000
Eri Okayama	68	70	67	205	4,675,000
Chae-Young Yoon	66	71	68	205	4,675,000
Mami Fukuda	69	67	69	205	4,675,000
Minami Katsu	68	67	70	205	4,675,000
Jiyai Shin	69	65	72	206	3,000,000
Mamiko Higa	68	71	68	207	1,992,000
Momoko Ueda	72	66	69	207	1,992,000
Haruka Morita	72	66	69	207	1,992,000
Mone Inami	67	69	71	207	1,992,000
Kaori Ohe	68	66	73	207	1,992,000
Karen Gondo	68	70	70	208	1,420,000
Kana Mikashima	69	69	70	208	1,420,000
Ah-Reum Hwang	70	68	70	208	1,420,000
Megumi Kido	67	70	71	208	1,420,000
Bo-Mee Lee	70	66	72	208	1,420,000
Erika Kikuchi	67	69	73	209	1,120,000
Miki Sakai	71	68	71	210	980,000
Hee-Kyung Bae	70	70	70	210	980,000
Na-Ri Lee	68	69	73	210	980,000
Serena Aoki	68	69	73	210	980,000
Reika Usui	70	65	75	210	980,000

Daio Paper Elleair Ladies Open

Elleair Golf Club, Matsuyama, Ehime
Par 36-36–72; 6,580 yards

November 21-24
purse, ¥100,000,000

	SCORES				TOTAL	MONEY
Hinako Shibuno	67	70	66	66	269	¥18,000,000
Ai Suzuki	71	65	67	67	270	8,800,000
Min-Young Lee	70	65	67	69	271	7,000,000
Ayaka Furue	68	68	68	68	272	5,500,000
Haruka Morita	65	69	67	71	272	5,500,000
Sayaka Takahashi	67	67	68	71	273	4,000,000
Seonwoo Bae	67	66	69	72	274	3,250,000
Minami Katsu	68	69	65	72	274	3,250,000
Saiki Fujita	70	70	68	67	275	2,250,000
Erika Kikuchi	69	74	63	69	275	2,250,000
Lala Anai	72	68	71	65	276	1,560,000
Saki Nagamine	72	70	68	66	276	1,560,000
Saki Takeo	71	70	69	66	276	1,560,000
Mami Fukuda	70	67	71	68	276	1,560,000
Eri Okayama	70	66	68	72	276	1,560,000
Jiyai Shin	67	69	66	74	276	1,560,000
Yui Kawamoto	68	69	70	70	277	1,160,000
Yuki Ichinose	69	69	69	70	277	1,160,000
Kana Mikashima	69	71	72	66	278	936,666
Erika Hara	72	69	69	68	278	936,666
Yumiko Yoshida	70	69	69	70	278	936,666

Japan LPGA Tour Championship Ricoh Cup

Miyazaki Country Club, Miyazaki
Par 36-36–72; 6,535 yards

November 28-December 1
purse, ¥120,000,000

	SCORES				TOTAL	MONEY
Seonwoo Bae	71	68	71	67	277	¥30,000,000
Ayaka Furue	69	72	71	69	281	14,700,000
Hinako Shibuno	70	70	71	70	281	14,700,000
Yui Kawamoto	73	70	72	67	282	9,396,000
Ai Suzuki	72	73	70	68	283	7,164,000
Bo-Mee Lee	71	69	69	74	283	7,164,000
Jiyai Shin	75	70	71	68	284	4,240,000
Hee-Kyung Bae	73	69	71	71	284	4,240,000
Eri Okayama	71	72	70	71	284	4,240,000
Mamiko Higa	71	77	68	69	285	1,872,000
Hikaru Yoshimoto	73	70	70	72	285	1,872,000
Min-Young Lee	71	73	71	71	286	1,316,000
Momoko Ueda	73	70	70	73	286	1,316,000
Sakura Koiwai	74	71	68	73	286	1,316,000
Erika Hara	72	75	69	71	287	788,000
Mi-Jeong Jeon	73	71	70	73	287	788,000
Teresa Lu	67	70	75	75	287	788,000
Hina Arakaki	76	68	73	72	289	624,000
Erika Kikuchi	75	73	71	71	290	600,000
Minami Katsu	75	69	74	72	290	600,000
Asuka Kashiwabara	70	76	69	75	290	600,000

Korea LPGA Tour

Taiwan Women's Golf Open

Hsin Yi Golf Club, Chinese Taipei
Par 36-36–72; 6,463 yards

January 17-20
purse, US$800,000

	SCORES				TOTAL	MONEY
Mi Jeong Jeon	71	67	66	72	276	KRW179,600,000
Min Sun Kim5	71	69	68	69	277	87,555,000
Pei-Ying Tsai	68	69	69	71	277	87,555,000
Yu-Ju Chen	72	71	67	68	278	40,410,000
A Lim Kim	69	67	68	74	278	40,410,000
So Yi Kim	72	72	64	71	279	31,430,000
Ji Hyun Oh	70	69	71	70	280	24,695,000
Ji Yeong Kim2	72	67	71	70	280	24,695,000
S. Langkul	71	70	69	72	282	15,715,000
Chae Yoon Park	69	71	67	75	282	15,715,000
Min Kyung Choi	72	73	69	69	283	10,192,300
Eun Soo Jang	74	68	71	70	283	10,192,300
So Young Lee	70	72	70	71	283	10,192,300
Ju Young Pak	71	70	70	72	283	10,192,300
Min Ji Park	73	69	69	72	283	10,192,300
Chonlada Chayanun	71	71	70	71	283	10,192,300
Shin Young Park	73	69	70	71	283	10,192,300
Hye Jin Choi	72	71	68	72	283	10,192,300
Hyo Rin Lee	71	72	71	70	284	8,486,100
Hana Wakimoto	73	70	71	70	284	8,486,100

Lotte Rent a Car Ladies Open

Sky Hill Jeju Country Club, Seogwipo, Jeju Island
Par 36-36–72; 6,301 yards

April 4-7
purse, KRW600,000,000

	SCORES				TOTAL	MONEY
Ayean Cho	71	70	71	67	279	KRW120,000,000
Jeongmin	69	72	70	69	280	69,000,000
Ellie Na	72	71	71	67	281	34,000,000
Ju Young Pak	68	75	68	70	281	34,000,000
Min Sun Kim5	67	71	71	72	281	34,000,000
Han Sol Ji	70	70	70	72	282	19,500,000
Ji Yeong Kim2	70	73	69	70	282	19,500,000
Jung Min Lee	67	72	72	72	283	15,000,000
Song Yi Ahn	70	74	73	67	284	9,700,000
Chae Yoon Park	70	73	73	68	284	9,700,000
Hye Jin Choi	68	71	70	75	284	9,700,000
Ha Na Jang	73	73	74	66	286	7,320,000
Min Kyung Choi	71	74	70	71	286	7,320,000
Somi Lee	70	76	74	67	287	6,290,000
Ji Hyun Kim	74	72	71	70	287	6,290,000
Carrie Park	72	76	71	68	287	6,290,000
Hyun Soo Kim	70	75	71	71	287	6,290,000
Gi Ppuem Lee	70	74	71	72	287	6,290,000
Suji Kim	70	73	69	75	287	6,290,000
Eun Bin Lim	66	76	74	72	288	5,288,571

626 / WOMEN'S TOURS

	SCORES				TOTAL	MONEY
Yoon Jung Cho	71	73	75	69	288	5,288,571
Hae Rym Kim	70	78	73	67	288	5,288,571
Gyo Rin Park	72	75	71	70	288	5,288,571
Min Song Ha	70	77	73	68	288	5,288,571
Eun Soo Jang	75	73	69	71	288	5,288,571
Hyo Rin Lee	72	73	72	71	288	5,288,571

Celltrion Queens Masters

Bora Country Club, Ulsan
Par 36-36–72; 6,674 yards

April 12-14
purse, KRW800,000,000

	SCORES			TOTAL	MONEY
Jeongmin Cho	67	70	72	209	KRW160,000,000
Seung Hyun Lee	69	70	71	210	78,000,000
Bo Ah Kim	68	71	71	210	78,000,000
HeeJeong Lim	69	71	71	211	40,000,000
Ayean Cho	74	74	66	214	30,000,000
A Lim Kim	72	75	67	214	30,000,000
Bo Bae Kim$_2$	72	70	73	215	24,000,000
Chae Yoon Park	75	73	68	216	13,760,000
Ju Young Pak	70	73	73	216	13,760,000
Hyun Soo Kim	73	72	71	216	13,760,000
Ji Hyun Kim	73	71	72	216	13,760,000
Min Ji Park	67	71	78	216	13,760,000
Ji Yeong Kim$_2$	71	77	69	217	8,502,857
Ji Hyun Kim$_2$	73	72	72	217	8,502,857
Gyo Rin Park	72	76	69	217	8,502,857
Yeun Jung Seo	74	72	71	217	8,502,857
Na Rin An	71	74	72	217	8,502,857
Ha Na Jang	70	75	72	217	8,502,857
Song Yi Ahn	69	71	77	217	8,502,857

Nexen Saint Nine Masters

Gaya Country Club, Gimhae
Par 36-36–72; 6,808 yards

April 19-21
purse, KRW600,000,000

	SCORES			TOTAL	MONEY
Seong Yeoun Lee	69	68	69	206	KRW120,000,000
Ye Rim Choi	71	67	69	207	69,000,000
A Lim Kim	72	68	68	208	48,000,000
Ji Hyun Lee$_2$	71	69	69	209	27,000,000
Ha Na Jang	71	70	68	209	27,000,000
So Yeon Park	71	69	70	210	12,942,857
Gayoung Lee	71	71	68	210	12,942,857
Chae Yoon Park	70	71	69	210	12,942,857
Ayean Cho	70	72	68	210	12,942,857
Min Sun Kim$_5$	73	69	68	210	12,942,857
Ji Hyun Kim$_2$	69	72	69	210	12,942,857
Seo Hyeon Youn	71	68	71	210	12,942,857
Somi Lee	75	68	68	211	6,990,000
So Young Lee	74	69	68	211	6,990,000
Ji Young Park	73	70	69	212	6,270,000
Eun Bin Lim	75	68	69	212	6,270,000
Seul Gi Jeong	69	73	70	212	6,270,000
Ellie Na	72	71	69	212	6,270,000

	SCORES				TOTAL	MONEY
Eun Soo Jang	73	67	73		213	5,730,000
Jung Min Lee	70	72	71		213	5,730,000

CreaS F&C KLPGA Championship

Lakewood Country Club, Seoul
Par 36-36–72; 6,610 yards
April 25-28
purse, KRW1,000,000,000

	SCORES				TOTAL	MONEY
Hye Jin Choi	69	69	67	70	275	KRW200,000,000
So Yeon Park	70	67	68	70	275	115,000,000

(Choi defeated Park on first playoff hole.)

	SCORES				TOTAL	MONEY
Da Yeon Lee	68	66	71	71	276	80,000,000
Jeongeun Lee$_6$	69	67	74	68	278	50,000,000
Ji Young Park	69	69	70	71	279	40,000,000
Ji Hyun Lee$_2$	73	70	69	68	280	32,500,000
So Young Lee	70	71	71	68	280	32,500,000
Suji Kim	71	68	72	70	281	18,375,000
A Lim Kim	70	66	75	70	281	18,375,000
Char Young Kim$_2$	70	69	70	72	281	18,375,000
Min Ji Park	71	70	71	69	281	18,375,000
Ye Rim Choi	71	71	72	68	282	10,666,667
Yul Lin Hwang	72	71	68	71	282	10,666,667
Ayean Cho	72	71	71	68	282	10,666,667
Ji Hyun Kim$_2$	71	70	73	68	282	10,666,667
Seul Gi Jeong	73	67	71	71	282	10,666,667
Yoon Kyung Heo	72	72	70	68	282	10,666,667
Ka Ram Choi	69	71	69	73	282	10,666,667
Gyo Rin Park	72	67	72	71	282	10,666,667
Hyun Kyung Park	71	72	69	70	282	10,666,667

Kyochon Honey Ladies Open

Ferrum Country Club, Yeoju, Gyeonggi
Par 36-36–72; 6,582 yards
May 3-5
purse, KRW500,000,000

	SCORES			TOTAL	MONEY
So Yeon Park	65	69	71	205	KRW100,000,000
Min Kyung Choi	70	69	67	206	48,750,000
Min Ji Park	72	69	65	206	48,750,000
Ellie Na	74	68	67	209	22,500,000
So Young Lee	69	69	71	209	22,500,000
Bo Bae Kim$_2$	72	68	70	210	17,500,000
Ji Hyun Oh	69	73	69	211	9,142,857
Ka Ram Choi	69	71	71	211	9,142,857
Ha Na Jang	74	71	66	211	9,142,857
Ye Rim Choi	70	70	71	211	9,142,857
Chae Yoon Park	77	67	67	211	9,142,857
Min Sun Kim$_5$	70	68	73	211	9,142,857
HeeJeong Lim	68	69	74	211	9,142,857
Somi Lee	72	71	69	212	5,450,000
Ji Hyun Lee$_2$	72	69	71	212	5,450,000
Sohye Park	69	71	72	212	5,450,000
Hae Rym Kim	67	71	74	212	5,450,000
Min Song Ha	70	70	73	213	4,780,000
Ji Hyun Kim	72	71	70	213	4,780,000
Cho Hui Kim	70	70	73	213	4,780,000

	SCORES	TOTAL	MONEY
Seul Gi Jeong	68 73 72	213	4,780,000
Seung Hyun Lee	70 69 74	213	4,780,000

NH Investment & Securities Championship

Suwon Country Club, Yongin, Gyeonggi
Par 36-36–72; 6,559 yards
March 10-12
purse, KRW700,000,000

	SCORES	TOTAL	MONEY
Hye Jin Choi	69 67 65	201	KRW140,000,000
Ha Na Jang	70 66 68	204	80,500,000
Hyo Joo Kim	69 68 68	205	56,000,000
Jung Min Lee	71 65 70	206	35,000,000
Yoon Kyung Heo	70 71 66	207	28,000,000
Chae Yoon Park	70 73 65	208	24,500,000
HeeJeong Lim	70 69 70	209	14,490,000
Eun Soo Jang	73 67 69	209	14,490,000
Ju Young Pak	71 70 68	209	14,490,000
Ji Hyun Kim$_2$	71 69 69	209	14,490,000
Seong Yeoun Lee	68 69 72	209	14,490,000
Carrie Park	72 68 70	210	8,540,000
Ka Ram Choi	68 70 72	210	8,540,000
Gi Ppuem Lee	69 72 70	211	7,160,000
Yun Kyo Kim	70 71 70	211	7,160,000
Ye Jin Kim	70 71 70	211	7,160,000
Ji Young Park	71 71 69	211	7,160,000
Min Ji Park	71 71 69	211	7,160,000
Eun Hye Jo	70 72 69	211	7,160,000
Yu Jin Sung	69 72 70	211	7,160,000

Doosan Match Play Championship

Ladena Country Club, Chuncheon
Par 36-36–72; 6,246 yards
May 15-19
purse, KRW700,000,000

ROUND OF 16

Jeongmin Cho defeated Ayean Cho, 1 up.
Shin Young Park defeated Bo Mi Park$_2$, 2 up.
Ka Ram Choi defeated Chae Yoon Park, 2 and 1.
Ji Hyun Kim$_2$ defeated Sohye Park, 3 and 2.
Ji Yeong Kim$_2$ defeated You Na Park, 3 and 2.
Hyun Soo Kim defeated Song Yi Ahn, 1 up.
Char Young Kim$_2$ defeated So Yeon Park, 20 holes.
Ji Hyun Kim defeated Inbee Park, 2 and 1.

(Each losing player received KRW9,248,820.)

QUARTER-FINALS

Ji Hyun Kim$_2$ defeated Ji Yeong Kim$_2$, 19 holes.
Hyun Soo Kim defeated Ka Ram Choi, 2 and 1.
Char Young Kim$_2$ defeated Shin Young Par, 1 up.
Ji Hyun Kim defeated Jeongmin Cho, 1 up.

(Each losing player received KRW22,750,000.)

SEMI-FINALS

Hyun Soo Kim defeated Char Young Kim$_2$, 3 and 2.
Ji Hyun Kim defeated Ji Hyun Kim$_2$, 1 up.

PLAYOFF FOR THIRD-FOURTH PLACE

Ji Hyun Kim$_2$ defeated Char Young Kim$_2$, 5 and 4.
(Ji Hyun Kim$_2$ received KRW56,000,000; Char Young Kim$_2$ received KRW35,000,000.)

FINAL

Ji Hyun Kim defeated Hyun Soo Kim, 6 and 4.
(Ji Hyun Kim received KRW175,000,000; Hyun Soo Kim received KRW80,500,000.)

E1 Charity Open

South Springs Country Club, Incheon
Par 36-36–72; 6,514 yards

May 24-26
purse, KRW800,000,000

	SCORES			TOTAL	MONEY
Eun Bin Lim	67	66	73	206	KRW160,000,000
So Yi Kim	70	65	71	206	65,333,333
Ji Hyun Kim	69	68	69	206	65,333,333
Somi Lee	64	68	74	206	65,333,333
(Lim won in playoff.)					
Min Ji Park	70	65	73	208	30,000,000
Hyun Kyung Park	70	68	70	208	30,000,000
Eun Soo Jang	72	71	67	210	18,000,000
Chae Yoon Park	67	72	71	210	18,000,000
Seong Yeoun Lee	67	70	73	210	18,000,000
Gyeol Park	72	68	70	210	18,000,000
Yeon Ju Jung	71	67	73	211	9,632,000
Ji Young Park	71	70	70	211	9,632,000
Jung Min Lee	69	70	72	211	9,632,000
Ji Hyun Kim$_2$	70	67	74	211	9,632,000
Min Kyung Choi	72	66	73	211	9,632,000
HeeJeong Lim	71	69	72	212	8,400,000
Na Rin An	70	70	73	213	7,428,571
Seo Hyeon Youn	71	72	70	213	7,428,571
Ha Na Jang	68	74	71	213	7,428,571
Yul Lin Hwang	72	70	71	213	7,428,571
Chae Eun Lee	64	75	74	213	7,428,571
So Young Lee	71	71	71	213	7,428,571
So Yeon Park	68	74	71	213	7,428,571

Lotte Cantata Ladies Open

Sky Hill Jeju Country Club, Seogwipo, Jeju Island
Par 36-36–72; 6,365 yards

May 31-June 2
purse, KRW600,000,000

	SCORES			TOTAL	MONEY
Bo Ah Kim	67	69	66	202	KRW120,000,000
Ji Yeong Kim$_2$	65	69	69	203	69,000,000
Chae Yoon Park	71	66	68	205	39,000,000
Na Rin An	69	66	70	205	39,000,000
Jeongmin Cho	68	68	70	206	24,000,000
Ran Hong	69	69	69	207	19,500,000
Somi Lee	66	68	73	207	19,500,000
Gayoung Lee	67	70	71	208	13,500,000
Ji Young Park	68	71	69	208	13,500,000
Sujin Lee	68	71	70	209	8,200,000
Bo Bae Kim$_2$	69	70	70	209	8,200,000

	SCORES			TOTAL	MONEY
Da Yeon Lee	71	66	72	209	8,200,000
Jung Min Lee	73	70	67	210	6,705,000
Seul A Yoon	69	69	72	210	6,705,000
Yul Lin Hwang	68	68	74	210	6,705,000
Ye Rim Choi	69	70	71	210	6,705,000
So Yeon Park	71	67	73	211	6,030,000
Hae Rym Kim	66	69	76	211	6,030,000
Ayean Cho	69	72	71	212	5,245,714
He Yong Choi	72	71	69	212	5,245,714
Eun Woo Choi	69	71	72	212	5,245,714
Yu Jin Sung	73	70	69	212	5,245,714
Ye Jin Kim	69	72	71	212	5,245,714
Uree Jun	67	73	72	212	5,245,714
Min Song Ha	65	72	75	212	5,245,714

S-Oil Championship

Elysian Jeju Country Club, Jeju Island
Par 36-36–72; 6,622 yards
(Tournament reduced to 36 holes—fog.)

June 7-9
purse, KRW700,000,000

	SCORES		TOTAL	MONEY
Hye Jin Choi	66	66	132	KRW140,000,000
Ji Young Park	68	65	133	68,250,000
Ha Na Jang	64	69	133	68,250,000
Uree Jun	69	65	134	35,000,000
Seo Hyeon Youn	69	66	135	22,750,000
Ayean Cho	65	70	135	22,750,000
Ji Min Jung	67	68	135	22,750,000
Dana Kim	67	68	135	22,750,000
Eun Soo Jang	67	69	136	10,206,000
Ji Hyun Lee$_2$	67	69	136	10,206,000
Chae-Lin Yang	66	70	136	10,206,000
Sujin Lee	68	68	136	10,206,000
Min Song Ha	65	71	136	10,206,000
Ye Jin Kim	69	68	137	7,280,000
Jeongmin Cho	69	68	137	7,280,000
Yoon Kyung Heo	70	67	137	7,280,000
Han Sol Ji	69	68	137	7,280,000
A Lim Kim	67	70	137	7,280,000
Seong Yeoun Lee	67	70	137	7,280,000
Kyu Jung Baek	69	69	138	5,833,333
Yul Lin Hwang	70	68	138	5,833,333
Su Yeon Jang	70	68	138	5,833,333
Ye Na Chung	67	71	138	5,833,333
Yoon Ji Cho	69	69	138	5,833,333
So Yeon Nam	68	70	138	5,833,333
Somi Lee	69	69	138	5,833,333
Ji Hoo Lee	68	70	138	5,833,333
Do Yeon Kim	69	69	138	5,833,333

Kia Motors Korea Women's Open Championship

Bear's Best CheongNa, Incheon
Par 36-36–72; 6,869 yards

June 13-16
purse, KRW1,000,000,000

	SCORES				TOTAL	MONEY
Da Yeon Lee	72	65	77	70	284	KRW250,000,000
So Young Lee	69	71	69	77	286	100,000,000
Jin Seon Han	74	71	69	73	287	75,000,000
Jung Min Lee	70	76	70	72	288	45,000,000
Jeongmin Cho	68	71	71	79	289	35,000,000
Ha Na Jang	74	70	77	69	290	30,000,000
A Lim Kim	70	72	74	75	291	25,000,000
HeeJeong Lim	74	73	73	72	292	15,940,000
Eun Soo Jang	69	66	81	76	292	15,940,000
Na Rin An	71	73	72	76	292	15,940,000
Ji Young Park	73	67	76	76	292	15,940,000
Min Ji Park	72	73	70	77	292	15,940,000
Gayoung Lee	73	73	77	70	293	12,900,000
Ji Hyun Kim	71	73	75	74	293	12,900,000
Seong Yeoun Lee	70	71	72	80	293	12,900,000
You Na Park	72	73	73	75	293	12,900,000
So Yeon Park	71	76	75	72	294	11,550,000
Somi Lee	71	77	72	74	294	11,550,000
Thitikul Atthaya [A]	76	73	71	74	294	
Do Yeon Kim	71	75	73	75	294	11,550,000
Bo Ah Kim	68	81	73	72	294	11,550,000

BC Card HanKyung Ladies Cup

Fortune Hills Course, Pocheon, Gyeonggi
Par 36-36–72; 6,550 yards

June 20-23
purse, KRW700,000,000

	SCORES				TOTAL	MONEY
Jeongmin Cho	67	72	70	67	276	KRW140,000,000
Ayean Cho	67	72	69	69	277	80,500,000
A Lim Kim	69	69	72	68	278	35,875,000
Ji Hyun Kim	72	67	71	68	278	35,875,000
Ji Young Park	68	70	67	73	278	35,875,000
Ye Jin Kim	69	67	69	73	278	35,875,000
Sanghee Han	68	65	69	77	279	21,000,000
Min Sun Kim$_5$	67	73	77	63	280	15,750,000
Hye Jin Choi	71	67	72	70	280	15,750,000
Ha Na Jang	74	68	70	69	281	9,257,500
Hyun Kyung Park	71	68	71	71	281	9,257,500
Yul Lin Hwang	68	73	71	69	281	9,257,500
Dana Kim	71	69	70	71	281	9,257,500
Yeun Jung Seo	70	72	72	68	282	7,280,000
Hae Rym Kim	70	72	71	69	282	7,280,000
Han Sol Ji	70	70	72	70	282	7,280,000
Min Song Ha	70	64	75	73	282	7,280,000
Ye Rim Choi	69	69	72	72	282	7,280,000
Seul A Yoon	69	69	68	76	282	7,280,000
Gi Ppuem Lee	72	70	70	71	283	6,440,000

McCol Youngpyong Resort Open

Yongpyong Resort, Birch-Hill Course, Pyeongchang
Par 36-36–72; 6,434 yards

June 28-30
purse, KRW600,000,000

	SCORES			TOTAL	MONEY
Hye Jin Choi	69	68	69	206	KRW120,000,000
So Young Lee	71	66	71	208	69,000,000
Chae-Lin Yang	69	70	70	209	39,000,000
Jin Seon Han	69	69	71	209	39,000,000
Seo Hyeon Youn	70	66	74	210	22,500,000
Seul A Yoon	70	72	68	210	22,500,000
Gyo Rin Park	71	72	68	211	15,000,000
Hyun Kyung Park	70	69	72	211	15,000,000
Min Song Ha	70	71	70	211	15,000,000
Hyun Soo Kim	72	71	69	212	8,200,000
HeeJeong Lim	70	71	71	212	8,200,000
Ji Yeong Kim$_2$	69	70	73	212	8,200,000
Ayean Cho	74	68	71	213	6,705,000
Yul Lin Hwang	71	69	73	213	6,705,000
Bo Mi Kwak	72	69	72	213	6,705,000
Bo Ah Kim	69	69	75	213	6,705,000
Cho Hui Kim	72	71	71	214	6,030,000
So Yi Kim	69	74	71	214	6,030,000
Yeon Song Kim	74	69	72	215	5,320,000
Ju Young Pak	72	70	73	215	5,320,000
Yoon Kyung Heo	71	70	74	215	5,320,000
Na Rin An	73	70	72	215	5,320,000
Ellie Na	73	72	70	215	5,320,000
Ye-Nah Hwang	73	65	77	215	5,320,000

Asiana Airlines Open

Weihai Point Course, Shandong, China
Par 36-35–71; 6,070 yards

July 5-7
purse, KRW700,000,000

	SCORES			TOTAL	MONEY
Da Yeon Lee	72	66	65	203	KRW140,000,000
Jeongmin Cho	71	69	69	209	80,500,000
Hye Jin Choi	74	68	68	210	56,000,000
Ayean Cho	70	71	71	212	35,000,000
Ran Hong	73	74	66	213	22,750,000
So Young Lee	73	73	67	213	22,750,000
Ji Young Park	74	69	70	213	22,750,000
Chae Yoon Park	71	73	69	213	22,750,000
Bo Ah Kim	69	74	71	214	14,000,000
A Lim Kim	72	72	71	215	9,975,000
Shin Young Park	73	71	71	215	9,975,000
Ju Young Pak	76	73	67	216	8,750,000
Char Young Kim$_2$	74	74	69	217	7,306,250
Han Sol Ji	74	72	71	217	7,306,250
Jin Seon Han	74	74	69	217	7,306,250
Min Sun Kim$_5$	71	77	69	217	7,306,250
Hee Won Na	69	74	74	217	7,306,250
Ji Hyun Oh	72	71	74	217	7,306,250
Weiwei Zhang	74	71	72	217	7,306,250
Min Song Ha	72	70	75	217	7,306,250

MY Moonyoung Queens Park Championship

Solmoro Course, Paju
Par 36-36–72; 6,527 yards

July 12-14
purse, KRW600,000,000

	SCORES			TOTAL	MONEY
A Lim Kim	66	71	63	200	KRW120,000,000
Bo Mi Kwak	67	69	67	203	69,000,000
Ha Na Jang	64	71	69	204	48,000,000
So Yeon Park	74	68	64	206	25,000,000
So Yi Kim	69	68	69	206	25,000,000
Seul Gi Jeong	67	72	67	206	25,000,000
Ji Yeong Kim₂	71	68	68	207	13,500,000
Da Yeon Lee	67	68	72	207	13,500,000
Jeongmin Cho	67	68	72	207	13,500,000
Jin Seon Han	72	65	70	207	13,500,000
Ji Hyun Lee₃	70	70	68	208	7,070,000
Dana Kim	68	70	70	208	7,070,000
Eun Woo Choi	68	70	70	208	7,070,000
Suji Kim	70	69	69	208	7,070,000
Ji Hyun Kim	67	71	70	208	7,070,000
Hye Jin Choi	73	65	70	208	7,070,000
Dabeen Heo	69	71	69	209	5,736,000
Ji Young Park	70	72	67	209	5,736,000
Min Song Ha	71	68	70	209	5,736,000
Song Yi Ahn	71	69	69	209	5,736,000
Ayean Cho	68	71	70	209	5,736,000

Jeju Samdasoo Masters

ORA Country Club, Jeju Island
Par 36-36–72; 6,666 yards
(Tournament reduced to 36 holes—rain.)

August 9-11
purse, KRW800,000,000

	SCORES		TOTAL	MONEY
Hae Ran Ryu	68	66	134	KRW160,000,000
Ji Yeong Kim₂	66	70	136	92,000,000
Seo Hyeon Youn	70	67	137	52,000,000
Ayean Cho	69	68	137	52,000,000
Ka Ram Choi	69	69	138	32,000,000
Ji Sun Kang	69	70	139	26,000,000
Jung Min Lee	64	75	139	26,000,000
Min Ji Park	70	70	140	13,760,000
Hyun Kyung Park	74	66	140	13,760,000
Suji Kim	72	68	140	13,760,000
Hee Won Na	69	71	140	13,760,000
Inbee Park	68	72	140	13,760,000
Jin Young Ko	73	68	141	8,940,000
Eun Woo Choi	68	73	141	8,940,000
Hyun Soo Kim	73	68	141	8,940,000
Carrie Park	69	72	141	8,940,000
Bo Mi Park₂	71	71	142	7,760,000
Ye Rim Choi	74	68	142	7,760,000
Gayoung Lee	72	70	142	7,760,000
Hye Jin Choi	69	73	142	7,760,000

Bogner MBN Ladies Open

Star Hue Country Club, Yangpyeong
Par 36-36–72; 6,629 yards

August 16-18
purse, KRW600,000,000

	SCORES			TOTAL	MONEY
Min Ji Park	67	63	69	199	KRW120,000,000
Da Yeon Lee	68	68	64	200	49,000,000
Ha Na Jang	66	66	68	200	49,000,000
Char Young Kim$_2$	65	67	68	200	49,000,000
Ju Young Pak	66	66	70	202	21,000,000
Ju Yeon In	64	68	70	202	21,000,000
Sujin Lee	67	66	69	202	21,000,000
Hye Jin Choi	67	70	66	203	15,000,000
Min Sun Kim$_5$	69	66	69	204	9,150,000
So Young Lee	67	68	69	204	9,150,000
JinHee Im	67	68	69	204	9,150,000
Jin Seon Han	68	68	68	204	9,150,000
Jung Min Lee	68	69	68	205	6,780,000
Min Song Ha	71	66	68	205	6,780,000
Kyu Jung Baek	72	66	67	205	6,780,000
Lee Ji Hyun Lee$_2$	69	68	68	205	6,780,000
So Yeon Park	71	67	68	206	5,892,000
Somi Lee	66	70	70	206	5,892,000
Shin Young Park	66	71	69	206	5,892,000
Hae Rym Kim	66	68	72	206	5,892,000
Min Kyung Choi	66	68	72	206	5,892,000

High1 Resort Ladies Open

High1 Country Club, Jeongseon
Par 36-36–72; 6,496 yards

August 22-25
purse, KRW800,000,000

	SCORES				TOTAL	MONEY
HeeJeong Lim	68	66	66	75	275	KRW160,000,000
Chae Yoon Park	67	73	70	69	279	92,000,000
Ju Young Pak	71	70	69	71	281	64,000,000
Suji Kim	74	68	70	70	282	28,800,000
Hyo Rin Lee	70	72	70	70	282	28,800,000
Min Ji Park	72	70	70	70	282	28,800,000
Hyun Kyung Park	68	71	70	73	282	28,800,000
Bo Mi Kwak	71	68	69	74	282	28,800,000
Song Yi Ahn	71	73	71	69	284	16,000,000
Sujin Lee	71	71	72	71	285	11,400,000
Ye Rim Choi	73	73	68	71	285	11,400,000
So Young Lee	70	73	75	68	286	9,546,667
Ran Hong	72	68	74	72	286	9,546,667
Hyo Joo Kim	76	68	71	71	286	9,546,667
Woo Jeong Kim	69	69	76	73	287	8,300,000
Bo Ah Kim	71	73	73	70	287	8,300,000
Ji Hoo Lee	73	72	71	71	287	8,300,000
Ji Hyun Kim	68	74	72	73	287	8,300,000
Hyun Soo Kim	74	71	72	71	288	7,184,000
Bo Bae Kim$_2$	71	72	70	75	288	7,184,000
Seul Gi Jeong	71	70	72	75	288	7,184,000
Jung Min Lee	73	71	68	76	288	7,184,000
Ji Hyun Kim$_2$	71	70	69	78	288	7,184,000

Hanwha Classic

Jade Palace Course, Gangwon
Par 36-36–72; 6,737 yards

August 29-September 1
purse, KRW1,400,000,000

	SCORES				TOTAL	MONEY
Chae Yoon Park	71	70	73	69	283	KRW350,000,000
Jung Min Lee	71	71	72	70	284	97,066,667
So Yi Kim	70	69	71	74	284	97,066,667
Nelly Korda	72	68	68	76	284	97,066,667
Hye Jin Choi	72	72	71	70	285	49,000,000
Gayoung Lee	69	70	72	75	286	39,900,000
MinYoung Lee$_2$	72	69	75	70	286	39,900,000
Ha Na Jang	71	73	72	71	287	25,725,000
Hyo Joo Kim	69	72	70	76	287	25,725,000
Shin Young Park	68	74	72	73	287	25,725,000
Somi Lee	75	72	67	73	287	25,725,000
Min Song Ha	69	74	74	71	288	16,706,667
Yui Kawamoto	75	71	73	69	288	16,706,667
Ye Rim Choi	70	73	72	73	288	16,706,667
HeeJeong Lim	69	74	74	72	289	14,020,000
Hikaru Yoshimoto	74	71	73	71	289	14,020,000
Chae Young Yoon	73	73	73	70	289	14,020,000
Uree Jun	72	74	72	71	289	14,020,000
In-Kyung Kim	72	74	70	73	289	14,020,000
Ju Young Pak	70	71	74	74	289	14,020,000
Yoon Kyung Heo	72	69	71	77	289	14,020,000

KG-Edaily Ladies Open

Sunning Point Country Club, Yongin
Par 36-36–72; 6,672 yards
(Tournament reduced to 36 holes—rain.)

September 6-8
purse, KRW600,000,000

	SCORES		TOTAL	MONEY
Gyo Rin Park	67	66	133	KRW120,000,000
Jeongmin Cho	66	68	134	69,000,000
Da Yeon Lee	67	68	135	48,000,000
Yeon Ju Jung	69	67	136	27,000,000
Hee Won Jung	69	67	136	27,000,000
Na Rin An	70	67	137	13,850,000
Char Young Kim$_2$	70	67	137	13,850,000
Gyeol Park	67	70	137	13,850,000
Woo Jeong Kim	69	68	137	13,850,000
Suji Kim	69	68	137	13,850,000
Dabeen Heo	68	69	137	13,850,000
Hye Jin Choi	69	69	138	6,740,000
Gayoung Lee	69	69	138	6,740,000
Min Song Ha	67	71	138	6,740,000
Sohye Park	68	70	138	6,740,000
Jung Min Lee	67	71	138	6,740,000
Song Yi Ahn	68	70	138	6,740,000
Somi Lee	69	70	139	5,316,000
Min Sun Kim$_5$	70	69	139	5,316,000
Ha Na Jang	69	70	139	5,316,000
Hyo Rin Lee	68	71	139	5,316,000
Jin Seon Han	67	72	139	5,316,000
Ju Young Pak	68	71	139	5,316,000
Ji Hyun Lee$_2$	71	68	139	5,316,000
Chae-Lin Yang	65	74	139	5,316,000

	SCORES		TOTAL	MONEY
So Yi Kim	68	71	139	5,316,000
Hae Rym Kim	67	72	139	5,316,000

All for You. Renoma Championship

South Springs Country Club, Incheon
Par 36-36–72; 6,654 yards

September 13-16
purse, KRW800,000,000

	SCORES				TOTAL	MONEY
HeeJeong Lim	65	70	70	71	276	KRW160,000,000
Ji Hyun Kim	61	72	73	70	276	92,000,000

(Lim defeated Kim on second playoff hole.)

Ayean Cho	69	70	72	68	279	64,000,000
Ye Rim Choi	66	72	72	70	280	36,000,000
So Yi Kim	69	70	69	72	280	36,000,000
Jin Seon Han	74	68	68	71	281	26,000,000
Min Ji Park	73	67	72	69	281	26,000,000
Song Yi Ahn	70	67	71	74	282	18,000,000
So Young Lee	68	68	72	74	282	18,000,000
Chae Yoon Park	70	72	71	71	284	12,000,000
Suji Kim	69	74	72	70	285	9,080,000
Ji Yeong Kim$_2$	68	71	75	71	285	9,080,000
Gayoung Lee	72	69	73	71	285	9,080,000
Yun Kyo Kim	74	69	73	69	285	9,080,000
Jeongmin Cho	76	69	68	72	285	9,080,000
Hye Jin Choi	73	66	74	72	285	9,080,000
Ji Young Park	70	72	68	75	285	9,080,000
Hae Ran Ryu	66	72	74	73	285	9,080,000
Jung Min Lee	71	72	74	69	286	7,280,000
Min Song Ha	68	72	76	70	286	7,280,000
Somi Lee	71	70	72	73	286	7,280,000
Ji Hyun Lee$_2$	75	71	69	71	286	7,280,000

OKSavingsBank Se Ri Pak Invitational

Elysian Gangchon Course, Gangchon
Par 35-36–71; 6,329 yards

September 27-29
purse, KRW800,000,000

	SCORES			TOTAL	MONEY
Ayean Cho	64	64	68	196	KRW160,000,000
A Lim Kim	67	66	63	196	78,000,000
Hye Jin Choi	66	62	68	196	78,000,000

(Cho defeated Kim on first and Choi on third playoff hole.)

Ji Yeong Kim$_2$	67	68	65	200	40,000,000
Ji Hyun Lee$_3$	69	67	65	201	26,000,000
Ha Na Jang	69	63	69	201	26,000,000
Char Young Kim$_2$	64	68	69	201	26,000,000
Seung Yeon Lee	68	64	69	201	26,000,000
Ji Young Park	69	65	68	202	12,200,000
Hae Ran Ryu	67	66	69	202	12,200,000
Min Sun Kim$_5$	65	67	70	202	12,200,000
Ju Young Pak	66	68	68	202	12,200,000
Jung Min Lee	67	68	68	203	8,940,000
Bo Ah Kim	71	65	67	203	8,940,000
Eun Hye Jo	68	65	70	203	8,940,000
Hyun Kyung Park	66	70	67	203	8,940,000
So Yeon Park	65	69	70	204	7,893,333

	SCORES			TOTAL	MONEY
Jin Seon Han	68	67	69	204	7,893,333
Shin Young Park	67	68	69	204	7,893,333
Ye Rim Choi	69	65	71	205	7,173,333
Gyeol Park	65	69	71	205	7,173,333
Seong Weon Park	69	66	70	205	7,173,333

Hana Financial Group Championship

Sky 72 Golf Club, Incheon
Par 36-36–72; 6,557 yards

October 3-6
purse, KRW1,500,000,000

	SCORES				TOTAL	MONEY
Ha Na Jang	69	65	72	70	276	KRW375,000,000
Ji Yeong Kim₂	68	71	66	72	277	122,250,000
Da Yeon Lee	70	69	68	70	277	122,250,000
Jin Young Ko	68	69	71	73	281	48,600,000
Hye Jin Choi	71	69	71	70	281	48,600,000
Jin Seon Han	70	70	68	73	281	48,600,000
Song Yi Ahn	70	71	69	71	281	48,600,000
Gayoung Lee	69	68	71	73	281	48,600,000
Ji Young Park	72	74	70	66	282	26,250,000
Minjee Lee	71	71	72	68	282	26,250,000
Danielle Kang	69	71	70	74	284	20,250,000
Yealimi Noh	75	67	75	68	285	17,512,500
Thitikul Atthaya [A]	73	69	73	70	285	
HeeJeong Lim	72	68	74	71	285	17,512,500
Bo Mi Kwak	70	73	71	71	285	17,512,500
Ji Hyun Kim	72	68	70	75	285	17,512,500
Alison Lee	74	70	70	72	286	15,300,000
Ju Young Pak	69	75	70	72	286	15,300,000
Jung Min Lee	68	71	72	75	286	15,300,000
Ji Hyun Oh	68	74	72	73	287	14,400,000

Hite Jinro Championship

Blue Heron Golf Club, Yeoju
Par 36-36–72; 6,736 yards

October 10-13
purse, KRW1,000,000,000

	SCORES				TOTAL	MONEY
Jin Young Ko	71	71	71	72	285	KRW200,000,000
Hye Jin Choi	68	75	72	71	286	71,250,000
Ji Yeong Kim₂	76	66	73	71	286	71,250,000
Somi Lee	70	74	72	70	286	71,250,000
Hee Won Na	72	68	76	70	286	71,250,000
Ayean Cho	73	75	70	69	287	25,000,000
Hyun Kyung Park	72	73	71	71	287	25,000,000
Eun Woo Choi	73	74	70	70	287	25,000,000
Chae Yoon Park	72	72	72	71	287	25,000,000
Hae Ran Ryu	73	70	71	73	287	25,000,000
Gayoung Lee	71	74	71	72	288	12,633,333
Min Ji Park	70	71	74	73	288	12,633,333
Han Sol Ji	74	70	70	74	288	12,633,333
Yoon Kyung Heo	72	69	76	72	289	11,400,000
Jee Hyun Ahn	75	74	72	70	291	10,533,333
Ye Rim Choi	73	73	73	72	291	10,533,333
Woo Jeong Kim	72	74	71	74	291	10,533,333
Gi Ppuem Lee	76	70	75	71	292	9,260,000

	SCORES				TOTAL	MONEY
Min Lee Jung	74	73	71	74	292	9,260,000
Ji Hoo Lee	73	73	74	72	292	9,260,000
HeeJeong Lim	72	71	75	74	292	9,260,000
Da Yeon Lee	75	71	74	72	292	9,260,000

KB Financial Group Star Championship

Black Stone Course, Incheon
Par 36-36–72; 6,660 yards

October 17-20
purse, KRW1,000,000,000

	SCORES				TOTAL	MONEY
HeeJeong Lim	65	69	69	70	273	KRW200,000,000
Min Ji Park	66	68	72	69	275	97,500,000
Da Yeon Lee	68	67	69	71	275	97,500,000
Somi Lee	73	65	72	67	277	50,000,000
So Young Lee	69	69	71	69	278	35,000,000
A Lim Kim	71	70	67	70	278	35,000,000
Ji Hyun Oh	72	65	72	69	278	35,000,000
Hyun Kyung Park	67	68	71	75	281	25,000,000
Dabeen Heo	67	70	75	72	284	20,000,000
Yoon Kyung Heo	74	69	74	68	285	14,250,000
Eun Woo Choi	68	68	73	76	285	14,250,000
Min Sun Kim$_5$	71	69	73	73	286	12,200,000
Hae Ran Ryu	69	66	74	77	286	12,200,000
Ju Yeon In	72	70	74	71	287	10,750,000
Bo Bae Kim$_2$	73	73	73	68	287	10,750,000
Ayean Cho	70	71	74	72	287	10,750,000
Ye Jin Kim	66	72	75	74	287	10,750,000
In Gee Chun	71	71	75	71	288	9,400,000
Suji Kim	71	69	77	71	288	9,400,000
Seung Yeon Lee	75	70	70	73	288	9,400,000
Eun Song Choi	68	73	71	76	288	9,400,000

BMW Ladies Championship

LPGA International Busan, Busan
Par 36-36–72; 6,726 yards

October 24-27
purse, US$2,000,000

	SCORES				TOTAL	MONEY
Ha Na Jang	69	67	68	65	269	KRW352,350,000
Danielle Kang	67	67	71	64	269	212,059,499

(Jang defeated Kang on third playoff hole.)

	SCORES				TOTAL	MONEY
Amy Yang	69	69	67	67	272	153,833,661
In Gee Chun	70	69	67	70	276	107,393,931
Somi Lee	68	68	67	73	276	107,393,931
Nanna Koerstz Madsen	70	69	71	67	277	67,144,991
HeeJeong Lim	68	70	69	70	277	67,144,991
Min Sun Kim$_5$	69	70	69	69	277	67,144,991
Min Ji Park	72	70	69	67	278	45,713,889
Jin Young Ko	67	69	71	71	278	45,713,889
Sei Young Kim	68	71	68	71	278	45,713,889
Seung Yeon Lee	67	68	68	75	278	45,713,889
Yu Liu	68	69	71	71	279	35,835,170
So Young Lee	72	67	68	72	279	35,835,170
Su Oh	68	70	67	74	279	35,835,170
Nicole Broch Larsen	72	71	69	68	280	29,025,419
Charley Hull	73	69	69	69	280	29,025,419

	SCORES				TOTAL	MONEY
Hee Won Na	68	67	73	72	280	29,025,419
Minjee Lee	66	70	73	71	280	29,025,419
Jeongeun Lee6	67	73	68	72	280	29,025,419
Jung Min Lee	69	71	72	69	281	23,939,834
Jing Yan	70	69	69	73	281	23,939,834
Mi Jung Hur	70	69	69	73	281	23,939,834
Hyun Kyung Park	70	68	71	72	281	23,939,834
Lydia Ko	69	71	68	73	281	23,939,834
Ji Hyun Kim	73	68	72	69	282	20,956,604
Ye Jin Kim	71	66	73	72	282	20,956,604
Nelly Korda	69	70	73	71	283	18,250,556
Alena Sharp	71	70	71	71	283	18,250,556
Megan Khang	74	72	67	70	283	18,250,556
Hye-Jin Choi	70	72	70	71	283	18,250,556
Caroline Masson	71	68	72	72	283	18,250,556

SK Networks Seokyung Ladies Classic

Pinx Golf Club, Jeju Island
Par 36-36–72; 6,638 yards

October 31-November 3
purse, KRW800,000,000

	SCORES				TOTAL	MONEY
Hye Jin Choi	66	68	70	69	273	KRW160,000,000
HeeJeong Lim	70	68	69	69	276	92,000,000
Da Yeon Lee	69	71	68	69	277	64,000,000
Song Yi Ahn	68	70	69	71	278	36,000,000
Bo Bae Kim2	70	69	68	71	278	36,000,000
Ayean Cho	73	69	68	69	279	28,000,000
Yeon Ju Jung	69	75	65	71	280	22,000,000
Ji Hyun Lee2	70	72	68	70	280	22,000,000
Kyu Jung Baek	74	70	70	67	281	12,933,333
Seul Gi Jeong	71	71	70	69	281	12,933,333
Hee Won Na	68	67	71	75	281	12,933,333
A Lim Kim	73	72	70	67	282	8,986,667
Gyo Rin Park	69	73	70	70	282	8,986,667
Somi Lee	71	72	71	68	282	8,986,667
Char Young Kim2	71	72	70	69	282	8,986,667
So Yeon Nam	66	72	72	72	282	8,986,667
Dabeen Heo	71	71	70	70	282	8,986,667
Ju Yeon In	72	69	71	71	283	7,110,000
Yu Jin Sung	71	73	71	68	283	7,110,000
Han Sol Ji	71	70	72	70	283	7,110,000
Hye Sun Kim2	73	67	72	71	283	7,110,000
Go Un Yu	71	75	69	68	283	7,110,000
Seung Yeon Lee	72	73	68	70	283	7,110,000
Ji Hyun Oh	70	71	71	71	283	7,110,000
Ji Young Park	65	70	77	71	283	7,110,000

ADT CAPS Championship

Woo Jeong Hills Course, Cheonan
Par 36-36–72; 6,632 yards

November 8-10
purse, KRW600,000,000

	SCORES			TOTAL	MONEY
Song Yi Ahn	67	69	71	207	KRW120,000,000
Gayoung Lee	68	69	71	208	69,000,000
HeeJeong Lim	73	67	70	210	34,000,000

640 / WOMEN'S TOURS

	SCORES			TOTAL	MONEY
Hyun Kyung Park	68	71	71	210	34,000,000
Min Ji Park	70	69	71	210	34,000,000
Chae Yoon Park	73	66	72	211	19,500,000
So Young Lee	70	69	72	211	19,500,000
Jin Seon Han	70	71	71	212	12,000,000
Seul Gi Jeong	70	71	71	212	12,000,000
Ha Na Jang	72	68	72	212	12,000,000
Ji Young Park	70	73	70	213	7,395,000
Ji Yeong Kim$_2$	70	73	70	213	7,395,000
Hee Won Na	72	69	72	213	7,395,000
Ju Young Pak	70	70	73	213	7,395,000
Han Sol Ji	72	70	72	214	6,320,000
Ayean Cho	71	70	73	214	6,320,000
Gi Ppuem Lee	71	69	74	214	6,320,000
Bo Mi Kwak	73	72	70	215	5,940,000
Bo-Mee Lee	72	72	72	216	5,182,500
Min Kyung Choi	71	71	74	216	5,182,500
Su Yeon Jang	75	71	70	216	5,182,500
Eun Soo Jang	74	69	73	216	5,182,500
Ji Hyun Kim	71	73	72	216	5,182,500
Woo Jeong Kim	73	72	71	216	5,182,500
Suji Kim	72	71	73	216	5,182,500
A Lim Kim	71	68	77	216	5,182,500

Hyosung Championship

Twin Doves Golf Club, Binh Duong, Vietnam
Par 36-36–72; 6,579 yards

December 6-8
purse, KRW700,000,000

	SCORES			TOTAL	MONEY
Da Yeon Lee	67	68	70	205	KRW140,000,000
Somi Lee	71	68	69	208	80,500,000
Eun Woo Choi	70	67	72	209	56,000,000
Jin Seon Han	74	70	66	210	29,166,667
So Young Lee	71	69	70	210	29,166,667
Jung Min Lee	71	68	71	210	29,166,667
Heejeong Lim	69	67	75	211	21,000,000
Ye Rim Choi	75	68	71	214	14,000,000
Gayoung Lee	71	72	71	214	14,000,000
Hye Jin Choi	70	71	73	214	14,000,000
Min Sun Kim$_5$	74	73	68	215	8,248,333
Woo Jeong Kim	72	68	75	215	8,248,333
Gyo Rin Park	73	70	72	215	8,248,333
Hye Lim Jo	74	68	73	215	8,248,333
Bo Mi Kwak	72	69	74	215	8,248,333
Hae Ran Ryu	69	70	76	215	8,248,333
Ju Young Pak	70	76	70	216	7,035,000
Na Rin An	72	71	73	216	7,035,000
Julie Kim	75	71	71	217	6,545,000
Shin Young Park	73	73	71	217	6,545,000

Australian Ladies Tour

Ballarat Icons ALPG Pro-Am

Ballarat Golf Club, Ballaret, Victoria
Par 36-36–72; 5,639 yards

February 2-3
purse, A$30,000

	SCORES		TOTAL	MONEY
Marianne Skarpnord	69	68	137	A$4,500
Celina Yuan	69	69	138	2,625
Kim Kaufman	71	67	138	2,625
Hannah Burke	68	71	139	1,500
Beth Allen	73	66	139	1,500
Pei-Ying Tsai	72	67	139	1,500
Robyn Choi	66	74	140	1,200
Cheyenne Knight	71	70	141	892.50
Hanee Song	71	70	141	892.50
Mio Kotaki	71	70	141	892.50
Xiyu Lin	76	65	141	892.50
Diksha Dagar	70	72	142	720
Ingrid Gutierrez Nunez	74	69	143	600
Charlotte Thompson	74	69	143	600
Lydia Hall	75	68	143	600
Rebecca Artis	70	74	144	450
Yu Eun Kim	72	72	144	450
Katelyn Must	75	69	144	450
Whitney Hillier	72	73	145	312.86
Sarah Schober	72	73	145	312.86
Mireia Prat	74	71	145	312.86
Amelia Lewis	75	70	145	312.86
Leticia Ras-Anderica	69	76	145	312.86
Chantelle Cassidy	71	74	145	312.86
Stephanie Na	74	71	145	312.86

ISPS Handa Vic Open

13th Beach Golf Links, Barwon Heads, Victoria
Par 36-36–72; 6,625 yards

February 7-10
purse, US$1,100,000

	SCORES				TOTAL	MONEY
Celine Boutier	69	71	69	72	281	US$165,000
Sarah Kemp	70	71	77	65	283	77,242
Charlotte Thomas	68	68	78	69	283	77,242
Su Oh	67	68	74	74	283	77,242
Azahara Munoz	72	72	74	66	284	38,191
Katherine Kirk	72	68	73	71	284	38,191
Haru Nomura	67	67	76	74	284	38,191
Lauren Stephenson	69	72	76	68	285	24,875
Jodi Ewart Shadoff	71	70	72	72	285	24,875
Kim Kaufman	66	66	75	78	285	24,875
Ashleigh Buhai	72	69	76	69	286	17,800
Alison Lee	68	71	78	69	286	17,800
Peiyun Chien	69	74	73	70	286	17,800
Ayako Uehara	71	72	72	71	286	17,800

	SCORES				TOTAL	MONEY
Marianne Skarpnord	71	69	75	71	286	17,800
Olivia Cowan	68	70	76	72	286	17,800
Wichanee Meechai	72	72	72	71	287	13,294
Thidapa Suwannapura	74	69	73	71	287	13,294
Isi Gabsa	70	73	72	72	287	13,294
Alena Sharp	69	69	77	72	287	13,294
Jane Park	68	76	70	73	287	13,294
Brittany Lang	71	73	73	71	288	11,019
Suzuka Yamaguchi	69	75	73	71	288	11,019
Karis Davidson	68	74	75	71	288	11,019
Yu Liu	74	71	70	73	288	11,019
Felicity Johnson	65	74	74	75	288	11,019
Christina Kim	74	71	73	71	289	9,077
Daniela Darquea	72	70	75	72	289	9,077
Nanna Koerstz Madsen	71	73	72	73	289	9,077
Xiyu Lin	70	74	70	75	289	9,077
Marissa Steen	68	70	76	75	289	9,077

ISPS Handa Women's Australian Open

Grange Golf Club, Grange, South Australia
Par 36-36–72; 6,648 yards

February 14-17
purse, A$1,800,000

	SCORES				TOTAL	MONEY
Nelly Korda	71	66	67	67	271	A$270,000
Jin Young Ko	68	72	69	64	273	167,919.73
Wei-Ling Hsu	65	69	74	68	276	121,813.83
Haru Nomura	70	67	70	70	277	85,039.66
Angel Yin	72	69	70	66	277	85,039.66
Alena Sharp	69	71	70	68	278	56,999.74
Azahara Munoz	72	71	70	65	278	56,999.74
Jodi Ewart Shadoff	65	73	70	71	279	43,210
Marissa Steen	70	71	70	68	279	43,210
Mi Hyang Lee	71	71	70	68	280	32,470.90
Sarah Kemp	72	71	68	69	280	32,470.90
Hannah Green	68	69	73	70	280	32,470.90
Jeongeun Lee$_6$	72	69	67	72	280	32,470.90
Amy Olson	70	76	66	68	280	32,470.90
Bronte Law	67	72	70	72	281	23,141.30
Moriya Jutanugarn	68	72	70	71	281	23,141.30
Kristen Gillman	68	74	70	69	281	23,141.30
Minjee Lee	71	70	71	69	281	23,141.30
Ashleigh Buhai	72	70	69	70	281	23,141.30
Mirim Lee	73	69	68	71	281	23,141.30
Teresa Lu	77	67	70	67	281	23,141.30
Marina Alex	72	68	75	67	282	18,258.55
Celine Boutier	71	70	74	67	282	18,258.55
Meghan MacLaren	73	69	73	67	282	18,258.55
Jaclyn Lee	72	71	71	68	282	18,258.55
Gaby Lopez	71	69	72	70	282	18,258.55
Jaye Marie Green	73	72	70	68	283	14,755.35
Tonje Daffinrud	72	73	71	67	283	14,755.35
Karis Davidson	71	70	73	69	283	14,755.35
Brittany Altomare	69	75	69	70	283	14,755.35
Yu Liu	69	70	70	74	283	14,755.35
Carlota Ciganda	68	72	73	70	283	14,755.35

Pacific Bay Resort Australian Ladies Classic

Bonville Golf Resort, Bonville, New South Wales
Par 35-37–72; 6,249 yards

February 21-24
purse, A$350,000

	SCORES				TOTAL	MONEY
Marianne Skarpnord	70	72	69	69	280	A$52,500
Hannah Green	69	72	70	71	282	26,250
Nuria Iturrios	69	67	75	71	282	26,250
Daniela Holmqvist	68	76	70	70	284	15,750
Doey Choi (A)	66	74	72	72	284	
Jenny Haglund	69	73	72	71	285	11,725
Madelene Sagstrom	68	74	68	75	285	11,725
Linnea Strom	72	70	75	69	286	9,800
Esther Henseleit	73	74	73	67	287	8,400
Nanna Madsen	72	71	72	72	287	8,400
Nicole Broch Larsen	75	69	72	71	287	8,400
Kim Kaufman	72	73	71	72	288	7,525
Ursula Wikstrom	72	76	68	72	288	7,525
Krista Bakker	71	75	73	70	289	6,825
Becky Morgan	71	74	72	72	289	6,825
Celine Herbin	71	75	67	77	290	5,906.25
Meghan MacLaren	73	73	74	70	290	5,906.25
Xiyu Lin	72	76	70	72	290	5,906.25
Anne van Dam	71	75	73	71	290	5,906.25
Sarah Schober	72	77	71	71	291	5,068
Munchin Keh	72	75	70	74	291	5,068
Linda Wessberg	75	75	69	72	291	5,068
Manon De Roey	73	72	75	71	291	5,068
Leona Maguire	73	75	68	75	291	5,068

ActewAGL Canberra Classic

Royal Canberra Golf Club, Canberra, ACT
Par 35-36–71; 6,196 yards

March 1-3
purse, A$150,000

	SCORES			TOTAL	MONEY
Anne van Dam	68	63	65	196	A$22,500
Katja Pogacar	67	64	68	199	13,500
Jiyai Shin	69	64	67	200	9,000
Carly Booth	67	65	70	202	6,750
Madelene Sagstrom	68	67	68	203	5,400
Manon De Roey	66	67	72	205	4,425
Meghan MacLaren	67	69	69	205	4,425
Hannah Green	68	68	70	206	3,547.50
Christine Wolf	68	72	66	206	3,547.50
Esther Henseleit	68	71	67	206	3,547.50
Lina Boqvist	71	66	69	206	3,547.50
Linnea Strom	68	70	69	207	3,180
Agathe Sauzon	70	68	70	208	3,030
Leona Maguire	69	68	72	209	2,677.50
Noemi Jimenez Martin	68	71	70	209	2,677.50
Kanyalak Preedasuttijit	71	68	70	209	2,677.50
Sarah Kemp	71	70	68	209	2,677.50
Karolin Lampert	70	68	72	210	2,232.50
Tonje Daffinrud	74	67	69	210	2,232.50
Felicity Johnson	71	69	70	210	2,232.50
Ursula Wikstrom	70	69	71	210	2,232.50
Ingrid Gutierrez Nunez	68	70	72	210	2,232.50
Daniela Holmqvist	69	69	72	210	2,232.50

Worrells NSW Women's Open

Queanbeyan Golf Club, Queanbeyan, New South Wales
Par 36-35–71; 6,065 yards

March 7-10
purse, A$150,000

	SCORES				TOTAL	MONEY
Meghan MacLaren	70	66	67	69	272	A$22,500
Lynn Carlsson	71	65	67	72	275	11,250
Munchin Keh	69	68	71	67	275	11,250
Christine Wolf	71	66	68	72	277	6,750
Diksha Dagar	72	67	69	70	278	4,765
Felicity Johnson	69	69	71	69	278	4,765
Valdis Thora Jonsdottir	63	70	72	73	278	4,765
Emma Nilsson	70	71	70	68	279	3,712.50
Karolin Lampert	70	65	70	74	279	3,712.50
Lejan Lewthwaite	71	72	66	71	280	3,435
Whitney Hillier	69	76	67	68	280	3,435
Laura Fuenfstueck	72	69	69	71	281	2,862.50
Gabriella Cowley	71	69	70	71	281	2,862.50
Carly Booth	69	72	71	69	281	2,862.50
Michele Thomson	68	69	73	71	281	2,862.50
Rebecca Artis	67	70	70	74	281	2,862.50
Noemi Jimenez Martin	74	70	68	69	281	2,862.50
Amelia Lewis	70	72	69	71	282	2,241.43
Lina Boqvist	74	69	73	66	282	2,241.43
Carmen Alonso	67	74	70	71	282	2,241.43
Manon Gidali	68	74	71	69	282	2,241.43
Manon De Roey	72	66	73	71	282	2,241.43
Amandeep Drall	73	70	70	69	282	2,241.43
Silvia Banon	73	67	70	72	282	2,241.43

Sheraton Deva New Caledonia Women's International Pro-Am

Sheraton Deva Resort, Bourail, New Caledonia
Par 72; 5,787 yards

March 14-15
purse, A$40,000

	SCORES		TOTAL	MONEY
Brooke Baker	73	71	144	A$6,000
Emilie Ricaud [A]	71	76	147	
Chizuru Ueda	73	75	148	4,000
Celina Yuan	72	77	149	2,550
Chantelle Cassidy	77	72	149	2,550
Miki Nishiyama	74	77	151	1,516.67
Viva Schlasberg	76	75	151	1,516.67
Robyn Doig	79	72	151	1,516.67
Kayla Jones	74	78	152	1,100
Breanna Gill	76	77	153	1,000
Nadine White	73	81	154	912.50
Tahnia Ravnjak	76	78	154	912.50
Georgia Clarke	77	77	154	912.50
Paige Stubbs	80	74	154	912.50
Montana Strauss	76	79	155	837.50
Grace St Just	77	78	155	837.50
Mathilde Guepy [A]	80	76	156	
Victoria Fricot	84	73	157	800
Kristalle Blum	79	79	158	750
Molly Lavercombe	80	78	158	750
Momo Sakuragi	82	76	158	750

Trust Golf Thailand LPGA Masters

Panya Indra Golf Club, Bangkok, Thailand
Par 36-36–72; 5,899 yards

September 4-6
purse, A$175,000

	SCORES			TOTAL	MONEY
Weiwei Zhang	65	70	69	204	A$26,250
P.K. Kongkraphan	70	67	69	206	17,500
Du Mohan	69	71	67	207	13,125
Chonlada Chayanun	69	70	70	209	10,500
Pavarisa Yoktuan	71	69	70	210	7,350
Chatprapa Siriprakob	69	71	72	212	4,900
Pannarat Thanapolboonyaras	69	70	73	212	4,900
Yifan Ji	72	70	70	212	4,900
Hanee Song	72	71	69	212	4,900
Kultida Pramphun	68	72	72	212	4,900
Mookharin Ladgratok	68	75	71	214	3,097.50
Yunjie Zhang	73	70	71	214	3,097.50
Trichat Cheenglab	72	73	69	214	3,097.50
Ornnicha Konsunthea	71	73	70	214	3,097.50
Prima Thammaraks	69	73	72	214	3,097.50
Monique Smit	70	74	71	215	2,747.50
Jienalin Zhang	72	70	73	215	2,747.50
Arpichaya Yubol	70	75	70	215	2,747.50
Wanchana Poruangrong	73	74	69	216	2,441.25
Aretha Pan	71	74	71	216	2,441.25
Ye Seul Lee	71	73	72	216	2,441.25
Liu Yan	71	71	74	216	2,441.25

New Zealand PWG Pro Am in Memory of Anita Boon

Remuera Golf Club, Auckland, New Zealand
Par 73; 5,910 yards

October 13-14
purse, A$36,500

	SCORES		TOTAL	MONEY
Breanna Gill	70	77	147	A$5,475
Whitney Hillier	74	74	148	2,859.17
Grace St. Just	74	74	148	2,859.17
Elmay Viking	74	74	148	2,859.17
Hanee Song	74	77	151	2,007.50
Kristalle Blum	77	76	153	1,825
Dee Dee Russell	78	76	154	1,460
Munchin Keh	77	79	156	1,204.50
Chizuru Ueda	76	81	157	985.50
Phillis Meti	82	75	157	985.50
Emma Fairnie	80	78	158	876
Lauren Hibbert	78	81	159	784.75
Kristen Farmer	82	77	159	784.75
Katelyn Must	81	79	160	730
Karen Pearce	79	82	161	638.75
Katy Jarochowicz	81	80	161	638.75
Jade Shellback	81	80	161	638.75
Jenna Hunter	82	79	161	638.75
Liv Cheng	75	87	162	547.50
Samantha Whittle	78	86	164	460.81
Victoria Fricot	78	86	164	460.81
Gennai Goodwin	81	83	164	460.81
Bree Arthur	82	82	164	460.81

Senior Tours

Mitsubishi Electric Championship

Hualalai Golf Course, Ka'upulehu-Kona, Hawaii
Par 36-36–72; 7,107 yards

January 17-19
purse, $1,800,000

	SCORES			TOTAL	MONEY
Tom Lehman	69	65	65	199	$305,000
David Toms	65	65	70	200	180,000
Jerry Kelly	71	64	67	202	120,000
Bernhard Langer	70	65	67	202	120,000
Fred Couples	72	66	66	204	85,000
Kevin Sutherland	69	72	63	204	85,000
Colin Montgomerie	69	66	70	205	70,000
Joe Durant	65	69	72	206	57,500
Brandt Jobe	69	69	68	206	57,500
Mark Calcavecchia	71	67	69	207	45,000
Marco Dawson	69	68	70	207	45,000
Tom Watson	71	67	69	207	45,000
Stephen Ames	71	65	72	208	34,000
Paul Goydos	69	68	71	208	34,000
Scott Parel	68	71	69	208	34,000
Jeff Sluman	69	67	72	208	34,000
Kirk Triplett	69	72	67	208	34,000
Scott McCarron	71	68	70	209	27,000
Kenny Perry	69	73	67	209	27,000
Paul Broadhurst	70	70	70	210	23,000
Olin Browne	70	68	72	210	23,000
John Daly	73	68	69	210	23,000
Lee Janzen	72	65	73	210	23,000
Rocco Mediate	71	68	71	210	23,000
Carlos Franco	72	71	68	211	18,500
Miguel Angel Jimenez	68	74	69	211	18,500
Corey Pavin	70	67	74	211	18,500
Ken Tanigawa	72	68	71	211	18,500
Gene Sauers	71	72	69	212	14,333.34
Steve Stricker	70	74	68	212	14,333.34
Woody Austin	71	70	71	212	14,333.33
Steve Flesch	71	72	69	212	14,333.33
Jay Haas	72	66	74	212	14,333.33
Vijay Singh	69	69	74	212	14,333.33

Oasis Championship

Old Course at Broken Sound, Boca Raton, Florida
Par 36-36–72; 6,807 yards

February 8-10
purse, $1,700,000

	SCORES			TOTAL	MONEY
Bernhard Langer	64	68	65	197	$255,000
Marco Dawson	66	67	69	202	149,600
Bob Estes	67	68	68	203	122,400
David Toms	67	67	70	204	102,000
Scott McCarron	68	70	67	205	70,266.67
Gene Sauers	65	71	69	205	70,266.67
Woody Austin	65	70	70	205	70,266.66

SENIOR TOURS / 647

	SCORES			TOTAL	MONEY
Fred Couples	67	69	70	206	51,000
Ken Tanigawa	65	71	70	206	51,000
Darren Clarke	67	75	65	207	39,100
Jeff Maggert	68	69	70	207	39,100
Corey Pavin	73	68	66	207	39,100
Tim Petrovic	65	74	68	207	39,100
Brandt Jobe	69	65	74	208	28,900
Colin Montgomerie	71	70	67	208	28,900
Jesper Parnevik	63	72	73	208	28,900
Tom Pernice, Jr.	71	71	66	208	28,900
Kevin Sutherland	66	70	72	208	28,900
Michael Allen	68	73	68	209	21,182
Tom Byrum	66	69	74	209	21,182
David Frost	70	68	71	209	21,182
Miguel Angel Jimenez	70	70	69	209	21,182
Tom Lehman	66	70	73	209	21,182
Stephen Ames	70	66	74	210	17,425
Retief Goosen	69	69	72	210	17,425
Paul Broadhurst	69	72	70	211	15,130
Bart Bryant	70	73	68	211	15,130
Paul Goydos	71	67	73	211	15,130
Scott Parel	70	70	71	211	15,130
Olin Browne	68	70	74	212	11,496.25
Chris DiMarco	70	71	71	212	11,496.25
Lee Janzen	68	72	72	212	11,496.25
Kent Jones	69	69	74	212	11,496.25
Sandy Lyle	69	72	71	212	11,496.25
David McKenzie	72	71	69	212	11,496.25
Mark O'Meara	72	72	68	212	11,496.25
Jeff Sluman	71	71	70	212	11,496.25

Chubb Classic

The Classics at Lely Resort, Naples, Florida
Par 35-36–71; 6,843 yards

February 15-17
purse, $1,600,000

	SCORES			TOTAL	MONEY
Miguel Angel Jimenez	68	66	66	200	$240,000
Olin Browne	68	66	66	200	128,000
Bernhard Langer	68	64	68	200	128,000

(Jimenez defeated Browne and Langer on first playoff hole.)

Woody Austin	67	65	69	201	86,400
Kevin Sutherland	70	62	69	201	86,400
Stephen Ames	63	68	71	202	51,840
Retief Goosen	68	65	69	202	51,840
Tom Lehman	67	70	65	202	51,840
Sandy Lyle	63	71	68	202	51,840
Colin Montgomerie	69	63	70	202	51,840
Glen Day	65	66	72	203	32,960
Bob Estes	66	68	69	203	32,960
David McKenzie	67	69	67	203	32,960
Steve Stricker	67	66	70	203	32,960
Ken Tanigawa	65	66	72	203	32,960
Darren Clarke	68	69	67	204	25,600
Jay Haas	64	70	70	204	25,600
Brandt Jobe	68	68	68	204	25,600
Kirk Triplett	68	69	68	205	19,413.34
Duffy Waldorf	68	68	69	205	19,413.34
Paul Broadhurst	69	66	70	205	19,413.33
Kent Jones	65	67	73	205	19,413.33

	SCORES			TOTAL	MONEY
Rocco Mediate	67	66	72	205	19,413.33
Dan Olsen	65	67	73	205	19,413.33
Jeff Maggert	67	70	69	206	13,351.12
Billy Andrade	67	68	71	206	13,351.11
Marco Dawson	67	67	72	206	13,351.11
Paul Goydos	69	68	69	206	13,351.11
Scott McCarron	69	67	70	206	13,351.11
Jose Maria Olazabal	68	69	69	206	13,351.11
Fran Quinn	70	66	70	206	13,351.11
Jerry Smith	69	65	72	206	13,351.11
David Toms	67	70	69	206	13,351.11

Cologuard Classic

Omni Tucson National, Tucson, Arizona
Par 36-37-73; 7,207 yards

March 1-3
purse, $1,700,000

	SCORES			TOTAL	MONEY
Mark O'Meara	66	70	66	202	$255,000
Darren Clarke	70	68	68	206	113,900
Scott McCarron	67	70	69	206	113,900
Kirk Triplett	68	69	69	206	113,900
Willie Wood	66	71	69	206	113,900
Brandt Jobe	68	71	69	208	57,800
Steve Stricker	66	72	70	208	57,800
Kevin Sutherland	73	67	68	208	57,800
David Toms	71	70	67	208	57,800
Lee Janzen	73	66	70	209	44,200
Scott Parel	73	69	68	210	39,100
Kenny Perry	65	73	72	210	39,100
Stephen Ames	71	72	68	211	33,150
Colin Montgomerie	70	72	69	211	33,150
Mark Calcavecchia	72	72	68	212	27,234
Tom Lehman	70	70	72	212	27,234
Billy Mayfair	68	74	70	212	27,234
Tim Petrovic	72	71	69	212	27,234
Duffy Waldorf	71	73	68	212	27,234
Fred Couples	73	70	70	213	20,485
Miguel Angel Jimenez	66	75	72	213	20,485
Kent Jones	72	71	70	213	20,485
Ken Tanigawa	72	74	67	213	20,485
Tom Byrum	68	75	71	214	17,000
Doug Garwood	73	70	71	214	17,000
Gibby Gilbert	71	68	75	214	17,000
Bob Estes	74	68	73	215	14,450
Dudley Hart	71	70	74	215	14,450
Wes Short, Jr.	72	71	72	215	14,450
Jerry Smith	72	73	70	215	14,450

Hoag Classic

Newport Beach Country Club, Newport Beach, California
Par 35-36–71; 6,584 yards

March 8-10
purse, $1,800,000

	SCORES			TOTAL	MONEY
Kirk Triplett	70	65	68	203	$270,000
Woody Austin	68	67	68	203	158,400
(Triplett defeated Austin on second playoff hole.)					
Jeff Maggert	76	63	65	204	118,800
Scott McCarron	64	72	68	204	118,800
Steve Flesch	69	67	69	205	74,400
Paul Goydos	69	68	68	205	74,400
Fran Quinn	64	67	74	205	74,400
Doug Garwood	66	71	69	206	54,000
Lee Janzen	71	70	65	206	54,000
Paul Broadhurst	71	69	67	207	41,400
Fred Couples	68	70	69	207	41,400
David McKenzie	68	66	73	207	41,400
Scott Verplank	73	64	70	207	41,400
Miguel Angel Jimenez	69	68	71	208	34,200
Billy Andrade	67	74	68	209	25,660
Marco Dawson	71	71	67	209	25,660
Bob Estes	71	69	69	209	25,660
Billy Mayfair	70	68	71	209	25,660
Mark O'Meara	71	73	65	209	25,660
Corey Pavin	67	71	71	209	25,660
Ken Tanigawa	69	74	66	209	25,660
Esteban Toledo	70	65	74	209	25,660
David Toms	67	67	75	209	25,660
Kevin Baker	71	68	71	210	16,087.50
Tom Byrum	70	69	71	210	16,087.50
Glen Day	70	70	70	210	16,087.50
Brandt Jobe	73	67	70	210	16,087.50
Rocco Mediate	69	72	69	210	16,087.50
Scott Parel	70	69	71	210	16,087.50
Tom Pernice, Jr.	70	68	72	210	16,087.50
Kenny Perry	75	67	68	210	16,087.50

Rapiscan Systems Classic

Fallen Oak Golf Club, Biloxi, Mississippi
Par 36-36–72; 7,088 yards
(Tournament completed on Monday—darkness.)

March 29-April 1
purse, $1,600,000

	SCORES			TOTAL	MONEY
Kevin Sutherland	65	69	75	209	$240,000
Scott Parel	68	72	69	209	140,800
(Sutherland defeated Parel on seventh playoff hole.)					
Billy Andrade	71	68	71	210	115,200
Marco Dawson	65	72	74	211	96,000
Bernhard Langer	71	72	69	212	66,133.34
Wes Short, Jr.	70	73	69	212	66,133.33
Steve Stricker	73	70	69	212	66,133.33
John Daly	71	71	71	213	45,866.67
Brandt Jobe	71	71	71	213	45,866.67
Kent Jones	69	72	72	213	45,866.66
Billy Mayfair	71	71	72	214	34,000
Colin Montgomerie	70	71	73	214	34,000
Vijay Singh	69	72	73	214	34,000

	SCORES	TOTAL	MONEY
Jeff Sluman	68 73 73	214	34,000
Tom Byrum	68 72 75	215	28,000
Kenny Perry	71 73 71	215	28,000
Olin Browne	71 73 72	216	22,624
Fred Couples	69 70 77	216	22,624
Tim Petrovic	70 75 71	216	22,624
Gene Sauers	72 70 74	216	22,624
Duffy Waldorf	71 69 76	216	22,624
Tom Gillis	73 71 73	217	17,653.34
Joe Durant	72 70 75	217	17,653.33
Ken Tanigawa	73 71 73	217	17,653.33
Michael Allen	71 72 75	218	14,592
Woody Austin	71 74 73	218	14,592
Cliff Kresge	71 73 74	218	14,592
Jeff Maggert	72 73 73	218	14,592
Rocco Mediate	72 73 73	218	14,592
Paul Broadhurst	71 74 74	219	12,320
Bob May	72 74 73	219	12,320

Mitsubishi Electric Classic

TPC Sugarloaf, Duluth, Georgia
Par 36-36–72; 6,987 yards

April 19-21
purse, $1,800,000

	SCORES	TOTAL	MONEY
Scott McCarron	68 70 71	209	$270,000
Joe Durant	72 70 69	211	120,600
Kent Jones	74 68 69	211	120,600
Jerry Kelly	71 73 67	211	120,600
Kirk Triplett	72 70 69	211	120,600
Stephen Ames	73 70 69	212	61,200
Ken Duke	73 71 68	212	61,200
Kenny Perry	77 69 66	212	61,200
Jeff Sluman	77 67 68	212	61,200
Stephen Leaney	74 70 69	213	41,400
Rocco Mediate	73 68 72	213	41,400
Colin Montgomerie	74 71 68	213	41,400
Willie Wood	73 72 68	213	41,400
Glen Day	73 71 70	214	31,500
Miguel Angel Jimenez	72 70 72	214	31,500
Bernhard Langer	77 69 68	214	31,500
Vijay Singh	72 73 69	214	31,500
Ken Tanigawa	73 73 69	215	26,190
Duffy Waldorf	76 67 72	215	26,190
Billy Andrade	76 69 72	217	23,760
Michael Bradley	72 73 73	218	20,475
Tom Gillis	73 75 70	218	20,475
Bob May	69 74 75	218	20,475
Kevin Sutherland	76 70 72	218	20,475
Jose Maria Olazabal	74 72 73	219	17,160
Dan Olsen	74 72 73	219	17,160
Wes Short, Jr.	74 73 72	219	17,160
Paul Broadhurst	76 73 71	220	14,256
Steve Flesch	77 70 73	220	14,256
Brandt Jobe	74 73 73	220	14,256
Tim Petrovic	73 73 74	220	14,256
Esteban Toledo	73 73 74	220	14,256

Bass Pro Shops Legends of Golf at Big Cedar Lodge

Top of the Rock: Par 27-27–54; 2,808 yards
Ozarks: Par 36-35–71; 7,036 yards
Ridgedale, Missouri

April 26-28
purse, $1,800,000

	SCORES			TOTAL	MONEY (Each)
Scott Hoch/Tom Pernice, Jr.	62	48	46	156	$171,000
Paul Broadhurst/Kirk Triplett	50	67	44	161	91,125
Vijay Singh/Carlos Franco	52	63	46	161	91,125
Jesper Parnevik/Jeff Maggert	51	62	49	162	58,500
Brandt Jobe/Scott McCarron	52	63	49	164	42,750
Paul Goydos/Kevin Sutherland	47	66	51	164	42,750
Lee Janzen/Rocco Mediate	51	65	49	165	26,280
Billy Andrade/Joe Durant	50	65	50	165	26,280
Michael Allen/John Daly	50	65	50	165	26,280
Olin Browne/Steve Pate	66	49	50	165	26,280
Roger Chapman/David Frost	63	51	51	165	26,280
Ken Tanigawa/Gene Sauers	46	69	51	166	19,800
Colin Montgomerie/Mark O'Meara	51	67	49	167	16,650
David Toms/Steve Flesch	50	68	49	167	16,650
Larry Nelson/Billy Mayfair	66	50	51	167	16,650
Bart Bryant/Brad Bryant	64	51	52	167	16,650
Retief Goosen/Mark McNulty	68	52	48	168	13,530
Scott Parel/Larry Mize	64	54	50	168	13,530
Shaun Micheel/Loren Roberts	63	52	53	168	13,530
Corey Pavin/Duffy Waldorf	68	51	51	170	11,880
Jose Maria Olazabal/Miguel Angel Jimenez	49	69	53	171	11,250
Fred Funk/Dana Quigley	70	52	50	172	10,125
Hale Irwin/Wes Short, Jr.	68	52	52	172	10,125
Peter Jacobsen/Jay Haas	50	70	52	172	10,125
Sandy Lyle/Ian Woosnam	51	67	54	172	10,125
Scott Verplank/Bob Tway	69	53	51	173	9,000
Brad Faxon/Dudley Hart	52	71	51	174	8,550
Bruce Fleisher/Tom Jenkins	71	52	52	175	8,100
Tom Watson/Andy North	50	75	51	176	7,695
Mark Brooks/John Huston	68	56	52	176	7,695

Insperity Invitational

The Woodlands Country Club, The Woodlands, Texas
Par 36-36–72; 7,002 yards

May 3-5
purse, $2,220,000

	SCORES			TOTAL	MONEY
Scott McCarron	67	65	67	199	$330,000
Scott Parel	67	68	66	201	193,600
Lee Janzen	70	67	67	204	158,400
Marco Dawson	72	65	68	205	118,800
Paul Goydos	68	67	70	205	118,800
Tom Lehman	67	71	69	207	88,000
Jerry Kelly	69	68	71	208	61,600
Jeff Maggert	71	69	68	208	61,600
Billy Mayfair	68	71	69	208	61,600
Colin Montgomerie	68	68	72	208	61,600
Vijay Singh	70	70	68	208	61,600
Ken Tanigawa	68	72	68	208	61,600
Retief Goosen	71	70	68	209	42,900
Kenny Perry	70	69	70	209	42,900
David Frost	69	75	66	210	35,244
John Huston	70	71	69	210	35,244

	SCORES			TOTAL	MONEY
Kent Jones	68	69	73	210	35,244
Bernhard Langer	69	70	71	210	35,244
David Toms	72	69	69	210	35,244
Clark Dennis	69	73	69	211	24,577.15
Joe Durant	71	71	69	211	24,577.15
Michael Bradley	71	68	72	211	24,577.14
Bart Bryant	69	72	70	211	24,577.14
Miguel Angel Jimenez	69	71	71	211	24,577.14
Gene Sauers	72	69	70	211	24,577.14
Kevin Sutherland	72	69	70	211	24,577.14
Tommy Armour	70	76	66	212	17,105
Tom Byrum	74	69	69	212	17,105
John Daly	71	71	70	212	17,105
Ken Duke	71	73	68	212	17,105
Steve Flesch	69	72	71	212	17,105
Brandt Jobe	68	75	69	212	17,105
Wes Short, Jr.	70	72	70	212	17,105
Kirk Triplett	73	68	71	212	17,105

Regions Tradition

Greystone Golf & Country Club, Birmingham, Alabama
Par 36-36–72; 7,277 yards
(Tournament completed on Monday—rain.)

May 9-13
purse, $2,400,000

	SCORES				TOTAL	MONEY
Steve Stricker	68	64	70	68	270	$360,000
Billy Andrade	68	67	69	72	276	176,000
Paul Goydos	70	67	69	70	276	176,000
David Toms	67	67	70	72	276	176,000
Tom Byrum	71	69	66	71	277	115,200
Paul Broadhurst	73	66	68	72	279	77,760
Lee Janzen	74	66	71	68	279	77,760
Bernhard Langer	69	67	68	75	279	77,760
Jeff Maggert	69	73	71	66	279	77,760
Willie Wood	69	71	70	69	279	77,760
Brandt Jobe	71	69	69	71	280	57,600
Steve Flesch	75	70	68	68	281	47,400
Jerry Kelly	71	70	69	71	281	47,400
Rocco Mediate	74	68	71	68	281	47,400
Ian Woosnam	72	71	70	68	281	47,400
Woody Austin	74	74	67	67	282	35,080
Glen Day	64	72	73	73	282	35,080
Tom Lehman	73	69	71	69	282	35,080
Shaun Micheel	73	68	71	70	282	35,080
Scott Parel	71	66	70	75	282	35,080
Kirk Triplett	73	67	74	68	282	35,080
Stephen Ames	71	71	67	74	283	25,248
Olin Browne	71	73	72	67	283	25,248
Dan Forsman	71	70	72	70	283	25,248
David Frost	73	68	72	70	283	25,248
Retief Goosen	74	67	71	71	283	25,248
Michael Bradley	71	68	71	74	284	20,880
Darren Clarke	72	71	71	70	284	20,880
Steve Jones	68	73	70	73	284	20,880
Marco Dawson	71	69	74	71	285	18,080
Joe Durant	74	69	69	73	285	18,080
Joey Sindelar	74	66	71	74	285	18,080
Tommy Armour	76	65	71	74	286	15,480
Gary Hallberg	73	65	73	75	286	15,480

SENIOR TOURS / 653

	SCORES				TOTAL	MONEY
Kent Jones	72	68	73	73	286	15,480
Billy Mayfair	72	68	77	69	286	15,480
Miguel Angel Jimenez	68	70	77	72	287	13,440
Kevin Sutherland	73	72	68	74	287	13,440
David McKenzie	79	67	72	70	288	12,000
Jose Maria Olazabal	71	72	73	72	288	12,000
Corey Pavin	73	70	73	72	288	12,000
Esteban Toledo	72	72	69	75	288	12,000
Bart Bryant	74	73	71	71	289	9,600
Mike Goodes	70	72	73	74	289	9,600
Spike McRoy	73	73	71	72	289	9,600
Vijay Singh	72	75	73	69	289	9,600
Jeff Sluman	73	73	69	74	289	9,600
Duffy Waldorf	72	72	71	74	289	9,600
Scott Hoch	73	71	73	73	290	7,440
John Huston	75	73	73	69	290	7,440
Wes Short, Jr.	75	72	72	71	290	7,440
Gene Sauers	72	74	70	75	291	6,480
Russ Cochran	75	73	70	74	292	5,640
Fred Funk	72	71	75	74	292	5,640
Doug Garwood	74	70	74	74	292	5,640
Mark McNulty	78	70	73	71	292	5,640
Mark Calcavecchia	77	71	74	71	293	4,320
Paul Lawrie	76	73	72	72	293	4,320
Len Mattiace	76	74	73	70	293	4,320
Tom Pernice, Jr.	79	69	73	72	293	4,320
Tim Petrovic	75	70	71	77	293	4,320
Ken Tanigawa	75	69	72	77	293	4,320
Tommy Tolles	72	75	73	73	293	4,320
Jerry Pate	70	74	76	74	294	3,360
Chris DiMarco	75	73	76	71	295	3,120
Scott McCarron	73	74	72	77	296	2,760
Fran Quinn	75	73	73	75	296	2,760
Carlos Franco	76	70	72	79	297	2,400
Steve Pate	78	72	73	75	298	2,256
Jerry Smith	80	71	77	71	299	2,112
Bob Gilder	78	74	75	78	305	1,968

KitchenAid Senior PGA Championship

Oak Hill Country Club, Rochester, New York May 23-26
Par 35-35–70; 6,896 yards purse, $3,250,000

	SCORES				TOTAL	MONEY
Ken Tanigawa	67	74	66	70	277	$585,000
Scott McCarron	72	69	67	70	278	347,000
Paul Broadhurst	70	67	67	75	279	215,000
Retief Goosen	67	72	67	74	280	150,000
Jerry Kelly	70	70	72	69	281	120,000
Scott Parel	66	73	74	69	282	104,000
John Riegger	69	71	69	74	283	94,000
Billy Andrade	72	75	71	66	284	84,033.33
Corey Pavin	69	74	66	75	284	84,033.33
Duffy Waldorf	69	74	71	70	284	84,033.33
Woody Austin	74	75	70	67	286	74,500
Tommy Armour	70	73	72	72	287	59,516.66
David Frost	72	71	73	71	287	59,516.66
Bernhard Langer	72	74	72	69	287	59,516.66
Rocco Mediate	71	71	72	73	287	59,516.66
Jesper Parnevik	68	74	70	75	287	59,516.66

	SCORES				TOTAL	MONEY
Esteban Toledo	70	67	74	76	287	59,516.66
Mike Goodes	72	69	71	76	288	43,333.33
Brandt Jobe	71	72	74	71	288	43,333.33
Taichi Teshima	69	77	69	73	288	43,333.33
Mark Brown	74	72	72	71	289	32,571.42
Lee Janzen	73	75	71	70	289	32,571.42
Paul Lawrie	69	72	74	74	289	32,571.42
Jeff Maggert	68	78	74	69	289	32,571.42
Colin Montgomerie	74	75	70	70	289	32,571.42
Vijay Singh	72	73	70	74	289	32,571.42
Bob Sowards	71	73	71	74	289	32,571.42
Bart Bryant	74	70	74	72	290	22,685.71
Steve Flesch	78	70	70	72	290	22,685.71
Carlos Franco	73	74	72	71	290	22,685.71
Stephen Leaney	74	72	73	71	290	22,685.71
Tom Lehman	75	73	69	73	290	22,685.71
Kirk Triplett	70	71	72	77	290	22,685.71
Thaworn Wiratchant	73	74	73	70	290	22,685.71
Stephen Ames	73	72	74	72	291	15,516.66
Peter Baker	72	72	74	73	291	15,516.66
Darren Clarke	68	74	74	75	291	15,516.66
Marco Dawson	67	74	77	73	291	15,516.66
Doug Garwood	70	73	75	73	291	15,516.66
Rafael Gomez	71	75	73	72	291	15,516.66
Peter Fowler	71	74	75	72	292	11,100
Cliff Kresge	73	75	72	72	292	11,100
Steve Stricker	76	72	72	72	292	11,100
Scott Dunlap	72	74	73	74	293	9,000
Greg Meyer	71	72	75	75	293	9,000
Shaun Micheel	74	74	72	73	293	9,000
Wes Short, Jr.	72	73	72	76	293	9,000
Dan Forsman	72	75	77	70	294	7,450
Billy Mayfair	75	74	73	72	294	7,450
David McKenzie	73	71	76	74	294	7,450
Tim Petrovic	71	73	77	73	294	7,450
Mark Brooks	71	76	74	74	295	6,700
Paul Goydos	72	74	73	76	295	6,700
Prayad Marksaeng	71	74	71	79	295	6,700
Chad Proehl	76	71	74	74	295	6,700
Toru Suzuki	77	70	74	74	295	6,700
Steve Pate	74	72	72	78	296	6,300
Tom Pernice, Jr.	76	72	72	76	296	6,300
Jerry Smith	71	74	72	79	296	6,300
Olin Browne	73	75	73	76	297	6,000
Scott Hoch	70	77	74	76	297	6,000
Bob May	71	71	81	74	297	6,000
Paul Eales	76	73	75	74	298	5,700
Gibby Gilbert	69	76	76	77	298	5,700
Jay Haas	74	74	75	75	298	5,700
Steve Jones	77	71	72	79	299	5,525
Stuart Smith	74	75	74	76	299	5,525
Mike Miles	69	75	74	82	300	5,425
Larry Mize	76	73	76	75	300	5,425
Paul McGinley	73	72	81	75	301	5,325
Mark Mielke	73	76	77	75	301	5,325
Jared Melson	76	73	75	78	302	5,225
Omar Uresti	70	76	78	78	302	5,225
John Huston	69	77	78	79	303	5,125
Thomas Levet	70	78	79	76	303	5,125
Gary Hallberg	72	74	79	79	304	5,050

Principal Charity Classic

Wakonda Club, Des Moines, Iowa
Par 36-36–72; 6,831 yards

May 31-June 2
purse, $1,850,000

	SCORES			TOTAL	MONEY
Kevin Sutherland	72	65	62	199	$277,500
Scott Parel	63	66	70	199	162,800
(Sutherland defeated Parel on second playoff hole.)					
Jerry Kelly	67	67	66	200	133,200
David Toms	67	68	68	203	111,000
Kent Jones	72	67	66	205	76,466.67
Corey Pavin	69	67	69	205	76,466.67
Gene Sauers	67	68	70	205	76,466.66
Jay Haas	71	68	67	206	53,033.34
Marco Dawson	69	65	72	206	53,033.33
Doug Garwood	68	68	70	206	53,033.33
Steve Flesch	71	67	69	207	35,942.86
Retief Goosen	71	69	67	207	35,942.86
Brandt Jobe	72	67	68	207	35,942.86
Jeff Maggert	68	72	67	207	35,942.86
Fran Quinn	71	70	66	207	35,942.86
Billy Andrade	66	69	72	207	35,942.85
Duffy Waldorf	67	71	69	207	35,942.85
Stephen Ames	71	68	69	208	26,085
John Riegger	68	74	66	208	26,085
Ken Tanigawa	72	70	66	208	26,085
Paul Goydos	74	66	69	209	19,583.58
Woody Austin	67	70	72	209	19,583.57
Mark Calcavecchia	72	68	69	209	19,583.57
Ken Duke	70	70	69	209	19,583.57
Stephen Leaney	70	69	70	209	19,583.57
Scott McCarron	70	67	72	209	19,583.57
Wes Short, Jr.	71	72	66	209	19,583.57
Olin Browne	72	70	68	210	14,652
Darren Clarke	67	70	73	210	14,652
John Daly	69	72	69	210	14,652
Glen Day	71	70	69	210	14,652
Esteban Toledo	71	70	69	210	14,652

Mastercard Japan Championship

Narita Golf Club-Accordia Golf, Narita, Chiba, Japan
Par 36-36–72; 7,140 yards

June 7-9
purse, $2,500,000

	SCORES			TOTAL	MONEY
Scott McCarron	69	67	67	203	$400,000
Billy Andrade	69	69	68	206	196,500
Kirk Triplett	69	68	69	206	196,500
Darren Clarke	68	70	69	207	135,000
Scott Parel	70	68	69	207	135,000
David Frost	72	69	67	208	100,000
Doug Garwood	67	73	69	209	80,000
Jerry Kelly	73	67	69	209	80,000
Tsuyoshi Yoneyama	71	70	68	209	80,000
Paul Goydos	68	74	68	210	60,000
Cliff Kresge	72	66	72	210	60,000
Colin Montgomerie	68	72	70	210	60,000
Tom Byrum	73	72	66	211	46,312.50
Joe Durant	69	71	71	211	46,312.50

	SCORES			TOTAL	MONEY
Corey Pavin	71	71	69	211	46,312.50
Jeff Sluman	70	71	70	211	46,312.50
Bart Bryant	70	72	70	212	36,312.50
Dudley Hart	67	74	71	212	36,312.50
Jeff Maggert	70	71	71	212	36,312.50
Gene Sauers	74	69	69	212	36,312.50
Steve Flesch	68	76	69	213	27,041.67
Prayad Marksaeng	75	69	69	213	27,041.67
David McKenzie	72	71	70	213	27,041.67
Tom Pernice, Jr.	72	71	70	213	27,041.67
Toshi Izawa	69	70	74	213	27,041.66
Ken Tanigawa	65	77	71	213	27,041.66
Mark Calcavecchia	76	69	69	214	20,291.67
Keiichiro Fukabori	74	68	72	214	20,291.67
Fred Funk	74	70	70	214	20,291.67
Jerry Smith	73	70	71	214	20,291.67
Woody Austin	73	69	72	214	20,291.66
Wes Short, Jr.	71	69	74	214	20,291.66

American Family Insurance Championship

University Ridge Golf Club, Madison, Wisconsin
Par 36-36–72; 7,083 yards

June 21-23
purse, $2,000,000

	SCORES			TOTAL	MONEY
Jerry Kelly	65	70	66	201	$300,000
Retief Goosen	69	66	66	201	160,000
Steve Stricker	67	67	67	201	160,000
(Kelly defeated Stricker on first and Goosen on third playoff hole.)					
Duffy Waldorf	67	67	68	202	120,000
John Daly	68	69	66	203	88,000
Kevin Sutherland	70	70	63	203	88,000
Billy Andrade	68	66	70	204	72,000
Woody Austin	69	67	69	205	55,000
Tom Gillis	67	71	67	205	55,000
Stephen Leaney	69	68	68	205	55,000
Scott Parel	68	71	66	205	55,000
Steve Flesch	68	65	73	206	44,000
Colin Montgomerie	70	68	69	207	35,000
Tom Pernice, Jr.	68	67	72	207	35,000
Ken Tanigawa	73	65	69	207	35,000
Esteban Toledo	69	69	69	207	35,000
David Toms	67	72	68	207	35,000
Kirk Triplett	67	70	70	207	35,000
Olin Browne	72	69	67	208	26,466.67
Kenny Perry	70	71	67	208	26,466.67
Ken Duke	70	69	69	208	26,466.66
Stephen Ames	73	69	67	209	21,550
Scott McCarron	71	67	71	209	21,550
Tim Petrovic	72	67	70	209	21,550
Omar Uresti	74	66	69	209	21,550
Paul Broadhurst	71	68	71	210	17,800
David Frost	66	74	70	210	17,800
Gary Hallberg	72	67	71	210	17,800
Cliff Kresge	69	71	70	210	17,800
Marco Dawson	73	69	69	211	14,440
Steve Jones	73	66	72	211	14,440
Bernhard Langer	69	73	69	211	14,440
Dan Olsen	72	67	72	211	14,440
Vijay Singh	72	71	68	211	14,440

U.S. Senior Open Championship

Warren Golf Course Notre Dame, Notre Dame, Indiana
Par 35-35–70; 6,943 yards

June 27-30
purse, $4,000,000

	SCORES				TOTAL	MONEY
Steve Stricker	62	64	66	69	261	$720,000
Jerry Kelly	64	64	70	69	267	350,440
David Toms	62	67	70	68	267	350,440
Bob Estes	67	65	68	70	270	188,477
Kirk Triplett	64	68	71	69	272	156,983
Stephen Ames	70	67	66	72	275	114,444
Chris DiMarco	66	66	73	70	275	114,444
Paul Goydos	67	69	69	70	275	114,444
Miguel Ángel Jimenez	66	71	67	71	275	114,444
Scott McCarron	72	69	70	64	275	114,444
Woody Austin	68	69	70	69	276	79,185
Paul Broadhurst	71	67	68	70	276	79,185
Tom Lehman	68	69	70	69	276	79,185
Doug Garwood	70	69	68	70	277	63,216
Retief Goosen	66	65	72	74	277	63,216
Fran Quinn	68	70	69	70	277	63,216
Ken Duke	70	70	66	72	278	46,359
Jeff Gallagher	69	67	72	70	278	46,359
Jay Haas	70	68	71	69	278	46,359
Kent Jones	70	67	69	72	278	46,359
Steve Jones	71	66	72	69	278	46,359
Duffy Waldorf	65	69	74	70	278	46,359
Tom Watson	69	68	73	68	278	46,359
Tom Byrum	73	67	72	67	279	28,798
Joe Durant	67	69	73	70	279	28,798
Lee Janzen	70	70	71	68	279	28,798
Bernhard Langer	66	68	70	75	279	28,798
Colin Montgomerie	68	72	68	71	279	28,798
Scott Parel	67	73	67	72	279	28,798
Phillip Price	72	68	70	69	279	28,798
Wes Short, Jr.	68	70	72	69	279	28,798
Vijay Singh	65	72	71	71	279	28,798
Billy Andrade	66	68	69	77	280	20,464
Roger Chapman	70	69	70	71	280	20,464
Gary Orr	70	68	72	70	280	20,464
Jeff Sluman	67	71	69	73	280	20,464
Ken Tanigawa	68	69	72	71	280	20,464
Clark Dennis	69	70	71	72	282	16,252
Prayad Marksaeng	72	69	69	72	282	16,252
Mark O'Meara	68	73	69	72	282	16,252
Corey Pavin	68	72	67	75	282	16,252
Kevin Sutherland	67	70	72	73	282	16,252
Mark Brown	66	69	72	76	283	12,633
Bart Bryant	72	68	73	70	283	12,633
Peter Fowler	71	68	70	74	283	12,633
Tom Werkmeister	72	67	70	74	283	12,633
Marco Dawson	72	68	70	74	284	9,935
Jeff Maggert	70	67	71	76	284	9,935
Rocco Mediate	72	69	72	71	284	9,935
Jean-Francois Remesy	70	69	74	71	284	9,935
Kirk Hanefeld	69	71	72	73	285	8,826
Billy Mayfair	68	72	73	72	285	8,826
Toru Suzuki	65	72	76	72	285	8,826
Brad Bryant	71	70	73	72	286	8,570
Paul Lawrie	70	71	71	75	287	8,449
Gary Nicklaus	68	71	75	73	287	8,449
Kohki Idoki	69	72	73	74	288	8,328

	SCORES	TOTAL	MONEY
Tim Petrovic	69 70 74 76	289	8,247
Scott Dunlap	71 70 78 72	291	8,169

Bridgestone Senior Players Championship

Firestone Country Club, Akron, Ohio
Par 35-35–70; 7,400 yards

July 11-14
purse, $2,800,000

	SCORES	TOTAL	MONEY
Retief Goosen	69 62 75 68	274	$420,000
Jay Haas	69 68 72 67	276	224,000
Tim Petrovic	71 68 69 68	276	224,000
Kent Jones	70 67 70 71	278	151,200
Scott Parel	66 72 67 73	278	151,200
Steve Stricker	64 70 73 72	279	112,000
Woody Austin	71 71 70 68	280	89,600
Scott McCarron	74 67 71 68	280	89,600
Kenny Perry	71 71 71 67	280	89,600
Steve Flesch	71 67 72 71	281	72,800
Michael Bradley	77 68 67 70	282	64,400
Tom Lehman	72 71 69 70	282	64,400
Ken Duke	69 71 70 73	283	50,400
Miguel Angel Jimenez	73 70 68 72	283	50,400
Brandt Jobe	69 65 73 76	283	50,400
Colin Montgomerie	71 68 71 73	283	50,400
Kevin Sutherland	70 70 71 72	283	50,400
Billy Andrade	73 69 71 71	284	38,290
Olin Browne	70 70 73 71	284	38,290
John Daly	70 73 69 72	284	38,290
Vijay Singh	70 70 70 74	284	38,290
Fred Couples	75 72 69 69	285	31,640
Doug Garwood	72 72 68 73	285	31,640
Bob Estes	71 69 72 74	286	26,768
Jerry Kelly	69 72 72 73	286	26,768
Wes Short, Jr.	71 70 70 75	286	26,768
Tommy Tolles	70 67 76 73	286	26,768
Duffy Waldorf	70 70 73 73	286	26,768
Gene Sauers	76 71 71 69	287	23,240
Paul Broadhurst	73 70 74 71	288	20,650
Marco Dawson	72 69 77 70	288	20,650
Paul Goydos	70 71 78 69	288	20,650
David McKenzie	70 74 73 71	288	20,650
Tom Byrum	74 70 75 71	290	16,856
Joe Durant	75 69 73 73	290	16,856
Lee Janzen	71 77 74 68	290	16,856
Steve Jones	71 75 70 74	290	16,856
Bernhard Langer	76 72 72 70	290	16,856
Stephen Ames	76 71 70 74	291	13,160
Scott Dunlap	73 68 74 76	291	13,160
John Huston	73 76 73 69	291	13,160
Jeff Maggert	71 74 75 71	291	13,160
Billy Mayfair	77 71 70 73	291	13,160
Corey Pavin	75 70 73 73	291	13,160
Scott Verplank	68 76 75 72	291	13,160
Bart Bryant	72 75 73 72	292	9,520
Mark Calcavecchia	72 75 72 73	292	9,520
Shaun Micheel	70 75 69 78	292	9,520
Tom Pernice, Jr.	71 73 77 71	292	9,520
Loren Roberts	76 72 73 71	292	9,520
David Toms	73 75 75 69	292	9,520

	SCORES				TOTAL	MONEY
Glen Day	72	73	74	74	293	7,280
Larry Mize	76	75	72	70	293	7,280
John Cook	77	73	72	72	294	6,440
David Frost	78	71	72	73	294	6,440
Jeff Sluman	76	70	73	75	294	6,440
Michael Allen	75	80	70	70	295	5,740
Tom Gillis	74	75	72	74	295	5,740
Dan Forsman	76	68	75	78	297	5,320
Russ Cochran	76	76	72	74	298	4,760
Sandy Lyle	72	78	75	73	298	4,760
Esteban Toledo	76	77	71	74	298	4,760
Rocco Mediate	76	73	77	73	299	4,060
Ken Tanigawa	78	76	74	71	299	4,060
Jerry Smith	75	74	79	72	300	3,500
Kirk Triplett	75	73	73	79	300	3,500
Carlos Franco	75	77	76	73	301	3,080
Willie Wood	74	75	78	75	302	2,800
Mark Brooks	74	83	77	72	306	2,464
Chris DiMarco	76	74	81	75	306	2,464
Joey Sindelar	73	78	76	79	306	2,464
Bob Gilder	75	84	79	74	312	2,128
Robert Gamez	81	77	79	76	313	1,960
Bobby Wadkins	81	82	76	76	315	1,848
Scott Simpson	82	80	81	77	320	1,736
Danny Edwards	88	81	78	86	333	1,624
Tommy Armour	74				WD	
Mark O'Meara					WD	

The Senior Open Championship presented by Rolex

See Staysure Tour section.

Dick's Sporting Goods Open

En-Joie Golf Club, Endicott, New York
Par 36-36–72; 6,994 yards

August 16-18
purse, $2,050,000

	SCORES			TOTAL	MONEY
Doug Barron	65	68	66	199	$307,500
Fred Couples	70	68	63	201	180,400
Woody Austin	68	68	67	203	147,600
Scott McCarron	69	66	69	204	110,700
Colin Montgomerie	70	68	66	204	110,700
Miguel Angel Jimenez	65	72	68	205	73,800
Scott Parel	66	69	70	205	73,800
Kevin Sutherland	67	70	68	205	73,800
Billy Andrade	67	70	69	206	51,250
Marco Dawson	66	69	71	206	51,250
Kenny Perry	68	73	65	206	51,250
Duffy Waldorf	68	69	69	206	51,250
Joe Durant	73	66	68	207	35,875
Retief Goosen	72	66	69	207	35,875
Paul Goydos	68	69	70	207	35,875
Jay Haas	68	68	71	207	35,875
Tim Petrovic	69	68	70	207	35,875
Tommy Tolles	68	68	71	207	35,875
Paul Broadhurst	71	66	71	208	26,291.25
Ken Duke	68	76	64	208	26,291.25
Steve Flesch	68	69	71	208	26,291.25

	SCORES			TOTAL	MONEY
Tom Lehman	68	72	68	208	26,291.25
Tom Pernice, Jr.	71	68	70	209	22,550
Chris DiMarco	68	71	71	210	19,598
Bernhard Langer	68	70	72	210	19,598
David McKenzie	67	69	74	210	19,598
Joey Sindelar	70	72	68	210	19,598
Ken Tanigawa	70	71	69	210	19,598
John Daly	71	70	70	211	16,195
Tom Gillis	70	70	71	211	16,195
Gary Nicklaus	69	73	69	211	16,195

Boeing Classic

The Club at Snoqualmie Ridge, Snoqualmie, Washington
Par 36-36–72; 7,217 yards

August 23-25
purse, $2,100,000

	SCORES			TOTAL	MONEY
Brandt Jobe	69	66	63	198	$315,000
Tom Pernice, Jr.	68	68	65	201	184,800
Fred Couples	65	63	76	204	138,600
Jerry Kelly	67	68	69	204	138,600
Tommy Tolles	69	68	68	205	92,400
David Toms	70	63	72	205	92,400
Doug Garwood	66	69	71	206	61,320
Miguel Angel Jimenez	70	67	69	206	61,320
Bernhard Langer	66	68	72	206	61,320
Stephen Leaney	66	68	72	206	61,320
Kevin Sutherland	71	67	68	206	61,320
Paul Broadhurst	66	67	74	207	41,475
Glen Day	69	68	70	207	41,475
Ken Duke	68	66	73	207	41,475
Tim Petrovic	70	65	72	207	41,475
Woody Austin	69	69	70	208	31,626
Gibby Gilbert	71	67	70	208	31,626
Retief Goosen	67	69	72	208	31,626
Paul Goydos	69	70	69	208	31,626
Rocco Mediate	74	65	69	208	31,626
Joe Durant	69	74	66	209	23,887.50
John Huston	69	69	71	209	23,887.50
Lee Janzen	71	66	72	209	23,887.50
Gene Sauers	67	72	70	209	23,887.50
Steve Flesch	69	71	70	210	19,582.50
David McKenzie	69	73	68	210	19,582.50
Colin Montgomerie	69	70	71	210	19,582.50
Jeff Sluman	73	70	67	210	19,582.50
Stephen Ames	70	69	72	211	15,540
Olin Browne	70	68	73	211	15,540
Marco Dawson	69	72	70	211	15,540
Kent Jones	68	71	72	211	15,540
Jeff Maggert	66	71	74	211	15,540
Kirk Triplett	68	71	72	211	15,540

Shaw Charity Classic

Canyon Meadows Golf & Country Club, Calgary, Alberta, Canada
Par 35-35–70; 7,086 yards

August 30-September 1
purse, $2,350,000

	SCORES			TOTAL	MONEY
Wes Short, Jr.	64	67	66	197	$352,500
Scott McCarron	64	69	65	198	206,800
Steve Flesch	62	68	69	199	169,200
Tom Gillis	67	64	69	200	141,000
Joe Durant	67	68	66	201	97,133.34
Billy Andrade	64	69	68	201	97,133.33
Tom Byrum	63	69	69	201	97,133.33
Ken Duke	65	68	69	202	67,366.67
Retief Goosen	64	70	68	202	67,366.67
Corey Pavin	66	67	69	202	67,366.66
Tim Petrovic	64	69	70	203	56,400
David McKenzie	68	69	67	204	47,783.34
Mark Brooks	64	70	70	204	47,783.33
Bernhard Langer	68	66	70	204	47,783.33
Woody Austin	68	67	70	205	35,485
Paul Broadhurst	71	67	67	205	35,485
Michael Campbell	66	71	68	205	35,485
Doug Garwood	66	68	71	205	35,485
Jeff Maggert	67	70	68	205	35,485
Rocco Mediate	68	67	70	205	35,485
Ken Tanigawa	66	70	69	205	35,485
Doug Barron	66	72	68	206	23,634.29
Jay Haas	68	69	69	206	23,634.29
John Huston	66	71	69	206	23,634.29
Mark O'Meara	67	69	70	206	23,634.29
Chris DiMarco	68	68	70	206	23,634.28
Lee Janzen	69	67	70	206	23,634.28
Scott Parel	70	65	71	206	23,634.28
Stephen Ames	67	71	69	207	17,020.72
Colin Montgomerie	67	71	69	207	17,020.72
Jesper Parnevik	69	68	70	207	17,020.72
Paul Goydos	69	67	71	207	17,020.71
Brandt Jobe	69	70	68	207	17,020.71
Jerry Kelly	74	66	67	207	17,020.71
Vijay Singh	68	69	70	207	17,020.71

Ally Challenge

Warwick Hills Golf & Country Club, Grand Blanc, Michigan
Par 36-36–72; 7,085 yards

September 13-15
purse, $2,000,000

	SCORES			TOTAL	MONEY
Jerry Kelly	67	65	68	200	$300,000
Woody Austin	68	65	69	202	176,000
Steve Flesch	68	70	66	204	120,000
Tim Petrovic	69	68	67	204	120,000
David Toms	70	66	68	204	120,000
Retief Goosen	66	73	66	205	80,000
Tom Byrum	70	67	69	206	58,400
Tom Gillis	66	69	71	206	58,400
Bernhard Langer	68	67	71	206	58,400
Tom Lehman	69	67	70	206	58,400
Wes Short, Jr.	69	67	70	206	58,400
Fred Couples	70	70	67	207	40,666.67

	SCORES	TOTAL	MONEY
Kenny Perry	70 66 71	207	40,666.67
Jerry Smith	67 68 72	207	40,666.66
Scott McCarron	66 67 75	208	35,000
Colin Montgomerie	69 70 69	208	35,000
Stephen Ames	70 71 68	209	29,150
Marco Dawson	72 70 67	209	29,150
Chris DiMarco	70 68 71	209	29,150
Brandt Jobe	71 68 70	209	29,150
Doug Barron	70 69 71	210	22,200
Angel Cabrera	72 72 66	210	22,200
Glen Day	70 71 69	210	22,200
Lee Janzen	71 72 67	210	22,200
Mark O'Meara	70 69 71	210	22,200
Stephen Leaney	68 70 73	211	17,800
Scott Parel	76 69 66	211	17,800
Gene Sauers	69 68 74	211	17,800
Ken Tanigawa	69 72 70	211	17,800
David Frost	70 71 71	212	15,066.67
Kirk Triplett	70 70 72	212	15,066.67
Bart Bryant	72 68 72	212	15,066.66

Sanford International

Minnehaha Country Club, Sioux Falls, South Dakota
Par 34-36–70; 6,729 yards

September 20-22
purse, $1,800,000

	SCORES	TOTAL	MONEY
Rocco Mediate	69 68 64	201	$270,000
Bob Estes	70 66 67	203	132,000
Colin Montgomerie	70 66 67	203	132,000
Ken Duke	69 65 69	203	132,000
Jay Haas	73 65 66	204	79,200
Steve Flesch	71 65 68	204	79,200
Retief Goosen	70 70 65	205	45,000
Woody Austin	68 71 66	205	45,000
Tom Byrum	70 68 67	205	45,000
Scott McCarron	70 68 67	205	45,000
Esteban Toledo	72 66 67	205	45,000
Jerry Kelly	70 67 68	205	45,000
Paul Broadhurst	67 69 69	205	45,000
Kirk Triplett	66 68 71	205	45,000
Paul Goydos	69 66 70	205	45,000
Wes Short, Jr.	69 69 68	206	29,700
Stephen Ames	70 68 68	206	29,700
Michael Allen	74 69 64	207	25,380
Tom Gillis	67 71 69	207	25,380
Marco Dawson	70 66 71	207	25,380
John Huston	71 71 66	208	20,475
Duffy Waldorf	71 69 68	208	20,475
Tommy Tolles	69 70 69	208	20,475
Darren Clarke	69 69 70	208	20,475
Tom Lehman	70 71 68	209	15,686
John Daly	72 71 66	209	15,686
Tommy Armour	71 70 68	209	15,686
Tom Pernice, Jr.	70 69 70	209	15,686
David McKenzie	70 69 70	209	15,686
Jesper Parnevik	69 69 71	209	15,686

PURE Insurance Championship

Pebble Beach Golf Links: Par 36-36–72; 6,864 yards
Poppy Hills: Par 35-36–71; 6,898 yards
Monterey Peninsula, California

September 27-29
purse, $2,100,000

	SCORES			TOTAL	MONEY
Kirk Triplett	70	69	67	206	$315,000
Billy Andrade	70	67	69	206	184,800
(Triplett defeated Andrade on first playoff hole.)					
Paul Broadhurst	72	67	68	207	151,200
Tom Gillis	69	70	69	208	126,000
Marco Dawson	67	71	71	209	81,900
Tom Lehman	67	73	69	209	81,900
Billy Mayfair	71	69	69	209	81,900
Tom Byrum	68	72	69	209	81,900
Bernhard Langer	67	72	71	210	50,400
Kent Jones	68	69	73	210	50,400
Steve Flesch	68	67	75	210	50,400
Wes Short, Jr.	68	72	70	210	50,400
Lee Janzen	71	69	70	210	50,400
Vijay Singh	72	69	70	211	38,850
Woody Austin	69	71	71	211	38,850
Greg Kraft	68	72	72	212	32,602
Rod Pampling	67	74	71	212	32,602
Jerry Kelly	67	74	71	212	32,602
Colin Montgomerie	72	71	69	212	32,602
Stephen Leaney	69	70	74	213	25,305
Joey Sindelar	67	72	74	213	25,305
Esteban Toledo	69	73	71	213	25,305
Duffy Waldorf	68	74	71	213	25,305
Retief Goosen	67	75	72	214	19,200
Glen Day	71	73	70	214	19,200
Doug Barron	67	73	74	214	19,200
Scott McCarron	69	73	72	214	19,200
Gene Sauers	68	74	72	214	19,200
Tom Pernice, Jr.	72	69	73	214	19,200
Tim Petrovic	74	67	73	214	19,200

SAS Championship

Prestonwood Country Club, Cary, North Carolina
Par 35-37–72; 7,237 yards

October 11-13
purse, $2,100,000

	SCORES			TOTAL	MONEY
Jerry Kelly	68	67	65	200	$315,000
David McKenzie	69	69	63	201	184,800
David Toms	71	68	66	205	126,000
Woody Austin	67	67	71	205	126,000
Doug Barron	66	68	71	205	126,000
Chris DiMarco	70	69	67	206	79,800
Gene Sauers	69	69	68	206	79,800
Scott McCarron	73	67	67	207	57,750
Joe Durant	71	69	67	207	57,750
Stephen Ames	71	66	70	207	57,750
Retief Goosen	69	68	70	207	57,750
Gibby Gilbert	70	71	67	208	39,200
Tim Petrovic	69	71	68	208	39,200
Bob Estes	70	69	69	208	39,200
Rocco Mediate	71	68	69	208	39,200

	SCORES			TOTAL	MONEY
Jeff Maggert	73	66	69	208	39,200
Rod Pampling	69	69	70	208	39,200
Brandt Jobe	72	71	66	209	30,555
Marco Dawson	70	71	68	209	30,555
Tommy Armour	70	72	68	210	26,880
Ken Duke	71	67	72	210	26,880
Scott Parel	73	69	69	211	23,170
Glen Day	71	69	71	211	23,170
Bernhard Langer	69	69	73	211	23,170
Paul Broadhurst	75	71	66	212	20,020
Skip Kendall	72	70	70	212	20,020
Steve Flesch	73	66	73	212	20,020
Mike Goodes	75	68	70	213	15,592
Fred Couples	74	70	69	213	15,592
Bart Bryant	71	72	70	213	15,592
Jay Haas	75	67	71	213	15,592
Vijay Singh	68	74	71	213	15,592
Tom Byrum	74	71	68	213	15,592
Billy Mayfair	71	71	71	213	15,592
Jeff Sluman	76	71	66	213	15,592

Dominion Energy Charity Classic

The Country Club of Virginia, Richmond, Virginia
Par 36-36–72; 7,025 yards
(Tournament completed on Monday—rain.)

October 18-21
purse, $2,000,000

	SCORES			TOTAL	MONEY
Miguel Angel Jimenez	67	68	63	198	$305,000
Tommy Tolles	65	67	68	200	180,000
Colin Montgomerie	66	67	68	201	144,800
Woody Austin	70	68	65	203	98,000
Bernhard Langer	70	65	68	203	98,000
Scott Parel	66	66	71	203	98,000
Wes Short, Jr.	69	68	67	204	72,000
Steve Flesch	70	67	68	205	60,000
Carlos Franco	68	69	68	205	60,000
Joe Durant	71	70	65	206	50,000
Retief Goosen	67	68	71	206	50,000
Bart Bryant	70	71	66	207	42,000
Marco Dawson	68	69	70	207	42,000
Stephen Ames	73	66	69	208	36,000
Glen Day	69	70	69	208	36,000
Kirk Triplett	72	68	68	208	36,000
Ken Duke	76	67	66	209	30,000
Scott McCarron	68	70	71	209	30,000
Vijay Singh	70	69	70	209	30,000
Jay Haas	69	71	70	210	25,400
Rocco Mediate	67	70	73	210	25,400
John Daly	68	72	71	211	22,066.67
Billy Mayfair	72	72	67	211	22,066.67
Doug Garwood	72	68	71	211	22,066.66
Darren Clarke	74	69	69	212	18,240
Tom Gillis	72	70	70	212	18,240
Lee Janzen	73	69	70	212	18,240
Jeff Maggert	72	68	72	212	18,240
Kenny Perry	71	69	72	212	18,240
Jerry Kelly	74	69	70	213	14,440
Stephen Leaney	71	70	72	213	14,440
Jesper Parnevik	71	69	73	213	14,440

	SCORES			TOTAL	MONEY
Gene Sauers	69	69	75	213	14,440
Jeff Sluman	72	68	73	213	14,440

Invesco QQQ Championship

Sherwood Country Club, Thousand Oaks, California
Par 36-36–72; 7,006 yards

November 1-3
purse, $2,000,000

	SCORES			TOTAL	MONEY
Colin Montgomerie	69	70	63	202	$305,000
Bernhard Langer	70	65	67	202	180,000

(Montgomerie defeated Langer on first playoff hole.)

Retief Goosen	68	66	69	203	131,900
Tommy Tolles	68	69	66	203	131,900
Billy Andrade	70	71	64	205	84,333.34
Miguel Angel Jimenez	66	70	69	205	84,333.33
Ken Tanigawa	72	68	65	205	84,333.33
Fred Couples	70	65	72	207	60,000
Scott Parel	70	66	71	207	60,000
Doug Garwood	70	70	68	208	50,000
Jerry Kelly	72	70	66	208	50,000
Gene Sauers	67	71	70	208	50,000
Tim Petrovic	72	68	69	209	46,000
Chris DiMarco	68	72	70	210	44,000
Ken Duke	69	71	71	211	31,666.67
David McKenzie	69	73	69	211	31,666.67
Mark O'Meara	70	72	69	211	31,666.67
Kenny Perry	72	70	69	211	31,666.67
Wes Short, Jr.	72	70	69	211	31,666.67
Jeff Sluman	70	70	71	211	31,666.67
Woody Austin	66	73	72	211	31,666.66
Joe Durant	71	69	71	211	31,666.66
Steve Flesch	71	68	72	211	31,666.66
Tom Gillis	67	72	73	212	20,500
Tom Lehman	73	70	69	212	20,500
Bart Bryant	70	75	68	213	17,400
Brandt Jobe	70	69	74	213	17,400
Corey Pavin	73	67	73	213	17,400
David Toms	74	71	68	213	17,400
Kirk Triplett	68	78	67	213	17,400

Charles Schwab Cup Championship

Phoenix Country Club, Phoenix, Arizona
Par 36-35–71; 6,763 yards

November 7-10
purse, $2,500,000

	SCORES				TOTAL	MONEY
Jeff Maggert	63	65	69	66	263	$440,000
Retief Goosen	66	67	66	64	263	250,000

(Maggert defeated Goosen on third playoff hole.)

Woody Austin	67	70	64	64	265	210,000
Joe Durant	69	66	65	68	268	137,812.50
Miguel Angel Jimenez	65	70	63	70	268	137,812.50
Bernhard Langer	64	68	69	67	268	137,812.50
Colin Montgomerie	67	69	67	65	268	137,812.50
Marco Dawson	67	67	69	66	269	81,250
Kevin Sutherland	67	72	66	64	269	81,250

	SCORES				TOTAL	MONEY
Paul Goydos	65	71	67	67	270	63,750
Jerry Kelly	66	74	64	66	270	63,750
Stephen Ames	69	67	66	69	271	60,000
Brandt Jobe	67	66	71	68	272	57,500
Billy Andrade	67	70	69	67	273	52,500
Steve Flesch	65	70	69	69	273	52,500
Wes Short, Jr.	68	67	68	70	273	52,500
Doug Barron	67	72	66	69	274	46,250
David Toms	68	73	66	67	274	46,250
Tom Byrum	68	68	69	70	275	37,500
Scott Parel	66	70	70	69	275	37,500
Ken Duke	67	70	70	69	276	27,500
Tim Petrovic	69	72	68	67	276	27,500
Ken Tanigawa	70	67	70	69	276	27,500
Rocco Mediate	67	70	70	70	277	23,750
Bob Estes	70	72	69	67	278	21,875
Tom Lehman	73	68	70	67	278	21,875
Lee Janzen	66	73	68	73	280	19,375
Scott McCarron	69	71	69	71	280	19,375
Jay Haas	72	67	72	70	281	17,812.50
David McKenzie	71	73	68	69	281	17,812.50

Staysure Tour

Jordan Mixed Open
See LET section of Women's Tours chapter.

KitchenAid Senior PGA Championship
See Champions Tour section.

Senior Italian Open

Villaverde Resort, Fagagna, Italy
Par 36-36–72; 6,980 yards

May 30-June 1
purse, €300,000

	SCORES			TOTAL	MONEY
Barry Lane	69	72	67	208	€45,000
Marc Farry	72	66	70	208	30,000
(Lane defeated Farry on second playoff hole.)					
Miguel Angel Martin	70	70	69	209	15,772.50
Jose Coceres	71	67	71	209	15,772.50
Jean-Francois Remesy	71	68	70	209	15,772.50
David Shacklady	71	69	69	209	15,772.50
Phillip Price	70	71	69	210	10,200
Paul Eales	72	69	69	210	10,200
Gary Wolstenholme	68	74	69	211	7,500
Jarmo Sandelin	71	69	71	211	7,500
Paul Streeter	71	69	71	211	7,500
Roger Chapman	72	70	69	211	7,500
Gary Orr	68	72	72	212	5,255
Gary Evans	68	74	70	212	5,255
Peter O'Malley	70	71	71	212	5,255
Andre Bossert	71	69	72	212	5,255
Rafael Gomez	71	71	70	212	5,255
Jose Manuel Carriles	71	73	68	212	5,255
Santiago Luna	70	73	70	213	4,140
Mark McNulty	71	71	71	213	4,140

Senior Open Hauts de France

Arras Golf Resort, Anzin-Saint-Aubin, France
Par 36-36–72; 6,510 yards

June 7-9
purse, €200,000

	SCORES			TOTAL	MONEY
Peter Baker	66	70	67	203	€30,000
James Kingston	71	71	66	208	20,000
Markus Brier	71	69	69	209	14,000
Miguel Angel Martin	66	73	71	210	8,815
Dan Olsen	68	69	73	210	8,815
Roger Chapman	70	70	70	210	8,815
Phillip Price	72	73	65	210	8,815
Santiago Luna	71	74	66	211	5,733.33
David Gilford	73	70	68	211	5,733.33

668 / SENIOR TOURS

	SCORES			TOTAL	MONEY
Stephen Dodd	74	70	67	211	5,733.33
Jonathan Lomas	68	74	70	212	4,600
Peter O'Malley	71	75	66	212	4,600
Paul Lawrie	68	79	66	213	3,800
Chris Williams	69	73	71	213	3,800
Gary Orr	71	72	70	213	3,800
David Shacklady	69	73	72	214	3,028
Gary Wolstenholme	70	70	74	214	3,028
Mauricio Molina	70	73	71	214	3,028
Juan Quiros	72	73	69	214	3,028
Rafael Gomez	72	76	66	214	3,028

Farmfoods European Legends Links Championship

Trevose Golf & Country Club, Padstow, England
Par 36-36–72; 6,821 yards

June 21-23
purse, €200,000

	SCORES			TOTAL	MONEY
Jean-Francois Remesy	68	71	67	206	€50,000
Barry Lane	67	73	67	207	17,647
Gary Evans	71	71	67	209	12,352.90
Jarmo Sandelin	66	73	71	210	8,849.97
Peter T. Wilson	68	73	69	210	8,849.97
Peter Baker	68	73	70	211	5,717.63
Carl Suneson	69	72	70	211	5,717.63
Cesar Monasterio	69	74	68	211	5,717.63
Mauricio Molina	70	73	68	211	5,717.63
Markus Brier	75	72	64	211	5,717.63
Tim Thelen	69	78	66	213	4,058.81
Jose Manuel Carriles	71	72	70	213	4,058.81
Stuart Little	67	76	71	214	3,264.70
David Shacklady	71	72	71	214	3,264.70
Mark McNulty	71	75	68	214	3,264.70
Paul Streeter	72	74	68	214	3,264.70
Andrew Oldcorn	68	73	74	215	2,523.52
Steen Tinning	68	78	69	215	2,523.52
Santiago Luna	70	76	69	215	2,523.52

U.S. Senior Open Championship

See Champions Tour section.

Swiss Seniors Open

Golf Club Bad Ragaz, Bad Ragaz, Switzerland
Par 35-35–70; 6,157 yards

July 5-7
purse, €320,000

	SCORES			TOTAL	MONEY
Jose Coceres	65	68	66	199	€48,000
Peter O'Malley	66	65	70	201	19,859.20
Peter Baker	66	67	68	201	19,859.20
Phillip Price	66	67	68	201	19,859.20
Chris Williams	68	67	66	201	19,859.20
Jean-Francois Remesy	71	66	64	201	19,859.20
Andrew Oldcorn	67	65	70	202	10,880
Rafael Gomez	70	68	64	202	10,880

	SCORES			TOTAL	MONEY
Ian Woosnam	66	72	65	203	8,320
Bob May	68	70	65	203	8,320
Roger Chapman	69	66	68	203	8,320
Clark Dennis	64	69	71	204	6,506.67
Simon P. Brown	67	67	70	204	6,506.67
Marc Farry	69	68	67	204	6,506.67
Magnus P. Atlevi	67	67	71	205	5,440
Mauricio Molina	67	70	68	205	5,440
Paul Eales	68	69	68	205	5,440
Miguel Angel Martin	68	69	69	206	4,554.67
Bill Longmuir	70	68	68	206	4,554.67
Tim Thelen	73	67	66	206	4,554.67

Bridgestone Senior Players Championship

See Champions Tour section.

European Tour Destinations Senior Classic

PGA Catalunya Resort, Girona, Spain
Par 36-36–72; 7,172 yards

July 12-14
purse, €250,000

	SCORES			TOTAL	MONEY
Jose Manuel Carriles	70	66	67	203	€37,500
Chris Williams	69	66	71	206	25,000
David Shacklady	67	71	69	207	14,191.67
Greg Turner	69	69	69	207	14,191.67
Mauricio Molina	72	67	68	207	14,191.67
Gary Wolstenholme	70	70	68	208	10,000
Paul Streeter	72	67	70	209	9,000
Santiago Luna	70	71	69	210	7,500
Philip Golding	71	73	66	210	7,500
James Kingston	71	69	71	211	6,000
Clark Dennis	72	71	68	211	6,000
Simon P. Brown	74	70	67	211	6,000
Magnus P. Atlevi	71	74	67	212	4,750
Peter O'Malley	72	70	70	212	4,750
Dan Olsen	72	73	67	212	4,750
Gary Evans	70	74	69	213	3,893.75
Barry Lane	72	68	73	213	3,893.75
Jonathan Lomas	73	68	72	213	3,893.75
Bob May	75	70	68	213	3,893.75
Steen Tinning	71	69	74	214	3,125
Jarmo Sandelin	72	68	74	214	3,125
Paul McGinley	72	69	73	214	3,125
Jose Coceres	72	71	71	214	3,125

WINSTONgolf Senior Open

WINSTONopen Course, Vorbeck, Germany
Par 36-36–72; 6,762 yards

July 19-21
purse, €350,000

	SCORES			TOTAL	MONEY
Clark Dennis	70	68	63	201	€52,500
Jose Maria Olazabal	66	66	70	202	35,000
James Kingston	69	69	66	204	24,500

	SCORES			TOTAL	MONEY
Jamie Spence	67	69	69	205	17,552.50
Bernhard Langer	68	68	69	205	17,552.50
Thaworn Wiratchant	66	71	71	208	12,600
Phillip Price	70	66	72	208	12,600
Andre Bossert	71	68	69	208	12,600
Peter Baker	66	72	71	209	8,400
Dan Olsen	66	76	67	209	8,400
Gary Wolstenholme	67	68	74	209	8,400
Magnus P. Atlevi	69	70	70	209	8,400
Jose Manuel Carriles	70	75	64	209	8,400
Philip Golding	70	69	71	210	6,650
Esteban Toledo	64	74	73	211	5,950
David Shacklady	68	71	72	211	5,950
Santiago Luna	70	71	70	211	5,950
Gary Orr	67	75	70	212	4,739
Steen Tinning	69	73	70	212	4,739
Gary Evans	71	71	70	212	4,739
Paul Streeter	71	72	69	212	4,739
Peter Fowler	71	72	69	212	4,739

The Senior Open Championship presented by Rolex

Royal Lytham & St. Annes, Lancashire, England
Par 34-36–70; 6,948 yards

July 25-28
purse, US$2,000,000

	SCORES				TOTAL	MONEY
Bernhard Langer	71	67	70	66	274	€281,632.47
Paul Broadhurst	67	71	67	71	276	187,787.83
Retief Goosen	70	67	74	66	277	95,085.57
Tim Petrovic	74	68	67	68	277	95,085.57
Doug Barron	69	69	73	67	278	65,370.49
David McKenzie	70	70	68	70	278	65,370.49
Wes Short, Jr.	67	67	73	72	279	43,577.34
Woody Austin	68	70	68	73	279	43,577.34
David Frost	72	67	73	67	279	43,577.34
Darren Clarke	68	68	73	71	280	28,601.08
Ken Duke	68	69	70	73	280	28,601.08
Roger Chapman	70	68	73	69	280	28,601.08
Bob Estes	70	71	74	65	280	28,601.08
Miguel Angel Jimenez	71	68	74	67	280	28,601.08
Thomas Levet	74	68	71	67	280	28,601.08
Paul Lawrie	70	69	72	70	281	23,178.93
Miguel Angel Martin	70	75	70	66	281	23,178.93
Colin Montgomerie	68	70	73	71	282	20,228.18
Bart Bryant	69	68	73	72	282	20,228.18
Stephen Dodd	71	68	69	74	282	20,228.18
Mauricio Molina	72	69	69	72	282	20,228.18
Stephen Leaney	73	66	73	70	282	20,228.18
Mark McNulty	73	67	73	69	282	20,228.18
Scott Parel	67	71	76	69	283	17,059.40
Magnus P. Atlevi	68	73	70	72	283	17,059.40
Dan Olsen	70	72	70	71	283	17,059.40
Billy Andrade	73	71	72	67	283	17,059.40
Paul Eales	74	69	66	74	283	17,059.40
Scott Dunlap	67	68	75	74	284	13,960.60
Tom Gillis	68	73	73	70	284	13,960.60
Jarmo Sandelin	70	75	69	70	284	13,960.60
Jerry Kelly	73	66	71	74	284	13,960.60
Billy Mayfair	73	69	72	70	284	13,960.60
Stephen Ames	74	69	71	70	284	13,960.60

	SCORES				TOTAL	MONEY
Thaworn Wiratchant	74	71	69	70	284	13,960.60
Tom Lehman	70	70	74	71	285	11,483.44
Phillip Price	71	67	70	77	285	11,483.44
Esteban Toledo	71	70	74	70	285	11,483.44
Ian Woosnam	72	72	69	72	285	11,483.44
Jeff Sluman	73	70	70	72	285	11,483.44
Dudley Hart	74	69	72	70	285	11,483.44
Peter Scott	70	75	72	69	286	9,866.95
Seiki Okuda	72	72	69	73	286	9,866.95
Jean-Francois Remesy	74	68	77	67	286	9,866.95
Chris DiMarco	76	66	74	70	286	9,866.95
Fred Funk	69	72	72	74	287	7,007.18
Peter Baker	69	73	71	74	287	7,007.18
Paul Archbold	70	70	75	72	287	7,007.18
Dicky Pride	71	68	74	74	287	7,007.18
Clark Dennis	72	69	77	69	287	7,007.18
Paul Streeter	72	71	72	72	287	7,007.18
Prayad Marksaeng	72	73	69	73	287	7,007.18
Paul McGinley	73	69	72	73	287	7,007.18
Barry Lane	73	69	74	71	287	7,007.18
Dennis Edlund	73	70	71	73	287	7,007.18
Joe Durant	73	71	71	72	287	7,007.18
Gary Wolstenholme	74	69	73	71	287	7,007.18
Gary Orr	74	70	76	67	287	7,007.18
James Kingston	75	70	71	71	287	7,007.18
Simon P. Brown	71	70	74	73	288	4,569.48
Shaun Micheel	71	72	67	78	288	4,569.48
Fred Couples	73	67	75	73	288	4,569.48
Tom Pernice	73	71	70	74	288	4,569.48
Glen Day	72	69	75	73	289	3,933.34
Gibby Gilbert	72	71	74	72	289	3,933.34
Tom Watson	74	70	72	73	289	3,933.34
Jamie Spence	71	73	76	70	290	3,431.59
Peter Fowler	72	70	77	71	290	3,431.59
Michael Clark	74	69	75	72	290	3,431.59
Dennis Hendershott	71	74	71	75	291	3,068.72
Peter O'Malley	72	70	74	75	291	3,068.72
David Morland	71	70	77	74	292	2,867.13
David Gilford	73	72	73	75	293	2,665.53
Andrew Oldcorn	74	71	71	77	293	2,665.53
Gene Elliott [A]	75	68	76	74	293	
Ken Tanigawa	74	71	71	81	297	2,463.94
Steven Kelbrick [A]	76	69	78	74	297	
Andre Bossert	72	67	78	81	298	2,329.54
Bob May	72	72	78	77	299	2,127.95
Mike Goodes	74	71	77	77	299	2,127.95

Staysure PGA Seniors Championship

London Golf Club, Ash, Kent, England
Par 36-36–72; 6,855 yards

August 1-4
purse, £400,000

	SCORES				TOTAL	MONEY
Phillip Price	67	66	71	67	271	€65,556
Michael Campbell	68	71	67	67	273	32,405.15
Peter Lonard	69	64	71	69	273	32,405.15
James Kingston	70	69	64	70	273	32,405.15
David McKenzie	65	69	68	72	274	17,282.75
Peter Fowler	67	73	64	71	275	16,306.40
Clark Dennis	70	66	73	66	275	16,306.40

	SCORES				TOTAL	MONEY
Thaworn Wiratchant	74	67	65	70	276	13,826.20
Chris Williams	66	73	70	68	277	11,233.79
Magnus P. Atlevi	67	70	71	69	277	11,233.79
Paul McGinley	69	69	67	72	277	11,233.79
Miguel Angel Martin	69	68	70	71	278	8,785.40
Colin Montgomerie	70	69	71	68	278	8,785.40
Tim Milford	71	65	71	71	278	8,785.40
Rafael Gomez	71	72	69	67	279	7,777.24
Jose Coceres	70	70	71	69	280	6,927.50
Barry Lane	72	67	68	73	280	6,927.50
Thomas Levet	73	66	70	71	280	6,927.50
Roger Chapman	70	72	69	70	281	5,818.52
Mauricio Molina	71	69	71	70	281	5,818.52
Gary Evans	73	72	66	70	281	5,818.52

Scottish Senior Open

Craigielaw Golf Club, Craigielaw, Longniddry, Scotland
Par 35-36–71; 6,601 yards

August 16-18
purse, £250,000

	SCORES			TOTAL	MONEY
Paul Lawrie	68	72	71	211	€40,833.75
Peter Baker	71	72	70	213	23,139.13
Peter Fowler	72	66	75	213	23,139.13
Markus Brier	70	71	73	214	13,652.08
David Shacklady	73	72	69	214	13,652.08
Phillip Price	72	71	72	215	10,344.55
Jean-Francois Remesy	74	70	71	215	10,344.55
Andrew Oldcorn	71	73	72	216	7,803.78
Ian Woosnam	72	72	72	216	7,803.78
Gary Evans	73	74	69	216	7,803.78
Paul Eales	71	70	76	217	5,444.50
Marc Farry	71	74	72	217	5,444.50
Roger Chapman	71	74	72	217	5,444.50
Jamie Spence	72	72	73	217	5,444.50
Jarmo Sandelin	72	77	68	217	5,444.50
Des Smyth	73	74	70	217	5,444.50
Paul Wesselingh	70	73	75	218	3,617.19
Rafael Gomez	70	73	75	218	3,617.19
Bill Longmuir	70	75	73	218	3,617.19
Barry Lane	70	76	72	218	3,617.19
Simon P. Brown	70	77	71	218	3,617.19
Magnus P. Atlevi	71	72	75	218	3,617.19
Philip Golding	74	74	70	218	3,617.19
Mauricio Molina	75	70	73	218	3,617.19

The Sinclair Invitational

Hanbury Manor Marriott Hotel & Country Club,
Ware, Hertfordshire, England
Par 36-36–72; 6,892 yards

August 30-September 1
purse, £400,000

	SCORES			TOTAL	MONEY
David Shacklady	68	71	66	205	€66,168
Markus Brier	69	69	68	206	44,112
Paul Streeter	68	68	71	207	30,878.40
Phillip Price	67	68	73	208	24,261.60

	SCORES			TOTAL	MONEY
Magnus P. Atlevi	68	67	74	209	19,982.74
Andrew Oldcorn	69	73	68	210	17,644.80
Stephen Dodd	67	69	75	211	14,115.84
Paul Lawrie	69	73	69	211	14,115.84
Mauricio Molina	70	69	72	211	14,115.84
Bob May	67	70	75	212	10,586.88
James Kingston	70	70	72	212	10,586.88
Jose Manuel Carriles	72	68	72	212	10,586.88
Gary Evans	66	70	77	213	8,381.28
Peter Fowler	69	75	69	213	8,381.28
Philip Golding	73	70	70	213	8,381.28
Jarmo Sandelin	70	71	73	214	7,072.62
Rafael Gomez	70	75	69	214	7,072.62
Joakim Haeggman	72	69	73	214	7,072.62
Thomas Levet	72	70	73	215	5,663.98
Steen Tinning	73	67	75	215	5,663.98
Peter Baker	73	69	73	215	5,663.98
Barry Lane	73	72	70	215	5,663.98
Jose Coceres	74	69	72	215	5,663.98

Paris Legends Championship

Racing Club de France la Boulie, Paris, France
Par 36-36–72; 6,470 yards

September 19-21
purse, €200,000

	SCORES			TOTAL	MONEY
David Shacklady	69	66	68	203	€30,000
Jean-Francois Remesy	70	66	67	203	20,000

(Shacklady defeated Remesy on first playoff hole.)

James Kingston	68	67	70	205	14,000
Peter Baker	69	69	68	206	11,000
Magnus P. Atlevi	70	69	69	208	8,530
Markus Brier	74	68	66	208	8,530
Jose Manuel Carriles	71	69	69	209	6,400
Thomas Levet	67	71	71	209	6,400
Phillip Price	69	73	67	209	6,400
Jose Coceres	70	70	70	210	4,800
Joakim Haeggman	68	72	70	210	4,800
Paul Streeter	71	71	68	210	4,800
Roger Chapman	70	67	74	211	3,800
Stephen Dodd	71	71	69	211	3,800
Chris Williams	73	71	67	211	3,800
Mark Davis	74	66	73	213	2,950
Peter Fowler	75	74	64	213	2,950
Santiago Luna	72	71	70	213	2,950
Miguel Angel Martin	72	74	67	213	2,950
Gary Orr	73	71	69	213	2,950
Paul Wesselingh	70	72	71	213	2,950

Murhof Legends – Austrian Senior Open

Golfclub Murhof, Frohnleiten, Austria
Par 36-36–72; 6,701 yards

September 27-29
purse, €250,000

	SCORES			TOTAL	MONEY
Jose Coceres	66	62	69	197	€37,276.34
Paul Lawrie	70	66	65	201	24,850.89
Phillip Price	67	67	68	202	17,395.62
Philip Golding	67	70	66	203	13,667.99
Stephen Dodd	64	71	69	204	10,598.91
Barry Lane	67	70	67	204	10,598.91
Gary Evans	65	74	66	205	7,952.29
Jarmo Sandelin	66	70	69	205	7,952.29
Miguel Angel Martin	68	68	69	205	7,952.29
Rafael Gomez	66	68	72	206	6,212.72
Peter Fowler	69	71	66	206	6,212.72
Mauricio Molina	67	72	68	207	4,908.05
David Gilford	68	70	69	207	4,908.05
James Kingston	69	67	71	207	4,908.05
Magnus P Atlevi	71	68	68	207	4,908.05
David Shacklady	68	70	70	208	3,984.42
Paul Wesselingh	68	73	67	208	3,984.42
Clark Dennis	71	69	68	208	3,984.42
Marc Farry	70	71	68	209	3,528.83
Jean-Francois Remesy	67	73	70	210	3,255.47
Juan Quiros	70	72	68	210	3,255.47

Farmfoods European Senior Masters

Forest of Arden Hotel & Country Club, Coventry, England
Par 36-36–72; 6,958 yards

October 4-6
purse, €200,000

	SCORES			TOTAL	MONEY
Thomas Levet	69	69	68	206	€50,000
Markus Brier	68	70	69	207	17,647
Jarmo Sandelin	68	71	69	208	10,017.61
Paul Lawrie	69	69	70	208	10,017.61
Ian Woosnam	70	68	70	208	10,017.61
Paul Broadhurst	69	68	72	209	7,058.80
James Kingston	71	69	70	210	6,352.92
Jose Manuel Carriles	70	70	71	211	5,647.04
Stephen Dodd	68	71	73	212	4,941.16
Peter Baker	66	74	73	213	3,917.63
Dan Olsen	67	74	72	213	3,917.63
David Shacklady	68	71	74	213	3,917.63
Peter Fowler	70	68	75	213	3,917.63
Gary Marks	71	71	71	213	3,917.63
Mauricio Molina	68	70	76	214	2,999.99
Carl Suneson	72	70	72	214	2,999.99
Jonathan Lomas	72	71	71	214	2,999.99
Phillip Price	69	73	73	215	2,585.28
Joakim Haeggman	74	70	71	215	2,585.28
Rafael Gomez	69	72	75	216	2,152.93
Chris Williams	70	71	75	216	2,152.93
Andre Bossert	72	71	73	216	2,152.93
Paul Streeter	75	68	73	216	2,152.93
Peter Wilson	76	69	71	216	2,152.93

MCB Tour Championship - Madagascar

International Golf Club Du Rova, Andakana, Madagascar
Par 36-35–71; 6,202 yards

November 29-December 1
purse, €275,000

	SCORES			TOTAL	MONEY
Barry Lane	70	71	69	210	€42,212.44
Juan Quiros	70	72	69	211	23,920.38
Jean-Francois Remesy	74	68	69	211	23,920.38
Gary Evans	68	73	71	212	13,160.90
Stephen Dodd	69	72	71	212	13,160.90
Clark Dennis	72	65	75	212	13,160.90
Jean Baptiste Ramarozatovo	69	75	69	213	8,217.36
Peter Wilson	71	71	71	213	8,217.36
Chris Williams	74	69	70	213	8,217.36
Mauricio Molina	74	70	69	213	8,217.36
James Kingston	74	73	66	213	8,217.36
Mark Mouland	72	72	70	214	6,191.16
Miguel Angel Martin	72	71	72	215	5,487.62
David Shacklady	74	72	69	215	5,487.62
Jose Manuel Carriles	69	72	75	216	4,784.08
Paul Eales	73	70	73	216	4,784.08
Cesar Monasterio	74	72	70	216	4,784.08
Stuart Little	72	73	72	217	4,122.75
Phillip Price	73	74	70	217	4,122.75
Gary Wolstenholme	70	73	75	218	3,686.55
Peter Fowler	77	70	71	218	3,686.55

MCB Tour Championship - Seychelles

Constance Lemuria, Praslin, Seychelles
Par 34-36–70; 6,135 yards

December 5-7
purse, US$350,000

	SCORES			TOTAL	MONEY
Peter Fowler	70	69	67	206	€48,370.34
James Kingston	69	66	72	207	32,246.89
Mauricio Molina	70	68	70	208	18,305.48
Phillip Price	71	68	69	208	18,305.48
Paul Eales	72	67	69	208	18,305.48
Joakim Haeggman	68	75	66	209	10,963.94
Miguel Angel Martin	71	67	71	209	10,963.94
Simon P. Brown	72	68	69	209	10,963.94
Peter Baker	73	66	70	209	10,963.94
Dan Olsen	69	74	67	210	8,061.72
Paul McGinley	72	70	68	210	8,061.72
Peter Wilson	69	67	75	211	6,771.85
Jonathan Lomas	72	69	70	211	6,771.85
Rafael Gomez	68	75	69	212	5,965.67
Andre Bossert	70	70	72	212	5,965.67
Magnus P. Atlevi	69	70	74	213	5,022.45
Cesar Monasterio	70	70	73	213	5,022.45
Paul Streeter	70	70	73	213	5,022.45
Santiago Luna	70	72	71	213	5,022.45
David Frost	68	73	73	214	4,030.86
Mark Mouland	69	72	73	214	4,030.86
Chris Williams	71	76	67	214	4,030.86
Jean-Francois Remesy	72	76	66	214	4,030.86

MCB Tour Championship - Mauritius

Constance Belle Mare Plage, Poste de Flacq, Mauritius
Par 36-36–72; 6,609 yards

December 13-15
purse, €400,000

	SCORES			TOTAL	MONEY
Jarmo Sandelin	69	70	65	204	€61,400
James Kingston	68	67	72	207	40,935
Jean-Francois Remesy	66	69	73	208	23,235.85
Clark Dennis	68	71	69	208	23,235.85
Phillip Price	71	68	69	208	23,235.85
Carl Suneson	70	72	67	209	16,373.31
Miguel Angel Martin	68	70	72	210	12,484.65
Paul Lawrie	68	74	68	210	12,484.65
Steen Tinning	69	69	72	210	12,484.65
David Shacklady	69	69	72	210	12,484.65
Tim Thelen	69	71	71	211	8,698.32
Jose Coceres	70	70	71	211	8,698.32
Peter Fowler	71	69	71	211	8,698.32
David Frost	72	70	69	211	8,698.32
Stephen Dodd	69	74	69	212	6,764.23
Peter Wilson	70	71	71	212	6,764.23
Mark Mouland	73	69	70	212	6,764.23
Cesar Monasterio	73	69	70	212	6,764.23
Stuart Little	69	76	68	213	5,382.73
Roger Chapman	70	71	72	213	5,382.73
Paul Streeter	71	73	69	213	5,382.73
Barry Lane	75	69	69	213	5,382.73

Japan PGA Senior Tour

Kanehide Senior Okinawa Open

Kanehide Kise Country Club, Kise, Okinawa
Par 36-36–72; 7,217 yards

April 12-13
purse, ¥27,000,000

	SCORES		TOTAL	MONEY
Taichi Teshima	67	68	135	¥4,500,000
Masayuki Kawamura	68	68	136	2,250,000
Thaworn Wiratchant	68	69	137	1,500,000
Masahiro Kuramoto	66	72	138	1,250,000
Yoshinori Mizumaki	73	67	140	983,333
Shinichi Akiba	72	68	140	983,333
Akio Nishizawa	67	73	140	983,333
Naoyuki Tamura	73	68	141	675,000
Yutaka Hagawa	72	69	141	675,000
Chien-Soon Lu	72	69	141	675,000
Wen-Teh Lu	73	69	142	475,000
Tsutomu Higa	73	69	142	475,000
Jong-Duck Kim	72	70	142	475,000
Masayoshi Yamazoe	75	68	143	339,375
Takeshi Sakiyama	73	70	143	339,375
Ken Hayano	73	70	143	339,375
Kohki Idoki	73	70	143	339,375
Shigehiko Washio	73	70	143	339,375
Katsumi Kubo	72	71	143	339,375
Masayoshi Nakayama	72	71	143	339,375
Gregory Meyer	70	73	143	339,375

Nojima Champion Cup Hakone Senior

Hakone Country Club, Kanagawa
Par 36-36–72; 7,056 yards

April 18-19
purse, ¥50,000,000

	SCORES		TOTAL	MONEY
Shinichi Akiba	68	67	135	¥10,000,000
Katsunori Kuwabara	67	69	136	5,000,000
Gregory Meyer	69	68	137	2,433,333
Shoichi Kuwabara	69	68	137	2,433,333
Jong-Duck Kim	67	70	137	2,433,333
Masayoshi Nakayama	71	67	138	1,340,000
Suk Joug Yul	69	69	138	1,340,000
Kiyoshi Murota	69	69	138	1,340,000
Takeshi Sakiyama	68	70	138	1,340,000
Masami Ito	62	76	138	1,340,000
Hiroshi Tominaga	73	67	140	892,500
Seiki Okuda	72	68	140	892,500
Kohki Idoki	71	69	140	892,500
Katsumi Kubo	70	70	140	892,500
Thaworn Wiratchant	70	70	140	892,500
Toru Suzuki	68	72	140	892,500
Yoshinori Mizumaki	73	68	141	610,000
Masayuki Kawamura	72	69	141	610,000

	SCORES		TOTAL	MONEY
Wen-Teh Lu	72	69	141	610,000
Chien-Soon Lu	70	71	141	610,000
Kazuhiro Takami	70	71	141	610,000
Hiroo Okamo	67	74	141	610,000

Fubon Yeangder Senior Cup

Linkou International Golf Club, Chinse Taipei
Par 36-36–72
(Tournament reduced to 36 holes—rain.)

April 26-28
purse, ¥40,000,000

	SCORES		TOTAL	MONEY
Eiji Mizoguchi	72	66	138	¥7,200,000
Takeshi Sakiyama	67	71	138	3,600,000
(Mizoguchi defeated Sakiyama on second playoff hole.)				
Chun-Hsing Chung	72	67	139	1,752,000
Kiyoshi Murota	72	67	139	1,752,000
Masayuki Kawamura	71	68	139	1,752,000
Chi Huang Tsai	69	70	139	1,752,000
Hiroshi Tominaga	69	70	139	1,752,000
Prayad Marksaeng	64	76	140	1,080,000
Wen-Teh Lu	70	71	141	880,000
Keiichiro Fukabori	70	71	141	880,000
Kazuhiro Takami	69	72	141	880,000
Masahiro Kuramoto	73	69	142	720,000
Chin-Sheng Hsieh	72	70	142	720,000
Jong-Duck Kim	69	73	142	720,000
Shinsuke Yanagisawa	77	66	143	541,333
Richard Backwell	76	67	143	541,333
Yuji Igarashi	73	70	143	541,333
Masayoshi Nakayama	72	71	143	541,333
Hideki Kase	69	74	143	541,333
Seiki Okuda	68	75	143	541,333

Sumaiida Cup

Eastwood Country Club, Tochigi
Par 36-36–72

May 30-June 1
purse, ¥50,000,000

	SCORES			TOTAL	MONEY
Masayoshi Yamazoe	68	69	65	202	¥10,000,000
Suk Joug Yul	68	68	67	203	4,750,000
Chien-Soon Lu	67	71	66	204	2,466,666
Prayad Marksaeng	71	64	69	204	2,466,666
Masahiro Kuramoto	69	65	70	204	2,466,666
Shintaro Iizuka	72	67	66	205	1,350,000
Tsuyoshi Yoneyama	68	71	66	205	1,350,000
Toshimitsu Izawa	67	70	68	205	1,350,000
Hiroshi Tominaga	66	70	69	205	1,350,000
Seiki Okuda	71	70	65	206	903,571
Kiyoshi Maita	74	65	67	206	903,571
Keiichiro Fukabori	72	67	67	206	903,571
Katsumi Kubo	69	70	67	206	903,571
Shinichi Akiba	69	66	71	206	903,571
Jong-Duck Kim	68	67	71	206	903,571
David Ishii	67	66	73	206	903,571
Wen-Teh Lu	72	68	67	207	609,000

	SCORES			TOTAL	MONEY
Akira Teranishi	70	69	68	207	609,000
Shoichi Kuwabara	70	69	68	207	609,000
Shinsuke Yanagisawa	68	71	68	207	609,000
Hidezumi Shirakata	71	65	71	207	609,000

Starts Senior

Starts Kasama Golf Club, Ibaraki
Par 36-36–72; 7,101 yards

June 14-16
purse, ¥60,000,000

	SCORES			TOTAL	MONEY
Masahiro Kuramoto	70	71	64	205	¥14,000,000
Toru Taniguchi	67	70	68	205	6,750,000
(Kuramoto defeated Taniguchi on first playoff hole.)					
Chien-Soon Lu	71	69	66	206	3,260,000
Prayad Marksaeng	65	71	70	206	3,260,000
Toru Suzuki	70	69	69	208	1,890,000
Kiyoshi Murota	73	70	66	209	1,674,000
Masami Ito	71	69	70	210	1,485,000
Thaworn Wiratchant	69	75	67	211	1,155,250
Taichi Teshima	68	76	67	211	1,155,250
Shinsuke Yanagisawa	71	72	68	211	1,155,250
Shinichi Akiba	68	75	68	211	1,155,250
Ikuo Shirahama	72	72	68	212	950,000
Eiji Mizoguchi	69	74	69	212	950,000
Katsunori Kuwabara	71	75	67	213	842,000
Hideki Kase	69	73	71	213	842,000
Jong-Duck Kim	74	73	67	214	642,571
Shoichi Kuwabara	71	75	68	214	642,571
Hiroshi Tominaga	72	73	69	214	642,571
Tsuneyuki Nakajima	71	73	70	214	642,571
Gregory Meyer	70	74	70	214	642,571
Suk Joug Yul	72	71	71	214	642,571
Hidezumi Shirakata	71	71	72	214	642,571

Kumamoto Aso Senior Open

Kosugi Resort Aso Highland Golf Club, Kumamoto
Par 36-36–72

August 3-4
purse, ¥20,000,000

	SCORES		TOTAL	MONEY
Gregory Meyer	64	68	132	¥3,600,000
Hidezumi Shirakata	68	65	133	1,500,000
Suk Joug Yul	67	66	133	1,500,000
Kiyoshi Murota	68	66	134	850,000
Jong-Duck Kim	67	67	134	850,000
Shinichi Akiba	70	66	136	660,000
Satoshi Higashi	70	66	136	660,000
Akira Teranishi	69	67	136	660,000
Hideki Kase	73	64	137	440,000
Masayoshi Yamazoe	71	66	137	440,000
Prayad Marksaeng	70	67	137	440,000
Takeshi Nakashima	69	68	137	440,000
Ryoken Kawagishi	69	68	137	440,000
Masami Ito	68	69	137	440,000
Katsunori Kuwabara	73	65	138	288,000
Kohki Idoki	71	67	138	288,000

	SCORES	TOTAL	MONEY
Yoshinori Mizumaki	70 68	138	288,000
Ikuo Shirahama	68 70	138	288,000
Yoshihiro Hori	68 70	138	288,000
Wen-Teh Lu	72 67	139	217,200
Tsuyoshi Yoneyama	71 68	139	217,200
Toru Suzuki	71 68	139	217,200
Takeshi Sakiyama	69 70	139	217,200
Yoichi Shimizu	68 71	139	217,200

Fancl Classic

Susono Country Club, Susono, Shizuoka
Par 36-36–72; 7,009 yards

August 23-25
purse, ¥72,000,000

	SCORES	TOTAL	MONEY
Prayad Marksaeng	68 67 72	207	¥15,000,000
Naoyuki Tamura	72 69 66	207	5,100,000
Suk Joug Yul	70 66 71	207	5,100,000

(Marksaeng defeated Yul on first and Tamura on third playoff hole.)

Kiyoshi Maita	71 70 67	208	1,950,000
Takeshi Sakiyama	72 68 68	208	1,950,000
Thaworn Wiratchant	71 69 68	208	1,950,000
Toshimitsu Izawa	67 69 72	208	1,950,000
Toru Suzuki	76 67 67	210	1,260,000
Akira Teranishi	69 70 71	210	1,260,000
Takeshi Nakashima	74 74 63	211	990,000
Seiki Okuda	70 74 67	211	990,000
Shinichi Akiba	72 71 68	211	990,000
Tsuyoshi Yoneyama	72 69 70	211	990,000
Satoshi Higashi	71 73 68	212	810,000
Kiyoshi Murota	71 72 69	212	810,000
Daisuke Serizawa	76 70 67	213	702,750
Taku Yamanaka	72 72 69	213	702,750
Keiichiro Fukabori	70 73 70	213	702,750
Hiroshi Tominaga	72 69 72	213	702,750
Yutaka Hagawa	77 68 69	214	595,200
Wen-Teh Lu	72 71 71	214	595,200
Masami Ito	72 71 71	214	595,200
Gregory Meyer	67 76 71	214	595,200
Mitsutaka Kusakabe	72 69 73	214	595,200

Hiroshima Senior

Hiroshima Country Club, Saijo Course, Hiroshima
Par 36-36–71

August 29-30
purse, ¥20,000,000

	SCORES	TOTAL	MONEY
Shinsuke Yanagisawa	67 65	132	¥3,600,000
Chien-Soon Lu	68 65	133	1,800,000
Wen-Teh Lu	70 64	134	1,050,000
Seiki Okuda	69 65	134	1,050,000
Yoshinobu Tsukada	68 67	135	695,000
Masayoshi Nakayama	68 67	135	695,000
Mitsutaka Kusakabe	65 70	135	695,000
Kiyoshi Murota	65 70	135	695,000
Yoshikatsu Saito	69 67	136	440,000
Kazuo Seike	68 68	136	440,000

	SCORES		TOTAL	MONEY
Jong-Duck Kim	67	69	136	440,000
Takeshi Sakiyama	67	69	136	440,000
Keiichiro Fukabori	67	69	136	440,000
Toru Suzuki	65	71	136	440,000
Katsumi Kubo	71	66	137	272,571
Gregory Meyer	70	67	137	272,571
Naoyuki Tamura	68	69	137	272,571
Masahiro Kuramoto	68	69	137	272,571
Akira Teranishi	67	70	137	272,571
Kohki Idoki	66	71	137	272,571
Tsuyoshi Yoneyama	66	71	137	272,571

Maruhan Cup Taiheiyo Club Senior

Taiheiyo Club, Rokko Course, Hyogo
Par 36-36–72; 6,915 yards

September 7-8
purse, ¥50,000,000

	SCORES		TOTAL	MONEY
Prayad Marksaeng	68	66	134	¥10,000,000
Hidezumi Shirakata	69	66	135	5,000,000
Katsunori Kuwabara	69	68	137	3,100,000
Nobumitsu Yuhara	70	68	138	2,100,000
Gregory Meyer	70	68	138	2,100,000
Toshimitsu Izawa	72	67	139	1,393,750
Chien-Soon Lu	70	69	139	1,393,750
Akira Teranishi	70	69	139	1,393,750
Wen-Teh Lu	70	69	139	1,393,750
Masahiro Kuramoto	72	68	140	956,250
Yoshinori Mizumaki	72	68	140	956,250
Masayoshi Yamazoe	71	69	140	956,250
Thaworn Wiratchant	71	69	140	956,250
Kiyoshi Maita	70	70	140	956,250
Shinichi Akiba	69	71	140	956,250
Naoyuki Tamura	74	67	141	628,928
Eiji Mizoguchi	73	68	141	628,928
Masami Ito	72	69	141	628,928
Katsumi Kubo	70	71	141	628,928
Yuji Igarashi	70	71	141	628,928
Yutaka Hagawa	69	72	141	628,928
Nobuo Serizawa	67	74	141	628,928

Komatsu Open

Komatsu Country Club, Komatsu, Ishikawa
Par 36-36–72; 6,917 yards

September 12-14
purse, ¥60,000,000

	SCORES			TOTAL	MONEY
Thaworn Wiratchant	69	68	65	202	¥12,000,000
Prayad Marksaeng	65	69	68	202	5,700,000

(Wiratchant defeated Marksaeng on first playoff hole.)

	SCORES			TOTAL	MONEY
Gregory Meyer	68	67	68	203	4,020,000
Ikuo Shirahama	68	70	66	204	2,730,000
Akira Teranishi	71	68	66	205	1,729,000
Hisashi Sawada	70	69	66	205	1,729,000
Yoshinobu Tsukada	69	66	70	205	1,729,000
Yuji Igarashi	69	66	70	205	1,729,000
Hiroshi Tominaga	67	67	71	205	1,729,000

	SCORES	TOTAL	MONEY
Chien-Soon Lu	68 65 72	205	1,729,000
Eiji Mizoguchi	69 70 67	206	1,221,000
Hiroo Okamo	69 67 70	206	1,221,000
Kazuhiro Takami	74 69 64	207	878,250
Kiyoshi Murota	71 70 66	207	878,250
Ryoken Kawagishi	71 69 67	207	878,250
Masahiro Kuramoto	70 69 68	207	878,250
Seiki Okuda	68 71 68	207	878,250
Tsuyoshi Yoneyama	70 68 69	207	878,250
Masayoshi Yamazoe	72 65 70	207	878,250
Takeshi Oyama	70 67 70	207	878,250

Japan Senior Open Championship

Hidaka Country Club, East-West Course, Saitama
Par 36-36–72; 6,977 yards

September 19-22
purse, ¥80,000,000

	SCORES	TOTAL	MONEY
Toru Taniguchi	66 70 72 72	280	¥16,000,000
Thaworn Wiratchant	68 71 71 71	281	8,800,000
Barry Lane	73 71 70 71	285	6,160,000
Naoyuki Tamura	74 66 74 72	286	4,000,000
Boo Won Park	68 78 69 72	287	2,660,000
Masahiro Kuramoto	71 71 73 72	287	2,660,000
Masami Ito	71 75 67 74	287	2,660,000
Gregory Meyer	71 71 71 74	287	2,660,000
Wen-Teh Lu	73 72 72 71	288	1,760,000
Toru Suzuki	73 71 75 70	289	1,394,666
Keiichiro Fukabori	74 72 72 71	289	1,394,666
Masayoshi Nakayama	69 77 71 72	289	1,394,666
Taichi Teshima	71 77 70 72	290	982,000
Katsumi Kubo	74 72 72 72	290	982,000
Yutaka Hagawa	71 74 72 73	290	982,000
Masayoshi Yamazoe	73 71 73 73	290	982,000
Yoichi Shimizu	67 73 72 79	291	840,000
Prayad Marksaeng	73 75 70 74	292	744,000
Clark Dennis	75 71 71 75	292	744,000
Eiji Mizoguchi	72 73 72 75	292	744,000
Suk Joug Yul	73 70 73 76	292	744,000

Seven Hills Cup KBC Senior Open

Seven Hills Golf Club, Fukuoka, Saga
Par 36-36–72; 6,607 yards

September 27-28
purse, ¥28,000,000

	SCORES	TOTAL	MONEY
Akira Teranishi	66 64	130	¥5,000,000
Kazuo Seike	67 64	131	1,820,000
Hiroo Okamo	64 67	131	1,820,000
Seiki Okuda	64 67	131	1,820,000
Thaworn Wiratchant	66 66	132	1,064,000
Shinichi Akiba	65 67	132	1,064,000
Masahiro Kuramoto	67 66	133	882,000
Suk Joug Yul	62 71	133	882,000
Yoichi Shimizu	66 68	134	759,600
Gregory Meyer	67 68	135	616,000
Kiyoshi Maita	67 68	135	616,000

	SCORES		TOTAL	MONEY
Keiji Teshima	66	69	135	616,000
Jong-Duck Kim	64	71	135	616,000
Tetsu Nishikawa	70	66	136	476,000
Masami Ito	70	67	137	371,700
Chien-Soon Lu	70	67	137	371,700
Masayoshi Yamazoe	70	67	137	371,700
Hideki Kase	69	68	137	371,700
Tsuyoshi Yoneyama	69	68	137	371,700
Katsumi Kubo	69	68	137	371,700
Yoshinobu Tsukada	68	69	137	371,700
Takeshi Oyama	68	69	137	371,700

Japan PGA Senior Championship

Summit Golf Club, Ibaraki
Par 36-36–72; 7,018 yards
(Tournament reduced to 54 holes—typhoon.)

October 10-13
purse, ¥50,000,000

	SCORES			TOTAL	MONEY
Hidezumi Shirakata	67	65	72	204	¥10,000,000
Masahiro Kuramoto	69	68	70	207	3,250,000
Prayad Marksaeng	67	70	70	207	3,250,000
Thaworn Wiratchant	69	66	72	207	3,250,000
Yoshinobu Tsukada	68	66	73	207	3,250,000
Chien-Soon Lu	68	69	71	208	1,500,000
Naoyuki Tamura	72	68	69	209	1,350,000
Yutaka Hagawa	71	72	67	210	1,150,000
Masayoshi Yamazoe	67	72	71	210	1,150,000
Takeshi Oyama	69	68	73	210	1,150,000
Masayuki Kawamura	72	69	70	211	975,000
Mitsuhiro Tateyama	71	73	68	212	825,000
Shinichi Akiba	71	69	72	212	825,000
Yoshinori Mizumaki	74	65	73	212	825,000
Gregory Meyer	67	71	74	212	825,000
Yuji Taguchi	74	69	70	213	608,333
Tsuyoshi Yoneyama	68	75	70	213	608,333
Kazuhiro Kinjo	70	70	73	213	608,333
Suk Joug Yul	68	72	73	213	608,333
Kiyoshi Murota	74	65	74	213	608,333
Shinsuke Yanagisawa	67	70	76	213	608,333

Trust Group Cup Sasabo Senior Open

Sasebo Country Club, Nagasaki
Par 36-36–72

October 19-20
purse, ¥25,000,000

	SCORES		TOTAL	MONEY
Shinichi Akiba	72	67	139	¥4,500,000
Masahiro Kuramoto	69	71	140	2,250,000
Suk Joug Yul	72	69	141	1,375,000
Yoshinori Mizumaki	72	69	141	1,375,000
Tsuyoshi Yoneyama	75	67	142	856,250
Masayuki Kawamura	73	69	142	856,250
Takeshi Sakiyama	71	71	142	856,250
Gregory Meyer	71	71	142	856,250
Katsunori Kuwabara	75	68	143	550,000
Naoyuki Tamura	72	71	143	550,000

684 / SENIOR TOURS

	SCORES		TOTAL	MONEY
Wen-Teh Lu	72	71	143	550,000
Ryoken Kawagishi	71	72	143	550,000
Toshimitsu Izawa	70	73	143	550,000
Kazuo Seike	73	71	144	412,500
Katsunari Takahashi	71	73	144	412,500
Yoichi Shimizu	74	71	145	350,000
Jong-Duck Kim	73	72	145	350,000
Keiichiro Fukabori	72	73	145	350,000
Masami Ito	72	73	145	350,000
Hidezumi Shirakata	75	71	146	265,625
Katsumi Kubo	75	71	146	265,625
Yasunobu Kuramoto	74	72	146	265,625
Chien-Soon Lu	73	73	146	265,625
Kohki Idoki	73	73	146	265,625
Thaworn Wiratchant	73	73	146	265,625

Fukuoka Senior Open

Fukuoka Country Club, Wajiro Course, Fukuoka
Par 36-36–72; 6,556 yards

October 26-27
purse, ¥35,000,000

	SCORES		TOTAL	MONEY
Toshimitsu Izawa	67	69	136	¥7,000,000
Yoshinobu Tsukada	70	67	137	3,500,000
Gregory Meyer	70	68	138	1,575,000
Yoichi Shimizu	69	69	138	1,575,000
Kiyoshi Murota	69	69	138	1,575,000
Prayad Marksaeng	66	72	138	1,575,000
Jong-Duck Kim	69	70	139	1,050,000
Shinichi Akiba	73	68	141	850,500
Shinsuke Yanagisawa	72	69	141	850,500
Kiyoshi Maita	72	69	141	850,500
Masahiro Kuramoto	71	70	141	850,500
Katsumi Kubo	69	72	141	850,500
Norio Shinozaki	74	68	142	570,000
Toshikazu Sugihara	74	68	142	570,000
Wen-Teh Lu	71	71	142	570,000
Naoyuki Tamura	70	72	142	570,000
Eiji Mizoguchi	70	72	142	570,000
Hiroo Okamo	70	72	142	570,000
Hidezumi Shirakata	65	77	142	570,000
Takeshi Sakiyama	73	70	143	376,250
Katsunori Kuwabara	73	70	143	376,250
Masami Ito	71	72	143	376,250
Toru Suzuki	70	73	143	376,250
Boo Won Park	70	73	143	376,250
Yoshikatsu Saito	66	77	143	376,250

Fujifilm Senior Championship

Edosaki Country Club, Ibaraki
Par 36-35–71

November 7-9
purse, ¥70,000,000

	SCORES			TOTAL	MONEY
Thaworn Wiratchant	68	64	68	200	¥14,000,000
Toru Suzuki	70	70	66	206	6,650,000
Barry Lane	69	69	69	207	4,900,000

	SCORES			TOTAL	MONEY
Prayad Marksaeng	70	68	70	208	3,045,000
Suk Joug Yul	70	66	72	208	3,045,000
Kiyoshi Murota	71	71	67	209	1,925,000
Keiichiro Fukabori	67	73	69	209	1,925,000
Wen-Teh Lu	71	72	67	210	1,540,000
Masahiro Kuramoto	70	71	69	210	1,540,000
Tsuyoshi Yoneyama	72	71	68	211	1,299,666
Shinichi Akiba	73	68	70	211	1,299,666
Gregory Meyer	68	72	71	211	1,299,666
Norio Shinozaki	69	73	70	212	1,155,000
Jong-Duck Kim	68	71	73	212	1,155,000
Katsunori Kuwabara	77	69	67	213	959,000
Ryoken Kawagishi	70	75	68	213	959,000
Kazuhiro Takami	75	69	69	213	959,000
Masayoshi Nakayama	74	68	71	213	959,000
Toshimitsu Izawa	71	70	72	213	959,000
Yoshinori Mizumaki	73	74	67	214	721,000
Masayuki Kawamura	72	72	70	214	721,000
Naomichi Ozaki	69	75	70	214	721,000
Kiyoshi Maita	72	71	71	214	721,000
Kohki Idoki	71	70	73	214	721,000

Elite Grip Senior Open

Naruo Golf Club, Hyogo
Par 35-35–70; 6,542 yards

November 15-16
purse, ¥20,000,000

	SCORES		TOTAL	MONEY
Eiji Mizoguchi	68	67	135	¥3,600,000
Norio Shinozaki	70	67	137	1,165,000
Suk Joug Yul	70	67	137	1,165,000
Akira Teranishi	69	68	137	1,165,000
Masayuki Kawamura	69	68	137	1,165,000
Tetsu Nishikawa	71	67	138	584,000
Yuji Igarashi	69	69	138	584,000
Masahiro Kuramoto	68	70	138	584,000
Gregory Meyer	68	70	138	584,000
Kazuhiro Takami	67	71	138	584,000
Katsumi Kubo	72	67	139	328,000
Shinichi Akiba	71	68	139	328,000
Yuzo Oyama	70	69	139	328,000
Masami Ito	69	70	139	328,000
Yoshinobu Tsukada	69	70	139	328,000
Hidezumi Shirakata	69	70	139	328,000
Yoshinori Mizumaki	67	72	139	328,000
Tsukasa Watanabe	67	72	139	328,000
Naoya Sugiyama	71	69	140	224,000
Katsunari Takahashi	70	70	140	224,000
Chien-Soon Lu	68	72	140	224,000

ISPS Handa Cup Philanthropy Senior

Hatoyama Country Club, Saitama
Par 36-36–72

November 19-20
purse, ¥20,000,000

	SCORES		TOTAL	MONEY
Suk Joug Yul	66	69	135	¥3,600,000
Katsumi Kubo	69	67	136	1,500,000
Kiyoshi Murota	68	68	136	1,500,000
Masahiro Kuramoto	68	70	138	900,000
Thaworn Wiratchant	72	67	139	760,000
Keiichiro Fukabori	69	70	139	760,000
Naoyuki Tamura	70	70	140	660,000
Takeshi Sakiyama	73	68	141	525,000
Colin Montgomerie	72	69	141	525,000
Yoichi Shimizu	70	71	141	525,000
Katsunori Kuwabara	70	71	141	525,000
Gregory Meyer	71	71	142	332,000
Chien-Soon Lu	71	71	142	332,000
Yoshinobu Tsukada	71	71	142	332,000
Hitoshi Kato	69	73	142	332,000
Tsuyoshi Yoneyama	69	73	142	332,000
Yoshikatsu Saito	68	74	142	332,000
Hidezumi Shirakata	68	74	142	332,000
Norio Shinozaki	70	73	143	248,000
Masayoshi Yamazoe	68	75	143	248,000